Ernst Karner and Barbara C Steininger (eds)

European Tort Law 2023

European Tort Law Yearbook

Edited by the
European Centre of Tort
and Insurance Law

together with the
Institute for European Tort Law
of the Austrian Academy of Sciences
and the University of Graz

European Tort Law 2023

Ernst Karner
Barbara C Steininger (eds)

With Contributions by

Ewa Bagińska • Marko Baretić • Elena Bargelli • Søren Bergenser • Agris Bitāns • Lucian Bojin • Sergiu Căileanu • Giannino Caruana Demajo • Rui Cascão • Michael Chatzipanagiotis • Andrea Cioni • Emanuel GD van Dongen • Simona Drukteinienė • Gregor Dugar • Anton Dulak • Isabelle C Durant • Andreas Bloch Ehlers • Sandra Friberg • Martin Hogg • Jiří Hrádek • Zoé Jacquemin • Anne LM Keirse • Jonas Knetsch • Bernhard A Koch • Päivi Korpisaari • Irene Kull • Janno Lahe • Peter Loser • Indrė Maculevičienė • Inês de Oliveira Martins • Colm Peter McGrath • Attila Menyhárd • David Messner-Kreuzbauer • André Pereira • Ronen Perry • Eoin Quill • Lawrence Quintano • Nicolas Riemann • Albert Ruda • Barbara C Steininger • Hristina Tancheva • Knut Martin Tande • Thomas Thiede • Viktor Tokushev • Zafeirios Tsolakidis • Corinne Widmer Lüchinger • Wolfgang Wurmnest • Paulina Wyszyńska-Ślufińska • David E Zammit

DE GRUYTER

European Centre of Tort and Insurance Law
Reichsratsstraße 17/2
1010 Vienna
Austria
Tel: +43 1 4277-29650
E-Mail: ectil@ectil.org

Institute for European Tort Law
of the Austrian Academy of Sciences
and the University of Graz
Reichsratsstraße 17/2
1010 Vienna
Austria
Tel: +43 1 4277-29651
E-Mail: etl@oeaw.ac.at

ÖAW

UNI GRAZ

ISBN 978-3-11-137612-7
e-ISBN (PDF) 978-3-11-137672-1
e-ISBN (EPUB) 978-3-11-137777-3

Library of Congress Control Number: 2024943284

Bibliographic information published by the Deutsche Nationalbibliothek
The Deutsche Nationalbibliothek lists this publication in the Deutsche Nationalbibliografie; detailed bibliographic data are available on the internet at http://dnb.dnb.de.

Printing and binding: CPI books GmbH, Leck

www.degruyter.com

MIX
Papier | Fördert gute Waldnutzung
FSC® C083411

Preface

Published jointly by the European Centre of Tort and Insurance Law (ECTIL) and the Institute for European Tort Law (ETL), this Yearbook provides information and analysis about tort law developments in Europe in 2023. It contains reports from all EU Member States except Luxembourg. Additionally, reports from Norway, England and Wales, Scotland and Switzerland, and an overview of developments in the field of EU law are included. Moreover, the Yearbook contains a report on developments in Israeli tort law. In conclusion, a comparative analysis evaluates selected highlights and identifies emerging trends.

The Yearbook is associated with the Annual Conference on European Tort Law, which is held each year in the week after Easter. The 23rd Annual Conference took place in Vienna from 4 to 5 April 2024. The next Annual Conference on European Tort Law is scheduled for 24 to 25 April 2025. Papers from the Special Session of the Conference appear each year in a special issue of the Journal of European Tort Law. This year, the theme was 'Product Liability'. The papers can be found in vol 15 no 2 of the Journal.

The editors express their gratitude to their colleagues on the ECTIL-ETL staff for their help with the Yearbook and Conference in myriad ways. Special thanks go to Lisa Zeiler for organising the Conference in a way that made meeting in Vienna so enjoyable, Julian Pehm and Samuel Loibl for taking care of technical aspects, Donna Stockenhuber for proof-reading the entire manuscript with expertise, fervour and sensitivity, Kathrin Karner-Strobach for handling the copy-editing in the same manner, Samuel Loibl and Luke Filan for formatting and coordinating the publication process and Samuel Loibl and Katarzyna Ludwichowska-Redo for compiling the Index.

Ernst Karner
Barbara C Steininger
Vienna, July 2024

https://doi.org/10.1515/9783111376721-001

Table of Contents

David Messner-Kreuzbauer and Barbara C Steininger
I. Austria — 1
A. Legislation — 1
B. Cases — 1
C. Literature — 33

Isabelle C Durant
II. Belgium — 39
A. Legislation — 39
B. Cases — 40
C. Literature — 57

Viktor Tokushev and Hristina Tancheva
III. Bulgaria — 61
A. Legislation — 61
B. Cases — 62
C. Literature — 83

Marko Baretić
IV. Croatia — 87
A. Legislation — 87
B. Cases — 91
C. Literature — 108

Michael Chatzipanagiotis
V. Cyprus — 111
A. Legislation — 111
B. Cases — 113
C. Personal Injury — 126
D. Literature — 131

Jiří Hrádek
VI. Czech Republic — 133
A. Legislation — 133
B. Cases — 134
C. Literature — 162

Søren Bergenser and Andreas Bloch Ehlers
VII. Denmark — 165
A. Legislation — **165**
B. Cases — **165**
C. Literature — **176**

Colm Peter McGrath
VIII. England and Wales — 179
A. Legislation — **179**
B. Cases — **179**
C. Literature — **207**

Janno Lahe and Irene Kull
IX. Estonia — 211
A. Legislation — **211**
B. Cases — **211**
C. Literature — **227**

Päivi Korpisaari
X. Finland — 229
A. Legislation — **229**
B. Cases — **230**
C. Literature — **241**

Jonas Knetsch and Zoé Jacquemin
XI. France — 243
A. Legislation — **243**
B. Cases — **243**
C. Literature — **259**

Wolfgang Wurmnest and Nicolas Riemann
XII. Germany — 263
A. Legislation — **263**
B. Cases — **267**
C. Literature — **284**

Zafeirios Tsolakidis
XIII. Greece — 289
A. Legislation — **289**

B. Cases — **290**
C. Literature — **315**

Attila Menyhárd
XIV. Hungary — 319
A. Legislation — **319**
B. Cases — **319**
C. Literature — **331**

Eoin Quill
XV. Ireland — 333
A. Legislation — **333**
B. Cases — **339**
C. Literature — **353**

Elena Bargelli and Andrea Cioni
XVI. Italy — 357
A. Legislation — **357**
B. Cases — **357**
C. Literature — **377**

Agris Bitāns
XVII. Latvia — 379
A. Legislation — **379**
B. Cases — **386**
C. Literature — **404**

Simona Drukteinienė and Indrė Maculevičienė
XVIII. Lithuania — 407
A. Legislation — **407**
B. Cases — **408**
C. Literature — **436**

G Caruana Demajo, L Quintano and D Zammit
XIX. Malta — 441
A. Legislation — **441**
B. Cases — **441**
C. Literature — **456**

Emanuel GD van Dongen and Anne LM Keirse
XX. The Netherlands — 459
A. Legislation — **459**
B. Cases — **461**
C. Literature — **480**

Knut Martin Tande
XXI. Norway — 485
A. Legislation — **485**
B. Cases — **485**
C. Literature — **506**

Ewa Bagińska and Paulina Wyszyńska-Ślufińska
XXII. Poland — 513
A. Legislation — **513**
B. Cases — **518**
C. Literature — **527**

Inês de Oliveira Martins, Rui Cascão and André Pereira
XXIII. Portugal — 529
A. Legislation — **529**
B. Cases — **531**
C. Literature — **550**

Lucian Bojin and Sergiu Căileanu
XXIV. Romania — 553
A. Legislation — **553**
B. Cases — **554**
C. Literature — **566**

Martin Hogg
XXV. Scotland — 575
A. Legislation — **575**
B. Cases — **575**
C. Literature — **595**

Anton Dulak
XXVI. Slovakia — 599
A. Legislation — **599**

B. Cases — 599
C. Literature — 605

Gregor Dugar
XXVII. Slovenia — 607
A. Legislation — 607
B. Cases — 614
C. Literature — 631

Albert Ruda
XXVIII. Spain — 633
A. Legislation — 633
B. Cases — 644
C. Literature — 663

Sandra Friberg
XXIX. Sweden — 667
A. Legislation — 667
B. Cases — 668
C. Literature — 683

Peter Loser
XXX. Switzerland — 689
A. Legislation — 689
B. Cases — 691
C. Literature — 719

Bernhard A Koch and Thomas Thiede
XXXI. European Union — 721
A. Legislation — 721
B. Cases on Infringements of the GDPR — 721
C. Other Cases — 734

Ronen Perry
XXXII. Israel — 753
A. Legislation — 753
B. Cases — 756

Corinne Widmer Lüchinger
XXXIII. Comparative Remarks — 779
A. Introduction — **779**
B. The Sweet Shop Selection — **780**
C. Final Comments — **794**

Contributors — 797

Index — 821

Publications — 827

David Messner-Kreuzbauer and Barbara C Steininger

I. Austria

A. Legislation

In 2023, there were no significant legislative developments in the field of tort law 1
in Austria.

B. Cases

1. Oberster Gerichtshof (Austrian Supreme Court, OGH)[1] 25 April 2023, 10 Ob 2/23a (final judgment):[2] Diesel Emissions Scandal, Part I: Cause of Action; Deduction of Benefits

a) Brief Summary of the Facts

This is a case in the current mass litigation against several car manufacturers in 2
the 'diesel emissions scandal'.[3] The claimant had bought a used VW Tiguan Lounge TDI BMT produced by the second defendant (VW Germany, 'the producer') for € 26,890 from the first defendant ('the seller'). It had approx 500 km and was powered by a diesel engine type EA189, which is the engine that had first triggered the scandal. The producer had rigged it with software which manipulated air pollution tests: the 'defeat device' recognised when the emissions test took place, in which case it switched to a test mode with reduced output. In use on the road, the car's emission levels were much higher and exceeded the permitted threshold. Although the producer offered an update deactivating the manipulation software

1 Cases are available at <http://www.ris.bka.gv.at/jus>.

2 ECLI:AT:OGH0002:2023:0100OB00002.23 A.0425.000; Evidenzblatt der Rechtsmittelentscheidungen (EvBl) in Österreichische Juristenzeitung (ÖJZ) 2023/196 with cmt by *R Kolbitsch-Franz* = Zeitschrift für Verbraucherrecht (VbR) 2023, 75 with cmt by *P Leupold* = Zeitschrift für Verkehrsrecht (ZVR) 2023/127 with cmt by *G Kathrein*. The case reported in the following must not be confused with OGH 21.2.2023, 10 Ob 2/23a (partial judgment) EvBl 2023/195 with cmt by *J Kepplinger* = ZVR 2023/83 with cmt by *G Kathrein*, which was issued in the same procedure with the same file number (on its content see below no 3).

3 <https://en.wikipedia.org/wiki/Diesel_emissions_scandal>.

https://doi.org/10.1515/9783111376721-002

once the scandal broke, this would not have mitigated a second problem, namely that the emissions only remain within the reported level under a temperature between 15 and 33°C (so-called 'thermal window', a second and less manifestly problematic circumvention of the emissions standards also used by other manufacturers at the time). The claimant refused to accept the software categorically because he had not intended to buy a manipulated car and would not have bought the vehicle absent the manipulation. He pursued a claim for damages of € 26,890 (the price he paid for the vehicle) against both the seller and the producer, as well as contractual remedies (recission on the basis of misrepresentation and warranty) against the seller.

3 The procedural situation prior to the judgment reported here requires some further explanation. The Court had already rendered a decision in favour of the claimant against the seller in an interim judgment,[4] which we do not report extensively here because it mainly relates to issues of contract law. Concerning the action against the producer, the Court had stayed proceedings, awaiting an imminent judgment of the Court of Justice of the European Union (CJEU) in a preliminary ruling requested by the Regional Court in Ravensburg (*Landgericht Ravensburg*), Germany. As far as relevant for the reported decision, the Regional Court in Ravensburg essentially asked: Is the EU regulatory framework[5] on the approval of motor vehicles 'intended to protect the interests of individual purchasers of motor vehicles' (Question 1)? If so, is this also true for the interest in *not* buying a manipulated car (Question 2)? In further questions (5 and 6), the *Landgericht Ravensburg* asked whether EU law permits setting off benefits – in particular, the use already made of the vehicle by a claimant – against the harm suffered by a claimant.

4 The CJEU's judgment on this request, *QB v Mercedes-Benz Group AG*,[6] followed on 21 March 2023 and is the basis of the decision we are reporting here. *Mercedes-Benz Group AG* holds that the regulatory framework 'must be interpreted as protecting, in addition to public interests, the specific interests of the individual purchaser of a motor vehicle vis-à-vis the manufacturer of that vehicle where that ve-

4 OGH 21.2.2023, 10 Ob 2/23a (partial judgment).

5 Art 18(1), art 26(1) and art 46 of Directive 2007/46/EC of the European Parliament and of the Council of 5 September 2007 establishing a framework for the approval of motor vehicles and their trailers, and of systems, components and separate technical units intended for such vehicles (Framework Directive) [2007] Official Journal (OJ) L 263/1, as amended by Commission Regulation (EC) No 385/2009 of 7 May 2009 [2009] OJ L 118/13, read in conjunction with art 5(2) of Regulation (EC) No 715/2007 of the European Parliament and of the Council of 20 June 2007 on type approval of motor vehicles with respect to emissions from light passenger and commercial vehicles (Euro 5 and Euro 6) and on access to vehicle repair and maintenance information [2007] OJ L 171/1, and of the second paragraph of art 267 TFEU.

6 CJEU 21.3.2023, C-100/21, *QB v Mercedes-Benz Group AG*, ECLI:EU:C:2023:229.

hicle is equipped with a prohibited defeat device.'[7] The CJEU did not specifically answer Question 2. Finally, the CJEU held that 'the detailed rules under which purchasers concerned by the acquisition of such a vehicle may obtain compensation [are] for each Member State to determine',[8] but – crucially – the purchaser 'has a right to compensation from the manufacturer of that vehicle where that device has caused damage to that purchaser.'[9] It must not be 'impossible or excessively difficult for the purchaser of a motor vehicle to obtain adequate compensation for the damage',[10] but rather 'adequate with respect to the damage suffered.'[11]

b) Judgment of the Court

The OGH upholds the claim against the producer. The Court assumes that the CJEU decision in *Mercedes-Benz Group AG*[12] already dictates that the claimant must, in principle, have access to a claim in tort against the producer. The Court, therefore, only discusses the nature and extent of that claim under Austrian law. 5

As to the nature, the Court concludes that, in light of *Mercedes-Benz Group AG*, the EU regulatory framework on the approval of motor vehicles is a protective norm (*Schutzgesetz*) which the producer breached. According to the OGH, that norm also specifically aims to protect the claimant from the harm in question (protective purpose of the rule, *Schutzzweck der Norm*). Finally, the Court holds that the breach in question shifts the burden of proof regarding fault, and since the defendant had not even disputed misconduct, fault could be inferred when assessing the evidence. 6

Regarding the assessment of damages, the Court first observes that restitution in kind takes precedence over a quantification in money. The claimant would, therefore, primarily have a right to a vehicle without a defeat device. However, since the update offered by the producer does not remedy the situation – as mentioned, the thermal window remains in place – he is entitled to claim the purchasing price (as paid to the seller) from the producer, though he would have to return the affected vehicle to the producer. The benefit received through the use of the car must also be deducted. As already in the decision against the seller, the OGH calculates the deductible benefit in the following, simple manner: the time of use by 7

7 C-100/21 *Mercedes-Benz Group AG* no 85 and Ruling 1.
8 C-100/21 *Mercedes-Benz Group AG* no 92.
9 C-100/21 *Mercedes-Benz Group AG* no 91.
10 C-100/21 *Mercedes-Benz Group AG* no 93.
11 C-100/21 *Mercedes-Benz Group AG* no 96 and Ruling 2.
12 See above no 4.

the claimant relative to the expected full lifespan of the vehicle is multiplied with the full price of the car (as paid to the seller). The OGH thus arrives at a figure of € 7,563, which it deducts from the claim, thus awarding a sum of € 19,326. According to the OGH, that sum fulfils the CJEU's 'adequacy' requirement in *Mercedes-Benz Group AG*.

c) Commentary

8 This is the OGH's first decision upholding a claim against a producer[13] in the diesel emissions scandal. It now serves as a precedent.[14] Before *Mercedes-Benz Group AG* and the present follow-up decision of the OGH, academics generally assumed that Austrian law – similar to German case law up to that point[15] – would (only) uphold a claim against the producer based on rather demanding causes of action, such as, in particular, intentional misrepresentation (§ 874 Austrian Civil Code, *Allgemeines Bürgerliches Gesetzbuch*, ABGB).[16] It seems very likely that without the CJEU's decision in *Mercedes-Benz Group AG*, the courts would have come to the same conclusion (which would arguably have sufficed to hold the defendant producer in the case, VW, liable). However, things turned out differently.

9 Given the decision in *Mercedes-Benz Group AG*, the OGH had little choice but take the CJEU's holdings as a starting point. However, taken *literally*, the EU Court's language of 'protected interests', adequacy, and the national law nature of the claim was open to many interpretations. For instance, a rather defiant reading of the judgment concluded that upholding the pre-*Mercedes* orthodoxy just sketch-

13 Noteworthy prior decisions: OGH 30.6.2022, 9 Ob 33/22a (held that there is no loss if claimant had already sold the car for market value before the scandal broke); 29.8.2022, 5 Ob 100/22z (held that 'abstract assessment' of damages might be open and quashes appeal court decision, which had rejected a claim *a limine* for lack of plausibility).

14 See, eg, OGH 27.6.2022, 6 Ob 150/22k; 19.9.2023, 2 Ob 5/23 h ZVR 2024/45 with cmt by *U Neumayr*; 19.10.2023, 8 Ob 88/22 g ZVR 2024/46 with cmt by *C Müller/A Wittwer.*

15 See BGH VI ZR 252/19, reported by *J Kleinschmidt*, Germany, in: E Karner/BC Steininger (eds), European Tort Law 2020 (2021) 206, no 34 ff.

16 See *A Kogler*, Falsche Abgaswerte – Rechtsfolgen, Der Sachverständige (SV) 2017, 71, 74 f; *A Riedler*, Irrtum, List, Gewährleistung und Schadenersatz – auch vor dem Hintergrund der BGH-E VI ZR 252/19, ZVR 2020, 320, 326; *R Franz*, Die Haftung des Herstellers im "Diesel-Skandal" aus der Perspektive des österreichischen Schadenersatzrechts, ZVR 2021, 129, 130 f; *Walter Doralt*, Dieselfälle und sogenannter Abgasskandal: Ansprüche der Käufer gegen den Hersteller nach österreichischem Recht. Expert opinion for Landgericht Braunschweig, Graz Law Working Paper No 13–2022, Available at SSRN: <https://ssrn.com/abstract=4252567> or <http://dx.doi.org/10.2139/ssrn.4252567> 40 ff; and OGH 18.6.2018, 5 Ob 62/18 f (obiter dictum: claim was dismissed on other grounds).

ed (intentional misrepresentation necessary for an action in tort) is still acceptable.[17] After all, that former solution does take *some* notice of individual interests, and protected interests do not mechanically entail an actionability under national tort laws, since Austrian (and German) law have developed tests that can exclude liability *in spite* of the breach of a relevant duty. Another, second option might have been to say that the CJEU did not really mean the *precise* loss of the purchasing price in question, but other types of harm.[18] Be that as it may, the OGH reasonably assumes that the CJEU wanted to make a different point in *Mercedes-Benz Group AG:* EU emissions law demands (at least) standard liability – that is, liability for negligence – and understands the acquisition of a 'problem' vehicle as relevant harm.

The choice to understand this liability as breach of a statutory duty (*Schutzgesetzverletzung*), however, is worth debating further. Breach of statutory duties (literally: violation of a protective statutory norm) is one of the main routes to establish wrongfulness and therefore one essential element of a tort claim under Austrian law.[19] However, understanding the violation of the EU regulatory framework as actionable in tort law does not fit well into the Austrian system.[20] Where only economic interests and consumer decisions are at stake, national law is not usually so generous in awarding individual rights of action.[21] Arguably, it would have been more fitting to classify the direct claim required by the CJEU as flowing from a different cause of action, namely information liability for generating spe- 10

17 In this sense – on German law – *HC Grigoleit*, Perspektiven der Schutzgesetzhaftung im Kontext des unionsrechtlichen Effektivitätsgebots – am Beispiel der Dieselklagen, Zeitschrift für Wirtschaftsrecht (ZIP) 2023, 221, 222 f, 232 f. Compare also *G Wagner*, Ersatz wegen Verletzung von Unionsrecht – Luxemburg locuta, causa aperta, Neue Juristische Wochenschrift (NJW) 20243, 1761, 1766 f. As Wagner acknowledges and criticises, the CJEU suggests otherwise: it specifically refers to § 823 (2) German Civil Code (Bürgerliches Gesetzbuch, BGB), and the whole answer must be seen in the context of the case and questions filed by the Landgericht Ravensburg.

18 Compare *A Kletečka*, Abschalteinrichtungen in Dieselfahrzeugen vor und nach EuGH C-100/21, ÖJZ 2023, 388, 395 ff.

19 See *E Karner*, Austria, in: B Winiger/E Karner/K Oliphant (eds), Digest of European Tort Law vol III: Essential Cases on Misconduct (2018) 1/3 no 3.

20 See, eg, *Kletečka*, ÖJZ 2023, 388, 395 ff. *M Lutschonig*, Neue Haftungs- und Beweisfragen in Dieselmassenverfahren, ZVR 2024, 103, 105 ff offers a more positive view.

21 See, eg, most recently OGH 14.7.2022, 1 Ob 91/22x, reported by *S Loibl/S Nitsch*, Austria, in: E Karner/BC Steininger (eds), ETL 2022 (2023) 1, no 67 ff; 12.10.2022 Der Gesellschafter (GesRZ) 2023, 201 with cmt by *M Oppitz*; 1 Ob 140/22b EvBl 2023/115 with cmt by *S Mock* (declining tort actionability for pure economic loss suffered through insufficient enforcement of criminal law and financial law in relation to a bank's insolvency). Compare also OGH 15 May 2023, 1 Ob 199/22d, reported below at no 22 ff, which denies actionability in tort even for personal injury.

cific reliance (*Vertrauenshaftung*).[22] Even then, granting a direct claim against the producer for the price paid to a seller in this case but not in others would have remained challenging to justify within the Austrian legal framework. It might have been a further option to (also) isolate the liability demanded by the CJEU as a special cause of action which only applies where there are pressing environmental or other instrumental concerns (similar to direct claims in unfair competition and cartel law). It remains to be seen whether admitting claims based on breach of statutory duty against the producer leaves enough room for a rational limitation of liability, or whether the floodgates are opened for direct claims against producers under Austrian law. In any case, it speaks against the European tort system that such an important result can be imposed without any substantial discussion on the advantages and – many – disadvantages of direct claims against producers.[23]

11 The remedy granted seems appropriate if one accepts the cause of action. It seems clear that the present decision assumes relevant harm to be the conclusion of an unwanted contract in itself.[24] Although it is worth noting that through this decision Austrian law deviates from current German practice (the latter does not allow recovery of the price paid to the seller where breach of the regulatory framework is the only cause of action[25]), it seems, in principle, consistent to protect someone from unwanted contracts by unwinding them.

12 We further suggest that deducting the claimant's benefits, and thus acting upon the discretion left by the CJEU, was justified. *Compensatio lucri cum damno* is, in principle, broadly accepted as necessary in European tort law,[26] and denying it would have produced a windfall profit for the claimant. Certainly,

---

22 In this sense *E Karner* (personal communication); see also – for Germany – *T Lobinger*, Die Fahrlässigkeitshaftung des Herstellers in den sogenannten Dieselfällen, Juristenzeitung (JZ) 2023, 769, 770 f; *A Spickhoff* in BeckOGK (1.12.2023) § 823 no 315. On this type of liability in Austrian law, see further *J Angyan*, Haftungsfreizeichnung gegenüber Dritten (2022) 186 ff, 199 ff; *H Koziol*, Obsoleszenzen im österreichischen Recht (2015) nos 69 ff, 142 ff, 194 ff.

23 Compare *Wagner*, NJW 2023, 1766 f, on the equivalent development in Germany. For an extensive and critical discussion of direct claims, see *H Koziol*, Mehrstufiger Warenverkehr (2021) 66 ff, 160 ff. For a more favourable view, *C Wendehorst*, Direkthaftung des Herstellers. Eine Machbarkeitsstudie für die Umsetzung der neuen Gewährleistungs-RL in Österreich, VbR 2020, 94 and 138.

24 Compare *Franz*, ZVR 2021, 131 f; *id*, EvBl 2023/196; *Lutschonig*, ZVR 2024, 106. At least by now, *Kletečkas* view (ÖJZ 2023, 389) that delivery of a manipulated car is the relevant harm does not seem defensible. The OGH says this even more clearly in a following decision, to be discussed below at no 32 ff.

25 BGH 26.6.2023, VIa ZR 335/21 JZ 2023, 769 with cmt by *T Lobinger* = NJW 2023, 2236 with cmt by *R Schaub* = Versicherungsrecht (VersR) 2023, 1117 with cmt by *M Birkholz*.

26 Compare *D Messner-Kreuzbauer*, Deduction of Collateral Benefits in European Tort Law, 14 (2024) Journal of Medical Law and Bioethics 1.

the modalities of this deduction could further be discussed. Case notes[27] have observed that establishing the deductible use-value by taking the price paid to the seller as the multiplicand (to be multiplied with the proportion between actual use and lifetime of the vehicle) does not adequately represent the relevant value factors. This price does not consider whether the use may legitimately be considered worth less to the claimant because of the manipulation. Whether this evaluation should be considered as relevant for an evaluation of pecuniary damages, or considered an immaterial aspect, is open to debate.

Finally, the decision leaves open a number of questions which were not relevant in the present case, such as what happens if the claimant does not wish to return the car, if they already resold it or if the deduction becomes too high. These issues then surfaced in further cases, one of which will be reported further below in the present report. 13

2. OGH 25 April 2023, 10 Ob 15/23p:[28] Tree Hazards; Omissions as Conduct Against Good Morals

a) Brief Summary of the Facts

The claimant and the defendant own neighbouring land in a forest. The ash trees on the defendant's forest property were affected by the symptoms of 'ash dieback',[29] a chronic fungal disease which may cause the infected trees to fall. Indeed, falling trees damaged the claimant's own young trees, and she and her husband spent 49 working hours on collecting fallen trees between 2017–2020. In 2020, 29 hazard trees, which posed an acute risk of falling, and 22 risk trees, which posed a latent risk of falling, were still identified on the defendant's property. The claimant alleged that she had already warned the defendant of the hazard in 2014. She claimed for compensation of her losses and efforts, and a preventive injunction against the disturbance of her property through further falling trees. 14

27 *Kolbitsch-Franz*, EvBl 2023/196; *U Neumayer*, ZVR 2024/45 (cmt on 2 Ob 5/23h); see also – on German law – *M Fervers/B Gsell*, Vorteilsausgleich und Nutzungsvorteil bei manipulierten Dieselfahrzeugen, NJW 2020, 1393, 1395. Others have argued that the market value did not fall through the scandal, which they take as evidence that the price paid correctly represents the use-value. See eg, *C Huber*, Viel Lärm um nichts oder doch wenig? Juristische Blätter (JBl) 2023, 205, 210.

28 ECLI:AT:OGH0002:2023:0100OB00015.23P.0425.000; EvBl 2024/147 with cmt by *E Karner* = Recht der Umwelt (RdU) 2024, 24 with cmt by *E Wagner*.

29 See eg, <https://www.forestresearch.gov.uk/tools-and-resources/fthr/pest-and-disease-resources/ash-dieback-hymenoscyphus-fraxineus/>.

The Court of First Instance dismissed the claims, because it saw no viable causes of action against a neighbour who leaves their forest property – albeit infected and dangerous – in a natural state. The Court of Appeal reversed that decision because it did identify a potential cause of action, namely § 1295 (2) ABGB[30] (intentional infliction of damage in a manner contrary to public morals). It therefore ordered the trial court to take further evidence.

b) Judgment of the Court

15 The OGH quashes the decision of the Court of Appeal and restores the first instance judgment. The Court explains that liability for omissions under § 1295 (2) ABGB is only conceivable under very narrow circumstances, which it considers to be manifestly lacking in the present case, even taking into account the possibility of admitting further evidence. The Supreme Court reminds that liability for omissions in tort, even apart from § 1295 (2), generally requires a duty to act, which only emerges under specific circumstances. Prior case law had identified such circumstances where the defendant had caused a dangerous situation, where the interests of the endangered party had a much higher standing than those of the inactive party, or in the presence of special contractual or legal obligations. The OGH does not take these criteria as even potentially fulfilled in the facts of the present case.

16 The Supreme Court adds that § 1295 (2) would further require 1) intentional misconduct, in the sense of taking harm as 'seriously probable' and accepting it, and 2) conduct against good morals. Even allowing that the defendant's omissions may have intended harm in this broad sense, the Supreme Court takes the second element to be absent. It notes that none of the various indicators established for immoral action in legal literature (abuse of a formal position, taking advantage of another, violation of fundamental ethical norms, etc) are perceptible in the present case. The OGH adds that 'good faith and fair dealing with respect to customs' could demand a different view in other cases, but not in this one: the natural hazards of the forest are not problematic. An intention to cause harm (in the broad sense of element 1 just mentioned) does not change this assessment by itself. Finally, the OGH briefly hints that the defendant might not have had a right to refuse

30 § 1295 (2) ABGB: 'A person who intentionally inflicts damage in a manner contrary to public morals is also liable; however, if the damage was inflicted in the exercise of a right, he is liable only if the exercise of the right clearly had the object of harming the other.' Translation by *BC Steininger* in: E Karner/K Oliphant/BC Steininger (eds), European Tort Law: Basic Texts (2nd edn 2018) 2.

the claimant entry on his land for the sake of protecting her own land, had the claimant asked for this.

c) Commentary

17 Tree liability has been much debated recently,[31] but the present case does not seem very problematic and is noteworthy mainly because of theoretical questions relating to § 1295 (2) ABGB. The judgment is in line with established case law, although its position on § 1295 (2) ABGB is not entirely clear.

18 The Supreme Court specifically underlines that it did not assess any basis of liability besides § 1295 (2). But even under other causes of action, it is true that the OGH has consistently denied landowners' responsibility for 'natural' hazards.[32] This is particularly clear for harmful events within a forest, which are the subject of the present case. It might be objected that there is a hint in the text of the judgment that the ash forest was originally planted by design.[33] However, the aim to limit the responsibility of those who leave something ordinarily found in nature more or less natural and to make foresting feasible must be considered even in this case (see in particular § 176 [2] Forestry Act, *Forstgesetz*, ForstG: no liability for condition of the forest). While a public law duty to act against infections (such as under § 44 ForstG) might potentially change this equation, the trial court had specifically denied the presence of such a duty. It is also worth noting that, although the lower courts in the reported case discuss a number of potential causes of action (§§ 1295 [1], 176 [4] ForstG, § 364a ABGB *per analogiam*), the classification of a disturbance as natural curtails all of these ordinary routes, because it means that the defendant did not interfere with the claimant's entitlement in the first place, considering the relevant test of neighbourhood law.[34]

---

31 See, eg, *B Borkowski*, Das HaftRÄG 2022: Eine Neuordnung der Haftung für Bäume, ZVR 2023, 57; *E Wagner*, Hurra – Ministerialentwurf zur Baumhaftung (endlich) da! RdU 2024, 4. In 2024, § 1319b ABGB on liability for trees was added to the ABGB.

32 A decision with an in-depth discussion of this stance was reported in 2018. See OGH 30.10.2018, reported by *J Pehm/S Nitsch*, Austria, in: E Karner/BC Steininger (eds), ETL 2018 (2019) 1, no 57 ff (with further refs). Compare also OGH 30.6.2022, 9 Ob 28/22s reported in ETL 2022 by *Loibl/Nitsch* (fn 21) no 55 ff; *E Karner*, Rechtliche Beurteilung des Konzepts für ein differenziertes Baumgefahren-Management in Österrreichs Nationalparks, in: E Karner/K Zsak (eds), Baumgefahren-Management in Österreichs Nationalparks (2023) 78 f.

33 It talks of the ash forest as (a result of) lawful timbering (Bestockung).

34 On this test in Austrian law, see *D Messner*, The Foundations of Civil Liability for Industrial Pollution 11 (2020) Journal of European Tort Law (JETL) 208, 221 ff.

19 The specific attention § 1295 (2) received in the reported case must also be seen in this context. As similar concepts in other jurisdictions,[35] it might conceivably be used to impose extraordinary obligations upon neighbours even where interferences are usual. It is more difficult, however, to imagine § 1295 (2) as a basis for an active duty to prevent harm. Norms such as this are based on the weight of improper *motives*,[36] which are manifest in actions not serving a comprehensible purpose. But for omissions – not taking an action – a defendant will usually have many innocuous reasons (eg, the defendant wanted to get on with his affairs rather than cutting trees).

20 If there is clear room for a duty to act under § 1295 (2), it must be because sometimes the action required of the defendant would have cost them so little effort that their failure to perform the action can only be explained through improper motives: such as not warning the endangered party of imminent and severe harm. If so, however, liability under § 1295 (2) for omissions is virtually identical with the very narrow general duty to rescue proposed by part of legal literature already under the general clause of § 1295 (1).[37] Others are more defensive in the first place and reject generally defined duties to act.[38] In the present decision, the OGH did not have to take a position as to which of the two views it would follow, because neither of them would support a duty to act. A duty under § 1295 (2) seems even less plausible, because academics agree this clause should be limited to specific classes of cases;[39] not concluding a contract in a monopoly situation appears to be the only clearly relevant omission case. The Court's brief statement *obiter dictum* that it might support liability for an omission in 'good faith and fair dealing with respect to customs' therefore seems misleading. It should not be taken as establishing a new and third view on the problem of a general duty to act.[40]

---

35 Compare the role of malice in the tort of nuisance, or the role of 'abus de droit' in the French law of neighbours.

36 *M Karollus*, Funktion und Dogmatik der Haftung aus Schutzgesetzverletzungen (1992) 51 f; *E Karner* in: P Bydlinski/S Perner/M Spitzer (eds), ABGB (7th edn 2023) § 1295 no 21.

37 *H Koziol*, Basic Questions of Tort Law from a from a Germanic Perspective (2012) 191 ff; see also *G Christandl*, The Duty to Prevent Harm in Challenging Times, 12 (2021) JETL 93, 94 ff.

38 *R Reischauer* in Rummel, ABGB (3rd edn 2007) § 1295 nos 54, 56; *K Spielbüchler*, Dankt der Gesetzgeber ab? JBl 2006, 341, 351.

39 *H Koziol*, Österreichisches Haftpflichtrecht I (4th edn 2020) A/4/10 ff; Rummel/*Reischauer* (fn 38) § 1294 no 3.

40 The Supreme Court supports this one sentence only rather apodictically by reference to a *Rechtssatz* – a line of judgments supposedly connected by the same constant reasoning – which really concerns a very different situation in competition law. See RS0037753 and the decisions assigned to it. More precisely, this string of case law answers the question when competitors must

Finally, the OGH's suggestion that the claimant in this case would have had the liberty to enter the defendant's land and cut the trees merits support.[41] As some authors have argued,[42] if faced with a denial of this right by the defendant, the claimant could even prepare for this entry by filing an injunction in advance, asserting a right not to be disturbed in protecting her property. 21

3. OGH 15 May 2023, 1 Ob 199/22d:[43] Failure of Public Authority to Protect Citizens from COVID-19 Infection

a) Brief Summary of the Facts

This case received much attention in the public, as it concerns an allegation of mishandling by the public authorities of the COVID-19 crisis in the Austrian skiing region of Ischgl, where the pandemic first hit the country. The claimant submitted that he came to the small town in Tyrol on 7 March 2020 for skiing, where he was infected with the virus. At that time, several infected tourists from Iceland had already stayed in the region. The claimant contends that the Icelandic authorities had informed their Austrian counterparts in time and that the latter therefore should have acted or at least have warned the public of the epidemiological danger already looming in the region. Rather than sharing their information, the authorities of the Land of Tyrol sent out placating messages. For instance, they claimed, without much evidence, that the Icelandic tourists had been infected on their flight home (5 March). They emphasised a statement of an expert member of the health 22

actively prevent the spread of misinformation about a product, which they had *caused through their own advertising*.

41 *Karner*, EvBl 2024/147. On the roots of this idea, see *F Baur*, Der negatorische Beseitigungsanspruch, Archiv für die civilistische Praxis (AcP) 160 (1961) 465, 475 ff (on German law).

42 *P Jabornegg/R Strasser*, Nachbarrechtliche Ansprüche als Instrument des Umweltschutzes (1978) 147; *E Karner*, Abwehransprüche bei naturgegebenen Immissionen, in: S Perner/O Riss (eds), Festschrift für Gert Iro zum 65. Geburtstag (2013) 17, 30 ff. *E Wagners* comment on the present decision in RdU 2024, 44 takes an opposing view.

43 ECLI:AT:OGH0002:2023:0010OB00199.22D.0515.000; EvBl 2023/189 with two cmts by *U Wagrandl* and by *I Vonkilch*. See further (with critique) *D Messner-Kreuzbauer*, Schutzzweck und Amtshaftung im Lichte der "Causa Ischgl", Recht der Wirtschaft (RdW) 2023/410; *T Rabl*, Oh nein – nicht schon wieder (keine) Amtshaftung, oder: OGH und Ischgl: Weil nicht sein kann, was nicht sein darf! Zeitschrift für Wirtschaftsrecht (ecolex) 2023, 549. The decision is welcomed by *M Paar*, COVID-19-Ausbruch in Ischgl im März 2020 und die Frage der Amtshaftung (Teil I), Recht der Medizin (RdM) 2024, 15; *id*, COVID-19-Ausbruch in Ischgl im März 2020 und die Frage der Amtshaftung (Teil II), RdM 2024, 60 who represented the defendant.

authority, who had considered an infection of the Icelanders at one particular bar as unlikely (with hindsight, it is now public knowledge that this bar was in fact a hotbed for infections). Moreover, the claimant alleged that the Federal Chancellor had prematurely announced a quarantine for Ischgl, causing infections in the resulting chaos of hasty departures. The claimant sought an award of pecuniary and non-pecuniary damages under the Public Authority Liability Act (*Amtshaftungsgesetz*, AHG) against the Federal State, which is constitutionally responsible for the prevention of epidemics and thus also the principal of the State authorities and agents on the ground in Ischgl.

23 The Court of First Instance denied all claims without taking evidence on the alleged misconduct. Even supposing the claimant's allegations to be true, it held, all potential causes of action still fail on questions of law. Crucially, it held that all possible breaches of the Epidemics Act (*Epidemiegesetz 1950*, EpiG) are irrelevant, because the statute's aim is the promotion of public health, whereas the protection of individuals is not within its scope of protection for the purpose of tort law. Yet the Court of Appeal reversed the decision. It found that, while the authorities' pure failure to act would indeed not be relevant for tort law, an *active* misrepresentation by the authorities – if proven at trial – could indeed justify an award of damages.

b) Judgment of the Court

24 The OGH sides with the Court of First Instance, restores the latter's judgment and denies any potential cause of action in tort. Still, the Supreme Court discusses several potential grounds of action at length. These are: (1) a claim based on the omission to enforce the Epidemics Act, (2) a claim based on the public authorities' failure to protect the claimant's human rights under arts 2 and 8 European Convention on Human Rights (ECHR); as well as arts 2, 3 and 7 of the Charta of Fundamental Rights of the European Union, (3) a claim based on the public authorities' misrepresentation of the danger in Ischgl, (4) a claim based on the commitment of a relevant public endangerment crime (§ 180 Penal Code, *Strafgesetzbuch*, StGB: endangerment through infectious diseases),[44] (5) a claim based on the Federal Chancellor's premature announcement of a quarantine in Ischgl, resulting in a chaotic departure from the town.

---

44 In theory, crimes impose statutory duties that can be actionable in tort as breaches of statutory duties (Schutzgesetzverletzungen). A criminal conviction is not necessary; indeed, the competent public prosecutor decided not to pursue potential crimes committed by the competent officials.

25 Most importantly for any further litigation related to public health, the Court reiterates the Court of First Instance's reasoning on cause of action 1. The OGH claims that the EpiG merely aims at protecting public health rather than individuals. Therefore, the Court concludes that the statute does not aim to protect individuals, and denies its protective purpose (*Schutzzweck der Norm*) for tort law purposes. The Supreme Court's arguments in this matter are predominantly textual and historical: they seek to document a perceived lack of concern for the individual expressed in the text of the EpiG (going back to 1913)[45] and the legislative protocols.

26 The Court declines to further consider the arguments based on fundamental rights (cause of action 2). On this cause of action, it holds that the direct addressee of the ECHR is the legislator rather than administrative authorities, while it denies that the Charta of the EU is applicable at all. Moreover, the Court dismisses the claim based on misrepresentation (cause of action 3), by referring to case law which limits this type of liability to scenarios with a specific prior relationship between public authority and claimant. Finally, the OGH denies causes of actions 4 (public endangerment crime) and 5 (premature statements), inter alia by holding again that all potentially relevant duties of the authorities are not actionable in tort law.

c) Commentary

27 This decision had immediate practical relevance because it abruptly ended ongoing mass litigation related to the Ischgl incident: shortly after its publication, the OGH dismissed 50 pending claims by reference to the present leading case, and the claimants withdrew a further 130 claims and one collective claim still pending at first instance.[46] Academics who wrote on the Ischgl case before the decision had not expected such a categorical rejection of any liability.[47] Moreover, the OGH's rea-

45 The bulk of the EpiG is still based on the Austrian Monarchy's Statute on the prevention and abatement of infectious diseases (Gesetz betreffend die Verhütung und Bekämpfung übertragbarer Krankheiten), Reichsgesetzblatt 1913, no 67.

46 <https://www.derstandard.at/story/3000000184026/-ischgl-alle-klagen-gegen-tirol-und-bund-am-lg-innsbruck-vom-tisch>. Other COVID-19 related litigation against the State had been less promising from the beginning, see, eg, OGH 18.5.2022, 1 Ob 75/22v reported in ETL 2022 by *Loibl/Nitsch* (fn 21) no 22 ff (ordinance violating procedural law).

47 *A Geroldinger*, Amtshaftung wegen Fehlern bei der Bekämpfung der COVID-19-Epidemie? JBl 2020, 523, 532 ff; *D Schindl/M Spitzer*, Beweiserleichterungen im Haftpflichtprozess. Überlegungen zu Amtshaftung und Beweisrecht am Beispiel Ischgl, ZVR 2021, 263, 265 f; *Christandl*, 12 (2021) JETL 107 f.

soning on the first cause of action (failure to enforce the EpiG) reflects a style of argument on which the Supreme Court seems to increasingly rely in its case law on public authority liability: the textual and historical approach for determining whether public law duties, enshrined in administrative law statutes, are relevant for tort law.[48] Tempting as this method may seem, in our view, it is rather unfortunate, while the result in the reported case remains debatable.[49]

28 As already indicated, the test as to what extent public law duties are relevant in tort law is considered part of the broader question of the protective purpose of the norm (*Schutzzweck der Norm*).[50] *Schutzzweck* is the most relevant limitation of liability generally and of particular importance in public authority liability. The general test is whether the duty or obligation breached by the defendant also aimed at protecting the claimant from the precise harm they suffered, and it can be helpful to break this scope down further into a personal, a substantive and a modal aspect.[51] Some authors argue that the question whether an individual action in tort is suitable at all merits a test of its own.[52] In substance, however, there are as many ways to interpret the protective scope as there are ways to interpret norms and their aims. Generally, the Supreme Court follows a pluralist approach, which it rhetorically refers to even at one point of the present decision. Thus, the finding of a protective purpose has often been based on 'systematic' and 'teleological' arguments, meaning arguments in principle (what are the affected rights, how likely is harm, how concerning is the defendant's conduct) or even functional arguments (is it reasonable to impose liability in light of the available resources?). Yet where statutory text is clearer and more indicative, textual and historical arguments receive more attention.

29 An influential basic idea, as shown in the present judgment, is that the legislator also *implies* more or less concern for individual claimants through their general statutory language when imposing duties. Two aspects may speak against this approach. First, it may not immediately be clear to readers from other jurisdictions why the legislator's rhetoric should be so relevant for tort law. This is arguably due to a comparatively strong appreciation of original intent in (part of) Austrian

48 It issued a second decision using this style on the same day as the one discussed: OGH 25.4.2023, 1 Ob 39/23a EvBl 2024/1 with cmt by *D Messner-Kreuzbauer.*

49 The following discussion relies on thoughts in *Messner-Kreuzbauer*, RdW 2023/410.

50 *BA Koch*, The Liability of Public Authorities in Austria, in: K Oliphant (ed), The Liability of Public Authorities in Comparative Perspective (2016) no 38 ff.

51 See *Koziol* (fn 37) no 7/15 ff.

52 On this idea, see *Karollus* (fn 36) 343 ff, 369 ff; *R Rebhahn*, Staatshaftung wegen mangelnder Gefahrenabwehr (1997) 245 ff.

scholarship.[53] Second, however, even if one generally shares this enthusiasm for uncovering the historical legislator's intentions, it remains questionable whether the present decision comes close to proving a relevant and weighty intention.[54] Does the reference to public health language used in 1913 really mean that 'the legislator' 'wanted' to bar claims under tort law, although such claims did not even exist against public authorities before the AHG was passed in 1949? Does public health language signal any lack of concern for the individual at all, or does it merely refer to issues where many, but nonetheless relevant, individuals are involved?

The decision is arguably least convincing where it denies even a potential liability for the authorities' alleged misrepresentations. While it is true that some case law limits information liability to individual relations inviting specific trust of the claimant,[55] this limitation was introduced for pure economic losses.[56] According to general tort liability principles, responsibility for misleading health information is not limited in this way – thus arguably, the OGH modified the rule instead of merely relying on it. It is also worth noting the bizarre situation that, following the recent developments in the diesel emissions scandal reported above,[57] vehicle manufacturers' misinformation on vehicle emissions creates a 'direct link' between individuals and car manufacturers and is thus actionable in tort, while public authorities' misinformation on health issues does not give rise to such a link, producing no action in tort. 30

The judgment leaves the impression that the Court did not debate what mattered most, namely, whether and under what circumstances imposing a tort law duty to protect from epidemics is reasonable considering an epidemic's potential to cause mass harm – a question which requires an open debate of analogous 31

53 The Austrian version of originalism (historical interpretation, historische Interpretation) tends to take the form of 'original intent', though aspects of 'original meaning' are not unknown. Generally, Austrian doctrine is pluralist, often placing greater emphasis on arguments based on coherence (systematic interpretation, systematische Interpretation) and functional arguments (teleological interpretation, teleologische Interpretation). For a pronounced preference for 'historical' arguments, see *F Kerschner/J Kehrer* in: F Kerschner/A Fenyves/A Vonkilch, Klang-Kommentar zum ABGB (3rd edn 2014) nos 15 ff, 32 ff, 99 ff; for the arguably more mainstream method leaning towards the other arguments, *F Bydlinski*, Juristische Methodenlehre und Rechtsbegriff (2nd edn 1991) 533 ff, 577 ff.

54 One of the most influential analyses of breach of statutory duties in Austrian law takes a skeptical view on the significance of such arguments. See *Karollus* (fn 36) 343 ff, 348, 359. See also *G Wagner*, Deliktsrecht (14th edn 2021) no 114 with reference to *G Williams:* 'looking for what is not there'.

55 See *E Karner*, Amtshaftungsansprüche des Kreditgebers bei unrichtiger Baulandbestätigung, Zeitschrift für das gesamte Bank- und Börsenwesen (ÖBA) 2001, 235.

56 *Karner*, ÖBA 2001, 237.

57 Above no 2 ff.

cases and of principle, as well as of deterrence and institutional concerns.[58] Finally, it should be briefly noted that the Court did not have to discuss the – likely – contributory responsibility of the claimant in light of its full rejection of any claim.

4. OGH 17 August 2023, 5 Ob 82/23d:[59] Wrongful Birth; Mental Harm Suffered by Sibling

a) Brief Summary of the Facts

32 The claimant in this case is a minor girl. The defendant is the obstetrician who treated the claimant's mother during her pregnancy with the claimant's younger brother. The defendant had failed to inform the claimant's mother about additional examination methods which would have substantially increased the likelihood of detection of the heart defect the claimant's brother was suffering from.[60] The claimant claims to have suffered mental harm reaching the level of an injury to health (*Krankheitswert*), which was due, on the one hand, to the level of care required for her brother having detrimental effects on the care provided to the claimant and, on the other hand, to the social isolation necessary to avoid health risks to her brother. Had the defendant informed the claimant's mother correctly, the claimant argues, her mother would have opted for the additional examination, the heart defect would have been detected and the claimant's mother would have opted for an abortion. Consequently, the mental harm suffered by the claimant would not have occurred.

---

58 *Messner-Kreuzbauer*, RdW 2023/410. This article concludes that, as in nervous shock and bereavement cases, a limitation of actionable losses to a defined class of first-order victims should be preferred to denying all liability. For further in-depth analyses of the principles and policies relevant for public authority liability from an Austrian perspective, see *F Bydlinski*, Methodological Approaches to the Tort Law of the ECHR, in: A Fenyves/E Karner/H Koziol/E Steiner (eds), Tort Law in the Jurisprudence of the European Court of Human Rights (2011) esp no 2/71 ff; *Rebhahn* (fn 52) 324 ff.

59 ECLI:AT:OGH0002:2023:0050OB00082.23D.0817.000; Zeitschrift für Familien- und Erbrecht (EF-Z) 2024/6 with cmt by *Schwarzenegger* = EvBl 2024/106 with cmt by *BC Steininger* = Recht der Medizin Leitsätze (RdM-LS) 2023/133 = Zeitschrift für Gesundheitsrecht (ZfG) 2023, 135.

60 The defendant's liability towards the mother was affirmatively dealt with in separate proceedings.

b) Judgment of the Court

The OGH's decision focuses on the question of whether the treatment contract between the claimant's mother also protected the claimant. According to Austrian law, third persons who are foreseeably at a greater risk of suffering harm due to the performance of a contract and who belong to the sphere of interest of one of the contracting parties are also protected. 33

The OGH argues that the claimant, as a minor child, is, in principle, included in the protective purpose of her mother's contract with the defendant. However, the 5th panel of the Court also holds that, in the case of a violation of contractual duties, liability will only arise if interests which the contractual duty aimed to protect are harmed. The OGH continues by examining the purpose of the treatment contract, arguing that a treatment contract on prenatal diagnosis also aims at detecting developmental disorders and malformations of the unborn child and at creating a basis for deciding how to proceed. In the view of the OGH, the doctor's duty is limited by objective foreseeability of a risk to the interests of the doctor's contractual partner. In the view of the Court, the parents' financial interests are covered by the protective purpose of the treatment contract, as it is foreseeable that, in the case of a serious disability, a termination of the pregnancy may also be performed because of the considerable expenses which will be incurred for a disabled child. 34

However, the mental harm reaching the level of an injury to health (*Krankheitswert*) suffered by the claimant is, in the view of the OGH, not covered by the protective purpose of the treatment contract, as the suffering of such harm as a consequence of a mere violation of duties to inform about possible examination methods is not foreseeable. The 5th panel continues by arguing that the risk to the claimant's interests did not result from the fact that her parents did not have a basis for a decision about terminating the pregnancy but would be the consequence of the existence of the (disabled) child. Finally, the Court holds that the child itself – irrespective of whether it is disabled or not – is not seen as damage but, quite to the contrary, as a non-material enrichment. Consequently, the OGH rejected the claimant's extraordinary appeal. 35

c) Commentary

The OGH focused its decision on the question of whether the claimant was covered by the protective purpose of the treatment contract between her mother and the 36 defendant.[61] We are, therefore, confronted with a grey area between tortious and contractual liability. By way of this concept of a contract with protective purpose in favour of third parties,[62] claimants can benefit from the advantages of contractual liability. However, to ensure that the dividing line between contractual and tortious liability is not blurred, the OGH has repeatedly stressed the need to define the circle of persons protected narrowly. It is, therefore, no surprise that the OGH denied the claimant's claim.

37 The core argument of the Supreme Court is the lack of foreseeability of the harm suffered by the claimant. As stressed elsewhere[63] the line of argumentation does not seem to be precise enough in this respect. After all, it is hard to see why it should be foreseeable that parents may opt for the termination of a pregnancy in the case of a severe disability of their unborn child for financial reasons, while it is not foreseeable that the wellbeing of elder siblings may also play a decisive role in this decision. It could, of course, be argued that an encroachment upon the sibling's wellbeing reaching the level of an injury to health could not be foreseen. However, earlier decisions on shock damage[64] suggest that changes to the care situation may have quite severe consequences, in particular for very young children. Moreover, it has to be taken into account that the harm suffered by the claimant is a violation of her health, a higher ranking good than the pure economic loss suffered by the parents. If information duties aim to protect the parents' pure economic interests, the same can be argued for a sibling's health.

38 We are certainly faced with a borderline case here, where arguments for both accepting and denying a protective purpose of the treatment contract can validly be put forward. However, the additional arguments of the Court, namely that the harm is the consequence of the child's existence and that a child cannot be considered damage, seem problematic, in particular because the OGH has rejected this line of argumentation in wrongful birth and wrongful conception cases concerning the compensation of maintenance costs for the unplanned child.[65] If a distinction can be made between the child and the maintenance costs for the child, the same distinction can be drawn between the child and a sibling's health.

61 A claim based on tort was only very briefly mentioned but not dealt with in any further detail.

62 See on this, *H Koziol*, Österreichisches Haftpflichtrecht II (3rd edn 2018) A/2/356 ff.

63 *Steininger*, EvBl 2024, 362 f.

64 Cf OGH 16.6.1994, 2 Ob 45/93; cf also 2 Ob 111/03t, EvBl 2004/1.

65 OGH 11.12.2007, 5 Ob 148/07m, reported by *BC Steininger*, Austria, in: H Koziol/BC Steininger (eds), ETL 2007 (2008) 134, no 61 ff.

5. OGH 9 September 2023, 2 Ob 126/23b:[66] Mental Shock Suffered by Stepfather of a Deceased 17-Year-Old Primary Victim

a) Brief Summary of the Facts

The claimant's stepson was killed in a car accident negligently caused by the first defendant in a car insured by the second defendant. The claimant had known his stepson since the latter was five years old, when he met the boy's mother in 2010. He moved in with the boy and his mother, whom he married in 2011, and, in 2012, a son of the claimant and the mother was born. From the beginning, the claimant had a warm relationship with his stepson, whom he treated as his first son. Together with his wife, he took care of the stepson's upbringing, and in all respects acted as a caring father. He looked after the boy's schooling and dealt with his drug problems. The stepson regarded the claimant as his father and only saw his biological father when visiting his grandmother abroad once a year. The stepson, his mother, his half-brother and the claimant lived together as a family. In 2019, the claimant changed his official residence to another apartment (employer-provided housing) in the same city and family life was lived in both apartments as the first was too small for the family. 39

After his stepson's death, the claimant suffered mental harm reaching the level of an injury to health (referred to as shock damage under Austrian law) and claimed compensation for the mental harm suffered (*Schockschadensschmerzengeld*). While the Court of First Instance awarded compensation, the Court of Appeal rejected the claim, arguing that the claimant was not part of the deceased's nuclear family and that awarding compensation to members of a stepfamily would open the floodgates of liability. 40

b) Judgment of the Court

The OGH starts by stressing that in shock damage cases, ie cases of mental harm reaching the level of an injury to health, § 1325 of the Austrian Civil Code, the 41

66 ECLI:AT:OGH0002:2023:0020OB00126.23B.0919.000; JBl 2023, 731 = ZVR 2024/6 with cmt by *BC Steininger* = EvBl 2024/82. See also *T Schoditsch*, Die schadenersatzrechtliche "Kernfamilie" im Licht des Art 8 MRK, ÖJZ 2024, 283.

ABGB, on bodily injury applies.[67] The wrongfulness of the tortfeasor's conduct is not based on the norm aimed at avoiding the harm caused to the primary victim, in the case at hand, the rules regulating motorised traffic, but derives from the violation of the secondary victim's absolutely protected right to bodily integrity. It is decisive that the conduct of the tortfeasor is highly apt to cause a mental shock to the secondary victim, which will typically be the case if the secondary victim witnessed or was informed of the death of a close relative. According to the OGH, in shock damage cases, the health impairment suffered serves as an objective indicator of the existence and extent of the non-pecuniary harm suffered. This speaks in favour of drawing the circle of persons entitled to compensation wider than in cases of mere bereavement not reaching the level of an injury to health.

42 The 2nd panel of the OGH then continues by referring to various provisions in the law in which a stepfamily relationship is referred to (eg § 139 sec 2 sentence 1 ABGB; art 8 ECHR) from which it derives a tendency of the legislator to equate the stepparent/stepchild relationship with the parent/child relationship under certain conditions. For the case at hand, the OGH concludes that stepfather, mother, minor stepson and, as of 2012, his half-brother lived in the same household for years. The fact that family life partly took place in another apartment does not change this result. The stepfather 'replaced' the biological father by taking care of his stepson as a caring father. In view of the relationship lived, the OGH considered the stepfather to be a relative entitled to damages for pain and suffering for shock damage.

c) Commentary

43 A decisive factor for assessing whether the conduct of the tortfeasor was highly apt to cause mental harm to the secondary victim typically is whether a close emotional relationship existed between the primary and the secondary victim. As there clearly was such a relationship between the claimant and his stepson, the result of the present decisions merits full approval. As far as the reasoning is concerned, some points do, however, remain unclear:[68] in particular, the OGH's reference to the tendency of the legislator to equate the stepparent/stepchild relationship with the parent/child relationship under certain conditions leaves open whether stepchildren/stepparents should generally be considered as members of the nucle-

67 According to this provision, the person harmed is entitled to compensation for healing costs and loss of earnings and can claim damages for pain and suffering.
68 See on the following *Steininger*, ZVR 2024, 22.

ar family[69]or whether a close emotional relationship needs to be proven in every individual case. One could also require additional objective indications such as a common household for classifying stepchildren/stepparents as members of the nuclear family. Compared to a mere reference to the stepchildren/stepparents relationship, such an approach is preferable as it would make it easier to identify scenarios in which a close emotional relationship typically exists.[70]

The OGH did not have to deal with the question of mere bereavement, ie suffering that does not reach the level of an injury to health (*Trauerschmerzengeld*). 44
For lack of a health impairment suffered, the objective indicator available in shock damage scenarios is lacking in such cases of mere bereavement and, therefore, the formal family relationship is more important.[71] Nevertheless, it has been held convincingly in literature that proof of a sufficiently close emotional relationship will justify compensation even if there is no formal family relationship.[72] Against this background, even compensation for mere bereavement would have been justified in the case at hand as a close emotional relationship existed. The stepchildren/stepparents relationship could therefore serve as an objective indicator for establishing a sufficiently close emotional relationship – in particular when combined with a common household over an appropriate period of time.[73]

6. OGH 28 September 2023, 10 Ob 27/23b: Diesel Emissions Scandal, Part II: Error of Law and Damages Without Loss[74]

a) Brief Summary of the Facts

This is another case in the current mass litigation against several car manufactur- 45
ers in the 'diesel emissions scandal' in Austria. In 2017, the claimant bought a used vehicle, produced by the defendant in 2024, for € 31,000. It had approx 94,500 km

69 On this term, see *K-H Danzl*, Handbuch Schmerzengeld (2019) no 3.70; *E Karner*, Zur Ersatzfähigkeit von Schock- und Trauerschäden, in: FS Danzl (2017) 99 ff.

70 *Steininger*, ZVR 2024, 22.

71 See *Karner* (fn 69) 99 ff.

72 *E Karner*, cmt on OGH 8 Ob 127/02p, ZVR 2002, 393, who provides the example of a distant relative who took in a child without formally adopting it.

73 *Steininger*, ZVR 2024, 22.

74 ECLI:AT:OGH0002:2023:0100OB00027.23B.0928.000; VbR 2023, 177 with cmt by *P Leupold/B Gelbmann* as well as *B Wallner*; ZVR 2024/46 with cmt by *C Müller/A Wittwer*. See further *Lutschonig*, ZVR 2024, 103 ff; *M Spitzer*, Schadenersatz ohne Schaden bei Dieselmotoren, ÖJZ 2024, 260; *A Riedler*, Schadensberechnung im Abgasskandal: Mindestschaden 5 % – Maximalschaden 15 % des jeweiligen Kaufpreises des absichtlich betrogenen Käufers? VbR 2024, 200.

and was powered by an engine type EA897. While this engine was not rigged with a defeat device sensitive to test modes, it only fulfilled the reported emission limits between 17 and 37°C: it had a 'thermal window'. The claimant would not have bought the car if he had known this, not even for a lower price. However, he apparently did not wish to return the vehicle later and only pursued a claim for € 9,300. He submits that this represents the value the car lost through the thermal window installation, which he alleged to be illegal. The Court of First Instance dismissed the claim, because it could not find the claimant to have suffered any harm. The Court of Appeal reversed this decision, finding that an 'abstract assessment' of harm is possible, so that the claimant may obtain compensation upon proof of the lost market value of the car. However, it also held that the defendant's negligence is not yet established.

b) Judgment of the Court

46 The OGH confirms the decision of the Court of Appeal. This confirmation relies, again, on the CJEU's judgment in *Mercedes-Benz Group AG*, but also on the leading case reported above,[75] as well as a landmark judgment of the German BGH.[76] The OGH's own leading case had already clarified the relevant cause of action in emissions scandal cases, and thus, in the present case, the OGH simply refers to the precedent. The reasoning on the present decision only discusses two central questions further, namely, (1) whether the defendant may defend itself by reference to an error of law, since it claimed not to have intentionally breached the regulatory framework, and (2) whether the claimant in the present case may claim the reduction in value from the producer (referred to as 'small compensation' in the Germanic discourse) instead of claiming the price versus return of the vehicle (referred to as 'large compensation').

47 The Supreme Court first notes that according to *Mercedes-Benz Group AG*, the 'unlawfulness' is 'liable to create uncertainty as to the possibility of registering, selling or entering into service that vehicle and, ultimately, to harm the purchaser of a vehicle equipped with an illegal defeat device.'[77] On the basis of this quote, the OGH assumes that the CJEU must mean that concluding an undesired contract (with the seller) is itself actionable harm. However, the Supreme Court confirms

75 No 2 ff.

76 BGH 26.6.2023, VIa ZR 335/21. The OGH tends to compare or even support its decisions on difficult cases with those of its German counterpart, provided that the legal context is similar (which in itself is of course often debatable).

77 C-100/21 *Mercedes-Benz Group AG* no 84.

that the defendant's negligence was not yet established since they had alleged an error of law. The OGH explained that this error may be a suitable excuse under certain circumstances, although the defendant bears the burden of proof of that error. The producer would have to prove that it could not reasonably be expected to understand the correct legal assessment of the framework. If there was not already a decision by a competent authority taking account of the specific issue (the 'thermal window') justifying its good faith, it would further have to show that the relevant authority, if duly confronted with the question, would have made the same mistake as the defendant.

Besides setting out these guidelines for relevant errors of law, the Court pro- 48
vides new criteria on how to assess damages in such a case should the defendant be liable. Again, referring to *Mercedes-Benz Group AG*, the Court quotes the CJEU (and art 46 of the Framework Directive) as saying that sanctions must be 'effective, proportionate and dissuasive'. Explicitly following the example of the German BGH,[78] the OGH comes to the conclusion that the claimant in a scenario such as this can at least claim 5% and at most 15% of the vehicle's value, whereas the trial court must infer the precise figure via an estimation of loss under § 273 (1) Civil Procedure Ordinance (*Zivilprozessordnung*, ZPO). The OGH specifically denies that this estimation may be called into question by way of evidence on the car's actual loss of value or even by *positive proof* that their vehicle did not lose *any* economic value, and that evidence such as expert opinions should not be accepted on this issue.

c) Commentary

This decision again quickly became a point of reference for other panels of the 49
OGH.[79] While the Supreme Court's position on errors of law is rather convincing, academics have heavily criticised the assessment of damages proposed in this decision,[80] with good reason.

The reported decision shows well how wrong an old assumption on errors of 50
law – namely that they are generally irrelevant (compare § 2 ABGB) – is.[81] The Su-

78 BGH 26.6.2023, VIa ZR 335/21.

79 OGH 19.10.2023, 8 Ob 88/22g; see also 23.1.2024, 2 Ob 3/24s.

80 *Lutschonig*, ZVR 2024, 106 f; *C Müller/A Wittwer*, ZVR 2024/46; *Riedler*, VbR 2024, 207 f; *Spitzer*, ÖJZ 2024, 264 ff.

81 On this assumption, and a (historical) lack of allowance for errors of law in Austrian tort law, *A Geroldinger*, Der mutwillige Rechtsstreit (2017) 749 ff; *H Koziol*, Rechtsunkenntnis und Schadenszurechnung (2022) no 10 ff (fittingly, with an example from CJEU case law).

preme Court convincingly refused to admonish everyone who did not foresee rather surprising findings of law by a competent court (such as the CJEU). However, the test proposed by the OGH for this defence may seem too heavily focused on the specific competent authority in charge. While trust in an actual decision merits protection, the relevance of trust in hypothetical decisions of the authorities remains more obscure. We suggest it must first be asked whether the defendant, if they acted otherwise in good faith, was under a duty to provide further information to the authorities. If so, it might still be open to them to defend themselves by reference to the hypothetical, mistaken decision (this is formally a question of alternative conduct, *rechtmäßiges Alternativverhalten*).[82]

51 Regarding the standard of care applied to legal knowledge, *Koziol* has argued that its strictness should depend on the extent to which the black-letter law in question already provides answers, and to what extent the courts must deliver new arguments for solving an interpretive problem.[83] Although the language of the regulatory framework was not overly clear before a number of CJEU decisions,[84] the OGH must assume that the defendant could have at least taken notice of the *potential* relevance of the thermal window, even if it were admitted that it could not foresee its violation of the regulatory framework. It would have to be carefully examined to what extent such an obligation is itself reasonable at which stage in time.

52 Concerning the problem of assessment, simply imposing on the trial court that it *must* find a range of 5–15 % of the car's value as damages is a clear challenge to the coherence of the Austrian tort system.[85] Where restitution in kind is not feasible and damages must be awarded in money, Austrian law generally acknowledges two 'methods' for calculating the award (*Berechnungsmethoden*).[86] First, as in other Germanic systems, the claimant's lost net worth sometimes constitutes the relevant loss ('difference principle', or 'concrete assessment of damages', *konkrete Schadensberechnung*), but this need not be further discussed because the OGH's 5–15 % award clearly does not attempt to define such a lost net worth. Second,

82 *Geroldinger* (fn 81) 779, 785 debates this question and argues against allowing a defence purely on this basis.

83 See *Koziol* (fn 81) no 256 ff, 276 ff, distinguishing between genuine and pseudo judge-made law, as well as between infringements of a clearly defined right and other types of wrongfulness. Roughly, Koziol argues that infringements of clearly defined rights demand the highest standards of care concerning the applicable law, while the standard for other types, especially in cases of genuine judge-made law, should be more lenient.

84 In particular CJEU 17.12.2020, C-693/18, *CLCV ua*, ECLI:EU:C:2020:1040.

85 See the refs in fn 80 above.

86 *E Karner*, Austria, in: B Winiger/H Koziol/BA Koch/R Zimmermann (eds), Digest of European Tort Law vol II: Essential Cases on Damage (2011) 2/3 no 3.

the Supreme Court and part of academia accept an 'abstract assessment of damages' (*abstrakte Schadensberechnung*), oriented at the market value of an infringed entitlement rather than the claimant's lost net worth – indeed proponents say this is the point of departure in Austrian law (compare § 1331 f ABGB).

One might assume some proximity between the 5–15% clause and the abstract assessment, because they are both an 'abstraction' from some potentially relevant facts. However, the assessment proposed in the present decision is not an abstract assessment in the Austrian sense for at least two reasons.[87] First, an abstract assessment requires the complete loss or diminishment of a clearly defined *entitlement* (*Rechtsgut*). As has often been remarked in relation to other cases, a mere loss of value or potential use is not sufficient, since the value or use in itself does not enjoy specific protection.[88] Second, in our view, an abstract assessment allows abstraction from aspects of the claimant's position but surely not any invention of harm. If the Supreme Court denies that there is any role for experts and other evidence to play in finding the relevant value, then that must mean that there are no facts to find (other than the initial purchasing price). This fact-free assessment of harm either boils down to an extreme oversimplification of a possible harm (uncertainty about future loss of use), or to harm which is nothing but 'normative' (ie, invented). It is quite astonishing to observe an award of such damages without regard to substantive and procedural principles on very thin grounds of efficiency and consumer protection. 53

To be fair, the OGH might be defended under the circumstances, for what other options remain if EU law (the CJEU) demands 'effective, proportionate and dissuasive' sanctions? Certainly, this decision was not easy to make, but we suggest that there could have been better options. First, as the decision reported above[89] held, an Austrian claimant who would not have bought the affected vehicle can generally claim their payment to the seller from the producer if they return the car and deduct the value of its use. That may already be 'effective, proportionate and dissuasive' enough, since the CJEU did not say that there must be 'schematic damages' in each and every case.[90] Second, even if one takes *Mercedes-Benz* 54

87 Similarly *Lutschonig*, ZVR 2024, 106 f; *Spitzer*, ÖJZ 2024, 267.

88 See *E Karner*, Fragen der objektiv-abstrakten Schadensberechnung in: S Perner/S Rubin/M Spitzer/A Vonkilch (eds), Festschrift für Attila Fenyves (2013) 189, 201 f; *H Koziol*, Objektiv-abstrakte und subjektiv-konkrete Schadensberechnung, JBl 2023, 758, 766 ff; on the present case *Spitzer*, ÖJZ 2024, 266 f.

89 No 2 ff.

90 *Lutschonig*, ZVR 2024, 107; *Riedler*, VbR 2024, 204, 207 ff; *Spitzer*, ÖJZ 2024, 265 f; see also *Birkholz*, VersR 2023, 1121 (on the analogous BGH decision).

Group AG as demanding damages without loss, it is arguably better to be clear and say this. Even if bound in terms of results, national law is still free to call such an imposition what it is: treating a loss that is very uncertain at best as certain and calculable for the sake of consumer protection and efficiency. And if the methods of Austrian law do not allow this, then the courts are not entitled to bend the rules, even at the risk of provoking a violation of EU directives.[91] In sum, reception of the German BGH's 5–15% rule was not the best possible way of upholding the integrity of the Austrian tort system against the challenging impulses from Luxembourg.

55 Finally, is a deduction of benefits convincing for such damages if one accepts them as a (questionable) premise? The consequential answer must be no.[92] Where an 'assessment' is insensitive to (nearly) all relevant facts, the assessment of benefits should follow the same level of abstraction (that is, it should be made without regard to any facts other than the purchasing price and the 5–15% formula).

7. OGH 21 November 2023, 3 Ob 9/23d:[93] Wrongful Birth

a) Brief Summary of the Facts

56 The defendant is an obstetrician who treated the first claimant during her second pregnancy. The second claimant is the first claimant's husband and father of the unborn child. In the course of the pregnancy, the defendant performed several ultrasound screenings, but negligently failed to detect that the claimants' daughter

91 On this methodological constraint, see *P Bydlinski*, Richtlinienkonforme "gesetzesübersteigende" Rechtsfindung und ihre Grenzen – eine methodische Vergewisserung anlässlich 20 Jahre EU-Mitgliedschaft, JBl 2015, 2, 3 ff.

92 Similarly, *Lutschonig*, ZVR 2024, 106 f. Compare also, before the present decision, *A Riedler*, Abgasskandal – KEIN Benützungsentgelt bei bloßer Preisminderung und "kleinem Schadenersatz", VbR 2022, 120 ff. By contrast, the BGH 26.6.2023, VIa ZR 335/21 accepted a limited deduction (similarly *Müller/Wittwer* in their cmt to the present decision, ZVR 2024/46).

93 ECLI:AT:OGH0002:2023:0030OB00009.23D.0707.000; EF-Z 2024/25 with cmt by *Schickmair* (EF-Z 2024/43) = EvBl 2024/49 with cmt by *E Karner* = Interdisziplinäre Zeitschrift für Familienrecht (iFamZ) 2024, 16 with cmt by *M Neumayer* = JBl 2024, 178 = Medizinrecht (MedR) 2024, 344 with cmt by *Bernat* = Österreichische Zeitschrift für Pflegerecht (ÖZPR) 2024/15 = RdM 2024/24 with cmt by *BC Steininger* = VbR 2024/11 with cmt by *Leitner* = Zivilrecht aktuell (Zak) 2024/57 = Zeitschrift für Versicherungsrecht (ZVers) 2024, 94. See on this also *S Oechsner/S Lagger-Zach*, "Wrongful birth", "wrongful conception" und Art 5 UN-BRK, Zak 2024, 68; *D Prisching/B Sommer*, Schadenersatzrechtliche Gleichstellung von "wrongful birth" und "wrongful conception", Zak 2024, 104; *P Schwarzenegger*, Wrongful birth und wrongful conception – weiterführende Überlegungen zu OGH (verstärkter Senat) 3 Ob 9/23d, JBl 2024, 366.

suffered from amelia, ie she lacks her left upper limb. The girl only has a rudimentary arm bud and her entire left chest and shoulder area is developed insufficiently, which results in reduced mobility, motor skills and participation in daily life. She has difficulties performing everyday activities, in particular those which are usually performed with both hands.

The claimants argue that, had they been informed of their daughter's disability, they would have opted for an abortion. The lack of the girl's arm should already have been detected during the first trimester screening, at a time when an abortion under § 97 sec 1 no 1 StGB would still have been possible. According to this provision, abortions are exempt from punishment if performed within the first three months of pregnancy (so-called *Fristenlösung*). At a later stage, abortions are permissible under Austrian law according to § 97 sec 1 no 2 StGB if there is a serious risk that the unborn child will be severely mentally or physically disabled. 57

The claimants argue that they would have opted for an abortion at any rate and they claim compensation for their daughter's entire maintenance costs since her birth and bring an action for a declaratory judgment concerning the defendant's liability for future harm caused by the diagnostic error (including future maintenance costs). Both the Court of First Instance and the Court of Appeal awarded the claimants compensation and declared the defendant liable. 58

b) Judgment of the Court

Unlike in earlier decisions, the OGH acknowledges that its past practice on compensation for maintenance costs in wrongful birth and wrongful conception cases was inconsistent. It therefore holds that an amplified panel[94] of the OGH should decide the case.[95] The amplified panel then carefully analyses the OGH's past practice and extensively examines the controversial literature on the topic. On this basis, it reaches the following conclusions: 59

While the child's birth or existence cannot constitute damage in the sense of the law, financial expenses resulting from the child's birth, in particular the cost of 60

94 According to § 8 Bundesgesetz über den Obersten Gerichtshof (Act on the Supreme Court, OGHG), a regular panel is to be amplified if its decision would depart from established practice of the Supreme Court or if the legal question has not been solved consistently in the OGH's practice.

95 OGH 7.7.2023, 3 Ob 9/23d, ECLI:AT:OGH0002:2023:0030OB00009.23D.0707.000; Zak 2023/510 = RdM 2023/60 with cmt by *C Kopetzki*. Critical from a procedural point of view *S Perner/M Spitzer*, ÖJZ 2023, 693.

maintenance, can. In the view of the amplified panel, this must apply to any unwanted child, regardless of whether it is born healthy or with a disability.

61 The OGH argues that prenatal diagnostics not least aim to detect disabilities of the unborn child and to enable parents to decide on opting for a legally permissible termination of pregnancy. The claimants' compensation claim presupposes that the first claimant, had she been adequately informed, could have had a lawful abortion. Although an abortion on the basis of § 97 sec 1 no 1 in the first three months of pregnancy is, according to common opinion, only exempt from punishment but nevertheless illegal, the child's disability would, according to the OGH, have justified an abortion under § 97 sec 1 no 2 StGB. In the view of the amplified panel, an abortion would, therefore, have been lawful – even if performed within the first three months of pregnancy.

62 The amplified panel further states that non-pecuniary advantages brought about by the child cannot reduce or eliminate a compensation claim of the parents. Moreover, it holds that damages cannot be limited to the additional maintenance costs brought about by the disability of the child. While it is clear that the defendant caused the entire maintenance costs, the OGH also stresses that the protective purpose of the treatment contract covers the entire maintenance costs, as the contract should have enabled the parents to take a decision for or against an abortion also from the point of view of avoiding financial burdens. In the view of the amplified panel, awarding only the additional costs brought about by the disability could only be reached by comparing the disabled child with a fictional healthy child, which would not only be incorrect from the point of view of tort law but would, moreover, emphasise the disability and thereby be discriminatory.

63 Both in the case of a medical intervention aimed at contraception as well as in the case of prenatal diagnostics, the financial interests of the mother (parents) to prevent conception or – if the prerequisites of § 97 sec 1 no 2 StGB are met – the birth of a (further) child, are covered by the protective purpose of the medical treatment contract. If the child would not have been conceived or born had the mother (parents) been treated or informed properly, the doctor – irrespective of any disability of the child – is liable in particular for the child's maintenance costs.

c) Commentary

64 In the past, the OGH was confronted with the question of whether maintenance costs for an unplanned child can be compensated on several occasions. Its practice was, however, inconsistent: one group of decisions concerned cases in which the unborn child's disability was not detected during pregnancy, which prevented parents from opting for an abortion. In these cases, referred to by the OGH as *wrong-*

ful birth cases, compensation was awarded for the entire maintenance costs of the child born with a disability.[96] In a second group of cases, the OGH held that maintenance costs for an unplanned child can be compensated only exceptionally in the case of an extraordinary burden on the parents, be it because of their limited financial resources or because of special needs of the child. This second line of cases relates to the birth of children whose conception should have been prevented by the defendant and who do not suffer from a disability (cases referred to by the OGH as *wrongful conception* cases).[97] These two lines of case law were based on two main strands of argumentation in doctrine, the first assuming that maintenance costs constitute pecuniary damage as the maintenance obligation placed on the parents reduces their patrimony and are, therefore, generally compensable (*Trennungsthese*), while the second argued that the tortfeasor's conduct does not merely cause maintenance costs but leads to a comprehensive family relationship, which can only be considered as pecuniary loss in exceptional cases, namely if an extraordinary burden is placed on parents (*gemäßigte Einheitsthese*).[98]

As the law lacks precise rules on this question, and the legislator failed to take action, court practice had to provide a solution. Both main positions set out in legal doctrine were based on legitimate arguments so either of them provided a viable solution.[99] What was, however, not an option was to follow both of them as this must lead to contradictory results: if, on the one hand, one assumes that maintenance costs can only be compensated exceptionally in the case of an extraordinary burden, it is not evident why the basic maintenance costs for a child with a disability should always be such an extraordinary burden. On the other hand, if the entire maintenance costs for a disabled child are compensated, it is hard to see why the maintenance costs for a child born without a disability cannot be compensated. Even more problematic than the contradiction between different decisions as such was that the OGH drew the line between the two groups of cases depending on whether the child was disabled or not, a discriminatory starting point which 65

---

96 OGH 7.3.2006, 5 Ob 165/05h, reported by *BC Steininger*, Austria, in: H Koziol/BC Steininger (eds), ETL 2006 (2008) 68, no 5 ff; 11.12.2007, 5 Ob 148/07m, reported in ETL 2007 by *Steininger* (fn 65) no 61 ff.

97 OGH 14.9.2006, 6 Ob 101/06f, reported in ETL 2006 by *Steininger* (fn 96) no 18 ff; 30.11.2006, 2 Ob 172/06t; 7.8.2008, 6 Ob 148/08w, reported by *BC Steininger*, Austria, in: H Koziol/BC Steininger (eds), ETL 2008 (2009) 108, no 55 ff; 29.1.2015, 9 Ob 37/14b, reported by *BC Steininger/J Pehm*, Austria, in: E Karner/BC Steininger (eds), ETL 2015 (2016) 1, no 6 ff; 25.5.2022, 8 Ob 69/21m, reported in ETL 2022 by *Loibl/Nitsch* (fn 21) no 33 ff. Cf also OGH 25.5.1999, 1 Ob 91/99k (for a summary of this decision in English see *Steininger*, ETL 2006 [fn 96] no 13 f).

98 For a comprehensive overview, see *Koziol* (fn 39) B/1/25 ff with further refs.

99 In this sense already, *Steininger*, ETL 2008 (fn 97) no 63 ff.

cannot be decisive for the basic question of whether maintenance costs are compensable or not.[100]

66 It is, therefore, a very positive development that the OGH abandoned its argument, according to which, its two lines of court practice are not contradictory as they concern different factual scenarios (namely, disabled children, on the one hand, and healthy children, on the other), and opts for a decision of an amplified panel.

67 The result reached by this amplified panel to award compensation for the child's maintenance costs irrespective of a disability also merits approval. Generally accepting that maintenance costs constitute compensable damage (*Trennungsthese*) admittedly does not map the complexity of the parent-child relationship, but it brings about a solution which can be handled more easily in practice, as no reference to the rather vague notion of an extraordinary burden is required and pecuniary and non-pecuniary aspects need not be set-off against each other. Moreover, by abandoning its contradictory practice and the differentiation based on disability, the OGH shifts the focus away from a disability of the child and, as such, provides a non-discriminatory and, therefore, much better solution. For the same reason, the amplified panel's argument according to which, the protective purpose of the treatment contract covers the entire maintenance costs and not only the additional expenses brought about by the disability is to be welcomed. When the contract aims to detect disabilities and to enable parents to opt for a legally permissible abortion, this decision entails financial consequences which the parents foreseeably also want to avoid. It is, therefore, not convincing why the fact that parents were willing to pay maintenance for a child when no reason for a permissible abortion existed should limit the protective purpose of the treatment contract.

8. OGH 14 December 2023, 2 Ob 208/23 m:[101] Mental Shock Suffered by the Best Friend of the Primary Victim

a) Brief Summary of the Facts

68 The claimant went on a moped ride with several friends. When a few members of the group stopped at the side of the road, the defendant crashed into the group

100 See *Steininger*, ETL 2008 (fn 97) no 65.
101 ECLI:AT:OGH0002:2023:0020OB00208.23M.1214.000; EvBl 2024/166 with cmt by *C Huber* = Zak 2024/62.

without braking, killing the claimant's best friend and another member of the group and injuring several others. The claimant, who witnessed the accident from a distance of approximately 45 to 50 metres, saw how his friends were thrown through the air. He was with the injured persons within seconds, tried to provide first aid but could not prevent his best friend's death on the spot. This led to the claimant suffering mental shock reaching the level of an injury to health and he claimed compensation for loss of earnings and for pain and suffering. Both the Court of First Instance and the Court of Appeal awarded the claimant compensation, the award for pain and suffering amounting to approximately € 4,000.

b) Judgment of the Court

The OGH refers to its practice on shock damage, ie mental harm reaching the level 69
of an injury to health, and differentiates between two groups of cases. First, close relatives suffering mental shock can claim compensation for pain and suffering irrespective of the question whether they witnessed the accident or were only informed about the death or most severe bodily injury of their relative. Secondly, third persons who are not close relatives of the primary victim but who were directly involved in the accident are also entitled to compensation for their pain and suffering.

The OGH starts by examining whether the claimant falls under the first group 70
and argues that the relationship between the claimant and the primary victim, though very close, is based on mere friendship, which is not a relationship recognised in a special way by the law. To avoid opening the floodgates, best friends like the claimant can, therefore, according to the OGH, not be considered as close relatives of the primary victim.

In a next step, the OGH deals more closely with the second group of cases: it 71
examines its earlier decisions in this field, makes reference to the practice of the German BGH and extensively cites statements in Austrian but also in German literature. Based on this, the OGH draws the conclusion that awarding compensation for mental shock reaching the level of an injury to health to third persons who are not close relatives of the primary victim presupposes a reason for imputation equivalent to the special relationship between close relatives. This prerequisite will be met if the third person was *objectively and in a serious manner directly ex-*

posed to the initial harm.[102] In the view of the OGH, this condition of an *involvement in the accident in a qualified manner* is not only met if the third person was directly involved in or endangered by the accident but may also be fulfilled in comparable scenarios.[103] The fact of a close relationship to the primary victim which does not lead to the third person being considered as a close relative may, according to the OGH, be taken into account in this respect.

72 For the case at hand the OGH holds that the claimant was neither directly involved in the accident nor endangered. Nevertheless, the claimant can, in the view of the OGH, not be considered as a mere uninvolved witness. The claimant had to watch the entire accident from close proximity; an accident which – due to the number of victims and the force of the collision – was particularly horrific. He was at the scene of the accident within seconds and tried to save his best friend's life but had to watch him die on the spot. The OGH concludes that the claimant was *involved in the accident in a qualified manner.* The Court adds that it was foreseeable from an ex ante perspective that driving into a group of moped drivers may cause mental shock to other group members. Therefore, the OGH holds the defendant liable.

c) Commentary

73 The OGH's decision and its careful analysis of potential factual scenarios merits approval. It is convincing that the OGH refrained from diluting the category of close relatives and denied considering even *best* friends as close relatives. This does not mean that the OGH is not willing to take a friendship between the primary and the secondary victim into account, but it does so in a far more appropriate way. While so far persons not being close relatives of the primary victim were only awarded compensation in cases in which they were directly involved in the accident eg as passengers or as the other party to the accident, the OGH now, in a dogmatically convincing way, defines this second group more comprehensively. The decisive question is whether, from a normative point of view, the situation is comparable to those involving close relatives of the primary victim. Starting point is whether the conduct of the first tortfeasor is highly dangerous towards the bodily integrity of the secondary victim.[104]

102 Here, the OGH refers to *E Karner,* Rechtsprechungswende bei Schock- und Fernwirkungsschäden Dritter? ZVR 1998, 182, 188.

103 In this respect, the OGH refers to the arguments put forward by *LB Beisteiner,* Angehörigenschmerzengeld (2009) 206 f.

104 See *Karner,* ZVR 1998, 182 (188); *idem* (fn 69) 94 f; *Koziol* (fn 62) A/5/185 ff.

While close relatives of the primary victim will typically be endangered by the tortfeasor's conduct, there are several other factors which may contribute to making the conduct of the tortfeasor highly dangerous also for the secondary victim.[105] The most prominent ones are, of course, direct involvement in the accident and an endangerment of the secondary victim in the accident. However, when referring to an involvement in the accident in a qualified manner, and completing this reference by addressing involvement in first aid measures, intense confrontation (bodies being thrown through the air) or a pre-existing close relationship (though not being related), the OGH finds a convincing instrument which sets the focus on the question of the risk caused to the secondary victim by the tortfeasor's conduct and at the same time remains flexible enough to deal with future factual scenarios. 74

9. Personal Injury

Apart from the two decisions already covered (cases 5 and 8 above), the OGH, in two further remarkable decisions, decided that a broken intrauterine device may cause psychological harm that is compensable as personal injury[106] and that the affected person may claim damages under the AHG from the Federal State where the public authority monitoring these products fails to exercise due care in its duties.[107] 75

C. Literature

1. *A Fenyves/F Kerschner/A Vonkilch*, Großkommentar zum ABGB – Amtshaftung und Staatshaftung (Verlag Österreich, 2023), with contributions by A Kahl, F Kerschner, E Wagner and T Müller

This book is a commentary on the AHG and the unwritten rules on public authority liability for the violation of EU law. As such it is welcome since Austria lacks an up-to-date academic treatise on public authority liability, and a substantial part of 76

105 Cf Rummel/*Reischauer* (fn 38) § 1325 no 5.

106 OGH 27.6.2023, 1 Ob 28/23h JBl 2024, 41 with cmt by *Schickmair* = Journal für Medizin- und Gesundheitsrecht 2023, 36 with cmt by *Rief* = RdM 2024, 27 with cmt by *Paar* = ecolex 2023, 1032 with cmt by *Pötz*.

107 OGH 25.4.2023, 1 Ob 39/23a EvBl 2024/1 with cmt by *Messner-Kreuzbauer*.

the literature – although without doubt valuable – is written from the view of the officials defending the State against such claims.[108] Some parts on § 1 AHG, on which this very brief review will focus, are authored by an expert in public law (*A Kahl*). This author provides much useful historical and systematic background and context to public authority liability in Austria (§ 1 no 1 ff) and on the problem of finding the right defendant and attributing an official's acts to it with references to public law doctrine (§ 1 no 73 ff). The remainder of the text on this central provision is written by an expert in private law (*E Wagner*), who adds helpful cross-references to general tort law in her part, such as on how the types of wrongs relevant for liability are transformed in public authority liability (§ 1 no 261 ff). Collecting the details on the flood of decisions on one of the crucial aspects of this field, the protective purpose of the norm, must have been hard work that can be very helpful for readers (§ 1 no 306 ff). The book offers a comprehensive documentation of relevant case law, with numerous excerpts from individual decisions. While a detailed analysis of the authors' views is not possible here for lack of space, the work is a very useful exposition of Austrian public authority liability.

2. *C Denkmaier*, Produkthaftung und Digitalisierung (Verlag Österreich) 2023

77 This book offers an analysis of the impact of digitalisation on current product liability rules. It discusses some of the most relevant questions in that area, eg whether data loss should be considered compensable harm (45 ff), whether software is a product (49 ff), who can be identified as a producer where a product is the result of several contributions to a 3D-printout (81 ff), and the relevant yardstick for defects in the case of software and AI products (104 ff). The author gives a good overview on established doctrine and how it struggles with the diminishing relevance of the original concepts and ideas, such as the tangible nature of products (56 ff) and the idea that they are final when placed on the market (123 ff). Moreover, the book addresses known weaknesses of the Austrian law (*Produkthaftungsgesetz*, PHG) transposing the Product Liability Directive, such as the problematic limitation of defendants to the Austrian concept of entrepreneurs (*Unternehmer*) (70 ff), which might become of greater significance in times where software and 3D-printouts are increasingly (co)-produced by non-professionals. In substance, the author argues for the inclusion of modern products and thus takes a relatively

---

108 See notably *M Paar*, Grundzüge des Amtshaftungsrechts (2021); *H Ziehensack*, Amtshaftungsgesetz: Praxiskommentar (2nd edn 2023).

claimant-friendly view. For instance, she argues for understanding software as a product and for comprehensive responsibility for updates. The results are generally convincing and the overview on the debate very useful. In some instances, the line of argumentation could have been expanded, in particular concerning the relation between the purpose of product liability and the risk of modern production and on the weaknesses of the consumer expectations test. Even though the draft Product Liability Directive will likely change the law, this book remains a good guide to some of the problems in the background of the expected new version.

3. Further Selected Literature

Data Protection, Personal Rights, IT and Technology: *I Faber*, Bewertungsplattformen und Persönlichkeitsrechte, in: T Garber (ed), Festschrift Neumayr (2023) 459; *A Gerhartl*, Fragen des Ersatzes immaterieller Schäden bei Datenschutzverletzungen, Zak 2023, 88 78

Environment: *C Huber/P Schultess*, Haftung von Klimaaktivisten: Schadenersatzpflicht bei Angriffen auf Kunstgegenstände, Flughafen-, Gleis- und Straßenblockaden? ÖJZ 2023, 260 79

General: *P Bydlinski*, Zur langen Verjährung auf Straftaten beruhender Schadenersatzansprüche (§ 1489 Satz 2 Fall 2 ABGB), RdW 2023, 318; *P Bydlinski/J Ulbrich*, Die Haftung mündiger Minderjähriger wegen culpa in contrahendo, in: T Garber (ed), Festschrift Neumayr (2023) 431; *M Dangl*, Die Richtlinie über Verbandsklagen zum Schutz der Kollektivinteressen der Verbraucher (2023); *JW Flume*, Zur gesetzlichen Ordnung des Leistungsstörungsrechts, ÖJZ 2023, *F Harrer*, Gehilfen im Deliktsrecht, in: T Garber (ed), Festschrift Neumayr (2023) 497; *C Huber*, Niemals Anrechnung künftiger Vorteile – wie weit reicht das Ausgleichsprinzip? Zak 2023, 24; *S Jahn/S Loibl*, Schadenersatzrechtliche Entwicklungen in Europa 2022 – Bericht über die 22nd Annual Conference on European Tort Law (ACET), ZVR 2023, 431; *G Kodek*, Zivilrechtliche Verantwortung für Lieferanten auf dem Boden der Rechtsdogmatik, in: P Lewisch (ed), Lieferkettenverantwortlichkeit: Wieso – woher – wohin (2023) 77; *H Koziol*, Ausufernder Ersatz für ideelle Schäden? in: T Garber (ed), Festschrift Neumayr (2023) 575; *H Koziol*, Objektiv-abstrakte und subjektiv-konkrete Schadensberechnung, JBl 2023, 758; *M Leitner*, Die zivilrechtliche Zurechnung qualifiziert strafbaren Verhaltens, in: T Garber (ed), Festschrift Neumayr (2023) 587; *M Leitner*, Objektiv-abstrakt berechneter Schadenersatz auch bei subjektiv-konkret geringerem Schaden? Neue Gedanken zu einem ewigen Streit, JBl 2023, 69; *E Ondreasova*, Haftung von juristischen Personen in der Rechtsprechung, in: T Garber (ed), Festschrift Neumayr (2023) 599; *M Pfeiffer*, Schadenersatzanspruch des Leasingnehmers auf das „Substanzinteresse"?! (Teil II), Zeitschrift für Finanz- 80 recht (ZFR) 2023, 121; *R Reischauer*, Schadenersatz wegen Nichterfüllung oder Flume und kein Ende? ÖJZ 2023, 330; *BC Steininger*, Haftung für Menschenrechtsverletzungen in Lieferketten nach österreichischem Recht, in: T Garber (ed), Festschrift Neumayr (2023) 703; *P Warto*, Zur Beweislastumkehr des § 1298 ABGB am Beispiel des „Sturzes im Supermarkt", in: T Garber (ed), Festschrift Neumayr (2023) 725; *L Werderitsch/MM Schweiger*, Der Freistellungsanspruch im Schadenersatzrecht, Zak 2023, 5; *A Wittwer*, Die unrichtige Unterscheidung von Erfolgs- und Sorgfaltsverbindlichkeiten bei der Beweislastumkehr des § 1298 ABGB, in: T Garber (ed), Festschrift Neumayr (2023) 735; *J Zehetner/T Haberer*, Verjährung kartellrechtlicher Schadenersatzansprüche, in: T Garber (ed), Festschrift Neumayr (2023) 749

81 **Investors and Banking:** *L Herndl*, Intertemporale Fragen der Haftung für fehlerhafte Finanzaufsicht, RdW 2023, 329; *C Müller*, Schadenersatzrechtliche Haftung echter Dritter bei Mitwirkung an Verstößen gegen das Einlagenrückgewährverbot? – zugleich eine Besprechung von OGH 23.6.2021, 6 Ob 61/21w, Österreichisches Juristisches Archiv (ÖJA) 2023, 129

82 **Medical Liability:** *A Birklbauer*, Grobe Fahrlässigkeit bei medizinischen Behandlungsfehlern, in: T Garber (ed), Festschrift Neumayr (2023) 2187; *I Harrer-Hörzinger*, Arzthaftung und Verjährung, in: T Garber (ed), Festschrift Neumayr (2023) 2201; *C Katzenmeier*, Neue Wege zur Patientenentschädigung – Beweisrechtliche und haftungsergänzende Lösungen in Österreich und Deutschland, in: T Garber (ed), Festschrift Neumayr (2023) 2251; *C Kopetzki/K Stöger*, Patientenwunsch und Stand der Wissenschaft (2023)

83 **Procedural Law:** *A Geroldinger*, Durchbrechung der Rechtskraft eines Schiedsspruches qua Schadenersatz? in: T Garber (ed), Festschrift Neumayr (2023) 1441; *C Huber*, Ersatzfähigkeit der Kosten eines VersBeraters bei einem verschuldeten Kfz-Unfall, ZVR 2023, 117; *S Perner/M Spitzer*, Schäden und ihre massenweise Geltendmachung, ÖJZ 2023, 513; *A Wilfinger*, Einschüchterungsklagen – Nationale Grundsätze und europäische Perspektiven, ÖJA 2023, 1

84 **Product Liability:** *C Huber*, Viel Lärm um nichts oder doch wenig? JBl 2023, 205; *A Kletečka*, Abschalteinrichtungen in Dieselfahrzeugen vor und nach EuGH C-100/21: Ersatzansprüche der Erwerber gegen die Hersteller? ÖJZ 2023, 388; *C Müller/T Keskin*, Dieselskandal – Zur (Un-)Zulässigkeit eines Thermofensters und zur Frage des Schutzgesetzcharakters einschlägiger europarechtlicher Normen, ZVR 2023, 3

85 **Professionals and Liability of Public Authorities:** *D Messner-Kreuzbauer*, Schutzzwecklehre und Amtshaftungsrecht im Lichte der „Causa Ischgl", RdW 2023/410; *M Paar*, Aktuelles vom OGH zur Abgrenzung zwischen Hoheits- und Privatwirtschaftsverwaltung, ÖJZ 2023, 138; *M Paar*, Die Rettungspflicht nach § 2 Abs 2 AHG, ÖJZ 2023, 696; *H Ziehensack*, Amtshaftungsgesetz: Praxiskommentar (2nd edn 2023)

Real Estate Law: *I Vonkilch*, Haftungsrechtliche Konsequenzen des Besteller- 86
prinzips, wobl 2023, 255

Transportation, Traffic and Infrastructure: *B Borkowski*, Das HaftRÄG 2022: 87
Eine Neuordnung der Haftung für Bäume, ZVR 2023, 57; *K-H Danzl*, Baumsicherungspflichten aus richterlicher Sicht, ZVR 2023, 60; *W Doralt/P Schwarzenegger* (eds), Steinschlag – Rechtlicher Rahmen und Haftung, Verlag Österreich, with contributions by FC Greinix, AS Neubauer and F-J Friedl (2023); *S Haiden*, Fluggastrechte-VO: Der Wortlaut ist nicht das Limit, wirtschaftsrechtliche blätter (wbl) 2023, 121; *E Karner*, Baum- und Wegehalterhaftung im Siedlungsraum sowie in Wald- und Naturgebieten, ZVR 2023, 67; *E Karner/K Zsak*, Baumgefahren-Management in Österreichs Nationalparks (2023); *B König*, Die Haftung der Pistenhalter nach „Pistenschluss", ZVR 2023, 423; *E Lindinger*, Vorteilsausgleich im Reiserecht, ZVR 2023, 300; *L Milacher/M Pfeiffenberger*, Verkehrssicherungspflichten auf der Skipiste, Zak 2023, 204; *F Parapatits/S Perner*, Haftung bei Sportveranstaltungen auf öffentlichen Straßen, in: T Garber (ed), Festschrift Neumayr (2023) 611; *B Pfurtscheller*, Die zivilrechtliche Haftung für Bäume, in: T Garber (ed), Festschrift Neumayr (2023) 627; *M Winzaurek*, Helmobliegenheit beim Rodeln? ZVR 2023, 459; *K Zsak*, Differenziertes Baumgefahren-Management: Möglichkeiten und Voraussetzungen zur Ausweisung naturbelassener Wege, ZVR 2023, 77

Isabelle C Durant

II. Belgium

A. Legislation[1]

1. Arrêté royal du 26 janvier 2023 portant des dispositions complémentaires relatives à l'information précontractuelle qui est fournie au consommateur sur les diamants naturels et synthétiques/Koninklijk besluit van 26 januari 2023 betreffende de nadere bepalingen inzake precontractuele informatie die aan de consumenten verstrekt wordt over natuurlijke en synthetische diamanten (Royal Decree of 26 January 2023 concerning Additional Provisions relating to the Pre-Contractual Information provided to Consumers on Natural and Synthetic Diamonds)[2]

The Belgian Code of Economic Law provides that, as a general rule,[3] before the 1
consumer is bound by a contract, the business must provide them, in a clear and comprehensible manner, with various information listed in art VI.2, para 2. For example, it must provide the main characteristics of the product, its identity, the total price of the product inclusive of all taxes, and any services to be paid compulsorily in addition by the consumer, where applicable, the arrangements for payment, delivery and performance, the date by which it undertakes to deliver the product and the arrangements made for dealing with complaints.

---

1 Belgian Acts, published in the Belgian Official Journal (Moniteur belge/Belgisch Staatsblad) (MB/BS), are available on the website of the Belgian Ministry of Justice: <http://www.ejustice.just.fgov.be/cgi/welcome.pl>.

2 Belgian Official Journal of 1 March 2023 25703 (MB/BS) (<http://ejustice.just.fgov.be/cgi/welcome.pl>).

3 This does not apply to distance contracts, off-premises contracts or the contracts referred to in art VI.66 para 1 of the Code of Economic Law (1° sales of foodstuffs, beverages and other everyday household goods physically delivered by a company on frequent and regular rounds to the consumer's home, place of residence or place of work; 2° insurance contracts; 3° certain sales organised as part of non-commercial events with an exclusively philanthropic purpose; 4° certain credit agreements).

https://doi.org/10.1515/9783111376721-003

2 The same legal provision stipulates that, for the products He designates, the King may specify the additional information that the business provides to the consumer and the manner in which this information is provided to them before the contract is concluded.

3 The King made use of this option in the commented decree of 26 January 2023 concerning planned sales to consumers of an unmounted natural diamond, an unmounted synthetic diamond or a piece of jewellery or watch incorporating one or more natural or synthetic diamonds. The additional information to be provided includes, in particular, information to the effect that the item contains a natural or synthetic diamond, information on the treatment the diamond has undergone, and the weight of the diamond.

4 Since the information must be provided before the contract is concluded, the failure to comply with this information obligation constitutes a tort.[4]

B. Cases[5]

1. Supreme Court (Cour de cassation/Hof van Cassatie) 15 December 2022, C.21.0003.F; Journal des tribunaux (JT) 2023, 614, cmt *F Bouhon/L Fontaine*; Revue de Jurisprudence de Liège, Mons et Bruxelles (JLMB) 2023, 523; Revue Générale des Assurances et des Responsabilités (RGAR) 2023, no 15945: State Liability – Faulty Conduct of the Legislator

a) Brief Summary of the Facts

5 The facts of this case are rooted in the adoption in 2006 by the Belgian federal legislator of an Act establishing the Commission for the Modernisation of the Judiciary.[6] [7] This Act was part of an ambitious reform the aim of which was the decentral-

4 Court of Appeal of Antwerp, 6 June 2023, Limburgs Rechtsleven 2023, 327 (this case concerns an architect contract). Cf *R Steennot*, Precontractuele informatieverplichtingen op grond van artikel VI.2 WER: inhoud, bewijslat en sanctionering, Journal des Juges de Paix/Tijdschrift van de Vrederechters 2021, 562–567.

5 Most of the decisions delivered by the Supreme Court are to be found on Juportal, the public database of Belgian case law (<https://juportal.be/moteur/formulaire>).

6 Loi du 20 juillet 2006 instaurant la Commission de Modernisation de l'Ordre judiciaire et le Conseil général des partenaires de l'Ordre judiciaire/Wet van 20 juli 2006 tot instelling van de Commis-

isation of the management of staff, the budget, equipment and legal costs, on the one hand, and increasing the accountability of the judicial authorities at district level, on the other hand.[8] According to the Act, the Commission was responsible for any action aimed at modernising the management of the judicial system.

After a few years of operation, SL was appointed chairman of the Commission 6
for the first three years of a six-year term of office starting on 1 March 2013, by Royal Decree of 26 February 2013; it was also planned that SL would act as vice-chairman of the Commission for the last three years of his term of office.[9] At the time of his appointment, SL was Deputy Director of a strategic entity of the federal public service responsible for implementing federal policy in the field of justice.

About one year after SL's appointment as chairman of the Modernisation Com- 7
mission, an Act of 8 May 2014 abolished the Commission, with effect from 1 July 2014.[10] This abolition was justified by the fact that the Commission had worked to develop various tools for strategic management and autonomous management of the judiciary and that the creation of new management bodies within the judiciary now made it possible to continue the development of management tools.[11]

---

sie voor de Modernisering van de Rechterlijke Orde en de Algemene Raad van de partners van de Rechterlijke Orde (Act of 20 July 2006 setting up the Commission for the Modernisation of the Judiciary and the General Council of Partners of the Judiciary).

7 The facts of the case are summarised in the request containing the appeal in cassation, published in the public database of Belgian case law (<https://juportal.be/moteur/formulaire>).

8 Parliamentary documents: Chambre des représentants de Belgique – Projet de loi du 10 juillet 2006 instaurant la Commission de Modernisation de l'Ordre judiciaire et le Conseil général des partenaires de l'Ordre judiciaire/Belgische Kamer van volksvertegenwoordigers – Wetsontwerp van 10 juli 2006 tot instelling van de Commissie voor de Modernisering van de Rechterlijke Orde en de Algemene Raad van de partners van de Rechterlijke Orde, Doc 51 2595/003, 3 (<http://www.lachambre.be>).

9 Belgian Official Journal of 28 February 2013 (3rd edn) 12938 (MB/BS) (<http://ejustice.just.fgov.be/cgi/welcome.pl>).

10 Art 133 de la loi du 8 mai 2014 portant modification et coordination de diverses lois en matière de Justice (I)/Art 133 van de wet van 8 mei 2014 houdende wijziging en coördinatie van diverse wetten inzake Justitie (I) (Act of 8 May 2014 Modifying and Coordinating various Acts relating to Justice).

11 Parliamentary documents: Chambre des représentants de Belgique – Proposition de loi du 12 février 2014 portant modification et coordination de diverses lois en matière de Justice/Belgische Kamer van volksvertegenwoordigers – Wetsvoorstel van 12 februari 2014 houdende wijziging en coördinatie van diverse wetten inzake Justitie, Doc 53 3356/001, 5–6 (<http://www.lachambre.be>).

8 The Act abolishing the Modernisation Commission stipulated that the members of this Commission would be assigned to one of the new management bodies, provided that they did not accept another position.[12]

9 SL, who accepted certain new functions with reservations, was not given a mission within the new management bodies, although he had questioned the Minister of Justice on the subject. Taking the view that the State had committed a fault which caused him damage, by terminating his office as chairman without providing him with an equivalent position, SL sued the Belgian State before courts in order to obtain compensation for the damage allegedly suffered, which he estimated at € 85,000. SL based his action on art 1382 of the old Civil Code,[13] which provides that any act whatsoever by man which causes damage to another person obliges the person by whose fault it occurred to make reparation for it.

10 At first instance, the French-speaking Court of First Instance of Brussels declared not founded SL's action, by a decision of 6 November 2015. Then, in a decision delivered on 28 February 2019, the Court of Appeal of Brussels declared SL's appeal not founded. According to the Court of Appeal of Brussels, it is true that the State may be held liable by virtue of its legislative power; however, it is not admissible to base State liability solely on the breach of the general duty of care.

---

12 Art 137 of the Act of 8 May 2014 (fn 10).

13 It is recalled that, by an Act of 13 April 2019, which came into force on 1 November 2020, a new Civil Code was adopted by the Belgian (federal) legislator. The Civil Code, inherited from the Napoleonic era, dated 21 March 1804, now referred to as the 'old Civil Code', is still in force. On the one hand, some of its parts will remain in force as long as the new books are not adopted. On the other hand, the rules of transitional law may have the effect that the old provisions still apply. On the reform of the Civil Code, cf *IC Durant*, Belgium, in: E Karner/BC Steininger (eds), European Tort Law (hereinafter ETL) 2019 (2020) 33, nos 1–17; for the second step, ETL 2020 (2021) 30, no 1; for the next step, *E De Saint Moulin/IC Durant*, ETL 2022 (2023) 35, nos 2–45. With regard to non-contractual liability, the Federal Parliament adopted the text of the new Book 6 of the Civil Code in plenary session on 1 February 2024 (Parliamentary documents: Chambre des représentants de Belgique – Projet de loi du 1 février 2024 portant le livre 6 'La responsabilité extracontractuelle' du Code civil'/Belgische Kamer van volksvertegenwoordigers – Wetsontwerp van 1 februari 2024 houdende boek 6 'buitencontractuele aansprakelijkheid' van het Burgerlijk Wetboek, Doc 55 3213/013 (<http://www.lachambre.be>). The Act is dated 7 February 2024 and was published in the Belgian Official Journal of 1 July 2024 79393 (MB/BS). The new provisions are due to come into force on the first day of the sixth month following publication in the Official Journal (which means on 1 January 2025). They will be commented on in the 2024 Yearbook. These new provisions repeal arts 1382 to 1386*bis* of the Napoleonic Code (and also the Act of 25 February 1991 on Liability for Defective Products, the provisions of which have now been incorporated into the Civil Code). Nevertheless, the old provisions will still apply. Under transitional law, the new provisions will apply to events liable to give rise to liability that occur after the entry into force of Book 6. They will not apply to events occurring before that time. Nor will they apply to the future effects of events having occurred before that time.

In this respect, the Court of Appeal points out that to date there has been no ruling by the Court of Cassation to the effect that the legislator should be liable before courts for breach of the general duty of care, where no breach of a higher standard (for example, a standard of European law) is invoked. Nor could any ruling of the Constitutional Court be invoked in this respect. Furthermore, according to the Court of Appeal, the possibility of holding the legislator liable solely for breach of the general duty of care and diligence would run up against obstacles in constitutional law, in particular the principle of the separation of powers, and would not be favourably considered by legal writers.[14] 11

SL lodged an appeal in cassation against the judgment of 28 February 2019, which resulted in the decision commented on. 12

b) Judgment of the Court

The judgment under review overturns the decision of the Brussels Court of Appeal of 28 February 2019, because it violated art 1382 of the old Civil Code by deciding that the State could not be held liable for breach of the general duty of care. 13

As a preliminary to this decision, the Supreme Court indicated that the legislator's fault that could give rise to State liability under art 1382 of the old Civil Code consists either in: 14

- conduct which can be analysed as an error of conduct which must be assessed according to the criterion of an ordinarily careful and prudent legislator, placed in the same conditions,
- or conduct which, subject to an invincible error or other ground for exoneration from liability, violates a norm of national or international law having direct effects in the internal order which requires it to abstain or to act in a certain way.

As a result of the cassation of the decision of 29 February 2019, the case was referred to another court of appeal, namely the Court of Appeal of Mons. 15

14 The decision of the Court of Appeal is not published but extracts from it are reproduced in the request containing the appeal in cassation.

c) Commentary

16 For more than a century, the Supreme Court has been building up the system of non-contractual public liability for fault, judgment after judgment. In the specific case of non-contractual State liability for fault committed in its function of legislating, the story began a little under twenty years ago.

17 Although the trial courts had already had to rule on the issue, the first judgments of the Supreme Court concerning the liability of the State as legislator date from 2006, the year in which two landmark judgments were delivered, one on 1 June[15] and the other on 28 September.[16] In these two judgments, which put an end to the dogma of the State's lack of liability for the wrongful acts or omissions of the legislator,[17] the Court reiterated that the State is subject to the rules of law, as are citizens. In particular, the State is subject to the rules governing compensation for damage resulting from wrongful interference with the subjective rights and legitimate interests of individuals. The principle of the separation of powers and the independence of the legislator does not mean that the State is exempt from the obligation to compensate damage caused to others by a fault committed in the exercise of the legislative function, and it is the task of the judiciary to protect civil interests.

18 In the case that gave rise to the judgment delivered on 28 September 2006, the Belgian State was found to have breached art 6 (1) of the European Convention on Human Rights – in other words, to have disregarded an international rule – by failing to 'take the legislative measures likely to ensure compliance with [this rule]', with the effect of 'depriving the judiciary of sufficient means to enable it to deal

15 Cour de cassation/Hof van Cassatie (Cass) 1 June 2006, C.05.0494.N; Pasicrisie (Pas) 2006, 1274; Arresten van het Hof van Cassatie (Arr Cass) 2006, 1267; Auteurs & Media (AM) 2006, 484; Journal des tribunaux (JT) 2006, 461, cmt *S van Drooghenbroeck;* Revue de Jurisprudence de Liège, Mons et Bruxelles (JLMB) 2006, 1534, cmt *Y Thiels/I Wouters*, cmt *J Wildemeersch*, cmt *M Uyttendaele*; Nieuw juridisch Weekblad (NjW) 2006, 559, cmt *I Boone*; Chroniques de Droit Public/Publiekrechtelijke Kronieken (CDPK) 2006, 905, cmt *E Maes*; Rechtskundig Weekblad (RW) 2006 – 07, 213, cmt *A Van Oevelen*; Tijdschrift voor Bestuurswetenschappen en Publiek Recht (TBP) 2006, 435, cmt *K Muylle.*

16 Cour de cassation/Hof van Cassatie (Cass) 28 September 2006, C.02.0570.F; Pas 2006, 1870; Arr Cass 2006, 1848; JT 2006, 594; JT 2018, 600, cmt *S van Drooghenbroeck*; JLMB 2006, 1548, cmt *J Wildemeersch*; cmt *M Uyttendaele*; Revue du notariat belge (Rev not b) 2006, cmt *D Sterckx*; RW 2006 – 07, 27, cmt *A Van Oevelen*; NjW 2007, 319, cmt *I Boone*; Rechtspraak Antwerpen Brussel Gent (RABG) 2007, 199; 320, cmt *C Verbruggen*; Revue critique de jurisprudence belge (RCJB) 2007, cmt *S van Drooghenbroeck*; Revue Générale des Assurances et des Responsabilités (RGAR) 2007, no 14242, cmt *P Moreau*; Revue de Droit judiciaire et de la Preuve/Tijdschrift voor Procesrecht en Bewijsrecht (RDJP/P&B) 2007, 98; TBP 2007, 546, cmt *E Maes.*

17 *S van Drooghenbroeck*, La responsabilité extracontractuelle du fait de légiférer, vue d'ensemble, in: D Renders (ed), La responsabilité des pouvoirs publics (2016) 331 – 393, no 7.

with the cases brought before it within a reasonable time'.[18] Because of the insufficiency of the number of Brussels judges, the victim of a medical fault had not been able to have her case heard within a reasonable time and she had sued the Belgian State before court in order to obtain compensation of the damage suffered as a result of the abnormally long proceedings she had initiated some fifteen years earlier. The purpose of the proceedings was to seek compensation for damage allegedly suffered as a result of a medical error committed during surgery.

Since there is no legal or constitutional provision exempting the legislative 19
power, in the exercise of its duties, from the obligations arising from art 1382 of the old Belgian Civil Code,[19] it is obliged to compensate the damage caused by its wrongful acts or omissions. This consequence applies both to the federal parliament and to the parliaments of the federated entities.[20]

With this first milestone established by the judgments delivered in 2006, the 20
rest of the construction required that the concept of fault be more clearly defined when it comes to the legislator's liability, even if it was reasonable to think that the general definition of fault, developed in the context of the application of art 1382, should apply to the legislator.[21] If this were indeed the case, that is, if the assessment of the fault of the legislator were to consist of a variation of the general definition of fault, some authors concluded that the fault of the legislator consists of conduct that either disregards a supra-legislative rule requiring it to act or refrain from acting in a specific manner, subject to invincible error or some other justification, or, in the absence of such a rule, constitutes an error of conduct that an ordinarily prudent and diligent legislator would not have committed in the same circumstances.[22] As we shall see, the judgments delivered by the Supreme Court after 2006 show that the general definition of fault effectively also applies to the legislator, in the absence of any derogatory legislative intervention.

---

18 Court of Appeal of Brussels, 4 July 2002, JLMB 2002, 1184, no 4.5. Free translation.

19 Art 1382 of the old Civil Code, which is the statutory provision for liability based on fault.

20 *B Dubuisson/S van Drooghenbroeck*, Responsabilité de l'État-législateur: la dernière pièce du puzzle? JT 2011, 801, fn 5; *P Van Ommeslaghe*, Les obligations, vol 1 (2013) no 866.

21 *B Dubuisson/V Callewaert/B De Coninck/F George/N Schmitz*, Droit de la responsabilité civile. Chronique de jurisprudence 2008–2020. Volume 1. Le fait générateur et le lien causal (2023) no 883.

22 *Dubuisson/van Drooghenbroeck*, JT 2011, 801, no 3. When these two authors speak of a supra-legislative rule, they are referring to the violation of the Constitution or of an international convention. Subsequently, one of them specified the first hypothesis as follows: violation of the Constitution or of a rule established under the Constitution to determine the respective competences of the State, the Communities and the Regions (*van Drooghenbroeck* [fn 17] no 22). In the same sense, cf *Van Ommeslaghe* (fn 20) no 865.

21 A judgment of 10 September 2010 was a first step towards defining the fault of the legislator,[23] but left some grey areas.[24] In this case, the Constitutional Court ruled that a tax provision was unconstitutional because it discriminated between taxpayers. Subsequently, one of the taxpayers argued that the legislator had committed a fault by adopting the tax provision, which was said to be unconstitutional. The decision of the Supreme Court (*Cour de cassation/Hof van Cassatie*) was handed down in the context of a liability dispute between this taxpayer and the State. The Court of Appeal of Brussels had deduced the State's fault from the mere finding of unconstitutionality. According to the Supreme Court, however, the fault of the legislator cannot be deduced from the mere existence of a decision by the Constitutional Court declaring an act (or a provision of an act) to be contrary to a provision of the Constitution. Any unconstitutionality (and, by extension, any inconsistency with an international convention) does not automatically constitute a fault. The legislator's liability requires the trial judge to make their own assessment, says the Supreme Court, without nevertheless elaborating further.

22 The commented decision, delivered on 15 December 2022 following up on the similar conclusions of the public prosecutor, removes the grey areas left by the judgment of 10 September 2010. Fault on the part of the legislator, which may give rise to State liability under art 1382 of the old Civil Code, is defined in two parts. Fault on the part of the legislator thus consists of:

- either conduct which can be analysed as an error of conduct to be assessed according to the criterion of the normally careful and prudent legislator, placed in the same conditions,
- or conduct which, subject to invincible error or some other ground for exoneration from liability, infringes a rule of national or international law having direct effect in the domestic order, which requires the legislator to refrain from acting or to act in a particular way.

It should be noted that this two-part definition is largely based on that suggested by certain authors following the 2006 and 2010 judgments, with the sole reservation that, in the part concerning the breach of a specific rule, reference is made not to a supra-legislative rule (the Constitution or an international rule, including Euro-

23 Cour de cassation/Hof van Cassatie (Cass) 10 September 2010, F.09.0042.N; Pas 2010, 2228; Arr Cass 2010, 2135; RABG 2010, 1263, cmt *J Vanden Branden*; RW 2010–11, 1726, cmt *P Popelier*; CDPK 2011, 291; JT 2011, 811; NjW 2011, 425, cmt *S Guiliams*; Fiscale jurisprudentie/Jurisprudence fiscale (FJF) 2011, 230; Revue générale du contentieux fiscal (RGCF) 2011, 125; Tijdschrift voor Fiscaal Recht (TFR) 2011, 196, cmt *S Guiliams*. Cf *IC Durant*, Belgium, in: K Oliphant/BC Steininger (eds), ETL 2011 (2012) 33, no 7 ff.

24 *Dubuisson/van Drooghenbroeck*, JT 2011, 801, no 8 ff.

pean law), but to a rule of national or international law having direct effects in the domestic order.

Each aspect of the definition of fault, as given by the Supreme Court in its decision of 15 December 2022, merits some comment. 23

According to the commented decision, the legislator's fault may, first of all, consist of conduct that the court considers is not that which a careful and prudent legislator would have adopted in the same circumstances. This assessment of the legislator's conduct will require the court not only to rely on a reference standard but also to adopt a retrospective approach. Academic writers have suggested a number of parameters that could guide the court in its assessment. For example, the fact that the legislator did not follow up on a reason for censure that the Legislation Section of the Council of State (*Conseil d'État/Raad van Staat*) had rightly pointed out during the process of drafting the law. It should also be borne in mind that where European Union law is at issue, the 'sufficiently serious breach' standard developed by the Court of Justice of the European Union (CJEU) will, at the very least, be respected. Finally, the court must look back to the time when the contested legislation was adopted. Assessing the legislator's conduct must therefore be seen in a historical perspective (except where the fault attributed to the legislator consists not in *having adopted* the legislation criticised, but in *having maintained* legislation declared unconstitutional or unconventional).[25] 24

The second type of fault that can be held against the legislative power is conduct that violates a norm of national or international law. This norm must have direct effects in the Belgian legal order and must require the State to abstain or to act in a specific way.[26] In other words, it is not enough for a legal norm to have been disregarded; that norm must also have imposed a specific order.[27] 25

---

25 *Dubuisson/van Drooghenbroeck*, JT 2011, 801, no 14.

26 For a case of violation of a European norm, cf also Cour de cassation/Hof van Cassatie (Cass) 30 April 2015, C.12.0637.F; Pas 2015, 1077; Arr Cass 2015, 1114; JLMB 2015, 1958. For a case of violation of a constitutional provision: cf recently, Court of Appeal of Mons, 22 September 2023, JT 2023, 614; Le Courrier Fiscal 2023, 480, cmt *L Kell*. In this case, a taxpayer reproached the Belgian State of having committed a fault by adopting a tax act on the basis of which a tax had been imposed on him. This tax act was subsequently annulled by the Constitutional Court on the grounds that the legislator had violated the principle of legality of taxation guaranteed by art 170 of the Constitution (the principle according to which, taxpayers must be able to determine, with a minimum level of predictability, the tax regime that will be applied to them). The taxpayer then claimed reimbursement of the tax paid under the annulled act, as compensation for his loss. The Court of Appeal of Mons considered that the State had committed a fault by adopting the annulled act because it had violated a constitutional provision requiring it to act in a specific manner (ie the abovementioned art 170). As a result, it ordered the Belgian State to reimburse the taxpayer the amount of money he had paid. The particularity of this case is that the refund was imposed

26 The judgment of 15 December 2022 has puzzled some commentators, particularly in that it states that the fault of the legislator may be analysed as an error of conduct assessed in accordance with the standard of an ordinarily prudent and diligent legislator.[28] Along with authors who had already expressed their views on the subject in the wake of the 2006 judgments,[29] these commentators wonder whether the principle of the separation of powers is not, this time, being put to too severe a test. This principle is not expressly mentioned in the Constitution, but it is inferred from several of its provisions (in particular art 33 ff). In application of this principle of separation, each of the powers of the State exercises part of its sovereignty and any concentration of powers in the hands of a single power is avoided. Thus, the judge cannot interfere in the functions of legislating or administering. These same commentators also point out that the legislative function involves assessing the appropriateness of adopting certain acts and making choices in a context of budgetary, economic, social and cultural constraints.

27 Despite the scepticism thus expressed by some authors, the Supreme Court has continued along the long-standing path of not exempting public authorities from ordinary tort law.[30] And this view is also the one recently adopted by the legislator itself.

28 On 1 February 2024, the Federal Parliament adopted the text of the new Book 6 of the Civil Code. This Book concerns the provisions governing extra-contractual civil liability. It will come into force six months after the new Act, dated 7 February 2024, is published in the Belgian Official Journal.[31] On the recommendation of the

even though the Constitutional Court had annulled the tax act while maintaining its (produced) effects (by application of art 8 of the special act on the Constitutional Court). According to the Court of Appeal of Mons, 'the Constitutional Court's use of article 8 of its special act cannot, … have the effect of exonerating the Belgian State from any liability, depriving the citizen of his right to be compensated for damage suffered as a result of a fault resulting from the adoption of an act contrary to higher standards' (free translation).

27 *S van Drooghenbroeck*, La responsabilité de l'État-législateur: une très remarquable construction jurisprudentielle, JT 2018, 602.

28 *F Bouhon/L Fontaine*, La responsabilité extracontractuelle de l'État législateur imprudent: un pas de plus, un pas de trop? JT 2024, 609–613, no 8.

29 *R Ergec*, Quelques doutes sur la soumission du législateur au droit commun de la responsabilité civile, JT 2007, 440, no 14; *P Van Ommeslaghe/J Verbist*, Responsabilité de l'État pour les actes du législateur/Overheidsaansprakelijkheid voor het optreden van de wetgevende macht, Avis/Advies, Doc 52 1627/001, 48 (<http://www.lachambre.be>).

30 *F Auvray*, (On)wettigheid binnen (overheids)aansprakelijkheid. Stellingname voor een uniforme toepassing van het gemeen recht (2023).

31 Cf fn 13.

experts who drew up the draft,[32] the legislator made a number of choices, two of which are of particular interest with regard to the commented decision:

1. Firstly, the legislator has chosen to treat natural persons and legal persons (under private and public law) in the same way.[33] This choice is clearly expressed in art 6.4: 'Unless otherwise provided by law, the provisions of this Book shall apply to legal persons, whether private or public, as well as to natural persons.'[34]
2. Secondly, the legislator has not called into question the approach taken by the Supreme Court of subjecting public authorities to the same rules of liability as private individuals.[35] Therefore, the new Book 6 does not provide for any derogatory regime concerning the liability of the State for the fault of the legislative authority.[36] However, the preparatory works take care to specify that the assessment of fault will have to be marginal whenever the act of which the public authorities are reproached results from the exercise of a discretionary power.[37] Only a manifest error of assessment may constitute a fault.[38]

2. Supreme Court (Cour de cassation/Hof van Cassatie) 14 December 2023, C.23.0032.N: Reparation in Kind – Award of a Periodic Sum of Money

a) Brief Summary of the Facts

In 2015, at the age of 64, HB, who had been a magistrate since 1992, after having 29
been a lawyer, took early retirement. She took this decision after obtaining infor-

32 Significantly, co-chairmen Prof Bernard Dubuisson (UCLouvain) and Prof Hubert Bocken (UGent). Cf Ministerial decree establishing the Civil Code Reform Commissions (Arrêté ministériel du 30 septembre 2017 portant création des Commissions de réforme du droit civil/Ministerieel besluit van 30 september 2017 houdende oprichting van de Commissie tot hervorming van het burgerlijk wetboek), Belgian Official Journal of 9 October 2017 91600 (MB/BS).

33 Parliamentary documents: Chambre des représentants de Belgique – Proposition de loi du 8 mars 2023 portant le livre 6 'La responsabilité extracontractuelle' du Code civil/Belgische Kamer van volksvertegenwoordigers – Wetsvoorstel van 8 maart 2023 houdende boek 6 'Buitencontractuele aansprakelijkheid' van het Burgerlijk Wetboek, Doc 55 3213/001, 8 (<http://www.lachambre.be>).

34 Free translation.

35 Doc 55 3213/001, 9.

36 Doc 55 3213/001, 48.

37 Doc 55 3213/001, 48.

38 *Dubuisson/Callewaert/De Coninck/George/Schmitz* (fn 21) no 894.

mation from the Federal Pensions Office (*Service fédéral des Pensions/Federale Pensioendienst*), and in particular after receiving a handwritten document from a civil servant which showed that waiting until the statutory pension age (67) before retiring would only have brought her a small increase in pension. This handwritten document was a third estimate requested by HB. HB had in fact already received two other estimates, which were in the form of estimates generated by a computer application.

30 Ultimately, upon retirement, it became apparent that HB was receiving a much lower pension than the one she had been told by the civil servant. She sued the Federal Pensions Office before court to seek compensation for her loss, arguing that if she had been correctly informed by the civil servant, she would not have retired until she reached the statutory age of 67, so that she would have received a full pension.

31 On appeal, the judges held that both the Pensions Office and HB committed a fault. The Office had been at fault because the civil servant had not only incorrectly estimated the amount of the pension (using incorrect premises as a starting point) but had also failed to express any reservations about the calculation in writing. HB, for her part, had also committed faulty negligence insofar as the estimate on which she based her decision as to whether or not to retire was in handwritten form, unlike the first two estimates generated by a computer application. As this handwritten estimate was more generous than the previous two, she should have asked some questions.

32 The appeal judges then considered that the two faults had contributed, for HB, to the loss of an opportunity to remain professionally active until the statutory pension age (67) and to obtain a higher pension. More specifically, they estimated the loss of opportunity at 90 %. The Pensions Office was ordered to compensate 90 % of the loss (ie 81 % of the loss actually suffered) and HB was ordered to bear 10 % of the loss (ie 10 % of the 90 %).

33 For the remainder, the appeal judges referred the case back to the first judge and confirmed the investigative measure taken by the latter, namely the appointment of an expert with the aim of calculating the difference between the retirement pension actually received by HB and the pension she would have received had she retired at the age of 67. The expert was asked to carry out the calculation using the capitalisation method.

34 The Pensions Office, which had offered to pay compensation in kind, criticised the decision of the appeal judges and appealed to the Court of Cassation.

b) Judgment of the Court

Article 1382 of the Old Civil Code obliges the person whose fault has caused damage to another to compensate for it in full, which implies that the injured party should be placed, as far as possible, in the condition in which they would have been had the fault not been committed. 35

Reparation in kind is the normal mode of compensation for damage. Consequently, the court is obliged to order the reparation of damage in kind when the victim asks for it or the liable party offers it and, moreover, when this mode of reparation is possible and does not constitute an abuse of rights. 36

If reparation of damage in kind is possible by awarding a payment due periodically and the liable party offers this mode of reparation, the court cannot, in principle, order the reparation of damage by equivalent (ie award of damages) through capitalisation. This also applies if liability has been established only for the loss of an opportunity. 37

In this case, the appeal judges imposed the use of the capitalisation method, whereas the Pensions Office had offered to compensate the damage in kind by increasing the amount of the pension paid each month. For this reason, their decision had to be quashed. 38

c) Commentary

When a person is responsible for damage, they must compensate it fully. Compensation is a consequence of liability. More specifically, when the damage is of a pecuniary nature, ie when the victim suffers economic consequences, the general objective of compensation is to restore the victim, as accurately as possible, to the situation they would have been in had the event giving rise to liability not occurred. In Belgian law, civil liability essentially plays a compensatory role and compensation tends to restore a hypothetical situation. 39

Compensation may take the form of reparation in kind. Reparation in kind is the most normal form of compensation[39] and takes precedence, in principle, over compensation in the form of damages.[40] Consequently, if the victim requests rep- 40

39 Cour de cassation/Hof van Cassatie (Cass) 3 April 2017, S.16.0039.N; Journal des tribunaux du travail (JTT) 2017, 293; RW 2017–18, 1414, cmt *P Dion/Y Stevens*; JLMB 2018, 1892, cmt *P Wéry*; RGAR 2028, no 15521; Chroniques de droit social (Chr DS) 2018, 303.

40 *P Colson*, La réparation des préjudices corporels en droit de la responsabilité extracontractuelle (2022) no 154; *P Wéry*, Les condamnations non pécuniaires dans le contentieux de la respon-

aration in kind, it must, in principle, be ordered by the judge, and if the liable person offers to make reparation in kind, the same will apply. Exceptions arise in a number of cases, in particular where reparation in kind is impossible or where it would be unreasonable to claim it.[41]

41 The new Book 6 of the Civil Code[42] takes up the principle of the primacy of reparation in kind and now formalises, in a somewhat extended manner, the exceptions to this principle (art 6.33 [2]):

> 'If the injured party so requests, reparation in kind shall be ordered, unless it is impossible or manifestly unreasonable, if it requires the use of coercion on the person liable or if it is contrary to human dignity. The liable person may offer to compensate the damage in kind. The injured party may nevertheless refuse this offer if they can show just cause'.[43]

42 As we have already observed, the fact that the exceptions to the principle have been conceived more broadly, in particular by recourse to the concept of just cause on the part of the injured party, weakens the principle somewhat.[44]

43 In the commented case, the liable person had offered to pay not a capital but a periodical supplementary pension, which the Supreme Court described as reparation in kind. Given the primacy of reparation in kind, the Supreme Court held that it was not possible to impose the use of capitalisation. This decision is traditional in that it recalls that reparation in kind is the normal method of compensation and that reparation in kind must be ordered if it is offered by the liable person. On the other hand, it once again generates a certain amount of confusion in that it qualifies as reparation in kind the payment (in this case periodic) of a sum of money.

44 In this respect, we will recall a decision delivered by the Supreme Court on 25 November 2020.[45] In this decision, the Supreme Court opted for a fairly strict definition of reparation in kind. It stated, for the first time, that reparation in

---

sabilité. Rapport belge, in: B Dubuisson (ed), Le dommage et sa réparation dans la responsabilité contractuelle et extracontractuelle. Etudes de droit comparé (2015) 64.

41 *P Wéry*, La réparation en nature du dommage extracontractuel: un équivalent non pécuniaire de l'intérêt lésé, et rien d'autre, JT 2022, 197, no 2.

42 Cf fn 13.

43 Free translation.

44 *IC Durant*, Belgium, in: E Karner/BC Steininger (eds), European Tort Law 2021 (2022) 31, no 78.

45 Cour de cassation/Hof van Cassatie (Cass) 25 November 2020, P.20.0808.F; Revue générale de droit civil belge/Tijdschrift voor Belgisch Burgerlijk Recht (RGDC/TBBR) 2021, 306, cmt *S De Rey/ P Wéry*; RGAR 2021, no 15756; JLMB 2023, 150, cmt *D P.* Cf *Durant* (fn 44) no 53 ff.

kind is *a non-pecuniary equivalent*. This judgment of 25 November 2020 marked a break with previous judgments.[46]

The issue arose as to whether this decision would remain unique[47] or become a precedent. This question is now being asked more than ever. The new Book 6 of the Civil Code states that 'reparation in kind is intended to remove in practice the harmful consequences of an event giving rise to liability' (art 6.33).[48] Although one author has seen in this text the mark of an adherence to a strict conception of reparation in kind (that is, a non-pecuniary equivalent),[49] it must be recognised that, formally, it does not require that the removal of the harmful consequences be non-pecuniary. 45

A reading of the preparatory works leaves some doubt as to how the text of art 6.33 should be interpreted. Did the authors of the reform opt for a restrictive vision of reparation in kind (a *non-pecuniary* equivalent) or, on the contrary, did they wish to leave room for possible pecuniary reparation in kind? On the one hand, we read that reparation for damage is made in kind or in the form of damages, ie in the form of a non-pecuniary equivalent or in money (or even a combination of the two).[50] But the authors do not really refute the case law prior to the decision of 25 November 2021 and seem, in another place, to endorse the idea that reparation in kind could consist in the payment of a sum of money.[51] Some hesitation therefore remains as to the exact scope of reparation in kind. 46

It should be recalled that advocates of a strict view of reparation in kind see the recovery by the victim of what they were entitled to not as reparation but as a measure of restoration.[52] [53] To make a clear distinction between reparation and a 47

---

46 Especially Cour de cassation/Hof van Cassatie (Cass) 22 January 2007, S.04.0088.N/S.04.0169.N; Pas 2007, 128; JTT 2007, 481, cmt *F Lagasse/M Palumbo*; RCJB 3008, 168, cmt *F Kefer*; Chr DS 2008, 443.

47 There was at least a second decision delivered in the same way: Cour de cassation/Hof van Cassatie (Cass) 26 November 2021, C.20.0578.F; Bulletin des assurances/Tijdschrift voor verzekeringen (Bull ass/T Verz) 2022, 500; JT 2022, 206; RGAR 2022, no 15858; RGDC/TBBR, 2023, 424, cmt *S De Rey.*

48 Free translation.

49 *P Wéry,* La réparation en nature en matière extracontractuelle: quelques nouvelles avancées jurisprudentielles, JLMB 2018, 1893, no 8. In favour of the definition of reparation in kind as non-pecuniary waiver of the consequences of the harmful event, cf *Colson* (fn 40) no 146. Some years later, P Wéry had, however, to recognise that the definition of reparation in kind included in the new Book 6 does not correspond exactly to the strict definition given by the Supreme Court in the decisions dated 25 November 2020 and 26 November 2021 because it does not expressly exclude the possibility to obtain a *pecuniary* reparation in kind (*Wéry,* JT 2022, 197, no 7).

50 Doc 55 3213/001, 148.

51 Doc 55 3213/001, 150.

52 *S De Rey/P Wéry,* La réparation en nature en matière extracontractuelle: un équivalent non pécuniaire de l'intérêt lésé, RGDC/TBBR 2021, 307, nos 3 and 4.

53 *Durant* (fn 44) no 68.

measure of restoration has various impacts. For example, the claim aiming at restoration is not subject to the same limitation rules.[54]

48 It was this strict view that prevailed when it came to defining the consequences of a breach of contract in the new Civil Code. Article 5.237 of the Civil Code provides that: 'In the event of non-performance attributable to the debtor, they are bound to fully compensate, in kind or in pecuniary form, for the damage suffered by the creditor'.[55]

49 In the present state of the law in the new Civil Code, the concept of reparation in kind may therefore possibly be understood a little differently in the two orders of liability.

3. Supreme Court (Cour de cassation/Hof van Cassatie) 15 December 2023, C.23.0156.F; JT 2024, 81: Concurrent Faults; Victim's Fault; Criterion of Shared Liability

a) Brief Summary of the Facts

50 A traffic accident occurred in which a police moped driven by JM collided with the car driven by JFD, who was insured with the defendant. Following the accident, JM sued the defendant for compensation. The Belgian State intervened in the case, as JM's employer and insurer.

51 At first instance, the court ruled that JM and JFD were jointly liable for the accident and ordered them to bear the consequences of their losses. On appeal, the court found that the two drivers had each committed a fault causally linked to the accident. However, the court noted that JFD's fault was one of inattention while performing a manoeuvre, whereas JM's fault was deliberate and wilful. In this case, as a police officer, JM had taken the liberty of driving the wrong way on the carriageway, without any real need to do so. The appeal judges therefore considered that the respective faults of the two drivers had not contributed equally to causing the damage, and they apportioned liability as follows: one-third to JFD and two-thirds to JM.

52 JM and the Belgian State criticised this decision. They pointed out that, according to the case law of the Supreme Court, liability between two parties whose fault contributed to the damage cannot be shared on the basis of the seriousness of the

54 *De Rey/Wéry*, RGDC/TBBR 2021, 307, no 7.

55 Free translation.

fault (carelessness versus wilful and deliberate fault). For this reason, they appealed to the Supreme Court.

b) Judgment of the Court

Where there is concurrent fault on the part of several persons, the court assesses not only whether the fault of each caused the damage, but also the extent to which it contributed to its occurrence. It is on the basis of the relative causal importance of each of the competing faults that the court then determines the share of the damage attributable to each of the tortfeasors. 53

In this case, the appeal judges considered that both drivers had committed a fault that was causally linked to the accident in question: JM had used the lane reserved for oncoming traffic and JFD, who had priority and was performing a U-turn manoeuvre, had not looked to his left. 54

They then transferred two-thirds of the liability to JM on the grounds that JFD had committed a fault of inattention in carrying out his manoeuvre, whereas JM had committed a deliberate and wilful offence. In other words, the appeal judges apportioned liability between the two parties according to the seriousness of their respective faults, without assessing the concrete impact of each of these faults on the occurrence of the damage. The appeal judges disregarded the rules applicable in this area. Their decision must be quashed. 55

c) Commentary

The Supreme Court has consistently held that where there are concurrent faults on the part of the liable party and the victim, the judge hearing the case must assess the extent to which each party's fault contributed to the damage when determining the share of damages between the liable party and the victim.[56] In other words, it is the *causal impact* of each fault on the damage that is the criterion to be taken into account when apportioning liability.[57] This same criterion is applied when the 56

56 However, the victim will not be entitled to compensation for the damage, by application of the principle, 'fraus omnia corrumpit' if they intentionally caused the damage.

57 Cour de cassation/Hof van Cassatie (Cass) 5 September 2003, C.01.0602.F/C.01.0604.F, Pas 2003, 1360; RGDC/TBBR 2005, 168; 9 October 2009, C.07.0080.F/C.07.0370.F, Pas 2009, 2195; 26 September 2012, P.12.0377.F; Pas 2012, 1737; 14 November 2012, P.11.1611.F; RGAR 2013, no 15009; 13 March 2013, P.12.1830.F; Pas 2013, 652; RGAR 2013, no 14994; RABG 2014, 65; 19 November 2014, P.14.1139.F; Pas 2014, 2583; RGAR 2015, no 15197.

victim is not at fault but several tortfeasors are at fault and the consequences of liability need to be apportioned between them.[58] The same applies where there is fault on the part of several tortfeasors as well as fault on the part of the victim.[59]

57 To proceed with a division according to the causal impact requires the judge to consider the role, preponderant or less preponderant, played by each fault in the occurrence of the damage.

58 Despite the case law of the Supreme Court, there is still sometimes a temptation to divide liability not on the basis of the causal power of each fault, but on the basis of the seriousness of the fault. Thus, as in the case under review, some judges divide the fault on the basis of whether it was intentional or unintentional.

59 It is true that the way in which the Supreme Court has sometimes defined the seriousness of fault muddies the waters.[60] For example, in a decision of 26 September 2012,[61] the Court states that seriousness is defined 'as the character of that which may lead to serious consequences'.[62] It therefore establishes a link between the ability of the fault to cause the loss and its seriousness, and recognises that the judge may refer to seriousness of the fault to assess the relative weight of two causal faults. And in 2013,[63] the Supreme Court did not sanction the judge who referred to the age and inexperience of the worker, which increased the risk of accident, to assess the impact of the worker's behaviour on the occurrence of the damage. On the other hand, a judgment of the Supreme Court of 26 May 2020 is much more orthodox:

> 'In cases of concurrence of faults, the court unquestionably judges the extent to which each person's fault contributed to causing the damage and, on that basis, determines each person's

---

58 Cour de cassation/Hof van Cassatie (Cass) 4 February 2008, C.06.0236.F; Pas 2008, 329; RW 2009–10, 1561, cmt *B Weyts*; 21 October 2008, P.08.0561.N; Pas 2008, 2319; Nullum Crimen (NC) 2009, 197; 2 October 2009, C.08.0168.F; Pas 2009, 2110; Bull ass/T Verz 2010, 440, cmt *B Weyts*; JT 2010, 538, cmt *A Lenaerts*; NjW 2010, 318, cmt *I Boone*; RABG 2010, 1287, cmt *E De Kezel*; RDJP/P&B 2010, 99; RGAR 2010, no 14671; RW 2010–11, 487, cmt *S Guiliams*; JT 2011, 291, cmt *T De Haan*; 16 May 2011, C.10.0214.N; Pas 2011, 1337; NjW 2011, 23, cmt *I Boone*; Circulation responsabilité assurances/Verkeer aansprakelijkheid verzekering (CRA/VAV) 2011/5, 298; RGDC/TBBR 2012, 355; 4 September 2014, C.12.0535.F; Pas 2014, 1731; JLMB 2015, 872; NjW 2015, 244, cmt *G Jocqué*; RGAR 2015, no 15177; RGDC/TBBR 2015, cmt *D Renders*; CRA/VAV 2015/1, 46, cmt *G Jocqué*; 9 September 2015, P.15.0653.F; Pas 2015, 1963.

59 Cour de cassation/Hof van Cassatie (Cass) 26 May 2020, P.20.0169.N; NC 2021, 36, cmt *S Guiliams*; RGAR 2020, no 15707; CRA/VAV 2020/4, 32.

60 *Dubuisson/Callewaert/De Coninck/George/Schmitz* (fn 21) nos 447 and 463.

61 Cour de cassation/Hof van Cassatie (Cass) 26 September 2012, P.12.0377.F; Pas 2012, 1737.

62 Free translation.

63 Cour de cassation/Hof van Cassatie (Cass) 13 March 2013, P.12.1830.F; Pas 2013, 652; RGAR 2013, no 14994; RABG 2014, 65.

share of compensation in their mutual relationship. Foreign to that causal relationship are the gravity of the respective faults and, in the case of intentional blows, the will of the perpetrator to cause certain damage or not'.[64]

C. Literature

1. Books and Collective Works

C Borucki, Buitencontractueel kostenverhaal door de overheid, coll Aansprakelijkheids en Verzekeringsrecht no 20 [Extra-contractual cost recovery by public authorities] (Antwerp, Intersentia 2023) 546 pp 60

A Carette/P Lefranc/T Malfait/E Rentmeesters/H Schoukens, Milieuzakboekje. Leidraad voor de milieuwetgeving in Vlaanderen [Environmental pocketbook. Guide to environmental legislation in Flanders] (Mechelen, Wolters Kluwer Belgium, 2023) 1300 pp 61

P Colson (ed), La prescription, coll Commission Université-Palais no 224 [Limitation periods] (Limal, Anthemis 2023) 180 pp 62

D de Callataÿ, Droit de la responsabilité civile. Chronique de jurisprudence 2008–2020. Volume 2. Le dommage (principes généraux et préjudice corporel), coll Les Dossiers du journal des tribunaux no 120 [Tort law. Case law 2008–2020. Volume 2. Damage (general principles and personal injury)] (Brussels, Larcier 2023) 1050 pp 63

J-Q De Cuyper ea (coord), Gouvernance et responsabilité. Mélanges à la mémoire de Didier Willermain [Governance and liability. Liber Amicorum in memory of Didier Willermain] (Brussels, Larcier 2023) 1350 pp 64

D Deferme, Bevrijdende verjaring in het privaatrecht, coll Recht en onderneming [Limitation periods in private law] (Brugge, die Keure 2023) 840 pp 65

B Dubuisson/V Callewaert/B De Coninck/F George/N Schmitz, Droit de la responsabilité civile. Chronique de jurisprudence 2008–2020. Volume 1. Le fait générateur et le lien causal, coll Les Dossiers du journal des tribunaux no 119 [Tort law. Case law 2008–2020. Volume 1. Damaging event and causal link] (Brussels, Larcier 2023) 1446 pp 66

B Gors/M Karolinski/F De Muynck (eds), Mémento de l'environnement (Régions wallonne et bruxelloise) [Memento of the environment (Walloon and Brussels Regions)] (Liège, Wolters Kluwer Belgium, 29th edn 2023) 1237 pp 67

64 Free translation.

68 *L Helsen*, Verkeerszakboekje. Verkeersrecht, verzekeringen en schadebegroting [Traffic booklet. Traffic law, insurance and damage assessment] (Mechelen, Wolters Kluwer Belgium, 27th edn 2023) 344 pp

69 *I Lutte* (ed), États généraux du droit médical et du dommage corporel. Tome 2. Questions d'actualité [General assembly on medical law and personal injury. Volume 2. Current Issues] (Limal, Anthemis 2023) 328 pp

70 *J Nounckele* (ed), La responsabilité du mineur et de ses parents: du fait dommageable à l'indemnisation de la victime, coll de la Conférence du Jeune Barreau de Bruxelles [The liability of minors and their parents: from the harmful event to compensation for the victim] (Brussels, Larcier 2023) 215 pp

71 *E Steen*, Bedrijfsjuristen en bedrijfsverantwoordelijkheid/Les juristes d'entreprise et les responsabilités de l'entreprise, coll Le Droit des affaires en évolution/Tendensen in het bedrijfsleven no 33 [Company lawyers and corporate liabilities] (Ghent, Larcier/Antwerp, Intersentia 2023) 186 pp

2. Articles and Collective Book Contributions

72 *C Borucki*, Buitencontractueel kostenverhaal door de overheid: een stappenplan voor de rechter en wetgever [Extra-contractual cost recovery by public authorities: a roadmap for courts and legislators], Rechtskundig Weekblad 2023–24, 43–56

73 *M Castermans*, De aansprakelijkheid van artsen wegens medisch niet noodzakelijke 'geslachtsnormaliserende' operaties van intersekse kinderen [Physicians' liability for medically unnecessary 'sexual normalising' surgeries of intersex children], Revue de droit de la santé/Tijdschrift voor gezondheidsrecht 2023–24, 252–255

74 *M Castermans*, La responsabilité de médecins pour opérations de 'normalisation sexuelle' médicalement non nécessaires d'enfants intersexes [Physicians' liability for medically unnecessary 'sexual normalising' surgeries of intersex children], Revue de droit de la santé/Tijdschrift voor gezondheidsrecht 2023–24, 256–259

75 *I Claeys/C Desmet*, Rechtstreekse aansprakelijkheid van de hulppersoon via de rechtstreekse vordering? [Direct liability of auxiliary persons through direct claims], Rechtskundig Weekblad 2023–24, 796–800

76 *D De Callataÿ*, Conflits d'intérêt: le zéro et l'infini [Conflicts of interest: the zero and the infinity], Revue générale des assurances et des responsabilités 2023, no 15942

77 *E De Saint Moulin*, La connaissance par la personne lésée de l'identité du responsable ou de son assureur au regard de la prescription [The injured party's knowledge of the identity of the liable party or their insurer with regard to the

limitation period], Revue générale des assurances et des responsabilités 2023, no 15941

B Dubuisson, Le dommage moral est-il un dommage corporel? [Is moral dam- 78
age a bodily injury?] Revue de jurisprudence de Liège, Mons et Bruxelles 2023, 1916–1918

J Hantson, Juridische aspecten van mobiele gezondheidszorg of mHealth [Legal 79
aspects of mobile healthcare or mHealth], Revue de droit de la santé/Tijdschrift voor gezondheidsrecht 2023–24, 294–304

C Hélas, Application anticipée de l'article 5.89 du Code civil: l'illicéité de la 80
clause exonératoire de responsabilité en cas d'atteinte à la vie ou à l'intégrité physique [Early application of article 5.89 of the Civil Code: the unlawfulness of a liability exemption clause in the event of injury to life or physical integrity], Revue générale des assurances et des responsabilités 2023, no 15934

C Jaumain, Crise sanitaire, choc des taux d'intérêt, pic d'inflation: conséquen- 81
ces sur la capitalisation des rentes indemnitaires [Health crisis, interest rate shock, inflation spike: consequences for the capitalisation of compensation annuities], Revue générale des assurances et des responsabilités 2023, no 15999

C Joisten, Causalité, incertitude et perte de chance: de nouvelles perspectives 82
[Causation, uncertainty and loss of a chance: new perspectives], Revue Générale de Droit Civil/Tijdschrift voor Belgisch Burgerlijk recht 2023, 458–481

G Lammens, Seksuele ongeschiktheid en schade: meerwaarde van een zeven- 83
delige schaal [Sexual unfitness and damage: added value of a seven-part scale], Circulation, responsabilité, assurance/Verkeer, aansprakelijkheid, verzekering 2023/3, 3–8

G Lammens, Genoegenschade: meerwaarde van een zevendelige schaal [Plea- 84
sure damage: added value of a seven-part scale], Circulation, responsabilité, assurance/Verkeer, aansprakelijkheid, verzekering 2023/4, 4–7

J Lentz, L'incidence de l'inconnue dans l'équation: 'véhicule embrasé propaga- 85
tion au véhicule voisin = responsabilité engendrée?' [The impact of the unknown factor in the equation: 'vehicle engulfed in flames spread to neighbouring vehicle = generated liability?'] Forum de l'assurance 2023, 111–112

S Lievens, Preuve par vraisemblance dans le Livre 8 du Code civil, perte d'une 86
chance selon le droit en vigueur et la théorie de l'équivalence à l'art. 6.19 du projet de loi [Proof by reasonableness in Book 8 of the Civil Code, loss of a chance under current law and the theory of equivalence in art. 6.19 of the bill], Revue de droit de la santé/Tijdschrift voor gezondheidsrecht 2023–24, 160–166

S Lievens, Perte de chances de survie et le concept de préjudice *ex haerede* 87
[Loss of a chance of survival and the concept of *ex haerede* damage], Revue de droit de la santé/Tijdschrift voor gezondheidsrecht 2023–24, 323–326

88 *I Samoy/S Van Eekert*, De terechte afschaffing van het samenloopverbod en de leer van de quasi-immuniteit van de hulppersoon: ander en beter [The rightful abolition of the concurrence prohibition and the doctrine of quasi-immunity of the auxiliary person: different and better], Rechtskundig Weekblad 2023–24, 437–440

89 *V Schollaert*, Het nieuwe buitencontractueel aansprakelijkheidsrecht. Een verkennende analyse [The new extra-contractual liability law. An exploratory analysis], Nieuw juridisch Weekblad 2023, 374–381

90 *V Schollaert*, Het tweeledige schadebegrip in het wetsvoorstel houdende boek 6 'Buitencontractuele aansprakelijkheid' van het Burgerlijk Wetboek [The dual concept of damage in the bill containing Book 6 'Extra-contractual liability' of the Civil Code], Revue Générale de Droit Civil/Tijdschrift voor Belgisch Burgerlijk recht 2023, 377–385

91 *V Schollaert/J De Bruyne*, Voorstel Richtlijn AI-aansprakelijkheid. Verkennende analyse vanuit Belgisch perspectief [Proposed AI Liability Directive. Exploratory analysis from a Belgian perspective], Nieuw juridisch Weekblad 2023, 574–587

92 *R Vanbergen*, L'actualisation des montants du tableau indicatif pour contrer l'inflation! [The updating of the amounts in the indicative table to counter inflation!], Assuropolis-L'Assurance au présent 2023/2, 13–16

93 *R Vanbergen*, L'indemnisation des incapacités permanentes [Compensation for permanent disability], Assuropolis-L'Assurance au présent 2023/5, 1–6

94 *G Van Daele*, Jeunes émeutiers: qui paie les dégâts? [Young rioters: who will pay for the damage?], Assuropolis-L'Assurance au présent 2023/7, 1–8

95 *A Van Oevelen/A Van Regenmortel/I Samoy/P Gillaerts/I Van Puyvelde/ M Schouteden*, Overzicht van rechtspraak. Aansprakelijkheid uit onrechtmatige daad. Schade en schadeloosstelling (2007–2021) [Overview of case law. Tort law. Damages and compensation (2007–2021)], Tijdschrift voor Privaatrecht 2023, 475–1081

96 *T Vansweevelt/B Weyts*, Fraus omnia corrumpit en in-solidum-gehoudenheid, in het bijzonder bij aanstellersaansprakelijkheid [Fraus omnia corrumpit and in-solidum-liability, in particular in the case of appellant's liability], Revue Générale de Droit Civil/Tijdschrift voor Belgisch Burgerlijk recht 2023, 420–423.

Viktor Tokushev and Hristina Tancheva

III. Bulgaria

A. Legislation

1. Protection of Persons Who Report or Publicly Disclose Information on Breaches Act (Promulgated SG No 11 of 2 February 2023)

1 This Act implements into Bulgarian law the provisions of Directive (EU) 2019/1937 of the European Parliament and of the Council of 23 October 2019 on the protection of persons who report breaches (whistle-blowers) of Union law. The Act establishes two new grounds of tort liability in Bulgarian law.

2 The first new tort, which is based on the principle of the prohibition of so-called retaliation against a person reporting a breach introduced by law, can be defined as liability for damage from retaliation against the person reporting a breach. This liability covers compensation for both pecuniary and non-pecuniary damage. The factual elements of liability include: the deed (the forms of retaliation are exhaustively listed in 15 points[1]), unlawfulness, damage and a causal link between the unlawful act and the damage. Fault is also an element and under the law it is presumed, but only in one of its possible forms, as intent. This gives rise to the argument that adoption of the Act introduces, into our law, tort liability only for intentional acts.[2]

3 The second new tort is liability for persons who intentionally report false information. The factual composition of this liability consists of the same elements – a deed (disclosure of information that is false), unlawfulness, damage and a causal link between the unlawful act and the damage. In this case, too, the fault must be established and, like the first constituent element, only an intentional act is sanctioned – the person must have known that the information was false or, under the circumstances, was bound to assume that it was false. The peculiarity here is that no presumption of guilt has been introduced and it must be proved by the party concerned.

1 The hypotheses of retaliation are listed in art 33 of the Act, which corresponds to art 20 of the Directive.

2 Thus, *P Goleva*, Interesting Regulatory Admission of Tort Liability in Our New Legislation, Commercial and Obligation Law 11 (2023) 5, see in more detail below no 97.

https://doi.org/10.1515/9783111376721-004

B. Cases

4 This year the subject of analysis will be new and significant case law in the Supreme Court of Cassation (SCC) and the Courts of Second Instance, interpretative decisions, rulings and decisions, and additionally, the issue of compensation in personal injury cases are discussed.

1. Supreme Court of Cassation, Interpretative Decision No 1 of 20 April 2023, Interpretative Case No 1/2022, General Assembly of Civil and Commercial Chambers: Tort or Unjust Enrichment

a) Brief Summary of the Facts

5 The factual grounds for the Interpretative Case are as follows: in 2014, by means of an explicit law, the State imposed a fee on revenue from renewable electricity generators by statute. This law was subsequently declared unconstitutional. Numerous producers sought compensation for the fee paid while the law was in force and the cases reached the Supreme Court of Cassation.

6 At the end of 2021, a panel of the SCC established contradictory case law and initiated an interpretative case intended to answer the question of what the correct legal grounds for a claim against the State for repayment are when a particular legal provision is declared unconstitutional and the National Assembly fails to rectify the unfavourable legal consequences of applying the said legal provision – is it compensation for damage or for unjust enrichment?[3]

7 The practical significance of clarifying whether the basis for the claim is tort or unjust enrichment lies in the fact that, in both cases, there is a different point from which interest for delay is due – from the demand for payment (in the case of unjust enrichment) or from the committing of the tort.

3 Specific solutions in both directions have been the subject of discussion in the 2020 and 2021 reports: see *V Tokushev*, Bulgaria, in: E Karner/BC Steininger (eds), European Tort Law (ETL) 2020 (2021) 53, nos 3–10 and *idem*, Bulgaria, in: E Karner/BC Steininger (eds), European Tort Law 2021 (2022) 54, nos 11–18.

b) Judgment of the Court

In its Interpretative Decision, the SCC ruled that the legal basis of a claim brought against the State for reimbursement of the amount of fee paid into the State budget by virtue of a law, given the subsequent declaration of the law to be unconstitutional and the failure of the National Assembly to remedy the adverse legal consequences of the application of this provision, is tort law. 8

The reasoning adopted by the SCC is based on constitutional legal theory and a recent decision of the Constitutional Court, Decision No 3 from 8 April 2020 in Constitutional Case No 5/2019. This Decision states that, according to the Constitution of the Republic of Bulgaria, the decisions of the Constitutional Court (CC) declaring a law unconstitutional have an *ex nunc* effect. The *ex nunc* effect is expressed in terms of the impossibility of applying, in the future, a law declared unconstitutional, and that no changes can occur with regard to previous legal relationships that were within the scope of the law at the time of its standing. 9

However, the future effect of the Decision on unconstitutionality has a more specific application in cases where litigation was pending *at the time of the decision* of the CC on the unconstitutionality of a terminated legal relationship which was governed by the unconstitutional law. In these cases, the CC held that the law declared unconstitutional should not be applied and the Court should resolve the dispute on the basis of the Constitution or on the analogous application of a current act or law. 10

In the light of these arguments and in view of the fact that the subject matter of the disputes on which the controversial practice is based is precisely the payment of a fee based on an act that was declared unconstitutional, the SCC ruled that the adoption, by the National Assembly (NA) of an act contrary to the Constitution is a tort, as is the failure of the NA to comply with its obligation to redress the effects of the act declared unconstitutional. In this sense, the legal basis for a claim brought against the State in this factual situation is tort law and the liability of the State is tortious, strict, no-fault based and is effective regardless of whether the conduct of the officials concerned was culpable. 11

There is a dissenting opinion to the decision, supported by a significant number of judges. It defends the thesis of 'unjust enrichment' as the legal basis of the claim in this case. The reasoning of the dissenting opinion is twofold: first, it is submitted that in torts, compensation is a substitute for the good(s) damaged , the reimbursement of the fee paid cannot be regarded as 'compensation', since it is equal to that which was paid. 12

Secondly, the dissenting opinion adopts a different interpretation of the constitutional arguments, contending that prohibiting a court from applying a law declared unconstitutional to a legal dispute over a completed legal relationship 13 means, in effect, that the payment made while the law was in effect is a payment without justification. In that sense, the legal basis for the claim of the renewable energy producers should also be 'unjust enrichment'.

c) Commentary

14 The conclusion reached in the Interpretative Decision must be supported, as those arguments set out in the dissenting opinion are not well founded. Thus, the criterion of whether compensation in tort is a substitute remedy is correct only in the case of non-pecuniary damage, but in the case of pecuniary damage, the compensation is equal to the damage suffered. Perhaps it is precisely the identical nature of what was paid and what was returned that justifies the argument of unjust enrichment (in the form of its initial lack of justification).

15 On the other hand, the view that declaring unconstitutional the law under which the payment was made is an argument that the payment was made while it was in effect is also inaccurate. In order to have a payment in the absence of a legal basis, that ground must not have existed at all, which is contrary to the concept of the effect of CC decisions on the unconstitutionality of an *ex nunc* law as set out above. Moreover, the unconstitutionality found by the CC is the operative fact that gives the plaintiff the right to seek payment from the State on the basis of the law being declared unconstitutional.

16 In conclusion, it should be emphasised that in the present case, all the elements for the establishment of tortious liability are present – the existence of an action by an organ of the State; unlawfulness – the adoption of a law contrary to the Constitution of the Republic of Bulgaria, combined with the failure on the part of the National Assembly to remedy the negative consequences of the application of the unconstitutional law, from which damage to private law subjects occurred as a direct and immediate consequence.

2. Supreme Court of Cassation, Decision No 50011 of 6 February 2023, Civil Case No 1364/2022, Civil Chamber, 1st Bench: Damage Caused by Chattels

a) Brief Summary of the Facts

17 The plaintiff sustained injuries while sliding down a waterslide at a water park owned by the defendant. The cause of the injuries was that the air mattress on

which he was sliding down tipped over and he hit the bottom of the pool. The plaintiff claimed non-pecuniary damages in the amount of € 5,000 from the company which owns the slide, insofar as its employees failed to exercise due care in operating it.

The Court of First Instance dismissed the appeal, holding that, in the present 18 case, the incident occurred due to an accidental and unforeseeable event, namely the rotation of the air mattress used, and therefore the occurrence of the damage could not be attributed to the fault of the defendant company's employees. Even if all the regulatory conditions are complied with, going down a fast waterslide is in itself a risky activity. The injured party should therefore bear the risk of any accident.

The Court of Second Instance also rejected the plaintiff's claim, but on differ- 19 ent grounds. According to the Sofia City Court, in this case, the plaintiff claimed that he had suffered damage due to the failure of the defendant's employees to exercise due care, but it was not proven what exactly that failure to exercise due care consisted of and what safety rules were not followed. In the Court's view, the mere fact of pain and suffering being occasioned does not imply that the defendant failed to act and hence, that compensation was justified.

The case was admitted to cassation on the issue of the legal classification of a 20 claim for damages arising from the use of a waterslide.

b) Judgment of the Court

The SCC overturned the decisions of the lower courts. The Court's main argument 21 is that the claim is incorrectly classified, and should, on the basis of the facts set out in the claim, be classified as a claim for damage from chattels. The incident occurred because of the properties of the chattel itself, an inflatable mattress that slides on an inclined water-logged surface, whereby it cannot be entirely predicted whether it will land in the pool in the usual manner or whether some unforeseen rotation will occur causing those descending to hit the bottom of the pool. Liability for damage from chattels is strict and does not depend on the acts or omissions of the property owner's employees.

Sliding down a waterslide carries risks of harm that cannot always be fore- 22 seen. At the same time, the strict liability for damage from chattels rests on the concept of risk – 'he who takes the benefits must bear the burdens'. It is the parties who organise the ride and who derive benefits from that activity who should be liable for damage arising from unforeseen circumstances in connection with the use of the slide, not the person who is injured in those circumstances.

23 In view of the consequences of the trauma suffered, the SCC held € 3,500 to be fair compensation.

c) Commentary

24 The decision of the SCC is correct. It is of interest because it deals with a borderline hypothesis between liability arising from the performance of employees and liability for damage from chattels. This is a rare case inasmuch as, in our current practice, damage from chattels most often concerns damage caused by pets.

25 The reasoning put forward regarding the bearing of risk should also be approved since, when a risky activity, such as going down a waterslide for pleasure, is organised in a commercial manner, this does not mean that the owner does not bear the risk of operating it.

3. Supreme Court of Cassation, Ruling No 3733, Civil Case No 1239/202, Civil Chamber, 1st Bench: Liability for Causing an Injury to a Dog

a) Brief Summary of the Facts

26 The plaintiff was walking his dog, a Pinscher, in a grassy area where the defendant was walking his two dogs, both American Staffordshire Terriers, without leads and muzzles. The defendant's two dogs lunged at the plaintiff's dog and began biting it. The plaintiff tried to protect his dog, which was, itself, bitten by the two dogs in the leg and neck area. He was also bitten by the dogs.

27 The plaintiff claimed non-pecuniary damages, both for the pain he suffered and for the suffering caused to him by the injury to his dog.

28 The Court of First Instance upheld the plaintiff's claim up to an amount of € 5,000, which was confirmed by the Court of Appeal. Claiming that the decision was incorrect and that the amount of compensation had been unjustifiably excessive, the defendant brought an appeal in cassation.

b) Judgment of the Court

29 The SCC did not allow the case to proceed to cassation. Its reasoning on the cassation issues raised is of interest. First of all, the SCC held that the objection that the

injured dog was not the chattel of the plaintiff but of his girlfriend, with whom he cohabited, was irrelevant, insofar as the dog had been kept by the two of them for two years and a deep emotional bond had been established between them.

As regards the amount of compensation, the SCC confirmed that the Court of Appeal correctly assessed the nature of the plaintiff's injuries and the other circumstances relevant to the compensation and, in determining the amount of compensation, the Court also took into account the negative experience in relation to the assault and injuries to the plaintiff's pet. 30

c) Commentary

The SCC's ruling is of interest in both of the above respects. Firstly, it is the first time that the SCC has ruled that damage can be suffered from harm to a chattel which is not the property of the plaintiff. On the other hand, the concept of non-pecuniary damage arising from harm to a pet (which Bulgarian law treats as a chattel) is also a novelty for the practice of the SCC. It remains to be seen whether these rulings will be accepted as constant practice. 31

4. Supreme Court of Cassation, Decision No 50038 of 25 May 2023, Civil Case No 1608/2022, Civil Chamber, 2nd Bench: Damage Arising from Insult and Defamation

a) Brief Summary of the Facts

An internet site posted an article taken from the defendant's public Facebook profile. It contained allegations that the plaintiff was a 'State Security Agent,' 'unacknowledged due to incompetence,' 'a caricature of our political life,' and 'ridiculous and pathetic.' The plaintiff filed claims in tort for non-pecuniary damages in a total amount of € 5,000 arising from the defendant's offensive and defamatory statements. 32

The Court of First Instance held that the statement made was defamatory of the plaintiff and that the information that he was an informer for the State Security agency was untrustworthy, ie a false fact had been circulated and this affected the plaintiff's honour and dignity, amounting to defamation. With regard to the other expressions: 'unacknowledged due to incompetence', 'a caricature of our political life', 'ridiculous and pathetic', the Court held that they were offensive terms, degrading the plaintiff's honour and dignity. 33

34 The Court decided that a tort had been committed through a post on the defendant's Facebook profile, which was accessible to an unlimited number of readers and which had been reproduced from another website and reached a wider audience. The Court took into account that, at the time of the tort, the plaintiff was a Member of the National Assembly and, as a public figure and politician, according to the consistent and uncontroversial case law of the European Court of Human Rights, should have a higher threshold of sensitivity to such statements by third parties, and therefore awarded damages in the amount of € 2,300.

35 The Court of Appeal found that the conclusion of the first instance court that the defendant had committed the offence of insult by writing the article was unfounded – the author had expressed an opinion on a political topic by giving his assessment, as none of the expressions in question contained obscene, vulgar or cynical words, nor any that contained derogatory judgements. However, the Court held that the allegation that the plaintiff was an agent/informer for the State Security agency constituted a defamatory assertion, since in Bulgarian society, claiming that a person was an agent/informer of the State Security agency has negative connotations, damaging and tarnishing a person's reputation in society, on the ground that the State Security agency was a repressive structure of the totalitarian regime of the Bulgarian Communist Party.

36 The second instance court took into account the short duration of the negative emotions experienced (only a few days), the fact that the plaintiff was a former Member of Parliament and political scientist, ie a public figure, the fact that it was not established in the case that the publication had reached a wide circle of people, and also that the defendant was a journalist who, although in violation of the Constitution of the Republic of Bulgaria, exercised his right to free opinion and its dissemination by speech and the defendant expressed his personal position in the article in question.

37 The Court found that fair compensation for the non-pecuniary damage suffered as a result of the tort amounts to € 130, taking into account the fact that the conviction of the defendant itself achieved moral compensation of the plaintiff.

b) Judgment of the Court

38 The Court of Cassation allowed an appeal on the question of whether it should be accepted, without proof (as a fact known to the Court) that the audience of those publications made freely available on the social network, Facebook, and the news (journalistic) sites on the internet is unlimited (objectively indefinable) or whether it is necessary for the parties to provide evidence to establish the actual number of persons reached by the publication in question. The issue is relevant to the Court's

reasoning in determining the amount of compensation for non-pecuniary damage, insofar as the Court took the view that the publication had not reached 'a wide range of people' without setting out any reasons as to how it established that fact and how it related to the plaintiff's negative experiences.

The SCC held that a statement contained in a post on a personal Facebook profile with the setting 'public' should be considered as a known fact and that the audience of the open access post is unlimited (apart from the number of users of the relevant online social network). It is not a matter of proof how many users were reached by the publication containing the defamatory statement. 39

The SCC upheld the decision, holding that the Court of Appeal had correctly applied the law by qualifying the expressions used by the defendant and distinguishing between those which constituted opinion about a public figure (who should accept greater interference in his private sphere) and those which were statements of fact, subjecting the latter to a test of their veracity, in the light of which it also upheld the merits of the claim only in respect of those written statements which constituted allegations of false facts of a defamatory nature. 40

c) Commentary

As long as the defendant's social network profile is public, it enables anyone, including those outside the social network, to access and share the posts. Therefore, the audience can be presumed to be broad, without any need to provide evidence of that fact. Indeed, it would be difficult to ascertain, by means of concrete evidence, what audience the publication had reached, so the Court was justified in finding that, since the profile was public, many individuals would have had access to it, especially since, in this case, the article was also published on an internet site. It was reasonably held that the value expressions used were not of such a nature as to materially affect a person who is a public figure and who should have a higher threshold of tolerance. The defendant was a journalist and therefore he used such expressions which reinforced suggestions, and since they were not vulgar or cynical but rather expressed a personal opinion, freedom of speech should not be restricted. On the other hand, false allegations of belonging to the former State Security Agency could be characterised as defamatory, given that that service was part of a regime which had been declared criminal by law and that it had not been established in the case that the plaintiff had been a member of it. 41

It is interesting to note the approach of the appellate court in awarding a symbolic compensation amount of € 130, assuming that, in addition to the fact that negative emotions are not particularly long-lasting and intense, the moral compensa- 42 tion is achieved by the defendant's conviction itself, which is why a lower compensation amount, almost nominal, was set.

5. Supreme Court of Cassation, Ruling No 1045 of 10 October 2023, Civil Case No 4346/2022, Civil Chamber, 1st Bench: Municipality's Liability for Pedestrian's Injuries

a) Brief Summary of the Facts

43 While walking along a pavement with a companion, because he was blind, the plaintiff tripped over one of the pavement barriers (bollards), as a result of which, he fell and sustained injuries (left shoulder joint contusion, extensive bruising with a deep abrasion on the anterior surface of the right lower leg). The victim was examined by a doctor, but after a week his condition deteriorated: he developed complications of the wound on his right leg – necrosis of the skin, which required surgical intervention. It took more than 40 days for the wound to heal. During this time, the plaintiff experienced pain, had difficulty moving around and was inconvenienced in his daily activities.

44 The victim brought claims against the municipality for compensation of non-pecuniary damage in the amount of € 7,500 and for compensation of pecuniary damage in the amount of € 310 for medical expenses.

45 The Court of First Instance upheld the claims for pecuniary and non-pecuniary damages in full, holding that the municipality, which owned the pavement, had failed to fulfil its obligation to provide the conditions necessary for uninterrupted, safe and comfortable transit, which was a prerequisite for its liability for damage resulting from that failure. The municipality is liable in tort for the acts and omissions of the persons to whom it has entrusted the performance of its duties – in this case the performance of repair work (including the installation of bollards) on the pavement where the accident occurred.

b) Judgment of the Court

46 The Court of Appeal upheld the finding that there was a basis for the municipality to be held liable. It was accepted that in this case, the purpose of the concrete bollards, which had been installed to ensure the safe passage of pedestrians by indicating the boundary of the pavement and thereby prevent, or at least reduce, the likelihood of pedestrians unsuspectingly entering a section in which trams were

running, was compromised by their colour, shape and size. The bollards were of a similar colour to that of the road surface, with sharp edges and a low height, thus making it likely that pedestrians who tripped and fell on them would suffer significant injuries, as in the plaintiff's case. The defendant's plea of contributory negligence on the part of the plaintiff was held to be unfounded.

The Court of Appeal, having regard to the time of the occurrence of the injury, 47
the economic situation in the country at that time, the age of the victim, the information from forensic medical examination on the type, nature and extent of the trauma suffered by the plaintiff, the duration of the healing process, and the manner and extent of recovery, held that the fair compensation for non-pecuniary damage amounted to € 5,000 and dismissed the remainder of the claim up to the full amount claimed. The Court also held that some of the costs representing pecuniary damage had not been proven and dismissed the claim in part.

The Court of Cassation held that there is no ground for cassation appeal. 48

c) Commentary

The Court referred to the Road Act, which provides that the construction, repair 49
and maintenance of municipal roads is the responsibility of the municipality, which includes the maintenance of pavements as part of the street road network. The municipality should ensure conditions necessary for safe and convenient transit, and failure to do so is a prerequisite for liability for damages. For this reason, and despite the fact that the bollards were included in the street construction designs, they turned out to be non-functional (they blend in with the pavement colour and are low), not in line with the requirements of the environment and create a nuisance for people. The unlawful conduct consists of action, namely, the placement of concrete bollards with sharp edges and low height, creating a risk of injury to pedestrians; and inaction, namely, the failure to remove these bollards.

The Court took into account the fact that the victim was a blind person to 50
whom society owed a duty of special care under the Persons with Disabilities Act. A provision of the same Act is cited, according to which, the identification and removal of all obstacles and bollards which hinder the accessibility of the urban environment must be undertaken. The Court held that the concrete bollards in place created obstacles to the free movement and risk of disability even for people with normal sensory perception and normal physical mobility.

The plea of contributory negligence was rightly rejected, since for contributory 51
negligence to exist, the injured party must be blameworthy for the acts or omissions which contributed to the damage, whereas in this case he had exercised due care in providing a reliable person to accompany him.

6. Supreme Court of Cassation, Decision No 50020 of 15 February 2023, Civil Case No 2340/2022, Civil Chamber, 4th Bench: Damage Caused by Failure to Implement EU Directive

a) Brief Summary of the Facts

52 The plaintiffs entered into a contract for the purchase of an apartment using a loan secured by a mortgage on the property in favour of the bank. The annual interest rate on the loan initially agreed between the parties was 10.45 %, but within one year, the monthly instalment on the loan increased due to a unilateral increase in the interest rate by the bank. Having become unemployed, the plaintiffs found themselves unable to repay the loan and the bank claimed for repayment of the loan. The creditor sued the debtors under the immediate procedure under art 417 of the Code of Civil Procedure (CCP) on the basis of an extract from the bank's books. The plaintiffs submitted an objection to the enforcement order, appealed against the order for immediate enforcement under art 419 of the CCP and sought a cease of enforcement under art 420 of the CCP, arguing that there was an unfair clause in the loan agreement allowing a unilateral change of the interest rate. The Court dismissed the appeal on the ground that, in ordering immediate enforcement, the Court only undertook a formal examination of the documents submitted in the payment proceedings, and the issue of the unfairness of the clauses should have been examined in the claim proceedings. In the meantime, the plaintiffs' apartment had been sold at a public sale in the enforcement proceedings brought by the bank and they were forced to leave.

53 Claim proceedings were subsequently initiated, in which the bank's claims were partially upheld, as the Court held that the provisions of the loan agreement allowing a unilateral change of the bank's interest rate were unfair and therefore null and void. The remainder of the claim was upheld, finding that the conditions for immediate repayment due to non-payment had been met.

54 On the basis of the Act on the Liability for Damage caused by the State and Municipalities, the plaintiffs claimed that the defendants, the National Assembly of the Republic of Bulgaria and the District Court of Plovdiv, were jointly and severally liable to pay compensation in the amount of € 23,000 for the pecuniary damage caused to them in the form of loss, representing the costs incurred in satisfying the claims of the bank in the claim and enforcement proceedings brought by the bank against them in connection with the loan agreement, together with statutory interest. They further sought compensation in the amount of € 27,500 for the pecuniary damage suffered by them in the form of loss of profit, representing the dif-

ference between the market value of their apartment at the time the claim was brought (€ 59,300) and the value of the outstanding loan debt (€ 31,800), together with statutory interest, as well as compensation in the amount of € 15,000 for non-pecuniary damage, representing compensation for the distress, frustration, financial and domestic concern caused as a result of the breach of European Union law.

The Court of First Instance held that the provisions of the loan agreement were unfair clauses, given that they enabled one party to the agreement – the bank – to change the value of the interest rate without this change in the price of the service having been the result of external factors beyond the control of the trader, or without being caused by the influence of the free market and/or a State regulator. The Court held that the District Court of Plovdiv was obliged to take into account the case law of the European Court of Justice (ECJ) requiring it to make an *ex officio* assessment of the unfairness of the relevant contractual clauses, which it failed to do. It also held that the National Assembly had not adequately transposed Directive 93/13/EEC on Unfair Terms, and that court proceedings were initiated under art 417 of the Code of Civil Procedure, which did not allow for an assessment on the merits of the unfairness of the clauses contained in the document submitted. It held that the infringement of European Union law was sufficiently substantial in view of the importance of the rights affected and the manner and extent of the infringement. 55

The Court of First Instance found that, as regards compensation for pecuniary damage, there was no direct and proximate causal link between the unlawful conduct and the damage suffered. With regard to the claim for non-pecuniary damages, the Court considers that, where a plaintiff claims compensation for the non-pecuniary damage resulting from a tort, ie where the harmful act has been proved and the claim is well-founded in its cause of action, no formal evidence is necessary to establish that damage, since that harm always results from the damaging conduct. In this case, the Court ordered the defendant to pay € 3,500 as non-pecuniary damages. 56

The Court of Appeal held that the principle of State liability for damage caused to private individuals by infringements of Community law applies in any case where a Member State infringes Community law, even if the infringer is the national legislature. 57

The appellate court held that the claim for compensation for non-pecuniary damage in the amount of € 5,000 for each plaintiff was justified, holding that the damage was caused jointly by the District Court of Plovdiv and the National Assembly, and that their liability was joint and several. As regards pecuniary damages, the Court held that they were not due, since the reduction of the plaintiffs' patrimony by the payment of the loan sums was lawful under the contract. The 58 sale of the property was also not a direct consequence of the defendant's unlawful conduct relating to the unfair contract terms. In the event that the plaintiffs had continued to make their repayments, without the increase formed on the basis of the unfair terms, the loan would not have been declared immediately repayable and the bank would not have had to be satisfied by means of a forced sale.

b) Judgment of the Court

59 The appeal is admissible only on a point of law concerning the Court's duty to ascertain whether a direct causal link between the infringement of EU law and the rights deriving therefrom and the damage allegedly suffered exists in the case.

60 In the present case, the alleged non-pecuniary damage is based on the plaintiffs' stress, frustration and worry of a financial and domestic nature from the real danger of losing their only home and its subsequent forced sale, as well as from the length of the court proceedings, during which period the plaintiffs were constantly worried about their future, in fear of being left homeless.

61 The Court held that the sale of the property was not a direct consequence of the plaintiffs' conduct in relation to the unfair terms, but was the result of the plaintiffs' complete cessation of payment under the loan agreement and its subsequent declaration as being immediately repayable, as a result of which the enforcement proceedings were initiated in which the property was sold to satisfy its claims. Only if the plaintiffs had continued to pay their instalments, without the increase following the bank's unilateral change in the base rate, but the loan had nevertheless been declared to be immediately repayable, could compensation have been claimed. Therefore, the Court held that there was no direct causal link between the infringement of EU law and the damage suffered by the plaintiffs. The claims for compensation for non-pecuniary damage were therefore rejected.

c) Commentary

62 Undisputedly, the case established wrongdoing. The Bulgarian State failed to fulfil its obligations under European Union law concerning the correct transposition of certain provisions of Council Directive 93/13/EEC of 5 April 1993 on Unfair Terms in Consumer Contracts. In the Code of Civil Procedure (promulgated, State Gazette No 59 of 20 July 2007, effective 1 March 2008), the legislator established proceedings for the immediate enforcement of a pecuniary obligation owed to a bank on the basis of an extract from the books of account only, without requiring the presentation of the loan agreement. This means that an unfair term in a consumer con-

tract cannot be established by courts in a timely manner, but only at a later stage, when enforcement may even have already been undertaken, as in the present case. Significantly, following an infringement found on the part of the Bulgarian legislator, the European Commission recommended the adoption of relevant legislative changes, which have been reflected in the amendment of Item 2, para 1 of art 417 of the Code of Civil Procedure (SG No 100 of 2019), which requires the abstract of the books of account to be accompanied by the document from which the bank's claim arose.

At the same time, according to the case law of the European Court of Justice, 63
the national court is obliged to assess *ex officio* the unfair nature of contractual clauses, regardless of the type of proceedings, where the necessary legal or factual circumstances are present, which was not so in this case. The Plovdiv District Court should have applied that principle in the proceedings before it, and its failure to do so, despite the explicit reference to the plaintiffs as appellants, is an infringement of Community law.

The dispute essentially concerns whether the damage suffered has a direct 64
causal link with the wrongdoing established. The Court rightly dismissed the claim for pecuniary damages for lack of a direct causal link. The plaintiffs had ceased to meet the loan obligations entirely because they had become unemployed and insolvent, which led to all the adverse consequences, and it could not be alleged that this had been caused solely by the existence of an unfair contract clause, ie the damage is indirect. It is only the increase in the interest rate which was unlawful, whereas the principal and interest before the increase were due and should have been paid, which, had it been done, could have prevented the plaintiffs from having been sanctioned and their property sold. Whether, if the plaintiffs had continued to pay the amount before the increase in interest, this would have deterred the bank from enforcing satisfaction for the difference between the amount paid and the amount charged by the bank is another question.

7. Supreme Court of Cassation, Ruling No 2565 of 18 September 2023, Civil Case No 4647/2022, Civil Chamber, 2nd Bench: Medical Malpractice

a) Brief Summary of the Facts

On 13 November 2019, the plaintiff underwent a surgical intervention, a vasectomy, 65
in a medical centre for which the amount of € 760 was paid. A few months later, the plaintiff's wife became pregnant, which upset their relationship and led to a

temporary separation. The plaintiff claimed the sum of € 760 in compensation for pecuniary damage suffered and the sum of € 4,350 in compensation for non-pecuniary damage from the clinic employing the doctor who had carried out the procedure.

66 The Court of First Instance did not find that the physician had deviated from medical standards and the rules of good medical practice in performing the procedure. It was found that it was very rare (a 0.2 % chance) that even a perfectly performed procedure could fail, of which the plaintiff had been informed. The latter signed an informed consent to the procedure, by which he declared that he was aware of his rights, the possible risks and dangers of the procedure, including the fact that he could not obtain a full guarantee of the outcome of the surgery.

67 The Court held that the plaintiff's allegations that, during the examination on 12 February 2020 and in a telephone call on 13 August 2020, he had received information from the doctor that the vasectomy had been successful and that he could no longer have children, and that his wife's pregnancy dated from 22–24 February, were unfounded. Since no documentary evidence had been provided about the doctor's conclusion, but only the testimony of the plaintiff's wife, who was an interested person within the meaning of art 172 of the Code of Civil Procedure, the Court dismissed the claims as unsubstantiated.

b) Judgment of the Court

68 The Court of Appeal held that the decision was incorrect. It pointed out that the expert witness found inconsistencies with the rules of good medical practice and established standards in the preparation of the medical records by the surgeon, which led to ambiguity and misinformation as to the type of surgery performed on the patient, as well as uncertainty as to the anaesthesia used.

69 The Court held that, having seen the first spermogram of 10 February 2020 (which showed 67 million spermatozoa with a norm of over 39), the doctor should have informed the patient and repeated the vasectomy. The Court found that there was non-performance of the professional duties of a doctor in the performance of a medical activity. The doctor breached medical standards as regulated under the Health Act and the Rules of Good Medical Practice, and the fundamental principles of medical care, namely, timeliness, sufficiency and quality of medical treatment regulated under the Health Act, which resulted in injury.

70 The Court held that, since the expert witness had concluded that the procedure was ineffective, the Court of First Instance failed to comply with the instruction in art 172 of the Civil Procedure Code to subject the testimony to an overriding assessment in the light of all the other evidence in the case against which the im-

pact of the 'interested party' factor is to be assessed. The Court of Appeal held that there was a substantial body of circumstantial evidence which formed a coherent and unbroken logical chain of facts corresponding to the factual allegations in the claim relating to specific omissions on the part of the doctor which were directly causally linked to the injurious result suffered by the plaintiff – pain, suffering, disruption of family relations, and material damage. It is accepted that there was a medical failure in the post-operative treatment process relating to the correct reading of the tests and the proper and timely informing of the patient about the effect and consequences of the vasectomy.

The Court held that the fair amount of compensation for non-pecuniary dam- 71
age in this case was € 1,000, given that no pain and suffering beyond that which is usual in the particular circumstances of the facts of the case was alleged, no lasting and irreparable consequences had occurred, but rather short-term emotional discomfort, tension and disappointment and a disruption of the normal functioning of his marital relationship experienced. Compensation in the amount of € 760 for pecuniary damage was also awarded.

The Court of Cassation dismissed the appeal against the decision, arguing that 72
it was not obviously incorrect, that the issues raised in the appeal were not determinative of the outcome of the dispute, nor was there a conflict with the case law referred to by the cassation appellant.

c) Commentary

The Court of Appeal was right to hold that a cumulative assessment of all the evi- 73
dence in the case led to the conclusion that the doctor at the medical centre had failed to provide the patient with due care after performing the operation, given that he should have followed up and ascertained whether it had been successful and informed the patient, who did not have the special knowledge to be able to assess the success of the procedure, in a timely manner. Even if the patient had been informed that the procedure might not have the desired effect, this did not remove the obligation to follow up and ascertain whether that was the case and, if necessary, to repeat it.

8. Supreme Court of Cassation, Ruling No 2565 of 18 September 2023, Civil Case No 4647/2022, Civil Chamber, 2nd Bench: Failure of Court to Rule on Request for Preliminary Ruling

a) Brief Summary of the Facts

74 The plaintiff requested the Criminal Court, which was examining his measure of restraint, to ask for a preliminary ruling from the European Court of Justice. At a hearing before the Criminal Court, the plaintiff's measure of restraint was examined, and the Court dismissed the application to vary it, but did not examine or rule on the plaintiff's request for a preliminary ruling. The plaintiff thereby alleged that the defendant had committed a denial of justice, which had upset him, and he brought an action for damages in the amount of € 13,000 against the Court.

75 The Court of First Instance pointed out that, where a party has filed a request for a preliminary ruling, the Court hearing the case must rule on that request. The Court may not grant, but must review, the request for a preliminary ruling. By failing to do so, the Court hearing the case committed a procedural breach.

76 However, the Court of First Instance held that it was unsubstantiated that the plaintiff had suffered damage as a result of the procedural breach described above. The request did not, in essence, raise any questions on the interpretation of EU law or of the compatibility of national law with EU law, but alleged breaches committed by the Court that examined the case, and therefore there was no ground for a preliminary ruling to be made. The failure of the Court Bench of the defendant court to consider the plaintiff's request for a preliminary ruling did not lead to an unlawful result and could not have caused the plaintiff any damage. The Court also did not accept the testimony of the witness in the case that, after the refusal of the Court to request a preliminary ruling, the plaintiff felt nervous and constantly talked about the matter. The Court rejected the claim on this point.

b) Judgment of the Court

77 The Court of Appeal found that the facts were correctly established by the Court of First Instance. It accepted that, notwithstanding the procedural breach committed from a formal point of view, the plaintiff did not suffer any damage, because, first, the questions raised in the request did not concern the interpretation of EU rules but were, essentially, objections to the Court's conclusions in relation to the mea-

sure of restraint and, secondly, no damage had been proved to be directly causally linked to the alleged breach.

Having found that there was no evidence of manifest error in the decision, the SCC issued a ruling which did not allow a cassation appeal against the decision of the Court of Appeal. 78

c) Commentary

In this case, the defendant unlawfully failed to rule on the plaintiff's request for a preliminary ruling. However, it was reasonably held that since the request was unfounded, even if the Court had ruled, it would not have led to a referral to the ECJ. The request for a preliminary ruling must concern the interpretation or validity of EU law and not the interpretation of national rules or questions of fact raised in the proceedings before the national court. There is testimony in the case that the plaintiff was 'irritated' that the Court had refused to refer the case for a preliminary ruling, which could in principle be regarded as damage suffered if there were grounds for referral to the ECJ, but in this case, even if the Court had ruled, the result would have been the same – the request would not have been granted and the plaintiff would have suffered negative emotions in this case as well. 79

9. Supreme Court of Cassation, Ruling No 50399 of 5 June 2023, Commercial Case No 1624 /2022, Commercial Chamber, 1st Bench: Non-Pecuniary Damage of the Brother of a Deceased

a) Brief Summary of the Facts

A passenger in a car was killed as the result of an accident and his mother and brother sought compensation for non-pecuniary damage. The first plaintiff claimed an amount of € 127,000 and the second the sum of € 76,000 from the third party liability insurer of the driver of the crashed car. 80

The Court of First Instance found that, on the date of the accident, a valid legal relationship existed between the driver and the defendant company under which the defendant insurer had undertaken to provide cover for any liability that might arise in connection with the use of the car. The Court established the unlawful act and the culpability of the insured driver. Therefore, the Court held that the driver 81 of the car committed a tort and the liability of the motor insurer should be recognised.

82 With respect to compensation for the deceased's brother, the Court found that exceptional circumstances had been proven in this case, which justified the payment of compensation. The testimony of witnesses and a social report established that, for the plaintiff, his deceased brother was like a father, given that his actual father had become uninterested in him. The bond between the two was extremely strong and the sudden death of the brother had a very negative impact on the plaintiff's psyche. As regards the mother, there was also a strong relationship with the deceased, whom she had brought up on her own.

83 The Court rejected the defendant's objection of contributory negligence on the part of a third party, the Road Infrastructure Agency. It was found that the stretch of road was passable in winter conditions, and the Court held that the state of the road surface at the time of the incident did not give rise to its occurrence.

84 In the light of the foregoing considerations, the Court found that the claims were well-founded and should be upheld for the full amounts claimed.

b) Judgment of the Court

85 The Appellate Court confirmed that the claims had merit, but also found the complaints in the appeal that the amount of the compensation awarded was excessive to be partly justified. The Court held that, without denying the immeasurable suffering of the plaintiff as the mother of the deceased, the amount of compensation awarded did not correspond to the established case law on the award of such compensation. In the Court's view, in this case, the fair amount of compensation payable was € 51,000.

86 The Court of Appeal agreed with the conclusion that persons outside the immediate family circle (parents, children and spouse) are recognised as victims and entitled to compensation for moral damage only where, due to specific life circumstances, the attachment had become so strong that the death of the relative caused the other moral pain and suffering exceeding the intensity and duration that would normally be present in the family relationship concerned. It was accepted that in the present case, an emotional relationship had been proved, different from 'usual' relationships in terms of type, intensity and duration, and in which a relationship similar and extremely close to that existing between the closest circle of persons had been established, and was not limited to 'normal' relationships in the traditional Bulgarian family, characterised by affection, moral support and emotional closeness.

The Court of Cassation dismissed the action against the appeal judgment, holding that the questions raised by the cassation appellant did not appear to be determinative of the outcome of the specific legal dispute, and that there was no contradiction between the answers of the Appellate Court in the contested decision and the case law of the SCC. 87

c) Commentary

The Court's decision is in line with established practice, following the rulings of 88
Interpretative Decision 1/2016 of the General Assembly of the Supreme Court of Cassation's Civil, Commercial and Criminal Chamber, which sets as criteria for the payment of compensation in the event of the death of a person other than the parents, children and spouse, the proof of a lasting and deep emotional relationship with the deceased. If no evidence of a particularly strong relationship between the deceased and the person claiming compensation (most often brothers, sisters, grandparents) is presented in the case, the claim is dismissed.[4] The idea is not to compensate all the close relatives who suffer negative emotions from someone's death, but only those closest who, as a rule, suffer the most (parents, children and spouse), and others who, in a particular case, due to special circumstances, suffer significantly and this suffering has been proven.[5] The opposite is also possible – persons who are normally deemed to be entitled to compensation may not be awarded it because, in a given case, it is established that they have not suffered at all or have not suffered to such an extent that they are entitled to compensation.[6]

4 Ruling No 50555 of 21 October 2023 in Commercial Case No 2011/2022 of the Supreme Court of Cassation, 2nd Commercial Chamber; Decision No 50078 of 26 October 2023 in Commercial Case No 2045/2022 of the Supreme Court of Cassation, 1st Commercial Chamber; Ruling No 50562 of 13 October 2023 in Commercial Case No 2078/2022 of the Supreme Court of Cassation, 1st Commercial Chamber; Ruling No 50434 of 19 October 2023 in Commercial Case No 2078/2022 of the Supreme Court of Cassation, 1st Commercial Chamber; Ruling No 50434 of 19 October 2023 in Commercial Case No 2045 /2022 of the Supreme Court of Cassation, 1st Commercial Chamber; Ruling No 50562 of 13 October 2023 in Commercial Case No 2078 /2022 of the Supreme Court of Cassation, 1st Commercial Chamber; Ruling No 50434 of 19 October 2023 in Commercial Case No 1924/2022 of the Supreme Court of Cassation, 1st Commercial Chamber, etc.

5 Ruling No 3479 of 13 November 2023 in Civil Case No 1011/2023 of the Supreme Court of Cassation, 3rd Civil Division.

6 Ruling No 910 of 31 October 2023 in Commercial Case No 2/2023 of the Supreme Court of Cassation, 1st Commercial Chamber.

89 In the case outlined above, the Court reasoned that there were exceptional circumstances in view of the fact that the deceased brother was proved to have been like a father to the plaintiff, helping the mother in raising and bringing him up.

10. Personal Injury

90 **Supreme Court of Cassation, Decision No 118 of 24 October 2023 in Civil Case No 953/2023, Civil Chamber, 4th Bench.** In this Decision, which was probably the subject of most debate in 2023 due to the amount of compensation awarded, the SCC awarded compensation in the amount of € 400,000 to the plaintiff who had suffered extremely serious injuries as a result of an incident. In effect, this Decision awarded additional compensation of € 200,000 to compensation of € 200,000 already awarded in a previous partial claim. The reason for the extraordinary amount of compensation is the exceptional nature of the injuries (described in detail in the Decision with relevant medical terms covering approximately one page). The Court also took account of the victim's young age of 21 at the time of the incident, the fact that she was a mother and that after the incident she is practically incapable of living independently. Unable to attend to herself, she is totally incapacitated and the prognosis for the development of her condition is unfavourable. It should be noted that the Court took into consideration not only her physical condition, but also her psychological state (insofar as the physical injuries had led to psychological changes), which in aggregate determined the amount of compensation. As a result, a record amount of compensation was awarded, with the SCC increasing the compensation awarded in this case from the € 100,000 awarded at first instance and € 200,000 at appeal.

91 **Supreme Court of Cassation, Decision No 50017 of 21 July 2023 in Commercial Case No 2643/2021, Commercial Chamber, 2nd Bench** – compensation of € 300,000. The plaintiff was injured in an accident, suffered a spinal cord injury which resulted in total paralysis of his lower body and partial paralysis of his arms. The SCC took into account the fact that the victim was 17 years old at the time of the accident, as a result of which he was completely immobilised and unable to attend to his affairs without assistance. It therefore increased the compensation awarded by the Court of Appeal from € 225,000 to € 375,000. The latter amount was also adjusted on the ground of contributory negligence on the part of the plaintiff, who was walking on the road in breach of traffic rules, thus awarding a final amount of € 300,000. Here, as in the previous case, in determining the amount of the compensation, the Court took into account not only the physical but also the psychological condition of the victim.

Supreme Court of Cassation, Decision No 50016 of 9 March 2023 in Commercial Case No 2691/2021, Commercial Chamber, 2nd Bench – compensation of € 65,000. In its Decision, the SCC stated that the amount of compensation was fair insofar as it was proportionate to the nature and extent of the injuries – a craniocerebral trauma resulting in partial hearing loss, and injuries to the body resulting in prolonged immobilisation. The SCC did not consider that contributory negligence could be alleged in this case and set aside the decision of the Court of Appeal insofar as it reduced the compensation. 92

On the basis of the above decisions, several general conclusions may be drawn: (1) compensation for an injury resulting in a drastic impairment of the quality of life is significantly higher than compensation payable to a victim's relatives in the event of a victim's death; (2) in addition to the severity of the injuries, a guiding criterion in determining the amount of compensation is the age of the victim, which allows an estimation of the period during which the person will be deprived of a normal or even tolerable quality of life; and (3) the SCC tends to award higher amounts of compensation than the appellate courts. 93

C. Literature

1. *Ivan Genchev*, Can Legal Persons Suffer Non-Material Damage and are they Subject to Compensation? Commercial Law 2023, No 2, 81–104

In the author's view, the possibility for a legal person to claim non-pecuniary damages can be found in the incentive function of civil liability and should therefore be recognised. The indirect reflection of adverse consequences in the economic sphere of the legal person does not constitute sufficient grounds for refusing to award compensation for non-pecuniary damage. Separate provisions of legal acts in Bulgaria also recognise a claim for such damages. Furthermore, it is unacceptable that Bulgarian law does not recognise the precedents of case law of the ECtHR and the ECJ in accepting an award of moral damages to legal persons. 94

The conclusion reached is that the concept of non-pecuniary damage is evolving and is not only expressed in pain and suffering. There are insufficient grounds to adopt a differentiated approach, recognising this possibility only for a certain type of legal person (those with a non-profit-making purpose), while denying it for another. 95

2. *Damyan Dimov*, Compensation for Non-Pecuniary Damage in the Case of Legal Persons, Commercial Law 2023, No 2, 105–122

96 The author considers that compensation for non-pecuniary damage should be dealt with in a differentiated manner, taking into account the nature of the legal person (entity) claiming the damage. A legal person that is a merchant cannot suffer non-pecuniary damage, whereas non-profit legal persons can. The latter differ, significantly, from legal persons that are merchants in that they do not distribute profits, which makes it impossible for reputational damage to have a negative impact on the company's financial position. A company's reputation is part of its commercial enterprise, conferring rights, obligations and factual relationships. The commercial enterprise may be an object of typical transactions of disposal – sale, will, pledge, etc. Therefore, in order to be able to be the object of financial transactions of disposal, a commercial enterprise is valued at its monetary worth, which implies that, in the case of commercial companies, goodwill, as part of the commercial enterprise, has a pecuniary dimension and its impairment results in pecuniary and not non-pecuniary damage.[7]

3. *Polya Goleva*, Interesting Regulatory Admission of Tort Liability in Our New Legislation, Commercial and Obligation Law 2023, No 11

97 The article deals with the new Protection of Persons Who Report or Publicly Disclose Information on Breaches Act, which sets out two sets of tort liability – for the reporting person (whistle-blower) and for the person subject to the report. The author considers that this Act introduces a new legal concept of fault in Bulgaria, providing for liability for damage caused to the reporting person only in the case of intent, which is presumed – negligence is excluded. It also provides for compensation of the person concerned by the report, the special feature being that the offence must also be intentional – the offender has knowingly disclosed by means of a report or has made public information that they know to be false or which, under the circumstances, they had to assume was false. However, as there is no

7 The two articles deal with the issue of whether legal persons are subject to compensation for non-pecuniary damage in connection with the Supreme Court of Cassation, Interpretation Case No 1/2023, General Assembly of the Civil and Commercial College, which addresses similar issues and will be considered after a decision has been reached.

presumption of intent in this form of liability, intent, as well as all the other elements of the factual constitution of liability, must be proved by the person that claims compensation. It is pointed out that the Act regulates those cases in which the reporting person is exempted from liability for compensation for the damage caused by them.

Marko Baretić

IV. Croatia

A. Legislation

1. Zakon o predstavničkim tužbama za zaštitu kolektivnih interesa i prava potrošača (Representative Actions for Protection of Collective Interests and Rights of Consumers Act) National Gazette (Narodne novine, NN) No 59/2023

This Act aims at transposing Directive (EU) 2020/1828 on representative actions for the protection of the collective interests of consumers into the Croatian legal system. Apart from injunctions, as a form of preventive relief, for the first time in Croatian legal history, this Act introduces the class action, as a sort of compensatory relief. 1

Pursuant to art 5, para 1, point 6 of the Act, a collective action is an action for the protection of collective interests and rights of consumers filed by a qualified entity in the name of consumers. This entity requests that the court establish the violation of laws aimed at the protection of consumers, that such violation be prohibited in the future, that compensation for material and non-material damage be awarded and/or that the restitution of benefits received from such violation be granted. 2

As implied in the above definition and as expressly defined in art 8 of the Act, a collective action can only be lodged by a qualified entity, ie an association established for protecting consumer interests and which is entered in the List of Qualified Entities, based on the Decision of the Ministry of the Economy. Hence, in order for a qualified entity to be entitled to appear as a plaintiff in a collective proceeding, an association must first lodge an application to be entered into the List of Qualified Entities and obtain a positive decision from the Ministry. Article 9 of the Act contains a rather voluminous and detailed list of conditions to be met by an association before it is entered into the List. For the time being, the Ministry of the Economy has not yet published the List of Qualified Entities, which means that currently there is no possibility to lodge this type of action before Croatian courts by domestic entities. However, pursuant to art 8, para 3 of the Act, apart from a domestic qualified entity, a collective action can also be filed by a qualified entity from any other EU Member State. 3

https://doi.org/10.1515/9783111376721-005

4 A collective action can be brought against a particular trader, a group of traders from the same economic sector, interest associations of traders and/or the holders of the codes of conduct which promote the use of unfair commercial practices (art 13, para 2).

5 In case a collective action is brought to seek compensatory relief, ie as a class action aimed at compensation for damage sustained, a qualified entity must attach to the claim the list of particular consumers on whose behalf a claim is being filed, together with a power of attorney of every single consumer included in the 'class'. Hence, Croatia obviously decided to introduce the so-called opt-in system of forming a 'class' of consumers engaged in a class action, meaning that, in a class action seeking compensatory relief, only consumers who expressly accepted to take part in the proceedings can be included (art 21). Pursuant to art 23 of the Act, a consumer who consented to take part in a class action cannot lodge an individual claim for compensation for the same damage nor can they be included in another class action initiated for compensation of the same damage.

6 As is apparent from art 19, para 2 of the Act, in a collective action seeking compensatory relief, the plaintiff must define a quantum of damages sought and, pursuant to art 5, para 1, point 5, compensation for both material and non-material damage can be sought.

7 By filing a collective action, the limitation period is suspended (art 30). Hence, Croatia decided to opt for suspension, rather than interruption of the limitation period in the case of filing a collection action, although, arguably, an interruption of the limitation period seems to be a more suitable solution for collective actions, at least those seeking injunctive relief.

8 The introduction of a collective action in the form of compensatory relief no doubt represents a rather significant development. It remains to be seen how often this novel concept will be used in Croatian legal practice. Apart from the fact that class actions are alien to the Croatian legal environment, challenges in the future application of this novel concept could also stem from a number of practical issues which are left unanswered in the new Act. Thus, for example, it is not clear whether a plaintiff must define an exact amount of compensation sought by each particular consumer or whether the designation of a lump sum sought for the entire group should be sufficient. Furthermore, the Act is silent as to how the compensation obtained is to be divided among the consumers included in the class action, especially if the claim is only partially sustained. This issue is closely related to the questions as to whether, in its decision, the court should define what part of the compensation is to be granted to which consumer or whether the division of the compensation among particular consumers should be left to the consumers themselves.

2. Zakon o mirnom rješavanju sporova (Amicable Dispute Settlement Act) NN No 67/2023

This Act introduces an interesting procedural requirement in cases involving liability for damage. Pursuant to art 9 of this Act, before initiating any court proceedings for compensation for damage, except those involving damage sustained in labour-related relations, the parties are required to attempt to settle the dispute amicably. 9

Pursuant to art 9, para 2 of this Act, it shall be deemed that this requirement is fulfilled if the conciliation procedure between the parties was unsuccessfully concluded or if the party informed the other party of their demands and objections and called the other party to fulfil those demands or to engage in conciliation procedure, and the other party refuses such a call or does not respond within 15 days. 10

A party intending to initiate a court proceeding for compensation for damage will not be required to attempt to resolve the dispute amicably if, due to any violence involved in a particular case, it is not to be expected that the dispute will be resolved amicably or if the party intending to initiate a court proceeding was unsuccessful in obtaining the address of the residence of the other party. 11

3. Zakon o mjerama ograničavanja (Restrictive Measures Act) NN No 133/2023

This Acts regulates measures implemented by the Government of the Republic of Croatia based on obligatory legal acts of the European Union, the United Nations and other international organisations, by which natural and legal persons, states, territories and entities, organisations and others are restricted for the reasons of the protection of democratic values, the rule of law, human rights and principles of international law, the preservation of peace, conflict prevention and strengthening of international security. 12

Pursuant to art 18 of this Act, the Republic of Croatia and other natural and legal persons and others implementing restrictive measures shall not be liable for damage sustained thereby, unless the damage is caused intentionally or with gross negligence. 13

4. Zakon o državnim službenicima (Public Servants Act) NN No 155/2023

14 This Act, which comprehensively regulates the legal status of public servants, contains special provisions on liability for damage public servants inflict on the governmental body in which they are employed.

15 Pursuant to art 129 of this Act, a public servant shall be liable for damage inflicted intentionally or with gross negligence, which also applies to recourse claims, by which the governmental body seeks reimbursement of what they paid to third parties as compensation for damage sustained by the public servant's wrongdoings.

16 Damage, its quantum and the circumstances under which the damage occurred shall be determined by the decision of the head of governmental body, or a person designated by them. If a public servant refuses to compensate the damage so determined, compensation shall be determined in accordance with general rules of the law of obligations.

17 Pursuant to art 132 of this Act, a public servant and the head of a governmental body may reach a settlement in which the quantum of damages and the method of compensation will be determined. Depending on the quantum of damages, the governmental body may decide, upon the request of the public servant, that the damages be refunded in instalments.

18 If the damage was inflicted on the governmental body's property, the public servant may be allowed to repair the damage by restitution. If restitution is not carried out as agreed, the head of the governmental body will issue a decision on compensation for damage in accordance with the provisions of this Act.

19 A public servant will be freed from liability for damage if they acted based on orders of the head of the body or other superiors, and the public servant informed their superiors in writing, before taking action, that acting as ordered may cause damage.

5. Pravilnik o naknadi štete od strogo zaštićenih životinja (Bylaw on Compensation for Damage from Strictly Protected Animals) NN No 97/2023

This Bylaw replaces the Bylaw on compensation for damage from animals belonging to strictly protected species of 2017, and regulates the issue of compensation for damage sustained therefrom along the same lines as the previous Bylaw.[1] 20

B. Cases

1. Presuda i rješenje Županijskog suda u Velikoj Gorici (Judgment and Decision of the County Court in Velika Gorica) No Gž 2587/2021-10 of 28 February 2023: Liability of the State for Passing the Law; Scope of Liability

a) Brief Summary of the Facts

This case represents a follow-up to the 'public enforcers' saga' that started in 2010. 21

As already reported in the Yearbook of 2015,[2] in 2010, the Croatian Parliament 22 passed the Public Enforcers' Act,[3] pursuant to which, the enforcement in civil matters was to be shifted from state bodies to public enforcers, ie natural persons appointed by the Minister of Justice vested with the power to perform enforcement in civil matters. Pursuant to this Act, the public enforcers' service was to be introduced on 1 January 2012. After the introduction of the service was postponed several times, the concept of public enforcers was finally abandoned even before it was introduced in practice by the Croatian Parliament passing the Act on the Cessation of Applicability of the Public Enforcers' Act of 28 September 2012.[4]

In 2011 and 2012, a number of individuals previously appointed as public en- 23 forcers filed a constitutional claim before the Constitutional Court of Croatia (the Constitutional Court) requesting that this Court proclaim the Act on the Cessation

1 See *M Baretić*, Croatia, in: E Karner/BC Steininger (eds), European Tort Law 2017 (2018) 73, nos 30–33.

2 See *M Baretić*, Croatia in: E Karner/BC Steininger (eds), European Tort Law 2014 (2015) 88, nos 24–28.

3 NN 139/10.

4 NN 112/12.

of Applicability of the Public Enforcers' Act as unconstitutional and to restore the situation that existed before this Act entered into force. In its Decision of 23 January 2013, the Constitutional Court dismissed the request but has, however, awarded to every person formally appointed as public enforcers a satisfaction in the amount of HRK 18,000 (approx € 2,350). The Constitutional Court also noted that the awarded satisfaction does not preclude previously appointed public enforcers from claiming compensation for sustained damage before competent civil courts and has emphasised that the awarded satisfaction should not be 'calculated into' compensation which could possibly be awarded by civil courts.[5]

24 Against this background, the victim, who practised law as an attorney before he was elected a public enforcer, initiated civil proceedings against the Republic of Croatia claiming material and non-material damage caused by the unexpected cessation of the public enforcers' service. The victim claims compensation for non-material damage in an amount of HRK 350,000.00 (€ 46,453) for violation of his right to honour and dignity and of his moral integrity, compensation for regular damage in an amount of HRK 129,097.25 (€ 17,134) consisting in the costs of education for public enforcers (ie taking a state exam for public enforcers), the costs of hiring business premises and the costs of office furniture, equipment and supplies, and compensation for lost profit in an unspecified amount consisting of the proceeds he would have gained in the period between 1 January 2012, when the public enforcers' service was supposed to commence, and 31 December 2014, when he resumed practising law as an attorney. These amounts were to be determined during the proceedings after the defendant submitted data on the overall number of enforcement proceedings conducted in the designated period before the Municipality Civil Court in Zagreb, the Municipality Court in Sesvete and the Commercial Court in Zagreb, the amount of claims enforced through those proceedings and the number of overall procedural activities taken in each of these cases.

25 As in the previous cases regarding the same subject matter,[6] the Republic of Croatia denied the existence of the conditions necessary for the establishment of tortious liability, particularly the lack of a wrongful act and the lack of unlawfulness of its actions. Thus, the Republic of Croatia opined that passing a legislative act can never by regarded as a wrongful act since passing laws represents a constitutional prerogative of Parliament. In addition, in a situation where a competent body – within its powers – adopts a legislative act by which it regulates certain

5 See the decision in joint cases U-I-5612/2011, U-I-6274/2011, U-I-178/2012, U-I-480/2012 of 23 January 2013 (NN 13/13).

6 See *Baretić* (fn 2) no 28.

matters in a constitutionally acceptable manner, there cannot be wrongfulness in actions of this body, opined the Republic of Croatia.

b) Judgment of the Court

The court of first instance partially sustained the victim's claim, awarding him HRK 20,000 (€ 2,654) for non-material damage and HRK 15,493.25 (€ 2,056) for 'regular' damage (ie decrease of the victim's assets). The court of first instance further dismissed the victim's claim for non-material damage in the remaining amount of HRK 330,000 (€ 43,799), the victim's claim for regular damage in the remaining amount of HRK 113,604 (€ 15,078) and the victim's claim for compensation for lost profit. 26

The County Court in Velika Gorica, acting as an appellate court, dismissed the victim's appeal and affirmed the first instance decision as to the awarded non-material damages and regular damages, and upheld the victim's appeal and quashed the first instance court's decision regarding the compensation for lost profit, remitting the case to the first instance court for re-examination regarding this issue. 27

Responding to the defendant's objections as to the lack of unlawfulness of their actions, the County Court in Velika Gorica largely repeated what the Constitutional Court reasoned in their decision of 23 January 2013, recalling that Parliament has a constitutional right to enact laws and, in this respect, to replace the concept of public enforcers with whatever concept it deems appropriate. However, this Court also opined that exercising discretionary powers of the State must not result in consequences which cannot be reconciled with basic constitutional values, the principle of justifiable balance between different interests being one of those values. On these grounds, the County Court in Velika Gorica recalled that the Constitutional Court held that by passing the Act on the Cessation of Applicability of the Public Enforcers' Act, the legislator failed to establish a justifiable balance between public interests (ie interests of society) and private interest of those who were previously appointed as public enforcers. In this respect, the County Court in Velika Gorica opined that the State was obligated to find appropriate solutions in the final provisions of the Act on the Cessation of Applicability of the Public Enforcers' Act, whereby the problems the victim encountered by virtue of passing this Act would be addressed. Since the State failed to do so, it violated the victim's legitimate expectations that were based on the valid legal acts of the State. Therefore, concluded the County Court in Velika Gorica, by failing to take into consideration legitimate expectations of this particular victim and other people in the same situation when passing the Act on the Cessation of Applicability of 28 the Public Enforcers' Act, the State acted unlawfully and is therefore liable for damage thus sustained by the victim.

29 Substantiating its decision as to the scope of damages, the County Court in Velika Gorica confirmed that, based on the full compensation principle, the victim is entitled to be compensated for any head of damage provided for in the Croatian legal system, which includes lost profit. Since the first instance court dismissed the victim's claim as to lost profit, holding that the victim is not entitled to this type of damage, the County Court in Velika Gorica quashed the first instance court's decision regarding this particular head of damage, and remitted the case for re-examination.

30 As regards the regular damage, the County Court in Velika Gorica confirmed, on a general level, that the victim is entitled to this head of damage, however, only to that portion of regular damage which is founded in evidence. In this respect, the County Court in Velika Gorica held that the victim is entitled to compensation of the expenses incurred for educational purposes in the course of obtaining necessary permissions for acting as a public enforcer because he successfully proved that he did in fact incur these expenses. For this reason, the County Court in Velika Gorica affirmed the first instance court's decision regarding the regular damage, up to the value of expenses incurred for educational purposes. As to the expenses for hiring business premises and buying office furniture, equipment and supplies, the County Court in Velika Gorica held that, by failing to submit to the case file any proof of actual payments made for these purposes, the victim failed to prove that he ever incurred any actual damage in this regard. In this respect, the County Court in Velika Gorica recalled that the mere possibility of damage occurrence is not sufficient, but rather a victim must prove the existence of the actual loss, ie a decrease of their assets.

31 Finally, as to the non-material damage, the County Court in Velika Gorica found that the victim's mental health was impaired by the State's actions and upheld the first instance court's position that the victim suffered 'certain psychic tension' because of the State's actions. For this reason, the County Court in Velika Gorica found the first instance decision regarding non-material damage well-substantiated, both as to the merits and the quantum of compensation. Regarding the quantum of non-material damages, the County Court in Velika Gorica confirmed that compensation for non-material damage in an amount of HRK 20,000 (€ 2,654) is appropriate, without providing any detailed reasons for such position.

c) Commentary

As already commented in the 2015 Yearbook,[7] the Constitutional Court's decision of 23 January 2013 was the first decision ever in the Croatian legal system in which it was confirmed that, as a matter of principle, the State can be held liable for their wrongdoings in the legislative branch, ie in passing laws. However, so far, no decision had been reached in which the regular courts took a position on the scope and quantum of damage thus sustained. Indeed, in the judgment of the County Court in Varaždin No Gž-5818/13–2 of 16 January 2014,[8] which dealt with a similar claim, the Court took a somewhat unexpected position and issued an interim judgment, by which it confirmed that the State is held liable for the damage sustained by persons following the Act on the Cessation of Applicability of the Public Enforcers' Act, but refrained from deciding on the scope and quantum of damage, thus obviously allowing the State appropriate time to settle this issue amicably with the victims, ie persons appointed as public enforcers. Since the State obviously did not make use of the given opportunity, cases before regular courts resumed. 32

This case represents one of the first cases in which the court took a clear position regarding the scope of damage inflicted by passing the Act on the Cessation of Applicability of the Public Enforcers' Act by which the public enforcers' service was abandoned. 33

Unsurprisingly, the County Court in Velika Gorica confirmed that the victim, ie a person who was appointed as a public enforcer, can in principle seek compensation under all heads of damage provided under Croatian tort law, namely material damage in the form of regular damage (ie a decrease of the victim's patrimony) and loss of profit (ie prevention of increase of the victim's patrimony) as well as non-material damage (violation of the victim's personality rights). In this respect, the County Court in Velika Gorica specifically invoked general provisions of the Civil Obligations Act (COA), namely arts 1045 and 1046, which define the types of compensable damage under this Croatian Law. Indeed, such position of the County Court in Velika Gorica is perfectly in line with the full compensation principle from art 1090 COA, pursuant to which, the court shall, taking into account the circumstances following the occurrence of damage, determine the amount of compensation required in order to return the victim's financial position to the state in which it would have been had the wrongful act or failure to act not occurred. 34

More precisely, the County Court in Velika Gorica confirmed that, as a matter of principle, any expenditure causally linked to the public enforcers' service, such 35

7 See *Baretić* (fn 2) no 30.

8 Commented by *Baretić* (fn 2) nos 30–34.

as expenditure incurred to obtain necessary permissions, to obtain appropriate business premises, and to buy office furniture, equipment and other supplies, are in principle suitable to be compensated. Moreover, the County Court in Velika Gorica expressly confirmed that the victim would, in principle, be entitled to compensation for lost profit consisting in proceeds the victim would have earned had they been allowed to act as a public enforcer.

36 Although the County Court in Velika Gorica expressly invoked the full compensation principle, thus confirming that, in principle, a victim is entitled to compensation of any type of damage sustained by passing the law, it also clearly established that only damage which actually occurred and the victim is capable of proving can be compensated. In this respect, the County Court in Velika Gorica clearly confirmed that the mere possibility of damage occurrence is not sufficient; when seeking regular damage, a victim is required to prove actual losses suffered. Therefore, the County Court in Velika Gorica rightly noted that the victim in this case is not entitled to compensation of those expenses the payment of which the victim failed to prove. In this respect, the Court was particularly clear regarding the question of what type of proof is needed to prove the existence of a certain type of expenditure. Thus, the County Court in Velika Gorica refused to award compensation for expenses the victim supposedly incurred for the purchase of office furniture, opining that these expenses cannot be proven with a sales contract, but only with actual invoices, which prove that the agreed price was actually paid. In this respect, the County Court in Velika Gorica confirmed that damage occurs only when particular expenditure is incurred, and not when an obligation to make this payment is taken.

37 As to the compensation for non-material damage, this judgment clearly defines the amount of compensation victims can generally expect in similar situations. Unfortunately, the County Court in Velika Gorica was rather tight-lipped regarding the criteria this Court used in the course of determining the amount of compensation for non-material damage. What can be said with a reasonable level of certainty is that the Court held the violation of the victim's personality rights not to be particularly serious, since, as the Court emphasised, the victim did not attach to the case file any medical documentation demonstrating any serious violation of their personality rights. Hence, the Court was obviously of the opinion that more serious violation of the victim's personality rights could possibly justify a higher amount of compensation, however a more serious violation of a victim's personality rights, on the other hand, would have to be proven with medical documentation. Be that as it may, somewhat more elaborate reasoning regarding the criteria based on which the quantum of compensation for non-material damage was assessed in this case would certainly allow a future position of the courts with respect to this issue to be predicted with more certainty.

Since a large number of factually identical cases are currently pending before Croatian courts, this judgment will no doubt be instrumental in shaping case law as to the scope and quantum of damage sustained by passing the Act on the Cessation of Applicability of the Public Enforcers' Act in particular, and passing laws in general. 38

2. Rješenje Vrhovnog suda Republike Hrvatske (Decision of the Supreme Court of the Republic of Croatia) No Rev 999/2021-4 of 1 March 2023: Medical Error; Conditions for Liability

a) Brief Summary of the Facts

On 29 October 2005, the victim underwent surgery in a hospital (A1), performed by a medical doctor (A2), on which occasion her urinary stress incontinence was successfully treated with the so-called sling method, involving the use of transobturator tape. On 26 June 2006, the victim underwent another operation with another doctor and institution, for bladder prolapse, in which case the doctor performing the surgery noticed that the transobturator tape, used in the course of the first surgery, had fused with the surrounding tissue and therefore could not be removed. 39

The victim sues A1 and A2 and claims compensation for material and non-material damage based on the alleged medical error committed by A2. 40

b) Judgment of the Court

The first instance court dismissed the victim's claim for lack of unlawfulness on the part of A1 and A2. The first instance court reasoned that A1 and A2 used a commonly accepted method of treating urinary stress incontinence, that the medical product used in the course of the treatment (ie transobturator tape) was in general use and that the victim was duly informed of the surgery procedure, including possible side effects and complications commonly associated with this kind of procedure. The first instance court further reasoned that the fact that the transobturator tape used in the course of the procedure was not entered into the register of medical products at the time of the surgery was of no consequence for the case at hand. In the course of making its decision, the first instance court took into consideration the expert witness report prepared by the Medical Faculty of the University of Zagreb, in which it was established that the victim was properly diagnosed and prop- 41 erly treated. However, the first instance court rejected the part of the expert witness report in which the Medical Faculty established that A1 and A2 failed to properly inform the victim regarding frequent complications associated with the sling operation and that they failed to remove the transobturator tape when permanent difficulties arose, holding that, in this part of the report, the Medical Faculty gave a legal and not a medical expert opinion.

42 The second instance court upheld the first instance decision on the merits.

43 The Supreme Court accepted the victim's request for revision and remitted the case to the second instance court for re-examination.

44 Supporting its decision, the Supreme Court gave a thorough explanation of the conditions necessary for the establishment of liability of medical services providers to arise, particularly focusing on the unlawfulness of medical services providers' actions and the causal relationship between their actions and the damage sustained.

45 The Supreme Court began by stating that, based on the applicable legislation, the concept of medical error is to be understood as to mean a procedure or behaviour which is contrary to the rules and methods of the medical profession and scientific knowledge, as a result of which, a human's life and health are endangered or by which moral or ethical principles of the medical profession are violated, whereby no cumulation of these conditions is necessary, but it is sufficient that only one of these conditions is fulfilled for a medical error to occur.

46 The Supreme Court further opined that civil liability for damage for negligent or inappropriate treatment presupposes individual error or omission on the part of medical personnel, which led to an unexpected and/or unusual worsening of the patient's medical condition. Therefore, continued the Supreme Court, it is necessary in each particular case to examine whether the doctor performing the procedure did everything that was possible in the given circumstances. In this respect, the Supreme Court explained that negligent behaviour on the part of the medical professional includes superficiality, carelessness, rashness and every other type of unintentional procedure undertaken in the course of performing a medical activity. According to the Supreme Court, a medical professional acts negligently (either by acting or refraining from acting) if, in the course of performing their activities, they do not respect the rules of the medical profession (ie generally accepted rules of medicine), lack appropriate equipment or instruments necessary for the successful performance of the procedure in question, or carelessly undertake procedures for which they are not properly trained or skilled.

47 Based on the foregoing, the Supreme Court concluded that in order for the medical error to be classified as an unlawful act, it is necessary to establish that the application of a particular mode of treatment can be assessed in the given case as obviously unsuitable, that is, it is necessary to establish a violation of pro-

fessional duties stemming from the generally accepted rules of the medical profession. In this respect, the Supreme Court recalled that medical professionals are obligated to act with an increased level of care (care of a good expert).

As to the question of causation, the Supreme Court took the stance that the medical error must be the cause of damage, ie, it must be established that the use of an alternative treatment method or an alternative medication or an alternative surgical procedure would not have resulted in damage. 48

The Supreme Court opined that the expert witness report prepared by the Faculty of Medicine of the University of Zagreb, in the part which was neglected by the first instance court, contains elements based on which unlawfulness of the tortfeasors' actions should be assessed. For this reason, the Supreme Court remitted the case for re-examination. 49

c) Commentary

This decision of the Supreme Court merits mention for an usually thorough explanation of some of the conditions necessary for liability for medical error to arise, particularly unlawfulness of the medical professionals' actions. 50

Thus, the Supreme Court firstly recalled some of the obvious and well-established facts about medical liability: first, the liability of medical professionals is fault-based, and second, in assessing whether medical professionals acted with due care, a special type of care – the so-called care of a good expert, should be applied. 51

By emphasising that a medical error represents behaviour contrary to the rules and methods of the medical profession and scientific knowledge by which human life and health is endangered or by which moral or ethical principles of the medical profession are violated, the Supreme Court appears to invoke the concept of protective purpose of the norm (in German: *der Schutzzweck der Norm*), opining that a medical error will occur only if those norms of the medical profession are violated whose purpose is either to protect human life and health or moral or ethical principles of the medical profession. *A contrario*, a violation of the norms of the medical profession which are not aimed at protecting these two sets or values would arguably fall outside the concept of medical error. 52

The Supreme Court further contributed to the general understanding of the concept of medical error by enumerating some actions which are typically associated with this specific type of professional wrongdoing, eg acting superficially, carelessly, hastily, neglecting the rules of the medical profession, lacking appropriate equipment or instruments, performing procedures without necessary training or skill. Moreover, the Supreme Court clearly established that the concept of med- 53 ical error is objective in nature. Hence, in each particular case, the behaviour of a medical professional is to be assessed from an objective point of view, meaning the courts should assess whether the conduct of the medical professional in question lived up to the expectations of the abstract concept of care of a good expert.

54 Finally, with respect to the Supreme Court's elaboration of the concept of medical error, it is certainly interesting to see how this Court approaches the issue of unlawfulness. By emphasising that medical error presupposes a violation of the norms of the medical profession and the lack of due care on the side of a medical professional, the Supreme Court obviously understands the concept of unlawfulness as a mixed objective-subjective concept, much like the French concept of *faute*. Hence, although Croatian jurisprudence and case law insist on the division between objective unlawfulness (ie violation of a legal norm) and subjective unlawfulness (ie fault, either in the form of intent or negligence), this decision of the Supreme Court clearly suggests that objective and subjective unlawfulness are merely different sides of the same coin, often impossible to separate.

55 Elaborating on causation in cases involving medical error, the Supreme Court argues in this decision that in order to conclude that a medical error caused the damage, it must be established that the use of an alternative treatment method or an alternative medication or an alternative surgical procedure would not have resulted in damage. Hence, although not explicitly mentioning the concept, it is obvious that, in this case, the Supreme Court applies the 'but-for test' of causation, holding that liability for medical error cannot be established unless it can be proven that alternative behaviour would have prevented the occurrence of the damage, hence that the sole reason for the damage occurring is the particular conduct of the medical professional.

56 Although this decision significantly contributes to an understanding of the complex concept of medical error, it is, however, not without controversy. Thus, for instance, one should be somewhat hesitant about the Supreme Court's suggestion that any lack of appropriate equipment or instruments should automatically imply medical error. This should certainly be true in situations in which a medical professional chooses to use inappropriate equipment or instruments, ie where the use of inappropriate equipment or instruments is the result of poor decision-making on the part of that medical professional. However, as is often the case in Croatia, medical professionals are forced to use outdated or even obsolete equipment for lack of more advanced or modern equipment. In these situations, a medical professional will inevitably be confronted with the dilemma of whether to provide medical assistance with inappropriate equipment or instruments or to abstain from providing medical assistance in the first place. If a medical professional chooses to provide medical assistance even though aware of the fact that the

only equipment at their disposal is deficient or in any other way substandard, holding them liable for medical error would, in my opinion, by utterly wrong.

3. Rješenje Vrhovnog suda Republike Hrvatske (Decision of the Supreme Court of the Republic of Croatia) No Rev 65/2023-2 of 18 April 2023: Statute of Limitations; Claim Against Attorney at Law for Professional Malpractice

a) Brief Summary of the Facts

The victim sues his attorney at law for alleged malpractice in representation be- 57
fore the court and claims damage, consisting of the litigation costs the victim was obligated to pay to the counterparty who prevailed in the proceeding.

b) Judgment of the Court

Before the first instance court, the issue of the statute of limitations arose. Since 58
the first instance court concluded that the victim's claim was time-barred, the court rejected the claim without discussing other disputed facts. The first instance court took the position that the limitation period starts to run as of the day when the victim was finally ordered payment of the opposing party's litigation costs, and that the victim's claim becomes time-barred after a period of three years.

The second instance court accepts the first instance decision as to the moment 59
from which the limitation period starts to run, but rejects the first instance court's position regarding the duration of the limitation period. The second instance court holds that, in this case, the general, five-year limitation period should be applied, since in this situation, the claim for damages should be qualified as a case of contractual liability. Since the COA does not provide for any special limitation period for a mandate contract (which was concluded between the victim and his attorney at law), the general five-year limitation period should apply.

The Supreme Court accepted the victim's request for revision, quashed both 60
lower courts' decisions and remitted the case to the first instance court for re-examination.

The Supreme Court accepts the second instance court's position regarding the 61
applicable limitation period. Thus, the Supreme Court confirms that this case should be decided based on the rules of contractual liability for damage, since the relationship between the victim and his attorney at law was based on the man-

date contract, and therefore, any possible damage would result from breaching this contract. Since the COA provides for no special limitation period to be applied to a mandate contract, the Supreme Court concludes that in this case, the general five-year limitation period should apply.

62 The Supreme Court, however, disagrees with the lower courts as to the moment from which the limitation period starts to run. The Supreme Court rejects the lower courts' position that the limitation period should start to run as of the day when the court decision ordering the victim to pay the other party's litigation costs became final, and concludes that the limitation period should start to run as of the day on which the victim actually paid these costs, since only at the moment of payment did the victim's patrimony for the amount paid decrease.

c) Commentary

63 This Supreme Court's decision certainly adds clarity to the issue of the statute of limitations in cases of legal malpractice. Since such cases are appearing before Croatian courts with increasing frequency, this decision will no doubt be instrumental for future litigation.

64 In this decision, the Supreme Court addressed two most important issues regarding the statute of limitations in client-attorney related cases. First, how to qualify this relationship and consequently, what liability rules to apply, ie the rules of contractual or extra-contractual (tortious) liability. Second, when the limitation period in cases of payment of the opposing party's litigation costs starts to run.

65 Regarding the first issue, the Supreme Court qualified the client-attorney relationship as contractual in nature, and therefore concluded that any potential liability issue arising out of this relationship should be assessed based on the rules of contractual liability.

66 Regarding the second issue, the Supreme Court opined that the limitation period for damage consisting in payments ordered by the court decision should start to run as of the day when the payment was actually made, and not as of the day when the court decision by which the payment is ordered became final. This stance certainly has merits. Pursuant to the COA, regular damage is defined as a decrease of the victim's patrimony. Since the victim's patrimony decreases only by making the payment, and not when the payment is ordered, this Supreme Court's position resonates well with the statutory concept of damage.

4. Rješenje Vrhovnog suda Republike Hrvatske (Decision of the Supreme Court of the Republic of Croatia) No Rev 79/2022-2 of 8 February 2023: Unlawfulness in Exercising Self-Help

a) Brief Summary of the Facts

The tortfeasor is a drinking water supplier that deprived the victim of their water supply by disconnecting the water meter in the victim's house for non-payment of due instalments for their water supply. The drinking water supplier undertook the disconnection of the water meter in the victim's house based on its own internal act, the Bylaw on General and Technical Conditions for Water Supply, enacted based on the Waters Act. 67

The victim claims compensation for material damage sustained thereby and for the non-material damage suffered, consisting in frustration, humiliation and the feeling of helplessness. 68

b) Judgment of the Court

The first instance court dismissed the victim's claim for lack of unlawfulness of the defendant's actions. This court reasoned that the Bylaw on General and Technical Conditions for Water Supply entitles the defendant to disconnect a client's water meter in the case of non-payment of due instalments for the supplied water. 69

The second instance court affirmed the first instance court's decision. 70

The victim filed a request for revision before the Supreme Court, asking the Supreme Court to allow revision regarding the legal question of whether the drinking water supplier has the right to disconnect the water supply to the user with whom it has concluded a contract on delivery of water by removing the water meter in the event that the user does not pay his due debt within eight days from the receipt of the warning, ie whether unlawfulness of such water supplier's action is excluded by the mere fact that it is based on the water supplier's internal act. 71

The Supreme Court accepted the request for revision, quashed the decisions of the first and second instance courts and remitted the case to the first instance court for re-examination. 72

Recalling its earlier decisions and decisions of the Constitutional Court of the Republic of Croatia regarding the same subject matter, the Supreme Court reasoned that, notwithstanding the fact that the supplier's Bylaw provided for the pos- 73 sibility of disconnecting the water supply in the case of non-payment of due instalments, the water supplier is not automatically (unconditionally) authorised to disconnect the water supply in an attempt to collect any due amounts. Such unconditional right to disconnect the water supply in any case the supplier sees fit would be arbitrary and as such, constitutionally unacceptable, especially if the supplier had at their disposal other, less intrusive measures of collecting their outstanding claims.

74 In this respect, the Supreme Court argues that in each particular case, before resorting to such a drastic measure such as depriving a customer of their water supply, a proportionality test must be carried out in order to ensure that the justified balance between the public interest (of ensuring the orderly settlement of accounts, thus ensuring the financial viability of the water supplier and the uninterrupted provision of water) and the client's constitutional right to access to drinking water is achieved.

75 The Supreme Court continued by asserting that, in carrying out the proportionality test, the courts must take into consideration all the relevant facts pertaining to the given case and, in this respect, the Supreme Court provided for some useful guidance as to different considerations to be taken into account when carrying out the proportionality test. Thus, the Supreme Court emphasised that every natural person has a constitutional right to access drinking water. However, the Court also emphasised that this right does not presupposes the access to unconditional quantities of water nor the right to the free use of drinking water. The Court also emphasised that the right to access drinking water relates only to private, and not commercial consumption. On the other hand, the Supreme Court recalled the need to ensure an uninterrupted water supply, which presupposes the need to ensure that the bills for water consumption are settled in a timely manner, thus ensuring the financial viability of the service.

76 Based on the foregoing, the Supreme Court concluded that in each particular case, the courts must assess whether disconnecting the water supply was really necessary or whether the supplier had at their disposal less intrusive measures, for example, initiating court proceedings in order to collect unsettled accounts. Since in this particular case the lower courts failed to perform such an assessment, the Supreme Court decided to remit the case for re-examination.

c) Commentary

77 This is just one of the recent decisions of the Croatian courts in which a significant shift in the understanding of the concept of unlawfulness can be discerned, presumably influenced by the European Court of Human Right's case law.

Not so long ago, it was almost undisputed that any provision, either in law or any bylaw, allowing someone to do something, would imply that the authorised person is free to choose any mode of exercising their right, without fearing that their actions might be assessed as unlawful; the mere fact that the law authorises a person to do something automatically removes any possibility of unlawfulness of the authorised person's actions, undertaken in the course of exercising prerogatives vested to them by law. 78

This, obviously, somewhat obsolete view has been recently refined under the influence of the concept of human rights and the legal institutes developed or promoted through the case law pertaining to international and domestic legal sources regulating human rights. In this respect, the Supreme Court clearly emphasised in this decision that statutory authorisation to do something does not automatically authorise the holder of the right to choose any mode of exercising their right. Instead, the holder of the right should choose the mode of exercise of their right which is the least harmful or intrusive towards the debtor or other person against whom the right is exercised. When deciding on how to exercise their rights, a rightholder must take into consideration legitimate interests and legitimate expectations of the persons against whom the right is exercised. This, of course, does not imply that a rightholder must refrain from exercising their rights just because this might prove to be inconvenient for the debtor. However, when being able to choose among different options of exercising their rights, a rightholder should opt for the option which strikes the right balance between their legitimate interests and those of the party against whom the right is exercised. The most drastic, most intrusive measures, should always be a last resort, as clearly suggested by the Supreme Court. 79

Although the concept of the proportionality test and the requirement to balance opposing interests, derived from this concept, gained prominence through the application of the legal sources aimed at human rights protection, they are certainly not alien to civil law. In fact, one could plausibly argue that the requirement of balancing opposing interests and the concept of the proportionality test are enshrined in the basic principles of civil law in general and tort law in particular, for instance, the good faith principle and the prohibition of abuse of right principle. As suggested by Croatian jurisprudence, the good faith principle requires from the parties to an obligation, among others, to take care of the legitimate interests of the other party. The prohibition of abuse of rights principle requires from the parties to an obligation to refrain from using their rights for purposes not intended by law. 80

Disregarding the legitimate interests of the parties against whom the right is exercised, thus causing damage to this party, is contrary to the general principles of civil law, such as the good faith principle and the prohibition of abuse of rights 81 principle, and therefore unlawful. Hence, this decision is a good example of how general principles of civil law actively contribute to shaping the contours of the general conditions for the establishment of tortious liability.

5. Personal Injury

a) Rješenje Vrhovnog suda Republike Hrvatske (Decision of the Supreme Court of the Republic of Croatia) No Rev 213/2022-2 of 18 April 2023: The Moment of Occurrence of Non-Material Damage

i) Brief Summary of the Facts

82 The victim, while employed with the tortfeasor, was exposed to asbestos dust, causing the gradual development of asbestosis, which evolved into malignant rib mesothelioma, the ultimate cause of the victim's death.

83 Before he died, the victim initiated proceedings against the tortfeasor for compensation for non-material damage, and after the victim died, the proceedings were taken over by his daughter.

84 During the proceedings, it was established that malignant rib mesothelioma is a progressive disease, which has no phase of stabilisation, but instead it progresses until a fatal outcome, causing more and more pain as it progresses.

85 In the course of the proceedings, the medical expert witness established that the consequences of the disease and the scope of damage caused thereby could not be determined at the moment when the disease was diagnosed, but only at the moment of death.

ii) Judgment of the Court

86 The first instance court took the position that the non-material damage occurred when the disease was diagnosed for the first time. Since, in the case at hand the disease was diagnosed in 2004, when non-material damage was regulated by the old COA of 1978, which did not provide for the possibility of inheriting claims for compensation of non-material damage, the first instance court suspended the proceeding after the victim died.

87 The second instance court affirmed the first instance decision.

88 The victim's daughter filed a request for revision before the Supreme Court, challenging the legal position of the lower courts and requesting from the Supreme Court that revision be allowed regarding the legal question of whether, in a case where a disease never stabilises but constantly progresses until the death of the victim, the moment of damage occurrence should be regarded as the moment

when the disease is diagnosed or the moment when the scope of damage can be finally determined.

The Supreme Court established that the legal position of the lower courts regarding the occurrence of damage is directly opposite to the well-established case law of the Supreme Court, according to which, the moment of occurrence of non-material damage should not necessarily coincide with the occurrence of the wrongful act (the moment of injury), but instead, as regards the moment of damage occurrence, when the process of healing is finalised, when the patient's medical condition is stabilised and when the final scope of damage can be determined should be taken as that moment. The Supreme Court further recalled that, in principle, the moment when the claim for compensation for non-material damage becomes due is the moment when the expert witness report is submitted, in which the final scope of damage is determined. 89

Since the lower courts' decisions departed from well-established case law, the Supreme Court quashed both decisions and remitted the case for re-examination. 90

iii) Commentary

This decision of the Supreme Court reaffirms the long-standing position of this Court that the moment of occurrence of damage is not necessarily the moment when the wrongful act (injury) takes place, but the moment when the patient's medical condition stabilises and the scope of damage can be finally determined, thus contributing to legal certainty regarding the issue of damage occurrence. 91

As is evident from the description of the facts of this case, in this proceeding, the lower courts quite inappropriately diverted from well-established case law. In this respect, it is certainly reassuring that the Supreme Court demonstrated a clear lack of willingness to accept any derailing from well-established case law. 92

The long-standing position that the damage occurs when the patient's medical condition stabilises and the scope of damage can be finally determined seems quite reasonable and well-founded. The time of maturity of the compensation claim should be the moment when the victim becomes fully aware of the tortfeasor and the damage, because only when the victim gains knowledge of these two facts will they be in a position to initiate legal proceedings. Before the damage is known, the victim simply cannot properly define the quantum of their claim. Hence, it certainly makes sense to insist on the position that damage occurs only at the moment when the scope of damage can be finally determined. 93

C. Literature

1. *Maja Bukovac Puvača/Sandra Winkler*, Naknada štete prouzročene povredom prava na poštovanje obiteljskog života [Liability for damage caused by violation of right to respect family life], Zbornik Pravnog fakulteta Sveučilišta u Rijeci 1 (2023) 107–131

94 In the opening section of this paper, the authors focus on the interplay between supranational and national legal sources aimed at the protection of family life, arguing that only a comprehensive and combined interpretation of these sources allows for some minimal standards of protection of family life to be deducted. Based on such an approach, the authors, using extensively the case law of the European Court of Human Rights and the Croatian Constitutional Court, emphasise in the second part of the paper some of the most common violations of the right to respect family life which will give rise to tortious liability, including a long-time failure to ensure contact between parents and their children and the length of proceedings in which a decision is made as to who a child will live with. In the third part, the authors examine the correlation between the gravity of violation of the right to respect family life and the amount of compensation awarded for non-material damage thereby sustained.

95 Bearing in mind the relatively high number of cases in which Croatian citizens seek protection of their right to family life before international tribunals, Croatian courts obviously, as the authors suggest, have failed in establishing efficient mechanisms of protection of these rights at the national level. In this respect, this article may contribute to establishing standards and mechanisms for a more efficient protection of the right to family life at the national level, thus contributing to a reduction of the number of tort cases resulting from violations of the right to family life.

2. *Zvonimir Slakoper/Saša Nikšić*, Dužna pažnja prema Zakonu o obveznim odnosima [Due care according to the Obligations Act], Zbornik Pravnog fakulteta Sveučilišta u Rijeci 1 (2023) 25–58

96 This article is a comprehensive analysis of the concept of due care under the COA, which is examined from substantive, temporal and personal aspects (*ratione materiae, ratione temprae, ratione personae*). Examining extensively domestic case

law and legislative acts, and to some extent comparative sources, the authors strive to fathom the meaning of, and the requirements imposed upon the parties by different types of due care, recognised in Croatian private law, notably, care of a good family father (*bonus pater familias*), care of a good businessman and care of a good professional. The authors particularly focus on drawing clear dividing lines between different types of due care, especially between the concepts of care of a good businessman and care of a good professional.

Although the concept of due care extends well beyond tort law, given the fact 97
that this concept represents a building block of negligence, this paper will certainly contribute to a better understanding and application of fault as one of the prerequisites for the establishment of tort liability.

Michael Chatzipanagiotis

V. Cyprus

A. Legislation

1. Civil Procedure Rules (CPR)

1 On 1 September 2023, the new Civil Procedure Rules (CPR), which replaced the old Civil Procedure Rules dating back to 1958, before Cyprus became an independent State, entered into force.

2 The new CPR are largely based on the English CPR of 1998, with slight modifications, to account for Cypriot practice, culture and customs. They consist of 60 parts and their overriding objective is to deal with cases justly and at a proportionate cost,[1] given also the huge delays in the administration of civil justice in Cyprus. In this regard, they provide the courts with extensive case-management powers and flexibility. They also lay emphasis on the cooperation of the parties with the judge and between themselves for time- and cost-efficient proceedings, as well as on alternative dispute resolution mechanisms.

3 Among the novelties of the new rules are the pre-trial protocols, ie a set of best practices for particular categories of cases, which aim at informing parties of their respective positions and facilitating a settlement. So far there are pre-trial protocols for claims for a specified monetary amount and for personal injury claims. Furthermore, a new small claims procedure has been introduced for which there were no provisions in the previous rules.

4 Of particular interest for the area of tort law are the provisions on representative parties to the trial. Section 20.7(1) provides that parties with the same interest in a cause or matter may be represented by one or more persons with the same interest in that cause or matter. Although this is an old common law rule, which enables opt-out collective actions,[2] in Cyprus there was an opt-in variation of

1 CPR, rule 1.2(1).
2 See *Lloyd v Google LLC* [2021] United Kingdom Supreme Court (UKSC) 50, para 34 ff; *J Sorajbi*, The hidden class action in English civil procedure, Civil Justice Quarterly (CJQ) 2009, 28(4), 498, 500 ff.

Acknowledgement: The author would like to thank Myrianthi Panayiotou, Attorney-at-Law, LL.M, Research Assistant at KOIOS Center of Excellence, University of Cyprus, for her kind assistance in the preparation of the case summaries of this report.

https://doi.org/10.1515/9783111376721-006

that rule in force, which rendered collective redress impractical. The newly introduced rule provides an additional procedural possibility for cases of mass harm.

5 The new rules are part of a wider overhaul of the Cypriot court system. Among others, a new Court of Appeals has been established.[3] As a result, there are now three instances: the first instance before the District Courts; the second instance before the Court of Appeals, which may review cases regarding both the merits and legal issues;[4] and the third instance before the Supreme Court, where a special permission by that Court is needed and which addresses only certain legal issues, ie departure from established case law; the need for correct interpretation of a substantive (ie non-procedural) statutory provision; or an issue of major public interests or general public importance or coherence of the law in case of conflicting/contradictory judgments of the Court of Appeals.[5] Furthermore, issues of constitutionality of legal provisions are now decided by a newly established (more accurately, revived[6]) Constitutional Court.[7]

2. Law on Injunctions and Representative Actions for the Protection of Collective Interests of Consumers of 2023 (Law 91(I)/2023)

6 The Law on Injunctions and Representative Actions for the Protection of Collective Interests of Consumers of 2023 (RAL) transposes the Representative Actions Directive (RAD).[8] It establishes an opt-out system of collective redress for consumers, while it does not differentiate between domestic and cross-border actions. The Law does not provide details regarding the procedure to be followed, as such questions fall under the competence of the Supreme Court, which issues procedural regulations. However, it is expected that the provisions of the new CPR on representative proceedings[9] will complementarily apply. Moreover, the RAL regulates lit-

3 Administration of Justice (Various Provisions) Laws of 1964 to 2023, sec 3 A.
4 See CPR, rule 41.12(1)-(2).
5 Administration of Justice (Various Provisions) Laws of 1964 to 2023, sec 9(3)(c).
6 There was a Constitutional Court in Cyprus from 1960 to 1964, but in 1964 its functions were transferred to the Supreme Court.
7 Administration of Justice (Various Provisions) Laws of 1964 to 2023, sec 3(8).
8 Directive (EU) 2020/1828 of the European Parliament and of the Council of 25 November 2020 on representative actions for the protection of the collective interests of consumers and repealing Directive 2009/22/EC [2020] Official Journal (OJ) L 409/1.
9 CPR, rule 20.7.

igation finance issues, which are of major importance in practice, only to the extent that the RAD regulates them.

B. Cases[10]

1. Supreme Court, 22 May 2023, *A Hadjiyianni v Pitsillides Trading Co Ltd and P Pitsillides*, Civil Appeal No 341/2014, ECLI:CY:AD:2023:A177: Defamation; Defamatory Meaning; Effect of Articles 12–14 E-Commerce Directive on Defamation Actions

a) Brief Summary of the Facts

The respondent/plaintiff 2 was a director and shareholder of the respondent/plaintiff 1, which was engaged in the distribution of the Red Bull energy drink in Cyprus. The distribution was entrusted to them by the Austrian company Red Bull GmbH ('Red Bull'). The partnership between respondent 1 and Red Bull began in 1998 and ended in 2007, at the initiative of the latter. In early 2008, respondent 2 received from a Red Bull official an e-mail, sent to Red Bull by the appellant/defendant who was 'brand manager' of Red Bull. The e-mail mentioned, among others, the following: 7

> 'Also it would be very useful to have the latest visibility master plan. As I have already told you, lots of fridges have disappeared from the market after orders from Pitsillides (Andreas can confirm that). It will be very useful to have the master plan in order to be able to track our posm and shelf space.'

The plaintiffs/respondents suggested that the e-mail contained false, unsubstantiated and malicious allegations that respondent 2 (or the employees of respondent 1) stole Red Bull fridges, thereby damaging the reputation, image and professional status of both. 8

The District Court accepted the action. It ruled that the publication was defamatory of both plaintiffs/respondents and that the actions of the defendant/appellant were characterised by malice. As a result, the District Court awarded general damages in the amount of € 5,000 to each of the plaintiffs/respondents. The defendants appealed. 9

10 In the cases cited, an ECLI is provided only where it is available.

b) Judgment of the Court

10 The Supreme Court affirmed the judgment of the District Court. It ruled that the District Court had to look at the totality of the facts, words and phrases, in order to interpret the statement at hand. The Supreme Court observed that the court evaluates whether a statement is defamatory taking into account the ordinary, natural meaning of the words or phrases, as perceived by the average reasonable person. The court considers neither whether a particular reader or even the plaintiff himself might deem the statement defamatory nor any testimony given as to how a publication was perceived in relation to its meaning. The plaintiff cannot himself attribute a defamatory meaning to the publication and consider himself aggrieved if the text is open to other innocent interpretations. During the judicial evaluation of the text, its entire content is considered, with reference to the time and place of the publication, as well as to the public opinion on the subject.

11 The Court also remarked that the District Court did not have to examine whether the requirements of *Stealing* under sec 255 of the Criminal Code were fulfilled, as there is no need to prove precisely what exactly the behaviour attributed to the plaintiff by the defendant amounts to. It suffices that the statement provides reasonable grounds to suspect the involvement of the plaintiff in the situations alleged by the defendant, considering also a balance between the presumption of the plaintiff's innocence under art 12(4) of the Constitution and the defendant's freedom of speech and expression according to art 19(1) of the Constitution.

12 Moreover, the Supreme Court referred to the judgment of the Court of Justice of the European Union (CJEU) on the case C-291/13 *Pappasavvas*,[11] according to which, the e-Commerce Directive[12] does not preclude defamation actions under national law. Hence, the Court rejected the appellant's/defendant's submission that the e-Commerce Directive precludes liability for defamation by electronic means.

13 Furthermore, the District Court was correct to point out that a necessary condition for the defence of 'qualified privilege' to apply is that the statement was not made in bad faith, that is, the defendant was not driven by improper motives, or did not know that his statement was false, or that he demonstrated complete disregard as to whether his statement was based on facts.

---

11 CJEU 11.9.2014, C-291/13, *Sotiris Papasavvas v O Fileleftheros Dimosia Etaireia Ltd and Others*, ECLI:EU:C:2014:2209.

12 Directive 2000/31/EC of the European Parliament and of the Council of 8 June 2000 on certain legal aspects of information society services, in particular electronic commerce, in the Internal Market [2000] OJ L 178/1.

Further, the Court briefly mentioned two other parameters of liability for defamation, affirming the judgment of the District Court. Although the defamatory statement referred personally to plaintiff/respondent 2, who was the director of plaintiff/respondent 1, the Court found that the circumstances of the case, namely that the statement concerned the conduct of business of the company, enabled the company to bring proceedings in its own name. Furthermore, the defendant/appellant had invoked the doctrine of intra-corporate immunity, since the statement had been made in the context of business operations of the same company. The District Court did not examine such defence and the Supreme Court summarily rejected the applicability of the defence under Cypriot law. The Court followed English authorities and implied that such defence could have the form of a qualified privilege, the requirements of which had sufficiently been examined by the District Court. 14

c) Commentary

Defamation cases are often the subject of Supreme Court judgments. This judgment summarises many of the principles applicable. 15

In an action for defamation under Cypriot law, it is established that whether a statement has a defamatory meaning is evaluated objectively, by reference to the ordinary meaning of a statement as this would be understood by the average reasonable person, without accounting for the subjective opinion and feelings of the claimant or the testimonies of any witnesses in this regard.[13] Among the factors to be taken into account are the circumstances surrounding the publication of the statement, to the extent that these would be known to the recipients of the statement, especially in the case of a true innuendo, in which the defamatory meaning arises in connection with extrinsic facts.[14] 16

The defence of a 'conditional/qualified privilege' to a defamatory statement is enshrined in art 21 of the Civil Wrongs Law. This defence is defeated if the claimant proves that the defendant did not act in good faith. Article 21(2) provides that such would be the case if: (a) the matter was untrue and the defendant did not believe it to be true; or (b) the matter was untrue and the defendant published it without having taken reasonable care to ascertain whether it was true or false; or (c) 17

---

13 *Papadopoulos v Kyrix Publishing Co Ltd et al* (1963) 2 Cyprus Law Reports (CLR) 290; *Galiniotis v Ekdotikos Oikos Dias et al* (2011) 1 Apofaseis Anotatou Dikastiriou (Supreme Court Reports, AAD) 474.

14 *Inomeni Ekdotiki Etaireia Dias Ltd v Hadjikosta* (1990) 1 AAD 244; *Attalidis v Rodouli* (2004) 1 AAD 1690.

that, in publishing the matter, he acted with intent to injure the plaintiff to a substantially greater degree or substantially otherwise than was reasonably necessary for the public interest or for the protection of the private right or interests in respect of which he claims to be privileged. In the case at hand, the District Court held, and the Supreme Court affirmed, that the defendant/appellant had acted with malice trying to undermine the claimant without any evidence in support of his statements, because he was trying to protect himself from an allegation by the claimant that he had been bribed by another company. Thus, the Court, affirming its position expressed in an earlier case,[15] found that malice arises from an improper motive, while the circumstances mentioned in art 21(2) are ways of establishing that the defendant acted with malice.[16]

18 Third, the Court reiterated, by reference to the case law of the CJEU,[17] that arts 12–14 of the e-commerce Directive, which release an information service provider from liability, do not preclude the application of civil liability for defamation. The Court rejected the appellant's/defendant's submission that the e-commerce Directive precludes liability for defamation by electronic means. It is noteworthy that such submission would in any case be without merit in the present case, since the liability restrictions imposed by the Directive apply to information service providers, not to drafters of e-mails.

19 Last, the case is an example of the legal standing of a company regarding defamatory statements against its officers.[18]

2. Supreme Court, 1 December 2023, *CD O'Dwyer v Karayianna et al*, Civil Appeal No 47/2015: Battery; Aggravated Damages; Punitive Damages

a) Brief Summary of the Facts

20 The plaintiff and the defendants had pre-existing disputes pending before the courts, regarding the purchase of a residence from the company of the defendants. On 14 January 2008, the plaintiff drove with a friend of his, in separate cars, to the area of the residence. The plaintiff's friend was carrying a video camera, while a

15 *Leonidou et al v Kyriakou et* al, Civil Appeal No 305/2013, 20.7.2021, ECLI:CY:AD:2021:A353.

16 See *Roberts v Bass* [2002] HCA 57, at [78]; *A Mullis/R Parkes* (eds), Gatley on Libel and Slander (12th edn 2013) para 17.4.

17 C-291/13 *Papasavvas*, para 36.

18 See Gatley on Libel and Slander (fn 16) para 8.17.

second camera was mounted on his hat. He stayed in his car and, following the plaintiff's instructions, he recorded the plaintiff, while the plaintiff was taking photos and measurements of the residence. At the same time, the plaintiff himself was carrying a small camera, specifically hidden in his jacket, with which he was filming himself. While outside the house taking pictures, he met the new buyer of the house, who complained to him about taking photos without her permission and then called someone on her phone. Immediately afterwards, the plaintiff received a call from his friend, who told him that his car had been blocked by the car of defendant 1. The plaintiff then started driving towards his friend. As he was driving, a car driven by defendant 2, and carrying defendant 3 as a passenger, collided with his car. Defendant 2 got out of the car and punched the plaintiff in the face. The plaintiff tried to use his mobile phone, but defendant 2 took it from his hands. Then defendant 1 appeared on the scene and shouted in a threatening manner. The plaintiff heard the word 'camera' and understood that defendants 1 and 2 had seen the small camera hidden in his jacket. The plaintiff took the camera in his hand and started running, but defendants 1 and 2 caught up with him, knocked him to the ground and defendant 1 stepped on his face. Defendant 2 hit him on his lower back and stomach, while defendant 3 was holding him down and trying to take the camera away from him, which he eventually did. After the incident, the plaintiff was transferred to hospital.

The District Court awarded special damages in the amount of € 285, general 21
and aggravated damages in the amount of € 13,000, but did not award any punitive damages. The plaintiff appealed on the grounds that, among others, punitive damages should have been awarded.

b) Judgment of the Court

The Supreme Court affirmed the judgment of the District Court. It ruled that puni- 22
tive damages are awarded in cases where the defendant's conduct is so reprehensible as to warrant punishment by a civil court. Conduct is reprehensible when it is accompanied by strong evidence of arrogance, insolence or improper motive, or when it tends to humiliate the victim. Punitive damages do not aim at restituting the victim. They are awarded to demonstrate the Court's repugnance at the defendant's conduct and aim at both punishing the defendant and setting an example. However, the Court also has discretion to award aggravated damages, which do not have a punitive character, if it finds damage to the plaintiff's feelings of dignity.

c) Commentary

23 This judgment reiterates the approach of Cypriot courts to punitive/exemplary damages. Although Cypriot courts generally follow English law, in awarding punitive damages, they tend not to apply the restrictive criteria of the House of Lords in *Brookes v Barnard*[19], according to which, punitive damages may only be awarded in three cases: (1) use of oppressive and unconstitutional conduct by servants of the State; (2) torts committed in gross disregard of the rights of the injured party, perpetrated in circumstances calculated to yield profit to the perpetrator; and (3) where the statute expressly permits an award of exemplary damages. Cypriot courts have not explicitly rejected *Brookes v Barnard*, but they refer mostly to the traditional common law approach, according to which, punitive damages are awarded where the defendant's conduct is so repugnant, in the sense of being extreme, arrogant or oppressive or tending to humiliate the plaintiff, as to justify the imposition of punishment by a civil court.[20] However, there is also (rather isolated) case law adopting the principles of *Brookes v Barnard.*[21]

24 In any case, courts in Cyprus are reluctant to award punitive damages, because the main purpose of tort law is restitution of the plaintiff, not punishment of the defendant.[22] As a result, they tend to emphasise the distinction between punitive damages and aggravated damages, which have a restitutionary character.[23] Nonetheless, there are contradictory authorities as to whether compensatory damages should be separated from punitive damages,[24] and whether punitive damages may be awarded even if the plaintiff has not explicitly requested such damages.[25]

---

19 [1964] All England Law Reports (All ER) 367.

20 See *S Eliades v V Lyssarides* (1979) 1 CLR 254; *A Constantinides v V Pitsillou et al* (1980) Judgments of the Supreme Court of Cyprus (JSC) 279; *Papakokkinou et al v Kanther* (1982) 1 CLR 65; *Kennedy Hotels Ltd v Indjirdjian* (1992) 1 AAD 400; *Phileleftheros Public Company Ltd v Christodoulou* (2012) 1 ΑΑΔ 1763; *Attorney General v Onoufriou*, 23 January 2018, Civil Appeal No 463/2012, ECLI:CY:AD:2018:A517.

21 *Erotokritou v Eirinarhou et al* (1997) 1 AAD 1800.

22 *T Yiallouros v E Nicolaou* (2001) AAD 558; *Attorney General v A Palma et al* (2015) 1 AAD 2489.

23 *S Eliades v V Lyssarides* (1979) 1 CLR 254;

24 Against such separation, *S Eliades v V Lyssarides* (1979) 1 CLR 254; *Papakokkinou et al v Kanther* (1982) 1 CLR 65. However, in *Attorney General v Onoufriou*, 23 January 2018, Civil Appeal No 463/2012, ECLI:CY:AD:2018:A517, it was ruled that punitive damages should be awarded separately, to underline the exemplary element. See also. *Constantinides v Pitsillou et al* (1980) JSC 279, *Tsivikou v Attorney General*, 29 May 2018, Civil Appeal No 350/2011, ECLI:CY:AD:2018:A255, *Alitheia Ekdotiki Etaireia et al v Alonefti* (2002) 1 AAD 1863, which awarded punitive damages as a separate head.

3. Supreme Court, 13 July 2023, *M Herodotou et al v M Panayidi*, Civil Appeal No 336/2014, ECLI:CY:AD:2023:A113: Trespass to Land by Co-Owners

a) Brief Summary of the Facts

TH was the father of appellant/defendant 1 and ex-husband of the appellant/defendant 2. He was the owner of a residence which also included ancillary buildings (ancillary residence). In 1996, he transferred 50 % of the residence to his daughter, appellant/defendant 1. In 1997, he signed an agreement with his ex-wife in which, among other things, (a) he granted her the right to lease the residence and manage the income therefrom; (b) he granted her the right to use the residence together with the then-minor appellant 1; and (c) these would be valid for the entire life of appellant/defendant 2 unless, when appellant 1 turned 18, she took away these rights. 25

TH subsequently married the respondent/plaintiff, with whom he had two children. In 2003, TH transferred to the respondent the remaining 50 % of the residence. Thus, the respondent became a co-owner of the residence with appellant 1. Both the latter and her mother (appellant 2) continued to live in the residence. The respondent asked the appellants to allow her to use the residence as well, but they refused. 26

The District Court issued an injunction in favour of the plaintiff/respondent obliging the appellants/defendants, among others, to allow the plaintiff/respondent to enter the residence freely and enjoy its use. 27

b) Judgment of the Court

The Supreme Court, in affirming the judgment of the District Court, ruled that a co-owner may bring an action against another co-owner for trespass to immovable property only if he has actually been evicted from or deprived of his property. A contrary view would deprive the co-owner of the enjoyment of his property, which is also guaranteed by art 23 of the Cypriot Constitution. 28

25 Against such possibility, *Attorney General v A Palma et al* (2015) 1 AAD 2489. However, according to *Kennedy Hotels Ltd v Indjirdjian* (1992) 1 AAD 400, punitive damages may be awarded nevertheless, since the court has discretion to decide on the appropriate remedy for each case.

c) Commentary

29 This judgment affirms that an action for trespass to land against a co-owner is possible if the plaintiff has actually been removed from or dispossessed of the land. It is interesting that the Court relates the right of action in such cases with the protection of the fundamental right to property under art 23 of the Cypriot Constitution. This is in line with the view of Cypriot courts that fundamental rights must be protected by the State through its courts also in relations between private persons.[26]

30 In such cases, apart from an injunction, the plaintiff may also claim damages. The measure of damages is not the actual profit that the trespasser gained or the plaintiff's actual loss, but the market rental value of the property occupied or used for the period of wrongful occupation (mesne profits), even if the plaintiff could not have used the land or rent it.[27] If actual damage of the (co-)owner is not proven, then the court may award nominal damages.[28]

4. Supreme Court, 28 March 2023, *A Stephanou v Agrowise Ltd* and *A Stephanou v A Stylianou*, Civil Appeals Nos 368/14 and 371/14, ECLI:CY:AD:2023:A113: Fire on Immovable Property; Negligence; Rule of *Rylands v Fletcher*; Effect of Illegal Contract

a) Brief Summary of the Facts

31 A fire burned premises and equipment of a livestock unit belonging to the respondent/plaintiff. The fire started from an adjoining field, which belonged to the appellant/defendant. The respondent/plaintiff had rented the field from the Ministry of the Interior for exclusively agricultural purposes.

32 The District Court ruled for the plaintiff, based on negligence and the reversal of the burden of proof established in secs 52 and 53 of the Civil Wrongs Law. Section 52 regards the 'onus of proof of negligence when damage is caused by dangerous things' and sec 53 the 'onus of proof of negligence when damage is caused by fire'.

26 *T Yiallouros v E Nicolaou* (2001) AAD 558.

27 *Attorney General v Bahchecioglou et al* (1998) 1 AAD 426; *Adrian Holdings Ltd v Attorney General* (1998) 1 AAD 1836.

28 *C Ttantis v G Hadjimichael et al* (1982) 1 CLR 301; *S Kakoullou et al v I Kakoulli* (1985) 1 CLR 355.

The defendants appealed, claiming, among others, that the District Court erroneously connected in its judgment the tort of negligence with secs 52 and 53 of the Civil Wrongs Law. 33

b) Judgment of the Court

The Supreme Court upheld the judgment of the District Court and clarified that, 34 depending on the content of the statement of claim, the legal basis of the claim for damages due to fire on immovable property may be negligence and/or the rule in *Rylands v Fletcher*.[29]

The main conditions for the application of the rule in *Rylands v Fletcher* are 35 that: (1) the defendant brought something into his premises that could cause damage if it escaped; and (2) those things occurred in the course of a non-physical use of the premises. This rule also applies to cases of fire. However, the owner of a dangerous object is not responsible if it escapes as a result of an independent act of a third person and there was no negligence of the owner.

As to the defence of illegality, the Supreme Court ruled that it is immaterial 36 that the injured party had concluded a contract with the Ministry of the Interior, under which, the property was leased to her for exclusively agricultural and not for storage purposes. There was no contract between the parties to the trial, so neither can plead the illegality of the other to obtain a benefit in the form of damages. There was only a relationship between neighbours, which entailed a duty of care. Although illegality may be a defence to an action in tort, a simple and formal illegality cannot eliminate the tortfeasor's duty of care, because it would provide the tortfeasor a form of immunity from the consequences of his wrong, thus excluding the restitution of the victim.

c) Commentary

This judgment clarifies two issues in Cypriot tort law. 37

First, it underlines the distinction between negligence and the rule in *Rylands* 38 *v Fletcher*, which is correct.[30]

---

29 This rule originates from the judgment of the House of Lords on the case *Rylands v Fletcher* (1868) Law Reports (LR) 3 House of Lords (HL) 330.

30 Regarding Cypriot law, see also *Partemis/G Erotokritou*, Civil Wrongs, vol 2 (2003) (in Greek) 47–50 and *P Polyviou*, Civil Wrongs in the Law of Cyprus, vol B (2020) (in Greek) 653 f.

39 The rule of *Rylands v Fletcher* is a special tort, based on strict liability and it is not included in the Civil Wrongs Law. Nevertheless, the provisions of the Civil Wrongs Law are not exhaustive. By virtue of art 29(1)(c) of the Court of Justice Law of 1960 (Law 14(I)/1960), the principles of common law and equity are applied by Cypriot courts, to the extent that they do not contradict the Constitution and the statutes of Cyprus. As a result, the rule of *Rylands v Fletcher* may be invoked instead of or alongside the tort of negligence. Older case law of the Supreme Court drew a distinction between the two torts.[31] More recent case law, including the present case, also distinguishes between the two torts, but considers that sec 53 of the Civil Wrongs Law incorporates *Rylands v Fletcher.*[32]

40 Section 53 is entitled 'Onus of proof of negligence when damage is caused by fire'. It provides that in any action brought regarding damage in which it is proved (a) that such damage was caused by or in consequence of any fire and (b) that the defendant started such fire, or was liable for starting such fire, or was the occupier of the immovable property, or the owner of the movable property on which such fire originated, the onus is upon the defendant to show that there was no negligence for which he is liable in connection with the origin or spread of such fire. Thus, sec 53 is an evidentiary rule regarding the tort of negligence. As such, it is distinct from the rule in *Rylands v Fletcher.*[33] The present judgment and the more recent case law of the Supreme Court mentioned above create unnecessary confusion.[34]

41 Second, this judgment elaborates on the role of an illegal contract as regards liability for a tort. The Supreme Court observed that an illegal contract concluded by the plaintiff may not affect the tortious liability of the defendant, unless the contract has been concluded between these two parties. In the case at hand, the plaintiff/respondent had concluded a contract with a different person. As a result, the Supreme Court affirmed the part of the judgment of the District Court that omitted to examine the effect of alleged illegality of the behaviour of the plaintiff/respondent regarding a contract concluded with the Ministry of the Interior on a particular use of the land destroyed by the defendant's behaviour. It is noteworthy that the alleged 'illegality' in this case did not refer to the contract as such, but to the plaintiff's behaviour in the sense that he had breached a contractual duty towards his contractual party. Another noteworthy detail is that the Supreme

31 *Hamza v Vlachos* (V21) 1 CLR 169; *Mouzé v Lampri* (1994) 1 AAD 216; *Christofi v Petrakis Exhaust Silencers Ltd & Anor* (1993) 1 AAD 543.

32 *Georghiou v Stylianou* (2009) 1 AAD 70. This case had been invoked by the defendants/appellants in the case at hand.

33 See also above fn 28.

34 Above fn 30 and the present judgment.

Court based its reasoning, apart from the Cypriot case law, on Canadian authorities,[35] contrary to its usual practice of drawing guidance from English cases.

5. District Court of Paphos, 11 December 2023, *A Tziamalis v Parthenon Tziamalis Mosaic Factory Ltd*, Action No 1870/2015: Employer's Liability; Liability of a Company towards its Director for a Labour Accident

a) Brief Summary of the Facts

The plaintiff was the sole director and shareholder of the defendant, which was a company engaged in the sale and processing of marble, and at the same time had the status of the defendant's employee. On 15 May 2014, while ET, who was also an employee of the defendant, was transporting a slab of marble with a lifting machine, he broke the marble and injured the plaintiff's knee. At the time of the accident, the plaintiff was giving instructions to ET for the installation of marble. 42

The plaintiff filed an action for employer's negligence, breach of statutory duties regarding safety at work, and vicarious liability for the conduct of ET. The plaintiff claimed that ET together with the other employees failed, among other things, to thoroughly check the large slab of marble for cracks or fissures before loading it onto a lifting machine, thus causing the marble to break and injure the plaintiff. They also failed to warn the plaintiff of the risk that the marble might break and injure him, and allowed him to work near what they knew was an unsafe and dangerous place. 43

The defendant suggested that the plaintiff, who was its sole director and shareholder, had the duty to take all necessary measures and ensure that the defendant fulfilled its duty of care and its legal duties to its employees. 44

It was undisputed that the fall of the marble was not due to mishandling of the lifting machine by ET or to any defect in the machine or any part thereof. Moreover, the plaintiff was near the lifting machine during the process of transporting the marble. 45

35 *Rankin (Rankin's Garage & Sales) v J J* [2018] Supreme Court of Canada (SCC) 19, para 63 and *Kim v Choi* [2020] British Columbia Court of Appeal (BCCA) 98, paras 33 and 43–49.

b) Judgment of the Court

46 The District Court observed that there were different causes of action in this case. First, there was an alleged breach of statutory duty arising from the Health and Safety at Work Law (Law 89(I)/1996). Such duty is non-delegable and the employer bears absolute liability for its breach, even if a person other than the employer was to blame therefor. The latter scenario could entail vicarious liability of the employer, although this is not a case of vicarious liability in strict legal terms. Moreover, there was alleged negligence under art 51 of the Civil Wrongs Law.

47 The Court noted that the company and its director are different persons. At the same time, the director of a company has a duty of care towards the company, when exercising his duties.

48 The Court then referred to what it called 'the Brumder defence', which has its origins in the case of *Brumder v Motornet Service and Repairs Ltd* [2013] Court of Appeal, Civil Division (EWCA Civ) 195. This defence applies to claims brought by a natural person against a company for violations of the regulations of health and safety at work. If the claimant is the sole director and shareholder of that company, they cannot assert that the company had not proved that it had done all it could to ensure compliance with such regulations, when it was only through their acts as director that the company itself could act. Otherwise, the policy reasons for the strict liability of employers under these regulations, namely, to protect employees and to encourage high standards of compliance by those responsible for the performance of the company's duties, would be significantly undermined. The Court observed that, following *Brumder*, where an employee brings a claim for personal injury against his employer and proves that their injury was caused by a breach of law which made the employer strictly liable, they need do no more. However, the employer may plead that the employee is themself liable and this defence applies: (a) where the claimant's act or omission had the legal effect of the defendant breaching a statutory duty, but (b) the employer proved that it had done all it could to ensure compliance with the duty.

49 The Court also referred to *Carr v Brands Transports Ltd*,[36] which held that the 'Brumder defence' could not apply to the extent that the plaintiff's fault was not coextensive (ie equal in scope) with the company's own fault, and the company's fault arose out of the independent contractor's errors for which the company was legally responsible. In *Carr* the court had concluded that there was contributory negligence on the part of the plaintiff to 40 %.

---

36 [2022] England & Wales High Court (Administrative Court) (EWHC) 3167 King's Bench (KB).

On the facts of the case, the Court accepted that the plaintiff, as the director of the defendant, had to ensure that the rules regarding health and safety at work were observed, and it was due to his omission that the defendant was primarily liable. As a result, the 'Brumder defence' applied. Nonetheless, the Court accepted that the defendant's employees had been instructed to check the marble for any fissures before lifting them, which they failed to do in that instance. Hence, the defendant was vicariously liable for such failure of its employees. At the same time, the Court found the plaintiff contributory negligent to 50 %, because he had been too close to the lifting of the marble, despite recognising the risk from a potential fall of the marble. 50

c) Commentary

This judgment regards the peculiar scenario of a company's sole director and shareholder bringing an action against that company for an accident sustained on the company's premises due to alleged negligence and violation of a statutory duty of the company. The ultimate aim of the action is to obtain coverage from the company's liability insurer. 51

The District Court noted the practical difficulties arising in such cases, given that, on the one hand, the company acts through its director and the director's decisions and choices are the decisions and choices of the company, while, on the other hand, the director and the company are separate persons and the director may be an employee of the company. At the same time, the employer's duties to their employees are not delegable. 52

The District Court followed English authorities as to the defence that a company can invoke regarding its (vicarious) liability for breach of a duty of care or of a statutory duty towards an employee, when such breach has been caused by the employee's behaviour: once the employee has established a prima facie breach of the employer's duty, it is up to the employer to prove that it had taken all necessary steps to fulfil its duty and the employee was solely to blame for the accident.[37] The Supreme Court of Cyprus had extended these principles to the liability of the company for behaviour of its sole director in a claim brought by the director against the company, albeit with brief reasoning and by reference to an analysis in *Clerk and Lindsell on Torts.*[38] However, it was more recent English authorities, 53

37 *Boyle v Kodak* [1969] 2 All ER 439; *Ginty v Belmont Building Supplies Ltd* [1959] 1 All ER 414.
38 *P Panayiotou v S Panayiotou and Sons Ltd* (2004) 1 AAD 1339. See also *Cyprus Linen Co Ltd v S Anthoulli* (2004) 1 AAD 679, which refers to these principles in an obiter.

namely *Brumder v Motornet Service and Repairs Ltd and another* [2013] EWCA Civ 195 and *Carr v Brands Transport Limited* [2022] EWHC 3167 (KB) that guided the District Court in its judgment.

54 As already mentioned, Cypriot courts have been called before to solve such issues.[39] This is explained by the fact that most companies in Cyprus are family businesses and their directors are very often their sole shareholders, while being formally employees of the company for tax reasons. The value of the present judgment lies in that, for the first time, it analyses in depth the arising legal challenges.

C. Personal Injury

55 **Preliminary remarks:** Only judgments of trial judges are presented, because of the often very long time between the filing of an action and rendering of the judgment (which can take up to nine years) and subsequently between the filing of appeal and delivery of an appellate judgment (which can take up to seven years). The judgments of trial judges are probably more appropriate to demonstrate the trends of the courts in awarding general damages,[40] given that they refer to more recent periods than the Supreme Court judgments and considering that the Supreme Court in principle does not interfere with the findings of trial judges.

56 A further issue is the date from which interest is awarded. This is left to the discretion of the judge under sec 58 A of the Civil Wrongs Law, but there is also non-binding guidance from the case law of the Supreme Court.[41] According to the latter, interest should be reduced if plaintiffs unreasonably delayed filing their actions.

---

39 See above fn 37.

40 This means compensation mainly for non-material damage, such as pain, suffering and loss of amenities.

41 Cyprus Supreme Court, 30 May 1991, *Foinikarides & Anor v Georgiou & Ors* (1991) 1 AAD 475; Cyprus Supreme Court, 28 September 2005, *Kampouris v Biochrom Ltd* (2005) 1 AAD 1246.

1. District Court of Nicosia, 31 October 2023, *Stephanidou et al v Attorney General et al*, Action No 6779/13: Medical Negligence; Infant

a) Brief Summary of the Facts

On 25 October 2010, plaintiff 1 gave birth to plaintiff 3 at a public hospital. The mother and the new-born girl remained in the hospital for four days before being discharged. Two years later, the girl was diagnosed by a private doctor with a congenital dislocation of the left hip. The diagnosis was followed by four surgeries. The parents of plaintiff 3 (plaintiffs 1 and 2) claimed that the congenital dislocation of the hip was present from birth and/or was caused during childbirth and/or as a result of treatment received at the public hospital. 57

After the second operation, the girl was placed in a physiotherapy programme and, since then, she has been clinically monitored and receiving medical guidance, especially for physiotherapy and restriction of activities at school. The problem with her hip has a series of consequences for plaintiff 3: unsteadiness in walking, fatigue, inability to participate in sports activities, special care during games, difficulty walking on stairs, reduced school and extra-curricular socialisation, and difficulty on uneven terrain or on the beach. Moreover, plaintiff 3 cannot participate in gym classes and needs a school escort to help her at school. She is also subject to discrimination and bullying from other children. 58

In an examination on 21 July 2016, the doctor found that there was persistent difficulty in walking due to weakness in the muscle around the left hip and, as a result, the little girl had difficulty standing for a long time, walking smoothly, balancing correctly, running, going up and down stairs or standing on her left leg, and she presented great instability and risk of falling. During the next examination on 26 February 2020, the doctor found that there had been an improvement and that the imbalance had been overcome. However, at the same time, he also found persistent muscle weakness in the left hip area, which still caused incomplete balance and difficulties in going up and down stairs and in running or jumping or walking for a long time, and there was an inability to perform a deep squat. Moreover, there was a decline in the function of the joint (by 20 degrees) and, in the long term, the dysfunction of the joint will intensify, which will affect her daily life. She will also need to undergo water therapy every year. Furthermore, an additional operation is more than likely to be required near the age of 60. 59

b) Judgment of the Court

60 The Court awarded to plaintiff 3 special damages in the amount of € 5,896, with interest from the date she had been discharged from the maternity clinic until the date of the judgment. However, the interest was reduced by 50 % to account for the fact that her loss did not arise from the beginning of her life. The Court also awarded general damages for pain and suffering in the amount of € 130,000, with interest from the date she was discharged from the maternity clinic. In addition, it awarded general damages in the amount of € 70,000 for loss of future income, € 10,000 for future expenses for surgery and € 18,000 for future water therapy (€ 600 x 30 years), all these with interest from the date of the judgment.

61 Moreover, the Court noted that there were consequences for the parents of plaintiff 3, namely restrictions regarding their previous activities, as well as sadness, anxiety, insecurity and concern about their child's health and life. The Court also accepted that, during the period of the surgeries, the child's mother experienced greater suffering and loss of personal comfort, as she had to resign from her permanent full-time job and choose a part-time job. As a result, the Court awarded general damages in the amount of € 10,000 to the father and € 20,000 to the mother, both with interest from the date of the discharge from the maternity clinic.

2. District Court of Nicosia, 2 June 2023, *Voskou v Stylianou & Son Auto Care Services Ltd et al*, Action No 6822/13, ECLI:CY:EDLEF:2023:A174: Labour Accident

a) Brief Summary of the Facts

62 The plaintiff was 25 years old and healthy at the time of the accident. Defendant 1 was a repair station for motor vehicles and defendant 2 was its owner. On 9 September 2013, the plaintiff helped defendant 2 to transport to the repair station a vehicle that needed to have its fuel immediately removed. Defendant 2 placed a plastic basin under the pump that collected the fuel, placed a car battery near the pump and connected the battery to the pump. He then instructed the plaintiff to hold the battery wires as he (defendant 2) had to leave the premises. While the plaintiff was under the vehicle, the plastic tube (rubber) came out of the tank, causing the pump wires that were attached to be stretched and sparked. The fuel was ignited while the plaintiff was under the elevated vehicle holding the

wires to the battery terminals, resulting in an explosion and a fire. As a result, the plaintiff suffered second and third degree burns to 24 % of his body.

The plaintiff was hospitalised for about six weeks, and was operated on three times. He was unable to work for about one year. He had to receive special medication to alleviate his pain, which was more intense when he was exposed to the sun. He also had concentration and sleeping difficulties. 63

The plaintiff's scars and itching pain are permanent. Furthermore, he suffers from permanent wounds on the left ankle. In the future, permanent wounds and even skin cancer may develop in the places of scars on the lower limbs. 64

In view of the above, the Court awarded special damages in the amount of € 2,130 and general damages in the amount of € 120,000 with interest from the date of the accident. 65

3. District Court of Nicosia, 27 October 2023, *ST v Kythera Developments Ltd*, Action No 2607/2013: Labour Accident

a) Brief Summary of the Facts

The plaintiff was a construction worker, 54 years old at the time of the accident, and an employee of the defendant, a construction company. The plaintiff was working in the outdoor area of a construction site, opening pits for tree planting, when he fell into an underground space 3.1 metres deep. Because the building complex was almost complete, no safety helmets were available at the work site, so the plaintiff was not wearing one. 66

The plaintiff suffered a skull injury and fractures to both arms. He was briefly hospitalised and then transferred to a rehabilitation centre, where he underwent physiotherapy and was discharged about two and a half months later. For many months he was bedridden and in a wheelchair. He could not use his arms or stand up to walk, had headaches, was confused, and experienced dizziness. After his discharge from the rehabilitation centre, he was able to walk short distances with a cane but because of the hand injury, it was also painful for him to use a cane. As a result, he spent all his time at home and his wife took care of him on a daily basis. 67

The plaintiff is no longer capable of manual work. He is unable to walk, stand, use stairs, and has significant mobility problems. He still feels dizziness, has many headaches, has memory and concentration problems and there is an increased chance of developing epilepsy. He suffers from weakness and/or difficulty using his upper limbs, holding objects, and lifting weights. His gait is unsteady. His toes feel numb, and he cannot stand for a longer period of time. His hands are 68 still weak, and he feels pain in his hands, especially when the weather changes. His disability is permanent, which causes psychological problems: he feels extreme pain and suffering and suffers from depression. Further medical treatment and expenses will be necessary in the future.

b) Judgment of the Court

69 The Court awarded special damages in the amount of € 1,110 for medical expenses plus € 130,938 for loss of earnings, with interest from the date when the final amount of these (recurrent) expenses could be determined. It also awarded general damages in the amount of € 175,000 for pain and suffering, with interest from the date of the accident.

4. District Court of Nicosia, 24 February 2023, *GP v GN et al*, Action No 4745/2013, ECLI:CY:EDLEF:2023:A43: Road Negligence; Injury of Pedestrian

a) Brief Summary of the Facts

70 The plaintiff was 52 years old at the time of the accident, and married, with two children. The defendant, while driving his motorcycle, hit, dragged, and injured the plaintiff who was crossing a road. The plaintiff was transferred to hospital in a comatose state, in a life threating situation, and underwent intensive treatment and a craniectomy. He was hospitalised in the intensive care unit for one month and then transferred to a specialised physiotherapy centre for rehabilitation. Four months after the accident, he underwent another operation to replace the bone which had been removed in the craniectomy.

71 After the accident, he was on sick leave for twenty months. When he returned to work, he was transferred to another department with reduced salary. He subsequently resigned and, since then, has been unable to work owing to his injuries.

72 The plaintiff suffers from permanent left hemiparesis (one-sided muscle weakness), permanent muscle weakness on his left side, muscle atrophy of the upper and lower limbs and an increased chance of developing epilepsy. He suffers from frequent and severe headaches, frequent dizziness, a permanent unsteadiness of gait, a permanent loss of smell and taste, and permanent dysphasia. Moreover, the plaintiff suffers from permanent neurological conditions: he has persistent binge eating, intense uncontrollable emotional arousals and outbursts, such

as tantrums and tremors, and suffers from pathological crying. He has almost no capacity for work and he is sexually impotent. He is unable to take care of himself and his health condition will continuously deteriorate. Caregiver assistance will be permanently necessary, while the treatment of permanent scars requires surgery, re-stitching, and laser treatment. Furthermore, he is highly uncomfortable with his appearance, since a large scar is visible on the right frontocentral part of the skull with an obvious groove due to the surgery.

b) Judgment of the Court

The Court awarded special damages in the amount of € 282,000 with interest from 73
the date of the accident, plus € 41,134 for loss of earnings with interest from the date of his resignation from his job. Moreover, the Court awarded general damages in the amount of € 150,000 with interest from the date of the accident.

D. Literature

1. *Polyvios Polyviou*, Κυπριακό Ενοχικό Δίκαιο, Τόμος II, Δίκαιο Αστικών Αδικημάτων [The Law of Obligations in common law and in Cypriot law, Volume II, The Law of Civil Wrongs] (Nomiki Vivliothiki 2023) 816 pp, ISBN 978-960-654-985-4

This book is part of a series of four volumes on the Law of Obligations by the au- 74
thor. Volume I is a General Introduction, Volume II regards the Law of Contracts and Volume IV the Law of Unjust Enrichment and Restitution. Volumes II-IV are concise versions of earlier books of the author on the same subjects.

The author, Polyvios Polyviou, is a renowned lawyer and a very experienced 75
legal practitioner, having published numerous books not only on Cypriot law, but also on the Cyprus Question. His books are often cited by courts. It is noteworthy that Cypriot courts sometimes adopt English case law by reference to both the judgments as such and to the part of Polyviou's books mentioning these judgments.

His book on Civil Wrongs includes a comprehensive analysis of torts under 76
Cypriot law and common law. It consists of the following parts: (1) an introduction to the law of torts in general and to the Cypriot tort law in particular, (2) trespass to person, (3) negligence, (4) breach of statutory duty, (5) nuisance, (6) the rule in *Rylands v Fletcher*, (7) vicarious liability, (8) economic torts, (9) defamation, (10) mis-

use of private information and (11) remedies. However, the book does not dedicate any chapter on torts related to property (save for a short chapter on unlawful detention), although the Cypriot Civil Wrongs Law contains special sections on trespass to immovable property, trespass to movable property and conversion (to which the author refers very briefly at the end of the chapter on unlawful detention).

77 The book analyses the law of torts regarding both its theoretical foundations and its practical application. A characteristic of the book is the frequent citation of exact excerpts of the judgments it refers to. Another important element is the comparative presentation of the law in other common law jurisdictions, such as Australia, Canada, England and New Zealand.

78 The book is a very good source of current Cypriot tort law, with interesting comparative observations. It is useful mainly for legal practitioners. Students especially undergraduate, will find it a little difficult to read and understand, given the extensive analysis of various issues and the limited use of subheadings.

Jiří Hrádek

VI. Czech Republic

A. Legislation

1. Act No 250/2023 Coll, on Public Auctions

Act No 250/2023 Coll, on Public Auctions,[1] is rather a procedural law which lays down procedural rules for selling things. The Act on Public Auctions lays down rules on public auctions followed by specific provisions on forced auctions. A forced auction is a public auction in which the bidder is the auction creditor, ie a person whose claim is secured by a lien or pledge. 1

The legislator's main goal when adopting the Law was to unify provisions on the transfer of ownership rights under the Act on Public Auctions and the Civil Code, which states in sec 1771[2] that an ownership title passes with the granting of the bid. Moreover, the legislator wanted to impose certain obligations on all persons connected with the auction. However, to ensure the legal position, it sets forth specific duties regarding damages. 2

As regards compensation for damage, the Act stipulates the following provisions: 3

- Pursuant to sec 28, if the auctioneer, ie a person who carries out the public auction, violates an obligation stipulated by the Act, they must compensate the damage caused thereby. However, the auctioneer will be released from this obligation if they prove that they exercised all reasonable care to prevent the occurrence of damage.
- Pursuant to sec 58, in the event of a forced auction, the auction creditor must compensate any damage that arose from the unauthorised application of a claim they made. They will be released from this liability if they prove that they exercised all reasonable care.
- If the auction creditor does not notify changes regarding the applied claims that occurred after its application without undue delay, it must compensate damage caused by the delay.
- Pursuant to sec 2, an auctioneer must conclude liability insurance for damage caused in connection with the execution of a public auction. The agreed

1 Zákon č. 250/2023 Sb., o veřejných dražbách.

2 At an auction, a contract is concluded by the fall of the hammer (Translation <www.aspi.cz>).

https://doi.org/10.1515/9783111376721-007

amount of the insurance limit must be at least CZK 500,000 (approx € 20,000) for each insurance event, and in case of multiple insurance events in one year, at least CZK 1,000,000 (approx € 40,000). However, the agreed amount of the insurance limit in case of forced auctions must be at least CZK 5,000,000 (approx € 200,000) for each insurance event, and in case of multiple insurance events in one year, at least CZK 10,000,000 (approx € 400,000).

B. Cases

1. Supreme Court of the Czech Republic (Nejvyšší soud České republiky) 31 August 2023, 30 Cdo 63/2023: State Liability for Crisis Measures Adopted During COVID-19 Pandemic; Unlimited Liability of the State

a) Brief Summary of the Facts

4 The claimant, a trading company in the retail sector, claimed damages of CZK 1,139,123 (approx € 45,600) that it incurred because of various crisis measures issued by the Czech Government in 2020 and 2021 that limited retail sales at certain specified times and later completely prohibited them, including business at the claimant's premises. The claimed damages represent lost profits.

5 The court of first instance rejected the claim. As part of the legal assessment, the court of first instance first excluded the application of Act No 82/1998 Coll, on Liability for Damage Based Either on Maladministration or on Illegal Decisions ('State Liability Act'),[3] as the cause of the damage was neither maladministration of a State body nor an illegal decision issued by it (maladministration and illegal decision are the only two reasons for establishing liability under the State Liability Act). Furthermore, the court of first instance proceeded according to the specific Law, namely Act No 240/2000 Coll, on Crisis Management ('Crisis Act').[4]

6 The court ruled that the conditions for the establishment of liability for damage caused in connection with the adopted crisis measures are laid down in sec 36

3 Zákon č. 82/1998 Sb., o odpovědnosti za škodu způsobenou při výkonu veřejné moci rozhodnutím nebo nesprávným úředním postupem a o změně zákona České národní rady č. 358/1992 Sb., o notářích a jejich činnosti (notářský řád).

4 Zákon č. 240/2000 Sb., o krizovém řízení a o změně některých zákonů (krizový zákon).

of the Crisis Act.[5] Such liability will be deemed strict with the possibility of exoneration if the injured party caused the damage to itself.

Liability established in this way is based on the principle of 'special victims', where a distinction must be made between an individual measure (as an intervention in the individual rights and property sphere of an individual in resolving a crisis), and a general restriction of certain rights and freedoms of an indefinite number of persons adopted by a generally binding legal regulation when dealing with a crisis. 7

However, the court concluded that the crisis measures in question had the nature of a generally binding legal act (legal regulation), which affected an indefinite number of people to whom they imputed legal obligations. Consequently, since the State does not bear liability for legislation, ie for the content of legal regulations and for harm caused to persons by fulfilling legal obligations, the court rejected the claim. 8

The court of second instance confirmed the decision. 9

The Supreme Court allowed an extraordinary appeal in order to assess whether State liability is possible under the Crisis Act. 10

b) Judgment of the Court

According to the Supreme Court, it is clear from sec 36 para 1 of the Crisis Act that the institute of liability for damage arising in causal connection with a crisis measure is a special norm containing the special factual basis of the State's liability, which is governed by this Crisis Act and not by the State Liability Act. At the same time, it establishes strict liability and, unlike the State Liability Act, does not require that the damage be caused by an illegal decision or maladministration. The State can release itself from liability if it proves that the injured party inflicted the damage upon itself. 11

It does not follow from the provision that the legislator intended to limit the State's liability for damage only to individually focused crisis measures. On the contrary, it was aware that emergency measures would be implemented to deal with large-scale emergencies. Finally, the fact that the legislator cannot, at the time of the adoption of a certain legal regulation, imagine all the situations to which this norm will be applied in the future, is not exceptional and can be resolved 12

5 (1) The State is obliged to compensate damage caused to legal entities and natural persons in causal connection with crisis measures and their exercises (sec 39, para 5) carried out in accordance with this Act. The State can only be released from this liability if it is proven that the injured person caused the damage himself.

by standard methods of legal interpretation, including analogy and teleological reduction. The argument regarding the unpredictability of an emergency, such as an epidemic of a highly contagious disease affecting the entire State territory, is thus unfounded.

13 Thus, the limitation of the State's liability according to sec 36 of the Crisis Act to situations where crisis measures are directed against specifically designated persons has no support in the law and cannot be deduced even by a teleological interpretation.

14 In its case law, the Supreme Court has not yet rendered an explicit opinion on when a crisis measure is implemented as one of the conditions for State liability. However, it is clear from the above that the State's duty to compensate damage caused by a crisis measure commences when such effects of the crisis measure may occur that led to the occurrence of damage. This moment must be assessed according to the specific circumstances of the case, since crisis measures may include a group of undetermined activities (reactions) of crisis management authorities to manage a crisis. For this reason, the liability of the State cannot be limited to only those measures that the State itself carries out (eg demolishing a house).

15 The fact that the claimant adhered to the crisis measures and that it respected them cannot be a disadvantage to it. Another opinion would mean that a person who did not respect the crisis measures would be entitled to compensation pursuant to sec 36 para 1 of the Crisis Act, while the claimant who acted in accordance with the law should not be. Such a conclusion is clearly incorrect.

16 The aforementioned conclusion is also supported by sec 36 para 3 of the Crisis Act.[6] This provision does not state that the damage or harm should have been caused by the implementation of the crisis measure but refers to the damage or harm caused as a result of the crisis measure.

c) Commentary

17 The Court decided on several fundamental issues in connection with the liability of the State. These issues took on a high profile during and after the COVID-19 pandemic, when the State began issuing a number of legislative and semi-legislative acts that fundamentally restricted people's rights and imposed new obligations and restrictions.

---

6 (3) Compensation for injury to health incurred during the performance of an imposed work obligation, work assistance or voluntary assistance performed as part of an organised activity is provided similarly according to the regulations on compensation for occupational accidents, if the right to compensation for this damage did not already arise from an employment relationship.

In the case at hand, the claimant was directly restricted in doing business when its retail sales were limited at certain specified times and later completely prohibited. Consequently, the claimant suffered damage in the form of lost profits. 18

The Supreme Court thus had to address several questions. There was the matter of whether liability for crisis measures issued based on the Crisis Act results from this law or from the State Liability Act. This latter Act establishes the general regime of State liability, governing any public liability, unless it is inferred that there is a special legal regulation. 19

Furthermore, the Court dealt with the question of liability for the crisis measure, which, by their nature, are neither individual administrative decisions nor legislative measures, but a legal regulation standing between these two legal acts. 20

Section 2 lit c) of the Crisis Act defines crisis measures as organisational or technical measures designed to resolve a crisis and eliminate its consequences, including measures that interfere with people's rights and duties. At the same time, it does not follow from the wording and language interpretation that the scope of persons whose rights and duties are affected by the crisis measures would have to be specifically defined or limited. 21

The Court came to the correct conclusion that the Crisis Act is the specific basis for the State's liability, and the State will always be liable for the measures issued if the victim did not cause the damage itself. Of course, such a cause cannot be that the victim suffered damage in connection with compliance with the measures. 22

The Court thus rejected the considerations that the State is not liable for damage caused by crisis measures, which are by their nature the product of legislative activity. First, the State is not liable for damage caused by normative acts only under the general regime laid down by the State Liability Act. This is because neither maladministration nor an illegal decision can be considered a legislative activity. However, under other laws, such liability remains unchanged. 23

Nevertheless, this conclusion that the State is also liable for legislative activity is not new. The doctrine that the State is not liable for damage caused by legislative activity, or its absence, was already challenged in the past. The Supreme Court held in 2012 that the State is liable for legislative errors in the case of a breach of EU law (File No 28 Cdo 2927/2010) and the Constitutional Court due to errors in legislative activity relating to rent regulation (File No I ÚS 92/94). 24

Secondly, the legislator has not been prevented from voluntarily accepting the obligation to compensate damage caused by various activities of bodies exercising public power, including the exercise of legislative activity, as was the case in sec 36 para 1 of the Crisis Act. 25

The liability of the State is not limited only to measures that are implemented by State bodies but also to those carried out by individual recipients of the norm. Therefore, the Court does not state that the damage or harm should have been 26 caused by the implementation of the crisis measures, as this is irrelevant. Instead, it refers to the damage or harm caused due to the crisis measures in general.

2. Supreme Court of the Czech Republic (Nejvyšší soud České republiky) 21 April 2023, 30 Cdo 414/2023: State Liability for Specific Type of Measures Adopted During COVID-19 Pandemic

a) Brief Summary of the Facts

27 The claimants filed a lawsuit demanding an apology from the respondent for the non-pecuniary damage that was caused to them by the measures issued by the Ministry of Health during the pandemic-induced state of emergency, which were subsequently declared null and void. As a result of those measures, the rights of the claimants to protect private and family life as well as the right to protect health and other rights were interfered with, as these extraordinary measures limited the possibility of free movement and also implemented other restrictions, such as the obligation to wear a mask or respirator.

28 The courts of first and second instance dismissed the claim.

29 The courts based their opinion on the State Liability Act and concluded that the assessed crisis measures were issued by the Ministry of Health based on sec 2 of Act No 94/2021 Coll, on extraordinary measures during the COVID-19 pandemic (the 'Pandemic Act').[7] Such laws represent measures of a general nature (*opatření obecné povahy*), ie a mixed legal act, which is neither a decision nor a legal regulation, and since the Pandemic Act does not contain any specific provision on liability, it remains subject to the general regulation set forth in Act No 82/1998 Coll, on State Liability. The State liability under the State Liability Act is conceived as liability for damage (injury) caused to an individual by an illegal decision or maladministration. Although the case law for some measures of a general nature has allowed the possibility of the State Liability Act to be applied, in the past such measures were of a general nature issued in zone planning proceedings and established the relationship between a public authority and a specific person. The measures of a general nature in question, however, had a general and nationwide impact.

7 Zákon č. 94/2021 Sb., o mimořádných opatřeních při epidemii onemocnění COVID-19 a o změně některých souvisejících zákonů.

b) Judgment of the Court

First, the Supreme Court dealt with whether the assessed extraordinary measures issued by the Ministry of Health, which are measures of a general nature, can be deemed decisions within the meaning of the State Liability Act, and answered in the affirmative. 30

A decision is generally considered to be an individual legal act that establishes, cancels, changes or declares the rights and obligations of a named person (Supreme Court File No 2 Cdon 129/97).[8] 31

A measure of a general nature generally represents an administrative act of a mixed nature with a specifically determined object of regulation and a generally defined scope of recipients. This is the result of public administration activity, which is neither an individual decision nor a legal regulation. It is not a decision because it is not directed towards a particular person or persons, but, on the contrary, towards an indefinite number of persons. On the other hand, it is not a legal regulation, because, like a decision, its object is the solution of a specific matter, not the establishment of a general rule of conduct applicable to all cases of the same kind.[9] 32

Since the extraordinary measures are issued without proceedings and thus there cannot be parties to the proceedings, any person whose rights and obligations were subject to the measure, ie a person whose rights were affected by the issuance of an illegal extraordinary measures, can have the status of a party to the proceedings within the meaning of sec 7 of the State Liability Act.[10] At the same time, however, it must be a person who has used the opportunity to file a lawsuit against the extraordinary measures within the statutory period (ie within one month from the effective date) pursuant to sec 13 of the Pandemic Act. 33

Thus, a party is not a person who remained passive despite being entitled to challenge the extraordinary measures in court, because only by using this means to protect their rights does the injured party make it clear that they perceive the relevant extraordinary measures as harmful and interfering with their rights and that they intend to defend themselves against their adoption by legal means. This conclusion remains unchanged regardless of whether such a lawsuit led to the cancellation of the extraordinary measures or not. 34

---

8 *P Simon*, Odpovědnost za škodu při výkonu veřejné moci [Liability for damage caused by exercise of public authority] (1st edn 2019) 71.

9 The same definition can be found in sec 171 of the Administrative Code.

10 The right to compensation for damage caused by an illegal decision belongs to the parties to the proceedings in which the decision was issued that caused them damage.

c) Commentary

35 This is the second important decision adopted in 2023 to deal with State liability during the COVID-19 pandemic.

36 The issue consists in the fact that the liability of the State based on the State Liability Act requires that damage occurs either because of maladministration or an illegal decision. However, there are also mixed legal acts that may cause damage. One of them is the measure of a general nature.

37 The decision is essential for assessing whether, if a measure of a general nature is adopted, the affected persons are entitled to compensation for damage.

38 The Court concluded that the affected person may claim damages, although the mentioned legal act falls outside the individual categories in which the law allows or, on the contrary, excludes the right to compensation for damage. This conclusion is made even though the State Liability Act, as a general regulation for compensation for damage caused by an illegal decision or maladministration, explicitly mentions the decision as the only option of a relevant legal act.

39 Although a measure of a general nature does not present a decision in the narrow sense, according to the explanatory report to Act No 160/2006 Coll,[11] which extensively amended the State Liability Act and which introduced new legal institutes, including measures of a general nature,

> '[i]t is indisputable that also for damage caused on the basis of these [new] institutes the State or territorial self-governing units should be liable. Measures of a general nature are explicitly subordinated under decision.'

40 Thus, the intention of the legislator was to deem measures of a general nature a decision.[12]

41 However, the Supreme Court laid down very important conditions for claims to damages. It clearly defined the conditions under which any person who feels that they have been harmed by the legal act may claim damages.

42 Since the extraordinary measures are issued without proceedings and thus there cannot be parties to the proceedings, any person whose rights and obligations were subject to the measure and who has used the opportunity to file a law-

---

11 See *J Hrádek*, Czech Republic, in: H Koziol/BC Steininger (eds), European Tort Law 2006 (2008) 123, no 18 ff.

12 *F Ištvánek/P Simon/F Korbel*, Zákon o odpovědnosti za škodu způsobenou při výkonu veřejné moci rozhodnutím nebo nesprávným úředním postupem, Komentář [Act on liability for damage caused by exercise of public authority by decision or maladministration, Commentary] (2017) 180.

suit against the measures in question can have the status of a party to the proceedings within the meaning of sec 7 of the State Liability Act.

No other person may currently claim damages from the State under the State Liability Act. 43

3. Supreme Court of the Czech Republic (Nejvyšší soud České republiky) 23 March 2023, 25 Cdo 455/2022: Scope of Liability for Damage to Health; Calculation under Methodology

a) Brief Summary of the Facts

On 12 March 2016, a traffic accident occurred in which the claimant, crossing the road outside a pedestrian crossing in a state of severe intoxication, was hit by a vehicle insured for liability for damage by the respondent. The claimant suffered severe injuries. The respondent, an insurance company, acknowledged its obligation to perform in the amount of 60 % and to this extent paid the claimant's claims for compensation for pain and treatment costs. However, according to the claimant, the respondent's obligation amounted to 70 %. 44

The court of first instance concluded that the calculation of the pain allowance made by the expert according to the Methodology for the Compensation of Non-Property Injury to Health (the 'Methodology') included items representing medical interventions that were incorrectly evaluated using an analogy. The court concluded that the medical procedures were carried out in a standard manner and that compensation for pain suffered during their performance is already included in the assessment of the pain associated with the claimant's injuries, which were the cause of the medical procedures. 45

The court of second instance confirmed the previous decision. In its opinion, it is necessary to distinguish between the pain caused by the injury while fully conscious from the pain caused by the medical treatment while deeply unconscious. The latter must be completely overruled by the first pain. 46

b) Judgment of the Court

The purpose of compensating for pain is to address not only the direct experience of discomfort but also the stress and challenges associated with the health damage suffered. This compensation acknowledges the intrusion into the personal sphere 47 of the injured party, particularly concerning the typical pain accompanying damage to health.

48 The interpretation of sec 2958 of the Civil Code[13] cannot lead to the conclusion that the term pain is now to be understood only as physical pain without connection to the mental aspects of painful conditions. Compensation for pain means compensation for pain in the broader sense, ie both physical pain and mental distress (Supreme Court File No 25 Cdo 2245/2017). Nor can the victim's perception of physical pain be separated from the negative perception of discomfort, stress and difficulty associated with healing. The degree of such difficulties must be considered when determining the amount of compensation for pain, since the assessment made by the doctor (expert) is only a starting point, based on which the court determines the final reasonable amount of compensation in view of the specific circumstances of each case.

49 If there is no explicit item in the pain overview for a certain type of damage, the item that is closest in nature and severity to the relevant damage is used for scoring purposes (analogous application). To determine the resulting value, points from individual pain conditions are summed up. The amount of compensation (ie point assessment) can be adjusted (increased) by the assessing expert depending on the complexity of the medical condition. This requires a more demanding method of treatment in relation to the items to which the complication relates if the basic assessment does not sufficiently describe the severity of the injury. Depending on the degree of complications, this increase usually does not exceed 20 %.

c) Commentary

50 To determine adequate compensation, the judicial practice since 2014 has been to use a non-binding aid for the interpretation of sec 2958 of the Civil Code. This aid is called the Methodology for the Compensation of Non-Property Injury to Health. The basis for determining the amount of compensation for pain is usually the opinion of an expert from the specific branch of health care. The expert opinion of a doctor is only satisfactory in simple cases. The purpose of the opinion of an expert in the relevant specialisation is to create a sufficiently detailed, structured and

13 Where harm to health is caused, the wrongdoer shall redress such harm by means of a monetary sum fully compensating the pain suffered and other immaterial loss; if the harm to his health interferes with the future prospects of the injured party, the wrongdoer shall also compensate him for the difficulties in attaining his proper social position. If the amount of compensation cannot be determined in this way, it shall be determined in accordance with the principles of equity.

comprehensible factual basis for the court, containing the appropriate expert medical conclusion.

However, the extent to which the pain from a primary injury is comparable to the pain induced by medical interventions is fundamentally a factual matter requiring expert evaluation. Therefore, the court should rely on a doctor's expert assessment to provide the necessary basis for determining this comparison. If the court does not find the expert assessment on the degree of pain and functional abilities in the case of health injuries to be sufficiently convincing, it should supplement the evidence with the expert opinion of a doctor with a suitable specialisation (expert or consultant). For instance, in the case of anaesthesia and intubation, this would most likely be an anaesthesiologist. 51

As regards the main issue of this case, the Supreme Court did not provide a clear answer on whether different types of pain deserve more compensation. It ruled that compensation for pain means compensation for pain in the broader sense, ie both physical pain and mental distress, and that such pain in the broader sense will be assessed by an expert. We deem this approach correct, since it allows the court to assess the particular case and compensate it, even under analogous application. 52

If extraordinary circumstances occurred during the treatment (even if caused by medical predispositions), which led to the prolongation of the treatment and increased the pain of the injury or its treatment, the court must take them into account in its final decision. For example, it can do so by increasing the amount, usually no more than 20 % in case of complications and a more demanding method of treatment (Supreme Court File No 25 Cdo 2207/2020). 53

4. Supreme Court of the Czech Republic (Nejvyšší soud České republiky) 23 March 2023, 25 Cdo 1152/2021: Liability for Dangerous Operational Activity

a) Brief Summary of the Facts

The claimant, an entity entrusted with the management of forests owned by the State, sought compensation for damage caused to the forests by emissions released into the air in 2014 by factories operated by the respondent. The share of the pollutants with harmful effect on the forests administered by the claimant was determined based on a deposition study prepared by an expert. 54

55 The courts of first and second instance assessed the claimant's claim in accordance with sec 2924 of the Civil Code,[14] as the adverse effects of emissions released into the air are a typical case of the influence of operational activity on the surroundings. In their opinion, there is no reason for all similar activities to be moved to the category of particularly dangerous operation under sec 2925 of the Civil Code,[15] as it is not assumed that it is impossible to prevent any harm, but only the occurrence of serious damage.

56 The Supreme Court allowed the extraordinary appeal, since the question of qualification of particularly dangerous operation under sec 2925 of the Civil Code has not been answered yet.

b) Judgment of the Court

57 An operation becomes particularly dangerous if the possibility of serious (ie specially qualified) damage cannot reasonably be excluded in advance, even with due care, which the operator is obliged to exercise. The special danger of the operation thus derives from the increased probability of the occurrence of damage, which cannot be removed completely. Subsequently, a rebuttable legal presumption of special danger is established where the activity is carried out in a factory manner (ie in a concentrated form with the organised use of technological procedures), and where dangerous substances such as explosives, chemicals, poisons, biologically active materials and the like are used.

---

14 A person who operates a business or other facility with the aim of making a profit shall compensate damage resulting from the operation, regardless of whether it is caused by the operational activity itself, by a thing used for it or by the effect of the activity on its surroundings. The duty shall not apply if the person proves that he made all reasonable efforts to prevent the occurrence of damage.

15 (1) A person who operates an extraordinarily dangerous business or other extraordinarily dangerous facility shall compensate damage caused by the source of the increased danger. An operation is considered extraordinarily dangerous if the possibility of serious damage occurring cannot reasonably be excluded, even with the exercise of due care. The duty to compensate shall not apply if it is proved that the damage was caused by force majeure, by the actions of the injured party or by the unavoidable actions of a third party. Other exclusions of liability that have been agreed shall not be taken into account. (2) If it is apparent from the circumstances that the operation significantly increased the risk of damage occurring, even though other possible causes can also be identified, the court shall require the operator to provide compensation for damage to an extent that corresponds with the probability of the operation having caused that damage. (3) An operation shall be deemed extraordinarily dangerous if it is operated as a factory or if it operates or deals with explosives or similarly dangerous substances.

The operation of facilities that burn fossil fuels for their work and production processes generally meets the characteristics of a particularly dangerous operation (especially the production of electrical or thermal energy, fuels and chemical compounds). There is no doubt about the factory method of such activities, as physical and chemical processes are used in an organised manner in complex and sophisticated devices following various technological procedures. Consumed and produced energy or other products can be considered hazardous substances in their quantity and concentration, just like waste substances permanently discharged into the air or waterways. 58

However, the liability of the operator according to sec 2925 of the Civil Code only arises if the source of increased danger caused the damage, ie the factors establishing the characteristics of a particularly dangerous operation. On the contrary, this type of liability does not arise if such circumstances (activities) that are not an essential feature of a particularly dangerous operation cause a harmful consequence, such as the movement of factory vehicles, the action of guard animals or construction defects of buildings. Such circumstances, even if they are related to the operation of particularly dangerous activities, are not a source of increased danger within the meaning of sec 2925 of the Civil Code. 59

In disputes about compensation for damage caused to forests by emissions originating from industrial plants, gaseous compounds of nitrogen and sulphur can reasonably be considered as a source of increased danger, as their release and action cannot be completely eliminated. Thus, even with proper care, it cannot be ruled out that in the aggregate and long-term, effects can lead to serious damage to forests and other vegetation or even to human health. 60

c) Commentary

In the given case, the Court decided for the first time whether emissions constitute a particularly dangerous operation within the meaning of sec 2925 of the Civil Code. Such a qualification is in favour of the injured party, as unlike the (standard) liability for operational activity under sec 2924 of the Civil Code, there is only a limited possibility to exonerate. Such exoneration is only possible if damage was caused by force majeure or by the injured party. 61

The Supreme Court considered this issue based on an evaluation of the impact of the operation on the surroundings, regardless of the time effect. In its opinion, as part of the objective determination of the danger, the overall potential of the given operation to cause damage should be considered, ie the damage cannot be measured only in relation to the specific claim asserted by the injured party, 62 but also considering the overall effects of the assessed activity. Only in this way is it possible to properly assess the risk of the operation.

63 The fact that damage is caused by a longer-term operation, as in the present case, should therefore not be sufficient to exclude the condition of seriousness of the damage.

64 This conclusion is further supported by legal doctrine, which states that it would be unreasonable and contrary to the principle of equality to link the 'severity' of the damage to situations in which damage occurs due to a sudden or massive operational impact such as an explosion or one-time release of a poisonous substance, as even gradual operational impacts or a gradually increasing volume of pollutants can have comparably negative consequences for the injured party.[16]

65 Nevertheless, despite the clear statement, there is an issue of the 'historic legislator'.[17] When adopting the current legal regulation, there was a clear statement in the legislative process that pollution or other long-term emissions do not represent a particularly dangerous operation. Thus, the historic interpretation would correspond with the opinion expressed by the general court that such cases must be considered under sec 2924. With this new case law, such an interpretation was clearly rejected as the purpose of the norm clearly protects both the short-term and the long-term influence on the surroundings.

5. Supreme Court of the Czech Republic (Nejvyšší soud České republiky) 25 October 2023, 25 Cdo 154/2023: Liability for Means of Transport

a) Brief Summary of the Facts

66 The claimant suffered health damage after falling in a tram owned and operated by the respondent.

67 After boarding the tram, the tram driver set the tram in motion, causing the claimant to fall backward, resulting in a fracture of the sacrum and pain in the lumbar region. The tram departure was routine, and at the time of the accident, the speed was approx 9 km/h.

68 The courts concluded that the claimant, as a passenger, suffered bodily harm during the transportation, the compensation of which is governed by sec 2927 of

16 *F Melzer/P Tégl et al*, Občanský zákoník, § 2894–3081, velký komentář [Civil Code, sec 2894–3081, Large Commentary] (2018) 487 f.
17 Ibid.

the Civil Code,[18] which lays down a strict liability regime. The courts did not identify any circumstances arising from the operation of the tram that would exclude the possibility of exonerating the wrongdoer, and since the tram was equipped with enough appropriately placed holding devices, the respondent was exonerated. Consequently, the court dismissed the claim.

The Supreme Court allowed for an extraordinary appeal to decide which cir- 69
cumstances are to be qualified as 'resulting from operation'.

b) Judgment of the Court

It is not important where circumstances resulting from operation come from, but 70
in what way and with what result they manifest themselves towards the means of transport (including its operator, technique or organisational measures) causing damage. In other words, it must first be clear that the damage was caused by the special nature of the operation (otherwise sec 2927 of the Civil Code does not apply at all), and only then can it be considered whether it was caused by circumstances originating directly in the operation (exoneration is excluded) or by other circumstances, ie not directly connected with the operation (exoneration comes into consideration). Thus, the concept of circumstances that do not originate in traffic is triggered only by those agents which act with such force or in such a way that they can cause negative manifestations of the special nature of traffic, which would not otherwise occur.

In terms of strict liability for damage caused by the special nature of traffic or 71
vehicles, this means that the negative effect of the movement of vehicles was commenced by external circumstances so strong that they prevailed over the normal characteristics of the operation. Examples are the falling of a tree or stone on the vehicle, landslide, attack on the driver by the person being transported, conflict between passengers, explosion or fire of substances carried by the passenger. Only in the case of such and similar circumstances can the operator of transport or means of transport be exonerated if they prove at the same time that they could not have prevented the damage even with all the efforts that could reasonably be expected of them, ie that they could not have prevented the circumstances that

18 (1) A person who operates a transport business shall compensate damage caused by the specific character of that operation. The same duty also pertains to any other operator of a vehicle, boat or plane, unless the means of transport is operated by human power. (2) An operator cannot be exempted from the duty to compensate damage if the damage was caused by circumstances that have their origin in the operation. Otherwise he shall be exempted from liability if he proves that he could not prevent the damage, even by exercising all due care.

caused the harmful effect and eliminate their effect on the operation of the vehicle.

72 Since the claimant fell during a routine driving manoeuvre of the tram upon departure from the stop, typical characteristics of tram operation such as accelerated movement and starting acceleration were evident. These were not circumstances outside the operation that would have had a more significant impact.

c) Commentary

73 The legal regulation of the obligation to compensate for damage caused in connection with the operation of means of transport is a case of strict liability. Therefore, liability is excluded only if specific reasons are present (sec 2927 para 2 of the Civil Code). The law thereby provides increased protection to the injured party and reflects the fact that vehicles are complex technical devices. As such, they are associated with increased demands on their control, usually move at higher speeds, and therefore present an increased risk of damage to the transported persons or to their surroundings.

74 Strict liability is associated with precisely these manifestations typical for the operation of the vehicle. Even the drive (movement) of the vehicle itself, during which the transported passenger fell, is a circumstance establishing the obligation to compensate for damage according to sec 2927 of the Civil Code. This liability is then related not to the person who directly controls (drives) the vehicle when the damage occurs, but to the operator (Supreme Court File No 25 Cdo 3434/2009).

75 The reason for exoneration is defined in sec 2927 para 2 of the Civil Code by the requirement to exert all the efforts that can be required from the operator to prevent the occurrence of damage during the transport activity. However, its application is limited only to cases where the damage was caused by circumstances not originating in the operation of the transport or vehicle. Under the rather vague concept of circumstances originating in traffic (which exclude exoneration from liability), existing jurisprudence includes, for example, the failure of the persons used, deficiencies or defects in the material. On the contrary, 'external' influences are circumstances that do not originate in operation (and therefore enable exoneration).

76 The mentioned concept of circumstances originating and not originating in traffic is rather unclear, because the distinction between internal and external circumstances is only general. The conclusion will always depend on the specific facts.

77 However, in the present case, the Supreme Court provides a rather clear guide to assessing the issue of which circumstances originate and which do not originate in traffic. The concept of circumstances that do not originate in traffic is triggered

only by those agents that act with such force or in such a way as to cause negative manifestations of the special nature of traffic that would not otherwise occur.

6. Supreme Court of the Czech Republic (Nejvyšší soud České republiky) 31 October 2023, 23 Cdo 3191/2022: Scope of Damages in Case of Pre-Contractual Liability; Termination of Negotiation

a) Brief Summary of the Facts

The claimant claimed damages caused by the respondent's dishonesty during pre-contractual negotiations about the conclusion of a contract for work. The court of first instance concluded that the claimant suffered the alleged damage due to the respondent's breach of the pre-contractual obligation when it unjustifiably terminated the negotiations. 78

The court of second instance agreed with the court of first instance that the respondent acted dishonestly within the meaning of sec 1729 para 1 of the Civil Code[19] when it terminated negotiations on the contract without just cause. During the negotiation process, the parties had come so far that the conclusion of the contract appeared highly probable. However, the court concluded that the claim for compensation for the lost profit resulting from the possible contract, which the claimant would have received had the contract for work been concluded, is unjustified. The court of appeal stated that the respondent is only liable to the claimant for the damage it incurred in connection with the respondent's pre-contractual conduct, and lost profit from a work contract that was not concluded cannot be included in such damage. 79

b) Judgment of the Court

According to sec 1729 of the Civil Code, if the parties reach such a stage in the negotiation of a contract that the conclusion of the contract appears highly probable, 80

---

19 (1) If contract negotiations between parties reach a point where the conclusion of the contract seems highly probable, the party which terminates the negotiations without a just cause despite reasonable expectations of the other party to conclude the contract acts unfairly. (2) A party who acts unfairly shall compensate the other party for the damage, but only to an extent not exceeding the loss from failing to conclude a contract in similar cases (Translation <www.aspi.cz>).

the party who, despite the reasonable expectation of the other party to conclude the contract, terminates the negotiations on the conclusion of the contract without having a just reason for doing so, acts dishonestly (para 1). The party that acts dishonestly (unfairly) must compensate the other party for damage, but at most to the extent that corresponds to the loss from the contract that was not concluded in similar cases (para 2).

81 The liability of the party that terminated the negotiations on the contract without just cause is conceived as responsibility for raising expectations in the injured party, not as responsibility for not concluding the contract. Hence, the compensation for damage to the injured party aims to bring it to a legally compliant state, which is one where the injured party knew that the contract would not be concluded, or does not have to be concluded, and not where the contract would have been concluded, while sec 1729 para 2 of the Civil Code only represents a limitation of compensation for such damage.

82 Therefore, the failure to conclude the contract itself cannot be considered illegal within the meaning of sec 1729 of the Civil Code. For that reason, it cannot even be regarded as the cause of the damage. Illegal conduct is the termination of the negotiation without just cause, ie behaviour that contradicts the principle of good faith. It is only in this behaviour, and not in the failure to conclude a contract, that the cause of the resulting damage must be sought.

c) Commentary

83 According to the Civil Code, liability for the termination of pre-contractual negotiations pursuant to sec 1729 of the Civil Code represents a special factual basis of compensation for damage, namely damage caused by the termination of negotiations without a just cause. The reasoning is based on the general rule that while respecting the principle of freedom of contract, the behaviour of one of the potential contractual partners can be considered illegal provided that the negotiations have reached a stage where, as a result of the other party's behaviour, one of the parties was in good faith that the contract would be concluded (the conclusion of the contract appeared to it to be highly probable) (Supreme Court File No 25 Cdo 856/2018).

84 The issue of pre-contractual liability has not been defined as a case of contractual liability by the Civil Code. Moreover, the Civil Code does not stipulate any legally defined pre-contractual relationship. The pre-contractual relationship is based on principles of good faith, prohibition of abuse of law and mutual protection of rights. In the case of a breach of these principles and values, liability arises

based on fault, as contractual liability would require a stipulation of contractual duties.

Consequently, the obligation to compensate damage arises because of the violation of a legal obligation according to sec 2910 of the Civil Code.[20] The obligation to compensate damage arises when all the requirements of this provision are met, ie illegal action, the occurrence of damage and the causal relationship between these two conditions, all of this in the case of presumed fault (Supreme Court File No 25 Cdo 1267/2020). 85

In the present case, the claimant claimed compensation for lost profit, which, according to her claim, she lost because the contract for work in question was not concluded and the claimant could not fulfil this contract. 86

However, the court refused the claim. The fact that the respondent acted dishonestly and terminated negotiations without just cause does not establish a causal relationship between those actions and the manner in which the respondent concluded the contract. 87

According to the court, a breach of negotiations and the lost profit resulting from it are not in a causal relationship. Thus, the consequence of the dishonest conduct of the party in such a case is not the failure to conclude a contract (and therefore not a situation where, in the case of honest conduct, the conclusion of a contract would have occurred), but the result of the other party's expectation that the conclusion of a contract would occur (ie a situation where, in the case of honest conduct, this expectation of the other party did not arise). Everyone can negotiate a contract freely and is not liable for not concluding it. 88

In legal theory, there is an opinion according to which, if the injured party proves that, in the absence of dishonest conduct, the contract would have been concluded, there is no reason to reject the right to compensation for damage in the form of lost profit from the contract that was not concluded.[21] 89

We do not agree with this minority opinion. If a contractual obligation is breached, ie the contractual legal relationship, the party that violates its obligation will be obliged to compensate the entire damage corresponding to the expected fulfilment of the obligation arising from the contractual relationship. On the other hand, if there is a breach of duty and there is no effective formation of a contract, 90

---

20 A wrongdoer who through his fault breaches an obligation set by law and in doing so interferes with an absolute right of the injured party shall compensate the harm he causes by doing so. The duty to provide compensation also applies to a wrongdoer who interferes with another right of the injured party by breaching through his fault a duty established by law for the protection of that right.

21 *M Hulmák et al*, Občanský zákoník, Závazkové právo. Obecná část. Komentář [Civil Code, Obligatory law, General part, Commentary] (2014) no 15.

especially in cases of *culpa in contrahendo*, then the injured party is entitled to be compensated for the damage resulting from their trust in the negotiation or the other party. It follows that the damage resulting from trust (negative interest or negative damage) may not always be lower than the damage resulting from the breach of the contractual relationship (positive interest or positive damage), as it depends on the specific circumstances of the case, and especially the function of a protective norm.

7. Supreme Court of the Czech Republic (Nejvyšší soud České republiky) 30 August 2023, 25 Cdo 3019/2022: Liability for Information and Advice

a) Brief Summary of the Facts

91 The claimant claimed compensation for damage caused to it by the fact that, as part of the expert opinion prepared based on the contract between the expert and the company F, it incorrectly verified the possibility of applying a deductible item of research project costs from the claimant's tax base in the accounting period 2014.

92 The claimant ordered expert advice from F, which was represented by a member of the board of directors (who also signed the contract), who is the respondent. The subsequent contract between F and the respondent was also signed by the respondent herself, both on behalf of the company and on her own behalf. It is therefore clear that both parties knew that it is the respondent who should provide the claimant with the requested information applicable for tax purposes, although the provision of this obligation was contained in two consecutive contracts concerning company F.

93 The court concluded that the claimant's claim is not based on a breach of the respondent's contractual obligation and applied sec 2950 of the Civil Code.[22] The court ruled that the provision of advice that turns out to be incorrect does not automatically constitute an obligation to compensate under this provision, because it

22 A person who presents himself as carrying on a specific profession or occupation required for a professional service, or who otherwise claims to be an expert shall provide compensation for damage caused by incomplete or incorrect information or harmful advice provided by him for a fee in a matter relating to his knowledge or skills. Except in these circumstances, only damage caused intentionally by information or advice shall be compensated.

is necessary to distinguish between obvious misconduct and a relevantly reasoned opinion, which is subsequently not accepted by the competent authority.

The court of second instance confirmed the judgment. However, in its opinion, sec 2950 of the Civil Code cannot be applied either, as the respondent, as an expert, did not provide any advice to the claimant against consideration. The respondent prepared the assessment according to the requirements of a third party, from whom she received remuneration for fulfilling the obligation arising from this contract, but in relation to the claimant she was not entitled to any payment. 94

The Supreme Court allowed an extraordinary appeal for the question under which conditions a party will be liable for advice provided. 95

b) Judgment of the Court

The wording of sec 2950 of the Civil Code chosen by the legislator clearly does not mention that there must be a direct contractual relationship between the provider of advice or information and the injured party as its addressee as a necessary condition. With this basic linguistic and systematic interpretation, it can be concluded that the conclusion of a contract is not a condition for the establishment of an obligation to compensate damage under sec 2950 of the Civil Code. 96

Even from the point of view of the meaning and purpose of the law, a contractual relationship cannot be considered an inevitable condition for the occurrence of an obligation to compensate damage according to sec 2950 of the Civil Code, although this circumstance will of course be very common when providing advice or information for a fee. If the relationship does not originate from knowingly caused damage by advice or information (second sentence of the examined provision), the information or advice must be provided for remuneration. The expectation of remuneration in exchange for information, ie the circumstance that the person in question provides information or advice with the knowledge of profit, will have to be supported by some relationship. 97

We can conclude that the obligation to compensate damage caused by a breach of the obligation to provide proper information or advice is not, within the meaning of sec 2950 of the Civil Code, reduced to a direct relationship between two contractors. 98

It is clear from the factual circumstances that there was a specific relationship between the participants in the proceedings. Although not a direct contractual relationship, it was fundamentally close to one, or essentially replaced it. Similarly, it follows from the continuity of two consecutive contracts that the information was provided for remuneration, which was shared between the company F and the respondent, although the performance was to be provided by F. It was therefore clear 99 to the expert that she would be remunerated by a certain entity, which, however, does not necessarily have to be the one to whose person or activity the advice is directed. The Constitutional Court came to a similar conclusion, which leaned towards the interpretation that it is not decisive who the wrongdoer receives the remuneration from, but that the wrongdoer did not act selflessly (File No III ÚS 3528/20).

c) Commentary

100 This case decided by the Supreme Court answers the question of whether liability for information or advice, as stipulated in sec 2950 of the Civil Code, must arise based on a contract. In particular, it addresses whether it is possible to demand compensation for damage from a person who provided advice without a direct contractual relationship with the victim and received payment for such advice from a person other than the one to whom the advice was addressed.

101 Based on a linguistic analysis of the text, the Supreme Court concluded that the wording laid down by the legislator clearly does not mention as a necessary condition a direct contractual relationship between the provider of advice or information and the injured party as its addressee. In addition, from the teleological interpretation, the obligation to provide proper information or advice is not, within the meaning of sec 2950 of the Civil Code, reduced to a direct relationship between two contractors. Nevertheless, a certain relationship must exist, since otherwise remuneration, which is an inevitable condition for liability, could not be provided.

102 However, the Supreme Court did not consider further what type of relationship it should be. For that, it is sufficient that there is a formal legal basis for providing the remuneration. One could say that for the Supreme Court it is important that the provision of information is not provided for free, ie selflessly.

103 This conclusion is correct and corresponds with the case law of the Constitutional Court, which ruled that it is not decisive who the wrongdoer receives the remuneration from, but that the wrongdoer did not act selflessly. This means that in the case of a selfless act, sec 2950 will not apply.

104 We can thus claim that the Supreme Court together with the Constitutional Court adopted the current Austrian concept, where instead of insisting on the existence of an obligation relationship, the essential issue is whether the advice is provided selflessly. In other words, whether the person providing the information or advice pursues their interests towards the injured party. The term for remuneration cannot therefore be clearly understood as payment.

Moreover, with this conclusion, the Court admitted that sec 2950 of the Civil Code is not a *lex specialis* to cases when damage is caused by information or advice but as an additional provision to the general factual basis of compensation for damage. Based on this, sec 2950 amends the general clause on contractual or non-contractual liability. This provision has its own normative scope only seldomly, when information or advice is provided outside of a contractual relationship or other legal obligation. 105

8. Supreme Court of the Czech Republic (Nejvyšší soud České republiky) 16 May 2023, 25 Cdo 2202/2021: Wrongful Birth

a) Brief Summary of the Facts

Claimants A and B are a couple whose first-born son was born in 2012. In 2014, claimant B became pregnant for the second time. The pregnancy proceeded without complications; claimant B underwent regular checks and examinations. When conducting the first trimester pregnancy screening, the examining physician did not correctly enter all the necessary data, and therefore biochemical markers were not included in the calculation of the risk of the most common congenital developmental defects of the foetus, even though they were detected in the claimant's blood sample. The result of the screening thus determined the risk of Down syndrome at a value of 1:1,834, with the overall conclusion of the screening of the first trimester as negative. However, when including the detected values of biochemical markers, the value of the resulting risk would be 1:172. Even during later checks and examinations, no indicator of Down syndrome was revealed. When the diagnosis of foetal Down syndrome is confirmed, 95 % to 98 % of parents decide to terminate the pregnancy. 106

On 28 February 2015, the claimants had a daughter. She was diagnosed with Down syndrome shortly after birth. The birth of a daughter with Down syndrome was a shock for the claimants. They claimed that if a higher risk of Down syndrome had been found, they would have undergone further testing and then made a decision based on the result, most likely terminating the pregnancy in such a situation. 107

The court of first instance concluded that the error in performing the first-trimester screening is a *non-lege artis* procedure. This error had a major impact on the further procedure in the provision of health care for claimant B during pregnancy, because, as a result of a poorly evaluated screening as a false negative, the claimants were not informed of the higher risk of the existence of a developmental defect in the foetus, and claimant B was not offered a consultation with a geneticist 108 or other supplementary examination. This also provides a causal link between the respondent's unlawful conduct and the claimants' harm, which the court identified in the fact that the claimants were denied the right to information about the actual state of the matter and were deprived of the possibility of choosing whether to give birth to a child with Down syndrome and accept the fundamental influence on their current and future planned life, or whether to undergo further examinations and possibly terminate the pregnancy. Nevertheless, the question of whether the claimants would have actually decided to terminate the pregnancy is irrelevant in the given case, as the claimed harm arises from the denial of the claimants' opportunity to exercise their choice in making such a decision.

109 When quantifying the non-pecuniary damage, it was analogously based on the procedure of the courts when awarding compensation in cases involving the death of a close person. The court considered the permanence of the harm, the attitude of the respondent and the traumatic shock of the claimants, who were expecting a healthy child and whose ideas about their future family and family life collapsed. It also considered the necessity of psychological intervention for claimant B, the social contribution of the claimants, their concerns about the future security of their daughter and their own future.

110 The court of second instance agreed with the awarding of monetary compensation, but found the amount of compensation to be incorrectly determined and lowered it. It deemed it reasonable to award CZK 300,000 (approx € 12,000) in the case of claimant A and CZK 600,000 (approx € 24,000) in the case of claimant B. However, the difference in the awarded amounts was not reasoned.

b) Judgment of the Court

111 One of the basic prerequisites for the success of similar lawsuits is a woman's right to undergo termination of pregnancy under the law. If a woman does not have the option of abortion, she does not have the choice of whether to keep the disabled child or not, and the result (the birth of the disabled child) would occur regardless of the procedure of the healthcare provider. At a certain stage of pregnancy, the Czech legal system prioritises the autonomy of the pregnant woman's will over the protection of the unborn child, which shows a liberal approach to this issue. At the same time, the protection of a woman's personal integrity does not take absolute priority over the protection of life before birth.

112 The claimants are entitled to adequate satisfaction for the interference with their personal right to reproductive self-determination. It follows from the factual statements that the claimants are demanding compensation for an interference

with their reproductive self-determination and compensation for life with a disabled child (interference with private and family life).

The claim for compensation for non-pecuniary damage caused by interference with private and family life, consisting of permanent concern about the development and future of a child affected by a genetic disease and the impact on the life of the entire family, is conditioned by the finding that, if not for the healthcare provider's error, the child would not have been born. Thus, it must be proven that if the prenatal diagnosis had been carried out correctly, claimant B actually would have undergone not only the recommended examinations, but also a termination of pregnancy (eg health reasons or her 'worldview' would not have ruled it out). 113

A claim for compensation for non-pecuniary damage caused by a healthcare provider's error during a prenatal examination, if a child is subsequently born with a genetic defect, is permissible in the Czech legal system. The prerequisite for this claim is proof of an error during the prenatal examination, followed by the occurrence of non-pecuniary damage, where the partial personal rights that have been interfered with must be distinguished. Finally, proof of a causal connection between an unauthorised interference with a specific partial personal right and non-pecuniary damage must be established. 114

Given that it may involve interference with different sub-personality rights, all three prerequisites must be met in relation to each sub-personality right. 115

c) Commentary

The court dealt for the first time with a wrongful birth claim and, therefore, had to set criteria for compensation. It must be emphasised that the present case is based on *non-lege artis* medical treatment by a healthcare provider, which establishes three possible breaches of personality rights: (1) non-pecuniary damage caused by interference with the parents' right to family planning, because they were not properly informed about the condition of the foetus; (2) non-pecuniary damage caused by the discovery of the child's actual state of health; (3) non-pecuniary damage arising from the fact that parents have to witness the life of their disabled child and that they experience fear about the child's development. 116

The Czech legal system does not contain an explicit legal regulation of non-pecuniary damage arising in this way, and the domestic judiciary has essentially never encountered this type of lawsuit. Czech doctrine deals with wrongful births such that non-pecuniary damage suffered by parents having insufficient information may consist in denial of the opportunity to decide autonomously, or in denying 117 parents the opportunity to terminate the pregnancy, but also in the emotional anxiety of the parents faced with taking care of a disabled child.[23]

118 The court explicitly concluded that a claim for compensation for non-pecuniary damage caused by a healthcare provider's error during a prenatal examination, if a child is subsequently born with a genetic defect, is permissible in the Czech legal system. The prerequisite for this claim is proof of an error during the prenatal examination, followed by the occurrence of non-pecuniary damage, where the partial personal rights that have been interfered with must be distinguished. Finally, proof of a causal connection between an unauthorised interference with a specific partial personal right and non-pecuniary damage must be established.

119 In the present case, the claimants claimed compensation for interference with their reproductive self-determination as well as compensation for life with a disabled child (interference with private and family life). The court acknowledged that such interference may occur as a result of the wrongful medical treatment.

120 As regards the first interference, the respondent's wrongful conduct, which involved an error during prenatal genetic examination, resulted in the failure to detect that the foetus was affected by a genetic disease, despite the high likelihood that it could have been detected. This is an interference with the claimants' right to self-determination represented here by the right to family planning. There is a causal connection between the unlawful conduct of the respondent and the interference with the personal rights of the claimants. Thus, all prerequisites for the emergence of a civil law obligation to compensate for this non-pecuniary damage are met. Moreover, it is irrelevant whether claimant B would have undergone a termination of pregnancy or not, since the damage already consists in the interference with the personal rights of the claimants.

121 The second interference, consisting of permanent concern about the development and future of a child affected by a genetic disease and the impact on the life of the entire family, is conditioned by the finding that, were it not for the healthcare provider's error, the child would not have been born. Thus, it must be proven that if the prenatal diagnosis had been carried out correctly, claimant B would have undergone not only the recommended examinations, but also a termination of pregnancy (eg health reasons or her 'worldview' would not have ruled it out).

122 If there is an unauthorised interference with a person's personality, under sec 82 of the Civil Code, the injured party has the right to demand that the unau-

23 *A Doležal*, Wrongful life, wrongful birth žaloby – etické a právní úvahy [Claims on wrongful life and wrongful birth, ethical and legal considerations], Časopis zdravotnického práva a bioetiky 2013, No 3.

thorised interference be stopped or that the consequences of this interference be removed. Alternatively, under sec 2951 of the Civil Code,[24] the injured party has the right to demand adequate monetary satisfaction.

In the present case, monetary satisfaction alone will not ensure real and sufficiently effective reparation for the harm caused to the claimants. The Civil Code does not provide a clear answer as to what amount is sufficient. In general, however, the court must proceed from both the overall nature and the individual circumstances of a specific case. It must take into account the intensity, nature and method of unauthorised interference or the character and the extent of the affected personality value. Moreover, the principal of proportionality will also apply. Based on this, we believe that the courts must award particular satisfaction for each breach separately, taking into account the above criteria for each claimant. In result, each parent can be awarded different satisfaction if conditions for this exist. 123

9. Constitutional Court of the Czech Republic (Ústavní soud České republiky) 23 May 2023, IV US 1126/22: Establishment of Condition of State Liability

a) Brief Summary of the Facts

The claimant claimed compensation of CZK 928,000 (approx € 37,120) consisting of compensation for non-pecuniary damage of CZK 180,000 (approx € 7,200) and for property damage of CZK 748,000 (approx € 29,920). He suffered damage due to the maladministration of a real estate eviction procedure by the district court. The procedure lasted an unreasonable amount of time – a total of five years and eight months – due to which he could not fully exercise his ownership right to the real estate during this time. This consisted mainly of renting it for CZK 11,000 (approx € 440) per month. The CZK 748,000 claim could not be asserted against the tenants, as both persons were insolvent and there were also enforcement proceedings against one of them for a claim of CZK 2,040,080.38 (approx 124

24 (1) Damage shall be compensated through restitution in kind. If this is not reasonably feasible or if requested by the injured party, the damage shall be compensated in money. (2) Immaterial loss shall be redressed by an award of reasonable satisfaction. Such satisfaction shall be provided in money, unless another means of satisfaction provides for actual and sufficient redress of the loss caused.

€ 81,600). Therefore, due to their financial situation, the judicial claim for this amount would only represent an unnecessary expenditure of legal costs.

125 The court of first instance concluded that the duration of the proceedings, which lasted five years and eight months, was disproportionate and caused the applicant non-pecuniary damage consisting of uncertainty regarding the outcome of the proceedings. Therefore, it awarded him financial compensation for both non-pecuniary damage and pecuniary damage.

126 According to the court of second instance, the claimant's claim as regards compensation for property damage of CZK 748,000 is completely unfounded. As the injured party, the claimant 'had the legal opportunity to achieve satisfaction of his claim due to unjust enrichment, and it is his responsibility that he did not do so, while this liability cannot be transferred to the State. The claimant's inaction in the sense of not filing a claim for the issuance of unjust enrichment results in a missing causal connection between the occurrence of damage on the one hand and the maladministration on the other'.

127 The Supreme Court dismissed the extraordinary appeal.

b) Judgment of the Court

128 The interpretation of Act No 82/1998 Coll, on State Liability submitted by the court of second instance, in which it concluded that the causal connection between maladministration and damage was interrupted by the claimant's failure to demand unjust enrichment from third parties through an action for performance, although it was obvious that even in the case of the issuance of a writ of execution, the claimant's claim would not be successful, or that the claimant would not be satisfied even with regard to compensation for the costs of the court proceedings, is impermissibly formalistic and even excessive.

129 After all, such a formalistic and constitutionally incompatible interpretation would not be admissible even in the case of compensation for damage caused by an illegal decision. The rule of exhaustion of procedural remedies requires that the claimant duly pursues those remedies that are available and sufficient to achieve redress of the alleged violations. The existence of effective remedies must be certain not only in theory but also in practice, and the claimant was therefore not obliged to use remedies that would be insufficient and ineffective.

c) Commentary

Under the State Liability Act, the State will be held liable if either an illegal decision or maladministration is causally connected with the damage incurred by a person. Liability for an illegal decision requires that the decision is declared null and void for its illegality, however, it also contains secondary conditions. A claim for compensation for damage caused by an illegal decision can only be granted if the injured party has used all procedural means provided to them by the law to protect their rights within the time limits set by law, such as appeal, extraordinary appeal and other procedural remedies for the protection of the right. This provision is based on the general principle of prevention, according to which, the party to the proceedings should use all the procedural means that the law provides to protect their rights, and which are also capable of removing an illegal decision, in the proceedings themselves. 130

This second condition does not apply to cases where damage is caused by maladministration. 131

In the case under consideration, the tenants who did not vacate the flat upon termination of the lease agreement did not provide compensation for the use of the flat to the claimant. However, the claimant could not even successfully and effectively file his claim from these people, as the amount of their obligations significantly exceeded their property. Both people living in the flat were insolvent and subject to enforcement proceedings. Formally, the claimant could claim recovery of the unjust enrichment, but it has to be assessed that, in the case of judicial enforcement of unjustified enrichment, the obtained execution title would be effectively 'irretrievable' and there would only be an increase in the damage incurred by the claimant for the costs of the court proceedings. 132

Thus, although theoretically possible, such a remedy would not have led to any result and would have led to more debts. 133

Therefore, the Constitutional Court correctly pointed out that compensation for maladministration consisting of an unreasonable length of court proceedings cannot be denied because the injured party did not use the legal means of protecting his right in the form of initiating court, administrative or other legal proceedings when they were ineffective in a specific situation. This conclusion is even more valid as sec 8 para 3 of the State Liability Act does not apply to compensation for damage caused by incorrect official procedures (maladministration). The opposite interpretation violates the injured party's right to compensation for damage caused by maladministration of a State body pursuant to art 36 para 3 of the Charter of Fundamental Rights and Freedoms. 134

10. Constitutional Court of the Czech Republic (Ústavní soud České republiky) 20 December 2023, I US 2410/23: Principle of Full Compensation

135 Pursuant to sec 7 para 3 of Decree No 440/2001 Coll, on Compensation for Pain suffering and Aggravated Social Position, in particularly exceptional cases worthy of special consideration, the court may reasonably increase the amount of compensation, determined in accordance with the Decree. The awarded amount of compensation must be based on objective and reasonable reasons, and there must be a relationship of proportionality between the awarded amount and the damage (injury) caused.

136 The assessment of the adequacy of compensation does not only result from the specific circumstances of the case. It also follows from the economic context of the time when compensation was awarded. Therefore, even where the courts proceed according to the old legislation (ie according to the old civil act and decree), it is not possible to disregard the Supreme Court's Methodology for the compensation of non-pecuniary damage to health.

137 Time plays an even greater role if the compensation is decided with a long time gap after the abolition of the point evaluation system according to the Decree.

C. Literature

1. Articles

138 *L Červinka,* Odpovědnost státu za škodu a autonomie Parlamentu: Kancelář Poslanecké sněmovny a Kancelář Senátu jako ústřední správní úřady [Liability of the State for damage and the autonomy of the Parliament: the Office of the Chamber of Deputies and the Office of the Senate as central administrative bodies], Právník 9/2023, 858–866

139 *P Bezouška,* Ušlý zisk – reflexe judikatury [Lost profit – a reflection of the jurisprudence], Právní rozhledy 10/2023, 343–347

140 *V Jirásko,* 'Uč se synu moudrým býti' aneb prospěch studenta jako aspekt podstatný pro určení náhrady za ztrátu na výdělku ['Teach your son to be wise' or the benefit of the student as an essential aspect for determining compensation for loss of earnings], Právní rozhledy 11/2023, 381–389

141 *J Bártů,* Jednání na vlastní nebezpečí a spoluúčast poškozeného v případě újmy způsobené zvířetem [Acting at its own risk and participation of the injured party in the case of damage caused by an animal], Právní rozhledy 18/2023, 611–618

V Kolmačka, Nad ústavností § 2944 ObčZ [On the constitutionality of sec 2944 of the Civil Code], Právní rozhledy 21/2023, 738–743 142

L Tichý/J Dubický, Náhrada nemajetkové újmy právnické osoby? [Compensation for non-pecuniary damage to a legal entity?], Bulletin Advokacie 11/2023, 24–33 143

E Karner, Odpovědnost za autonomní systémy: stávající předpisy, návrhy reformy EU a potřeba inovativních koncepcí [Liability for autonomous systems: existing regulations, EU reform proposals and the need for innovative concepts], Bulletin Advokacie 12/2023, 44–48. 144

Søren Bergenser and Andreas Bloch Ehlers

VII. Denmark

A. Legislation

No relevant legislation was introduced in the field of tort law in Denmark in 2023. 1

B. Cases

1. Højesteret (Supreme Court) 20 November 2023, UfR (Ugeskrift for Retsvæsen, Weekly Law Report) U 2024.746 H: Law Firm Liable for Damages for Tax Authority's Loss

a) Brief Summary of the Facts

In 2014, a lawyer (A) employed with the law firm of Bech Bruun advised the German bank, North Channel Bank, on the bank's potential liability by participating in transactions with Danish listed shares. The transactions involved the bank issuing dividend notes that could be used when submitting applications to the tax authority for refunds of dividend tax. In 2014 and 2015, North Channel Bank issued the said dividend notes which were attached to dividend tax refund applications. Based on the applications, the tax authority paid out approx DKK 1,135 billion. The refund applications subsequently turned out to be entirely unjustified, as the applications were based on fictitious transactions. 2

The main question of the case was whether Bech Bruun was liable for the advice given by A to North Channel Bank based on the argument that said advice had contributed to the fraud committed by the North Channel Bank and consequently the loss suffered by the tax authority (due to the unjustified refunds of dividend tax). 3

b) Judgment of the Court

The Supreme Court first stated that, in order for a lawyer to become liable in said situation, the lawyer must have 'unreasonably disregarded the interests of the tax authority'. According to the Court, a central element in this assessment was wheth- 4

https://doi.org/10.1515/9783111376721-008

er the lawyer had advised on transactions that had a real commercial purpose and that were not suspicious in nature.

5 The Supreme Court found that A should have realised that there was an imminent risk that the North Channel Bank (together with others) was involved in preparing a model for unjustified reimbursement of dividend tax. Therefore, A had disregarded the interests of the tax authority by advising the bank. In this regard, the Court particularly stressed that A, in his legal opinion, had stated that the bank 'should not be subject to civil or criminal liability for its participation.'

6 Further, the Supreme Court found that there was a sufficient causal connection between A's negligent advice and the loss of approx DKK 700 million suffered by the tax authority. In addition, the Supreme Court found that there was no contributory negligence or relevant assumption of risk on the part of the tax authority. However, based on considerations of adequacy (proximate cause), the Supreme Court found that Bech Bruun's liability should be limited to DKK 400 million (and thus not the tax authority's full claim of approx DKK 700 million).

c) Commentary

7 The decision by the Supreme Court raises several questions. First of all, the Court seems to set the bar for lawyers becoming liable in such cases quite low when saying that unreasonable disregard of the interests of the tax authority is sufficient for liability to arise. Thus, a tax lawyer such as A who advises a client on tax matters must act in the interests of his client and not the tax authority. It is clear that a tax lawyer becomes liable if he is aware that a client will commit fraud but to say that an 'unreasonable disregard' of the tax authority's interests is sufficient for liability to arise must be considered excessive and open to discussion. Moreover, Danish courts rarely determine culpability by examining whether the claimant's interests have been infringed upon. Normally, culpability is assessed by examining whether the tortfeasor acted in accordance with how his peers would have acted in the same situation. This is an entirely different standard whereby the tortfeasor, in accordance with the whole idea of the concept of *culpa*, is only held liable if they did not observe the applicable standards of care within their (professional) field.

8 With regard to the question of (factual) causation, it is also quite difficult to follow the court's ruling. According to the test of factual causation (the *conditio sine qua non* test), the advice given by A must have been a necessary condition of the loss suffered by the tax authority. In this regard, the Court found that A's advice was indeed a necessary condition for said loss. The Court's main reason for saying so seems to be that the first wrongful claim for dividend tax was made not long after the advice was given by A. Time is often an important factor

when proving causation but the question at hand was essentially not said time gap but whether the tax authority would have suffered said loss 'but for' the advice of A. Put this way, it seems clear that the legal opinion of A made no difference at all. In this connection, the Supreme Court also seems to ignore that the other participants acted with intent to commit fraud. In such situations, one might say that a break in the chain of causation occurs. In conclusion, it is quite difficult to see that the advice of A (submitted in a rather brief legal opinion for which the bank paid approx € 13,000) was a relevant cause of the loss suffered by the tax authority.

As developed above, the Court did not find that the entire loss of approx DKK 700 million was foreseeable, and therefore the liability of Bech Bruun was limited to DKK 400 million. The Supreme Court (and Danish courts in general) is usually very reluctant to award compensation to indirectly harmed parties. In this case, it was A's advice to the North Channel Bank that (according to the Supreme Court) caused said loss of the tax authority whom are thus to be regarded as an indirectly harmed third party. Nevertheless, the Court apparently was not reluctant to find A liable. 9

In summary, the decision of the Supreme Court begs several questions and the result does not seem to be correct. 10

2. Vestre Landsret (High Court, Western Division) 27 October 2022, UfR (Ugeskrift for Retsvæsen, Weekly Law Report) U 2023.409 V: Work-Related Injuries and the Issue of a Right of Recourse

a) Brief Summary of the Facts

This decision concerns liability for work-related injuries and the right of recourse against the tortfeasor. In this case, a carpenter (A) needed help cutting down a number of trees. His girlfriend's brother (B) assisted him. When the chainsaw A was using got stuck in some branches, he pulled it to free it, and, by so doing, struck B on the leg, resulting in tendon and muscle damage. B was unable to work and had to go on sick leave. He received sick pay from the municipality. 11

The municipality filed a recourse claim against A for the sick pay paid to B in accordance with the Danish Act on Sick Pay art 78 (1.1). A's insurance company acknowledged liability and refunded part of the sick pay to the municipality. *Arbejdsmarkedets Erhvervssikring* (the Labour Market Insurance) subsequently acknowledged that the injuries occurred in a work-related accident and thus the insurance 12 company refused further refunds referring to the Danish Act on Sick Pay, art 78 (1.2).

13 *Arbejdsmarkedets Erhvervssikring* had found that B had provided A with a 'helping hand'. This was based on the fact that B received no payment for his assistance and A would have had to engage another professional to cut down the trees if B had not helped. Thus, the help was considered an actual work effort, which was beyond what A could expect of his girlfriend's brother and was thus covered by the Danish Workers' Compensation Act. The municipality maintained its recourse claim against A while A's insurance company demanded a refund of the sum already paid.

b) Judgment of the Court

14 The district court found that the municipality could not assert a recourse claim against A as the work-related injury was covered by the Workers' Compensation Act. Furthermore, the insurance company could claim a refund of the money already paid to the municipality on the basis of the municipality's recourse statements. On these grounds, the claim raised by the municipality against A was rejected.

15 The High Court found that A was the only one who had an interest in cutting down the trees on the land owned by him, and on which he intended to build two homes. Thus, at that time, B had no prospect of receiving any financial gain, nor did he receive any form of remuneration. With this remark, the High Court, for the reasons stated by the District Court, accepted that the matter is covered by art 78 (1.2) of the Danish Sickness Benefits Act, including that there is no basis to reach a result other than that of the *Arbejdsmarkedets Erhvervssikring* regarding the question of whether the case concerned a work-related injury. The High Court thus found that the municipality had no recourse claim against A and that the insurance company could claim a refund of the sum already paid.

c) Commentary

16 This case illustrates the extent of art 78 (1.2) of the Danish Sickness Benefits Act by stating that an injured party who provides a helping hand without any prospect of financial gains is covered by art 78 (1.2).

17 Furthermore, as regards the issue of when an injury can be considered a work-related injury, the court stated that cases where the injured provides a helping hand are also covered.

3. Højesteret (Supreme Court) 1 December 2022, UfR (Ugeskrift for Retsvæsen, Weekly Law Report) U 2023.945 H: Liability of a Former CEO of a Bank for Losses on Stock Credits

a) Brief Summary of the Facts

This case concerns the assessment of liability of the former director A and board members B, C, D and E of the Roskilde Bank. 18

Roskilde Bank was declared bankrupt in 2009. Prior to that, the business of the bank was taken over by *Finansiel Stabilitet* (an independent public company owned wholly by the Danish State) that filed a compensation claim against several of the bank's former directors and board members. The High Court acquitted the defendants. The case before the Supreme Court was limited to the question of liability of the former director A and four board members partly due to six loans in connection with the sale of the bank's own shares to four of its biggest customers, and partly due to its business activities with H as a borrower. 19

b) Judgment of the Court

The High Court found that three of the loans were authorised without any immediately preceding credit assessment and that the reason for this was that director A had decided that the bank should reach out to its largest corporate customers with the purpose of selling the bank's own shares and that the bank should offer finance loans for the share purchases without any prior credit assessment. The High Court stated that a credit authorisation without any prior credit assessment must be considered reckless. Thus, director A was found liable and sentenced to pay damages to *Finansiel Stabilitet.* 20

The Supreme Court did not find that the board members had knowledge of the fact that the share credits were granted without prior assessment. The Supreme Court also did not find sufficient grounds to hold the board members liable regarding the approval of the authorised loans. Therefore, the claims against the board in relation to the loans for the shares were rejected. Regarding the involvement with H, the Supreme Court found that both director A and the board members who had authorised the loan to purchase shares in the bank in March 2006 were liable. However, they had been entitled to assume that the bank's staff would follow the development of the share price and ensure that an agreed stop loss clause was used if necessary. 21

22 The Supreme Court did not find it proven that the stop loss clause could not have been used when the share price of the Roskilde bank share dropped mid-2007, so that the bank's loss could have been prevented.

23 Thus, the Supreme Court did not find grounds to establish the liability of director A or the board members regarding the authorisation in March 2006. The board approved another authorisation to H in a board meeting on 25 October 2007. The Supreme Court found that it was not – regarding the caution that must be exercised in overriding a management's business judgement when granting a loan – proven that the board's approval of loans covered by the authorisation was a liable offence.

c) Commentary

24 This case highlights the Court's reluctance to overrule a management business judgement, by stating that caution must be exercised in cases that concern a management's business judgement.

4. Østre Landsret (High Court, Eastern Division) 10 January 2023, UfR (Ugeskrift for Retsvæsen, Weekly Law Report) U 2023.1282 Ø: EIK Banki P/F Liability of Directors and Officers

a) Brief Summary of the Facts

25 The main issue in this case concerns the liability of the directors and managers of EIK Banki P/F.

26 A subsidiary of *Finansiel Stabilitet* took over the bank's assets in 2010 as the bank was unable to meet the requirements set by the Danish Financial Supervisory Authority for the bank's solvency.

27 *Finansiel Stabilitet* subsequently brought a suit against two board members (A and B) and two members of the board of directors (C and G) for the financial losses of the bank regarding six different loan commitments.

28 The Faroese Court found that A, B and C were jointly liable for DKK 150 million on loan commitments in Germany while they were acquitted in regard to other commitments. G was acquitted on all accounts.

29 The main issue addressed by the High Court was whether the defendants A and B, as former members of the bank's management board, and C in his capacity

as CEO, had acted negligently and therefore must compensate the bank's loss in relation to three loan commitments – one regarding German shopping centres operated as a limited liability partnership, one regarding housing construction on the Faroe Islands and one regarding constructions in Denmark.

b) Judgment of the Court

The High Court found that one of the authorisations for the German shopping centres was made on an inadequate basis as the usual credit assessment was not performed and no further verification measures regarding several uncertainties were undertaken. 30

The High Court thus overruled the bank's business judgement concerning the authorisation's soundness and suitability to prevent or minimise the risk of loss on the commitment. 31

C had knowledge of or access to the available information and the inadequate basis, while C had not considered information that emerged after the board's decision, but before the authorisation was final. 32

C was thus found liable while A and B were acquitted. Furthermore A, B and C were acquitted regarding the two housing commitments. 33

In the *Capinordic* case, the Supreme Court expressed the view that members of a management board of a bank are subject to a common fault-based negligence standard, and that there is no basis for establishing a stricter standard of liability. 34

In the *Capinordic* case, the Supreme Court further found that a decision to grant a loan is largely based on a business judgement, in particular on the basis of a credit rating of the borrower, and that this business judgement must be made on reasonable grounds. In the credit rating, the bank should include factors such as the purpose of the loan, the borrower's financial circumstances, the security provided for the loan and the borrower's ability to run their business, namely considering the common economic cycles. 35

The *Capinordic* case also showed that the assessment of whether the granting of a loan is reasonable should be made on the basis of the information available to the individual manager at the time of the loan. In addition to this, significance should also be attached to whether the managers had ensured that further information was provided prior to the loan commitment, if there was cause to do so. 36

Moreover, the *Capinordic* case also showed that one should be reluctant to second guess the bank's assessment of the business judgement that the management and direction exercise when granting a loan. In the *Eik Bank DK* case the Supreme Court also stated that caution must be exercised in setting aside the bank management's assessment of whether the available information constitutes a sufficient 37 basis for the credit rating or whether there is a need to obtain, for example, an external assessment.

38 The caution that must be exercised in setting aside the business judgement in connection with a loan must not be exercised if it must be assumed that the authorisation has not only been made on the basis of business considerations for the bank but also on the basis of other considerations – irrelevant to the bank.

39 The High Court found that the directors and managers of the bank were not generally liable for granting the loan. However, the High Court overruled the bank's business judgement concerning the authorisation's soundness and suitability to prevent or minimise the risk of loss in the transactions.

40 The High Court stated that C was the person who handled the transaction on behalf of the bank and prepared the recommendation to the board of directors. C had access to all the bank's information, including an external consultant's notes on valuation and cashflow. The High Court thus found that C had knowledge of or access to the available information and the inadequate basis for its authorisation

41 The High Court found that C did not take any further action after receiving information that emerged after the Board's decision, but before the authorisation was final. C was thus found liable while A and B were acquitted.

42 Furthermore A, B and C were acquitted in the case of the transactions regarding the loans for the two housing projects.

c) Commentary

43 This case concerns possible claims against C in his capacity as CEO of EIK Bank FO regarding some specified authorisations. The *EIK Bank DK* case concerned possible claims against C in his capacity as chairman of the board of directors of Eik Bank DK concerning other authorisations. These cases are alike, however, not identical.

44 To a large extent, the Supreme Court followed the lines they had drawn in the *Capinordic* case regarding the business judgement rule. In the *Capinordic* case, however, the Supreme Court did not test the basis for the directors' business decision. In the *EIK Bank DK* case as well as this case, they seemed to go further, as the Supreme Court in their business judgment rule assessment also examined the directors' basis for their business decisions. The Supreme Court assessed whether the directors had enough information before they made their business decision and whether they took into account information that emerged after the board's decision, but before the authorisation was final.

5. Højesteret (Supreme Court) 20 September 2023, UfR (Ugeskrift for Retsvæsen, Weekly Law Report) U 2023.5380 H: Right to Compensation for Lost Earnings following Work-Related Injuries

a) Brief Summary of the Facts

This decision concerns the right to compensation for work-related injuries. 45

A suffered a shoulder injury following a work-related injury in 2015. His employer's insurance company acknowledged liability and paid ongoing compensation for loss of earnings. 46

In 2018, the insurance company stated their temporary estimate of A's final loss of earning capacity at 25 % and in February 2019 paid the compensation for loss of earnings in full and stopped the ongoing compensation payments. 47

The question in this case was whether the insurance company could terminate the obligation to pay compensation for loss of earnings by estimating A's future permanent loss of earning capacity and paying compensation in accordance with this estimate. 48

b) Judgment of the Court

The Supreme Court stated that the preparatory works to the Law of Liability for Damages Rules on Loss of Earnings states three ways in which the obligation to pay compensation for loss of earnings can be terminated. 49

The Supreme Court stated that these preparatory works include cases that are also covered by the Workers' Compensation Act. 50

The Supreme Court stated that previous Supreme Court cases on this matter had established that if a tortfeasor or its insurance company finds that it is impossible to – possibly temporarily – estimate the injured's future loss of earning capacity and thus believes their obligation to pay loss of earnings is terminated, it may either make a reasonable assessment of the loss of earning capacity and pay this or request that the *Arbejdsmarkedets Erhvervssikring* provides an opinion. 51

Thus, the obligation to pay compensation for loss of earnings exists until the submission of an opinion by the *Arbejdsmarkedets Erhvervssikring* or until the tortfeasor or insurance company has provided a reasonable estimate on a sound basis and paid compensation accordingly. 52

The preparatory works to the Act on Liability for Damages art 2 lists three ways that the obligation to pay compensation for loss of earnings can be terminat- 53 ed. One of the three ways includes the situation where the tortfeasor or their insurance company on a reasonable basis makes a reasonable estimate of the future (permanent) loss of earning capacity and pays compensation in accordance with this estimate. This also includes cases which are covered by the Workers' Compensation Act.

On this basis, the Supreme Court found that the insurance company could terminate its obligation to pay compensation for lost earnings assessing the injured party's future (permanent) loss of earning capacity on a reasonable basis and awarding compensation in accordance with this estimate.

c) Commentary

54 This case clarifies provisions of the Workers' Compensation Act art 2 (1.2) and provides tortfeasors with an opportunity to terminate the obligation to pay ongoing compensation for lost earnings when it is possible to reasonably assess the injured party's future (permanent) loss of earning capacity on a reasonable basis once and for all. This opportunity can be used by the tortfeasor to finally settle the matter instead of waiting until the *Arbejdsmarkedets Erhvervssikring* provides an opinion and paying compensation until this point.

6. Højesteret (Supreme Court) 11 October 2023, UfR (Ugeskrift for Retsvæsen, Weekly Law Report) U 2024.249 H: Employer's Liability in the case of a Work-Related Injury

a) Brief Summary of the Facts

55 This decision concerns liability for work-related injuries.

56 An insurance company brought an action against the National Social Appeals Board claiming that A's personal injury should not be recognised as a work-related injury. On 3 October 2016, A was sitting at her desk at work working on her PC when she suddenly fainted. A fell and hit her head on the floor, causing her to suffer a post-traumatic headache.

57 In a decision of 7 June 2019, the National Social Appeals Board had recognised A's personal injury in the form of post-traumatic headaches as a work-related injury. The case concerned whether the injury A sustained when she fainted at her workplace was an occupational injury under art 5, cf art 6 of the Danish Work Injury Insurance Act, and thus a consequence of the work or the conditions under

which it was carried out. The parties agreed that the feeling of uneasiness that caused A to faint was not a consequence of the work or the conditions of the work. It was also agreed that A would have suffered the same consequences if the incident had occurred under exactly the same physical circumstances at her home or in another place.

b) Judgment of the Court

The High Court stated that, according to art 1 of the Work Injury Insurance Act, the purpose of the Act is to provide compensation and reimbursement to the injured or their survivors in the event of a work-related injury and that the injury must have been caused by the work or the conditions under which the work was carried out (arts 5–7) However, there is no requirement for *culpa* on the part of the employer. 58

In the preparatory work to art 5 of the Work Injury Insurance Act, it is stated that, for an injury to be regarded as work-related, it is necessary that the injured person was working for an employer when the injury occurred and that the injury was caused by the work or the conditions under which it was carried out. For example, if the injury occurred during private errands or during the injured party's free time, or if the injury occurred on the way to a fixed place of work or on the way home from work, the injury would normally not be recognised as a work-related injury, even if the conditions were otherwise met. As A was working on her PC at her desk at work when she fainted and hit her head on the floor, the High Court found that A's post-traumatic headache was a consequence of her work or the conditions under which it was carried out, and that the injury was thus a work-related injury according to art 5, cf art 6, of the Work Injury Insurance Act. 59

The fact that A felt unwell and fainted and that A would have suffered the same consequences if the incident had occurred somewhere else could not lead to a different result. There was thus no basis for setting aside the National Social Appeals Board's decision of 7 June 2019, and the High Court upheld the claim for acquittal. 60

The decision was appealed to the Supreme Court, which found that regardless of the reason for A fainting, it must be attributed to her work or the conditions under which it was carried out. There was no need to make a probability assessment of whether the injury would have been as bad if she had suffered the injury anywhere other than at work. On these grounds, the Supreme Court upheld the decision of the High Court. 61

c) Commentary

62 This case concerns the question of when an injury can be considered a work-related injury. The High Court found that although the injured party could have suffered the same injury anywhere else, the fact that she suffered the injury at the workplace is sufficient to be considered a work-related injury.

C. Literature

1. *Laura Tholstrup/Karsten Høj*, Offererstatningsloven – med kommentarer [Compensation Act – with comments] (DJØF Forlag, Jurist- og Økonomforbundets Forlag, 2nd edn 2023)

63 This book is an updated version of the previous editions. It is updated with the latest case law, legislation and literature.

64 Since the publication of the first edition, the law has undergone significant changes in several key areas. In recent years, the Board of Compensation has increasingly been involved in several cases of general public importance and the review of specific decisions. In addition to annotations to the Compensation Act, this second edition also provides an overview of court decisions and the latest administrative practice. The issue concerning the extent of damages for personal injury that hold particular significance for the decisions of the Board of Compensation are reviewed.

2. *Søren Halling-Overgaard/Birgitte Sølvkær Olesen*, Skatterådgiverens erstatningsansvar [The tax advisor's liability] (Karnov Group Denmark A/S, 1st edn 2023)

65 The book contains a brief overview of the different types of tax advisors and a determination of the standard of liability applicable to them, including a thorough breakdown of the important factors that decide this fault-based standard of liability.

66 Furthermore, a number of different types of cases where the assessment of the tax advisor's advice is relevant in a tort law context are analysed, divided into business-related tax advice and non-business-related tax advice. Firstly, business-related tax advice is reviewed, including liability for tax advice in connection

with the transfer of assets, tax-free business transaction, mergers, demergers, share exchanges, termination of cohabitation/divorce, assistance in the preparation of tax returns, etc. Finally, the requirements for the existence of the other conditions for awarding compensation in cases where there is a basis for tax advisors' liability are analysed.

3. *Thomas Riis*, Mellemmænds direkte ansvar i varemærkeretten efter EU-Domstolens afgørelse i de forenede sager C-148/21 og C-184/21 (*Louboutin*) [Direct liability of intermediaries in trademark law following the decision of the ECJ in the joined cases C-148/21 and C-184/21 (*Louboutin*)], Ugeskrift for Retsvæsen (UfR) U2023B.63

This article examines the decision of the ECJ in the joined cases C-148/21 and C-184/ 67
21 and the result hereof. According to the joined cases, a trading platform is subject to direct trademark liability under certain specific conditions. The author examines the conditions for an intermediary to incur direct trademark liability for the acts of third parties.

Colm Peter McGrath

VIII. England and Wales

A. Legislation

Alas there were no major legislative developments relating to tort law in England and Wales in 2023. 1

B. Cases

1. *Fearn and others v Board of Trustees of the Tate Gallery* [2023] United Kingdom Supreme Court (UKSC) 4, [2024] Appeal Cases (AC) 1:[1] Private Nuisance; Visual Intrusion; Property Rights

a) Brief Summary of the Facts

As with many cases involving the tort of private nuisance, the facts of *Fearn* are 2
admirably straightforward. Alas, the legal analysis would prove rather different. On the south bank of the Thames in central London lies the Tate Modern, a modern art museum of international renown that attracts a sizeable number of visitors from around the world each year. Part of the museum's footprint on the site comprises the Blavatnik Building which is itself a major attraction by reason of the fact the top floor of the building is a public viewing gallery from which a panoramic vista of London can be enjoyed by up to three hundred people at a time. And enjoyed it certainly was, given around half a million visitors would do so each year.

The claimants in this case lived in flats in a building that formed part of the 3
Neo Bankside development that was a little more than 30 metres (100ft) away. The nature of the flats was such that, to enjoy the spectacular view that the location and height of the building would allow (as with the Blavatnik Building), the outer walls were comprised largely of floor to ceiling glass panels. Aggrieved by what they regarded as the inappropriate, indeed allegedly unlawful, extent to

1 Judgment available online at <https://www.supremecourt.uk/cases/docs/uksc-2020–0056-judgment.pdf>. Noted by *J Lee* (2023) 139 Law Quarterly Review (LQR) 535; *M Lee* [2023] 82 Cambridge Law Journal (CLJ) 208; *J Hariharan* (2024) 87 Modern Law Review (MLR) 697.

https://doi.org/10.1515/9783111376721-009

which their lives were visually intruded upon, with many visitors to the gallery waving and taking pictures for social media of their living quarters, the claimants brought suit seeking an injunction or, in the alternative, substantial damages.

4 At first instance, the claim was framed as one sounding in breach of the rights guaranteed under art 8 of the Convention for the Protection of Human Rights and Fundamental Freedoms alongside, or in combination with, the tort of private nuisance.[2] Although the former failed as a freestanding claim, on the basis that the defendants were not a public authority, the claim in private nuisance could be deployed to protect the relevant interest in the absence of sufficient protection being available through either the planning process or the action under the Protection from Harassment Act 1997.[3] On the facts however, Mann J held there was no actionable nuisance given the nature of the defendant's activity was not inherently objectionable and, ultimately, that the claimants' building could have been designed so as to prevent such intense visual intrusion. In the give and take of everyday life at the heart of nuisance, there was no protection available in a situation where they could have taken steps to protect themselves.

5 The Court of Appeal upheld the result, but on a rather different basis.[4] For a start, the relevance of the Convention here was doubtful. There was, noted Etherton MR, no case in which art 8 had been extended to mere overlooking,[5] nor were there sound reasons to overlay the tort of private nuisance with the interests and protections offered by art 8. The former offers a narrower degree of protection, focused as it is on interests in land, with a concurrent limitation on who can actually bring an action in the tort.[6] Similarly there were important substantive differences between how each form of action was assessed such that any running together was inapt.[7]

6 Rather, the judgment of the Court of Appeal focused on the fundamental and long-established requirements of the tort of private nuisance. The bulk of the judgment acted as a rehearsal of these fundamentals and gave rise to the following clear principles, whose application to the case left the result in no doubt. Private nuisance was confirmed to require an interference with the real property rights of the claimant, it is, at heart, a tort against land.[8] The manner in which the defendant may unlawfully interfere with such rights is not limited or subject to fixed cat-

2 [2019] England & Wales High Court (EWHC) 246 Chancery (Ch).
3 Para 174.
4 [2020] Court of Appeal (Civil Division) (EWCA Civ) 104.
5 Para 90.
6 Ibid.
7 Paras 92–94.
8 Para 31.

egorisation, as useful as that may be to organise and structure the voluminous case law here.[9] To the extent that the claimant must show damage, that concept was a 'highly elastic' one, and certainly physical damage was not necessary in the context of a classic claim for interference with the amenity of the land.[10] The key threshold question here was whether being overlooked by a neighbour was even the sort of interference that might, if unlawful, constitute private nuisance in the first place?

The Court of Appeal concluded that it was not. In a judgment of admirable clarity and structure, the court first considered previous authority, searching for any ground on which it might be said such an interest had previously been protected by private nuisance. It found none convincing and, indeed, identified a number in which the courts appeared to have rejected such a cause of action.[11] As they put it, 'the overwhelming weight of judicial authority, particularly in this jurisdiction, is that mere overlooking is not capable of giving rise to a cause of action in private nuisance.'[12] Approaching the matter from first principles, the court was adamant that the action in private nuisance could not extend to the facts in *Fearn* as a matter of broader policy.[13] To do so in the context of mere overlooking would render the objective test of whether an interference was material too difficult to apply.[14] Equally, the existence of planning regulations and controls already afforded aggrieved claimants a degree of protection such that tort did not need to be called upon to close the gap.[15] Finally, given the real gist of the interference here was the claimants' privacy rather than their interest in their property, again there were both other protections available and the matter was more appropriate for a legislature to balance than the court.[16] The claimants appealed to the Supreme Court. 7

9 Para 32 f.

10 Para 34.

11 Para 53 ff. Including the classic Australian authority provided by *Victoria Park Racing and Recreation Grounds Co Ltd v Taylor* (1937) 58 Commonwealth Law Reports (CLR) 479, see para 66 ff.

12 Para 74.

13 Para 80.

14 Para 81.

15 Para 82.

16 Para 84.

b) Judgment of the Court

8 Across two lengthy judgments the UK Supreme Court split by a bare majority in favour of allowing the appeal. Having fought to the highest court in the land, the claimants triumphed.

9 Delivering the judgment of the majority Lord Leggatt JSC started by emphasising the nature of the tort itself. Private nuisance is wrongful interference with the enjoyment of rights over land, constraining who can bring an action, and ruling out recovery for mere personal discomfort.[17] Rather the gist of the action itself is diminution in the 'utility and amenity value of the claimant's land.'[18] Given the varied nature of ways in which this might be interfered with, the majority confirmed there was 'no conceptual or a priori limit to what can constitute a nuisance',[19] nor that there be any physical emanation from the defendant's land or invasion of the claimant's land.[20] Indeed, in principle the mere sight of the defendant's activities could suffice if the appropriate standard was met.[21] Turning then to the facts at hand, it was obvious that such activity could not be ruled out as being a private nuisance without more. The Court of Appeal had, it turned out, been wrong to suggest that there was in fact some *a priori* limitation on what could constitute a nuisance.

10 To reach their ultimate conclusion, the majority clarified the structure of private nuisance given the absence of any such prior question beyond whether the claimant held a sufficient legal connection to the relevant land and the correct interest was being interfered with by the defendant. From there, the substantive question of whether the defendant had committed an actionable nuisance required the court to ask itself the following question: '... whether the defendant's use of land has caused a substantial interference with the ordinary use of the claimant's land.'[22] Upholding previous authority, this was an objective test and was to be judged by the standard of the ordinary person in the claimants' position.[23] Likewise, reflecting that nuisance bites harder on uncommon uses of land, a judge must consider whether the claimant's use of their land is an ordinary use.[24] If the claimant satisfies this bar, then failing any response, the defendant

17 Para 9 f.
18 Para 11.
19 Para 12.
20 Para 13.
21 Para 15 f.
22 Para 21.
23 Para 22 f.
24 Para 26.

will be liable for an actionable nuisance. That is to say, the question of substantial interference with the ordinary use of land – with no *a priori* limit on the behaviours that might satisfy this – now supplies the definition of actionable nuisance.

As Lord Leggatt clarified, in order to avoid this result, the defendant must demonstrate that their use of their own land is 'no more than an ordinary use'.[25] Recognition of this converse proposition was a means of fully honouring the principle of reciprocity, of 'give and take, live and let live', that lies at the heart of the tort of private nuisance,[26] and was captured in the old test set out in *Bamford v Turnley*[27], that 'those acts necessary for the common and ordinary use and occupation of land and houses may be done, if conveniently done, without subjecting those who do them to an action.'[28] One important conclusion that flowed from the re-emphasis on this principle was that the question of whether the defendant is behaving reasonably in the use of their land plays no role in the assessment of whether they have an answer to the charge of having created a substantial interference with the claimant's land.[29] In assessing both elements of the tort, and again in line with well-settled principles, Lord Leggatt confirmed the locality of the area in question was central to understanding whether the respective parties were using their land in an ordinary fashion.[30] 11

Having established this framework, the task was then to apply this to the facts at hand, a task Lord Leggatt felt, with respect to the lower courts, was 'entirely straightforward'.[31] Given the persistent nature of the overlooking and the behaviour of many of the spectators in taking pictures of the interior of the claimants' flats, he characterised the situation of the claimants as akin to 'being on display in a zoo'.[32] It was, beyond a doubt, sufficiently intrusive to pass the bar of a substantial interference with the claimants' ordinary use and enjoyment of the land. This marked a clear point of departure from the assessment in the Court of Appeal, who had not properly appreciated the extent to which, by inviting members of the public to look out from the viewing gallery, the activity being imposed on the claimants by the defendants went well beyond *mere* overlooking.[33] 12

---

25 Para 27
26 Para 34.
27 (1862) 3 Best & Smith's Reports (B & S) 66, 83.
28 Para 27 f.
29 Para 30.
30 Paras 38–40.
31 Para 48.
32 Para 48.
33 Paras 89–92.

13 On the question of whether the Tate could avoid liability by pointing to the ordinary and convenient use of their own land, the majority was, again, clear. Although at trial Mann J had characterised the locality as one used for a 'mixture of residential, cultural, tourist and commercial purposes', and that as a result any occupier might expect less privacy than in a rural area,[34] Lord Leggatt noted that there was no finding that there were any other viewing platforms in that part of London, nor did he regard operating one was either a common and ordinary use of the Tate's land in general or a natural incident of running an art museum.[35] Were it otherwise, then the claimants would be expected to put up with it, but on the characterisation favoured by the majority, it was then inevitable that the claimants would succeed.

14 For the dissenting minority of Lord Sales and Lord Kitchin JJSC, the matter was, again, whether there was an actionable nuisance on the facts. Like the majority, they agreed that the activity in *Fearn* was capable of constituting an actionable nuisance in principle. Taking an approach closer to that of the Court of Appeal, the minority canvassed previous authority and broader policy before concluding that the core assessment of give and take at the heart of private nuisance was both capable and well-attuned to the task of policing the boundaries of the tort, rather than seeking to identify an *a priori* list of interferences against which nuisance might, in principle protect.[36] Like the majority, the relevance of art 8 was downplayed in favour of a focus on tort as the appropriate vehicle to resolve the competing interests here, indeed, the minority doubted whether in any case the Tate were even the correct defendants had the case been put in those terms.[37] Rather, it was in relation to the core matter of whether, applying the principle of reciprocity, the activity amounted to an actionable nuisance on which the minority dissented, a question that they regarded as requiring a balanced assessment rather than merely the question of whether the claimant was suffering a substantial interference.[38]

15 Here, the minority regarded it as appropriate, as had Mann J, to take into account in the overall balancing of interests between the parties whether there were reasonable self-help measures the claimants could have undertaken.[39] This was parsed as part of the general expectation of tolerating new and even unusual uses of their land by the defendant, assuming such use to be within the bounds

34 Para 50.
35 Para 50.
36 Para 155 ff; para 198.
37 Para 206 ff.
38 Para 225.
39 Para 214 ff.

of the ultimate objective bounds of reasonable use. Nor ultimately did the minority feel that the manner in which the Neo Bankside development had been designed could be regarded as a common and ordinary use of their own land. Rather, in choosing to do as they had done, they had exposed themselves to a 'heightened degree of sensitivity to the ordinary feature of being overlooked', and thus it was reasonable, in balancing the respective rights, to pay heed to reasonable self-help measures (in this case, say, curtains), which were open to them.[40]

As the nature of the case before the court went only to liability and the relevant findings on available remedy had not been made at trial, the matter of what remedy would be available would require a re-hearing on the point before the first instance judge. 16

c) Commentary

Fearn has been heralded as a landmark decision in the law of private nuisance, but one that surprised many commentators and, indeed, the general public. The spectacle of well-off flat owners – not all of whom were actually in occupation – deploying private law to deny the public access, at least in part, to the sort of view that was central to the design of their residences is, to put it mildly, an awkward social result for the majority to have arrived at. Equally, the tenor of both judgments, each of which is lengthy by the standards of modern tort decisions, smacks of each initially having been written as the leading judgment, and are a powerful reminder of the fine margins on which final results can turn. Nevertheless, *Fearn* has both clarified a number of important questions in the modern law of private nuisance and, more importantly, reoriented the internal architecture of the tort. 17

Centrally here, and obvious in the division between the majority and the minority, was the role of public utility and what it is that those with property interests can expect tort to protect them against. The majority can be supported in the decision to reject the idea of a fixed list of ways that one can commit nuisance. Viewed thus, it re-asserts and expands on the proprietary interests that lie at the heart of the right to bring the tort in the first place,[41] but the latter, chosen path is one that risks the need for more substantive decision making case-to-case rather than the clarity that the former would have brought in some, and po- 18

40 Para 272; para 273.
41 See, for instance, Lord Leggatt at para 122.

tentially some hard, cases.[42] By adopting their broader analytical structure, the majority likewise ruled out the relevance of public utility on the question of actionability, confirming suggestions in the previous leading case of *Lawrence*[43] that this is only relevant to the question of what remedy is available.

19 *Fearn* also acts as a good reminder of the breadth and scope of private nuisance and the power of normative judgment within that. The naturally gritty and factual nature of a first instance trial gave way in the Supreme Court to two central questions on which there is little to rely beyond the decision of the judges themselves. One may take into account planning information and other available data about the nature of the locality, but ultimately the question of whether either party is using their land in a common and ordinary fashion, and whether, if so, the defendant's activity is, in the favoured cant of *Bamford*, 'conveniently done' is for the court to decide. The latter, damming decision for the defendant's case appears little more than a policy decision about a whole area of London where, as the minority so powerfully pointed out, many buildings are designed to take advantage of the view on offer. Should the result appear to so clearly hinge on whether, say, the infringement is a viewing gallery *at the top* of a modern art museum, or whether as part of an exhibit in the museum guests are invited to peer out and reflect on the world around them?

20 Of clear lasting importance is the reshaping of the tort itself. Whilst both Lords Leggatt and Sales placed great emphasis on the idea of reciprocity that traditionally lies at the heart of private nuisance – that private nuisance is tasked with policing the give and take necessary between neighbours – it is fair to say that it is the minority approach that better resembles the approach adopted in previous authorities. The idea that there is an initial threshold over which the defendant's activity constitutes an actionable nuisance is clearly novel. Not least in that it lowers the bar on that finding. Rather than a balancing act across a range of factors that focused on the relationship *between* the parties, the majority now leaves us with a bi-partite tort which focuses sequentially on each of them. This has two immediate, inelegant doctrinal consequences beyond moving away from that traditional – if somewhat soupy at times – bilateral focus.

21 The first is that, in effect, many of the factors that might previously have been considered going to liability must now be treated as, in effect, defences. This both stretches the idea of what constitutes a defence in the abstract,[44] and places a burden on the defendant to overturn a prior finding that leaves them in that position

42 See the comments, at para 36, on the television reception (in)famously at stake in *Hunter v Canary Wharf Ltd* [1997] AC 655.

43 Para 129 ff, see *Lawrence v Fen Tigers Ltd* [2014] Appeal Cases (AC) 822.

44 The quintessential modern work here is *J Goudkamp*, Tort Law Defences (2013).

in the first place. Inertia matters and the approach of the majority can fairly be viewed as, in general, a claimant-friendly stance. Equally, it is clearly a challenge to suggest that the traditional defences (properly understood) that are available against a claim in private nuisance share much in common with those of the re-ordered tort. Acquiring a right to conduct the nuisance by prescription, or having the nuisance authorised by statute are different in flavour and nature from a finding that the defendant's behaviour is common and ordinary in the locality.

The second is that some of the matters that would have fed into the bilateral 22
assessment of whether there is an actionable nuisance at hand must now be stretched somewhat to fit this new architecture. The old cases suggest that even if what was done would otherwise have fallen short of actionability, if done with malice (admittedly a tough bar for the claimant to meet), the behaviour becomes actionable.[45] What is the rubric now? That it is not common and ordinary to use one's land in a malicious fashion? No doubt the principle is undisturbed, but the manner in which it is engaged has shifted around it, and in a tort so slippery as private nuisance the need for clarity as to how and why arguments can be deployed is all the more pressing.

Although the case was treated by the Supreme Court as a quintessential appli- 23
cation of the tort of private nuisance, the very fact that it fell to be treated by this tort at all is an issue that bears further scrutiny. As the approach in the first instance court demonstrates, it was not wholly obvious that this was the best or only means of addressing the facts. Mann J's judgment dove in depth into the relevance of human rights and the long-established protection found in that domain for privacy-related interests. Where X visually intrudes on Y's private life in a sufficiently serious manner, it might be expected that some remedy is available. All the more surprising then that, as had the Court of Appeal, the majority in the Supreme Court dismissed the attempt to engage art 8 as an 'unnecessary complication and distraction in this case'.[46]

Yet from the practical perspective of the claimants, if what was sought was an 24
injunction, the natural remedy in the case of an ongoing nuisance, then at least one other option might have been available in the form of the action provided under the Protection from Harassment Act 1997. As with some of the suggestions on art 8, perhaps the correct answer here is that one is not responsible for the intrusive acts of others who you enable but do not procure. Perhaps the better answer is simply that the standard of behaviour falls short of the high bar usually

45 See the suggestion in argument before the lower courts – discussed at para 155 – that such would be the case for malicious overlooking of any facts.
46 Para 113.

demanded before behaviour can be regarded as harassment under the act.[47] But certainly the latter is hard to square with the idea that the Court of Appeal were wrong to regard this as just a regular overlooking case and, in fact, what was going on was such a level of intrusive scrutiny so as to cross the line into an actionable nuisance under the new rubric.

25 Finally, it bears mentioning that, alongside the fifth decision reported below, *Fearn* represents another step in the increasing tendency to retrench seemingly orthodox principles of English tort law whilst, arguably, expanding or otherwise developing the scope of liability. Such development does not necessarily, as it does in *Fearn*, widen that scope, as *HXA*, below, demonstrates. Rather, it serves to act as the means for a re-presentation of the fundamental architecture of the respective part of tort doctrine and confirmation of the underlying normative interests being protected. Whether one agrees with the choices made by an apex court, or the recurrent tone that suggests there are in fact no choices being made at all and existing legal structures are simply being applied to a particular/hard set of facts, one purported benefit of this tendency is clarity for both claimants and defendants. Clarity over the scope of what an individual tort protects should limit the extent to which litigation is needed. In this sense, *Fearn* at least appears to have been successful in that it has not opened the floodgates for further litigation over visual intrusion, for now.

2. *Jalla v Shell International Trading and Shipping Co Ltd* [2023] UKSC 16, [2023] 2 Weekly Law Reports (WLR) 1085:[48] Private Nuisance; Continuing Nuisance; Limitation Periods; Accrual of Cause of Action

a) Brief Summary of the Facts

26 *Jalla* concerned an oil spill that took place in the Bonga oil field, off the coast of Nigeria in December 2011. A substantial amount of crude oil leaked from an underwater pipe that was being used to transport it to a ship offshore. This lasted for around six hours and the claimants alleged that the escaped oil had then washed

47 See *Majrowski v Guy's and St Thomas's NHS Trust* [2007] 1 AC 224 applied in *Ferguson v British Gas Trading Ltd* [2009] EWCA Civ 46 [2010] 1 Weekly Law Reports (WLR) 785.

48 Judgment available online at <https://www.supremecourt.uk/cases/uksc-2021–0050.html>. Noted by *JLT Chu* (2024) 140 LQR 192; *E Bond/J Chu* (2023) Conveyancer and Property Lawyer (Conv) 297.

up on land they owned on the shore, that this was still present and had not been removed.

These claims were pertinent as the issue at stake in the case was, having applied to procedurally amend the relevant defendant in an action for private nuisance after a period exceeding six years from the spill, the claimants had been met by an objection that the relevant limitation period had now lapsed. Their argument in response was that, given the continuing nature of the interference, there was, in fact, a continuing cause of action that accrued on an ongoing, daily basis. They lost at first instance, with Stuart-Smith J holding that the event was a single escape, which did not constitute a continuing nuisance. As such, the action had accrued initially, but was now barred. An appeal was dismissed by the Court of Appeal. 27

On a set of assumed facts – which would have to be investigated at trial if the appeal was granted – the claimants appealed further to the Supreme Court on the sole issue of whether there was a continuing nuisance such that the application to amend was not barred by reason of limitation. 28

b) Judgment of the Court

The Supreme Court unanimously dismissed the appeal. In a single judgment, authored by Lord Burrows, the Court held that, on the facts as assumed, there was not, and indeed could not be a continuing nuisance such that the cause of action accrued afresh. 29

In the Court of Appeal, Coulson LJ had based the decision on a range of reasons. A continuing nuisance in the sense required by the claimant would usually involve repetition of the act that gave rise to the original cause of action. In this case, there was, by contrast, a single one-off event, the oil spill, which gave rise to a single cause of action when, as assumed, the tort of private nuisance was completed.[49] Rather, he regarded the earlier *Delaware Mansions* decision as an example of a situation that *could* be regarded as giving rise to a continuing accrual of the cause of action. There, the cause of the relevant nuisance was the root of the defendant's tree, which had grown so as to cause cracks in the claimant's building.[50] Unlike in *Delaware Mansions*, where the root itself was still present, in *Jalla*, the oil that remained was the consequence of the single event represented 30

49 Para 16.

50 *Delaware Mansions Ltd v Westminster City Council* [2001] United Kingdom House of Lords (UKHL) 55; [2002] 1 AC 321.

by the spill. Equally, the fact that there might be continuing harm – given the oil had not been cleaned up – was not the same, for these purposes, as the nuisance itself being ongoing, not least given this would risk extending the potential for an action in the case of such a one-off spill long into the future. Likewise, it was untenable to regard the nuisance as continuing until removed or cleaned not least as the defendants lost control over it once it had reached the claimants' land.

31 In the Supreme Court, Lord Burrows upheld much of this reasoning, noting that a continuing nuisance in the legal sense was a common occurrence in the case law. Starting from a matter of principle, he defined such a nuisance as one where, '...outside the claimant's land and usually on the defendant's land, there is repeated activity by the defendant or an ongoing state of affairs for which the defendant is responsible which causes continuing undue interference with the use and enjoyment of the claimant's land. For a continuing nuisance, the interference may be similar on each occasion but the important point is that it is continuing day after day or on another regular basis'.[51] Where this was the case, damages could not be recovered for future causes of action that are yet to accrue, but could only be granted for causes of action that have already accrued.[52] The facts in *Delaware Mansions* were evidently then an example of this sort of situation, with a fresh cause of action accruing every day, and spoke to why, in the ordinary course of events, the standard remedy in many nuisance cases was an injunction: to prevent such continuance.[53] The defendant's continued conduct, rather than its effect is key.

32 Applying this to the assumed facts, Lord Burrows held it was plain that there was not a continuing nuisance in a legal sense. The suggestion that the assumed continued presence of oil could be regarded as a continuing nuisance was incorrect.[54] Not only would this appear to convert the tort into being actionable (continually!) upon failure to repair the claimant's land, it also risked creating formidable problems for the assessment of damages, which is ordinarily to be done on a once and for all basis.[55] Likewise, were this to be otherwise, it would also risk undermining the broader policies underpinning the law on limitation more generally by allowing a situation to extend indefinitely into the future.[56]

51 Para 26.
52 Para 29.
53 Para 30; para 28.
54 Paras 34–37.
55 Para 36.
56 Para 39 f.

c) Commentary

Jalla is a narrow but interesting decision and one on which, as Lord Burrows noted,[57] there appeared to be no authoritative statement in English law. The result is to be supported and it has certainly not raised controversy, but there are a number of collateral points onto which *Jalla* has shone light. 33

It is regrettable that the court was able to side-step the question, assumed on the facts, that a one-off event could constitute a private nuisance at all. As highlighted by some of the responses, this is not at all clear.[58] Indeed, there have been suggestions in the case law that in cases of a one-off event, the claimant would either have to satisfy the more stringent requirements of the so-called rule in *Rylands v Fletcher* – an ersatz strict liability for the escape of something likely to do mischief from the defendant's land – or, less prosaically, demonstrate the usual requirements of negligence.[59] 34

As a case notionally about the tort of private nuisance, *Jalla* also afforded the opportunity to offer broader insights into the operation of the tort. The decision in *Fearn*, above, was deployed to provide, as one might expect, exposition of the 'core principles' of the tort, confirming its place as a touchstone authority in the field.[60] Beyond this, central to the argument was the idea that nuisance is not actionable per se and, as a result, any cause of action does not accrue until damage results. In this sense, it is plainly wrong, as Stuart-Smith J noted, to describe a state of affairs on a defendant's land that has the *potential* to result in harm as a nuisance until such damage occurs.[61] 35

Likewise, in response to an ambitious argument from counsel for the defendants, the Supreme Court rejected the idea that the defendant must necessarily have control over the situation for there to be a continuing nuisance.[62] Self-evidently one could remain liable for a situation they had created, even if they no longer had control over it.[63] 36

Finally, as Lord Burrows pellucidly noted, the sense in which a 'continuing' nuisance was being interrogated in *Jalla* was, of course, importantly distinct from another similar use of the term in this area. To 'continue' a nuisance is nor- 37

57 Para 17.

58 See *E Bond/J Chu* (2023) Conv 297.

59 *Northumbrian Water Ltd v Sir Robert McAlpine Ltd* [2014] EWCA Civ 685, per Moore-Bick LJ at 24.

60 Para 18.

61 Para 13.

62 Para 43 f.

63 Para 45.

mally deployed as a means of explaining why a defendant who did not create a nuisance may be sued for it, on the basis they have, with knowledge of the situation, allowed it to continue.[64] This was of no relevance for explaining whether there was a nuisance that continued in the required sense of an accruing cause of action. In a similar vein, and perhaps demonstrating the drawbacks of a legal system built around judicial decisions where conceptual and contextual language comingle in the construction of legal consequences, it is, of course the case that the consequence of an actionable nuisance may be regarded as a continuing nuisance as a matter of ordinary language. It is plainly a continuing nuisance to you in that sense if there is still oil on your land, but, alas for the claimants' hopes of recovery here, such ordinary language does not, in this instance, map onto the doctrine as they might have hoped.[65]

3. *McCulloch v Forth Valley Health Board* [2023] UKSC 16, [2023] 3 WLR 321:[66] Medical Disclosure Duties; Disclosure of Alternative or Variant Treatments

a) Brief Summary of the Facts

38 In this decision, that originated in the Scottish courts, the pursuer's husband had been twice admitted to hospital where the same consultant cardiologist, Dr Labinjoh had treated them. The day after the second visit, having been sent home on a watching brief, he suffered a cardiac arrest and died as a result of idiopathic pericarditis. The pursuer and other family members sued the defendant for the negligence of the consultant, alleging that she ought to have advised her patient of the option of non-steroidal anti-inflammatory drugs (NSAIDs) as a treatment for his condition. Dr Labinjoh had neither prescribed this, nor disclosed it and discussed the benefits and risks of undertaking such treatment, as in her professional medical opinion, it was not appropriate to do so given the patient was not in pain and there was no clear diagnosis of pericarditis at the time.

39 The pursuer had failed in her claim before the lower courts, who held that NSAIDs were not a reasonable alternative which was required to be disclosed to

64 See *Sedleigh-Denfield v O'Callaghan* [1940] AC 880; [1940] 3 All England Law Reports (All ER) 349.
65 Para 24.
66 Judgment available online at <https://www.supremecourt.uk/cases/docs/uksc-2021–0149-judgment.pdf>. Noted by *K Amirthalingam* (2024) 140 LQR 11; *J MacLeod* (2024) 28 Edinburgh Law Review (Edin LR) 130; *L Austin* (2024) 32 Medical Law Review (Med LR) 1.

and discussed with a patient. The point on appeal to the UKSC was the scope and basis of the duty to disclose alternative treatments. The pursuer contended that the relevant test here was for the court, not medical practitioners to decide, and that all reasonable variant or alternative treatments so judged had to be disclosed.

b) Judgment of the Court

The UKSC unanimously dismissed the appeal. **40**

41 The starting point for analysis was the existing acknowledged division between the standard of care as it relates to medical practice. This formed the doctrinal battleground on which *McCulloch* would be fought, and the solutions that could be deployed in response.

42 Where a case concerns a matter of diagnosis and treatment, the test focuses on whether a clinician has acted in accordance with a practice accepted as proper by a responsible body of medical opinion. This, the court termed the 'professional practice test'.[67] Where it concerns the clinician's advisory role, the UKSC in *Montgomery* in 2015 held that the relevant test was not to be found in professional practice, but rather in a quasi-subjective test that required them to take reasonable steps to ensure the patient was aware of 'any material risks involved in any recommended treatment, and of any reasonable alternative or variant treatments'.[68] Whilst the test of whether a risk was material was identified in *Montgomery* to be a quasi-subjective test focused on what the reasonable person in the position of the patient would regard as significant, the question of what constituted a reasonable alternative or variant treatment had been left open and now called for direct scrutiny.

43 A number of lower courts subsequent to *Montgomery* had adopted the view that the test in such a situation was the same as that in cases of diagnosis and treatment, the professional practice test. In particular the English and Welsh Court of Appeal had, in the *Duce* decision in 2018, held that a clinician was not under a duty to disclose risks that would not have been known to the medical profession in connection with the given treatment.[69] Such a question was to be tested against the professional practice test. This would then identify the basket of risks on which the test set out in *Montgomery* might then bite, judged against the patient-focused standard set out there. It was the pursuer's argument in *McCulloch*

67 Para 1.
68 Para 2.
69 Para 50 ff.

that the question of what constituted a reasonable alternative or variant treatment was attuned not to professional knowledge, but to patient preference.

44 The Supreme Court confirmed the relevant test here was that of professional practice. As the medical evidence had demonstrated that Dr Labinjoh's decision that prescribing NSAIDs was not appropriate was supported by a responsible body of medical opinion, there was no failure to meet the standard of care upon which a claim in negligence could be hung. She could not be liable for failing to advise a patient of an alternative that, in her medical judgement, she did not regard as an alternative for a patient in that situation.

45 Plural reasons were given for this decision. The first was consistency with *Montgomery* itself. The line drawn there between matters which fall to the clinician and matters which fall to the patient to decide identified the former as the appropriate test here. Indeed, the Supreme Court regarded their decision as upholding the basis of the reasoning in *Montgomery* itself.[70] Secondly, in line with *Duce*, it would be inconsistent to have a separate test for whether risks were enlivened in regard of a given treatment and whether one treatment was a reasonable alternative.[71] Thirdly, the external professional guidance from leading medical bodies within the UK – the foremost of which had intervened before the court in *McCulloch* itself – regarded the identification of options for treatment as falling within professional expertise.[72] Fourthly, it was inappropriate to enact a legal standard that would require a clinician to advise a patient of an option that they did not, in fact, regard as clinically supported or reasonable in the circumstances.[73] Finally, allowing clinical judgement to draw the line around what may need to be disclosed served the important aim of preventing patients from being bombarded by medical information without any filter. This would not serve the broader goal of supporting patients to make appropriate decisions for themselves. Likewise, setting the standard thus would support clinicians to better understand when their advisory role was engaged and, as such, what was required of them.[74] This amounted to a decision that a patient-focused standard in relation to identifying reasonable alternatives would be, simply, too confusing for both courts and clinicians to enforce.

46 Two final matters were clarified. Once the filter of professional practice has been applied to the state of the patient before them and the reasonable alternative treatments identified, all such alternatives must be disclosed to the patient, and,

---

70 Paras 59–62.
71 Paras 63–65.
72 Paras 67–70.
73 Para 71 ff.
74 Para 74 ff.

per *Montgomery*, the material risks discussed.[75] On the other hand, where a clinician does not, in her professional opinion, regard a treatment to be a reasonable alternative in the situation, but knows that other clinicians *would* so regard it, she is not obliged to disclose that fact to the patient. The justification for this latter stance was, again, the difficulty for clinicians in applying this standard, and the risk of leading to the same conflicting set of legal and ethical responsibilities that the Court was trying to avoid in choosing the professional practice standard in the first place.[76]

c) Commentary

The decision in *McCulloch* brings to a close a persistent issue in the case law that stood to highly disrupt the smooth functioning of the law in this area. Again, clarity of analytical result stands out as the hallmark, matched in this instance by explicit recognition of the need for a *workable* test for clinicians on the ground. 47

Nevertheless, it may be said that the decision represents a regressive choice in a developing area of the law. Having adopted a – unique for English tort law – standard focused on the patient in *Montgomery*, the idea that the patient is simply irrelevant when it comes to what treatments they may wish to undertake is difficult to swallow. 'Patients' Rights! (within the bounds of what *we* think is suitable)' is, after all, a difficult banner to rally behind. Nothing in the law following *Montgomery* has undermined the idea that a clinician does not have to actually provide a given treatment for the patient. Rather, the advisory duty is exactly that, a duty to ensure that the patient understands the options open to them and the risks so involved. A more expansive duty here may well lead patients to take decisions that their clinician regards as irrational, dangerous or, to be blunt, stupid. But if the values that underpinned *Montgomery* are to be taken seriously, then that must be respected. *McCulloch* reads as a decision to enshrine a narrower model of patient choice at the cost of reducing such results in practice. 48

Moving from principle to authority, certainly it is not wholly convincing to point to lower authority and decide that a higher court must feel itself beholden. It would have been in the power of the Court to simply overturn *Duce* or distinguish it on the basis that the risks in *Duce* were genuinely unknown, whilst the question of whether treatment X is relevant to condition Y is a matter on which a patient may well have an opinion. 49

75 Para 80.
76 Para 81.

50 This is particularly hard to stomach given the variegated approach to clinical authority. On the one hand, they are clinical experts, yet on the other their role is, it seems, not to help patients understand the broader landscape of what treatment options are available, but only the ones that they themselves regard as suitable. In a public healthcare system, the luck of the draw ought not so greatly constrain the menu with which the patient is presented. If there is to be a conflict between recommending a treatment known to be relevant but not favoured by a given clinician and the patient's right to decide, it is hard to see what justifies favouring the former. On the one hand, matters of medical disclosure are rooted in patients' rights to self-determination, not medical expertise, but if medical expert bodies regard something as a matter that falls within their responsibility, that is persuasive for the courts? Hardly a convincing indication that the courts have successfully, or are as willing as *Montgomery* might have suggested, to break with a historical, path-dependent reliance on medical expertise in medical matters.

51 What is clear, however, is that having broken with a unitary standard of professional practice for all matters medical, the court would inevitably have had to tackle this question one way or the other. Perhaps the true challenge lies in the paucity of options that present themselves. The choice appears to be, and has been treated as, binary. The test is either patient-focused or clinician-focused and the manner in which the competing normative values underpinning each make it hard to reconcile or develop a hybrid or more nuanced test. As such, we end up with a nested set of standards of care depending on precisely how the claim is framed. What alternatives would have been available here? Had the court in *Montgomery* been brave enough to enact a fully subjective test as to what risks ought to be disclosed, perhaps in *McCulloch* a court-policed objective test of what options the reasonable patient would want to know may have provided a middle ground. As it is, in a choice between a binary of greater or lesser certainty, the court can be forgiven for plumping for the former.

52 Finally, whilst *McCulloch* can be thought of as naturally paired with *Montgomery* in providing the central tests in matters of medical disclosure, the area represents an excellent example of the foibles of common law law-making. The conceit after *McCulloch* is that *Montgomery* managed to enact a test that, in part, the court was not clear on as to what it actually meant. This is not the only such matter that still remains unclear and must be addressed by future decisions. Not least, if the duty set out in these cases is owed in the context of treating a patient, when is one actually doing that? Is that an initial, trapdoor decision, as in ordering from a menu in a restaurant, or, is it a choice that must be canvassed at each stage of a given treatment pathway? As in *Montgomery* and, now, *McCulloch*, the underlying normative values in this area of the law will be as determinative as the practical policy consequences.

4. *BXB v Trustees of the Barry Congregation of Jehovah's Witnesses* [2023] UKSC 15, [2023] 2 WLR 953:[77] Vicarious Liability; Sexual Assault; Relationship of Employment; Close Connection Test

a) Brief Summary of the Facts

The claimant was an adult practicing member of the Jehovah's Witnesses who suffered rape at the hands of Mark Sewell, an elder (the designation of a spiritual leader within that church) with whom she had been close friends, having come to know him through the church. Indeed, the claimant's family had regularly socialised and holidayed with Sewell and his family in the past. 53

Around the same point at which Sewell's own marriage had been in difficulty, his behaviour had changed, abusing alcohol and becoming overtly romantic with the claimant. The claimant had consulted Sewell's father, another elder in the church, who had explained that he was depressed and needed love and support, encouraging the claimant to provide him with extra support. Had it not been for that encouragement, the evidence in the case demonstrated that their friendship would have ended around that time. As it was, their connection continued and having spent time that day carrying out door-to-door evangelising, the families found themselves together in Sewell's house. The claimant tried to speak to Sewell privately about seeking help for his depression and, in the course of that interaction, he pushed her to the floor and raped her. 54

Both the trial judge and Court of Appeal held the defendant religious organisation vicariously liable for Sewell's acts, awarding £62,000 in damages. The defendant appealed to the Supreme Court. 55

b) Judgment of the Court

In a unanimous judgment delivered by Lord Burrows, the Supreme Court allowed the appeal, the defendant escaped vicarious liability for Sewell's actions. Lord Burrows confirmed the settled structure of vicarious liability that has emerged in recent years. This is a two-stage process, each with its own respective test. Each must be satisfied for the defendant to be vicariously liable. 56

77 Judgment available online at <https://www.supremecourt.uk/cases/docs/uksc-2021–0089-judgment.pdf>. Noted by *J Letwin/W Peck* [2023] 82 CLJ 388; *P Giliker* (2024) 44 Legal Studies (LS) 191; *A Bell* (2023) 39 Journal of Professional Negligence (PN) 169.

57 The first stage involves asking whether the relationship between the defendant and the tortfeasor is one of employment or can be viewed as one that is akin to employment. The second stage then turns to ask whether there is a sufficiently close connection between the acts that the tortfeasor had been authorised to do and the relevant wrongful act that it could be fairly regarded as having been done in the course of the tortfeasor's employment or quasi-employment.[78]

58 As to the first stage, Lord Burrows emphasised that whilst in many cases of employment, where the classical indicia will be obvious, this will be straightforward, in the akin to employment category, a court must carefully consider the extent to which the relationship differs from that classical model. This may involve looking at a range of factors: how integral the tortfeasor's work is, whether the defendant had control over the tortfeasor, whether the work furthers the aims of the defendant, the situation in regard to appointment and termination, and whether there is a hierarchy of seniority into which the tortfeasor's role fits. As confirmed in the *Barclays Bank* decision in 2020, the traditional rule that there can be no vicarious liability for independent contractors forms a converse bulwark of safety for defendants in contrast to either the employment or akin to employment situations.[79] The approach adopted in *BXB* does nothing to undermine that.

59 Applying the first stage here, and upholding the lower courts, it was clearly a relationship that was akin to employment.[80] Lord Burrows emphasised that Sewell was clearly carrying on work on behalf of the Jehovah's Witnesses, the work was integral to the furtherance of their organisation and he had both been subject to an appointment process (and could be the subject of a removals process) and fitted into an established hierarchy. Stage one was satisfied.

60 As to stage two, Lord Burrows here noted that the so-called 'close connection test', developed in the aftermath of the *Lister* decision at the turn of the century by Lord Nicholls in the *Dubai Aluminium* decision and subsequently approved in *Morrison* in 2020, remained authoritative. Where appropriate, this needed to be adjusted to focus on the close connection between the wrong and what had been authorised in the course of the relationship of quasi-employment, rather than traditional employment, and that there was no value to parsing that link as being in the 'ordinary' course of employment (or quasi-employment). As he rightly noted, there could be no sense in which, to take an example, the sexual abuse of children in some of the past cases could be described as within the 'ordi-

78 Para 58.
79 Ibid.
80 Para 65.

nary' course of employment there.[81] Whilst the application of this test is fact-specific, previous cases suggested that where the claim involved the abuse of children in the care of the tortfeasor, this test would be satisfied. To the contrary, where the wrong is in pursuit of a personal vendetta against the employer, the test will not be satisfied.[82]

Applying the second stage here, the Supreme Court identified errors in the ap- 61
plication of the law by both lower courts and, in doing so, reached the opposite result on the facts. The claimant would not be able to demonstrate the second stage had been satisfied and, as such, the defendant would not be vicariously liable for Mr Sewell's actions.[83] It was insufficient to suggest that 'but for' Sewell's position as an elder the claimant would likely have ceased to socialise with him, nor was it relevant that Tony Sewell, again an elder himself, had encouraged her to provide support and, in doing so, remain in contact.[84] That such a factual causal link is necessary is obvious, but could not substitute for the separate, substantive assessment of whether the close connection test was satisfied on the given set of facts.[85]

What proved decisive here for the Supreme Court were the following matters. 62
The rape had not been committed whilst carrying out activities on behalf of the Jehovah's Witnesses. Rather Sewell was in his own home and not performing any work related to his role as an elder. This rendered the facts 'significantly different' from the institutional sexual abuse cases, where the abuse occurred in the context of ongoing care.[86] Likewise, at the time of the rape, Sewell did not have control over the claimant in his role as an elder. What brought them together that day was personal friendship rather than anything to do with their religious affiliation.[87] The Supreme Court did not regard him as still wearing his 'metaphorical uniform' at the time, nor was there any analogy between the gradual grooming of children in the child abuse cases and the progression from Sewell's romantic infatuation and the subsequent assault.[88]

In a final, brief cross-check on the answer arrived at by application of each 63
relevant stage, and the disposition of the case that arose as a result, Lord Burrows considered the underlying policy of enterprise liability that he had identified as

---

81 Para 58.
82 Ibid.
83 Para 70, para 72.
84 Para 70.
85 Para 77.
86 Para 74.
87 Para 75.
88 Paras 76–79.

broadly capturing the overall justification for vicarious liability in English law. From this vantage point, there was clearly no convincing reason to hold the defendant liable for the acts of the tortfeasor.[89]

c) Commentary

64 This is an area that has seen much development in recent years and what is notable first and foremost about *BXB* is that it appears to honour the avowed position of the Supreme Court that the outer boundaries of the law in this area have now been reached.[90] One might say that, certainly given the claimant won in the lower courts, this is, in part, evidenced by the reversal before the Justices, but in hard cases a plausible argument can often be made either way, so instead the better evidence here lies elsewhere in two features of the decision.

65 The first is the emphasis placed by Lord Burrows on the need for rules not policy reasons in this area.[91] Whilst there has been much effort in the English courts to identify a convincing justification for what can often be an unconvincing and anomalous form of liability, the focus is on applying clear legal tests (which is not to say that their *application* is at all clear itself) rather than simply reverting to look at underlying policy reasoning and then somewhat flabbily apply it to the facts at hand. Given the final paragraph of the decision and the light-touch policy cross-check deployed there, this must be taken with a pinch of salt – even as one says it, it is obviously not unhelpful at times to revert to asking oneself what the underlying aim of the law is in a given area – but it may yield greater clarity over time and strengthen the utility of previous decisions in an uncertain area, to be able to point to how the two stages have been applied rather than why a result was arrived at. Even then, the Court is to be commended for so clearly identifying a sense of enterprise risk as the underpinning value here,[92] with greater clarity than previous courts have managed.[93]

66 The second, flowing from the first, is the somewhat narrower view taken of the overall situation, leading to the conclusion on stage two. It is both analytically helpful and a powerful reminder for lower courts – who, one feels, had been some-

89 Paras 42–47, 82.

90 See in particular, *Barclays Bank Plc v Various Claimants* [2020] UKSC 13, [2020] AC 973; *WM Morrison Supermarkets Plc v Various Claimants* [2020] UKSC 12, [2020] AC 989.

91 Para 58.

92 Paras 47, 58, 82.

93 Most notably and influentially, Lord Phillips' five policy reasons in *Various Claimants v Catholic Child Welfare Society* [2013] 2 AC 1 at para 35.

what overtaken by the heartrendingly appalling nature of the facts here – that the law requires more than a 'but for' test here. Yet clearly given a relationship squarely rooted in the church and having returned earlier that day from proselytising, the situation was hardly unrelated to their church link. That the happenstance of being assaulted whilst walking between houses during proselytising rather than having returned home can so differently characterise the legal result will, as in other difficult decisions at stage two,[94] strike many as distasteful. If the justification is indeed enterprise liability, then how one frames the benefit gained by the defendant can just as easily frame the breadth of the risk that they must bear.

Yet there is cause for optimism in the continued arrest of years of expansion 67
in the law here. As the English courts had not previously had to wrestle with vicarious liability in the context of religious orders before this expansionary era, where the traditional test of vicarious liability naturally becomes challenging to apply, some degree of development here might have been thought inevitable. Likewise, even had the string of cases involving religious orders not emerged, the gig economy may well have prompted the same need to expand the category of relationships in which vicarious liability might arise. On this front, *BXB* can be applauded as clear and well-reasoned. If, at the second stage, the initial decision in *Lister* to expand the types of behaviour for which a defendant may be vicariously liable means that one will struggle to identify something beyond a circular policy test,[95] then the attempt to emphasise a rule-based approach must again be encouraged as a step in the right direction.

In further confirmation of a general trend in the case law here, Lord Burrows 68
confirmed a unitary analytical framework and set of normative values for the law. There was not, as had potentially been one option open to the court, one approach within the enclave of sexual abuse cases, and one approach in situations outside that enclave.[96] Again, if the law here is to move towards a more settled and predictable nature for all concerned, firmly basing one set of rules on one, if a general, set of values is an encouraging move.

Finally, *BXB* provided an interesting insight into the challenge of these cases in 69
practice. There had been some discussion in the lower courts as to whether the defendant here was in fact the correct 'relevant' defendant against whom an ac-

---

94 *Mohamud v Wm Morrison Supermarkets plc* [2016] UKSC 11; [2016] AC 677; *Bellman v Northampton Recruitment Ltd* [2018] EWCA Civ 2214; [2019] 1 All ER 1133.

95 As Lord Burrows put it, at para 58, 'The test at stage 2 (the "close connection" test) is whether the wrongful conduct was so closely connected with acts that the tortfeasor was authorised to do that it can fairly and properly be regarded as done by the tortfeasor while acting in the course of the tortfeasor's employment or quasi-employment.'

96 Para 58.

tion in principle could be brought – a particular challenge in the case of religious orders where the nebulous and independent functioning of branches of an order can frustrate traditional analysis – and Lord Burrows confirmed that it was not clear the named defendants in the appeal were actually the correct defendants. In any case, the worldwide governing body of the Jehovah's Witnesses had initially been joined as another defendant and had agreed at all times to satisfy any judgment against the named defendant in the appeal. Indeed, as he noted, neither counsel had raised the issue themselves in argument.[97] And so the case proceeded.

5. *HXA v Surrey County Council*; *YXA v Wolverhampton City Council* [2023] UKSC 52, [2024] 1 WLR 335:[98] Public Authority Liability; Negligence; Duty of Care in Relation to Children Suffering Abuse

a) Brief Summary of the Facts

70 Reported in the Yearbook 2022, this decision concerned two cases brought against the respective local authority with responsibility for social services. The claimants were both children who had suffered abuse from a family member and were suing the defendants for negligence in failing to prevent this abuse by taking them into care. In each case, albeit to different degrees, the claimants were known to the respective defendants and had been in ongoing contact with them connected to the safety and wellbeing of the children.

71 The issue at hand was a purely legal question as to whether the defendants could owe a duty of care in principle. If so, a full trial would be required. At first instance, the claims had been struck out on the basis that recent Supreme Court authorities had settled the law in this area and that public authorities would not owe a duty of care, all things being equal, if they had simply failed to confer a benefit on the claimants. This had been overturned in the Court of Appeal on the dual footing that the law in this area was not settled and was, in fact, still developing, and that on the facts, it could not be ruled out that the defendants had, in their respective dealings with the claimants, assumed responsibility to them, creating a duty of care in the tort of negligence. The defendants appealed this result to the Supreme Court.

---

97 Para 63.

98 Judgment available online at <https://www.supremecourt.uk/cases/docs/uksc-2022–0148–0149-judgment.pdf>.

b) Judgment of the Court

The Supreme Court unanimously allowed the appeal. There was no duty of care in such circumstances. 72

In a single judgment, authored by Lords Burrows and Stephens, the Supreme Court reiterated the fundamental tenets of the law in this area. There is no special or different approach to assessing duties of care in the tort of negligence as it relates to public authorities than to individuals.[99] The general position is that no duty of care is owed for the mere failure to confer a benefit, as had indeed been recently and directly clarified in the social service context in *N v Poole Borough Council* in 2020.[100] Likewise, despite the fact that there was a statutory background to the powers that the defendants were exercising in their dealings with the respective claimants, this alone was insufficient to generate a private law duty of care.[101] 73

Whilst it generally remained the case that a duty of care might be owed by reason of the fact that the defendants had created the relevant danger, had control over a third party who had caused the danger, or had assumed responsibility to the claimants through their dealings,[102] only the latter had been pleaded in the courts below. Rejecting the logic of the Court of Appeal, the Supreme Court held that there was no such assumption of responsibility in this case towards either claimant. 74

In relation to the first claimant, the fact that the defendant had carried out internal preparatory work or investigated the position of the claimant would not amount to, as it would need to, providing a service to the claimant on which they could then rely, nor was seeking legal advice sufficient, given that rather than for the claimant's benefit, it was instead intended as advice for and to the benefit of the local authority in coming to their decision.[103] In relation to the second, where the claimant had at various points been taken into care for brief periods with the consent of the parents, whilst there was undoubtedly a duty of care owed during these periods, the fact that such periods were always attended by a duty to return the child to their parents prevented an ongoing assumption of responsibility from arising.[104] The case was, ultimately, indistinguishable from *Poole*, to the same result.[105] 75

---

99 Paras 44–49.

100 [2019] UKSC 25; [2020] AC 780; reported in *K Oliphant*, England and Wales, in: K Oliphant/ BC Steininger (eds), European Tort Law (ETL) 2019 (2020) 141, no 6 ff.

101 Para 21.

102 Paras 49, 88.

103 Paras 93–95.

104 Paras 96–99.

105 Para 101.

c) Commentary

76 The judgment in *HXA* is both straightforward and perplexing. On the one hand, the result is inarguably in line with the tenor and direction of recent leading authorities in negligence as it relates to the duty of care, and, viewed thus, is simply another in a continuing trend of reliance on principled reasoning in this area. On the other, whilst the crux of the issue was settled in the decision to reject the view of the Court of Appeal that this was a developing and unsettled area of the law,[106] it is inevitably open to question whether the law in this area is ultimately amenable to such apparently principled simplicity. Whilst counsel for the claimants was admonished for setting out a 'long chronology' of the dealings between the parties,[107] in cases such as this, there will be, by necessity, a history of interactions that may need to be scrutinised in a more granular fashion before coming to a conclusion on the duty issue. The Supreme Court's desire for principled simplicity, and the certainty this should bring lower courts,[108] may ultimately prove too reductive for the potential complexity and subtlety of the analogical reasoning they are so keen to rely on.

77 From a broader comparative perspective, *HXA* represents an incontestably clear rebuttal of suggestions that the burden of decision making here could be shifted from the conceptual question of whether there is a duty of care, to the question of whether the defendant's behaviour evidences fault. Such an approach, akin to that under a French-style system without an obvious analogue to English law's duty concept, had been canvassed in some of the preceding academic commentary on the Supreme Court's decision here. This was explicitly rebuffed, doubling down on English law's long-standing preference to treat such questions as going to a preliminary duty concept.[109]

78 Finally, whilst there was clearly ultimately no hope of a duty of care on the facts in these cases, nothing in the judgment should be understood as ruling out the *potential* for a duty of care owed by reason of an assumption of responsibility to children in their dealings with social services. The Supreme Court noted that an obvious example would be obtaining a care order such that the local authority had

---

106 Paras 102–104.

107 Para 15.

108 As discussed, positively in *HXA*, see *DFX v Coventry City Council* [2021] Personal Injuries and Quantum Reports (PIQR) P18. There the trial judge, as in *HXA*, regarded the law as settled such that the claims could be dismissed for want of a duty of care in the context of children and social services.

109 Paras 85, 104.

parental responsibility over a child.[110] Likewise, they took the opportunity to clarify that, in this general context, whilst a common hallmark of an assumption of responsibility as the ground for a duty of care is reliance by the claimant, that was not necessary in cases such as this. As Lords Burrows and Stephens put it, '...in a case like YXA, where one has a vulnerable young child with learning difficulties, it would be inappropriate to insist on specific reliance by the child in order to find that there was an assumption of responsibility triggering a duty of care during the respite period.'[111] This offers not only a valuable insight into the development of the broader concept of an assumption of responsibility, but confirms that it has different indicia in different contexts.

6. Personal Injury

a) Trends in Personal Injury Claims

Previous annual reports have noted the general decline in personal injury actions, 79
and the role of the Government's efforts to tackle the perceived problem of compensation culture through both regulation of personal injury actions and, in some limited cases, direct intervention in the quantum of damages recoverable in common cases.[112] The effect of the pandemic has also become clear since the 2020/2021 year, where there was a reduction in actions (itself already part of an overall trend of decline) from 829,252 in 2019/2020 to 564,359 in 2020/2021.[113] The same trend continued in 2022/2023 with 484,330 claims. Of this, and without surprise, road traffic accident claims continue to represent the bulk of all claims brought but were down somewhat, numbering 367,535 over the same period. Across the other categories of collected data, there was a slight drop in clinical negligence claims, from 15,549 to 14,443 and a slight climb in public cases from 52,724 to 53,403, such that it is the drop in road traffic accident claims that represents most of the year-on-year decline here.

---

110 Para 106 f.

111 Para 108.

112 The details of the most relevant reforms can be found here, *A Morris/K Oliphant*, England and Wales, in: K Oliphant/BC Steininger (eds), European Tort Law (ETL) 2012 (2013) 186, no 1 ff.

113 Statistics on the number and type of claims pursued each year are publicly available from the Department for Work and Pensions' Compensation Recovery Unit: <https://www.gov.uk/government/publications/compensation-recovery-unit-performance-data/compensation-recovery-unit-performance-data>.

b) Significant Decisions

80 In the pairing of *Rabot v Hassam* and *Briggs v Laditan*[114] the Court of Appeal had to parse the award of damages for pain, suffering and loss of amenity where some, but not all of the injuries suffered by the pair of claimants fell within the scope of sec 3 of the Civil Liability Act 2018, which was introduced to limit the award of damages recovered for whiplash. Such damages are now considerably smaller than at common law and now attract a tariff award calculated in line with the Whiplash Injury Regulations 2021. Injuries not falling within the scope of that legislation are not subject to such tariffs, but are generally awarded in line with informal guidelines published from time to time by the Judicial College. Section 3(8) envisages such cases of 'mixed' injuries but provides no guidance on how to actually then calculate the award. Here, all relevant loss of amenity from both injuries was covered by the whiplash injury, which was the longer lasting of the relevant injuries. A split court held that the combined legislation had done nothing to alter the longstanding principle that full damages should be recovered for non-whiplash injuries. Faced with such 'mixed' injuries, the court must assess the tariff awards as appropriate under the legislation, assess the non-tariff awards in line with ordinary common law principles and then 'step back' from those individual components and adjust the combined sum to ensure it reflected the overall pain, suffering and loss of amenity endured, conscious that the whiplash award would be smaller than it would have been at common law and subject to the caveat that the award could not be smaller than that awarded for the non-tariff injuries if that was all that had been suffered. A dissenting judgment from the Master of the Rolls would have awarded only the tariff damages in such cases, treating the 2018 Act as having lowered general damages recoverable for non-whiplash injuries where whiplash has been sustained. Permission to appeal has been granted.

81 The liability of occupiers continues to play an important role in personal injury litigation as visible in a pair of decisions from the lower courts. In *Juj v John Lewis Partnership Plc,*[115] where an 83-year-old suffered personal injury when his foot clipped the top edge of the kerb marking the disabled parking bay where his wife had parked their car on a shopping trip, the Court of Appeal upheld a finding that there was no duty to warn of obvious dangers under the Occupiers Liability Act 1957 in relation to something that was clearly visible. Nor was it reasonable to expect the defendant supermarket to either flag concerns to a more appropriate co-occupier of the premises, or to erect signage to the effect

114 [2023] EWCA Civ 19; [2023] King's Bench Division (KB) 171.
115 [2023] EWCA Civ 1507.

that a parking bay designated by the co-occupier as a disabled parking bay, was, potentially, not suitable. In *Apres Lounge Ltd v Wade*,[116] the claimant suffered personal injury when she slipped on a drink outside the defendant's bar. Evidence demonstrated that, whilst there was not a specific plan for such instances, the bar had a proactive system which saw a number of staff roving around throughout the night collecting glasses and keeping an eye on any safety issues – such as broken glass or spilt liquid – that might arise. Rejecting the approach taken below, the court held that the duty under the 1957 Act – to take reasonable care to ensure a visitor was reasonably safe – did not require a system of continual monitoring such that no liquid could ever end up on the floor that a patron might slip on. As such, the duty had been discharged.

Finally, in *Mathieu v Hinds*,[117] the High Court was provided with an opportunity to tackle some interesting issues in the calculation of damages for personal injury. There, on the issue of quantum, the court had to assess what could be awarded in various common categories for traumatic brain injury suffered by a 29-year-old art student. He had gone on to recover well and, resident now in Canada, his art had been exhibited round the world, but, he argued, his overall productivity had been hampered. Despite the challenges of assessing evidence as to the extent and reception of any artist's future works, the court proved capable of deploying the customary multiplicand/multiplier method, settling on an appropriate sum of £2,108,909. 82

C. Literature

1. *Mauro Bussani/Anthony Sebok/Marta Infantino*, Common Law and Civil Law Perspectives on Tort Law (Oxford University Press, 2023)

Authored by a team of scholars bridging the traditions to which this work attends 83
itself, this volume focuses on England, the United States, France, Germany and Italy. The work addresses a broad range of both theoretical and contextual issues in tort law, starting from the place of tort law in each of those systems before branching out into classic chestnuts such as pure economic loss or psychiatric injury, or more abstract challenges such as causation.

116 [2023] EWHC 190 (KB); [2023] PIQR P13.
117 [2022] EWHC 924 Queen's Bench Division (QB).

2. *Anna Beckers/Gunther Teubner*, Three Liability Regimes for Artificial Intelligence (Hart Publishing, 2023)

84 Responding to a pressing challenge in law and society, the authors of this short but stimulating interdisciplinary work draw on information technology and the sociology of risk in framing three distinct approaches to questions of liability across a spectrum of individual, hybrid and collective machine behaviour. Drawing broadly on legal systems and legal reasoning in doing so, this is an impressive work that offers an important provocation.

3. *John Murphy*, The Province and Politics of the Economic Torts (Hart Publishing, 2023)

85 Attempting to bring coherence to the economic torts in English law is a task which has frustrated many scholars and judges alike. The author, an undoubted expert in this field with an eye for exploring and reframing common assumptions about the law of tort, offers a novel and penetrating argument *against* seeking such efforts. Rather than unity, he posits that the sought common core in this area is an illusion and the path to improving this area lies in taking that seriously rather than continuing current trends.

4. *James Goudkamp/Mark Lunney/Leighton McDonald* (eds), Taking Law Seriously Essays in Honour of Peter Cane (Hart Publishing, 2023)

86 A hefty tribute to the honouree, this *Festschrift* for Peter Cane brings together a plethora of scholars to consider a broad range of topics across the span of Cane's sizable interests. To do justice to Cane's contributions to common law legal thought is a substantial task for any group, but all involved in the project are to be commended and for civilians interested in the common law of tort, there is undoubtedly something to be enjoyed in this volume.

5. *James Goudkamp/Eleni Katsampouka* (eds), Landmark Cases in the Law of Punitive Damages (Hart Publishing, 2023)

Another volume in the ever-engaging Landmark Cases series, this work will be of 87
interest to those who regard the availability of punitive damages as one of the common law's signal characteristics. The cases selected range widely around the common law tradition as a whole, not simply English law, and, indeed, touch on relevant issues in both German and French law.

6. *Donal Nolan*, Questions of Liability Essays on the Law of Tort (Hart Publishing, 2023)

Rounding out a bumper year for collectors of hardback tort works is this offering 88
from one of English tort law's leading modern thinkers. Collecting together a series of articles from the author's career to date, as well as a new essay aimed against strict liability in the context of defective products and a reflective overview of the whole collection by the author himself, this covers a range of central issues in tort law and will reward anyone interested in the subject.

7. Selected Journal Articles

Tort Law in General: *S Steel*, Damages without loss (2023) 139 Law Quarterly Re- 89
view (LQR) 243; *J Goudkamp*, Rethinking fault liability and strict liability in the law of torts (2023) 139 LQR 269; *A Phang*, The importance of comparative common law – a view from Singapore (2023) 7 Journal of Business Law (JBL) 538; *J Murphy*, Anomalies in Tort Law: A Cause for Concern? (2023) 86 MLR 872; *E Descheemaeker*, Against Normative Damages (2023) 76 Current Legal Problems (CLP) 35.

Negligence: *S Bogle*, Involuntariness in negligence actions (2023) 43 Legal Stud- 90
ies (LS) 122; *J Gardner*, Rethinking risk-taking: the death of volenti? [2023] 82 CLJ 110; *J O'Sullivan*, Gambling Disorder, Financial Loss and Suicide – A Journey to the 'Outer Reaches' of the Common Law (2023) 76 CLP 173.

Other Torts: *MJR Crawford*, Contract as property: triangles and tragic choices 91
[2023] 82 CLJ 83.

Privacy: *NA Moreham*, Privacy, freedom of expression and legitimate audience 92
interest (2023) 139 LQR 412; *J Ainslie*, Intrusion of privacy and the actio iniuriarum (2023) Juridical Review (Jur Rev) 139; *J Skillen*, Exemplary damages and misuse of private information (2023) 28 Communications Law (Comms L) 158.

93 **Damages:** *N Sinanis*, The North Briton No. 45 and the doctrinal origins of exemplary damages [2023] 82 CLJ 321.

94 **Vicarious Liability:** *J Brown*, The vicarious liability of sports governing bodies and competition organisers (2023) 43 LS 221; *M Campbell*, Vicarious liability: analysing relationships akin to employment (2023) 39 PN 153.

95 **Clinical Negligence:** *S Fulham-McQuillan*, Infringement of autonomy as damage in medical negligence (2023) 139 LQR 126; *ME Tumelty*, Plaintiff aims in medical negligence disputes: limitations of an adversarial system (2023) 31 Med L Rev 226; *M Prictor*, Where Does Responsibility Lie? Analysing Legal and Regulatory Responses to Flawed Clinical Decision Support Systems when Patients Suffer Harm (2023) 31 Med L Rev 1; *A Mackley/K Liddell/JM Skopek/I Le Gallez/Z Fritz*, The frontiers of medical negligence and diagnosis: an interview-based analysis (2023) 31 Med L Rev 485.

96 **Artificial Intelligence:** *EWK Lim*, Law by algorithm (2023) 43 Oxford Journal of Legal Studies (OJLS) 650; *O Dheu/J De Bruyne*, Artificial intelligence and tort law: a 'multi-faceted' reality (2023) 31 European Review of Private Law (ERPL) 261; *C Jones/J Thornton/JC Wyatt*, Artificial intelligence and clinical decision support: clinicians' perspectives on trust, trustworthiness, and liability (2023) 31 Med L Rev 501.

Janno Lahe and Irene Kull

IX. Estonia

A. Legislation

No amendments or changes to main legislative acts of tort law can be reported. 1

B. Cases

1. Ruling in Criminal Case no 1-23-691 of the Supreme Court, 24 November 2023: Pecuniary Damage from Unlawful Deletion of Data from a Storage Medium

a) Brief Summary of the Facts

The plaintiff was convicted under the Penal Code for the production and facilitation of child pornography. The court ordered that the laptop and mobile phone taken from the plaintiff as evidence during the search be returned to him, after deleting any videos or photos of a person under the age of 18 in a pornography situation. 2

The plaintiff later applied to the Public Prosecutor's Office for compensation for the damage suffered in the criminal proceedings, pointing out that, contrary to the decision of the District Court, the prosecutor had erased all the data on the media. The plaintiff claims compensation of € 1,446 for the estimated cost of recovering the deleted data. 3

The District Court dismissed the appeal on the grounds that the plaintiff had not suffered any damage, as no evidence had been submitted to the court that the value of the laptop and mobile phone had been reduced as a result of the deletion of the data. The District Court upheld the order of the County Court. 4

b) Ruling of the Court

The Supreme Court annulled the decisions of the lower courts and sent the case back to the County Court for review. The Supreme Court noted that the courts had misapplied substantive law in holding that the preconditions for compensation 5

https://doi.org/10.1515/9783111376721-010

for damage in criminal proceedings set out in § 7(1) of the Compensation for Damage in Criminal Proceedings Act[1] (SKHS) were not met, as the cost of restoring the data could not be regarded as pecuniary damage. Paragraph 7(1) of the SKHS provides that, where a procedural law is infringed culpably by a person who is the subject of proceedings, thereby causing damage to a person, that person is entitled to claim compensation for that damage, irrespective of the outcome of the proceedings in which the damage was caused. For a claim for damages to be upheld, it is therefore necessary to establish the existence of a culpable breach of a procedural rule by the liable person and the damage suffered, and the causal link between them.

6 By deleting all the data from the information media, the prosecutor failed to comply with his obligation to ensure the preservation of evidence. The Supreme Court did not agree with the lower courts that the cost of restoring the data cannot be regarded as a loss: the harmful consequence of deleting data is generally not the diminution in the value of the information medium, but the cost that the person must incur to reach the status *quo ante* (ie to restore or re-obtain the data).

7 The extent of compensation for damage in the event of destruction, loss of or damage to a thing is governed by § 132 of the Law of Obligations Act[2] (LOA). In a new hearing of the case, the District Court must determine the extent to which the claim for damages by the plaintiff relates to the restoration of the data and whether it concerns the reasonable costs of repairing the object.

c) Commentary

8 The Supreme Court had not previously dealt with a claim for compensation for damage caused by the unlawful erasure of data from a storage medium. Although this is a decision of the Criminal Chamber, the LOA had to be applied in the case. The same questions as to the nature of the damage would arise in a similar tort claim.

9 Regarding the pecuniary damage, we have to agree with the position of the Supreme Court that, in the case of deletion of data from a mobile phone or a computer, the cost of restoring the data can be considered as compensable damage, because, in most cases, the value of the data carrier itself is indeed not affected by

---

1 Süüteomenetluses tekitatud kahju hüvitamise seadus (Compensation for Damage Caused in Offence Proceedings Act) of 5 November 2014, available in English at <https://www.riigiteataja.ee/en/eli/530102023002/consolide>.

2 Võlaõigusseadus (Law of Obligations Act, LOA) of 26 September 2001, available in English at <https://www.riigiteataja.ee/en/eli/ee/527122023005/consolide/current>.

the deletion of the data. A separate question is, however, what this cost is in any event in the specific case. It is also clear that the recovery of certain files may not be possible at all (eg personal photos, videos).

The Supreme Court also rightly pointed out that the scope of the claim in such a situation is governed by § 132(3) of the LOA, which deals with compensation for damage in the event of damage to property.[3] Computer programmes or files are not things in their own right in the civil law sense. Therefore, it would not have been correct in this case to refer to § 132(1) of the LOA, which deals with compensation for damage in the event of the destruction or loss of a thing. 10

Theoretically, § 131 of the LOA, which provides that in the event of the existence of an obligation to compensate for damage caused by unlawful deprivation of liberty, defamation of person or other violation of personal rights, the injured person must be compensated for the expenses caused to them, as well as for the damage caused by the reduction of their income or further economic opportunities, could also be relevant with regard to pecuniary damage. The application of this provision is subject to the condition that the deletion of files, in particular those of a personal nature, constitutes an infringement of a personal right. 11

The plaintiff did not seek compensation for non-pecuniary damage in this case. Such a claim may also be relevant in the event of erasure, for example, if photos or videos of holidays, birthdays, etc are unlawfully deleted from a person's data storage medium. In such a case, a claim for compensation of non-pecuniary damage cannot be brought on the basis of § 134(4) of the LOA, which provides that, in the case of destruction or loss of a thing, the aggrieved person has, taking into account exceptional circumstances, the right to claim a reasonable amount of money as compensation for non-patrimonial damage in addition to compensation for patrimonial damage, regardless of the usefulness of the thing, if the person had a special interest in the destroyed or lost thing primarily for personal reasons. This is because the deletion of the files does not constitute destruction or loss of the thing, since they are not things. 12

However, as mentioned above, it is not excluded that files of a personal nature are protected by personal rights (§ 1045(1)(4) of the LOA). If this is the case, the relevant norm for a claim for damages would be § 134(2) of the LOA, which provides that where there is an obligation to compensate for damage resulting from the deprivation of liberty of a person, the infliction of bodily injury or damage to health of a person or the infringement of other personal rights, including defama- 13

3 LOA § 132(3) provides: 'If damage is caused to a thing, compensation for the damage shall cover, in particular, the reasonable costs of repairing the thing and the potential decrease in the value of the thing. If repairing the thing is unreasonably expensive in comparison to the value of the thing, compensation shall be paid pursuant to subsection 1 of this section.'

tion of a person, a reasonable sum of money shall be paid to the injured person to compensate for non-pecuniary damage.

14 In summary, the erasure of data from a storage medium raises quite a few legal issues. In Estonia, the relevant case law has not yet developed, but this judgment is a start.

2. Judgment in Civil Case no 2-21-5449 of the Supreme Court, 23 March 2023: Non-Pecuniary Damages for Defamation

a) Brief Summary of the Facts

15 The plaintiff is a well-known person in Estonia, and an article about how the plaintiff celebrated her birthday appeared in the online edition of the newspaper 'Õhtuleht'. In the comment section of that article, the defendant wrote the comment 'the wallet is between her two legs'. The phrase 'the wallet is between her two legs', in the opinion of the plaintiff, means, for the average reasonable reader, that she earns money by prostitution, by selling her body and by providing sexual services. This is an incorrect statement of fact and an inappropriate value judgement. The plaintiff sought compensation for non-pecuniary damage from the defendant at the court's equitable discretion.

16 The defendant did not agree to pay damages, claiming that it had apologised to the plaintiff by sending her a message via Facebook. The defendant also asked the newspaper to delete the comment.

17 The County Court dismissed the action. The District Court noted that the defendant's use of the term was inappropriate and disparaging, but in a situation where the plaintiff is publicly exposing herself for profit, the threshold for tolerating criticism should be higher. In view of the seriousness of the infringement and the defendant's conduct and attitude after the infringement, an award of monetary damages for non-pecuniary damage is not justified. The District Court upheld the decision of the County Court.

b) Judgment of the Court

18 The Supreme Court overturned the decisions of both the County and District Courts and sent the case back to the County Court for reconsideration. The Supreme Court noted that the courts found that the defendant in this case made an implied statement of fact about the plaintiff that the plaintiff earned money through the intimate use of her body.

The courts should have first assessed whether the implied statement of fact made by the defendant was defamatory, ie damaging to the reputation of the plaintiff. If the implied statement of fact published was detrimental to the plaintiff's reputation, the defendant had the burden of proving the veracity of that statement of fact pursuant to § 1047(2) of the LOA. It cannot be lawful in the public interest, and therefore also within the meaning of § 1046(2) of the LOA, to defame a public figure (or any other person) by knowingly publishing false information. 19

The Supreme Court maintains its previous position that, in order to obtain financial compensation for non-pecuniary damage, it is sufficient to establish that the defendant is liable for the infringement of the plaintiff's personal right, ie the plaintiff does not have to prove the existence of non-pecuniary damage. The Supreme Court also disagrees with the view of the courts that the judicial proceedings themselves and the judicial decision are sufficient to remedy the negative consequences of defamation. 20

The courts also wrongly based their dismissal on the fact that the defendant had apologised to the plaintiff and that this was sufficient to compensate the plaintiff for the consequences of the publication of a comment which had offended her honour and dignity. The Supreme Court explains that an apology may be important in determining the amount of financial compensation for non-pecuniary damage in a situation where the defendant has sincerely acknowledged its wrongdoing and has done everything reasonable to remedy the consequences of its wrongdoing. 21

c) Commentary

The present judgment of the Supreme Court confirms in general that the personal rights of public figures are also protected, ie the rights of a public figure who exhibits their person and body to the public. The Supreme Court rightly noted that the plaintiff does not have to prove the existence of non-pecuniary damage in order to claim compensation. In the case of a statement of fact in support of a claim for non-pecuniary damages, it is sufficient to establish the unlawfulness of the statement of fact under §§ 1046 and 1047 of the LOA. The decision of the Supreme Court that judicial proceedings and a judicial decision cannot be sufficient to remedy the negative consequences of defamation can also be supported. 22

The courts also based their rejection on the fact that the defendant had apologised to the plaintiff. According to the position of the Supreme Court, an apology cannot exclude a claim for compensation for non-pecuniary damage suffered by the injured party, but the apology and the remedying of the consequences of the wrongdoing may affect the amount of compensation. In the past, however, the Su- 23 preme Court has considered the significance of the apology to be even more important: in its judgment of 13 May 2005, the Supreme Court stated that, in addition to the court proceedings and the court decision, the court may also consider that the moral damage caused by defamation may be remedied in monetary terms by an apology to the victim (no 3-2-1-17-05).

3. Judgment in Civil Case no 2-20-1836 of the Supreme Court, 5 April 2023: Liability for Violation Committed by Other Persons

a) Brief Summary of the Facts

24 Defendant I (City of Narva) had a 279 m long street built on its property, which directly borders the property belonging to the plaintiff. Defendant I did not inform the plaintiff (a company) of the preparation of the project or of the commencement of the works. The construction work was carried out by defendant II (a company) on the basis of a contract for work concluded with defendant I.

25 During the construction work, a section of reinforced concrete fence, approximately 30 m long, collapsed on the plaintiff's property, separating the plaintiff's property from that of defendant I. The fence was made of reinforced concrete panels. Defendant II then installed a temporary fence in place of the collapsed part of the fence.

26 According to the plaintiff, it suffered pecuniary loss as a result of the defendants' actions, consisting of the cost of rebuilding the fence. According to the price quotation submitted by the plaintiff, the cost of the restoration of the reinforced concrete panel fence was € 27,699 (including VAT). The plaintiff was of the opinion that both defendants are liable for the damage suffered by it.

27 The County Court dismissed the action because, in the court's view, the plaintiff suffered no loss because defendant II installed a temporary fence to replace the collapsed fence. The fence on the plaintiff's property was dilapidated and in danger of collapsing. The District Court partially upheld the action and ordered the defendants jointly and severally to pay € 10,645 plus default interest. The District Court held that the County Court's finding of no damage was not properly reasoned. Defendant II is liable for the plaintiff's damage under the general tort claim, and defendant I is liable for defendant's II violations under § 1054(3) of the LOA as a person at whose request the act was performed.

b) Judgment of the Court

The Supreme Court overturned the decisions of both the County and District Courts and sent the case back to the same County Court for reconsideration. As regards the liability of defendant I, the Supreme Court noted that the courts failed to properly clarify and verify the presumptions for the application of § 1054(3) of the LOA. According to § 1054(3) of the LOA, where a person performs an act at the request of another person, the person giving the request is liable for the damage unlawfully caused in the course of the performance of the request as if it had been caused by itself, if the damage was caused or made possible by the performance of the request and the person giving the request had control over the conduct of the person causing the damage in accordance with the relationship between the person giving the request and the person causing the damage. Thus, in order to apply § 1054(3) of the LOA, the District Court first had to find that defendant II was liable for the damage caused to the plaintiff under § 1043 ff of the LOA and then examine whether the additional prerequisites for the liability of defendant I as the contracting entity under § 1054(3) of the LOA were met, including that defendant I as the contracting entity had control over the conduct of defendant II in the relationship between itself and defendant II as the contractor. 28

The fact, referred to by the District Court, that defendant II carried out the excavation work on the basis of the contract concluded with defendant I and the instructions (ie the construction project) received from defendant I within the framework of the contract is not sufficient to establish that defendant I had control over the conduct of defendant II within the meaning of § 1054(3) of the LOA. The Supreme Court explains that, in order to establish the existence of control within the meaning of § 1054(3) of the LOA, it is not sufficient for the contracting authority to be able to control the conduct of the contractor, including the giving of instructions to the contractor, in accordance with the legal relationship with the contractor. What is important is that the contracting authority has control over the contractor. The control of the contracting entity over the contractor may consist in giving the contractor specific instructions as to the manner in which the work is to be carried out or the conditions under which it is to be carried out, such as an obligation to use certain materials, techniques or methods. 29

However, the fact that the contracting entity has ordered and handed over to the contractor the construction project required for the execution of the works does not mean that the contracting entity has control over the contractor's conduct within the meaning of § 1054(3) of the LOA. This condition cannot be deemed to be fulfilled even if the contracting entity is under an obligation to ensure that the owner is performing the duty to supervise required by the law. Control by the contracting authority over the conduct of the contractor within the meaning of 30

§ 1054(3) of the LOA presupposes that the contracting authority has given specific instructions as to the way the work was to be carried out, in respect of the activity which caused unlawful damage to a third party, and that the contractor has complied with those instructions.

31 The Supreme Court further explained that in the given situation, defendant I may also be liable for breach of the ordinary duty of care and, in addition, since the damage was caused by excavation works, as alleged in the action, it may also be considered damage caused by a major source of danger (§ 1056(1) and (2) of the LOA) and defendant I, as the contracting authority for the works, may be liable as the owner of the dangerous structure. The Supreme Court has previously clarified that the repair of a road can be regarded as a major source of danger under § 1056(2) of the LOA (see the judgment of the Supreme Court of 9 March 2011 in civil case no 3 2-1-169-10, at 12).

c) Commentary

32 According to the § 1054 of the LOA, a person who engages another person to perform its economic or professional activities or to fulfil its duties may be liable for the delict caused by that person. The application of § 1054(3) of the LOA presupposes that the service provider had control over the conduct of the person who caused the damage. The Supreme Court has not previously clarified what is meant by the fact that the person giving the entrustment has control over the conduct of the person causing the damage within the meaning of that provision. In the view of the Supreme Court, it is not sufficient for control to be present if the person who caused the damage did so while acting within the terms of a contract concluded with the contracting authority and, in so doing, complied with the construction project received from the contracting authority. Nor is it sufficient that the contracting authority guaranteed the owner's duty to supervise the construction, and that the contracting authority was in principle able to control the conduct of the contractor. What is important is that the contracting authority actually exercised control over the behaviour of the person who caused the damage, which may take the form of specific instructions given by the contracting authority to the contractor as to the manner in which the work was to be carried out or the conditions under which it was to be carried out, for example by requiring him to use certain materials, techniques or methods. It is also important that the contractor followed these instructions.

33 According to one of the provisions of § 1054(3) of the LOA, the recipient of a service is not liable for damage caused by an independent contractor. The service provider is not an independent contractor if the recipient of the service has con-

trol over its activities. The same principle follows from art 6:102 (2) of the Principles of European Tort Law (PETL).

It can be concluded from the judgment of the Supreme Court that, in this case, the presumptions of § 1054(3) of the LOA are not fulfilled. This does not mean, however, that defendant I should certainly not be liable for the plaintiff's damage. The Supreme Court pointed out that the County Court must, in a new review of the case, examine the liability of defendant I based on defendant I's own tort (breach of ordinary duty of care), but also based on risk liability (road construction as a major source of danger). 34

4. Judgment in Administrative Case no 3-19-1565 of the Supreme Court, 3 October 2023: Compensation of Non-Pecuniary Damage for Defamation caused by Public Authority

a) Brief Summary of the Facts

The two plaintiffs were deputy mayors of Tartu. They were both arrested on 18 October 2017 as suspects in unrelated criminal cases, but were both suspected of, among other things, taking bribes. At a press conference on the same day, the Special Prosecutor of the Southern District Prosecutor's Office stated, inter alia: 35

> 'The city of Tartu is one of the most influential and largest municipalities in Estonia, and therefore I find it extremely unfortunate that two deputy mayors involved in the governance of Tartu are, figuratively speaking, to be bought off.'

One of the plaintiffs was ultimately acquitted, while the criminal proceedings against the other were closed because there were no grounds at present. 36

Both parties then lodged appeals with the Administrative Court, claiming, among other things, compensation for non-pecuniary damage. The Administrative Court dismissed the appeals. The District Court quashed the decisions of the Administrative Court, stating that the press conference had to be considered as a whole and that, on balance, it had to be clear from the press conference that the plaintiffs were only suspected of bribery. Even though the press conference used unfortunate wording on one occasion, the average reasonable person would understand that mere suspicion was being expressed. 37

b) Judgment of the Court

38 The Supreme Court left the resolutions of the District Court's decisions unchanged but changed the reasons for the decisions. The Supreme Court noted that it agreed with the courts that the disputed sentence could not properly be viewed out of context of the entire statement made at the press conference. Indeed, taken in isolation, the disputed sentence has the characteristics of a statement of fact. However, it was clear from what was said at the press conference that the plaintiffs had only been suspected of, inter alia, taking bribes. In the present case, the Supreme Court considered the prosecutor's disputed sentence to be a value judgement and considered it to be inappropriate and unlawful.

39 According to § 7(1) of the State Liability Act (SLA)[4], a person whose rights have been violated by an unlawful act of a public authority in a public law relationship may claim compensation for damage caused to them if the damage could not have been avoided and cannot be eliminated. According to § 9(1) of the SLA, a natural person may claim pecuniary compensation for non-pecuniary damage caused by wrongful acts, including defamation of honour or reputation. The Chamber concluded that the plaintiffs suffered emotional pain and suffering as a result of the initiation of the criminal proceedings and their disclosure to the public. However, it is beyond doubt that emotional pain and suffering would have occurred even without the statement of the prosecutor which is the subject of the present case. In the view of the Supreme Court, the prosecutor's disputed sentence – one carelessly uttered, albeit unlawful, sentence – could not have given rise to separate consequences (additional pain and suffering) which would have been more intense than the consequences arising from the normal publicity.

c) Commentary

40 This is not directly a tort case, as, in the present case, the liability of the prosecutor (the State) is based on the STA (§ 7). According to § 9(1) of the STA, a public authority is also obliged to compensate non-pecuniary damage. § 9(1) of the STA provides that:

> 'A natural person may claim financial compensation for non-patrimonial damage upon wrongful degradation of dignity, damage to health, deprivation of liberty, violation of the in-

4 Riigivastutuse seadus (State Liability Act) of 2 May 2001, available in English at <https://www.riigiteataja.ee/en/eli/520032023005/consolide>.

> violability of home or private life or the confidentiality of messages or defamation of honour or good name of the person.'

At the same time, §§ 1046 and 1047 of the LOA must also be applied in the case of State liability for defamation. 41

In the present case, the Supreme Court found that the prosecutor's statement was unlawful, but nevertheless dismissed the plaintiffs' claim on the ground that the unlawful statement did not cause them any additional suffering (harm) compared to the negative consequences of criminal proceedings in general. 42

It should be noted that one of the three judges disagreed with this judgment, considering that the complaints should have been upheld. He found that the prosecutor's sentence caused additional hardship to the plaintiffs: the prosecutor's unlawful sentence, which violated the plaintiffs' presumption of innocence, caused the plaintiffs to suffer separate consequences. In the light of the foregoing, the Supreme Court should have assessed the amount of the damage suffered and awarded compensation accordingly. 43

It can be concluded from the present judgment that the 'bar' for claiming compensation for non-pecuniary damage is set higher in the context of State liability than in civil law in general. In civil law, it is sufficient to establish the unlawfulness of the defamation to obtain compensation. Thus, for example, in Civil Case no 2-21-5449 of 23 March 2023, the Civil Chamber of the Supreme Court reiterated the view it had previously expressed that, in order to obtain financial compensation for non-pecuniary damage, it is sufficient to establish that the defendant is liable for the infringement of the plaintiff's personal right, ie the plaintiff does not have to prove the existence of non-pecuniary damage. 44

5. Judgment in Civil Case no 2-20-5869 of the Supreme Court, 9 August 2023: Compensation for Non-Pecuniary Damage to Legal Persons

a) Brief Summary of the Facts

An employee published posts on Facebook about her employer (a legal entity), which gave the impression that several employees had been fired without notice and without justification at the employer's initiative, that the employer's management insulted, humiliated and treated employees in an inappropriate and disrespectful manner, and that the employer had an abnormally high turnover of employees due to the attitude of the management towards the employees, ie they did 45 not care about the opinion of the latter. The employer brought an action against the former employee who had made the postings, claiming € 7,200 in damages for the harm caused.

46 In the alternative, the plaintiff requested that if the court finds that the damage has been established, but that the exact amount of the damage cannot be determined, the court should itself determine the amount of the damages and order the defendant to pay them, together with the pre-litigation legal costs. In the defendant's view, the plaintiff failed to prove the existence of direct pecuniary damage and damage to reputation.

47 The County Court partially upheld the action and ordered the defendant to pay to the plaintiff € 1,493 in compensation for pecuniary damage on the basis of § 1043, § 1045(1)(6) and (8), § 1047(1), (2) and (3) of the LOA. The Court held that the post on Facebook must be considered a publication within the meaning of § 1047 of the LOA.

48 False information about a person can also be implied statements of fact, ie sets of factual statements (the veracity of which is verifiable) and value judgements (the veracity of which is not verifiable) that give rise to a statement of fact. Also, to give the impression that some facts existed was already a statement of fact. In conclusion, the County Court held that the posts were emotional and made without verification of specific facts, which gave rise to the finding that they were unlawful. The Court found that, although the plaintiff had submitted an expert opinion which found that a communication plan, costing € 7,200, was needed to compensate for the damage caused, this does not prove damage of the same amount. The Court held that the amount of damages should be based on § 127(6) of the LOA, which entitles the court to take as a basis the amount of damages awarded in similar cases, and awarded the plaintiff damages of € 800 to compensate for the loss of reputation caused by the postings.

49 The District Court dismissed the appeals of the defendant and the plaintiff. The District Court held that the County Court correctly found that the defendant's act was unlawful. It also found that the County Court's findings regarding the expert's opinion were proper and agreed that the amount of damage could not be determined. The Circuit Court added that, although Estonian case law does not recognise the reputational damage of a legal person, the County Court was not prohibited from following the case law on the award of compensation for non-pecuniary damage to natural persons by analogy and dismissing the action.

b) Judgment of the Court

The Supreme Court found that the judgments of both courts should be annulled on the grounds of misapplication of substantive law and substantial breach of procedural law and remitted the case to the District Court for a new hearing. The Supreme Court clarified that a legal person cannot, by its very nature, be the subject of a claim for compensation of non-pecuniary damage caused by the defamation of its honour and referred to its earlier judgment.[5] However, a legal person may have a claim for compensation of pecuniary damage against a person who unlawfully and negligently publishes incorrect information (§ 1043 ff of the LOA). Damage caused by the publication of inaccurate information about a legal person may be unlawful if the publication of such information interferes with the economic or professional activities of the legal person (§ 1045(1)6) and § 1047(1–3) of the LOA), violates a statutory obligation (§ 1045(1)7) and (3) of the LOA), or if it was intentionally published in bad faith (§ 1045(1)8) of the LOA). 50

The Supreme Court explained that the courts failed to qualify the legal basis of the unlawfulness of the defendant's act in their judgments. Namely, the statutory grounds of unlawfulness are 'alternative' in the sense that the unlawfulness of the defendant's act can be established on only one ground at a time. The courts ought to have ascertained the nature of the interference with the plaintiff's economic and professional activities as a result of the publication of the incorrect factual statements, including whether there was a publication of a fact which was economically detrimental to the plaintiff within the meaning of § 1047(2) of the LOA. Both the unlawfulness of the publication and the apportionment of the burden of proof depend on the foregoing. 51

The Supreme Court held that the damage had not been established. The Supreme Court instructed that, on a new examination of the case, the plaintiff must prove the damage allegedly suffered as a result of the defendant's misrepresentations (eg loss of turnover, customers leaving the company, difficulties in obtaining new contracts, including recruitment) and establish whether there was a causal link between the misrepresentations and the damage suffered. 52

c) Commentary

The judgment of the Supreme Court raises several questions. Firstly, the question arises as to whether the Supreme Court was justified in adhering to the judgment 53

5 Judgment of the Civil Chamber of the State Court of 27 March 1997 in civil case no 3-2-1-35-97.

of 1997 or whether it could have taken a different position in the circumstances of the case. In its judgment of 27 March 1997, the Supreme Court held that only natural persons could claim compensation for moral damage in cases of defamation. At the time of the decision, § 42 of the General Part of the Civil Code Act was in force, worded as follows:

> 'A legal person shall have the right to apply to the courts for an injunction to stop defamation, for the refutation of defamatory statements made by the defamer if the defamer fails to prove their accuracy, and for compensation for any moral damage caused by the defamation.'

54 Thus, the law (in force in 1997) explicitly provided that a legal person could only claim compensation for pecuniary damage caused by defamation and not for moral damage. The Supreme Court clarified that, since a legal person has no inherent moral character, compensation for moral damage cannot be claimed. The new General Part of the Civil Code Act (in force from 1 July 2002) does not contain such a provision as it was replaced by § 134(2) of the LOA. According to § 134(2) of the LOA, every person who suffered from the violation of personal rights, including defamation, must be paid a reasonable sum of money as compensation for non-pecuniary damage. Also, the law no longer uses the expression 'moral damage', which would give rise to a debate on whether a legal person has morals.

55 The commentary[6] on § 1045 of the LOA states that, after the entry into force of § 134 of the LOA, the question of the personal rights of legal persons remains open, and it is therefore not clear whether a legal person could be entitled to claim compensation for non-pecuniary damage in the event of damage to its reputation and good name, in particular in the event of the publication of incorrect information or an incorrect value assessment. Reputational damage can take the form of pecuniary damage, such as the cost of advertising and information campaigns, discounts, surveys or loss of turnover. In addition, a legal person may also seek the termination of the infringement under § 1055 of the LOA. If one accepts that, in the case of a legal person, the damage to reputation may also consist of non-pecuniary damage, then, in accordance with the principle of full compensation for damage, compensation of non-pecuniary damage should also be justified. Compensation of non-pecuniary damage to legal persons should be based on the same criteria as those used to determine the non-pecuniary damage caused to natural persons.

56 Although the plaintiff did not explicitly seek compensation of non-pecuniary damage, the County and District Courts held that compensation has to be awarded not for the necessary costs of restoring the reputation, but for abstract damage cor-

6 *Paul Varul et al*, Võlaõigusseadus IV. Kommenteeritud väljaanne [Law of Obligations Act IV. Commented Edition] (2020) 755 f.

responding to the average amount of compensation of non-pecuniary damage awarded to natural persons in similar circumstances. As the Supreme Court clearly stated its position that non-pecuniary damage caused to a legal person is not compensable in Estonia, there is likely no possibility to change this position soon, even if the lower courts seem to be ready to accept this concept in Estonian law.

The position of the Supreme Court is surprising as compensation of non-pecuniary damage caused to a legal person has been recognised by the European Court of Human Rights (ECtHR)[7] and the European Court of Justice (CJEU)[8] in their case law. Several countries[9] such as Belgium, England, France, Italy, Spain, and Switzerland have also done so either in law or in practice. Having regard to the increasing influence of social media on the reputation of companies and the fact that damage to the reputation of a legal entity may have far-reaching consequences for the company's economic activities as well as for the company management, the compensation of non-pecuniary damage to a legal person appears to be an appropriate remedy. 57

Finally, the standard of proof of causation set by the Supreme Court also raises questions. Finding that the courts had not established that there was a causal link between the fact on which the liability of a person is based and the occurrence of the damage (§ 127(4) of the LOA), the Supreme Court failed to analyse whether, in certain circumstances, a causal link could be presumed between the fact underlying the breach and the damage caused. 58

6. Personal Injury

In 2023, the Supreme Court conducted an analysis of the case law of 2020–2022, where compensation for non-pecuniary damage was claimed (authors Kätlin Piho and Karolyn Krillo). The authors point out that the maximum amounts of 59

7 See eg EctHR *Comingersoll SA v Portugal*, 6.4.2000, no 35382/97: 'Non-pecuniary damage suffered by companies may include heads of a claim that are to a greater or lesser extent "objective" or "subjective". Among these, account should be taken of the company's reputation, uncertainty in decision-planning, disruption in the management of the company (for which there is no precise method of calculating the consequences) and lastly, albeit to a lesser degree, the anxiety and inconvenience caused to the members of the management team.'

8 Eg CJEU 13.12.2018, T-558/15, *Iran Insurance Company v. Council of the European Union*, ECLI:EU:T:2018:945; CJEU 13.12.2018, T-559/15, *Post Bank Iran v Council of the European Union*, ECLI:EU:T:2018:948.

9 See more in *A Fenyves et al*, Tort Law in the Jurisprudence of the European Court of Human Rights (2011) 701. Comparative analysis can also be found in *C von Bar*, The Common European Law of Torts, vol 1 (1998) 61 ff.

compensation in cases of violations of personal rights have increased significantly (almost tripled) compared to previous periods, but the average compensation has increased only slightly, and the median compensation has even decreased. The authors explain this by the fact that the nature of the infringements of personal rights for which compensation for non-pecuniary damage is awarded has changed over time. In previous years, claims were primarily brought against media companies, but in the period analysed, damages were awarded in half of the civil cases in situations where the defamatory posts were made on Facebook or other social media platforms (ie the defendants were natural persons). In the case of personal injury or damage to health, the awards have remained broadly unchanged compared to the previous period.[10]

60 The increase in compensation amounts in defamation cases is also illustrated by the judgment of the Harju County Court of 26 April 2023, whereby the court ordered a lawyer who, in the opinion of the court, made an incorrect factual statement about the incumbent prime minister to pay € 15,000 to the latter. The judgment has not yet entered into force. However, a legal person may have a claim for compensation of pecuniary damage against a person who causes pecuniary damage by unlawfully and negligently publishing incorrect information (§ 1043 ff of the LOA). Damage caused by the publication of inaccurate information about a legal person may be unlawful, in particular if the publication of such information interferes with the economic or professional activities of the legal person (§ 1045(1)(6) and § 1047(1–3) of the LOA), violates a statutory obligation (§ 1045(1)(7) and (3) of the LOA), or if it was published intentionally in bad faith.

10 The analysis is available in Estonian at: <https://www.riigikohus.ee/sites/default/files/analyys/Mittevaraline_kahju_2020-2022.pdf>.

C. Literature

1. *Janno Lahe/Irene Kull*, Lähedaste võimalus saada mittevaralise kahju hüvitist. Kas Riigikohtu diskretsioon või seadusandja võimalus? [The possibility for close persons to receive compensation for non-pecuniary damage. Is it the discretion of the Supreme Court or an option for the legislator?] 7 Juridica (2023) 544 – 553

The article analyses the claim for compensation for non-pecuniary damage of persons close to direct victims, which is based on § 134(3) of the LOA. The authors note that the scope of application of § 134(3) of the LOA has so far been rather limited in Estonian case law, precisely because of the criterion of exceptional circumstances. On 7 October 2022, however, the Criminal Chamber of the Supreme Court issued a decision clarifying the criterion of exceptional circumstances and extending the scope of the provision. The article discusses what the significance of the Supreme Court's ruling could be for future case law. It also raises the question of whether the Estonian legislator should consider abandoning the exceptional circumstances criterion contained in § 134(3) of the LOA. 61

2. *Age Värv*, Kas vabandada või maksta? Kommentaar Riigikohtu tsiviilkolleegiumi 23. märtsi 2023. a otsusele asjas 2-21-5449 [Apologise or pay? Commentary on the judgment of the Civil Chamber of the Supreme Court of 23 March 2023 in case no 2-21-5449] 7 Juridica (2023) 554 – 557

In the article, the author discusses § 134(2) of the LOA and the judgment of the Supreme Court of 23 March 2023 in Civil Case no 2-21-5449. The same judgment is also discussed above. 62

3. *Karl Joonas Kendla/Irene Kull,* Hagi tagamisega tekitatud kahju hüvitamise nõue: kas unustuse hõlma vajunud õiguskaitsevahend või võlgniku hädavajalik tagatis? [Claiming damages by way of security: a forgotten remedy or an indispensable security for the debtor?] 2 Juridica (2023) 14–159

63 The legislator has provided for the obligation of the party who brings an action to compensate the other party for the damage caused. This means that the risk is placed on the party who brings the action. In the article, the authors analyse the case law on compensation for damage caused by a claim. German legal literature and case law are examined for comparison.

Päivi Korpisaari

X. Finland

A. Legislation

1. Amendments of the Tort Liability Act, TLA

The Tort Liability Act (*vahingonkorvauslaki*, 412/1974 TLA) applies both to tort liability and the question of the quantum of damages. It does not apply to contractual liability or to liability arising in any other act, unless the contrary is provided. The latest amendment to the TLA entered into force in 2006 and it concerned compensation for personal injuries. 1

On 17 August 2021, the Ministry of Justice appointed a working group to prepare a reform of the regulations regarding liability for damage caused by public corporations. The working group presented its proposal on 19 January 2023[1] and received statements on the report by 15 March 2023.[2] 2

The working group proposed some changes which were reported on in the 2022 European Tort Law Yearbook. A general election was held in Finland after the proposal was made, and, as a result, there was a change in both the Government and the Minister of Justice. No political decision has as yet been taken on the implementation of the reform, and it is currently uncertain whether the regulation will be reformed. The pressure for reform is likely to be reduced by the fact that the proposed reforms were in part simply a codification of existing case law. 3

1 Julkisyhteisön vahingonkorvausvastuu. Työryhmän mietintö. Oikeusministeriön julkaisuja 2023:4. Available here: <https://api.hankeikkuna.fi/asiakirjat/82adb403-91ad-4abf-95ec-5141df404872/d1090963-0592-447a-bf3d-ac688aac5f5c/MIETINTO_20230119131606.pdf> (accessed on 15 February 2024).

2 Statements can be found here: <https://www.lausuntopalvelu.fi/FI/Proposal/Participation?proposalId=018621f8-eab9-40cb-8e6f-575bdd295957> (accessed on 15 February 2024).

Acknowledgement: The author thanks research assistants, Sade Mäntylä and Sanna Korpi for help with this contribution.

https://doi.org/10.1515/9783111376721-011

B. Cases

1. Supreme Court Case (Korkein oikeus, KKO) 29 March 2023, KKO 2023:24: State Liability; Amount of Damage, ECLI:FI: KKO:2023:24

a) Brief Summary of the Facts

4 The police arrested A on suspicion of gross tax fraud and, in the course of his arrest, € 4,865 was found and confiscated from A. The police informed the enforcement authority of the confiscation of the funds.

5 The enforcement authority seized the funds and used them to pay A's debts under enforcement. A argued that he had suffered damage equal to the amount of funds seized and claimed damages from the State.

b) Judgment of the Court

6 The question to be resolved by the Supreme Court was whether the police had the authority to report the confiscation to the enforcement authority on its own initiative, or whether this was an erroneous action by the police. If the police had acted incorrectly, the Supreme Court had to decide whether, when making the report, the police had failed to comply with the requirements reasonably set for its function, as required by ch 3, sec 2, subsec 1 of the TLA on the liability for damage caused by public corporations. If there were a basis for liability, the Supreme Court still had to assess whether A had suffered damage due to the conduct of the police.

7 The Supreme Court held that the police could interfere with an individual's rights or obligations only if the intervention was based on law, and that the police has the right to use their authority only for purposes that are specified in specific provisions. Chapter 7, sec 2, subsec 1 of the Police Act (872/2011) does not provide for the authority of the police to hand over information on their own initiative. Since the provision in question is of a general nature and the authority of the police is stipulated precisely and with given limits, it is not justified to interpret the provision in such a way that the police would be considered to have the authority to hand over information to the enforcement authority on their own initiative for the purpose of an enforcement.

8 In addition, the Supreme Court stated that, according to the applicable provisions of the Enforcement Code (705/2007), the enforcement authority's right of ac-

cess to confidential information only applies to information deemed necessary by the enforcement authority, and the police's obligation to give information is 'tied' to the request for it.

Since the functions of the police involve the exercise of public power, the Supreme Court next had to assess whether the police's incorrect conduct met the conditions for liability laid down in ch 3, sec 2, subsec 1 of the TLA, ie whether the conduct of the police failed to comply with the reasonable requirements set for it, taking into account the nature and purpose of the function. 9

The Supreme Court referred to the preliminary works of the TLA, according to which, any deviation from the reasonable requirements set for a task or a function does not establish liability for compensation. In addition, it referred to its own jurisprudence, according to which, in evaluating compliance with the reasonably set requirements, the importance of the proper performance of official duties must be taken into account, specifically from the point of view of the entity whose rights are affected by the action. The conduct of the police was based on a general practice in the police. In spite of this, it had overstepped its authority provided by the law. As a public corporation, the police could reasonably be expected to refrain from making an unjustifiably broad interpretation of its authority. The matter also had to be considered from the point of view of the object of the use of power, ie, A. 10

On these grounds, the Supreme Court held that the conduct of the police did not meet the requirements reasonably set for it, taking into account its nature and purpose, and that the State was liable to compensate A for any damage caused by the police's conduct. 11

Regarding the amount of damages, the Supreme Court considered that A's financial position had not worsened as a result of the seizure, since the seized funds had been used to reduce his enforcement debts. Consequently, A had not suffered any damage due to the negligent conduct of the police and thus had no right to compensation. 12

c) Commentary

In the decision, the Supreme Court interpreted the obligations of public corporations quite strictly, which is justified considering the subordinate position of citizens. The police exercise power over the persons they arrest, and therefore high standards must be set for the appropriateness of their conduct. 13

In a recent report of the working group of the Ministry of Justice on the regulation of the liability of public corporations, it is proposed that the above-mentioned ch 3, sec 2, subsec 1 of the TLA concerning the liability of public corpora- 14 tions be repealed. On the one hand, setting a higher threshold for the liability of authorities than for others is not justified. On the other hand, the liability of public corporations has never been considered restricted in jurisprudence based on that provision, and thus it is redundant. As mentioned above, it is not certain whether the legislation will be changed in this regard.

15 Rejecting the claim for compensation was the correct decision because A did not suffer any damage due to the conduct of the police. This case differs from case KKO 2022:18 reported last year, where, due to an error made by the enforcement authority, funds paid to the claimant as compensation for permanent harm caused by an assault had been erroneously seized.[3] The payments did in fact reduce the claimant's debts, but without the erroneous seizure, he could have used the funds himself. The Supreme Court stated that the entity that caused the damage was liable to compensate the damage to the extent that the person who suffered the damage would be in the same position that they would have been in if the damage had not been caused. In this case, the claimant would have been allowed to use the funds himself. Moreover, he did not benefit from the reduction of his debts, as, soon after the events, he concluded a debt arrangement, in which he only paid a part of his debts, according to his ability to pay.

2. Supreme Court (Korkein oikeus, KKO) 12 October 2023, KKO 2023:73: Gross Dishonesty of the Debtor and the Amount of Damage

a) Brief Summary of the Facts

16 From 10 August 2011 to 20 January 2012, B, a deputy member of the Board of Directors of C Ltd, withdrew a total of € 161,500 from the company's bank account. B had given the withdrawn funds to A, who effectively controlled the company. Of these funds, A had used € 116,595 for purposes other than the benefit of the company. Receivables corresponding to this amount were therefore entered in the company's accounts.

17 The company had been declared bankrupt on 10 September 2012, leaving it with debts of € 106,132 and assets of € 1.43. The bankruptcy of the company had been pursued by way of a public inquiry, which had established the amount of the creditors' claims at € 73,843. As this amount shows, not all creditors had enforced their claims in the bankruptcy proceedings relating to C Ltd. Therefore,

3 See *P Korpisaari*, Finland, in: E Karner/BC Steininger (eds), European Tort Law 2022 (2023) 201.

the amount of the creditors' claims was lower than the total amount of the company's debts.

A was considered to have caused the company's insolvency by the aforementioned money withdrawals and was convicted of aggravated dishonesty of a debtor. B was convicted of aiding and abetting A's gross dishonesty. 18

In accordance with the bankrupt estate's request, the District Court had ordered A and B jointly and severally to pay the bankrupt estate € 116,595 plus interest for the funds wrongly withdrawn from the company. The Court of Appeal did not alter the decision of the District Court. The question before the Supreme Court was whether the bankrupt estate was entitled to damages in excess of the total amount of the creditors' claims. 19

b) Judgment of the Court

The Supreme Court stated that according to ch 39, sec 9(2) of the Criminal Code (*rikoslaki*, 39/1889), the injured parties in cases of dishonesty of a debtor, aggravated dishonesty of a debtor and favouring a creditor are the creditors known at the time of commission of the act by the debtor. According to para 3 of the same section, if the bankrupt estate of a debtor has been placed under administration pursuant to the Bankruptcy Code , the administration exercises the right of the injured parties to be heard in a case concerning an offence by the debtor. However, an individual creditor is entitled to exercise an independent right to be heard on their own behalf. 20

The bankrupt estate had entitled its claim as a claim by the plaintiff, representing the company's creditors, and asked the defendants to be ordered jointly and severally to pay the bankrupt estate the sum of € 116,595, the amount which had been wrongly withdrawn from the company's account. The bankrupt estate was considered as having presented its claim on the basis of a criminal offence and as a plaintiff in a criminal case. It was not a claim for repayment of undue payments on behalf of the company. 21

A and B were liable to compensate the damage caused by the offence. The Supreme Court held that where the obligation to perform was based on compensation for damage caused to creditors, the amount of the obligation could not exceed the total amount of the debts of the estate. The bankrupt estate's claim was therefore unfounded insofar as it exceeded the total amount of the claims of the company's creditors. The Supreme Court had assessed the total amount of the debts at € 69,550 instead of the € 73,843 previously mentioned. Consequently, the liability of A and B was reduced, and they were ordered jointly and severally to pay the bank- 22 rupt estate of C Ltd € 69,550 plus interest, instead of the € 116,595 ordered by the Court of Appeal.

c) Comments

23 It is clear from the case that the claimant should state the basis of their claim precisely and rather too broadly than too narrowly. The Supreme Court suggested in its reasoning that a claim for compensation in excess of the amount of the creditors' claims might have succeeded if it had been brought on behalf of the company (rather than the creditors) as a claim for restitution based on an illegal distribution of assets. The Supreme Court also referred to the fact that the amount of withdrawals in excess of the creditors' claims could have been forfeited to the State as an illegally obtained criminal gain if it had been claimed.

24 Since the liquidator represented the creditors, it was quite logical that the amount of compensation awarded could not exceed the amount of the debts on which the claim was based.

3. Supreme Court Case (Korkein oikeus, KKO) 15 November 2023, KKO 2023:85: Compensation for the Suffering Caused to the Relatives of a Deceased, ECLI:FI:KKO:2023:85

a) Brief Summary of the Facts

25 Some teenagers drove by car from Tampere to Pori, a journey of approximately 100 kilometres. Before the return trip, the teenagers had been drinking alcohol. At the time, 17-year-old A had a driver's licence but he drove under the influence of alcohol. A test revealed that the alcohol concentration in his blood after driving was measured at 1.68 parts per thousand.

26 On the days of the drive, on 15 and 16 August 2020, A's friends, B, C and D, accompanied him. The car driven by A ran off the road near their destination in a gentle curve of the road to the left. After running off the road, the car hit a tree with its right front side, and the car had been ripped in two from behind the front seats. As a result of hitting the tree, B and C, who were passengers on the back seat of the car, and D, who was a passenger on the front seat next to the driver of the car, were killed.

27 A's driving speed had increased to at least 170 km/h before the accident. The speed of the vehicle had been about 120 km/h when the car ran off the road,

while the speed limit on the road in question was 100 km/h. At the point where the car left the road, there was a gentle curve to the left in relation to the direction of travel. The accident had taken place around 1:09 am, when it was dark. Driving conditions had otherwise been normal, and the road surface had been bare and dry.

A was sentenced to three years and nine months in prison for three grossly negligent homicides committed as a young person. In terms of damages, the question was whether the parents of B and D had the right to receive compensation for the suffering caused by the death of their children. 28

b) Judgment of the Court

The Supreme Court stated that about 14 minutes before the car ran off the road, A had sent a Snapchat message from his mobile phone, which included an image of the car's driving panel showing a speed of about 140 km/h. A had attached the message 'I will kll myself' to the picture. In addition, about five minutes before the accident, A had sent a Snapchat message with a picture of the car's driving panel at a speed of about 170 km/h. A had attached the message 'Citica's peaks' to the picture. Between these messages, B, who was a passenger in the car, had sent his friend a video from inside the car and a message stating 'I'm probably going to die'. 29

A had used his mobile phone while driving and also sent messages other than those described above. There is no knowledge of whether A was using his mobile phone when the accident happened. 30

According to ch 5, sec 4 a, subsec 1 of the Tort Liability Act (412/1974 TLA), the parents, children and spouse of the person killed, as well as other comparable persons who are particularly close to the person killed, have the right to receive compensation for the suffering caused by the death if the death was caused intentionally or by gross negligence and the compensation is considered reasonable, taking into account the closeness of the relationship between the person killed and the person claiming compensation, the nature of the act, and other circumstances. 31

The parents of B and D had demanded compensation of their suffering. It is undisputed that the parents of a person killed who claim compensation are considered particularly close to the deceased. The deaths were also caused by gross negligence. In this respect, the conditions for awarding compensation for suffering were thus fulfilled. 32

In ch 5, sec 4 a of the TLA, it is further stipulated that the awarding of compensation must be considered reasonable. The consideration takes into account the closeness of the relationship between the deceased and the party claiming compensation, the nature of the act, and other circumstances. 33

34 The Supreme Court stated that the purpose of the compensation is to compensate for the suffering that the relatives of the deceased feel due to the death of a person who was important to them. The provision regarding compensation is intended as an exception, according to which, relatives of victims of mainly only gross homicide are entitled to compensation.

35 Although deaths following road traffic accidents are not typically intentional, they may still have features that support the awarding of compensation for suffering (see eg KKO 2002:83 and KKO 2004:48). However, when it comes to such deaths, the awarding of compensation must be more restrained than in intentional homicides. When considering the reasonableness of awarding compensation, paying special attention to the closeness of the relationship between the deceased and the claimant is justified (see KKO 2008:79, para 16).

36 Regarding the closeness of the relationship between the deceased and the claimant, the Supreme Court stated that B had lived with his parents and D alternated between his parents. The closeness of the relationships thus supported awarding compensation.

37 Regarding the nature of the act and other circumstances, the Supreme Court stated that the accident was not due to A's momentary gross negligence, but that he had driven the car for part of the roughly 100 kilometre journey and had been heavily intoxicated. Even before driving off the road, he had repeatedly exceeded the speed limit, and the texting that took place while he was driving showed a disregard for traffic safety. In addition, the message of B, who was a passenger, showed the fear they experienced.

38 However, it was justified to take a more cautious approach to awarding compensation for suffering for deaths in road traffic accidents than for deaths caused by intentional homicides. Thus, the above-mentioned facts could not be considered to support awarding compensation for suffering in particular.

39 It was also necessary to take into account the fact that all the teenagers had been drunk and that they had gone on the car trip knowing that the driver was intoxicated. In the course of the trip, the driver had also been switched. All those on board had thus known, at the very least, that there was an increased risk of a traffic accident due to the driver's intoxication. These facts spoke against awarding compensation for suffering.

40 The Supreme Court concluded that ch 5, sec 4 a of the TLA on the right to compensation in the event of death was intended as an exception, according to which, relatives of victims of mainly intentional homicides are entitled to compensation. Taking into account in particular that the case did not involve an intentional homicide, and the other circumstances as explained above, the Supreme Court considered that awarding compensation in this case was not reasonable, despite the par-

ticularly close relationship between the parents and the victims, as referred to in ch 5, sec 4 a of the TLA.

A should thus be released from the liability to compensate as decided by the Court of Appeal. The charge of three second-degree murders committed as a young person was also dismissed, and A was convicted of three grossly negligent homicides committed as a young person (vote 4–1). The dissenting judge would have awarded compensation to the parents of the 18- and 17-year-old victims who lived with their parents. 41

c) Comments

Finnish law has a very restrictive approach to compensating suffering to the relatives of deceased persons. Moreover, if compensation is awarded, its amount is rather low. In this case, the Court of Appeal had awarded € 6,000 as compensation for suffering to each parent who had claimed compensation. The compensation is thus rather symbolic. In the government bill of the TLA, it is considered that the main purpose of compensation is to facilitate mourning and to help the bereaved to cope with the sudden loss of a loved one. The compensation could be used to finance, for example, therapy costs or additional free time from employment.[4] Therefore, the intention behind the compensation is not to compensate for all the suffering and grief caused by the loss of a close one. 42

The Supreme Court had considered in its earlier decision KKO 2008:79 that awarding compensation based on a death in a road traffic accident must be approached more cautiously than would be the case of an intentional homicide. In this earlier case, the children, who were of age and had already moved away from home, had no right to compensation for the suffering caused by the death of their parent. 43

On the other hand, in the jurisprudence of the Supreme Court, compensation for suffering has been awarded to a victim's relatives even when the death was caused by grossly negligent conduct in traffic. The cases have had in common the fact that the victim was unknown to the perpetrator, and they had no reason to foresee the accident (KKO 2002:83 and KKO 2004:48). 44

The Supreme Court has stated in its previous precedents that the reasonableness of awarding compensation for suffering is primarily assessed from the perspective of the claimant (KKO 2008:79, para 14 and KKO 2004:48, para 13). In this case, however, the Supreme Court seems to have paid attention to the objective as- 45

4 Government Bill 116/1998, 110.

pects of the course of events. Emphasis was placed on the fact that the victims were not bystanders but had gone on a car trip together with the driver, knowing that he was intoxicated. The dissenting judge, who would have awarded compensation, emphasised the atmosphere in the car, which – taking into account the messages sent by B – had been very anxious and that A had been drinking while driving.

46 The decision is once again an indication of the restricted approach of Finnish law and jurisprudence to compensation for suffering.

4. Supreme Court Case (Korkein oikeus, KKO) 23 November 2023, KKO 2023:91: Amount of Damage, ECLI:FI:KKO:2023:91

a) Brief Summary of the Facts

47 A had worked for B Ltd as an offset pressman. A was injured in an occupational accident on 27 January 2016, in such a way that the soft tissue of the skin of the II-V fingers of his right hand was completely peeled from the knuckles to the tip of the fingers. The nerve and blood vessel structures of the fingers were torn. The injured fingers had to be amputated up to the area of the middle digits. A was 47 years old at the time of the accident.

48 The district court had sentenced C, the chief executive officer of B Ltd, and its production manager D to pay a fine for negligence in occupational safety and injury and had ordered B Ltd to pay a community fine.

49 Based on the Occupational Accidents and Diseases Act (*työturvallisuuslaki,* 459/2015), A was paid insurance compensation in periodical payments due to the injury in question. In 2017, the amount of compensation was € 167 per month. Increases according to the yearly index were added to the amount.

50 On the basis of the Tort Liability Act, A demanded that B Ltd, C and D be jointly liable to compensate him € 15,000 plus penalty interest for permanent damage.

51 A argued that the insurance compensation he received could not be considered as full compensation for the permanent harm he had suffered. Taking into account the periodical payments, a reasonable amount of compensation was € 15,000.

52 B Ltd, C and D demanded that the claim should be dismissed. In their opinion, the insurance compensation fully compensated for the permanent harm caused by the injury.

b) Judgment of the Court

A was 47 years old at the time of the occupational accident. Under the Occupational Accidents and Diseases Act, A was granted compensation corresponding to the disability category 12, which was paid to him as a periodical payment. The amount of the allowance in 2017 was € 167 per month. 53

According to ch 5, sec 7, subsec 2 of the TLA, permanent harm is compensated with a one-off payment. However, the compensation can be ordered to be paid partly or totally in periodical payments if it is appropriate, taking into account the circumstances of the person who suffered the injury, the amount of compensation, and the financial circumstances of the person liable for compensation. 54

Compensation for permanent harm caused by an occupational accident or occupational disease is regulated in ch 11 of the Occupational Accidents and Diseases Act. According to sec 83, subsec 1 of the Act, compensation is paid to the injured party for permanent general harm caused by the injury and illness caused by the accident. 55

According to subsec 2 of the same section, general harm refers to the weakening of the functional capacity (functional impairment) caused by an accident. Functional capacity is measured according to the functional capacity of a healthy person of the same age. Thus, the limitations that the disability or illness, considering its nature and the degree of difficulty, usually cause in everyday life are taken into account. When assessing functional capacity, occupation, living conditions, and other individual circumstances of the injured person are not considered. 56

According to subsec 3 of the section, in order to assess the magnitude of the general harm, the harms caused by various injuries and illnesses are related to each other by dividing the injuries and illnesses into 20 categories of harm based on their medical nature and degree of severity. 57

The Supreme Court stated that compensation should not result in the injured party receiving an unfair advantage from the compensation (the so-called prohibition of enrichment, see eg, KKO 2021:87, para 10). 58

The compensation for permanent harm according to the TLA and the insurance compensation for permanent harm according to the Occupational Accidents and Diseases Act cover the same consequences of a personal injury. Both compensate only for so-called intangible damage. Both aim to compensate for the loss of quality of life that the injured party will suffer for the rest of his life. 59

Chapter 5, sec 2 c, subsec 2 of the TLA provides for the possibility to take into account a particular impairment of the quality of life caused by a personal injury as a factor increasing the amount of compensation, while, according to the Occupational Accidents and Diseases Act, the individual circumstances of the injured party are not taken into account when determining the amount of compensation. 60

Therefore, the amount of compensation according to the TLA may in some cases be higher than that according to the Occupational Accidents and Diseases Act.

61 The Supreme Court held that if the conditions for awarding compensation in accordance with both Laws are present, the injured party's right to compensation according to the Occupational Accidents and Diseases Act is not an obstacle to compensation awarded in accordance with the TLA. However, the compensation paid according to the Occupational Accidents and Diseases Act has to be deducted from the compensation paid according to the TLA.

62 The Supreme Court stated that A was 47 years old at the time of the accident and that the one-off compensation payment corresponding to the category 12 harm in the Occupational Accidents and Diseases Act had been € 52,610 at the time.

63 In the 2023 compensation standards confirmed by the Traffic and Patient Injury Board,[5] compensation for permanent harm of category 12 was € 52,800 for an 18-year-old. This amount should have been reduced for A because of his advanced age. Thus, the Supreme Court held that the compensation for permanent harm under the TLA should not be greater than the capital value of the compensation determined under the Occupational Accidents and Diseases Act. If the periodical payments are sufficient compensation for the permanent harm caused to A, A is not entitled to the additional compensation he sought.

c) Comments

64 The Supreme Court's decision can be considered justified as it states that additional compensation can be granted under the TLA if it would lead to a higher compensation amount than that determined under the Occupational Accidents and Diseases Act.

65 Utilising the standards of the Traffic and Patient Injury Board to define the amount of compensation results in the same amount of compensation being paid for similar injuries and harms. This promotes equality of victims of damage. On the other hand, these standards also keep the compensation level constantly low. In my opinion, the compensation of € 52,610 for the permanent harm caused by the amputation of four fingers and nerve pain is too low, and the level of compensation in Finland should be raised. In this case, the Supreme Court's reference to the prohibition of enrichment appears rather absurd.

5 Tilapäisen haitan, pysyvän haitan sekä pysyvän kosmeettisen haitan korvausluokat 1.1.2023 alkaen. Soveltamisohje 3/2022. Liikenne- ja potilasvahinkolautakunta 12.12.2022 [Compensation categories for temporary harm, permanent harm and permanent cosmetic harm from 1 January 2023. Instructions for application 3/2022. Traffic and Patient Injury Board 12.12.2022].

C. Literature

1. *Katri Havu/Timo Havu*, EU-esitykset tuotevastuudirektiiviksi ja tekoälyn aiheuttamiin vahinkoihin soveltuviksi säännöksiksi: edistysaskeleita ja ongelmia [EU proposals for the revised product liability directive and for an AI liability directive: progress and problems] Lakimies 2023/1, 104–115

This article discusses the EU proposals (2022) for an AI liability directive and for a revised product liability directive. The authors argue that the new proposals would create clarity and uniformity of applicable laws across the EU on a number of issues. However, the proposals are neither simple nor easy to read. National courts would also be left with a considerable margin of discretion on certain issues. 66

2. *Sofia Heikkonen/Katri Havu*, Liability for Medical Devices – How Clear and Harmonised Is It? Europarättslig tidskrift 2023/4, 651–668

Civil liability for defective medical devices is not regulated comprehensively by European Union law. The current EU product liability rules cover a significant proportion of the cases that concern the liability of manufacturers, but the national laws of EU Member States remain relevant. The liability of parties other than manufacturers is largely left to national laws. Given the vagueness of EU law, case outcomes vary, and the law is uncertain. Economic operators need clear liability rules to gauge the risks of introducing innovations to the market. Predictable liability rules are also important for individuals and for the uptake of new technologies. At present, interpreting EU and national law can be difficult, in particular in the context of intelligent medical devices. EU legislators are eager to promote the use of beneficial artificial intelligence (AI). Accordingly, they have published two proposals that, if passed into law, would affect liability for medical devices. One of the proposals concerns a revision of the EU product liability framework. The other deals with liability for harm caused by AI. In the article, the writers ad- 67 dress the problems of contemporary EU law and discuss developments in the Union-level regulation of liability for medical devices.[6]

6 Description is written by the authors of the article.

Jonas Knetsch and Zoé Jacquemin

XI. France

A. Legislation

No new tort law legislation was introduced in 2023. 1

B. Cases

1. Cour de cassation, Chambre sociale (Cass Soc) 8 February 2023, no 21-14451: The Appalling Saga of the Asbestos Litigation; Reparation for the Violation of an Employee's Dignity

a) Brief Summary of the Facts

In France, the use and the manufacturing of material containing asbestos was banned in 1997. However, under certain circumstances, industrial companies could apply for an exception allowing them to use asbestos until 2001. This was the case of a chemical company, which even continued the use of asbestos illegally from 2002 to 2005. 2

After disclosure, with the help of trade unions, several workers of this company claimed damages for their permanent anxiety over the risk of developing an asbestos-related pathology. In addition, they sought compensation of the loss arising from the breach of their employer's duty of loyalty (*devoir de loyauté*) towards them. 3

b) Judgment of the Court

The trial judges held that the claimants could not obtain damages for the fear of future illness (*préjudice d'anxiété*), the compensation claim being time-barred. However, they decided to grant damages on the basis of the violation of the employer's duty of loyalty. 4

The Court of Cassation confirmed the trial judgment, holding that 'the violation of an employee's dignity is to be regarded as a breach of the employer's 5

https://doi.org/10.1515/9783111376721-012

duty to execute in good faith the contract of employment' and that the employees could invoke, in support of their claim, a loss distinct from the fear of future illness. In its press release accompanying this judgment, the Court of Cassation was even more explicit in detailing the solution.[1] According to the press service, 'employees whose right to compensation for fear of future illness is time-barred are entitled to damages for the violation of their dignity if their employer has used asbestos illegally, and may claim the compensation of a non-economic loss, independently of a loss of anxiety'.

c) Commentary[2]

6 This judgment is a continuation of the French legal solutions, both case law based and statutory, on compensation for victims of asbestos. A specific compensation scheme (*Fonds d'indemnisation des victims de l'amiante*) was established in 2001 in order to award full compensation to employees (and their relatives) who were exposed to asbestos in their workplace and who are suffering from asbestos-related diseases.[3] In 2010, the Court of Cassation decided to recognise anxiety as a specific head of damage for employees whose work had involved contact with asbestos, even in cases where no specific disease could be diagnosed. Over the years, the prerequisites for compensation of this specific head of loss have eased substantially; nowadays, employees who are in a situation of constant worry and have to undertake medical tests in order to detect asbestos-related path-

1 It is not unusual, yet highly questionable, that the Court of Cassation delivers more detailed explanations in press releases than in its judgments. On this issue, see eg *F Guiomard*, Sur les communiqués de presse de la chambre sociale de la Cour de cassation, Revue de droit du travail 2006, 222.

2 See also *P Adam*, La dignité (bafouée) des travailleurs de l'amiante, Semaine sociale Lamy 2023, no 2034, 13 f; *M Keim-Bagot*, Atteinte à la dignité du salarié et réparation d'un préjudice distinct: une consécration de la distinction entre dommage et préjudice moral en droit social? La Semaine Juridique: Juris Classeur Périodique (JCP) S 2023, no 12, 32; *J Knetsch*, Le préjudice d'atteinte à la dignité des travailleurs de l'amiante: les errements de la chambre sociale de la Cour de cassation, JCP G 2023, no 13, 668; *J Morin*, Nouvelle voie de droit pour l'indemnisation des salariés de l'amiante: de l'idéologie de la réparation à celle de la sanction? Revue de jurisprudence sociale 2023, no 6, 21; *C Willmann*, Réparation du préjudice d'atteinte à la dignité, exit le préjudice d'anxiété, Droit social 2023, 367.

3 Art 53 of the Act no 2000-1257 of 20 December 2000. See *A Thébaud-Mony*, Justice for Asbestos Victims and the Politics of Compensation: The French Experience, 9 (2003) International Journal of Occupational and Environmental Health 280; *C Manaouil/M Graser/O Jardé*, Compensation of Asbestos Victims in France, 25 (2006) Medicine and Law 435.

ologies may seek compensation of *préjudice d'anxiété* even if they did not work in one of the industrial sites listed by public authorities.

The 2023 judgment takes a step further, enabling asbestos workers to claim damages on alternative legal grounds, even in cases in which the limitation period for the compensation of *préjudice d'anxiété* has expired. The distinction made by the Court of Cassation judges between the duty of employers to provide safety (*obligation de sécurité*), used for the compensation of *préjudice d'anxiété*, and their duty to perform the employment contract in good faith (*obligation de loyauté*) has not yet proved to be very consistent. The reasoning seems rather driven by policy considerations, sanctioning a company that voluntarily disclosed to its personnel the use of asbestos beyond the limited authorisation period. 7

This policy-based approach is also discernible when it comes to the concept of employees' dignity which, according to the judges, was violated by the employer. While there is an isolated case from 2001, in which the infringement of an employee's dignity was the legal basis for a compensation claim,[4] it seems rather excessive to consider that the mere fact of exposing employees to a harmful substance violates human dignity. The context in which the concept of human dignity was elaborated refers to the post-Second World War period when it was deemed crucial to prevent genocides, experiments on human beings and eugenic practices. 8

In any case, this judgment also reveals the growing importance of tort law in the context of labour law. While workplace accidents and occupational diseases are not subject to civil liability rules under art L 422-1 of the Social Security Code,[5] actions in tort have increased rapidly over the last years in areas left open by the specific compensation scheme operated by social security.[6] 9

4 Cour de Cassation, Chambre Sociale (Cass Soc) 7 February 2012, no 10-18686 (in this case, an employee was insulted by extremely degrading remarks made by her employer, who asserted that her body would give off 'foul odours' arising from 'gangrene' or 'incontinence').

5 For more details, see eg *S Carval*, France, in: U Magnus (ed), The Impact of Social Security Law on Tort Law (2003) 74.

6 For a detailed assessment of the blind spots of the dedicated compensation scheme, see *M Keim-Bagot*, De l'accident du travail à la maladie: la metamorphose du risqué professionnel (2015) 112.

2. Cour de cassation, Chambre commerciale (Cass Com) 24 May 2023, no 21-25081: 'Non-Cumul' Principle and Liability for the Act of Employees

a) Brief Summary of the Facts

10 A consulting firm contracted with a security company for the upkeep of its premises and various handling and maintenance tasks. In the course of his duties, an employee of the security company stole boxes of vouchers. He was ordered to pay more than € 240,000 in damages to the consulting company but turned out to be insolvent. The consulting firm sued the security company for damages on the basis of vicarious liability.

b) Judgment of the Court

11 The Versailles Court of Appeal dismissed the claim. The judges ruled out the liability of employers for the acts of their employees under art 1242(5) of the Civil Code (formerly art 1384(5)) on the grounds that a contract had been concluded between the consulting company and the security firm and that the employee's theft had occurred during the performance of his contractual duties. The 'non-cumul' (or rather 'non-option') rule applicable in France[7] prevents the plaintiff from claiming damages on an extra-contractual basis where contractual liability applies. Hence the dismissal of the extra-contractual claim. However, the claim could not succeed on a contractual basis either, as the Court of Appeal held that the plaintiff had failed to prove that the security company had breached one of its contractual obligations. A key factor appears to have been that the theft occurred when the employee was not, strictly speaking, providing the services agreed between the parties, but was handling other boxes at the company's request.

12 Such arguments did not convince the Court of Cassation, which overturned the decision. It held that the lower court had violated art 1384(5) (now art 1242(5)) of the Civil Code, as well as former art 1147 of the same Code (on contractual liability). According to the Court of Cassation, 'it follows from these texts that the creditor of a contractual obligation may invoke the rules of delictual liability against the debtor of that obligation in order to claim compensation for damage resulting from a distinct act (*fait distinct*) committed by the debtor's employee'. Insofar as the Court of Appeal found that it was not the breach of contract, but solely the employee's

7 On this rule in English, see *J Knetsch*, Tort Law in France (2021) 55.

'distinct criminal act' (*fait délictuel distinct*) which had caused the damage to be compensated, it should have concluded that the employer was vicariously liable, all the more so as the employee had committed the theft on the premises and in the course of his duties (*sur les lieux et à l'occasion de ses fonctions*).

c) Commentary[8]

It is worth noting that the present decision has not been published in the official bulletin. Yet it received remarkable attention from the doctrine. Indeed, it deals with a question that is still unclear, namely the application – or not – of the 'non-cumul' rule to the liability of the employer for the acts of their employees. Some authors have pointed out that trial judges tend to apply art 1242(5) of the Civil Code even between contract parties, without paying attention to the option prohibition. The Court of Cassation itself, in landmark decisions during the 1980s, applied former art 1384(5) of the Civil Code between contractual parties, sometimes without even mentioning the *non-cumul* rule.[9] In other decisions though, the 'non-cumul' principle served to rule out the extra-contractual liability of the employer,[10] leading to much uncertainty as to the state of the law. Unfortunately, the Contract Law Reform 2016[11] did not seize the occasion to clarify the sit- 13

8 See also *P Jourdain*, Le fait délictueux d'un préposé du débiteur distinct de l'exécution du contrat engage la responsabilité délictuelle de celui-ci en qualité de commettant, Revue Trimestrielle de Droit Civil (RTD Civ) 2023, no 4, 896; *J Knetsch*, Relativisation de la règle dite de "non-cumul" en présence d'un dommage causé par le salarié d'un débiteur contractuel, JCP G 2023, no 46, 1992; *O Robin-Sabard*, Responsabilité du fait d'autrui – Option entre responsabilité contractuelle et responsabilité des commettants du fait des préposés, Responsabilité civile et assurances (RCA) 2023, nos 7–8, 181.

9 See especially Cour de Cassation, Assemblée plénière (Cass Ass plén) 15 November 1985, no 84-12601 (regarding an employee of a surveillance company who deliberately set fire to the factory that he was supposed to be supervising) and Cass Civ 1, 18 January 1989, nos 87-16269 and 87-17595 (with similar facts and also decided on the grounds of extra-contractual vicarious liability).

10 See eg Cass Civ 1, 18 January 1989, no 87-18081 deciding that the service provider was 'contractually obliged' to guarantee its client, whose premises it had undertaken to provide surveillance and guarding services for, against damage caused by the fault of the employee he had placed there (curiously the same court and on the very same day as the contrary decision quoted in the previous note).

11 Ordinance no 2016-131 of 10 February 2016, on which see *J Knetsch/Z Jacquemin*, France, in: E Karner/BC Steininger (eds), European Tort Law 2016 (2017) 191, nos 1–3.

uation, but rather relegated civil liability as a whole to a later reform to come (which has still not happened).[12]

3. Cour de cassation, Première chambre civile (Cass Civ 1) 5 July 2023, no 22-13457: French Slavery on Trial

a) Brief Summary of the Facts

14 In 2014, three civil rights associations and fifty individual claimants based in the French overseas department, Martinique brought an action in tort against the French State, seeking compensation of 'past, present and future losses arising from slave trade and slavery committed by French public authorities', the funding of 'the repatriation to Africa of all descendants of deportees who wish to do so', 'a judicial expertise of the loss suffered by the Martinican people' as well as the establishment of a € 20 billion provision to cover future damages.

b) Judgment of the Court

15 The trial judges of both the First Instance Court and the Court of Appeal rejected this action, holding that there was no legal standing (*intérêt à agir*) for some of the claimants, that the action was time-barred and that there was no relevant legal basis for it. In particular, it was considered that the 21 May 2001 Act qualifying slave trade and slavery as a crime against humanity (the so-called 'Taubira Act'), invoked by the claimants, does not entitle the claimants to a right of compensation.

16 The Court of Cassation confirmed the Court of Appeal judgment on two different issues. First, regarding the starting point of the limitation period, the present judgment considered that descendants of slaves were in a position to file a claim as soon as the French State ratified, during the post-Second World War period, international conventions recognising slavery as a crime against humanity and that there are no indications that they were hindered from doing so at that time. Second, the Court of Cassation held that the claimants did not establish any 'certain, direct and personal loss linked to slave trade or slavery, notwithstanding the references made to academic work on transgenerational losses due to the influence of

12 On the reform attempts, see *Knetsch/Jacquemin* (fn 11) nos 13–21; *J Knetsch/Z Jacquemin*, France, in: E Karner/BC Steininger (eds), ETL 2017 (2018) 187, nos 1–8; *J Knetsch/Z Jacquemin*, France, in: E Karner/BC Steininger (eds), ETL 2019 (2020) 186, nos 1–5; *J Knetsch/Z Jacquemin*, France, in: E Karner/BC Steininger (eds), ETL 2020 (2021) 178, nos 1–5.

environment on human genetics and to the transmission of collective dehumanising traumata in the past and notwithstanding economic and non-economic losses suffered by every descendant of slaves'.

c) Commentary[13]

This case is remarkable in a number of respects. First of all, it is one of the few examples in French case law where civil courts had to face compensation claims related to historical injustice. While there is a growing tendency in other jurisdictions (mostly in Common Law countries) to seek reparation of historic wrongdoing through tort law actions,[14] the situation in France is slightly different. Public authorities have created specific compensation schemes for victims of the confiscation of Jewish property during the Second World War, and for victims of child abuse in religious institutions and public health scandals. One of the aims of these ad hoc solutions is precisely to keep compensation claims out of court, by paying lump sum settlements rather than full compensation. French media report that an avalanche of procedures is currently pending before civil and administrative courts, mostly in the overseas territories in the Caribbean.[15] The future will tell us how the courts will deal with these politically sensitive issues although there is no tradition of 'political justice' in France. 17

In the present case, the Court of Cassation judges carefully avoid putting themselves in a situation where the judgment could be interpreted as a political statement. The appeal to the Court was dismissed on the grounds of limitation of actions, the judges insisting on the possibility of descendants, at least since the 2001 Taubira Act, to file a compensation claim against the State. As actions against the State are time-barred after four years,[16] the Court had no choice but to confirm the decision of the trial judges on this point. It is rather up to the legislature to include (or not) in the 1968 Act on Limitation of Actions against the State a provi- 18

13 See also *J Knetsch*, La réparation de l'esclavage devant la Cour de cassation: manque d'audace ou orthodoxie bienvenue? JCP G 2023, no 40, 1738; *M Eliphe/B Moron-Puech/M Cormier*, L'introuvable réparation des préjudices liés à la traite négrière et l'esclavage, Dalloz 2023, 1954.

14 See eg *M Loth*, How does tort law deal with historical injustice? On slavery reparations, postcolonial redress, and the legitimations of tort law, 11 (2020) Journal of European Tort Law 181; *D Butt*, Rectifying International Injustice: Principles of Compensation and Restitution Between Nations (2008) 97.

15 *J-M Hauteville*, Aux Antilles, une cascade de procès contre l'État sur la question de l'esclavage, Le Monde 26 January 2022.

16 On this point, see in English *D Fairgrieve/F Lichère*, The Liablity of Public Authorities in France, in: K Oliphant (ed), Liability of Public Authorities in Comparative Perspective (2016) 155, 159.

sion extending the criminal law-relevant imprescriptibility to compensation claims.[17]

19 As for the legal assessment of the reparable loss, the Court of Cassation refuses to acknowledge in legal terms the existence of a 'transgenerational loss', implying that such a concept would be inconsistent with the requirement to prove a 'personal loss'. It is indeed a rather complicated endeavour to implement into tort law the idea of a transferable loss for claimants whose ancestors lived almost ten generations earlier and in a context where interracial relations, rather forced than consensual, were more frequent than we think, leading to societies marked by *métissage*. It is indeed more than likely that some of the individual claimants had not only ancestors living in slavery, but also masters. The Court's choice to not recognise the loss as reparable is probably also driven by the desire to let the French Parliament decide on the issue of compensating (or not) slavery and colonisation.

4. Cour de cassation, Première chambre civile (Cass Civ 1) 18 October 2023, no 22-11492: Compensation for the Anxiety Caused by a Risk of Personal Injury (Diethylstilbestrol-Based Drugs)

a) Brief Summary of the Facts

20 A woman facing infertility problems sued the manufacturers of diethylstilbestrol-based drugs (DES), known in France as 'Distilbène', which her mother took during her pregnancy. As mentioned in previous editions of this Yearbook,[18] there have been a number of cases dealing with the consequences of the medical use of DES, a drug which was widely prescribed to pregnant women in the 1970s, but which turned out to cause infertility and various cancers in women who had been exposed *in utero*.[19] The causal link between these harmful effects on the 'woman-to-be' and the drug was scientifically established in the 1990s and the drug withdrawn from the market.

21 In this case, the woman claimed compensation on two grounds: firstly, for her infertility and, secondly, for the anxiety caused by having to undergo regular med-

17 An appeal to the Constitutional Council (Conseil constitutionnel) was found inadmissible on this point by the Court of Cassation (Cass Civ 1, 8 November 2018, no 18-13894).

18 *Knetsch/Jacquemin*, ETL 2019 (fn 12) nos 21–28 and *Knetsch/Jacquemin*, ETL 2017 (fn 12) no 37 f.

19 See beyond France in English *R Goldberg*, Causation and Drugs: The Legacy of Diethylstilbestrol (1996) Anglo-American Law Review 286 (with further refs to American law).

ical check-ups due to the increased risk of developing cancer as a result of exposure to DES *in utero.*

b) Judgment of the Court

The Paris Court of Appeal dismissed the plaintiff's claims on both grounds. First, it ruled that the existence of a causal link between the exposure and the infertility was doubtful in the specific case. Medical evidence showed that the woman did not have the genital anomalies usually associated with DES exposure and that another cause could also explain the infertility, namely chlamydia infection. Because of this uncertainty, the Court of Appeal ruled that causation had not been sufficiently demonstrated and denied compensation. With regards to anxiety, the Court of Appeal held that since it could not be proven that the DES had caused any bodily harm, no subsequent prejudice of anxiety could be inferred from a personal injury. It therefore refused compensation on this ground as well. 22

The Court of Cassation overturned the decision of the Court of Appeal on both grounds. Firstly, on causation, the Court of Cassation held that fault liability under the French Civil Code (art 1240 reproducing former art 1382) provided for compensation whenever the damage was causally linked to a fault, even if the fault was not the sole cause of the damage. The Court of Appeal could therefore only have excluded liability if it had established that exposure to DES could in no way have contributed to the plaintiff's infertility. 23

Secondly, with regard to the prejudice of anxiety, the Court of Cassation refused to make such prejudice dependent on the existence of a personal injury. Referring once again to the French Civil Code, it held that 'the anxiety resulting from exposure to a risk of harm is a compensable damage' under art 1240. In its view, the prejudice of anxiety must be derived from the exposure to DES itself and the risks it entails. The Court of Cassation therefore quashed the decision and referred the case back to the Paris Court of Appeal (in a different composition) to decide on both heads of compensation. 24

c) Commentary[20]

Two preliminary remarks: first, it should be noted that, although the decision quotes the Civil Code's liability for fault, art 1240 – formerly art 1382 – does not 25

20 See also *V Mazeaud*, Lien de causalité et préjudice d'anxiété, Gazette du Palais (Gaz Pal) 2024,

define causation, nor loss. It is a (quite famous) 'general clause' which provides that 'any human action whatsoever which causes harm to another creates an obligation in the person by whose fault it was caused to make reparation for it'.[21] Second, the more 'natural' ground for action in such cases today would be product liability rather than fault liability. However, the facts of the case predate the transposition of the Product Liability Directive into French law, hence the recourse to fault liability.

26 The reasoning concerning causation is not exempt of criticism. French courts apply the theory of 'equivalence of conditions', meaning that every cause which contributes to produce the damage is considered as satisfying the causation test (also referred to as the *conditio sine qua non* test). This theory allows a consideration of a plurality of causes and to hold jointly liable a plurality of debtors. Nevertheless, this theory is not so extensive as to consider that every *possible* cause satisfies the causation test. This is the difference between *plural* causation and *alternative* causation. In the present case, it seems that the Court of Appeal was unable to ascertain whether the infertility had been caused by the exposure to the DES or by the chlamydia infection. Who should then bear the risk of the doubt? Usually, it should be borne by the party who bears the burden of proof – thus the plaintiff. By ruling that the Court of Appeal failed to establish that exposure to DES could in no way have contributed to the plaintiff's infertility, the Court of Cassation implies that the only way to exonerate the defendant of liability would have been to show that its product could not have been the cause of the pathology. By doing so, the Court thus seems to apply a reversal of the burden of proof to the benefit of victims exposed *in utero* to DES and who later show symptoms of infertility. Such presumption would go quite far, especially in cases where a concurrent cause of infertility had been identified, with even more probability (the medical expertise identified a probability of only 40 % of DES being responsible).

27 As regards the choice to compensate the damage caused by anxiety, irrespective of any physical injury that may have occurred, the decision also raises a number of questions. It is true that the plaintiff has to undergo regular medical check-ups because of the increased risk of developing cancer. This is what causes her anxiety – not the infertility. Consequently, it would have been unfair to make the former dependent on the latter. On the other hand, there is an obvious risk

no 2, 3; *S Hoquet-Berg*, Exposition au Distilbène: la réparation n'implique pas la faute exclusive du laboratoire, RCA 2023, no 12, 282; *L Vitale*, L'exposition fautive au Distilbène ouvre droit à réparation même si elle ne constitue pas la cause exclusive du dommage, JCP G 2023, no 49, 1405; *C Quezel-Ambrunaz*, Lien de causalité – deux causes possibles, Dalloz 2024, 34.

21 Translation of art 1240 – *Knetsch* (fn 7) no 45.

of going too far by recognising the possibility of compensating immaterial loss for a mere risk of personal injury. Do French courts really want to grant compensation for immaterial losses in the absence of proof of any personal injury? Is it not too 'risky' to compensate for a mere 'risk' of personal injury? In any case, by accepting compensation for anxiety without any correlated personal injury, the decision clearly paves the way for compensation for what could be called 'pure immaterial loss'.

5. Cour de cassation, Première chambre civile (Cass Civ 1) 15 November 2023, nos 22-21174, 22-21178-22-21180: What is Left of Fault-Based Liability in case of Harm Caused by a Defective Product?

a) Brief Summary of the Facts

From 1976 to 2009, a French pharmaceutical company, Servier, manufactured and marketed Benfluorex, a drug sold under the brand name Mediator. It was marketed as an antidiabetic, but was widely used off-label for obesity on prescription from general practitioners. Due to a risk of heart valve disease, the drug was withdrawn after a recommendation of the European Medicines Agency. While Servier denied any knowledge of Mediator's side effects, a criminal court fined the company € 2.7 million after finding it guilty of manslaughter, the drug being linked to the deaths of up to 2,000 patients. 28

Along with the criminal procedures (highly publicised, even in international media),[22] the legislature implemented a specific compensation procedure for patients suffering personal injury due to Mediator.[23] Servier being reluctant to grant compensation on the basis of negligence, the French compensation office for medical accidents, ONIAM, was requested to facilitate the award of damages, replacing the drug company in the case of a refusal to pay. 29

In all four cases, patients had received a compensation offer from Servier. Considering that the amounts proposed were insufficient, they sued the drug company 30

22 See eg *A Mullard*, Mediator scandal rocks French medical community, The Lancet 12 March 2011, 890.

23 Art L 1142-24-1-1142-24-8 of the French Public Health Code (Code de la santé publique). See in the English language *J Knetsch*, The French Medical Accident Compensation Scheme. A Critical Assessment of the Patients' Rights Act of 4 March 2002, in: D Bach-Golecka (ed), Compensation Schemes for Damages Caused by Healthcare and Alternatives to Court Proceedings (2021) 179, 184.

in tort in order to receive full compensation of their losses. However, according to art 1245-16 Civil Code (transposing art 10-1 of the 1985 EC Directive), the limitation period for actions based on product liability is three years, with the starting point being 'the day on which the plaintiff became aware, or should reasonably have become aware, of the damage, the defect and the identity of the producer'. As the claimants were aware of this information earlier, their action was time-barred. The central question was thus the possible legal basis of the compensation claim. The claimants argued that, even with an action being time-barred under the product liability regime, they could file a compensation claim on the grounds of fault according to the common rules of civil liability.

b) Judgment of the Court

31 The Versailles Court of Appeal dismissed the claimants' actions on the grounds that Servier's lack of vigilance was not distinct from a 'defect' in the sense of the 1985 EC Directive and that a claim based on such fault could not be admitted. The trial judges were simply applying the rule established by the CJEU in the 2002 *Gonzalez Sánchez* case interpreting art 13 of the Directive (the application of other contractual or non-contractual liability regimes is only possible if they are 'based on other grounds').[24]

32 The Court of Cassation quashed the Court of Appeal judgment holding that 'victims of a loss attributed to a defective product may hold liable the producer on the basis of art 1382 (now art 1240) if they prove that their loss results from a fault of the producer, such as keeping on the market a product whose defect is known or the violation of the duty of vigilance regarding the product's risk'.

c) Commentary[25]

33 Over the last twenty years, there has been a significant increase in product liability litigation before French civil courts, and it is expected that the introduction of dif-

24 CJEU 25.4.2002, C-183/00, *María Victoria González Sánchez v Medicina Asturiana SA*, ECLI:EU:C:2002:255.

25 See also *V Rivollier*, L'option entre le régime de responsabilité du fait des produits défectueux et le droit commun de la responsabilité délictuelle pour faute. Vers l'abandon de l'exigence d'une faute détachable du défaut du produit ? Dalloz 2024, 150; *C Radé*, La responsabilité du producteur résultant d'un défaut de suivi de ses produits, Responsabilité civile et assurances (Resp civ assur)

ferent types of class actions in 2014 and 2016 will accentuate this trend in the future. This explains why today, more than 25 years after the transposition act came into force, the Court of Cassation is still dealing with the interpretation of specific issues related to the product liability regime. In particular, the interrelationship with the common rules of civil liability has played an important role in recent case law.

In 2010, the Court of Cassation decided, in a product liability case, that liability for fault under art 1240 Civil Code could only be relied on if the claimant characterises 'a fault distinct from the defect'.[26] By doing so, it required claimants to identify a distinct conduct attributable to the producer, which could not qualify as a defect in the sense of the 1985 Directive. As the European and national case law takes a rather extensive approach to the concept of defect, it seemed almost impossible to base a compensation claim on fault-based liability. 34

In the present case, the First Civil Chamber overruled this restrictive approach and decided to open up the applicable liability regimes in cases in which a defective product caused loss. The Court of Cassation judges did not refer to a 'fault distinct from the defect' any more, implying that *any* fault may give rise to a compensation claim based on the common rules. While this interpretation is consistent with art 13 of the 1985 Product Liability Directive (which 'shall not affect any rights which an injured person may have according to the rules of the law of contractual or non-contractual liability'), it is not clear however to what extent it complies with the 2002 *Gonzalez Sánchez* case. Some authors argue that, from now on, a distinction should be made between 'simple defects' and 'defects with fault'. However, it is also clear that the broad definition of *faute* under French tort law makes it difficult to not qualify as a fault the simple fact of marketing a defective product. 35

The examples given in the judgment, that is 'keeping on the market a product whose defect is known (and) the violation of the duty of vigilance regarding the product's risk', refer to cases in which fault-based liability with extended limitation periods and without specific defences can be seen as a sanction of a particularly improper conduct. 36

Earlier in 2023, the Court of Cassation issued another judgment on the interrelationship of product liability with other liability and guarantee regimes, holding that the guarantee against latent defects (*garantie des vices cachés*) only applies to damage caused by the defective product itself, whereas the product liability regime may cover consequential losses.[27] The extensive case law of recent years shows the 37

2024, no 1, 35; *L Vitale*, Affaire Médiator: la Cour de cassation facilite l'action en justice de la victime d'un médicament défectueux, Gaz Pal 2024, no 2, 22.

26 Cour des Cassation, Chambre commerciale (Cass Com) 26 May 2010, no 08-18545.

27 Cass Civ 1, 19 April 2023, no 21-23726.

importance of this issue under French law, where the open approach of *faute* leads claimants to rely on the common rules of civil liability, more favourable to consumers, rather than on the EU law-based product liability regime. It is high time that the CJEU addresses this issue, especially since the draft directive of 2022 on a new product liability regime leaves the provisions unchanged on this point.

6. Personal Injury

a) Cour de cassation, Assemblée plénière (Cass Ass plén) 20 January 2023, nos 21-23947 and 20-23673: Compensation of Occupational Diseases; Interplay between Tort Law and Social Security Law in Cases of Gross Misconduct of the Employer

38 As in other continental jurisdictions, in France, the compensation of work-related accidents and diseases falls under a specific scheme carried out by semi-public health insurance funds (*caisses d'assurance maladie*). According to art L 422-1 of the Social Security Code, workers are not eligible to full compensation of their losses, but only to allowances on a fixed basis (*forfaitaire*) depending on the seriousness of the personal injury and the level of professional income.[28] Those allowances only (partially) cover loss of income in the form of daily benefits and invalidity pensions as well as health expenses. Workers are not even allowed to sue their employers in tort for additional damages since an 1898 Act, establishing a so-called 'concrete-solid deal' (*deal en béton*) between trade unions and employers, which was designed to smoothen working relations inside factories.

39 However, in the case of gross misconduct of an employer (*faute inexcusable de l'employeur*), the worker is entitled to an increased invalidity pension and to additional compensation covering non-economic losses, for example aesthetic loss (*préjudice esthétique*) or loss of enjoyment of life (*préjudice d'agrément*), provided that the Social Security allowances do not already cover those losses. Until the 2023 cases, judicial courts considered that invalidity pensions compensate, under certain circumstances, 'functional impairment' (*déficit fonctionnel permanent*),[29] precluding claimants from seeking damages under this head of loss. This solution was abandoned in the present judgments, allowing victims of work-related accidents and diseases to obtain more generous compensation. As there is a growing discrep-

---

28 For a presentation of this compensation scheme, see in particular *F G'Sell/I Veillard*, France, in: K Oliphant/G Wagner (eds), Employers' Liability and Workers' Compensation (2012) 203, 206–234.
29 A presentation of the different heads of losses in English is given by *Knetsch* (fn 7) no 336.

ancy with the principle of full reparation, more and more voices speak up for a comprehensive reform of the occupational injuries compensation scheme, encountering considerable resistance from employers' associations.[30]

b) Cour de cassation, Deuxième chambre civile (Cass Civ 2) 19 January 2023, nos 21-12264 and 21-12270: Calculation of the Economic Loss of a Child of Divorced Parents

In France, the calculation of compensation is a matter for the lower courts. However, the Court of Cassation can provide general guidelines. This is what happened in this case. A woman was murdered. She was the mother of two girls who lived with her. The father, who used to pay the mother a contribution towards the children's maintenance and education, took custody of the daughters following her death. The daughters then applied for compensation from the Guarantee Fund for Victims of Terrorism and Other Offences (*Fonds de garantie des victimes des actes de terrorisme et d'autres infractions*, FGTI) and a dispute arose over how to calculate the economic loss they had suffered. The Court of Cassation took this case as an opportunity to clarify how economic compensation due to children following the death of a divorced parent should be calculated. The Court of Cassation begins by laying down a general principle of equal treatment, holding that, 40

> 'the economic loss suffered by a child as a result of the death of one of their parents must be assessed without considering the separation or divorce of the parents, since these circumstances have no bearing on their obligation to contribute to the maintenance and education of the child or on the child's place of residence'.

It then offers a ready-to-use formula: 41

> 'in the event of the death of the parent with whom the child was living, the economic loss suffered by the child must be assessed by reference to the annual income of the parents before their death, taking into account, on the one hand, the proportion of their own consumption and the fixed costs they bore in their respective households and, on the other hand, the proportion of the surviving parent's income that could be devoted to the child'.

This is the first time that the Court of Cassation has ruled on this issue, which is crucial in today's society, where parental separation and divorce are commonplace. 42

---

30 See already *G Lyon-Caen*, Les victimes d'accidents du travail, victimes aussi d'une discrimination, Droit social 1990, 737–739.

c) Cour de cassation, Deuxième chambre civile (Cass Civ 2) 9 February 2023, no 21-21217: Calculation of the Economic Loss resulting from a Bodily Injury Suffered by an Entrepreneur

43 This decision of the Court of Cassation did not concern a liability action, but a claim for compensation brought by the victim of a private accident against his insurer under an 'accident of life' policy. Nevertheless, such compensation is based on the same principles as civil liability under ordinary law and the decision raises an interesting question, namely how to calculate the economic loss resulting from a bodily injury suffered by an entrepreneur. In this case, the victim of an accident had decided to keep his job but to take on an employee (a groom) to help him with the tasks he could no longer do alone. How should the losses suffered and/or the lost profit be calculated then? As for the loss of earnings (which is more than mere loss of a chance since it is a loss that is certain and not only hypothetical), the Court of Appeal set the damages at € 112,146. But then, the Court also granted € 737,000 for the economic impact (*retentissement économique*) corresponding to the additional costs incurred in hiring the employee to help him after the accident.

44 The Court of Cassation quashed the decision on the grounds that the same economic loss had been compensated twice. The decision reminds us that, although the French Court of Cassation normally refuses to control the amount of compensation awarded by judges (as it is a factual and not a legal question), it occasionally invokes principles such as full compensation without loss or profit to the victim (cited in the decision) when it deems it necessary to review a compensation award that appears to unjustly enrich the victim or, on the contrary, to not cover all the victim's losses.[31] In the present case, the risk of overcompensation was all the greater because the hourly cost of hiring the employee turned out to be much higher than the victim's own loss of future earnings. In such cases, is it legitimate to allow the victim to choose the most expensive solution to remedy the damage? In the absence of a mitigation duty under French law, the answer is clearly yes.[32] Nevertheless, the compensation of both measures seemed, indeed, excessive.

---

31 See eg *Z Jacquemin*, La réparation sans perte, ni profit selon la Cour de cassation ou l'art de transformer une maxime en instrument de contrôle, Revue des contrats (RDC) 2019, 187.

32 The Civil Liability Reform Bill 2017 considers the introduction of a mitigation rule, but excludes it for personal injury (art 1263).

C. Literature

1. Doctoral Theses and Monographs

B Darmois, Crise de l'expression au public en ligne et responsabilité civile extra-contractuelle [Civil liability and crisis of online speech] (Paris, Mare & Martin 2023) coll Bibliothèque des thèses, préface *M-É Ancel* 45

A Hacène-Kebir, La co-responsabilité dans les droits de la responsabilité civile et administrative [Joint tortfeasors in civil and State liability] (Paris, Mare & Martin 2023) coll Bibliothèque des thèses, préface *C Ophèle* 46

G Wester, Les principes de la réparation confrontés au dommage corporel [Personal injuries and the principles of compensation for damage] (Paris, LGDJ 2023) coll Bibliothèque de droit privé, préface *S Porchy-Simon* 47

2. Textbooks

P Brun, Responsabilité civile extracontractuelle [Extra-contractual tort law] (Paris, LexisNexis 6th edn 2023) 48

P le Tourneau (ed), Droit de la responsabilité et des contrats [Tort law and contracts] (Paris, Dalloz 13th edn 2023) coll Dalloz Action 49

C Quézel-Ambrunaz, Le droit du dommage corporel. Caractérisation, évaluation et indemnisation des préjudices [Personal injury law] (Paris, LGDJ 2nd edn 2023) coll Avocat & pratique professionnelle, préface *P Brun* 50

3. Symposium Proceedings and Collective Works

O Gout/J Knetsch (eds), Covid-19 et droit de l'indemnisation – La prise en charge des dommages liés à la crise sanitaire [Covid-19 and the law of compensation: the reparation of losses related to the health crisis] Proceedings of 19 – 20 November 2022 Franco-Japanese Conference at the Tokyo University, Cahiers Louis Josserand 2023, no 3 51

F Guiomard (ed), Le droit social et les désordres de la réparation [Social security law and the chaos of compensation for damage] Proceedings of 30 September–1 October 2022 Conference of the Association française de droit du travail, Droit social 2023, no 4, 284 – 329 52

L Mayaux/S Porchy-Simon (eds), Les grands risques: aspects d'assurance et de responsabilité [Large risks: insurance and civil liability aspects] Proceedings of 53

7 April 2023 Conference at the Lyon 3 University, Revue générale de droit des assurances 2023, no 9, 33–72 and no 10, 22–40

54 *L Morlet-Haïdara/S Hocquet-Berg/T James* (eds), Le risque médical entre solidarité et assurance 20 ans après la loi About du 30 décembre 2002 [Medical risk between insurance and national solidarity 20 years after the About law of 30 December 2002] Proceedings of 12 January 2023 Conference at the Paris-Cité University, Resp civ assur 2023, dossier 15–25

55 *J Travard* (ed), La protection des droits fondamentaux par le recours en responsabilité [Protection of fundamental rights through tort litigation] Proceedings of 18 June 2021 Conference at the Lyon 3 University (Paris, Mare & Martin 2023) coll Droit public

4. Articles

56 *M Bacache*, Regard civiliste sur la loi du 27 mars 2017 relative au devoir de vigilance des sociétés mères et entreprises donneuses d'ordre [A private law view on the Act of 27 March 2017 on the corporate due diligence duty of parent companies] Mélanges en l'honneur d'Isabelle Urbain-Parleani (Paris, Dalloz 2023) 253–280

57 *J-S Borghetti*, L'adaptation du droit des contrats spéciaux à la réforme à venir du droit de la responsabilité civile [The adaptation of the rules regarding specific contracts to the future tort law reform] C-É Bucher/M-A Daillant (eds), La réforme du droit des contrats spéciaux (Paris, Dalloz 2023) 69–78

58 *C Bloch*, De l'application de la responsabilité du fait des produits au dommage causé au produit fini par un de ses composants défectueux [The application of product liability rules in cases of damage to property caused by a defective component] Homme de foi, homme de droit. Mélanges en l'honneur d'Alain Sériaux (Paris, Mare & Martin 2023) 39–46

59 *T Bonneau*, La responsabilité de l'ESMA en raison d'un dommage causé par un défaut de surveillance [The liability of the European Securities and Markets Authority for losses caused by a lack of supervision] Mélanges en l'honneur d'Isabelle Urbain-Parleani (Paris, Dalloz 2023) 413–422

60 *W Bourdon*, Les nouvelles figures de la responsabilité : des outils précieux face à l'obsession de l'irresponsabilité [New liability patterns: useful tools in response to the obsession of irresponsibility] Cheminer avec Mireille Delmas-Marty. Mélanges ouverts en l'honneur de Mireille Delmas-Marty (Paris, Mare & Martin 2023) 517–522

W Chaiehloudj, La percée de la responsabilité civile dans le droit des pratiques anticoncurrentielles [The breakthrough of civil liability in antitrust law] RTD civ 2023, no 1, 21 – 43 61

A Danis-Fatôme, La sanction de la vigilance par la responsabilité civile [Civil liability and the sanction of diligence] La Semaine Juridique. Edition entreprise (JCP E) 2023, no 31 – 35, 44 – 49 62

A Danis-Fatôme, La porosité entre compliance et responsabilité civile : progrès ou régression? [The permeability between compliance and civil liability: progress or setback?] États de droit. Mélanges en l'honneur de Dany Cohen (Paris, Dalloz 2023) 205 – 223 63

D Dibie, Le contentieux civil de la réparation des dommages numériques en matière de santé [Tort litigation for digital losses in healthcare] Dalloz IP/IT 2023, no 3, 151 – 154 64

T Duchesne, La responsabilité pour faute de l'actionnaire [Fault-based liability of stakeholders] Revue trimestrielle de droit financier 2023, no 3, 57– 61 65

M Eliphe, La responsabilité civile de l'employeur sur le fondement de son obligation de sécurité: contractuelle ou délictuelle? [Civil liability of employers under their obligation to provide safety to their employees: is it contractual or extra-contractual?] Revue de droit du travail 2023, no 4, 355 – 366 66

A Fournier, La responsabilité des constructeurs et réputés constructeurs dans l'avant-projet de réforme du droit des contrats spéciaux [The liability of builders and quasi-builders in the draft reform of rules regarding specific contracts] Revue Lamy Droit civil 2023, no 218, 47– 52 67

G Gil, La responsabilité civile du géomètre-expert [The liability of land surveyors] Annales des loyers 2023, no 6, 27– 37 68

F Gonthier, Les caractères du préjudice réparable [The prerequisites of reparable loss] Mélanges en l'honneur du Professeur Philippe Conte (Paris LexisNexis, 2023) 399 – 410 69

L Grynbaum, La future 'Législation sur l'IA' à l'aune de la responsabilité civile [The future AI Act in the light of tort law] JCP G 2023, no 28, 1349 – 1352 70

M Keim-Bagot/J Knetsch, (Ré)concilier les inconciliables. Regards croisés sur la réparation des AT-MP [Reconciling the irreconcilable: confronting views on the compensation of workplace accidents and occupational diseases] Droit social 2023, no 7– 8, 629 – 636 71

J Knetsch, Que restera-t-il de l'obligation de sécurité de l'employeur après la réforme de la responsabilité civile? [What will be left of the employer's duty to provide safety to its employees after the tort law reform?] Itinéraires d'un juriste. Mélanges en l'honneur de Marc Véricel (Paris, Mare & Martin 2023) 231 – 247 72

J Knetsch, L'influence du droit des personnes sur la responsabilité civile : une révolution silencieuse? [The influence of the 'law of persons' on tort law: a quiet 73 revolution?] in: B Teyssié (ed), Les métamorphoses du droit des personnes (Paris, LexisNexis 2023) 401–426

74 *C Mangematin*, Responsabilité du fait des produits défectueux et intelligence artificielle : une proposition presque parfaite [Product liability and artificial intelligence: an almost perfect proposal] Resp civ assur 2023, no 6, étude 8

75 *B Parance/J Rochfeld*, Discussions sur les conditions des actions en conformité au devoir de vigilance [Reflections on the prerequisites of due diligence litigation] JCP G 2023, no 46, 1983–1987

76 *B Plessix*, La responsabilité administrative de demain : vers un dépassement de sa fonction réparatrice? [State liability of tomorrow: overcoming the sole compensatory function?] Droit administratif 2023, no 10, 67–71

77 *S Porchy-Simon*, Le dommage corporel face au temps [Personal injury and the passage of time] Resp civ assur 2023, no 9, étude 10

78 *C Quézel-Ambrunaz*, Et si l'arrêt Blanco avait été différent? Réflexions uchroniques sur la dévolution du contentieux de la responsabilité de la puissance publique aux juridictions civiles [What if the Blanco case had had another outcome? Uchronial remarks about the jurisdiction of civil courts for State liability cases] in: F Blanco/S Gilbert/A Jacquemet-Gauché (eds), Autour de l'arrêt Blanco (Paris, Dalloz 2023) 325–334

79 *V Rivollier*, Le droit commun de la réparation comme complément au régime AT-MP en cas de faute inexcusable [Common rules of civil liability as an additional layer to the workplace accident and occupational disease compensation scheme in cases of gross negligence] Resp civ assur 2023, no 5, étude 6

80 *A Tardif*, Responsabilité civile et rupture du couple [Civil liability and relationship breakdown] Droit de la famille 2023, no 3, étude 5

81 *L Thibierge*, Perte de chance: un peu de sérieux? [Loss of chance: taking it more seriously?] Revue de jurisprudence de droit des affaires 2023, no 6, 7–15.

Wolfgang Wurmnest and Nicolas Riemann

XII. Germany

A. Legislation

1. Implementing Representative Actions

1 While no relevant legislative developments on tort law itself can be reported for 2023, it is worth noting that the German legislature strengthened the enforcement of consumers' rights. A new type of 'collective redress mechanism' was adopted when implementing the Directive on representative actions for the protection of the collective interests of consumers.[1] The adoption was a last-minute endeavour in October 2023[2] after the European Commission had announced it was considering initiating infringement proceedings against Germany for failure to implement the Directive.[3]

2 The Directive aims at a harmonisation of collective redress. To implement it, the German *Verbandsklagenrichtlinienumsetzungsgesetz* created a new statute, the *Verbraucherrechtedurchsetzungsgesetz* (VDuG) and further amended pre-existing procedural rules. As outlined in § 1 (1) VDuG, there are two types of *Verbandsklagen* (representative actions) under German law: firstly, the *Abhilfeklage* (action for redress) and, secondly, the *Musterfestellungsklage* (model declaratory relief). Both proceedings must be brought before the *Oberlandesgericht* (Higher Regional Court, OLG) at the defendant's place of business.

3 The so-called *Abhilfeklage* shall enable consumer organisations to bundle multiple claims by consumers and small businesses seeking compensation from traders (*Unternehmer*) regarding contractual disputes or matters of tort. This is a significant improvement for collective redress in Germany which so far was essentially based on the *Musterfeststellungsklage*. The latter did not help consumers extensively when attempting to enforce their rights as consumer organisations could only sue for declaratory relief on certain disputed matters. As a consequence, each registered consumer had to lodge a follow-on action in their own right for compensation after the consumer organisation had clarified certain

1 Directive (EU) 2020/1828 of 25 November 2020 on representative actions for the protection of the collective interests of consumers [2020] Official Journal (OJ) L 409/1.

2 Verbandsklagenrichtlinienumsetzungsgesetz, Bundesgesetzblatt (BGBl) I 2023 No 272.

3 Announcement 27 January 2023 by the Commission <https://ec.europa.eu/commission/presscorner/detail/en/inf_23_262>.

https://doi.org/10.1515/9783111376721-013

key aspects of the litigation in the *Musterfeststellungsverfahren.* The newly introduced *Abhilfeklage* allows consumer organisations to sue for compensation that is then paid out to the persons registered. In other words, to the individuals on behalf of which the organisation became active or which joined respectively.

4 Whereas the European Directive limited the scope of representative actions to the application to those instruments of EU law listed in its Annex I (Directive on product liability, the General Data Protection Regulation, etc), the German legislature went further. According to § 1 (1) VDuG, a representative action is permitted in all private law disputes that involve claims of multiple consumers against a trader ('In bürgerlichen Rechtsstreitigkeiten, die Ansprüche und Rechtsverhältnisse einer Vielzahl von Verbrauchern gegen einen Unternehmer betreffen ….'). Thus, generally speaking, all private law disputes are covered, which broadens the scope significantly. In addition, small companies, and not only consumers, may benefit from this form of collective redress. Small businesses are considered to be equivalent to consumers if they have fewer than ten employees and an annual turnover or an annual balance of not more than € 2 million.[4] However, this equality between consumers and small businesses only applies from a procedural perspective. On its merits, the law often confines special rights to consumers only. The latter do not benefit from consumer law protection rules.

5 Only qualified consumer associations named in a list (cf § 4 UKlaG) that do not receive more than 5 % of their funding from businesses[5] are entitled to bring representative actions.[6] The Federal Ministry of Justice (*Bundesministerium der Justiz*) publishes the list of qualified associations online.[7] Furthermore, there is a consumer quorum determining that at least 50 consumers must be affected by the representative action.[8]

6 A financing of the collective action by third parties is possible to a certain extent. The German legislature has established certain limitations in § 4 (2) VDuG to prevent conflicts of interests and to avoid incentives for actions that are deemed to be unfair. The most important restriction is that third party funders may not re-

---

4 Cf § 1 (2) VDuG.

5 This restriction is derived from recital 25 of the Directive, which states: 'They [the qualified consumer associations] should be independent and should not be influenced by persons other than consumers who have an economic interest in the bringing of a representative action, in particular by traders or hedge funds, including in the event of funding by third parties.'

6 Cf § 2 (1) VDuG.

7 This list can be accessed via <https://www.bundesjustizamt.de/DE/Themen/Verbraucherrechte/VerbandsklageregisterMusterfeststellungsklagenregister/Verbandsklagenregister/Verbandsklagen/Verbandsklagen_node.html>.

8 Cf § 4 (1) VDuG.

ceive more than 10 % of the compensation that was awarded to the consumers or small businesses.[9]

The *Abhilfeklage* constitutes a new type of proceeding within the German civil procedure system. It can be divided into two sub-groups. 7

First, a claim can be brought on behalf of named consumers. Hence, in the case of success, the defendant will need to pay the awarded amount directly to the named consumers (and/or small businesses).[10] In light of the wording, this model is limited to monetary claims.[11] However, the purpose of this model seems to enable judgments relating to outcomes that may be generalised such as replacement of a specified product, even though that was not made clear during the drafting process.[12] It remains to be seen if courts will stick to the wording or will consider an analogous application. 8

Second, the consumer association can also sue traders on behalf of unnamed consumers (and/or small businesses). The persons benefitting from this legal action will later be determined by a set of general criteria laid down by the court. Therefore, this model consists of more than one proceeding. In a first trial, the court must award a judgment in favour of consumers. The suing association and the defendant shall then negotiate a settlement to fulfil consumers' claims.[13] If these negotiations fail, the court will decide on the fulfilment, which then will lead to the second phase, the implementation procedure.[14] This procedure aims to identify affected consumers and settle their claims. Some sections of the implementation procedure are modelled on insolvency proceedings and distribution proceedings under maritime law.[15] The implementation proceedings are led by an appointed trustee who is controlled by a court.[16] 9

Consumers must join the representative action by registering their claims with a public register. However, consumers may also withdraw from the register and proceed with their claims individually. Withdrawal as well as registering are permitted up to three weeks once the oral hearing in first instance has ended. A valid 10

9 Cf § 4 (2) VDuG.

10 § 16 (1) 2 VDuG.

11 *G Bayat*, Die Verbandsklage und das Umsetzungsverfahren, Zeitschrift für Internationales Wirtschaftsrecht (IWRZ) 2023, 258, 261.

12 *Bayat*, IWRZ 2023, 258, 261.

13 § 17 VDuG.

14 § 22 ff VDuG.

15 *Bayat*, IWRZ 2023, 258, 262.

16 Cf § 30 VDuG.

registration of a claim in the public register suspends the limitation period for the claim.[17]

11 In sum, Germany has considerably strengthened the enforcement of consumers' rights. Nonetheless, the new type of collective redress will compete with so-called 'cession models' in which consumers use specialised legal companies to claim damages. This model is more open to financing by third parties while still being able to bundle claims against the defendant.[18] In recent years, the cession model has gained much importance especially in the area of flight passenger rights.

2. Federal Ministry for Digitalisation and Transport will not Initiate Proceedings against Former Minister

12 After several investigations including a committee of inquiry in the *Bundestag* (German parliament) and a closer look at criminal charges by a public prosecutor,[19] the Federal Ministry for Digitalisation and Transport has finally decided not to claim damages from the former German Federal Minister of Transport, Andreas Scheuer. Scheuer implemented a road toll system for cars in Germany which – despite massive doubts on its legality – submitted only non-German residents to pay for road usage (whereas car owners based in Germany would be 'paying' by their vehicle taxation). In 2019, the European Court of Justice (CJEU) had rendered this scheme unlawful.[20] However, by then Scheuer had already signed contracts with the designated road toll operator. These contracts had to be cancelled after the judgment resulting in a € 243 million settlement at the expense of the German taxpayers.[21] Additionally, Germany had to pay more than € 26 million for legal and expert fees caused by the 'road toll disaster'.[22]

13 After the election in 2021, the new Minister commissioned an expert opinion from a Berlin-based law firm on the question of the personal liability of his pre-

---

17 § 204a (1) no 3, no 4 BGB.

18 *Bayat*, IWRZ 2023, 258, 265.

19 In Berlin, the 'Staatsanwaltschaft' initiated investigations against Scheuer regarding false testimony in the committee of inquiry.

20 CJEU 18.6.2019, C-591/17, *Austria v Germany*, ECLI:EU:C:2019:504.

21 Cf Gutachten zu Haftungsansprüchen gegenüber Bundesminister a. D. Andreas Scheuer wegen der von der Bundesrepublik Deutschland zu tragenden Entschädigungszahlungen aus dem Betreibervertrag zur Erhebung der Infrastrukturabgabe ('Pkw-Maut') – legal opinion commissioned by the Federal Ministry for Digitalisation and Transport, para 21 (<https://bmdv.bund.de/SharedDocs/DE/Anlage/K/gutachten-haftung-maut.pdf?__blob=publicationFile>).

22 Schriftliche Frage Nr 71, 18 November 2022, cf Bundestags-Drucksachen (BT-Drs) 20/4515, 44.

decessor for the damage caused. The expert opinion argued that the federal government does not have the right to claim damages from Scheuer based on the rules for State liability because these rules were introduced for claims of a third party against the (public) employer of civil servants and not for public authorities itself. Notwithstanding that Scheuer was as Federal Minister somewhat 'employed' (ministers are in an administrative relationship [*Amtsverhältnis*] to the Federal State)[23] opening him arguably up for contractual liability according to § 280 BGB, the legal opinion counselled against legal proceedings given the substantial litigation risks and doubts about the enforceability of a potential award against the former minister in light of the high amounts at stake. Therefore, no proceedings were initiated.

Against this background, a debate has started on the basis and limitations of civil liability of ministers for their professional conduct.[24] So far, only civil servants may be held liable in case of breach of duties. Ministers can merely be judged politically. Solely, the Federal State of Bavaria – Scheuer's home state – provides for a special ministerial liability scheme since 1961.[25] It is, however, very unlikely that the federal law will change in the near future as the risk of liability might also deter politicians from taking decisions. 14

B. Cases

1. BGH 17 January 2023, VI ZR 203/22:[26] Contributory Negligence of the Keeper of a Car that is Owned by the Financing Bank

a) Brief Summary of the Facts

Two cars were involved in an everyday accident: The claimant had parked his car in a car park. When reversing his car in order to drive to the car park's exit lane, 15

---

23 Cf § 1 Bundesministergesetz (Act governing Federal Ministers).

24 *J Lindner*, Schadensersatzpflicht für Politiker? Zeitschrift für Rechtspolitik (ZRP) 2023, 161; *W Bader*, Verfassungsblog <https://verfassungsblog.de/scheuers-missgluckte-pkw-maut/>.

25 Cf art 7 (2) Bayerisches Ministergesetz (Act governing Bavarian Ministers).

26 ECLI:DE:BGH:2023:170123UVIZR203.22.0; Neue Juristische Wochenschrift (NJW) 2023, 1361; recht und schaden (r+s) 2023, 265; Zeitschrift für Bank- und Kapitalmarktrecht (BKR) 2023, 401; Wertpapiermitteilungen (WM) 2023, 422; BeckRS 2023, 2055.

he collided with another car that was insured by the defending insurer. The latter car was also reversing out of a parking space.

16 At the time of the accident, the claimant was the keeper (*Halter*) and driver of the vehicle, the purchase of which he had financed via a bank. To secure the loan, he had transferred the property of the vehicle to the bank (*Sicherungsübereignung*). In addition, the claimant had ceded all claims arising out of future car accidents to the bank and the bank had entitled the claimant to claim damages resulting from such accidents on behalf of the bank in his own name. Hence, the legal owner of the car was the bank, but the claimant was entitled to use the car and to claim compensation on behalf of the bank in case the car was damaged in an accident.

17 The lower courts' judgments assumed that both, the claimant and the driver of the car that was insured with the defendant, acted negligently and therefore the defendant should only bear 50 % of the compensable costs. The claim was, amongst others, based on § 823 (1) BGB as the bank's property was damaged.

18 The dispute between the parties before the *Bundesgerichtshof* (BGH) essentially centres on the question as to which claims are claims of the bank and which claims are claims of the car's keeper and on the question to what extent the contributory negligence of the claimant as collateral provider reduces the bank's claim for damage to its property resulting from the accident.

b) Judgment of the Court

19 The *Bundesgerichtshof* upholds the finding by the *Landgericht* (LG) with regard to the claimant's contributory negligence. The court approves the application of the traffic rules as laid down in § 9 (5) and § 1 (2) Road Traffic Regulation (*Straßenverkehrsordnung*, StVO) to driving in a public car park (even though it is not a proper road). While reversing his car, the claimant had to drive in such a way that he could stop the vehicle immediately, if necessary. Due to the circumstances in a car park, he had to expect at any time that other vehicles would cross his way. He, therefore, had to drive at low speed in order to be able to react swiftly to stop his car.

20 The *Bundesgerichtshof* reiterates that the bank's collateral property constitutes genuine property within the meaning of § 823 (1) BGB. Therefore, the bank has a claim against the defendant based on the fault-based liability rules of the BGB as well as under § 7 Road Traffic Act (*Straßenverkehrsgesetz*, StVG), which establishes a strict liability of the car's keeper. With regard to the claim under § 7 StVG, the claimant's contributory negligence cannot be attributed via § 17 (2) StVG, as the bank itself is not liable in accordance with the provisions of

the StVG (for lack of any breach of the traffic rules). Thus, the application of § 17 (2) StVG is precluded. The contributory negligence of the claimant must, however, be attributed to the bank via § 9 StVG which states: 'If the injured party was at fault when the damage occurred, the provisions of § 254 BGB shall apply with the proviso that the fault of the person who has actual control over the damaged object is deemed to be the fault of the person who has actually suffered the damage'.[27]

There is, however, no corresponding rule for attributing the claimant's contributory negligence to the bank for the claim under § 823 (1) BGB. In a previous judgment, the *Bundesgerichtshof* had already held that § 9 StVG is not applicable to cases of fault-based liability under the BGB (neither directly nor analogously).[28] Accordingly, this rule cannot be relied upon. Also, an attribution according to § 254 BGB was excluded. In contrast to § 9 StVG, the latter rule does not attribute the fault of the party exercising actual control over the (damaged) object to the injured party. In addition, an attribution via § 254 (2) 2 BGB fails as the claimant was not the bank's agent (*Erfüllungsgehilfe*) within the meaning of § 278 BGB when driving the car. Therefore, the collateral taker (bank) can claim full compensation for the damaged car from the defendant without having to deduct a certain amount for the contributory negligence by the collateral provider (driver). 21

The fact that it was not the bank claiming damages but the (negligent) collateral provider on behalf of the bank does not alter this finding. The *Bundesgerichtshof* held that the *dolo agit* defence does not apply to the case at hand. Although § 242 BGB prevents the enforcement of a claim if the claimant would have to return what he obtained from the debtor immediately thereafter, the *Bundesgerichtshof* underscores that it is the bank that has the claim against the tortfeasor even if he authorises the keeper (collateral provider) to act in the bank's place. In other words, the bank's claim is not affected by the tortfeasor's claim against the claimant. 22

---

27 § 9 StVG states: 'Hat bei der Entstehung des Schadens ein Verschulden des Verletzten mitgewirkt, so finden die Vorschriften des § 254 des Bürgerlichen Gesetzbuchs mit der Maßgabe Anwendung, dass im Fall der Beschädigung einer Sache das Verschulden desjenigen, welcher die tatsächliche Gewalt über die Sache ausübt, dem Verschulden des Verletzten gleichsteht.'

28 BGH NJW 2007, 3120, no 11 ff.

c) Commentary[29]

23 Transferring property of vehicles to secure loans is a common way to finance the purchase of vehicles in Germany. The concept of *Sicherungsübereignung* leads, however, to rather complicated legal issues resulting from everyday car accidents. The judgment deals with typical issues with regard to cars that were transferred to a financier as collateral in the form of a *Sicherungsübereignung* and is also of importance for car leasing models. It covers complex issues of German civil law ranging from tort law, collateral property, joint and several liability, and the *dolo agit* defence. Three points of the judgment are of particular importance.

24 First, the collateral taker's (ie the bank's) rights to the collateral (in this case the property of the vehicle) do not relate to all claims arising from the damaging event such as a car accident. Therefore, claimants that are keepers of the car whose ownership belongs to a third party have to carefully distinguish which heads of damages are claims in their own right (for example, the cost of renting a car during the time in which the damaged car is under repair, expert costs to assess the damage, or claims for personal injury) and which heads of damages are claimed on behalf of the collateral taker. The latter merely has the right to claim damages flowing from the damage to the car itself, unless the keeper has ceded his claim to the collateral taker, which rarely happens in practice.

25 Second, even though it seems odd at first glance that the keeper's contributory negligence can only be attributed to the bank for the claim based on strict liability and not for the fault-based claim under § 823 (1) BGB, this difference can be explained: § 9 StVG and § 254 BGB have a different wording and an analogous application of § 9 StVG is not permissible given that the legislature has not opted for a different wording by accident (so that there is no '*planwidrige Regelungslücke*' which would allow an analogy). The difference laid down in the two attribution rules reflects the varying liability regimes they were made for. § 9 StVG was introduced to soften the effect of strict liability, as do the liability caps laid down in § 12 StVG, whereas § 254 BGB was drafted for fault-based claims, as the *Bundesgerichtshof* had already pointed out in a previous judgment.[30] Therefore, the bank is entitled to claim full compensation for claims under § 823 (1) BGB with regard to the damaged car. This is, however, only the case for claims of the collateral taker (ie the bank) against the defendant. As far as the keeper has ceded his claims to the bank,

---

29 See the case notes by *U Gail*, NJW 2023, 1368; *M Vollmerhausen*, BKR 2023, 407; *D Figgener/ F Quaisser*, NJW-Spezial 2023, 266; *G Toussaint*, Fachdienst Zivilverfahrensrecht (FD-ZVR) 2023, 456118; *H Eimler*, Immobilien- und Baurecht (IBR) 2023, 220; *J Oechsler*, Wirtschafts- und Bankrecht 2023, 204.

30 BGH NJW 2007, 3120, no 11 ff.

and the bank asserts these claims (which are claims of the keeper), the defendant can invoke all defences that he could have invoked vis-à-vis the keeper (cf § 404 BGB).

Third, the *Bundesgerichtshof* has clarified to what extent the *dolo agit* defence flowing from § 242 BGB can be invoked against the bank's claim that is asserted by the claimant. Against the background that the claimant acts on behalf of the bank and the latter is entitled to the full amount due to the lack of a rule that attributes the claimant's contributory negligence for claims under § 823 (1) BGB to the bank, the defendant argued that paying full compensation to the claimant would violate the principle that no one shall be entitled to claim a sum of money or an object that ought to be returned immediately thereafter. The defendant pointed out that the keeper of the car and the defendant are – as they both negligently contributed to the car's damage – jointly and severally liable vis-à-vis the bank (which is the car owner). If two tortfeasors are jointly and severally liable, the injured person can claim the entire amount of damages from one of the tortfeasors (cf § 426 (1) BGB). This tortfeasor can then recover from the other tortfeasor the amount of damage caused by his negligence (cf § 426 (2) BGB). In the case at hand, the claimant's contributory negligence was set at 50 %. The defendant pointed out that if one of the tortfeasors acts on behalf of the injured person – as the car's keeper did on behalf of the bank – the other tortfeasor – the defendant in the case at hand – can – after having paid the entire amount of damages to the keeper – recover half of the sum due to the keeper's contributory negligence. The defendant argued in line with some scholars and lower courts[31] that in such a scenario the defendant should be able to raise the *dolo agit* defence so that the keeper cannot claim full compensation on behalf of the bank given that he would have to return 50 % of the sum to the defendant after having received it. 26

The *Bundesgerichtshof* rightly rejected the application of the *dolo agit* defence. It correctly pointed out that the car's keeper as collateral provider and the bank as collateral taker are two distinct (legal) persons and that the bank has an interest in obtaining full compensation. If the bank claimed damages from the defendant in court, the defendant could not rely on the *dolo agit* defence. The fact that the bank entitled the keeper to act on its behalf does not alter this finding, as it is still the bank's claim and the bank does not owe anything to the defendant. 27

31 OLG Nürnberg 19 July 2017, BeckRS 2017, 145249; *F Pardey*, Haftungsverteilung bei Unfallschäden eines geleasten oder sonst fremdfinanzierten Kfz, Straßenverkehrsrecht (SVR) 2019, 7, 9 f.

28 As a consequence, a counter action (*Widerklage*) needs to be lodged to recover any amount from the tortfeasor (the keeper) under § 426 (2) BGB.[32] This will limit the risk that the collateral provider will default payment.

2. BGH 24 January 2023, VI ZR 1234/20:[33] Keeper's Liability for Explosion of a Removed Vehicle Battery

a) Brief Summary of the Facts

29 An electric scooter was taken to a garage for inspection. An employee of the garage removed the battery and began to charge it. Once he realised that the battery was heating up, he disconnected it from the power supply and placed it on the floor to cool down. Nonetheless, the battery exploded and set the entire building on fire. The building insurer indemnified the house owner and claimed compensation from the liability insurer of the electric scooter.

b) Judgment of the Court

30 In this judgment, the *Bundesgerichtshof* had to decide on the scope of the liability under § 7 (1) StVG, which submits the keeper (*Halter*) to a strict liability for damage caused 'during the operation' ('beim Betrieb') of the vehicle. The *Bundesgerichtshof* tends in general to interpret the term 'during the operation' broadly, but held in this judgment that it does not cover damage arising from batteries that were entirely removed from the vehicle.

31 First, the *Bundesgerichtshof* recalls the basic considerations of strict liability under § 7 (1) StVG and the term 'during the operation'. It is decisive for liability that the vehicle must have had an impact on the event causing the damage. Therefore, a close local and temporal nexus between the cause of the damage and the process of operating the vehicle is needed to impose strict liability on the vehicle's keeper. As pointed out in previous cases, strict liability can also apply if a vehicle was brought into a garage for inspection or repair and burst into flames causing

32 *U Gail*, NJW 2023, 1368.

33 ECLI:DE:BGH:2023:240123UVIZR1234.20.0; NJW 2023, 2279; BeckRS 2023, 3235; Monatsschrift für deutsches Recht (MDR) 2023, 563; Versicherungsrecht (VersR) 2023, 538.

damage.[34] One of the specific consequences and intentions of the strict liability under § 7 (1) StVG is to indemnify victims whose life, health or property are impaired by a vehicle in operation. Thus, from a legal perspective, there is no difference whether a fire occurs before, during or after the vehicle was driven. Otherwise, cases in which solely a technical defect causes damage might not be covered.

There are, however, limits to strict liability if the damage was caused when the 32
car was not 'in operation'. In the case at hand, the *Bundesgerichtshof* held that the damage was caused by an incident that had no local and temporal nexus to the battery and the vehicle's operation. The battery had already been completely removed and was not connected to the vehicle anymore in any other way. Thus, the battery itself was not part of the vehicle and could not be part of its operation. That the battery was once part of the scooter is not sufficient to construct a link between the damage and the operation of the scooter.

c) Commentary[35]

The judgment is a welcome clarification of the term 'during the operation' of a ve- 33
hicle according to § 7 (1) StVG for cases in which batteries cause damage. The *Bundesgerichtshof* confirms its reading that this term must be interpreted in a broad manner. Damage caused by batteries that are connected to the vehicle fall within the scope of § 7 (1) StVG. That a vehicle is stationed in a garage for repair or inspection at the time the damage is caused does, therefore, not exonerate the keeper from liability under § 7 (1) StVG. However, if the battery is completely detached from the vehicle and there is no other nexus to it, one cannot argue that the damage was caused 'during the operation' of the vehicle. The *Bundesgerichtshof* pointed out that this case is similar to the case where the battery has not even been built in, for example if the damage occurs when the battery was being charged before being connected to the vehicle. This argument is convincing.

However, if the battery had been removed from the vehicle but had still been 34
connected to it via cables when causing the damage, it seems most likely that the *Bundesgerichtshof* would have held that the damage was caused during the operation of the scooter under § 7 (1) StVG.

34 BGH 20 October 2020 – VI ZR 158/19, NJW 2021, 1157; VI ZR 374/19, BeckRS 2020, 31471; VI ZR 319/18, MDR 2021, 232. BGH 20 October 2020 – VI ZR 374/19, BeckRS 2020, 31471; BGH 20 October 2020 – VI ZR 319/18, MDR 2021, 232.

35 See the case notes by *N Biller-Bomhardt*, Neue Zeitschrift für Verkehrsrecht (NZV) 2023, 314; *D Figgener/F Quaisser*, NJW-Spezial 2023, 169; *O Kääb*, Fachdienst Straßenverkehrsrecht 2023, 456338; *H Schüle*, r+s 2023, 567; *P Steinert*, SVR 2023, 180.

35 The judgment shows that the reach of the 'operation requirement' to cases of electromobility is still not clarified entirely. The *Bundesgerichtshof* added some clarity. However, it can be predicted that this judgment was not the last judgment on the scope of § 7 (1) StVG regarding damage caused by batteries. The judgment does not contain any indications as to where to draw the line between removed but still connected (eg wireless) batteries and those that are completely disconnected.

3. OLG Hamm 15 August 2023, 7 U 19/23:[36] No Monetary Compensation after Facebook Data Leak

a) Brief Summary of the Facts

36 The claimant, a user of the Facebook network, claims, amongst others, monetary compensation from Meta, the operator of Facebook, for violations of various data protection rules that led to a very significant 'scraping' incident. As a consequence, data of around 500 million users was published in the so-called 'darknet' in 2021. The data published included real names and telephone numbers of Facebook users. Unknown persons had collected this information over a period of time, initially by utilising Facebook's search functions. At that time, it was possible to identify users via the search function by entering a telephone number, even though the display of the user's telephone number was not activated. The 'scrapers' exploited this leak by generating telephone numbers and retrieving data for the purpose of storing. After realising this leak, Facebook sought to modify this function before finally restricting it significantly.

37 The claimant sued Meta for non-pecuniary loss and claimed at least € 1,000 arguing that the violations of various data protection rules caused 'feelings of loss of control, being watched and helplessness'. The *Landgericht* dismissed the claim as the claimant had not substantially pleaded nor proven the occurrence of non-pecuniary loss.

36 ECLI:DE:OLGHAM:2023:0815.7U19.23.00; Gewerblicher Rechtsschutz und Urheberrecht (GRUR) 2023, 1791 = Computer und Recht (CR) 2023, 655.

b) Judgment of the Court

The *Oberlandesgericht* Hamm upholds the finding that the claimant was not entitled to damages. Even though the defendant had breached the law, the claimant had not pleaded and proven that these violations caused non-material loss. 38

According to the CJEU,[37] a claim for compensation based on art 82 (2) General Data Protection Regulation (GDPR) must meet three requirements: processing of personal data that infringes the provisions of the GDPR, damage suffered by the data subject, and a causal link between that unlawful processing and that damage. 39

The first requirement was met. After clarifying the scope of the GDPR, the *Oberlandesgericht* held that Facebook's data processing infringed the GDPR and was therefore unlawful. Article 5 (1) GDPR lays out certain principles relating to the processing of personal data. When violations are alleged, it is up to the controller, according to art 5 (2) GDPR, and, thus, the defendant to demonstrate compliance with these principles. 40

Facebook's data processing regarding the visibility of user profiles via their phone number using the search and contact import function was not necessary for the functioning of the social network and, thus, for the performance of the contract with the network users. Therefore, the data processing was not justified according to art 6 (1) (b) GDPR. Referring to the recent CJEU judgment in *Meta Platforms et al*, the *Oberlandesgericht* Hamm pointed out that the processing of personal data can be regarded as necessary for the performance of a contract if it is 'objectively indispensable for a purpose that is integral to the contractual obligation intended for the data subject. The controller must therefore be able to demonstrate how the main subject matter of the contract cannot be achieved if the processing in question does not occur.'[38] That 'such processing may be referred to in the contract or may be merely useful for the performance of the contract is, in itself, irrelevant in that regard. The decisive factor for the purposes of applying the justification set out in art 6 (1) (b) GDPR is rather that the processing of personal data by the controller must be essential for the proper performance of the contract concluded between the controller and the data subject and, therefore, that there are no workable, less intrusive alternatives.'[39] 41

Against this background, the *Oberlandesgericht* pointed out that there were less intrusive alternatives. In fact, Facebook required that only certain personal data must be 'always public', ie visible and searchable for the purpose of network- 42

37 CJEU 4.5.2023, C-300/21, *Österreichische Post*, ECLI:EU:C:2023:370, para 36.
38 CJEU 4.7.2023, C-252/21, *Meta Platforms et al*, ECLI:EU:C:2023:537, para 98.
39 CJEU C-252/21, *Meta Platforms et al*, para 99.

ing. For other personal information, Facebook allowed network users to decide whether and to whom it should be disclosed. This indicates that not all data was objectively indispensable for Facebook's networking purposes. Moreover, the *Oberlandesgericht* held that the processing was also not justified by effective consent given by the claimant to the searchability of her user profile via a phone number according to art 6 (1) (a) GDPR. In addition, the incriminating function was terminated after the abuse was discovered and was, therefore, not necessary for purposes of legitimate interests of the controller according to art 6 (1) (f) GDPR.

43 Despite the violation of the GDPR rules, the court held that the claimant was not entitled to any compensation as the second requirement was not met, ie the suffering of damage. The *Oberlandesgericht* found that the claimant was not able to plead reasonably why she had suffered non-material damage caused by the infringement, and in any case did not meet the standard of proof required.

44 Liability under art 82 GDPR requires that the infringement of data protection rules causes – pecuniary or non-pecuniary (in the words of the GDPR: material or non-material) – damage. Referring to the *Österreichische Post* judgment by the CJEU[40] the *Oberlandesgericht* reiterated that – unlike in German tort law – there is no threshold of seriousness for awarding damages. The lack of such a threshold can, however, not mean that any infringement of the GDPR constitutes non-material damage within the meaning of art 82 GDPR. The mere infringement of the GDPR itself does not necessarily entail compensable injury. Rather, the *Oberlandesgericht* was convinced, it has to be pleaded and proven that the infringement caused real and certain damage.

45 The *Oberlandesgericht* argued that the unauthorised disclosure of data through 'scraping' and the loss of control caused by it poses a general risk for all data subjects. This kind of loss is an inevitable and general consequence of unlawful data processing by Facebook. Nonetheless, the claimant did not show an impairment beyond this general risk. The claimant's general references to her 'feelings of loss of control, being watched and helplessness' were not regarded as sufficient for assuming that real damage occurred with reasonable certainty. Rather, it is indispensable to explain the concrete circumstances of how the claimant was negatively affected by the violation of the law. This has to be done in a manner that relates individually to the claimant. As the claimant had merely described her feelings in a very abstract manner and had not even changed her telephone number even though it was disclosed in the darknet, the *Oberlandesgericht* held that the claimant did not plead the existence of damage sufficiently ('nicht

40 CJEU C-300/21, *Österreichische Post.*

schlüssig dargelegt'). Apart from that, the claimant did not meet the standard of proof set out in § 286 Code of Civil Procedure (*Zivilprozessordnung*, ZPO).

c) Commentary[41]

Tech companies are facing an increasing number of law suits relating to violations of data protection rules. Following the discovery of this Facebook data leak, numerous civil law suits were filed against Meta.[42] The judgment of the *Oberlandesgericht* Hamm, which is the first judgment of a higher court in Germany regarding the data leak, is of importance for two reasons: 46

First, the court clarified that a scraping event as such does not make the data controller liable. It is carried out by third parties and a breach of law in the sense of art 82 (2) GDPR requires that the controller itself violated its obligations under the GDPR. That Facebook did not process the data in line with the GDPR and must, thus, bear the consequences of the breach of data protection rules was meticulously elaborated by the court in its very well drafted opinion. 47

Second, and far more important to the readers of the European Yearbook, is the court's interpretation of the *Österreichische Post* judgment of the CJEU. In *Österreichische Post*, the CJEU had, on the one hand, dismissed a seriousness threshold as being part of European law.[43] As a consequence, courts cannot deny an award of damages because the loss sustained by the claimant was not severe enough to constitute a compensable injury. On the other hand, the CJEU had made clear that not every infringement of the GDPR qualifies as damage. The 48

41 See case notes by *E Noske*, Gewerblicher Rechtsschutz und Urheberrecht in der Praxis (GRUR-Prax) 2023, 646; *T Wybitul*, Betriebsberater 2023, Heft 41, I; *G Thüsing/J Zhou*, Zeitschrift für Datenschutz (ZD) 2024, 3. Case notes CJEU C-252/21, *Meta Platforms et al: U Schnelle*, GRUR 2023, 472; *P Picht*, GRUR 2023, 1169.

42 LG Lübeck 25 May 2023 – 15 O 74/22, Gewerblicher Rechtsschutz und Urheberrecht – Rechtsprechung (GRUR-RS) 2023, 11984; LG Duisburg, 14 June 2023 – 10 O 126/22, GRUR-RS 2023, 14602; LG Bochum 5 June 2023 – 6 O 86/22, GRUR-RS 2023, 14580; LG Aachen 26 May 2023 – 8 O 267/22, GRUR-RS 2023, 13773; LG Dortmund 22 May 2023 – 24 O 20/23, GRUR-RS 2023, 14600; LG Bonn 3 February 2023 – 18 O 127/22, GRUR-RS 2023, 4565; 3 February 2023 – 2 O 170/22, GRUR-RS 2023, 4566; 8 March 2023 – 17 O 165/22, GRUR-RS 2023, 3854; 30 March 2023 – 3 O 208/22, GRUR-RS 2023, 14581; LG Frankfurt am Main 2 March 2023 – 2-03 O 164/22, GRUR-RS 2023, 4571; LG Berlin 7 March 2023 – 13 O 79/22, GRUR-RS 2023, 3826; LG Baden-Baden 9 March 2023 – 3 O 248/22, GRUR-RS 2023, 3862; LG Konstanz 28 April 2023 – D 6 O 98/22, GRUR-RS 2023, 13796; LG Aurich 17 March 2023 – 5 O 227/22, ZD 2023, 636; LG Augsburg 2 May 2023 – 031 O 1709/22, ZD 2023, 639; cf in the context of another data leak: AG Essen 2 May 2023 – 130 C 135/21, BeckRS 2023, 9399.

43 CJEU C-300/21, *Österreichische Post*, para 49.

CJEU held that the claimant is not 'relieved of the need to demonstrate that [negative consequences caused by the infringement] constitute non-material damage within the meaning of art 82 [GDPR]'.[44] However, the CJEU did not give national courts much guidance on when an impairment can be seen as non-material damage. The *Oberlandesgericht* Hamm held that merely general references to impairments without any individualisation to the concrete situation of the claimant do not suffice to demonstrate that the claimant has suffered damage. Thus, one must recognise that the *Oberlandesgericht* based its rejection entirely on procedural grounds and did not rule out that a loss of control over personal data may constitute compensable damage. Therefore, the judgment is in line with EU law as the CJEU has stated in a judgment concerning the posting of financial data that was handed down after the *Oberlandesgericht's* decision, that 'fear experienced by a data subject with regard to a possible misuse of his or her personal data by third parties as a result of an infringement of that regulation is capable, in itself, of constituting "non-material damage" within the meaning of [art 82 GDPR]'.[45] However, claimants will still have to demonstrate and prove a negative impact on their well-being through anger or similar negative feelings to receive compensation.[46] These requirements were, according to the *Oberlandesgericht* in the case at hand, not met. It is noteworthy that the lawyer representing the claimant seems to have also represented many other claimants suing Meta for damage caused by the data leak. This lawyer had apparently used similar or even identical descriptions of the negative consequences in all complaints and briefs without individualising them. Therefore, the *Oberlandesgericht* could dismiss the claim on procedural grounds.

4. Landgericht (LG) Köln 13 June 2023, 5 O 197/22:[47] State Liability for Sexual Abuse by Clerics

a) Brief Summary of the Facts

49 In recent years, various investigations of sexual abuse scandals within the church were conducted and victims of such abuses have started to sue for damages when offered compensation was regarded as insufficient. The *Landgericht* Köln dealt

44 CJEU C-300/21, *Österreichische Post*, para 50.
45 CJEU 14.12.2023, C-340/21, *VB/Natsionalna agentsia za prihodite*, ECLI:EU:C:2023:353, para 86.
46 See *M Robak*, Gewerblicher Rechtsschutz und Urheberrecht (GRUR-Prax) 2024, 18.
47 ECLI:DE:LGK:2023:0613.5O197.22.00; NJW 2023, 2496; Neue Zeitschrift für Verwaltungsrecht (NVwZ) 2023, 1524.

with such an abuse case. One of the victims claimed compensation from the church, precisely an archbishopric (*Erzbistum*), for numerous cases of sexual abuse by a priest he endured as a child. The claim for damages was based on principles of State liability according to § 839 (1) BGB, art 34 German Constitution (*Grundgesetz*, GG).

The church had essentially not denied the allegations of abuse by the deceased priest. The claimant had been sexually abused numerous times from 1972 to 1979. After abuse allegations made by a stepfather of another child in 1980, the church removed the priest from his position and transferred him to a hospital where he continued to provide pastoral care. Further abuse investigations did not occur. The claimant later underwent a number of therapies which were paid for by the defendant. Following an application, he was also compensated with initially € 5,000 and later additional € 20,000 by a conciliation commission appointed by the church. 50

As a result of the abuse, the claimant developed severe neurodermatitis, suffered physically from severe migraine attacks with aura (visual impairment) and hypertension, and he also suffered from post-traumatic stress disorder. In 2004, a degree of disability of 50 % was officially recognised. 51

Although the abuse happened more than 40 years ago, the church had waived their defence of limitation allowing this judgment that otherwise may have been time-barred. 52

b) Judgment of the Court

The *Landgericht* Köln finds that the rules of State liability are applicable to breaches of official duties by clerical servants, and, under these rules, the claimant is entitled to compensation. 53

It was disputed whether the general rules of tort law (§ 823 ff BGB) apply to the case at hand or the rules of State liability (§ 839 BGB, art 34 GG). The court argued that the rules for State liability apply even if the tortfeasor did not act in an official capacity to represent the defendant, as far as he acted within the framework of church tasks that lie outside the purely fiscal activities and whose fulfilment therefore constitutes the exercise of a public office within the meaning of art 34 GG.[48] As the defendant has a public law status and certain sovereign pow- 54

48 BGH 30 January 1961 – III ZR 227/59, Leitsatz 1, juris.

ers,[49] the court found that church bodies and clerics have a close proximity to the German State. Thus, even outside their areas of sovereign powers granted to the Roman Catholic church (church tax, cemeteries, etc) they are required to comply with the law to a greater extent than an average citizen. Although these bodies are not directly bound by the German constitutional fundamental rights (*Grundrechte*), they act in a public sphere due to their status as a public body and given their power and influence on society. Against this background, the *Landgericht* applied the rules of State liability.

55 By abusing the claimant in a situation related to church work, for example during the preparation of services, the priest had infringed his official duties that he bore towards third parties including the claimant. But the court did not go so far to argue that priests always act in their official capacity. The claimant argued that he was also abused on holiday trips, to which the cleric had invited him. In this respect, the claimant did not succeed. The *Landgericht* held that there was not a sufficient connection between the cleric's holiday and his clerical duties. In addition, the claimant did not substantively plead and prove the allegation relating to abuse during holidays.

56 The claimant also did not succeed with his claim that the archbishopric must have gained knowledge about the cleric's abusive behaviour prior to 1979. Rather, the *Landgericht* pointed out that once the allegations against the cleric emerged in 1980, the priest was transferred to a new position and that it was not demonstrated that the archbishopric should have acted earlier.

57 The defendant had not disputed most actions by the priest so the court could assume he acted intentionally.

58 As the general prerequisites for claims under the State liability rules were met, the court assessed for which damage the claimant could claim compensation. The court pointed out that money for pain and suffering has to be awarded for suffering in the past but the amount must also reflect possible future developments. As the abuse happened many years ago, the court held it most unlikely that (further) follow-on injuries (apart from those that have already manifested itself) would occur.

59 When assessing the amount of damages to be awarded, the *Landgericht* pointed out that other judgments in which courts have awarded damages against the church for sexual abuse by their clerics do not exist as a comparative basis. So, the court looked at judgments which dealt with the sexual abuse of minors as a

49 Art 140 GG incorporates certain articles from the 'Weimarer Reichsverfassung' that grant certain religious communities, such as the Roman Catholic Dioceses and Protestant Regional churches, certain powers and rights.

reference. In addition, the court considered that the abuse took place over a longer period and affected the victim's mental health severely. As a result, the claimant was awarded € 300,000. This is a very high amount according to German standards. The defendant did, however, not lodge an appeal so the judgment became final.

c) Commentary[50]

The judgment met with an enormous press reaction – even though it was decided by a lower court. For the first time, a church was ordered by a German State court to pay compensation for abuse by one of its clerics. 60

Generally speaking, the principle of State liability under German civil law according to § 839 (1) BGB and art 34 GG requires that 'a public servant intentionally or negligently breaches an *Amtspflicht* (public duty) vis-à-vis a third party protected by the duty breached'. Thus, when applying this rule to the actions of a cleric of the church, two questions arise, namely whether the rules for State liability can be applied to the Roman Catholic church and, if so, to what extent actions of employees can be attributed to their employer. The answer to these two questions depends on the interpretation of 'public duty'. 61

Under German law, the main Christian churches (as well as certain other religious communities) exercise certain public functions, for example with regard to (church) tax, which is collected by the State on behalf of these bodies. Less clear is the question whether a cleric performing pastoral care has an *Amtspflicht* vis-à-vis members of the Christian community or other third parties in the sense of § 839 (1) BGB. The *Landgericht* Köln takes this position by referring to a judgment rendered by the BGH in which the State liability rules were applied (analogously) to a traffic accident caused by an employee of the church who was driving a car to reach an event that was related to church activities other than purely fiscal matters.[51] The *Landgericht* Köln affirms this approach by referring to the position of the incorporated religious institutions. The *Landgericht's* reasoning and broad interpretation of the *Amtspflicht* concept is to be commended. 62

In the judgment to which the *Landgericht* Köln referred, the *Bundesgerichtshof* had discussed the conditions for an analogous application of the State liability rules convincingly.[52] Certain religious communities, like the Roman Catholic and Protestant churches, enjoy a broad autonomy not only with regard to religious af- 63

50 See the case notes by *L Jaeger*, VersR 2023, 1193; *A Janssen*, NJW 2023, 2459; *S Rixen*, NVwZ 2023, 1481.

51 BGH 30 January 1961 – III ZR 227/59, VersR 1961, 437.

52 BGH 17 December 1956 – III ZR 89/55, NJW 1957, 542.

fairs but also with regard to organising their affairs, such as labour conditions etc. Even though they are not State bodies, they are public corporations (*Körperschaften des öffentlichen Rechts*) bound by the rule of law that limits their autonomy. In the absence of specific church liability rules, the BGH has held that the churches are liable under the State liability rules for wrongdoings of their representatives or employees as far as these persons violate an *Amtspflicht*. As churches are not part of the German State, these rules apply (at least) analogously.[53]

64 However, there has not been a judgment regarding sexual abuse perpetrated by priests. This led to the question as to whether the rules for State liability apply or whether these acts must be judged under the general rules of tort law because no *Amtspflicht* was breached. The *Landgericht* Köln argued that the Catholic church and therefore its representatives have a distinguished position not just in society but also under the German Constitution. Although, the Constitution's underlying concept of secularism distinguishes between church and State, one cannot leave the corporation of certain churches under the *Grundgesetz* out of consideration. As pointed out by the *Landgericht*, corporated churches have a 'State-like status' from a State liability perspective. Priests have a superior status in society when acting on behalf of the church, which includes church-related duties with regard to minors. For these reasons, it is not convincing to distinguish between the sacral chiming of bells as a State-like activity[54] and pastoral care as a church-only one, excluded from State liability, which is sometimes advocated.[55] Therefore, it is reasonable to establish an *Amtspflicht* vis-à-vis minors and apply the concept of State liability to the core of churches' activities such as pastoral work. As a result, the *Landgericht* Köln correctly distinguishes between abusive acts related to church work for which the church is liable and abuse in the context of private events of the priest which are not covered by the State liability rules.[56]

65 Differing from the *Landgericht* Köln's approach, *Janssen* argues that in the case at hand, the church is only liable under the general rules of tort law under §§ 823, 89, 31 BGB.[57] However, this would mean that claimants would have to demonstrate and prove an organisational fault by the church. As long periods of time can pass between the abuse and the court proceedings, the question of fault in such cases is much more difficult to establish.

---

53 BGH 17 December 1956 – III ZR 89/55, NJW 1957, 542; *H Wöstmann* in: J von Staudinger, Kommentar zum Bürgerlichen Gesetzbuch (2020) § 839 no 751.

54 See BVerwG 28 January 1994 – 7 B 198/93, NJW 1994, 956.

55 In favour of this seperation, *B Eicholt*, Neue Juristische Online-Zeitschrift (NJOZ) 2022, 993.

56 LG Köln, NJW 2023, 2496, 2498.

57 *A Janssen*, NJW 2023, 2459 no 10.

In sum, the judgment sets out the first precedent for other clerical abuse proceedings that will certainly reach German courts in the near future. Given the gravity of abuse over a long period of time and the severe effects on the claimant's mental health, also the relatively high amount of damages awarded is reasonable. 66

5. Personal Injury

Regular readers of this Yearbook may have noticed the numerous, important decisions on personal injuries in 2022, especially on damages for non-material loss.[58] For 2023, fewer decisions can be reported, but this does not mean they are less noteworthy. 67

The *Bundesgerichtshof* ruled on compensation for secondary victims (*Hinterbliebenengeld*) under § 844 (3) BGB. Following a tragic traffic accident, the dispute arose on the amount of the *Hinterbliebenengeld.* The BGH made clear that the lower courts possess a broad margin of appreciation to assess the amount of damages based on § 287 ZPO. As a point of reference, the BGH further approves an amount of € 10,000 that has been stated in the legislative materials.[59] However, one may argue that this figure may be reassessed given the inflation that has occurred over the last years.[60] Regarding the factors to be included when calculating the amount to be paid to the victim, the *Bundesgerichtshof* points out two aspects: first, the financial situation of the secondary victim is only relevant as far as it significantly influences the emotional distress suffered. Second, indirect consequences, such as the changed behaviour by the claimant's autistic brother in the case at hand, may influence the emotional effects and therefore may constitute a relevant factor when calculating the proper amount of damages. 68

In a case of workplace bullying, the *Bundesverwaltungsgericht* (BVerwG) specified the requirements for unlawful bullying in a civil servant relationship that entitle the victim to claim compensation and also dealt with possible heads of damages.[61] First, civil servant's compensation for a breach of duty of care may include non-material damages. Second, the court held that the assessment of a potential breach of the duty of care with regard to various individual acts must take the overall context into account. 69

58 See *J Kleinschmmidt*, Germany, in: E Karner/BC Steininger (eds), European Tort Law Yearbook 2022 (2023) 203 ff.

59 BGH 23 May 2023 – VI ZR 161/22, NZV 2023, 510, no 12 referring to BT-Drs 18/11397, 11.

60 *C Huber*, NZV 2023, 512.

61 BVerwG 28 March 2023, 2 C 6.21, LKV 2023, 216; see also the case note by *K Friederichs*, NVwZ 2023, 1349.

70 Various decisions concern compensation for loss of housekeeping services (*Haushaltsführungsschaden*). In principle, compensation under German law relates to reparation in kind, ie the injured party is to be treated as if the damaging event had not occurred, cf § 249 (1) BGB. Since every person generally runs a household, compensation must also be paid for the damage suffered by the injured party as a result of the fact that they are no longer able to carry out previous activities relating to their household or are impaired in these activities due to the consequences of the damaging event. Claimants have to plead and prove precisely what kind of household activities are executed by them and to what extent these activities have been affected. These requirements were set out in a recent decision by the *Oberlandesgericht* Brandenburg according to which, a mere tabular presentation of the activities does not suffice.[62] Another aspect concerning the damage relating to housekeeping that was considered by the *Oberlandesgericht* Saarbrücken is the obligation to minimise damage.[63] This responsibility especially includes the use of technical assistance and possibilities of re-organisation. The burden of proof for the failure to do so lies with the tortfeasor.

71 When determining compensation for personal injuries, two basic forms can be considered, namely the award of a lump sum or a payment of an annuity. The *Oberlandesgericht* Rostock stated that in the event of the most severe health impairments suffered during birth, which have led to physical and mental impairments as well as considerable psychological stress, the injured person may also be entitled to a payment of an annuity as compensation for pain and suffering in addition to a lump sum.[64] In the case at hand, the claimant needed constant care and assistance from third parties, which makes it impossible for the claimant to live without help. This led the court to award an annuity of € 750 per month until the claimant's death and (additionally) a lump sum of € 200,000.

C. Literature

72 **Artificial Intelligence and Autonomous Systems:** *T Dötsch*, Außervertragliche Haftung für Künstliche Intelligenz am Beispiel von autonomen Systemen (Springer Gabler, Wiesbaden 2023); *P Hacker/A Berz*, Der AI Act der Europäischen Union – Überblick, Kritik und Ausblick, ZRP 2023, 226; *R Konertz*, Urheberrechtliche Fragen

62 OLG Brandenburg 6 July 2023 – 12 U 28/22, BeckRS 2023, 20321; see also the case note by *D Figgener/F Quaisser*, NJW-Spezial 2023, 553.
63 OLG Saarbrücken 20 April 2023 – 3 U 7/23, r+s 2023, 521; see also the case notes by *D Figgener/F Quaisser*, NJW-Spezial 2023, 394; *O Kääb*, Fachdienst Straßenverkehrsrecht 2023, 457313.
64 OLG Rostock 2 June 2023 – 5 U 91/17, BeckRS 2023, 30736.

zur Textgenerierung durch Künstliche Intelligenz: Insbesondere Schöpfungen und Rechtsverletzungen durch GPT und ChatGPT, Wettbewerb in Recht und Praxis 2023, 796; *R Schaub*, Nutzung von Künstlicher Intelligenz als Pflichtverletzung? NJW 2023, 2145; *D Staudenmayer*, Haftung für Künstliche Intelligenz, NJW 2023, 894; *G Wagner*, Die Richtlinie über KI-Haftung: Viel Rauch, wenig Feuer, JuristenZeitung (JZ) 2023, 123.

Automated Driving: *H Steege*, Haftung für künstliche Intelligenz im Straßen- 73
verkehr, SVR 2023, 9; G *Wagner*, Produkthaftung für autonome Fahrzeuge – die zweite Spur der Straßenverkehrshaftung, NJW 2023, 1313.

Capital Markets: *P Buck-Heeb*, Whitepaper-Haftung nach MiCAR, BKR 2023, 74
689; *K Fohrer*, Die Entwicklung der neueren BGH-Rechtsprechung zur Anspruchskonkurrenz im Prospekthaftungsrecht, BKR 2023, 597; *K Knops/C Fromm/J Patz*, Die Abschlussprüferhaftung nach § 826 BGB, BKR 2023, 442; *G Nebel*, DCF-Prinzipien im Kollektivanlagen- und Schadensrecht, Schriften zum Unternehmens- und Kapitalmarktrecht 110 (Mohr Siebeck, Tübingen 2023); *R Litten*, ESG – Wind of Change im Kapitalmarktrecht, BKR 2023, 569; *M Weber*, Die Entwicklung des Kapitalmarktrechts 2022/2023, NJW 2023, 963; *A Wilhelm*, Konkurrenzprobleme im Prospekthaftungsrecht, BKR 2023, 341.

Climate Change: *P Abel*, Zukunftsgerichtete zivilrechtliche Klimaklagen und 75
Grundgesetz, NJW 2023, 2305; *C Behme*, Haftung fürs Haften – Deliktsrechtliche Verantwortlichkeit der 'Letzten Generation', NJW 2023, 327; *M-C Gruber*, Die Cupola im Anthropozän: Klimahaftungsklagen der Zukunft, JZ 2023, 417; *L Patros/A Pollithy*, Zivilrechtliche Haftungsfolgen von Sitzblockaden zu Protestzwecken – welche Verantwortung trifft die Klimaaktivisten, NJOZ 2023, 1; *J Schirmer*, Haftung für künftige Klimaschäden, NJW 2023, 113.

Collective Redress: *M Lerch/C Valdini*, Herausforderungen an den Zivilprozess 76
bei Massenverfahren, NJW 2023, 420; *H Schläfke/TB Lühmann*, Kollektiver Rechtsschutz nach der Umsetzung der EU-Verbandsklagen, NJW 2023, 3385; *S Thönissen*, ESG-Klagen und kollektiver Rechtsschutz, NJW 2023, 945.

Company Law: *S Fischer*, Die Haftung des Vorstands einer Aktiengesellschaft 77
bei Cyberangriffen, Düsseldorfer Rechtswissenschaftliche Schriften 180 (Nomos, Baden-Baden 2023); *C König*, Unternehmenshaftung (Mohr Siebeck, Tübingen 2023); *S Röß*, Die Frage der Haftungsbeschränkung bei der GbR nach dem MoPeG, Neue Zeitschrift für Gesellschaftsrecht (NZG) 2023, 727; *R Stagat*, Die Haftung von Vorstand und Geschäftsführern für Kartellbußen, Gesellschafts- und Wirtschaftsrecht (GWR) 2023, 291; *D Weidlich/C Federle*, Haftungsfragen bei einem Gesellschafterwechsel unter Geltung des MoPeG, NJW 2023, 1993.

Competition Law: *D Beck*, Keine Organhaftung für Kartellbußgelder... oder 78
etwa doch? Neue Zeitschrift für Kartellrecht (NZKart) 2023, 654; *R Mallmann/F Leinemann*, Sonderzivil(prozess)recht für kartellrechtliche Schadensersatzansprüche?

Zeitschrift für Wettbewerbsrecht (ZWeR) 2023, 44; *M Mevißen*, Die Haftung für Kartellschäden im System des allgemeinen Deliktsrechts, Kölner Schriften zum Europarecht 74 (Nomos, Baden-Baden 2023); *C Thole*, Beweisrecht und Kartellschadensprozess – aktuelle Fragen und Entwicklungen, NZKart 2023, 447; *J Tolkmitt*, Die Kunst der Schadensberechnung – Die erste Entscheidung des UK Competition Appeal Tribunal in Sachen LKW-Kartell, ZWeR 2023, 309.

79 **Data Privacy Law:** *S Assion*, Die Entwicklung des Datenschutzrechts, NJW 2023, 2619; *P Gola/C Klug*, Die Entwicklung des Datenschutzrechts, NJW 2023, 658; *A Golland/T Kriegesmann*, Zivilprozessuale Fragen zum datenschutzrechtlichen Schadensersatzanspruch, Zeitschrift für IT-Recht und Digitalisierung (MMR) 2023, 733; *L Stegemann*, Der immaterielle Schadensersatz bei Datenschutzverstößen, Frankfurter Studien zum Datenschutz 70 (Nomos, Baden-Baden 2023); *G Thüsing/J Zhou*, Ersatz immaterieller Schäden wegen Datenschutzverstößen nach Art. 82 DS-GVO: Wer trägt die Darlegungs- und Beweislast? ZD 2024, 3.

80 **Diesel:** *T Horacek*, Der Abgasskandal und der BGH – a (never) ending story? Verbraucher und Recht (VuR) 2023, 337; *R Schaub*, Die Diesel-Problematik zwischen europäischem und nationalem Recht, NJW 2023, 2236; *C Syrbe*, Die zivilgerichtliche Aufarbeitung des 'Diesel-Abgasskandals' – ein weiterer Zwischenstand, NZV 2023, 529.

81 **General:** *D Looschelders*, Reparaturkostenersatz beim Haftpflichtschaden, ZfS: Verkehrsrecht, Schadensrecht, Versicherungsrecht (ZfS) 2023, 364; *G Spindler/M Meyer*, Digitale Assets im Deliktsrecht, MMR 2023, 907; *M von Rochow*, Kein Abzug 'neu für alt' bei Beschädigung öffentlicher Sachen, NJW 2023, 2381.

82 **Legal History:** *G Schiemann* (ed), Mediävistik und Schadensrecht (Mohr Siebeck, Tübingen 2023).

83 **Medical Liability:** *S Göpfert*, Anwendung der Beweislastumkehr beim groben Behandlungsfehler im Gesamtschuldregress, VersR 2023, 1268; *H-W Laumen*, Die Beweislastregeln des § 630 h BGB, VersR 2023, 1481; *J Prütting/D Heyn/R Stubenrauch*, Eltern als Schaden? – Patientenautonomie bei ärztlicher Behandlung und am Lebensende, NJW 2023, 321; *J-R Schmidt*, Die Auswirkungen der Nutzung von KI-Software auf die ärztliche Haftung, GesundheitsRecht 2023, 341; *A Spickhoff*, Die Entwicklung des Arztrechts 2022/2023, NJW 2023, 1629.

84 **Personal Injury:** *C Fellner*, Die Haftung bei sog. Schockschäden, MDR 11/2023, 680; C *Huber/R Kornes/M Mathis/A Thoennеßen* (eds), Fachtagung Personenschaden 2023 (Nomos, Baden-Baden 2023); *H Karlsfeld/M Nugel*, Sechs Jahre Hinterbliebenengeld – ein erstes Fazit aus der Praxis, VersR 2023, 1416; *L Jaeger*, Rechtsprechung zum Schockschaden kehrt zur Normalität zurück, VersR 2023, 358; *L Jaeger*, Die Bemessung des Schmerzensgeldes nach sexuellem Missbrauch – Die Bewertung der Verletzung des sexuellen Selbstbestimmungsrechts und der Dauerschäden, VersR 2023, 1193; *L Jaeger*, Bemessung des Schmerzensgeldes nach Vergewaltigung und sexuellem Missbrauch Minderjähriger durch Kleriker, VersR 2023, 209; *G Koch*, Zur

Schmerzensgeldfindung bei doppeltem Mitverschulden des Geschädigten, ZfS 2023, 604; *F Schwepcke*, Die 'taggenaue Berechnung' des Schmerzensgeldes – ein Fehlgriff? VersR 2023, 294; *T Tomas-Keck*, Hinterbliebenengeld, Studien zum Privatrecht 113 (Mohr Siebeck, Tübingen 2023).

Personal Rights: *J Kahl/R Zimmer*, Identitätsdiebstahl – Rechtsgrundlagen und Rechtsdurchsetzung, Zeitschrift für Urheber- und Medienrecht 2023, 374; *J Lennartz*, 'Digitale Puppenspieler' – die Nachbildung von Körper und Stimme durch KI, NJW 2023, 3543. 85

Prescription: *P Aligbe*, Das neue Impfschadensrecht 2024, NJW 2023, 3457. 86

Product Liability and Product Safety: *A Kapoor/T Klindt*, Aktuelle Entwicklungen im Produktsicherheits- und Produkthaftungsrecht, NJW 2023, 1862; *P Reusch*, KI und Software im Kontext von Produkthaftung und Produktsicherheit, Recht Digital 2023, 152; *G Wagner*, Produkthaftung für das digitale Zeitalter – ein Paukenschlag aus Brüssel, JZ 2023, 1; *G Wagner*, Schadensersatz wegen Verletzung von Unionsrecht – Luxemburg locuta, causa aperta, NJW 2023, 1761. 87

Road, Railway, Waterways and Air Traffic: *T Almeroth*, Schadensersatz bei Verkehrsunfällen (CH Beck, München 2023); *N Biller-Bomhardt*, Die Erstattungsfähigkeit von Standkosten eines Kfz nach einem Verkehrsunfall, NZV 2023, 101; *M Heile*, Das Comeback des Interlining: Herausforderung für Haftung und Fluggastrechte, NZV 2023, 545; *JL Kemperdiek*, Der Fußgängerunfall im Straßenverkehr, ZfS 2023, 544; M *Müller*, Der Anspruch auf Ersatz von Kfz-Bergungs- und Abschleppkosten sowie dessen Deckung durch die Kfz-Versicherung, VersR 2023, 943; *T Schulz*, Vorschäden in der Unfallregulierung, NJW 2023, 565. 88

State Liability: *P Itzel*, Neuere Entwicklungen im Amts-, Staatshaftungs- und Entschädigungsrecht, MDR 2023, 261; *A Janssen*, Amtshaftung der katholischen Kirche in Fällen sexuellen Missbrauchs? Juristische Rundschau 2023, 209; *K-O Knops*, Der unionsrechtliche Staatshaftungsanspruch wegen fehlerhafter Richtlinienumsetzung, NJW 2023, 2225; *M Hippeli*, Staatshaftung im Kapitalmarktaufsichtsrecht, BKR 2023, 357. 89

Supply Chain (Corporate Due Diligence): *AE Frincke/M Christiansen/L Brunswick*, Dogmatische Fragen des Lieferkettengesetzes, Young Academics: Corporate and Business Law 1 (Tectum Verlag, Baden-Baden 2023); *M Kroll*, Der Einfluss von Multistakeholder-Initiativen auf deliktische Haftungsansprüche unter Geltung des Lieferkettensorgfaltspflichtengesetzes, Studien zum Handels-, Arbeits- und Wirtschaftsrecht 216 (Nomos, Baden-Baden 2023); *MM Sharei*, Lieferkettenrechtliche Sorgfaltspflichten und Bemühenspflichten, NJW 2023, 3462; *B Steinbrück/S Traub*, Lieferkettensorgfaltspflichten: Die besondere Prozessstandschaft nach § 11 LkSG, MDR 2023, 1083; *P Tschäpe*, Die Sorgfaltspflicht des Lieferkettengesetzes – Rechtsnatur, Inhalt und Haftung, Zeitschrift für deutsches und internationales Bau- und Vergaberecht 2023, 423. 90

Zafeirios Tsolakidis

XIII. Greece

A. Legislation

1. Law 5023/2023 Principle of equal treatment regardless of disability or chronic disease, update of the terminology of the Civil Code .... and other provisions to facilitate access to justice for persons with disabilities[1]

Article 5 of Law 5023/2023, which replaced art 917 of the Greek Civil Code (hereinafter GrCC), provided for cases of limited imputability. The amended version of art 917 GrCC reads as follows: 'A person who is above ten years of age but below fourteen is liable for the damage he has caused unless he has acted without discretion.' Acting 'without discretion' means acting without having the capacity to discern the unlawful character of one's behaviour. The second sentence of art 917, according to which, 'The same rule applies to deaf-mute people' has been abolished. 1

The treatment of deaf-mute people in the same way as minors under the age of 14 was based on the (outdated) notion that a person who had been deprived of the ability to hear and speak from an early age was also mentally impaired, so that they should be relieved of liability. However, today deaf-mute people are able to communicate with their environment and cannot be considered mentally impaired. For this reason, Greek theory had proposed the amendment of art 917 GrCC in order to be able to hold deaf-mute people liable in tort.[2] 2

1 Published in the Official Gazette (FEK) A' 34/17.02.2023.

2 Indicatively *G Georgiades* in: A Georgiades (ed), Short Commentary of the Greek Civil Code I (2nd edn 2023) (in Greek) art 917 no 11.

https://doi.org/10.1515/9783111376721-014

B. Cases

1. Areios Pagos (Greek Supreme Court, AP) 13 January 2023, no 41: Limitation Period for Tortious Claim

a) Brief Summary of the Facts

3 The plaintiff, after suffering from pain in her left arm, called upon an orthopaedic surgeon, who suggested that she undergo an operation. The surgeon offered to undertake the operation himself with the assistance of a medical team at a privately owned hospital, which, as he informed the plaintiff, was equipped with the most modern infrastructure as well as with specialised medical and nursing staff. The plaintiff was admitted to the aforementioned hospital and underwent the indicated operation on the same day.

4 After the operation was completed, at 2:30 pm, the doctor visited her and after having clinically examined her, he ascertained that she was functional, being able to move her arms and legs naturally and to breathe normally. Afterwards, the surgeon provided both the patient and the nursing staff with the necessary after-care instructions, including checking the mobility of the patient's limbs every hour and monitoring her vital signs, among which the patient's breathing was also included, every three hours. He then left the patient and medical staff to perform another scheduled operation.

5 At around 3:40 pm, the patient developed difficulty in swallowing as well as shortness of breath, about which her husband informed the nursing staff. At around 4 pm, the nurse appeared, checked the patient's vital signs, which were found to be normal, and reassured the patient and her visitors that the observed discomfort was common in operations of such nature. However, a few minutes after the nurse left, the patient's shortness of breath symptoms deteriorated and at around 4:20 pm, it became more difficult for her to breathe. The patient's husband sought a member of the nursing staff once again, also by using the relevant call button in the ward, but the nurses on duty reassured him, without seeing the patient, that a doctor would be called and advised him not to use the call button without good reason. Shortly thereafter, the patient's breathing become almost impossible. After that, the nurses found that the patient had lost consciousness, and they then notified the doctor on duty.

6 From the medical examination she underwent, it was diagnosed that, as a result of the surgery, a haematoma had formed, which gradually caused suffocating phenomena and obstruction of the respiratory tract. Because of this, the patient

suffered permanent and irreversible damage to her health and was left in a vegetative state, with a 95 % disability rate for life.

The Supreme Court ruled in cassation proceedings, following a lawsuit filed by the patient against the three nurses and the company that owned the hospital. 7

b) Judgment of the Court

Article 937 GrCC provides that a tort claim is time-barred five years after the victim became aware of the damage and the person liable for compensation, but in any case, a claim is time-barred twenty years after the tortious action took place. The condition for the application of the five-year limitation period, under art 937 para 1 GrCC, is the lapse of a time period of five years since the injured party became aware of the damage as well as of the person liable for compensation. 8

More specifically, the second part of the requirement, namely the knowledge of the victim, is justified, since it is only from the point where the victim is aware of the damage and the liable person that a lawsuit can be filed with chances of success. It is considered that the victim or the beneficiary of the claim in general is aware of the person liable for compensation when they are aware of so many facts that, based on them, they file a lawsuit against a specific person with chances of success. Mere guesses, suspicions or negligent ignorance are not sufficient. The time when this happens is a matter of fact, which depends on the overall assessment of the specific case. If the name and the address of the person liable for compensation can be ascertained, then the victim is considered to know that person at the time when they were able to find this out by investigating the matter. From the same provisions in combination with the provision of art 338 of the Greek Code for Civil Procedure, it follows that the burden of proof that the beneficiary of the compensation knew from a certain point in time of the damage and the person liable for compensation is on the person who invokes the limitation period of the claim, namely the defendant, whereas the argument of the plaintiff that they became aware of the person liable for compensation at a subsequent time, is a specific denial of the limitation defence and not a counter-defence. 9

The Court of Appeal held that the plaintiff was aware of the damage, namely her severe physical injury, from the very time it occurred on 18 April 2008, but only from 24–30 October 2014 did she become aware of the facts that constituted the basis of the tortious behaviour of the nursing staff, on which the vicarious liability of the company owning the hospital could be established, namely the facts that identified those liable for compensation as well as the legal reason for their liability, without which it was not possible to establish knowledge of the persons liable in this particular case, since several persons with different responsibilities and du- 10 ties were involved in dealing with the complication. Due to this fact, the damaging result could have been caused as a result of completely different incidents and specifically by different behaviour and culpable acts or omissions of any of those involved. In particular, it was held that the plaintiff became aware of the above-mentioned incidents during the criminal trial initiated after she submitted a complaint as well as a lawsuit against the treating surgeon. The patient believed (due to her negligence) that the surgeon was liable for the physical damage caused to her as a result of his negligence relating to the monitoring of her post-operative course, because (as she believed) he had been notified by the three defendant nurses to visit the patient due to the appearance of a possible complication and he failed to do so. The mere fact that the nurses did not respond to the calls of the patient's husband would not be sufficient to establish their negligence if what they told him was true, namely that they had notified a doctor, who would come to examine the patient. However, this was not true as they failed to do so, thus not showing the due care required by the circumstances and their status.

11 The Court of Appeal also held that the claim against the company which owned the hospital, under art 922 GrCC, had not been time-barred either. The basis of the company's liability and therefore their status as liable for compensation due to the actions of the three nurses, which could establish a certain action against the company with hopes of success, such as the one judged, was held to have come to the knowledge of the plaintiff only from 24–30 October 2014. This period of time can be explained by the fact that, while dealing with the complication which arose, several people with different responsibilities, qualities and duties were involved, and the damaging result could have been caused by completely different incidents and specifically by different behaviour and culpable acts or omissions of each of them. It was not possible for the patient to file a claim against the company, because such claim would have included completely unclear or even contradictory facts regarding the legal basis for liability (as to the cause of the damage: insufficient post-operative care by the assigned treating doctor, neglect of actions imposed by medical science or delay of the doctor on call to deal with the incident, delay in the surgical attempt to restore the haematoma by the doctors who intervened, omissions by the nurses assigned). Because of the lack of clear knowledge of such incidents on the part of the plaintiff, that came to her knowledge in 2014, a lawsuit against other persons or even against the company itself could not be filed with chances of success before she became aware of the facts that established, under the provisions regulating vicarious liability, the strict liability of the company as having assigned to the nurses the performance of their services. The case under consideration, due to its aforementioned peculiarities, differs from other, more common cases, in which strict liability can be attributed to the master or the person who has assigned another without specifying the assignee,

in view of the fact that several auxiliary persons have similar responsibilities and are charged with the same duties, during the execution of which more or just one of them demonstrated the illegal and culpable behaviour described in the lawsuit (through their act or omission) which caused the damage.

The Supreme Court upheld the judgment of the Court of Appeal. 12

c) Commentary

The decision clarifies two distinct issues related to the statute of limitations for a 13 tort claim.

Under art 937 para 1 GrCC, 14

> 'A tort claim is time-barred five years after the victim became aware of the damage and the person liable for compensation, but in any case, the claim is time-barred twenty years after the tortious action took place'.

Knowledge of the person liable for compensation means knowledge of the facts, 15 from which the obligation of a certain person for compensation arises. The injured party is considered to know the liable person when they know so many facts that they are able to bring an action against that person with chances of success.[3]

In the case under consideration, the plaintiff was informed of the damage (her 16 disability after the operation) on 18 April 2008. The plaintiff brought an action against the doctors, believing that her disability was due to their negligence. However, her claim was dismissed, and at the trial held in 2014, the plaintiff became aware of the fact that her disability was due to the negligence of the nurses after the operation. The plaintiff then filed a lawsuit on 10 November 2014 against the nurses. The Court of Appeal ruled that the plaintiff's claim was not subject to the statute of limitations, because she was informed that the nurses were liable for compensation only in 2014 and the Supreme Court upheld the decision.

Article 922 GrCC reads as follows: 17

> 'A master or a person who has assigned to another the performance of a service shall be liable for the damage incurred by a third party due to breach of law by the servant or the assignee while performing such service'.

Pursuant to this provision, anyone who uses auxiliaries to conduct their af- 18 fairs is jointly and severally liable for their torts with them in damages. It is settled

3 AP 866/2017; AP 379/2017; *P Kornilakis*, Law of Obligations, Special Part (3rd edn 2023) § 237 no 9.

case law in Greek jurisprudence that a private clinic is liable for both the doctors (even for those who are not employees, but external collaborators), and the rest of their staff assigned.[4] Regarding the statute of limitations for a claim based on art 922 GrCC, it is generally accepted that 'knowledge of the injured party' exists even when the exact person who caused the damage is not known, but it is known that the damage was caused by one of the persons employed on behalf of the principal.[5] Therefore, the statute of limitations starts from this point in time. The Supreme Court deviated from the above position in the case under consideration, because it considered that several auxiliary persons with different capacities and duties had been involved and that the damaging result could have been caused by completely different incidents (negligence of the doctor during the operation, negligence or delay in dealing with the incident by the doctor on call, negligence in monitoring by the nurses, etc). It considered, therefore, that crucial to the initiation of the limitation period against the master, without regard to the person of the assistant, is whether all assistants have similar responsibilities and are charged with the same duties. For this reason, it ruled that, in the case under consideration, the claim against the hospital, based on art 922 GrCC, was not time-barred.

2. AP (Greek Supreme Court) 31 August 2023, no 13277: 'The Victim's Family'; Entitlement to Monetary Satisfaction due to Pain and Suffering

a) Brief Summary of the Facts

19 Due to a road traffic accident, X died. Because the car that caused the accident was not insured for civil liability, relatives of the victim filed a claim for compensation against the 'Supplementary Capital for Car Accident Liability Insurance'. With the lawsuit, they sought, among other things, monetary satisfaction due to pain and suffering. The wives of the victim's two brothers were also included as relatives who filed the lawsuit. The Court of First Instance and the Court of Appeal considered their claim well-grounded and awarded € 13,000 to each of them.

4 Indicatively AP 418/2018; AP 427/2015; AP 687/2013; AP 1429/2012.

5 AP 659/2018; AP 72/2007; AP 160/2001; Athens Court of Appeal 46/2019.

b) Judgment of the Court

According to art 932 para 3 GrCC, in the case of wrongful death, monetary satisfaction due to mental anguish can be awarded to the victim's family. In this provision, the meaning of the term 'victim's family' is not defined, obviously because the legislator did not want to set in a binding way the boundaries of an institution which, by its nature, is necessarily affected by social changes over time. However, according to the clear meaning of the above provision, which derives from the purpose of its enactment, the victim's family includes close relatives who experienced emotional pain as a result of their loss. Compensation should serve to alleviate their pain, regardless of whether or not they lived together with the victim (AP in plenary session no 21/2000), a fact which is only taken into account when determining the amount of monetary satisfaction. As a result, the 'victim's family' within the meaning of the above provision and according to the ruling jurisprudence of the Supreme Court, includes, among others, the first-degree by affinity relatives of the victim, that is the husband of the victim's daughter (son-in-law), or the wife of the victim's son (daughter-in-law), but not relatives by affinity in a further degree, such as the husband of the victim's sister, or the wife of the victim's brother (brother-in-law and sister-in-law, respectively), who are second-degree by affinity relatives and indeed regardless of whether there are other closer relatives or whether they are the only relatives of the victim. This conclusion is reinforced by the provisions of art 57 para 2 and art 59 GrCC, which regulate in a restrictive way the persons who are entitled to request the protection of the personality of the deceased person and the award of monetary satisfaction due to moral harm, among whom the brother-in-law and sister-in-law of the deceased are not included based on their mere family relationship with the victim. 20

The Court of Appeal of Athens, with its contested decision, held that the lawsuit in which the sisters-in-law of the victim, based on their own family relationship, requested monetary satisfaction due to mental anguish for his death was substantively well-grounded, adopting the view in its contested decision, as the first instance court also did, that these respondents fall under the concept of the 'family' of the victim in question and have legal standing in such a lawsuit. With its aforementioned judgment, the Court of Appeal, holding that the above claim of the respondents has a legal basis and that they are entitled to monetary satisfaction due to mental anguish for the victim's death in the car accident, directly violated the aforementioned substantive legal provision of art 932 para 3 GrCC. The Court held that this provision was incorrectly interpreted and incorrectly applied, since these respondents, as sisters-in-law of the victim, are second-degree by affinity relatives, namely relatives by affinity beyond the first degree and, therefore, they are not included in the 'family' of the deceased. 21

c) Commentary

22 In the case of wrongful death, art 932 GrCC provides that monetary compensation due to 'mental anguish' is awarded to the 'family' of the victim. The law deliberately did not list specific persons as beneficiaries, but used the concept of 'family' in order to allow the interpreter to adapt the circle of entitled persons to changing perceptions. It is necessary to establish that these persons were connected by a close family bond with the deceased, so that they experienced mental pain from their death. Apart from the family relationship, the existence of a close bond is a fact which must be judged on a case-by-case basis.[6]

23 In addition to very close relatives (spouse, ascendants, descendants, siblings), who are consistently considered to be members of the family, Greek jurisprudence has also recognised the betrothed as a beneficiary,[7] while it does not consider that uncles, nieces and nephews or cousins are entitled to monetary satisfaction. After a series of rejective judgments by the Supreme Court regarding those who live in a free union,[8] it was recently decided that 'family' can also include free unions of two persons without marriage, where children have been born,

> 'provided that the determining criterion of the real existence of close personal ties between them is met and their symbiosis is the result of love and devotion and a serious and firm intention for companionship and common life.[9]

24 This decision deals with the issue of the relatives by affinity of the deceased person. In this regard, it confirms the settled case law of the Supreme Court that only the *first-degree by affinity relatives*, that is the parents of the surviving spouse and the spouses of the deceased's children, can be considered as 'family' of the victim.[10] In the case under consideration, the plaintiffs were the spouses of the victim's brothers, ie second-degree by affinity relatives. The Supreme Court considered that they did not fall under the concept of family according to art 932 GrCC and overturned the decision of the Court of Appeal that had awarded monetary satisfaction to them.

---

6 AP (plenary session) 21/2000. For a brief summary in English of the facts and the judgments of the said decisions as well as a commentary thereof, see *E Dacoronia* in: H Koziol/BC Steininger (eds), European Tort Law 2001 (2002) 269, nos 41–56. AP 51/2018.

7 AP 1918/2022; AP 43/2012; AP 995/2009.

8 AP 454/2018; AP 775/2011; AP 1541/2009; AP 1141/2007; AP 1735/2006.

9 AP 1159/2022.

10 AP (plenary session) 21/2000; AP 957/2022; AP 253/2020; AP 51/2018; AP 442/2017; AP 602/2015; AP 652/2014; AP 382/2013; AP 1503/2012; AP 581/2010.

3. Court of Appeal of Athens, 17 January 2023, no 277: Liability of a Bank towards Third Parties due to Breach of Obligations towards its Customers

a) Brief Summary of the Facts

Company X entered into a factoring agreement with the defendant bank. X assigned to the bank their claims against their customers, derived from the sales of goods to them on credit. X transmitted to the bank a complete 'file', which contained the legal documents of the sale (invoices, etc), sales contract, contract of assignment of the claim from the sale, announcement of the assignment to the buyer-debtor, and an application for granting credit and opening a bank account in the name of the buyer. The factoring contract also included terms under which X's assignees were responsible for verifying the identity of the person appearing before them and the person listed as the buyer-debtor and for verifying signatures on all applications and contracts of the 'file'. Further, the contract also provided for the express release of the bank's liability. 25

The bank undertook the obligation to acquire the claims of X against their customers at its discretion. The bank would check the creditworthiness of the prospective buyers by accessing interbank data files relating to financial behaviour ('Teiresias', 'Thalis', etc). If the bank were interested in acquiring the claim, it would proceed to discount it, paying to the supplier, according to the terms of contract, an amount equal to the amount of the claim (from the sale price), after deducting the (bank's) fee plus interest and expenses. 26

X transmitted to the bank a complete 'file' in the plaintiff's name, which contained sales contracts (between X and the plaintiff), an application for credit and an application for a credit card with signatures which turned out not to be genuine. It was proven that the plaintiff never carried out the above transactions, neither the purchase (sale) of consumer goods from X, nor requested, or received, or in any way used loan or credit card money from the bank, but his signature was forged. 27

The plaintiff sued 'everyone responsible and every principal or accomplice', for forgery and fraud against him. According to the content of the lawsuit, a person unknown to the plaintiff appeared in a store of company X, under the name of the plaintiff, and bought consumer goods on credit, receiving loans from X, for a total amount of € 7,000, having forged the signature of the plaintiff and having included in the relevant contracts, among other things, false information, alleged to be true information. The fraudster's aim was to mislead the bank, to avoid paying debts and to rather burden the plaintiff with these debts. 28

29 The bank terminated the loan agreement and called on the plaintiff to pay the principal of the loan, plus interest and costs, as his debt on the loan.

b) Judgment of the Court

30 The unlawful and culpable infringement of personality rights constitutes a tort, under the provisions of arts 914, 919, 920, 932 GrCC. An unlawful infringement of one's personality by an act or omission of another disturbs one or more aspects of the physical, mental, spiritual and social individuality of the injured person at the time of the infringement. A disruption of the social personality of the person is, among others, their defamation or the questioning of the person's personal or professional honesty, even when these simply make others suspect them of using dishonest methods, during the exercise of their professional duties or during their social activity.

31 Banks exercise a public function (in the broadest sense of the term), since their activity reflects directly on the national economy. Moreover, a bank, when fulfilling its obligations towards its customers, as good faith and commercial usages require (art 288 GrCC), has a 'duty of care' (in particular the obligation to protect its clients' assets, especially when these assets may be put at risk as a result of the bank's performance), because it has an increased ability to intervene in the property sphere of its clients. Furthermore, as an exception to the doctrine of privity, contracts may, under certain conditions, have a protective effect in favour of third parties, who are closely related to the object of the performance or are involved in the scope of the existing trust relationship. Persons who are not in a transactional relationship with the bank and are not included in the protective field of this relationship are entitled to request compensation, according to the provisions of the GrCC on torts (arts 914 and 919 GrCC), in the event that the bank, during the performance of its service to its customers, culpably violates the legal interests of these persons. This is because, in such a case, the bank breaches the general duty of every social person (also of any entity similar to a person under the law) not to culpably cause harm to another. Such a duty has special weight when it is infringed by a credit institution, in view of the strong intervention of the latter in the economic landscape and hence, as mentioned, in view of the exercise of a public function *lato sensu*.

32 In particular, in the case of concluding a loan agreement in which, due to flawed control by the bank's employees, a person who has not transacted with the bank is listed as the debtor due to the forgery of their signature (which was not reviewed as required by the circumstances), it is appropriate and fair for the bank to bear the risk. Such a risk is within the professional sphere of control

of the bank. The bank is able to organise its professional banking activities (recruitment and special training of experienced employees, etc) in order to exclude or reduce to a minimum the risk of concluding contracts with persons who have not actually entered into them. It is socially, economically and logically correct that liability rests with the bank and not with the alleged counterparty, who, as a rule, is financially weaker and presumably less experienced in transactions.

During the process of final approval of the 'file' transmitted to the bank by company X, as the bank was supposed to acquire the claim of X against its customer, the bank's employees were grossly negligent. They failed to carry out the check imposed by good commercial practice and specifically (failed) to compare the plaintiff's (genuine) signature, as it appears on the photocopy of his original ID card, with the (non-genuine) signatures that were placed on the applications and the other aforementioned contracts and sales documents. The consequence of the aforementioned omission of the due check by the defendant bank's employees was the conclusion of the contracts (loan and credit card agreements) for a total amount of € 7,000, with the plaintiff listed as debtor. The plaintiff, however, neither requested nor received, nor used, in any way, financing for the purchase of consumer products. 33

Both the conclusion of the contracts in question for a cumulative amount of € 7,000, a debt which the plaintiff still has, and the subsequent entry of the debt in the interbank data file of financial behaviour 'Teiresias' at a time (2005) before the bank was notified of the forgery (12 March 2007), stem from the negligence of the bank's employees, who carried out a flawed check of the signatures on the above documents transmitted to them. This conduct of the employees does not correspond to the reasonably expected security of banking transactions, namely to the bank's relative duty of care for the security of its transactions, in the professional sphere of which the risk of error during their execution is included. In this way, via its employees, the bank breached the general duty of every person not to culpably cause harm to another. 34

At the time of the hearing of the lawsuit, the alleged debt against the plaintiff, amounting to a capital of € 7,000, on the one hand, still existed with a consequent risk to his property, and, on the other, still registered as an unfavourable financial element against him in the database 'Teiresias'. This resulted in (a) the appearance of the plaintiff among a wide circle of persons as an insolvent debtor, and (b) the loss of his creditworthiness and his trading freedom, which (both the creation of the alleged debt, and its 'Teiresias' entry) infringed his personality rights. 35

Through the above conclusion of the loan and credit card agreements, the defendant, due to the negligence of its employees, consisting, as stated above, in the failure to check the signature of the buyer-debtor with the photocopy of his ID card, on the one hand, and with the application and contract documents, on the 36 other hand, rendered the plaintiff the debtor for the above capital amount of € 7,000, without having any right to do so. In this way, the defendant, through its employees, on the one hand, endangered the property of the plaintiff and, on the other, put him in the extremely difficult position of investigating and proving, as detailed above (by submitting requests for copies of the loan contract file, checking and investigating them, drawing conclusions, filing a lawsuit and monitoring the criminal proceedings, submitting written information to the defendant and exchanging correspondence and a series of out-of-court statements, etc) that he was never involved. The above conduct of the defendant's employees, in the performance of their duties, namely the unlawful (without the defendant's right to infringe the plaintiff's interests) and culpable (negligent) omission of due legal action, constitutes a tort against him, as a consequence of which the latter suffered moral harm, since he experienced intense mental disturbance, stress and anxiety.

37 The Court, weighing the circumstances of the tort, the exclusive culpability of the defendant's employees regarding the infringement to the personality rights of the plaintiff, aged 25 at the time of the tort, as well as the financial and social status of the parties and the mental suffering of the plaintiff as a result of the tort, considers it reasonable to award the plaintiff the amount of € 5,000 as monetary satisfaction for his moral harm.

c) Commentary

38 The decision establishes the bank's liability *towards third parties*, due to a breach of the duty of care, which the bank had contractually undertaken towards its counterparty. For this purpose, the decision recalls the 'general duty' of care and safety which every person bears, according to Greek jurisprudence, and with the aim of strengthening its reasoning, it also invokes additional considerations, which are not always convincing.

39 In the factoring contract concluded between the defendant bank and company X, it was agreed that X would sell goods to its customers on credit, would agree with them that the price would be paid through bank loans or credit card, would collect the applications of customers for entering these contracts and would transmit them to the bank, which would check the customers' authorisation and creditworthiness in order for them to receive the credit. The bank had an obligation to carry out these tasks diligently, both in its own interest and in the interest of its counterparty, X, since it had been agreed that, in case of default on the part of the customers, the bank could turn to X.

X transmitted to the bank applications for loans and for a credit card, accompanied by supporting documents, with a forged signature of the alleged applicant (the plaintiff). The employees of the bank did not correctly compare this with the signature sample they had and did not discover the forgery, as a result of which the loan contracts were drawn up in the plaintiff's name. By so doing, they breached their obligation towards X to diligently check prospective clients. 40

As a result of the negligent behaviour of the bank's employees, the plaintiff appeared as a defaulting debtor and was registered in the relevant file kept by banks to evaluate future debtors. However, the bank was not bound by a contractual relationship with the plaintiff, nor had it undertaken an obligation towards him to check the applications submitted. The issue, therefore, was whether there was a legal basis to establish the plaintiff's claim for monetary satisfaction of moral harm. 41

The Court uses parallel reasoning to establish the bank's liability in tort against third parties who are not its customers. First, it refers to the special position that banks have in economic life, and to the ability that their conduct has to affect the financial status of their customers. From such position, duties of care, loyalty and protection arise, the aim of which is to prevent unduly burdensome consequences for them.[11] Subsequently, the Court attempts to extend the above duty of care to third parties, non-contracting parties, through the doctrine of the 'contract with protective purpose for third parties' (*Verträge mit Schutzwirkung für Dritte*).[12] In such contracts, it could be recognised that duties of care and protection also arise in favour of third parties, who, however, have a link with the contract, as long as the debtor could objectively discover the involvement of third parties in the fulfilment of their performance. It is, however, doubtful whether in this case the contract between X and the bank can be considered to have a protective purpose in favour of X's customers. Finally, the decision refers to the well-known position of Greek jurisprudence that a general duty is accepted 'not to culpably cause harm to another' (*neminem laedere*). However, such a general duty could not be recognised towards everyone, since in fact in this way the condition of the 'unlawful' occurrence of damage, which is expressly provided for in art 914 GrCC, is overlooked.[13] 42

11 This perspective has been consistent in the jurisprudence of the Supreme Court in recent years. See indicatively AP 476/2021; AP 323/2021; AP 1188/2021; AP 1185/2019; AP 1352/2011.

12 For these contracts, see, in Greek theory, *M Stathopoulos*, Law of Obligations, General Part (5th edn 2018) § 4 no 63 ff. For the recognition of this doctrine in Germany, see *K Larenz*, Lehrbuch des Schuldrechts, vol I (14th edn 1986) § 17 II, 224 ff.

13 See indicatively *A Karabatzos*, Compensation for damage suffered by a third party, in particular, liability of specialists towards third parties (Expertenhaftung, liability of experts), Chronicles of

43 The decision is part of a series of court decisions that tend to expand the tortious liability of banks, recognising obligations of care and safety not only towards their customers, but also towards third parties. A characteristic example is decision no 1768/2009 of the Supreme Court (*Areios Pagos*), which considered that a bank that grants a block of cheques to an insolvent person is liable for compensation to the bearers of the checks that are not paid.[14]

4. Court of Appeal of Athens, 24 January 2023, no 444: Liability of a Minor's Parent towards Third Parties because of Damage Suffered by the Minor

a) Brief Summary of the Facts

44 X was driving his car, which was insured against damage to third parties in the defendant insurance company, on Avenue A, heading towards Athens. The plaintiff, who was five years old at the time, had crossed the road on foot, accompanied by his mother, and both of them were standing on the dividing island. Their intention was to cross the road towards Athens, in order to reach the opposite pavement, from a point where there were no designated pedestrian crossings or traffic lights.

45 The mother of the minor victim, after having fulfilled her obligation to check the movement of vehicles, left the dividing island, holding her minor son by the hand. The mother, suddenly seeing X's car, stopped. X, due to driving incompetence, although he perceived at least from a distance of 70 metres the pedestrians crossing the left lane of the road where he was driving, failed to brake as he had the opportunity and sufficient time to do. He reacted recklessly and entered the right lane to avoid the pedestrians. The plaintiff, acting instinctively, let go of his mother's hand and quickened his pace in order to run to the right-hand side of the pavement, with the consequence that he suddenly entered the path of the oncoming car. Driver X, who was driving in excess of 70 kilometres per hour, failed to

Private Law (Chronika Idiotikou Dikaiou, Journal in Greek) 2018, 409 f; *Z Tsolakidis*, Illegality as a prerequisite for tortious liability in case of an infringement of environmental goods, Chronicles of Private Law 2016, 96.

14 Regarding this decision, see *M Stathopoulos*, The illegality in art 914 GRCC and the specification of good faith (on the occasion of a critical commentary of AP 1768/2009), Essays in honour of E. Kounougeri-Manoledaki (2016) 825 ff; *K Karagiannis*, The granting of a block of cheques by a credit institution to an 'untrustworthy-insolvent' person as a 'source of risk' giving rise to tortious liability? Applications of Civil Law (Efarmoges Astikou Dikaiou, Journal in Greek) 2014, 443 ff.

stop his vehicle, as a result of which he hit the minor with the front part of his vehicle. The minor was seriously injured and required long-term hospitalisation.

b) Judgment of the Court

From the provision of art 300 GrCC, which stipulates that, if the injured party contributed to the damage through their own fault, the court may not award compensation or may reduce its amount (contributory negligence), in conjunction with the provision of art 916 GrCC, under which, whoever has not reached the age of ten is not liable for the damage they cause, it is clear that, regarding damage caused by the fault of a third party against a person who has not reached the age of ten, the minor's (contributory) fault cannot be countered against the minor plaintiff, nor against their parents as legal representatives, for the consequences against the tortfeasor to be mitigated, since the imperative rules of law are not addressed to a minor who lacks capacity. 46

In the case of a minor under the age of ten who was injured by a car and seeks compensation for the damage or monetary satisfaction due to moral harm, the defendant cannot claim the negligence of his parents supervising him, that is to attribute to the minor the fault of his legal representatives in relation to the supervision exercised by them. This is because, on the one hand, the wrongful third party and the minor's supervising parents are jointly and severally liable towards the minor for the damage suffered due to his injury, and on the other hand, the legislator would be contradicting itself if the minor in need of guardianship, to whom the legislator provides protection in multiple ways, was attributed liability for the actions of others, especially the acts or omissions of his parents. Parents are obliged by law to care for and represent a minor, taking into account the fact that the imperative rules of law are not addressed to a minor who lacks capacity but to his legal representatives. 47

Parents represent the minor when, as the minor's legal representative, they bring an action in the name and on behalf of the minor, seeking compensation for the minor's damage. On the contrary, *if the legal representative of the minor directly harmed by the tort brings an action*, in which they request compensation of the damage *which they suffered indirectly from the tort*, then the defence of contributory negligence of the legal representative (parent of the minor), who breached their supervision duties (art 923 GrCC), may be permissible, since they seek compensation for their own damage. 48

It is also possible, when the accident is also due to a breach of supervision duties by the minor's parents (art 923 GrCC), that the person who compensated the minor turns to the parents, under art 927 GrCC, to demand what they paid, alleging 49 and proving that the minor's injury was due to a breach of the duty of supervision on their part. According to the provision of art 923 para 1 GrCC:

> 'Whoever has the supervision of a minor or an adult, who is under judicial support, is liable for the damage that these persons unlawfully cause to a third party, unless they prove that they exercised the appropriate supervision or that the damage could not have been prevented.'

50 Supervision, in the sense of the above provision, is the control, supervision and protection of the minor, depending on the circumstances, and it is exercised, in principle, in the case of a minor, by those with parental care, in accordance with the provision of art 1510 GrCC. With the aforementioned provisions, a rebuttable presumption is established against the parent (supervisor) regarding the existence of their fault in the exercise of supervision, the measure of which depends on the totality of the circumstances and, in particular, the age, maturity, education as well as the state of health (physical and mental) of both the parent and the minor. This presumption establishes fault-based liability with a reversed burden of proof, that is, the presumption can be overturned if the supervising parent pleads that they exercised appropriate supervision in this particular case or that the damage could not have been prevented despite the exercise of appropriate supervision. However, the purpose of the above provision, as it emerges from the provision itself, is *the protection of third parties against minors* or persons who are under judicial support (who are usually insolvent or unable to be imputed) for damage that they suffer due to the neglect of their supervision, and not the protection of the supervised person themselves. Thus, if, as a result of the breach of the duty of supervision, the minor suffers damage due to a tort committed by a third party, the parents' liability towards the minor will not be based on this provision (of art 923 GrCC) but either on the provisions that regulate the special relationship (legal or contractual) from which the obligation of supervision originates, or possibly on the provision of art 914 GrCC, as a consequence of a breach of the duty of supervision. As far as the damage of the minor is concerned, the third party and the parent are held jointly liable, according to the relevant provisions.

51 Furthermore, under the provision of art 927 GrCC, the person who, according to the previous article, paid full compensation has a right of recourse against the others. According to the above provision, one of the jointly liable tortfeasors who paid all the compensation can demand that the other tortfeasors pay a part of or all the compensation. The right of recourse within the internal relationship between the jointly liable tortfeasors is, as a rule, exercised by means of a legal action. The plaintiff must plead the degree of fault of the defendant and the facts that establish it and if they claim that they were not at fault and the damage must be

borne exclusively by the defendant, the plaintiff must also plead and prove the facts on which this allegation is based. In the event that they are unable to prove their claims or the defendant presents facts that justify the assertion that the degree of culpability and causality of each of the tortfeasors cannot be ascertained, the court will apply the rule of art 927 sec 3 GrCC and will distribute the loss among all jointly liable persons in equal parts.

It was proved that the minor's mother, who had joint custody of the minor and 52 accompanied him at the time of the accident, did not show due care and diligence regarding the supervision of her minor child while crossing the road, the supervision being a more specific content of custody, according to art 1518 para 1 GrCC, since she should, in view of his very young age (five years old), have paid particular attention, so as to monitor and supervise him anytime, in order not to put his life and physical integrity at risk, especially in view of the fact that they were crossing a road without a pedestrian crossing. Therefore, *she is jointly and severally liable to 30 %*, due to not exercising the proper supervision of her minor son. Accordingly, she was ordered to pay the defendant 30 % of the capital, plus interest and court costs awarded by this decision from the minor's lawsuit.

c) Commentary

The decision of the Court of Appeal follows the settled jurisprudence of the Su- 53 preme Court, regarding the liability of parents in the event that *through their own fault they have contributed to the damage caused by a third party to their child.*

As it is accepted in Greek jurisprudence, when the child's damage is caused, *in* 54 *addition* to the unlawful and culpable action of the tortfeasor, also due to the negligence of the parents (as a rule, failure to provide adequate supervision), the tortfeasor cannot claim the contributory negligence of the parents (art 300 GrCC) to defend against the minor's lawsuit, because the provision refers to the fault of the injured party, who is incapable of imputation in such cases.[15]

If, on the contrary, the parents bring an action for the damage they suffered 55 themselves due to the injury of their child, the tortfeasor can allege their own contribution to the damage.[16] The jurisprudence even accepts that the contributory negligence of the parents is sufficient to reduce the claims of other beneficiaries such as siblings or grandparents.[17] In order to determine whether the parent is re-

15 AP 1004/2021; AP 276/2019; AP 532/2012; AP 1446/2009; AP 1676/2006.

16 AP 276/2019; AP 861/2012; AP 1743/2007.

17 AP 132/2019; AP 1261/2007; AP 1676/2006.

sponsible for the injury, art 923 GrCC, which establishes fault-based liability with a reversed burden of proof, namely it provides for a presumption that the parent is at fault for the improper supervision, which the parent bears the burden of rebutting, shall not apply. In the case under consideration, the wrongdoer will bear the burden of proving that the parent is culpable for the damage caused to their child.[18]

56 According to art 926 GrCC, when more than one person is liable for a tort in parallel, they are jointly and severally liable to the injured party. If one of them pays the compensation, they have the right to turn to the others, in order to demand the share of the compensation attributed to them (art 927 GrCC). The distribution is based on the degree of each person's fault.[19] When the injury of a minor is due to the fault of both a third party and their parents, the third party/defendant can bring an action against the parents, in which they request payment of the proportion of the compensation, based on the percentage of fault that is determined to be borne by the parents. Such a lawsuit was brought by the insurance company in the case under consideration against the mother, and the company was awarded 30 % of the compensation that they would be required to pay to the minor.

5. One-Member Court of First Instance of Thessaloniki, 26 September 2023, no 12947: Liability of a Bank because of Digital Fraud (Phishing)

a) Brief Summary of the Facts

57 The plaintiff, a teacher, maintained a payroll account with the defendant bank, in which, at the same time, he saved money derived from his work. On 17–18 December 2017, the plaintiff was a victim of digital fraud, through 'phishing'. Unknown perpetrators managed, among other things, in three individual transactions to extract and transfer a total amount of € 14,687 from the aforementioned account and without the plaintiff's consent, to a Dutch bank account.

58 The plaintiff received an SMS message on his mobile phone, in which he used to receive, until then, all the notifications on his account movements as well as the one-time codes, every time he had to approve a money transfer and through which he was asked to re-register his mobile phone number, through the link '……–help.-

18 AP 48/2016.

19 On the distribution of the damage, see, indicatively, *A Georgiades*, Law of Obligations, General Part (2nd edn 2015) § 64 no 28 ff.

com' in the defendant's online banking system. The plaintiff, being mistaken regarding the fact that the relevant request came from his bank, activated the link in the message, thus opening a website controlled by the malicious third parties/ perpetrators of the fraud. He entered his username and password, as requested, while still believing that he was updating his personal information. The bank then sent a message to the plaintiff's mobile phone, containing a six-digit code, the immediate (within two minutes) entry of which is required for the completion of the transaction carried out through the electronic banking service. The plaintiff proceeded to enter the six-digit code, as a result of which the process of his identification as a user was completed.

When the plaintiff discovered that three transfers had taken place, he contact- 59
ed the defendant bank, on the phone number that the latter had indicated to him, informing the defendant's representative that the transfers in question had not been made by him or with his consent, giving an explicit order for them to be withdrawn and requesting his bank to take the measures necessary in order to stop the illegal process and return the money.

The defendant addressed the foreign bank to which the money was trans- 60
ferred and requested the cancellation of the transfers. However, the expected credit of the money, in the amount of € 14,687, was never carried out, despite repeated verbal and written complaints by the plaintiff to his bank. Finally, the bank informed him that he had to communicate with the representatives of the foreign bank to locate his money himself.

b) Judgment of the Court

According to the provision of art 71 of Law 4537/2018, which incorporated Direc- 61
tive 2015/2366/EU on payment services into Greek legislation, the payment service provider shall restore an unauthorised or incorrectly executed payment transaction to the payment service user only if the latter notifies, without undue delay, the payment service provider as soon as they become aware of any such payment transaction that gives rise to a claim for compensation. Under art 73 para 1, in the case of an unauthorised payment transaction, the payer's payment service provider, upon discovery or notification, shall immediately and in any case no later than the end of the next business day, return the amount of the unauthorised payment transaction to the payer. Paragraph 3 of art 73 of Law 4537/2018 provides that:

> 'in case of unauthorised payment, further compensation is not excluded, as long as a relevant right is established in the law governing the contract concluded between the payer and the

payment service provider or in the law governing the contract concluded between the payer and the payment initiation service provider'.

62 Pursuant to art 72 para 2, if a payment service user denies having authorised an executed payment transaction, the use of a payment instrument recorded by the payment service provider shall not necessarily, in itself, be sufficient to prove either that the payment transaction was authorised by the payer or that the payer acted fraudulently or failed with intent or gross negligence to fulfil one or more of the obligations under art 69 and the payment service provider shall provide evidence to prove fraud or gross negligence on the part of the payment service user. The term 'authenticity of the payment transaction' refers to a transaction that was performed with the actual consent of the user of the payment services, namely either by him or with his knowledge by a third party, to whom he had provided relevant permission. There is no genuine transaction when the user is unaware of it and it was acted upon by a third party, without a right to do so, even if the user's consent was allegedly given in the form agreed between the parties. Furthermore, under the provision of art 96 paras 1 and 3, payment service providers shall have in place customer identification measures where the payer: (a) accesses their payment account online, (b) initiates an electronic payment transaction, and (c) carries out any action through a remote channel which may imply a risk of payment fraud or other abuse.

63 In addition, the liability of payment service providers is also established in the provision of art 8 of Law 2251/1994 ('Liability of the service provider'), as amended by Law 4512/2018 and in force, which is in accordance with the provisions of Law 4537/2018. The aforementioned provision stipulates, among others, that the service provider is liable for any property damage or non-pecuniary loss caused unlawfully and culpably, by their act or omission, when providing services to the consumer. The term 'service providers' also includes banks, which have transactional obligations of protection and security towards the consumers Therefore, if, in the context of the provision of services by the bank, conduct that does not meet the standard of the reasonably expected security, ie the transactional obligations of protection and security, occurs, this behaviour is unlawful and, at the same time, culpable, since both conditions of unlawfulness and culpability are met based on the consideration of negligence as a form of fault and as a form of illegality as well (AP 974/2018, AP 1849/2017, AP 1284/2017, AP 535/2012).

64 The mere breach of a contractual obligation, given that the existence of a contractual relationship between the provider of the service and its recipient is the norm, is not sufficient to establish tortious liability, but illegality is required, in the sense of the provision of art 914 of the GrCC. In this case, the provision applies, regardless of the existence of a contract. It is possible, however, that a damaging

action, either an act or an omission, by which the contract is breached, may at the same time establish liability in tort. This arises when this action, in itself, even without the pre-existing contractual relationship, would be illegal, as contrary to the general duty imposed by the provision of art 914 of the GrCC, not to culpably cause harm to another (AP 1228/2019, AP 1028/2015, AP 1738/2013). If there is also a breach of contract and, in particular, defective performance, it will be a case of concurrence of claims. Given that the observance of the rules of professional diligence is also a contractual obligation of the service provider and that these rules of professional diligence, internationally, are formed as a single framework, whether there is a contractual link or not, a service that violates these rules shall constitute, at the same time, both an illegal act, according to the provision of art 914 of the GrCC, and a contractual violation. The above provision also applies to contracts in which the counterparty is a supplier bank (AP 254/2018, AP 884/2018, Athens Court of Appeal 662/2018).

The Court is convinced that the three disputed transactions do not meet the 65 requirement of authenticity, within the meaning of Law 4537/2018, as the plaintiff had not given his consent to the transfers. The plaintiff entered his personal codes on the counterfeit website, but he was never informed, before the completion of the disputed transaction, of the amount that would be transferred from his account to a third party's account, nor did he receive on his mobile phone through a message or in any other way, the six-digit one-time code, which was required to be entered for the payment transactions to be completed and for him to be identified. Thus, the defendant is liable for the payment of the aforementioned amount, in accordance with the provisions of arts 71, 73 and 92 of Law 4537/2018, which provide for liability of the service provider and for exemption only for unusual and unforeseen circumstances, which are beyond the control of the party invoking them and which could not be avoided, despite all efforts to the contrary. These provisions introduce mandatory law (*jus cogens*) in favour of users.

Furthermore, the liability of the defendant to compensate the plaintiff is also 66 based on the provision of art 8 of Law 2251/1994, as well as on the provisions of arts 288 and 914 GrCC. Thus, given that the commission of electronic fraud by means of the 'phishing' method was already, during the time in question, widespread and the defendant banking company itself characterises it in its pleadings as the 'most usual and known method used by third parties', the latter, as a provider of services to consumers being subject to transactional obligations of protection and security, did not show due diligence in ensuring the required security in electronic transaction services, which was encroached by the fraudulent interception of money. The bank did not meet all the required high security standards in the execution of their services, failing to implement the process of verifying the identification of the customer and checking the authenticity of the account, to which the funds were sent, thus not realising the 'suspicious' character of the transaction. Further, the bank did not take well-developed and improved means of protection in order to fully protect its customers from malicious attacks and online fraud and in order to prevent the intrusion of unauthorised third parties and did not comply with its obligations to enlighten, properly inform and warn its customer, as it failed to inform him, sufficiently, of the attempts to intercept his personal information by sending an informative email or SMS, ensuring the increased surveillance of his interests. While the plaintiff responded immediately and informed the bank on the same day and indeed even at a time prior to the third transfer, the bank did not act immediately, regarding the investigation of the fact and the seizure of the remittances from the foreign bank, so that to thwart its client's loss, but it waited for more than one month until it responded to the foreign bank. In addition to being culpable in the form of gross negligence, such behaviour was also illegal, since, even without the contractual relationship, it would have been contrary to the provisions of Law 4537/2018 and Law 2251/1994. These provisions relate not only to the level of security of the services that the consumer is legitimately entitled to expect, but also to the building of the trust necessary in banking transactions, which the bank had to offer within the sphere of the services provided, but also subject to the principles of good faith and common usage (art 288 GrCC), as well as in the general duty imposed by art 914 GrCC not to culpably cause harm to another.

67 Because of the above, the plaintiff, in addition to his positive damage, also suffered moral harm, consisting of his mental suffering and the agitation, anxiety and distress he experienced from the funds not being credited to his account immediately and especially despite the continuous assurances from the defendant that everything was under control and going well. Taking into account all the circumstances of the case in general, the extent of the plaintiff's damage, the gravity of the defendant's fault, the mental suffering of the plaintiff, the insecurity he felt regarding his savings, the distress he experienced and the stress he suffered because of his financial loss as well as the financial and social status of the parties, compensation must, at the discretion of the Court, be awarded, as monetary satisfaction, due to his moral harm. The amount of € 1,000, was considered reasonable and fair.

c) Commentary

68 In the case under consideration, it is obvious that there was, primarily, a breach of the bank's contractual obligation towards its customer. Subject to both Law 4537/2018 and Directive 2015/2366/EU, payment transactions are based either on a framework contract or on an individual order granted by the payer to the payment

service provider. Consequently, the liability provided for in art 88 of Law 4537/2018 (and art 89 of Directive 2015/2366/EU), although not specified in the provision, constitutes liability for the defective performance of the bank's obligation.

However, the decision adopts a view which is common in Greek jurisprudence. 69
According to it, a violation of the rules of professional diligence constitutes unlawful behaviour, under art 914 GrCC. The reasoning is as follows: as it is established, unlawful conduct exists not only when a specific, peremptory or prohibitive rule of law is violated, but also when the obligations of care and security imposed by good faith are violated.[20] Observance by professionals of the rules of diligent and appropriate exercise of their profession is imposed by the principle of good faith (art 288 GrCC). Therefore, a violation of the rules of professional diligence constitutes a tort and entails (in addition to contractual) tortious liability, which implies an obligation to compensate and restore the moral harm.[21] In fact, it is held by jurisprudence that in these cases, when the injured party has the status of a consumer, art 8 para 1 of Law 2251/1994 applies as well,[22] as long as 'behaviour has been manifested that does not correspond to the reasonably expected safety that is, to the transactional obligations of care and security'.[23]

First of all, it could be questioned whether the violation of rules of law estab- 70
lishing obligations in the context of a specific contract constitutes a tort.[24] Even more questionable is whether it can be considered that the violation of rules of professional diligence (of a doctor, engineer, etc) constitutes an illegal act. The reasonable counterargument to this opinion[25] is that, with such an approach, every breach of a contractual obligation by a professional is ultimately equated to a tort. In other words, any violation of the standards of appropriate service provision is considered to constitute not only a breach of contract, but also illegal behaviour. This not only constitutes an excessive expansion of the scope of tort law, but ultimately sets aside the rules for breach of contract, which, among others, do not

20 Indicatively AP 2061/2022; AP 1185/2021; AP 1355/2019; AP 54/2019; AP 1359/2018.

21 AP 2061/2022.

22 'The service provider is liable for any property damage or moral harm caused unlawfully and culpably, by his/her act or omission, when providing services to the consumer. A service provider means anyone who, in the context of exercising a professional activity, provides a service independently'.

23 AP 1024/2022; AP 1047/2020; AP 1439/2019; AP 1028/2015.

24 According to Greek jurisprudence, the violation of laws which incorporate the Directives known as MiFiD I and MiFiD II into Greek legislation establishes tortious liability of the credit institution. See indicatively AP 1182/2021; AP 342/2021; AP 1228/2019; AP 974/2018; AP 1028/2015; AP 2212/2014; AP 1738/2013.

25 See, indicatively, *Z Tsolakidis*, The expansion of tort liability and the commercial enterprise, Applications of Civil Law 2019, 850 f.

allow the recovery of non-pecuniary loss in the case of breach of contractual obligations (art 299 GrCC).

6. Personal Injury

a) Notable Decisions

71 Article 931 GrCC reads as follows: 'The disability or disfigurement caused to the injured party shall be taken into account when awarding compensation if it affects his/her future'. Decisions no **303/2023** and no **415/2023** of the **Supreme Court** confirmed the settled case law[26] that this provision provides for awarding a victim suffering from disability or disfigurement a reasonable amount of compensation, precisely because of the disability or disfigurement, without connection to specific property damage, which, after all, cannot be determined. Therefore, the amount to which the victim is entitled according to art 931 GrCC, is calculated at the discretion of the judge who will determine in a fair judgment a reasonable amount of money, based, on the one hand, on the type, extent and the consequences of the disability or disfigurement of the victim and, on the other hand, on the age, sex, special abilities of the victim and the degree of their contributory negligence. The claim established on art 931 GrCC is different from the claim under art 929 GrCC, which refers to compensation for the victim's loss of income, which is necessarily linked to proof of specific property damage due to the victim's inability to work. Further, it also differs from a claim for monetary satisfaction due to moral harm, according to the provision of art 932 GrCC. All the above claims can be brought, either cumulatively or individually, since they are independent claims and the foundation of each does not necessarily presuppose the existence of the others.

72 Questions of contributory negligence (art 300 GrCC) were considered in decision no **7/2023** of the **Dodecanese Court of Appeal.** The plaintiff was riding a moped, entered the oncoming traffic lane and collided with the car of the defendant, who was driving at normal speed, but did not have time to stop his vehicle. In addition, the plaintiff was not wearing a protective helmet. According to art 300 GrCC, compensation can be reduced or excluded if the injured party contributed to their damage or to the extent thereof. The Court held that the provision introduces two distinct elements, namely a contribution to the occurrence of the damage and a contribution to the extent of the damage. It was held that the plaintiff

26 Indicatively AP 931/2021; AP 485/2021; AP 1106/2019; AP 419/2019.

was jointly liable for the collision, and therefore for the occurrence of the damage to the extent of 80 %, a percentage by which the compensation should be reduced. Next, the resulting amount must be further reduced by 50 % because the plaintiff contributed to the severity of her injury, thus to the extent of her damage, by not wearing a protective helmet.

In decision no **517/2023** of the **Athens Court of Appeal**, it was held that the motorcycle passenger was jointly liable to 20 % for his damage due to a car accident because, although he would have been able to avoid risk to his health by not getting on the vehicle, he did so. Although he was aware that the motorcycle driver was under the influence of alcohol and narcotic substances, he nevertheless chose to board the above vehicle, knowing of the driver's reduced ability to drive. The fact that he (the passenger) was in the same situation, that is under the influence of alcohol and narcotic substances, does not negate either his contributory negligence comprising in getting onto a vehicle whose driver had a reduced ability to drive, or his decision to get on board without wearing a helmet, as his state did not completely exclude him from realising the danger of driving under the influence of alcohol and riding a motorcycle without wearing a helmet. 73

In decision no **1462/2023** of the **Athens Court of Appeal**, it was held that the final decision issued on an action for compensation, due to death or injury to the body or health of a person, constitutes *res judicata* in the new trial for compensation with the same historical and legal cause, regarding: a) the circumstances under which the tort took place; b) the liability of the tortfeasor; c) the possible joint liability of the tortfeasor and the victim; d) the causal connection between the damaging event and the damage; and e) the damage suffered by the plaintiff, for the period of time mentioned in the first action, but not for the subsequent time, during which the tort may continue to have damaging effects, because they had not been raised, nor had been made the subject of investigation in the first action. Therefore, when loss of profit is claimed due to incapacity to work due to a lifelong disability resulting from an injury in a traffic accident, the final judgment on an action between the same parties, with the same subject matter for an earlier time, produces *res judicata* that the victim became disabled for life and is also entitled to claim loss of profit for a later period, since the examination of this issue was necessary to support the original decision. On the contrary, the *res judicata* of the final decision, which was issued in the first action of the victim due to a tort and specifically due to physical or health damage, does not include adverse consequences that constitute a deterioration of the existing situation, which, in the beginning, could not have been foreseen to occur in the ordinary course of events. 74

b) Compensation of Non-Pecuniary Damage

75 The plaintiff, as a result of errors in the diagnosis and during the operation for the removal of a tumour, suffered a partial and irreversible (permanent) disability. The Court of Appeal of Thessaloniki awarded her monetary satisfaction due to moral harm amounting to € 150,000,

> 'in view of the circumstances of the tort, namely the type of infringement, the degree of culpability of the assignee's doctors, the non-existence of contributory negligence, her age (69 years old), as well as of the social and financial status of the parties'.

76 The **Supreme Court**, in its decision no **55/2023**, ruled that the Court of Appeal

> 'did not violate the principle of proportionality nor did it exceed the extreme limits of its discretion, given that this amount, according to common experience, judicial practice and conscience of fairness, does not lag in an obvious way behind those that are usually awarded in similar cases of monetary satisfaction based on the determining criteria mentioned in the decision'.

77 The Court of Appeal of Nafplio awarded the family of a person who died in a work accident monetary satisfaction due to mental anguish as follows: it awarded to his wife, his minor daughter and his parents the amount of € 50,000 each and to his brother the amount of € 30,000. The **Supreme Court**, in decision no **61/2023**, ruled that with regard to the wife and daughter, the Court of Appeal did not exceed the extreme limits of its discretion, nor did it include insufficient reasoning in its decision, because the amount awarded is the amount reasonably awarded by the courts in cases of work accidents of similar gravity and consequences to that of the victim, also taking into account the liability of the appellants (the tortfeasors) at a rate of 80 % and the joint liability of the victim himself at a rate of 20 %. On the contrary, with regard to the other relatives, the Court of Appeal violated the principle of proportionality and exceeded the extreme limits of its discretion, since the amounts awarded to them, according to common experience, judicial practice and conscience of fairness, patently exceeded those which are usually awarded in similar cases for monetary satisfaction, without justifying why the amounts in question are reasonable, in view of the acknowledgment that the victim had already created his own family and at the time of death he was living with his wife and his child outside the parental residence.

78 The Court of Appeal of Athens awarded the family of a traffic accident victim monetary compensation due to mental anguish: (a) to each of his brothers the amount of € 15,000, (b) to his wife the amount of € 40,000 and (c) to each of his minor children the amount of € 50,000. The **Supreme Court**, in decision no **162/**

2023, held that the Court did not violate the principle of proportionality, nor did it exceed the extreme limits of its discretion, given that these amounts, according to common experience, judicial practice and conscience of fairness, do not exceed in an obvious way those that are usually awarded in similar cases of monetary satisfaction.

The plaintiff entered a construction site in a port area riding his motorcycle. 79
The vehicle overturned causing him to suffer permanent disability. He was found to be 30 % co-responsible for causing the accident. The Court of Appeal of Thessaloniki awarded him compensation due to disability, according to art 931 GrCC, in the amount of € 40,000, and monetary satisfaction due to moral harm, according to art 932 GrCC, in the amount of € 50,000. The **Supreme Court** in decision no **303/2023** ruled that the Court of Appeal did not violate the provisions of arts 931 and 932 GrCC and the principle of proportionality and did not exceed the extreme limits of its discretion, given that these amounts, taking into account the significant degree of his contributory negligence in the occurrence of the accident and the seriousness of his injury from it, according to common experience, judicial practice and the conscience of fairness, are reasonable and do not lag behind, in an obvious way, those that are usually awarded in similar cases.

The victim of an accident suffered multiple fractures, required operations, 80
hospitalisation and a long post-operative rehabilitation period, and developed depression. The Court of Appeal of Athens awarded him the amount of € 18,000 as monetary satisfaction due to moral harm. The **Supreme Court**, in decision no **1341/2023**, ruled that the Court of Appeal did not violate the principle of proportionality, nor did it exceed the extreme limits of its discretion, given that this amount, according to common experience, judicial practice and conscience of fairness, does not exceed, in an obvious way, what is usually awarded in similar cases of monetary satisfaction due to moral harm.

C. Literature

1. *K Foundedaki/M-E Gerasopoulou/V Maroudas*, Civil Medical Liability (Nomiki Vivliothiki, Athens 2023)

The book comprehensively presents all issues related to civil medical liability, with 81
references to Greek theory and jurisprudence, also including a comparison with developments in German and French law. The scope of the study is not only limited to tortious liability but also refers to contractual liability (medical treatment contract). In the field of tort law, the following should be highlighted: the study of med-

ical error (fourth chapter), where, among other things, the criteria for the recognition of the error and the measure of diligence required are examined, the study of the doctor's liability as a service provider (fifth chapter) and the examination of issues related to causation (seventh chapter). Tortious medical liability because of a breach of obligations regarding the patient's consent and the lack of adequate information are also investigated in detail.

2. *A Xynopoulou*, Duties of Care in the System of Tortious Liability (Sakkoulas, Athens-Thessaloniki 2023)

82 The author examines the notion of illegality under art 914 GrCC, in particular through the recognition of due diligence obligations (duties of care). The study of the problem under Greek law is presented together with a comparative examination of English and German law, as well as a historical review of the roots of the institution. The fourth chapter of the book is devoted to Greek law. The author examines the crucial issue of the expansion of illegality, addressing both the extensive discussion in Greek theory (regarding the limits of the expansion of tortious liability) and the jurisprudence, which seem to accept a general principle not to harm others (*neminem laedere*). In order to limit the extent of such a general principle, the author examines several cases which justify the grounding of special duties of care (invitation to the public to visit a place; previous creation of a hazardous situation; circulation of a product, etc). In this sense, she examines the specific conditions which may ground a duty to control and a duty to interfere.

3. *E Kinini*, Joint and Several Liability and Recourse in the Law of Free Competition (Nomiki Vivliothiki, Athens 2023)

83 The book deals with the specific issue of the liability of a company which secured immunity in the context of a 'leniency programme', provided by the legislation for the protection of free competition (Law 4529/2018, which incorporated Directive 2014/104/EU). Initially, the joint and several liability of more than one enterprise is investigated, not only towards those damaged by their actions, but also their internal liability due to recourse. Next (fourth chapter) the liability of the company that secured immunity is examined: on the one hand, the limitation of its liability towards the injured parties and, on the other, the relationship with other companies which took part in the infringement of competition law.

4. *K Christakakou-Fotiadis*, The Liability of Minors and their Supervisors in the Law of Torts (PN Sakkoulas, Athens 2nd edn 2023)

The first chapter of the study deals with the tortious liability of minors. The capacity to impute and the liability of a minor between the ages of 10 and 14, who is liable, unless they can prove that they acted 'without discretion', is considered. Furthermore (second chapter), the liability of the minor for reasons of leniency, that is, their obligation to pay reasonable compensation when the damage they caused cannot be covered from another source, is also investigated. The third chapter studies the liability of third parties for damage caused by minors. In particular, the concept of supervision, its neglect, and the possibility for supervisors to be exonerated if they prove that they exercised adequate supervision over the minor are explored. 84

Attila Menyhárd

XIV. Hungary

A. Legislation

There was no new legislation in tort law in Hungary in 2023. 1

B. Cases

1. Supreme Court, Curia Pfv.III.20.287/2022/5, BH2023. 8., January 2023: Loss of a Chance; Medical Malpractice

a) Brief Summary of the Facts

In 2002, the mother of the first plaintiff and the spouse of the second plaintiff was 2
diagnosed with a benign tumour for which she underwent several operations. In October 2016, the plaintiffs' relative consulted her doctor due to an increased occurrence of occipital neuralgia (a headache disorder that can cause sudden, sharp head pain). The doctor recommended infiltration treatment and the procedure was performed at the defendant's neurosurgery clinic on 21 October 2016 at 1pm. After administering Lidocaine and Midazolan, the treating physician left the patient alone and did not arrange for her observation. On returning to the ward at 1.20pm, the second plaintiff noticed that his spouse was unconscious and that her lips were blue. Following resuscitation, the plaintiffs' relative was admitted to the intensive care unit. A CT scan of the skull performed on 21 October 2016 and an MRI scan of the skull and cervical spine performed on 23 October 2016 confirmed brain damage due to oxygen deprivation. The plaintiffs' relative died on 31 October 2016. In the case of infiltration treatment, one to two hours of observation is recommended, and this includes the monitoring of the patient's consciousness, blood pressure, pulse, and respiratory functions every 10–15 minutes. The monitoring of a patient's respiratory functions is mandatory after administration of the drug Midazolan, as one of the possible side effects of taking this drug is respiratory paralysis.

https://doi.org/10.1515/9783111376721-015

b) Judgment of the Court

3 In their claim, the plaintiffs sought compensation of their non-pecuniary loss. The defendant pleaded that there was only a direct causal link between the failure to act and the reduction in the patient's chances of recovery and survival which cannot be qualified as an unlawful act vis-á-vis the plaintiffs. Further the defendant argued that the alleged conduct threatened, at most, to interfere with the plaintiffs' right to privacy in the family as a whole. He also argued that private law provides for damages as a remedy only in case the interference with a right has already occurred, but not if there is only a threat of interference with such a right. The court of first instance awarded HUF 5,000,000 (€ 12,500) to each plaintiff as compensation for their non-pecuniary loss. The court of second instance, reduced the amount to HUF 2,000,000 (€ 5,000) per person. The Supreme Court, however, reversed this judgment and confirmed the judgment of the court of first instance.

c) Commentary

4 The question of loss of a chance is an issue which has been approached in different ways in Hungarian tort law. It has procedural aspects in the context of evidence or allocating the burden of proof, while solutions provided in substantive law include – varying from case to case – establishing a causal link or proportional liability on the grounds of partial causation. It seems to be a well-established court practice that, in the context of non-pecuniary damages in medical malpractice cases, a finding of the loss of a chance is sufficient to establish a causal link. All courts have followed this approach. The difference in this case is that, while the court of second instance concluded that the sum awarded as non-pecuniary damages should be proportionate to the established probability, the court of first instance and the Supreme Court did not apply such a proportionality test. The central issue in the case was that if the court establishes the defendant's liability on the basis of an increase in the probability of the victim's death, should the sum awarded in the form of *solatium doloris* be proportionate to the probability of surviving? The lower courts inclined to this approach and awarded *solatium doloris* in an amount proportionate to the probability that the death of the plaintiff was increased by the negligence of the defendant's doctors. The Supreme Court, however, responded that if a wrongful interference with inherent rights was established, the interference shall determine the sum but not the manner in which causality is established. Thus, the full sum, approx € 12,500, should be awarded.

2. Supreme Court, Curia Pfv.III.21.589/2019/6, BH 2023. 9., January 2023: Compensation for Loss of a Relative

a) Brief Summary of the Facts

5 BS, the father-in-law of plaintiff 1, was the father of plaintiff 2 and the spouse of plaintiff 3. His medical history included, among other things, chronic obstructive pulmonary disease, ischemic heart disease, reduced left ventricular function, aortic and bicuspid valve disease, and Parkinson's disease. On 15 December 2008, BS was admitted to the defendant hospital and, two days later, was transferred to the National Institute of Cardiology, where an ultrasound examination of the heart confirmed an artificial valve blockage. However, despite immediate treatment with anticoagulant therapy, his clinical condition deteriorated and he died on 20 December 2008, suffering from septic shock. In their action, the plaintiffs sought compensation for the material and non-material damage they suffered as a result of the loss of a relative.

b) Judgment of the Court

6 In its judgment, the court of first instance awarded HUF 1,000,000 (€ 2,500) in non-pecuniary damages to plaintiff 1 and HUF 2,500,000 (€ 6,250) in non-pecuniary damages to plaintiff 2. The defendant's liability was based on the fact that the plaintiffs' relative had not been properly informed about the use of anticoagulant injections when he was discharged from hospital following his surgery in November 2008 and that he was not properly informed about the use of anticoagulant injections on 15 December 2008 and 17 December 2008. While the patient was in hospital between 15 November 2008 and 17 December 2008, the defendant did not carry out appropriate examinations in accordance with the patient's complaints and the medical condition in question. As a result, the defendant's diagnosis was either incorrect or delayed and this led to the death of the plaintiffs' relative. In assessing the claims for non-pecuniary damages, it was considered that the plaintiffs had had a close family relationship with their relative and that the loss of this relationship violated their right to a family life. In the case of plaintiff 2, the equally close parent-child relationship was taken into account. This judgment was finally confirmed by the Supreme Court.

c) Commentary

7 The Supreme Court confirmed that if the death of a spouse's direct relative results in the severance of a close family bond, which reaches the level of a parent-child relationship, that relative may also be entitled to non-pecuniary damages for the interference with the right to live in an intact family The main conclusion of the judgment is that in every case, it has to be assessed whether there has been a breach of family integrity and whether there has been a loss in connection with that breach, which may give rise to non-pecuniary compensation. The sum of compensation should be determined on the basis of the particular circumstances. It is clear from this judgment that even a son-in-law can be entitled to compensation for the loss of his father-in-law.

3. Supreme Court, Curia Pfv.III.20.110/2020/6, BH2023. 36., February 2023: Assessment of Damages

a) Brief Summary of the Facts

8 On 3 June 2012, in a road traffic accident caused by the defendant's insured in Germany, the plaintiff suffered concussion, a neck sprain, bruising all over his body, a head injury (8 cm cut) and a laceration above his right eyebrow. He developed an acromioclavicular dislocation associated with a contusion of his left shoulder, which healed but left the plaintiff with reduced mobility of his left shoulder joint, a moderate functional atrophy of the deltoid muscle, and shoulder impingement syndrome. The plaintiff developed post-traumatic stress disorder as a result of the accident, and the psychological trauma contributed to the emergence of symptoms of anxiety and depression, which he had suffered from prior to the accident due to a genetic predisposition. He required specialist medical treatment for his mental illness. He has a 21% overall impairment to his mental health as a result of the accident and is not expected to improve.

9 Prior to the accident, the plaintiff worked as a truck driver and occasionally took on work as a crane operator in order to earn extra money. As he was unable to perform his work due to the accident, his employment was terminated by mutual agreement. The plaintiff is unable to work in his original occupation because of his condition and has been receiving disability benefits since 24 February 2014. The plaintiff claimed non-pecuniary damages and also compensation for lost income in the form of a monthly income replacement allowance. In order to determine the amount of this allowance, the defendant sought to take into account, first, job advertisements attached to the application to prove the level of income possi-

ble in a similar job and, second, data provided by the Ministry of the National Economy.

b) Judgment of the Court

In its judgment, the court of first instance awarded HUF 4,000,000 (€ 40,000) in non-pecuniary damages and HUF 134,692 per month as the income replacement allowance. In assessing the merits of the claim for non-material damages, the court assessed that the plaintiff had enjoyed an active life before the accident, but that the accident had completely changed his life, he had lost his previous job, he was unable to find a job because of his condition and age, he needed specialist medical assistance and he was unable to look after his household properly on his own. The court further took into account the fact that the plaintiff requires rehabilitation treatment and medication, and he suffers from recurrent pain and sleep problems. The Court of Appeal upheld the judgment. Both courts awarded the income replacement allowance only until the plaintiff's retirement age. The Supreme Court confirmed the judgment as to the part awarding non-pecuniary damages and also the amount of the income replacement allowance but without the time limit. 10

c) Commentary

Court practice does not consider the reaching of the retirement age as the final deadline for the payment of income replacement benefits if there is no proof beyond reasonable doubt that the victim will no longer work in the given circumstances. If the period of the obligation to pay an annuity cannot be limited, it can be established without a time limit. Reaching retirement age can only be the final date for the obligation to pay an income replacement pension if it can be foreseen with certainty that it will lead to the termination of an individual's earning capacity. 11

4. Supreme Court, Curia Pfv.III.20.604/2022/5, BH2023. 96., March 2023: Loss of a Chance

a) Brief Summary of the Facts

12 On the basis of a contract of appointment concluded on 21 November 2011, defendant 1 represented the plaintiff in an action for damages brought against the latter. Defendant 1 was represented by defendant 2. The judgment ordering the plaintiff hunting company to pay HUF 9,131,199 in damages (plus default interest and costs) was served on 9 March 2017 on defendant 1's law firm. On 24 March 2017, the law firm lodged an appeal by electronic means with the Nyírbátor District Court, which, after transmission, was dismissed *ex officio* by this court as being submitted too late. The decision dismissing the application for failure to comply with the time limit within which an appeal could be lodged was upheld by the Debrecen Court of Appeal, which upheld the decision dismissing the appeal. As a result, the judgment of the court of the first instance that became final was served on 7 December 2017 on the defendant, who did not notify the plaintiff. On 6 December 2017, the application for an enforcement order was filed at the district court, and in January 2018 HUF 17,272,712 (€ 42,500) was withdrawn from the plaintiff's bank account by a bailiff. The plaintiff claimed HUF 1,336,849 plus HUF 15,878,385 (approx € 42,000) in damages as compensation for the money lost as a result of the court's decision becoming final due to the defendant's negligence.

b) Judgment of the Court

13 In its judgment, the court of first instance awarded HUF 668,424 plus HUF 4,763,515 in damages (a total of approx € 13,250). The court established that the legal basis for the claim for damages is the failure to meet the deadline for appeal, as a result of which, the legal representative deprived the plaintiff of the legal remedy provided for in the Fundamental Law. According to consistent judicial practice, this Law must be examined in the context of a violation of an individual's personality rights and can be compensated by damages. The court of second instance partially altered the judgment of the court of first instance in the appealed part, and reduced the amount of damages to HUF 1,500,000. The court of second instance pointed out that the damages are based on the interference with the plaintiff's inherent rights. It stressed that the duty of the law firm providing the legal representation was to handle the case to the best of its ability in accordance with the law and to promote the rights of its client in a conscientious manner and in a manner befitting the legal profession. As admitted by the defendants (and the insurer as intervener),

the appeal against the judgment of the court of first instance in the main proceedings before the District Court, which found against the plaintiff in the present action, was erroneously lodged by the defendant in the first instance, as a result of an administrative error, and was consequently dismissed for being out of time. As a result, the plaintiff lost the chance of having his application for a stay of proceedings dismissed, ie he lost the chance of winning his case. The fact that the defendant's failure to act prevented the plaintiff from exercising his fundamental right guaranteed by art XXVIII (7) of the Fundamental Law, and from making use of the possibility to seek a legal remedy as regulated in the Civil Code is assessed as an interference with the plaintiff's inherent rights, which is the basis for a claim for damages. The court of second instance stressed the fact that the failure of defendant 1 was not the failure to lodge an appeal but rather an administrative error, the lodging of the appeal with the wrong court. After becoming aware of the error, the legal representative, using all the possibilities available under the procedural rules (request for certification, appeal against the rejection of the application), did everything possible to correct his error, but his actions were not effective. In the light of this, the Court of Appeal established the amount of damages at HUF 1,500,000. The Supreme Court upheld the judgment of the court of second instance. The Court established that, in the case of a lawyer's failure to meet a deadline for legal remedies, the severity of the infringement and the degree of fault are of particular importance as criteria when determining the amount of damages. However, the uncertain factor of the amount of the pecuniary loss suffered by the victim in connection with the failure to pursue the appropriate legal remedy cannot be considered a non-pecuniary loss suffered by the victim.

c) Commentary

This case is a typical loss of a chance case in the context of the professional liability 14
of lawyers. Hungarian courts are reluctant to apply any consistent and general doctrine in cases of loss of a chance. Solutions to address the problem, in the context of causation if probabilities but not certainty can be established, vary depending on whether uncertainty is inherent or not. If uncertainty emerges in the context of evidence, a reversal of the burden of proof or simply the discretionary power of the court in the course of weighing evidence can be options. In cases of inherent uncertainty, that is, when there is no potential evidence to establish causation, such as in cases of medical malpractice, increasing the risk of injury is considered as establishing a causal link and resulting in liability. In such cases, liability is not proportional. In other cases, partial causation can be a means to establish proportional liability. As regards the liability of lawyers for professional negligence, none

of these solutions can prevail. Courts have 'invented' a special way of providing satisfaction – but not damages – to victims of such negligence. According to this view, access to justice is denied in such cases by the negligence of the legal service provider, which is an interference with the client's fundamental rights. This line of thought enables the courts to qualify the result of such negligence as an interference with inherent rights of the person and to award non-pecuniary damages (or *solatium doloris*) with the aim of providing just satisfaction to the victim. This doctrine is rather inconsistent from the point of view of protecting the inherent rights of the person, because the underlying paradigm is that inherent rights shall be derived from human dignity. The right to access the justice system, however, should not be qualified as an inherent right derived from human dignity. It is inconsistent for Hungarian courts to consider the chance of losing a case as an interference with the right to access justice and to award non-pecuniary damages, insofar as access to justice should not be qualified as a personality right. This is a way for the courts to avoid the application of the doctrine of loss of a chance, while at the same time not wanting to leave the wrongful conduct of the defendant without consequences. The Supreme Court explicitly stressed that the loss suffered by the victim as a result of the defendant's fault is irrelevant when determining the sum to be paid as *solatium doloris.*

5. Supreme Court, Curia Pfv.III.21.258/2021/6, BH2023. 130., May 2023: Interference with Personality Rights

a) Brief Summary of the Facts

15 On 11 June 2019, while the plaintiff was still breast feeding her third child, the plaintiff went to the defendant's private clinic because she felt a lump the size of a walnut in her left breast. The defendant, after investigating the complaints, classified the lump as a symptom associated with breastfeeding, noting in the medical file: 'intact lactating breasts, several tender, non-inflamed lumps on the left side. Diagnosis: lactation, suggestion for control.' The defendant did not order any further tests, but verbally informed the plaintiff that she should return for a check-up although the lump in her left breast was already painful and red. On 26 August 2019, the plaintiff attended a private clinic of another gynaecologist, where further examinations were ordered. On 9 September 2019, the plaintiff was diagnosed with malignant tumours of the left breast and lymph nodes of the axilla and upper limb. She subsequently underwent mastectomy surgery. The plaintiff claimed HUF 1,000,000 (€ 2,500) in damages from the defendant clinic. She argued that the defendant's doctor had infringed her rights to life, mental

and bodily integrity and health by his conduct during the examination. She claimed that she had suffered psychological trauma and injury because, until the expert opinion was provided in the notarial procedure, she had lived in the knowledge that, had the defendant acted properly and carried out the necessary tests without delay, her condition would not have progressed to a metastatic stage.

b) Judgment of the Court

The court of first instance ordered the defendant to pay HUF 700,000 (€ 1,750) in damages. The court of second instance reversed the judgment and rejected the claim. This judgment was upheld by the Supreme Court. 16

c) Commentary

The issue in this case was whether an interference with the personality right to bodily and mental integrity can be established also in the absence of an apparent illness. The courts agreed that this should be answered in the affirmative. The different approaches meant that while the court of first instance established an unlawful interference with the plaintiff's personality rights *per se,* the upper courts concluded that psychological impairment requires proof when they established that psychological impairment that does not rise to the level of illness may also constitute an injury to personality. However, here, the burden of proof lies with the victim. § 2:52 of the Hungarian Civil Code provides that, beyond the fact of unlawful interference, evidence of injury should not be required as a precondition for awarding *solatium doloris.* In spite of this, courts tend to require proof of actual harm. 17

6. Supreme Court, Curia Pfv.III.20.371/2022/5, BH2023. 156., July 2023: Non-Pecuniary Damages

a) Brief Summary of the Facts

The plaintiff attended the defendant's neurosurgery outpatient clinic on 27 May 2013 with a history of lower extremity weakness that had begun one and a half to two years prior to the treatment. Imaging studies confirmed a dislocation of the cervical V vertebra, disc herniation and consequent spinal cord compression, and a block in vertebrae VI-VII. During the surgery performed on 13 June 2013, the 18 cervical discs IV and V, hernia and bony outgrowths were removed and vertebrae IV-VI were fixed by the implantation of metallic material. An MRI scan taken on 21 January 2014 showed moderate degeneration of the intervertebral discs II-III, III-IV and compression of the spinal cord at the level of the cervical vertebra VI. The defendant's physician recommended a laminectomy of the cervical vertebra VI on 27 January 2014. During the pre-operative examination at the cardiology ward of the hospital in Kiskunfélegyhaza, it was decided not to administer the anticoagulant (Warfarin) due to the previously inserted artificial valve but rather to change to an anticoagulant with a low molecular weight heparin (LMWH), from 14 March 2014. After some preliminary treatment, the plaintiff was admitted to the defendant's neurosurgery clinic on 17 March 2014. The use of the LMWH (Clexane) was recorded on the fever chart and medication order form on that day. The surgical procedure (CV-VI laminectomy) was performed on 18 March 2014. A follow-up MRI scan on 23 March 2014 confirmed the presence of a haematoma in the spinal canal. As the degree of spinal cord compression was significantly increased compared to the previous examination, another surgery was performed on the same day to remove the hematoma located above the hard capsule and in the soft tissues. The plaintiff was treated in a hospital rehabilitation ward from 7 April 2014 to 1 August 2014. At the time of discharge, he was wheelchair-bound, could walk 10–15 metres with the aid of a walker, and was experiencing faecal and urinary problems. During his repeated rehabilitation in-patient treatment from 22 August 2014 to 22 October 2014, he became independently mobile with two crutches. An MRI scan on 7 October 2014 did not confirm spinal cord compression, but there were signs of spinal cord damage at the level of the cervical vertebra VI. The condition that the plaintiff developed, and still has, is causally related to the bleeding that occurred as a complication of the spinal surgery performed by the defendant on 18 March 2014 and the spinal cord damage caused by the resulting spinal cord compression.

19 The plaintiff claimed HUF 1,500,000 (€ 3,750) in damages, plus HUF 9,250,238 (€ 23,125) in overdue compensation, HUF 4,794,652 (€ 12,000) in overdue income replacement and HUF 195,750 (€ 490) per month in lost income. The basis of her claim for a cost-replacement allowance is that she also needs help with household and domestic chores.

b) Judgment of the Court

20 In its judgment, the court of first instance decided for the plaintiff and awarded damages according to the claim. The court of second instance set aside this judgment. The Supreme Court upheld the judgment of the court of first instance.

c) Commentary

The primary conclusion of the judgment is that the question of whether the injured party generates the financial resources necessary to cover the material losses resulting from the damage suffered from his own income or property or whether they are advanced to him by third parties outside his control, and whether they are provided free of charge, are matters outside the scope of liability. The free material or non-material (active) assistance of a family member does not serve to relieve the tortfeasor of liability for damages in whole or in part, and the tortfeasor is liable for the compensation of these losses. 21

7. Supreme Court, Curia Pfv.III.21.160/2022/6, BH2023. 298., August 2023: Awarding General Damages

a) Brief Summary of the Facts

On 25 April 2018, the plaintiff, as the driver of a large motorcycle, collided with a car. The defendant was the insurer of the car owner/tortfeasor. As a result of the accident, the plaintiff suffered a concussion, fractures in his right arm, a hyperextension injury of the humerus, a subclavian artery injury, combined with complete loss of sensation in the right hand, a circulatory blood supply disturbance and a pulse deficit in the right upper limb. During emergency vascular reconstructive surgery, it was discovered that the right common carpal nerve was severely damaged and that the plaintiff suffered further bodily harm. The right dominant upper limb is completely impaired in movement and sensation due to damage to the common carpal nerve. The plaintiff has lost all sensation in his right side and movement in his fingers, wrist, elbow joint and shoulder. The plaintiff can only move his shoulder. His pain is persistent and requires strong pain relief. The plaintiff's physical and physiological condition results in an overall health impairment of 64 %, corresponding to a 78 % reduction in working capacity. The plaintiff claimed pecuniary as well as non-pecuniary damages. 22

b) Judgment of the Court

The court of first instance decided for the plaintiff and awarded damages. A part of the total sum was awarded as general damages. The court of second instance reversed the part of the judgment of the court of first instance that awarded general damages. According to the court of second instance, there was a procedural barrier 23 to awarding compensation in the form of general damages as the plaintiff did not specify such damages in his claim. The Supreme Court reversed the judgment of the court of second instance and established that if the court applies general damages without the plaintiff having requested in its claim that the amount of damages be determined on that basis, it does not interfere with the principle of the claim to be determined (art 2(2) of the Civil Procedure Act). The Court also established that when determining the benefits that may be included in the income covered by the income replacement allowance, the purpose of the benefits must be taken into account. A benefit given as reimbursement of expenses should be taken into account as remuneration for work if its real purpose is to remunerate work.

c) Commentary

24 As far as the impact of civil procedural rules to substantive law is concerned, in one case, the court awarded an annuity as general damages although there was no claim for compensation in the form of general damages. General damages shall be awarded, according to § 6:531 of the Hungarian Civil Code, if the extent of compensable loss cannot be established. Their amount shall be calculated by the court on a discretionary basis in an amount which the court finds appropriate for compensating the victim. In this case, the court awarded such compensation without it having been requested by the plaintiff. The defendant argued in its appeal that awarding damages as general damages was not in line with civil procedural rules that require courts to address the claims brought by the parties. The Supreme Court, however, established that there is no violation of the procedural rules concerning the disposition of claims if the court awards general damages without the plaintiff having requested that the amount of damages be determined on that basis.

C. Literature

1. *Réka Pusztahelyi*, Néhány gondolat a párhuzamos kártérítési igények törvényi kizárásáról [Some thoughts upon the non-cumul rule] Salus vocalis Csegöldi indulás – Győri érkezés (Universitas-Győr Nonprofit Kft, Győr 2023) 629 – 640

In this article, the author addresses in a detailed analysis the implications of ap- 25
plying the rule of the Hungarian Civil Code which provides that the aggrieved party shall enforce a claim for damages according to the rules of liability for breach of contract even if the claim could also be established in tort.

Eoin Quill

XV. Ireland

A. Legislation

1. The Courts and Civil Law (Miscellaneous Provisions) Act 2023 (No 18 of 2023)

Part 6 of the Act amends the Occupiers' Liability Act 1995.[1] Section 3 of the 1995 Act 1
provided that the duty owed to visitors was a duty of reasonable care; the Act explicitly noted the care a visitor could provide for themselves, or the care that could be expected of a person supervising the visitor, as relevant factors. This standard equates to the common law standard of care in negligence cases.[2] The definition of reasonable care in sec 3 of the 1995 Act now has a number of more explicit factors to be taken into account in determining whether the duty to visitors was breached. It provides:

> Without prejudice to the generality of subsection (2), in determining the extent of the common duty of care of an occupier towards a visitor, and whether it has been complied with by the occupier, regard shall be had, as appropriate, to all of the circumstances and matters referred to in that subsection, which shall include but are not limited to the following:
>
> (a) the probability of a danger existing on the premises;
> (b) the probability of the occurrence of an injury to, or of damage suffered by, a visitor by reason of a danger existing on the premises;
> (c) the probable severity of an injury to a visitor that might result from a danger existing on the premises;
> (d) the practicability, and the cost, of precautions or preventative measures;

1 Commenced by the Courts and Civil Law (Miscellaneous Provisions) Act 2023 (Commencement) Order 2023 (Statutory Instrument (SI) No 389 of 2023), art 3(f). Irish legislation can be accessed on the website of the Attorney General's Office (AG), <http://www.irishstatutebook.ie/home.html> and on the British and Irish Legal Information Institute website (BAILII), <http://www.bailii.org/>.
2 See *Vega v Cullen* [2005] Irish High Court (IEHC) 363 (Peart J); *O'Flynn v Cherry Hill Inns Ltd Trading As The Oliver Plunkett Bar* [2017] Irish Court of Appeal (IECA) 211, [37] (Irvine J for the court). Most of the 21st century Irish cases cited can be found on BAILII (fn 1) and the Courts Service of Ireland's judgments database, <https://beta.courts.ie/judgments>.

https://doi.org/10.1515/9783111376721-016

(e) where applicable, the social utility of the activity or conduct that gives rise to the risk of injury or damage referred to in paragraph (b).[3]

2 The change is cosmetic, as the listed factors are ones that a court would be inclined to look at in any event in determining reasonableness. The factors are similar to some of those in sec 4 of the 1995 Act, governing the reckless disregard standard owed to recreational users and trespassers, though one would expect the interpretation to vary as between a negligence and recklessness standard. The factors in sec 4 that are related to the occupier's state of knowledge have been slightly rephrased by the 2023 Act to whether the occupier 'knew of, or was reckless as to whether' the various factors were present; the older phrasing was whether they 'knew or had reasonable grounds for believing that' the factors were present. A more significant issue in respect of recklessness as a standard of care, highlighted in the Irish Supreme Court (IESC),[4] is the lack of clarification as to whether recklessness under sec 4 is to be determined by an objective gross negligence standard or by a more subjective determination; this issue is not addressed in the amending legislation. The degree of change in the 2023 Act on the recklessness standard is slight and is probably more cosmetic that substantive and fails to address a more important factor that could carry some significance.

3 The 2023 Act also makes two changes aimed at the exclusion of certain claims. The first is a change to the existing provision on dismissal of claims by criminal entrants and the second is a new voluntary assumption of risk defence. Section 4(3) of the 1995 Act provided for the exclusion of claims by an entrant who 'enters onto premises for the purpose of committing an offence' or a person who commits an offence on the property, unless the court found that allowing the action to proceed was 'in the interests of justice'. The discretion to allow a claim to proceed may now only be exercised 'in exceptional circumstances, having regard to matters such as the nature of the offence, the extent of the recklessness on the part of the occupier, or the fact that the person was not a trespasser', rather than a simple 'interests of justice' test. On the face of it, this narrows judicial scope to allow such actions to proceed, but given the lack of superior court consideration of the earlier provision, it is not clear if it makes s significant difference. The absence of cases also suggests

---

3 The same factors are also added to the standard of reasonable care in respect of the maintenance of structures provided for use primarily by recreational users in sec 4(4) of the 1995 Act (with 'recreational user' substituted for 'visitor' in factors b and c).

4 *Weir-Rogers v The SF Trust* [2005] Irish Supreme Court (IESC) 2; [2005] 1 Irish Reports (IR) 47, noted by *W Binchy* (2005) 1(1) Quarterly Review of Tort Law (QRTL) 1; *R Ryan/D Ryan* (2005) 23 Irish Law Times (ILT) 59; *R Byrne/W Binchy*, Annual Review of Irish Law 2005 (2006) 685 ff; *E Quill*, Ireland in: H Koziol/BC Steininger (eds), European Tort Law (ETL) 2005 (2006) 348, no 14 ff.

it is not a major issue of contention.[5] Nonetheless, the change of wording may give some additional tactical advantage to insurers in a limited number of cases.

4 Section 34(1)(b) of the Civil Liability Act 1961 extended the remit of the contributory negligence defence to situations that would have been governed by the common law defence of voluntary assumption of risk and went on to provide a narrower defence based on consent.[6] The 2023 Act introduces a new sec 5 A into the 1995 Act, providing that the duties imposed in respect of visitors or recreational users do not apply to injury from risks 'willingly accepted' where the entrant 'is capable of comprehending the nature and extent of those risks'. For the purposes of this provision, sec 34(1)(b) of the 1961 Act does not apply and willing acceptance does not require any communication or interaction with the occupier.[7] This effectively restores a voluntary assumption of risk defence that may be implied from the circumstances in occupiers' liability cases. It is not clear what this defence will achieve, since the courts have been taking self-responsibility into account in determining the standard of care in numerous cases in recent years, both under the Act and in other circumstances and it is expressly provided for in the 1995 Act as part of the standards of care.[8] In many instances, claims have been entirely rejected, based on the entrant's ability to appreciate the risk and protect themselves. Thus, the objective sought by the new provision seems to have already been achieved by the courts through an alternative mechanism.

5 Perhaps the amendments do not change much of any practical significance, given what the courts were already doing. It provides the appearance of change to improve the position of occupiers in response to widespread publicity on 'compensation culture' in this area and complaints by representative groups, but will

---

5 Apart from occupiers' liability cases, public policy exclusion of claims due to the claimant's criminal behaviour at the time of being injured is possible, but exceptionally rare. One of the few examples in recent years is *Anderson v Cooke* [2005] IEHC 221, [2005] 2 IR 607, noted by *R Ryan* (2005) 1(1) QRTL 16; *Byrne/Binchy* (fn 4) 711 f; *Quill* (fn 4) no 25 ff.

6 See *BME McMahon/W Binchy*, The Law of Torts (4th edn 2013) [20.68] ff; *E Quill*, Torts in Ireland (4th edn 2014) 446 ff.

7 The waiver defence under the 1961 Act has been held to require communication between the parties – *O'Hanlon v ESB* [1969] IR 75; *McComiskey v McDermott* [1974] IR 75.

8 See *E Quill*, Ireland in: E Karner/BC Steininger (eds), ETL 2021 (2022) 282, no 39 ff; *E Quill*, Ireland in: E Karner/BC Steininger (eds), ETL 2020 (2021) 302, no 34 ff; *E Quill*, Ireland, in: E Karner/BC Steininger (eds), ETL 2019 (2020) 289, no 34 ff; *E Quill*, Ireland, in: E Karner/BC Steininger (eds), ETL 2018 (2019) 299, no 37 ff. In exceptional circumstances, self-responsibility has been considered as a factor excluding a duty of care in negligence, eg *PMcD v The Governor of X Prison* [2021] IESC 65, [2022] 1 IR 741, noted by *R Byrne/W Binchy*, Annual Review of Irish Law 2021 (2022) 480 f; *Quill*, ETL 2021, no 3 ff. Section 3(2) and sec 4(2)(g) of the 1995 Act make explicit provision for this factor in the standards of care towards the various categories of entrant.

make little, if any, difference to the outcome of court decisions. The same could be said of the original 1995 Act, but that seemed to have some practical effect – at least in terms of reducing the media coverage of the issue and assuaging representatives of occupiers and entrants. It may also have encouraged insurance companies to change settlement practices in respect of claims against occupiers. Perhaps this legislation will have similar effects.

2. Protected Disclosures (Amendment) Act 2022 (Commencement) Order 2022 (SI No 510 of 2022)

6 This statutory instrument commenced the 2022 Act from 1 January 2023, bringing into force the new causes of action in that Act – an action for wrongful disclosure of the identity of whistle-blowers and an action for damage caused by knowingly making a false disclosure. These actions are intended to fill gaps left by the original provisions in the Protected Disclosures Act 2014.[9]

3. Garda Síochána (Compensation) Act 2022 (Commencement) Order 2023 (SI No 163 of 2023)

7 Article 2 of this statutory instrument commences the 2022 Act from 10 April 2023. The Act provides a new scheme of compensation for police officers suffering personal injuries or death, maliciously inflicted in connection with their duties; it replaces the scheme established in the Garda Síochána (Compensation) Acts 1941–45 and associated regulations. Section 5 of the Act provides transitional arrangements for claims in process at the time of commencement of the new scheme. One of the key features of the new scheme is that the eligible claims will be referred to the Personal Injuries Resolution Board (PIRB) for assessment of damages.[10]

---

9 Noted by *E Feldman*, Whistleblower Protection, in: R Byrne/W Binchy (eds), Annual Review of Irish Law 2014 (2015) 708 ff; *E Quill*, Ireland in: E Karner/BC Steininger (eds), ETL 2014 (2015) 263, no 2.

10 The Board was formerly known as the Personal Injuries Assessment Board (PIAB), see no 25 below on the change of title and functions.

4. Remediation of Dwellings Damaged by the Use of Defective Concrete Blocks Act 2022 (Commencement) Order 2023 (SI No 321 of 2023)

The 2022 Act commenced on 22 June 2023, bar one provision on the indemnifica- 8
tion of building professionals conducting duties under the Act. The Act is not a tort provision, but it was introduced to deal with potential difficulties in using tort or contract actions to resolve problems with a widespread construction defects problem.[11] This legislation now provides for grants administered by local authorities to meet the costs of repairing affected houses.[12] House owners do not have to establish the damage; this issue is to be determined by the Housing and Sustainable Communities Agency.[13]

5. Patient Safety (Notifiable Incidents and Open Disclosure) Act 2023 (No 10 of 2023)

This expands the disclosure system for medical incidents, established in the Civil 9
Liability (Amendment) Act 2017.[14] The Act changes the system from one of voluntary disclosure to mandatory disclosure on the part of health service providers to patients, or their representatives, and to the Health Information and Quality Authority. The patient, or their representative (where applicable), can refuse to attend a meeting to receive disclosure.[15] As with the earlier legislation, disclosure and apology do not amount to an admission of liability and are not admissible as evidence in tort proceedings in relation to the incident; neither do they invalidate any insurance cover for the incident, or any indemnity provided by a medical defence organisation.

11 Mainly concrete blocks with excessive pyrite or mica.

12 The scheme applies to four counties – Clare, Donegal, Limerick and Mayo – where the problem is most pronounced. Section 5 of the Act provides that the government may designate other local authorities as coming within the provisions.

13 Sections 15 and 16. Part 5 of the Act provides an appeals process.

14 Noted by *R Byrne/W Binchy*, Annual Review of Irish Law 2017 (2018) 624; *E Quill*, Ireland, in: E Karner/BC Steininger (eds), ETL 2017 (2018) 283, no 2. The 2023 Act has not been commenced at the time of writing.

15 Section 19; sec 20 makes provisions concerning a health service provider's inability to contact the patient or their representative.

6. Representative Actions for the Protection of the Collective Interests of Consumers Act 20232 (No 22 of 2023)

10 This Act is intended to implement the EU Collective Redress Directive,[16] having missed the implementation deadline of 25 December 2022. The Act commenced on 30 April 2024.[17] Ireland has chosen an opt-in mechanism; consumers must notify a qualified entity of their wish to be represented in order to benefit from any redress obtained through the representative action and that notification must be made prior to the determination of the admissibility of proceedings.[18]

7. Mother and Baby Institutions Payment Scheme Act 2023 (No 20 of 2023)

11 This establishes a long promised statutory compensation scheme for women and children that suffered as a result of the operation of institutions for unmarried pregnant women and girls. The institutions were ostensibly for the provision of care, but in fact often involved physical abuse and forced adoptions. The introduction of a statutory scheme was recommended by an official report in 2021.[19] The scheme was formally established on 20 March 2024 and will run for up to five years.[20] The scheme is to be run by a new official within the Department for Children, Equality, Disability, Integration and Youth – the Chief Deciding Officer;[21] immunity from suit has not been included in the Act, so liability for loss or injury caused by the running of the scheme could arise in due course. The scheme of payments and services is set out in Part 3 of the Act; children resident in relevant institutions for not less than 180 days will be eligible for payments, set out in a

16 Directive (EU) 2020/1828 of the European Parliament and of the Council of 25 November 2020 on representative actions for the protection of the collective interests of consumers and repealing Directive 2009/22/EC [2020] Official Journal (OJ) L 409/1.

17 Representative Actions for the Protection of the Collective Interests of Consumers Act 2023 (Commencement) Order 2024 (SI No 181 of 2024) art 2.

18 Section 24, exercising the discretion contained in art 9(2) of the Directive.

19 *Department of Children, Equality, Disability, Integration and Youth*, Final Report of the Commission of Investigation into Mother and Baby Homes (2021), noted by *Quill*, ETL 2021 (fn 8) no 42.

20 The establishment date is set out in the Mother and Baby Institutions Payment Scheme Act 2023 (Commencement) Order 2024 (SI No 67 of 2024). The five-year limit is set out in sec 6 of the Act; the scheme may be ended sooner by ministerial order.

21 Part 2 of the Act.

Schedule to the Act.[22] The pregnant girls and women in the institutions are eligible for general payments without a minimum threshold length of stay; for those that stayed longer than 89 days, there is an additional work-related payment.[23] Under certain conditions, eligible persons may also be entitled to certain free health services or a health support payment. Where payments are made under the scheme, the recipient or their personal representatives may not pursue civil proceedings in respect of the facts forming the basis of the payment.[24] A general or work-related payment under the scheme may not be made in respect of a person who has received compensation in civil litigation in respect of the stay in the institution. The additional benefits are not available to those participating in a similar system of eligibility for services under the Redress for Women Resident in Certain Institutions Act 2015.[25]

B. Cases

1. *McGee v The Governor of Portlaoise Prison*, Irish Supreme Court (IESC) 25 May 2023, [2023] IESC 14: Limitation of Actions in Claims for Violation of Constitutional Rights

a) Brief Summary of the Facts

P was incarcerated between 2000 and 2004 and had to engage in the process of slopping out.[26] He commenced the present action in December 2014 and only delivered a detailed statement of claim in August 2020. The High Court (IEHC) found the claim was statute barred by sec 11(2) of the Statute of Limitations Act, 12

22 Schedule 2 lists the amount of payments for various specified lengths of stay. The relevant institutions are listed in Schedule 1; the Minister has the power to add further institutions to the list.

23 Schedule 3 sets out the scale of general and work-related payments

24 Section 32.

25 See *E Quill*, Ireland in: E Karner/BC Steininger (eds), ETL 2015 (2016) 282, no 1. The restrictions on eligibility are set out in sec 18(6) & (7) of the 2023 Act.

26 For detailed consideration of unlawfulness in relation to conditions of incarceration, see *Simpson v The Governor of Mountjoy Prison* [2019] IESC 81, [2020] 3 IR 113 noted by *R Byrne/W Binchy*, Annual Review of Irish Law 2019 (2020) 694 ff; *Quill*, ETL 2019 (fn 8) no 4 ff.

1957 – the provision providing the limitation periods for tort actions.[27] P was granted leave to appeal directly to the IESC.[28]

b) Judgment of the Court

13 The IESC noted that while numerous IEHC cases had treated actions for damages for the violation of constitutional rights as a claim in tort for the purposes of the 1957 Act, there was no definitive IESC ruling on the issue in respect of what may be termed horizontal claims.[29] In the leading previous IESC case on the issue,[30] two of the five judges indicated the action was one in tort for the purposes of the Act and two offered alternative bases for finding the claim to be time-barred.[31] The fifth member of the court agreed with all three judgments, thereby giving no clear support for any particular one of the three reasons offered to explain why the claim was time-barred.

14 After detailed consideration, O'Donnell CJ for the Court held that a private law action for damages for violation of constitutional rights was a claim in tort for the purposes of the 1957 Act and the IEHC was correct to dismiss the claim.

c) Commentary

15 It is useful to have IESC clarification on this issue, confirming the position that lawyers have long understood to be the correct position with respect to the limitation

27 *McGee v The Governor of Portlaoise Prison* [2022] IEHC 210 (Barr J). Tort claims, other than personal injuries claims, generally have a limitation period of six years from the accrual of the cause of action. The present case had accrued at least ten years prior to commencement of the action.

28 *McGee v The Governor of Portlaoise Prison* [2022] IESC Determination (IESCDET) 123.

29 O'Donnell CJ suggests that *Blehein v Minister for Health* [2018] IESC 40, [2020] 2 IR 164 considered a constitutional violation claim to be a tort for limitation of action purposes, but he classified the *Blehein* case as a public law one (State liability for unconstitutional legislation), so not directly on point (though it was of persuasive value in reaching the ultimate conclusion in *McGee*). This perhaps stretches the interpretation of *Behein*, since McKechnie J (Charleton concurring) at [58] acknowledges that there are differing views on the issue; the point did not need to be determined to decide the case. On various sub-categories of constitutional rights claims, see [4]-[10] of O'Donnell CJ's judgment in the present case.

30 *McDonnell v Ireland* [1998] 1 IR 134.

31 Although the case was pleaded as one for breach of constitutional rights, Barrington J considered the case to be one for loss of office, while Barron J considered it to be a breach of contract case. Keane J (O'Flaherty J concurring) considered the action to be one in tort.

period for horizontal or private law claims of damages for violation of constitutional rights.[32] P had made a superficially logical argument that the action for damages for violation of constitutional rights was only available if tort law was ineffective in protecting the right, therefore it could not itself be a part of tort law. This decision recognises that the constitutional action is a way of plugging gaps in the existing law of tort, but that the development of new claims to fill such gaps as are identified are sufficiently similar in nature and purpose to tort claims, so that they should be treated as tort claims (at least for the purposes of procedural issues, such as time limits for the initiation of proceedings).[33]

2. *Davey v Sligo County Council*, Irish Court of Appeal (IECA) 23 February 2023, [2023] IECA 39: Employers' Liability; Affirmative Duty of Care

a) Brief Summary of the Facts

The plaintiff was a council worker; he was one of a crew working on the hard 16
shoulder of a road cutting hedges and clearing debris when he was injured in a collision caused by a 15-tonne lorry that crashed into the crew of workers and their vehicles; the driver had fallen asleep and had the cruise control set at 88 km/h travelling in an 80 km/h zone. There were two tractors and a digger being used by the council crew and three workers, including the plaintiff, on foot picking litter.[34] Behind these vehicles, there was a 3-tonne pickup truck with flashing lights and a large illuminated sign, with an arrow pointing to the carriageway. There were also three sets of warning signs on the road before traffic

---

32 See *M Canny*, Limitation of Actions (3rd edn 2022) [24.02] f; *McMahon/Binchy* (fn 6) [46.02] & [46.173]; *Quill* (fn 6) 360; *G Hogan/DG Morgan/P Daly*, Administrative Law in Ireland (5th edn 2019) [20.99].

33 The court took a broad general view of tort claims as being in the nature of private law actions for vindicating personal and property rights. O'Donnell cited a passage from *RFV Heuston/RA Buckley*, Salmond & Heuston on the Law of Torts (20th edn 1992) § 2.2 (cited by Keane J in *McDonnell*); the court also considered *Savickis v Governor of Castlerea Prison (No 2)* [2016] IECA 372, [2016] 3 IR 292, treating the constitutional action as a tort for the purposes of the jurisdiction of the Circuit Court (IECC) and *Bailey v Commissioner of An Garda Síochána* [2017] IECA 220, which followed Keane J in *McDonnell*.

34 One of the three workers on foot was killed and the third one was also injured; some of the workers in the vehicles were also injured. It was agreed by the parties that the present hearing would determine the principles applicable to all eight cases arising out of the incident.

reached the works convoy. The issue arising was whether the alleged failures of the council, as the plaintiff's employer, to provide sufficient protective measures contributed to the accident and ensuing injuries, such that it could be considered as a concurrent wrongdoer alongside the driver and his employer. The driver's employer alleged numerous failures by the council, including a lack of risk assessment and oversight, numerous traffic management issues and, perhaps most importantly, that a much larger vehicle than the pickup truck should have been used as a buffer. The IEHC found that the council was negligent in a number of respects, but that its errors were not a legal cause of the injuries. While a greater distance should have been in place between the council vehicles and the carriageway, the purpose of such a precaution was to prevent workers or equipment straying into traffic, not to prevent traffic coming into the hard shoulder. The use of heavier buffer vehicles was confined to dual carriageways and motorways, not single carriageway roads such as the one in the present case. In any event, they are usually placed further back than the pickup truck in this case and would probably have been overlooked by the lorry, which would have hit the convoy anyway.[35] The driver's employer appealed.

b) Judgment of the Court

17 The IECA held that there was no liability on the part of the council; the driver was the sole legal cause of the incident and the injuries.[36] The trial judge had characterised the driver's behaviour as a *novus actus interveniens*, but the IECA disagreed; the council's behaviour would have to be a cause of injury in some sense before one could consider a later event as intervening to break the causal chain. The IECA was satisfied that none of the suggested precautions that could be regarded as plausible examples of breach of duty would make the behaviour of the council a cause of the accident.[37]

---

35 *Davey v Sligo County Council* [2021] IEHC 707 (Coffey J, Ex Tempore).

36 Noonan J (Costello J concurring); Ní Raifeartaigh J issued a separate judgment, concurring with Noonan J's conclusions and he agreed with Ní Raifeartaigh J's judgment. As an aside, Ní Raifeartaigh J has been elected to serve as the next Irish judge on the European Court of Human Rights.

37 Noonan J [44]; Ní Raifeartaigh J [40] ff. Each possibility was carefully examined and plausible reasons were offered as to why the precautions would not have averted this accident (or at least not in a way sufficient to make the behaviour of the employer a legal cause).

c) Commentary

While a traffic accident might seem too routine a case to comment on, the discussion of principle is interesting. Ní Raifeartaigh J notes the interchangeability of concepts – one can frame the issue as an affirmative duty to protect workers, as a question of the scope of duty of care, or a question of the standard of care, as a matter of legal cause or the subset of legal cause described as *novus actus interveniens* – but a different framing of the issue does not change the result. While a sleeping driver is a foreseeable event – in that it is rare, but is known to happen – precautions against it are almost impossible to devise and implement, so an employer of a third party victim should not be readily held liable for failing to prevent injury caused in this manner. Ní Raifeartaigh J also notes that we should not overly stretch an employer's obligations to impose liability for highly improbable combinations of circumstances,[38] even if each step in the combination is individually a known risk, as this would move us towards strict liability and the common law only applies a negligence standard.[39] 18

> The duty of care and the range of precautions required are not infinitely elastic; a line must be drawn somewhere. The Council is not an insurer of its employees.[40]

3. *McCarthy v The Commissioner of An Garda Síochána*, IECA, 20 September 2023, [2023] IECA 224: Battery, Dismissal for Delay

a) Brief Summary of the Facts

The plaintiff claimed the police used excessive force against him during some public unrest at a Halloween bonfire in 2008. A plenary summons was issued two years later.[41] This was followed by a period of slow but regular interaction between the parties until late November 2013. There was a seven-year period of al- 19

38 In the present case, there was also the question of excessive speed and failure to react to earlier warnings of the presence of the works. The excess speed was only slight, but the size of the vehicle made it a significant issue for the judges.
39 Statutory occupational safety legislation sometimes demands higher levels of precaution from employers, but these were not raised in the case.
40 [2023] IECA 39 [27].
41 Apparently, there was an application to PIAB before this, but the date is not specified in the judgment.

most total inactivity in the litigation.[42] The IEHC dismissed the case, citing prejudice to the police officers by way of having allegations of misconduct hanging over them.[43] The plaintiff appealed.

b) Judgment of the Court

20 The IECA allowed the appeal; reputational damage was not a sufficient prejudice to justify dismissal. While there was unreasonable delay, the balance of justice favoured allowing the case to proceed, as there was no concrete prejudice to the defendants. The defendants' inactivity during the seven years of delay was not particularly blameworthy, but it was relevant; if the defendants were concerned about their reputation, they had opportunities to progress the case, which they chose not to take. The IECA felt this tactical choice was a relevant factor in balancing the parties' interests in reaching a decision on dismissing or allowing the case to proceed.

c) Commentary

21 The principles governing dismissal for delay are well established and have considered many issues over the years, but this case still manages to raise a novel point, not clearly determined in this context.[44] The plaintiff accepted that the delay was inordinate and inexcusable; however, in such cases the courts are required to consider the balance of justice. The reputational interest of a defendant in respect of litigation alleging significant malpractice in their work and having this hang over them for a protracted period, due to the litigation not being resolved in a timely manner, has been considered in the past and differing views can be found in the cases.[45] The IECA here has clearly indicated that such an effect alone is not

42 In March 2017, the plaintiff's lawyers served a notice of intention to proceed and in July 2017 the plaintiff's lawyers notified the defendants that they believed the discovery made by the defendants in October 2013 was not satisfactory.

43 Reynolds J, 23 March 2022, (*Ex Tempore*).

44 The key principles were set out in *Ó Domhnaill v Merrick* [1984] IR 151 and *Primor plc v Stokes Kennedy Crowley* [1996] 2 IR 459. See *Canny* (fn 32) ch 4; *McMahon/Binchy* (fn 6) ch 46 part VI; *Quill* (fn 6) 473 ff.

45 Prejudice to police officers was treated as relevant in *Flynn v The Minister for Justice* [2017] IECA 178, though it was only one of a number of factors; a strong criticism of reputational damage as a prejudicial factor was voiced by Collins J, *obiter*, delivering judgment for the court in *Cave Projects Ltd v Kelly* [2022] IECA 245, [36].

a strong factor in defeating a plaintiff's interest in access to justice for an alleged wrong, even though the plaintiff has been the primary culpable party in the delay. The decision also clarifies that although the defendants were not obliged to take any steps in the period of inactivity and, therefore were not particularly culpable or acquiescent, they had opportunities to address their concerns about reputational effects, so their inactivity could not be entirely ignored by the court in the balancing exercise. The decision seems particularly generous to a tardy plaintiff, but does serve to warn defendants that inactivity on their part is not without risk.

4. *The Board of Management of Wilson's Hospital School v Burke*, Irish High Court (IEHC) 16 March 2023, [2023] IEHC 144: Trespass; Breach of Injunction

a) Brief Summary of the Facts

The defendant, a teacher, has been involved in a long-term protest against his em- 22
ployer in respect of perceived discrimination against his religious beliefs. During the course of disciplinary proceedings, he was placed on paid administrative leave. Due to his continued presence at the school, an injunction was obtained to restrain him from trespassing on the school premises.[46] In January 2023, the IEHC imposed a fine of € 700 per day for civil contempt, due to continual breaches of the injunction.[47] The present case is one of many court proceedings in respect of the dispute: it dealt with costs issues in respect of earlier proceedings and the issue of interest to us here – a review of the civil contempt, including the appropriate remedy for breach of the injunction to desist entering school property.

b) Judgment of the Court

O'Moore J, who set the daily fine in January, now had to consider how to address 23
the defendant's continuing breach of the injunction. Evidence showed breach on every working day from the order setting the level of fine until 1 March, so he fixed the amount at € 23,800. He then considered whether the fine should be in-

---

46 Barrett J, IEHC, 7 September 2022. An appeal against this injunction was rejected in *The Board of Management of Wilson's Hospital School v Burke* [2023] IECA 52 (7 March 2023).

47 *The Board of Management of Wilson's Hospital School v Burke* [2023] IEHC 36 (O'Moore J). The fine was prospective only; past breaches were not included for reasons of procedural fairness.

creased, since setting it had not had any deterrent effect. He determined that an increase was not necessary at this point, but crystallising the amount due, permitting the school to take appropriate enforcement steps and collect the fines, would suffice for the present.

c) Commentary

24 The case is a highly unusual one, involving a concerted refusal by the defendant, assisted by his family in some instances, to comply with judicial processes and court orders. The particular issue of imposing a daily fine for civil (as opposed to criminal) contempt rarely arises. The jurisdiction clearly exists,[48] but has rarely been exercised and the earlier cases are unclear on the destination of such fines.[49] The payment of a fine to a party in civil proceedings is something of a novelty in Ireland. The object of the exercise is to encourage respect for court orders and it is coercive and possibly punitive in nature.[50] Thus, the plaintiff in civil proceedings gets something of a windfall since the fine is not aimed at compensating them for the harm they suffered and is independent of any award of damages. In this it has some similarities with punitive damages, though the two are distinct and the use of civil fines is much rarer.[51] The school subsequently obtained a permanent injunction and damages of € 15,000.[52] The defendant's continued refusal to

48 *Phonographic Performance Ltd v Amusement Caterers (Peckham) Ltd* [1964] 1 Law Reports, Chancery Division (Ch) 195; *Keegan v De Burca* [1973] 1 IR 223; *Flood v Lawlor* [2001] IESC 100, [2002] 3 IR 67; *Shell E & P Ireland Ltd v McGrath* [2006] IEHC 108, [2007] 1 IR 671; *Irish Bank Resolution Corporation Ltd v Quinn Investments Sweden AB* [2012] IESC 51

49 *Curley v Galway Corporation* [2001] IEHC 53 is one of the few cases involving the imposition of a fine, but Kelly J does not discuss enforcement and does not indicate who the recipient of the fine should be.

50 O'Moore J indicates that the Court has (subject to fair procedures) a broad discretion in deciding on the appropriate measures to be put in place to ensure respect for its Orders. *The Board of Management of Wilson's Hospital School v Burke* [2023] IEHC 36, [24]. See also the obiter discussion of the purpose of civil contempt by Fennelly J in *Irish Bank Resolution Corporation Ltd v Quinn Investments Sweden AB* [2012] IESC 51, reviewing the varying view expressed in the Irish superior courts on the matter.

51 Awards of punitive damages are rare, but civil fines are extremely rare. The present case is the first I have seen giving the plaintiff the benefit of the fine and control over enforcement, though this practice may be inherent in the jurisdiction and simply not have been discussed in the earlier cases. The issue is not even mentioned in the *Law Reform Commission* (LRC), Consultation Paper on Contempt of Court (LRC CP 4–1991) ch 6 dealt with civil contempt.

52 *The Board of Management of Wilson's Hospital School v Burke* [2023] IEHC 288; Owens J expressly indicated that the damages were in addition to the daily fines, [33].

abide by court decisions resulted in subsequent committal to prison for contempt.[53]

5. Personal Injury

a) Structural Change

25 The Personal Injuries Assessment Board (PIAB) has been renamed as the Personal Injuries Resolution Board (PIRB);[54] its new functions include a mediation service – initially this is provided for employers' liability claims, with the intent to roll it out to other classes of claim in 2024.[55] It also has a new research function and it published an analysis of employers' liability claims and awards from 2019 to 2022 (discussed in the general statistics section below). It also now provides assessments in respect of Garda (police) compensation claims.[56]

b) General Statistics

26 The PIAB Annual Report 2022 indicates that the volume of PIAB claims in 2022 was down 14 % on 2021;[57] the average value of claims was € 15,857, down 34 % on the 2020 average, and down 18 % on the 2021 average.[58] It should be noted that the

53 *The Board of Management of Wilson's Hospital School v Burke* [2023] IEHC 528 (Heslin J, 8 September 2023).

54 Personal Injuries Resolution Board Act 2022 (No 42 of 2022), the change of title took effect on 12 December 2023 by art 2 of the Personal Injuries Resolution Board Act 2022 (Commencement of Certain Provisions) (No 3) Order 2023 (SI No 626 of 2023). The Board styles itself as the 'Injuries Resolution Board', see <https://www.piab.ie/eng/>. Other provisions of the Act were brought into force during the year by the Personal Injuries Resolution Board Act 2022 (Commencement of Certain Provisions) Order 2023 (SI No 28/2023), the Personal Injuries Resolution Board Act 2022 (Commencement of Certain Provisions) (No 2) Order 2023 (SI No 354 of 2023) and the other articles in SI No 626 of 2023.

55 Commenced for employers' liability claims on 14 December 2023 by art 4(e) of SI No 626 of 2023. Extended to actions in respect of the use or occupation of premises by art 2 of the Personal Injuries Resolution Board Act 2022 (Commencement) Order 2024 (SI No 187 of 2024).

56 See no 7 above.

57 Available at <https://www.injuries.ie/eng/about-injuries-resolution-board/reports/piab-annual-report-2022.pdf>, accessed 2 May 2024. There were 18,453 claims in 2022, compared to 21,410 claims in 2021.

58 Though the highest award was significantly higher – € 655,678 compared to € 360,522 in 2021.

2022 average was 12 % above the average for April-December 2021;[59] new Personal Injury Guidelines, with mainly lower amounts of general damages for non-material loss, came into effect in April 2021.[60] The distribution of claims showed a slight variation, with a drop in the proportion of motor claims.[61] The acceptance rate for awards rose slightly to 48 %.

27 The Courts Service Annual Report 2022 also records a drop in the volume of cases filed and a significant increase in the use of the District Courts (IEDC).[62] Overall compensation levels dropped also. The IEHC awarded € 253,486,344 in 354 cases; the IECC awarded € 15,041,482 in 794 cases; the IEDC awarded € 2,801,164 in 450 cases; all of these are down on 2021 awards. Medical negligence cases increased in number, but not generally in value.[63]

28 Reviews of 2022 figures have produced some interesting information on trends, confirming some points made in my Yearbook reports over recent years. The PIAB Annual Report 2022 shows that since 2016 both the number and value of PIAB awards have generally been falling.[64] Under its new research function, the Board has produced a detailed study of employers' liability claims from 2019 to 2022 and it also shows decreasing claims volumes and values.[65] Data from Na-

---

59 This figure was reported in the PIAB Personal Injuries Award Values 2022 (Dec 2023), but this report is no longer available online at the time of writing.

60 The guidelines are noted by *Quill*, ETL 2021 (fn 8) no 35 ff; for comment on a particular aspect of the guidelines, see *E Deering*, Lack of Insight (2022) 27 The Bar Review (Bar Rev) 73. Some of the impact of the guidelines is noted by *E Quill*, Ireland in: E Karner/BC Steininger (eds), ETL 2022 (2023) 307, no 29 ff; see also *R Byrne/W Binchy*, Annual Review of Irish Law 2022 (2023) 564 ff. The constitutionality of the new guidelines was upheld in *Delaney v The Personal Injuries Assessment Board* [2024] IESC 10.

61 Motor claims were down 4 % to 65 % of claims, with a 2 % rise each in employers' liability (15 %) and public liability (20 %).

62 Available at <https://www.courts.ie/acc/alfresco/8adf9153-bfec-4402-9c2b-cc3d51b83da5/The%20Courts%20Service%20Annual%20Report%202022%20FINAL.pdf/pdf#view=fitH>, accessed 2 May 2024. 12,459 personal injury suits were filed in 2022, a 17 % decrease on 2021. The distribution was 3,766 in the High Court, a 26 % decrease on 2021; 7,151 in the Circuit Court, a 19 % decrease on 2021; 1,542 in the District Court, a 44 % increase on 2021.

63 € 178,711,076 awarded in 107 cases, compared to € 203,600,714 in 84 cases in 2021. The lowest award in 2022 was € 10,000, compared to € 7,000 in 2021; the highest award in 2022 was € 19,000,000, compared to € 30,000,000 in 2021.

64 There was a significant increase in the number (but not value) of claims in 2022, compared to 2021, but otherwise the trend has been in decline. The total value of 2016 awards was € 315 million; in 2022 it was down to € 141 million.

65 PIRB, Analysis of Employer Liability Claims & Awards: Workplace Personal Injury Accidents 2019–2022 (2023). This records a 38 % decrease in the total volume of claims in the period. A comparison of 2020 to 2022 shows a 26 % drop in the average award, with a 38 % drop in non-pecuniary damages. The report provides excellent detail in sectoral analysis.

tional Claims Information Database confirm the trend of claims falling in both number and value; however, insurance premiums in the commercial sector have increased by 8 %.[66]

The fifth Private Motor Insurance Report based on the National Claims Information Database shows a 7 % decrease in motor insurance premiums from 2021 and a 20 % increase in the cost of claims per policy, though the cost is still 2 % below 2019 levels.[67] Claims as a percentage of premium increased to 61 % in 2022 from 47 % in 2021; the average over the periods from 2009 to 2022 is 65 %. There was a precisely equal division between claims resolved under the new Personal Injury Guidelines and the previous Book of Quantum. As more claims fall under the new guidelines, further reductions in damages can be anticipated going forward. 29

c) Cases: Quantum of Damages

There were several cases clarifying aspects of the processes involved in determining general damages for non-pecuniary loss in 2023. In *Zaganzyck v John Pettit Wexford Unlimited Company*,[68] the IECA reduced an IEHC general damages award of € 90,000 to € 60,000. A gas explosion in the workplace burned and traumatised a worker. Noonan J for the court reiterated that the correct approach to multiple injuries was to work out the value of the most serious injury and give an uplift to account for the additional injuries – as opposed to simply calculating the value of each individual injury and adding them all together, as this risks overcompensating due to overlapping effects of the various injuries.[69] He also noted that there should be a global check for proportionality to ensure the total award is fair to both parties. This harks back to an approach established in the 1980s, 30

66 *Central Bank of Ireland*, Employers' Liability, Public Liability and Commercial Property Insurance Report 3: National Claims Information Database (2024), available at <https://www.centralbank.ie/docs/default-source/statistics/data-and-analysis/national-claims-information-database/ncid-employers-liability-insurance-report-3.pdf?sfvrsn=bfc1631a_8>, accessed 2 May 2024.

67 *Central Bank of Ireland*, Private Motor Insurance Report 5: National Claims Information Database (2023), available at <https://www.centralbank.ie/docs/default-source/statistics/data-and-analysis/national-claims-information-database/private-motor-insurance-report-5.pdf>, accessed 2 May 2023. The report analyses data from 2009 to 2022 and reiterates the trends shown in earlier reports and provides an update to show how 2022 fits in the patterns.

68 [2023] IECA 223.

69 *Meehan v Shawcove* [2022] IECA 208, noted by *Quill*, ETL 2022 (fn 60) no 34.

but not seen much in recent years[70] – after all the elements of damages are individually calculated, the total amount is considered as a whole to assess whether it is fair. In practice, this was almost always used for the purpose of reducing plaintiffs' awards in cases of serious injury with high damages levels and there is a dearth of cases involving any awards being raised on global review for being insufficient. Noonan J used an earlier IEHC case on somewhat similar injuries as a comparator for review and also noted a range of other injuries attracting sums at either end of the figures under consideration here in order to address the proportionality issue.[71]

31 In *McHugh v Ferol*,[72] the plaintiff suffered multiple injuries in a head-on collision while driving her car. The IEHC considered the assessment of multiple injuries; in particular the principles governing the uplift of damages for the dominant or principal injury to account for the additional injuries.[73] The court noted that nothing in the Personal Injuries Guidelines required the amount of uplift to be less than the amount assessed for the dominant injury. The court noted that there could be scenarios in which the range of additional injuries were enough to support an uplift higher than the amount for the dominant injury. The case itself was not found to be one of these and the court awarded € 60,000 for the dominant foot injury and an uplift of € 32,500 for the other injuries. Noonan J, in *Zaganzyck*, noted Murphy J's dictum on the possibility of an uplift exceeding the value of the dominant injury, but expressly reserved his position until it arises for direct consideration.[74] We shall have to await a suitable case to definitively determine the issue, but Murphy J's approach looks sound in principle.

32 *Wolfe v The Personal Injuries Assessment Board* involved a judicial review of a PIAB decision on multiple injuries.[75] The applicant claimed that the basis for calculation was not sufficiently clear, leaving the plaintiff unable to make an informed judgement on accepting or rejecting the assessment; rejection would put them at risk of incurring costs under sec 51 A of the Personal Injuries Assessment

---

70 *Reddy v Bates* [1983] IR 141, see *McMahon/Binchy* (fn 6) [44.133] ff; *Quill* (fn 6) 540. It should be noted that proportionality is expressly included in the Guidelines as a general factor in the determination of damages and consideration of 'the overall award' as an aspect of proportionality is expressly included in the narrative guidance on multiple injuries.

71 *Lipinski (A Minor) v Whelan* [2022] IEHC 452 (Coffey J) involved a somewhat more serious level of PTSD, but somewhat lesser physical injury – € 60,000 was awarded in that case.

72 [2023] IEHC 132 (Murphy J).

73 Following the PIGC Guidelines and the decision in *Lipinski* (fn 71).

74 *Zaganzyck* (fn 68) [24].

75 [2023] IECA 245.

Board Act 2003.[76] The information provided to the claimant listed the dominant injury as 'Back', the severity category as 'Minor' and the sub-category as 'Substantial recovery 1–2 years'. This was accompanied by a statement that:

> The assessors also considered where appropriate the presence or absence of other lesser injuries. The assessors considered the range and severity of other injuries and the additional pain, discomfort and limitations arising from the claimant's lesser injury/injuries. The assessors having regard to the Guidelines have considered an uplift if appropriate.

A figure of € 11,000 in general damages for the dominant injury was provided and 33
no uplift was included. The assessors' affidavits indicated that the additional injuries were included in the figure of € 11,000, as they would have given somewhat less for the dominant injury if it had been the sole injury. O'Regan J in the IEHC rejected the judicial review application.[77] On appeal, the IECA accepted that while the information on the classification of the dominant injury was rudimentary, one could compare the evidence to the narratives and factors in the Guidelines and reach a view on whether the findings were appropriate. However, the absence of any detail on how the lesser injuries were accommodated in the assessment meant that the assessment was flawed. An order quashing the assessment and requiring a new assessment, with an adequate explanation, was ordered. The IECA noted that the information on the valuation of the additional injuries did not need to be very detailed – a simple statement of a lower figure for the dominant injury and a total, showing the value of the additional injuries would suffice. On balance, the decision supports a fairly light administrative burden on assessors, but does require a sufficient minimum level of clarity for claimants in order to understand the decisions on every aspect of their claim.

In *O' Daly v Bus Éireann (Irish Bus),*[78] Noonan J considered how the court 34
should assess personal injuries complaints which are unsupported by medical evidence; in this instance some of the suffering described by the plaintiff was at odds with the expert medical testimony. Noonan J said:

> ...while the vast majority of plaintiffs are honest and truthful about their complaints, that is not invariably the case...Some will be of a stoic disposition and wish to be seen not to complain unduly. Some...may complain bitterly about things that most would take in their stride. But the law must treat everyone fairly and equally. Fairness means being consistent in one's approach to particular injuries, even if...they may affect different people differently.

---

76 This section provides that the costs of a court hearing can be awarded against a plaintiff that does not get an award higher than the PIAB assessment.
77 *Wolfe v Personal Injuries Assessment Board* [2022] IEHC 370.
78 [2023] IECA 232.

35 On one reading, this involves an objective view of the assessment of pain and suffering, which runs counter to the long-established principle that such suffering is subjective and peculiar to each individual. On another reading, Noonan J may just be considering whether the plaintiff is malingering or overstating the degree of suffering. It would be preferable that the statement is treated as one on the credibility of the witness and not one changing the entire focus of damage assessment to an objective basis. There is some support for the latter interpretation in the opening paragraphs of the judgment, where Noonan J acknowledges that there is a subjective element to pain and suffering and notes that witness credibility is a difficult matter.

d) Cases: Medical Negligence

36 In *Mitchell v The Health Service Executive*;[79] O'Connor J held that the HSE did not owe a duty of care to parents in respect of psychiatric injuries in a case involving their daughter's cervical cancer diagnosis and death. In doing so, he relied on an earlier IEHC decision that it was not reasonably foreseeable that negligence towards a patient would lead to a medically recognised psychiatric injury being suffered by a close relative.[80] O'Connor J noted that the outcome is similar to recent England and Wales Court of Appeal (EWCA) decisions.[81] While the result is consistent with the decisions cited, the cases are based on a very narrow view of the duties owed by hospitals, laboratories and medical practitioners generally. It is difficult to see why close relatives are sufficiently proximate and foreseeable victims in the case of various accidents, such as traffic collisions, inflicting catastrophic injuries on their loved ones, but not in the case of terminal illness where the terminal nature of the condition results from medical negligence.

37 In *McLaughlin v Dealey*,[82] Ferriter J was asked to attach less weight, as a matter of principle, to the expert medical evidence introduced on behalf of the plain-

79 [2023] IEHC 394

80 *Morrissey v Health Service Executive* [2019] IEHC 268, Cross J. This aspect of the case was not appealed and so did not form any part of the appellate decision considered in *Quill* (fn 8) ETL 2020, no 3 ff.

81 *Paul v The Royal Wolverhampton NHS Trust* [2022] Court of Appeal (Civil Division) (EWCA Civ) 12, [2023] Law Reports, Queen's Bench Division (QB) 149 and *Taylor v A Novo (UK) Ltd* [2013] EWCA Civ 194, [2014] QB 150. The English approach is premised on lack of proximity, rather than lack of foreseeability. It has subsequently been endorsed by the United Kingdom Supreme Court (UKSC) in *Paul v Royal Wolverhampton NHS Trust* [2024] UKSC 1, [2024] 2 Weekly Law Reports (WLR) 417.

82 [2023] IEHC 106; € 60,272 was awarded for a soft tissue injury that had no physical manifestation in an MRI; € 57,500 of the total was for general damages (ie, non-pecuniary loss).

tiff on the basis that the plaintiff was referred directly to a consultant by her solicitor rather than by her general medical practitioner. After carefully considering the law on expert witnesses, Ferriter J decided that no such special rule was needed and it was a matter for the judge in each particular case to weight the evidence on factors such as the objectivity of the witness and the quality of information provided to them on which to base their expert opinion. This is one of a number of cases in recent years involving direct referrals to medical practitioners by lawyers. While some negative commentary has been expressed in the cases, Ferriter J is correct in determining that no special rules of evidence arise out of this practice, though it does require an element of care by trial judges in assessing whether it has had any practical adverse effects on the quality of the evidence adduced. The Law Society of Ireland has subsequently issued a new protocol for solicitors commissioning medical reports.[83]

C. Literature

1. *Law Reform Commission*, Consultation Paper: Third-Party Litigation Funding (LRC CP 69 – 2023)

This consultation paper provides an explanation of the current law in Ireland on 38
maintenance and champerty and its restrictive effect on third-party funding for the conduct of litigation. In light of concerns with modernising litigation funding mechanisms in the context of access to justice, it explores three models for law reform; one each from England and Wales, Hong Kong and New Zealand, with limited consideration of the use of those models in further jurisdictions. It poses questions for reform options and seeks stakeholder responses that will feed into a follow up report making recommendations to government.

---

83 The protocol is available at <https://www.lawsociety.ie/globalassets/documents/committees/litigation/medical-report-protocol.pdf>, accessed 7 May 2024.

2. *Caoimhe Daly/Patrick Treacy*, Medical Negligence Litigation in Ireland: Current Issues and Approaches (Clarus Press, 2023)

39 This provides an extensive and up to date exposition of the law of medical negligence claims in Ireland.

3. *Simon Shire*, Entertainment and Media Law in Ireland (Clarus Press, 2023)

40 Part I, titled 'Business Management, Regulation and Risk Mitigation' includes two aspects of tort law – occupational safety and defamation. Part VI, titled 'Journalism Law, Regulation and Ethics' includes coverage of privacy.

4. *Glen Gibbons*, Gibbons on Trade Marks Law (Clarus Press, 3rd edn 2023)

41 Chapter three discusses passing off and other tort actions that may be used in the protection of trade marks.

5. *Frances Meenan*, Employment Law (Round Hall, 2nd edn 2023)

42 Chapter 17 considers safety, health and welfare at work. It includes sections on statutory duties, vicarious liability, workplace bullying and a brief one on volunteers.

6. Articles

43 *S Reid/R Murray*, Two Trains Stuck at the Same Platform: The Case for Clinical Negligence to be Decoupled from Personal Injuries Actions (2022) 28 Medico-Legal Journal of Ireland (MLJI) 63; *V Corbett*, Third-Party Litigation Funding – Time for a Rethink? (2023) 69 The Irish Jurist (Ir Jur) 12; *JP Byrne*, Regulating AI (2023) 28 Bar Rev 13; *M Nutley*, Statute Barred (2023) 28 Bar Rev 62; *C Smith/A Farrelly*, Mediating Personal Injuries Disputes (2023) 28 Bar Rev 139; *A Staunton*, Liability for Medical Products under Revised EU Product Liability Directive Proposal (2023) 30

Commercial Law Practitioner (CLP) 91; *T Murphy*, Data Protection – Data Breach Claims – Recent Developments (2023) 30 CLP 134; *P O'Malley*, Concurrent Wrongdoer – Who Me, Couldn't Be! (2023) (2) Construction, Engineering and Energy Law Journal 37; *M Canny*, A Discussion of Judgments on Limitation Issues Delivered in the Last Six Years of Relevance to Property Lawyers (2023) (1) Conveyancing and Property Law Journal 9; *J Gleeson*, Medical Negligence Doctrine and the Road to Systems Thinking in Response to Medical Error: Facilitating or Frustrating (2023) 22 Hibernian Law Journal (Hibernian LJ) 1; *M MacMahon*, The EU's Digital Services Act: An Analysis of the Updated Conditional Intermediary Liability Regime (2023) 25 Irish Journal of European Law (IJEL) 107; *O Kelleher*, Possibilities for a Right to Clean Air After Case C-61/21 *JP v Ministre de la Transition Écologique and Premier Minister* (2023) 25 IJEL 133; *JP Byrne*, Getting the Intelligence into Artificial Intelligence Liability (2023) 41 ILT 86; *L Kierans*, It's Nothing Personal: The Ineffective Exclusion of Personal Grievances in the Protected Disclosures Act 2014 – *Baranya v Rosderra Irish Meats Group Ltd* (2023) 5 Irish Supreme Court Review (ISCR) 81; *N Cox*, *Higgins v Irish Aviation Authority* [2022] IESC 13 (2023) 5 ISCR 105 (Defamation); *P Kenna*, *Clare CC v Bernard and Helen McDonagh and IHREC* [2022] IESC 2 (2023) 5 ISCR 145 (Trespass, Constitutional Rights); *R Condon*, Shadow Constitutionalism: *P McD v The Governor of the X Prison* [2021] IESC 65 (2023) 5 ISCR 165 (Damages, Prisoners' Rights); *T McInerney*, Shock Therapy (2023) 117 (1) Law Society of Ireland Gazette (Gaz) 20 (Negligently Inflicted Psychiatric Injury); *E Pentony/E Murray*, 2 Fast, 2 Frivolous (2023) 117(3) Gaz 26 (Dismissal of Claims); *B Barton*, Runaway Jury (2023) 117(4) Gaz 38 (Defamation); *J Roche*, Broadcast News (2023) 117(8) Gaz 38 (Defamation).

Elena Bargelli and Andrea Cioni

XVI. Italy

A. Legislation

In 2023, there were no significant legislative developments in the field of tort law in Italy. 1

B. Cases

1. Corte di Cassazione Sezioni Unite [Grand Chamber, GC] (Cass SS UU) 1 February 2023, no 3077: Environmental Damage; Directive 2004/35; Liability of the Owner of a Site of National Interest[1]

a) Brief Summary of the Facts

The owner of the site of national interest known as 'Litorale Domizio flegreo ed Agro aversano' appealed against the administrative measure ordering him to implement, within ten days, emergency safety measures in relation to the aquifer found contaminated in the vicinity of the quarry, where the waste collected was stored, and to adopt preventive and remedial measures for the soil and the water table. The owner denied its liability according to the Environmental Code and objected that the tortfeasor had not been identified by the competent authority. The Tribunal rejected the claim and affirmed the owner's liability according to 'the polluter pays' principle. It further emphasised that environmental liability is strict. 2

Note: Elena Bargelli authored nos 2–44, Andrea Cioni authored nos 45–88.

1 In IUS Responsabilità Civile, 17 March 2023, with comment by *F Agnino*, Danno ambientale ed individuazione dei soggetti responsabili.

https://doi.org/10.1515/9783111376721-017

3 The plaintiff appealed to the Court of Cassation challenging the 'polluter pays' principle stated by Directive 2004/35/CE[2] if the author of the contamination has not been identified.

b) Judgment of the Court

4 The Grand Chamber recalled the legal framework in matters of environmental damage, starting from art 3 para 3 Treaty on the European Union (TEU) and art 191 Treaty on the Functioning of the European Union (TFEU), whereby the Union's policy contributes to the pursuit, among others, of the preservation, protection and improvement of the quality of the environment, the protection of human health, and the prudent and rational utilisation of natural resources.

5 It further recalled that Directive 2004/25/EC,[3] in affirming the liability of operators whose activity caused environmental damage or the imminent threat of such damage, encourages the adoption of measures and the development of practices aimed to minimise the risks of environmental damage, and, therefore, pursues the objective of eliminating environmental damage rather than imposing the payment of monetary damages. Accordingly, the operator (art 2[6]) is defined as a person who exercises or controls a professional activity or to whom decisive economic power over the technical operation of that activity is delegated.

6 The Italian legislator implemented the above-mentioned Directive in the Environmental Code (*decreto legislativo* [d lgs] 3 April 2006, no 152). Article 311 of the Environmental Code thus establishes the strict liability of those who carry out specific listed professional activities and the fault-based liability of anyone who causes environmental damage (para 2).

7 The Court further cited the Court of Justice of the European Union (CJEU)'s judgment *MATTM v Fipa Group*,[4] which clarified that Directive 2004/25/EC

> 'does not preclude national legislation ... which, in the event that it is impossible to identify the person responsible for the contamination of a site or to obtain remedial measures from that person, does not allow the competent authority to require the preventive and remedial measures to be carried out by the owner of that site, who is not responsible for the contamination, who is liable only to reimburse the costs relating to the measures taken by the competent authority up to the market value of the site'.

---

2 Dir 2004/35/CE of 21 April 2004 on environmental liability with regard to the prevention and remedying of environmental damage [2004] Official Journal (OJ) L 143/56.

3 Dir 2004/25/EC of 21 April 2004 on takeover bids [2004] OJ L 142/12.

4 CJEU 4.3.2015, C-534/13, *Ministerio dell'Ambiente e della Tutela del Territorio e del Mare (MATTM) v Fipa Group srl*, ECLI:EU:C:2015:140.

The Court concluded that, although the Directive does not preclude Member States from maintaining or adopting more stringent measures to prevent or remedy environmental damage, there must be a national legal basis for the strict liability of the landowner whenever the latter did not cause such damage. To this end, the general aims proclaimed by arts 191 and 192 TFEU could not be invoked to impose such liability. 8

The Court further investigated whether national law allows the landowner's strictly vicarious liability for the environmental damage caused by someone else. It quoted the decisions of the Plenary Assembly of the *Conseil d'Etat* (State Council) no 21 of 2013 as well as those by Section VI of 5 October 2016, no 4099 and no 4119, which clarified that the Ministry cannot impose on the owner of a contaminated area (not responsible for the pollution) the obligation to perform emergency safety and remediation measures. Moreover, the Court made clear that the obligation to be imposed on the owner might not exceed what is provided for by art 253 of the Environmental Code (reimbursement of costs related to interventions carried out by the competent authority within the limits of the market value of the site determined after execution). 9

The Court stressed that the owner would only be required to take the appropriate preventive measures to minimise an event that has created an imminent threat to health or the environment and is held as a source of sufficiently probable risk, according to the doctrine of causation (art 253). In turn, the administration would have the obligation to carry out investigations to identify the person responsible for the contamination and request them to take remedial action (art 244, para 2 of the Environmental Code), whereas the owner is required to comply with a specific obligation to notify when it discovers an actual or potential contamination (art 245, para 2 of the Environmental Code). If neither the liable party nor any other interested party intervenes, the preventive activities and reparation are carried out *ex officio* by the competent administration (art 250), while – as anticipated – the owner not responsible for the contamination is in any case granted the right to voluntarily carry out the remediation works (art 245, para 1). 10

According to the Court, art 245 of the Environmental Code, in requiring the owner of the area to implement preventive measures in accordance with the procedure referred to in art 242, does not intend to extend their liability beyond the emergency measures in order to deal with a potential risk. This limited obligation must be kept separate from security measures, which presuppose an actual contamination of the area. 11

The Court reminded that several precedents and most authors had excluded the obligation of the owner to contribute to remove, prevent and adopt emergency safety measures. Conversely, other decisions had required the owner to carry out safety and restoration work. This conflicting interpretation culminated in the Plena- 12 ry Assembly of the Council of State submitting two preliminary references to the Court of Justice in 2013. The CJEU (C-534/13 *MATTM*) clarified that Directive 2004/35/CE must be interpreted as not precluding national legislation '... which, in the event that it is impossible to identify the party responsible for the contamination of a site or to obtain remedial measures from that party, does not permit the competent authority to require the preventive and remedial measures to be carried out by the owner of that site who is not responsible for the contamination and is liable only to reimburse the costs of the measures taken by the competent authority up to the market value of the site, as determined after the carrying out of those measures.'

13 The Court further recalled that this doctrine was followed by subsequent judgments of the Council of State (eg, that of 4 August 2021, no 5742, which denied the owner's obligation to adopt the emergency safety and reparation measures referred to in art 245, para 2, subparas [m] and [p]). Conversely, other decisions, by referring to the precautionary principle, admitted that emergency safety measures would also be included in the preventive measures to be taken by the owner (Council of State, Sec IV, 12 July 2022, nos 5863 and 5864).

14 The Court, however, observed that qualifying the emergency safety measures as a type of preventive measure would not be in line with the cited CJEU *MATTM* judgment (C-534/13) and would impose an obligation to repair actual damage on a party who is not responsible for the contamination that caused it.

15 The Court further made clear that environmental liability falls entirely under the Environmental Code, with the consequence that the general rules on tort liability enshrined in the Civil Code do not apply to environmental damage. As a consequence, arts 2050 (dangerous activity) and 2051 (damage caused by a thing) of the Civil Code are not applicable and are replaced by the detailed rules of the Environmental Code.

16 The Grand Chamber upheld the appeal.

c) Commentary

17 The present decision deals with the sphere of application of the strict liability for environmental damage provided for by Directive 2004/35/CE. After defining environmental damage as any significant and measurable deterioration, direct or indirect, of a natural resource or the utility provided by it, the Code states that, if such damage is caused by operators whose activities are listed in annex 5 to part 6, their liability is strict. As a consequence, they have to adopt the remedial measures listed in annex 3 to part 6 of the Code. If the damage is caused by any other person, the same obligation arises if they acted with intent or negligence. In case the nec-

essary measures are not (wholly or partially) adopted, the Minister of the Environment and of the Protection of the Land and Sea shall determine the costs of such activities and claim damages from the tortfeasor.

Against this background, the Court stated that if the owner did not cause any environmental damage, their liability may not exceed that stated by art 253 of the Environmental Code. 18

As clarified by the Grand Chamber, the regime of environmental damage is wholly enshrined in the Environmental Code, while both the general tort law rule and the liability for dangerous activities (art 2050 CC) and damage caused by a thing (art 2051 CC) are not applicable. Nevertheless, causation plays a crucial role as an essential requirement of both fault and strict liability stated by the Environmental Code. As a consequence, the mere ownership of the land may not lead to any liability if it is not accompanied by the causing of damage. 19

A specific question the Grand Chamber deals with is whether the clean-up and safety obligations may be imposed on the owner who did not cause the pollution. The Grand Chamber makes clear that the owner may be required to perform only emergency preventive measures. 20

2. Cass SS UU 5 December 2023, no 33954: Unjust Enrichment and Tort Law Claims; Subsidiarity Rule

a) Brief Summary of the Facts

A company bought land upon which buildings could be erected and filed an application for a building permit. The municipal administration had changed in the meantime, and the new administration decided to change the building regulations. As a consequence, the destination of the land changed from residential to agricultural. 21

Since the municipality needed to bury high-voltage cables in the ground, the company offered to do it in exchange for the change of the building regulation. However, although the service was performed by incurring € 150,000, the regulation remained unchanged. 22

Therefore, the company filed an application against the municipality and claimed both pre-contractual damages and unjust enrichment. 23

While the Tribunal of Udine rejected the claim for pre-contractual damages and upheld that for unjust enrichment, the Court of Appeal of Trieste confirmed the denial of the claim for damages while declaring the unjust enrichment claim as inadmissible according to the subsidiarity rule stated by art 2042 CC. 24

25 The company appealed to the Court of Cassation, Third Chamber, which, however, suspended the proceeding and referred the matter to the Grand Chamber.

b) Judgment of the Court

26 The question the Grand Chamber dealt with focuses on the subsidiarity of the unjust enrichment claim when a prior action for damages has been filed and rejected.

27 According to the plaintiff, the subsidiarity rule aims at preventing the *cumul* of actions. Therefore, it should apply wherever the prior action has a contractual or legal ground, as, in both cases, the court checks whether its requirements exist *in abstracto*. Conversely, if the prior claim is based on a general clause – such as in case of pre-contractual or extra-contractual damages – the court would need to examine whether it is actually grounded and, in case it is rejected, the unjust enrichment claim might be examined.

28 Conversely, according to the Third Chamber of the Cassation, the rationale of the subsidiarity rule is quite the opposite, as its aim is to prevent the plaintiff from claiming for enrichment after losing the main action. This would explain why the unjust enrichment claim would be excluded if the main claim was time-barred, as affirmed by Cass 30614/2018. According to this view, the subsidiarity rule would apply even where the main action is based on pre-contractual or extra-contractual liability.

29 The Grand Chamber upheld the appeal by embracing an 'in-between' approach.

30 It started by reminding that, according to the traditional view, the subsidiarity rule applies if an alternative remedy remains at the disposal of the plaintiff, regardless of whether it has been actually sought or rejected for any reason. This abstract concept of subsidiarity aims at both providing legal certainty and preventing a duplication of remedies. This view was upheld by the Grand Chamber in 2008 (decision no 28042) and 1996 (decision no 9531). In particular, the unjust enrichment claim has been excluded if the alternative action (eg for damages) is prescribed (Cass no 30614/2018).

31 The Grand Chamber further recalled the opposite concept of subsidiarity *in concreto*, which grants the unjust enrichment action if the alternative has been rejected (eg, on grounds of prescription), or even where it does not cover what the plaintiff could be awarded by filing an unjust enrichment claim (for instance, if the enrichment is more than the suffered damage). According to this perspective, the aim of the subsidiarity rule would be to prevent the *cumul* of actions and, therefore, a duplication of remedies.

As the Grand Chamber reminded, several judgments of the Court of Cassation had limited the sphere of application of the subsidiarity rule over the last twenty years by admitting the unjust enrichment claim when the alternative action, instead of being based on a contractual or legal ground, was grounded on a general clause, such as the general tort law rule (see, Cass no 843/2020). 32

The Grand Chamber did not uphold the appellant's arguments and expressed a restrictive view on subsidiarity by referring to its historical background and emphasising the need to grant legal certainty. As a consequence, it confirmed that the unjust enrichment claim should be excluded where any alternative action is at the disposal of the plaintiff. At the same time, it denied the interpretation of the subsidiarity rule established by several judgments of the Court of Cassation (see above no 32) by denying the restitutionary claim even where the alternative remedy is grounded on a general clause like pre-contractual or extra-contractual liability. As a consequence, it further made clear that the victim should neither be allowed to choose the most convenient remedy nor cumulate enrichment and damages claims by asking for enrichment exceeding the amount of damage. Finally, it confirmed that the unjust enrichment claim should not be admitted wherever the main action has been rejected for lack of evidence or prescription. 33

Nevertheless, the Grand Chamber admitted the unjust enrichment remedy in two main situations. Firstly, where the main action is aimed at the enforcement of a contract, which turned out to be void, unless it is illegal due to a violation of a mandatory rule or public order (Cass no 13203/23). Secondly, wherever the main action is rejected as groundless for lack of substantial requirements (for instance, in the case of an extra-contractual claim, if fault, causal link, violation of a legally relevant interest or damage are lacking). 34

The Grand Chamber further clarified that the plaintiff may, alternatively, submit both tort and unjust enrichment claims or even only the latter by explaining the reasons why the main action for damages would be groundless. In this second scenario, the court must *ex officio* verify whether the subsidiarity rule has been respected. 35

As to the present case, the Grand Chamber concluded that the Court of Appeal had violated the above reported doctrine as the pre-contractual claim had been rejected by the court as groundless. This statement, according to the Grand Chamber, would make the unjust enrichment claim admissible. 36

c) Commentary

The present decision has attracted much attention as the meaning of the subsidiarity rule stated by the Civil Code (art 2042 CC) has been quite controversial. 37

Whereas several authors have embraced more liberal approaches by admitting the unjust enrichment rule where the alternative action has been rejected for any reason,[5] or confining the subsidiarity rule to indirect enrichment cases,[6] the opposite view holds such claims inadmissible whenever the plaintiff, in principle, has a different remedy at its disposal. While the latter view has remained the minority view in the literature,[7] it has been followed by case law since the entry into force of the Civil Code.

38 The Grand Chamber took an 'in-between' position between the *in abstracto* and *in concreto* view of subsidiarity by reasoning that the unjust enrichment claim is not precluded when, although an alternative remedy is at stake, it has been rejected as groundless. This approach is not absolutely new in the Cassation's recent case law, being adopted by several precedents.[8]

39 The Court's reasoning is convincing as far as it expressly rejected the strictest approach to subsidiarity, which, in preventing the unjust enrichment claim whenever an alternative one is conceivable, results in a reduction of the protection of the damaged party without any reasonable ground.

40 Its statement apparently seems to take a step back from the doctrine according to which, the subsidiarity rule would apply whenever an action grounded on a contract or a specific legal provision is at the plaintiff's disposal, whereas it would not come into play if the damaged party may avail themselves of a claim based on a general rule such as that on tort or pre-contractual liability.

41 At a closer look, however, the precedents affirming such milder interpretation revolved around disputes concerning executed void contracts concluded with the Public Administration, where the restitutionary claim was admitted even if the damaged party could file an action for damages against the public servant whose illegal act caused the invalidity.[9] Conversely, no precedent focused on drawing the boundary between unjust enrichment and tort law claims. Indeed, the relationship between these claims is far from being clarified.

42 The Grand Chamber denied the plaintiff the opportunity to cumulate both actions by claiming for enrichment exceeding the amount of damage suffered by the damaged party. This general statement, however, does not preclude the right to file

5 *P Sirena*, La sussidiarietà dell'azione generale di arricchimento senza causa, Rivista di diritto civile 2018, 379 ff.

6 *U Breccia*, Gestione d'affari, ripetizione dell'indebito, arricchimento senza causa (1982).

7 *P Schlesinger*, Arricchimento, azione di (diritto civile), in: Novissimo Digesto Italiano I (1958) 1008.

8 See eg, Cass 13 June 2018, no 15496.

9 Cass 17 January 2020, no 843; Cass 22 November 2017, no 27827.

both claims cumulatively in specific fields if this is allowed by certain legal provisions (ex, art 940 CC; art 125 of the Intellectual Property Code).

Compared with the approaches followed by most authors, the doctrine of the Grand Chamber remains restrictive. Indeed, while overcompensation or duplication of remedies should be prevented, a more liberal concept of subsidiarity would help the unjust enrichment claim to develop and better shape the general tort law rule. For instance, in the case of unlawful exploitation of someone's land, the unjust enrichment claim might theoretically apply wherever the owner suffered no real loss.[10] Conversely, the Italian case law is keen to interpret the tort law requirements broadly and award damages as a consequence of the impairment of land use, regardless of whether an actual loss has been suffered by the owner. It is unlikely that this trend will be changed after the commented decision of the Grand Chamber. 43

Finally, although tort law and unjust enrichment claims might overlap, overcompensation concerns are baseless as the plaintiff could not be allowed to receive duplicate damages. 44

3. Cassazione civile (Cass civ) 6 March 2023, no 6568: Concept of the Apparent Manufacturer of the Defective Product

a) Brief Summary of the Facts

Following a road accident, a driver reported personal injuries caused by the malfunctioning of the airbag in his Ford Mondeo. He brought an action under Directive 85/374/EEC against Ford Italia Ltd, claiming that it was the manufacturer of the vehicle. Ford Italia Ltd contested the claimant's version of events, arguing that it was the supplier and not the manufacturer of the car, which was in fact manufactured by *Ford Werke Aktiengesellschaft*. 45

---

10 Cass 15 November 2022, no 33645, Responsabilità civile e previdenza (Resp civ e prev) 2023, 84, with comments by *G Alpa*, Danno in re ipsa e tutela dei diritti fondamentali (diritti della personalità e diritto di proprietà); *E Bargelli*, Occupazione abusiva come specie di illecito: dall'agevolazione probatoria alla lesione della facoltà di godimento; *M Franzoni*, Occupazione sine titulo nella decisione delle SS. UU.; *CM Nanna*, Sezioni Unite e danno da occupazione sine titulo, tra inutilità di "astrazioni concettuali" ed esigenze di semplificazione; *C Scognamiglio*, Danno e risarcimento nel problema dell'occupazione abusiva di un immobile; *Pietro Sirena*, Danno-evento, danno-conseguenza e relativi nessi causali. Una storia di supefetazioni interpretative e ipocrisie giurisprudenziali.

46 On 6 November 2012, the Court of Bologna upheld the claim, finding that the damage suffered was due to a manufacturing defect in the airbag, and ordered Ford Italia Ltd to pay compensation. Ford Italia Ltd appealed the decision, reasserting its role as a mere vehicle supplier, but the appeal was rejected. Ford Italia Ltd then appealed to the Court of Cassation on various grounds. In particular, Ford Italia Ltd disputed its characterisation as the vehicle manufacturer. While deciding the case, the Court of Cassation referred a preliminary ruling on Directive 85/374/EEC[11] to the Court of Justice.

b) Judgment of the Court

47 The question to be addressed by the Court was whether Ford Italia Ltd can be regarded as the apparent manufacturer of the defective vehicle simply because it has a name that is wholly or partially identical to the real manufacturer's name and trade mark.

48 According to art 3(1) of Directive 85/374/EEC,[12] in addition to the manufacturer of the finished product, raw materials or components, any person who, although not actively involved in the production of the goods, 'by affixing his name, trade mark or other distinctive sign to the product, presents himself as its manufacturer' is to be regarded as the manufacturer.

49 The Court considers that there are grounds for considering Ford Italia Ltd as the apparent manufacturer of the vehicle, even though it is undisputed that it was the supplier of the defective product. This possibility would arise from the factual 'coincidence, wholly or predominantly perceptible to the consumer, of the trade mark or business name of the actual manufacturer with the trade mark or business name of the distributor/supplier'.[13] In other words, the fact that the signs and distinctive elements of the actual producer, on the one hand, and the distributor/supplier, on the other, overlap to such an extent that there is confusion on the part of the consumer as to the actual identity of the producer could be sufficient to justify 'the extension of the producer's liability to a person who is not the actual producer'.[14]

---

11 Council Directive 85/374/EEC of 25 July 1985 on the approximation of the laws, regulations and administrative provisions of the Member States concerning liability for defective products [1985] OJ L 210/29.

12 In Italy, the article of the Directive was transposed first in art 3(3) of Legislative Decree No 224/1988 and then in art 103, para 1, letter d) of the Consumer Code.

13 Cass 7 December 2017, no 29327.

14 Cass 6 March 2023, no 6568, commented here.

However, being aware that the text of the Directive requires active action on the part of the person wishing to be regarded as the producer, the Court questioned the possibility of interpreting the term 'affixing' in art 3 of the Directive in a broad sense and therefore asked the Court of Justice for an interpretation. In particular, the Court of Cassation asks the Court of Justice: 50

> 'whether an interpretation which extends the producer's liability to the supplier, even if the latter has not physically affixed his name, trade mark or other distinctive sign to the goods, solely because the supplier has a name, trade mark or other distinctive sign which is wholly or partly identical to that of the producer, is compatible with art 3(1) of Directive 85/374/EEC – and if not, why not'.

c) Commentary

In order to better understand the legal issue at stake, two aspects must be borne in mind. Firstly, the case is only the latest in a series of court decisions in which compensation claims under Directive 85/374/EEC have been brought against vehicle suppliers/distributors rather than the actual manufacturers.[15] In a situation very similar to the one that gave rise to the present case, the Court of Cassation laid down the following principle of law: under art 3(1) of Directive 85/374/EEC, 51

> 'the distributor or importer is liable for damage caused by a defect in the construction of the product if he has a trade mark or business name which is wholly or substantially identical to that of the manufacturer and has marketed the product under such distinctive signs'.[16]

Secondly, it is also important to consider the interaction between the doctrine of the apparent manufacturer and the commercial reality of corporate groups. In large multinational groups, the parent company, which owns the reference brand, often organises the group's activities at a continental level, designating certain affiliates for the production and others for the distribution of branded products in each national market. This supply chain model is the same as that used by the Ford Motor Company: Ford Motor Company US holds the Ford trade mark, which is then used to brand cars produced in Europe by Ford Werke and then distributed in Italy by Ford Italia Ltd. 52

15 Cass 7 December 2017, no 29327; Cass 20 May 2009, no 11710, Rassegna di diritto farmaceutico 2010, 11.

16 Cass 7 December 2017, no 29327.

53 Against this picture, it is possible to say that the Court of Cassation's guideline is questionable for several reasons and is likely to be rejected by the Court of Justice.

54 First of all, if such an interpretation were to prevail, suppliers/distributors would inevitably be forced to take out insurance policies, the cost of which would then be passed on to consumers, leading to an increase in the price of the products. However, this result would explicitly contradict the intention of the European legislator, which deliberately chose not to extend the liability of suppliers excessively in order to avoid increased costs and a surge in litigation.[17]

55 Furthermore, in the case of groups where the controlled companies regularly use the parent company's brand, the assessment of the national distributor as the apparent manufacturer should take into account the information in the user manual and instructions for use, as well as what is stated on the label and additional communications from the company about the product. Suppose the controlled undertaking explicitly informs the consumer by any of these means that it is the supplier of the product and discloses the name of the actual manufacturer. In that case, it should not be considered as an apparent manufacturer, notwithstanding the use of the trade mark.

56 However, there is another reason why the interpretation of art 3(1) proposed by the Court of Cassation does not seem convincing. The Court of Cassation constructs its entire argument around the consumers' perception and their confusion caused by the supplier/distributor. In doing so, the Court fails to identify the actual inter-individual relationship contemplated by the norm. In a nutshell, the norm is not concerned with the relationship between the consumer and the apparent manufacturer but rather with the relationship between the manufacturer and the supplier/distributor that attaches its distinctive signs to the product. Given that the objective of the Directive is to ensure the safety of products placed on the market, it seems correct to consider that the category of apparent manufacturer stems from the desire to hold accountable not only those who physically manufacture the products, but also those who are in a position to influence production decisions and ensure the safety of the products.[18] As can be seen from the preparatory

---

17 CJEU [GC] 13.1.2006, C-402/03, *Skov Æg v Bilka Lavprisvarehus A/S e Bilka Lavprisvarehus A/S v Jette Mikkelsen and Michael Due Nielsen*, ECLI:EU:C:2006:6 – Responsabilità civile 2006, 506, with comment by *L Villani*, La responsabilità del produttore-fornitore: nuovi casi italiani ed europei; also in CJEU 25.4.2002, C-52/00, *Commission of the European Communities v French Republic*, ECLI:EU:C:2002:252 – Resp civ e prev 2002, 997 ff, with comment by *di S Bastianon*, Responsabilità del produttore per prodotti difettosi: quale tutela per il consumatore?

18 *O Troiano*, Sub art 3, in: R Pardolesi/G Ponzanelli (eds), Commentario. La responsabilità per danno da prodotti difettosi, Nuove leggi civili commentate 1989, 525.

acts of the Directive, the European legislator had in mind the practices of large distribution or mail order companies, which typically have their goods produced by small local manufacturers, then brand them and distribute them on a large scale under their own name.[19] In these cases, the manufacturer typically has very little remaining autonomy, as it usually only follows the instructions of a party with a stronger contractual and market position and lacks effective control over production to ensure and improve the safety of the products placed on the market.[20] In this way, the European legislator, aware of the power dynamics in the market, wanted to make liable for damage caused by a defective product also those who, although not the actual manufacturer, wished to exploit their reputation by marketing the product under their brand while being able to guarantee its safety effectively.[21]

The Court of Cassation's interpretation, which completely ignores the power 57 dynamics between companies and focuses exclusively on consumers' perceptions, deviates from the real objectives of the Directive. Indeed, it is clear that, in the case in question, in which Ford Italia Ltd is a controlled company solely responsible for the distribution of the product on the Italian market and unable to intervene in its quality, the extension of the scope of the apparent manufacturer concept would not bring any real benefits in terms of consumer safety.

Finally, the Directive already seems to be able to guarantee the consumer the 58 possibility of establishing the passive legitimacy of an action for damages without the need to extend the scope of the notion of apparent producer. Indeed, in order to ensure that the consumer is able to identify a legitimate defendant within a reasonable time, it provides for the subsidiary liability of the supplier of the defective product if the producer cannot be traced.[22]

19 Proposal for a Council Directive relating to the approximation of the laws, regulations and administrative provisions of the Member States concerning liability for defective products, COM(76) 372 23 July 1976; *U Carnevali*, voce Responsabilità del produttore, Enciclopedia del diritto, Aggiornamento II, 1998, 941; *Troiano* (fn 18); *D Fairgrieve/G Howells/P Møgelvang Hansen/G Straetmans/ D Verhoeven/P Machnikowski/A Janssen/R Schulze*, Product liability directive, in: P Machnikowski (ed), European Product Liability: An Analysis of the State of the Art in the Era of New Technologies (2016) 63–65.

20 CJEU C-402/03 *Skov Æg v Bilka Lavprisvarehus A/S e Bilka Lavprisvarehus A/S v Jette Mikkelsen and Michael Due Nielsen.*

21 *Troiano* (fn 18).

22 See art 3(3) of Directive 85/374/EEC.

4. Cass SS UU 6 July 2023, no 19128: Establishment of the Causal Link between a Blood Transfusion and the Onset of a Disease

a) Brief Summary of the Facts

59 After a car accident, a man underwent surgery, including a transfusion of blood, in a private hospital. In September 2004, the man was diagnosed with HIV. He claimed damages for personal injury from the hospital and the Italian Ministry of Health, the latter being responsible for monitoring the safety of blood bags used for transfusions under the law.

60 He also filed a request for indemnity against the Ministry of Health under Law 210/1992. The Law allows a person irreversibly injured by compulsory vaccinations, transfusions, and administered blood derivatives to claim indemnity from the State. According to the procedure established by Law 210/1992, indemnity is granted regardless of fault if a medical committee establishes a causal link between the transfusion or vaccine and the disease of the injured person.

61 The committee confirmed the existence of a causal link, and the indemnity claim was accepted. The Court of Rome also ordered the private hospital and the Ministry of Health to pay damages under art 2043 of the Civil Code. After the rejection of its appeal, the Ministry referred the case to the Court of Cassation, arguing that the causal link between the blood transfusion and the pathology had not been proven during the civil proceedings and that the Court of Appeal had based its decision solely on the determination of the causal link made by the medical committee outside the court proceedings.

62 Within the Court of Cassation, there was a difference of opinion as to the evidential value, in the context of an action for damages, of assessments made in indemnity proceedings under Law No 210 of 1992. In order to resolve this conflict, the Third Session, by order of 31 October 2022, no 32077, referred the question to the Grand Chamber.

b) Judgment of the Court

63 The decision of the Court of Cassation concerns the value to be attached, in civil court proceedings, to the establishment of the causal link between a blood transfusion and the onset of a disease, which was carried out during the administrative proceedings as laid down by Law 210/1992.

According to a first opinion, dating back to the judgment of the Grand Chamber no 577 of 11 January 2008, findings made during administrative proceedings do not constitute legal evidence.[23] Therefore, the judge may take them into account at the trial as mere indications, but cannot give them the value of full and irrefutable evidence. On the other hand, according to a recent directive, since the medical committee consulted during the indemnity procedure is a governmental body, the establishment of the causal link between the transfusion and the disease during the administrative procedure must be considered an indisputable fact that does not require proof in determining the compensation in front of a judge.[24] 64

In the decision at stake, the Plenary Session first clarifies the ontological difference between the social indemnity procedure under Law 210/1992 and the right to damages under art 2043 of the Civil Code. According to the Plenary Session, the right to compensation is based on a wrong, ie blameworthy behaviour causing a loss, whereas the right to indemnity does not depend on fault. The latter is based, in particular, on the duty of social solidarity as defined in art 2 of the Constitution, which calls on the community to contribute to remedying certain types of harm to health, which would otherwise remain the sole responsibility of the injured party. 65

On the main issue, the Plenary Session considers reaffirming the previous position of the Court. The decision states that the establishment of a causal link during the indemnity procedure does not amount to a confession or legal proof (evidence that cannot be contradicted) in civil court proceedings. However, it specifies that what has just been stated does not mean that, in an action brought against the Ministry of Health for compensation for damage caused by a transfusion, the administrative finding of a causal link between the transfusion and the onset of the disease cannot be used by the injured party to prove the link. In particular, for the Plenary Session, once the indemnity has been granted, the establishment of the causal link in administrative proceedings may be used by the injured party in civil proceedings as presumptive evidence under art 2729 of the Civil Code. Therefore, the Ministry of Health cannot limit itself to a general denial of the causal link in the compensation judgment, but must present specific facts, which could not be assessed in the indemnity proceedings, which are likely to overturn the presumptive evidence. 66

---

23 Cass [GC] 11 January 2008, no 577, with comment by *M Gorgoni*, Dalla matrice contrattuale della responsabilità nosocomiale e professionale al superamento della distinzione tra obbligazioni di mezzo/di risultato, Resp civ e prev 2008, 856 ff.

24 Cass 15 June 2018, no 15734; Cass 5 October 2018, no 24523; Cass 30 June 2020, no 13008; Cass 17 November 2021, no 34885.

67 Finally, the Plenary Session specifies that if the Ministry of Health has not challenged the outcome of the administrative procedure and it has therefore become *res judicata*, the finding of causality made in the indemnity procedure must also be considered as finally established in the indemnity procedure before the court.

c) Commentary

68 The problems related to the interaction between the findings gathered during the compensation and indemnity proceedings arise from the fact that, unlike in other countries, in Italy, the two types of protection are neither alternative nor mutually exclusive.[25] Although some aspects of the decision have been criticised,[26] it has the merit of highlighting both the similarities and differences between the two different procedures. However, in addition to what is expressed in the decision, there is another difference between the two procedures: the amount of indemnity is generally much lower than the actual loss suffered by the injured party, whereas the amount of damages awarded in civil proceedings under art 2043 of the Civil Code compensates the actual loss.[27]

69 The Plenary Session seeks a middle ground between the two opposing views mentioned above. On the one hand, it affirms that the administrative finding on the causal link does not have the effectiveness of legal proof; on the other hand, however, it argues that if the injured party is indemnified, then the administrative finding does not have the value of a mere indication but is valid as presumptive evidence.

70 This seems to be a compromise to reduce the claimant's burden of proof in civil proceedings without depriving civil judges of their decision-making powers. However, there may be another reason why the court preferred not to consider the administrative finding as irrefutable evidence: the idea that medical committees establish the existence of a causal link between the transfusion and the

25 *V Carbone*, Danni da sangue infetto: il Ministero della Sanità risponde per omessa vigilanza e non per esercizio di attività pericolosa, Corriere giuridico 2001, 1209 ff.

26 *F Greco*, Diritto all'indennizzo e diritto al risarcimento: comunanze e discordanze congiunte al verbale della commissione medico ospedaliera, Resp civ e prev 2023, 1494 ff.

27 *R Breda*, Danno da vaccinazione tra indennizzo e risarcimento del danno, Rivista italiana di medicina legale (Riv it med leg) 2018, 289 ff.

onset of the disease with a lower standard of proof than that applied by the courts.[28]

5. Cass civ 23 October 2023, no 29387: Dangerous and Defective Products

a) Brief Summary of the Facts

An elderly woman fell while using a disabled lift and suffered serious injuries. The lift stopped 20 cm below floor level but, in spite of the height difference, the doors still opened, allowing the elderly woman to enter the lift and then fall due to the height difference. The victim's daughter decided to pay damages of her own accord, considering herself responsible for the accident as the owner and custodian of the lift. In 2013, she brought an action against the manufacturer under art 117 of the Italian Consumer Code, which transposes art 3 of the Directive 85/374/EEC, claiming that the product was defective and seeking compensation for the costs incurred. The claim, rejected in the first instance, was upheld in the second one. 71

In its appeal to the Court of Cassation, the manufacturer contested the finding that the lift was defective, arguing that it complied with the safety standards laid down in the sectoral technical regulations. 72

b) Judgment of the Court

The Court of Cassation ruled in favour of the manufacturer. The decision revolves around the concept of a defective product and what needs to be proven for a product to be considered as defective. According to art 6(1) of Directive 85/374/EEC, 'a product is defective when it does not provide the safety which a person is entitled to expect, taking into account all the circumstances.' 73

The Court states that the Court of Appeal was wrong in its finding that, for the lift to be considered safe, it should not have been possible to open the doors unless the lift was level with the floor. The Court points out that it is not for judges to dictate and assess how a particular product should have been designed. Furthermore, 74

28 However, although many assume that the committees apply a lower standard of proof, Law 210/1992 does not allow any lowering of the standard of proof. See *A Parziale*, Sanno da vaccinazione e incertezza del nesso causale: il ruolo della prova per presunzioni, Riv it med leg 2017, 1067 ff.

the mere existence of safer products, on the market or in theory, is not a sufficient reason to consider the product defective.

75 In addition, the Court makes it clear that art 117 is not intended to equate the absence of defects with the safety of the product. There may be defective products that are not dangerous, and there may be dangerous products that are not defective. The Court provides the example of a circular saw designed and sold without protection for the rotating parts. Although it is undoubtedly a dangerous product, it should not be considered defective for that reason alone.

76 Finally, the Court links the assessment of the defect to the compliance with the minimum safety standards set out in the sectoral technical regulations. Since the official technical consultancy had ruled out any non-conformity of the lift with the recognised standards of construction technology, the Court of Cassation considers that the Court of Appeal erred in condemning the manufacturer.

77 Against this background, the Court of Cassation upheld the appeal and referred the case back to the District Court. The Court of Cassation established the following legal principle: 'The assessment of the defectiveness of a product, according to art 117 of the Italian Consumer Code, does not consist in assessing the dangerousness of the product (since dangerous products are not defective in themselves), nor does it allow the judge to determine how he thinks the product should be designed or manufactured. On the contrary, the determination of whether a product is defective should be made by determining whether it has been designed and manufactured in compliance with the minimum standards required by sector-specific regulations or the rules of common prudence'.

c) Commentary

78 The decision has the merit of distinguishing the categories of dangerous and defective products. The difficulty in drawing the line lies in the very close relationship between the concept of defect and that of lack of safety.[29] Indeed, as mentioned above, a product is defective if it does not have the safety that a person reasonably expects. Some products are dangerous but are still marketed because of the benefits they bring to society. These products are unavoidably unsafe, so they cannot be considered defective simply because they cause harm.[30] Medicines are an example of this type of product: they have side effects that can be serious, but they cannot

29 *E Bellisario*, Il danno da prodotto conforme tra regole preventive e regole risarcitorie, Europa e Diritto Privato 2016, 841 ff.

30 *U Carnevali*, Prevenzione e risarcimento nelle Direttive comunitarie, Resp civ e prev 2005, 12 ff.

be considered defective for that reason alone.[31] Obviously, in such cases, consumers must be adequately informed of the dangerousness of the product.[32]

On the other hand, the claim that manufacturing choices, and in particular alternative product designs, should not be considered when assessing the defect of a product is unusual and not convincing. In fact, the concept of design defect precisely lies in this aspect. Especially, 'challenging a product's design challenges the decision of the manufacturer's engineers and managers to develop and sell a product containing a particular type and level of danger'.[33] Moreover, in the present case, the product was not an ordinary lift but one specifically designed for persons with motor disabilities, so it can be reasonably assumed that it should have been designed to prevent this type of accident. It is also questionable whether a disabled lift is a dangerous product. On closer inspection, it does not have the intrinsic and ineradicable danger that is typical of some products such as medicines and weapons. 79

However, the most critical and questionable point of the decision relates to the role of the minimum standards required by sectoral regulations or the rules of common prudence. Italian scholars are divided on this point. Some, inspired by the theory of pre-emption, consider that if the product complies with the standards, it cannot be considered defective;[34] others, on the contrary, argue that the standards are only minimum rules necessary to allow products to be placed on the market, but that, as minimum rules, compliance with them does not absolve the producer from liability under Directive 85/374/EEC.[35] Previously, the Court of Cassation had held that compliance with the standards was only one of the many aspects to be considered by the court in the complex assessment of the de- 80

31 *A Querci*, Sicurezza e danno da prodotti medicali (2011) 174 ff.

32 *D Wuyts*, The Product Liability Directive – More Than Two Decades of Defective Products in Europe (2014) 5 Journal of European Tort Law 8 ff.

33 *DG Owen*, Design Defects, Missouri Law Review 2008, 6.

34 *E Al Mureden*, Il danno da 'prodotto conforme'. Le soluzioni europee e statunitensi nella prospettiva del transatlantic trade and investment partnership (T.T.I.P.), Contratto e impresa 2015, 388 ff; *U Carnevali*, Prevenzione e risarcimento nelle Direttive comunitarie, Resp civ e prev 2005, 11 ff; *A D'Alessio*, La responsabilità del produttore di alimenti tra difetto e sicurezza del prodotto, Resp civ e prev 2018, 2016 ff.

35 *Bellisario*, Europa e Diritto Privato 2016, 841; *A Fusaro*, Quale modello di responsabilità per la robotica avanzata? Riflessioni a margine del percorso europeo, Nuova Giurisprudenza Civile (Nuova Giur Civ) 2020, 1344 ff; *J Di Rosa*, Sulla difettosità di un prodotto sicuro, Danno e Responsabilità (Danno e Resp) 2018, 773 ff; *A Luminoso*, Certificazione di qualità di prodotti e tutela del consumatore-acquirente, Europa e Diritto Privato 1999, 43 ff.

fectiveness of the product.[36] Instead, in the decision at stake, proof of compliance with the minimum standards required by sectoral regulations is sufficient for exemption from liability. However, this approach runs the risk of unlawfully creating a new exemption from liability in addition to those already provided for in art 7 of Directive 85/374/EEC.

6. Personal Injury

81 In 2023, the Court of Cassation dealt with several personal injury cases, specifically regarding the definition and quantification of non-pecuniary damages.

82 In judgment no 18442/2023, the Court clarified how to assess damage to health in cases of subsequent impairments, ie, when 'new' harm is added to previous harm. According to the Court, the assessment of subsequent impairments should be carried out in three stages. First, the total impairment resulting from both the pre-existing impairment and the current unlawful act must be estimated in percentage points. Then, the pre-existing impairment must be estimated in percentage points, and both percentages must be converted into a monetary amount. Finally, the amount corresponding to the pre-existing impairment must be subtracted from the total amount. This is without prejudice to the exercise of the judge's discretion to assess damages equitably if appropriate in the case in question, in tune with so-called corrective or integrative justice. Behind such a method of calculation lies the idea that it is not the degree of the impairment but the vital functions lost by the victim and the resulting deprivations that constitute the compensable damage. In this view, the deprivations (and the associated suffering) do not grow proportionally to the level of impairment: the former increases more than the latter.

83 With regard to the quantification of non-pecuniary damages, the most interesting innovation is the modification of the tables drawn up by the Tribunal of Rome, which increasingly serve as a parallel reference to those of the Tribunal of Milan. The modification was necessary to update the amounts of compensation and to adapt them to the rapid increase in the inflation rate that began in 2019. For this reason, too, the report accompanying the new tables announces that, from now on, the values will be automatically updated each year based on Istat (Istituto

---

36 Cass civ 10 May 2021, no 12225, with comment by *A Fusaro*, Effetto avverso del farmaco: obblighi informativi e responsabilità, Nuova Giur Civ 2021, 1145 ff; Cass 20 November 2018, no 29828; Cass 29 May 2013, no 13458, with comment by *C Baldassarre*, Responsabilità del produttore: danno risarcibile, onere della prova e logica giuridica, Danno e Resp 2014, 489 ff.

Nazionale di Statistica, Italian National Statistics Institute) indicators. In addition, the new tables introduce several innovations concerning the criteria for assessing parental damages, subjective moral damages, and catastrophic damages.[37]

The Court of Cassation also ruled on the reimbursement of medical treatment costs incurred as a result of biological damage. In particular, in its decision no 29308/2023, the Court stated that the compensation for pecuniary loss corresponding to the medical expenses incurred by the injured party, under art 1227, para 2 of the Civil Code, cannot be reduced for the sole reason that the injured party chose to be treated in a private facility rather than in a public one. There is no obligation to use the national health system. 84

The Court of Cassation also dealt, once again, with the nature of non-pecuniary damage, confirming that they are not *in re ipsa.* In a very specific case,[38] where a son was unable to attend his father's funeral because his flight had been wrongly cancelled by the airline, the Court confirmed that non-pecuniary damage does not coincide with the infringement of the interest protected by the law, but with the consequences of such an infringement. It follows that the existence of non-pecuniary damage must always be alleged and proved, even by presumptions. In this context, the Court held that the inability to attend the funeral of a parent as a result of an unlawful act or omission justifies compensation for non-pecuniary damage, where proven. 85

C. Literature

1. *Massimo Franzoni*, Dalla colpa grave alla responsabilità professionale [From gross negligence to professional liability] (Giappichelli Turin 2023)

This book, now in its fourth edition, examines the intellectual professions and focuses on how they have evolved. The author's interest is to show how the relationship between client and professional has changed over the years. The essay examines the main intellectual professions, from the most known to legal research to the least studied. The new edition takes into account the innovations introduced by Legislative Decree No 14 of 12 January 2019, recent case law developments on 86

37 *L Berti,* Le tabelle aggiornate del Tribunale di Roma, Diritto e giustizia, 16 November 2023.
38 Cass 29 November 2023, no 33276.

personal rights, interventions by the European Union, and some new issues raised by technological innovations.

2. *Stefano Rodotà*, Il problema della responsabilità civile, ristampa inalterata con prefazione di Guido Alpa [The problem of civil liability, unchanged reprint with a preface by Guido Alpa] (Giuffrè Milan 2023) Series Università Di Roma – Facoltà di Giurisprudenza Studi di Diritto Civile

87 Sixty years after its publication, Stefano Rodotà's book is still relevant: the use of comparative methodology and the attention paid to the dialogue between sources make the work a true masterpiece of legal scholarship. The impact of this book on Italian legal thought and practice has been immense. In particular, through the use of the comparative method and the direct application of the provisions of the Constitution to private relationships, Rodotà dismantled the prevailing dogmas and innovated the system, allowing the extension of the field of protected interests and promoting a fairer assessment of unjust damage.

3. *Emiliozzi Enrico Antonio*, La Responsabilità Medica [Medical liability] (Giuffrè Milan 2023) Series trattato di diritto civile e commerciale Cicu-Messineo

88 The book deals with medical liability, taking into account the latest legislative and case law developments. In particular, the author examines in detail informed consent and the possible infringement of the patient's right to therapeutic self-determination. The book also considers the liability of the medical practitioner for negligent failure to diagnose malformations or foetal pathologies. Finally, given the close connection with medical liability, the book also analyses liability for damage arising from vaccines and blood transfusions, including blood products.

Agris Bitāns

XVII. Latvia

A. Legislation

1. Amendments to Consumer Rights Protection Law (Grozījumi Patērētāju tiesību aizsardzības likumā) Latvijas Vēstnesis no 190, 2 October 2023

These amendments to the Consumer Rights Protection Law, which was adopted on 1
20 January 2022 and entered into force on 14 September 2023, transposes provisions of Directive (EU) 2020/1828 of the European Parliament and of the Council of 23 October 2019 on representative actions to protect the collective interests of consumers and repealing Directive 2009/22/EC.[1]

The purpose of the amendments is to provide consumers with an effective and 2
efficient procedural mechanism for collective claims, therefore, simultaneously with these amendments, amendments to the Law on Civil Procedure were adopted accordingly.

The amendments introduced a new law institute in Latvia – the collective ac- 3
tion – for the protection of consumers' rights. The provisions of the consumers' collective action are applicable to consumers' claims also in cases of cross-border infringements, including when these infringements were terminated before the submission or consideration of the consumers' collective action or the administrative process for the prevention of the infringement was terminated (part 10 art 4^1).

A consumers' collective action may be filed in court only by a qualified insti- 4
tution that has obtained such status by the Consumer Rights Protection Centre's (CRPC) decision (part 1 art 23^1) or it has been approved in another European Union Member State (part 6 art 23^4). The CRPC grants the status of a qualified institution permanently or for bringing specific consumer collective claims if the association (NGO) meets the requirements specified in part 1 art 23 of the Law.

The list of qualified institutions approved in Latvia is maintained by the CRPC 5
(art 23^2), while the list of qualified institutions approved in each Member State of the European Union and notified to the European Commission is maintained and made publicly available by the European Commission (art 23^3). The qualified institution can bring the collective consumers' claim in court for the benefit of consum-

1 [2020] Official Journal of the European Union (OJ) L 409/63.

https://doi.org/10.1515/9783111376721-018

ers (part 1 art 26^{19}). The court, the CRPC or another relevant supervisory and control institution can recognise a violation of the collective interests of consumers (part 2 art 26^{19}).

6 The qualified institution is entitled, for the benefit of those consumers who have been harmed due to a particular violation of the collective interests of consumers, to demand and receive compensation for the harm from the manufacturer, seller or service provider, including compensation, repair, exchange, price reduction, termination of the contract or refund of the amount paid (part 1 art 26^{20}). As indicated in the annotation of the amendments to the Law, the harm (which is compensable under this Law) should be understood as the harm as provided by art 1635 of the Civil Law, which also includes non-pecuniary (moral) damage. Compensation of the harm does not affect other consumer claims that are not covered by the specific consumer collective claim (part 2 art 26^{20}).

7 The qualified institution has an obligation to publish information inviting consumers to apply for participation in the consumers' collective claim and inform the CRPC about the published call, which is published on its website and social networks (part 1 art 26^{21}).

8 The consumer can submit a signed application for participation in the consumers' collective claim to the qualified institution (part 1 art 26^{22}). The consumer should attach documents that substantiate the claim, including a copy of a transaction and payment document (cheque or other proof of payment) and other evidence that substantiates their right to compensation for damage in the specific consumer collective claim (part 2 art 26^{22}). The consumer's application for participation in the consumers' collective claim at the same time confirms the authority of the qualified institution to perform all actions under this Law and the Civil Procedure Law in connection with the relevant consumers' collective claim.

9 Article 26^{23} determines certain requirements for the evaluation of the consumers' application and the consequences related to it. The qualified institution has an obligation to evaluate the received consumers' applications within a reasonable period of time (part 1). Consumers who have given their consent to be represented in a consumers' collective claim cannot be represented in another consumers' collective claim with the same basis and against the same manufacturer, seller or service provider, nor can they individually bring a claim with the same basis and against the same manufacturer, seller or service provider. This limitation does not apply to those consumers who have withdrawn from the consumers' collective action in accordance with art 26^{29} of this Law. Consumers are not entitled to receive compensation for damage more than once for the same cause of action from the same manufacturer, seller or service provider (part 2). If the consumer's application does not meet the requirements of art 26^{22} of this Law, or if all the necessary documents are not attached to it and they are not corrected within the specified period,

the consumer shall be informed that participation in the consumers' collective claim is refused (part 3). If the consumer's participation in the consumers' collective claim is approved, the qualified institution informs the consumer about the procedure for paying the registration fee if such a fee is provided for in the specific consumers' collective claim (part 4). If the consumer has not paid the registration fee for participation in the consumers' collective claim within the specified term, the qualified institution shall inform the consumer that participation in the said claim is refused (part 5).

The qualified institution, after collecting consumers' applications, applies to 10
the manufacturer, seller or service provider with a demand for the termination of the violation and compensation for the damage caused to consumers or with a claim for compensation for the damage caused to consumers and warns about going to court with a consumers' collective claim if the relevant requirements are not met (part 1 art 26^{24}). The qualified institution and the manufacturer, seller or service provider may agree on the settlement and its terms. Such settlements are binding on the manufacturer, seller or service provider and the respective individual consumers who will enter into the settlement (part 2 art 26^{24}). The manufacturer, seller or service provider shall bear the costs of publishing the contents of the settlement (part 3 art 26^{24}). The qualified institution informs those consumers who have been approved in the consumers' collective claim about submitting the complaint to the manufacturer, seller or service provider, as well as about the progress of such a claim, the proposed settlements and the procedure for their conclusion (part 4 art 26^{24}). If the manufacturer, seller or service provider does not fulfil the requirements referred to in the first part of this section in full within the period specified by the qualified institution (which must not be shorter than 14 days), or if no other agreement has been reached, the qualified institution is entitled to bring a consumers' collective action in court in accordance with the Civil Procedure Law (part 5 art 26^{24}).

The qualified institution may apply to the court if: (1) at least five consumers 11
have been approved in the consumers' collective claim; (2) claims of the consumers are directed against the same defendant or defendants; (3) claims of consumers are based on the same or similar factual and legal circumstances (part 1 art 26^{25}). In the consumers' collective action, in addition to compensation for damage, the consumers may ask to determine one or more of the following remedies for the manufacturer, seller or service provider: (1) terminate the violation immediately or within a specified period; (2) inform other consumers who have suffered from the violation in question about the final court ruling and about any approved settlements and consumers' rights to claim compensation, including, if necessary, by publishing information in a means of communication appropriate to the circumstances of the case (part 2 art 26^{25}). Consumers are not obliged to cover the costs

of legal proceedings in connection with the consumers' collective action, since the qualified institution is the plaintiff in the consumers' collective action (part 3 art 26^{25}). However, the law provides that a qualified institution has rights to claim compensation from consumers for losses suffered as a result of wilful actions or negligence in connection with a consumers' collective action (part 4 art 26^{25}). If during legal proceedings or until the execution of the judgment, the qualified institution that brought the consumers' collective action loses its status, another qualified institution may be its successor (part 5 art 26^{25}).

12 The qualified institution is obliged to inform consumers in a timely manner about the progress of the consumers' collective action and the proposed settlements (part 1 art 26^{28}). If the consumer does not agree to the settlement proposed by the qualified institution and the manufacturer, seller or service provider, the consumer has the right to withdraw from the consumers' collective action by submitting a relevant signed application to the qualified institution. In this case the consumer shall not be included in the settlement agreement (part 1 art 26^{29}).

13 The limitation period for those consumers who are affected or could be affected by the specific violation is terminated at the moment when the manufacturer, seller or service provider receives a warning from the qualified institution about going to court with a consumers' collective action or at the moment when the supervision and control institution receives a notice from the qualified institution of the application for prevention of violation of consumer rights (art 26^{30}).

14 Article 26^{31} regulates the issue of third-party financing of the qualified institution, including the obligation to disclose information about its funding sources in general, in order to avoid a conflict of interests between the financier and the work of the qualified institution in the consumers' collective claim and its outcome.

15 During legal proceedings, until the examination of the merits of the case has been completed, the qualified institution has the right to ask the court with a final ruling to oblige the manufacturer, seller or service provider to compensate the expenses incurred by the qualified institution in connection with the consumers' collective action. These expenses are related to informing consumers in the process of bringing collective action and conducting the case (part 1 art 26^{33}). Expenses related to a consumers' collective claim must be proportionate and objectively justified (part 2 art 26^{33}). The allowable amount of expenses related to the consumers' collective claim and expenses that are not reimbursable are determined by the Cabinet of Ministers (part 4 art 26^{33}).[2]

2 On 12 December 2023, the Cabinet of Ministers issued Regulation no 729 on 'Granting funding to the qualified institution for bringing collective claims'.

The qualified institution shall pay consumers the awarded sums of money in the consumers' collective claim. If the awarded amount is not enough to satisfy all the consumers' claims, this amount shall be paid among the consumers proportionally (part 1 art 26[34]). 16

2. Amendments to the Law on Mandatory Social Insurance in Respect of Accidents at Work and Occupational Diseases (Grozījums likumā 'Par obligāto sociālo apdrošināšanu pret nelaimes gadījumiem darbā un arodslimībām') Latvijas Vēstnesis no 57 A, 21 March 2023

On 8 March 2023, the Latvian Parliament adopted amendments to the Law on Mandatory Social Insurance in Respect of Accidents at Work and Occupational Diseases, which has been in force with amendments since 1 January 1997. The amendments became effective from 1 July 2023. 17

The main goal of these amendments is to determine the methodology for calculating the minimum amount of compensation for so-called breadwinner's losses, tying it to a percentage value of the median monthly minimum income published on the website of the Central Statistics Office, which corresponds to the defined minimum income thresholds as defined in the Law on Social Security. The amendments were necessary to fully implement the judgments of the Constitutional Court of the Republic of Latvia. The Constitutional Court in its judgments in cases no 2019-24-03, no 2019-25-03, no 2019-27-03 and no 2020-07-03 emphasised that the State is obliged to regularly assess the adequacy of the amount of social assistance provided to guarantee that it is respectful, corresponds to social reality and to ensure that citizens with low incomes are provided with the help they need. 18

In relation to the minimum amount of compensation for the loss of a provider for each child, the new wording of part 10 art 23 of the Law foresees the transition from the numerical value of the minimum income in terms of euros (which was € 136 and € 163 until now) to a percentage value and rounded to whole euros from the minimum income median per one equivalent consumer per month (the income median) published on the website of the Central Statistical Bureau of the median income of households. Thus: 19

1) for a child up to the attainment of seven years of age – in the amount of 25 % of the income median;
2) for a child from seven years of age – in the amount of 30 % of the income median.

3. State Defence Service Law (Valsts aizsardzības dienesta likums) Latvijas Vēstnesis no 75, 18 April 2023

20 This Law was adopted on 5 April 2023 and entered into force on 19 April 2023. The purpose of this Law is to ensure the preparation of Latvian citizens for the performance of national defence tasks, as well as to strengthen the resilience and response capabilities of the State and society as part of a comprehensive system of national defence (art 1).

21 The Law also provides regulations related to tort liability. For instance, art 18 determines the liability of a soldier of the national defence service. A soldier of the national defence service who has behaved in an illegal manner may be subjected to disciplinary liability, administrative liability or criminal liability. Further, they can be held liable for the material damage caused in relation to the procedures specified in the regulatory acts. The reference to pecuniary loss indicates that the liability of a soldier of the national defence service is limited only to pecuniary loss and not to non-pecuniary loss.

22 Likewise, para 1 art 24 also determines the liability of the person performing the national defence civil service or alternative service (persons who cannot perform the national defence military service due to their thoughts, conscience or religious beliefs) only for the direct damage caused to the institution in which they perform such alternative service, due to their illegal, culpable action.

4. Amendments to the Law on the Rights of Patients (Grozījumi Pacientu tiesību likumā) Latvijas Vēstnesis no 214, 3 November 2023 and Latvijas Vēstnesis no 226, 22 November 2023

23 On 26 October 2023, the Latvian Parliament adopted amendments to the Law on the Rights of Patients, which has been in force with amendments since 1 March 2009.[3] With these amendments, which became effective from 1 January 2024, the Law has been amended with art 17^1.

24 The main goal of this amendment was to ensure that compensation will continue to be paid to those who suffered serious or moderately serious harm to their health or life due to confirmed adverse effects caused by the COVID-19 vaccination after the Law on the Management of the Spread of COVID-19 Infection and art 49^7

3 See the brief description and my comments in *A Bitāns*, Latvia, in: E Karner/BC Steininger (eds), European Tort Law (ETL) 2009 (2010) 361, nos 3–8.

lost its force on 31 December 2023. Accordingly, the Cabinet of Ministers' Regulations Regarding Compensation for Serious or Moderately Serious Harm to the Health or Life of a Patient due to Adverse Effects Caused by the COVID-19 Vaccination also lost their force.

This article states that the Cabinet shall determine[4] the requirements and pro- 25
cedures for the requesting, granting, and disbursement of compensation or for a refusal to grant it, and also shall determine the amount of compensation to be awarded according to the severity of harm. Total compensation shall not exceed € 142,290 (part 1 art 17^1).

Part 2 art 17^1 determines the time period during which a compensation claim 26
for the serious or moderately serious harm to a person's health or life due to confirmed adverse effects caused by the COVID-19 vaccination shall be examined and a decision shall be taken. This should occur within six months after receipt of the compensation claim. This time period may be extended for up to one year, if necessary, to request, collect and evaluate additional information to examine the compensation claim and to arrive at a decision.

A request for compensation shall be submitted not later than two years from 27
the day of discovering the harm, however, not later than three years from the day of vaccination (part 3 art 17^1).

If the patient has already received compensation for the harm to their life or 28
health within the scope of civil proceedings, they are not entitled to receive compensation under this article (part 3 art 17^1).

In accordance with art 17^1, Cabinet of Ministers' Regulations no 812 on Com- 29
pensation for Serious or Moderately Serious Harm to the Health or Life of a Patient due to Adverse Effects Caused by the COVID-19 Vaccination are effective from 1 January 2024. These Regulations are similar to Regulations no 272 on Compensation for Serious or Moderately Serious Harm to the Health or Life of a Patient due to Adverse Effects Caused by the COVID-19 Vaccination, which was effective from 7 May 2022.[5]

---

4 See the brief description and my comments below under no 31 ff.

5 See the brief description and my comments in *A Bitāns*, Latvia, in: E Karner/BC Steininger (eds), European Tort Law (ETL) 2022 (2023) 349, nos 15–28.

B. Cases

1. Judgment[6] of the Senate of the Republic of Latvia, Department of Civil Cases, 2023, no SKC-[H]/2023 ECLI:LV: AT:2023: Separation of Pecuniary and Non-Pecuniary Loss; Liability for Unauthorised Using of Picture in Advertising[7]

a) Brief Summary of the Facts

30 The claimant, A, brought an action against company B (the defendant) for compensation of non-pecuniary loss in the amount of € 150,000. The claim was brought because the defendant repeatedly published (processed) the claimant's personal data on its branded Facebook and Twitter websites for advertising purposes between 2015 and 2016, namely, photographs had been published 20 times and video material nine times.

31 The State Data Inspectorate confirmed that the processing of the claimant's personal data was carried out without his consent and without any other legal basis. The Data State Inspectorate recognised the claimant as a victim within the meaning of part 1 art 261 of the Code of Administrative Offenses of Latvia and imposed the maximum fine of € 11,400 on the defendant. Such a decision is confirmation of the gravity of the violation committed against him and the significance of the violation of his rights.

32 The claimant stated that such illegal data processing can significantly harm the claimant's career and reputation as a professional athlete, as it may mislead the public to thinking that the claimant advertises gambling on behalf of the defendant, and such a situation caused a negative experience for the claimant and his family.

33 Due to the defendant's illegal actions, the claimant has simultaneously suffered moral damage and damage related to the violation of his rights due to the violation of the Personal Data Protection Law and the Advertising Law. According to the claimant, these violations cannot be separated and distinguished, because they are related to the same illegal action of the defendant, therefore the legal basis of the damage caused, and its extent can be seen in the context of both Laws.

34 The claimant stated that, when determining the amount of compensation for moral damage (non-pecuniary loss), in addition to art 5 of the Civil Law, the prin-

6 Status of closed case.
7 See on the Latvian Supreme Court website: <https://www.at.gov.lv/downloadlawfile/9498>.

ciples set out in part 3 art 69^1 of the Copyright Law can also be applied, ie taking into account the hypothetical licence fee for permission to use one's image, and the amount should not be lower than the amounts already determined in contracts concluded by the claimant for the use of his name and image in advertisements (€ 258,362). At the time when the defendant committed the violation, the claimant was a well-known athlete in both Latvia and worldwide. At the time of the defendant's violation, the claimant had signed a brand ambassador and representative contract with JSC (company) for the amount of € 44,679. The claim was based on arts 5, 1635, 1770 and 1772 of the Civil Law, arts 19, 32 of the Personal Data Processing Law, para 4 part 2 art 4 and art 18^1 of the Advertising Law.

The first instance court partially satisfied the claim and awarded € 100,000 as compensation. The regional court, as a court of second instance, satisfied the claim in part and awarded € 50,000 as compensation. With the 2020 judgment of the Senate, the judgment of the regional court was annulled in the part regarding determination of the amount of damages and in the part concerning the recovery of legal costs. As regards this latter part, it was decided that the case should be sent for re-adjudication to the appellate court. In the Senate's judgment, it was pointed out that the amount of compensation for non-pecuniary loss determined for the claimant does not correspond to the case law that has developed in similar cases. 35

The regional court, having reviewed the case again, partially satisfied the claim and awarded the claimant € 50,000 as compensation and € 4,398 to compensate his legal costs. 36

The defendant filed a cassation complaint, which challenged the judgment of the second instance court. 37

b) Judgment of the Court

The Senate decided that the judgment of the second instance court should be set aside and that the case should be sent for re-adjudication to the appellate court. 38

The Senate concluded that the court had erred in using the method of 'case comparison and typifying'. In determining the amount of compensation for non-pecuniary loss, it used examples from case law that were not comparable to the case under consideration in terms of the violated non-property rights (values), and only partially applied criteria applicable to the compensation of material damage to motivate the judgment. Therefore, the court incorrectly applied the provisions of arts 1635 and 5 of the Civil Law. 39

By ignoring the instructions given in the 2020 judgment of the Senate regarding the interpretation of the law, the court violated the provisions of art 476 of the 40

Civil Procedure Law. In the opinion of the Senate, the error was manifested in the fact that the court based its judgment mainly on comparisons with cases from the practice of Latvian courts, other countries' courts and the European Court of Human Rights (ECtHR), the actual circumstances of which were significantly different from the actual circumstances of the case under consideration.

41 The Senate reiterated the previously expressed position that compensation for non-pecuniary loss should not be excessive, that it has a satisfactory function, and the court should take into account exactly what non-property rights (values) were violated.

42 The Senate pointed out that the claimant, when formulating his claim, did not draw a clear line between non-pecuniary loss and pecuniary loss. In the case under consideration, the claimant's arguments were dominated by considerations related to the possible non-pecuniary loss (moral damage) that could have occurred as a result of the violation of the claimant's non-property rights, including the unauthorised use of his name and image.

43 The Senate did not see a problem with referring to examples of case law that were not directly applicable to the case under consideration if they only illustrate the court's position on the issue of the importance of the affected non-material values and help to find an understanding of the criteria to be used in determining just compensation. However, problems arise, since these examples of case law are not used to justify the special nature of the specific case and justify the compensation for non-pecuniary loss in the amount awarded in the appealed judgment.

44 The Senate recognised that even in terms of factual circumstances, the circumstances mentioned in similar civil legal disputes tend to be different to a greater or lesser extent, and therefore in cases of non-pecuniary (moral) damage, even in cases where the same non-property rights or non-property values are violated, various circumstances affecting persons may impact on the severity and intensity of suffering.

45 At the same time, the method of 'case comparison and typifying' does not mean that comparable cases from case law should be completely or almost identical. Within the framework of the mentioned method, the cases compared should be as similar as possible, but they do not have to be completely uniform in terms of legal and factual circumstances. In the appealed judgment, the court did not take into account the similarity and importance of the violated rights and interests, for comparison also referring to such examples from case law, which obviously could not be used in the adjudication of the case (cases of compensation for non-pecuniary loss for health injury or death of a person).

46 The Senate rejected the defendant's argument that the severity and duration of the violation established in the case under consideration did not increase the claimant's suffering, as he did not suffer negative consequences in the field of

his professional activity, as the severity and duration of the violation of non-property rights or values can be criteria used when determining the amount of compensation in accordance with arts 1635 and 5 of the Civil Law.

At the same time, the Senate found that the appealed judgment did not provide an assessment of how exactly the mentioned factors increased the claimant's suffering. The Senate agreed with the defendant's argument that the criteria intended for the compensation of material damage cannot be used to determine the amount of compensation for moral damage, because the court's reference to the brand ambassador and representative contract concluded by the claimant with JSC (firm) and its amount (in the amount of € 44,679, which is close to the amount of compensation awarded by the court) indicates the use of the licence fee method known in intellectual property law. The claim was not filed for pecuniary loss (in the form of lost profit or unearned income) due to the actions of the defendant, which in some way prevented the claimant from fulfilling the contract or was an obstacle to concluding similar contracts with other companies. Also, the hypothetical licence fee method is only a method of calculating compensation for material damage and is not applicable for determining compensation for non-material damage. 47

Also, the court did not provide a more detailed justification for referring to several examples from foreign court practice, in which well-known athletes were awarded a significant amount of compensation for the unauthorised use of their image in advertisements. The Senate pointed out that the amount of compensation for non-pecuniary loss cannot be based on the circumstances related to the compensation of pecuniary loss, or based on examples from judicial practice, which use criteria or methods of compensation of pecuniary loss. 48

c) Commentary

It is positive that the Senate explained that the method of 'case comparison and typifying' does not require that the comparable case law should be completely or almost identical, therefore they may not be completely uniform in terms of legal and factual circumstances. The Senate did not see a problem with the use of examples from case law that were not directly applicable to the case under consideration if they were only used to illustrate the court's position on the issue of the importance of the affected non-material values and to help to find an understanding of the criteria to be used in determining just compensation. 49

Also, the Senate accepted the possibility of referring to cases from other countries' courts and the ECtHR if the circumstances in these cases are similar to the case under consideration and the courts' approach to determining compensation 50 does not differ from the criteria recognised in Latvian case law regarding the determination of compensation for non-pecuniary loss.

51 Accordingly, courts are not limited to references to existing Latvian case law. However, reiteration that compensation for non-pecuniary loss should not be excessive seems to limit courts in relation to determining just and appropriate compensation for non-pecuniary loss, because the Senate used as a comparison judgments which were more than ten years old.

52 The Senate did not assess whether the amount of compensation for non-pecuniary loss determined in past judgments is still adequate. Namely, whether they meet the criteria of fair and adequate compensation for the damage caused to the person, and whether they fulfilled the function of reconciliation or prevention. This is very important because the courts mainly referred to judgments which were handed down only recently after the amendment of art 1635 of the Civil Law in 2006, when the general institution of non-pecuniary loss was introduced into the Civil Law. Since the non-pecuniary loss institute was recognised relatively recently, the courts have not had sufficient experience in determining the amount of compensation for non-pecuniary loss. And secondly it is time to re-evaluate amounts of compensation awarded ten and more year ago at least because of inflation. For instance, according to the Central Statistics Office, inflation in the last ten years was at an average of 49.5 % but the inflation rate has been at 92.2 % since January 2007. Therefore, it is not a surprise that Latvian case law regarding maximum compensation amounts for non-pecuniary loss, including, personal injury, lags far behind in comparison to EU case law. These findings were presented at the 21st Annual Conference on European Tort Law in 2022.

53 Also, it is unclear why a court, when determining compensation for non-pecuniary loss for the unauthorised use of a person's image, should not examine the argument regarding the victim's commercial publicity (existing licence or advertising contracts). In order to determine just and appropriate compensation for non-pecuniary loss, all reasons or arguments should be evaluated, and there is no reason to exclude arguments of a commercial or material nature from a potential evaluation since Latvian courts have awarded compensation for non-pecuniary loss even in cases of violations of property rights or for material damage.[8]

8 See the judgment of the Riga Regional Court case No CA-2062–17/32 of 27 December 2017 and the Senate judgment case No SKC-82/2012 of 22 February 2012.

2. Judgment of the Senate of the Republic of Latvia, Department of Civil Cases, 15 March 2023, no SKC-11/2023 (C33454219) ECLI:LV:AT:2023:0315.C33454219.12.S: VAT and Damages; Determination of Pecuniary Loss in the Case of Damaged Property[9]

a) Brief Summary of the Facts

54 The claimant (a company) brought an action against the defendant (employee of the claimant) for the recovery of pecuniary loss in the amount of € 21,017 caused by him. The defendant was intoxicated during the performance of work duties outside of Latvia. In February 2019, the defendant caused a traffic accident, as a result of which the claimant's truck and a rented refrigerated trailer belonging to Vitrans SIA were damaged. The insurance company refused payment of insurance indemnity due to significant violations of the terms of the insurance contract.

55 According to a report, which the defendant did not contest, the possible market value of the truck, including value added tax (VAT), is € 7,000 – 9,000. The claimant paid both the purchase price and the VAT calculated for the purchase of the truck, therefore the defendant must compensate the value of the truck and the VAT, a total of € 8,000. The lessor of the trailer, Vitrans handed over the trailer for the claimant's disposal, receiving payment for its residual value of € 1,000. The claimant paid Vitrans compensation of € 9,600, which is the difference between the actual value of the trailer and the funds received for its disposal.

56 The defendant did not dispute the expenses of € 3,417 for the removal of the vehicle and trailer, hotels, fuel and employee business trips, which are proven by the payment documents in the case.

57 The Vidzeme Regional Court, as an appellate court, with its judgment of 3 December 2020, satisfied the claim for recovery of € 21,017 as damages for the loss caused in a road traffic accident, which consists in the value of the truck (€ 8,000), the value of the trailer (€ 9,600), removal costs and other expenses related to preventing the consequences of the accident (€ 3,417).

58 The defendant filed a cassation complaint, which challenged the judgment of the second instance court.

9 See on the Latvian Supreme Court website: <https://www.at.gov.lv/downloadlawfile/9498>.

b) Judgment of the Court

59 The Senate partly quashed the appeal court's judgment. Since the cassation complaint did not contain any arguments regarding the contested damages of € 3,417 for the removal of the vehicle, hotel, fuel and employee business trips, the judgment of the appeal court was left unchanged in this part. The Senate concluded that the rest of the appealed judgment should be quashed.

60 The Senate pointed out that, according to art 1779 of the Civil Law, everyone has an obligation to compensate the loss caused by their actions or inactions, therefore the claimant has an obligation to prove the amount of the loss caused, which was directly causally related to the defendant's illegal actions. Whereas VAT is a consumption tax that is included in the value of a good or service, for the company, which is the payer of the relevant tax, the tax is financially neutral, that is, the tax paid for the purchased item, which is used to ensure its economic activity, is included in the tax declaration as input tax and deducted from the tax amount payable in the budget. In other words, the claimant himself can take the steps reasonably expected of any merchant to recover the tax paid to the State.

61 The court's conclusion that the defendant did not prove that the input tax paid by the claimant for the purchase of the truck would have been returned from the State does not establish the defendant's obligation to pay as damages the VAT paid by the claimant. Accordingly, the Senate pointed out that the court, when determining the value of the truck that should be compensated, included the VAT paid by the claimant at the time of purchase and that art 1779 of the Civil Law was incorrectly applied.

62 While the claimant kept the damaged truck and requested compensation equal to the value of the damaged truck in order to restore the condition that existed before the traffic accident, it is important, when assessing the amount of damages, to take into account the scrap value of the truck, which remains at the claimant's disposal.

63 According to the circumstances established in the judgment, the first instance court did not take into account that the damaged trailer was not owned by the claimant, and the claimant paid compensation to Vitrans for the damage caused to the rental object. Although the mentioned circumstance may play a role in determining the amount of the damages, the agreement between the claimant and Vitrans does not create a presumption of the existence of a causal connection between the entire amount of money paid and the defendant's unlawful conduct, as well as regarding the amount of money paid under agreement as the amount of loss.

64 Whether the restoration of the trailer was technically and economically more advantageous, as well as what actions were subsequently carried out with the trail-

er by third parties are important. Therefore, it is necessary to find out whether the restoration of the trailer was really not possible, and it was handed over for disposal for the remaining value, or whether the trailer was repaired after the accident and passed a technical inspection for participation in road traffic. Accordingly, in the event that property is completely destroyed or its restoration is impossible, according to the legal framework of arts 1789 and 1791 of the Civil Law, the amount of damages shall be determined according to the value of the object at the time of the damage, while if the damage does not reach such a degree, the damages are made up of the amount of necessary repair expenses.

c) Commentary

This judgment shows that it is important to correctly determine the actual amount 65
of pecuniary loss regarding partly damaged or fully 'lost' objects. For a claimant who pays VAT, it is necessary to exclude paid VAT from the value of lost property, since VAT is financially neutral.

In order to fulfil the requirements of arts 1779, 1789 and 1791 of the Civil Law, it 66
is important to exclude from pecuniary loss the residual value of the damaged object if it stays at the claimant's disposal. Also, the amount of damages shall be determined according to the value of the object at the time of the damage, while if the damage does not reach such a degree, the damages are made up of the amount of necessary repair expenses.

3. Judgment of the Senate of the Republic of Latvia, Department of Civil Cases, 28 September 2023, no SKC-368/2023 (C33275321) ECLI:LV:AT:2023:0928. C33275321.19.S: Liability of Board Member for Lost Profit[10]

a) Brief Summary of the Facts

The claimant (a company) brought an action against the defendant (former board 67
member) for the recovery of lost profit in the amount of € 33,648 and statutory interest of € 5,742. The claim was based on parts 1 and 2 art 169 of the Commercial Law and the following circumstances.

10 See on the Latvian Supreme Court website: <https://www.at.gov.lv/downloadlawfile/9528>.

68 During the time when the defendant performed the duties of a board member in SIA (company A), two transactions were concluded: (1) a lease agreement, by which SIA, as a lessee, was given warehouse premises with an area of 2,760 m^2 and an office with an area of 180 m^2. The rental fee for the warehouse premises was set at € 2.89 per square metre and for an office at € 3.94 per square metre, as well as an additional fixed management fee of € 0.50 per square metre; (2) a sublease agreement for these premises with another company – SIA C for a warehouse with an area of 638 m^2 and an office with an area of 140 m^2, setting the sublease fee for the warehouse premises at € 2.89 per square metre and for the office at € 3.94 per square metre, as well as an additional specified management fee of € 0.50 per square metre. The sublease was terminated early.

69 When the defendant concluded a sublease agreement on behalf of the company, he accepted the sublease fee, which did not include a mark-up. The claimant thus incurred losses of € 16,706 in the form of lost profit. When the defendant left his position as a board member, he did not inform the claimant that the sublease agreement had been terminated and the leased premises were not being used. This resulted in losses of € 16,042. The defendant, as a board member, did not fulfil his duties as a reasonably prudent and careful manager.

70 The claim was rejected by the judgment of the court of first instance of 17 March 2022. The Riga Regional Court, as the court of second instance, also rejected the claim with its judgment of 21 November 2022.

71 The claimant filed a cassation complaint, which challenged the judgment of the second instance court.

b) Judgment of the Court

72 The Senate quashed the appeal court's judgment.

73 The Senate stated that when deciding on the liability of a board member according to art 169 of the Commercial Law, the court must first check the validity of the company's argument about the existence of losses. Only after this has been verified does the court then have to check the existence of other prerequisites to assess if any losses have been caused.

74 In the case of a claim against a board member for compensation for losses in the form of lost profits, the court must take into account the legal regulation of lost profits (arts 1786 and 1788 of the Civil Law), as well as findings of case law in relation to the application of the relevant legal regulation.

75 When a claim has been brought against a member of a board for the recovery of lost profits, the court, when determining the existence of losses (lost profits), must consider whether there are reliable and sufficient circumstances in the

case that allow it to conclude that, if the member of the board had acted as a reasonably prudent and careful manager, the profit claimed would certainly have been made. The obligation to indicate such circumstances and to prove them as far as possible rests with the claimant.

The Senate agreed with the cassation complainant that the court's motives, on which its conclusion that the damage was not proven, were erroneous. 76

When examining a dispute of this kind, the court must assess whether the defendant's conduct (action or inaction) has been established, what is its nature (whether it meets or does not meet the requirements set for the actions of a reasonably prudent and careful manager), whether there has been a reduction of the claimant's property as a result of not making a profit, and whether the relevant consequences were caused by the actions of the board member. With regard to the fact that the sublease fee did not include a mark-up, the court did not analyse the evidence to determine whether the defendant's actions caused the consequences claimed ie the reduction of the claimant's property without making a profit from the transaction for the reason stated in the claim, ie due to the adjustment of an economically unjustified fee. Therefore, the Senate recognised that the court applied part 2 art 169 of the Commercial Law incorrectly. 77

The Senate additionally indicated that it is generally in the interests of the company to conclude profit-making transactions, and it is expected that the board member, representing the capital company in business relations, will take all reasonable measures so that transactions concluded on behalf of the capital company are profitable. However, this does not mean that the company always has real chances and manages to conclude profitable transactions. 78

c) Commentary

The Senate correctly described the order of applicability of art 169 of the Commercial Law. First, a company should prove the existence of a loss and only then should a board member provide arguments as to why they arrived at the decision that no loss was actually incurred or that they acted as a reasonably prudent and careful manager. 79

In the present case, it is possible to show the existence of loss in the form of lost profit. However, this does not mean that the claim should be satisfied after a second review by the second instance court. As the Senate rightly pointed out, although the purpose of commercial activity is to make a profit, this does not mean that the company always has real prospects and succeeds in concluding profitable transactions. The claimant has an obligation to prove that there is reasonable ground to believe that such profit could have accrued. 80

4. Judgment of the Senate of the Republic of Latvia, Department of Civil Cases, 23 March 2023, no SKC-100/2023 (C33366121) ECLI:LV:AT:2023:0323.C33366121.9.S: Unethical Behaviour of Insolvency Administrator as Wrongful Act[11]

a) Brief Summary of the Facts

81 The claimant (a chairman of company A) brought an action against the defendant, B (insolvency administrator) of the company C for the recalling of information that injured his reputation and dignity and compensation for non-pecuniary loss (moral damage), based on arts 1, 1635 and 2352[1] of the Civil Law.

82 The claimant particularly requested: (1) payment of € 1 as compensation for non-pecuniary loss for the dissemination of false information which harmed his honour and dignity; (2) to impose on the defendant an obligation to recall information which the defendant, as an insolvency administrator, wrote on 24 September 2020 and which is offensive to the claimant's honour and dignity; (3) to pay € 1 as compensation for non-pecuniary loss for violation of the claimant's personal rights.

83 The claimant repeatedly wrote letters to the defendant in order to ensure the proper conduct of the insolvency proceedings. On 10 March 2020 and 10 April 2020, he was given answers that contained statements which insulted his honour and respect. They had an arrogant tone, used sharp remarks, for example, mocking the fact that the claimant did not distinguish between the creditor's statement and the creditor's claim, an indication of a lack of legal education, the incorrectly used word *coldest*. The answer also contained the humiliating text '10.03.2020. The creditor was already understood, unambiguous, simplified extended sentences, indicated in the official language'.

84 The moral damage caused to the claimant manifested as shame and irritation for the treatment experienced, a decrease in self-esteem, emotional suffering and negative experiences. The defendant committed a violation of para 1 art 2.5 of the Code of Professional Ethics of Administrators and Supervisors. This violation was also confirmed by the letter of the Insolvency Control Service dated 19 January 2021. Also, by providing the Insolvency Control Service with deliberately false information about the claimant's alleged pressure, the defendant has insulted the claimant's honour and respect also in the written explanation of 24 September 2020, as this gave third parties the impression that the claimant was dishonest.

---

11 See on the Latvian Supreme Court website: <https://www.at.gov.lv/downloadlawfile/9013>.

The claim was rejected by the judgment of the court of first instance of 11 October 2021. The Riga Regional Court, as the court of second instance, satisfied the claim in part with its judgment of 2 February 2022. The court awarded € 1 as compensation for non-pecuniary loss for violation of the claimant's personal rights, while the remainder of the claim (recall of information insulting the claimant's honour and dignity and compensation of non-pecuniary loss for dissemination of such false news) was rejected. 85

The defendant filed a cassation complaint, which challenged the judgment of the second instance court. 86

b) Judgment of the Court

The Senate quashed the appeal court's judgment. 87

The violation of the claimant's personal rights, as it follows from the claim, was expressed in three statements included in the administrator's letter addressed to the claimant as legal representative of the creditor company. It follows from the judgment of the appellate court that the basis for drawing a conclusion about the illegality of the defendant's actions was the fact found in the letter of the Insolvency Control Service of 19 January 2021 that 'the administrator's actions regarding the information about the "price temperature" indicated to the applicant were not correct and ethical under art 2.5 of the Code'. In addition, in the opinion of the court, the defendant's wrongful activity was also manifested in a contemptuous attitude towards the claimant due to his inability to distinguish between the creditor's statement and the creditor's claim, as well as mockery, indicating to him in the letter the need to explain the situation repeatedly and in a simplified manner. 88

The Senate agreed with what was indicated in the cassation complaint that the mentioned grounds revealed in the judgment are not sufficient in the specific situation to draw a conclusion about the defendant's wrongful activity within the meaning of art 1635 of the Civil Law. The feature of the legal composition of the 'wrongful act' in part 1 art 1635 of the Civil Law is an open legal concept, the content of which must be clarified by the person applying the legal norm in the context of the law and the specific case. The wrongful act must be linked not only to the action itself, but also to its purpose, the motives of the perpetrator and to the circumstances of the specific case, as it can significantly affect the perception of the true nature of the activity. 89

Responding to letters from creditors is the responsibility of the insolvency administrator. The use of sarcastic statements in correspondence with clients may be considered as behaviour inconsistent with the ethical canons of the profession, 90 however, it cannot be recognised as unlawful in the sense of part 1 art 1635 of the Civil Law, since the requirements of professional ethics are always higher than those regulated by law.

91 With regard to statements and actions that may offend a person's honour and dignity and that may be qualified as unlawful, the legislator has formulated the prerequisites for liability in art 2352[1] of the Civil Law. If the defendant's statements do not comply with the provisions of this article or do not infringe any other legally protected non-property values, such as privacy, they cannot be recognised as unlawful within the meaning of part 1 art 1635 of the Civil Law. However, the Senate pointed out that even if the appellate court had recognised in its judgment that the defendant's conduct (derogatory attitude) corresponds to the content of a wrongful act in the sense of part 1 art 1635 of the Civil Law, this in itself does not constitute a basis for recovery of compensation for non-pecuniary loss. Since the purpose of such compensation is to compensate the consequences of the non-material damage caused to the person, it is necessary to establish the existence of the moral damage itself. The Senate also pointed out that only in the cases indicated in part 3 art 1635 of the Civil Law is the injured person exempted from proving the existence of moral damage, while, in all other cases, the victim, as an injured person, must prove the moral damage or adverse consequences. No evidence was presented in the case that the claimant suffered any adverse consequences as a result of the defendant's actions. The Senate also reiterated the opinion established in case law that not every violation of rights gives rise to the right to compensation.

c) Commentary

92 The Senate correctly mentioned that not every violation of rights gives rise to the right to compensation. However, the requirement to prove the existence of moral damage (non-pecuniary loss) shows that the Senate still continues to interpret part 3 art 1635 narrowly. It is unclear how the claimant should prove that non-pecuniary loss has been caused. In general, non-pecuniary loss is based on a presumption that a particular wrongful act could create unpleasant feelings or emotional consequences for a reasonably sensitive person.

93 Also, it is at least a disputable conclusion that professionally unethical behaviour cannot be recognised as unlawful in the sense of part 1 art 1635 of the Civil Law, since the requirements of professional ethics are always higher than those regulated by law. Since particular professions have higher standards than ordinary persons, this means that professionals also have a higher threshold for liability.

5. Personal Injury

a) Riga City Court Judgment, criminal case[12]

On 6 December 2023, the Riga City Court delivered a summary judgment, which found the accused person guilty of committing a criminal offence and sentenced him to 90 hours of community service. The accused person was found guilty of deliberately infecting a person with the human immunodeficiency virus (HIV) in the period from 2013 to 2014. 94

Upon discovering the HIV infection, the accused person confirmed with his signature that he was informed and acquainted with the rights and obligations of an infected person, and undertook to comply with them, namely, to ensure that the disease does not spread further and to encourage contacts or sexual partners to take an HIV test. Instead, the accused person did not warn his girlfriend about being infected with HIV, with whom he repeatedly had sexual intercourse without using the necessary contraceptives. As a result of the actions of the accused person, the girl also became infected with HIV. 95

The accused person has regretted his actions in relation to the victim. The motivation for his actions was 'love for this person, whom he was afraid to lose.' 96

The victim applied for compensation of moral damage (non-pecuniary loss) in the amount of € 135,000. The court partially satisfied it and obliged the accused to pay the victim a total of € 50,000 in damages. 97

There is no information on whether the judgment has entered into force, since it was possible to appeal it in the Riga Regional Court. 98

This is the first case in Latvia which resulted in finding a person both criminally liable but also legally liable for deliberately infecting a person with HIV. The amount of the awarded compensation amount corresponds to that currently awarded within the existing case law of Latvia. 99

12 Not published. Summary published – Pirmā lieta Latvijā par personas apzinātu inficēšanu ar HIV, Jurista Vārds, 19.12.2023, No 51/52 (1317/1318) 4.1.

b) Judgment of the Senate of the Republic of Latvia, Department of Civil Cases, 22 October 2022, no SKC-8/2022 (C33642915) ECLI:LV:AT:2022:1004.C33642915.14.S: Building Owner's Obligation to Maintain a Building in a Safe Condition; Liability for a Mistake in the Selection of Employees (Executors) (*culpa in eligendo*); Construction Process Participants' Civil Liability; Amount of Compensation for Non-Pecuniary Loss[13]

100 On 21 November 2013, the roof of a supermarket building collapsed and 54 people, including three rescue workers and a further 41 individuals were injured (the Zolitude disaster). As a result of the collapse of the roof of the store building, one claimant lost his mother, two claimants lost their father, one claimant lost his daughter and another lost his sister, one claimant lost his wife, and one claimant lost his mother. The claimants initiated several civil proceedings against several defendants and requested compensation for non-pecuniary loss due to the death of loved ones. The initiated civil cases were combined into one legal proceeding with the number C33642915.[14]

101 On 28 November 2019 the Zemgale Regional Court, as the Court of Appeal, rejected the claim.

102 The cassation complaint against the judgment was filed by only two claimants. The claimants asked the Senate to submit questions for a preliminary ruling to the CJEU regarding Directive 2001/95/EC of the European Parliament and of the Council of 3 December 2001 on general product safety and Council Directive 85/374/EEC of 25 July 1985 on the approximation of the laws, regulations and administrative provisions of the Member States concerning liability for defective products.

103 The Senate did not see a reason to address the ECJ, because in the case under consideration, it was not established that the reason for the collapse of the shopping centre was an unsafe movable item that was used in the collapsed building.

104 The Senate provided very extensive interpretation regarding a building owner's liability for maintaining a building in a safe condition also during the construction of this building, as well as regards the separation of liability between involved parties and the determination of the amount of damages.

105 Part 1 art 1084 of the Civil Law defines the legal obligation of a building owner to maintain a building in a safe condition, and failure to do so is one of the prerequisites for the application of general liability under arts 1635, 1646, 1649 and 1779 of the Civil Law. The owner is liable to any person who has suffered damage

---

13 See on the Latvian Supreme Court website: <https://www.at.gov.lv/downloadlawfile/8606>.

14 For a brief description and my comments, see *A Bitāns*, Latvia, in: E Karner/BC Steininger (eds), European Tort Law (ETL) 2015 (2016) 325, nos 108–113 and *idem* in: E Karner/BC Steininger (eds), European Tort Law (ETL) 2013 (2014) 361, nos 104–110.

to themselves or to their property as a result of improper maintenance of the building. Wrongful inaction (omission) of the owner of the building in relation to the fulfilment of the obligation specified in part 1 art 1084 can manifest itself not only as a failure to fulfil an obligation directly defined in the regulatory act, but also as a failure to perform such an action which is not directly provided for by the regulatory acts, but which is necessary to maintain the building in a safe condition. However, the fulfilment of the obligations set out in the regulatory acts does not in itself release a person from liability if a reasonably prudent and careful owner should have foreseen the possibility of damage and taken appropriate measures to prevent the risk from occurring. When evaluating the performance of the owner of the building's duty as a prudent and careful owner, objective considerations are taken into account and subjective considerations, such as the actual knowledge, skills, etc of the relevant person, are not taken into account. In general, measures of care should be proportionate to the possibility of harm and the extent of the possible harm (greatest care should be shown in the case of possible harm to human life or health and if the probability of its occurrence is high). The building owner's duty of care manifests itself not only as a reaction to any visible signs that could indicate a danger, but also as taking measures to detect potential dangers in time, for example, a technical survey of the building or some of its elements, etc. Therefore, the owner of a building may be held liable for damage caused by the collapse of the building due to construction defects, based on part 1 art 1084 of the Civil Law, only if the owner of the building, failing to show the necessary care in the process of its maintenance, did not detect the relevant defect in time and failed to take the necessary measures to prevent possible damage.

In the case of a building collapsing, the burden of proof regarding the fulfil- 106
ment of the obligation specified in part 1 art 1084 of the Civil Law lies on the owner of the building, while the burden of proof regarding the damage, the event that caused the damage, and the causal relationship between the event and the damage rests with the victim.

Article 1782 of the Civil Law provides liability (*culpa in eligendo*) for errors in 107
the selection of employees (executors) and not attributing the activity of another person to the assignor. Liability for a mistake in the selection of employees (executors), where a person is liable for their own culpable conduct, manifested as a lack of due diligence in selecting an employee or supervising their work, should be distinguished from liability for the culpable conduct of another person in cases where the action of another person is imputed to the person whose obligations it fulfils.

The Construction Law provides individual liability of each participant in the 108
construction process (namely, a special regulation in relation to the provisions

of the Civil Law). Thus, the initiator of the construction (owner of the building) was liable only for their actions, including a possible error in the selection of other participants in the construction process, and not directly for their actions. The construction initiator's participation in the commissioning of the building does not increase the scope of their liability, that is, they are thus not liable either for other construction participants or for the mistakes made by the construction board. Also, at this stage of the construction process, the initiator of a construction can rely on the professional knowledge of certified construction specialists, as well as on the competence of construction board specialists.

109 If another person (who is not the defendant in the case) makes voluntary payments to the victim, then in general they are not included in the damages if they are not intended to relieve the wrongdoer from liability, but only to benefit the victim. However, if the purpose of these payments is to relieve the wrongdoer from liability (which is a question that can be clarified by considering the merits of the case), then they are included in the damages.

c) Information Regarding State Compensation for Victims[15]

110 This article also provides a summary of the statistics of the Legal Aid Administration, which is responsible for paying State compensation to victims of crime. According to the Law on State Compensation to Victims adopted on 18 May 2006,[16] State compensation to victims of criminal offences is paid from the State budget.

111 Number of adopted decisions on the payment of State compensation according to the consequences of the criminal offence:

	2018	2019	2020	2021	2022
Death of a person	97	106	64	106	87
Violation of a person's virtue or sexual integrity	214	218	185	165	211
Serious bodily injury	120	114	107	76	82
Moderate injuries	318	316	300	254	261

15 See *A Turlaja*, Valsts kompensācija cietušajiem: iestāžu sadarbība, kompensācijas apmērs un informatīvais atbalsts [State compensation for victims: cooperation between institutions, amounts of compensation and informative support] Jurista Vārds, 18.7.2023, No 29 (1295) 32–36.

16 For a brief description and my comments, see *A Bitāns*, Latvia, in: H Koziol/BC Steininger (eds), European Tort Law (ETL) 2006 (2008) 325, nos 108–113 and *idem* in: E Karner/BC Steininger (eds), ETL 2013 (2014) 311, nos 11–20.

Continued

	2018	2019	2020	2021	2022
Human trafficking	4	4	2	14	10
HIV, hepatitis B and C	0	0	0	0	1

Maximum State compensation amounts paid: 112

Year	Minimal monthly wage €	Number of maximum State compensation awards	Amount of maximum state compensation in €
2006	128	5	640
2007	171	5	854
2008	228	5	1,138
2009	256	5	1,281
2010	256	3	768
2011	285	3	854
2012	285	3	854
2013	285	4	1,138
2014	320	5	1,600
2015	360	5	1,800
2016	370	5	1,850
2017	380	5	1,900
2018	430	5	2,150
2019	430	5	2,150
2020	430	5	2,150
2021	500	5	2,500
2022	500	5	2,500
2023	620	5	3,100

C. Literature

1. Medicīnas tiesības [Medical law] (Tiesu Namu Aģentūra, 2022) 701 pp

113 This book is a second, supplemented edition of the book 'Medical Law', which was published seven years ago. The book provides a scientific review of medical law in the protection of patients' human rights and the organisation of healthcare in Latvia.

114 The Medical Law textbook is written by 15 authors with expert knowledge in their fields. It covers the basic principles of law in every health situation, including the right to medical treatment, patients' rights and the professional obligations of medical practitioners in various contexts, medical treatment of a special group of patients, legal challenges as regards the development of artificial intelligence technologies in the health sector, the right to sexual and reproductive healthcare, the legal aspects of transplantation and issues related to healthcare at the end of life.

115 The final part of the book – Chapters 14 to 18 – is dedicated to issues of protection of patients' rights and legal liability of medical practitioners and healthcare institutions. Chapter 14 provides an overview of the mechanisms for protecting patients' rights. Besides disciplinary (Chapter 15), administrative (Chapter 16) and criminal liability (Chapter 17) of medical practitioners, Chapter 18 of the book provides an overview of the patient's right to compensation for personal injury.

2. Legal Articles

116 **Damages for Violation of Competition Law:** *L Rasnačs*, Karteļa radītu zaudējumu atlīdzība, ja nav piemērojama zaudējumu esamības vai apmēra prezumpcija [Compensation for losses caused by a cartel if presumption of existence or amount of damage is not applicable] Jurista Vārds, 24.10.2023, No 43 (1309) 9–12; *L Rasnačs/B Petrone*, Iepriekš novērtēti zaudējumi konkurences tiesību pārkāpuma gadījumā [Liquiated damages in the case of infringement of competition law] Jurista Vārds, 24.10.2023, No 43 (1309) 36–42

117 **Artificial Intelligence and Civil Liability:** *V Soņeca*, Mākslīgais intelekts un civiltiesiskā atbildība [Artificial intelligence and civil liability] Jurista Vārds, 28.2.2023, No 9 (1275) 2; *R Purmalis/J Kārkliņš*, Viedo sistēmu operatoru vainojamības modelis [Intelligent system operators' culpability model] Jurista Vārds, 2.5.2023, No 18/19 (1284/1285) 15–21; *S Kaprāne*, Mākslīgais intelekts un pamattiesību aizsardzība [Artificial intelligence and protection of fundamental rights] Jurista

Vārds, 2.5.2023, No 18/19 (1284/1285) 40–45; *S Kaprāne*, Mākslīgā intelekta un digitalizācijas ietekme uz intelektuālā īpašuma tiesībām [The impact of artificial intelligence and digitisation on intellectual property rights] Jurista Vārds, 5.9.2023, No 36 (1302) 23–28

Protection of a Company's Reputation: *D Gertmans*, Kapitālsabiedrības reputācija un tās civiltiesiskās aizsardzības tiesiskais pamats [A company's reputation and the legal basis for its civil protection] Jurista Vārds, 13.6.2023, No 24 (1290) 8–13; *K Losāns*, Zaudējumu atlīdzināšanas pamats komercsabiedrības reputācijas aizskāruma gadījumā [The basis for compensation for losses in the case of violation of a company's reputation] Jurista Vārds, 20.6.2023, No 25/26 (1291/1292) 20–25 118

Compensation for Loss: *R Ivanovs*, Tīri ekonomisku zaudējumu atlīdzināšana [Compensation for pure economic loss] Jurista Vārds, 4.7.2023, No 27 (1293) 23–30 119

State Compensation for Victims: *A Turlaja*, Valsts kompensācija cietušajiem: iestāžu sadarbība, kompensācijas apmērs un informatīvais atbalsts [State compensation for victims: cooperation between institutions, amount of compensation and informative support] Jurista Vārds, 18.7.2023, No 29 (1295) 32–36. 120

Simona Drukteinienė and Indrė Maculevičienė

XVIII. Lithuania

A. Legislation

1. Amendment of the Law on the Rights of Patients and Compensation of Damage to Patients' Health, 15 November 2022, No 2022 – 22951[1]

The amendments to the Law on the Rights of Patients and Compensation of Damage to Patients' Health (the Law), briefly discussed in previous years,[2] took effect on 1 January 2023. One significant change was the expansion of the concept of 'unavoidable damage to health,' encompassing harm to a patient's health not only resulting from the provision of healthcare services but also arising from the conduct of a low-intervention clinical trial of a medicinal product or any other biomedical trial. This includes circumstances beyond the foresight, control, or prevention of the healthcare professional or institution involved. According to the amendments, disputes arising from such unavoidable damage to health, like other cases of damage to patients, fall within the jurisdiction of the Commission for the Determination of Damage to Patients' Health (the 'Commission').[3] 1

The amendments also clarify that the Commission is not a mandatory pre-trial authority when a civil action for damages is initiated during a pre-trial investigation or criminal trial. 2

The list of cases in which the Commission may refuse to handle patients' claims for compensation has been expanded. Specifically, when the claim pertains to harm with only minor adverse temporary effects (except for harm caused by biomedical research) or harm caused by services other than healthcare services, or when the statutory limitation period of three years has elapsed from the date when the patient became aware of the harm or should have become aware of it. 3

1 Lietuvos Respublikos pacientų teisių ir žalos sveikatai atlyginimo įstatymo Nr. i-1562 2, 24, 25, 26 ir 27 straipsnių pakeitimo įstatymas (TAR 2022 – 11 – 15, No 2022 – 22951).

2 See discussed by *L Šaltinytė* in: E Karner/BC Steininger (eds), European Tort Law (ETL) 2022 (2023) 383, nos 1 – 4.

3 See discussed by *S Drukteinienė/L Šaltinytė* in: E Karner/BC Steininger (eds), European Tort Law (ETL) 2020 (2021) 379, no 3 ff.

https://doi.org/10.1515/9783111376721-019

4 Another amendment specifies that, when a patient appeals a decision of the Commission to the court, the court shall not assess the fault of the healthcare institution or the healthcare professional who caused the damage.

5 Given that in court disputes between patients and healthcare service provider, the State is represented by the authorised governmental authority, one more amendment confers the right upon this authority to obtain all necessary information required for the State's representation in court. Moreover, it imposes an obligation on individuals addressed by this governmental authority to provide the requested information, emphasising that such information must be treated as confidential.

B. Cases

1. *UAB 'Aukštaitijos implantologijos klinika' v the Republic of Lithuania,* Represented by the Government of the Republic of Lithuania and the Ministry of Health of the Republic of Lithuania, Supreme Administrative Court of Lithuania (SACL) 19 April 2023, no eA-1193–525/2023: Lost Income due to the Banned Commercial Activity during COVID-19-Related Quarantine

a) Brief Summary of the Facts

6 A company offering dental and health services filed a public liability claim in the administrative court seeking compensation for a lost profit of € 34,000. This loss was incurred due to the restrictions imposed on its activities by the Resolution of the Government of the Republic of Lithuania during the COVID-19 pandemic-related quarantine. The claimant argued that, as a result of the quarantine-related restrictions, it was prohibited from engaging in any commercial activity for a total of 63 days, from 16 March 2020 to 17 May 2020.

7 According to the claimant, the Resolution, which banned beauty services and postponed dental services, except for ensuring essential medical assistance, was adopted in violation of the Constitution of the Republic of Lithuania, laws, and their hierarchy. The claimant also asserted that the restrictions were clearly disproportionate. According to the claimant, during the Resolution's adoption, the Law on Prevention and Control of Communicable Diseases (the Law on Communicable Diseases) and the Civil Protection Laws granted the right to the Government

to establish special conditions for economic activities and services during quarantine. However, these Laws did not authorise the imposition of restrictions on economic freedom and a ban of the provision of public and administrative services. The amendments of the Law on Communicable Diseases and the Civil Protection Laws allowing for such restrictions only became effective on 8 April 2020, and 1 May 2020 respectively. These provisions were not in place when the quarantine was announced by Resolution. According to the claimant, the Lithuanian Parliament (*Seimas*), by amendments of the mentioned Laws, attempted to retrospectively legitimise the Government's actions.

The first instance court, relying on the linguistic interpretation of the initial 8
version of the Law on Communicable Diseases, dismissed the claimant's claim. The claimant filed an appeal.

b) Judgment of the Court

The SACL decided to address the Constitutional Court of the Republic of Lithuania 9
(the Constitutional Court) with a request to examine whether the provisions of the Resolution which banned the provision of beauty services and postponed dental services, except for ensuring essential medical assistance, contradicted the constitutional principle of the rule of law, art 46 of the Constitution of the Republic of Lithuania,[4] and the provisions of the Law on Communicable Diseases.

The Constitutional Court on 24 January 2020 adopted a Ruling,[5] in which it ac- 10
knowledged that the mentioned provisions of the Resolution did not violate the specified legal acts.

First of all, the Constitutional Court noted that the freedom of economic activ- 11
ity is protected under art 16 of the Charter of Fundamental Rights of the European

4 Art 46 of the Constitution of the Republic of Lithuania provides:
The Lithuanian economy is based on the right to private ownership, the freedom, and initiative of individual economic activities.
The State supports economically beneficial efforts and initiatives for the benefit of society.
The State regulates economic activities in a way that serves the overall well-being of the nation.
The law prohibits monopolising production and the market, safeguarding the freedom of fair competition.
The State protects consumer interests (authors' translation).

5 Ruling No KT8-N1/2023 of the Constitutional Court on the restriction of freedom of economic activity following the declaration of quarantine, 24 January 2023. The texts of all rulings of the Constitutional Court are available in English at <http://www.lrkt.lt>.

Union[6] (the Charter). The Court of Justice of the European Union (CJEU), interpreting art 16 of the Charter, has found that it provides protection, among other things, for the freedom to engage in economic or commercial activities, and the freedom to pursue a professional activity is one of the fundamental principles of Community law; this also applies to the freedom to conduct business, coinciding with the freedom to pursue a professional activity. However, the CJEU has also emphasised that the freedom to carry out a professional activity is not absolute and must be evaluated in light of its social function, so the exercise of this freedom may be restricted if such restrictions fundamentally correspond to the common interests of the European Union and, considering the intended purpose, are not disproportionate and do not constitute an impermissible interference violating the essence of this right. One of such common interest goals recognised in CJEU jurisprudence is the aim to protect health arising from art 35 of the Charter. On the other hand, any restriction on the implementation of rights and freedoms recognised by the Charter must be provided for by law and not alter the essence of these rights and freedoms. Moreover, based on the principle of proportionality, it must be necessary to protect other rights and freedoms. Additionally, the CJEU, when assessing restrictions on fundamental rights, has noted that the requirement that any restriction on the implementation of fundamental rights must be provided for by law, as understood by the relevant provisions of the Charter and the European Convention on Human Rights and Fundamental Freedoms, not only means that the measure providing for the restriction must have a legal basis in national law but also that this legal basis must possess certain accessibility and predictability characteristics to avoid arbitrariness.

12 Secondly, the Constitutional Court analysed the jurisprudence of constitutional courts of foreign countries and found that, for example, the Constitutional Court of the Republic of Austria, the Constitutional Court of the Republic of Latvia, the Constitutional Court of the Republic of Slovenia, and the Federal Constitutional Court of the Federal Republic of Germany justified various restrictions imposed by States on the freedom of economic activity in order to manage the COVID-19 pandemic.

13 Finally, the Constitutional Court proceeded to examine the compatibility of the contested provisions of the Resolution with art 46 of the Constitution and the constitutional principle of the rule of law.

14 Relying on its settled case law, the Constitutional Court stated that the freedom of economic activity, established in art 46(1) of the Constitution, is not absolute. It can be restricted when necessary to protect the values enshrined in the Constitu-

6 Art 16 reads: The freedom to conduct a business in accordance with Community law and national laws and practices is recognised.

tion. Restricting economic freedom is permissible if the following conditions are met: (1) the restrictions are imposed by law; (2) the restrictions are necessary in a democratic society to protect the rights and freedoms of others, as well as the values enshrined in the Constitution; and (3) the restrictions do not deny the essence of rights and freedoms. It must also comply with the constitutional principle of proportionality. Human and public health are among the most important values of society. The protection of people's health is a constitutionally important goal and a public interest, and ensuring people's health is a function of the State.

In this case, the contested measures of the Government, temporarily restricting the freedom of economic activity for individuals engaged in the provision of beauty or dental services, were established considering the unfavourable epidemiological situation of COVID-19 (coronavirus infection) and aimed at limiting the spread of this infection. Therefore, the contested legal regulation aimed to achieve a constitutionally important goal and a public interest – the protection of people's and public health. 15

Assessing whether the economic activity-restricting measures were established by law, the Constitutional Court found that, according to the Law on Communicable Diseases, the Government had the authority in the field of prevention and control of communicable diseases, including the power to declare a quarantine and establish quarantine regime measures. Having systematically evaluated the provisions of the Law on Communicable Diseases, which stipulated under what conditions the Government could establish specific measures during quarantine, including those related to the conditions of specific economic activities and the provision of services, as well as the purpose for which such special conditions and procedures for economic activities were to be established (to limit the spread of infectious diseases) and for how long they could be applied (only until quarantine was declared or for a shorter period), the Constitutional Court concluded that there is no basis to claim that the law did not establish essential conditions for the Government to declare a quarantine during which specific conditions for economic activities could be established. 16

Therefore, by adopting the Resolution, the Government temporarily restricted the freedom of economic activity for individuals engaged in the provision of beauty or dental services, implementing the legislative mandate set by the Law on Communicable Diseases, which empowered the Government, after declaring a quarantine due to COVID-19, to detail special conditions and procedures for economic activities as part of the measures for the prevention and control of infectious diseases, thereby aiming to limit the spread of the COVID-19 disease. Subsequent amendments to the Law on Communicable Diseases did not fundamentally change the regulatory framework. 17

18 Moreover, the contested quarantine regime measures were applied only temporarily. The Government constantly reviewed them and, when their application was no longer necessary, lifted them.

19 Furthermore, the Government, after declaring a quarantine by the Resolution on 14 March 2020, and establishing quarantine regime measures, approved the Economic Incentive and Mitigation Plan for the Consequences of the Spread of Coronavirus (COVID-19) on 16 March 2020. This plan set out measures to, among other things, help preserve jobs and income for residents, help businesses maintain liquidity, including by providing tax loans and deferring certain tax payments, and stimulate the economy. Since the Government set the plan to compensate for the losses incurred due to the quarantine declaration and its measures, it cannot be argued that the essence of the freedom of economic activity was negated by such legal regulation.

20 The applied measures were proportionate, taking into account the special information available at that time about the spread of the infectious COVID-19 virus, which was scarce and rapidly changing. The situation was new and unpredictable, and the consequences of the COVID-19 infection were unexplored. When establishing the contested legal regulation, the Government did not have a basis to believe that achieving a constitutionally significant goal and implementing a public interest – protecting people's and public health, including ensuring the provision of healthcare services not only to those affected by COVID-19 but also to other individuals who might need such services – could be achieved with less restrictive measures than those stipulated.

21 Therefore, although the legal regulation established by the Government's Resolution temporarily restricted the freedom of economic activity for individuals engaged in the provision of beauty or dental services, it adhered to the principle of balancing the interests of individuals and society, and the measures were aimed at protecting people's and public health, seeking the common good of the nation. Thus, there is no basis to claim that the legal regulation established by the Government's Resolution violated art 46 of the Constitution or the constitutional principle of the rule of law.

22 Having resumed the trial of the case, the Court commenced the examination of the conditions for public liability. The Court specified that the State's obligation to compensate arises under art 6.271 of the Civil Code (CC), based on three conditions: unlawful actions or omissions, damage, and a causal link. If at least one of these pre-conditions for public liability is not established, the State is not obligated to compensate for damage.

23 Initially, the Court examined unlawful acts as a prerequisite for public liability. Relying on the Constitutional Court's explanations, the Court easily determined that, in these circumstances, the actions of the Government were lawful and,

therefore, do not give rise to liability. Since no unlawful actions were established, the claimant's appeal was dismissed.

c) Commentary

The outcome of the case is well-founded and not surprising. Though the first instance court mostly relied on the linguistic interpretation of the Law on Communicable Diseases, the Court left no room for doubt when it decided to turn to the Constitutional Court and made its decision based on its interpretation. 24

2. *AM v AA*, Supreme Court of Lithuania (LSC) 12 January 2023, no e3K-3-600-684/2023: Pecuniary Damages for Contamination of Farmer's Organic Field and Contributory Negligence of the Plaintiff

a) Brief Summary of the Facts

The plaintiff, a farmer, filed the lawsuit arguing that due to the defendant's, another farmer's, unlawful and faulty actions, she suffered damage. This happened when the defendant sprayed glyphosate-containing substances on his adjacent field, which was separated from the plaintiff's field by a 15 m wide ditch, leading to contamination of her field with this substance. As a result, in May 2019, glyphosate and the residue of the glyphosate degradation product amino methyl phosphonic acid were found in her field. This led to the revocation of a document allowing her to sell the produce grown in this field as organic. Consequently, she sold her non-organic wheat at a lower price than planned. 25

The first instance court determined that the defendant's field was sprayed with herbicides on 6 September 2018 and 9 May 2019. It was more likely that the plaintiff's wheat was affected by the glyphosate-containing chemicals while it was germinating, as the defendant sprayed his field on 9 May 2019. The court held that the defendant performed unlawful and faulty actions, causing damage to the plaintiff. The court recalculated the quantity of organic wheat that the plaintiff would likely have grown, taking into account the drought in the summer of 2019, and established that she suffered damage in the amount of € 40,510 as the price difference between organic and non-organic wheat. Since the plaintiff did not take sufficient measures to inform the defendant working on the adjacent field that her cultivated land was organic, nor took protective measures to prevent 26 her wheat from being contaminated with prohibited substances used in organic farming, she assumed 30 % of the risk of possible pollution. Therefore, the court awarded € 28,357 for lost profit and € 427 for soil testing expenses, along with 6 % annual procedural interest on the awarded amount until the complete execution of the judgment.

27 The Lithuanian Court of Appeal examined the plaintiff's and defendant's appeals.

28 The appellate court found that the defendant sprayed his field with glyphosate-containing herbicides only on 6 September 2018. On 9 May 2019, he sprayed the field with herbicide that did not contain glyphosate. According to the court, the plaintiff did not prove that the defendant's behaviour during the spraying on 6 September 2018 deviated from the requirements for a professional user of plant protection products, ie that the weather conditions were unsuitable, or the defendant sprayed too close to the plaintiff's field, or used unauthorised chemical preparations.

29 Assessing the defendant's behaviour using the *bonus pater familias* standard, the court considered the conclusion presented by an expert of the Institute of Agriculture and Food Sciences of the Faculty of Agronomy at Vytautas Magnus University. The conclusion was provided after the faculty's scientists conducted a model test to evaluate the possible influence of side wind on the spraying of glyphosate into an adjacent field. After conducting the test, the experts concluded that, given the layout of the fields and the wind blowing towards the defendant's field on the day of spraying, the probability of spraying a 20 m wide drainage ditch and even more than 200 m along the field boundary is extremely low.

30 Having established these facts, the Lithuanian Court of Appeal overturned the decision of the first instance court and adopted a new decision, dismissing the claim. The plaintiff filed a cassation claim.

b) Judgment of the Court

31 The LSC, based on the circumstances established by lower instance courts, decided that the most probable source of pollution to the plaintiff's field is the defendant's activity in the adjacent field, as the pollution spread precisely from the edge of the plaintiff's field bordering the defendant's field. No other source of pollution, from which glyphosate-containing plant protection products could have spread, was identified, and it was not established that another source of pollution existed. Therefore, the LSC concluded that the defendant, by spraying his field with plant protection products, contaminated the adjacent plaintiff's field.

In determining whether the defendant's actions were illegal and culpable, as provided in arts 6.246(1)[7] and 6.263(1) CC,[8] the Court assessed the duties imposed on the defendant by the Plant Protection Law. Firstly, the Court emphasised that the defendant is a farmer who, in his professional activity, uses plant protection products intended for professional use, as defined by the Plant Protection Law. Therefore, he is considered a professional user of plant protection products, and higher standards of professional care and diligence apply to him. Article 14(2) of the mentioned Law outlines the duties for professional users of plant protection products, namely: (1) to adhere to the requirements specified on the plant protection product label, which also complies with the requirements indicated in the product's registration certificate; (2) to comply with the legal regulations establishing the legal regime of protection zones for underground and surface water bodies, as well as the legal requirements for the protection of shore zones of surface water bodies, and other environmental protection requirements specified in laws and other legal acts; (3) to apply risk management measures specified on the plant protection product label; (4) to adhere to the requirements specified in the Rules for the Import, Transportation, Storage, Supply to the Market, and Use of Plant Protection Products. 32

Having assessed these duties, the Court concluded that, when using a chemical preparation, it is necessary to follow good practices in plant protection and ensure that such use does not violate the rights and legitimate interests of third parties. Since the defendant did not control the risk of contamination of the adjacent field, he acted unlawfully and was at fault. 33

When assessing the contribution of the plaintiff herself to the occurrence of the damage, the Court evaluated the regulatory provision stating that farmers, having assessed the risk of pollution with unauthorised materials used in the ecological production of agricultural land and/or crops, bordering with arterial roads and/or land worked in a non-ecological way, shall choose such a protective strip that the certified areas and/or crops in them are not contaminated with unauthorised materials used in ecological production. According to the Court, although the installation of protective strips in ecological fields is not mandatory for an organic farmer, they must assess the risk of contamination of certified areas and/or crops 34

---

7 Art 6.246(1) CC states that civil liability shall arise from non-performance of a duty established by laws or a contract (unlawful refrainment from acting), or from performance of actions that are prohibited by laws or a contract (unlawful acting), or from violation of the general duty to behave with due care (official translation).

8 Art 6.263(1) CC is the general delictual clause and reads: Every person shall have the duty to abide by the rules of conduct so as not to cause damage to another by his/her actions (or omission) (official translation).

in fields bordering with land worked in a non-ecological way and take measures to prevent contamination with unauthorised materials used in ecological production. The absence of protective strips can increase the likelihood of damage. Since the plaintiff did not do so, her actions were grossly negligent, which, according to art 6.282(1)[9] CC, is a basis for reducing the awarded damages. Taking this into account, the lower instance court reasonably allocated 30 % of the damages to the plaintiff herself.

35 Based on these arguments, the Court decided to confirm the decision of the first instance court.

c) Commentary

36 In Lithuanian law, under fault-based liability, unlawfulness is determined by the behaviour of the tortfeasor. The concept of unlawfulness shifts to result-based unlawfulness in strict liability cases.[10] In this case, the Court assessed the violation through the lens of negative outcome. The Court did not identify any specific legal provision prohibiting or recommending certain behaviour in the violation, but it established unlawfulness and fault. It can be concluded that the farmer's liability regime was brought closer to a strict liability regime.

9 Art 6.282 (1) CC provides: If the aggrieved person's gross negligence contributed to causing or increasing damage, depending on the degree of the aggrieved person's fault (and on the degree of the fault of the person by whom the damage was caused, in the event of the existence of such fault), the extent of the compensation can be reduced or the claim for the compensation dismissed unless the laws provide for otherwise (official translation).

10 *S Drukteinienė/S Palevičienė*, Lithuania, in: B Weyts (ed), International Encyclopaedia for Tort Law (2017) no 53.

3. *The plaintiff (data not disclosed) v the defendant (data not disclosed),* LSC 29 June 2023, no e3K-3-196-421/2023: Responsibility of a Healthcare Institution for the Leakage and Public Disclosure on the Internet of Sensitive Personal Data

a) Brief Summary of the Facts

The patient filed a claim against the provider of medical services to her. The plaintiff argued that the defendant failed to take necessary precautionary measures to ensure that the personal data about the plaintiff's health was sufficiently protected. Because of this failure, unidentified persons gained access to the defendant's database in which sensitive information about the plaintiff's health was stored and made this information available publicly. 37

The plaintiff asked the court to award compensation of € 20,000 from the defendant for failing to take necessary precautionary measures to ensure the protection of personal data. 38

The first instance court and the court of appeal upheld the claim and awarded € 20,000 in compensation for non-pecuniary damage. The courts determined that, even though the defendant did not transfer the plaintiff's personal data to third parties or make it publicly available, it violated the requirements concerning the protection of personal data and the general duty to exercise due care and diligence. 39

As a business professional, the defendant neglected to implement basic security measures, such as regularly changing the access passwords of its employees. This failure facilitated the unauthorised disclosure of the plaintiff's personal data. The defendant's unlawful conduct, specifically the failure to safeguard the plaintiff's personal data and the negligence, was confirmed by the facts indicating that all users of the personal data (defendant's employees) connected to its servers with the same accounts. These accounts had full administrator rights, providing access to absolutely all the plaintiff's personal data. 40

Furthermore, it was established that the defendant was aware of these deficiencies in its system from the previous audit report of its IT systems but failed to take necessary security measures. The courts concluded that, although the defendant had adopted rules governing the processing and protection of personal data, such measures did not ensure the necessary level of security for processing personal data. The defendant neglected critical measures like systematically changing passwords, determining the complexity level of passwords (the defendant used 41 simple and highly predictable passwords, such as names of employees), and restricting access to such personal data for employees without proper authorisation.

42 The courts determined that the defendant's unlawful conduct was causally linked to the damage suffered by the plaintiff. Specifically, due to the defendant's failure to implement necessary measures in processing the plaintiff's personal data, it was leaked and made public.

b) Judgment of the Court

43 The LSC found that, in essence, the courts correctly decided on the questions of the qualification of the unlawful actions and the fault of the defendant. Nevertheless, the LSC reduced the non-pecuniary damages to € 15,000.

44 Regarding the assessment of the causal link, the LSC found that the defendant's unlawful omission caused the damage to the plaintiff due to a failure to comply with data protection obligations. In this case, the legal causal link between the defendant's unlawful actions and the damage suffered by the plaintiff was not considered too remote. This conclusion considered foreseeability, as the defendant, being a professional businessman, should have understood the possible consequences of not complying with personal data processing requirements.

45 Additionally, as the defendant handled sensitive patient data, utmost care and constant attention to proper data processing were required. The defendant's conduct did not meet these necessary standards.

46 Article 2.23(4) CC establishes that unlawful public disclosure of facts on one's private life is grounds for compensation. The right to privacy may be infringed when a data controller fails to process personal data properly. The decisive criterion for assessing non-pecuniary damages is the legal value infringed. The amounts awarded by the LSC in similar cases range from € 1,000 to € 4,344.

47 The courts rightly considered factors such as the defendant's grossly negligent conduct, the sensitivity of the published personal data, and the fact that this data was not only stolen but also published on the internet. The plaintiff was found to be subjected to a double violation, involving both data disclosure and a cyber-violation, constituting violence against women according to the case law of the European Court of Human Rights. However, the lower instance courts did not adequately consider the applicable case law regarding non-pecuniary damages, leading to an award exceeding established precedents. Nonetheless, considering changes in the economy, including the national currency and inflation rate, the LSC justified the € 15,000 award.

c) Commentary

Article 6.247 CC stipulates that only damage directly related to actions (acts or omissions) establishing civil liability of the debtor can be compensable. The damage must be imputable to the debtor based on the nature of the actions and civil liability. To establish a causal link, firstly a factual causal link shall be established using the *conditio sine qua non* test. In the second stage, the legal causal link, determining if the consequences are not too remote from the unlawful acts, shall be established. 48

In this case, the defendant's failure to adequately protect and process personal data, combined with third parties' disclosure of the plaintiff's data, resulted in the damage. All instance courts rightly concluded that the relevant causal link was not too remote. 49

Moreover, the courts recognised that the actions of the third party, who leaked and published the private information, would not have occurred if not for the actions of the defendant. This interdependence facilitated the establishment of full liability on the part of the defendant for the entire damage suffered by the plaintiff. Since the plaintiff initiated legal action against only one defendant, the courts did not address the liability of the third person who leaked and published the plaintiff's personal data on the internet. 50

The LSC also cautioned against blindly applying past compensation amounts for non-pecuniary damage, emphasising the need for careful assessment considering economic changes in both law and the economy. 51

4. *JS v UAB (data undisclosed), AS and the German Company 'GmbH BHC'*, LSC 20 April 2023, no e3K-3-123-1075/2023: Liability for the Health Injuries of an Employee of a Company Accepting Workers from Another Company on a Contractual Basis

a) Brief Summary of the Facts

The plaintiff sought joint civil liability from three defendants, the Lithuanian company (the Employer), its director and the German company 'GmbH BHC' ('GmbH BHC'), for the compensation of approx € 43,000 until June 2021 for loss of earnings due to health injury; from July 2021, compensation of € 1,663 per month for loss of earnings, paid as periodic payments; € 1,618 for direct damage, and € 30,000 for non-pecuniary damage. 52

53 On 3 January 2019, the plaintiff concluded a temporary employment contract with the Employer. From January 2019 to 18 February 2019, the plaintiff, ordered by the Employer, worked at the construction site of 'GmbH BHC' in Germany. On 18 February 2019, the plaintiff suffered a workplace accident, falling from a hoist approximately 4–5 metres high. The plaintiff suffered personal injuries, resulting in a 40 % loss of working capacity.

54 In the first instance, the court partially granted the claim, ordering the Employer to pay the plaintiff € 30,000 as non-pecuniary damages and nearly € 10,000 as pecuniary damages covering lost income for the period until June 2021. The court dismissed the plaintiff's claim to award periodic compensation for lost earnings from July 2021. The court stated that there were changes in working capacity of the plaintiff and therefore the court lacked proof to assess the damage. Nevertheless, the court stated that the plaintiff has the right to seek compensation for pecuniary damage from the Employer in the future. Assessing the liability of 'GmbH BHC', the court found a contractual relationship between the defendants, as the Employer performed construction work for 'GmbH BHC', which paid for the services. The Employer failed to ensure a safe working environment for the plaintiff, neglecting to properly organise the performance of hazardous tasks mentioned in the employment contract, leading to the damage suffered by the plaintiff. The court imposed liability on the Employer based on general tort law and labour law rules.

55 The court absolved 'GmbH BHC' of liability, emphasising that the Employer is responsible for damage caused to employees. The court also dismissed the claim against the director of the Employer because she did not commit any unlawful actions against the plaintiff.

56 The court disagreed with the plaintiff's assertion that 'GmbH BHC' should be subject to strict civil liability under art 6.270 CC. This article stipulates strict liability for damage caused by a source of increased danger. The court reasoned that the plaintiff's job functions were associated with potential hazards, thus challenging the applicability of strict civil liability in this case. Article 6.270 CC applies to damage caused to third parties not connected with the operation of the source of increased danger.

57 The court of appeal agreed with the first instance court.

58 The plaintiff filed a cassation claim seeking to establish the liability of 'GmbH BHC' and the director of the Employer, as well as contesting the courts' conclusions regarding pecuniary damage. Concerning 'GmbH BHC's' liability, the plaintiff argued that it arises under several grounds. First, Directive (EU) 2018/957 of the European Parliament and the Council, amending Directive 96/71/EC on the posting of

workers,[11] regulates the obligation to ensure for posted workers the same employment conditions regarding health, safety, and hygiene as for employees working in the host State. Second, the Law on Occupational Safety and Health of the Republic of Lithuania regulates the obligation for multiple employers whose employees work together to cooperate in implementing occupational safety and health requirements. Third, it shall be liable under art 6.270 CC.

b) Judgment of the Court

Concerning the alleged liability of 'GmbH BHC', the LSC firstly analysed the regu- 59
lation by the applied Directive (EU) 2018/957. The LSC stated that the requirements under the Directive concerning the guarantee of working conditions for posted workers apply to the companies posting the workers but not to the undertakings receiving them.

According to the LSC, art 30 of the Law on Occupational Safety and Health ap- 60
plies only upon establishing the following conditions: first, employees of two or more employers performed common work; second, the work was carried out at the same workplace or workplaces. In this case, the lower instance courts did not establish the fact that the Employer's and 'GmbH BHC's' employees had been working together in one location. Therefore, the mentioned article is not applicable.

Examining the plaintiff's argument that the defendant 'GmbH BHC' is liable 61
for the damage as a lawful hoist operator, while the Employer is an unlawful operator,[12] the Court found that 'GmbH BHC' had legally transferred the hoist to the plaintiff's Employer, making the Employer the operator of the hoist during the relevant period. The Employer then made it available for use by its employees on the construction site. The voluntary transfer of the hoist by 'GmbH BHC', without any established breaches of public law, indicated that the possession of the hoist by the Employer was legal and therefore 'GmbH BHC's' liability under art 6.270 CC did not arise.

Moreover, the Court determined that there were no circumstances justifying 62
the direct liability of the director of the Employer because the case did not establish any unlawful or criminal actions by it against the plaintiff, nor did it demon-

11 Dir of 28 June 2018 [2018] Official Journal of the European Union (OJ) L 173/16.

12 In such a case, the lawful operator and the unlawful operator would be jointly liable under art 6.270(3) CC.

strate a failure to perform duties adequately or actions causing the plaintiff's damage.

63 The Court returned the question regarding the assessment of the amount of pecuniary damages to the court of appeal for reconsideration.

c) Commentary

64 The case is significant because it analyses the provisions of Directive (EU) 2018/957 of the European Parliament and the Council, amending Directive 96/71/EC on the posting of workers. It also develops the case law of the LSC on the criteria under which it is considered that employees of multiple employers worked together, and accordingly, both employers are responsible for their employment conditions. Furthermore, it confirms the LSC case law regarding the concept of the possessor of an object of increased danger.

5. *KB v the Republic of Lithuania, Represented by the General Prosecutor's Office and Vilnius County Police Headquarters,* LSC 14 December 2023, no e3K-3-306-969/2023: State Liability in Non-Pecuniary Damages for Unlawful Actions of a Prosecutor

a) Brief Summary of the Facts

65 The plaintiff sought € 5,000 in non-pecuniary damages from the State, represented by the Prosecutor General's Office and the Vilnius County Police Headquarters.

66 The plaintiff had faced charges under art 284 of the Criminal Code of the Republic of Lithuania (Criminal Code), which criminalises breach of public order. Despite the completion of the pre-trial investigation, the court, during the criminal trial, concluded that the plaintiff had not committed the alleged crime. Instead, the court determined the plaintiff's actions as a minor breach of public order, qualifying as a misdemeanour rather than a criminal offence.

67 Claiming non-pecuniary damage, the plaintiff argued that the prosecutor incorrectly classified his actions, resulting in an unjust pre-trial investigation and court proceedings. The plaintiff claimed that the pre-trial investigation officers unlawfully detained him for six hours and 30 minutes, did not provide the opportunity to seek legal assistance, and partially and incorrectly assessed the situation, leading to wrongful charges for criminal acts he had not committed.

The first instance court partially upheld the claim, awarding the plaintiff compensation from the State, represented by the General Prosecutor's Office. The court reasoned that the plaintiff's acquittal resulted from the prosecutor's incorrect legal assessment of the facts as a criminal offence, noting that all relevant facts were known when the indictment was prepared. The court found that the plaintiff suffered non-pecuniary damage due to the unfounded accusation and awarded compensation of € 2,000 in non-pecuniary damages. 68

Having assessed the appeals of both parties to the case, the court of appeal affirmed the judgment of the first instance court. 69

b) Judgment of the Court

The Court annulled the decisions of the lower instance courts and dismissed the claim. 70

According to art 6.272(1) CC, the State is obliged to compensate for damage caused by the actions or omission of law enforcement officials in the field of criminal proceedings. The CC specifies that damage resulting from unlawful conviction, unlawful arrest as a measure of suppression, unlawful detention, or the application of unlawful procedural measures of enforcement, or unlawful infliction of administrative penalties shall be fully compensated by the State, irrespective of the fault of officials in preliminary investigation, prosecution, or court. This article outlines a non-exhaustive list of unlawful acts committed by officials in pre-investigation, prosecution, and court. 71

The Court emphasised that when determining the civil liability of the State for the actions of law enforcement officials, it is essential to assess whether the criminal prosecution of an individual was initiated based on sufficient evidence to suspect their involvement in an offence. To establish that the prosecutor acted unlawfully, it must be demonstrated that the prosecutor made a mistake that was decisive for violating the plaintiff's rights in the criminal proceedings. 72

It was found that the plaintiff was acquitted in the criminal proceedings without establishing one of the necessary elements of the objective aspect of the criminal offence, namely the consequences. Therefore, the prosecutor did not adequately assess the evidence regarding the determination of the consequences of the offence. Consequently, the prosecutor's assessment was not entirely unfounded and clearly had a legal basis. The act was wrongly classified as a criminal offence but could be qualified as an administrative offence due to the incorrect identification of one of the constituent elements of a criminal offence during the pre-trial investigation. As such, this conduct cannot be considered a fundamental error within the meaning of art 6.272 CC. The mere fact that the prosecutor did not prop- 73 erly assess the evidence collected regarding the existence of one of the elements (consequences) of a criminal offence does not warrant deeming their actions negligent and in violation of the general duty of care and diligence.

74 The Court concluded that if one of the necessary conditions (unlawful acts) was not established, there was no justification for imposing civil liability on the defendant.

c) Commentary

75 The LSC upheld its settled case law that when assessing the civil liability of the State for the actions of law enforcement agents (prosecutor, pre-trial investigation authorities), it is crucial to determine if their actions were unlawful. A prosecutor's incorrect assessment of the facts, in the absence of fundamental irregularities in the pre-trial investigation, does not give rise to civil liability.

6. *RŠ v Seimas of the Republic of Lithuania*, LSC 20 April 2023, no e3K-7-41-943/2023: Protection of Honour and Dignity when Data Contained in an Official Document were Obtained in the Course of Intelligence Activities and Disseminated by the Intelligence Services Institution; State Secrets as Proof in Civil Proceedings

a) Brief Summary of the Facts

76 The plaintiff, former Minister of the Interior and Health, argued that the information about him revealed in the certificate 'On the provision of information' (the Certificate) by the State Security Department (the Department), presented in the legislative information system as an appendix to a legislative act, was false and discredits his honour and dignity. The plaintiff alleged that, on 5 June 2018, the *Seimas* of the Republic of Lithuania (the Parliament) adopted a Resolution endorsing the conclusions of a parliamentary inquiry on undue influence in political processes. The annexed Certificate contained statements alleging that representatives of a Lithuanian business conglomerate had coordinated with State politicians and public officials, portraying the plaintiff as a candidate suitable for high-ranking positions in the State, and then passed this information on to the plaintiff. The Parliament disseminated the Certificate submitted by the Department as an annex to the Resolution publicly.

Based on art 2.24 CC,[13] the plaintiff sought a declaration that the published information was false and defamatory. 77

The first instance and appeal courts upheld the claim, determining that the Certificate's upload to the Parliament's electronic information system on legal acts constituted information dissemination under art 2.24 CC. The contested disputed statements were considered statements, not mere opinion. There was no evidence supporting the truthfulness of the information about the plaintiff in the disputed statements. Considering the content, context, and the plaintiff's public position, the public could have formed a negative opinion about the plaintiff. 78

The Parliament of the Republic of Lithuania and the Department filed a cassation claim. 79

b) Judgment of the Court

One of the main legal issues raised in the present case through cassation appeals was whether the plaintiff, under art 2.24 CC, has the right to challenge in court the data as false and discrediting his honour and dignity when (a) the data is recorded in an official document of a State authority (the Certificate), and (b) the Certificate is part of the annexes to the Parliament Resolution, made public in a specialised electronic information system on legal acts. 80

The Court, sitting in its extended composition of seven judges, having analysed the aims of the Department as the intelligence institution, which acted as the third party in the case, stated that the institutional goals and tasks set to the Department, as well as the general and special principles applied in its activities, determine peculiarities when dealing with potential liability for defamation. The general competence of court control in this area, when examining individuals' lawsuits in civil proceedings regarding possibly false data specified in an official intelligence institution document, allegedly discrediting the honour and dignity of individuals, is limited. Therefore, the courts shall firstly evaluate whether the person's violated rights can be remedied through an action for the State's civil liability under art 6.271 CC. Only if such a remedy is deemed ineffective, as in this case, can a plaintiff rely on art 2.24 CC to protect their infringed rights. In the latter case, the court must assess whether the application of the remedy established in art 2.24 CC will not have a negative impact on the activities carried out by intelli- 81

13 Art 2.24 CC grants the right to demand refutal and compensation for pecuniary and non-pecuniary damage resulting from the public dissemination of false information discrediting honour and dignity.

gence institutions, considering the special tasks assigned to such institutions and the goals set for their activities. The refutal of data contained in documents issued by such institutions is only possible if the court determines that such an institution acted *ultra vires* or unlawfully included in an official document facts obtained illegally and not supported by facts.

82 In addition, the specific nature of the delict allegedly committed by the intelligence service institution also determines the particularity of the remedy applied. In other cases, once it is established that the data is false and discredits one's honour and dignity, the defendant is obliged to deny it in the same way that the information was disseminated. In cases like this at hand, the courts dealing with the case must assess whether the violated rights might be defended by recognising the violation by a court decision. The court also has the right, at the request of the plaintiff, to obligate the defendant to publish information about the court decision at their own expense, including the publication of the entire or part of the court decision in the media or in another way. The court decision or information about the court decision shall be published when the decision becomes final and binding unless the court decides otherwise. The court, evaluating the circumstances of the case, may also decide on the removal of the document containing such information from the website or other publicly accessible sources.

83 In addressing the question of whether the information in the Certificate should be considered as a statement for which liability under art 2.24 CC applies or as an opinion for which it does not, the Court concluded that the lower instance courts were correct in stating that the information provided in the Certificate cannot be qualified as an opinion. This is because it is based on factual data obtained through legal means in the collection of intelligence information as defined by law.

84 After establishing that statements about the plaintiff had been disseminated, the Court must assess whether they were true. The Court noted that it cannot comment on the veracity of the disseminated statements since the rules of evidence were violated in the case. As a result, it is not possible to assess whether the disseminated statements discredit the plaintiff's honour and dignity and what method of refutal shall be applied. Article 2.24(1) CC establishes a presumption that disseminated data is false until the person who disseminated it proves otherwise. According to the presumption, the burden of proof lies with the defendant; the plaintiff has the right to present evidence supporting the untruthfulness of the data.

85 Initially, the burden of proof in the case fell on the defendant, the *Seimas*, even though the contested statements were specified in the Certificate by the Department, which acted as the third party in the case. During the proceedings, the Department sought to prove that the statements in the Certificate corresponded to reality by filing classified information to the court. However, the court of first

instance rejected the Department's request, stating that such information could not be evidence in the case. The court relied on art 177(4) of the Code of Civil Procedure of the Republic of Lithuania (the CCP), stating that factual data constituting a State secret generally cannot be admitted as evidence in civil proceedings until declassified according to the procedure established by law.

The Court admitted that its case law in interpreting and applying art 177(4) CCP 86
is not abundant, and all explanations provided to date have related to cases of a different nature than this one. Therefore, the Court provided a comprehensive assessment of the use of classified information in this case. Firstly, the Court thoroughly analysed the Constitutional Court's doctrine and concluded that the law does not specify the nature of the circumstances the court must establish and evaluate when deciding on the admissibility of classified information. Secondly, in interpreting and applying art 177(4) CCP, the court must consider the concept of evidentiary privileges known in legal doctrine. The confidentiality, secrecy, or significance of certain information is considered more valuable than its use as evidence in the evidentiary process. However, privileges can be absolute or qualified. In the opinion of the Court, the CCP establishes limitations on the admissibility of evidence of a dual nature. Some restrictions are of an absolute nature (for example, data obtained during mediation cannot be used as evidence in civil proceedings), while others are relative (for example, data constituting a State or service secret [a professional secret, referring particularly to public service]).

The wording used in the said article of the CCP implies that this norm estab- 87
lishes a relatively limited prohibition on the use of factual data constituting a State or service secret as evidence in civil proceedings. Such a prohibition is limited in time – according to the procedure established by law, classified information can be used as evidence in civil proceedings once it is declassified. In assessing the possibility of the use of classified information as evidence in civil proceedings, it is necessary to establish the relationship between the legal goods protected by such regulation – the protection of a State or service secret and the establishment of truth in the case. Therefore, to resolve the dispute regarding the use of data constituting a State secret in the case as evidence, the court must: (1) determine whether the circumstances essential for the correct resolution of the case can only be confirmed by proof constituting a State or service secret; (2) evaluate whether classified information cannot be declassified according to the procedure established by law.

In this case, the lower instance courts, applying the limitations on the admis- 88
sibility of evidence set out in art 177(4) CCP, prevented the defendant and the third party from proving the correctness of the disseminated information. Since art 2.24(1) CC presumes that disseminated data is untrue until proven otherwise, and the defendant and the third party were unable to prove the veracity of the

data due to the limitations imposed on them, the lower instance courts' conclusion that the disseminated statements were false is inadequately reasoned.

89 Due to this reason, the case should be returned for reconsideration to the court of first instance, which must assess whether there is sufficient evidence to decide the case, based on the proof that is not classified information and, if not, evaluate the possibility of declassifying the data sought by the Department.

90 Finally, the Court ruled that the *Seimas* of the Republic of Lithuania does not have legal personality and therefore cannot independently participate in the case: the respondent must be the State itself.

c) Commentary

91 This was a high-profile case stemming from a widely discussed parliamentary inquiry into the possible undue influence of certain businesses on the actions of Lithuanian politicians and public officials.

92 In this extensive ruling, the Court resolved two difficult legal questions: first, the inter-relation of remedies available to the plaintiff, who was a former high ranking public official, when the plaintiff claims that the data revealed and published in an official document of an intelligence institution was not true and undermined his honour and dignity. Second, the court clarified whether information constituting a State secret, not accessible to all parties in the case, can be used as evidence in civil proceedings.

93 Examining the first question, the Court established a hierarchy of remedies. First and foremost, violated rights must be protected by filing a claim for damages against the State. Only when this method is inefficient can there be a demand to refute untrue information damaging an individual's honour and dignity. However, the decision does not provide criteria to determine whether a claim for damages would be inefficient. In this regard, the Court's practice will be developed.

94 Furthermore, the case highlights the problems associated with the use of information that constitutes a State secret. On the one hand, filing such information in civil proceedings may have a negative impact on the exercise of the exclusive powers of the State. On the other hand, without the use of such information, the proper conduct of civil proceedings is hardly possible. Therefore, the courts must be careful in finding a balance between these two conflicting interests.

7. *RA* v *the Republic of Lithuania, Represented by the National Health Insurance Fund under the Ministry of Health*, LSC 15 June 2023, no e3K-3-24-421/2023: Compensation for Damage to Patient's Health due to Alleged Contamination with COVID-19 while in Hospital

a) Brief Summary of the Facts

The plaintiff sought compensation from the Republic of Lithuania, claiming € 3,223 for pecuniary damage and € 15,000 for non-pecuniary damage. The case resulted after the death of the plaintiff's mother (the patient) at the Vilnius City Clinical Hospital (the Hospital). 95

The patient was admitted to the Hospital on 3 April 2020, for suspected sepsis, and her treatment was initially successful. However, on 9 May 2020, the plaintiff learned that the patient had been diagnosed with COVID-19 and transferred to another hospital, where her condition rapidly deteriorated, leading to her death on 14 May 2020. The plaintiff contended that the patient contracted COVID-19 at the Hospital due to its failure to comply with health and safety legislation. 96

In the first instance, the court partially upheld the claim. The court established that the patient, who did not exhibit symptoms of COVID-19, was admitted to a room alongside another patient experiencing fever, coughing, and breathlessness. These actions were deemed non-compliant with the stipulations outlined in Decision No V-387 issued by the Minister of Health on 16 March 2020. The court considered that these actions were causally linked to the patient's infection with the COVID-19 virus and subsequent death. In addressing the issue of damages, the court considered that healthcare services were rendered during a unique period when an epidemic status was declared in the Republic of Lithuania and globally. Consequently, the irregularities committed by the hospital, which might have led to the patient's infection, were deemed not to qualify as irregularities in the provision of healthcare services under standard circumstances and treatment conditions. Therefore, the court granted the plaintiff € 5,000 in non-pecuniary damages and € 1,000 in pecuniary damages. 97

The Court of Appeal (the CoA) overturned the judgment, dismissing the plaintiff's claim. The CoA emphasised that it was likely that, even in the absence of the breach, the harm to the patient would not have been averted. Establishing the precise origin of the illness and evaluating potential sources of infection is challenging. Additionally, considering the patient's age, multiple illnesses, and her pre-coronavirus condition, these circumstances were deemed the direct cause of her death. In cases following the new strict liability model, damages are granted if 98 there is evidence of a failure to adhere to a professional standard of care, and the harm could have been prevented by complying with that standard based on the prevailing state of medical science. The Court of Appeal determined that the patient's COVID-19 infection could not have been prevented even with all preventive measures in place.

b) Judgment of the Court

99 The Court annulled the decision of the CoA and increased the pecuniary damages to € 3,223. The calculation of the non-pecuniary damages was remitted to the CoA for further consideration.

100 Having analysed the regulation set out by the Law on the Rights of Patients and Compensation for Damage to Patients' Health,[14] the Court stated that the following conditions must be met for the right to compensation for damage to a patient's health: (1) the patient's health has been harmed, including death; and (2) the harm was not unavoidable. The existing regulation on compensation does not require fault as a prerequisite but is a strict liability regime. The criterion of unavoidability implies that damages should be granted if the harm was preventable in light of medical science and good medical practice in the course of the provision of services. Establishing a causal link between the actions of the healthcare provider and damage is crucial.

101 According to the Court, since the law does not require the identification and compensation for the unlawful acts or omission of healthcare institutions during the provision of healthcare services, the conclusion of the CoA that liability for harm to a patient's health arises only when the unlawful acts of the healthcare institution are established is legally unfounded.

102 The Court decided that, contrary to the conclusions of the CoA, there was no proof that the patient had contracted COVID-19 elsewhere. The first instance court made a justified conclusion that the harm to the patient's health during the provision of healthcare services does not qualify as unavoidable, therefore, it must be compensated.

103 However, the first instance inaccurately determined the amount of non-pecuniary damages, leading the Court to seek reassessment of this aspect by the CoA.

14 See *Drukteinienė/Šaltinytė* (fn 3) nos 1–6.

c) Commentary

An intriguing aspect of this case is the consideration by the courts of pecuniary and non-pecuniary damage suffered by the relative of the patient when health services were provided to the patient during the COVID-19 pandemic. 104

This decision is also significant for the Lithuanian legal system since it is the first in which the new no-fault liability model set out in the Law on the Rights of Patients and Compensation for Damage to Patients' Health was applied. 105

8. Personal Injury

There were no particularly noteworthy developments in the area of personal injury claims in 2023. Below, we discuss compensation amounts for non-pecuniary damage caused by criminal conduct, liability for personal injury resulting from traffic accidents, and inmates' personal injury claims against the State. 106

a) Compensation of Non-Pecuniary Damage Inflicted by Criminal Conduct

In cases of intentional and unintentional deprivation of life, compensation amounts for non-pecuniary damage were as follows: € 20,000 for the spouse or permanent partner of the deceased; € 30,000 for minor children; from € 15,000 to € 20,000 for the mother in the case of the loss of an adult child; € 15,000 for adult children, and € 10,000 for an adult sibling. 107

For example, € 20,000 was awarded in non-pecuniary damages to the cohabitant of the deceased for the intentional killing of her partner.[15] In another case, € 15,000 was awarded to each of the two adult children of the deceased, and € 20,000 was awarded to the mother of her adult son for his intentional killing.[16] 108

€ 30,000 was awarded to each of the two minor children of the deceased, € 20,000 to the spouse, € 15,000 to the mother, and € 10,000 to the adult sibling in non-pecuniary damages from a company as the civil respondent in a criminal case. These compensation amounts were granted due to the death of a company's employee, which resulted from the company's failure to ensure safe working conditions at a construction site.[17] 109

15 LSC 7 March 2023, case no 2K-55–387/2023.
16 LSC 21 February 2023, case no 2K-15–387/2023.
17 LSC 13 April 2023, case no 2K-100–387/2023.

110 In cases of minor or insignificant health impairments or breaches of personality rights, compensation amounts for non-pecuniary damage remained rather modest.

111 € 4,000 was awarded in non-pecuniary damages for a minor intentional health impairment when, under the influence of alcohol in a park, the accused intentionally struck and punched the victim's head and chest at least five times with his fist. This resulted in subcutaneous bleeding in the back of the nose, lower eyelid of the left eye, and inner corner of the right eye, as well as injuries in the nasal area, chest, fractures of the nasal bones, and a fracture of the root of one tooth. Additionally, € 300 was awarded in non-pecuniary damages to another victim of the same accused person who was intentionally pushed strongly with his hands, causing her to fall to the ground and thus inflicting physical pain.[18]

112 A sum of € 3,000 was awarded in non-pecuniary damages to compensate the victim when the accused person, out of revenge for a previous conflict, punched him once in the lower part of the face. As a result, the victim lost his balance, fell to the ground, and suffered a dislocation of the right acromioclavicular joint, contusions to the head and left forearm, a fracture of two upper front teeth, and injuries qualified as a minor health impairment.[19]

113 A sum of € 1,000 was awarded in non-pecuniary damages to the victim for the minor health impairment caused by her spouse, who, during a conflict, grabbed her by the shoulders and threw her to the ground when she attempted to stand up. Subsequently, he pushed her again and, while she was on the ground, kicked her in various parts of the body. When the victim managed to stand up, he pushed her out of the room. Upon her return to retrieve personal belongings, he struck her multiple times in the face, causing injuries and physical pain.[20]

114 € 3,000 was awarded to the mother, and € 1,500 to her minor daughter in non-pecuniary damages for the public announcements by the accused claiming they provide sexual services. The announcements included pictures of the minor and sexual organs of the mother. The latter pictures were taken by the accused without the knowledge of the mother during their communication via Skype.[21]

---

18 LSC 18 October 2023, case no 2K-207–628/2023.

19 LSC 8 June 2023, case no 2K-175–489/2023.

20 LSC 14 March 2023, case no 2K-29–648/2023.

21 LSC 12 December 2023, case no 2K-278–697/2023.

b) Liability for Personal Injury Inflicted during Traffic Accidents

In fatal traffic accident cases, compensation amounts for non-pecuniary damage were differentiated based on the relationship of the secondary victims to the deceased and the nature of the tortfeasor's actions. 115

For example, € 50,000 was awarded in non-pecuniary damages to each of the parents for the death of their 10-year-old child in a traffic accident. The traffic accident occurred when the accused's vehicle collided with a deer crossing the road. It was established that the driver failed to observe all necessary precautions upon encountering the obstacle, did not slow down, and did not stop. Compensation of € 15,000 was awarded for non-pecuniary damage to each of the two victims who suffered severe injuries during the same traffic accident. It was the employer of the driver, who was the possessor of the source of increased danger, who was ordered to pay these damages. In determining the amount of non-pecuniary damages to the parents, consideration was given to the close relationship between the deceased child's parents and the child, causing them emotional pain, distress, and the need for psychological assistance. When assessing the non-pecuniary damage to the injured individuals, it was considered that they underwent multiple surgeries, prolonged treatments, experienced pain, emotional distress, and ongoing consequences that they continue to endure. Additionally, the good financial condition of the employer was also taken into account.[22] 116

€ 15,000 was awarded to each of two minor children, € 5,000 to the adult sibling, and the same amount to each of the parents, and to the spouse of the deceased in non-pecuniary damages. This occurred due to the accused's actions while driving a car and approaching an unregulated pedestrian crossing where he did not slow down, failed to stop at the pedestrian crossing, and ultimately struck the victim causing fatal injuries.[23] 117

Another case stands out due to its exceptional circumstances. Two individuals suffered fatal injuries when the accused, operating a vehicle without a valid driving licence and highly intoxicated, intentionally accelerated his car for the purpose of causing disorder, exceeding the speed limit by 40–50 km/h. Disregarding the pleas of his passengers to slow down, he changed lanes in front of a vehicle in the same lane without ensuring a safe distance or confirming a safe return to his lane, leading to a collision with the vehicle ahead. This collision caused the latter vehicle to veer into oncoming traffic and collide with an approaching truck, resulting in the loss of lives for both the driver and passenger of the oncoming car. 118

---

22 LSC 21 June 2023, case no 2K-183–628/2023.

23 LSC 10 January 2023, case no 2K-72–654/2023.

Compensation of € 30,000 each was awarded in non-pecuniary damages to the two adult daughters and the mother of one of the deceased (including the amounts already paid by the insurer). The adult sister of the deceased received € 10,000 (including the insurer's payment). When determining the compensation amounts, the close relationships between the daughters and their mother were taken into consideration, along with the sister's somewhat more distant connection with the deceased. For the parents of the other deceased, non-pecuniary damages were set at € 10,000 each, and for the brother, € 5,000 (including amounts already paid by the insurer). It was observed during the proceedings that the deceased had resided in Hong Kong for the previous 15 years, returning to Lithuania only occasionally. As a Buddhist nun dedicated to spiritual activities, her spiritual and emotional connections with her parents and brother were not very close; relationships were maintained only periodically and, except for rare exceptions, were distant.[24]

c) Inmates' Personal Injury Claims against the State

119 As in previous years, a substantial category of cases examined in administrative courts concerning public liability for damage caused by violations in the field of public administration[25] is comprised of cases initiated by inmates and detainees alleging various violations they endured. Although these cases do not fall into the narrow sense of personal injury cases, it is worth briefly discussing them.

120 A considerable number of complaints from inmates and detainees that reached the SACL were dismissed. For example, it was determined that an inmate unjustifiably complained that his right to long-term family visits was restricted during the quarantine imposed to manage the COVID-19 pandemic.[26]

121 The claim was filed by a former soldier, who participated in a special international military operation. His assertion that he should be considered a public serv-

24 LSC 6 April 2023, case no 2K-118–788/2023.

25 In Lithuania, State liability is regulated by three articles in the Civil Code (arts 6.271–6.273). The first regulates damage caused in the field of public administration. Furthermore, while the matter is still controversial, legal doctrine acknowledges that this article also governs the liability of the State for damage caused in the field of legislative authority. However, case law is less clear on this latter issue. Article 6.272 of the Civil Code regulates cases where damage is caused by the State while performing judicial functions during pre-trial investigation or in the examination of civil or criminal cases. Article 6.273 CC regulates issues of representing the State in cases of compensation for damage. When the damage is caused in the field of public administration, cases are heard in administrative courts. In other cases, courts of general jurisdiction handle cases related to compensation for damage caused by State actions.

26 SACL 8 February 2023, No eTA-228–822/2023.

ant and, therefore, should be isolated from other convicts in detention, was also rejected because the legal acts do not grant him the rights of a public servant.[27]

122 A claim by an inmate regarding the alleged failure to determine the maximum allowable number of convicts in communal-type premises and compensation for the damage caused by it was also dismissed. The court concluded that, at the relevant time, the laws in force established the minimum living space per person in communal premises of correctional institutions. However, no imperative national or international laws, including the European Convention on Human Rights and Fundamental Freedoms, specifically set the number of convicts who could share communal-type premises.[28]

123 A claim for compensation of damage by an inmate who was not released for his wife's funeral when he informed the prison authorities about the funeral location and time only 2.5 hours in advance of the scheduled ceremony was also dismissed.[29]

124 The claim of a detainee to compensate for the damage when his request for a remote meeting with his half-brother, serving a sentence in another correctional institution was denied, was also rejected. The SALC decision was motivated by the fact that the laws of the Republic of Lithuania do not provide for the right of detainees to meet with other inmates remotely (the right is granted to inmates who are spouses, subject to certain conditions).[30]

125 Upon establishing that the catering in the correctional facility was organised in accordance with legal requirements, the claim for compensation for damage caused by inadequate nutrition was also dismissed.[31]

126 In several cases, violations were identified, and compensation for damage was either awarded or the SACL limited itself to an acknowledgment of the violation. For example, € 200 was awarded in non-pecuniary damages to an inmate, finding that the correctional institution administration failed to ensure the applicant's right, as an alternative to phone calls, to communicate with his spouse via video calls for almost two months.[32]

127 € 1,000 was awarded in non-pecuniary damages to an inmate because, while serving a sentence in a prison hospital, the required living space was not ensured.

27 SACL 31 May 2023, No TA-413–629/2023.
28 SACL 7 June 2023, No TA-306–556/2023.
29 SACL 14 June 2023, No TA-374–662/2023.
30 SACL 8 November 2023, No eTA-585–525/2023.
31 SACL 11 October 2023, No eTA-486–815/2023.
32 SACL 25 January 2023, No TA-127–492/2023.

For over seven months, he lived in a room that measured 5.075 sq m instead of the required 5.1 sq m.[33]

128 € 70 was awarded in non-pecuniary damages to a detained person who was held for two days in a detention cell equipped with a surveillance camera that recorded him using the toilet. The SACL found that the defendant, by monitoring the detention cell through video devices and, although technically obscuring the person's face using the toilet, violated the provision of the law that the inner part of toilets should not be recorded and did not ensure the applicant's privacy while using the toilet.[34]

129 The SACL granted the claim of an inmate who spent a week during the summer in a prison hospital and awarded him € 100 in non-pecuniary damages. The hospital management violated the hygiene norm by not installing curtains on the window, which requires protecting the patient from direct sunlight. Additionally, the rights of this inmate were violated when law enforcement officers attended psychiatric consultations six to seven times without a medical professional's request, hindering the possibility of consulting with a psychiatrist.[35]

130 € 140 was awarded in non-pecuniary damages to an inmate who was deprived of the opportunity to take prescribed medication for 11 days, which he must take continuously without interruption throughout his life.[36]

131 A violation was established, without awarding non-material damages, for the infringement of an inmate's right to privacy when, during a drug test, he was brought to urinate with the toilet doors open, while being observed by an officer.[37]

C. Literature

1. *S Drukteinienė*, Lithuania, in: K Kremens/W Jasiński (eds), Compensation for Wrongful Convictions: A Comparative Perspective (Routledge 2023)

132 This book provides a comprehensive comparative examination of the substantive and procedural aspects of compensating wrongful convictions in European coun-

33 SACL 8 March 2023, No TA-339–1047/2023.
34 SACL 19 April 2023, No TA-479–492/2023.
35 SACL 17 May 2023, No TA-480–520/2023.
36 SACL 7 June 2023, No TA-382–789/2023.
37 SACL 14 June 2023, No TA-453–552/2023.

tries and the USA, along with the standards derived from the case law of the European Court of Human Rights.

The Lithuanian report suggests that the regime of State liability for wrongful convictions, introduced in the 2000 Civil Code of the Republic of Lithuania, a decade after Lithuania's independence restoration, is modern. State liability for unlawful convictions arises from three prerequisites – unlawfulness, damage, and a causal link. However, while it is evident that the personal fault of a public official is not a condition for liability, the consideration of organisational fault is less clear. The Lithuanian report shows that although the State's liability for unlawful convictions is widely argued to be strict, the settled case law of the Supreme Court of Lithuania indicates that an exculpatory judgment does not automatically imply unlawfulness. This prerequisite may only be established in cases where the person was convicted due to breaches of criminal procedure provisions. Both pecuniary and non-pecuniary damage resulting from unlawful actions may be compensated. Pecuniary damage is assessed concretely, while non-pecuniary damage is evaluated based on various criteria, including the gravity of the unlawfully imposed penalty, severity of breaches in criminal proceedings, and mental suffering of the individual. Damage may also be compensated through an extra-judicial procedure, although it is not mandatory, and the victim can always directly address the court. The unpopularity of the extra-judicial procedure is attributed to the low amounts of damages set as maximum by the law. 133

The collection of the reports compares various jurisdictions with the aim of identifying both similarities and differences, and to assess the efficiency of national compensation systems. This analysis contributes to the design of an ideal compensation model that is both accessible and effective for victims of miscarriages of justice. According to the editors, the model aims to be acceptable across jurisdictions with diverse legal traditions, including common law and civil law systems, as well as inquisitorial and adversarial criminal processes. 134

2. *O Shevchenko*, Civilinės atsakomybės už incidentus, susijusius su automatizuotų transporto priemonių valdymu Europos Sąjungoje, reglamentavimas [Regulation of civil liability for incidents related to intelligent connected driving in the European Union] (Doctoral dissertation, Vilnius University 2023)

The author proposes a regulatory approach, termed 'synergetic regulation', to address civil liability arising from damage caused by automated transport vehicles. 135

The study argues for a liability model the aim of which is to prevent adverse effects on victims in cross-border incidents. It analyses the feasibility and suitability of implementing the synergetic regulation model in the European Union and its Member States. This analysis is conducted through the prism of its alignment with existing legal regulations.

3. *F Gennari*, Internet of Things: Legal Liability of IOE Devices in the Home (Doctoral dissertation, Mykolas Romeris University 2023)

136 This thesis focuses on the concept of the smart home, an interconnected environment designed to assist people in leading more environmentally sustainable lives and empowering vulnerable groups to live more autonomously, primarily through the widespread adoption of Internet of Things (IoT) technology. The central lens through which the research unfolds is the issue of civil liability related to the smart home's malfunctions.

137 The study delves into an examination of whether existing legal liability frameworks are adequately equipped to adapt to the challenges posed by this evolving connected environment, particularly in the context of IoT-enabled smart homes. By meticulously mapping both the technical and legal landscape, the thesis contends that the current European Union rules governing product liability, as outlined in the Product Liability Directive (PLD), can consistently apply to these technologically advanced objects.

4. *M Šalčius/C Herke*, Problems Regarding Compensation for the Breach of the Right to Criminal Proceedings within a Reasonable Time, International Comparative Jurisprudence 2023, No 9 (1) 111–122

138 The authors discuss the compensation for the violation of the right to criminal proceedings within a reasonable time, exploring different mechanisms in European countries. In several European nations, including Germany, Norway, Denmark, and Hungary, the reduction of sentences serves as compensation for prolonged criminal proceedings, aligning with international legal acts and the European Court of Human Rights (ECtHR) practice. However, the situation regarding monetary compensation in Lithuania, when a violation of art 6 (1) of the European Convention on Human Rights (ECHR) is established, is more complex. The legal regu-

lation does not expressly provide for compensation for damage caused by excessively long criminal proceedings, and this has been criticised in legal doctrine and international jurisprudence.

The article highlights that the resolution of this issue has been found in case law. In a ruling dated 15 October 2013, the ECtHR acknowledged that Lithuania's jurisprudence has developed effective remedies,[38] enabling individuals to demand compensation from the State for damage resulting from prolonged criminal proceedings. 139

Nevertheless, the article suggests that Lithuania should improve its legal regulation. According to the authors, compensation for damage due to prolonged criminal proceedings should be clearly and unambiguously established in legal acts, aligning with the recommendations of international institutions, and enhancing the consistency and clarity of the Lithuanian legal system. 140

5. *G Armalis*, 'Pinigų mulai': civilinės atsakomybės kilimo pagrindai, sąlygos ir forma ['Money mules': grounds, conditions and form of civil liability], Teisės apžvalga 2023, No 1 (27) 106–127

The author analyses the civil liability of individuals engaged in a recently emerging form of money laundering referred to as the 'money mule' phenomenon. In this scenario, individuals, when asked by their acquaintances or an 'employer', accept funds obtained from criminal activities related to money laundering. They proceed to deposit these funds into their bank accounts, launder the money, and subsequently deliver the laundered money to the ultimate recipient – the individual responsible for the criminal acts. 141

The study focuses on situations where 'money mules' remain unaware of the criminal origin of the assets. Consequently, in Lithuania, they may not be subjected to criminal liability. However, the author argues that they should be held accountable for delictual liability based on the breach of a general duty of care. The determination of breach of this duty hinges on whether a 'money mule' exercised due diligence in probing their 'employer', assessing its credibility, investigating the origin of the funds deposited into their account, scrutinising the intended recipients of the laundered funds, and considering other relevant circumstances. 142

38 See the LSC decision of 6 February 2007, No 3K-7–7/2007 by *H Gabartas/G Bžozeckaitė* in: H Koziol/BC Steininger (eds), European Tort Law (ETL) 2007 (2008) 400, nos 7–16.

G Caruana Demajo, L Quintano and D Zammit

XIX. Malta

A. Legislation

No legislation of direct relevance to tort law was enacted during 2023. 1

B. Cases

1. *Nathalie Bartolo v Jeffrey Pullicino Orlando*, Court of Appeal, Second Chamber, 31 May 2023, Application no 302/2011: Medical Malpractice; Causation

a) Brief Summary of the Facts

The first defendant, a dentist, extracted two molars, attached a dental bridge and 2
also performed root canal treatment on the plaintiff. The treatment was carried out on separate occasions over four months. The plaintiff complained of pain after the treatment. The first defendant attempted to treat the cause of the pain but without success. The plaintiff then sought the advice of another dentist, who advised that the bridgework and the root canal treatment had to be redone, and referred her to the second defendant, also a dentist.

The second defendant repeated the root canal treatment but the plaintiff still 3
complained of pain. The second defendant then performed a bone biopsy wherefrom it resulted that the plaintiff was suffering from chronic osteomyelitis, a bone infection.

The plaintiff sought the help of yet another dentist who suggested cryotherapy 4
but advised that, since he could note that the mental nerve had been damaged during the previous treatment, he could not guarantee a successful result. He also reported that the plaintiff suffered from permanent disability, which he assessed at 25 %.

In fact, notwithstanding the cryotherapy, the pain did not subside and the 5
plaintiff now suffers from chronic pain.

Alleging that the treatment at the hands of the first two defendants was neg- 6
ligently and unprofessionally performed, and that as a result she suffers from permanent disability, the plaintiff sued both defendants and also the chief govern-

https://doi.org/10.1515/9783111376721-020

ment medical officer, who is responsible for the State hospital, since the second root canal treatment and the biopsy had been performed at the State hospital.

b) Judgment of the Court

7 The first instance court appointed a dental expert who reported that the first root canal treatment had not been carried out correctly because it was 'short', ie did not reach the apex of the root. This was due to the fact that the dental root was curved and the first defendant had failed to notice this anomaly. Nevertheless, the expert concluded that the chronic pain complained of by the plaintiff could not be due to the short treatment since, at most, this could only give rise to acute, not chronic, pain. Nor could it be due to the second treatment or to the biopsy since the plaintiff had been complaining of the same pain before those episodes.

8 The court, however, observed that, notwithstanding the expert's opinion, it had been established that the first root canal treatment had not been correctly performed and had caused an infection which, according to *ex parte* evidence submitted by the plaintiff, could very well be the cause of chronic pain such as that complained of by the plaintiff. Although there were other possible causes, the pain was localised in the area which had been subjected to treatment and it was therefore probable that the treatment was the cause of the pain.

9 The court also noted that, before the expert's report was published, the first defendant himself had admitted that the treatment was not completely successful and that it was possible that, as a result, the plaintiff suffered a permanent disability, which he assessed at 12.5 %.

10 Another fact which transpired from the evidence was that the mental nerve had been damaged, possibly as a result of the bone biopsy but also possibly due to the bone infection. In view of this uncertainty, the court concluded that there was no conclusive evidence that the biopsy had been performed negligently.

11 Since the procedures conducted by the second defendant at the State hospital were not the cause of the plaintiff's disability, the claims against the second and third defendants were dismissed.

12 The first instance court, therefore, found the first defendant solely liable. It observed that the court-nominated expert had not furnished sufficient information to enable it to apply the usual multiplier formula and it therefore assessed damages *arbitrio boni viri* for loss of earnings as a result of the disability at € 15,000, in addition to a further € 721 for the costs of medical treatment and all judicial costs.

13 The first defendant appealed and the plaintiff entered a cross-appeal. The first defendant claimed that the court ought to have relied on the conclusions of its own expert and that, for this reason, the judgment against him should be overturned.

Moreover, the first instance court had expressly stated that the cause of the pain could not be ascertained and therefore it should have concluded that there was no proof of a causal link between the pain and the root canal treatment performed by him or, for that matter, by the other dentist; the more likely cause of the pain was the bone biopsy procedure. Moreover, the first defendant argued that the damages awarded were excessive.

The plaintiff, on the other hand, claimed that both dentists were to blame and 14 that judgment should be delivered also against the second defendant. She also claimed that, since the first instance court had not followed the normal multiplier formula, the damages awarded were inadequate and should therefore be increased.

The Court of Appeal observed that the first instance court was not bound by 15 the expert's report, and it was within its power to rely on other experts, albeit *ex parte*, whom it considered to be more convincing particularly since the evidence showed that the first root canal treatment had not been performed correctly and it was objectively ascertained and also acknowledged by the court-appointed expert that the plaintiff suffered chronic pain.

As regards the causal link between the first root canal treatment and the dis- 16 ability, the Court of Appeal observed that this need only be proved on a balance of probabilities. On the evidence, the court was satisfied that the inadequate treatment by the first defendant did cause or, at least, contribute to the disability suffered by the plaintiff because the 'short' root canal treatment probably caused the infection. The court stressed that the first defendant's liability arose not from the fact that the treatment was not successful but rather because it had not been carried out with proper care.

The first defendant's appeal was therefore dismissed. 17

Turning then to the plaintiff's cross appeal, the court disagreed with the first 18 instance court's conclusion that the second defendant was also not to blame. In addition to pain, the plaintiff also complained of numbness of the lip. This was a symptom of mental[1] nerve damage, and clinical examination revealed that the incision line for the biopsy was directly across the mental nerve on the gumline. It was therefore highly probable that the incision had damaged the nerve. This, in the view of the court, was evidence of gross negligence in the performance of the biopsy. It concluded therefore that the second defendant had been grossly negligent in carrying out the procedure.

At this point the court observed that, even if it was the biopsy procedure per- 19 formed by the second defendant that had damaged the nerve, this did not exoner-

1 'Mental' ie relating to the chin.

ate the first defendant because the need for the biopsy had arisen because of the shortcomings of the first root canal treatment.

20 The plaintiff's cross-appeal, insofar as it concerned the liability of the second defendant, was therefore upheld and both the first and the second defendants were held jointly liable.

21 On the assessment of damages, the Court of Appeal observed that, notwithstanding the insufficiency of the official expert's report, the evidence tendered by the *ex parte* experts was nevertheless sufficient to enable it to apply the multiplier formula. However, this gave a result which was less than that reached by the first instance court, and the damages were reduced to € 13,409.

c) Commentary

22 At one point when considering the liability of the second defendant as a result of the biopsy procedure, the Court of Appeal observed that,

> 'although a bone infection in the jaw can damage the nerve, in the present case this was just a possibility whereas on the other hand it was objectively proved that the mental nerve had been damaged during the biopsy and that this damage brought about the symptoms complained of by the plaintiff.'

23 Since, therefore, the first root canal procedure could only possibly have caused the harm, whereas the biopsy was the more probable cause, it would seem that the second defendant was more probably at fault than the first one.

24 In *Paul Pullicino v Director General, Works Department* (Court of Appeal of 30 March 2022, Application no 538/2009) on which we reported in the 2022 Yearbook, the Court of Appeal had observed that, since liability is based on probability, and mere possibility is not sufficient, where either of two defendants had probably caused the harm, liability is to be apportioned according to the degree of probability that the harm was caused by one or the other defendant.

25 Had this doctrine of alternative causation been applied in the present case, the possibility that the harm was caused also by the first defendant would have been insufficient to entail liability. Moreover, even if it were probable that the short root canal treatment had caused an infection which damaged the nerve, liability would have been apportioned, not necessarily in equal portions and certainly not joint.

26 Equally worthy of note is the appellate court's observation that, even if the cause of the harm were the biopsy procedure, this did not exonerate the first defendant, because the need for the biopsy had arisen as a result of the consequences of the first treatment. This reasoning would seem to not only extend liability for a

more remote albeit possibly dependant cause, but also to equate the remote cause with the more proximate cause in apportioning liability. This marks a departure from the more traditional view both as regards liability for a remote cause and also mere possibility as a ground of liability.

2. *Amanda Bilocca v Chief Government Medical Officer and another*, Court of Appeal, Second Chamber, 15 November 2023, Application no 27/2012: Medical Malpractice

a) Brief Summary of the Facts

After performing an ultrasound test on the plaintiff, the second defendant, a radiologist, reported that she suffered from chronic calculous cholecystitis, ie gallstones. Acting on the radiologist's report, the referring surgeon (who is not a party to the proceedings) recommended a keyhole laparoscopy on the gallbladder. 27

However, during surgery, the surgeon could not locate the gallbladder. A more invasive procedure was therefore performed to gain access to the organ, and what ought to have been a keyhole procedure turned into major surgery taking four hours at the end of which it transpired that the plaintiff had agenesis of the gallbladder, a rare congenital anomaly characterised by absence of the gallbladder. The whole procedure had been unnecessary because there was no gallbladder to treat! 28

Claiming that the resultant eighteen centimetre scar was a cause of permanent disability due to psychological distress, the plaintiff sued the hospital authorities and the radiologist for damages. 29

b) Judgment of the Court

The first instance court appointed a radiology expert who reported that no image of the gallbladder was present on the ultrasound radiography, and that what had been mistaken for gallstones was in fact gas in the duodenum. He concluded that the diagnosis of chronic calculous cholecystitis was wrong and that, in view of what appeared from the radiography, further tests ought to have been made. 30

Observing that the defendants had submitted no convincing arguments to rebut the expert's report, the court concluded that the radiologist had failed to exercise proper care and skill and was therefore responsible for the harm. It also held that since the relationship between the hospital authorities and the patient was contractual in nature, and the radiologist was an employee of the hospital, 31 the plea of lack of *culpa in eligendo* was not applicable in the context of that relationship. It therefore held that the hospital authorities were jointly liable for the harm caused to the plaintiff.

32 On the matter of damages, the plaintiff stated that she terminated her employment some time after this episode to help her husband in his business of handyman without being formally employed. She submitted no evidence of the income generated by her but showed that the total income from the family business was around € 55,000 per annum. The plaintiff therefore submitted that half this amount should be taken as the multiplicand.

33 The court rejected this argument, stating that there was no evidence to show that the plaintiff did generate half the income from the business. It considered that a more objective basis for assessing loss of earnings was the plaintiff's previous employment which she held at the time of the episode. Applying the usual multiplier method, the court assessed loss of earnings at € 18,681. It held both defendants jointly liable to pay the plaintiff this amount plus a further € 45 medical expenses and judicial costs.

34 Both defendants appealed and the plaintiff entered a cross-appeal.

35 On the liability of the radiologist, the defendants argued that an incorrect interpretation of the ultrasound image did not necessarily imply negligence or malpractice. Congenital absence of the gallbladder is an extremely rare condition and, according to normal practice, the radiologist is not expected to conduct further diagnostic tests for that condition. The correct test for negligence is whether a competent practitioner would have acted differently in the circumstances, which was not the case.

36 The Court of Appeal dismissed the defendants' arguments, observing that in the present case, the misdiagnosis was not due to an excusable error of judgement but due to failure on the radiologist's part to proceed with the proper care, skill and diligence expected of a professional practitioner. The official expert had highlighted two 'gross' errors in the radiologist's report: (i) the 'echogenic shadows' (due to gas in the duodenum) which appeared in the radiography were of the wrong shape to be interpreted as gallstones; and (ii) the radiography showed no signs of a thickened gallbladder wall, which would have been indicative of chronic calculous cholecystitis, leading the expert to conclude that 'the gallbladder was not seen with certainty' and that further examinations were indicated because 'agenesis of the gallbladder should be highly suspected when the gallbladder is not visualised on ultrasound'. Under the circumstances, the 'unequivocal' diagnosis of the radiologist was imprudent and injudicious.

37 The appeal, insofar as it concerned the liability of the radiologist, was therefore dismissed.

On the liability of the hospital authorities, the defendants argued that the radiologist was a qualified practitioner and therefore there was no *culpa in eligendo* in his appointment. Moreover, the hospital was fully equipped with the equipment required for all further tests that may have been necessary. 38

The court observed that *culpa in eligendo* is not to be interpreted as narrowly as suggested by the defendants and the fact that the radiologist was qualified in that speciality is not sufficient to exonerate the hospital as his employer. The court observed that whoever employs another to perform a particular task is liable if that other person performs that task negligently and with lack of skill. Since the radiologist had acted with lack of proper diligence while performing his duties in the employment of the hospital, the hospital was answerable for the harm caused by him. 39

For these reasons, the Court of Appeal confirmed that both defendants were jointly and severally liable. 40

The defendants' final ground of appeal concerned the assessment of damages. They argued that the plaintiff had not suffered any disability as a result of the surgery and her earning capacity was unaffected, so much so that she was now earning more than before. The court observed that the surgical procedure had left an eighteen centimetre scar on the plaintiff and that 'this scar caused a permanent disability on the plaintiff's body because the skin is part of the body'. Moreover, the episode left a profound psychological effect on the plaintiff. This part of the appeal was also dismissed. 41

The plaintiff's cross-appeal concerned the assessment of damages, but the Court of Appeal found no convincing reason to overturn the first instance court's decision in this regard, and the plaintiff's cross-appeal, like the principal appeal, was dismissed. 42

c) Commentary

Unlike the first instance court, which concluded that *culpa in eligendo* was not necessary or relevant in the context of a contractual relationship such as that between hospital and patient, the Court of Appeal founded liability on what it termed a 'wider' interpretation of *culpa in eligendo.* This is unusual and, in the circumstances, unnecessary because, as the first instance court correctly pointed out, liability for incorrect performance of a contractual obligation does not depend on *culpa in eligendo*; the test is more properly applied in tort, not in contract. 43

Also somewhat unusual is the comment that damage to the skin is tantamount to disability because 'the skin is part of the body'. This may be relevant if damages are awarded for cosmetic impairment, but not for purposes of compensation for 44 loss of earnings unless it is shown that the impairment affects earning capacity, either because appearance is important for the purpose of the victim's economic activity, eg a model, or because the psychological effects of disfigurement affect performance and earning capacity. In the present case, the psychological effect was proved so that the earlier comment on damage to the skin was not necessary unless the court is moving towards opening the way to awarding compensation for cosmetic harm, which it had decisively rejected in earlier cases[2].

45 One may also add that the award of damages for loss of future earnings when the plaintiff's economic condition actually improved after the incident goes to show that, notwithstanding the 'official' position that non-patrimonial damages are not awarded except in exceptional cases specifically provided for by law[3], the multiplier method adopted by the courts does in fact award non-patrimonial damages.

3. *Simon Grech v Dominic Humphreys*, Court of Appeal, First Chamber, 25 October 2023, Writ no 2224/1998: Medical Malpractice

a) Brief Summary of the Facts

46 The plaintiff had suffered an injury to his neck during a sports event, and was admitted to hospital where X-rays revealed the loss of the normal curvature of the neck. The plaintiff, however, discharged himself before completing treatment. Subsequently he went to the defendant who runs a clinic as chiropractor. The plaintiff alleged that the defendant had vigorously manipulated his neck and arms without having first examined the radiographic images. There were further sessions and the plaintiff used to complain that he was suffering intense pain during and after the sessions. His condition worsened; he was examined by a neurologist and went to London several times for treatment and surgery. He has to undergo physiotherapy sessions and to forego all sports with the exception of swimming.

2 See eg *Linda Busuttil v Dr Josie Muscat et*, Court of Appeal, 27 June 2014, reported by *G Caruana Demajo/L Quintno/D Zammit*, Malta, in: E Karner/BC Steininger (eds), European Tort Law 2014 (2015) 369, no 100 ff.

3 Damage caused by a wilful criminal offence against the person or affecting the dignity of persons subject to imprisonment of at least three years.

The neurologist advised that physical manipulation was contraindicated in a case of whiplash injury. He also confirmed that the pain felt by the plaintiff was due to the state of his spine. 47

Alleging that his condition was the result of the technique applied by the defendant, the plaintiff sued for damages. 48

The defendant disclaimed liability. He stated that he had advised the plaintiff that he could not guarantee success. He admitted that he had been informed about the X-rays taken in hospital but said that he had been informed by the plaintiff that these had not revealed anything wrong. For this reason, he had not insisted on consulting the X-rays before commencing treatment. 49

He declared further that he had commenced treatment by a technique of gentle traction and mobilisation, which could have brought about the desired results without any consequences. He also used orthopaedic and neurological testing to assess the pain the patient was suffering. 50

b) Judgment of the Court

The first instance court observed that the medical expert appointed by it had established a 25 % permanent disability. However, although the report was exhaustive on the plaintiff's medical condition, it did not clearly establish a connection between the treatment and the harm. On the other hand, the plaintiff's neurologist confirmed that the manipulation administered by the defendant was contraindicated in the plaintiff's case. The court further considered that the defendant should have examined the X-ray results, which had revealed the loss of the normal curvature of the plaintiff's neck. 51

For these reasons, the court concluded that the causal link between treatment and injury was sufficiently established and it found for the plaintiff. Applying the traditional multiplier method, it ordered the defendant to pay damages of € 75,647. 52

The defendant appealed, arguing that the first instance court had erred in its interpretation of the law and also made an erroneous appreciation of the facts. He argued that the medical expert appointed by the court had remarked that, in the absence of an MRI scan made prior to treatment, it was impossible to state whether the plaintiff's cervical disk herniation was due to the treatment. Consequently, the causal link between treatment and injury had not been established, particularly in view of the fact that the plaintiff had already suffered an injury for which he had been hospitalised before seeking treatment from the defendant, and the degree and nature of that injury was unknown because the plaintiff had discharged himself from hospital before receiving full treatment. There is, therefore, no evi- 53 dence that the chiropractic therapy had made the condition of the plaintiff any worse.

54 The Court of Appeal held that, although the court is not bound by the conclusions of its own experts, it will nevertheless disregard expert reports only for very serious reasons, which should be stated in the judgment. The expert had reported that,

> 'whether Mr Grech's cervical disc herniation became worse after the therapy cannot be objectively established in the absence of an MRI scan of the cervical spine before and after the treatment. He was suffering from intense pain before and after the therapy. Mr Grech, however, alleges that the symptoms were much worse immediately after the first manipulation of the neck'.

55 Although the court agreed with the first instance court's assessment that the defendant was wrong not to insist on seeing the X-ray results before commencing treatment, and that he should not have accepted the plaintiff's statement that these had revealed nothing wrong, this does not amount to proof that the treatment had caused the harm. There was no objective evidence to refute the expert's conclusion that the causal link 'cannot be objectively established'. The fact that the plaintiff was already in severe pain and that the radiography showed that there was already a loss of the normal curvature before he visited the defendant point to a strong possibility that the plaintiff was suffering from a severe disability even before the treatment.

56 The court observed further that the plaintiff had failed to file a copy of the X-rays in the records of the case. Hence, there is no evidence that, had the defendant seen the radiography results, he would have chosen a different method of treatment. In any case, the medical expert had observed that, in such situations, X-rays are not conclusive, in the sense that, notwithstanding the pathology, X-rays can still look normal; confirmation of the diagnosis can only be objectively established by an MRI scan of the neck.

57 Given all the circumstances of the case, the Court of Appeal held that it could not put aside the opinion of its own expert who had quite clearly reported that there is no reliable evidence to show a connection between the treatment given by the defendant and the damage suffered by the plaintiff. Hence the court upheld the defendant's appeal.

c) Commentary

58 Without the basic element of evidence showing a causal link between the defendant's acts or omissions and the harm, the action was bound to fail. In a case such as

this one, the evidence of the medical expert is of paramount importance. In civil proceedings in Malta, it is possible for the parties to submit *ex parte* expert reports even when experts have been appointed by the court. The court may appoint expert referees of its own motion or it may do so on the request of the parties or of one of them. However, the court is not bound to adopt the report of the referees against its own convictions.

In this case, the first instance court in effect rejected the conclusions of its own 59 expert. Although it was entitled to do so, the reason given therefor – namely, that the defendant had not consulted the radiography results before deciding on treatment – was deemed insufficient by the Court of Appeal and not conclusive for proving liability. At the same time, the Court of Appeal did not state that the report of a court-appointed expert should necessarily always prevail over the opinion of an *ex parte* expert witness. In fact, the Court of Appeal gave due weight also to the opinion of the plaintiff's neurologist, but considered it insufficient to prove the plaintiff's case. Significantly, in his testimony the neurologist had not in any way contradicted what the court-appointed expert had reported; he only said that chiropractic treatment was contraindicated in the plaintiff's case.

4. *Louis Cassar Pullicino on behalf of others v Director of Psychiatric Services and others*, Court of Appeal, Second Chamber, 15 November 2023, Writ no 12/1993: Medical Malpractice

a) Brief Summary of the Facts

After a suicide attempt while on holiday in Malta, the plaintiffs' wife and mother 60 was admitted for treatment to the general hospital. After her physical condition improved, she was transferred to the mental health hospital later that day. The patient's husband, who accompanied her to hospital, explained to the hospital authorities that she suffered from paranoid schizophrenia with a history of violent episodes, and had previously been hospitalised in the Netherlands, where they lived. He further explained that she was still undergoing psychiatric treatment in the Netherlands and was administered a dose of Fluanxol, a drug used in the treatment of schizophrenia, every two weeks.

On admission at the local mental hospital, she was again examined by a senior 61 house officer and appeared calm and co-operative, showing no signs of depression or psychosis. Indeed, she told the house officer 'I have no suicidal wishes; I want to see my only child grow'.

62 The dose of Fluanxol regularly administered to the patient in the Netherlands was relatively low; for this reason, her condition was not deemed to be serious. Moreover, since she had overdosed on pills, and less than fifteen days had lapsed since she had received the last dose of Fluanxol in the Netherlands, it was decided to wait until blood test results were available before administering a new dose. She was placed under general collective supervision – two or three nurses for between four and eight patients – with freedom of movement and not under constant watch.

63 A few hours after admission, and some 30 minutes after her husband left her side, during which time she had not manifested any deterioration in her mental state, the patient was allowed to go to the bathroom, where, according to normal practice, she would be unsupervised. In fact, she had not gone to the bathroom but to an adjacent room where she committed suicide by hanging herself using her belt.

64 Alleging that, in view of her mental condition, the patient ought not to have been left unsupervised, the plaintiffs sued the hospital authorities and also the senior house officer blaming them for her death. All defendants disclaimed liability.

b) Judgment of the Court

65 The first instance court appointed an independent psychiatric expert, who reported that the hospital authorities had correctly followed standard procedure and there was no evidence of negligence. The decision to postpone treatment by Fluanxol until blood tests were available was justified in view of the fact it was necessary first to determine whether there might be any adverse reaction with the pills on which the patient had overdosed. Moreover, even if Fluanxol had been administered immediately on admission, its effects would not have been felt until days later and certainly not by the time of the patient's suicide. Furthermore, even if the patient had been under constant supervision, she would still have been unsupervised in the bathroom to respect her dignity.

66 Adopting the expert's report, the court dismissed the plaintiffs' claims.

67 The plaintiffs appealed, claiming that in view of the patient's medical history and her latest suicide attempt a few hours before, the house officer's decision to rely on her verbal assurances and not to place her under constant watch was wrong and had facilitated the suicide.

68 The Court of Appeal agreed with the appellants that the events showed that the senior house officer's conclusion that the patient did not pose a danger to herself was erroneous. Moreover, the decision to allow her to retain her outdoor clothes, particularly the belt with which she had hanged herself, was not prudent.

However, this of itself was not sufficient to attach liability: errors of diagnosis after a clinical examination are not *ipso facto* equivalent to fault. It is for the plaintiff to show that the error of judgement was due to a failure to exercise proper care with the diligence expected of a competent practitioner. The court stressed that the standard of care was measured against an objective criterion, namely that of a 'normal' practitioner having the expected degree of skill and exercising the care required in the proper exercise of his profession.

Applying these principles to the present case, the court concluded that it had 69 not been shown that the house officer's judgement was the result of negligence or lack of proper skill. The fact that in the time between admission and the suicide the patient had not manifested any erratic behaviour, and also that her husband, who was familiar with her behaviour when leading to acute episodes, had not noted any alarming signs until he left her only 30 minutes before the event, showed that the decision not to place her under constant watch, although wrong in this case, was not unreasonable.

The court therefore dismissed the appeal insofar as it concerned the liability 70 of the house officer.

Turning then to the question of liability of the hospital authorities, the court 71 observed that the appeal centred on two points, namely (i) *culpa in eligendo* of the hospital authorities in selecting the nursing staff and (ii) lack of measures to ensure the safety of patients.

The first complaint concerned the failure of the duty nurse (i) to remove all 72 potential instruments for suicide, in particular the patient's belt, and (ii) to ascertain that the patient did indeed go to the bathroom after declaring her intention to do so.

The court observed that the 'record of patient's valuables on admission' 73 showed that the nurse had searched the patient for potentially dangerous objects which, according to usual practice, comprised 'hard, pointed objects, arms, drugs'. The decision to allow the patient to retain her belt had been taken not by the nurse but by the senior house officer who, for the reasons given above, had already been absolved of blame. Likewise, the decision not to place the patient under constant watch and to allow her freedom of movement had also been taken by the senior house officer.

There was therefore no reason to conclude that the nurse had not acted pro- 74 fessionally and that the hospital authorities had been at fault in selecting her for the duties of her office.

The Court of Appeal, however, observed that the measures in place to ensure 75 the patient's safety and to eliminate foreseeable risks were not adequate. In particular, access by patients to the room where the suicide took place – a sluice room or 'dirty utility' room – ought to have been permanently blocked since that room was intended for use by hospital staff not by patients. That should have been the case particularly in a ward where the patients were not under constant watch. The room contained an attachment just over two metres above the ground from which it was easy for the patient to hang the belt. Access to this room greatly facilitated the suicide.

76 The court observed that the contractual relationship between the hospital and patient made it incumbent upon the hospital not only to provide medical care but also to do so in an environment which eliminated foreseeable risks. In the present case, the hospital had signally failed in this duty.

77 Finally, the court observed that the plaintiffs had failed to provide reliable evidence of material loss, whether loss of earnings or expenses incurred. The only evidence produced was the husband's sworn statement wherein he stated that his wife was a housewife and a casual teacher earning approximately f (= Florins, Dutch Guilders) 10,000 (approx € 5,000) per annum. Moreover, he had to send his minor son to a day care centre for 26 months at a cost of f 23,000 (approx € 11,500). However, this was not supported by documentary evidence – such as payslips and receipts – and could not therefore be deemed to satisfy the best evidence rule. The court acknowledged that unpaid housework also had economic value, but some objective criterion against which it could be measured – such as evidence of the national minimum wage in the Netherlands – had to be provided to enable it to reach an assessment, and this was not made available by the plaintiffs.

78 The Court of Appeal, therefore, overturned the first instance judgment only insofar as it had exonerated the hospital authorities, but it did not award damages.

c) Commentary

79 This unfortunate case could indeed have gone either way insofar as the liability of the house officer is concerned; indeed, the reasoning exculpating the officer is not entirely convincing since prudence surely required that a suicidal patient ought not to have been allowed to retain her belt even though at the time she appeared calm and co-operative.

80 In any case, this judgment is noteworthy only because the court articulated in detail the principles governing liability for medical malpractice. In particular the court reaffirmed the position adopted in more recent cases that the relationship between the patient, on the one hand, and the hospital authorities and the attending medical practitioner, on the other, is contractual in nature, although it did also consider the possibility of liability for *culpa in eligendo*, which is not really relevant in a contractual relationship.

Of interest also is the comment concerning the economic value of housework, although the view that it is equivalent to the minimum wage may be questioned. Also of interest is the comment that, had the relative evidence been provided, the court would have been prepared to rely on the minimum wage criterion of the patient's country of residence rather than on the court's own national criterion. 81

5. Personal Injury

In general – with one notable exception which was, however, overturned on appeal – judgments on personal injury consolidated the trends of earlier years, albeit with some inconsistencies. 82

Thus, on the matter of when interest starts to run, in *Anthony Rapa and another v Anthony Chircop and another* (Court of Appeal, 25 January 2023), a fatality as a result of a traffic accident, in *Silvio Frendo and another v Rudolph Gatt* (Court of Appeal, 10 October 2023), a traffic accident case, in *Fleur Debono v Shanylee Reed and others* (Court of Appeal, 15 November 2023), another traffic accident case, and in *Antoine Spiteri v Mario Vella and another* (Court of Appeal 15 November 2023), a case of injuries due to assault, interest was to run from the date of the first judgment. 83

On the other hand, in *Samuel Leone Ciantar v Fahrenheit Freight Forwarders Co Ltd* (Court of Appeal, 12 July 2023), an industrial accident case, and in *Michael Sammut v Johan Dimech and another* (Court of Appeal, 25 October 2023), a case of injuries due to assault, interest was to run only from the date of the appeal judgment. One would have expected a more victim-friendly approach in the latter case where the harm was due to *dolus* rather than to mere negligence. 84

Surprisingly, in *Atlas Insurance PCC Ltd v GasanMamo Insurance Ltd* (Court of Appeal, 27 April 2023), *GO plc v Angelo Schembri and another* (Court of Appeal, 31 May 2023) and *GO plc v Schembri Infrastructures Ltd and others* (Court of Appeal, 5 October 2023), all cases of damage to property, interest was to run from the date of the filing of the judicial act commencing proceedings. It would appear therefore that, insofar as the running of interest is concerned, the defendant-debtor is treated more leniently – and the victim less favourably – in personal injury cases than in cases of damage to property. 85

Interestingly, in the *Atlas Insurance* case, the Court of Appeal adopted the principle that *lite contestata usuræ currunt*, rather than the arguably less correct *in illiquidis non fit mora* principle, which is usually followed. 86

On the matter of assessment of damages, the courts continue to apply the usual age-based multiplier and lump-sum deduction methods based respectively 87 on the degree of the victim's disability as assessed by medical experts and lapse of time between the accident and the date of judgment.

88 One notable exception is the first instance judgment in *Trevor Grech v Lawrence Agius* (Court of Appeal, 15 June 2023). The court expressly stated that in assessing the amount of damages, it will not rely on the experts' reports but rather on the difference in the victim's income before and after the incident. Deliberately departing from the traditional method of assessing loss of future earnings, it awarded a sum of € 635,713 by way of damages. No deduction was made to account for the fact that a lump sum was being awarded: the court did not consider that this would be justified in the present economic environment in view of the negligible interest paid on bank deposits. It also awarded *arbitrio boni viri* a further sum of € 30,000 for future expenses that may become necessary as a result of the accident. The Court of Appeal, however, reversed the judgment and re-assessed the damages on the basis of the traditional criteria, namely the degree of disability as assessed by experts, the victim's age at the time of the accident, and his pre-accident gross earnings taking future inflation into account. The damages for loss of earnings were therefore reduced to £ 256,024 after deducting 2 % on account of the lump-sum payment. Interest was to run from the date of the first judgment. The award of £ 30,000 for future expenses was confirmed.

C. Literature

1. *Amy Saliba*, Establishing a Duty of Care in Maltese Tort Law and Jurisprudence – A Critical and Comparative Analysis (Dissertation, University of Malta 2021)

89 The writer starts with an analysis of the common law requirement of duty of care in finding liability for negligence. The key concepts are analysed, with particular reference to specific tests which have arisen in order to determine when a duty is owed in one case but not in another.

90 The writer then moves to Maltese tort law, and examines whether the concept has been viably integrated in Maltese law, which is not based on a system of nominate torts but rather relies on general provisions establishing liability for *culpa.*

91 Finally, the writer questions the potential role which the duty of care has within Maltese tort law and jurisprudence, and whether the national interpretation reflects the common law understanding, reaching the conclusion that, although the duty of care holds fundamental importance within the common law world, this may not necessarily be the case under Maltese law.

2. *Katrina Maya Jo Borg Ferrando*, Pre-Implantation Genetic Diagnosis in Malta: New Legal Challenges within the Realm of Medical Liability (Dissertation, University of Malta 2021)

Pre-implantation genetic diagnosis is a rapidly evolving area of medicine within the field of medically assisted procreation, which provides prospective parents with information about their expected child to avoid having a child with a genetic abnormality, especially when one or both parents are carriers of a monogenic condition themselves. As a result, courts have been called upon to adjudicate a wide range of conflicts emerging from reproductive genetics, one of which being the liability of a medical professional working within the field of genetic testing. In other legal systems, an area of tort law which has originated from such practices is commonly referred to as prenatal tort, in which the child or parents themselves allege that, had it not been for the negligence of the medical practitioner, their child would not have been born in a world full of pain and suffering. Claims of this nature give rise to a range of ethical and legal conflicts, which have yet to be faced by Maltese courts. 92

3. *James Vella*, Attributing Legal Personality to Artificial Intelligence: A Possible Solution? (Dissertation, University of Malta 2021)

This dissertation seeks to determine the possibility of vesting artificially intelligent (AI) entities with legal personality, and its adequacy as a means of regulating the technology. 93

The first chapter serves to introduce the subject by discussing artificial intelligence and its rapid development, with particular emphasis on its disruptive nature. This is supplemented by a number of case studies to highlight the need for legislation dealing with AI. Furthermore, a section of the chapter is dedicated to developing a proper definition of AI for the purposes of its legal regulation. 94

The second chapter introduces the challenges posed by AI to existing legal principles, with particular emphasis being placed on what is referred to as the 'responsibility gap' caused by AI. In carrying out this exercise, a number of possible liability regimes that have been suggested by several authors are explored. The purpose of this exercise is to show the inadequacy of these legal frameworks whilst laying the foundation for a discussion on vesting legal personality to AI in the remaining chapters. 95

96 The next chapter introduces the concept of legal personality with the aim of discussing whether AI can be vested with such personality. The fourth chapter considers a number of arguments in favour of and against the approach of vesting AI with legal personality. The following chapter centres around practical challenges relating to its implementation and any possible solutions to such concerns.

97 Finally, the writer provides his own views on whether AI should be vested with legal personality on the basis of a cost-benefit analysis of implementing such an approach.

Emanuel GD van Dongen and Anne LM Keirse

XX. The Netherlands

A. Legislation

1. Representative Consumer Claims: Wet van 2 november 2022 tot wijziging van Boek 3 van het Burgerlijk Wetboek en het Wetboek van Burgerlijke Rechtsvordering in verband met de omzetting van Richtlijn (EU) 2020/1828 van het Europees Parlement en de Raad van 25 november 2020 betreffende representatieve vorderingen ter bescherming van de collectieve belangen van consumenten en tot intrekking van Richtlijn 2009/22/EG (PbEU 2020, L 409) (Implementatiewet richtlijn representatieve vorderingen voor consumenten, Stb 2022, 459) [Directive (EU) 2020/1828 of the European Parliament and of the Council of 25 November 2020 on representative actions for the protection of the collective interests of consumers and repealing Directive 2009/22/EC]

As mentioned in the previous Yearbook, this Act sets out rules for the implementation of Directive (EU) 2020/1828, allowing citizens across the EU to bring a (cross-border) collective action for consumer harm (as consumers of goods, passengers or patients). The implementation of this Directive in Dutch law resulted in a number of changes to the Redress of Mass Damage in a Collective Action Act (*Wet afwikkeling massaschade in collectieve actie*, WAMCA) now approved.[1] As discussed in previous Yearbooks, the WAMCA, which provides a legal basis for collective dam- 1

Note: Dr Emanuel GD van Dongen and Prof Dr Anne LM Keirse are Associate Professor and (part -time) Professor at the Molengraaff Institute, Utrecht University, and researchers at the Utrecht Centre for Accountability and Liability Law. Anne Keirse is also a judge at the Court of Appeal, Amsterdam, and Emanuel van Dongen a deputy judge at the Court of Appeal, Arnhem-Leeuwarden.

1 *EGD van Dongen/ALM Keirse*, The Netherlands, in: E Karner/BC Steininger (eds), European Tort Law (ETL) 2022 (2023) 437, no 1.

https://doi.org/10.1515/9783111376721-021

ages actions, entered into effect on 1 January 2020.[2] Subsequently, a number of amendments to some provisions of the WAMCA had to be made, since the harmonised law laid down in the Directive has supremacy over national law. The main changes concern the requirements for organisations in order to be qualified for collective actions in another Member State, as well as provisions on the admissibility of a cross-border collective action, eg with regard to the financing of organisations, and conditions set to the binding ties to a collective action under the Directive in the Netherlands of non-domiciled citizens. The legislator also applied some technical changes to the WAMCA, including the obligation to give notice under art 1018c(2) of the Code of Civil Procedure (*Wetboek van Burgerlijke Rechtsvordering*, Rv). As a result, it is no longer necessary to sign a copy of the summons in the register, only an extract is required.[3] The amended Law became effective on 25 June 2023.

2. Wetsvoorstel Wijziging van de Wet milieubeheer (implementatie richtlijn milieuaansprakelijkheid) [Legislative Proposal Amendment of the Environmental Management Act (Implementation of the Environmental Liability Directive)]

2 A discussion between the European Commission and the Dutch government regarding the (un)just implementation of art 12(1) of Directive 2004/35/EC, the European Environmental Liability Directive, has given rise to this bill, which proposes an amendment to art 17.15 of the Dutch Environmental Management Act and the insertion of a new art 20.2 in this Act. After being issued a notice of default by the European Commission due to the incomplete implementation of art 12 (1) of the Environmental Liability Directive, the Dutch government has taken the position that, from a legal perspective, the Directive has been fully implemented. The European Commission has noted that although this position may not be incorrect, parts of the Dutch legislation require further interpretation. The proposed amendment to art 17.15 of the Environmental Management Act clarifies the circle of persons who can request the competent authority to take measures in the event of (threatening) environmental damage. The new art 20.2 of the Environmen-

---

2 See *EGD van Dongen/ALM Keirse*, The Netherlands, in: E Karner/BC Steininger (eds), European Tort Law (ETL) 2019 (2020) 409, no 2; *EGD van Dongen/ALM Keirse*, The Netherlands, in: E Karner/BC Steininger (eds), European Tort Law (ETL) 2020 (2021) 429, nos 2 and 47.
3 Information taken from *van Dongen/Keirse* (fn 1) no 1.

tal Management Act provides an additional appeal option for those who are at risk of suffering environmental damage, so as to prevent them for not being received in their appeal as non-interested parties. Interested parties can already appeal to the administrative court under art 8:1 of the General Administrative Law Act. In alignment with art 12(1) of the European Environmental Liability Directive, this bill ensures that appeals are taken into consideration also from those individuals who may suffer environmental damage but are not directly involved and are considered to be interested parties.

B. Cases

1. Hoge Raad (Supreme Court, HR) 20 January 2023, ECLI:NL:HR:2023:62: Acquisition of Ownership of Land by a Possessor in Bad Faith on the Basis of Prescription (*Land Grabbing II*)

a) Brief Summary of the Facts

In 1991, an individual purchased a plot of land with a house in a vacation park that 3
was still undergoing development. During this period, the demarcation of property lines was not clearly defined, leading to discussions with the broker. Although the matter was eventually clarified in May 1993, the owner planted conifers in a curved hedge that extended beyond the actual boundary lines. It was later revealed that this encroachment amounted to an excess of 46 square metres of land. In 2000, a new owner bought the adjacent land and, upon his request, a border line of demarcation was conducted in 2014. This disclosed that the position of the boundary lines was different from the position of the conifer hedge.

The individual who planted the hedge and had taken possession of the addi- 4
tional land over the years argued that the twenty-year prescription period for the owner's right to challenge his possession expired. Consequently, having maintained possession, he had become the legal owner from 20 years after the initial acquisition in 1991 onwards. So, he claimed ownership of the land that had been encroached upon. The neighbour contended that the possessor ('land grabber') acted unlawfully, taking and maintaining possession of the land in bad faith. As a remedy, the neighbour claimed, as compensation in kind, the transfer and delivery of the strip into ownership. This claim was granted by the court of first instance as well as by the Court of Appeal. By doing so, both referred to a for-

mer judgment of the *Hoge Raad*, that was quite sensational and was discussed at the Annual Conference on European Tort Law in 2018.[4]

b) Judgment of the Court

5 The neighbour seeks a declaratory judgment asserting that the hedge planter acted unlawfully by initially taking possession and subsequently maintaining control of the strip of land in bad faith for all those years. The request also includes an order to compel him to provide compensation in kind by transferring the property of the strip.

6 Article 3:105 *Burgerlijk Wetboek* (Dutch Civil Code, DCC) states that the person who holds property in possession at the moment when the 20-year prescription period of the right of action of the owner to terminate this possession expires, acquires the property even if his possession was not in good faith. The rationale is that, at some point in time, the legal situation must be in line with the factual situation. This improves legal certainty. This means that the landgrabber became the owner of the grabbed land. A long time, it was widely assumed that a liability procedure based on tort against a landgrabber would be time-barred at the same time as the claim for restitution of the land and thus after 20 years following the grabbing of the land.

7 But no, it turns out that, after losing ownership of the property and the expiry of the prescription period, the legal race is not over yet. For the *Hoge Raad* found in a ground-breaking decision in 2017, in the case *Land Grabbing I*, that 20 years after the grabbing of the property, a new claim can emerge: a tort claim with a new prescription period, lasting a minimum of five years and a maximum of 20 years. [5] A party that takes something into possession and holds it, while knowing that another person rightfully owns it, is acting unlawfully towards this other person – the (previous) owner. This previous owner who has lost his property due to prescription can claim damages from the possessor, being the new owner. And since he can ask for compensation in kind, the transfer of the property can be ordered and the property has to be returned. For this claim, a new prescription period starts running: five years following the awareness of the loss of ownership or

4 HR 24 February 2017, ECLI:NL:HR:2017:309. See *ALM Keirse/T Bouwman*, The Netherlands, in: E Karner/BC Steininger (eds), European Tort Law (ETL) 2017 (2018) 412, no 10 ff; *ALM Keirse*, Land grabbing as a tort; balancing legal certainty with justice in individual cases, blog at <http://blog.ucall.nl/index.php/2018/04/land-grabbing-as-a-tort-balancing-legal-certainty-with-justice-in-individual-cases/>.

5 HR 24 February 2017, ECLI:NL:HR:2017:309. See on this case, *Keirse/Bouwman* (fn 4) no 10 ff.

20 years after the loss of ownership (and thus adding up to a maximum of 40 years after the initial loss of possession).

This judgment is repeated in this case. The aim of *Land Grabbing II* was to 8
challenge *Land Grabbing I,* but it ended in a confirmation of this unexpected turn. Consequently, after losing ownership of the property, a new claim arises, ie a tort claim. A new prescription period then begins, lasting at least five years and a maximum of 20 years (pursuant to art 3:310 subsec 1 DCC). According to the *Hoge Raad,* in this scenario, the subjective five-year prescription period of the tort claim (based on art 6:162 DCC) commences the moment the neighbour became aware of the loss of his ownership. In any case the claim prescribes 20 years after the possessor acquires ownership, by means of acquisitive prescription. Neither terms had passed at the moment the neighbour brought his claim.

Thus, the prescription of the right of action to terminate possession may have 9
expired, but the same is not true for the prescription of the right of action to claim damages for losing ownership.[6] Dutch law recognises indemnification in kind (pursuant to art 6:103 DCC) as a form of damages. Thus, the transfer of ownership of the disputed lot may be claimed, as the Court decided in this case. Consequently, the lot must be returned to its original owner (who, incidentally, are different neighbours at the moment of the procedure in cassation, as the new neighbours only moved in in 2000).

c) Commentary

In cassation, an attempt was made to have the *Hoge Raad* reconsider its case law,[7] 10
especially considering the substantial amount of criticism raised against the controversial judgment. The unexpected turn in 2017 raised eyebrows in legal circles. Prevailing literature and case law had not anticipated such an equitable resolution. It was believed that a claim for damages prescribes no later than the reclaiming of possession itself, which is the principal obligation.[8] The *Hoge Raad* introduced this novel insight in 2017 as an *obiter dictum.*[9] The most far-reaching complaint in cassation entails that the turn of the Supreme Court in *Land Grabbing I* was not well thought through, was claimed to be unjust and puts the Netherlands

6 Based on *Keirse,* Land grabbing as a tort (fn 4) 16 April 2018.

7 HR 24 February 2017, ECLI:NL:HR:2017:309.

8 See, amongst many others, *JE Jansen,* Schadevergoeding uit onrechtmatige daad na verkrijging door artikel 3:105 BW, RM Themis 2018–1, 8 f.

9 *Keirse* (fn 4) <http://blog.ucall.nl/index.php/2018/04/land-grabbing-as-a-tort-balancing-legal-certainty-with-justice-in-individual-cases/>.

in a unique position because in no other country that accepts the shift of ownership due to prescription, is it assumed that the landgrabber is liable in any way. And even the Grand Chamber of the European Court of Human Rights ruled in the *Pye* judgment that losing property due to prescription is not in itself an infringement of art 1 First Protocol to the European Convention for the Protection of Human Rights and Fundamental Freedoms.

11 In the current 2023 judgment, the *Hoge Raad* dismissed the complaints and saw no compelling reason to overturn its previous stance, instead it was upheld. The decision is based on legal policy. The rulings, both from 2017 and 2023, have been severely criticised, but others have applauded the rulings, pointing out the fairness of the outcome and the chastising of unlawful landgrabbing. We concur with the latter. Sure, the plaintiff failed to file an action on the claim for restitution of possession during the running of the first term of 20 years. But first of all this was due to the surreptitious behaviour of the landgrabber and more importantly the plaintiff was still in time for filing an action on the claim for losing ownership. So, besides moral grounds that can be put forward, we acknowledge a legal justification to support the outcome by distinguishing two tort claims, one reclaiming possession and another reclaiming ownership, each of them giving rise to two separate prescription periods.

12 This case law and the discussions it has invoked illustrate the struggle of finding a good balance between legal certainty, on the one hand, and justice in individual cases, on the other hand. We believe that the current balancing act of the *Hoge Raad* strengthens the trust and credibility of the legal system and its fairness, but we realise that others may have another standpoint.[10]

2. HR 17 March 2023, ECLI:NL:HR:2023:428: Liability of a Pension Advisor towards the Insured Third Party (*Employee/Employer and Pension Advisor*)

a) Brief Summary of the Facts

13 An employer makes a commitment to an employee to provide that the agreed-upon pension would involve a final salary scheme (*eindloonregeling*). However, the pension advisor engaged by the employer establishes a target money scheme (*streefgeldregeling*) for the employee. As a consequence, upon his retirement, the

10 See amongst others: *E van Wechem/J Rinkes*, Kroniek van het vermogensrecht, Nederlands Juristenblad (NJB) 2023/1076, 11.

employee receives a significantly lower amount than expected, resulting in a damages claim. The employee seeks to hold the pension advisor responsible for this, filing a claim based on tort, since there is no direct contractual relationship between the employee and the pension advisor. Initially, the legal action involves two claims: the employee holds both the employer and the pension advisor accountable. However, the Court of Appeal determines that, in order to establish unlawful conduct towards the employee, more than a breach of contract by the pension advisor towards the employer is required.

b) Judgment of the Court

In cassation, the main appeal revolves around the question under what circumstances the pension advisor is liable for conduct which causes harm to third parties. 14

The *Hoge Raad* rules that if the interests of the third party, in this case the employee, are so closely involved in the proper execution of the agreement that the third party can suffer damage or other disadvantages if a contractor fails in that execution, the standards of unwritten law pertaining to proper social conduct imply that the contractor must also adjust their behaviour according to those interests. When answering the question in a concrete case whether the standards of unwritten law pertaining to proper social conduct entail such consideration of the interests of a third party, the judge will have to take the relevant circumstances of the case into account in their assessment.[11] The facts established by the court in this case show that the employee's interests were so closely connected to the work performed by the pension advisor that the pension advisor had to observe his duty of care towards both the employer and the employee. The contractual task of the pension advisor, in relation to the employer, was to give advice on a supplementary pension for the employee. Failure to fulfil the duty of care is therefore in general also unlawful to the employee.[12] 15

The finding of the court of appeal that the employee had not made sufficient statements to conclude that the pension advisor had acted unlawfully did not hold up before the *Hoge Raad*. The pension advisor's duty of care implies, among other things, that his efforts should be aimed at ensuring a pension that is as close as possible to the agreements between the employer and the employee. Furthermore, the pension advisor was also accused of having failed to fulfil his duty to inform. 16

---

11 Cf HR 24 September 2004, ECLI:NL:HR:2004:AO9069.

12 Cf HR 22 September 2017, ECLI:NL:HR:2017:2444.

Against this background, the *Hoge Raad* ruled that the judgment of the court of appeal was not understandable.

17 The Court of Appeal had dismissed the claims, stating uncertainty about the existence of damage, and refused to refer the case to a claims assessment procedure. However, the *Hoge Raad* deems that the uncertainty is insufficient to reject the claims. With reference to its previous ruling, the *Hoge Raad* considers that, in order to grant a claim for compensation for damage to be assessed in a claims assessment procedure, it is sufficient that the possibility that damage has been or will be suffered is plausible, which does not mean that it is plausible that any damage has been suffered. Because the possibility of damage was left open, the Court of Appeal should not have based its rejection of the claim on its opinion that it is uncertain whether the employee suffered damage. Consequently, the *Hoge Raad* sets aside the judgment of the Court of Appeal and refers the case to another Court of Appeal for further proceedings.

c) Commentary

18 If it is impossible or difficult to determine the precise amount of loss, or if the claimant does not provide enough information to do so, it does not mean that the damages claim can be dismissed. This follows from the general rule that the court must assess the damage in a manner most appropriate to its nature and estimate the extent of the damage in case it cannot be determined precisely. Dismissing a claim for damages on the ground that the claimant's propositions are ambiguous as to the extent of the damage is not justified.[13]

19 If an event, such as a breach of contract or a tortious act, results in liability, the subsequent inquiry involves determining whether damage has occurred and to what extent. If the proceedings do not sufficiently clarify the presence or extent of damage, the judge cannot summarily dismiss the case. Instead, in such circumstances, the judge is obligated to investigate further. This may involve seeking input from experts, engaging parties, or estimating the extent of the damage. Alternatively, the judge may opt to refer the case to the damages assessment procedure, either on their own initiative or upon request. They may also declare that an unlawful act has occurred if such a declaration in law was demanded by the claimant. The judge cannot dismiss the referral to the damages assessment procedure, as in this case, by arguing that it is not yet certain that damage has been suffered. The *Hoge Raad*

13 HR 10 December 2021, ECLI:HR:2021:1842; see *EGD van Dongen/ALM Keirse*, The Netherlands, in: E Karner/BC Steininger (eds) ETL 2021 (2022) 408, no 54 ff.

asserts that, to grant a claim for compensation for damage, it is sufficient that the possibility that damage has been or will be suffered is plausible. It is not required that it is plausible that any damage has (already) been suffered.

This case further highlights that a contractor may also have a duty of care towards a third party when carrying out an assignment if the interests of that third party are so closely connected to the execution of the assignment that the third party may suffer damage as the result of the inadequate execution by the contractor. For a considerable period of time, it was established that contractual duties of care pertain to parties to the contract. Nevertheless, there is a discernible trend towards an expansion of the duties of care beyond them, encompassing obligations towards third parties. The *Hoge Raad* previously ruled on this matter, and the present judgment reaffirms that a contractor, while undertaking a task, may also bear a duty of care towards a third party if its interests are intricately linked to the task's execution, potentially leading to harm if the contractor fails in a proper execution. It is noteworthy that in this instance, the error made by the pension advisor predates the enactment of the Financial Services Act (*Wet financiële dienstverlening*) and the Financial Supervision Act (*Wet op het financieel toezicht*). According to these laws, a direct duty of care towards the employee has to be presumed on the part of the pension advisor.[14] 20

3. HR 28 March 2023, ECLI:NL:HR:2023:485: Shock Damages (*Cook's knife*)

a) Brief Summary of the Facts

The current procedure pertains to a criminal case in which the accused is charged with taking someone's life by stabbing the victim in the chest with a knife. A witness to the manslaughter joined the proceedings claiming compensation for shock damage but had no relationship with the victim, being a 'good acquaintance', both living in a small village. The court of first instance and the Court of Appeal rejected the claim, stating that the witness was not a victim within the meaning of art 51 of the Code of Criminal Procedure (*Wetboek van Strafvordering*, Sv) and did not have a particularly close emotional relationship with the victim. 21

14 Snijders, conclusion in ECLI:NL:PHR:2022:703.

b) Judgment of the Court

22 The legal question was whether a relationship between the victims (primary and secondary) is required to award shock damages. The *Hoge Raad* ruled that it is not. It ruled, referring to its decision on 22 February 2002,[15] that a person who kills or injures another by a wrongful act may also act unlawfully towards a person to whom the confrontation with that act or its consequences causes severe emotional shock (the secondary victim). Whether compensation of such secondary victim is justified depends on a weighing of the circumstances of the case. Points of view that play a role in this assessment are: (a) the nature, the circumstances and the consequences of the unlawful act committed against the primary victim, including the intention of the perpetrator and the nature and severity of the inflicted suffering; (b) the manner in which the secondary victim is confronted with the unlawful act committed against the primary victim and its consequences; and (c) the nature and closeness of the relationship between the primary and the secondary victim (in this regard, in the absence of a close relationship, unlawfulness cannot be readily assumed).[16] The court must assess the (un)lawfulness towards the secondary victim on a case-by-case basis, taking into account, inter alia, these points of view in their interrelationship, without giving *a priori* decisive importance to any of them. If one of these points of view does not provide a clear indication to assume unlawfulness, unlawfulness may nevertheless be assumed if the relevant circumstances, from other points of view, are sufficiently substantial.[17]

23 In its clarification in the current decision of 2023, the *Hoge Raad* emphasises that it is not mandatory to satisfy all three criteria. Therefore, if one of the three criteria is not met during the assessment, it does not automatically preclude the possibility to award compensation for shock damage. Contrary to the Court of Appeal's decision, which rejected the claim on the grounds that the witness lacked a relationship with the primary victim and, therefore, lacked intimacy and a relevant nature of the relationship, the *Hoge Raad* overturns this ruling. The *Hoge Raad* does not explicitly assert that compensation is warranted or should be granted but reiterates that the specific circumstances of the case play a crucial role in determining whether shock damage can be compensated. It underscores the necessity to thoroughly examine the details of the incident. While the three criteria remain important, their relative weight may differ from case to case and it is up to an overall assessment. The judge must weigh these circumstances and is given the

15 HR 22 February 2002, HR:2002:AD5356.
16 HR 28 June 2022, ECLI:NL:HR:2022:958; see ETL 2022, *van Dongen/Keirse* (fn 1) no 38 ff.
17 Ibid.

necessary freedom in doing so. Unlawfulness is less likely to be assumed if there is no close relationship with the primary victim or if the secondary victim had to be professionally aware of such a shocking event. However, it is not ruled out.

c) Commentary

This ruling is a reaffirmation of the existing case law. It was already decided by the Amsterdam Court of Appeal in 2022[18] and by the *Hoge Raad* in the same year,[19] that a confrontation with the crime in one way or another is deemed to be imperative but does not necessarily need to involve a direct and immediate confrontation with the crime itself. Also witnessing the consequences of the event at a later stage (for example in the mortuary) could be included. In this case, the *Hoge Raad* articulates a similar perspective, not about the criterion of confrontation but about the criterion of (close) relationship. Both judgments illustrate how the points of view-approach operates in situations where the secondary victim's perspectives of confrontation and relationship do not strongly support a claim for compensation. 24

The right to shock damages is limited to the damage resulting from mental injury determined according to objective standards. The *Hoge Raad* ruled in 2022 that it must concern mental suffering that is serious in view of its nature, duration and/or consequences, and can be sufficiently objectified, not necessarily limited to recognised psychiatric disorders but always diagnosed by an appropriately qualified and competent expert, such as a general practitioner, a psychiatrist or psychologist. If such mental injury is established, both material and immaterial damage caused by this injury are eligible for compensation. 25

4. HR 21 April 2023, ECLI:NL:HR:2023:653: Commencement of the Short Limitation Period (*Client/building consultant*)

a) Brief Summary of the Facts

In the spring of 2009, an agricultural company commissioned a structural design firm to provide an architectural design for the construction of a storage shed on its premises. In December 2009, the client then commissioned a building consultant to perform the static calculations for the design, among other things necessary to 26

18 Hof Amsterdam 31 May 2022, ECLI:NL:GHAMS:2022:1607.

19 HR 28 June 2022, ECLI:NL:HR:2022:958; see *van Dongen/Keirse* (fn 1) no 38 ff.

apply for a building permit. The calculations were submitted in February 2010. In June 2010, the client commissioned a contractor to build the shed, which was completed in September 2010. Subsequently, issues arose about the construction, presenting cracks and subsidence. To address the problems, the client engaged a research firm to investigate the matter, leading to a written report in December 2014. For this investigation, the structural consultant made new static calculations. In 2017, the client initiated legal proceedings against the architectural design office, alleging damage due to mistakes in the static calculations. The basis for the claim was art 6:76 DCC (liability for auxiliaries), asserting that the architectural design office is liable for its mistakes. However, in 2018, the court of first instance rejected the claim, stating that the construction consultant is not an auxiliary of the construction design office. In a letter dated 28 January 2019, the client's attorney held the construction consultant liable for the damage suffered due to static calculations errors made in 2010.

27 The court of first instance dismissed the claim as it was deemed to be prescribed. The Court of Appeal upheld this decision, pointing out that the client had contacted the structural consultant in 2012 due to subsidence, demonstrating awareness of the damage and identifying the person responsible. In 2012, the construction consultant reportedly downplayed or denied the existence of damage over the phone, asserting that some subsidence was normal. It is reasonable that the client could rely on this reassuring message. However, the situation changed in 2013, after issues with the shed escalated, manifesting in bulging walls and leaks. By 2013, no later than 1 January 2014, the client had sufficient certainty about the existence of damage and the liable party. Subsequently, the short five-year limitation period commenced, leading to the claim being time-barred on 28 January 2019.

b) Judgment of the Court

28 In cassation, the client challenged the prescription of the claim, asserting that they became sufficiently aware of damage resulting from deficient or wrongful acts of the person in question only after having read the architectural report in December 2014. In line with art 3:310 DCC, a subjective prescription period of five years begins the day after the plaintiff is aware of both damage and the liable person. According to established case law of the *Hoge Raad*, the awareness must be actual, while a mere presumption of a claim is insufficient. Furthermore, the prescription period under art 3:310 DCC only starts after the injured party becomes sufficiently certain, not necessarily absolutely certain, that their damage was caused by the

person deemed liable. Sufficient certainty is established depending on the circumstances of the case.[20]

The lack of knowledge or insight may mean that the injured party is still not sufficiently certain that their damage was caused by inadequate or faulty actions of the person held liable. In determining if the injured party obtained sufficient certainty, it may be crucial to consider whether the injured party, in its relationship with the sued person, had the right to rely on their expertise and had no reason (yet) to doubt the soundness of their work. Additionally, it may be of importance if the sued person mentioned different possible causes for the loss or damage, not within their sphere of risk, or otherwise reassured the injured party about their performance or about loss or damage to be expected.[21] The *Hoge Raad* also clarifies that courts, when invoking the statute of limitations, are not obligated to always check whether the injured party had knowledge and insight, in order to assess whether the performance delivered was sound. That is required only when the circumstances of the case and the arguments presented by the parties on these points give reason to do so. 29

In the present case, it was sufficiently certain that the other party had committed a fault. It became evident as early as in 2013, when the damage to the shed became increasingly apparent, that the contractor had failed. The fact that the client had engaged the building consultant himself to perform the calculations and that the building consultancy had already informed the client in 2012 that they were responsible for faulty strength calculations played a role in establishing this certainty. Consequently, the prescription period did not commence at a later date. Therefore, the appeal in cassation made by the injured party was unsuccessful. The damage incurred was a result of an error on the part of the contractor, but the injured party brought the case to trial too late. The argument put forth by the injured party, claiming an inability to bring a claim earlier due to an inability to assess the soundness, as the contractor asserted that the job was well done, did not hold up in Court. Since the injured party had obtained sufficient certainty that the damage was caused by the contractor's breach of contract but waited more than five years to bring his claim, it became time-barred. 30

---

20 Cf HR 9 October 2020, ECLI:NL:HR:2020:1603; HR 31 March 2017, ECLI:NL:HR:2017:552. See also van *Dongen/Keirse*, ETL 2020 (fn 2) 448 ff.

21 HR 9 October 2020, ECLI:NL:HR:2020:1603.

c) Commentary

31 Unfamiliarity with the legal assessment of facts and circumstances does not impede the commencement of the (subjective) short limitation period.[22] The question of whether one will win or lose a legal proceeding has no influence on the commencement period because one must abstract from the legal knowledge of the injured party, and a legal error is at the expense of the injured party. Even if the law changes over time, that will be at the expense of the injured party. However, an exception exists if a lack of legal knowledge prevents the injured party from understanding that the other party failed to fulfil its obligations. For the limitation period to start running, the injured party must have had a genuine possibility to bring a claim. The injured party can, of course, only file a claim when they are sufficiently certain that the damage was caused by someone's mistake. If an injured party cannot assess that another party made a mistake, they cannot file a claim. It must understand well enough that the counterparty has failed. This is the key issue of the current judgment, very much like the 2020 judgment, which we discussed in the Yearbook 2020.[23]

32 The starting date of the short limitation period depends on the knowledge and insight required to assess the soundness of the performance delivered. Therefore, the injured party must know whether a performance is (un)acceptable. The absence of knowledge or insight (in order to assess soundness) can mean that the injured party does not have sufficient certainty that the damage was caused by a mistake of another, and then the term does not commence yet. Trust in the expertise of the advisor and reassuring statements about other causes are relevant in this regard. There is no extensive duty of investigation on the part of the injured party, but under certain circumstances it may not be permissible to entirely rely on reassuring words from a building consultant.

33 The present case leaves a bitter taste for the injured party, given that the lawyer's notice of interruption of the prescription period arrived less than a month too late, delaying the procedure preceding the trial in a situation where potentially responsible parties were pointing fingers at each other. On the other hand, it is advisable to carefully consider the exact relationships, especially given the time that elapses while, in hindsight, litigating against the wrong parties.

22 HR 26 November 2004, Nederlandse Jurisprudentie (NJ) 2006, 115.

23 *van Dongen/Keirse*, ETL 2020 (fn 2) nos 38–42.

5. HR 23 June 2023, ECLI:NL:HR:2023:956: Deduction of Benefits in the Event of Property Damage (*Evides/GKB*)

a) Brief Summary of the Facts

During dredging works in 2017, contractor GKB Realisatie B.V. (hereinafter: GKB) 34
damaged a water pipeline owned by Evides N.V. (hereinafter: Evides). The water pipeline, dating back to 1972, was laid approximately 60 cm below the water surface of a ditch. Initially, Evides repaired the pipeline temporarily, using an above-ground pipeline. Subsequently, in accordance with the rules of the water board not applicable at the time but now prescribed, Evides installed an entirely new, deeper underground pipeline (at a depth of 1.30 m from the bottom), using directional drilling. The drinking water company Evides claims damages from contractor GKB, which caused the damage, including a judgment for payment of the full restoration costs. The court of first instance ruled that GKB is liable and grants the claim in full. However, the Court of Appeal overturns the judgment insofar as it relates to the calculation of damages (and confirms the remaining part of the judgment). It accepts GKB's argument as to the allocation of benefits for Evides because the new water pipeline provides advantages for the drinking water company. The new pipeline now complies with the applicable regulations. It lies deeper in the ground, minimising the risk of future damage. The Court of Appeal considers this a (future) benefit for Evides. The Cout of Appeal therefore applies a 'new for old' deduction and deducts 30 % from the damage suffered.

b) Judgment of the Court

In appeal in cassation, Evides' lawyer argues that benefit allocation (*voordeelstoer-* 35
ekening) should not apply in cases of property damage. In the case of property damage, the court should abstract from the specific circumstances of the case and apply abstract compensation. This involves relying on repair costs determined by objective standards. Such compensation is granted irrespective of whether repairs are actually carried out and how they are conducted.

In the law of damages, the aim is to restore the injured party as much as pos- 36
sible to the position they would have been in had the damaging act not occurred. This requires a comparison of the current situation with the situation in which the injured party would have been without the breach of duty: a comparison of finan-

cial positions, taking into account all the circumstances of the case.[24] The difference must be compensated. Additionally, it is conceivable that the occurrence, alongside the damage, may also bring some benefit to the injured party.

37 The *Hoge Raad* refers to its 2016 decision, in which it ruled that there are two conceivable ways to incorporate a cost allocation in damage calculation: either by benefit allocation (art 6:100 DCC) or calculation of the extent of the damage (ie, in the context of damage calculation, art 6:95–97 DCC). Ultimately, when comparing the actual situation with the situation that (presumably) would have existed if the norm violation had not occurred, it must be assessed which disadvantages and advantages are so closely related to the event on which the tortfeasor's liability is based that they can reasonably be attributed to them as a consequence of the event.[25] Both advantages and disadvantages need to be identified and an assessment made as to the extent to which they can be attributed to the event.

38 In the current case, the *Hoge Raad* reiterates the two steps already distinguished in the 2016 decision. Firstly, a causal relationship (*conditio sine qua non*) between the breach of duty and the alleged benefits (ie that one (benefit) would not have occurred without the other (breach of duty)) is required. Secondly, in view of the standard of art 6:98 DCC, it must be reasonable to take those benefits into account when determining the amount of compensation (reasonableness test).[26] What is new is that the *Hoge Raad* also indicates that, when assessing what is reasonable, it is important to protect the injured party from being forced into a certain spending pattern.

39 All this also applies to the compensation of repair or replacement costs in the case of damaged objects (considering abstract damage calculation). Although the cassation argument fails on this point, the part of the complaint regarding the judgment of the 30 % reduction succeeds because there are valid objections to be made. The extent to which a 30 % deduction is reasonable remains yet an unanswered question, since that will be determined by another Court of Appeal after referral.

---

24 See eg HR 10 February 2017, ECLI:NL:HR:2017:208 (*Arubaanse taxi*).

25 HR 8 July 2016, ECLI:NL:HR:2016:1483 (*TenneT/ABB*). See also *JM Emaus/ALM Keirse*, The Netherlands, in: E Karner/BC Steininger (eds), ETL 2016 (2017) 393, no 29 ff.

26 Ibid.

c) Commentary

A benefit can be described as an improvement in the (financial) position of an injured party as a result of a damaging event.[27] This pertains to actual benefits or benefits expected to be genuinely enjoyed in the reasonable future.[28] In this judgment, the criteria for the application of benefit allocation as decided by the *Hoge Raad* in 2016[29] are affirmed. It is acknowledged that there are two possible approaches when dealing with the reduction of the damage extent, namely through the concept of damage and by benefit allocation, because they are not fundamentally different. This aligns with the legislative history of art 6:100 DCC.[30] The court is thus free to choose, taking into account the arguments put forward by the parties, which approach it follows, as long as the manner in which the standard of art 6:98 DCC is applied is verifiable.[31] 40

This judgment clarifies that benefit allocation may also take place in the case of property damage. In instances of property damage, according to established case law, the judge calculates the damage abstractly, meaning that they abstract from the individual case (and thus whether or not repair has taken place). The Advocate-General emphasises that in cases of 'new for old', in which an object is worth more after repair or replacement, doctrine accepts that such appreciation can be deducted from the compensation. However, most authors advocate a certain restraint, as this involves a forced expenditure, and it is questionable whether a real benefit is enjoyed. Lower court decisions on this point vary.[32] The *Hoge Raad* rules that the principle of 'new for old' in the case of property damage can lead to benefit allocation, and thus to a reduction of compensation. Furthermore, in line with literature and the Advocate-General, it rules that, when determining what is reasonable, it is important to prevent the injured party from being forced into a certain spending pattern. The *Hoge Raad* also found that the Court of Appeal in this case had not adequately responded to the reasoned arguments of Evides, which had already been advised by Advocate-General Lindenbergh. The Advocate-General argued that there can be no actual benefit on the part of Evides. The semantic discussion about the concept of benefit, where the judge is given a 41

27 *AT Bolt*, Voordeelstoerekening, bij de begroting van de schadevergoeding in geval van onrechtmatige daad en wanprestatie (1989) 5.

28 HR 1 February 2022, ECLI:NL:HR:2022:AD667.

29 HR 8 July 2016, ECLI:NL:HR:2016:1483.

30 TM, Parlementaire Geschiedenis van Burgerlijk Wetboek (Parl Gesch BW) Boek 6, 348.

31 Cf *Lindenbergh*, T&C BW, Commentary ad art 6:100 DCC.

32 *AG Lindenbergh*, conclusion in ECLI:NL:PHR:2022:1132; see also *IMG Bakker*, 'Nieuw voor oud' in de context van voordeelstoerekening (art 6:100 BW)', Bedrijfsjuridische Berichten (Bb) 2023/53.

considerable degree of freedom, is thus deferred to the Court of Appeal for further consideration.[33]

6. HR 31 October 2023, ECLI:NL:HR:2023:1495: Assessment of Damages Resulting from Emotional Shock and Affection Damages

a) Brief Summary of the Facts

42 A man murdered his ex-girlfriend in her home, while her two-year-old daughter was sleeping in the same house. The morning after the murder, the mother of the victim unexpectedly visited and found the lifeless body of her daughter. In the criminal case, the defendant was initially convicted for the murder of his ex-girlfriend and sentenced to a prison term of 18 years, from which pre-trial detention time was deducted. On appeal, the defendant was convicted to the same prison term. The father, mother, and daughter joined proceedings as aggrieved parties, pursuant to art 51f Sv, requesting material damages as well as immaterial damages. For the daughter, material costs included loss of parental maintenance. Although the court of first instance had also sentenced the defendant to pay shock damages to the mother, the Court of Appeal decided otherwise.

43 The Court of Appeal declared the mother's claim for shock damages inadmissible and determined that she could only bring the claim before the civil court. It considered that, in principle, the requirements for granting shock damages were met. The mother suffered mental injury as a result of the crime in the form of anxiety and post-traumatic stress disorder. However, based on the submitted (medical) documents and the given explanation, the Court of Appeal considered that an insufficient distinction could be made between the mental issues she faces as a surviving relative that are (solely) the result of the death of her daughter due to the criminal act and the damage that is the direct result of the confrontation with her daughter's remains. Therefore, it cannot be determined exactly which part of the mental injury arose from the confrontation with the serious consequences of the criminal act (shock damage) and which part was caused by missing her daughter (bereavement damage). This means that, according to the Court of Appeal, the consideration of the claim would disproportionately burden the criminal proceedings as specified in art 361 para 3 Sv.

---

33 Thus *KK Bink*, Nieuw voor oud; is er sprake van voordeel? Tijdschrift voor de Procespraktijk 2023-5, 182.

b) Judgment of the Court

The criminal judge can partially make a substantive decision in the form of an award of damages, and declare the claim of the injured party not admissible for the remaining part. Such a division of the claim allows the criminal judge to decide on that part of the claim for which the consideration does not disproportionately burden the criminal proceedings, while the injured party can submit the remaining part of its claim to the civil court. However, this does not mean that the criminal judge, based on their provisional judgment, can entirely or partially grant the claimed (damages) amount as an advance, pending a definitive judgment from the civil judge.[34] 44

In addition to a claim for shock damages, a secondary victim, as a close relative of the primary victim, may also be eligible for a claim for fixed compensation under art 6:107 para 1 introduction and under b and art 6:108 para 1 jo 3 DCC (bereavement damages). In the case of concurrent claims, the court must, based on the circumstances, reasonably estimate the extent to which the bereavement damages claim is taken into account when it determines the amount of compensation for immaterial damage resulting from the severe emotional shock-induced mental injury. 45

With the implicit decision that a claim for shock damages is only admissible if it is possible to precisely determine which part of the mental injury can be considered as damage resulting from shock and which part as bereavement damage, the Court of Appeal overlooked the fact that, in the event of a combination of these forms of damage, the judge must, based on the circumstances, fairly estimate the extent to which affection damage is taken into account when it determines the amount of shock damages. The fact that a precise delineation between these forms of damage will generally not be possible does not prevent the court from determining, on an estimated basis, what amount is eligible for an award as compensation of shock damage, contrary to what the Court of Appeal decided. The *Hoge Raad* overturns the decision and refers the case back to the Court of Appeal. 46

c) Commentary

Claims for shock damages are dealt with not only by the civil court, but also by the criminal court, since injured parties can join the criminal proceedings. The legislator wanted to provide a simple and accessible procedure within the criminal 47

34 Cf HR 28 May 2019, ECLI:NL:HR:2019:793.

process to compensate injured parties as much as possible. When the assessment of the claim for damages is difficult and the handling of the claim would place a disproportionate burden on the criminal proceedings, the criminal court may declare the claim (partly) inadmissible. In such a case, the injured party can claim damages in a civil court.

48 The *Hoge Raad* first accepted the possibility of compensation for shock damage in 2002 (*Taxibus*), and the possibility to compensate bereavement damage was introduced into Dutch law in 2019. In 2022, the question arose as what to decide in the case of concurrence of claims of both kinds of damage. When determining the amount for immaterial damages resulting from a mental injury caused by a severe emotional shock, the courts will have to weigh the extent to which the claim for bereavement damages has to be taken into account, based on the circumstances of the case and in a fair and reasonable manner using estimates.[35] Critical remarks were made in the literature about this decision, as this weighing and assessment is considered to be very complicated and thus difficult.[36]

49 The *Hoge Raad* now reiterates that it is important to weigh such considerations and that the court must indicate how these considerations were taken into account. Furthermore, it reminds that, in a criminal court, a partially substantive decision can be taken, by partially awarding compensation for damage resulting from shock and declaring the remainder of the claim inadmissible (due to undue burden, in accordance with art 361 para 3 Sv). However, such judgment cannot be based on the assertion that the damage cannot be precisely demarcated in the specific case. Although this standpoint may be subject to criticism, it is consistent with what the *Hoge Raad* has stated before, more than once. Finally, the *Hoge Raad* reiterates once again that the (criminal) court must estimate the extent of the damage when it cannot be precisely determined.[37]

7. Personal Injury

50 As last year, compensation for damage caused by unlawfully induced emotional shock is at the core of discussion in the legal field. The leading case dates back to 2002, when the *Hoge Raad* ruled that a person who kills or injures another by a wrongful act may also act unlawfully towards the person to whom the confrontation with that act or its consequences causes severe emotional shock (the

---

35 HR 28 June 2022, ECLI:NL:HR:2022:958; see *van Dongen/Keirse* (fn 1) no 38ff.

36 See on the concurrence of both kind of immaterial damages, extensively, Advocate Generals TNBM Spronken & SD Lindenbergh, conclusion dated 22 February 2022, ECLI:NL:PHR:2022:166.

37 See already, HR 28 May 2019, ECLI:NL:HR:2019:793, para 2.8.7 and art 6:97 DCC.

secondary victim). Whether this is justified depends on a weighing of the circumstances of the case. Serious psychological effects resulting from being confronted with this unlawful act can lead to patrimonial damage as well as 'other disadvantages' (cf art 6:95 DCC).

Claims resulting from confrontations with shocking events do not appear to be 51
exceptional in case law from the lower courts. In 2022, it was decided that the point of view ('requirement') of direct confrontation was applied too strictly in case law. Although confrontation is still a relevant aspect, it could also encompass witnessing something similar at a later stage or occurring in a different manner. In 2023, the *Hoge Raad* clarified that the aspect of a close relationship with the victim is not a necessary element. Close relationship, as direct confrontation, are criteria to be weighed in their interrelationship, without giving, *a priori*, decisive importance to either of the criteria. If one criterion is not met during the assessment, it does not automatically preclude the possibility of awarding compensation for shock damage.

It has been shown that in case law from the lower (criminal) courts, shock 52
damage is often only treated as immaterial damage.[38] This is relevant, because of another head of immaterial damage, ie bereavement damage. Although that damage has been discussed or advocated for in doctrine for years, claiming affection damages under Dutch law only became possible on 1 January 2019, applying only to injuries or deaths which occurred after 31 December 2018[39], and only for certain relatives up to a certain amount determined by a governmental decree (cf art 6:107 (1) together with art 6:108 (3) DCC). Claims for shock damage are, however, also often instigated by relatives (*naasten en nabestaanden*).[40]

The question is how these two types of immaterial damage, shock damage and 53
bereavement damage, should be calculated in practice when compensation for both are claimed and awarded. It is not easy to make a distinction between mental harm as the result of a confrontation with an act seriously wounding or killing a relative on the one hand and the mental harm suffered due to losing (the health of) a loved one. Nevertheless, this is what is required according to the *Hoge Raad* case law. In the case law from the lower civil courts, the instruction to

---

38 Cf Spronken § Lindenbergh, conclusion dated 22 February 2022, ECLI:NL:PHR:2022:166, no 4.1.3.

39 Cf arts 68 and 69 Transitional law New Civil Code (Overgangswet NBW).

40 A research study is currently being conducted, under the guidance of the Dutch Research and Data Centre, to evaluate this legislation and the decision and to determine to what extent they have achieved the objective intended when the law was introduced, whether relatives experience the compensation as recognition of suffering and as a form of compensation. In addition, the research will provide insight into the advantages and disadvantages of possibly changing the scope of compensation and the circle of beneficiaries.

make a distinction between the causes is handled in different ways, while criminal courts usually pay no attention to this distinction and simply assign both without further motivation.[41]

54 In 2022, in a case before the *Hoge Raad*, the question arose as to how, in cases of concurrent claims for both types of damages, courts should weigh, based on the circumstances of the case and in a fair and reasonable manner using estimates, the extent to which the claim for bereavement damages should be considered when determining the amount for immaterial damages resulting from a mental injury caused by a severe emotional shock. As the case underlying the *Hoge Raad*'s judgment in 2023 demonstrates, making a distinction between the mental issues a person faces as a surviving relative solely due to bereavement on the one hand, and the moral damage resulting from the confrontation with the victimisation or criminal offence against a relative, on the other, can be challenging. Nevertheless, the *Hoge Raad* reiterates the importance of weighing such considerations and emphasises that courts must indicate how these considerations were taken into account.

55 Furthermore, the 2023 case reminds us that, as in a criminal court, a partially substantive decision can be made by partially awarding compensation for damage resulting from shock and declaring the remainder of the claim inadmissible. However, this judgment cannot be based on the assertion that the damage cannot be precisely demarcated in the specific case. The *Hoge Raad* reiterates once again that the (criminal and civil) courts must estimate the extent of the damage when it cannot be determined precisely.

C. Literature

1. *EAL van Emden*, Toerekening van externe kennis bij onrechtmatige daad [Imputation of external knowledge in tort law] (Wolters Kluwer 2023)

56 Knowledge is often essential in determining behaviour as unlawful. If the wrongdoer is unaware and, reasonably, could not have been aware of something, this lack of knowledge often means that their conduct is not unlawful. In such cases, no duty to pay financial compensation can be imposed. However, it is common for individuals in the wrongdoer's circle to have relevant knowledge (so-called external knowledge), such as assistants (*hulppersonen*), advisors, or family members

41 Spronken & Lindenbergh, conclusion dated 22 February 2022, ECLI:NL:PHR:2022:166, no 4.4.29.

of the wrongdoer. In a 2005 ruling, the *Hoge Raad* held that under certain circumstances, it is possible to attribute the knowledge of a third party to the wrongdoer.[42] By attributing (external) knowledge in this way, the conduct of the wrongdoer can still be considered unlawful. However, the ruling did not clarify when the attribution of knowledge is possible nor the applicable criteria. This dissertation provides guidance in this regard. As the title suggests, the criteria for attributing external knowledge are derived from the legal tort law system. It also provides a criterion to attribute knowledge of a third party to the injured party when assessing contributory negligence. It gives detailed information about which circumstances are relevant for the assessment and which arguments the parties must present to argue whether knowledge of a third party should or should not be attributed to the wrongdoer or the injured party.

2. *MA Loth*, Stemmen door de tijd; over intergenerationele zorgplichten in het aansprakelijkheidsrecht [Voices through time; on intergenerational duties of care in tort law] (Studio 2023)

In this farewell address, the author argues that everyone has a general legal duty 57
to take into account the legitimate (life-transcending) interests of future and past generations, and that this general duty, under certain circumstances, can solidify into specific enforceable duties of care. However, past generations faced serious obstacles in civil courts. On the one hand, we have doctrine on duties of care and liability, but these are not or are only barely developed for intergenerational relationships. On the other hand, we have the theory on 'intergenerational justice,' but this is not tailored to private law relationships. The author provides an initial approach by (1) first investigating under what conditions we can speak of duties of care towards future generations and then (2) addressing duties of care towards past generations. In his narrative, 'voices through time' resonate from the future or the past. These voices include examples, not only to clarify the narrative but also to offer perspectives for the normative interpretation of intergenerational duties of care. These voices have grown louder over time, even in tort law. The author argues that it is important for these voices to be heard and that they carry weight in tort law. Compliance with duties of care towards future and past generations represents an ultimate way to transcend ourselves. Loth believes that we have an obligation to take these duties of care seriously.

42 HR 11 November 2005, NJ 2007/231, with note by *JBM Vranken*.

3. *MWK Reijntjes*, Aansprakelijkheid voor onrechtmatige rechtspraak. Een rechtshistorisch en -vergelijkend onderzoek [Liability for unlawful judicial acts. A historical and comparative study] (Universiteit van Groningen 2023)

58 The rule that whoever causes damage to another must compensate that damage under Dutch law hardly applies when a court renders an incorrect judgment. The State is in principle not liable, nor are judges in person. The author studies the historical background of Dutch views on liability for unlawful judgments. Rules on liability of judges have existed for over two thousand years. In primitive legal systems, holding a judge liable was the only way to oppose a judgment. However, specific rules on the liability of judges continued to exist after it became possible to appeal a judgment. Reijntjes begins his study with Justinian law, arriving via Salian law, *gemeine recht* in Holland and Friesland, common law, to judicial liability in the Netherlands and ECHR and EU law standards. According to the author, accepting that the doctrine of unlawful acts fully applies to judicial acts would be an appropriate conclusion to the historical development. Considerable personal blame on the part of the judge is required for liability, albeit objectified to some extent, under the heading of 'gross dereliction of duty' or 'manifest gross disregard of what constitutes the proper performance of duties'. Only then can it be said that the judge did not administer justice in good conscience, making his judgment wrongful.

4. *R Rijnhout et al*, Haalbaarheid van een database ten behoeve van schadeverhaal door asbestslachtoffers [Feasibility of a database for the purpose of damage recovery by asbestos victims] (Boom juridisch 2023)

59 This book is the result of a study conducted by a collaboration between Utrecht University and Maastricht University, on behalf of the Institute for Asbestos Victims. The reason for the research was the desire to retrieve more insurance policies from liable (former) employers of asbestos victims or their surviving relatives. One proposed solution is a database, similar to the Employee Liability Trading Office (ELTO) in the United Kingdom. The central question focuses on the functioning of the ELTO within the broader legal framework of compensation for asbestos damage and how a database for the Netherlands could be established. The research consists of a doctrinal and comparative legal study on compensation in as-

bestos cases in the Netherlands and the UK, as well as a technical study on a database for insurance policies.

5. *FM Ruitenbeek-Bart*, En de veroorzaker dan? Een empirisch-juridisch onderzoek naar de plaats van de veroorzaker in de civiele letselschadepraktijk [And what about the perpetrator? An empirical-legal study on the position of the perpetrator in the practice of civil personal injury cases] (Boom juridisch 2023)

This dissertation reports on an interview study conducted among injury-causing 60
parties in cases of medical and traffic liability, as well as among personal injury professionals who handle damages claims on their behalf. The study aligns with the ongoing attention to personal injury victims and their immaterial needs, but takes the personal perspective of the person held responsible. Relevant questions, inter alia, are: How does it feel to have caused injury to someone else or to be held liable for it? How do injury-causing parties relate to 'their' victim? How do they perceive the settlement of personal injury claims? What further effects do injury-causing events have on them? And what can personal injury lawyers learn from the experiences of those responsible? The interview study reveals that there are possibilities for the person responsible to contribute to the immaterial recovery of the victim. Furthermore, it becomes evident that injury-causing parties also have immaterial needs. These findings raise new questions about the appropriate place of and approach to persons held responsible in personal injury cases.

6. *PWJ Verbruggen*, Productieaansprakelijkheid: Over zorgplichten in internationale productienetwerken [Production liability: On duties of care in international production networks] (Studio 2023)

In this inaugural lecture, the question of the legal responsibility companies in the 61
global North bear for negative external effects of their global production chains on workers, bystanders, or members of the local community is discussed. According to the author, cracks have appeared in the fortress of limited liability for damage caused within international production networks. He explores how duties of care are evolving in case law and legislation for multinational corporations to consider

or protect the identifiable interests of workers, bystanders, members of local communities, and other vulnerable individuals in international production networks. He also examines the foundations and limits of liability for damage in international production networks outlining the contours of a dynamic domain of civil liability. From the perspective of Dutch law, he argues that multinationals intentionally organise their networks to have an overview of the conditions under which production by their network partners takes place as well as its effects on people and the environment. To this effect, they use complex private systems of rules, supervision, and technology. These systems both increase knowledge and understanding of structural hazards and risks of production activities performed in their network and provide the ability to monitor the actions of network partners and to intervene when problems arise. If multinationals can take into account the interests of others, they have a duty of care to consider or protect these interests. According to the author, violation of this duty can lead to production liability.

7. *TE de Wijkerslooth-van der Linden*, Voor risico van de ondernemer. Over de betekenis van het ondernemersrisicobeginsel in het aansprakelijkheidsrecht [At the risk of the entrepreneur. On the significance of the entrepreneurial risk principle in tort law] (Wolters Kluwer 2023)

62 To establish liability, is it relevant whether the damage is caused by an entrepreneur or an individual? This question is particularly relevant, as entrepreneurs play a crucial role in society. Entrepreneurship is often equated with progress, but it also carries risks. Conducting a study on the role of entrepreneurs in non-contractual liability law (tort law), this dissertation addresses a gap. The research resulted in a new theory on the position of entrepreneurs within Dutch non-contractual liability law. Through an analysis of literature and case law, De Wijkerslooth-van der Linden not only clarifies how the requirements of ‘act’, ‘tortfeasorship,’ ‘unlawfulness’, and ‘attributability’ can be interpreted when the liable party is an entrepreneur, but also demonstrates how the status of being an entrepreneur can lower the threshold of liability. This dissertation is a significant addition to literature on the foundations of tort law, as it draws attention to a principle that has been underemphasised in Dutch legal literature: the entrepreneurial risk principle.

Knut Martin Tande

XXI. Norway

A. Legislation

There was no new legislation in tort law in Norway in 2023. 1

B. Cases

1. Norges Høyesterett (Norwegian Supreme Court, HR) 9 February 2023, HR-2023-268-A: Insurance Deduction in a Case of Patient's Injury

a) Brief Summary of the Facts

A spouse and two children had been awarded damages for loss of a provider by the Norwegian System of Patient Injury Compensation (*Norsk Pasientskadeerstatning*, NPE). The deceased had been covered by a life insurance policy, and the Patients' Injury Compensation Board (*Pasientskadenemda*) deducted approx 20 % of the insurance payment based on sec 3-4, subsec 2 of the Norwegian Compensatory Damages Act, which refers to sec 3-1 in the same Act. The spouse and the two children brought the case before the court. The question before the Supreme Court was if the insurance deduction should be made for each individual survivor, or if it should be based on the total insurance payment, before the payment was distributed to the survivors. 2

b) Judgment of the Court

The Supreme Court started by analysing the wording of the deduction rule in the Damages Act sec 3-1, subsec 2, finding that it provides for a discretionary assessment regarding the deduction of insurance payments but no further guidance. The preparatory works were then examined in detail, indicating a restrictive approach to deductions, especially for more common life insurance benefits. A deduction is only relevant for more significant insurance payments, and, even for such payments, the deduction should be limited. The courts should show generosity in 3

https://doi.org/10.1515/9783111376721-022

their assessment of the deduction for insurance payments, the Supreme Court argued

4 Prior Supreme Court case law was also carefully reviewed by the Court. While some cases in the 1990s had allowed deductions, this was because the insurance amounts were considered high based on the conditions at the time. However, the Court found no clear thresholds could be deduced from those judgments that were relevant for the case at hand.

5 The Supreme Court gave little weight to the Patient Injury Compensation Board's practice of making standardised deductions for insurance payments over a certain amount. The Court noted that there was criticism of this approach in legal theory.

6 The Supreme Court also took into consideration the insurance coverage that is common today through group life insurance. It referred to data showing that 10 to 15 times the basic amount in the National Norwegian Insurance Scheme (G, amounting to € 10,000), which equals € 100,000 to € 150,000 coverage, is now normal for adults. The Supreme Court more specifically found that no deductions should be made for life insurance payments of 15G or less for adults and 5G or less for children.

7 Only for individual payments substantially exceeding these levels should a discretionary assessment of a possible deduction under sec 3-1 be considered, the Court stated. Even then, the Court emphasised, considerable caution should be exercised in making deductions, in line with statements in the preparatory works.

8 Applying these principles to the specific case, the Supreme Court found it clear that no deductions should be made. The insurance payment to the spouse corresponded to 15G, while the children each received an amount equivalent to 2G. This was well within the levels where the Court's guidelines state that deductions are not to be made.

c) Commentary

9 In summary, the Supreme Court verdict provides important principles and guidance for the discretionary assessment of whether life insurance payments should be deducted from survivors' compensation in personal injury cases. The key factor is the level of insurance payments compared to what is considered common coverage today.

10 At the same time, the Court did not completely rule out deductions in cases where the insurance payments are substantially above common levels today. The discretionary assessment under sec 3-1 remains available in such cases, although subject to a high threshold and exercise of considerable caution.

The verdict provides important clarifications for the practice of compensation law in cases of survivors' losses. By largely rejecting deductions within the levels of common life insurance coverage today, it ensures more adequate compensation to survivors in many cases. The 15G/5G thresholds give clear guidance, while still retaining some flexibility for substantially higher payments. 11

The verdict also indicates that the 15G/5G thresholds should be adjusted over time if common insurance coverage levels change substantially in the future. 12

Despite these minor openings for potential future development, the Supreme Court's decision in HR-2023-268-A provides welcome clarifications to a previously uncertain area of compensation law, especially considering the deduction practices of the Patient Injury Compensation Board that have been criticised. It ensures fair and reasonable compensation to surviving family members in cases where insurance exists, while still leaving some flexibility for outlier situations. 13

2. HR 10 May 2023, HR-2023-877-A: Statute of Limitations for Damage not Related to a Contract

a) Brief Summary of the Facts

Two taxpayers running a business had their VAT and surtax reassessed in 2011. After an appeal, the reassessments were reversed in 2014. In 2015, the Tax Office decided to carry out a reassessment for 2009 for the two. After another appeal, these reassessments were reversed in 2017. In 2019, the taxpayers then filed a claim for compensation from the Norwegian State before the court for economic loss due to the invalid reassessment. 14

The legal question before the Supreme Court was if the two taxpayers had, or should have had, the 'necessary knowledge' about the damage and the responsible party, according to the Norwegian Statute of Limitations Act sec 9, subsec 1. 15

b) Judgment of the Court

The majority of the Supreme Court rejected the argument that there is a general rule that the limitations period does not start until the final administrative appeal decision. 16

The statutory language of the Norwegian Act Relating to the Limitation Period of Claims (*Foreldesesloven* (fl) sec 9, subsec 1) is clear in that the decisive factor is when the injured party had or should have had the 'necessary knowledge' about the damage and the responsible party. There is no reservation or exception for 17 claims against public authorities. Neither the preparatory works nor Supreme Court precedents supported reading in such an exception.

18 While practical considerations like avoiding unnecessary litigation before a final decision by the tax authorities can be valid, the statutory language did not allow adjusting the rule for such reasons where the necessary knowledge exists, the Supreme Court found. There was no basis in the sources of law for a categorical rule delaying the period until the final administrative decision. The assessment had to be specific to each case based on when the necessary knowledge was gained.

19 The majority then applied the condition of necessary knowledge to the specific facts of the case.

20 For the claims based on the VAT decision, the two taxpayers had the necessary knowledge by October 2014 at the latest when they filed for compensation. Thus, these claims were time-barred.

21 For the tax reassessment claims, the taxpayers knew the tax authorities had incorrectly applied a two-year deadline rule when issuing the reassessments in 2015. By October 2015, they also had the necessary knowledge of the alleged loss/damage and causal link based on their income loss, asset devaluation and interest losses due to the handling of their tax case. Based on this, the taxpayers had knowledge of all the factual and legal conditions for liability by October 2015 at the latest. The final appeal decisions did not bring any new significant information.

22 Thus, the majority of the Supreme Court concluded that the tax claims were also time-barred under fl sec 9, subsec 1.

23 The majority rejected the arguments based on the statute of limitations being interrupted by the appeals to the administrative appeal boards under fl sec 16, subsec 1. Also, the majority rejected the argument that claims should accrue successively rather than being time-barred collectively. In addition, the application of fl sec 9, subsec 1 was not found to violate the right to a fair trial under art 6, subsec 1 of the European Convention on Human Rights (ECHR).

24 The dissenting judge argued that in tax cases, the taxpayer typically lacks the 'necessary knowledge' of the unlawful grounds for their claim until the reasoned appeal decision clarifies the unlawfulness of the initial decision. It is difficult for a party to have grounds or reasonable cause to bring a lawsuit while their appeal is still pending, as the appeal decision and reasoning are usually key to properly assessing the grounds for liability.

25 The Supreme Court minority argued that the requirement in fl sec 9, subsec 1 regarding necessary knowledge, based on previous Supreme Court decisions, implies that the injured party must have knowledge of all the factual and legal conditions for liability, ie the grounds for liability, the loss, and the causal link between the two with prospects of a positive outcome.

According to previous Supreme Court practices, the minority judge stated, the injured party objectively must have sufficiently certain information to submit a claim for compensation with prospects of a positive outcome. 26

The minority judge argued that in an administrative case, the injured party generally lacks reasonable grounds to have the liability issue tried before the courts until the appeal decision clarifies the grounds for liability. 27

While necessary knowledge requires knowledge of all the conditions for compensation, the injured party may have reasonable grounds for a lawsuit at an earlier point. Still, the minority argued, this typically does not occur until the appeal decision has been handed down in administrative cases. 28

Based on this, the dissenting judge stated that even though the two taxpayers took steps which indicated their belief that they had been wronged, it was still essential for them to know the outcome and reasoning of the appeal before filing suit. Thus, the period of the statute of limitations should generally not start until the appeal decision in tax cases, unless special circumstances indicate earlier knowledge. 29

c) Commentary

In essence, the majority of the Supreme Court took a fact-specific approach, focusing on the actual or imputed knowledge of the claimants, while the dissenting judge argued that taxpayers generally lack such knowledge until the reasoned appeal decision clarifies the unlawfulness. 30

Firstly, there are no general rules delaying limitations period. The Court rejected establishing a general rule that the three-year limitation period does not start to run until the final administrative appeal decision. Each case requires a concrete assessment based on when the injured party had, or should have had, the necessary knowledge according to fl sec 9, subsec 1. 31

Secondly, the decisive factor is when the claimant obtained, or should have obtained, the necessary knowledge about the damage and the responsible party, regardless of the status of the administrative appeals process. 32

Thirdly, whether the claimant had the necessary knowledge for the limitation period to start depends on a fact-specific assessment of the circumstances in each case. 33

Fourthly, the majority rejected reading any categorical exceptions or reservations into fl sec 9, subsec 1 for claims against public authorities based on negligent administrative decisions. 34

The dissenting judge argued for a more claimant-friendly general premise, arguing that in tax cases, the necessary knowledge is typically lacking until the rea- 35 soned appeal decision clarifies any unlawfulness. In many ways, this appears to be a reasonable approach. It can be considered illogical that a claimant must bring a case before the court to stop the claim from being time-barred while an administrative appeal organ is still considering the case. Also, one can argue, as the minority judge did, that the claimant does not have the necessary knowledge to bring a case before the court until the administrative appeal organ has considered the case.

36 However, there is a tension between the reasoning of the dissenting judge, making exceptions from what follows directly from the wording of fl sec 9, subsec 1, and the need for predictability. In cases relating to the statutes of limitiation, it can be argued, as the majority of the court does, that predictability and following the wording of the law is most important.

3. HR 14 June 2023, HR-2023-1108-A: Patient Injury Compensation; Foreseeability of the Damage

a) Brief Summary of the Facts

37 A father claimed compensation from the Norwegian System of Patient Injury Compensation based on the Patient Injury Compensation Act sec 2, subsec 1, letter a, which provides for compensation in cases of failure in health care.

38 The father's 20-year-old daughter had committed suicide while she was receiving treatment for mental health problems. As a result, the father suffered mental injuries causing a financial loss (loss of income).

39 The NPE dismissed the claim for compensation, a dismissal that was later confirmed by the Patient Injury Committee. The case was then brought before the ordinary courts, the father seeking a declaratory judgment regarding the liability of the Norwegian State represented by the Patient Injury Committee.

40 The parties agreed that there had been a fault in the treatment of the daughter, that the suicide would have been avoided with better diagnosis and treatment, and that the father had suffered a financial loss. The question before the courts was if the father's mental injury was foreseeable or, more specifically, if there was sufficient proximity between the failure of the treatment of the daughter and the mental injury of her father.

41 The District Court and the Appeal Court answered this in the affirmative, but the Patient Injury Committee appealed to the Supreme Court.

b) Judgment of the Court

With reference to two Supreme Court cases in HR-2017-172 and HR-2020-1332-A, the Court presented the main question in the case at hand: Was there an adequate causal link between the actions to make the tortfeasor liable for the damage to the victim? 42

According to the Court, this was both a question of foreseeability of the damage, and a question of proximity between the damage and the action making the tortfeasor liable. 43

The main Supreme Court decision regarding cases that involved a parent's loss of a child because of failed health treatment, the Court stated, was a quite recent Supreme Court case in HR-2018-208-A, where the question was if a mother could be awarded damages due to her son's death after a failure in treatment at a hospital. 44

This previous case was referred to by the Supreme Court as a starting point for considerations in the case at hand. 45

In HR-2018-208-A, the Court referred to the preparatory works of the Patient Injury Compensation Act, which state that liability for the economic loss of persons other than the patient is based on the common rules of tort law, as developed by the Supreme Court. 46

Thus, the Supreme Court stated that the general principle of adequate causality had to be applied in the case at hand, but with the necessary adjustments regarding injured third parties. 47

One such adjustment was illustrated by four older Supreme Court cases (Rt 1938, 626, Rt 1960, 367, Rt 1966, 163 and Rt 1985, 1011), which established very narrow criteria for awarding damages to family members suffering mental injuries after the death of the primary victim. 48

The previous cases, the Court stated, appeared to award damages even for parents and spouses only when they observed an accident directly or the accident was especially dramatic or terrifying. 49

Referring to the Supreme Court in HR-2018-208-A, the Court stated that there were still arguments to restrict the awarding of damages in such cases, especially regarding which family members could be awarded damages. Only family members belonging to the 'inner circle" of the deceased could be awarded compensation. 50

However, with referral to the same case, the Court argued that there were grounds for some adjustment of the threshold for awarding damages to those family members. 51

52 According to the Supreme Court in HR-2018-208-A, mental injuries for parents are foreseeable when a child dies or is seriously injured even if the parent does not observe the death or injury directly.

53 However, the Court in HR-2018-208-A emphasised, there must be elements related to the damage or the circumstances of the damage that represent a particular burden for the parent, beyond the loss of the child or the damage to the child. The proximity between the actions of the tortfeasor and the parent's mental injury was relevant in this regard.

54 Based on these statements in HR-2018-208-A, the Court stated that mental injuries in general are foreseeable when a parent loses a child, although the duration and extension of the injury could be of relevance in this regard.

55 In addition, the Court emphasised that the statements regarding a 'particular burden' for the parent, beyond the loss of the child or the damage to the child, meant that it was necessary to consider if there was an adequate causal link based on the proximity between the mental injury and the tortfeasor's actions. Also, the degree of negligence was to be considered.

56 The Supreme Court emphasised that the personal connection between the daughter and the father in the case at hand was of the same strong type as in HR-2018-2080-A. Even if the daughter was 20 years old (the son in HR-2018-208-A was 15 years old), she lived at home, and the parents followed her treatment closely. In both cases from the Supreme Court, the injured third party was a parent.

57 Thus, the Court stated, the mental injury of the father was foreseeable, even if it mainly manifested itself a long time after his daughter committed suicide.

58 Regarding the question of adequate causality, based on the consideration of whether the death of the child represents a particular burden to the parent, the Court emphasised that the consideration included the proximity between the mental injury of the father and the failure of the treatment of the daughter in the health system.

59 Even if the suicide in the case at hand would have been avoided with the correct diagnosis and treatment, the failure in treatment was not the immediate cause of the death of the daughter. A suicide depends on the actions of the deceased.

60 Thus, the Supreme Court argued, the proximity between the failure of the health care system to the mental injury of the father was reduced due to the complex chain of causal elements leading to the father's injury.

61 Also, the Court stated, even if it was considered a failure to permit the daughter to leave the health institution without supervision, the Court of Appeal found that there was no gross negligence in the case at hand that could lower the threshold for awarding damages. The Supreme Court stated that it could not overrule this consideration.

The Supreme Court acknowledged that the father did not know about his daughter leaving the institution and thought that his daughter was in safe hands. This made the death of the daughter especially sudden and unexpected to him. Still, the Court argued, the family had known about the underlying risk of suicide for several years. 62

In addition, the father was not the one that found his daughter dead, in contrast to the mother in HR-2018-208-A, who found her son dead in his hospital bed. The death was communicated to the father by a priest and a policeman. 63

The father argued that one had to consider that the failure of treatment had lasted a long time and that the father had witnessed an attempted suicide by the daughter ten months earlier. 64

The Supreme Court replied that there was no doubt that the father had experienced a heavy burden for a long time due to his daughter's situation. However, the Court of Appeal did not consider this burden an important causal element regarding the mental injury of the father. Based on this, the burden could not be of importance in the legal consideration of adequate causality. 65

Based on this, the Supreme Court concluded (with one dissenting judge) that the mental injury of the father was foreseeable, but that the suicide and the surrounding circumstances did not represent a particular burden for the father beyond the loss of his daughter, especially because of the lack of proximity between the father's injury and the failure in the health system. Thus, the Court did not award damages. 66

The lack of professionalism by the police related to the identification of the daughter, and the fact that the health system did not acknowledge any fault for a long time were not considered relevant. 67

The dissenting Supreme Court judge agreed with the majority on the legal starting points in the case but found that the circumstances surrounding the daughter's suicide constituted a particular burden for the father beyond just losing his daughter. The judge made the following arguments supporting the conclusion that the mental injury of the father was sufficiently connected to the failures in the treatment of his daughter: 68

The suicide happened suddenly and unexpectedly while the father thought his daughter was safe in the closed ward at the hospital. This imposed an extra burden. 69

There was a close connection between the decision to allow the daughter to leave the hospital, which was acknowledged as negligent, and the burden it imposed on the father that the suicide happened when he thought she was safe. 70

The failure in treatment lasted many years, and with proper diagnosis and treatment, the outcome for the daughter could likely have been different as late as 2011 or early 2012. 71

72 The traumatic way in which the identification of the body was handled by the police added to the trauma experienced by the father.

c) Commentary

73 The conclusion of the majority of the Supreme Court in this case appears to be in line with the previous Supreme Court in HR-2018-208-A.

74 Even considering the lower threshold for awarding damages to parents after HR-2018-208-A, the case at hand appears to deviate too much from the necessary restrictions to awarding damages to third parties that have experienced an economic loss based on the primary damage.

75 The decisions of the health system in this case were based on difficult medical considerations, and treatment over a long period of time. In contrast to the case in HR-2018-208-A, there was no specific incident that the parent was exposed to that caused the mental injury of the parent. Awarding damages would open the floodgates for litigation by third parties not only in cases related to the suicide of patients, but also in other cases of death and serious injuries among patients caused by treatment in the health care system.

76 This is exactly the situation that the proximity rule, as a part of the consideration of the condition of causality in Norwegian tort law, aims to avoid.

77 In my opinion, the dissenting judge did not take this last aspect of the case sufficiently into consideration.

4. HR 22 June 2023, HR-2023-1172-A: Assessment of Aggravated Damages Related to Children

a) Brief Summary of the Facts

78 In a case involving a rape which had been committed while the victim was asleep, the Court of Appeal had imposed a youth sentence on the tortfeasor in addition to NOK 220,000 in compensatory damages. The tortfeasor was 15 years and nine months old, while the victim was 16 years and four months old.

79 The question before the Supreme Court was if the standard compensation according to the Norwegian Compensatory Damages Act (*Skadeserstatningsloven* (skl) sec 1-1) should be reduced further because the tortfeasor was a minor. The standard compensation according to skl sec 3-5 for rape was 2G or NOK 240,000.

b) Judgment of the Court

The majority of the Supreme Court stated that skl sec 1-1 on children's liability regulates both the basis and scope of liability. In determining the scope, the majority noted, the minor tortfeasor's interests shall be given greater weight than for adults. For serious crimes, considerably more is required to mitigate or waive liability. 80

Skl sec 3-5, which regulates compensation for the non-pecuniary loss of adults, emphasises the objective severity of the case, the tortfeasor's guilt, the injured party's subjective experience, and the nature and extent of the injuries. The significance of skl sec 1-1, the Court emphasised, lies in the special weight given to the tortfeasor's age. 81

The 2G standard compensation according to skl sec 3-5 has less direct relevance under skl sec 1-1, the Court majority argued. Case law has increased the standard amount of compensation according to skl sec 3-5 when the victim is a child. 82

In determining the amount of compensation under skl sec 1-1, the child's best interests shall be given great weight but may not be decisive, the Court argued. The standard 2G compensation for rape is a starting point before adjusting for the ages of both the tortfeasor and the victim. Thus, it takes less to deviate from the standard when the tortfeasor or the victim is a child than for adults. 83

Regarding the concrete assessment of the case at hand, the Supreme Court found that the conditions for ordering the tortfeasor to pay compensation according to skl secs 1-1 and 3-5 were undoubtedly met. The issue was what amount of compensation was reasonable considering the tortfeasor's age, development, conduct, financial capacity and the circumstances of the case in general. 84

The fact that the victim was a child, the Court majority noted, indicated that the amount should be increased to compensate for the greater burden on her. NOK 260,000 was an appropriate compensation amount before adjusting for the tortfeasor's age. 85

The majority of the Supreme Court argued that the tortfeasor's age of 15 years and 9 months pointed towards a reduction in comparison to what an adult tortfeasor would pay, as a 15-year-old has limited life experience, maturity and ability to understand consequences. The younger the child, the more reason to limit liability. 86

The tortfeasor had no current financial capacity to bear liability as a student without income or assets, the Court majority noted. His future earning potential was difficult to assess, and he had been notified of potential deportation. The tortfeasor's difficult upbringing and particular vulnerability as a Syrian refugee also indicated a reduction. 87

Thus, the Court majority noted, the interest in the tortfeasor's rehabilitation, suggests a more limited liability so that the liability did not become too burdensome and hinder his reintegration into society after the youth punishment. How- 88 ever, caution should be shown in reducing liability for serious crimes. On balance, the Court stated, the seriousness of the case at hand did not preclude a reduction considering all the circumstances.

89 After an overall assessment, the compensation was set at NOK 160,000, approx 60 % of what an adult tortfeasor would pay under the same circumstances, and the appeal to the Supreme Court succeeded. According to the court majority, this reasonably balanced the competing interests – providing the victim with significant compensation while reducing the amount based on the tortfeasor's age and finances. Compensation was still adequate to express society's condemnation of the offence committed.

90 Two Supreme Court justices dissented and found no basis to reduce the standard compensation amount because the tortfeasor was a minor. There should be a significant threshold before reducing the standardised compensation amount due to the tortfeasor's age alone, especially for a serious crime like rape, the minority argued. The tortfeasor's young age was already considered in sentencing him to a juvenile correction institute rather than prison.

91 In addition, the dissenting judges argued, previous Supreme Court cases in HR-2018-1014-A and HR-2022-980-A did not reduce the standard compensation amounts despite the tortfeasors being minors. The previous cases had older minor defendants (15.5 and 17.75 years old) and younger minor victims (14 years old in HR-2022-980-A).

c) Commentary

92 In summary, the Supreme Court's decision in the case at hand substantially reduced the compensatory damages for the 15-year-old, both based on age and other factors. By doing so, the Court went further than in previous Supreme Court cases involving minor tortfeasors who had committed serious offences.

93 The view of the dissenting judges cautioning against an extensive reduction appears more consistent with the earlier rulings. The majority of the Supreme Court argued for reduced compensatory damages based on specific facts related to the tortfeasor in this case, facts that differed from previous cases. However, it is not obvious how these specific facts can justify the deviation from previous Supreme Court cases.

94 Based on this, it can be difficult to decide if this case represents an arbitrary deviation from the previous court cases, or if the case indicates a more permanent liberal approach regarding the reduction of compensatory damages related to skl sec 1-1.

5. HR 8 September 2023, HR-2023-1796-A: Question of Reducing the Amount of Compensation due to the Injured Party's Contribution

a) Brief Summary of the Facts

This case concerned an insurance broker's professional liability for damages due to insufficient advice and whether that liability should be reduced due to the insured company's alleged contributory negligence in not thoroughly reviewing the insurance terms and conditions. 95

The case arose after a fire severely damaged a woodwork factory's leased production premises, equipment, machines and inventory. The factory had insurance policies, including one specifically for machines, inventory and movable property (MIL). However, the insured amounts under the MIL policy were too low to cover all economic losses related to the property. The factory owner had incorrectly assumed that permanently installed machines and equipment were covered by the landlord's building insurance policy. 96

In the lower courts, the factory owner successfully argued that its insurance broker, Pareto, was liable for the uninsured losses due to negligent advice regarding the scope of coverage and failure to clarify what each policy covered. The key issue before the Supreme Court was whether Pareto's liability should be reduced due to the factory owner's alleged contributory negligence in not diligently reviewing the voluminous insurance conditions. The Court of Appeal had reduced the compensation by about one-third on this basis. 97

b) Judgment of the Court

In assessing whether there were grounds to reduce liability under sec 5-1 of Norway's Compensatory Damages Act, the central question was whether the insured party could have reduced or eliminated the risk of insufficient coverage if it had carefully reviewed the insurance conditions. 98

Skl sec 5-1, subsec 1 states that where the victim has negligently contributed to the damage, the liability of the tortfeasor can be reduced to the extent that is considered just, having regard to the claimant's contributory conduct, its influence on the occurrence of the harm, the magnitude of the damage and the circumstances in general. Skl sec 5-1, subsec 2 states that it is also to be considered contributory conduct when the victim or claimant has neglected to eliminate or reduce the risk of harm or damage to the extent that could be reasonably expected. The Supreme 99

Court found both subsec 1 and subsec 2 relevant in the consideration of the victim's negligence in the case at hand.

100 The Supreme Court first noted that a broker's strict professional liability does not automatically mean a higher threshold for finding contributory negligence on the part of the insured client. However, the Court stated that whether the insured can be blamed must be evaluated based on the reasonable expectations of the insured's conduct in the situation. Those expectations differ depending on whether an insurance broker is involved or not.

101 Considering both the broker's and insured's actions, the Supreme Court emphasised that Pareto's negligence, as established by the Court of Appeal, related to the core of a broker's duties – identifying the client's insurance needs and mapping risk areas that could fall outside the scope of coverage. This was the very expertise the insured was paying for in hiring a broker.

102 It was undisputed that no one at the insured factory had read the full insurance conditions. While Pareto claimed it had explicitly instructed the insured to do so, the Supreme Court found this was not the case. Furthermore, the Court noted it would be challenging for an ordinary insured to locate all the relevant terms across the factory's and landlord's policies, in total around 160 pages. The Court pointed out the difficulty for a typical insured in understanding how the various types of coverage aligned and interacted with each other.

103 The Supreme Court reasoned that the very fact that insurance conditions can be so complex is a key reason why an insured is willing to pay for a broker's expertise. The Court stressed that the broker, as the insurance expert, was in the best position to prevent errors and gaps in coverage. And while the insured factory was a professional enterprise, it was a mid-sized company without specialised insurance knowledge. Moreover, Pareto had developed a good understanding of the insured's operations over several years of working together.

104 Although insurance conditions are a critical part of any policy, and there are valid arguments that insured companies should review them carefully, the Supreme Court concluded that the factory owner could not be faulted for not discovering the insufficient coverage in this case. The Court found no specific red flags that should have prompted the insured company to scour the policies and no evidence that the factory owner deliberately accepted the risk of underinsurance to save on insurance premiums.

105 The Supreme Court found that by hiring an insurance broker, the owner of the factory had contracted and paid for Pareto to handle the very tasks the owner would otherwise have to do itself, including identifying risks and ensuring proper coverage. There was a legitimate division of roles and responsibilities between the parties. While prevention of errors in general was a duty also for the insured

party, this duty applied most strongly to the broker as the party with the greatest expertise and ability to avoid mistakes.

In conclusion, the Supreme Court held the factory was not negligent in relying on Pareto's advice and services without independently verifying every detail of the insurance conditions. The broker breached its core obligations and the insured's reasonable expectations in the relationship. A reduction of liability for contributory negligence was therefore not warranted, and Pareto was held responsible for the full uninsured losses. 106

c) Commentary

While the decision of the Supreme Court depended heavily on the specific facts, roles and conduct of the parties, it demonstrates that when an insurance customer engages a broker, the broker bears primary responsibility for diligently investigating the client's needs and ensuring proper coverage is obtained. The insured is entitled to rely in good faith on the broker's expertise and advice. Only in cases of clear 'red flags' or explicit instructions to review the policy details is the insured likely to be found negligent for not spotting errors or inadequacies in the insurance coverage arranged by the broker. 107

The Supreme Court's ruling incentivises brokers to thoroughly perform their core duties as insurance professionals, since they bear liability if the client suffers an uninsured loss due to gaps in coverage. The decision may lead brokers to more clearly instruct insureds to review policy conditions in detail. However, the Court made clear that even if such an instruction is given, this does not automatically absolve the broker if the error was one the broker should have detected and avoided in the first place given its expertise and the nature of its engagement. 108

Insureds, especially businesses, have a responsibility to provide accurate information to brokers, carefully review policy declarations and terms, and raise any questions or concerns. Retaining a broker is not an excuse for an insured to completely abdicate its role in the insurance process. However, the Supreme Court's decision states that when an insured has a reasonable, good faith belief that it has hired a skilled, diligent broker to analyse its risks and obtain appropriate coverage, the insured will not be penalised for gaps in coverage due to the broker's negligent failure to deliver on those core responsibilities. The ruling upholds the reasonable expectations of insureds in the insurance broker relationship. 109

In terms of key legal principles, the Supreme Court confirmed that the threshold for an insured's contributory negligence is not automatically higher in cases when the defendant is subject to strict professional liability. However, the specific 110 nature of the professional's duties and the client's reasonable expectations in the relationship are highly relevant in assessing whether the client was negligent.

6. HR 2 November 2023, HR-2023-2069-A: Patient Injury Compensation related to Premature Baby

a) Brief Summary of the Facts

111 This case concerns a claim for patient injury compensation under the exception provision in the Norwegian Act on Patient Injury Compensation (Lov om pasientskaderstatning (pskl)) sec 2, subsec 3.

112 The patient was born extremely prematurely at 24 weeks gestation in 2017, weighing only 530 grammes. As part of the intensive care treatment, a peripheral arterial catheter was inserted into the patient's left arm to monitor blood pressure and blood values. This catheter led to reduced blood circulation, which in turn caused extensive tissue damage in A's left hand, which resulted in A losing all fingers and a medical disability degree of 40%.

113 The key question was whether, under an overall assessment based on pskl sec 2, subsec 3, there were grounds to award compensation for the injury.

b) Judgment of the Court

114 Pskl sec 2, third paragraph provides an exception allowing compensation to be awarded even if there are no grounds for liability under the first and second paragraphs. It states:

> 'Even if there are no grounds for liability under the first and second paragraphs, compensation may exceptionally be paid when a patient injury has occurred that is particularly severe or particularly unexpected, and which cannot be considered a materialisation of a risk that the patient must accept. Emphasis shall be placed on whether sufficient information was provided in advance.'

115 According to a previous Supreme Court verdict in HR-2013-653, the provision aims to provide compensation in some cases where it would be offensive not to award compensation, the majority stated. It does not provide for a completely discretionary assessment by the judge. The assessment shall be specific to the case and according to certain criteria. The majority refered to a previous Supreme Court verdict in HR-2022-2356-A, and emphasised that the key factors in the assessment are:

the importance of the procedure, often referred to as the 'indication', the frequency of injury and the extent of the injury.

According to the same previous Supreme Court verdict, the majority stated, the assessment culminates in an overall assessment of whether there is a marked disproportion between the injury and the patient's illness, which thus lies outside of that which the patient must accept. This can be formulated as a question of whether the tolerance threshold has been exceeded. 116

Where treatment is adequate and necessary to save the patient's life, an injury resulting from the treatment will normally be considered the materialisation of a risk that the patient must accept. However, patients with life-threatening conditions are not generally exempt from the provision. 117

The majority first addressed the question of how to assess the 'indication', ie the importance of the treatment. In the case of this victim, it was argued that the relevant treatment was the use of the arterial catheter specifically. However, the majority found that it would be too narrow to assess the indication based on the method for monitoring blood pressure and blood values. 118

Rather, the majority stated, the indication must be assessed with reference to the condition being treated, which was prematurity. All necessary measures included in the intensive care treatment must be considered as a whole. Since the premature treatment was necessary to save A's life, the tolerance threshold is very high in this case. 119

Regarding the extent of the injury, the patient's medical disability was set at 40 %, which is in the lowest category where it may be appropriate to award compensation as a guideline. The injury was therefore not so minor that it could be used as an argument against awarding compensation in itself, the majority stated. On the other hand, the disability was not so great that it was a particularly strong argument for compensation in the overall assessment. 120

Concerning whether the injury was 'particularly unexpected', the majority noted that while the general risk of necrosis injuries was known and thus 'in the direction of the risk', the risk of such a severe injury as A suffered was very low, with no known comparable cases. Although there was some uncertainty, the majority considered that the risk of an injury of this extent was so minimal that it must be considered 'particularly unexpected', even though the risk of injury was known. 121

However, in the overall assessment of what the patient had to tolerate, the majority placed great weight on the fact that the treatment of the premature baby – which must be considered as a whole – was necessary to save her life. The tolerance threshold is thus high. 122

After a comprehensive assessment of the indication, the extent of the injury and how unexpected the injury was, the majority concluded that there is not a suf- 123 ficiently marked disproportion between the injury and the condition that necessitated the intensive care treatment, so that the tolerance threshold for what the patient had to accept had been exceeded.

124 The dissenting judge agreed with the majority on the legal starting points, but disagreed on how the existing case law should be understood regarding which risk the provision refers to, and thus when the tolerance threshold should be raised.

125 In the dissenting judge's view, it is primarily the risk associated with the injury-causing treatment measure that determines how much a patient must tolerate. If the risk of the treatment in question is low, there are no grounds for raising the tolerance threshold, the judge argued, and this applies even if the patient suffered from a life-threatening illness.

126 The dissenting judge placed great emphasis on the Court of Appeal's factual assessment that the risk of such a serious necrosis injury from an arterial catheter was very low and atypical, not 'in the direction of the risk'. When a commonly used, recommended and preferred treatment measure that is generally considered to involve a low risk affects a patient in such an unexpected way as in this case, there is no basis for an elevated tolerance threshold, the dissenting judge argued.

127 Applying the normal tolerance threshold, the dissenting judge considered it clear that the injury was so severe and unexpected that, based on an overall assessment, it cannot be considered the materialisation of a risk that the patient must accept. Thus, the dissenting judge wanted to dismiss the appeal.

c) Commentary

128 The case illustrates the challenging medical, legal and ethical considerations involved in determining the limits of patient injury compensation in the context of life-saving treatment of extremely premature infants. It highlights the importance of the specific facts and medical evidence in each case when applying the legal norms and principles.

129 While the majority's elevation of the tolerance threshold based on the necessity of the treatment considered as a whole has support in the case law, the dissenting judge raises valid points about the relevance of the risk profile of the specific injury-causing measure.

130 Ultimately, the majority's reasoning prevailed, resulting in the State not being held liable to pay compensation, but the case underscores the difficult balance between compensating patients who have been especially unfortunate, while recognising that some injuries are an unavoidable risk of life-saving treatment that patients must accept. Where that line is drawn depends on a careful weighing of medical, legal and ethical factors considering the evidence in each case.

7. HR 6 December 2023, HR-2023-2303-A: Statute of Limitations for Damage not Related to a Contract

a) Brief Summary of the Facts

Three brothers who had been victims of extensive neglect in their childhood in the 1960s and 1970s brought an action against a municipality, claiming that the municipality was liable for damages due to the failure of the child welfare service to intervene and implement measures. The Court of Appeal found that the claims were time-barred, as the exception to the 20-year rule in fl sec 9, subsec 2 did not apply. The brothers then brought the case before the Supreme Court. 131

The 20-year rule in fl sec 9, subsec 2 states that compensation claims are time-barred no later than 20 years after the damaging act or other basis for liability ceased. However, this does not apply to personal injury if: a) the damage was caused in commercial activity or equivalent activity, or while the injured party was under the age of 18, and b) the responsible party knew or should have known this could entail a risk to life or serious health damage. 132

In this case, the brothers claimed the municipality was liable for damages because the child welfare service did not intervene to improve their care situation, which involved severe neglect and abuse. The damage occurred in the 1960s and 1970s when the brothers were minors. 133

The key question was whether the child welfare service's failure to act falls under a commercial activity or an equivalent activity. If not, the 20-year limitation applies and the claims would be time-barred, as over 20 years had passed since the brothers turned 18. 134

b) Judgment of the Court

The Supreme Court noted that the parties agreed that the basis for liability ceased at the latest when the brothers came of age, in 1975, 1979 and 1981 respectively. This means that the 20-year deadline for submitting a claim expired in the period 1995–2001. 135

The term 'commercial activity' includes, according to the most obvious linguistic understanding, activities with an economic purpose of some scope and intensity, the Court noted. The Court referred to HR-2018-577-A, para 41, where the corresponding expression in the Damage Compensation Act sec 4-2 is understood in this way. 136

137 What is meant by 'equivalent activity' is less clear. But as can be seen from the mentioned judgment, the wording of para 42, indicates activities that 'lie quite close to' a commercial activity, even if they do not have an economic purpose.

138 An obvious example is the provision of services by the public sector – the State and municipalities. Some services are provided both by private companies and by the public sector. Then it is natural to equate them, even if the public sector does not provide such services for economic purposes.

139 On the other hand, it seems difficult in my opinion to equate the exercise of public authority with a commercial activity. The exercise of authority essentially involves making decisions that affect citizens by virtue of publicly delegated authority. This cannot in principle be done for commercial purposes and is both in principle and in practice of a different in nature to a commercial activity.

140 The Supreme Court found that the legislative history largely confirmed this understanding of the wording and referred to the preparatory works in the Cabinet's Proposition to the Parliament (Ot prp no 46 (1987–1988)).

141 The Proposition also showed that the main purpose of adding this exception in the Norwegian Limitation Act sec 9, subsec 2 was to strengthen the protection of the injured party in so-called late injury cases, ie in cases where the injury only becomes apparent many years after it was inflicted. The delimitation to 'commercial activity and equivalent activity' is justified in the Proposition (point 4.2).

142 The Supreme Court could not see that the legislative purposes pointed out here indicated that the condition should be understood in such a way that the exercise of public authority is also included. Nor can further considerations, such as that the injured party should be ensured protection against late injuries also in the case of errors in such activities, in my opinion be decisive. In this connection, the Supreme Court referred to HR-2023-1637-A, para 39. It shows, the Court noted, with reference to previous case law, that the positive legal nature of the Limitation Act indicated that caution should be exercised in deviating from the wording of the Act. The discretion of the court is limited.

143 There is, therefore, a boundary between cases of damage where liability is linked to a public service, and cases of damage where it is linked to the exercise of public authority, the Court argued.

144 The Supreme Court noted that some public actors – such as schools, universities, hospitals, other health services and child welfare services – carry out activities with elements of both public service and public authority. In such cases, the Supreme Court indicated that the boundary has to be drawn in consideration of what the basis for liability is linked to. If the basis is errors and deficiencies in a service provision, the relevant exception in the Limitation Act sec 9, subsec 2 letter was applicable in principle. For the child welfare service, an example could be neglect in a public child welfare institution. But if the basis for liability is essen-

tially errors and deficiencies in the exercise of authority, the Supreme Court found that the exception did not apply, with the consequence that the 20-year limitation period applied.

In this case, the Court noted, the brothers had alleged that the municipality is liable for damages because the child welfare service did not intervene and implement measures to improve their care situation at home. Thus the case concerns a lack of measures in the form of omitted investigations, preventive measures and caretaking, according to the Norwegian Child Welfare Act 1953 secs 17 to 19. 145

Some such measures may be of a voluntary nature and could possibly have been implemented without a decision. But both investigations and preventive measures are implemented in accordance with rules that essentially required decisions by virtue of publicly delegated authority, and which – if necessary – would have led to the brothers being taken forcibly into the care of the authorities. 146

The basis for liability that the brothers had invoked was, therefore, essentially the deficient exercise of public authority. This cannot be equated with a commercial activity, with the consequence that the 20-year rule in the Limitation Act sec 9, subsec 2 applies. Thus, the compensation claims were time-barred. 147

The appeal was therefore rejected. 148

c) Commentary

The key implication that can be drawn from this Norwegian Supreme Court case (HR-2023-2303-A) is that the exercise of public authority cannot be equated with a 'commercial activity or equivalent activity' under the exception to the 20-year limitation rule. 149

Also, there is a distinction between deficiencies in public services, which may fall under the 'equivalent activity' exception, and deficiencies in the exercise of public authority, which do not. The boundary should be drawn based on what the alleged basis of liability relates to. 150

In addition, a restrictive interpretation of exceptions to statutory limitation periods is warranted due to the positive law nature of the act. Policy considerations have limited weight when considering a deviation from the wording of the law. 151

8. Personal Injury

The most important cases regarding personal injury in this year's report are the Supreme Court decisions referred to above (HR-2023-268-A, HR-2023-1108-A, HR-2023-1172-A and HR-2023-2069-A). 152

C. Literature

1. *Anne Marie Frøseth*, Erstatningsansvar for brukere av kunstig intelligens [Liability for users of Artificial Intelligence in tort law] Tidsskrift for erstatningsrett (TfE) 1–2 (2023) 7–62

153 The article discusses liability issues for users of Artificial Intelligence (AI) based on proposals from the European Parliament and the European Commission. AI has certain characteristics, such as complexity, unpredictability, and interconnectedness with external systems, which create challenges for liability.

154 The European Parliament proposes strict liability for high-risk AI systems, combined with mandatory insurance. For normal-risk systems, fault-based liability applies with a presumption of fault. The Commission's AI Liability Directive is based on national fault-based liability, with rules on access to evidence and a presumption of fault for non-compliance. It also proposes a general presumption of causation with different conditions for different categories of tortfeasors.

155 The article analyses the content of the proposals and their relationship to Norwegian law. It discusses whether the general fault-based rule falls short, and to what extent the proposals address the challenges. It also considers whether the Norwegian unwritten strict liability model has a broader scope than the European Parliament's strict liability model.

156 The author starts the article with an analysis of the characteristics of AI that create challenges regarding liability in tort law (pp 7–11).

157 AI systems have certain characteristics that create challenges for liability: complexity, unpredictability, and interconnectedness with external systems. The self-learning process that changes the logical structure is difficult to explain and control, leading to uncertainty about whether and how the technology can cause damage.

158 AI systems can respond independently to new information to perform tasks, but their decision-making process is often a 'black box'. The training data and algorithms determine the system's behaviour in ways that are not always transparent or predictable. This autonomy and adaptability make it challenging to foresee potential risks and harms.

159 Moreover, AI systems are often interconnected with other digital systems and rely on external data sources. A failure or vulnerability in one component can propagate through the system in complex ways. Determining the root cause of an AI-related incident and attributing liability can be difficult.

These characteristics – complexity, unpredictability, autonomy, and interconnectedness – are at the heart of the liability challenges posed by AI. Traditional legal concepts and liability rules may struggle to adequately address these novel risks. Policymakers are grappling with how to adapt liability frameworks to ensure adequate protection for individuals and society, while still encouraging innovation in AI technology. 160

The author then gives an overview of the proposed user liability regulations from EU bodies (pp 18–38). The European Parliament and Commission proposals aim to address the challenges of AI by introducing new liability rules and evidentiary presumptions specifically tailored to AI systems. However, as the article discusses, these proposals have their own limitations and potential drawbacks that need to be carefully considered. 161

The European Parliament proposes a strict liability regime for 'high-risk' AI systems. Under strict liability, the operator of the AI system would be liable for damage caused by the system, regardless of fault. This is intended to provide stronger protection for victims and shift the burden of AI risks onto the operators who benefit from the technology. 162

However, the author notes, the Parliament's definition of 'high-risk' AI systems seems problematic. It covers systems with 'significant potential to cause harm or damage to one or more persons in a manner that is random and goes beyond what can reasonably be expected'. This definition appears quite broad and vague, potentially encompassing a wide range of AI applications. 163

There are concerns that such a sweeping definition could lead to over-deterrence and chill innovation. It may fail to provide a clear and harmonised framework for strict liability across the EU. The Parliament's proposal also seems to focus mainly on risks from physical mobile machines like robots and vehicles, neglecting other types of harm which could be caused by AI. 164

Moreover, the author notes, the Parliament's strict liability rule could potentially limit the scope of existing national strict liability regimes. Many EU countries already have sector-specific or risk-based strict liability rules that may be broader than the Parliament's 'high-risk' category. It is unclear whether the EU rule would take precedence and constrain these national laws. 165

For 'normal-risk' AI systems, the Parliament proposes a fault-based liability rule with a presumption of fault. However, this presumption can be rebutted on extensive grounds that have similarities to a regular fault-based rule in practice. Based on this, it is questionable whether this presumption would significantly improve the position of claimants, the author argues. 166

Finally, the Parliament's complex definition of 'operator' liability seems to overlap with the existing Product Liability Directive. Operators are divided into frontend users and backend providers, the latter potentially including producers 167 and sellers. This raises concerns about expanding product liability 'through the back door' without directly amending the Product Liability Directive.

168 In summary, while the Parliament's proposal attempts to address the challenges of AI liability, it suffers from an overly broad and vague definition of 'high-risk' systems, it has the potential to conflict with national laws, it contains a rebuttable fault presumption of questionable value, and overlaps with the product liability regime. These issues may undermine the proposal's goals of harmonisation and effective victim protection.

169 In contrast to the Parliament's approach, the European Commission's proposed AI Liability Directive takes national fault-based liability rules as its starting point. Rather than introducing a new strict liability regime, it focuses on evidentiary rules to facilitate proving liability for AI-related harms.

170 The Directive includes two key features:

171 Firstly, the Directive establishes a duty to disclose evidence, with a presumption of fault for non-compliance. Providers and professional users of high-risk AI systems would be required to disclose certain evidence about the system upon court order. Failure to comply would lead to a rebuttable presumption that the non-disclosure contributed to the AI malfunction. This aims to address the black box problem and information asymmetries in AI liability cases.

172 Secondly, the Directive establishes a presumption of causation between the AI fault and the damage, with different conditions for providers, professional users, and private users of high-risk systems. Claimants would need to prove a breach of duty, likelihood that the breach influenced the AI output, and a causal link. The exact conditions vary depending on the category of defendant. This presumption is intended to ease the burden of proving the causal chain from human fault to AI failure to resulting damage.

173 However, the Directive's approach also has significant limitations. The duty to disclose evidence is restricted to data retention obligations for high-risk systems under the AI Act. This narrow scope may leave many AI liability cases without improved access to evidence.

174 The causation presumption is also quite limited in practice. For providers, it mainly applies to breaches of specific safety requirements in the AI Act. For professional users, only breaches of monitoring obligations are relevant. For private users, the presumption has little practical significance. Moreover, the presumption still requires the claimant to establish several elements, including a breach of duty and likelihood of influence on the AI output, which may be challenging to prove.

175 Overall, while the Commission's proposal neglects some of the issues addresses by the Parliament's strict liability approach, its impact may be constrained by the limited scope of the disclosure duty and causation presumption. It remains

to be seen whether these evidentiary rules will make a major difference for claimants in AI liability cases.

The Directive's reliance on the AI Act's definition of high-risk systems also raises concerns. As discussed earlier, this definition is complex and currently quite narrow. Tying liability rules to this same definition could unduly restrict their application. 176

In conclusion, the Commission's AI Liability Directive represents a more cautious approach focused on evidentiary issues within existing fault-based regimes. But its effectiveness may be hampered by the limitations of its disclosure and causation rules, as well as its dependence on the AI Act's high-risk definition. Further refinements may be needed to truly address the liability challenges posed by AI and provide meaningful redress for victims. 177

Frøseth then analyses the challenges in applying fault-based liability to AI (pp 38–40). 178

The article highlights several difficulties in applying traditional fault-based liability rules to AI systems. These challenges arise from the unique characteristics of AI discussed earlier, particularly its complexity, unpredictability, and autonomy. 179

One key issue is the difficulty of foreseeing and controlling the behaviour of AI systems that can learn and adapt in unexpected ways. Even with extensive testing, it may not be possible to anticipate all potential failure modes or unintended consequences. This makes it harder to determine whether an AI developer or operator has breached a duty of care. 180

Another challenge is the lack of general knowledge in society about the specific risks posed by different AI systems. Unlike established technologies, there is not yet a clear understanding of what constitutes reasonable care in the design, deployment and monitoring of AI. This can make it difficult for courts to assess fault by reference to industry standards or best practices. 181

The article notes that under Norwegian law, the level of knowledge required for the establishment of fault liability is generally limited to publicly available information. However, this standard may be higher for professionals working with AI, given their specialised expertise. This raises questions about what duties of care can reasonably be expected from AI developers and operators. 182

Relatedly, there are open questions about what counts as an acceptable level of residual risk for AI systems. Some degree of uncertainty and unpredictability may be inherent in the technology. Demanding that AI operators eliminate all possibility of harm could be unrealistic and overly burdensome. 183

These challenges suggest that fault-based liability rules alone may struggle to adequately address the risks of AI. Courts may have difficulty assessing whether an AI operator has taken appropriate precautions or breached a duty of care considering the technology's inherent unpredictability. 184

185 At the same time, the article cautions against setting the bar for reasonable care so high that it effectively imposes strict liability in practice. Doing so could overly deter socially beneficial innovation and deployment of AI systems.

186 Ultimately, the application of fault-based liability to AI will require careful consideration of what duties and standards of care are appropriate for different types of systems and contexts. A combination of industry standards, regulatory requirements, and case-by-case judicial assessments may be needed to strike the right balance between victim protection and encouraging responsible AI development.

187 The challenges highlighted here underscore the need for a comprehensive and nuanced approach to AI liability that goes beyond simply applying existing fault-based rules. The EU proposals discussed earlier attempt to address some of these challenges through modifications to evidentiary burdens and presumptions. But, as the article argues, their scope and effectiveness remain uncertain.

188 The article then compares the European Parliament's proposed strict liability rule for high-risk AI systems to the unwritten strict liability doctrine recognised in Norwegian law. This doctrine allows for strict liability to be imposed based on a judicial assessment of the nature and severity of the risk, among other factors.

189 The author questions whether this unwritten strict liability rule might have a broader scope of application than the Parliament's proposal. The latter is limited to predefined categories of high-risk AI systems, whereas the Norwegian doctrine allows for a more flexible, case-by-case determination of strict liability.

190 Under the Norwegian approach, courts can consider factors like the probability and severity of harm, the nature of the activity, the ability to prevent or insure against the risk, and the social value of the activity. This enables a more nuanced assessment of whether strict liability is appropriate for a particular AI system or context.

191 In contrast, the Parliament's proposal relies on a rigid classification of high-risk systems that may not capture all AI applications that warrant strict liability. Its focus on physical mobile systems like robots and vehicles could leave out other types of AI harms.

192 The Norwegian doctrine's flexibility also allows it to evolve and adapt as AI technology advances and new risks emerge. Courts can extend strict liability to novel AI applications based on their specific risk profiles. The Parliament's predefined categories, on the other hand, may quickly become outdated.

193 However, the article does not delve into a detailed comparison of the two approaches. It is possible that the open-ended nature of the Norwegian doctrine could also lead to uncertainty and inconsistency in its application to AI. Clear guidelines for assessing AI risks under the doctrine may be needed.

Moreover, the Norwegian approach is a unique feature of Norway's legal system. It may not be feasible or desirable to transpose it directly to the EU level, given the diversity of legal traditions among Member States. 194

Nonetheless, the comparison highlights the potential limitations of the Parliament's categorical approach to strict AI liability. It suggests that a more flexible, risk-based assessment akin to the Norwegian doctrine might be better suited to the evolving challenges of AI. 195

Of course, any strict liability regime for AI would need to be carefully designed to balance victim protection, legal certainty, and innovation incentives. The article's concluding observations emphasise the need for a comprehensive and coherent EU liability framework that encompasses both fault-based and strict liability rules, as well as product liability, in a transparent manner. 196

In the concluding section of the article (p 41 f), the author expresses skepticism about the need for special liability rules for users of AI, as proposed by the EU Parliament and Commission. 197

The author argues that such special rules may not be necessary, given the extensive product safety regulation already under development. This includes the proposed changes to the Product Liability Directive and the new AI Act. These instruments will impose mandatory safety standards and technical requirements on AI systems, particularly those classified as high-risk. Compliance with these standards will shape the duties that users have under the general liability rules. 198

The author suggests that a comprehensive regulation of the liability regime as a whole, designating certain cases to the rules of product liability in a clearer way where appropriate, could provide a more transparent solution. Instead of introducing special user liability rules, consideration should be given to whether product liability can be expanded to cover more situations where users play a substantial role in creating or controlling the risk. 199

The article also points out that the EU Parliament's proposal for strict user liability for high-risk systems seems to have a narrower scope of application than the Norwegian unwritten rule on strict liability. The Norwegian rule is more flexible and allows for a broader assessment of whether strict liability is reasonable based on the risk in the specific situation. The EU Parliament's model, on the other hand, is limited to predefined categories of high-risk systems. 200

Regarding the EU Commission's proposed AI Liability Directive, the author believes that it does little to alleviate the situation for injured parties in the form in which it was presented in 2022. The Directive's procedural tools, such as the duty to disclose evidence and presumptions of causation, have significant limitations that may undermine their effectiveness in practice. 201

Overall, the author suggests that a more comprehensive and coherent approach to AI liability is necessary, rather than introducing fragmented special 202 rules for users. Such a holistic regulation should encompass both fault-based liability, strict liability, and product liability in a way that balances the interests of victim protection, legal certainty, and innovation incentives. It should also be flexible enough to adapt to the rapid technological developments in the AI field.

203 In my opinion, this article represents a necessary and very welcome analysis of the development regarding the regulation of AI in the EU and its relation to Norwegian tort law. The author is thorough in the various analyses in the article and contributes to important interpretations and clarifications of the complex regulation of AI systems in the EU.

Ewa Bagińska and Paulina Wyszyńska-Ślufińska

XXII. Poland

A. Legislation

1. Amendment of arts 24 and 448 of the Civil Code [KC] by the Act of 28 July 2023 (Journal of Laws of 2023, item 1615): Protection of Personal Interests; Compensatory Claims of Direct and Indirect Victims; Concurrence, and Inheritance of Claims for Non-Pecuniary Loss

Before the revision, art 448 KC read: 1

> 'In the case of an infringement of personal interests, the court may, independently of other measures necessary to remove the results of the infringement, award the injured person an appropriate sum as compensation for non-pecuniary harm or (may at his request) award an appropriate sum to a social cause chosen by him.'

This version of art 448 KC was introduced in 1996, following the decision of the legislator to exclude intentional fault as a premise of the claim as well as to allow all social causes indicated by the victim as beneficiaries of an award (previously the law indicated the Polish Red Cross). 2

After the revision, art 448 now has three paragraphs instead of one: 3

> § 1. In the case of an infringement of personal interests, the court may, independently of other measures necessary to remove the results of the infringement, either award the injured person an appropriate sum as compensation for non-pecuniary harm or award (at his request) an appropriate sum to a social cause chosen by him.
>
> § 2. In the cases specified in Article 445 § 1 and 2 and Article 446^2, the person whose personal interest has been infringed may, in addition to (irrespective of) monetary compensation for non-pecuniary harm, demand that an appropriate sum of money be awarded to a social cause chosen by him.
>
> § 3. Article 445 § 3 shall apply to the claims referred to in § 1 and 2 above.

A parallel to the change to art 448 § 1 KC has been made in art 24 § 1 KC, according to which: 4

https://doi.org/10.1515/9783111376721-023

'Whosoever's personal rights are threatened by another person's action may demand that the action ceases, unless it is not unlawful. In the case of infringements already committed, he may also require the wrongdoer to remove the results of the infringements and in particular to make an appropriate declaration in an appropriate form. *Pursuant to the rules of this Code, he may also claim compensation for non-pecuniary loss or demand that the wrongdoer pay an appropriate sum of money to a specific social cause.*[1] The third sentence now reads: Pursuant to the rules of this Code, he may also *either* claim compensation for non-pecuniary loss *or* demand that the wrongdoer pay an appropriate sum of money to a specific social cause.'

5 The amendment significantly altered the structure of the provision of art 448 and its relation to the provisions governing some other claims. Its ramifications are threefold.

6 Firstly, as the correlative conjunction 'either, or' (Polish: *albo*) was used in art 448 § 1 (and also in art 24 § 1), instead of the conjunction 'or' (Polish: *lub*), the linguistic rules dictate that the claims are alternative claims. Thus, the injured may claim either compensation for themselves, or for a social cause chosen by them, but not both (whether in part or in whole). Consequently, the cumulation of claims described in art 448 § 2 constitutes an exception to this rule.

7 Secondly, a new normative content in art 448 § 2 has been expressed in a rather awkward manner. An additional claim for the adjudication of an appropriate sum for a social cause is now expressly granted to the person whose personal interest has been infringed and who, in the hypotheses specified in arts 445 § 1, 445 § 2[2] or 446^2 KC[3] is entitled to claim compensation for their own benefit. Thus, both the direct victim (whose claims are governed by art 445 § 1 and § 2), as well as the closest person (next of kin) of the seriously injured yet surviving victim (having a claim under art 446^2 KC) will be entitled to an additional claim under new art 448 § 2 KC – a sum to be paid to a social cause.

8 Thirdly, the content of the hitherto existing sentence 2 of art 448 has been marked as § 3 and it has been specified that art 445 § 3 applies to claims referred

1 Emphasis (italics) added by the authors.

2 Art 445 § 1. In the cases specified in the foregoing article, the court may award to the injured person an appropriate sum as compensation for non-pecuniary harm.
§ 2 The above provision shall also apply in the case of a deprivation of liberty and where a person has been induced by deceit, violence or the abuse of a relationship of dependency to submit to an illicit sexual act.
§ 3 A claim for compensation for non-pecuniary harm shall pass to the heirs of the deceased only if this was agreed in writing or the action was commenced when the deceased was still alive.

3 'In the event of a serious and irreversible personal injury or disorder of health resulting in the inability to establish or continue a family relationship, the court may award the injured party's immediate family members an appropriate sum by way of financial compensation for the non-pecuniary harm suffered.'

to in § 1 or § 2. The reference to the provision of art 445 § 3 KC confirms the admissibility and the conditions for inheritance of the victim's claims for compensation, regardless of whether paid to the victim or to a social purpose.

The amendment of the Code entered into force on 15 September 2023. The Act 9
does not contain transitional provisions, and therefore, in light of the prohibition of retroactivity (art 3 KC) and in accordance with the *tempus regit actum* rule, legal events occurring before 15 September 2023 leading to obligations arising before that date shall be governed by the previous provisions. The latter determine whether a given event constitutes a tort and what is the content of the resulting obligation to pay damages.

The motives behind the decision of the legislator are unclear and must be de- 10
ciphered from the text of the rules. It is futile to seek the reasons for the change in the explanatory memorandum of the amending bill because the latter in fact concerned alterations to the substantive and procedural rules on succession and selected family law rules. The changes to the provisions on the protection of personal rights were added in further stages of the legislative process, with no justification offered, but not entirely coincidentally prior to the upcoming parliamentary elections.

On a more general and policy level, the changes are significant. The present 11
wording of arts 24 § 1 and 448 § 1 KC may be interpreted as the introduction of a general rule that the victim of a tort has only one claim for compensation for non-pecuniary loss. They are now obliged to choose between monetary compensation for themselves and the payment of an appropriate sum to a designated social cause. This alternative is, however, limited to the situation of the violation of personal rights other than those protected under art 445 § 1 in conjunction with art 444 (ie health, physical and mental integrity), or under art 445 § 2 (personal freedom, sexual integrity). Hence, the cumulative concurrence of claims is permitted in the case of the violation of health, physical and mental integrity, personal freedom, sexual integrity and the family bond.[4]

A brief glimpse of the history of the interpretation of art 448 KC sheds some 12
light on the importance of the legislative change. The claim for the payment of a sum of money for a social purpose has its origin in art 165 of the Polish Code of Obligations (1933), which was inspired by art 49 of the Swiss Code of Obligations. In cases of bodily injury or health damage as well as violations of other rights, the earliest legislator allowed the compensation to be granted to the injured party or to an institution designated by them. In this way, the victim had the possibility to

4 A new entitlement for indirect victims of a tort was only introduced in art 446^2 KC in 2021, reported in *E Karner/BC Steininger* (eds), European Tort Law 2021 (2022) 467, nos 1–5.

obtain satisfaction of their choice. Under the Civil Code (1964), the claim for the benefit of the Red Cross (art 448) was not considered as compensation for non-pecuniary loss, but rather a sort of private penalty (sanction) that had to be paid to the Red Cross. It must be stressed that non-pecuniary damage arising from the violation of personal interests (when no physical or psychological damage to persons was at stake) was not otherwise compensated. Following the ruling of a full Civil Chamber of the Supreme Court on 8 December 1973,[5] the judicature emphasised that compensation paid to the Red Cross played an explicit preventive role, as well as served to punish the wrongdoer for their intent (malice) in an interference with personal interests of another. However, after the legislative change in 1996, case law and doctrine were divided on the issue of whether the claimant whose personal interests have been violated may demand only one form of compensation to be paid, either for their benefit or for the designated social purpose. In the minority view, art 448 KC regulated one, indivisible claim for redress of non-pecuniary loss. Therefore, consequently, some courts have held that the norm contained an alternative excluding a cumulation of claims. A major part of the doctrine took the same position. However, the Supreme Court followed the opposite view, which eventually prevailed in the recent decade both in the jurisprudence and in court practice.[6]

13 The prevalent interpretation was based on the following major arguments. First of all, the linguistic interpretation (the use of the word 'or') suggested a cumulative choice, and this conclusion was not superseded by the functional and systematic construction of art 448 KC. The fact that both claims are embraced by one provision and are based on the same premises does not mean that they are identical. Secondly, although both claims provide for pecuniary redress, the means of reparation of moral harm varies, and hence they are not identical, but separate claims. The money paid to the injured is a different means of redress than the satisfaction they feel by making the wrongdoer pay a sum of money to a charitable institution. Furthermore, the Supreme Court emphasised the difference in functions and structure between the claims (sanctions) embraced by art 448 KC: compensation for non-pecuniary loss plays a compensatory role, as it purports to make the plaintiff whole. Conversely, the sum awarded to a social cause serves as a private (civil) penalty as it aims at punishing the perpetrator as well as having preventive and deterrent functions. Finally, art 448 KC has always been considered a discretionary tool for a judge. If the claimant wishes to have a

5 Orzecznictwo Sądu Najwyższego (Decisions of the Supreme Court, OSN) 1974, 145.
6 See Sąd Najwyższy (Polish Supreme Court, SN) 17 March 2006, I CSK 81/05, OSP 3/2007, item 30.

part of the damages paid for their account and another part for a social purpose, it would be against the nature of such regulation to limit this possibility.

In the light of the above remarks, the claim for the payment of a sum of money to a social cause should be seen as a continuation of the institution expressed in the original regulation of art 448 KC. This means that the legislator seems to subscribe to the classic, yet forgone, views on the functions of the provisions of arts 448 and 445 KC (the minority view on the construction of art 448 KC), leading to a disjunctive alternative of claims expressed in what is now §1 of art 448. By way of an exception, the legislator has maintained the cumulative concurrence of claims in art 448 § 2. The debate, nevertheless, is certainly not over as the exclusion of cumulation of claims constitutes a reduction in the protection of the injured. By opting against the possibility of a cumulation of the claims specified in art 448 § 1 KC, the legislator's intention seems to focus on narrowing the scope of compensation in cases other than personal injury cases. On the other hand, in personal injury cases, providing the compensation to a social cause has not been limited to intentional and therefore particularly reprehensible violations, which would suggest that its main functions are deterrence and punishment. This additional sanction can be claimed even in the case of negligence or strict liability. Finally, the motives lying behind the granting of the additional claim to the injured person's next of kin pursuing a claim for compensation under art 446^2 for the discontinuation of a family bond with the seriously and irreversibly injured victim are unclear. 14

2. Amendment of art 1050 of the Civil Procedure Code [KPC] by the Act of 9 March 2023 (Journal of Laws of 2023, item 614): Protection of Personal Interests; Judicial Enforcement of Non-Compensatory Claims

By virtue of art 1(p 145) of the Act of 9 March 2023, a new § 4 was added to art 1050 of the Code of Civil Procedure. According to this rule, if in cases of an infringement of personal rights the debtor fails to make a statement of appropriate content and in an appropriate form, despite a time limit for its submission under the pain of a fine having been set, the court shall impose on the debtor a fine of up to PLN 15,000 (approx € 3,330) and shall order it to publish in Monitor Sądowy i Gospodarczy, at the debtor's expense, an announcement corresponding to the content of the required declaration and in an appropriate form. The publication of such an apology shall – to the extent covered by it – result in the expiry of the claim stated in the enforceable title. The amendment of art 1050 § 4 KPC was intended to change the line of case law, relating to the manner of enforcement of enforceable titles, in 15 which the debtor was obliged, pursuant to art 24 § 1 KC, to remove the consequences of the infringement of personal interests by making an apology.[7] This provision was politically motivated and may result in a significant limitation of the effective protection of personal rights through the non-pecuniary measures despite having obtained a judicial order by the plaintiff. The change was later followed by the amendment of the Civil Code reported above at nos 3–14.

B. Cases

1. Sąd Apelacyjny w Warszawie (Court of Appeals in Warsaw) I Civil Department, 22 June 2023, I ACa 352/23:[8] Violation of the General Data Protection Regulation (GDPR) and Violation of Personal Interests

a) Brief Summary of the Facts

16 When checking her first name and surname on the internet, the plaintiff discovered that her name was not anonymised in a judgment of the Supreme Administrative Court, published in the Central Database of Administrative Court Judgments. The judgment confirmed the denial of entry on the list of bailiffs as the plaintiff had been given a disciplinary punishment in the past. The plaintiff sued the State Treasury – Supreme Administrative Court, demanding payment of compensation in the amount of PLN 30,000 for moral damage, claiming that the lack of anonymisation in the judgment and the fact that the judgment was available to an unlimited number of people on the internet led to the violation of her personal interests (arts 24 and 448 KC). The court of first instance awarded compensation in the amount of PLN 20,000, indicating that the claimant's personal interests, ie her good name and the right to privacy and the provisions on personal data protection regulations, had been violated. The defendant filed an appeal.

7 See the resolution of the Supreme Court of 28 June 2006, III CZP 23/06, OSNC 2007, no 1, item 11 and the judgment of 6 October 1972, I CR 274/72.
8 Published at <orzeczenia.ms.gov.pl>.

b) Judgment of the Court

The Court of Appeals indicated that in the case, the basis for the plaintiff's claims are arts 24 § 1 and 448 KC and art 82 of the GDPR. The court pointed out that, under art 82 of the GDPR, both pecuniary and non-pecuniary damage is subject to compensation. It was underlined that the provisions on personal data protection are similar in nature to the tort liability regime, and due to the lack of a comprehensive regulation, to the extent not regulated by the GDPR, the provisions of the Civil Code should be applied. 17

The court held that personal data is not the same as personal interests, but in the case at hand, the violation of data protection regulations violated the plaintiff's personal interest in the form of her good name and right to privacy. The court underlined that a component of the right to privacy is the principle of informational autonomy of the individual, which manifests itself in the individual's right 'to decide independently to disclose to others information concerning his or her person, as well as the right to exercise control over such information in the possession of others'. 18

The conduct of the defendant fell within the sphere of the broadly understood exercise of public authority (*imperium*). The legal basis for the State Treasury's liability is, in addition to the provisions on the violation of personal rights, art 417 § 1 (strict liability for public authorities). Hence, the condition for awarding compensation for non-material damage is not, contrary to general principles, the fault of the tortfeasor, but it is sufficient to demonstrate the unlawfulness of the violation of personal interests. 19

The court reduced the compensation, indicating the plaintiff did not face any negative consequences from the disclosure of her data in the professional environment, or from those involved in her enforcement proceedings. The Court of Appeals also bore in mind that although the primary cause of the plaintiff's harm was the unlawful act (and then several years of inaction) of the defendant, the extent of the dissemination of the non-anonymised justification of the judgment, and thus the extent of the plaintiff's harm, was also affected by the conduct of a third party. 20

c) Commentary

The commented ruling is interesting as it attempts to explain the relationship between the provisions on the protection of personal interests provided for in KC and the regulations on the protection of personal data. The judgment is another exam- 21 ple of the view present in Polish court practice[9] according to which, if there is a violation of personal interests, the provisions of the GDPR referring to compensation for non-pecuniary damage are not sufficient. The Polish Civil Code shall be applicable to the extent that the matter is not regulated by the GDPR. Unfortunately, the court failed to take note of the boundaries between an infringement of personal interests and of the GDPR. It reduced its consideration only to the statement that the GDPR is not a sufficient ground for claiming compensation.

22 Nevertheless, it is worth noting that in the Polish doctrine, two views can be presented on the issue in question. According to the first, a violation of the GDPR is not a sufficient ground and such a violation must result in the violation of personal interests. The second provides that a violation of the GDPR is enough to claim damages and there is no need to indicate the violation of personal interests.[10] The second view seems to be more correct, as the legislator does not require the violation of personal interests. Nevertheless, to the extent not regulated in the GDPR, domestic provisions shall apply.

23 It can be added that there are not many cases on the violation of the GDPR in the context of seeking recovery for non-pecuniary loss. If such cases occur, the claimants most often invoke the regulation on violation of personal interests (arts 24 and 448 KC) as the basis of their claim.

2. The Supreme Court Resolution, 3 October 2023, III CZP 22/23:[11] Compensation for Moral Harm caused to a Legal Person

a) Brief Summary of the Facts

24 The defendant posted a negative opinion about the plaintiff's business conduct, alleging that the company sells poor quality products. The company sued the defendant for violation of personal interests (rights), demanding: the correction of information, the removal of the opinion from the internet and the payment of compensation for moral damage (Polish: *krzywda*) in the amount of PLN 22,000.

25 The first instance court upheld the claim, awarding compensation in the amount of PLN 5,000. The respondent appealed. The Court of Appeals had doubts

9 See also judgment of the Regional Court in Warsaw, 6 June 2020, file no XXV C 2596/19.

10 See *A Pązik*, Szkoda wynikająca z naruszenia przepisów RODO. Wybrane problemy, Zeszyty Naukowe Uniwersytetu Jagiellońskiego 3 (2020) 141 ff.

11 Published at <www.sn.pl>.

as to whether a legal person can claim compensation for moral harm. Pursuant to art 43 KC, the provisions on the protection of the personal interests of natural persons shall be applied accordingly to legal persons. The Court recalled two views. According to the first, in the light of art 43 KC, a legal person is entitled to claim compensation for moral damage (the view formed by the jurisprudence of the Supreme Court). According to the second view, a legal person is not capable of suffering moral harm, so it is not entitled to compensation (the position expressed by some courts of appeals).

The Court of Appeals asked a preliminary question to the Supreme Court: 26

> 'Can a legal entity demand that a person who has violated its personal interests pay compensation for the moral harm it has suffered under art 448 KC in conjunction with art 43 KC?'

In the proceedings before the Supreme Court, the Prosecutor General and the Ombudsman requested a resolution on the Court of Appeal's question. 27

b) Judgment of the Court

The Supreme Court ruled that the provisions of art 448 KC (now art 448 § 1 KC – compensation in case of violation of personal interests) apply accordingly to legal entities (art 43 KC), making it possible to award compensation. 28

Firstly, the Court pointed out that the amendment of the provisions of art 24 § 1 KC (protection of personal interests) and art 448 KC (compensation in a case of violation of personal interests) in 2023 is not relevant in the case at hand (see nos 1–13 above). 29

The Court presented the case law of the Supreme Court. The justification of the resolution is long and at times chaotic. In order to make it easier for the reader, we will group the arguments in the following sections: the personal interest of a legal entity, the meaning of non-pecuniary harm of a legal entity and the non-pecuniary and pecuniary means of protection. 30

Legal entities have personal interests. First of all, the Court pointed out that in the light of its case law, the provisions on the personal interests of natural persons and the means of their protection apply to legal entities only via the reference in art 43 KC. Unlike the interests of natural persons, whose interests are inherent to a human being, personal interests of legal persons are to be understood as non-material values that enable a legal person to function in accordance with its scope of activities. Since the interests of natural and legal persons are not the same, they have different functions. In addition, the Supreme Court stressed that the assessment of the personal interests of legal persons should be made ob- 31 jectively, irrespective of the subjective elements of feelings and emotions which are present when the personal interests of natural persons are violated. The Court pointed out that a distinction should be made between violations of the interests of legal persons, and the interests of natural persons who are members of a legal entity. A legal person is a separate legal entity, and therefore a violation of interests affects the entire substrate of the legal entity, not the natural persons who are its members.

32 In further consideration, the Court found that art 43 KC also refers to art 23 KC (the catalogue of personal interests of natural persons). As a result, it should be noted that legal persons can be considered to have personal interests. At the same time, the Court noted that such a statement that legal entities have personal interests is a simplification, as it is more correct to say that 'civil law grants protection to certain values of a non-material nature, which have significance not for an individual person, but for a certain separate legal entity'. The Court added that if a legal person is recognised as an entrepreneur, there is a clear connection between certain personal interests and the pecuniary sphere of the entity.

33 According to the Supreme Court, the personal interests of legal entities are non-material values that enable a legal entity to function in accordance with the scope of its activities. Such values must be recognised by society. In addition, it was pointed out that art 43 KC does not indicate what interests are subject to protection, and since art 23 KC provides for an open catalogue of personal interests, the catalogue of personal interests of legal entities is also open. Some personal interests of natural persons have no counterpart as regards the interests of legal persons, while others do. For example, the equivalent of a name and surname is the good name or business name of a legal person or of its identifying brands. The Court pointed out that the most common personal interest of a legal entity is considered to be its good reputation (good name). The infringement of this interest occurs in the case of negative opinions, which – objectively assessed – can lead to the loss of trust, which is essential for its functioning.

34 Based on art 43 KC, the provisions on the protection of personal interests of natural persons shall be applied accordingly, which means that there is no limitation on the scope of protection for a legal entity. This includes the possibility of claiming compensation on the basis of art 448 KC.

35 **The concept of moral (non-pecuniary) damage.** It is worth noting the arguments of the Court that define the concept of non-pecuniary harm of legal entities. According to the Court, the concept of harm indicated in art 448 KC does not exclude the application of this provision to legal entities, since the concept of harm cannot be equated solely with the experience of physical and mental suffering.

> 'For obvious reasons, legal entities do not experience either physical or mental suffering, but they suffer non-pecuniary damage as a result of the violation of their personal rights, which cannot be measured in money.'

As a further argument justifying the award of compensation to a legal entity, the Court considered the functions of compensation, stressing that it does not only have a compensatory function, but also satisfying, punitive and deterrent functions. The Supreme Court cited its Resolution of 9 November 2017, according to which, art 448 KC applies in conjunction with art 43 KC also to claims for compensation asserted by legal entities in the case of a violation of their personal interests.[12] The Supreme Court stressed that legal entities, by their very nature, cannot suffer harm, but all three functions of compensation support the need to grant them such compensation. 36

According to the prevalent doctrinal opinion, a legal entity is entitled to claim compensation due to the language of art 448 KC, which in 1996 replaced the term 'injured party' with the phrase 'one whose personal interests have been violated'. Moreover, the possibility of granting compensation for non-pecuniary damage has been recognised by the European Court of Human Rights (ECtHR). 37

The main argument against the application of art 448 KC to legal entities is the concept of moral harm used in the Code: the harm is considered to be the pain and suffering resulting from the violation of personal interests of a person. Such a definition of harm cannot be applied to legal entities. Due to the lack of a statutory definition of moral harm in the Code, it is necessary to refer to the common meaning of 'moral harm'. This allows, in the context of art 448 KC, the application of a broader meaning of harm, hence encompassing not only physical and mental feelings of a person, but also other negative non-material effects, such as the formation and preservation of false information about an entity in the public. 38

In order to assess whether there has been a violation of the personal interests of a legal entity and whether it has suffered harm, it is necessary to use objective rather than subjective criteria. Consequently, compensation for a legal entity is not intended to provide satisfaction or compensate for its physical and mental suffering, but to protect its objectively understood interests related to its personal interests. 39

Means of pecuniary and non-pecuniary protection. There is no reason to distinguish between the situation of natural and legal persons in the event of a violation of personal interests. They should be afforded the same level of protection. *Lege non distinguente* all means of protection can be applied. Nevertheless, greater 40

---

12 III CZP 43/17, OSNC 5/2018, item 49, reported by *E Bagińska/I Adrych-Brzezińska* in: E Karner/BC Steininger (eds), European Tort Law 2018 (2019) 474, nos 58–66.

caution should be exercised in the context of awarding compensation for non-pecuniary harm to legal entities. In order to award compensation, the court should take into account the type of business conducted by the legal entity, the personal interest that was violated, the scale of the violation and, consequently, the degree of impact on the conduct of the legal entity's business. The Supreme Court pointed out that, in the case of legal entities conducting business, in the event of a violation of their personal interests, the effects of the violation will affect the pecuniary sphere, so it seems more appropriate to apply pecuniary protection in addition to non-pecuniary means of protection (art 24 § 1 KC sents 1 and 2). On the other hand, for non-business legal entities, the violation might impede their current business and justify art 448 in conjunction with art 43 KC.

41 Finally, the Court emphasised that the constitutional argument concerning the limitation of freedom of expression can constitute an argument against the misuse of art 448 KC in specific factual situations.

c) Commentary

42 In recent years, there has been a clear tendency for legal persons (entities) to sue for non-pecuniary damage caused by an infringement of their personal interests (personal rights). *Prima facie* it might seem that the *Comingersoll*[13] case heard by the European Court of Human Rights opened up the possibility for legal persons to seek redress for non-pecuniary harm. Although the problem of compensation for moral harm caused to physical persons was broadly commented on both in Polish and foreign literature, the possibility of compensation for non-pecuniary damage caused to a legal person still raises much controversy.[14]

43 It should be noted that, so far, both doctrine and jurisprudence have lacked an unambiguous position on the possibility of compensation for this type of damage.[15] Unfortunately, the commented judgment, albeit of a great practical value, does not eliminate the doubts expressed in doctrine and case law.

44 First and foremost, the Court attempted to answer the question of whether a legal person can suffer non-pecuniary harm and, if so, what is the extent of the damage to be compensated. As there is no legal definition of damage, two doctrinal positions developed regarding the understanding of damage. According to the first,

---

13 ECtHR *Comingersoll SA v Portugal* [GC], 6.4.2000, no 35382/97.

14 On the other legal systems, see *V Wilcox*, A Company's Right to Damages for Non-Pecuniary Loss (2016).

15 See *A Szpunar*, Zadośćuczynienie za szkodę niemajątkową (Bydgoszcz 1999) 209; *Z Radwański*/ *A Olejniczak*, Zobowiązania (2020) 264.

damage is the mere violation of a given good or interest protected by law. The second view restricts the damage to the consequences of a certain event.[16] In a traditional concept of non-material damage, it includes negative experiences of the injured party in the form of mental and physical suffering.[17]

It is not clear whether the Supreme Court understands non-pecuniary harm as a mere fact of violation or as a result of the violation. It appears that, for the Court, the violation of a personal interest of a legal entity is equated to the occurrence of non-material damage. This view should be more precisely justified. 45

The Court noted the difference between an infringement of the interests of those entities which are entrepreneurs and those which are not, but failed to make a clear distinction of their harm and of the scope of the means of protection provided in arts 24 and 448 KC. If there is a violation of personal interests of the entrepreneurial entity, it can sustain pecuniary damage. The argument that the damage is difficult to quantify does not mean that the damage, which is of a pecuniary nature, cannot be determined. The view that when there is pecuniary damage, the pecuniary means of protection (including compensation for non-pecuniary harm) are more appropriate seems to be incorrect. It can be argued that if the infringement of personal interests leads to pecuniary damage, the claim for compensation for non-pecuniary loss should, lacking such (additional) harm, be dismissed. 46

Moreover, the Court failed to answer the question as to why, in a case of the infringement of personal interest of a legal entity, other (non-pecuniary) means of protection provided by the legislator are not sufficient. 47

The boundaries between legal entities' personal rights to good name and the right of individuals to express their own opinions (freedom of speech) should be established. The problem relates not only to private legal persons, but also to public entities. It can be underlined that in some judgments, municipal legal persons received the recognition of their own personal interests.[18] Therefore, the question of whether it is justified that public legal persons (municipalities, State entities, as well as political parties) are entitled to protection to the same extent as private legal persons should be asked. If such were the case, the risk of abusing the use of pecuniary means of protection of personal interests of public legal entities could occur. In our opinion, the extension of the effects of the commented judgment to legal persons of a public nature, for example State agencies or constitutional organs of the State (eg the National Central Bank, the National Broadcasting 48

---

16 *M Kaliński* in: System Prawa Prywatnego (2014) 101.

17 *Kaliński* (fn 16) 93.

18 SN of 21.9.2006, I CSK 118/06, OSP 10/2009, item 107, reported in ETL 2009, 475, no 62 fn 27.

Council, KRRiT) is incorrect, as State legal persons are not vested with personal interests.

3. Personal Injury

49 The concept of family bonds as a personal interest is still the subject of consideration of the Supreme Court. In one of the most recent judgments (SN, 13 October 2023, II CSKP, 991/22),[19] the Supreme Court again adhered to the view that the bond with a child constitutes a personal interest protected by arts 24 and 448 KC. It held that the violation of the family bond between the parent and the child also occurs when the child's state of health, caused by the harmful event, makes it impossible to maintain the family bond with the child in its proper manifestations, thwarts expectations and plans, and exposes the child to the need to be accompanied in suffering.

50 The Court held that a person by their nature is a social being and derives from a family. The family shall be defined as a natural and basic social group, and its establishment at a certain stage of life is an expression of self-realisation of a human being and the determination of their position among other people, an expression of activities immanent to the essence of humanity and the nature of a human. The Court referred to its judgment of 27 March 2017 (III CZP 60/17) according to which, the need to remain 'bonded' to another person, which is manifested in the sense of closeness and attachment to a loved one, is an inherent characteristic of human beings. The status of parent-child gives a sense of security and support to children, and over time, to parents. Its achievement is an expression of human self-realisation. Thus, the family bond shall be recognised as a personal interest and as such shall be protected by civil law. The way of granting protection to a personal interest such as the status of a parent to a child (family bond) is no different from that which would be used to obtain protection of health, bodily integrity, and identity.

51 The Court also observed that it is neither necessary nor justified to consider the parent as an indirectly injured party and the child as directly injured, because each of the persons mentioned here are directly affected in their own personal interests. The prerequisite for liability under arts 23–24 KC and art 448 KC is the violation of personal interest by unlawful conduct.

19 Published at <www.sn.pl>.

C. Literature

1. *N Baranowska/J Kuźmicka-Sulikowska/P Machnikowski/ R Strugała/M Wilejczyk* – P Machnikowski (ed), Prawo deliktowe wobec nowych technologii [Tort law in the face of new technologies] (Wolters Kluwer 2023)

The main aim of the book is to indicate the role of tort law in a society that uses 52
digital technologies, particularly those of artificial intelligence. The authors of the book address the following issues: characteristics of digital technologies relevant to the application of tort law; liability for damage caused by a dangerous product; the concept of fault in Polish law and foreign legal systems; functions of tort liability for violations of human rights; contribution of the injured party to the occurrence or worsening of the damage; liability of multiple entities for the same damage; ways of redressing property damage.

One of the attractive features of the book is that the authors critically appraise 53
the EU legislative preparatory works. They also indicate which elements of the tort law system need to be modified in connection with the spread of digital technologies.

2. Articles

S Koczur, Prawna kwalifikacja "odszkodowania" z tytułu rozwiązania umowy o 54
pracę i jej wpływ na zasądzenie odszkodowania cywilnego [Legal qualification of 'compensation' for terminating an employment contract and its impact on the award of civil compensation], Przegląd Sądowy 6 (2023) 68–81

B Kucharski/W Matysiak, Polemicznie o dopuszczalności uwzględnienia rabató 55
w i upustów przy ustalaniu odszkodowania kosztorysowego z ubezpieczenia odpowiedzialności cywilnej posiadaczy pojazdów mechanicznych [Polemical about the admissibility of taking into account discounts and rebates when determining cost compensation from motor vehicle liability insurance], Wiadomości Ubezpieczeniowe 1 (2023) 41–52

P Marczyk, Podmiotowe granice odpowiedzialności deliktowej władzy publicz- 56
nej [Subjective limits of tort liability of public authority liability for damages], Transformacje Prawa Prywatnego 1 (2023) 75–99

P Marczyk, Charakter prawny i przesłanki determinujące wysokość renty ure- 57
gulowanej w art 446 § 2 kodeksu cywilnego [Legal nature and prerequisites deter-

mining the amount of the pension regulated by art 446 § 2 of the Civil Code], Kwartalnik Prawa Prywatnego 2 (2023) 251–286

58 *K Mularski/K Grzesiowski*, Compensatio lucri cum damno w prawie prywatnym. Zakres odniesienia, podstawa prawna, sposoby rozumienia, krytyka [Compensatio lucri cum damno in private law. Scope of application, legal basis, interpretation approaches, critique], Kwartalnik Prawa Prywatnego 4 (2023) 655–720

59 *M Rożnowska*, Dobra osobiste sztucznej inteligencji a doktrynalna konstrukcja ochrony dóbr osobistych – czy sztuczna inteligencja może być podmiotem dóbr osobistych [Personal rights of artificial intelligence in the context of doctrinal construction of protection of personal rights – can artificial intelligence be a subject of personal right?], Transformacje Prawa Prywatnego 2 (2023) 177–207

60 *M Szaraniec*, Profiling and automated decisions concerning consumers in the insurance market and threats to their right to privacy and the right of disposal over their personal data, Wiadomości Ubezpieczeniowe 1 (2023) 25–40

61 *K Tokarz*, Więzi rodzinne – definicja, funkcjonowanie i w status w systematyce dóbr osobistych polskiego prawa cywilnego [Family bonds: definition, existence, and status in the systematics of personal interests of Polish civil law], Państwo i Prawo 10 (2023) 142–157.

Inês de Oliveira Martins, Rui Cascão and André Pereira

XXIII. Portugal

A. Legislation

1. Law no 22/2023, 25 May 2023 (Medically Assisted Death Act)

This Act makes provision for the conditions in which medically assisted death is not a punishable offence and amends the Penal Code accordingly[1]. Insofar as the appropriate procedure is followed, an adult person suffering unbearably from a serious incurable disease, or an injury of extreme seriousness, may seek medically assisted suicide or euthanasia. 1

Article 29 is of particular significance to tort and insurance law, as it provides that, for the purposes of life insurance contracts, medically assisted death is not grounds for exclusion of coverage. However, the procedure must be duly recorded as the cause of death in the death certificate. Furthermore, once the formal procedure requesting assisted death is started, the insured person is precluded from modifying the clauses that designate beneficiaries. 2

In contrast, art 191 of Decree-Law no 72/2008, 16 April (Insurance Contract Law)[2] provides that, unless otherwise agreed by the parties to a life insurance contract, the risk of death, in case of suicide within one year after the contract was concluded, is not covered. While the intention of the legislator is clear (averting the person seeking assisted suicide from being discouraged from doing so due to succession planning concerns), the drafting of the provision of art 29 of the Medically Assisted Death Act is not very clear. As such, there is a risk of potential interpretation loopholes or future insurance market practices that might undermine or circumvent the protection afforded by this provision[3]. 3

1 Official Journal (OJ) No 101, 1S, 25.5.2023, 10–20.

2 *AG Dias Pereira*, Portugal, in: H Koziol/BC Steininger (eds), European Tort Law (ETL) 2008 (2009) 526, no 8 ff.

3 Parliament carried out a comparative law study on this issue for the 'travaux préparatoires' of this Act: *Assembleia da República (DILP)*, Morte medicamente assistida e seguros de vida: Enquadramento internacional (2020). Art 15 of the Belgian Euthanasia Act, 28 May 2002, analysed in this study, is likely to have influenced this provision: 'a person who dies as a result of euthanasia performed in accordance with the conditions laid down in this Act is deemed to have died of natural

https://doi.org/10.1515/9783111376721-024

2. Decree-Law no 66/2023, 8 August 2023 (Implementation of Regulations on Financial Services and Partial Transposition of Directive (EU) 2021/2118, on Motor Insurance)

4 Directive (EU) 2021/2118 of the European Parliament and of the Council amended Directive 2009/103/EC of the European Parliament and of the Council relating to insurance against civil liability in respect of the use of motor vehicles, and the enforcement of the obligation to insure against such liability introduces a mechanism aiming at compensating injured parties in respect of the damage resulting from accidents in the case of insolvency of the responsible insurance company. In this respect, Member States are obliged to appoint compensation bodies to process claims emerging from such accidents. The compensation bodies in the different Member States are further required to conclude agreements between themselves regulating the settlement of cross-border claims. As such, injured parties will be able to file a claim with the compensation body of their Member State of residence (*front office*), which will subsequently seek redress from the compensation body of the Member State of origin of the responsible insurance undertaking (*back office*).

5 Decree-Law no 66/2023[4] transposed Directive (EU) 2021/2118 to domestic law, following a letter of formal notice by the European Commission, pursuant to art 258, to Portugal (and 15 other Member States), regarding the failure to notify the transposition of the Directive.[5] Article 9 of this Act designates the Insurance and Pension Funds Supervision Authority[6] as the national compensation body for this purpose.

causes with regard to the performance of the agreements to which he was a party, and in particular insurance contracts'.

4 Official Journal (OJ) No 153, 1S, 8.8.2023, 2–29.

5 European Commission – Infringement decisions. Non-transposition of EU legislation: Commission takes action to ensure complete and timely transposition of EU directives, Brussels, 20 July 2023, INF/23/3889.

6 Autoridade de Supervisão de Seguros e Fundos de Pensões (ASF).

B. Cases

1. Supreme Administrative Court, 7 September 2023, ECLI:PT:STA:2023:01435.12.1BELRA.59 (*Suzana Tavares da Silva*): Extra-Contractual Liability of the State; Cliff Beach Collapse; Contributory Negligence

a) Brief Summary of the Facts

On 4 August 2005, two young Spanish tourists died in an unsupervised cliffside beach near Peniche, a coastal resort in central Portugal, as a result of injury sustained due to the partial collapse of a cliff under which the couple were taking shelter from the sun. A similar fatal accident had occurred in the same location in 2003, taking the life of a German tourist. The 2003 event triggered inquiries by several relevant administrative entities and a significant risk to people and goods due to erosion was identified; therefore, while it was deemed impractical and disproportionate to permanently prohibit access to the location to the public, warning signs were placed at the location alerting visitors to the risks. For unknown reasons, these signs were no longer posted at the location on the day of the accident. 6

b) Judgment of the Court

This decision reverses a decision by the Central Administrative Court (South), confirming the decision in first instance by the Leiria Administrative and Tax Court. The plaintiffs were the bereaved parents of both victims and the defendants were the Portuguese State and the Portuguese Environmental Agency.[7] 7

The decision in first instance by the Leiria Administrative and Tax Court held the State and the Portuguese Environment Agency liable for non-performance or defective performance of a duty of care for risk management emerging from natural elements. However, the court deliberated that there was contributory negligence on the part of the victims, considering that, in spite of the fact that it was not forbidden to access the beach and that the risks were not clearly signposted at the location, they ought to have been aware, on the basis of the experience and caution expected from the average person, of the potential risks they would 8

7 Agência Portuguesa do Ambiente, IP (APA).

be exposed to by entering an unguarded cliffside beach.[8] Consequently, compensation was reduced by 50 % in proportion to their contribution to the accident. Each plaintiff was therefore awarded € 100,000 in damages (€ 40,000 for the death and € 60,000 for pain and suffering).

9 The plaintiffs, disagreeing with this decision, argued that there were no grounds for attributing contributory negligence to the victims and appealed to the Central Administrative Court (South). The defendants also appealed. The appellate court partially confirmed the decision in first instance, adjusting nevertheless the damages awards to € 140,000 to each plaintiff, reducing the allocation of contributory negligence to the victims from 50 % to 30 %, thus allocating 70 % of the extent of contribution to the defendants. In this decision, Judge Alda Nunes gave a dissenting opinion, arguing that there was no conduct by the victims that contributed to the accident and therefore the plaintiffs should be awarded full compensation.

10 The defendants accepted the verdict in second instance and did not appeal. However, the plaintiffs, still disagreeing with the attribution of contributory negligence, appealed to the Supreme Administrative Court, which overturned the appellate court's decision and reaffirmed the decision in first instance (50/50 % allocation), arguing that, considering the low threshold of culpability of the public entities, combined with the lack of foresight and prudence by the victims, such an 'excessive' allocation of fault was an error of judgement by the Central Administrative Court.

c) Commentary

11 This decision of the Supreme Administrative Court supported the dissenting vote of Judge Cláudio Ramos Monteiro, who disagreed with the Court as regards the contributory negligence of the victims. The fact that the victims were under the cliff at the time of the collapse is, as such, insufficient to apportion them any culpability for the accident, considering that there was no reason to consider their behaviour by entering the beach reckless or imprudent, as they neither had a reason to be aware of the risks, nor were they made aware by the competent public entities (by posting signs, for instance) of the risks, which were well known to them, preventable, and had caused fatal accidents in the past.

8 *C Amado Gomes/M Assis Raimundo*, Topicamente – e a quatro mãos… – sobre o novo regime da responsabilidade civil extracontratual do Estado e demais entidades públicas, Revista de Direito Público e Regulação CEDIPRE 5/3 (2010), 16.

Judge Monteiro's judgment echoes a recurring concern amongst several judges, translated in several dissenting opinions, that the Supreme Administrative Court tends to be lenient to the State and public entities in cases concerning extra-contractual liability, while unreasonably blaming victims who were merely at the wrong place at the wrong time.[9] 12

2. Supreme Administrative Court, 14 September 2023, ECLI:PT:STA:2023:0533.11.3BEPRT.96 (*Ana Celeste Carvalho*): Extra-Contractual Liability of the State; Medical Injury; Unlawfulness; Fault; Burden of Proof; Medical Activity

a) Brief Summary of the Facts

On 5 February 2007, the plaintiff underwent a surgical procedure to treat a C5-C6 herniated disc at the Vila Nova de Gaia/Espinho Hospital Centre (defendant).[10] The plaintiff had consented to medical treatment, despite a remote risk of tetraplegia. While the treatment was successful, the patient developed chronic hoarseness due to vocal cord paresis as an adverse effect. 13

b) Judgment of the Court

The plaintiff filed an extra-contractual liability lawsuit against the defendant with the Porto Administrative and Fiscal Court, which ruled in favour of the defendant. The plaintiff appealed to the Central Administrative Court (North), which reversed the previous decision, ruled in favour of the plaintiff and awarded him € 22,515 in damages. The defendant appealed to the Supreme Court, which reversed the appellate decision and quashed the damages award. 14

The court held that the hoarseness was legally relevant damage and that there was a causal link between the action (treatment) and the damage. However, the court considered that the other requirements for the establishment of extra-contractual liability (unlawfulness and fault) were not demonstrated by the plaintiff, who bears the burden of proof thereof. 15

---

9 Eg, Dissenting opinion of Judge Carlos Medeiros de Carvalho in Supreme Administrative Court 16 November 2017 (ECLI:PT:STA:2017:0484.17.8B: Extra-Contractual Liability of the State; Contributory Negligence; Link of Causation; Damages Awards for Death).

10 Centro Hospitalar de Vila Nova de Gaia/Espinho, E.P.E.

16 The court further stressed the difference between the concepts of unlawfulness and fault: while unlawfulness is the external infringement of the law and is an external judgement of censure anchored in the breach of an objective standard of care (*lege artis*), fault is considered as the internal psychological evaluation of the conduct of the tortfeasor, who will be at fault if they failed to act with diligence under the concrete circumstances of the case.

17 The court agreed that it can happen that there is legally relevant damage and a causal link between treatment and an adverse medical event, without the possibility of allocating unlawfulness or fault. Furthermore, it acknowledged that, under some specific circumstances, when medical treatment activities can be considered a dangerous activity or have an associated risk, the burden of proof of unlawfulness and fault might be shifted from the plaintiff to the defendant. The court found no reason to do so in this case.

18 The court applied to this case the legal regime of extra-contractual liability of the State and public entities of Decree-Law no 48051, 21 November 1967, meanwhile replaced by Law 67/2007, 31 December (Extra-Contractual Liability of the State and Other Public Bodies).

19 While the latter did not apply retroactively to this case, in this respect, the court stated that the new law does not point towards a shift of paradigm of compensation of personal injury, or an abandonment of the principle of liability and the 'dogma of fault' (sic). According to this prospective reflection by the court, the new Law will rather introduce an extension of the concept of unlawfulness to duties of care, in particular as regards the duties concerning information, consent and documentation (health records).

c) Commentary

20 This decision reaffirms the status quo of a fault-based liability system for adverse medical events and clarifies that there has been no major shift in the compensation of adverse medical events: and that is likely to remain unchanged with the 'new' 2007 Act. However, the court has left open the prospect of 'stretching' the concept of unlawfulness in a more creative, plaintiff-friendly fashion.

21 Due to the long delays in administrative procedures, forensic expertises, and the significant case backlog of extra-contractual liability cases in the administrative justice system, many cases are still being tried under the old legal framework.[11]

11 For instance, Portugal was liable for breach of art 13 European Convention on Human Rights

In the 2007 Yearbook, this report considered that this Act is 'generous' to the individual and very demanding to the State, not only in its administrative functions, but also in respect of judicial and legislative powers. Only its interpretation and application through case law will give us insight into its 'fair balance'. This case is a good 'teaser' as regards future trends in extra-contratual liability of the State and public bodies.[12] *À suivre...* 22

3. Supreme Court of Justice, 27 April 2023, ECLI:PT:STJ:2023:4017.20.0T8GMR.G1.S1.F3 (*João Cura Mariano*): Self-Defence; Disproportion; Mental State Excluding Fault

a) Brief Summary of the Facts

On 19 March 2019, at noon, A received a phone call from his wife, warning that a stranger had entered their house. A drove to his home, entered through the kitchen door and found a hooded man, B, standing in his living room. Upon noticing A's presence, B fled through a back door and began running down the street. At the time, B was 19 years old, while A was 46 and dealing with mobility issues due to a recent surgery. 23

A chased B in his car, with the purpose of stopping him and recovering any objects that he might have stolen from A's house. As B was running along the left side of the road, A, under nervous strain, drove towards him and struck him with the left side of his car. B was hit in his lower limbs and then projected against the car and onto the ground. The impact resulted in fractures to B's lower limbs and head injuries from contact with the vehicle's glass. After falling to the ground, B returned two silver medals, valued at € 680, taken from A's house during the burglary attempt. As a result of his injuries, B underwent surgery and was unable to work for 250 days. He also suffered a permanent loss of 5 percentage points in functional capacity, meaning that he could perform his former professional activities, albeit with increased effort. Additionally, he sustained per- 24

(ECHR – right to an effective remedy) in European Court of Human Rights (ECtHR) *Valada Matos das Neves v Portugal*, 29.10.2015 [Section I], no 73798/13, for a delay of nine years in the adjudication of extra-contractual liability of the State lawsuits. Longer delays are well known in the Portuguese legal community.

12 *AG Dias Pereira*, Portugal, in: H Koziol/BC Steininger (eds), European Tort Law 2007 (2008) 476, no 17; *Amado Gomes/Assis Raimundo*, Revista de Direito Público e Regulação CEDIPRE 5/3 (2010) 4.

manent aesthetic damage from scars left by the surgery on his legs. B was later convicted for attempted burglary.

25 B filed a claim against A's motor insurer, seeking compensation for both pecuniary and non-pecuniary damage. A was brought into the proceedings by the insurance company as an accessory intervenor. The first instance court ruled in favour of B, awarding compensation of € 353 for pecuniary damage and € 30,000 for non-pecuniary damage. Both A and B appealed the decision. The Appellate Court reduced the compensation for pecuniary damage to € 195 but increased the compensation for non-pecuniary damage to € 40,000, considering it under two independent heads of damage: € 20,000 for permanent incapacity and € 20,000 for moral suffering.

26 A then appealed to the Supreme Court seeking exoneration from liability, on the grounds of self-defence. Subsidiarily he requested the reduction of the amount of compensation established both for permanent incapacity and for moral suffering.

b) Judgment of the Court

27 The Court clarified that even if A were deemed to have acted in self-defence, and thus lawfully, he would still be liable under the strict liability regime for road traffic accidents. The request to consider self-defence was nonetheless relevant, as the amounts of compensation are higher in the case of fault-based liability. The decision turned on the requirements for self-defence under civil law, as set out by art 337(1) and (2) of the Civil Code.

28 The Court began by explaining art 337(1) of the Civil Code, recounting the debate surrounding its interpretation. Under art 337(1) of the Civil Code, an act is deemed justified when it aims to repel a present and unlawful act of aggression to the person or property of the agent or a third party, provided that resorting to ordinary means of defence is not possible and the damage resulting from the defence does not manifestly exceed the damage that would result from the aggression. Such a requirement of proportionality is absent from the provision on self-defence of the Criminal Code (art 32), enacted more than a decade later. Thus, disproportionate defensive actions are lawful under criminal law yet unlawful under civil law. From the point of view of criminal law, this can lead to the undesirable result of justifying self-defence against what was a lawful response in self-defence but had been rendered unlawful by the limitations of civil law. One significant viewpoint in scholarship holds that the Criminal Code revoked the part of the civil provision that requires proportionality between the harm caused and the harm prevented. Criminal or civil self-defence should instead be limited by the

principle of necessity of the defence.[13] This principle would preclude scenarios where there is a crass disproportion between the overall consequences of the offence and those of the defence, rendering the latter an abuse of the right of defence. Other authors consider that the provision of the Criminal Code should be read in light of the Constitution, and thus subject to some limit of proportionality.[14]

The Supreme Court recognised the need to harmonise the criminal and the civil provision, but without challenging the requirement of proportionality set out by the Civil Code. A coherent application of both provisions could be achieved by limiting criminal self-defence through the doctrine of the abuse of right and by limiting the right to respond to disproportionate defence, although it qualifies as a tort. 29

After this initial clarification, the Court went on to verify the general requirements for civil self-defence, which, apart from the aspect just mentioned, largely overlap with those of criminal self-defence. 30

First, the Court considered that there was an act of aggression, that is, ongoing at the time of the defence, since the theft had not been yet completed. B had not yet acquired 'peaceful possession' of the stolen items, for he had been continuously pursued by A since he left the house. Additionally, the means used for the defence were necessary. Assessing the situation objectively from the moment the aggression occurred, there were no alternative means available to A that would have been less detrimental to the interests of B. In this regard, the Court did not assess the conduct of A when he drove his car into B, but rather A's conduct in using his car to pursue B and prevent the completion of the theft. As A was impaired in his mobility due to a recent surgery, no other less onerous yet equally effective means were available to him. The Court then considered whether the defence was proportionate, according to the controversial standard of manifest disproportion as set out in art 337(1) of the Civil Code. The Court compared the harm caused by the aggression, the theft of silver medals worth € 680, with the harm caused by the defence, corresponding to fractures to B's lower limbs and head injuries, and found a 31

13 In criminal law, *J de Figueiredo Dias*, Direito penal, Parte geral (2019) 513 f; *MC Valdágua*, Aspetos da Legítima Defesa no Código Penal e no Código Civil, in: Jornadas de Homenagem ao Professor Doutor Cavaleiro Ferreira. In private law: *MG Trigo*, Art 337, Comentário ao Código Civil – Parte Geral (2014) 800; *A Menezes Cordeiro*, Artigo 337 in: Código Civil Comentado (2020) 963–965; *R Ataíde*, Direito das obrigações: introdução, conceito e características, modalidades, fontes das obrigações (2022) 372 f.

14 *MF Palma*, A Justificação por Legítima Defesa como Problema de Delimitação de Direitos (1990) 575–589; *T Quintela de Brito*, Justificação por Legítima Defesa e por Direito de Necessidade no Código Civil e no Código Penal, in: Estudos Comemorativos do 150.º Aniversário do Tribunal da Boa-Hora (1995) 47 ff.

manifest disproportion between the two harms, rendering A's action unjustified under art 337(1) of the Civil Code.

32 The Court then turned to art 337(2), which justifies excessive self-defence if caused by non-culpable fear or emotional disturbance. Interpreting the norm as requiring proportionality between the intensity of the emotion and the excess of means used or of harm caused, it concluded that the norm does not apply to this case. In light of the proven facts, A had acted in a state of tension, and not in a state of fear. There was, thus, no excuse for the disproportion between the interests preserved and those sacrificed.

33 Finally, the Court considered whether the amounts of compensation established for permanent incapacity and for moral suffering should be reduced. Both are cases of non-pecuniary damage, which should be assessed in accordance with arts 496(4) and 494 of the Civil Code on the basis of equity, considering the degree of culpability of the tortfeasor, the economic situations of the tortfeasor and the victim and the overall circumstances of the case. Concerning compensation for permanent incapacity, the Appellate Court had considered the age of the plaintiff and his degree of permanent incapacity, as well as the fact that the tortfeasor had acted with *dolus eventualis*. Regarding compensation for moral suffering, the Appellate Court considered the pain and suffering, as well as the nuisance, experienced by the plaintiff until recovery, and also his permanent aesthetic damage. In regard of both heads of damage, the Supreme Court found that the Appellate Court had not properly considered the fact that the victim had acted unlawfully, which had elicited an excessive reaction from the tortfeasor. As a result, the Supreme Court reduced the compensation amounts by one quarter for each head of damage to € 15,000 in each case.

c) Commentary

34 This decision by the Supreme Court provides one of the rare examples of enforcement of the civil provision on self-defence by the courts and can thus be particularly influential to future decisions of the lower courts on the matter. Self-defence has predominantly been applied and discussed in the realm of criminal law. However, due to the impact of civil self-defence upon its criminal counterpart, the discussion regarding criminal law trickles down to the interpretation of civil law.

35 At the centre of the decision lies one of the most controversial aspects of criminal self-defence: the requirement of proportionality between the interests defended and those sacrificed. The traditional approach views self-defence as an instrument to ensure the effectivity of law against infringements, thus exempting it from the constraints of proportionality. Conversely, more recent approaches have em-

phasised that self-defence is, at least concurrently, an instrument for the protection of individual interests and have highlighted that law only requires protection against conduct that is contrary to its values.[15] This has led to a limitation of the cases where self-defence is justified, further supported by several statutes on the use of firearms, that establish strict requirements of proportionality for their use in self-defence.[16]

The criminal provision on self-defence does not offer any clear indication as to 36
the overall limits of adequacy of the defence, which has led to varying perspectives in scholarship, all pleading for some sort of limitation to self-defence. However, these limitations do not amount to requiring proportionality between the interests defended and those sacrificed, which, according to most authors, would disregard the unlawfulness of the initial aggression.[17] This element is indeed what separates self-defence from the state of necessity. The acceptance of general limitations to self-defence therefore reduces the scope of the dissonance between the criminal and the civil provisions but does not eliminate it. Now, this dissonance, which the court does not see as overly problematic, raises two different questions.

The first question regards the implications *for the defensive action*, which, 37
when disproportionate, will be a tort, but not a crime. From the perspective of the overall coherence of the legal system, it is not problematic for conduct to entail consequences under civil law without incurring criminal law sanctions. This aligns with the subsidiary nature of criminal law, which imposes the most severe sanctions. Where this dissonance appears particularly troubling is in its potential to further diminish the role of self-defence even within criminal law. The risk of the victim having to pay compensation if they sacrifice interests that are deemed manifestly superior to the interests safeguarded can serve as a strong deterrent for self-defence, especially in cases where defending property involves sacrificing personal interests. To decide whether and how to react, the victim will have to make a difficult assessment in a context of tension, where an unlawful act of aggression is ongoing. Now, the criterion that applies here compounds the deterrent effect even further, since the court ascertains proportionality from an objective and *ex post* perspective, rather than from the moment in which the defence is undertaken.

---

15 *J de Figueiredo Dias* (fn 13) 474 f; *A Taipa de Carvalho*, Direito penal, Parte geral (2022) 361; *M Fernanda Palma*, Direito penal, Parte geral (2020) 292–294; *J Faria Costa* Direito penal (2017) 310 f.

16 Decree-Law no 457/99, of 5 November 1999, on the use of firearms and explosives by security forces and services; Law 5/2006, of 23 February 1999, providing the legal framework of firearms and ammunition.

17 *J de Figueiredo Dias*, Direito penal, Parte geral (2019) 475 f, 489 f, 494 ff; *Taipa de Carvalho* (fn 15) 361–363; *Faria Costa* (fn 15) 311 f.

This is manifest in the present decision, where the Supreme Court considered the actual value of the goods stolen, disregarding the fact that A did not know which objects could have been stolen when he acted in self-defence.

38 The second question concerns the implications of such dissonance for *further reactions* under self-defence, inquiring under which conditions a *reaction against a first disproportionate defence should be lawful*. This question was not raised by the present case, but it has been particularly underscored in support of an implicit repealing of a part of the civil provision requiring proportionality. It would not be acceptable to consider that the reaction against a disproportionate defence would be illegitimate for criminal law (which holds the first defence as lawful), but legitimate for civil law, since it would run against the principle of subsidiarity of criminal law. A first acceptable solution would be to hold the defensive reaction as admissible for both criminal and civil law. This would imply that, for these purposes, the first disproportionate defence was held as unlawful, and the requirement of proportionality would prevail. A second acceptable solution would be to reject the defensive reaction for both criminal and civil law. This would imply that, for these purposes, the first disproportionate defence would be held as lawful, and the requirement of proportionality would be set aside.

39 Apart from favouring scholarship that gives prevalence to arguments of proportionality even in criminal law, which reduces the extension of the problem, the court is not very clear on how the two provisions should be reconciled. However, it seems to limit the defensive reaction, treating the first disproportionate defence as lawful, at least when such defensive reaction would qualify both as a tort and as a crime. The more serious cases of counter-reaction would thus be disallowed, whereas the defensive reaction qualifying only as a tort and not as a crime would be admitted.

4. Supreme Court of Justice, 17 January 2023, ECLI:PT:STJ:2023:3.21.1T8VRL.G1.S1.4C (*Maria Clara Sottomayor*): Insurance Contract; First Party Insurance; Insurer's Delay

a) Brief Summary of the Facts

40 Company A, the plaintiff, operates a stone works factory, and entered into an all-risks industrial insurance policy with the defendant, insurance company B. On 10 May 2020, a heavy thunderstorm occurred in the town where A's premises are located. As the stone cutting machine used at the factory would not function on the following morning, a technician was called to inspect the machine. A

week later, the technician issued an expert report stating that the breakdown was caused by electrical power fluctuations during the storm. A proforma invoice attached to the report indicated that the cost of replacing the damaged components of the machine amounted to € 7,749. A forwarded the expert report and invoice to B, the insurer, on 18 May 2020, and requested compensation for the damage. B sent an expert to inspect the machine on 22 May 2020. On this occasion, the plant manager informed the insurance company expert that the stone cutting machine was essential for fulfilling contractual obligations with clients, with impending deadlines, and requested a prompt response from the insurer.

As the machine was indispensable for A's factory operations, on 20 June 2020, A decided to repair the machine at its own expense, totalling € 7,749. Meanwhile, production at the factory was halted for a total of 47 days. As a result, A was unable to meet the delivery deadlines for two contracts, which led to the cancellation of the contracts by its clients, and the loss of the right to payments in the amount of € 23,850. One contract required delivery by 1 June 2020, and the other by 10 June 2020. On 24 July 2020, over two months after receiving notice of the claim, B, the insurance company, communicated its decision to decline coverage, citing exclusion clauses in the policy's 'General and Special Conditions'. These clauses excluded coverage for damage to machines manufactured more than ten years ago, and the stone cutting machine in question was 19 years old. 41

A brought an action against its insurer, arguing that it had never received the 'General and Special Conditions', only the 'Special and Particular Conditions', which did not entail such an exclusion. A claimed it would not have entered into the contract under these conditions, as all machines used in its stone works were by then over ten years old. A contended that, under the Act on General Contract Terms and the Insurance Contract Act,[18] the undisclosed conditions could not be enforced against it, and therefore, the damage to the machine should be covered. Furthermore, A argued that the insurer's unreasonable delay in responding had prevented A from addressing the damage in a timely manner, in particular having the machine repaired earlier, resulting in lost business revenue of € 23,850. As the insurer's decision to decline coverage was based on information available since receiving the expert report, this delay was unjustified and amounted to a breach of the duty of good faith, making the insurance company liable for the loss of profits it caused. The insurer maintained that the exclusion was applicable and no amount was due under the insurance policy. 42

18 Law-Decree no 446/85, of 25 October 1985, on general contract terms, and Law-Decree no 72/2008, of 16 April 2008, which approved the Insurance Contract Act.

43 The trial court partially upheld A's claim, ruling that the undisclosed 'General and Special Conditions' could not be enforced against A. In consequence, the exclusion clause did not apply and the damage to the machine was covered by the insurance contract. However, the court rejected the claim for compensation for loss of profit, on the grounds that, under the Insurance Contract Act, there is no coverage for loss of profit unless the parties specifically agree to it, which was not the case. A appealed to the Appellate Court, which upheld the trial court's decision on different grounds. The Appellate Court ruled that there was no right to compensation for loss of profit because the insurer's delay did not cause such damage to occur, since the deadline for performance in both the cancelled contracts had expired before the insurance payment became due under the Insurance Contract Act. Under its art 102(1), the due date occurs only thirty days after the insurer has confirmed the occurrence of the insured event and ascertained its circumstances, causes and consequences.

44 A then appealed to the Supreme Court, arguing that the right to compensation for loss of profit stemmed from the breach of the insurer's duty to act in good faith, as set out by the Civil Code (art 762), and stated in the insurance contract entered into (clause 5). It was thus irrelevant whether the insurance contract provided for the coverage of lost profits. Moreover, the thirty-day term set out in the Insurance Contract Act did not apply to compensation for breach of the duty to act in good faith. The defendant did not present counterarguments

b) Judgment of the Court

45 The Supreme Court started by concurring with the Appellate Court's decision. The judgment asserted that, as generally held in case law, despite the absence of an agreement on the cover of loss of profit, the insurer that failed to promptly settle a claim without any reasonable justification breached the duty of good faith and should therefore compensate all resulting damage, including loss of use or loss of profit.

46 However, the Supreme Court diverged from the Appellate Court regarding the absence of a causal link between the insurer's breach of good faith and the insured's loss of profit.

47 The Court referred to art 102 of the Insurance Contract Act and set the beginning of the thirty-day deadline on 18 May 2020. On this date, the insurer, having access to the 'General and Special Conditions' it had drafted, received notice of the insured event and also a report from the technician who had inspected the machine. Therefore, the insurance payment would become due one month later, on 18 June 2020, only after the dates where performance should have occurred

under the contracts – 1 June and 10 June. Since the damage would have occurred even if the insurer had complied with the legal deadline set by law, it could not be attributed to the insurer's delay. However, the Court noted that, given the circumstances of the case, the insurer had a duty to promptly inform company A that it would not cover the damage. The insurer was aware that A urgently needed clarity on its rights, as production would be halted until the machine was repaired. Moreover, the insurer had all the necessary information to reach its decision to refuse coverage, at the latest when its expert visited the plant.

Regarding causation, the Court considered that, unless the insurer's failure to promptly communicate its refusal of coverage did not in any way influence A's client's decision to terminate their contracts, causation should be upheld under the standard of adequate causation in its negative formulation, generally applied to civil liability. Although it could not be said with certainty that the contracts that could not be fulfilled would have been maintained if the insurer had promptly communicated its refusal, there was at least some probability of that outcome. Thus, a causal link could be established. To address the uncertainty regarding the actual contribution of the insurer to the damage, the Court relied on equity to determine the compensation amount. 48

Considering the likely impact of the insurer's conduct on A's loss of profits, the Court awarded A compensation in the amount of € 10,000, slightly less than half of the amount A had claimed. 49

c) Commentary

It seems indisputable that the insurer that breached its duty to settle the claim promptly should be liable for compensating the loss of profit, irrespective of whether coverage for loss of profit was stipulated in the contract. The right to compensation for loss of profit does not arise from the contract, but from its breach. Therefore, a clause on the scope of insurance coverage is irrelevant in this context; only a clause addressing the consequences of breaching the insurance contract could, when lawful, be relevant in determining the compensation owed. 50

The crux of the judgment lies in its second part, concerning the causal link between breach of duty and loss of profit. The Court had to address art 102 of the Insurance Contract Act, which grants the insurer an inexplicable thirty-day period after completing its inquiries before the insurance payment becomes due. This provision, greatly tilted in favour of insurers, lacks parallels in neighbouring jurisdictions, that sometimes go as far as establishing a deadline for claims settlement, or at least mandate that insurers pay as soon as possible after completing their inves- 51 tigations.[19] The Portuguese regime not only neglects the urgency that insureds have in receiving insurance compensation after experiencing an insurance event, but also strengthens insurers' incentives to delay the settlement and payment of claims.[20]

52 The Court addresses this issue by considering that good faith may impose on insurers the duty to communicate their decision not to cover before the expiration of the one-month period. This is a significant decision, clarifying that insurers are not free to keep the insured in the dark throughout this time frame. When the insurer's decision is straightforward and it is aware of the insured's urgent need to obtain a final decision, then it should communicate its decision promptly. The Supreme Court's decision mitigates some of the adverse effects of an unfair provision without blatantly contradicting the provision's wording. Since the one-month period refers to the date when the insurance payment becomes due, it does not directly address cases where the insurer deems no payment to be due. It can be argued that the norm leaves out these latter cases, in which the insurer should simply communicate its decision as soon as possible after completing its investigations.

53 However, the rationale applied to this case also applies to cases where the insurer is aware that the damage is covered, and also that the insured urgently needs to receive compensation. Under the duty to act in good faith, which played a prominent role in this case, the insurer would be obligated to act expeditiously. Given the frequency with which persons who have suffered insured events require prompt compensation, this solution would significantly restrict the scope of application of the one-month period in art 102(1), which, considering that the provision is flawed in terms of policy, would be an outcome to salute.

---

19 See, generally, Project Group 'Restatement of European Insurance Contract Law', Principles of European Insurance Contract Law (PEICL) (2015) 231–234.

20 *KS Abraham*, Liability for bad faith and the principle without a name (yet), Connecticut Insurance Law Journal 1 (2012–2013) esp 7 ff; *WH v Boom*, Do insurers have to pay for bad behaviour in settling claims? Legal aspects of insurers' wrongful claims handling, Journal of European Tort Law (JETL) 2 (2011) 77–79; *MI Oliveira Martins*, El derecho de contrato de seguro en Portugal. Un régimen en la encrucijada, in: El contrato de seguro y su distribución en la encrucijada (2018) 2.2.

5. Appellate Court of Porto, 12 July 2023, ECLI:PT:TRP:2023:2467.20.1T8MTS.P1.3B (*Maria da Luz Seabra*): Liability of Keepers of Movable or Immovable Goods; Presumption of Fault; Presumption of Unlawfulness and Causation

a) Brief Summary of the Facts

A and B, the plaintiffs, lived together in an apartment above a discount shop and corresponding warehouse, operated by company C. On 6 June 2017, around 8 pm, A noticed smoke coming out of one of the doors on the ground floor, and quickly evacuated the house with his children, dog, wallet and cell phone. At 8:30 pm, the fire alarm of the shop went off; a few seconds later the lighting system failed, plunging the shop and warehouse into darkness. Company C's staff attempted to use the available fire extinguishers to contain the fire, but they were soon forced to leave the building due to its intensity. Although they alerted the firefighters at 8.35 pm, it took several hours to bring the situation under control. 54

It was determined that the fire originated at the back of the shop and spread to the other premises. However, the cause of the fire could not be established. There were no signs of a short circuit or anomalies in the lighting or electrical system, nor at the fuse box near the fire's point of origin. Company C initiated a criminal procedure against two individuals suspected of setting the fire, but the investigation did not yield conclusive results. The premises were equipped with a fire alarm, portable fire extinguishers and a video surveillance system, all of which were operational at the time of the event. 55

As a result of the fire, the plaintiffs incurred damage to their home and its contents and were unable to occupy their residence for a period of 35 months, during which they stayed with relatives and acquaintances. Consequently, they filed a claim against C and its insurer, seeking compensation for pecuniary damage, regarding loss of use, incurred expenses and direct damage to property, as well as for non-pecuniary damage regarding emotional distress suffered by the wife. 56

The trial court applied art 493(2) of the Civil Code, which holds the person conducting an inherently dangerous activity, by its own nature or by the nature of the means used, liable for the resulting damage it causes, unless they can prove the absence of fault or that the damage would have occurred even with due care. The court found the defendants liable and ordered them to immediately pay a portion of the requested sum to the plaintiffs, with the remaining amount to be determined in a subsequent procedure. The defendants appealed to the Appellate Court of Porto. Company C argued that the court should have declared as established the 57 fact that the fire had been deliberately set by unidentified individuals who had entered the shop shortly after the incident. Furthermore, C claimed it was not at fault, since it had not caused the fire, and had diligently tried to prevent and extinguish it. The insurer concurred that the fire had been deliberately set by third parties and claimed that, since this triggered a risk exclusion set out in the insurance policy, it was not obligated to indemnify the plaintiffs.

b) Judgment of the Court

58 The court initially addressed the appeal concerning matters of fact, finding that the testimonies provided by witnesses and experts did not support the conclusion that the fire had been deliberately started by third parties. Regarding matters of law, the Appellate Court disagreed with the lower court's application of the provision on liability for inherently dangerous activities (art 493(2)). The operation of a discount shop did not present a likelihood of causing damage exceeding normal levels compared to other activities. The case should rather be judged under art 493(1) of the Civil Code, which holds the person responsible for the custody of a movable or immovable thing liable for the damage it causes, unless they can prove absence of fault or that the damage would have occurred even with due care.

59 The Court explained that there was some debate on how this norm should be interpreted. Traditionally, it was viewed as entailing a mere presumption of fault, requiring the plaintiff to prove unlawful conduct by the defendant and that this conduct had caused the damage. However, the prevailing opinion in scholarship and in higher courts now views the norm as entailing a presumption of unlawfulness and fault. The plaintiff should demonstrate that there was a harmful event connected with the thing under custody, that they suffered damage, and that such damage was caused by the event. The Appellate Court endorsed this latter view and considered that the defendants had not rebutted the presumption of unlawfulness and fault. Indeed, they failed to demonstrate that C fulfilled its duties to guard the business premises (unlawfulness), or that it had diligently fulfilled such duties (fault). Notably, according to the court, the fact that C had set in place a video surveillance system, a fire alarm and fire extinguishers did not suffice to fulfil the duty of guarding the premises.

60 Furthermore, as the cause of the fire could not be determined, the risk exclusion put forth by the insurer did not apply, rendering it liable to indemnify the plaintiffs under the insurance policy.

61 Consequently, the Appellate Court rejected the appeal presented in regard of the duty to pay damages, while upholding a request made by the insurer regarding the distribution of process costs.

c) Commentary

The present decision serves as a striking example of the stringent approach taken by Portuguese courts regarding art 493, which sets out tort liability for custodians of things or animals (art 493(1)), or those engaged in dangerous activities (art 493(2)), based on presumed fault. 62

As is clear from this decision, the prevailing interpretation of the norm in scholarship and in courts takes the norms as entailing a presumption not only of fault, but also of the requirements of liability that logically precede it – causation of harm (in the sense of *haftungsbegründende Kausalität*) and unlawfulness. In other words, when presuming the fault of the defendant concerning damage caused by the thing or animal under custody, or by the dangerous activity in question, the provision also presumes that the plaintiff's conduct (an action or omission) caused the harm to occur and that such conduct violated the law. 63

The liability regime for custodians allows the defendant to avoid liability by demonstrating that the harm would have occurred even if due care had been taken. As generally the individual who acted unlawfully cannot avoid liability by establishing that hypothetical chains of events would have nonetheless caused the harm (doctrine of hypothetical causation),[21] this possibility is seen as a compensation for the overall stringency of the norm. Such a possibility is not set out in regard of dangerous activities, which are seen as a more severe source of liability. According to a considerable number of authors, liability for dangerous activities could not even be avoided by proving adoption of a normal degree of diligence; instead, the defendant would have to prove compliance with standards of enhanced diligence. 64

The present decision is particularly noteworthy regarding the defendant's burden of proof under the provision for liability of custodians. Concerning liability for dangerous activities, courts have stated that the defendant must prove compliance with all legal and technical standards aimed at preventing harm caused by the activity, as well as with the rules recommended by common experience. Whether such norms were adhered to has been at the centre of several decisions on liability of custodians or for dangerous activities. In some instances, courts have debated whether the applicable standards were complied with;[22] in others, they have 65

21 *P Mota Pinto*, Interesse contratual negativo e interesse contratual positivo, vol I (2008) 620–623, 691 f; *F Pereira Coelho*, O problema da causa virtual na responsabilidade civil (1998) 7–10. The traditionally restrictive approach towards the doctrine of hypothetical causation is not easy to reconcile with the relative openness towards the defence based on alternative lawful action.

22 See the decision of the Supreme Court of Justice of 25 May 2023, Proc no 366/13.2TNLSB.L2.S1, applying the rule on liability for dangerous activities to maritime navigation, for vessel testing and

based their decisions on the defendant's failure to establish which standards apply to the activity, or that they were met.[23]

66 In the present case, the defendant C did not present evidence to the court regarding the measures required for fire prevention in the context of operating its shops. Nonetheless, it did demonstrate that it had implemented a set of measures that would *ex ante* seem adequate for fire prevention – installation of a fire alarm system, of fire extinguishers and of a video surveillance system, all of which were functional. Moreover, there were no anomalies detected in the electrical installation.

67 Nevertheless, the court did not address the issue of determining the sufficiency of such measures to establish compliance with the standard of diligence required – not even to alert to the fact that defendant C itself had not proved which measures would be required. Instead, the court merely stated that defendant C failed to prove it had acted with all the diligence required, which seems to require that the defendant not only proves the adoption of measures *ex ante* adequate for prevention of harm, but is also able to explain all the causation process leading up to the damage, and to prove that all due diligence was adopted throughout this process.

68 In any case, custodians should be more shielded from liability than persons undertaking dangerous activities. If assessment of diligence on an *ad hoc* and *ex post* basis applies to the former, it should also apply to the latter; mere proof of *ex ante* compliance with legal and technical standards will not suffice. This places a significant burden of proof on defendants, exacerbating the kinship between these regimes of liability for presumed fault and strict liability.

6. Personal Injury

69 The Supreme Court of Justice decision of 21 June 2022 (Isaías Pádua, Proc no 1633/18) condemned the insurance company to pay compensation to the victim. Following a traffic accident, in which the plaintiff was a passenger, 26-year-old A, was injured and suffered severe injuries: tetraplegia; became dependent on assistance from third persons; *quantum doloris* 7/7, aesthetical damage of 6/7. He was awarded compensation of € 709,000 in pecuniary damages and € 500,000 in non-pecuniary

fishing net experience; or the decision of the Appellate Court of Guimarães of 12 October 2023, Proc no 353/21.7T8GMR.G1, applying the rule on liability for dangerous activities to the operation of an amusement park for children.

23 See the decision of the Appellate Court of Porto of 27 June 2023, Proc no 2481/21.0T8PRT.P1, in regard of the activity of transportation of vehicles by road.

damages. The Court stated that, in the equitable determination of this future pecuniary damage to the injured party, there is a range of topics or referential elements that could/should also be considered, such as: the age of the injured party at the time of the accident; the monthly remuneration received by the injured party on the date of the accident and/or other income received by the injured party; the prospective professional development, or not, and the consequences in terms of remuneration, whether you work for yourself or someone else, or even simultaneously; the average inflation rate and the rate of return on capital, based on a judgement of predictability; the severity of the injuries and their consequences, and the attribution of the degree of disability or functional deficit; all future capital/income that is anticipated.

Due to a traffic accident, the Supreme Court (decision of 27 September 2022; 70
Isaías Pádua, Proc no 253/17) ordered the insurance company to pay compensation. A 41-year-old woman died and left behind a young daughter of 11 and her husband. The court awarded compensation of € 258,000 for the pecuniary damage of the husband and € 103,000 for the pecuniary damage of the daughter (due to the maintenance duty until she reached the age of 25). Concerning non-pecuniary damages, the Court awarded € 95,000 for the (victim's) death damage, to be divided between the father and the daughter. Moreover, it awarded € 7,500 for the moral damage of suffering of the victim in the time between the accident and death. Finally, the Court awarded € 40,000 for the non-pecuniary loss of her husband and another € 40,000 for the daughter's non-pecuniary losses. To justify pecuniary damages, based on the duty to provide maintenance, the Supreme Court stated: All those to whom the deceased victim provided food or who were in a legal position to demand it from them have the right to demand compensation for future property damage. Hence, as stated in para 3 of art 495 of the CC, compensation for future property damage is limited, in essence, to the maintenance obligation of which the person who benefitted from it or could benefit from it in the foreseeable future was deprived. Among these people are surviving spouses and minor descendants (as a rule), the former as a result of the marital duty of assistance to which the deceased was bound while the conjugal society lasted, covering food and normal life expenses family (cf arts 1672, 1675, 1676, 2015, and 2009, no 1 al a) of the CC), and the latter as a result of the parental responsibilities to which the parents are subject and which involve the obligation to provide for the maintenance, health and education/instruction of children until they reach the age of majority, but which can continue beyond that, eg up to the age of 25, that is, until they complete the process of their education or professional training (see arts 1874, 1877, 1878, no 1, 1879, 1880 and 1885 and 1905, no 2, 2003 and 2009, no 1 al c) oft he CC). As the family of the deceased victim was made up of her, her husband and a daughter under 11 years of age, in the absence of factual elements, it is to be as-

sumed that the salary/income earned by the deceased victim would have been spent in the same proportion (1/3) on expenses for each of them.

C. Literature

1. *Jorge Sinde Monteiro*, Questões Prejudiciais de Portugal em Matéria de Acidentes de Trânsito, in: Estudos de Homenagem ao Professor Doutor António Pinto Monteiro, vol I (2023) 743–758

71 This article is a critical analysis of some European Court of Justice (CJEU) decisions[24] concerning problems regarding the concurrence between risk liability and fault in general and the concurrent behaviour of children in traffic accidents in particular. In fact, since 2007, case law and literature argue in favour of an interpretation in accordance with European Directives, according to which, the fault of the victim and the behaviour of a child (notably under the age of seven) could only exclude liability in concrete cases, and not as a general exclusion of no-fault liability. Some recent cases of the CJEU – in preliminary ruling – may thwart this humanistic and adequate interpretation. In fact, in some cases, the Portuguese courts did not award compensation to children and other injured parties, based on some decisions of the Court of Justice.

72 The author, the leading academic in the field of tort law, makes clear that although those Court of Justice decisions were unfortunate, they do not put aside the adequate interpretation of Portuguese law, according to which, there may be concurrence between fault of the victim (or a third party) and no-fault of the owner of the vehicle and – specially – that minors (under the age of seven) are not imputable, or they shall not be considered at fault. Thus, they shall – as a rule – be compensated in case they are injured by a vehicle.

24 CJEU 17.3.2011, C-484/09, Manuel Carvalho Ferreira Santos v Companhia Europeia de Seguros SA, ECLI:EU:C:2011:158 and CJEU 9.6.2011, C-300/10, *Marques Almeida v Companhia de Seguros Fidelidade-Mundial SA*, ECLI:EU:C:2012:656.

2. *Joaquim Sousa Ribeiro*, O Direito ao Bom nome e reputação ainda é reconhecido?: algumas reflexões críticas sobre o Acórdão do Tribunal Europeu de Direitos Humanos, no caso Freitas Rangel v Portugal, in: Estudos de Homenagem ao Professor Doutor António Pinto Monteiro, vol I (2023) 743–758

This article ('Is the Right to Good Name and Reputation still recognised? – Some reflections on the Judgment of the European Court of Human Rights, in the case of Freitas Rangel v Portugal') provides a critical overview of the ECtHR case law regarding the conflict between freedom of expression and the right to good name and reputation. According to the author, a former President of the Portuguese Constitutional Court, the ECtHR does not adequately balance the proportionality between these two conflicting human rights. The *Freitas Rangel* case is a significant example of this lack of proportionality. 73

3. *André Dias Pereira*, As "declarações de escusa de responsabilidade" dos profissionais de saúde: análise jurídica, in: Estudos de Homenagem ao Professor Doutor António Pinto Monteiro, vol I (2023) 915–954

Some healthcare professionals (doctors and nurses) claim an exemption of liability, complaining that the human or technical resources are not sufficient for a quality service, especially in the National Health Service. This paper provides a legal analysis of its validity. The brief conclusion is that healthcare professionals cannot exempt themselves from civil (disciplinary or criminal) liability with external effects, that is, vis-à-vis the patients. However, these statements can be legally relevant in ascertaining the degree of fault of the professional and the organisation in the case of medical error. 74

Lucian Bojin and Sergiu Căileanu

XXIV. Romania

A. Legislation

1. Law no 203/2023 amending the Criminal Procedure Code and other laws (Monitorul Oficial no 618 of 6 July 2023)

Law no 203/2023 introduced a series of amendments to the Criminal Procedure Code, among which, of interest for our topic, are the new legal provisions concerning the liability of the State for unlawful arrests (art 539 of the Criminal Procedure Code). The previous legal provisions were declared unconstitutional in 2021 and thus they had to be replaced. 1

The new art 539 provides that the person subject to a measure of deprivation of liberty (arrest, etc) has the right to obtain compensation if the measure has been ascertained as unlawful or if the person has been acquitted (except for the case when acquittal is due to decriminalisation). It also provides that the proof of fulfilling the conditions that give rise to the right of compensation (ie unlawfulness of the measure or acquittal) is given with the judgments or the prosecutor's decrees revoking the measure of deprivation of liberty or judgments or decrees of acquittal. 2

The amendment is of great practical interest. According to the previous rule, the right to obtain compensation was conditional upon a judgment confirming the unlawful character of the arrest or other similar measure. This meant that requesting compensation was a two-step procedure: first, obtaining the judgment confirming the unlawfulness of the measure and only then submitting the request for compensation of damage. Moreover, the right to compensation was limited to cases where the arrest or similar measure did not comply with legal requirements. In the case of a person arrested and then acquitted, the right to compensation existed only if the measure of the arrest had previously been declared as unlawful. For these reasons, in particular for the second, the law was declared unconstitutional.[1] 3

The new rule certainly improves the access to justice for this type of reparation measure, but it is likely to come with its own disadvantages. In particular, according to the new rule, the right to compensation is 'automatic' in the case of a 4

1 Decision no 136 of 3 March 2021 of the Constitutional Court, Monitorul Oficial no 494 of 15 May 2021.

https://doi.org/10.1515/9783111376721-025

person arrested and then acquitted. In such cases, only the amount of the compensation is discussed. Although in most cases, probably, an arrest followed by an acquittal would easily be qualified as a wrongful arrest, there can be situations in which such assessment is not at all clear.[2] This has to be understood in the context of the many changes in the criminal and criminal procedure legislation in the last decade and of the many interventions of the Constitutional Court in this field. For example, following the intervention of the Constitutional Court, some rules on collecting evidence were declared unconstitutional and then replaced or the rules on time limitations of criminal responsibility were reinterpreted. In some case, acquittals followed due to these changes in the rules. In such cases, in the light of the rules in force at the moment of the arrest, such measures might not have been considered as unlawful, although the person arrested was ultimately acquitted.

B. Cases

1. Înalta Curte de Casație și Justiție, Civil Section 1, Decision no 1012 of 7 June 2023:[3] Moral Damages for Death of a Relative; Amount of Moral Damages; Discrimination

a) Brief Summary of the Facts

5 In the autumn of 2016, claimant A and her deceased spouse D, while driving in their car, were hit by a tree falling to the ground. The tree which fell was in a row of trees at the side of the road and it was established that the fall was due to the advanced age of the tree. As a matter of fact, the defendant, *Compania Națională de Administrare a Infrastructurii Rutiere* (National Company for administering the road infrastructure, CNAIR), started a campaign of cutting down the trees in the area in July 2016, it stopped for a few months and then resumed the works of cutting a few days after the incident.

6 Claimant A, together with her sons, B and C, filed a lawsuit against the defendant CNAIR, seeking compensation for the material damage incurred by A (the value of the destroyed car assessed at € 883) and for moral damages for all

2 See the Decision of the High Court of Cassation and Justice no 356 of 1 March 2023, commented below no 23 ff.

3 Published online at <https://www.scj.ro/1093/Detalii-jurisprudenta?customQuery%5B0%5D.Key=id&customQuery%5B0%5D.Value=205612#highlight=##>.

three claimants, following the death of D, spouse and, respectively, father of the claimants. The Arad Tribunal granted in part the request and ordered the defendant to pay the amount of € 883 as material damages to A and € 80,000 as moral damages to A and, respectively, € 100,000 as moral damages to each of the sons B and C. This judgment was upheld on appeal by Timișoara Court of Appeal, but was annulled by the High Court of Cassation and Justice on 12 April 2022, which sent the case for retrial in appeal. When sending the case for retrial, the High Court instructed the appeal court to make its own assessment of the criteria based on which the amount of moral damages was established. It also requested the appeal court to take into account that the amount of the moral damages awarded should not be excessive in comparison with the life conditions of the victims and with the national standard of living, because the events giving rise to moral damage should not become a source of enrichment for the victim.

In retrial, the Timișoara Court of Appeal essentially maintained its previous 7 decision and confirmed the granting of the previously mentioned amounts as moral damages. Defendant CNAIR presented a request for review against this decision before the High Court of Cassation and Justice.

b) Judgment of the Court

By its Decision no 1012 of 7 June 2023, the High Court granted the request for re- 8 view and ordered that the case be returned for a second retrial before the Timișoara Court of Appeal.

The High Court noted that, while the Court of Appeal did make its own assess- 9 ment of the criteria for granting moral damages, it did not pursue the principle that such damages should not become an occasion for unjust enrichment. In particular, the Court of Appeal refused to relate the amount of moral damages to the earnings of the deceased, arguing that, in establishing the amount of moral damages, 'economic criteria such as the revenues earned by the deceased' cannot be taken into consideration.

The High Court also criticised the tendency of some courts (seemingly joined 10 by the Court of Appeal) to establish the compensation 'towards the same high amount'.[4] According to the High Court, this way of approaching moral damages threatens to 'break the balance between emotional injury and the compensation

4 See also Decision no 2010 of 8 November 2023 of the High Court of Cassation and Justice, below no 39.

granted' and to derail moral damages from their function, which is that of 'equitable satisfaction' (and should not be confounded with material damages).

11 The High Court concluded that 'by maintaining the same amount of the moral damages awarded in first instance' without testing it against the requirements indicated by the High Court in its first decision, the Court of Appeal manifestly breached its duty to observe in retrial the instructions provided by the Supreme Court.

c) Commentary

12 The judgment raises several interesting issues, of law, but also of policy. To fully understand the policy issues in this case, it should be recalled that the insurance industry in Romania was confronted with a significant crisis: between 2016 and 2023, no less than four major insurers went bankrupt,[5] with their debts taken over by the public Fund for Guaranteeing the Insured, so ultimately by the State. In this context, a certain concern for the overall financial stability of the system is understandable.[6] Since most insurance activity is related to cars and traffic, most of the debts taken over are in this field. And among such debts, the amount of those related to moral damages following the death of a relative or severe physical injury are still the less foreseeable due, in part, to diverse case law on this matter. Consequently, it is reasonable to assume that the stance taken by the High Court with regard to the amount of the moral damages in the present case is not unrelated to the general picture presented above.

13 Essentially, the High Court was dissatisfied that the Court of Appeal, in deciding the amount of moral damages to be granted to the relatives of the deceased, refused to relate this amount to the living conditions of the deceased and his family. All other legal issues in the case are not contested. The liability of defendant CNAIR was accepted even by the defendant itself (as strict liability, without fault, based on art 1376, para (1) of the Civil Code).[7] Also the entitlement of claimants to receive moral damages as a result of the death of their relative (spouse and

5 <https://www.euronews.ro/articole/probleme-in-piata-rca-firmele-de-asigurari-care-au-falimentat-in-ultimii-ani.>.

6 See also Decision no 2010 of 8 November 2023 of the High Court of Cassation and Justice, below no 39.

7 Art 1376, para (1) of the Civil Code provides: 'The custodian of a thing is obligated, regardless of any fault, to repair damage caused by things in his custody.'

father), based on art 1391, para (2) of the Civil Code,[8] was not disputed. Thus, the only issue in dispute remained the amount of the moral damages to be granted.

The living conditions of the victim were not, until recently, recognised as a criterion to assess the compensation of non-pecuniary loss due to emotional pain and suffering. As a matter of fact, the High Court, even in this judgment, mentions its 'blueprint checklist' of criteria to be considered when deciding the amount of moral damages: the negative consequences borne by the victim, the intensity of the perception of such negative consequences, the importance of the social values affected, the negative consequences and the extent to which family, professional and social lives were affected.[9] Additional to these criteria, there was, traditionally, the requirement that moral damages do not become a source of unjust enrichment, which could be interpreted as a prohibition of the abuse of the right to obtain compensation for moral damage. The commented judgment seems, instead, to include the reference to the living conditions of the victim as a proper, separate element in the 'checklist'. 14

The Court of Appeal explained its reluctance to use this criterion by qualifying it as an 'economic criterion' which, in its view, could not be used. It did not explain, however, why it could not be used. Economic reasoning is somehow inherent in establishing amounts of damages to be granted. The Court of Appeal likely had in mind that economic criteria are adequate for assessing the amount of material damages, but inadequate for moral damages. This is certainly a valid guiding principle, but not an absolute rule. The very idea of 'monetising' emotional suffering has an economic underlying. The High Court ignored the argument of the alleged impossibility to use economic criteria, although it could have been an opportunity to provide a convincing answer to this objection. 15

Instead, the High Court tried to justify the reference to the living conditions by emphasising the purpose of granting moral damages: that of allowing the victim to enjoy some advantages that might alleviate the emotional suffering. It added that, in the case of death of a relative, the emotional injury is 'major' and 'incommensurable'. For this very reason, the damage related to such injuries cannot be 'properly compensated', but the victim may be provided with an 'equitable satisfaction'. According to the Court, it is equally essential not to divert the purpose of moral 16

8 Art 1391, para (2) of the Civil Code provides: 'The court may also grant compensation to ascendants, descendants, brothers, sisters or a spouse for pain and suffering caused by the death of the victim, and to any person who can prove the existence of such pain or suffering.'

9 See eg *C Alunaru/L Bojin/S Căileanu*, Romania, in: E Karner/BC Steininger (eds), European Tort Law (ETL) 2021 (2022) 515, no 30; *C Alunaru/L Bojin*, Romania, in: E Karner/BC Steininger (eds), European Tort Law (ETL) 2017 (2018) 507, no 18.

damages into an unjust enrichment and not to confuse their purpose and function with the purpose and function of material damages.

17 All this is true, but it does little to clarify the relevance of the living conditions of the victims in order to decide the amount of moral damages. It might be, although the Court was not explicit on this point, that a high discrepancy between the living conditions of the victim and the moral damages granted could be an indicator of the excessive character of the damages. In other words, reference to the living conditions of the victims would work as a test for the amount of damages with the aim of preventing them from becoming an unjust enrichment. Is this really the case? In this dispute, so the defendant argued, the deceased victim had annual earnings of around € 7,000. The defendant even made calculations that the victim would have needed 40 years to earn the amounts granted to his relatives (a total of € 280,000). Is this an indication of unjust enrichment? The defendant concluded it was. The High Court did not explicitly validate this reasoning, but the judgment it issued, insisting on the necessity to relate the two figures, strengthened the defendant's argument.

18 However, the relevance of the comparison is limited. Precisely because the role of moral damages is not to compensate a pecuniary loss, reference to the loss of earnings for the family of the deceased is irrelevant. The High Court underlined the different purposes (and logic) of material and moral damages. But its insistence on referring to the living conditions of the victim seems to ignore its own argument. The loss of life is reduced to a loss of future earnings of the deceased. On the other hand, and above all, the High Court failed to provide the answer to the question its argument begged: how is the suffering of the children that lost their father related to the earnings of the father?

19 The 'check' function on the amount of damages that the High Court sought with its reference to the living conditions of the victims is, actually, much better realised by the reference (also underlined by the Court) to the national standard of living, which is an objective and impersonal criterion. A reference to the national standard of living would have sufficed for the Court's purpose and would have not created the presupposition of discrimination between victims as a function of their wealth.

20 Indeed, the most problematic part of the Court's reasoning is the fact that its insistence on referring to the living conditions of the victims might give the green light to higher amounts of moral damages for richer persons. The victim in this case would have needed 40 years to earn the amounts granted as compensation to his heirs. But what if the victim had been an executive with annual earnings of € 60,000 or even € 120,000? The moral damages awarded in this case would have passed the 'check' test by the High Court without a problem.

21 The media was quick to speculate on this possible consequence of the High Court's judgment.[10] And speculation is reinforced by an uninspired phrase used by the High Court: 'the tendency to establish the compensation towards the same high amount of the damages becomes a factor that breaks the balance (between the emotional injury and the compensation)'. In other words, there are cases in which a high amount of compensation might be due. However, they should be rather rare, there should not be a general tendency towards such amounts. And in order to curb this tendency, reference to the living conditions of the victim is a useful instrument. Such formulation is dangerously close to a licence for social inequality in granting moral damages.

22 It is certainly a legitimate aim to deter transforming cases on moral damages into a business seeking excessive compensation. But this is not enough to justify plain discrimination based on wealth criteria. The same purpose could have been better (and more justifiably) attained by the reference to the national standard of living. To our mind, the insistence of the High Court in the case discussed on the reference to the living conditions of the victim is a plain mistake in choosing its words.

2. Înalta Curte de Casație și Justiție, Civil Section 1, Decision no 356 of 1 March 2023:[11] Moral Damages for Unlawful Arrest

a) Brief Summary of the Facts

23 Claimant A was the subject of a criminal investigation starting in early 2011 and a warrant for his arrest was issued on 14 March 2011, valid for 29 days (15 March – 12 April 2011). The warrant was challenged and confirmed by the appeal court. After the expiry of the 29 days, the period was not extended. The investigation against the claimant was based on interceptions of phone calls during February and early March 2011. Between 2016 and 2018, the Romanian Constitutional

10 Eg <https://www.juridice.ro/712002/iccj-nivel-de-trai-mic-daune-morale-mici.html>, <https://www.stiripesurse.ro/justitie-pe-dos-la-iccj-o-viata-de-om-valoreaza-mai-putin-daca-ai-venituri-mici-si-familia-nu-merita-daune-morale_3122223.html>, <https://www.fanatik.ro/decizie-ciudata-a-inaltei-curti-daunele-morale-acordate-proportional-cu-situatia-financiara-a-victimei-pierderea-unei-vieti-nu-poate-fi-evaluata-matematic-20520788>.

11 Published online at <https://www.scj.ro/1093/Detalii-jurisprudenta?customQuery%5B0%5D.Key=id&customQuery%5B0%5D.Value=203220#highlight=##>.

Court issued three decisions (nos 51/2016, 22/2018 and 91/2018), the practical effect of which was the impossibility of using the interceptions of phone calls as evidence in criminal cases. As a consequence, on 20 April 2020, the said interceptions were removed from the criminal file and, on 6 May 2020, the Prosecutor's Office issued a decree of A's acquittal.

24 On 3 December 2020, A filed a lawsuit against the Romanian State, represented by the Ministry of Finance, requesting compensation for the moral damage suffered as a result of his arrest, amounting to € 100,000. The court of first instance, the Maramureș Tribunal, granted in part the request and ordered the defendant to pay moral damages in an amount of € 1,000. The Cluj Court of Appeal dismissed the appeals against this judgment: the appeal of the claimant was considered as time-barred and the appeal of the defendant as without merit. The defendant, the Romanian State, filed a request for review of this decision before the High Court of Cassation and Justice. The defendant argued that the arrest was not unlawful, despite the subsequent acquittal of the claimant. It also argued that the claimant did not prove an injury due to the period when he was under arrest for one month, in particular given the fact that he did not allege such injury in the nine years following his release from arrest.

b) Judgment of the Court

25 The High Court of Cassation and Justice dismissed the request for review on both points raised by the defendant.

26 Concerning the unlawfulness of the arrest, the High Court recalled the Constitutional Court Decision no 136/2021 in which it declared as unconstitutional (in part) the provisions of art 539 of the Criminal Procedure Code which regulate State liability for wrongful arrests. In its Decision, the Constitutional Court noted the distinction between an 'illegal arrest' and an 'unjust arrest'. The former category covers cases when the arrest warrant was issued in violation of the rules regulating it. Such 'illegality' of the measure would subsist irrespective of the judgment on the merits of the criminal case (ie irrespective of the guilt of the accused). The latter category covers cases when the arrest measure was taken in accordance with legal provisions but, following the acquittal, the arrest becomes 'unjust', since the criminal accusations have been denied. The Constitutional Court concluded that an 'unjust' arrest is a 'wrongful arrest' and entitles a victim to compensation of damage.

27 The High Court applied this reasoning of the Constitutional Court to the case discussed, acknowledged that the claimant was acquitted and concluded, based on

that, that his ‘arrest’ was ‘unjust’, according to the terminology of the Constitutional Court. Consequently, it was also wrongful.

Concerning the proof of injury, the High Court recalled that moral damage does not have to be proved in the same manner as material damage, instead compensation of moral harm has to be ‘justified’. Because moral damage implies that a value without economic content has been affected, the existence of the damage is subject to a ‘reasonable assessment’ on a basis of equity and observing the principle of proportionality. The fact that the claimant did not allege the injury for nine years following his release from arrest is, according to the Court, an element that may be useful when assessing the amount of the moral damages, but does not preclude him from claiming them. For these reasons, the High Court considered that the determination made in the first instance is in accordance with the law. 28

c) Commentary

This case raises a number of issues, some of theoretical interest and some of immediate practical relevance. The latter are related to the institutional context and history of the ‘anti-corruption campaign’ in Romania, that started in the late 2000s and is generally considered to have ended as a relevant political phenomenon in the years following the COVID-19 pandemic. 29

The ‘anti-corruption campaign’, ie a set of legislative and institutional measures, together with publicly visible action from the responsible institutions, was implemented, as a way of ensuring the continuous fulfilment after the 2007 EU accession by Romania, of the ‘rule of law’ criterion, a fundamental requirement in the pre-accession period.[12] In practice, it was realised through an increased autonomy of two investigative structures, the National Anti-Corruption Direction (*Direcția Națională Anticorupție*, DNA) and the Directorate for Investigating Organised Crime and Terrorism (*Direcția de Investigare a Infracțiunilor de Criminalitate Organizată și Terorism*, DIICOT). These organisations were prominent in initiating investigations against established politicians, with great media impact, but also in the midst of accusations of performing ‘political revenge’. Many of the criminal accusations were based on interceptions of phone calls. Such interceptions were performed in cooperation with the Romanian Intelligence Service (*Serviciul Român de Informații*, SRI), based on agreements signed between these institutions. The peri- 30

12 See EU Commission Decision 2006/928/EC of 13 December 2006 establishing a mechanism for cooperation and verification of progress in Romania to address specific benchmarks in the areas of judicial reform and the fight against corruption [2006] Official Journal (OJ) L 354/56.

od coincided with the entry into force of the new Criminal Procedure Code. Against this background, the carrying out of these investigations was influenced by repeated interventions of the Constitutional Court, which declared the unconstitutionality of various provisions in the criminal and criminal procedure legislation. One of the most significant interventions of the Constitutional Court was in declaring the invalidity of the phone interceptions obtained by SRI as evidence, due to breaching the separation of powers principle. After such invalidation, indeed a great number of the investigations were closed or, when the cases were at the trial stage, the accused were ultimately acquitted, due to insufficiency of the other evidence upon which to base a criminal charge.

31 The case discussed follows a criminal investigation opened by DIICOT and closed by the latter, nine years later, due, indeed, to the need to eliminate from the criminal files the evidence consisting in phone calls interceptions. The argument of the defendant was that the conditions for State liability for unlawful arrest were not fulfilled because, against the legal background in force at the time the arrest warrant was issued, the arrest could not be qualified as 'unlawful'. In other words, the State argued that its tort liability cannot be triggered because the essential requirement, ie the existence of a wrongful act, is not met in the case.

32 The analysis of the condition of the existence of a wrongful act provides an interesting insight into the intersections between private law and criminal procedure law. This argument is also linked with the previous regulation of liability for unlawful arrests that was declared unconstitutional and was replaced with new legislation in 2023.[13]

33 Article 539 of the Criminal Procedure Code, in its original form, provided that the 'unlawful deprivation of liberty' through arrest had to be acknowledged autonomously by a prosecutor's decree or by a judgment (either a judgment related to the warrant arrest procedure or a judgment on the merits of the criminal case). The essential point was that the judge called to decide on the State's liability did not have the autonomy to decide whether a wrongful act (wrongful arrest) existed or not, but was bound by the decision of a criminal court or by the decree of the prosecutor on this issue.[14] A second specific issue of this regulation was that the 'unlawful' character of the arrest measure was independent of the judgment on the merits of the criminal case. This means that the 'unlawfulness' of the arrest measure was intrinsic to the measure and, at least in theory, even an accused who was subsequently charged could still have been subject to an 'unlawful' arrest.

---

13 See Law no 203/20023, commented above no 1 ff.

14 To this effect, the Decision no 15 of 18 September 2017 of the High Court of Cassation and Justice, published in Monitorul Oficial no 946 of 26 November 2017, issued in the interpretation of law and mandatory for all ordinary courts.

The opposite was also true: the arrest of an accused that was subsequently acquitted could still be a 'lawful' arrest.[15]

These specific characteristics of the original regulation were tackled by the Constitutional Court in its previously mentioned Decision no 136/2021. The Constitutional Court acknowledged that, according to the regulation, a person that was subject to arrest and then acquitted would not be entitled to compensation because the measure of arrest could be qualified as 'lawful'. However, the Constitutional Court asserted that such an arrest measure could prove to be 'unjust' following the acquittal of the accused and that the latter should have the possibility to request compensation for damage caused by the arrest measure. The Constitutional Court stated that such a possibility is provided by art 52 para (3) of the Romanian Constitution regarding liability for judicial errors, despite two of the members of the Court issuing a separate opinion according to which, liability for judicial errors does not cover liability for an arrest that is followed by an acquittal. Based on this reasoning, the Constitutional Court declared as unconstitutional in part the provisions of art 539 of the Criminal Procedure Code and decided that an 'unjust' arrest must be treated similarly to an 'unlawful' arrest and entitles the person subject to the arrest measure to compensation of the damage caused due to such arrest. 34

In the case discussed, the High Court took over the distinction made by the Constitutional Court. The defendant was seeking to demonstrate that, despite the subsequent acquittal, the arrest was 'lawful'. It was so not only in the narrow sense, meaning it observed all the legal provisions in force at the date of the arrest. But, according to the defendant, it was 'lawful' also in the broad sense, of being 'just'. The defendant argued that the criminal investigation was closed due to changes in the legislation concerning evidence in criminal trials and not because the claimant would have been found not guilty. It recalled that, after his arrest, the claimant allegedly recognised the criminal accusations brought against him. Briefly, the defendant alleged that, in the given case, the requirement of wrongfulness of the arrest is not met. However, the High Court noted that, according to Decision no 136/2021 of the Constitutional Court and to the subsequent Decision no 1 of 16 January 2023 of the High Court of Cassation and Justice issued in the interpretation of law,[16] the mere judgment of acquittal is sufficient to prove the 'unjust' 35

15 To this effect, the Decision no 11 of 17 April 2019 of the High Court of Cassation and Justice, published in Monitorul Oficial no 613 of 24 July 2019, issued in the interpretation of law and mandatory for all ordinary courts.

16 Decision no 1 of 16 January 2023 of the High Court of Cassation and Justice – formation to decide on preliminary rulings, published in Monitorul Oficial no 142 of 20 February 2023. The preliminary rulings are a specific type of judgments issued by the High Court of Cassation and Justice de-

character of the arrest measure. Consequently, only the other requirements for triggering State liability may be discussed in similar procedures.

36 The second argument discussed by the High Court was the proof of injury due to the arrest. The defendant argued that the claimant did not prove an injury, in particular given the fact that he did not allege such injury in the nine years following his release. The assessment of evidence is, usually, not considered by the High Court, since its judicial reviews are deemed as being 'legality reviews' (ie reviews concerned with the application of law) and not 'merits reviews' (ie reviews concerned with the factual qualifications and assessment of evidence). However, in this case, the Court replied to the defendant's argument by recalling its established case law according to which,[17] in order to grant moral damages, a 'reasonable' and 'proportional' assessment is required, as opposed to the way evidence in the field of material damages is assessed. The High Court concluded that the defendant's criticism of the judgments of the lower courts from this angle is without merit. It mentioned that the circumstances underlined by the defendant may be elements that contributed to the decision on the amount of the moral damages (ie lowering the amount), but in themselves they do not deprive the claimant of his right to be compensated.

37 We believe that the High Court's second argument is open to criticism. The core of the defendant's criticism was that, even if the arrest was deemed unlawful following the claimant's acquittal, the latter still did not prove any injury due to his arrest. The reasoning behind the Court's view seems to be that, in such cases, not only wrongfulness, but also the injury is presupposed, while only the amount of moral damages is open to discussion. With this, the High Court went far beyond what was decided by the Constitutional Court. Although it is not easy to imagine cases in which persons subject to arrest did not suffer an injury, in theory, all conditions for the establishment of tort liability must be proven, including the injury. At least in theory, it is possible to have a case in which wrongfulness exists, but not the injury. Otherwise, all cases concerning damages for arrests followed by acquittals would be reduced to cases in which only the extent of the damages is discussed and not the existence of the damage itself.

ciding on unitary interpretations of the law and mandatory for all courts, according to art 519 ff of the Civil Procedure Code.

17 See eg *Alunaru/Bojin* (fn 9) ETL 2017, no 18 ff.

3. Personal Injury

2023 brought a few interesting judicial decisions in the field of personal injury. As the two judgments selected for comments illustrate broader trends in the Romanian judicial practice, some other judgments with similar concerns are also of interest. 38

Decision no 2010 of 8 November 2023 of the High Court of Cassation and Justice deals with the issue of the amount of moral damages granted due to the loss of a close relative (parents). In this case, the amount of the damages granted was around € 8,000 for each of the descendants of the victim following a request pointing towards an amount of € 100,000. The High Court was satisfied with the judgment in appeal and denied the request for review. It stressed again that the case law should not evolve in the direction of granting a similar amount for each person in a similar situation, because it would infringe the idea that each injury is personal and individual and compensation should be assessed according to the circumstances of each case. It also emphasised that moral damages 'cannot repair the irremediable'. Consequently, the guiding principle in granting them is that they should not 'constitute excessive sanctions for the authors of the damageable facts and, implicitly, for the insurers, nor unjustified enrichment for the victims', but should not be merely symbolic either. In this judgment, the High Court openly voiced its concern for the financial stability of the national insurance system. 39

Decision no 214 of 19 January 2023 of the High Court of Cassation and Justice, Section of Administrative Law deals with an issue related again to the moral damages of relatives of victims who were killed in car accidents. It involves a request filed by the relatives of a victim who died in an accident against the Fund for Guaranteeing the Insured (*Fondul de Garantare a Asiguraților*, FGA), a public guarantee scheme put in place to cover damages in the case of insolvency of the insurer. Since four of the largest Romanian insurers went bankrupt in the last eight years, many claims of victims came to be resolved by the FGA. The case discussed is a dispute of administrative law between a claimant and the FGA in which the claimant challenged the fact that the decision issued by the FGA concerning his request granted him material damages for injuries following an accident, but did not reply to his request for moral damages, arguing that a response will be given after the enactment of some internal proceedings in the course of discussion at the time, intended to homogenise the procedure for recognising moral damages. Such internal proceedings were being promoted in relation to concerns of the FGA related to the amounts of moral damages to be granted. The High Court deemed this defence as without legal basis and ordered the FGA to issue a decision on moral damages, as well. 40

41 Finally, Decision no 286 of 16 February 2023 of the High Court of Cassation and Justice dealt with the interesting issue of moral damages for acts of genocide. It regarded a request for moral damages from the State for the psychological suffering of a person subject to a measure of deportation in the USSR during the communist regime, for ethnicity reasons. The claimant attempted to claim that crimes of genocide could not be subject to any prescription periods. However, the High Court stated that the fact that crimes of genocide are not subject to any prescription periods from the perspective of criminal liability does not mean that tortious liability is not subject to the rules of time limitation. On the contrary, the civil time limitation remains in place for this kind of claim. The Court accepted that during the communist regime, it was impossible to file such a request, so the limitation period could not start to run, but it did commence to run after the fall of the communist regime. Therefore, 33 years after such event, a similar request was considered time-barred by the High Court.

C. Literature

1. *Marius Chelaru,* Răspunderea juridică în materia internetului obiectelor (IOT) [Legal liability in the field of the Internet of Things (IoT)], Revista Dreptul no 11/2023, 45–51

42 Law is, by its nature, conservative. It reacts only to the social and technological innovations that can change the status quo of the environment and tries to regulate them as best as possible, considering the existing knowledge of that time. However, since the emergence of the internet, it has become clear that law must reinvent itself and adopt a proactive approach, at least in the law-making process. Nowadays, this necessity has become even more urgent given the robotics' development, AI technology and the Internet of Things (IoT). Starting from this challenge, Chelaru's article contains a brief analysis of the current legislation in Romania on the topic of liability in the field of IoT, viewed as a part of the new EU regulations.[18]

43 The analysis starts with the definition of IoT: a network of connected digital devices, sometimes known as 'smart' devices, with its related research encompassing domains such as AI, 5G, cloud computing, blockchain, and micro- or nano-sys-

18 In this respect, see the European Commission White Paper (Artificial Intelligence – a European approach centred on trust and excellence) adopted on 19 February 2020.

tems.[19] Then, it approaches the particularities of civil liability in the case of damage caused by IoT. The paper is organised in several sections, each focusing on: (a) the relation between IoT and personal data protection regulations; (b) the safety guarantees required by law for IoT products; and (c) the legal liability regime for damage caused by IoT, as it is regulated by Romanian civil law.

Taking into account that IoT covers such a wide area and that it is strongly connected with other domains, the author correctly emphasises that, *de lege lata*, a complete regulation of IoT cannot be found either in Romania, or in the EU. Thus, in order to solve a dispute, the parties and the courts must consider the legislation of a particular domain and, if such legislation is not sufficient, they turn to the general regulations in the field of e-commerce of products. Consequently, in the case of damage caused by IoT, to establish the legal regime of the liability, one must consider the particularities of the product involved in the respective case. For example, in the case of a breach of personal data regulations, the civil liability regime shall be determined in accordance with GDPR regulations.[20] However, despite all these practical difficulties, the author outlines a methodology that can be used for the purpose of establishing the legal regime of liability in the case of damage caused by IoT. The formula includes both objective and subjective elements. 44

Regarding the subjective elements, Chelaru highlights that, when it comes to the field of IoT liability, more than two persons are generally involved. On the one hand, there is the victim, whose identity should not be very difficult to establish. However, on the other, there can be two or more of the following persons: (a) the seller of the IoT; (b) the manufacturer of the IoT; (c) the authority which establishes the safety standards of products, including IoT; and/or (d) a hacker. Identifying the hackers and determining their number can be problematic but they are essential for establishing the legal regime of civil liability. 45

Consequently, the author shows that it is very important to establish these subjective frameworks because there are numerous consequences arising from them. Firstly, if there are at least two persons responsible for the damage inflicted on the victim, they can be held jointly liable for the respective damage, based on art 1382 of the Romanian Civil Code, which provides that: 'Those responsible for an unlawful act are jointly liable to provide compensation to the victim.' Secondly, in almost 46

19 In the same way, see <https://digital-strategy.ec.europa.eu/en/news/iot-and-future-edge-computing-europe>.

20 Regulation (EU) 2016/679 of the European Parliament and of the Council of 27 April 2016 on the protection of natural persons with regard to the processing of personal data and on the free movement of such data, and repealing Directive 95/46/EC (General Data Protection Regulation) [2016] OJ L 119/1.

all cases, the seller and the manufacturer of the IoT are professionals. Therefore, their fault would be assessed in relation to a superior standard of diligence, according to art 1358 of the Romanian Civil Code, which provides that: 'In assessing fault, account shall be taken of the circumstances in which the damage was caused, which are unrelated to the person of the perpetrator and, where appropriate, of the fact that the damage was caused by a professional operating an undertaking.'

47 Regarding the objective elements, Chelaru notes that there are two major aspects that must be taken into consideration in order to establish the civil tort liability of the perpetrator. Firstly, one must determine if the victim concluded a sale-purchase agreement with the person responsible for the safety of the IoT involved in causing the damage or concluded another type of contract that gave the victim the right to use the respective IoT. In this case, liability will be contractual, given the fact that art 1350 para (3) of the Romanian Civil Code prohibits the victim from choosing between tortious and contractual liability ('Unless otherwise provided by law, neither party may waive the application of the rules of contractual liability in favour of other rules which are more favourable to them').

48 Furthermore, this objective element is important not only to establish if the liability, in a certain case, is contractual or tortious in nature. It is important also to establish which type of tort liability is applicable. In this respect, it must be determined what type of unlawful deed caused the damage. For example, if the IoT is hacked by a third party, which steals credit card information and uses it to withdraw money from the victim's bank account, the perpetrator's liability will be established under art 1357 of the Civil Code, which stipulates the following: '(1) A person who causes damage to another person by an unlawful deed, found guilty thereof, has the duty to compensate the damage. (2) The perpetrator shall be held liable for the slightest fault.' However, even if the legal regime is clear from a theoretical point of view, in practice the victim will face serious difficulties when trying to identify the perpetrator. In this respect, the author stresses that such identification is impossible, in most cases, as the perpetrator is usually a person from another part of the world, connected to a device that is not even registered in their name.

49 On the other hand, if the person liable for the damage is the manufacturer of the IoT, the victim can obtain compensation based on art 1376 para (1) of the Civil Code (Liability for damage caused by Things), which stresses that: '(1) Every person has the obligation to offer compensation, regardless of any fault, for the damage caused by the thing in their custody'. In such a situation, the identification of the person responsible for the damage is simple, but the victim can face difficulties when trying to prove the IoT did not function correctly. For this reason, Romanian law reverses the burden of proof. It exempts the victim from the burden of proving the defects and it states that the owner of the IoT, or the manufacturer, will have to

demonstrate that the respective IoT complies with safety regulations, and that it functions normally, without any flaws.

The second objective element that is required to assess the civil tort liability for the IoT is that the respective thing failed to comply with the applicable security standards. Regarding this second requirement, the author notes that a product shall be considered to comply with security standards if it meets the requirements stipulated by the relevant European standards and the standards in the country in which the product is sold, if it complies with the product's security good practices and if it takes into account the current state of the art in technical and scientific knowledge and the reasonable expectations of consumers, in general, regarding the security of products. Although we agree with the author's above mentioned considerations, we note that this duty of compliance with security standards is not relevant for the civil tort liability of the owner of the IoT, but only for the contractual liability of this owner towards the manufacturer of the IoT, because the terms of the contract concluded between the manufacturer and the owner of the IoT cannot be opposed to the victim. 50

In the final part of the study, the author analyses the possibility of filing a lawsuit, based on civil tort liability, against the public authority designated to establish the security standards for a certain type of products. To this question, Chelaru responds in the affirmative, noting that such liability could be established for the wrongful acts attributable to the authority, according to art 1357 of the Romanian Civil Code. Although we agree with this conclusion, as a general principle, we must specify that such an authority could be held liable only if all the conditions provided by law for State liability are met, given the fact that this authority is the representative of the State. 51

As a conclusion of his study, the author emphasises that the IoT regulations are incomplete and because of this, a victim could have serious difficulties if they suffer damage and want to obtain compensation from the perpetrator. In most situations, these difficulties lie in identifying the perpetrator and/or in providing proof of the defect of the IoT. Therefore, Chelaru concludes that swift legislative interventions are required, both at national and European levels, to ensure real protection in the case of civil liability in the field of IoT. 52

2. *Marta Claudia Cliza/Constantin-Claudiu Ulariu,* Responsabilitatea în domeniul protecției datelor cu caracter personal [Responsibility in the field of general data protection], Revista Dreptul no 7/2023, 35 – 52

53 The article by Cliza and Ulariu deals with a subject that is, currently, one of the most discussed topics in Romanian legal literature, namely, the general data protection regulation. This topic has led to many debates between private law authors who are interested in how personality rights (or human rights) evolve in the era of digitalisation and how adequate the legal protection of these rights currently is. Although the topic is not very new, as the authors point out in the second section of their paper, it was brought back to the attention of the legal world after the EU adopted the well-known General Data Protection Regulation (GDPR) in 2016.[21] This Regulation was adopted as a response to the abundant case law of the European Court of Human Rights (ECtHR) in the field of data protection[22] and it is seen as a major step forward in the quest for finding the most suitable protection of the confidentiality of personal data. The strongest point of this Regulation is that it brings clear and comprehensive rules that shall apply across all Member States of the European Union, rules whose violation shall be drastically sanctioned.

54 Personal data are defined as:

> 'any information relating to an identified or identifiable natural person ('data subject'); an identifiable natural person is one who can be directly or indirectly identified, in particular by referring to an identifier such as a name, an identification number, location data, an online identifier or to one or more factors specific to the physical, physiological, genetic, mental, economic, cultural or social identity of that natural person'.[23]

55 Regarding their legal nature, Romanian literature[24] emphasised that personal data cannot be qualified as a tangible or intangible 'asset', and must be included in the

---

21 Regulation (EU) 2016/679 of the European Parliament and of the Council of 27 April 2016 on the protection of natural persons with regard to the processing of personal data and on the free movement of such data, and repealing Directive 95/46/EC (General Data Protection Regulation) [2016] OJ L 119/1.

22 In this respect, see The Guide to the Case-Law of the of the European Court of Human Rights in the field of Data Protection, available at <https://www.echr.coe.int/documents/d/echr/Guide_Data_protection_ENG>.

23 Art 4 (1) of Regulation (EU) 2016/679.

24 *V Stoica*, Ce sunt datele cu caracter personal? Revista Română de Drept Privat no 1/2018.

category of personality rights regulated by the Romanian Civil Code,[25] being a part of the right to private life, as the ECtHR established in its case law.[26]

These theoretical considerations are very important because, as the authors stress, they are elements that give shape to the legal regime of civil liability in the field of data protection, especially regarding the types of damage that can be inflicted and the means of compensation. 56

Starting from these considerations, Cliza and Ulariu explain the legal regime of the civil liability regulated by Romanian law in the case of damage caused by an unlawful disclosure of personal data, and its particularities. The paper is divided into three major parts. In the first part, the authors present the legislative framework applicable in this field. The second part contains a history of data protection regulations at an international level and the final part deals with the topic of civil liability and the particularities of this liability in the field of data protection. 57

The first question raised by the authors concerns the legal nature of the civil liability that is applicable in the case of unlawful disclosure of personal data of a natural person. Namely, in such a case should tortious or contractual liability be applied? This debate starts from the fact that art 6 para (1) of the GDPR stipulates that: 'Processing shall be lawful only if and to the extent that at least one of the following applies: (a) the data subject has given consent to the processing of his or her personal data for one or more specific purposes.' Thus, some scholars emphasise that, since the law refers to an acceptance, liability should be contractual. However, the two authors of the study state that such an acceptance should not lead to the conclusion that in all cases the liability for breaching the provisions of data protection regulations will be contractual in nature. They justify this with two arguments. Firstly, they show that the acceptance provided by art 6 para (1) of GDPR is not the acceptance of an offer provided by Romanian law because this acceptance is not given in consideration of a counter-performance offered by the other party, but a simple acceptance for the operator to process their personal data, outside the framework of an agreement. Secondly, the authors invoke art 1355 para 4 of the Romanian Civil Code, which stipulates that 'a declaration of acceptance of the risk of injury shall not in itself constitute a waiver of the victim's right to compensation.' 58

Although we agree with the authors that liability in the case of violation of data protection regulations should be tort liability, we cannot accept the reasoning on which this conclusion is based. In this respect, our main objection towards the 59

25 Arts 58–103 of the Civil Code.

26 ECtHR *S and Marper v United Kingdom*, 4.12.2008, nos 30562/04 and 30566/04.

first argument is that not all contracts are synallagmatic. On the contrary, there are also so-called unilateral contracts, which are defined by the Romanian Civil Code as a type of contract that does not imply reciprocal and interdependent obligations (art 1171). Thus, according to Romanian law, in order to have a contract, it is not mandatory that every person involved in the respective legal relationship has to obtain a counter-performance or an advantage, be it pecuniary or non-pecuniary, from the other persons. What is essential for having a contract is to have, in accordance with art 1166 of the Romanian Civil Code, 'an agreement of wills between two or more persons with the intention of constituting, amending, or terminating a legal relationship'. If we analyse the acceptance provided by art 6 para 1 of the GDPR through the filter of art 1166 of the Romanian Civil Code, we will be able to observe that this acceptance does not aim to constitute, amend, or terminate a legal relationship, but it is only a permission. In other words, this acceptance is given outside of any contractual framework and independently of the rights and obligations implied by a contract. Consequently, in this situation, it cannot be said that a contract exists.

60 However, we note that there can be situations in which the acceptance given based on art 6 para 1 of the GDPR can be linked to contractual liability. This is the specific case of banking contracts or mobile phone service contracts. In these situations, contractual liability is justified by the fact that the acceptance for processing personal data is directly connected with the duties and obligations assumed by the bank or by the phone network company towards the customer (ie the phone number and the bank account number are personal data directly linked with the name of a natural person). Furthermore, we emphasise that the second argument raised by the authors is also ill-grounded, because art 1355 of the Romanian Civil Code, in general, and in particular its para (4), refers to damage caused in both contractual and tort liability situations.

61 Regarding the characteristics of this tort liability, the authors stress that there are several particularities which must be considered. Firstly, the two authors note that, although we are dealing with liability for personal actions, based on art 1357 of the Romanian Civil Code, the victim shall be exempted from the duty to prove the fault of the responsible person. This is because the tort liability subjected to this analysis is an objective form of liability, regardless of fault and based on a legal guarantee owed by the entity entitled to process the personal data of other persons. Therefore, the victim will have to prove only the wrongful act (which, in accordance with art 82 of the GDPR can be any infringement of the Regulation), the inflicted damage and the causal link between the wrongfulness and damage.

62 Secondly, the two authors are of the opinion that the victim is entitled to compensation for both pecuniary and non-pecuniary damage, given the fact that personal data is a part of a natural person's right to private life. This conclusion is ex-

pressly provided by art 82 para (1) of the GDPR, which stipulates that 'any person who has suffered material or non-material damage as a result of an infringement of this Regulation shall have the right to receive compensation from the controller or processor for the damage suffered.' Consequently, a disclosure of personal data could lead not only to a financial loss, but also to emotional distress and suffering. This distinction is important not only because it offers the victim the possibility to seek compensation for all the inflicted damage, but also because it offers the possibility to obtain a variety of remedies in order to compensate the damage and stop/reverse the effects of disclosing the personal data. In particular, the victim can rely on and request the enforcement of the remedies provided by art 253 para (1) of the Romanian Civil Code, which provides the following:

> '(1) A natural person whose non-pecuniary rights were violated or threatened may apply to the court at any time for: a) the prohibition of committing the unlawful act if it is imminent; b) the cessation of the violation and its prohibition for the future if it still continues; c) the ascertainment of the unlawful nature of the act if the disturbance it produced subsists.'

In addition, the victim can request the enforcement of the remedies provided by 63
para (3) of the same provision, which provides that:

> 'at the same time, the person who suffered a violation of such rights may apply to the court to order the perpetrator to perform any act deemed necessary by the court for restoration of the violated right, such as: a) to order the perpetrator to publish the judgment of conviction at their expense; b) any other measures necessary to put an end to the unlawful act or for the compensation of the damage caused.'

The final part of the study is devoted to the persons that can be held responsible 64
for the damage caused by the disclosure of personal data of a natural person. In this respect, the two authors state that the main responsible party is the operator, which is the entity that collects, stores and/or process in any other form the personal data of any other natural third party and which is authorised by the State in this regard. The operator shall be held liable even if the disclosure is the result of conduct of another person, but which was authorised by the operator to process the personal data of the victim. In reality, in such a case, the operator and its agent can be held jointly liable, according to art 1382 of the Romanian Civil Code. The operator and its agent should not be held liable for any damage inflicted on the victim if they prove that they are, in any way, not responsible for the event giving rise to the damage. In this latter situation, the authors stress that the victim could file a lawsuit against the public entity designated to supervise the personal data collection process, which holds a subsidiary responsibility.

65 As a conclusion of their study, Cliza and Ulariu report that the rules regarding data protection have become much clearer as a result of the GDPR and that, *de lege lata*, there is a general comprehensive framework on civil liability in the case of unlawful disclosure of personal data, which offers effective remedies to the victim.

Martin Hogg

XXV. Scotland

A. Legislation

There was no new legislation in the field of delict in 2023. 1

B. Cases

1. *Paterson v Lanarkshire Health Board*, Court of Session (Outer House) 6 January 2023, [2023] Court of Session Outer House (CSOH) 1, 2023 Scots Law Times (SLT) 67: Liability of Health Provider to Family Members for Breach of Duty of Care Owed to Relative who Committed Suicide

a) Brief Summary of the Facts

2 The pursuer was the mother of a deceased woman who, aged thirty-five, had committed suicide a month after having been discharged from psychiatric care in hospital. The mother (together with the deceased's siblings and children) raised an action for damages against the local health authority, who were the employers of a consultant psychiatrist who had discharged the deceased from hospital and overseen arrangements for her post-release care. The deceased had a long history of psychiatric illness and had been hospitalised repeatedly (sometimes voluntarily, sometimes compulsorily) over an extended period of time. The psychiatrist had arranged for the deceased to be referred to a community psychiatric nurse after her release from hospital and had provided her with telephone contact numbers in case she needed further help. Two days before the scheduled appointment with the nurse, the deceased had taken her own life.

3 The pursuer claimed damages in respect of the deceased's death, arguing that it was negligent of the consultant psychiatrist to have released the deceased from hospital without an appropriate care plan which would have provided her with support, supervision, and potential intervention during the period between discharge and the scheduled appointment with the nurse. It was argued that the deceased's suicide was a foreseeable consequence of her release from hospital without such an appropriate care plan. Damages were sought by the relatives under the

https://doi.org/10.1515/9783111376721-026

statutory provisions governing recovery of damages by family members of a deceased person.

b) Judgment of the Court

4 The judge agreed with the pursuer's argument that the consultant psychiatrist had been negligent (this being in breach of a duty of care owed to her), holding that the deceased was foreseeably at risk of deterioration in respect of her psychiatric health following her discharge. The approach adopted by the psychiatrist of leaving her 'to fend for herself' with phone numbers only did not take into account the significant risk of deterioration applicable in her case. There had been a failure to provide appropriate care and treatment to the deceased, which carried with it the foreseeable risk of self-harm, attempted suicide, or suicide. Had the deceased's state of mental health been maintained by appropriate post-discharge follow-up and care, her deterioration and consequent suicide would likely have been avoided. The suicide of the deceased was therefore a direct consequence of the deterioration of her psychiatric condition following her discharge. The judge awarded the deceased's mother £ 100,000 in damages, her siblings £ 50,000 each, and her children £ 70,000 each, in each case for the grief, distress, and sorrow they suffered.

c) Commentary

5 Medical practitioners owe a duty of care to their patients in respect of their diagnosis and treatment. Direct harm caused by negligence on the part of the practitioner will sound in damages to the patient (and, in some circumstances, their relatives). However, where a patient's own conduct is a cause of the harm suffered by them, liability on the part of the practitioner may be reduced or excluded.

6 A patient's own conduct will not, however, always dimmish the responsibility of the medical practitioner for negligent diagnosis or treatment. In particular, where a patient is in a fragile or disturbed state of mind, the patient may not be deemed responsible for the consequences of their own actions, and the medical practitioner may be required, by virtue of the duty of care owed to the particular patient, to have special regard to the care which may be needed to prevent foreseeable self-harm by a patient in such a state of mind. In this decision, the judge narrated the multiple admissions and discharges of the deceased from hospital, noting 'an elevated risk of suicide for those with her condition following their discharge and indeed that suicidal behaviour was part of the diagnostic description of that

condition'.[1] The foreseeable risk of self-harm or suicide was a risk falling within the scope of the duty of care owed to the patient, and a consequence therefore for which the medical practitioner was liable given the failure to ensure adequate care of the patient following her release from hospital.

The decision in this case is consistent with the established rules and authorities relating to the duty of care resting upon a medical practitioner. The damages awards to the deceased's relatives were made in application of the provisions of sec 4 of the Damages (Scotland) Act 2011, which regulates and provides for such claims. 7

2. *X v Y & the Lord Advocate*, Court of Session (Outer House) 2 March 2023, [2023] CSOH 17, 2023 Session Cases (SC) 235, 2023 SLT 293: Whether the Crown was Vicariously Liable for Alleged Assaults Committed by a Judge

a) Brief Summary of the Facts

The pursuer, who was a legal practitioner, sought damages of £ 120,000 based upon an alleged series of sexual assaults and harassment in 2018 said to have been committed by the first defender, who was a judge (a sheriff), for which the second defender (the Crown) was said to be vicariously liable. The four separate incidences of assault were claimed to be individual delictual acts at common law and, taken together, to also constitute a chain of harassment under the Protection from Harassment Act 1997. 8

On the issue of the vicarious liability of the Crown for the judge's alleged conduct, the Lord Advocate argued that there was an insufficient relationship between the Scottish Ministers and a sheriff and insufficient closeness of connection between that relationship and the wrongdoing for there to be any vicarious liability. Arguments were raised regarding the terms of the Crown Proceedings Act 1947, sec 2, which concerns the liability of the Crown for delictual conduct,[2] and as to 9

1 Para 52 of the judgment.

2 Sec 2(1) of that Act provides that: 'Subject to the provisions of this Act, the Crown shall be subject to all those liabilities in tort to which, if it were a private person of full age and capacity, it would be subject:– (a) in respect of torts committed by its servants or agents; ... Provided that no proceedings shall lie against the Crown by virtue of paragraph (a) of this subsection in respect of any act or omission of a servant or agent of the Crown unless the act or omission would apart from the provisions of this Act have given rise to a cause of action in tort against that servant or agent or his estate.' Sec 2(5) further provides that: 'No proceedings shall lie against the Crown by virtue of this

whether, were the Crown to be liable vicariously, its correct representative was the Lord Advocate or the Advocate General for Scotland (a matter not discussed further here).

b) Judgment of the Court

10 The court held that sec 2(1) of the 1947 Act plainly applied vicarious liability for delictual acts of Crown servants. There would be no need for sec 2(5), which excluded vicarious liability where responsibilities of a judicial nature were being discharged by a judge, if a judicial office-holder were not a Crown servant. For that reason, the pursuer was not bound to fail in her contention that a member of the judiciary is a Crown servant for the purposes of sec 2(1) of the Act. That section provided that the Crown could be subject to vicarious liability, but only in the same way as applied to other liable parties. That being so, the test of the relationship being akin to that between an employer and employee still required to be met. The key features of Crown and government involvement in the position and payment of sheriffs met this part of the test, and the independence of the judiciary did not negate that relationship.

11 Whether there was a close connection between that relationship and the alleged incidents was fact specific. Judges had a degree of authority and control over legal practitioners, so that the relationship between judge and Crown went beyond merely providing the opportunity for the wrongful conduct: it allowed a judge, in certain circumstances, to abuse the special position in which the Crown had placed the judge. The fact specific question would have to be explored at a trial of the facts (a 'proof'), though it was already clear that two of the alleged incidents of assault occurred in contexts (on a train and by means of an attempted video call) which did not fall within even a broad view of the sheriff's functions or field of activities and did not show abuse of the special position in which the Crown had placed him. They were thus not fairly and properly to be regarded as occurring while the sheriff was acting in the ordinary course of his duties but were personal matters.

12 The court ordered a proof before answer (a trial of the facts before a debate on the law).

---

section in respect of anything done or omitted to be done by any person while discharging or purporting to discharge any responsibilities of a judicial nature vested in him, or any responsibilities which he has in connection with the execution of judicial process.'

c) Commentary

This judgment is notable for two main reasons. First, the court takes the view that the party responsible for the judiciary (the Crown) can be vicariously liable for delicts committed by a judge; second, that in determining whether vicariously liability of the Crown arises for such delicts, the standard test developed in recent leading cases in the context of the employer-employee relationship is equally applicable in the case of the Crown's vicarious liability for a judge's delictual conduct. 13

The first substantive outcome is a welcome one. It would be invidious if a judge were able to commit delicts while working for the Crown, which appoints judges and sets standard for their conduct, to be able to disclaim responsibility for such wrongful conduct. Whether or not a judge is to be considered a 'servant', 'agent', or 'employee' of the Crown more generally (a matter of some dispute), the terms of the 1947 Act adequately answer the specific question of vicarious liability of the Crown for the delicts of judges: because there is a Crown exemption in sec 2(5) of the Act in relation to 'anything done or omitted to be done by any person while discharging or purporting to discharge any responsibilities of a judicial nature' (broadly speaking, for acts undertaken by the judge when adjudicating on matters before the court), this implies that there is no such exemption in respect of other conduct of judges. As regards the instant case, there would thus be no Crown exemption from liability of alleged assaults committed by the judge occurring within the precincts of a courthouse. That of course merely tells us there is no Crown exemption from liability, should such liability arise: it does not address whether such liability does arise on the facts of any particular case. Determination of that matter requires application of the test for vicarious liability. 14

As to the second substantive outcome, concerning application of the test for vicarious liability of the Crown for delicts committed by a judge, there have in the last quarter century been a number of important cases handed down by Scottish (and English) courts on the test for establishing vicarious liability in the field of employment (some of which involved alleged vicarious liability for acts which were criminal as well as delictual/tortious). In this case, the court considered those authorities equally applicable to the judge-Crown relationship.[3] These authorities have developed a test of 'close connection', requiring that the conduct of the employee have a close connection with his or her employment, albeit 15

3 The court refers to (among others) the decisions in *Wm Morrison Supermarkets plc v Various Claimants* [2020] United Kingdom Supreme Court (UKSC) 12, *Vaickuviene v J Sainsbury plc* [2013] Court of Session (Inner House) (CSIH) 67, *Catholic Child Welfare Society v Various Claimants* [2012] UKSC 56, and *Lister v Hesley Hall Ltd* [2001] United Kingdom House of Lords (UKHL) 22.

with some modification in cases where sexual abuse is alleged. In one Supreme Court case, Lord Phillips observed of cases of abuse that:

> 'Vicarious liability is imposed where a defendant, whose relationship with the abuser put it in a position to use the abuser to carry on its business or to further its own interests, has done so in a manner which has created or significantly enhanced the risk that the victim or victims would suffer the relevant abuse. The essential closeness of connection between the relationship between the defendant and the tortfeasor and the acts of abuse thus involves a strong causative link.'[4]

16 In this case, the judge observed (rightly, it is suggested) that such circumstances can arise in relation to the contact which judges have with legal practitioners:

> 'The vast majority of judicial office-holders will certainly not pose a risk. However, in principle the risk does arise for individuals coming into contact with judicial office-holders and who are subject to their authority or control. Authority and control have been relied upon for vicarious liability in cases of sexual abuse. Such an office-holder could, in certain circumstances, abuse the special position in which the Crown has placed him.'

17 It will be for further procedure in this case to determine whether any delicts were indeed committed by the judge and, if so, whether the test for vicarious liability developed in the recent case law has been met on the facts.

3. *Moray Offshore Renewable Power Ltd v Bluefloat Energy UK Holdings Ltd*, Court of Session (Outer House) 9 May 2023, [2023] CSOH 29, 2023 SLT 263: Whether Alleged False Claims in a Consortium's Contract Bid Constituted Unlawful Means Conspiracy against Another Bidder

a) Brief Summary of the Facts

18 The pursuer, a wind farm development company, sought damages of £ 400 million from the defender. The pursuer claimed to have suffered this loss by being deprived of a contract (or at least a material chance of securing the contract) as a result of an unlawful means conspiracy amongst the defender and other parties, or from unlawful means deployed by the defender. The contract concerned lease options over areas of the seabed (owned by the Crown) to be developed as offshore wind farms.

4 *Catholic Child Welfare Society v Various Claimants* [2012] UKSC 56, at para 86.

The pursuer had submitted a bid in relation to five lease sites, which included a floating wind farm. A consortium of bidders consisting of the defender and ten other parties was the successful bidder for the site. The consortium's bid included claims about its members' expertise and experience, including in relation to a previous offshore wind farm project. Bidders were held to warrant the truth and accuracy of information provided in their bids. The pursuer claimed that the claims made by the consortium were variously materially inaccurate, grossly exaggerated, false and misleading, and that the conduct of the consortium had constituted the actionable delicts pled by it. 19

b) Judgment of the Court

The court dismissed the pursuer's action. As to causing loss by unlawful means, to state a relevant case on the basis of that delict, the pursuer required to aver that: (i) the defender had the intention to cause economic harm to the pursuer; (ii) the defender acted unlawfully in relation to a third party; and (iii) such unlawful action affected that third party's freedom to deal with the pursuer.[5] The court held that there were relevant averments supporting elements (i) and (iii). However, as to element (ii), an unlawful action in relation to a third party, the pursuer had pled that (i) the defender's false statements had furnished the relevant third party (the Crown) with an action for breach of contract. However, the statements in the defender's bid did not themselves amount to a contract but merely to a pre-contractual statement. As such, no relevant unlawful action had been pled; and (ii) that the guidance notes for bidders had reserved to the Crown an entitlement to take such steps as it considered necessary where the bidding process had been distorted or a bid had not been made in good faith. Again, this statement in the guidance notes did not of itself create any contractual right but was merely a statement of what the Crown might, as a matter of fact do, in certain circumstances. An actionable wrong might possibly have been pled by the pursuer, but this had not been the case. The court was also not persuaded that causation was made out, given that even if the defender's bid had not been tainted by an arguable unlawful means, it could not be shown that the pursuer would have been successful or even that it had been deprived of a chance of winning, which could be reasonably estimated. 20

---

5 As to these requirements, see *McLeod v Rooney* [2009] CSOH 158, *Global Resources Group v MacKay* [2008] CSOH 148, and *OBG Ltd v Allan* [2007] UKHL 21.

21 As to the alleged unlawful means conspiracy, while it is conceivable that an examination of the facts of the case might support evidence of a conspiracy, this claim also failed because it could not be proved that, in the absence of any conspiracy, the loss would have been avoided (for the same reasons noted in the previous paragraph).

c) Commentary

22 This decision must have been a frustrating one for the pursuer: the judge hints that, had a different tack been taken to arguing what constituted element (ii) of the delict of causing loss by unlawful means – the requirement that the defender acted unlawfully in relation to a third party – the claim might have made it to the next stage of the court process. The judge suggests that, had the pursuer claimed that the defender's statements in its bid amounted not to breach of contract but instead to misrepresentation, the claim might not have been dismissed:

> 'Given the general antipathy of the law to misrepresentation, it seems at least possible that a characterisation of the relevant wrong as other than a breach of contract might have been found relevant, perhaps along the lines of the theory of a continuing responsibility upon the maker of a pre-contractual representation in situations where there is an interval of time between the making of the representation and the conclusion of a contract in reliance upon it … However, no attempt was made to argue that Crown Estate Scotland had a right of action against the defender other than one based on breach of contract, and it is not for the court to suggest any such argument or to speculate on what the outcome of an assessment of it might have been.'[6]

It does indeed seem curious that no alternative ground of argument was advanced on that basis, something which the pursuer might well have raised with its legal representatives after dismissal of the claim.

23 However, the judge's argument that the ground which was advanced – that the false and misleading statements of the defender amounted to a breach of contract by the defender towards the Crown – could not be maintained requires a little further examination. The judge's opinion that (i) a statement in a bid is pre-contractual and not a contract term, and (ii) a statement in an invitation to tender is similarly pre-contractual are, stated in those simple terms, unobjectionable.[7] That approach takes the relevant time for judging the nature of the statement as the

6 Para 64.

7 Of course, some precontractual statements can be actionable as freestanding promises, but that does not appear to have been the parties' intentions here.

pre-contractual stage. But a successful bid (such as the defender's in this case) turns a pre-contractual document (the bid) into part of a concluded contract comprising the bid (the offer) and the acceptance of it. At that point, statements in the bid have the potential of becoming contractual terms/warranties (and indeed, as noted earlier, in this case bidders were held to have made warranties when submitting information in their bids). If false information were provided in the defender's contract, then that would indeed seem to give rise to the possibility of an actionable breach of a contractual warranty. Unfortunately, that line of argument does not seem to have been clearly advanced in the written pleadings or argued before the court. The pleadings contained statements such as '(t)here is a breach of contract' and 'it would have been, and would be open to (the Crown) to take action against the defender and its consortium partners based on this contractual right' without clearly explaining the nature of any contractual claim as a breach of warranty.[8] It is regrettable that this line of argument was not developed more explicitly, given that the pursuer's claimed losses could not have occurred until it lost the bid (by virtue of the defender's bid being accepted), meaning that the relevant time for assessing the nature of the defender's allegedly false claims should presumably have been the moment when the contract was formed and not the time at which the defender's claims were still only precontractual statements.

The above points, if addressed in the pursuer's pleadings, would not necessa- 24
rily have got it any further, however, given the judge's findings on causation. In a case where a party inviting bids for a contract is not bound to accept the lowest or any other kind of bid, there is no guarantee that the pursuer's bid would have been successful even had the defender not behaved in an (arguably) wrongful fashion. This is where arguments based on loss of a chance can assist an aggrieved party. The pursuer in this case appears to have included a lost chance argument into its pleadings (arguing that a 'material chance' was lost), but without sufficient development of the argument to allow the court to believe that a relevant case had been pled. The judge highlights in particular

> 'the high-level nature of the averred primary facts and the absence of any indication of how the similarly high-level scoring rules were in fact interpreted and applied by Crown Estate Scotland in its evaluation of every bid put forward.'[9]

8 At para 63, the judge appears to distinguish a breach of warranty claim from a breach of contract claim, so it is not entirely clear what the court considered the nature of a warranty to be (some form of non-contractual liability?).

9 Para 69.

One may speculate as to whether, with greater development of the lost chance claim, together with action taken to address the points made earlier about the elements of the unlawful means delict, the pursuer might have been able to have persuaded the court to allow this claim to reach the next stage of the process (which would have been a fuller examination of the facts of the case).

4. *C & S v Shaw & another*, Court of Session (Inner House) 13 October 2023, [2023] CSIH 36, 2023 SLT 1327: Whether Employer was Vicariously Liable for Employee's Acts of Sexual Abuse

a) Brief Summary of the Facts

25 Two brothers raised an action for damages in delict against, firstly, a man who had sexually abused them when they were children and, secondly, the operators of a sports centre where the man had been employed as a caretaker during a part of the period of time when the abuse had taken place. The abuse had taken place on some occasions at the sports centre premises and on others in the brothers' family home. Prior to the damages claim being raised by the brothers, the caretaker had been criminally convicted of the abuse and sentenced to a term of imprisonment.

26 At first instance, the judge dismissed the claim against the man's employers. He held that the vicarious liability of the employer had not been established because there had not been a sufficiently close connection between the acts of abuse and his employment as a caretaker at the sports centre. None of the tasks for which the man was employed had created or enhanced a risk of harm to the pursuers, and before he had been employed, he had already been able to have close and private access to the pursuers (through his friendship with their mother). Moreover, the acts of abuse had commenced prior to the man's taking up employment at the sports centre.

27 The pursuer appealed against the decision of the judge at first instance.

b) Judgment of the Court

28 The appeal bench upheld the decision at first instance, dismissing the appeal. The court considered the leading authorities relating to vicarious liability of employ-

ers,[10] though noting that in all cases of vicarious liability, the 'circumstances which present themselves are of such infinite variety that there can be no one test, nor one list of factors which will always be relevant'.[11] While the abuser was *in loco parentis* towards the pursuers when they were children, that situation had not come about because of his employment, the nature of his duties, or his occupation of the caretaker's house on his employer's premises.

The judge at first instance had therefore not reached the wrong decision in relation to the matter of whether there was a sufficiently close connection between the acts of abuse and the employment to justify a finding of vicarious liability on the part of the employer. On the contrary, the facts of the case indicated that it was the abuser's relationship with the pursuers' mother which had facilitated the acts of abuse. The abuser had not obtained any authority over the pursuers by virtue of his role as a caretaker, it had derived from his familiarity and ingratiation with the family. The risk of his sexually abusing the pursuers was not created, nor significantly enhanced, by what he was authorised to do by his employer. 29

c) Commentary

The judgment in this case reinforces the very fact specific nature of judgments relating to vicarious liability, a point which was made in the discussion above in the case of *X v Y & the Lord Advocate*.[12] In this case, the facts that the abuser had first gained access to the two children through their mother and not through his employer, that the abuse had begun before he took up his employment at the sports centre, and that that employment had not (so the court thought) created or enhanced the risk of acts of abuse (a consideration emphasised in the earlier case of *Catholic Child Welfare Society v Various Claimants*[13]), were largely determinative of the rejection at both first instance and on appeal of any vicarious liability on the part of his employer. In reaching this conclusion, the appeal court made reference to the similar fact Canadian case of *Jacobi v Griffiths*,[14] in which vicarious liability had also been denied. 30

10 Some of which was adverted to above, in the discussion of the judgment in *X v Y & the Lord Advocate:* see above nos 8–17.

11 Para 18.

12 See above no 11.

13 [2012] UKSC 56. See comment of Lord Phillips in that judgment, quoted above at no 15.

14 (1999) 2 Supreme Court Reports (SCR) 570, (1999) 174 Dominion Law Reports (DLR) 71. In the present case the appeal bench noted that the claimants in *Jacobi* 'were, in fact, on stronger ground. For

31 Given that the outcome of this litigation was predominantly the result of findings of fact, upheld on appeal, it seems unlikely that there will be any further appeal.

5. *Ronnie O'Neill Freight Solutions Ltd v Macroberts LLP*, Court of Session (Outer House) 2 November 2023, [2023] CSOH 75, 2023 SLT 1196: Professional Negligence – Whether it was Negligent for a Solicitor not to Give Advice about Arguments which the Solicitor thought could be Advanced in Litigation but which were Likely to Fail

a) Brief Summary of the Facts

32 The pursuer, a freight delivery company, entered into a contract with a haulier (UP Logistics) for the transportation of freight pallets. The contract contained no express provision for termination, but UPL purported to unilaterally terminate the contract in April 2020. UPL emailed the pursuer's two largest customers informing them of the termination and inviting them to continue trading with UPL (which they did).

33 The pursuer sought legal advice about the purported termination from the defender, its legal agents. The defender's advice was that the agreement was terminable subject to reasonable notice being given and that, rather than litigate immediately, the pursuer should pursue a commercial settlement. Settlement was reached with UPL in the sum of £ 40,000, of which about £ 10,000 represented unpaid invoices and the balance damages. However, the pursuer was unable to persuade many of its existing customers to switch hauliers and it ceased trading in 2021.

34 The pursuer subsequently claimed to be dissatisfied with the legal advice which it had received from the defender. It argued that the defender ought to have given advice to seek interim remedies from the outset; that the agreement was arguably non-terminable; and that the defender's failure to tender such advice was negligent, in that it was advice which no ordinarily skilled solicitor exercising ordinary care would have failed to give. The pursuer argued that, had non-negligent advice been given, the pursuer would have achieved a better outcome than

example, there, the abuser was encouraged to form relationships with children at the club, which was not so in the instant case'.

it did. It valued its loss at some £ 232,500, claiming this amount in damages from the defender.

The defender argued that (i) the advice given by it was not negligent; (ii) even if it was negligent, that advice had no causative effect on the pursuer's position in that ultimately the action would have settled on the same basis as was in fact achieved; and (iii) if a legal claim by the pursuer against UPL had proceeded (on the grounds of non-terminability), it would have failed, meaning that the pursuer had failed to establish any loss. 35

b) Judgment of the Court

The judge dismissed the pursuer's claim. Whilst there might be a divergence of professional opinion on the advice to be given, applying the test for determining professional negligence, the advice given by the defender had not been negligent. It was advice which a reasonable body of legal professionals might also have given in the circumstances. The court rejected the pursuer's argument that there was a practice among solicitors of advising a client involved in a contentious situation about all stateable arguments which might be deployed: such a practice would be virtually meaningless and unworkable. The depth of advice given had to necessarily depend on the circumstances in which it was given and was ultimately a matter of professional judgement. Where a solicitor had formed a view (rightly or wrongly) on the meaning and effect of a contract, the solicitor was not under a duty to advise the client of counter arguments, as that would run contrary to the notion that a client paid for the solicitor's advice, rather than their doubts or a dissertation. 36

Given this finding by the court that there had been no breach of the defender's professional duty of care to the pursuer, it was not strictly necessary for the court to reach any conclusion on the arguments concerning causation of loss. However, the court stated that, even if advice had been given about the possibility of the non-terminable argument being made, a failure to give that advice had not resulted in any loss because the defender would have given the same overall recommendation of how to proceed, and the outcome would have been the same. 37

c) Commentary

38 There is a well-developed doctrine of professional negligence in Scots law, traceable back to the seminal decision in *Hunter v Hanly*.[15] That decision required three pre-requisites for the establishment of professional liability: (1) that there be a usual and normal practice in the profession in relation to the matter in contention; (2) that, where such a practice exists, it was not adopted by the practitioner; and (3) that the course of action which was adopted was one which no practitioner exercising ordinary skill would have taken had they been acting with ordinary care. The *Hunter* case was one of medical negligence, but the test it established has been applied across professions, including within the legal profession.

39 In this case, in applying the test for professional negligence to the facts before it, the court did not simply come to its own decision as to how a practising solicitor ought to have conducted himself in the circumstances: the judge's role is not the same as the practising solicitor's role, so the court heard expert evidence from two solicitors, who gave conflicting evidence. In such instances of conflicting evidence as to professional practice, as the judge in this case noted:

> '(i) the court's function is not to prefer one school of thought over another; (ii) if a defender leads evidence that other responsible professionals would have done what the impugned professional did, that does not necessarily lead to a finding that there was no negligence; (iii) that is because, exceptionally, a practice perpetuated by the second body of opinion may not stand up to rational analysis.'[16]

40 Where the professional practice in question is a legal one, a court is (so the judge asserted in this case), without supplanting the role of the experts, able to test the expert evidence against its own view of the law.[17] Here, the judge took the view that there was no rational basis for rejecting the evidence of one of the expert solicitors that not all ordinarily competent solicitors would advise a client about all arguments which were merely stateable, and that the non-terminability argument was sufficiently weak that advice need not have been given about it. This seems a perfectly reasonable conclusion for the court to have reached (given it did not doubt the competency of the expert witness), one which determined the finding on professional negligence in relation to the claim that alternative courses of action should have been advised.

---

15 1955 SC 200, 1955 SLT 213.
16 Para 51.
17 Para 52.

The judge's view that the failure to recommend interim interdict was not negligent also seems a reasonable finding on the facts: as the judge noted, 'seeking interim orders is attendant with risk; not only the risk of being found liable in expenses should interim interdict not be granted; but the risk of being found liable in damages to the interdicted party, should interim interdict be granted which was ultimately found not to have been warranted'.[18] 41

The outcome in this case is a reminder of the latitude given to practitioners in relation to the exercise of their professional judgement: if evidence suggests that there is a reasonable body of practitioners who would have adopted the same practice, the professional conduct at issue is unlikely to be held negligent unless the court deems the practice unreasonable and irrational. As the judge put it in very practical terms in relation to the facts of this case: a client is obtaining advice from a solicitor, not a dissertation. 42

6. *Miller v J W Wheatley & Son*, Court of Session, 28 November 2023, [2023] CSOH 84: Injured Worker Owed no Duty of Care by Electrical Contractors as he was not in a Relationship Akin to Employment

a) Brief Summary of the Facts

Algo Blairgowrie Ltd ('Algo') was constructing a storage building at a golf course in Fife. It subcontracted the electrical works to the defender, J W Wheatley & Son, which in turn further subcontracted part of the works (for the installation of solar roof panels) to MMS Building Services Ltd ('MMS'). The pursuer, Mr Miller, a solar panel engineer, was the sole director of MMS. He was personally responsible for fitting the panels. He submitted a risk assessment to Algo, in which he identified adverse weather as a hazard. 43

Mr Miller visited the golf course to fit the solar roof panels. No-one from the defender was present. Access to the roof was gained using equipment belonging to Algo. Because of adverse weather, the metal roof was wet. As a result, Mr Miller slipped and fell. He sustained a fracture to the left femur which required surgery. He sued the defender, arguing that it had breached a duty of care at common law owed to him, claiming damages amounting to £ 38,500. He argued that the relationship between him and the defender was akin to employment and that therefore the same protection ought to be afforded to him at common law as would be ap- 44

18 Para 65.

plicable under employment legislation had he had a formal contract of employment with the defender, relying on recent authorities such as *Uber BV v Aslam.*[19]

45 The defender argued that the pursuer worked for MMS (which was an independent contractor) and that it exerted no control over when and how the work was done by the pursuer. The pursuer's situation was not similar to that of Uber drivers: the transportation service provided by Uber drivers was very tightly defined and controlled by Uber, and their remuneration was fixed by Uber. The present case was wholly different. The defender was under no obligation to assess the risk of the work to be done by the pursuer, who was solely responsible for assessing the risks and deciding on how the work should be done.

b) Judgment of the Court

46 The judge dismissed the pursuer's claim. This was not one of those cases where it was difficult to decide whether a claimant was an employee to whom a duty of care was owed or an independent contractor: MMS were specialist independent contractors hired by the defender under a contract for services to perform the solar panel work. The pursuer was employed by MMS, not the defender, and it was MMS and not the pursuer which supplied services to the defender.

47 The court added that there was no comparison between the circumstances of the present case and the position of Uber vis-à-vis Uber drivers. The pursuer had not undertaken to do or perform personally any work or services for the defender: the pursuer was working for MMS and it was MMS which had agreed to install the panels. His position was unlike that of Uber drivers (who do personally provide services) and he did not have a relationship akin to employment with the defender. The pursuer was solely responsible for the accident.

c) Commentary

48 The decision in the *Uber* case has, as this litigation indicates, clearly given rise to attempts by independent contractors to paint their position as being comparable to Uber drivers and thus as entitling them to benefit from rights akin to those enjoyed by employees. However, that argument will not be successful where an individual is employed by a company to undertake work for which the *company* rather than

19 [2021] Industrial Case Reports (ICR) 657. That judgment held that Uber drivers constituted 'workers' for the purposes of a number of employment legislation provisions.

the individual is contractually obliged toward another. It would be necessary to treat the employee and the company as one person to enable such an argument to succeed, thus ignoring the separate legal personality of corporate bodies. A court will not do that, even where the employee also happens to be the sole director of the company.

As the court in this case was not persuaded that the pursuer was in the same position as an Uber driver, it was not willing to treat him as being in a relationship akin to employment with the defender and thus rightly concluded that the defender did not owe to him a common law duty of care which would have been the equivalent of duties afforded to employees under employment protection legislation. 49

7. *Davie v Powerteam Electrical Services (UK) Ltd*, Court of Session (Outer House) 19 December 2023, [2023] CSOH 94: Whether an Occupier of Land was Liable for Damage Sustained by a Member of the Public who Fell from the Roof of a Portacabin at a Construction Site

a) Brief Summary of the Facts

The pursuer, Mr Davie, sustained a catastrophic injury in the early hours of 29 September 2017. He had been socialising with friends in a pub, where he had been drinking alcohol. On his way home, he came across a temporary construction site under the control of the defenders. A pedestrian route running through the site passed two portacabins, one of which was stacked on top of the other. Barriers and traffic cones separated the pedestrian path from the lower portacabin. 50

Walking along the pedestrian route, the pursuer arrived at the portacabins. He found that a gate in the barriers at the foot of a stairway allowing access to the upper portacabin was not closed. Wanting a quiet place to sit and think, he climbed the stairway onto the roof of the upper portacabin. After sitting for a period of time, he attempted to descend from the roof and make his way home. While descending, he lost his footing and fell approximately eighteen feet (five and a half metres) onto the road. The injuries he sustained resulted in tetraplegia. 51

The pursuer raised a claim in damages against the defenders based on breach of a duty of care arising both at common law and under the Occupiers' Liability (Scotland) Act 1960. The pursuer argued that (i) the defenders ought to have had an effective barrier preventing access to the stairway from which further access could be gained to the roof of the portacabin; (ii) they ought to have known that 52 the site constituted an attraction and allurement to members of the public; (iii) it was known that licensed premises were in the locality; and (iv) that the stairway provided a ready climbing frame and means of access to the roof of the portacabin.

53 The defenders argued: (i) the stairway and the portacabin did not present a danger in themselves, and intoxication on the part of the pursuer did not turn something which was not dangerous into a danger; (ii) even if there was a danger on the premises, the authorities demonstrated that there is no general duty to fence off dangerous parts of premises where the danger is well known to a pursuer and there is no risk of inadvertently coming into contact with the danger; (iii) the pursuer was an adult who must have been fully aware of the risk of falling from the roof; and (iv) the pursuer had failed to aver facts that, if proved, would establish that the accident was caused by any failure in reasonable care on the part of the defenders.

b) Judgment of the Court

54 The court dismissed the pursuer's claim, noting that this was one of those rare and exceptional cases in which an action for personal injuries fell to be dismissed without any further examination of the facts. The judge noted that there was no defect in the roof itself, nor had any actions or omissions (such as a failure to maintain or inspect the state of the portacabin roof) on the part of the defenders created any danger. The danger of falling from the roof was created solely by the pursuer climbing onto the roof. While it could be said in general terms that adult members of the public might seek to gain access to the roof of a portacabin on a construction site (or indeed almost any building), the pursuer's pleadings did not set out any basis on which the defenders ought to have reasonably foreseen that an adult member of the public would climb onto the roof of the portacabin on this site.

55 Furthermore, the court noted that authorities referred to established that the exercise of reasonable care does not require an occupier to fence off a danger on its land where that danger is obvious to the pursuer.[20] In this case, the risks attend-

20 Reference was made to the decision in *Devlin v Strathclyde Regional Council*, which had concerned a 14-year-old school pupil who fell to his death from a school building's roof. In that case, the judge had stated that there was an obvious risk of a pupil falling and being seriously injured if he gained access to the school roof, adding however that the defenders were under no duty to make the roof inaccessible since there had been no accidents from the roof of the school building over the years.

ant upon the pursuer's conduct were obvious ones of which he must have been aware at the time.

c) Commentary

The judge in this case, reviewing the various authorities on occupiers' liability, lists nine different factors which he considered important to the specific duty advanced by the pursuer. A number of these have been highlighted already (the pursuer was an adult, the roof was not a danger in itself, the risks were obvious, and no similar incidents known to the defenders were averred in the pleadings). These cumulatively contributed to the court's conclusions that the injury to the pursuer was not foreseeable and that any duty resting on the occupiers should not be held to have extended to providing a barrier preventing the pursuer from engaging in dangerous activities. 56

Given prior decisions concerning injuries caused by objectively dangerous activities, the result in this case looks to be justifiable. One aspect of the decision which might however be open to question is the judge's observation that climbing onto a roof while intoxicated presents an obvious risk of which the pursuer must have been aware (one of the nine features of the case highlighted by the judge). Given that this judgment did not involve a trial of the facts, the judge's remark on this issue must have been reached without any judicial assessment of the precise level of the pursuer's intoxication. That is a point worth raising, because while a somewhat intoxicated person might well be expected to appreciate the dangers of climbing onto a roof while intoxicated, the greater the degree of intoxication, the greater the likelihood that an individual's rational appreciation of risks involved in dangerous activity will be diminished. One might question whether a stage of intoxication could be reached where the level of appreciation of risks were so negligible as to constitute a risk no longer being 'obvious' to the injured party. If such a stage were to be reached, that would not necessarily mean that an occupier ought to come under a duty which would not exist in relation to a less intoxicated party, but it might raise questions as to the validity of a justification for excluding a duty of care based upon a danger being obvious to someone entering the premises. 57

8. Personal Injury

58 The main body of case law in the field of personal injuries in 2023 was of a similar type to other years, with road traffic injuries, employment injuries, and medical negligence claims constituting the bulk of reported decisions.

59 One reported case, *Depuy Int Ltd v Gilchrist*,[21] follows in the footsteps of other litigation reported in earlier yearbooks, in considering defective products for prosthetic implants. A prior case of this sort was reported in the 2021 Yearbook.[22] The appeal level judgment in *Depuy* concerned the management of what are called in some jurisdictions 'class actions' but in Scotland 'group proceedings'. The high number of claims being raised in relation to allegedly defective prosthetics is an indicator of the magnitude of the potential liability for such (problematic, it would seem) products.

60 The Outer House judgment in *Rose v WNL Investments Ltd*[23] is worth noting in passing, in that it raised the issue also discussed in the case of *Miller v Wheatley*, reported in the main text at nos 43–49, namely of whether the pursuer was an employee or an independent contractor and whether he was therefore owed a duty of care by the defender.

61 The Sheriff Appeal court decision in *McCallum v Morrison*[24] upheld the decision at first instance that a patient who suffered a shock when reading a communication (sent fourteen months after his treatment) indicating that poor hygiene at his dental practice had exposed him to a low risk of infection by blood-borne viruses could not claim damages for nervous shock: his psychiatric injury was caused by fear of a harm which did not materialise, and was thus excluded following the approach taken to nervous shock by the House of Lords in *Rothwell v Chemical Insulation Co and Another.*[25] The dismissal of a further claim that the unhygienic treatment amounted to an instance of the *actio iniuriarum* was also upheld.

62 Finally, one may note that the first instance judgment in *Watt v Lend Lease Construction (Europe) Ltd*,[26] holding there to be no liability for causing mesothelio-

21 [2023] CSIH 47.

22 *Hastings v Finsbury Orthopaedics Ltd* [2021] CSIH 6, reported in *M Hogg*, Scotland, in: E Karner/BC Steininger (eds), European Tort Law (ETL) 2021 (2022) 539, nos 10–16.

23 [2023] CSOH 49.

24 [2023] Sheriff Appeal Court, Civil ([SAC] Civ) 23.

25 [2007] UKHL 39, [2008] 1 Appeal Cases (AC) 281.

26 [2022] CSOH 23.

ma at a time when the dangers of asbestos were unknown to the defender (referred to in the 2022 Yearbook[27]), was upheld on appeal.[28]

C. Literature

1. *Jonathan Brown*, Obtaining the 'main keys to wisdom': distinguishing 'damages' from other pecuniary remedies in Scots law, Edinburgh Law Review 2023, 77–82

In this article, the author cautions against equating English and other common law jurisdiction authorities on the topic of 'damages' with damages as understood in Scots law. While in the common law, the term 'damages' refers broadly to any pecuniary remedy, in Scots law the term has a narrower meaning, namely that of a remedy for the compensation of loss caused by wrongful conduct. There are other pecuniary remedies available in Scots law, but these are not to be treated as damages. 63

The author's cautious advice is to be commended, as the relevant authorities support the view that Scots law does indeed ascribe a narrower meaning to 'damages' than English law does. 64

2. *Jonathan Ainslie*, Intrusion of privacy and the *actio iniuriarum*, Juridical Review 2023, 139–159

In this article, the author argues that the recent emphasis on common law constitutional rights has renewed attention on the extent to which the rights arising under art 8 of the European Convention on Human Rights are adequately expressed through the existing common law authorities of the Scots law of delict. He argues that the inadequacy of existing delictual protections is particularly acute in the case of the non-informational aspects of privacy, where English law provides little guidance. 65

The article goes on to examine the viability of the *actio iniuriarum* as a means for protecting non-informational privacy. It outlines the emerging judicial framework for developing common law constitutional rights, discusses the distinction 66

27 *Hogg* (fn 22) no 45.
28 [2023] CSIH 19.

between informational and non-informational privacy (as well as judicial and scholarly treatment of the *actio iniuriarum*), before finally applying this framework to examine how far a modern *actio iniuriarum* might be developed to protect art 8 rights. Comparative reference is made by the author to the law of South Africa, where the *actio iniuriarum* covers all forms of privacy intrusion.

3. *Eleanor Russell*, Revisiting Pure Psychiatric Injury – *Weddle v Glasgow City Council*, Juridical Review 2023, 75–96

67 In this article, the author reconsiders the law concerning the recovery of damages for pure psychiatric injury with particular reference to the decision of the Sheriff Appeal Court in *Weddle v Glasgow City Council* (2023) SAC (Civ) 17. She concludes that the decision in Weddle (to the effect that the pursuer was not a primary victim) was not surprising in light of the key findings of fact which had been made by the sheriff and which remained undisturbed by the Sheriff Appeal Court. The author goes on to consider whether a claim as a secondary victim might have been advanced successfully on the basis of certain dicta in the English decision in *Alcock v Chief Constable of South Yorkshire* (1992) 1 AC 310 concerning bystanders.

4. *Craig Anderson*, Do we need spuilzie? Scots Law Times 2003, 43–47

68 In this article, the author argues that the old Scots delictual action of 'spuilzie',[29] which had fallen into disuse for some considerable period of time, is still required in the modern law. The action of spuilzie may be brought by the lawful possessor of property who has been wrongfully dispossessed of the property by another party. The author argues that, whether or not the action has largely fallen out of usage, it is still needed, or else parties may be encouraged to take the law into their own hands by depriving others of the possession of property.

29 Pronounced 'spool-ee'.

5. *Francis McManus*, *C v Shaw* (Case Comment), Scots Law Times 2023, 224–226

In this case comment, the author discusses the judgment of the Inner House in *C & S v Shaw and another*, discussed earlier in this report at nos 25–31, briefly comparing and contrasting it with other recent decisions. 69

Anton Dulak

XXVI. Slovakia

A. Legislation

There was no new legislation in the area of tort law in 2023. 1

B. Cases

1. Resolution of the Supreme Court of the Slovak Republic of 30 November 2021, Case No 5Cdo/162/2019, published in Collection 3/2023: Liability for Auxiliaries

a) Brief Summary of the Facts

Plaintiff 1 (the victim's wife) and plaintiffs 2 and 3 (the victim's children) claimed 2
compensation for non-pecuniary damage suffered as a result of the death of their husband and father. The victim fell off his bicycle into an unmarked sewer trench and died on the spot as a result of head injuries. It was found that the person (defendant 4) who was working on the excavation had breached safety regulations in marking the work on the road and his unlawful conduct caused the victim's death.

Defendant 4, however, did not perform the work independently, but for anoth- 3
er. The contractor (defendant 1) performed his duties through a helper (defendant 2), who performed through another helper (defendant 3), who contracted defendant 4 to do the work.

The District Court dismissed the action against defendants 1 to 3 (lack of stand- 4
ing of the defendants). The Regional Court upheld the judgment of the court of first instance. The applicants appealed against the judgment. The Supreme Court, as the Court of Appeal, found that the appeal was well-founded.

b) Judgment of the Court

The provision of sec 420(2) of the Civil Code, which regulates the liability of a nat- 5
ural or legal person for damage caused in the course of its activities by those whom it has used for its activities, also applies to the case of a chain of actions

https://doi.org/10.1515/9783111376721-027

of several potentially liable natural or legal persons. In order to determine the entity which is liable for the damage in such a case, the decisive criterion is the factual, local and temporal link between the activity which caused the damage and the final result of that activity.

c) Commentary

6 The current legislation in sec 420(2) CC expresses the rule that if someone causes damage in the course of carrying out an activity which they carried out for another person, they are not liable for this damage, but the person for whom they carried out this activity is liable. In essence, this is not general liability for damage, but a special situation in which one is liable for another. Thus, the law shifts the liability from the subject who caused damage to a third party by their actions (the auxiliary as a person used in someone else's activity) to another subject, the principal, ie the person who used the auxiliary for the performance of their activity. As a rule, there are two reasons for the transfer of this liability, namely the protection of employees against direct tort claims by third parties, which also applies to auxiliaries, and the obligation of the principal to bear the negative consequences arising from the risk of their activity, ie a similar reason to that used to justify strict liability under specific facts (eg secs 420a and 421a of the Civil Code).

7 It is clear from the content of the appeal that the applicants raised the issue of the interpretation of the concept of a person who was used for the activity of a natural or legal person in the context of which the damage occurred within the meaning of sec 420(2) of the Civil Code. The question is whether the person concerned can be any person who was partly involved in the work. The second question is whether the existence of a direct contractual relationship between the contractor and the person who was partly involved in the work is necessary for liability to arise under sec 420(2) of the Civil Code.

8 In the decision-making practice of the Court of Appeal, the question of interpretation of the concept of a person who was used for the activity of a natural or legal person in the context of which the damage occurred within the meaning of sec 420(2) of the Civil Code has already been dealt with. The case law is constant in the view that if an employee has been used by the employer to carry out their activity, such interference is deemed to be directly caused by the employer. The same conclusion is shared by the case law in the case of a person with whom the contractor has a direct contractual relationship. The issue of another person who has not entered into a direct contractual relationship with the contractor has not yet been addressed in the Court of Appeal's decision-making.

Any person who carries out an activity for the principal is not an assistant within the meaning of sec 420(2) CC. Legal theory sometimes distinguishes between independent and non-independent auxiliaries, treating only non-independent auxiliaries as auxiliaries within the meaning of sec 420(2) CC.[1] 9

Independent assistants carry out activities for the principal, but do so without significant interference from the principal, independently, at their own risk and responsibility. The principal does not exercise control over the performance of the activities of the independent assistant/auxiliary, nor do they give instructions to such an extent that it is fair to impute to them responsibility for the unlawful conduct of the assistant/auxiliary. Therefore, the principal is not to be held liable for the unlawful conduct of the assistant. A non-independent auxiliary is an auxiliary used in the activities of the principal who acts under the control and direction of the principal and who, even from the point of view of third parties, does not act independently and at their own risk. The legal relationship on the basis of which it carries out this activity for the principal is irrelevant. In such a case, the damage caused by the non-self-employed helper's breach of duty shall be attributed to the principal. 10

The distinction between independent and non-independent auxiliaries is also highlighted in sec 420(2) CC by the condition that the auxiliary must be an auxiliary who has been used in the activities of the principal. Thus, the assistant is not only to carry out the activity for the principal, but also, from the point of view of third parties, it is to carry out the activity of the principal in which the damage was caused. The decisive criterion for liability under sec 420(2) of the Civil Code is the factual, temporal and local connection between the activity which caused the damage and the subject of the final work. The existence of a direct contractual relationship between the contractor and the person who partially participated in the execution of the work is not decisive. What is relevant is whether, in carrying out the activity in which the damage was caused, the auxiliary was pursuing, both objectively and subjectively, the performance of the tasks of the principal. 11

The applicability of sec 420(2) CC is also possible in the case of a chain of several potentially liable entities. A non-dependent auxiliary brought in by another auxiliary is deemed to be a person used for the activity of the principal, provided that the principal at the end of the chain is aware of their inclusion in or invitation to the activity, and their implied consent is sufficient. 12

---

1 *V Trojčáková*, Zodpovednosť za škodu voči tretím osobám spôsobenú pomocníkom a poistenie zodpovednosti za škodu, Súkromné právo 6/2019, 244–250.

2. Resolution of the Supreme Court of the Slovak Republic of 27 November 2023, Case No 9Cdo/182/2022: Victims and Determination of the Compensation Amount for Non-Pecuniary Damage

a) Brief Summary of the Facts

13 The victim AL died in a traffic accident. Plaintiffs 1 to 25 brought an action for compensation for non-pecuniary damage caused by the death of a loved one against the insurance company with which the owner of the vehicle had an insurance policy.

14 The District Court awarded plaintiff 1 (the deceased's mother) € 20,720 and plaintiff 2 (his wife) € 51,800 instead of the € 120,000 claimed for each. For plaintiffs 3 to 5 (the children), the court awarded financial compensation of € 20,720 instead of the claimed € 100,000 each. The Court dismissed the claims of plaintiffs 6 to 12 (the deceased's brothers) for € 100,000 each, the claim of plaintiff 13 (brother-in-law), the claim of plaintiff 14 (daughter-in-law), the claim of plaintiff 15 (mother-in-law), and claims of plaintiffs 16 to 20 (grandchildren) for € 20,000 each.

15 The Regional Court, as Court of Appeal, disagreed with the amount of compensation awarded to plaintiffs 1 to 5 and set aside the judgment of the Court of First Instance in that regard.

16 The plaintiffs appealed against the decision of the Court of Appeal. The Court of Appeal upheld the grounds of extraordinary appeal and set aside the judgment of both the Court of Appeal and the Court of First Instance. The Court of First Instance and the Court of Appeal are bound by the legal opinion of the Court of Appeal (art 455 Act No 160/2015 Coll, Code of Civil Dispute Procedure [*Civilný sporový poriadok*, CSP]).

b) Judgment of the Court

17 The criterion of the family link between the plaintiff and the person whose death caused the plaintiff non-pecuniary damage is decisive for the award of non-pecuniary damages, but it is not the only criterion. In addition, the court must examine and take into account the intensity of the plaintiff's relationship with the deceased, the age of the deceased and of the plaintiff, the question of the plaintiff's dependence on the deceased, the moral satisfaction in the form of a legal penalty on the part of the injured party, the degree of fault or the degree of complicity of the deceased, the attitude of the injured party (regret, compensation, apology), the im-

pact of the event on the injured party's sphere of life and the injured party's financial circumstances.

The personality of each natural person is broad, multi-layered and internally diverse, with the result that the relationships that arise between them and their family members are highly individual and unique. It is undeniable, then, that the violent severance of family ties has an individual and varied effect, different for each individual, because each person, their very nature, their emotions, their relations with others, are highly individual. People do not always perceive the circumstances of the outside world in the same way, and even their relationships with others show signs of individuality, non-repetitiveness and uniqueness.[2] 18

c) Commentary

In view of the fact that the harmful event occurred on the territory of the Czech Republic, the tort was judged according to the law of the Czech Republic. 19

What remained in dispute between the parties in the proceedings was whether the pecuniary compensation for non-pecuniary damage claimed by the plaintiffs was adequate and whether it took account of the principle of fairness. 20

The district court awarded compensation to plaintiffs 1 to 5, the next of kin of the accident victim. It reasoned that the deceased had actually cared for his mother, that his wife was dependent on his income, that she had to repay the mortgage loan that had been taken out by her and the deceased, and that, as a wife, she had experienced psychological harm and trauma from her husband's death. The court awarded compensation to the children on the ground that they were having a difficult time coping with the death of their father, who was still employed and helping them, and that his death had caused them psychological harm. 21

The court did not award compensation to plaintiffs 6 to 20 on the ground that they all had their own families and were gainfully employed and therefore could not be found to have experienced the deceased's death as an injury of their own. 22

The Court of Appeal also emphasised the very closest family relationships, ie those between parents, children and spouses. It also noted that this did not deny family relations to other relatives as well. According to the Court of Appeal, it was not possible to find that plaintiffs 6 to 20 experienced the deceased's death as an intrinsic injury, which is essential for the award of non-pecuniary damages. According to the Court of Appeal, the Court of First Instance rightly dismissed the ac- 23

2 Similarly, the judgment of the Supreme Court of the Slovak Republic of 22 June 2016, Case No 3Cdo/18/2016.

tion against the original plaintiffs 6 to 20, including plaintiffs 16 to 20, who, as grandchildren of the deceased, do feel an emotional loss as a result of their grandfather's death, but, given their age, the compensation of any non-pecuniary damage is of no practical significance.

24 In this connection, the Court of Appeal emphasised that non-pecuniary damages are not intended to serve as financial security for the survivors, but only as a form of compensation for the damage. It is intended, for example, to restore mental health or to ensure the standard of living which the survivors had enjoyed during the lifetime of the deceased, who had also contributed to a large extent to the financing of the household.

25 The Court of Appeal pointed out that the criterion of the family link between the plaintiff and the person as a result of whose death the plaintiff suffered non-pecuniary damage is decisive for the award of non-pecuniary damages, but is not the only criterion. In addition to family ties, there are other criteria for compensation. The error is that the Court of Appeal did not deal, in the grounds of its decision, with the extent and intensity of the damage caused to the individual plaintiffs 16 to 20 by the loss of the deceased family member individually, ie in relation to each of the plaintiffs.

26 According to the Court of Appeal, the District Court's blanket assertion that non-pecuniary damages are not intended to serve the financial security of the survivors, even over a long period of time, but is merely intended to compensate for the damage in some way, serving, for example, to restore the survivors' mental health or to ensure the standard of living achieved by the survivors during the lifetime of the deceased, who had also contributed to a considerable extent to the financing of the household, is not sufficient in itself.

27 Only the reasoning of the Court of Appeal which, having regard to the relevant findings of fact, takes into account the individual nature of the consequences of the interference with the personality of each of the plaintiffs 1 to 9, 11 to 12 and 21[3] can satisfy the attributes of a proper statement of reasons.

3. Personal Injury

28 The author found no significant personal injury decisions from 2023.

3 The Court of Appeal did not address the claims of plaintiffs 22 to 25 due to a procedural error on the part of counsel (lack of power of attorney).

C. Literature

1. *Ľubomír Zlocha*, Niekoľko úvah k určovaniu výšky náhrady nemajetkovej ujmy v peniazoch [Some considerations on the determination of the amount of pecuniary compensation for non-pecuniary damage], Právny obzor 4/2023

The article deals with the issue of determining the amount of compensation for 29
non-pecuniary damage for unjustified interference in the immaterial sphere of the person. Determining the amount of compensation is problematic. The Slovak legislation provides almost no guidelines in this respect, and no limits or boundaries within which the court can operate when awarding compensation. In practice, therefore, court case law and the established decision-making of the courts, which have more or less developed a system of aspects that may influence the amount of compensation awarded, are of great importance. The author provides an insight into the established case law and individual criteria, interpreting these from a legal-theoretical perspective.

Gregor Dugar

XXVII. Slovenia

A. Legislation

1. Zakon o spremembah in dopolnitvah Zakona o odškodnini žrtvam kaznivih dejanj (ZOZKD-B)[1] – Amending Act to the Crime Victim Compensation Act (ZOZKD-B)

1 The Crime Victim Compensation Act (hereinafter ZOZKD)[2] regulates the right to compensation for victims of intentional violent acts and their relatives, the procedure for exercising these rights and the authorities that decide and participate in the decision-making process regarding these rights. This Law also regulates the competent authorities and the procedure in cross-border cases in accordance with Council Directive 2004/80/EC of 29 April 2004 on compensation for victims of crime. The Amending Act to ZOZKD (hereinafter ZOZKD-B) contains mainly editorial changes, but among content changes it is worth noting that proof of citizenship is no longer required to be attached to a claim for compensation (art 4 ZOZKD-B) and that the decision on compensation becomes legally binding on the day on which the applicant waives the right to file a lawsuit in an administrative dispute after being served with the decision in writing or orally on the record at the ministry responsible for justice (art 5 ZOZKD-B).

1 Uradni list Republike Slovenije (RS) (Official Journal) No 76/2023. The Act entered into force (27 July 2023) 15 days after publication (12 July 2023) in the Official Journal.

2 Uradni list RS (Official Journal) No 101/2005. The Act entered into force (12 November 2005) one day after publication (11 November 2005) in the Official Journal, and has been applicable since 1 January 2006.

https://doi.org/10.1515/9783111376721-028

2. Zakon o spremembah in dopolnitvah Zakona o nadzoru državne meje (ZNDM-2H)[3] – Amending Act to the State Border Control Act (ZNDM-2H)

2 If for performing tasks under the State Border Control Act (hereinafter ZNDM-2)[4] that are carried out along the State border, a more permanent and uninterrupted use of land is required, which makes the regular use of this land more difficult and this has already lasted longer than 24 months, the property right on such land is temporarily encumbered with an easement for the public benefit (art 8.c ZNDM-2). The Amending Act to the State Border Control Act (hereinafter ZNDM-2H) establishes new rules for the assessment of compensation if an easement for public benefit is not established because the reasons for the establishment of an easement for public benefit cease before the establishment of the easement. In this case, the owner of the land is entitled to compensation for the period from the expiration of 24 months from the beginning of the use of the land that makes the regular use of the land more difficult until the termination of such use of the land. Within six months of the cessation of land use, the ministry responsible for internal affairs must make an offer to the landowners to conclude an agreement on compensation, which is formed in accordance with a special methodology (see para 6 art 8.b ZNDM-2). If the owner of the land does not agree with the proposed amount of compensation or if they do not receive an offer within six months of the termination of the use of the land, they can propose that the competent court decide on the compensation in an informal procedure. When determining compensation, the provisions of the law governing the expropriation and limitation of property rights for the public benefit are applied *mutatis mutandis*. The compensation is paid by the ministry responsible for internal affairs to the personal or business account of the landowner. Funds for the payment of compensation are provided in the budget of the Republic of Slovenia as part of the financial plan of the ministry responsible for internal affairs (art 8.g ZNDM-2H).

3 Uradni list RS (Official Journal) No 76/2023. The Act entered into force (27 July 2023) 15 day after publication (12 July 2023) in the Official Journal.

4 Uradni list RS (Official Journal) No 60/2007. The Act entered into force (12 November 2005) one day after publication (11 November 2005) in the Official Journal, and has been applicable since 1 January 2006.

3. Zakon o zaščiti prijaviteljev (ZZPri)[5] – Reporting Persons Protection Act (ZZPri)

The Reporting Persons Protection Act (hereinafter ZZPri), for the purpose of protecting the public interest, determines the methods and procedures for reporting violations of regulations that individuals have learned about in the work environment, and their treatment, as well as the protection of individuals who report or publicly disclose information about the violation. The Law also determines the powers of the Commission for the Prevention of Corruption and protective and supportive measures to prevent or eliminate retaliatory measures (art 1 ZZPri). 3

An individual who reports or publicly discloses information about violations in accordance with the ZZPri does not violate any restrictions or prohibitions on the disclosure of information and does not bear any liability related to such reporting or public disclosure, provided that they have not reported or publicly disclosed false information and, on the basis of reasonable grounds, considered that the reporting or public disclosure of such information was necessary for the disclosure of the violation under the ZZPri. This rule does not apply to restrictions on the disclosure of information determined by regulations in the field of the protection of classified information, the professional secrecy of lawyers, medical professionals and medical associates, the confidentiality of judicial deliberations and the rules of criminal procedure. Regardless of the provisions of the law governing trade secrets, the reporting or public disclosure of information that includes trade secrets is not illegal if the applicant reports or discloses it in accordance with the ZZPri. The applicant bears no responsibility in connection with the acquisition or access to the information that they report or publicly disclose if such acquisition or access is not an independent criminal act. In any proceedings against the applicant due to insult or defamation, violation of copyright, violation of confidentiality of information in accordance with the above, violation of data protection rules or compensation claims, the applicant bears no responsibility for reporting or public disclosures based on the ZZPri and may, in the motion to reject the claim against them, refer to the reporting or public disclosure if, on the basis of valid reasons, they considered that the reporting or public disclosure was necessary for the disclosure of a violation based on the ZZPri (art 21 ZZPri). 4

The applicant may seek legal protection from retaliatory measures before the competent court. If the applicant in the procedure for issuing a temporary injunction proves that they submitted the application before the retaliatory measure, it is 5

5 Uradni list RS (Official Journal) No 16/2023. The Act entered into force (22 February 2023) 15 days after publication (7 February 2023) in the Official Journal.

considered that there is a risk that enforcement of the claim will be impossible or significantly more difficult. If a judicial protection procedure is necessary, the applicant is exempted from paying court fees. In proceedings before a court or other authority, in relation to damage suffered by the notifier, it is assumed that the damage is the result of retaliatory action due to the reporting or public disclosure if the notifier proves that they filed a report or publicly disclosed information about the violation and that they suffered damage. In such cases, the person who took the action must demonstrate that the action was lawful and appropriate and unrelated to the application (art 22 ZZPri).

4. Zakon o spremembah in dopolnitvah Zakona o finančnem poslovanju, postopkih zaradi insolventnosti in prisilnem prenehanju (ZFPPIPP-H)[6] – Amending Act to the Financial Operations, Insolvency Proceedings and Compulsory Dissolution Act (ZFPPIPP-H)

6 The Financial Operations, Insolvency Proceedings and Compulsory Dissolution Act (hereinafter ZFPPIPP-H) amends the rules on management's liability for compensation to creditors in bankruptcy proceedings. According to these rules, management is liable to creditors for damage they have suffered because they did not receive full payment in bankruptcy proceedings if bankruptcy proceedings were initiated against the company and if the management: (1) did not submit a proposal for the initiation of insolvency proceedings in time under art 38 of the Financial Operations, Insolvency Proceedings and Compulsory Dissolution Act[7] or (2) acted contrary to art 34 (made payments and assumed new obligations that were not necessary for the company's operations or treated creditors who were in the same position in relation to the company unequally) or art 39 ZFPPIPP (the company must comply with orders in a timely manner and must not violate the prohibitions set forth in Chapter 4 of the ZFPPIPP on a forced settlement procedure). If the management does not prove otherwise, it is considered that the creditor suffered damage due to the mentioned omissions or actions of the management, which shall be equal to the difference between the total amount of their claim

6 Uradni list RS (Official Journal) No 102/2023. The Act entered into force (8 November 2022) one day after publication (7 November 2022) in the Official Journal.
7 Uradni list RS (Official Journal) No 126/2007. The Act entered into force (15 January 2008) 15 days after publication (31 December 2007) in the Official Journal, and has been applicable since 1 October 2008.

and the amount up to which this claim was paid in the bankruptcy procedure. If the management has two or more members, all members are jointly liable to the creditors for the damage caused. The members of management are fully or partially exempt from liability for damages if they prove that all or part of the damage was caused by events or actions of persons other than management, although acting in accordance with the professional diligence of the business, financial and management professions and the profession of corporate management, could neither prevent nor deter or limit their harmful consequences. An individual member of management is exempt from liability for compensation for damage from the first paragraph of this article if they prove: (1) that they could not perform the act referred to in art 38 of the ZFPPIPP independently and proposed that it be done at a meeting of the management, but other members of the management opposed it, or (2) that they did not know about the violations of art 34 or art 39 ZFPPIPP or could not have prevented them, although they acted in accordance with the professional diligence of the business-financial profession and the profession of corporate management (art 25 ZFPPIPP-H).

ZFPPIPP-H also amended the condition in relation to the indemnity insurance 7 of an administrator in proceedings due to insolvency or forced liquidation. The function of the administrator can only be performed by a person who has a valid permit from the minister responsible for justice to perform the function of administrator in proceedings due to insolvency or forced liquidation. The minister responsible for justice issues a licence to perform the function of administrator to a person who also fulfils the condition of concluded insurance, which covers their liability for damage caused by a breach of their obligations, for the minimum insurance sum of € 500,000 in an individual year, whereby the insurance must also cover compensation claims filed after the termination of the insurance period if the cause of the damage or the occurrence of the damage originated within the duration of the insurance, although this period can be limited, but not to less than five years after the expiration of the insurance period (art 40 ZFPPIPP-H).

5. Zakon o interventnih ukrepih za odpravo posledic poplav in zemeljskih plazov iz avgusta 2023 (ZIUOPZP)[8] – Act Determining Intervention Measures for Recovery from the Floods and Landslides of August 2023 (ZIUOPZP)

8 With the Act Determining Intervention Measures for Recovery from the Floods and Landslides of August 2023 (hereinafter ZIUOPZP), necessary interventional, remedial and preventive measures and procedures are determined in order to eliminate the consequences of the floods and landslides of August 2023 (hereinafter: floods and landslides) and for the implementation and monitoring of these measures. The ZIUOPZP amended and supplemented the provisions of numerous laws for the purpose of the above-mentioned measures. Among them, it is worth mentioning the amendment to the Natural Disaster Recovery Act (hereinafter ZOPNN),[9] which regulates encroachments on property rights for the purpose of renovating public energy infrastructure and compensation for such encroachments. According to this regulation, for the purpose of the renovation of public energy infrastructure, the investor may take possession of land necessary for the implementation of constructions under art 106 (maintenance works for the public benefit) and para 1 art 107 (construction of replacement economic public energy infrastructure) ZIUOPZP, with effect from the day when they deposit with a notary or a court a sum in the amount of the estimated compensation for these lands and a security deposit in the amount of one half of the estimated compensation for any other damage, if before that the government or the municipal council has determined by decision that public benefit has been established on these lands for the implementation of economic reconstruction measures of the public energy infrastructure according to ZIUOPZP. The proposer of the decision to determine public benefit is the ministry responsible for energy. In the notarial record or record of taking over the above-mentioned amount for safekeeping, the term of safekeeping must be specified, until the condition for the payment of compensation is fulfilled, or at least five years, whichever occurs first. The submission of an agreement on compensation or the submission of a final decision on expropriation or limitation of property rights must be specified as a condition for payment to the entitled person. The deposited amount is an undisputable part of the compensation. The as-

8 Uradni list RS (Official Journal) Nos 95/2023, 117/2023, 131/2023. The Act entered into force (2 September 2023) one day after publication (1 September 2023) in the Official Journal.

9 Zakon o odpravi posledic naravnih nesreč (ZOPNN), Uradni list RS (Official Journal) Nos 114/05, 90/07, 102/07, 40/12, 17/14, 163/22, 18/23, 88/23, 95/23, 117/23. The Act entered into force (2 August 2003) one day after publication (1 August 2003) in the Official Journal.

sessment of compensation is made by an authorised real estate appraiser, appointed in accordance with regulations governing auditing and valuation, or a judicial real estate appraiser, or a judicial appraiser in the agricultural profession or a judicial appraiser in the forestry profession, appointed in accordance with regulations governing the operation of courts. An investor in the renovation of the economic public energy infrastructure, who has taken over the property, must immediately, or at the latest within six months after depositing the amount, initiate the procedure for acquiring real rights in accordance with the regulations governing expropriation and limitation of property rights. If, in order to acquire real rights on these lands, it is necessary to carry out a process of expropriation or acquisition of easement for public benefit, regardless of other regulations, it is considered that public benefit is demonstrated by a decision of the government or the municipal council, and by depositing an amount by which it is considered that the condition regarding the transfer of ownership has been fulfilled despite an appeal against the expropriation decision. If the investor takes possession of the land, the owner is entitled to pecuniary compensation due to a restriction of its use for the time from taking possession until the time when the investor acquires ownership or other real right to the land in question. Pecuniary compensation is agreed in a contract for the purchase or establishment of an easement if the real estate is acquired or encumbered by agreement, or as part of compensation in accordance with the regulations governing the expropriation and limitation of property rights, whereby such compensation may not exceed the amount of this compensation. Before depositing the amount, the investor informs the owner of the land about the intended takeover of the property and that, no later than six months after the start of construction, the procedure for acquiring property rights will be initiated in accordance with regulations governing the expropriation and limitation of property rights, and that for the period of use of this land, compensation will be paid. Contracts for the limitation of property rights are concluded for the duration of the operation of the infrastructure and for the benefit of each individual investor or owner of individual infrastructure or for the benefit of the dominant land whose owner is the investor or owner of the infrastructure (art 108 ZIUOPZP).

The ZIUOPZP also supplements the ZOPNN with a provision according to 9
which, consumers of gas and district heat who, due to damage to the public energy infrastructure because of floods or landslides, are unable to supply or ensure the energy supply, are not obliged to pay contractual penalties, are not liable for damages due to the inability to implement supply and access contracts, and have no other obligations arising from an existing contractual relationship (para 2 art 116 ZIUOPZP).

10 The ZIUOPZP complements the rules of the ZOPNN with a provision on the replacement of a facility for removal. Accordingly, the State provides the owner of the property owner with a facility whose ownership rights are to be removed with an equivalent property, unless said owner requests compensation. If the said owner proposes a replacement property, the State buys the property and transfers it to that owner if a valuation of the two properties establishes their equivalence. If the value of the assessed replacement real estate is lower than the value of the assessed real estate with the facility to be removed, and the owner of the real estate with the facility to be removed agrees to such compensation, the State pays that owner the difference in value between the two properties in money. If the value of the appraised replacement property with the facility to be removed is higher than the value of the appraised property with the facility to be removed, the State buys the replacement property if the owner of the property with the facility to be removed pays the difference in value between the properties (art 151.č ZIUOPZP).

B. Cases

1. Decision of the Supreme Court VIII Ips 14/2023, 24 October 2023: Polygraph Testing of Workers

a) Brief Summary of the Facts

11 The defendant (an employer) received an anonymous letter about irregularities in the work of her personnel department, with the threat of public publication if the irregularities were not eliminated. Because she wanted to discover who was responsible for disclosing the data and to prevent their leakage, she conducted a polygraph test on the female workers, among whom were the two plaintiffs. In addition to compensation for mistreatment at the workplace, the plaintiffs also demanded compensation from the defendant for interference with their personal rights because of the implementation of polygraph testing. The court of first instance ruled in favour of the plaintiffs regarding the damage caused by the polygraph test and awarded each of them € 2,000 in compensation for non-pecuniary damage. The illegality of the defendant's conduct was established by the fact that polygraph testing is based on the examinee's responses of the automatic nervous system, which is not under the control of their will, which means excessive interference with the employees' personal rights. The court of first instance took the position that polygraph testing should not be used in an employment relationship,

even with the consent of the employee, who is in a subordinate position in relation to the employer. The second instance court agreed with the first instance court and added that polygraph testing is a task of the police authority that the employer does not have, and that the testing took place without a legal basis and only in the interest of the employer. In relation to the disputed consent of the plaintiffs, it added that the consent of an injured party can exclude the illegality of conduct and damage if it includes consent to a violation of rights and a waiver of the right to assert a claim due to the violation, which is not evident from the evidence presented in the specific case. However, since in the opinion of the court of second instance, the court of first instance did not fully establish the factual situation regarding the alleged mistreatment in the workplace, it annulled the decision of the court of first instance and returned the case to this court for retrial.

b) Judgment of the Court

The Supreme Court ruled on two questions based on the permitted revision: 12
(1) whether the performance of polygraph testing of an employee by an employer constitutes illegal conduct or a disproportionate interference with the employee's personal rights, despite the employee's prior written consent; (2) whether an employee is entitled to compensation solely for psychological discomfort during the polygraph test and to what extent. The Supreme Court emphasised that particularly strict criteria apply to polygraph testing of an employee by an employer, since polygraph testing represents an invasive interference with the employee's personal rights, and it must also be taken into account that the employee is subordinate to the employer. It emerged from the factual findings of the lower courts that the plaintiffs had concerns about consenting to the testing due to a sense of indirect coercion, such that, in the event of refusal of consent, they would appear to be the anonymous authors. The Supreme Court therefore concluded that the consent of the plaintiffs to the polygraph test was not free and the use of the polygraph was inadmissible. In relation to compensation for mental discomfort, the Supreme Court emphasised that, in order to award pecuniary compensation for non-pecuniary harm, such a disturbance in a person's emotional perception must be established as to disrupt their mental balance. Mere short-term impairment or psychological discomfort due to the curtailment of personal rights does not constitute legally recognised harm. The plaintiffs sought compensation for mistreatment at the workplace, and the polygraph test was only one of a series of mistreatment practices alleged by the plaintiffs. According to the Supreme Court, the lower courts excluded damages from the polygraph testing from the broader context of maltreatment damages, so the damages were not determined as uniform dam-

ages. The Supreme Court approved the revision and returned the case to the court of first instance with the instruction that when determining uniform compensation in the retrial, the circumstances of the polygraph test should also be taken into account.

c) Commentary

13 In Slovenian legislation, the use of a polygraph is provided for in the process of detecting perpetrators of criminal acts. The implementation of the polygraph procedure is defined as one of the police powers that police officers have when performing police tasks (art 33 of the Act on Tasks and Powers of the Police (hereinafter ZNPPol)[10]). According to art 48 of ZNPPol, police officers may carry out a polygraph procedure as an aid in the investigation of criminal offences, taking into account the circumstances of the criminal offence. At the start of the procedure, the police officers must inform the person of the purpose and method of conducting the polygraph procedure and the operation of the polygraph machine, that the polygraph procedure may only be performed with their consent and that the results of the polygraph procedure cannot be used as evidence in criminal proceedings (para 1 art 48 ZNPPol). The polygraph procedure may only be carried out with the written consent of the person (para 2 art 48 ZNPPol). The police officer must interrupt the polygraph procedure if the person withdraws their consent or if the police officer finds that the person is in a psychophysical state that is not suitable for this procedure (para 3 art 48 ZNPPol). Other than in the ZNPPol, the possibility of polygraph testing is not regulated in other laws.[11]

14 Although no legal regulation expressly prohibits an employer from using a polygraph in an employment relationship, according to the Supreme Court, this does not mean that the use of a polygraph is permissible. The Supreme Court therefore assessed the admissibility of implementation on the basis of art 140 of the Code of Obligations,[12] according to which, the consent of the injured party excludes the illegality of the conduct and damages.[13] Consent, which by its legal nature is a declaration of will, is valid only if it is free and sincere (para 2 art 18 of the Code of Obligations).[14] The Supreme Court emphasised that polygraph testing is an invasive

10 Uradni list RS (Official Journal) Nos 15/13, 23/15, 10/17, 46/19, 47/19, 153/21.
11 Decision of the Supreme Court VIII Ips 14/2023, 24 October 2023.
12 Uradni list RS (Official Journal) Nos 97/07, 64/16, 20/18.
13 *D Jadek Pensa* in: N Plavšak/M Juhart (eds), Obligacijski zakonik s komentarjem – Splošni del I [Code of Obligations with commentary – General part I] (2003) 817.
14 Ibid.

intervention in a person's mental integrity, privacy and dignity. In addition, it should also be taken into account that, in an employment relationship, the employee is subordinate to the employer, so the employee's consent to polygraph testing must be assessed particularly strictly.[15]

In addition to the position of the Supreme Court in relation to an employee's 15
consent to polygraph testing, the case is also important from the point of view of the possibility of non-pecuniary harm arising from an interference with personal rights through polygraph testing. According to para 1 art 179 of the Code of Obligations, an injured party is entitled to fair pecuniary compensation for mental pain suffered due to an infringement of personal rights if the circumstances of the case, in particular the degree of pain and its duration, justify it. Mental pain and its duration must reach a certain level, otherwise legally recognised damage does not arise.[16] Although the Supreme Court in the case under consideration did not find a particular intensity or prolonged duration of mental pain due to the polygraph testing, it allowed the possibility that the polygraph testing of an employee may lead to such a degree of interference with personal rights that the employee is entitled to compensation for non-pecuniary harm.

2. Decision of the Supreme Court II Ips 10/2023, 19 July 2023: Start of the Limitation Period for the Payment of Pecuniary Compensation for Non-Pecuniary Damage

a) Brief Summary of the Facts

In October 2015, the plaintiff had a traffic accident in which, in addition to damage 16
to the car, she suffered a minor concussion, strained neck muscles and injuries to the forehead, lumbosacral region, left shoulder and left knee. She demanded that the defendant pay her € 35,337 for property damage, € 13,000 for physical pain and inconvenience suffered during treatment, € 3,000 for fear, € 10,000 for mental pain due to reduced life activity and € 4,000 for mental pain due to disfigurement, a total of € 65,337, and payment of a monthly annuity of € 450. The court of first instance rejected the plaintiff's claim in its entirety on the grounds that the statute of limitations for the compensation claim began to run at the end of January 2016 (for non-property damage) or at the beginning of February 2016 (for property damage), since the treatment of the plaintiff's injuries was completed at that time. Because

15 Decision of the Supreme Court VIII Ips 14/2023, 24 October 2023.

16 *Jadek Pensa* (fn 13) 1024.

the plaintiff only filed the lawsuit in June 2019, in the opinion of the court of first instance, her claim, taking into account the three-year limitation period under art 352 of the Code of Obligations, was time-barred. The second instance court partially upheld the plaintiff's appeal and overturned the first instance court's judgment in the part regarding payment of compensation for mental pain due to a reduction in life activity in the amount of € 4,300 with statutory default interest, on the grounds that the first instance court incompletely established the factual situation regarding the statute of limitations. The plaintiff stated in the lawsuit that her life activity was reduced due to fear and nightmares. It emerged from the expert opinion that the treatment of physical injuries was stabilised at the end of January 2016, while the post-traumatic stress disorder lasted for one year, ie, until October 2016. In the opinion of the second instance court, therefore, a claim for non-pecuniary damages related to physical harm, was time-barred. However, according to the court of second instance, the claim for payment of compensation for mental pain due to the reduction of life activity as a result of the claimed symptoms of post-traumatic stress disorder was not time-barred.

b) Judgment of the Court

17 The Supreme Court allowed revision in relation to the issue of whether the statute of limitations for non-pecuniary damage originating from the same historical damage event runs separately from damage due to physical injuries and separately for other health impairments (diseases, disorders). It emphasised that every person is a unique whole of an individual physical and spiritual being, therefore, for the victim, all the consequences of interference with their personal integrity are a single whole, and compensation for non-pecuniary damage is awarded in one total monetary amount. By splitting the beginning of the limitation period, so that the limitation period for individual forms of non-pecuniary damage would occur separately, contrary to the principle of legal certainty, the uncertainty of the injured party's legal position would disproportionately increase. Regardless of the fact that law and science demarcate different forms of mental suffering, from the point of view of life, the individual perceives them as a whole. Different forms of non-pecuniary damage can be intertwined, in individual cases even to such an extent that it is impossible to distinguish between them. Each case must therefore be considered as a whole, and therefore the final amount of compensation for the entire non-pecuniary damage is important (and not just the amounts of compensation for individual forms of this damage). Based on the stated reasons, the Supreme Court adopted the position that art 352 of the Code of Obligations should be interpreted in such a way that the beginning of the limitation period for all

forms of non-material damage is generally linked to the same moment; that is, when the injured party became aware of the scope and amount of the entire non-pecuniary damage. The Supreme Court therefore approved the revision in full, annulling the judgment of the court of second instance (in addition to the part relating to the payment of compensation for mental pain due to a reduction in life activity in the amount of € 4,300, which had already been annulled by the court of second instance), and also annulled the payment of compensation for fear in the amount of € 1,800 and in relation to physical pain and inconvenience during treatment in the amount of € 6,400 and returned the case to the court of first instance for retrial. It instructed the court of first instance that it must clarify the factual situation regarding the question of when the injured party learned about the scope and amount of the damage.

c) Commentary

The Code of Obligations sets subjective and objective time limits for the limitation of compensation claims. The subjective term is three years and begins to run when the injured party becomes aware of the damage and of the person who caused it (para 1 art 352 of the Code of Obligations). The objective term is five years from the occurrence of the damage (para 2 art 352 of the Code of Obligations). The injured party claims compensation for damage in a timely manner if they file the lawsuit in compliance with both deadlines.[17] 18

The case under consideration is important from the point of view of the development of court practice regarding the beginning of the limitation period for compensation claims. In the case under consideration, the Supreme Court referred to its previous position that the extent of non-pecuniary damage is known when the injured party's condition is stabilised and treatment that can realistically be expected to eliminate or reduce the damage is completed.[18] This also means that the beginning of the limitation period is not necessarily linked to the completion of treatment, although this may be the most tangible circumstance from the point of view of the injured party's diligence, but to the moment when the injured party became aware of the scope and amount of the damage.[19] Determining the moment when the limitation period starts to run can be difficult when the injured party 19

17 *V Kranjc* in: N Plavšak/M Juhart (eds), Obligacijski zakonik s komentarjem – Splošni del II [Code of Obligations with commentary – General part II] (2003) 478.

18 Eg, Judgment of the Supreme Court II Ips 330/2015, 7 September 2017; Judgment of the Supreme Court II Ips 237/2012, 4 December 2014.

19 Decision of the Supreme Court II Ips 143/2018, 16 January 2018.

has suffered several different forms of non-pecuniary damage. In the case under consideration, the Supreme Court adopted the important position that, in the event of the occurrence of several different forms of non-pecuniary damage, the statute of limitations does not run for each of these forms separately, but the beginning of the limitation period for all forms of non-pecuniary damage is generally linked to the same moment, ie, when the injured party discovered the scope and amount of the total non-pecuniary damage.[20]

3. Decision of the Supreme Court II Ips 69/2022, 5 April 2023: Liability of an Employer

a) Brief Summary of the Facts

20 The plaintiff was a truck driver and, in July 2016, he went to pick up a load at a factory in Austria. At the factory, they loaded his truck with sheet metal for the automotive industry, which he had to secure with bands so that it would not move while driving. When the plaintiff was installing the band under the pallet base, he cut his right finger on the sharp edge of the load. The plaintiff did not use protective gloves when installing the band, which would have prevented a cut if the plaintiff had taken appropriate care. The plaintiff was properly instructed about the correct way of securing the load and he undertook this task correctly, although he did not receive any prior information from the employer about what kind of load he was going to pick up, nor any specific instructions regarding the loading of this load. The plaintiff demanded compensation for the damage from the insurance company with which his employer had concluded a liability insurance contract. The court of first instance decided that the claim was not justified based on the provisions of the Code of Obligations on objective tort liability but that the employer's culpable tort liability was given. It concluded that the accident occurred mainly because the employer did not provide the plaintiff with protective gloves, thus neglecting the necessary safety measures. According to the court of first instance, the plaintiff also contributed to the occurrence of the damage by negligent behaviour, namely in the amount of 30 %. The court of second instance granted the defendant's appeal and changed the judgment of the court of first instance by rejecting the claim. It emphasised that the case concerned an everyday task of a truck driver and that the demand of the court of first instance that the employer should have instructed the plaintiff for such a simple task, provided pro-

20 Decision of the Supreme Court II Ips 10/2023, 19 July 2023.

tective gloves and ensured that the plaintiff used them, was excessive. It drew attention to the fact that the plaintiff had completed appropriate training and was independent in deciding how to perform his work.

b) Judgment of the Court

The Supreme Court allowed revision against the decision of the court of second instance regarding the question of whether the decision of the court of second instance was substantively correct, that in the case in question there was no duty of the plaintiff's employer to provide the plaintiff with personal protective equipment. The Supreme Court did not agree with the position of the court of second instance that the plaintiff should provide himself with protective equipment. It emphasised that art 12 of the Occupational Safety and Health Act (hereinafter ZVZD-1)[21] obliges a worker to respect and implement measures to ensure safety and health at work, but this does not mean that the worker is obliged to provide themselves with protective equipment. According to para 3 art 12 ZVZD-1, it is the employee's duty to use work equipment, safety devices and personal protective equipment in accordance with their purpose and the employer's instructions, to handle them carefully and to ensure that they are in perfect condition. According to art 5 and 9 ZVZD-1, the employer is obliged to provide protective equipment. The Supreme Court also emphasised that the employer's duty to provide the worker with protective equipment does not depend on whether it is a simple work task or not. Even simple tasks can become dangerous without the use of protective equipment. To secure a load, an employer must provide a truck driver with protective gloves and inform them of their obligation to use protective gloves. Only after the employer has fulfilled this obligation can the employee's duty to fulfil their obligations under art 12 ZVZD-1 begin. The Supreme Court thus concluded that, due to the erroneous application of substantive law, the factual situation was incompletely established, since the court of second instance, because of its substantive legal starting point, did not decide on an evidentiary assessment of whether the employer had provided the plaintiff with gloves. It therefore annulled the judgment of the court of second instance and returned the case to this court for retrial. 21

21 Uradni list RS (Official Journal) No 43/11.

c) Commentary

22 The Employment Relationship Act[22] stipulates in para 1 art 179 that an employer must compensate an employee for damage caused to them during work or in connection with work, and refers to the general rules of civil law. According to para 1 art 131 of the Code of Obligations, an employer must compensate an employee for damage if this is the result of the employer's illegal conduct and the employer is not relieved of the presumption of guilt. Exceptionally, when it comes to work with increased risk, in accordance with para 2 art 131 of the Code of Obligations, the employer is responsible for the damage objectively, ie, regardless of fault.[23]

23 The case under consideration is important because of the development of court practice in relation to an employer's liability for damage caused to workers due to insufficient protection at work. In its practice, the Supreme Court has emphasised that the employer must implement the measures necessary to ensure safety and health at work, including the prevention of hazards at work, informing and training workers, with appropriate organisation and the necessary material resources. They must also implement such preventive measures and choose such work and production methods as will ensure a higher level of safety and health at work. An employer must therefore constantly monitor whether an employee, before and during the work process, complies with appropriate protective measures, norms, standards and technical regulations and whether they are used correctly. In relation to the provision of protective equipment, the Supreme Court particularly emphasised that the employer does not relieve themselves of their legal obligations to ensure safety at work simply by providing protective equipment or aids for safe work, but must ensure that they are used, because only by using safe tools is safe work ensured.[24] In the case under consideration, the Supreme Court supplemented its practice with a clear position that an employer's duty to provide a worker with protective equipment does not depend on whether it is a simple work task or not.

---

22 Uradni list RS (Official Journal) Nos 21/13, 78/13, 47/15, 33/16, 52/16, 15/17, 22/19, 81/19, 203/20, 119/21, 202/21, 15/22, 54/22, 114/23, 136/23.

23 *D Možina*, Odškodninska odgovornost delodajalca [An employer's liability for loss], Pravni letopis 2017, 155.

24 Judgment of the Supreme Court II Ips 792/2006, 26 February 2009.

4. Judgment of the Supreme Court II Ips 62/2022, 5 April 2023: Damages for Loss of Profits

a) Brief Summary of the Facts

The plaintiff bought a plot of land in 2005, on which he planned to plant a walnut plantation in 2007. He did not plant the walnut grove in 2007, since he was prevented from doing so by the defendant, who unjustifiably took possession of the plot by driving building material, sand and soil onto it and placing sculptures on it, installing concrete blocks and moving a hedge. The plaintiff initiated several legal proceedings against the defendant, by which he obtained that the defendant must return the property to him, remove the material and other things from it, and restore the previous condition by moving the hedge and planting grass. In the present case, the plaintiff demanded compensation from the defendant for the lost profit that he would have obtained from the walnut plantation. In the repeated proceedings, a claim for the payment of € 22,325 with statutory default interest from 21 December 2016 was contested before the court of first instance. The court of first instance granted the claim. It concluded that the plantation was not created because of the defendant's actions, and the defendant's interventions would potentially damage the existing plantation so that half of the plantation (0.5 ha) would have to be restored. Nevertheless, it was considered that the plaintiff suffered damage in the amount of 1 ha, because an expert concluded that the contested plot was suitable for planting walnuts. The court of second instance partially granted the defendant's appeal and amended the judgment of the court of first instance by reducing the compensation amount by € 11,163 (ie, by half). The second instance court agreed with the finding of the first instance court that the plaintiff did not realise his intention in relation to the walnut plantation because the defendant made it impossible for him through his illegal actions. However, it criticised the first instance court for the fact that when calculating the amount of damages, it should have taken into account that the plaintiff could have planted walnuts on the remaining 0.5 ha suitable for agricultural cultivation. The issue of the area of influence (ie, the area on which the plaintiff could not plant walnuts in 2007) is a legally important issue that the court of first instance, due to the erroneous position (that the plantation was not actually made, therefore it should be considered that the plaintiff suffered damage to the extent of 1 ha), was not taken into account when calculating the damage. 24

b) Judgment of the Court

25 The Supreme Court approved revision and amended the judgment of the court of second instance by rejecting the remaining part of the defendant's appeal and confirming the judgment of the court of first instance. It emphasised that the assessment of lost profit takes into account the profit that could reasonably be expected in the normal course of events or given special circumstances, but which could not be achieved due to the tortfeasor's act or omission. The Supreme Court therefore assessed whether, given the actual situation established at the time of the damage event, it would be normal to expect the injured party to make an investment on half the size of the plot than planned. In doing so, it took into account the actual situation in the spring of 2007, when the plaintiff had intended to plant walnuts. At that time, there was already material in the middle of the plot that the defendant had brought in 2006. In addition, due to legal proceedings in relation to the existence of the property right and subsequent enforcement proceedings against the defendant, the plaintiff did not receive possession of the plot until June 2009. According to the Supreme Court, under such circumstances, it was unreasonable to expect the plaintiff to plant a part of the walnut plantation on the vacant part of the land already in April 2007, when the defendant still owned the property. On the contrary, the plaintiff's expectation was reasonable and normal that he would assert his rights most efficiently and quickly in court proceedings and then start planting the plantation in its entirety. The implementation of the planting of an intensive walnut plantation, as planned by the plaintiff, would be more optimal and expedient on a larger area and at once. According to the Supreme Court, therefore, the court of second instance did not make a correct decision, since its interpretation of the normal course of events included the requirement of unreasonable behaviour of the plaintiff during litigation.

c) Commentary

26 The Code of Obligations defines in art 132 property damage as a decrease in property (ordinary damage) or prevention of an increase in property (lost profit). When assessing the lost profit, the profit that could reasonably be expected based on the normal course of events or based on special circumstances, but which could not be achieved due to the tortfeasor's act or omission, is taken into account (para 3 art 168 of the Code of Obligations). Conclusions are drawn about what kind of profit the injured party would have achieved if there had been no loss event, mainly from expectations based on the normal course of events, for example based on the

volume of the injured party's business in the past.[25] According to the practice of the Supreme Court, compensation for damage is therefore decided on the basis of assumptions about the normal course of events, viewed from the perspective of the moment of the damage event, as a result of which, the standard of proof of certainty is not required, but of objective probability, as to whether the injured party had suffered a lost profit and in what amount or the threshold of a sufficient, above-half probability.[26]

In the case under consideration, the position of the Supreme Court in relation to the interpretation of the concept of profit applies. Although profit is an economic (financial) category, this does not mean that only an entity that would generate profit on the market with 'increased wealth' is entitled to this profit and thus obtain (direct) financial benefit from it. The Supreme Court pointed out that the fact that the plaintiff had no intention of making money from the walnuts does not mean that the increase in his assets was not prevented. The walnut crop can be valued monetarily, and if the plaintiff had wanted to produce it in the normal course of events, but was unable to do so because of the defendant's actions, he is entitled to compensation for this damage. The distinction between whether the plaintiff would have sold the crop on the market or whether he would have used it for other purposes is therefore not relevant for the existence of lost profit. 27

5. European Court of Human Rights (ECtHR) *Dolenc v Slovenia*, 20.10.2023, no 20256/20: Damage due to a Failure to Guarantee the Right to a Fair Trial

a) Brief Summary of the Facts

In May 1992, the applicant, an internationally renowned neurosurgeon, performed surgery on an Israeli citizen, EM, at Ljubljana University Hospital. Following the surgery and/or post-operative care, EM was left severely disabled. In May 1995, EM's lawsuit, in which he sought damages for medical negligence from the applicant, was served on the latter during his visit to the State of Israel (hereinafter Israel). The proceedings were subsequently conducted before the Tel Aviv District Court (hereinafter the Israeli district court). The applicant submitted his defence 28

25 *B Novak*, Osnove neposlovne odškodninske obveznosti [Bases of non-commercial tortious liability], in: M Juhart (ed) D Možina/B Novak/A Polajnar-Pavčnik/V Žnidaršič Skubic, Uvod v civilno pravo [Introduction to civil law] (2011) 237.
26 Judgment of the Supreme Court II Ips 62/2022, 5 April 2023.

statement, a medical opinion by neurosurgeon R, statements of eleven witnesses who worked at Ljubljana University Hospital and an opinion by a Slovenian legal expert who was to testify about the applicability of Slovenian law to the dispute. The applicant never appeared before the Israeli district court himself but was represented in the proceedings by an Israeli lawyer until he cancelled his representation.

29 On 22 September 1999, the applicant declined to participate via video link and requested that he and his witnesses be examined before a Slovenian court, in accordance with the Hague Evidence Convention. He pointed out that Israel and Slovenia had both signed the Hague Evidence Convention (hereinafter HEC) and that, pursuant to Slovenian law, witnesses would receive a court summons to appear. He repeated this request on 6 December 2000. On 27 August 2001, the Israeli district court, after a hearing, rejected the applicant's request, finding that the decision to examine him and the witnesses via video link struck an adequate balance between the interests of the parties. This was upheld on 18 July 2002 by the Israeli Supreme Court, which held that the position could be reconsidered by the district court if there were practical obstacles to organising the proceedings via video link. The applicant made another, his fourth, request for his witnesses to be examined by a Slovenian court, claiming that it was practically impossible to hold the proceedings via video link. On 26 December 2002, the Israeli district court rejected this request, holding that it was technically possible to examine witnesses that way. The applicant then asked that his scheduled testimony via video link be cancelled and for the court to decide how his witnesses would be questioned. On 6 February 2003, the Israeli district court upheld its decision of 26 December 2002, finding that the applicant's refusal to be questioned via video link did not arise from the lack of practical possibility of conducting such proceedings. The court then asked the applicant to reconsider his position and warned him that his main statement (written statement in lieu of his direct examination) would otherwise have to be excluded from the case file. Since the applicant maintained his position, on 4 June 2003 the court excluded his main statement from the case file. At the hearing on 7 November 2004, no one appeared on behalf of the applicant. He was then given several additional deadlines to submit his concluding statement. He disputed that he had ever been informed of these additional opportunities. In the absence of any response from the applicant, the Israeli district court reached its decision on the basis of the evidence submitted but excluded his witnesses' statements and the opinion of the Slovenian legal expert in line with Israeli law, finding that these witnesses had not been directly questioned owing to the applicant's conduct. On 9 June 2005, the applicant was found fully liable for the damage caused to EM. Referring to the applicant's 'attempts to prevent the court from enforcing the law and justice', the Israeli district court ordered him to cover the costs of the proceedings

and legal fees. On 19 January 2006, EM was awarded compensation for pecuniary and non-pecuniary damage in an amount equivalent to approximately € 2.3 million. The Slovenian Government submitted a number of documents relating to attempts, sometimes successful, sometimes not, to serve certain court documents from Israel on the applicant in Slovenia, but there is nothing to suggest that they relate to the above-mentioned proceedings.

On 29 June 2011, EM requested that the Ljubljana District Court recognise the above-mentioned judgments. The court allowed the request on 13 August 2012. The applicant lodged an objection and appeal, followed by a supplement to appeal lodged out of time, in which he complained that the proceedings in Israel had not been fair. He was not successful with these remedies. However, further to a constitutional complaint by him, the Constitutional Court on 3 March 2016 remitted the case to the Ljubljana District Court for reconsideration, essentially because it found the lower courts' reasoning concerning the Israeli district court's jurisdiction and the admissibility of uncertified translations to be inadequate. The Constitutional Court dismissed the complaints concerning the alleged unfairness of the proceedings in Israel because the applicant had failed to raise them in the remedies before the lower courts in a timely manner. 30

On 12 September 2017, the Ljubljana District Court reconsidered the case, also taking account of the applicant's arguments concerning the alleged non-compliance of the Israeli judgments with Slovenian public policy in a substantive and procedural sense. It dismissed EM's request to recognise the Israeli judgments, finding that there was a lack of reciprocity and a breach of the right to equality of arms related to the exceptionally high award for pecuniary damage. It dismissed the applicant's remaining arguments, including those concerning his alleged inability to have his evidence examined, the exclusion of evidence and statements, and the lack of a remedy in the proceedings in Israel. In assessing whether the applicant's procedural rights had been respected in Israel, the court held that proceedings conducted under the common law tradition (such as those in Israel) were different from proceedings in Slovenia but that this did not mean that they were *a priori* incompatible with the guarantees of a fair trial. It considered it crucial to determine whether, before excluding the evidence from the case file, the Israeli district court had reasonably done enough to secure the applicant's right to a fair trial. It further held that bad faith conduct aimed at avoiding the proceedings should not enjoy protection and that it was therefore necessary also to consider the applicant's actions in the Israeli proceedings. EM lodged an appeal, to which the applicant responded. On 5 March 2018, the Supreme Court found in favour of EM. The applicant lodged a constitutional complaint in which he disputed, inter alia, that he had waived his right to participate in the Israeli proceedings. On 28 October 2019, the Constitutional Court, by five votes to two, decided in a rea- 31 soned decision not to accept the applicant's constitutional complaint for consideration. As regards his complaint relating to his failure to be examined by the Israeli district court, the court found that not only in common law systems, but also in continental legal systems, the parties are responsible for gathering procedural material. This applies in particular when the party proposes his own testimony as evidence. In relation to the witnesses' failure to be examined by the Israeli district court, the Constitutional Court likewise considered that the applicant's opportunity to give evidence had not been disproportionately restricted. In the Constitutional Court's opinion, the Israeli district court could not be criticised for ultimately deciding that the examination of witnesses should take place in Israel. It observed that the Slovenian court had had difficulties complying with the request for international legal assistance regarding the cross-examination of witnesses. As regards the exclusion of written statements, the Constitutional Court observed that this was a logical consequence of the fact that the plaintiff had had no opportunity to cross-examine them and that the exclusion had been meant to secure the plaintiff's right to adversarial proceedings. As regards the service of the decisions, the Constitutional Court found it important that the applicant had known about the proceedings before the Israeli district court and had had an opportunity to appoint a representative, including one for serving court documents on him if he had so wished. In the Constitutional Court's view, the Israeli district court had had justified reasons for not serving the court documents at a foreign address and had rightly assumed that by serving them via his former lawyer, the applicant would have had reasonable opportunities to continue participating in the proceedings. The Constitutional Court, referring to the case *Pellegrini v Italy* (20.10.2001, no 30882/96), concluded that the domestic courts' review of the Israeli judgments had complied with the requirements under the HEC. Lastly, it found that the applicant had been able to give his view relating to the Supreme Court's decision on appeal during the earlier proceedings, as well as in his response to EM's appeal.

b) Judgment of the Court

32 The European Court of Human Rights (hereinafter ECtHR) emphasised that its case law underscores the obligation for domestic courts to undertake a certain level of review before enforcing a foreign decision. The case of *Pellegrini v Italy* clarified that, in the context of art 6 of the European Convention on Human Rights (hereinafter ECHR), the review might need to extend to the compliance of the foreign proceedings with the guarantees of this provision, especially where the implications of a declaration of enforceability were of paramount importance for the parties. As to the present case, the Court noted that the Israeli judgments had caused serious fi-

nancial and reputational damage for the applicant, finding him directly and exclusively liable for the serious damage to EM's health, which allegedly resulted from the medical care provided to him at Ljubljana University Hospital. The applicant was liable to pay to EM over € 2 million in damages. These judgments could, therefore, be deemed to be of paramount importance to the applicant. Moreover, the Slovenian courts themselves interpreted domestic law as requiring them to review whether the judgments to be recognised had been handed down in proceedings complying with the guarantees of a fair trial. The ECtHR, having regard to the foregoing and noting that it had not been argued that a presumption of equivalent protection should apply in the present case, saw no reasons to depart from the approach set out in *Pellegrini v Italy*. It thus had to assess whether, before recognising the Israeli judgments, the national authorities duly satisfied themselves that the relevant proceedings in Israel fulfilled the guarantees of para 1 art 6 of the ECHR. The Slovenian courts also did not attach sufficient weight to the consequences that the non-examination of the witnesses (including the expert on Slovenian law) via the HEC procedure and the ensuing exclusion of their statements had for the applicant's right to present evidence. This right is a fundamental component of the principle of a fair hearing and the Slovenian courts should have satisfied themselves that it had been respected in the proceedings in Israel before recognising the Israeli judgments. In view of the foregoing, the ECtHR found that the Slovenian courts, by failing duly to satisfy themselves that the trial in Israel had been fair before recognising the Israeli judgments, breached their duty under para 1 art 6 of the Convention. There had thus been a violation of this provision. The ECtHR therefore held that the respondent State must pay the applicant € 9,600, plus any tax that may be chargeable, in respect of pecuniary damage and € 6,000 plus any tax that may be chargeable, in respect of costs and expenses. The ECtHR dismissed the remainder of the applicant's claim for just satisfaction in respect of non-pecuniary damage and costs and expenses incurred up to the adoption of this judgment.

c) Commentary

Although in 2023 Slovenia was recognised as violating the ECHR in only two cases, 33
in both (*Dolenc v Slovenia*, 20.1.2023, no 20256/20 and *Rutar and Rutar Marketing d.o.o. v Slovenia*, 15.3.2023, no 21164/20), it violated para 1 art 6 of the ECHR because it did not ensure compliance with the principle of a fair trial. This principle, in the case of *Rutar and Rutar Marketing d.o.o. v Slovenia* was violated because the domestic court failed to provide reasons for the refusal to accede to the applicant's request to seek a preliminary ruling from the Court of Justice of the European

Union. The ECtHR emphasised in this connection that the right to a reasoned decision serves the general rule enshrined in the ECHR that protects an individual from arbitrariness by demonstrating to the parties that they have been heard and obliges the courts to base their decision on objective reasons. As the ECtHR has often noted, the rule of law and the avoidance of arbitrary power are principles underlying the ECHR. In the judicial sphere, those principles serve to foster public confidence in an objective and transparent justice system, one of the foundations of a democratic society. The ECtHR awarded the applicants in the case of *Rutar and Rutar Marketing d.o.o. v Slovenia* the amount of € 5,000, covering costs and expenses (the applicants did not make any claim in respect of pecuniary or non-pecuniary damage). The decisions in both cases, although there are only two cases, are worrying because violations of para 1 art 6 of the ECHR have been among the most frequent Slovenian violations of the ECHR for years.[27]

6. Personal Injury

34 In 2023, the courts followed the same basic principles in calculating pecuniary compensation for non-pecuniary damage as in 2022.[28] The basic principles for calculating pecuniary compensation for non-pecuniary damage are individualisation of the level of compensation and objective conditionality of the level of compensation. In 2023, two cases from the field of domestic violence should be highlighted, which complement court practice in such cases, especially from the point of view of the principle of objective conditionality of the amount of compensation. In the first case, in the period from July 2014 to March 2015, the defendant inflicted mental and physical violence on the plaintiff, for which he was legally convicted of the crime of violence. During this period, the defendant beat the plaintiff several times and inflicted injuries on various parts of her body. He also abused her several times, spat in her face, threatened her with murder and suicide. The plaintiff suffered bumps and abrasions on her face and body, as well as light injuries to the back of her left shoulder, the inside of her right shin, her left buttock, her right ear, under her left knee, her right elbow socket, her upper lip and her ear. The Supreme Court agreed with the courts of first and second instance that the plaintiff

27 We have already drawn attention to this problem in a past report: *B Novak*, Slovenia, in: E Karner/BC Steininger (eds), European Tort Law (ETL) 2020 (2021) 588, no 29; and previously *B Novak/G Dugar*, Slovenia, in: E Karner/BC Steininger (eds), European Tort Law (ETL) 2016 (2018) 550, no 34; *B Novak*, Slovenia, in: E Karner/BC Steininger (eds), European Tort Law (ETL) 2018 (2019) 599, no 35.
28 *B Novak*, Slovenia, in: E Karner/BC Steininger (eds), European Tort Law (ETL) 2022 (2023) 585, no 40.

was entitled to compensation for non-pecuniary damage in the total amount of € 7,500, namely for physical pain € 2,000, for fear € 1,500, for reduction of life activity € 3,000 and for violation of dignity € 1,000.[29] In the second case, during a marriage, the defendant treated the plaintiff badly, in addition to threats, insults and mental abuse, the plaintiff also suffered physical violence. During several harmful incidents, the defendant grossly insulted the plaintiff, often in front of their children, and threatened to kill her. She was often forced to leave home and even sleep in a garbage can. The defendant's behaviour made the plaintiff feel like an animal; she was humiliated and she could not defend herself but endured the blows. She was ashamed of what was happening in the family. She was often bruised and could not go to work for a month due to an injury to her nose. Even today, she feels humiliated and relives the events. She has lost her sense of security, self-respect, self-confidence and feels worthless. She lives in isolation, is distrustful of people and avoids contact. The consequences of the violence have left her with a depressive disorder. The plaintiff suffered several physical injuries, namely in the event of 2004, a fracture of the nasal bone, abrasions on the root of the nose and bruising of both eyelids of the left eye; in the event of 2005, several blows and bruises on the ribs and legs; in the event of 2012, an impact to the left shoulder and in the event of 2014, an injury to the scalp, face, a bite on the right upper arm and a blow to the hand. The Supreme Court agreed with the courts of first and second instance that the plaintiff was entitled to compensation for non-pecuniary damage in the total amount of € 20,000, namely for physical pain in the amount of € 5,000, for fear € 5,000 and for violation of dignity € 10,000.[30]

C. Literature

1. *V Žnidaršič Skubic,* Nekrivdna odškodninska odgovornost: primerno zdravilo za slovensko zdravstvo ali njegova stranpot? [No-fault tort liability: a suitable medicine for Slovenian healthcare or a wrong direction?], Podjetje in delo 6–7 (2023) 949–961

The paper deals with the issue of tort liability in Slovenian healthcare and suggests 35
possible solutions for the future. The author cites the implementation of a no-fault

29 Decision of the Supreme Court II DoR 506/2022, 1 March 2023.

30 Decision of the Supreme Court II DoR 18/2023, 15 March 2023.

compensation system as one of the possible solutions, although he is more in favour of gradual reform in the direction of additions and improvements to the existing fault system, whereby, following the French example, it is also possible to consider adding individual elements of a no-fault compensation scheme. He warns that the patient's rights, their safety and protection and the consideration of the specific characteristics of the Slovenian legal system must be at the forefront of any reform. These specific characteristics of the Slovenian legal system are that there is no effective compensation scheme for patients in Slovenia, that the regulation does not deter bad medical practice, that Slovenian compensation law is expensive and ineffective and that it contributes to the culture of covering up errors. Comprehensive reform therefore requires, in addition to the reform of tort law, a comprehensive reform of professional liability in healthcare, together with the modernisation of the quality and safety system.

2. *A Mohorič Kenda,* Sodno varstvo pravic v zdravstvu: nepremoženjska odškodnina ne pomeni pravičnega zadoščenja [Judicial protection of rights in healthcare: non-pecuniary damages are not just satisfaction], Javna uprava 1–2 (2023) 45–59

36 The article shows the international foundations on the basis of which the countries of the European legal area are obliged to implement judicial protection of rights in healthcare. In this light, it presents the jurisprudence on the assessment of just satisfaction under art 41 of the ECHR. At the same time, it notes that Slovenia does not fully fulfil the positive obligations under art 2 of the ECHR, according to which, it is obliged to establish appropriate mechanisms for the award of just satisfaction. In its internal legal order, it has not established the institution of just satisfaction, but recognises just pecuniary compensation for interferences with personal rights only if the consequences of the interference are physical pain, mental pain or fear.

Albert Ruda

XXVIII. Spain

A. Legislation

1. Exposure to Asbestos

In 2024, the Spanish Parliament amended the statutory regime on the protection of the victims of asbestos,[1] which had created a compensation fund for them.[2] The statutory modification took place through a final provision (no 10) included in the new Employment Act[3] and for which the legislature gives no explanation in the Act's Preamble. 1

At first sight, the changes may appear to be merely cosmetic or of an organisational nature and not to affect the substance of the previous statutory framework. So, for instance, the provision on who is entitled to receive compensation (art 6) is left unchanged. However, the detail of the amendments may provide a hint of the legal rationale behind them. To start with, the original statute stated that the fund as such had no legal personality (art 1.1).[4] This rule has disappeared as a result of the statutory amendment. However, the new statute (art 1) also does not state that the fund has legal personality, so the amendment may seem confusing. This suggests that, in reality, there should never have been a 'compensation fund' as such. In fact, using such terminology was confusing from the start. The victims had already pointed out that the best way to satisfy their needs was through compensation provided by the Social Security System.[5] This may be the reason why the new statute expunges any reference to a 'compensation fund' from the former text. For instance, when referring to the procedure applicable to claims for compensation, it is no longer provided that payments are made 'by the fund' (former art 7) but it is provided that payment is made 'from the account opened in the name of 2

1 Act (*Ley*) 21/2022, of 19 October, *de creación de un fondo de compensación para las víctimas del amianto* (Boletin Oficial del Estado [BOE] 252, 20.10.2022).

2 See *A Ruda*, Spain, in: E Karner/BC Steininger (eds), European Tort Law (ETL) 2022 (2023) 613, no 5.

3 Act 3/2023, of 28 February, *de Empleo* (BOE no 51, 1.3.2023).

4 On legal persons in general, now see *J Alfaro Águila-Real*, La persona jurídica (2023).

5 See *Deia*, José Luis Escrivá asegura que el fondo del amianto estará en funcionamiento en junio, 8 March 2023, <https://www.deia.eus/economia/2023/03/08/jose-luis-escriva-asegura-fondo-6538626.html>.

https://doi.org/10.1515/9783111376721-029

the Social Security General Treasury where the funds are held' (new art 7). In a similar vein, the original statutory drafting provided (former art 2) that: 'The compensation fund for asbestos victims shall be responsible for the full compensation of damage' resulting from exposure to asbestos. However, the amended provision (art 2) now states: 'The compensation for asbestos victims is intended to provide full compensation for damage' … . It may be suggested, then, that the reason why these and several other new statutory rules omit any reference to the fund as such is because the statute wants to avoid giving the impression that there is an autonomous compensation fund providing relief to the victim, instead of the Social Security System doing so according to a special procedure laid down in the statute. This may also explain why, as to the financial resources of the scheme, the previous statute established that the scheme would be financed, among others, by the 'income or products of the fund itself' (art 4.d), but such rule has disappeared from the new statutory framework.

3 In accordance with the previous amendment, the Monitoring Committee which was created pursuant to the Act in 2022 as an organ providing advice to the fund and which was attached to the National Institute for Safety and Health at Work has now been attached to the State Secretariat for Social Security and Pensions instead (art 5.1). Moreover, the Committee is no longer to be informed about the manner in which the fund actually operates (former art 5.3) but on the manner in which 'compensation is managed' (new art 5.3). This makes sense since there is no fund as such operating or managing any compensation. Similarly, it is not the fund, but the Social Security System that is subrogated to the actions and rights of the beneficiaries who have been awarded compensation (art 8.3; cf former art 8.4 2nd para).

4 The new statutory (art 8.1) text clarifies that whenever workers exposed to asbestos apply for compensation, they have to provide a report from the so-called PIVISTEA, the Integral Plan of Health Surveillance Plan for workers who are or were exposed to asbestos.[6] The old statutory provision only referred to the initials of this plan, without clarifying what it was. The new provision (art 8.2) retains the deadline for the Social Security System to decide on the application, which is six months. However, the rule that the Social Security System had to make a proposal for a decision on the application within three months (former art 8.3) has disappeared.

6 Such workers are monitored according to a protocol of the Spanish Health Ministry. See *Ministerio de Sanidad,* Protocolo de vigilancia sanitaria específica Amianto (3rd edn 2003) <https://www.sanidad.gob.es/ciudadanos/saludAmbLaboral/docs/ProtoVigiAmianto1.pdf>.

It is quite surprising that such statutory amendments should take place only a few months after the original law was passed. The legislature's erratic behaviour suggests a certain improvisation. Certainly, the fact that compensation is provided by the Social Security System instead of a compensation fund may entail some benefits for the victims, eg from a tax law perspective.[7] However, this change of course is actually detrimental for the victims, as the 'fund' should have been operational since 17 January 2023. The processing of the statutory reform has also meant that the drafting of the governmental regulation that was to develop the previous one has also been delayed. Spanish victims surely deserve better than this. In any case, this statutory reform represents a Spanish singularity with respect to the policy option adopted in other countries such as France, where a separate fund (the *Fonds d'Indemnisation des Victimes de l'Amiante*, FIVA) has been created. 5

2. Whistle-blowers

Another statute which was passed in 2024 is that related to the protection of whistle-blowers in the context of the fight against corruption,[8] through which the EU Directive (EU) 2019/1937 of the European Parliament and of the Council of 23 October 2019 on the protection of persons who report breaches of Union law[9] is transposed into Spanish law. The Act prohibits reprisals against whistle-blowers (art 36.1). The Act considers as a case of reprisal causation of damage to the whistle-blower, including 'damage to reputation, or financial loss, coercion, intimidation, harassment or ostracism' (art 36.3.b), among others. The terminology used by the statute is somewhat strange, as the expression used in the original Spanish version 'daño reputacional' is a mistranslation of the original English one.[10] 6

---

7 Trade unions had criticised the Spanish government for considering victims as 'second class', not least because they would have to pay taxes on compensation. See UGT, El Gobierno ningunea a las víctimas del amianto retrasando la entrada en vigor de su Fondo de Compensación, 4 October 2023, <https://www.ugt.es/el-gobierno-ningunea-las-victimas-del-amianto-retrasando-la-entrada-en-vigor-de-su-fondo-de>.

8 Act 2/2023, of 20 February, *reguladora de la protección de las personas que informen sobre infracciones normativas y de lucha contra la corrupción* (BOE no 44, 21.2.2023).

9 Official Journal of the European Union (OJ) L 305/17.

10 It would have been more correct to speak of 'damage to reputation' (*daño a la reputación*), although the traditional legal concept in Spanish is that of non-pecuniary loss (*daño moral*). However, the Spanish translation of the Directive (art 19.k) uses the right expression in Spanish (*daños a su reputación*). On non-pecuniary damage in general, see *F Gómez Pomar/I Marín García* (eds), El daño moral y su cuantificación (3rd edn 2023).

7 Leaving this aside, it is provided that administrative acts aimed at preventing or hindering the submission of communications and disclosures, as well as those that constitute retaliation or cause discrimination following the submission of communications and disclosures under this Act, shall be void and give rise, where appropriate, to corrective disciplinary or liability measures, which may include the corresponding compensation of damage to the victim (art 36.5).

8 The Act establishes a reversal of the burden of proof that the harm suffered by the victim is retaliation for having reported or publicly communicated a statutory violation (art 38.4). Whistle-blowers will be protected against liability claims in court proceedings (art 38.1), including 'defamation, copyright infringement, breach of secrecy, breach of intellectual property, breach of secrecy, breach of data protection regulations, disclosure of trade secrets, or to claims for compensation based on employment or statutory law' (art 38.5). Such protection is provided on the condition that whistle-blowers had 'reasonable grounds' to believe that the act of information or communication was necessary to bring to light a statutory violation (art 38.5).

3. Prospectus Liability

9 In 2023, the Spanish Parliament passed a new Act on the Securities Markets and Investment Services.[11] As regards liability, the new statute provides that entities responsible for the administration of the recording and registration of securities represented by means of systems based on distributed ledger technologies shall be liable to those who are harmed by the failure to make the corresponding registrations, by inaccuracies and delays in the same and, in general, by the intentional or negligent failure to comply with their statutory obligations. Compensation for damage caused shall, where possible, be made in kind (art 8.6). This is a statutory novelty which refers to the kind of technologies used, among others, in the case of blockchain-based networks. Leaving this aside, as regards the information requirements for admission to trading on a regulated market (art 37), the new statute provides for the liability of certain persons[12] for damage caused to the holders of the

11 Act 6/2023, of 17 March, *de los Mercados de Valores y de los Servicios de Inversión.* (BOE no 66, 18.3.2023).

12 Namely: (a) the guarantor of the transferable securities in relation to the information it is required to provide; (b) the lead manager in respect of the verification work it carries out, and c) any other persons who agree to assume responsibility for the prospectus, provided that this is stated in the same, and any other persons not included among the above who have authorised the contents of the prospectus (art 38.1).

securities acquired as a result of false information or omissions of material information in the prospectus or in the document to be drawn up by the guarantor (art 38.2).

Regarding multilateral trading facilities (*sistemas multilaterales de negociación*, SMN) and organised trading systems (*sistemas organizados de contratación*, SOC), the new statute lays down the duty of the governing bodies of such systems, where appropriate, to provide or ensure that information is publicly available to enable users to form a view on the instruments traded, taking into account both the nature of the instruments traded and the nature of the users (art 69.2). In case damage is caused to the holders of the financial instruments, in accordance with commercial law regulations, because of the information not giving a true and fair view of the issuer, liability may arise. Those liable will be, 'at least', the issuer and the members of its governing body (pursuant to art 71.1). The claim to enforce liability shall be barred three years after the claimant could have become aware of the fact the information does not give a true and fair view of the issuer (art 71.2). The fact that the rule considers for the start of the prescription period not only the fact that the victim knows, but could reasonably have known, is in accordance with other rules of Spanish law on prescription.[13] The new statute also provides for prospectus liability of securities issues in general (art 104.2) and the prescription period is the same (art 104.3). 10

4. Animals

In 2023 a new statutory regime on the protection of the 'rights and welfare of animals' was passed.[14] Its Preamble points out that the statute 'does not regulate animals as just another element in our economic activity to which conditions are owed because of their ability to feel but regulates our behaviour towards them 11

13 See *M Martín-Casals/A Ruda*, Spain, in: I Gilead/B Askeland (eds), Prescription in Tort Law. Analytical and Comparative Perspectives (2020) 579 ff.

14 Act 7/2023, of 28 March, *de protección de los derechos y el bienestar de los animales* (BOE no 75, 29.3.2023). That Act comes with a new statutory framework of crimes consisting in animal abuse: Organic Act (Ley Orgánica, hereinafter LO) 3/2023, of 28 March, *de modificación de la Ley Orgánica 10/1995, de 23 de noviembre, del Código Penal, en materia de maltrato animal* (BOE no 75, 29.3.2023). On tort liability for acts amounting to a crime, in legal literature, now see *FJ Rodríguez Almirón*, Aspectos jurídico-dogmáticos y jurisprudenciales en torno a la responsabilidad civil ex delicto (2023). On damage caused by animals, *V Magro Servet*, ¿Hace falta un seguro obligatorio individual que asegure la responsabilidad civil por daños causados por perros al margen del seguro de hogar?: (Ante el aseguramiento obligatorio de las responsabilidades por daños y lesiones causados por perros desde el 29 de septiembre), Diario La Ley 10339 (2023) <https://diariolaley.laleynext.es>.

as living beings in our living environment'. The aim of the Law is therefore to increase the level of animal protection and to prevent the large number of animals being abandoned on a regular basis in Spain. To this end, a series of animal rights is provided, namely, the right to 'good treatment, respect, and protection, inherent in and derived from their nature as sentient beings' (art 1.2). Therefore, animals are not considered as just a thing. The new Act is thus a step further in the way that started in 2021, when the Spanish Parliament acknowledged that animals are 'living beings endowed with sentience' (*seres vivos dotados de sensibilidad*).[15] Accordingly, property law rules are applicable to animals inasmuch as they are compatible with the nature of animals and the provisions which protect them (new art 333 bis.2 CC).

12 However, the 2023 Act provides for certain exceptions, in the sense that some kinds of animals are considered to be outside of the scope of application of the same. The first exception consists in animals used in bullfighting shows (art 1.3.a). This may certainly come as no surprise in a country like Spain, but it is a regrettable restriction of the recognition of animals' rights. Once it is accepted that animals as such have rights – and this is quite a step – it is a shame that the legislature keeps providing a legal cover to practices involving animals which are sanguinary and retrograde.[16] To put animal torture disguised as a show above animals' rights reveals a curious hierarchy of values for a statute whose ultimate goal allegedly is 'to achieve the maximum protection of animal rights and animal welfare' (art 2.1).

13 The new statute lays down a set of 'general obligations' with regard to pet animals and wild animals in captivity (art 24), the first one of which is to treat them 'in accordance with their status as sentient beings' (art 24.1). However, the 'person in charge of an animal' (*persona responsable de un animal*) also has some obligations. In particular, that person 'shall also be liable for any damage, harm or disturbance that, without provocation or fault (*negligencia*) on the part of a third party, it may cause to people, other animals or things, public roads and spaces and the natural environment, in accordance with the applicable legislation'

---

15 Art 7 of the Act 17/2021, of 15 December, *de modificación del Código Civil, la Ley Hipotecaria y la Ley de Enjuiciamiento Civil, sobre el régimen jurídico de los animales* (BOE no 300, 16.12.2021), which amended the Spanish Civil Code (new art 333.1 bis). See Royal Decree (Real Decreto, RD) 24 July 1889, *por el que se publica el Código Civil* (Gazette of Madrid no 206, 25.7.1889). For an unofficial translation of the Civil Code (hereinafter, CC) and other main tort law provisions in Spain see *A Ruda*, Spain, in: E Karner/K Oliphant/ BC Steininger (eds), European Tort Law: Basic Texts (2nd edn 2018).

16 Other exceptions are animals for the use of experimentation and animals used for sports or professional purposes (such as rescue dogs, art 3.j), among others.

(art 24.3). This is in line with the general rule of the Spanish Civil Code (art 1905), according to which the possessor (*poseedor*) of an animal is liable for damage caused. There are some differences between the two provisions, since the Spanish Civil Code establishes that liability is excluded in case of force majeure (*fuerza mayor*) in addition to the case of contributory negligence of the victim, and the 2023 Act does not. The liable person is also different in each case: the possessor of the animal or the person who makes use of the animal (art 1905) versus the 'responsible person' in the case of the 2023 Act. The latter is defined as 'any natural or legal person who, without being the owner, is, on a circumstantial or permanent basis, in the care, custody or guardianship of the animal' (art 3.bb). It may be suggested that the 'responsible person' will almost always be a possessor in the technical sense but there may be situations where both concepts do not match entirely. For instance, if someone brings their pet for a check-up to a vet, the possessor will be the first whereas the doctor may be considered to act in the animal's care.

Apart from the above, the new statute provides that dog owners must, for the 14
whole life of the animal, take out and maintain in force civil liability insurance for damage to third parties, which includes in its cover the persons responsible for the animal, for an amount sufficient to cover the possible expenses derived, which shall be established by regulation (art 30.2). In spite of the language of the provision, which refers to 'civil liability insurance for damage to third parties', this seems first-party insurance which covers the 'expenses' (*gastos*) which arise for the dog owner in the case of damage to others. If this interpretation is correct, victims have no direct claim against the insurer, unlike what happens in the case of third-party insurance (pursuant to art 76 of the Insurance Contract Act).[17] It may be submitted, however, that this is probably not what the legislature intended and that such direct claim should be available.[18]

Finally, the 2023 Act establishes an extensive catalogue of sanctions for non- 15
compliance with its provisions. However, accountability for these infringements is compatible with tort liability (art 79.1). Furthermore, it is established that the liability of a plurality of tortfeasors is solidary (art 79.2). In spite of the restrictive stance of the Civil Code (art 1137), solidarity has actually become the rule when special laws regulate the liability of multiple tortfeasors.

---

17 Act 50/1980, of 8 October, *de Contrato de Seguro* (BOE no 250, 17.10.1980).

18 On the contract of insurance generally, see *AB Veiga Copo*, Tratado del contrato de seguro, vol II (2023).

5. LGTBI Persons

16 The Spanish Parliament also improved the legal protection of LGTBI people through a new statute.[19] Although it does not establish specific rules on tort law, it does contain some provisions that may have an impact on the same. For instance, the Act establishes that trans and LGTBI persons who allege discrimination on the basis of sex or gender and provide 'well-founded indicia' (*indicios fundados*) of such discrimination will enjoy a reversal of the burden of proof in administrative proceedings (art 66.1).

17 Moreover, without prejudice to the individual standing of the persons concerned, political parties, trade unions, employers' organisations, trade union organisations, professional associations of self-employed persons, associations of consumers and users, and legally constituted associations and organisations whose aims include the defence and promotion of LGTBI people or their families, will have legal standing to defend the rights and interests of affiliated or associated persons in civil, administrative, or work-related legal proceedings, provided that they have express authorisation, and to sue in court for the defence of diffuse interests when the affected persons are an indeterminate or difficult to determine plurality (art 65). It seems that such legal standing, combined with the reversal of the burden of proof mentioned above, could facilitate claims for compensation for damage caused by discrimination.[20]

6. Nuclear Liability

18 The previously existing special statutory regime on nuclear liability was amended in 2023.[21] The new Act's Preamble does not provide any background for the amend-

19 Act 4/2023, of 28 February, *para la igualdad real y efectiva de las personas trans y para la garantía de los derechos de las personas LGTBI* (BOE no 51, 1.3.2023).

20 Causing damage or tarnishing movable or immovable property belonging to LGTBI persons or their families because of their sexual orientation and identity, or intended for the protection of the rights of LGTBI persons, including monuments or commemorative plaques, amounts to an administrative violation for which fines may be imposed (art 79).

21 Act 11/2023, of 8 May, *de trasposición de Directivas de la Unión Europea en materia de accesibilidad de determinados productos y servicios, migración de personas altamente cualificadas, tributaria y digitalización de actuaciones notariales y registrales; y por la que se modifica la Ley 12/2011, de 27 de mayo, sobre responsabilidad civil por daños nucleares o producidos por materiales radiactivos* (BOE no 110, 9.5.2023).

ment except for the fact that it was necessary to adapt domestic legislation[22] to international conventions signed by Spain. It is now provided that Title I ('Tort liability for nuclear damage') of the Nuclear Liability Act applies to nuclear damage as defined in art 3(1)(h) of the same, occurring in the territory of; or in the maritime zone established under international law belonging to; or, except for those States not party to the Paris Convention which do not meet the requirements of subparagraphs (b), (c) and (d) of this Article, on board a ship or aircraft registered by one of the States provided for in the Act (art 2.1). Therefore, the provision no longer mentions the requirement that damage is caused 'during storage, handling, processing, use in any form or transportation'.

The new Act also adds a definition of 'nuclear facilities' (*instalaciones nucleares*) (art 3.2.b) bis) with regard to 'accidents' where damage is caused by radioactive material which is not a nuclear substance. The same expression was already defined with regard to 'nuclear accidents' (art 3.1.b) so the new definition merely refers to the previously existing one. From the point of view of legal drafting, it would have probably been better to include just one definition which would be applicable to both kinds of accidents, but this would have required to rethink the structure of the Act again and the legislature just opted for the easy way. **19**

The remaining amendments are of a nature similar to the ones explained above in the sense that they are micro-adjustments carried out to align the domestic Act with the international conventions on the topic. Thus, changes affect the definition of the operator of a nuclear facility (art 4.1), transportation of nuclear substances (art 7.2 and 10), payment of compensation awards (art 11.1, 11.2 and 11.d), liability of the operators of radioactive facilities (arts 16 and 18), damage which is not compensable (art 17.1), liability of multiple operators or shippers (art 20), the right to claim in contribution (art 22), and liability for environmental damage (art 23).[23] **20**

Interestingly enough, in the case of claims for nuclear damage, it is now provided that the Nuclear Safety Council (*Consejo de Seguridad Nuclear*) will issue a technical report at the request of the court and such report will be binding (*preceptivo*) for the court. Moreover, the court itself is bound to request such a report (new art 14.1). This may seem a departure from the general rules on the civil court procedure, where it is up to the parties to bring evidence to the court according to the so-called adversarial principle (*principio dispositivo*). The Spanish judge usually **21**

---

22 In particular, the Act 12/2011, of 27 May, *sobre responsabilidad civil por daños nucleares o producidos por materiales radiactivos* (BOE no 127, 28.5.2011).

23 In legal scholarship, see *J M Beltrán Castellanos,* El concepto de daño medioambiental, in: G García-Álvarez García et al (eds), Observatorio de políticas ambientales (2023) 381–399 <https://www.boe.es/biblioteca_juridica/anuarios_derecho/abrir_pdf.php?id=ANU-O-2023-10038300402>.

assesses technical opinions according to the so-called 'rules of sound judgment' (*reglas de la sana crítica*) (art 348). However, the Council is a public entity; therefore, the law recognises a higher force to the reports issued by the same. According to procedural law, documents issued by public agencies and departments are considered 'public documents' (art 317 of the Act of Civil Procedure)[24] and are awarded a full 'evidentiary effect' (*fuerza probatoria*) (art 319.1 LEC).

7. Other Provisions

22 In 2023, the Spanish Parliament passed the statutory regime governing development cooperation.[25] The new Act provides that the General Public Administration and the Spanish Cooperation Offices have a duty of care (*deber de cuidado*) as regards all persons working in Spanish cooperation (art 46.1). Such duty of care includes obligations of information, protection, and consular assistance and, where appropriate, the assistance and the adoption of recommendations and other supportive measures that will contribute to the safety of such personnel in the field, in particular for those personnel engaged in humanitarian action (art 46.2).

23 One long-awaited legal reform is that of the right to housing (*derecho a la vivienda*). The Spanish Constitution[26] (art 47) enshrined such a right in 1978 but it had remained underdeveloped at the statutory level until last year. The new statute[27] deals, among many other topics, with the regulation of property managers (*administradores de fincas*). They are defined as the 'natural persons who are engaged on a regular and gainful basis in the provision of administration and consultancy services to owners of real estate and to homeowners' associations' (Additional Provision [*Disposición Adicional*, DA][28] no 6.1 of the Act). According to the same Act, they have a duty to behave in a careful manner (DA 6.3). Moreover, the Act provides the obligation of such professionals to have a tort liability insurance policy, which they may agree upon on an individual or collective basis (DA 6.4). However,

---

24 Act 1/2000, of 7 January, *de Enjuiciamiento Civil* (BOE no 7, 8.1.2000) (hereinafter LEC).

25 Act 1/2023, of 20 February, *de Cooperación para el Desarrollo Sostenible y la Solidaridad Global* (BOE no 44, 21.2.2023).

26 Constitución Española (BOE no 311, 29.12.1978) (hereinafter, CE). English translation by the Spanish Official Gazette available at <https://www.boe.es/legislacion/documentos/ConstitucionINGLES.pdf>.

27 Act 12/2023, of 24 May, *por el derecho a la vivienda* (BOE no 124, 25.5.2023). On this Act, generally, see *C Argelich Comelles*, Ley por el derecho a la vivienda (2nd edn 2023).

28 Additional Dispositions are just one type of the provisions which are usually found in the final part of statutes in Spain. It is not always clear why they are not simply included in the main body of the statute in the form of normal provisions (*artículos*).

the aim of such an insurance policy is to 'guarantee the rights of consumers' only (pursuant to the same DA 6.4). Since, pursuant to the Consumers Act,[29] consumers are 'natural persons who are acting for purposes which are outside their trade, business, craft or profession' (art 3.1) and 'legal persons and unincorporated entities acting on a non-profit basis outside a trade or business' (art 3.2), such policy insurance may not cover damage caused to professionals and entrepreneurs.

In 2023, a new statutory framework on universities was passed by the Spanish **24** Parliament.[30] The Act includes an Additional Disposition (DA 16) on the 'Principle of no significant harm'. According to the same, and in line with EU legislation, all actions to be carried out in compliance with this Act must observe the principle of no significant harm to the environment.

Moreover, in 2023, the Spanish legislature amended the statutory framework **25** of sexual life and reproductive life of women and the voluntary termination of pregnancy.[31] The new Act reverts some policy decisions adopted by the former, conservative, Government[32] and aims at expanding and better protecting mostly women's rights. In particular, it protects the right to terminate a pregnancy in the terms laid down in the Act (new art 24) as well as the right and autonomy of a woman to take decisions on her reproductive health (new art 27.a), bearing in mind that persons with disabilities may require some support to that end (DA 1). Surrogacy or surrogate pregnancy are explicitly forbidden (new art 32). In the case of advertising which violates the statutory provisions, eg because it depicts women in a humiliating manner, and is therefore deemed illegal, several persons – such as the Public Prosecutor of the Government's Delegate for Gender Violence – are acknowledged legal standing to sue according to the provisions of the Act on Unfair Competition[33] (art 32.1–4). Accordingly, they may request the cessation of the advertising, among other measures. However, they are not entitled to claim compensation for damage (art 32.5).

---

29 Royal Statutory Decree (Real Decreto Legislativo, RDleg) 1/2007, of 16 November, *por el que se aprueba el texto refundido de la Ley General para la Defensa de los Consumidores y Usuarios y otras leyes complementarias* (BOE no 287, 30.11.2007).

30 LO 2/2023, of 22 March, *del Sistema Universitario* (BOE no 70, 23.3.2023).

31 LO 1/2023, of 28 February, *por la que se modifica la Ley Orgánica 2/2010, de 3 de marzo, de salud sexual y reproductiva y de la interrupción voluntaria del embarazo* (BOE no 51, 1.3.2023). Shortly after that, the LO 4/2023, of 27 April, *para la modificación de la Ley Orgánica 10/1995, de 23 de noviembre, del Código Penal, en los delitos contra la libertad sexual, la Ley de Enjuiciamiento Criminal y la Ley Orgánica 5/2000, de 12 de enero, reguladora de la responsabilidad penal de los menores* (BOE no 101, 28.4.2023) was also passed, to address further criminal law aspects of the same reform.

32 The LO 2/2010, of 3 March, *de salud sexual y reproductiva y de la interrupción voluntaria del embarazo* (BOE no 55, 4.3.2010) is accordingly amended.

33 Act 3/1991, of 10 January, *de Competencia Desleal* (BOE no 10, 11.1.1991).

26 Finally, the Spanish Government passed a regulation on the Supervisory Agency on Artificial Intelligence.[34] Surprisingly, it did not wait until the EU passed its new Regulation on AI.[35]

B. Cases

1. Sentencia del Tribunal Supremo (Supreme Court Decision, STS) Civil Chamber, 217/2023, 13 February 2023, ROJ STS 350/2023,[36] ECLI:ES:TS:2023:350: Nudism

a) Brief Summary of the Facts

27 The majority of members in a residential area decided to establish some restrictions to access certain common areas of the same, namely the garden and the swimming pool. According to the statutes allegedly approved by the owners' council (*junta de propietarios*), access and use of those areas was possible provided that the members were naked only. Eight co-owners who disagreed filed a claim against the council on the basis of a violation of their fundamental rights and requested compensation for damage suffered.

b) Judgment of the Court

28 It is not possible to arbitrarily, by acts of force, by contracting private security services, prevent the claimants from enjoying the rights to which they are entitled under the condominium (*propiedad horizontal*) regime over common elements if they do not practise nudism, which is a perfectly respectable and legitimate per-

34 RD 729/2023, of 22 August, *por el que se aprueba el Estatuto de la Agencia Española de Supervisión de Inteligencia Artificial* (BOE no 210, 2.9.2023).
35 On the legal aspects of AI, see, among others, *L Rebollo Delgado*, Inteligencia artificial y derechos fundamentales (2023); *I Beltrán de Heredia Ruiz*, Inteligencia artificial y neuroderechos: la protección del yo inconsciente de la persona (2023), and *M Jorqui Azofra*, Responsabilidad por los daños causados por productos y sistemas de inteligencia artificial (2023). See also *A Zornoza Somolinos*, Vehículos automatizados y seguro obligatorio de automóviles: estudio de derecho comparado (2021).
36 ROJ stands for the register number for the search of court decisions in the database of the Center of Judicial Documents (Centro de Documentación Judicial, CENDOJ) <https://www.poderjudicial.es/search/indexAN.jsp>.

sonal choice, but whose practice cannot be demanded without any basis for the same. Therefore, such a decision would have required a unanimous agreement of the co-owners, which did not exist.

c) Commentary

The co-owners in a residential housing established the obligation for the members 29 of the same to be naked to access certain common areas. The Supreme Court concludes that the nudist majority has violated fundamental rights of the minority which is against nudism.[37] The decision does not exclude that co-owners may establish being naked as a requirement to access common areas, but it has to be a unanimous decision.[38] In the case at stake, the defendants failed to produce evidence that even a majority decision had been reached. As regards compensation, the court states that it is 'evident' that non-pecuniary damage has been caused to the claimants. Therefore, a compensation award of € 1,000 to each of the claimants is deemed to be adequate in the circumstances.

2. STS Civil Chamber, 1516/2023, 2 November 2023, ROJ STS 4609/2023, ECLI:ES:TS:2023:4609: Product Liability

a) Brief Summary of the Facts

In 2015, the owner of a bar business suffered the loss of an eye as a result of an 30 exploding beer bottle when he was handling a plastic crate that had just been supplied to him at the premises in question. He sued the manufacturer (Damm, SA) and its insurer (AIG Europe Ltd). The manufacturer argued in its defence that it was not at fault, that the accident was possibly the victim's fault, and that the product had passed all quality controls.

---

37 On the liability of companies for human rights violations generally, see *N Magallón Elósegui*, La ley aplicable a la responsabilidad civil extracontractual de empresas por abusos de los derechos humanos (2023).

38 See *AJ Martín Martín*, Nudistas a la fuerza, 102 Revista Registradores 2023 <https://revistaregistradores.es/nudistas-a-la-fuerza>.

b) Judgment of the Court

31 The Court of First Instance dismissed the claim because it considered that the special product liability rules, which are objective in nature, only apply to consumers. With regard to the general rule of liability for fault (art 1902 CC), it also dismissed the claim because the plaintiff did not prove the negligence of the manufacturer. According to the hospital report, the explosion occurred when the plaintiff was washing bottles; according to the manufacturer's expert, the explosion could only have been caused by a fall or an impact of the bottle. The witness evidence was dismissed as inconclusive. However, the Court of Appeal gave more weight to that witness evidence, consisting of the testimony of a customer who was eating with the victim at the time when the transporter arrived with the crate of beer. On that basis, the Court of Appeal concludes that the bottle exploded spontaneously, and that this can only be due to the fact that it did not offer the safety that could legitimately be expected. It therefore concluded that the bottle was defective, overturned the lower judgment and found the defendants jointly and severally liable.

32 In the cassation appeal to the Supreme Court, the defendant highlighted the contradiction between the witness evidence and the hospital report. However, the victim had already pointed out that he never said that he was washing the bottles. Moreover, according to the Court, it does not make sense that the victim got up in the middle of the meal to wash the bottles. Besides, a bottle would not have to explode even if it was being washed.

33 As regards the applicability of the rules on defective products to non-consumers, the Consumers Act 2007[39] is the transposition of EC Directive 374/1985.[40] That Directive does not define a consumer, nor does it require that the victim of the damage be considered a consumer. The scope of application of the transposition law is defined according to the type of damage, but does not exclude victims who suffer damage in the course of their business or professional activity. Therefore, consumers, professionals, workers, employers or other third parties who are not consumers are protected. It is true that the aforementioned Law defines the consumer, but it makes it clear that this definition is without prejudice to the provisions of Book III of the same Law, which is where product liability is regulated, and there is no reference to consumers.

---

39 See fn 29 above.

40 Council Directive 85/374/EEC of 25 July 1985 on the approximation of the laws, regulations and administrative provisions of the Member States concerning liability for defective products [1985] OJ L 210/29.

c) Commentary

The Spanish Supreme Court declares that the strict liability regime laid down in the Consumer Act 2007 is applicable to personal injury suffered by a professional as a result of a beer bottle explosion, even though he was not a consumer in the statutory sense. It is true that the legal regime on product liability is included in a 'Consolidated text' (*texto refundido*) on consumers and users. Moreover, there is no book or treatise on consumer law in Spain that does not include at least one chapter on product liability.[41] However, the defendants' theory, which sought to exclude liability on the grounds that the victim was not a consumer, is based on a flawed reading of the legal text. It is the clumsiness of the Spanish legislator that gives rise to that misinterpretation, since the regulation on defective products, by not requiring the victim to be a consumer, does not, properly speaking, form part of consumer law, and therefore should not have been included in the aforementioned consolidated text. 34

3. STS Civil Chamber, 3458/2023, 21 July 2023, ROJ STS 3538/2023, ECLI:ES:TS:2023:3538: Thalidomide

a) Brief Summary of the Facts

An Association of Victims of Thalidomide (*Asociación AVITE Víctimas de la Talidomida*) sued Grünenthal GmBH and its Spanish subsidiary, Grünenthal Pharma SA, in order to be ordered to compensate three victims with various amounts of money, as well as to pay them benefits equivalent to those received by pensioners in Germany from the Contergan Stiftung. The victims suffered damage as a result of exposure to thalidomide *in utero*. They argued that the defendant companies knew that other Spanish companies were manufacturing medicines with the same active ingredient as thalidomide and thus infringing their patents, but did nothing to prevent it. As a result, the victims did not know against whom they had to file their claims in tort. 35

41 In legal scholarship now, see *M R Martínez Pérez*, La responsabilidad del fabricante por daños causados por un producto médico implantable defectuoso: contexto de la regulación europea, in: E Muñoz/JC Bórquez Castillo/LG Delgado Páez (eds), Desarrollos recientes en el Derecho de daños (2023) 191–225. On consumer law generally, see *C Lasarte/Á Juárez Torrejón*, Manual sobre protección de consumidores y usuarios (2023); *Á Carrasco Perera* (ed), Derecho de consumo: materiales, fundamentos, aplicaciones (2023) and *P Pajín Echevarría* (ed), GPS Consumo (2023).

b) Judgment of the Court

36 The Madrid Court of First Instance partially upheld the claim, rejecting the defendants' argument that the claim was time-barred. The Spanish company (only) appealed the judgment on appeal. The Madrid Provincial Court held that the claim was time-barred because the effects of exposure to thalidomide had been known since 1962. The fact that the Spanish government approved a regulation[42] in 2010 to recognise the right of victims to obtain various public aid did not interrupt the statute of limitations, as these are social measures, which are irrelevant for the purposes of the civil statute of limitations. The claimant association argued that this was 'late damage' (*daños tardíos*) and therefore the statute of limitations did not apply, but the court found that this damage had not been proven. In a previous case,[43] the Spanish Supreme Court had already rejected a similar action, on the basis of the statute of limitations. The claimants were different in the case under discussion.

37 From a strictly theoretical point of view, there are two models for determining the initial day of calculation of the limitation period which, for reasons of legal certainty, prohibits the exercise of legal actions after a certain period of time has elapsed. The objective model identifies the initial day of the limitation period with the birth of the claim without paying attention to the subjective circumstances of the person of the claimant; whereas the subjective model expressly contemplates them insofar as it requires weighing up the knowledge or, better said, the reasonable possibility of the injured party knowing the conditioning elements of the birth of their tortfeasor's claim. As the object of the proceedings is an action for tortious fault of art 1902 CC, art 1968.2 CC is applicable which, inspired by a subjective criterion, states that actions for compensation for damage of this nature are subject to a limitation period of one year, the calculation of which will begin 'from the time the injured party knew of the damage' (*desde que lo supo el agraviado*). Therefore, in order for the legal time limit to start running, the victim has to know not only the harmful consequences of the unlawful act, but also the identity of the perpetrator, among other aspects. However, a criterion of potential knowledge (cognizability) applies, according to which the computation of the limitation period begins when the claimant should have acquired this knowledge. This implies acting with the required care which, in certain cases, even requires the

42 RD 1006/2010, of 5 August, *por el que se regula el procedimiento de concesión de ayudas a las personas afectadas por la talidomida en España durante el periodo 1960–1965* (BOE no 190, 6.8. 2010).

43 STS Civil Chamber, 544/2015, 20 October 2015, ECLI:ES:TS:2015:4149. See *A Ruda*, Spain, in: E Karner/BC Steininger (eds), European Tort Law (ETL) 2015 (2016) 600, no 39.

consultation of an expert, and also weighing up the debtor's conduct aimed at concealing his identity.

However, in this particular case, this doctrine cannot be invoked, as the plaintiffs took more than 50 years to file the lawsuit since the identity of the tortfeasor became known. In fact, in the claim that gave rise to the aforementioned Supreme Court decision, the claimants did not allege an impossibility of identifying the perpetrator, but rather the doctrine of continuous damage. In 2011, the plaintiff even initiated a negotiation process with Grünenthal to obtain some compensation, which shows that it was not unaware of that identity. Moreover, given the horrific effects of thalidomide, the applicant cannot claim ignorance. Finally, the patent in favour of Grünenthal was on the public record, so that it cannot claim ignorance either, given that the applicant is an association that provides legal advice and was formed in 2003 to defend the victims. 38

c) Commentary

The case is a follow up of a previous one on damage caused by the drug thalidomide. As in the previous case,[44] the discussion revolves on the issue of prescription. Once again, the Spanish Supreme Court closes the door to victims' compensation in considering that the action is time-barred. The Court does not apply either an objective test or a subjective test, but an intermediate one, according to which time starts to run whenever the victim could have known about the identity of the liable persons. In the case at stake, it is obvious that the claimant knew who the tortfeasor was, and therefore there is no doubt that the prescription period had expired, so liability is excluded. 39

In this regard, the fact that the Spanish Government passed a regulatory framework on the procedure for the recognition of public aid to the victims of thalidomide did not have any impact on the application of the statute of limitations.[45] 40

44 See previous fn.

45 RD 574/2023, de 4 de julio, *por el que se regula el procedimiento de concesión de ayudas a las personas afectadas por la talidomida en España durante el período 1950–1985* (BOE no 159, 5.6.2023). According to its Preamble, the regulation 'aims to respond to the need for recognition and solidarity support for people affected by the active substance "thalidomide" during the period 1950–1985, according to the different personal situations of each of them'. The amounts of aid granted range from € 30,000 to € 100,000. It can be considered a follow-up of the previous RD 1006/2010, of 5 August, *por el que se regula el procedimiento de concesión de ayudas a las personas afectadas por la talidomida en España durante el período 1960–1965* (BOE no 190, 6.8.2010).

41 Already in 2015, part of the doctrine affirmed that the Supreme Court decision issued in that year was impeccable from a technical point of view.[46] The same could now be said with respect to this other ruling. The victims certainly deserve support and are in a terrible situation, but it is worth suggesting that bringing claims when the Supreme Court has already said that the claim is time-barred only adds unnecessary suffering to them. It may seem cruel, but the Spanish Supreme Court may be sending AVITE a strong message by sentencing the same to pay the entire costs of the appeal proceedings, instead of dividing them between the two parties, as is generally the rule in civil proceedings when the factual or legal issue at stake is deemed dubious (pursuant to arts 398 and 394.1 LEC).

4. STS Civil Chamber, 924/2023, 12 June 2023, ROJ STS 2472/2023, ECLI:ES:TS:2023:2472: Truck Cartel

a) Brief Summary of the Facts

42 In 2023, the Spanish Supreme Court for the first time decided on the issue of liability for damage caused by the so-called truck cartel. The claimant had bought a truck at an alleged overprice of approximately 20 %. When he discovered the overprice, he sued Fiat Chrysler Automobiles NV and another company, CNH Industrial NV, as manufacturers. The claimant submitted an expert report to prove damage. However, a judge in Valencia considered the same inconclusive. Certainly, the report contained statistical data related to the cartel at stake but it was insufficient to establish damage in the particular case. In spite of the lack of evidence, since there was not any other report available, the court found for the claimant. As to the assessment of damage, it considered that damage could be estimated on a discretionary basis at 5 % of the sales price (ie € 1,835). Both the claimant and defendants challenged that decision on appeal. The Court of Appeal of Valencia found for the claimant and awarded him the legal interest in addition to the sum already awarded by the lower court. The defendants challenged that second decision on cassation before the Supreme Court.

46 See *M Yzquierdo Tolsada*, Comentario de la Sentencia del Tribunal Supremo de 20 de octubre de 2015 (4149/2015), in: M Yzquierdo Tolsada (ed), Comentarios a las Sentencias de unificación de doctrina (civil y mercantil) vol 7 (2015) 651–664, at 655.

b) Judgment of the Court

The existence of a truck cartel was beyond any doubt. The European Commission 43
had concluded through a decision already in 2016[47] that most truck manufacturers (15 in total) had agreed on price increases. Although the defendants argued in their favour that truck manufacturers had merely 'exchanged information' – as if that was not enough to hold them accountable for an antitrust violation – the EC decision was clear in that regard: prices had indeed been raised. In addition to that, the Damages Directive from 2014[48] provides a legal basis for such type of claim. As it happens, the Directive is not applicable to the case since the facts happened before the same entered into force, but the solution would have been the same should the Directive have been applicable.

It poses no problem that the claimant had failed to prove damage. The defend- 44
ant had argued in this regard that, since the claimant's expert report had been rejected, the Court was not allowed to conclude that there had been any damage at all. Otherwise, the Court would be behaving arbitrarily. However, the Spanish Supreme Court rejects that line of reasoning. The claimant had actually done its best to establish damage; what happened was only that the proof provided was deemed not sufficient. Nevertheless, given that a decision of the European Commission had established the cartel, damage could be deemed to have been proven by presumptions. Proof by presumptions is provided for on a general basis in Spanish procedural law (art 386 LEC). The case at stake did not revolve on a burden of proof issue, the Court adds: such burden lies undoubtedly on the claimant. But he seems to have done everything he could, given the circumstances. Therefore, it is concluded that damage has indeed been established, and that the damages award can be assessed on a discretionary basis as the lower courts had done.

47 *European Commission* (EC), Settlement Decision of 19.07.2016 (AT.39824), available at <https://competition-cases.ec.europa.eu/cases/AT.39824>.

48 Directive 2014/104/EU of the European Parliament and of the Council of 26 November 2014 on certain rules governing actions for damages under national law for infringements of the competition law provisions of the Member States and of the European Union [2014] OJ L 349/1 <https://eur-lex.europa.eu/legal-content/EN/TXT/PDF/?uri=CELEX:32014 L0104>.

c) Commentary

45 In 2023, there was a series of Spanish Supreme Court decisions dealing with the so-called 'truck cartel' (*cártel de camiones*).[49] Several truck producers agreed to artificially increase the sales price of their trucks, thereby causing damage to consumers. The cases revolve on the proof of the price increase.[50] The Supreme Court has decided that it can be established based on a judicial presumption on the ground of the circumstances in which the cartel operated. As to an assessment of the damage, it is decided that if damage is extremely difficult or even impossible to establish, the court may assess the same because of its discretionary powers, provided that the claimant has effectively attempted to prove the same in an adequate manner.

46 When establishing the compensation award, the defendant must pay compensation plus the legal interest (*interés legal*). The issue is whether such interest starts to accrue from the moment when the claim was filed or when the judicial decision is finally issued. The Court decides that the right solution is the first one, since interest accrues because of damage caused, and not because the defendant is in a situation of delayed payment (*mora debitoris*).

47 As to the prescription period, it is five years (pursuant to art 74.1 of the Antitrust Act).[51] Such prescription period was laid down as a result of a statutory re-

---

49 STS 923/2023, 12 June 2023 (ROJ STS 2492/2023, ECLI:ES:TS:2023:2492); 925/2023, 12 June 2023 (ROJ STS 2495/2023, ECLI:ES:TS:2023:2495); 927/2023, 12 June 2023 (ROJ STS 2475/2023, ECLI:ES:TS:2023:2475); 926/2023, 12 June 2023 (ROJ STS 2473/2023, ECLI:ES:TS:2023:2473); 928/2023, 12 June 2023 (ROJ STS 2474/2023, ECLI:ES:TS:2023:2474); 940/2023, 13 June 2023 (ROJ STS 2477/2023, ECLI:ES:TS:2023:2477); 941/2023, 13 June 2023 (ROJ STS 2497/2023, ECLI:ES:TS:2023:2497); 942/2023, 13 June 2023 (ROJ STS 2478/2023, ECLI:ES:TS:2023:2478); 948/2023, 14 June 2023 (ROJ STS 2493/2023, ECLI:ES:TS:2023:2493); 946/2024, 14 June 2023 (ROJ STS 2479/2023, ECLI:ES:TS:2023:2479); 947/2023, 14 June 2023 (ROJ STS 2480/2023, ECLI:ES:TS:2023:2480); 950/2023, 14 June 2023 (ROJ STS 2496/2023, ECLI:ES:TS:2023:2496), and 949/2023, 14 June 2023 (ROJ STS 2494/2023, ECLI:ES:TS:2023:2494). In legal scholarship see *JI Ruiz Peris/C Rodilla Martí*, Formación intensiva en acciones de daños por infracción de las normas de defensa de la competencia (2023) and *FJ Orduña Moreno* (ed), Derecho de consumo y correcto funcionamiento de los mercados (2023).

50 On access to information in this context, see *A Guerra Fernández/E Sevilla Soto*, Posición de los juzgados españoles en relación con las medidas de acceso a fuentes de prueba previstas en la Ley de enjuiciamiento civil para reclamaciones de daños derivadas de infracciones de las normas de defensa de la competencia, Anuario de derecho de la competencia (2023) 167–177. Also see *N Noms Heredia*, Estimación judicial del daño y costas procesales en litigios "antitrust": Sentencia del Tribunal de Justicia 2ª 16 de febrero de 2023, as. C-312/2021: Tráficos Manuel Ferrer, S.L., D. Ignacio y Daimler, AG, La Ley Unión Europea 117 (2023) <https://diariolaley.laleynext.es>.

51 Act 15/2007, of 3 July, *de Defensa de la Competencia* (BOE no 159, 4.7.2007) (hereinafter, LDC). In legal scholarship, see *S García López/JA Pérez García*, El Supremo y los primeros recursos del "car-

form in 2017,[52] through which the aforementioned EU Damages Directive was transposed. The previous statutory text did not establish any prescription period.[53] Transposition by EU Member States should have taken place before 27 December 2016 (pursuant to art 21.1 of the Directive), so the Spanish transposition was late. The Spanish Supreme Court has decided that the five-year prescription period can be applied on a retroactive basis provided that the claim was not yet time-barred when the transposition deadline elapsed. Moreover, as the Court of Justice of the European Union (CJEU) has pointed out,[54] the claimant lacks necessary information to decide whether to file a claim at the moment in which the EU Commission punishes the cartel members. It is only when the press release including all the details of such a decision is published that the claimants can be deemed to possess all the information they need and thus the prescription period starts running.

The Supreme Court takes into account that, lacking a specific prescription pe- 48
riod, the general one was applicable, but this was rather short: only one year (pursuant to art 1968.2). In such a brief time period, it is rather difficult for the claimant to gather all the evidence needed to prove damage in a case like this. The brevity of the prescription period is taken by the court as an element that allows proof by presumptions to be applied. This is interesting, since as a result of the transposition of the EU Directive (new art 74.1 LDC), the prescription period is currently much longer, as has been said. Therefore, it remains to be seen whether courts will be equally sensible with the claimant in the future when the Directive becomes applicable. It may be open to question whether having four more years to file a claim in a case like this really makes a difference.

The decision under comment is also relevant since, according to the Directive 49
and the Spanish Transposition Act, the national courts should have the power to estimate damage (arts 12.5 and 17.1 of the Directive) and damage may be presumed (art 17.2 of the Directive, art 76.3 LDC). This is remarkable since in many other settings the lack of evidence of damage would have led to the claim being dismissed by a Spanish court.[55] In a sense, it could be said that the decision under comment

tel de camiones": la prescripción de la acción y el alcance del daño, Diario La Ley 10330 (2023) <https://diariolaley.laleynext.es>.

52 Art 3.2 of the Royal Decree-Act (Real Decreto-ley) 9/2017, of 26 May, *por el que se transponen directivas de la Unión Europea en los ámbitos financiero, mercantil y sanitario, y sobre el desplazamiento de trabajadores* (BOE no 126, 27.5.2017).

53 The only one established referred to prescription of administrative violations (former art 68).

54 CJEU 22.6.2022, C-267/20, *AB Volvo and DAF Trucks NV v RM*, ECLI:EU:C:2022:494.

55 Similarly see *GA Martín Martín*, Cuantificando daños por ilícitos antitrust, ¿quo vadimus? Cuadernos de derecho transnacional (2022) 14(1) 387–404 <https://e-revistas.uc3m.es/index.php/CDT/article/view/6690>, at 390.

applies the Directive *avant la lettre*. This may remind us of Molière's 'bourgeois gentleman' – who had always been speaking in prose without knowing it. If the Court is right, then some of the Directive's provisions actually add very little to Spanish law. At any rate, this decision may turn out to be important in other scenarios where damage may also be difficult to prove.

50 Apart from the previous, the Supreme Court very subtly criticises the lower courts for having applied the doctrine of *res ipsa loquitur*. This doctrine is used by Spanish courts to facilitate proof, whenever it can be said that the facts 'speak for themselves'. Similar doctrines do exist in other legal systems – *Anscheinsbeweis, faute virtuelle,* etc. However, the Spanish Supreme Court suggests that such doctrine should not have been applied in this case.

51 Moreover, the Supreme Court relies on an earlier cartel case, where the overpriced contracts did not refer to trucks but to sugar (STS 651/2013, 7 November 2013).[56] In that previous case, the same Court had stated that Solomonic decisions are not acceptable: when establishing damage, it has to justify its reasoning and provide the actual basis for the assessment of damage. However, there is no explanation as to why compensation given is 5% of the sales price and not 20%, as the claimant requested in the present case.

52 Finally, it may be added that the solution reached in this case is in line with the Principles of European Tort Law drafted by the European Group on Tort Law:[57] according to the same, when damage is practically impossible or very difficult to prove, the court can estimate it (art 2:105). Although the Principles are not mentioned by the Court, they could have provided an additional foundation for the decision.

---

56 ROJ STS 5819/2013, ECLI:ES:TS:2013:5819. On which, see *F Marcos*, Las indemnizaciones de daños derivadas del cártel del azúcar, Osservatorio Permanente sull'Applicazione delle Regole di Concorrenza 25 June 2014 <https://www.osservatorioantitrust.eu/es/las-indemnizaciones-de-danos-derivadas-del-cartel-del-azucar/>; also available at Anuario de la Competencia (2014) 185–200 <https://anuariocompetencia.fundacionico.es/files/original/5f5d8c9b9f1d8a50f2817bdd6604094dc708ebd4.pdf>.

57 *European Group on Tort Law*, Principles of European Tort Law. Text and Commentary (2005).

5. STS Civil Chamber, 129/2023, 20 July 2023, ROJ STS 3472/2023, ECLI:ES:TS:2023:3472: Defamation

a) Brief Summary of the Facts

A person, resident in the municipality of Salamanca, disclosed in a TV report that her neighbour in the upper floor had been administratively sanctioned for excessive noise levels caused by banging and bed noises. The neighbour sued the former and the public corporation in charge of the TV channel (*Corporación Radiotelevisión Española*) for unlawful interference with the right to honour and privacy, due to the rebroadcasting of the report on a national television programme. The downstairs neighbour complained that the noise and vibrations were such that things on her bookshelf were continuously falling down, that she could not sleep because of the plaintiff's fieriness, that cracks were even appearing in the walls, and that the claimant was a prostitute. 53

Although the Court of First Instance of Salamanca had dismissed the claim, the Court of Appeal of the same city ordered the defendants to pay compensation to the plaintiff, amounting to € 10,000,[58] in addition to having to publish the judgment in a local newspaper, and to read it out on the television programme in question. Of the two defendants, only the neighbour of the flat below lodged an appeal in cassation. 54

b) Judgment of the Court

According to case law, in order to respect freedom of expression, which is necessary for the formation of a pluralistic public opinion in a democratic state, the news in question must be of general interest or public relevance, either because of the persons involved, or because of the subject matter, or both; in addition, a test of proportionality is applied. 55

As for the identification of the person, there is unlawful interference with the right to honour if the news item makes it possible to identify the person to whom it refers, even if it is in relation to people in the victim's closest circle, due to indirect references, or due to the circumstances of the case. 56

Although the appellant claims that the noise pollution is noxious, and therefore of public relevance, the fact is that we are dealing with a conflict between neighbours, with little public relevance. The report did not focus on noise pollution 57

58 The claimant had requested € 20,000.

as such, but on noise from the appellant's sexual activity. The way in which the statements were made in this regard infringed both the appellant's privacy and her personal reputation. In conclusion, the judgment under appeal is upheld.

c) Commentary

58 As every year, the Spanish courts handed down a large number of rulings on the protection of the right to honour and other personality rights. With regard to defamation, to name just a few cases, criticism of a university professor's performance was held not to be defamatory if it has a true basis, given that there was no overreaching (it was made at a departmental meeting) and there is a public interest in the matter (STS 1574/2023, 14 November 2023).[59] In relation to entertainment or 'social chronicle' television programmes, although they cannot properly be said to contribute to the formation of public opinion, they do have a certain interest for a sector of society; therefore, the broadcast of a TV report in which the applicant was described as a person who worked at events where women wore provocative clothes, without going so far as to say that she was engaged in prostitution, is not defamatory (STS 1504/2023, 27 October 2023).[60] Nor does the publication of a news item about an alleged scheme for the diversion of public subsidies by the Kingdom of Morocco in Spain, carried out through a series of 'shell companies' or 'front companies', constitute defamation (STS 1441/2023, 18 October 2023).[61] In a different case, it is concluded that the defendant's comments on the claimant's alleged use of her mental illness to benefit from the distribution of her father's inheritance, or the consideration of the claimant as a financially ambitious person are subjective perceptions and opinions of the defendant, which are protected by her freedom of expression (STS 1370/2023, 5 October 2023).[62] Nor does the assertion by a regular contributor to an entertainment programme that the claimant twice failed to attend his son's doctor's appointment constitute defamation. The

---

59 ROJ STS 4649/2023, ECLI:ES:TS:2023:4649. With regard to defamation due to the undue inclusion of the debtor's personal name in a solvency file, see *JR García Vicente*, Daño moral y función disuasoria de la responsabilidad civil en los daños al honor: el caso de los ficheros de solvencia; jurisprudencia del Tribunal Supremo, Actualidad Civil 1 (2023) <https://web.laley.es/>.

60 ROJ STS 4529/2023, ECLI:ES:TS:2023:4529. The Court also rejects that there is an invasion of privacy, since the claimant had signed a representation contract under which she had participated in several television programmes comparable to the one complained of. Similarly, see STS 488/2023, 17 April 2023 (ROJ STS 1568/2023, ECLI:ES:TS:2023:1568).

61 ROJ STS 4417/2023, ECLI:ES:TS:2023:4417.

62 ROJ STS 4231/2023, ECLI:ES:TS:2023:4231.

contributor was merely repeating what he had been told by a nurse and it did not necessarily follow from that statement that the claimant had failed to provide his son with the necessary medical care, as there were many possible reasons for the non-attendance (STS 1363/2023, 4 October 2023).[63] Nor is there defamation when a journalist accuses a judge of falsifying various documents in the context of an investigation of a corruption case if the facts turn out to be true, even if they are ultimately found not to constitute a crime (STS 2940/2023, 20 September 2023).[64] Also it is not defamation per se to merely share the debtor's data with a debt collection company (STS 809/2023, 26 May 2023).[65]

There have also been several cases of violation of the right to someone's per- 59
sonal image, where the image was taken from the Internet without permission. According to case law, it is not allowed to take the claimant's image from a social network on the Internet (STS 964/2023, 14 June 2023).[66] According to another decision, the Internet is not a 'public place' from which images may be taken. Therefore, the use of someone's private images found through Google search is not allowed (STS 1037/2023, 27 June 2023).[67]

The case under discussion is curious for several reasons. First, it considers 60
noise pollution (*contaminación acústica*) and noise from sexual activity to be two different things. In this regard, it criticises the defendant for having talked in the report about noise of sexual origin and not about 'noise pollution'. This is a somewhat forced distinction, as it seems unnatural to speak of a noise in the abstract without referring to its origin. Moreover, what is newsworthy in this case is precisely the sexual nature of the activity, given that there are usually many excessive noises, but those of a sexual nature that result in an administrative sanction do not seem to be very frequent.

Second, the defendants were sentenced for a double interference with both 61
the right to honour and the right to privacy. While the infringement of the latter right is clear (since no one is interested in the identity of the person sanctioned), it is more debatable whether there is a real infringement of the right to honour. The reason is (a) that it is a true fact (*exceptio veritatis*) and, as has already been shown, there is no defamation where the statements are true;[68] and (b) that

63 ROJ STS 3974/2023, ECLI:ES:TS:2023:3974.

64 ROJ STS 3690/2023, ECLI:ES:TS:2023:3690.

65 ROJ STS 2506/2023, ECLI:ES:TS:2023:2506.

66 ROJ STS 2596/2023, ECLI:ES:TS:2023:2596.

67 ROJ STS 2894/2023, ECLI:ES:TS:2023:2894.

68 See also STS 1044/2023, 27 June 2023 (ROJ STS 2893/2023, ECLI:ES:TS:2023:2893) with regard to the publication of pictures of commercial premises with regard to the observance of the sanitary regulations in the context of the Coronavirus (Covid-19) pandemic. However, there is liability if some-there is nothing denigratory *per se* in indulging in intense sexual activity.[69] The problem, in reality, is only one of privacy.[70]

62 Thirdly and finally, it is unclear how compensation is actually determined. As usual, the court awards half of the sum requested by the claimant. However, this is an arbitrary criterion, which may lead to an upward determination of the compensation requested in civil claims.

6. STS Administrative Chamber, 1360/2023, 31 October 2023, ROJ STS 4431/2023, ECLI:ES:TS:2023:4431: Coronavirus

a) Brief Summary of the Facts

63 As discussed in a previous report, the Spanish government decreed several lockdowns during the Covid-19 pandemic. A commercial company (Alhambra Palace SA) that ran a hotel in Granada sued the State for so-called 'liability of the State as legislature' (*responsabilidad del Estado legislador*) according to art 3.2 of Organic Law on states of alarm, exception and siege,[71] for damage derived from having had to close the hotel during the first lockdown. According to the claim, damage (quantified at more than € 400,000) was not due to the pandemic itself but to the abnormal functioning of the administration, which omitted the health alerts and emergencies that would have prevented the subsequent confinement.

---

one is mistakenly depicted as a 'prisoner on furlough' (STS 1008/2023, 21 June 2023 [ROJ STS 2728/2023, ECLI:ES:TS:2023:2728].

69 This assessment is more debatable as regards the suggestion that the applicant was in the oldest profession in the world. However, and bearing in mind that this is a highly complex issue, it is worth suggesting that even in this respect social perceptions may be changing. See eg, *C Meneses-Falcón/O García-Vázquez*, Prostitución, violencia y migraciones femeninas en España, CIDOB 2023 <https://www.cidob.org/publicaciones/prostitucion-violencia-y-migraciones-femeninas-en-espana>. However, there is defamation if it is stated that a city mayor spent public money with prostitutes (STS 776/2023, 22 May 2023 [ROJ STS 2198/2023, ECLI:ES:TS:2023:2198]).

70 In a different case, it is concluded that the communiqué from a trade union to the workers informing them that the claimant, a representative of another trade union, suffers from COVID, amounts to a privacy violation (STS 617/2023, 25 April 2023 [ROJ STS 1674/2023, ECLI:ES:TS:2023:1674]).

71 Organic Act (*Ley Orgánica*, LO) 4/1981, of 1 June, *de los estados de alarma, excepción y sitio* (BOE no 134, 5.6.1981).

b) Judgment of the Court

64 The rule on the liability of the State as legislature derives from the responsibility of public authorities (art 9.3 CE). But it is not constitutionalised as such, unlike the liability of the Public Administration (art 106.2) and therefore the legislature may exclude liability for damage caused by the same by way of a statute. The current statutory regime is found in the Act on the Public Sector (art 32.3 and 4),[72] according to which there is liability provided that the victim 'does not have the legal duty to endure' (arts 32.1 and 34.1). The statutory regulations that decreed the confinement and other restrictions due to the pandemic situation generate a duty to bear the measures imposed, in a general way, to preserve public health. The measures taken were necessary and proportionate, which excludes wrongfulness. The precautionary principle exempts the State from liability when the measures adopted are reasonable and proportionate, even if it later turns out that they were unnecessary, since they were taken in a context of uncertainty. Given the risks to public health, the restrictions on the freedom to conduct a business (art 38 CE) were justified. It cannot be said that the claimant suffered a special sacrifice, which would entitle him to claim compensation, given the generality with which the measures were ordered. For the same reason, it also cannot be said that the claimant was the victim of a compulsory expropriation. Whether the administration worsened the damage through mismanagement should be judged on the basis of the knowledge that was available at the time the measures were taken, not the current knowledge. The claim is therefore dismissed.

c) Commentary

65 This is the first case in which the Supreme Court has ruled on claims of State liability for the management of the pandemic. Given that there are currently thousands of similar claims before the Spanish courts, it is certain that other rulings will follow suit[73] – also because the liability potential in this scenario would

---

72 Act 40/2015, of 1 October, *de Régimen Jurídico del Sector Público* (BOE no 236, 2.10.2015). In legal scholarship now, see *S Alcaraz Zabala*, Responsabilidad patrimonial vs Principio de indemnidad (El Estado ante las F.C.S.E.) (2023).

73 See *Luisja Sánchez*, El fallo del Supremo marca el devenir para que cientos de recursos pendientes sobre responsabilidad patrimonial sean desestimados, Economist & Jurist 1.11.2023 <https://www.economistjurist.es/articulos-juridicos-destacados/el-fallo-del-supremo-marca-el-devenir-para-que-cientos-de-recursos-pendientes-sobre-responsabilidad-patrimonial-sean-desestimados/>.

have been simply impossible to assume even by the State.[74] Although this one is very clear on the absence of State liability, it does not resolve why the claimant company is considered not to have suffered a 'singular patrimonial sacrifice', which would have justified compensation. Although the pandemic measures were indeed general as the Court suggests, it is clear that they affected certain economic sectors (such as the hotel industry) much more than others.

7. Personal Injury

66 As is well known, the main characteristic of Spanish law in the area of personal injury is the application of the so-called *baremo*, as the existing compensation scheme is commonly known.[75] In this respect, the Supreme Court has clarified that under the previous statutory regime (ie the previous *baremo*), and until the reform introduced by Act 21/2007,[76] compensation included all medical and related expenses. However, from the entry into force of this reform, and with respect to claims occurring during its validity, only the following were to be compensated: 'the costs of medical, pharmaceutical and hospital care in the necessary amount until the healing or consolidation of sequelae, provided that the expense is duly justified in view of the nature of the care provided' (STS 1226/2023, 14 September 2023).[77] Also in relation to the previous *baremo*, another decision concludes that the correction factor of 10% is not applicable to aesthetic injury (STS 513/2023, 18 April 2023).[78]

---

74 Similarly, see *C Yáñez Díaz,* Responsabilidad patrimonial derivada del estado de alarma. La previsible sentencia del Tribunal Supremo de 21 de septiembre de 2023, Blog Sepin 7.11. 2023 <https://blog.sepin.es/responsabilidad-patrimonial-estado-alarma>.

75 See Act 35/2015, of 22 September, *de reforma del sistema para la valoración de los daños y perjuicios causados a las personas en accidentes de circulación* (BOE no 228, 23.9.2015). In legal scholarship see *E Agüero Ramón-Llín,* Las indemnizaciones de las víctimas de accidentes de tráfico: el nuevo sistema de valoración de los daños y perjuicios personales: Ley 35/2015 de 22 de septiembre (BOE 23 de septiembre de 2015) (3rd edn 2023).

76 Act 21/2007, of 11 July, *por la que se modifica el texto refundido de la Ley sobre responsabilidad civil y seguro en la circulación de vehículos a motor, aprobado por el Real Decreto Legislativo 8/2004, de 29 de octubre, y el texto refundido de la Ley de ordenación y supervisión de los seguros privados, aprobado por el Real Decreto Legislativo 6/2004, de 29 de octubre* (BOE no 166, 12.7.2007).

77 ROJ STS 3691/2023, ECLI:ES:TS:2023:3691. On medical malpractice, see *L Corpas Pastor,* La responsabilidad del médico por la prescripción de medicamentos de uso compasivo y fuera de ficha técnica, DS: Derecho y salud 1 (2023) 8–36. On personal injury par ricochet see *L Molina Martínez,* El daño indirecto o por rebote por causa de lesiones (2023).

78 ROJ STS 1484/2023, ECLI:ES:TS:2022:1484.

Apart from this, the Supreme Court has modulated or clarified its previous 'cross-convictions doctrine' (*doctrina de las condenas cruzadas*), established by STS 536/2012, 10 September 2023.[79] According to the latter, when there has been a traffic accident with a reciprocal collision resulting in personal injury, proportional compensation is only applicable when a specific percentage or degree of causal incidence of each of the vehicles involved can be accredited. Otherwise, both drivers are liable for the total damage caused to the other victim.[80] In 2023, the Supreme Court decided on liability resulting from a collision between, yet again, a motorbike and a car. According to this decision, the cross-convictions doctrine is not applicable to the case because the Court of Appeal had been able to determine, after assessing the evidence adduced,[81] the specific dynamics of the collision, as well as the causal contribution of each of the drivers involved in causing the damage (STS 987/2023, 20 June 2023).[82] 67

In another case, the interpretation of a rule of the Insurance Contract Act[83] concerning interest for late payment by an insurance company is raised. Two people on the same motorbike were involved in an accident when the vehicle slid off the road due to mud accumulated on the road after heavy rains the previous day. The insurance company claimed that the victim was committing fraud because she was not the actual driver at the time of the accident, but the passenger was. The Supreme Court concludes that such an allegation does not allow the insurer to delay the payment of compensation.[84] The same decision excludes that the aforementioned mud constitutes force majeure (*fuerza mayor*), the effect of which would be to exclude the applicability of the rule of strict liability for personal in- 68

79 ROJ 7647/2012, ECLI:ES:TS:2022:7647.

80 In the case at stake, it was dubious whether the bike involved in the accident had crossed into the oncoming lane of the road. Such doctrine was applied again by STS 312/2017, 18 May 2017 (ROJ STS 1903:2017, ECLI:ES:TS:2017:1903). In legal scholarship, with regard to motor vehicle accidents caused by alcohol consumption, see *AM de Toro Negro*, Responsabilidad civil y aseguramiento en los accidentes de tráfico que tienen su causa en el consumo de alcohol (2023).

81 Taking into account the drag marks on the carriageway, it was presumed that the bike at stake had indeed crossed into the oncoming lane. The party at stake challenged on cassation the application of the proof by presumptions, to no avail.

82 ROJ STS 2712/2023, ECLI:ES:TS:2023:2712.

83 Art 20 of the Act 50/1980, of 8 October, *de Contrato de Seguro* (BOE no 250, 17.10.1980) (hereinafter LCS).

84 In a different decision, the Supreme Court states that it is up to the insurance company to prove that the insured person did not notify it of the claim; see STS 1322/2023, 27 September 2023 (ROJ STS 3983/2023, ECLI:ES:TS:2023:3983).

jury caused by motor vehicle accidents.[85] According to the Court, the presence of such mud as a result of rain is a circumstance of the road which is neither unforeseeable, nor unavoidable, nor 'unrelated to driving' (STS 1506/2023, 27 October 2023).[86]

69 A similar restrictive stance has been adopted with regard to the other defence provided for in the strict liability regime for personal injury caused by motor vehicle accidents, as is the victim's contributory negligence. For such negligence to exclude liability, it has to be 'exclusive' (*culpa exclusiva del perjudicado*).[87] In the case in question, a motorist collided with a car that had stopped to turn, and which had exited from a road with a stop sign shortly before. Interestingly, when analysing whether the motorist was at 'fault', the court also analyses whether the driver was at fault himself, despite the fact that the driver's liability is in theory strict. The court concludes that the motorcyclist was not speeding, although he was actually surprised by the car's manoeuvre, as the car, among the different (correct) possibilities available to it when the motorbike approached, opted for the less diligent one.

70 Finally, it is well known that Spanish courts apply the *baremo* to cases of accidents not caused by motor vehicles, as a guideline for determining compensation for personal injuries.[88] One such case is the German Wings plane crash in 2015, where – as will be recalled – the pilot deliberately crashed the plane in the French Alps. Spanish law provides that, in exceptional cases, the amount resulting from the application of the scale may be increased. The Court of Appeal had not only applied the statutory increase, but also applied an additional increase (not specifically provided for by the *baremo* statutory regime) of between 10% and 20%, which it justified by the circumstances of the accident. [89] According to the Supreme Court, that increase is too small, since it does not take into account the pathological grief inherent in the loss of a loved one in an accident of this nature, which is catastrophic and involves extremely painful circumstances – especially in a case where the incident was not accidental, but was due to the deliberate action of one of the

---

85 Pursuant to art 1.1 II of the RDLeg 8/2004, of 29 October, *por el que se aprueba el texto refundido de la Ley sobre responsabilidad civil y seguro en la circulación de vehículos a motor* (BOE no 267, 5.11.2004).

86 ROJ STS 4601/2023, ECLI:ES:TS:2023:4601.

87 See fn 85 above. In legal scholarship see *N Subuh Falero*, Autopuesta en peligro en el tránsito motorizado y en la práctica deportiva (2023).

88 See *V Magro Servet*, Indemnizaciones por accidentes en el mar con motos acuáticas o embarcaciones marítimas y baremo indemnizatorio: (Análisis de la STS 704/2023 de 9 de mayo de 2023), Tráfico y seguridad vial 286 (2023) <https://revista.dgt.es/es/>.

89 The court refers to the catastrophic nature of the plane crash, as well as to public confidence in the safety of air traffic.

crew members (STS 704/2023, 9 May 2023).[90] Although this decision can be seen as an echo of the criterion adopted in a previous case (the 2008 Spanair accident), it is open to debate whether the court duly takes into account the particular circumstances of the case[91] or rather it implies privileged treatment of air navigation accident victims compared to others.[92]

C. Literature

1. *Klaus Jochen Albiez Dohrmann/José Antonio Castillo Parrilla*, Handbook on Spanish Civil Law: Obligations and Contracts (Atelier, 2023)

The book (in two volumes)[93] fills a gap in relation to English language expositions 71
of the Spanish law of obligations.[94] Although the text is aimed mostly at students, it can be very informative for the foreign legal scholar or lawyer who is approaching Spanish law for the first time. It includes chapters on tort law in general, called 'The right of damages' (Chapter 9), the conditions of tort liability (Chapter 10) and liability for the acts of another (Chapter 11).[95]

---

90 ROJ STS 1855/2023, ECLI:ES:TS:2023:1855.

91 As suggested by *E Domínguez*, ¿Cómo se indemniza el duelo patológico por la pérdida de un ser querido? Expansión, 12 June 2023 <https://www.expansion.com/juridico/opinion/2023/06/12/64873fca468aebd36e8b4627.html>.

92 See *E Navarro/H Gallego*, Las indemnizaciones de Germanwings: el TS trata con privilegios a las víctimas de siniestros aéreos, Expansión, 20 June 2023 <https://www.expansion.com/juridico/opinion/2023/06/20/6491d1b0468aeb015a8b456d.html> and *S Martínez Gómez*, Criterios privilegiados para la cuantificación del daño resultante de un accidente aéreo, Centro de Estudios de Consumo (CESCO), 12 July 2023, <https://centrodeestudiosdeconsumo.com/images/Criterios_privilegiados_para_la_cuantificacion_del_dano.pdf>. Also see *E Monterroso Casado*, El resarcimiento de daños en los accidentes aéreos. Más allá del baremo, Revista Crítica de Derecho Inmobiliario (RCDI) 800 (2023) 3567–3588.

93 Volume I: General Theory of Obligations and Contracts; Volume II: Contracts in Particular. Quasi-Contracts. Non-contractual liability.

94 However, see previously *T Rodríguez de las Heras Ballell*, Introduction to Spanish Private Law: Facing the Social and Economic Challenges (2009) and *Y Bergel Sainz de Baranda*, Handbook on Spanish Civil Patrimonial Law (2019); also see *S I Strong/K Fach Gómez/L Carballo Piñeiro*, Comparative Law for Spanish-English Speaking Lawyers: Legal Cultures, Legal Terms and Legal Practices (2016).

95 For a general treatment of Spanish tort law also, see *P Álvarez Olalla*, Manual de Derecho de daños (3rd edn 2023); *M Yzquierdo Tolsada*, Responsabilidad civil extracontractual. Parte general:

2. *Efrén Pérez Borges,* El lucro y el daño: ¿qué ocurre cuando dañar merece la pena? [Disgorgement of profits] (Aranzadi, 2023)

72 In this monograph, which is the result of a doctoral thesis, the author starts from the premise that it is unethical for the tortfeasor to be able to enrich himself as a result of committing a tort; therefore, he analyses the legal mechanisms through which this result may be avoided.[96]

3. *Andrés Marín Salmerón,* El defecto de diseño en los productos digitales [Design defect in the case of digital products] (Thomson Reuters Aranzadi, 2023)

73 This monograph is the result of the doctoral thesis submitted by its author at the University of Murcia. The author questions whether the 'classical' criteria for the concept of product defect still apply when dealing with digital products.[97]

Delimitación y especies. Elementos. Efectos o consecuencias (9th edn 2023) and *E Llamas Pombo,* Manual de Derecho civil, vol VII, Derecho de daños (2021). As regards liability for building defects, see *MY Puga Pérez,* La acción de responsabilidad civil por daños ocasionados por vicios de la construcción. Aspectos sustantivos y procesales (2023).

96 On unjust enrichment from a comparative perspective, see *R Fariña Fariña,* La restitución del enriquecimiento sin causa: un reto para el derecho español (2022). Also see, from a philosophical perspective, *DM Papayannis,* The Morality of Compensation through Tort Law, Ratio Juris 36(1) 3–25 <https://onlinelibrary.wiley.com/doi/10.1111/raju.12369>.

97 Also see *G Izquierdo Grau,* Software y algoritmos defectuosos. algunas consideraciones sobre la responsabilidad del desarrollador de software o de sistemas de inteligencia artificial, IDP: revista de Internet, derecho y política 38 (2023) 1–12 <https://dialnet.unirioja.es/descarga/articulo/9087345.pdf>.

4. *Esther Hernández Sainz/Loreto C Mate Satué/M Teresa Alonso Pérez* (eds), La responsabilidad civil por servicios de intermediación prestados por plataformas digitales [Liability for intermediation services provided by digital platforms] (Colex, 2023)

This is a timely collection of papers by several experts on the EU regulatory regime 74 on liability for intermediation services provided by digital platforms and its implementation into Spanish law.

5. *Francisco José Rodríguez Almirón,* Aspectos jurídico-dogmáticos y jurisprudenciales en torno a la responsabilidad civil ex delicto [Tort liability derived from crime] (Dykinson, 2023)

Spanish legal literature is already abundant with regard to the statutory regime of 75 tort liability for acts constituting an offence under the Criminal Code, which provides a separate set of rules on the same.[98] Therefore, it is legitimate to ask why there is yet another book on the topic. In this case, it is a monograph by a criminal lawyer who takes up the work previously started by another professor of the University of Granada (J Martínez Ruiz), who was unable to finish it due to a terrible accident that led to his death. The book is a very thorough study, especially of the case law.

98 Among the last, see *CD Delgado Sancho,* Responsabilidad civil ex-delicto. Paso a paso (2nd edn 2023); *M Pantaleón Díaz,* Delito y responsabilidad civil extracontractual. Una dogmática comparada (2022) and *JA Posada Pérez,* La responsabilidad civil ex delicto (2022), with further references. Also see *L Álvarez Suárez,* La carga de la prueba en materia de responsabilidad civil derivada de delitos de estafa cometidos mediante Phising (2023) La Ley Probática 13 (2023) <https://tienda.laley.es/la-ley-probatica>.

6. *Amelia Sánchez Gómez,* Responsabilidad civil extracontractual de las personas con discapacidad psíquica o intellectual [Tort liability of persons with psychical or intellectual disabilities] (Reus, 2023)

76 This book is a study of the statutory reform of 2021 that affected various articles of the Civil Code relating to the legal situation of persons with disabilities. Among other aspects, it delves into the debate on whether attributability (*imputabilidad*) – understood as the capacity to govern oneself – is still a requirement for fault-based liability after such a reform.

Sandra Friberg

XXIX. Sweden

A. Legislation

There were no changes in Swedish tort law in 2023. 1

In June 2023, the government decided to appoint an inquiry with the task of reviewing the rules on compensation of criminal damage.[1] The aim is to strengthen the position of crime victims and reduce the harmful effects of crime. An investigator will also review the rules on the right of persons deprived of liberty to compensation,[2] in order to achieve a more reasonable system for compensation to persons deprived of liberty. In order to strengthen parental responsibility, the investigator will also review the rules on guardians' liability for damage caused by their children through crime.[3] 2

The investigator shall, among other things, decide whether: 3

- victims of crime must have a right to compensation for criminal damage already when a judgment on damages has legal effect,
- the rules on prohibitions against the seizure of damages must be changed so that enforcement to a greater extent is enabled for the benefit of crime victims,
- the right to compensation for injuries suffered by police officers and other professional groups with special preparedness for criminal violations must be strengthened,
- guardians' liability for damage caused by their children by crime should be stricter, and
- the right to compensation for deprivation of liberty should be limited.

The investigator shall propose the necessary constitutional amendments. The assignment is to be reported no later than 24 February 2025. 4

1 Directive 2023:94.

2 The law on compensation in the event of deprivation of liberty and other coercive measures (1998:714).

3 The rules on guardians' liability are to be found in the Tort Liability Act (TLA), ch 3, secs 5 and 6 (para 2).

https://doi.org/10.1515/9783111376721-030

B. Cases

1. Supreme Court (Högsta domstolen) 14 March, 2023, Nytt Juridiskt Arkiv (NJA) 2023, 114: The Easter Riots 'Sabotage of Blue Light Activities' and the Right to Damages

a) Brief Summary of the Facts

5 The 'Easter riots' in Sweden in April 2022 were a series of riots that broke out in several different cities in Sweden. The chairman of the Stram Kurs party, Rasmus Paludan, planned a number of demonstrations in various places in Sweden over Easter, which coincided with the Muslim fasting month of Ramadan, to burn Islam's holy book, the Koran.

6 At one of these places where Paludan had been given permission to demonstrate, a public gathering took place before he arrived. The crowd started to attack the police by, among other things, throwing stones at them. Several police officers and police dogs were injured, police cars were badly damaged, several of which were set on fire, and the police were forced to leave the area.

7 The riots led to a number of court cases in which one of the questions was how to apply a rather new piece of legislation – 'the sabotage of blue light activities' ('*blåljussabotage*')[4] – and if this crime could entitle police officers to damages.

b) Judgment of the Court

8 In the Supreme Court ruling from 2023, two people were convicted of gross sabotage of blue light activities. They were considered criminally responsible only for those events that could be concretely linked to their own actions. When assessing the seriousness of the acts, however, great importance was attached to the fact that they were carried out in a context where many other people also attacked the police.

9 Regarding the question of damages to the police officers, the Supreme Court stated that in the case of crimes that are primarily aimed at public interests, there is normally no right to compensation. Even such a crime can, however, in

4 The Criminal Code (BrB) ch 13, sec 5c.

some cases, appear to be directed in such a way at one or more specific persons that there may be reason to make exceptions to this general rule.[5]

Beyond the stone throwing for which A had been convicted as violence against an official and for which he had already been ordered to pay damages in connection with this charge, the investigation did not show that any of the other acts for which he was convicted were specifically targeted against police officer X. 10

Hence, there was no reason to depart from the general rule that crime which is directed against public interests does not give a right to non-pecuniary damages for such violation. The Court added that even though the situation as a whole had clearly been deeply unpleasant and terrifying for X, as well as for other officers who were on the scene, this did not change anything. 11

c) Commentary

The protected interest of the penalty provision on sabotage of blue light operations is primarily the blue light operations as such (the societal interest in blue light operations – police, fire and ambulance services – being carried out) and not the interests of the individuals responsible for performing these activities. It follows from this that individuals normally do not have a right to damages following such a crime. 12

Depending on *how* the crime in question was committed, it may sometimes be appropriate to charge the perpetrator with the crime of assault and battery (ch 3 or 4 of the Criminal Code, BrB) if one or more people were injured. 13

The same applies to crimes according to ch 17, sec 1 of the Criminal Code, ie violence or threats against an officer, which includes violence and threats against persons but whose protected interest alongside the individual is also a societal interest in a broader sense. 14

The Supreme Court exemplified this general rule that crime which is not directed against individuals does not give a right to non-pecuniary damages for such violation, by referring to a previous court case, NJA 1998, 310. In this case, a person who caused an explosion in a school toilet was *not* held liable for damages towards a person who was in his office, directly opposite where the explosion took place. According to the Court, a crime that is primarily aimed at harming public interests can give right to damages under certain conditions. 15

5 This is exemplified by the Supreme Court case, NJA 1998, 310.

16 If, for instance,

(a) no one has indeed been injured, but the crime was directed at a specific person: if *the intention was to intimidate or threaten* one or more specific people, victims may be entitled to compensation;
(b) the perpetrator *deliberately* exposed one or more particular persons to a *tangible risk*, this should also be considered to mean that the crime was directed against them in such a way that damages should be payable;
(c) there are other circumstances which are such that compensation for violations should be awarded even if the act cannot be considered to have been directed at a particular person.

17 In the literature,[6] it has been argued that there are a number of parameters to consider when assessing if a certain crime gives right to compensation for violations. These are:

(1) 'clear cases', crimes where the criminal classification shows that the crime violated one of the interests protected by tort law (a person's physical or mental integrity, freedom, peace or honour);
(2) cases where factors internal to the crime – how the crime was committed – correspond to a 'clear case', ie the execution of the criminal act has its counterpart in a crime from the above category;
(3) the nature and severity of the risked injury gives right to damages for violations: eg in a case of arson (ch 13 sec 1 BrB), the interest protected by criminal law is public order but for criminal liability it is also required that the act entailed danger to life or health. If someone has been injured, it is a 'clear case' (cf (1) above), but when it was only a matter of someone being exposed to danger, it is required that the victim was exposed to *concrete* danger (not just *abstract* danger), and that the dangerous situation was qualified, eg that the fire developed suffocating smoke or that the victim was forced to make a life-threatening jump to escape the fire;[7]
(4) cases where the act is a violation of a person in that it contained degrading or shameful elements or is of a particularly reckless nature, eg when someone's home has been ransacked in connection with a burglary or by targeting someone who is particularly vulnerable (the elderly, sick, or disabled);
(5) cases where the perpetrator intended to harm or offend the victim or showed a clear lack of respect for the life or health of other people. What has been said

6 See *S Friberg*, Kränkningsersättning (2010) ch 10, particularly ch 10.5. and *H Andersson*, Ersättningsproblem (2017) chs 5.6 and 5.7 (with special analytical focus on Supreme Court cases concerning crimes against police and other uniformed civil servants).
7 Cf NJA 1998, 310.

can also be expressed as the perpetrator has shown a more severe degree of guilt in the form of a certain attitude towards (the risk of) certain severe consequences.

Not all of these parameters are, of course, necessary to consider in each and every case, but they can be weighed and assessed by the courts in their judgment concerning claims of damages for criminal infringements. This is clear in the 2023 case, where there were no such circumstances that could be argued in favour of the police. 18

2. Supreme Court (Högsta domstolen) 22 March 2023, Nytt Juridiskt Arkiv (NJA) 2023, 162: Right *in rem* and Right to Damages – When is a Claim Time-Barred?

a) Brief Summary of the Facts

A man worked from 2004–2007 at one of the State's historical museums – the coin cabinet. In 2009, 2010 and 2013, the man sold at auctions coins stolen from the coin cabinet. Between 2010–2013, the man held and handed over two other coins – also stolen from the coin cabinet – to a coin dealer. 19

The prosecutor demanded that the man be sentenced for dealing with stolen goods in relation to these coins, and the museum claimed damages totalling almost four million SEK[8] as compensation for the coins. 20

The action was brought on 12 December 2018 and the man was served with the indictment and the compensation claims on 14 December of the same year. 21

The man denied wrongdoing and opposed the claim for damages. He made several objections, inter alia that he had had the coins in his possession before December 2008 – ie more than ten years before the criminal action against him – and that the statutory limitation period had expired for both the criminal acts and the claim for damages. 22

The question to the Supreme Court was from what date the limitation period regarding the damages claim must be calculated. 23

8 Approx € 400,000.

b) Judgment of the Court

24 The Supreme Court initially reiterated that the circumstances relied upon by the museum for the damages claim are mainly deduced from the description of the criminal act. One such circumstance is that, from 2009 – 2013, on several occasions, the man handed over coins stolen from the museum to others and that he committed the acts with intent. Such a circumstance may give rise to liability for damages.

25 According to the Supreme Court, the damages claim that the museum submitted was based on the fact that the man allegedly handed over the coins, thus making it impossible for the museum to get the coins back. In the course of the case, it emerged that none of these events took place more than ten years before the action was brought and the claim for damages is therefore not time-barred.

26 The Supreme Court concludes by stating that how long the man may have had the relevant coins in his possession before handing them over is of no significance.

c) Commentary

27 In its ruling, the Supreme Court points to the fact that the limitation period for a claim for damages due to the committing of a crime normally starts to run from the day the crime was committed. However, the starting point for the time periods for limitations of claims and limitations of prosecution does not always coincide.

28 For a person who hands over stolen property to be liable for damage which arises through the transfer, it is not necessary that they committed a crime. According to the TLA ch 2 sec 1, it is sufficient that the person acted intentionally or negligently when their action means that the owner cannot get their property back; the loss of property corresponds to damage to property.

29 In the event that someone is in possession of stolen goods, without having become the owner of them, the real owner of the stolen property has the right to have the stolen goods returned to them – a right *in rem*. This claim is not subject to the statute of limitations. Thus, at this point, the owner has two civil claims: one based on a right *in rem* and one claim for damages.

30 If the stolen property, however, can no longer be reclaimed because the holder of the property has disposed of it by selling it or giving it away, the owner can claim damages according to the TLA ch 2 sec 1. This is the claim on which the statute of limitations is applicable. Therefore, as can be seen in the ruling from the Supreme Court, the important date to consider is when the property was disposed of in such a way that the property can no longer be returned to the rightful owner and thus a claim for damages arises. The limitation period is calculated from this date.

This is a practical way of protecting the rightful owner of stolen goods and the corresponding right to have one's property returned from the thief. Once this right has become extinct because of the thief's own handling of the property (eg selling or destroying the property), it would be unsatisfactory if the rightful owner's right to damages became extinct at the same time merely because it was impossible to claim the right *in rem* for ten years, when the property's whereabouts were unknown to the owner. Otherwise, the thief would benefit twice. 31

3. Supreme Court (Högsta domstolen) 11 July, 2023, Nytt Juridiskt Arkiv (NJA) 2023, 630: Insurance Claims Following the Pandemic (Covid-19)

a) Brief Summary of the Facts

Following the outbreak of the Covid-19 virus in Sweden, the Public Health Authority issued a number of regulations that applied to, among others, restaurants and bars. According to the regulations, the businesses concerned had to ensure that there was no crowding on their premises. Limitations regarding the number of visitors in the same group were also gradually introduced (initially a maximum of eight and then a maximum of four people). 32

Due to these limitations, a night club closed its business on 25 March 2020 and requested compensation for the interruption in the club's operations from their epidemic interruption insurance. The insurance company announced that the insurance could not be claimed since the expression in the insurance conditions – 'intervention by an authority' – only refers to an authority's decisions that are aimed directly at a policyholder. 33

Both the district court and the court of appeal judged that the expression does not cover general regulations and dismissed the club's action. 34

b) Judgment of the Court

The interpretation of epidemic interruption insurance must, according to the Supreme Court, take its starting point in the wording of the insurance condition's terms. The term 'authority intervention' seems to be a question of an individual decision, but can, from a purely linguistic perspective, not be considered to exclude that the condition is also applicable when the interruption follows general regulations issued by an authority. Further guidance must therefore be sought in the as- 35 sessment of how the insurance conditions are otherwise designed, ie a contextual interpretation must be made.

36 The Supreme Court then states that the general wording of the terms and conditions largely supports the insurance company's interpretation. The fact that the insurance applies to interventions at a specific insured location speaks for itself for the insurance not to cover interruptions due to general regulations but measures aimed directly at the insured business.

37 Another condition that speaks in favor of this interpretation is that the policyholder, in the case of compensation claims through a document, issued by an appropriate authority, must substantiate the time that the business could not be pursued as a result of the decision taken by the authority.

38 The Supreme Court therefore found that the club did not have a right to compensation from their insurance.

c) Commentary

39 This case was, of course, important for all those insurance companies that received compensation claims from their policyholders due to the Covid-19-related restrictions on the operation of hotel and restaurant businesses. The Swedish government took a series of measures to both limit the spread of the Covid-19 virus and at the same time alleviate the effects for companies that were hit hard by the restrictions, such as, among others, adjustment support, short-term lay-off, postponement of tax payments and turnover support for individual traders.

40 However, despite this, a large number of companies in, for example, the restaurant industry were greatly affected by the pandemic and were forced into bankruptcy. Some of these would probably have been put out of business anyway due to poor financial stability and failing demand, but the pandemic was a hard blow to the restaurant industry.

41 To extend the interpretation of the insurance conditions could perhaps have been another measure to 'save' businesses that suffered from the public health authority's decisions, but this would of course have had negative consequences on the insurance companies' financial situation and unforeseeable consequences in the future.

42 The calculated risk that insurance companies take in providing business insurance could, and should not, be overridden by the Supreme Court without good reasons. The pandemic, however, showed that society needs to, by different means, be better prepared for different types of crisis, and it remains to be seen if special pandemic insurance will be provided. For insurance companies, it is evident

from this judgment that it is necessary to improve their communication and information on the contents of their insurance policies to policyholders.

4. Supreme Court (Högsta domstolen) 14 November 2023, Nytt Juridiskt Arkiv (NJA) 2023, 830: Liability in Maritime Matters

a) Brief Summary of the Facts

A ship anchored – due to an engine failure – at a location in the Baltic Sea between Sweden and Germany, waiting for technicians and spare parts. In the district court and the Court of Appeal, it was established that the ship, by anchoring, had caused damage to an underwater cable, property of the company, Baltic Cable. 43

Baltic Cable claimed damages from the registered owner of the ship, SS, and two companies, who all had ownership connections to one another; SS was a full partner in company A, and company B was a limited partner in company A. SS was also the owner of a third company, company C, which had some form of employment contracts with the the captain, first mate and the chief engineer. 44

In the Supreme Court proceedings, the defendants accepted that the ship's anchor had caused the damage to the cable and that the captain and crew of the vessel caused the damage to the cable through fault or dereliction of duty. They also agreed on the level of damages. Thus, the remaining questions for the Supreme Court judges to consider were: 45

(a) Who should be considered the shipowner (*redare*)[9] and thus responsible for the damage according to the rules in ch 7 sec 1 of the Maritime Act (1994:1009)?;

(b) What can constitute 'qualified gross negligence' (gross negligence with knowledge that damage will probably result)? (The reason why this was of particular interest in the case is that the right to limitation of liability that exists in maritime law is 'lost' in the event of qualified gross negligence.)

b) Judgment of the Court

According to the Maritime Code, ch 7 sec 1, first paragraph, a shipowner is liable for damage that the master, a member of the crew or a pilot cause through fault or 46

9 For clarity: in the following, 'shipowner' will be used for the Swedish term 'redare', while the owner of the ship will be called 'vessel owner'.

negligence in the line of duty. The shipowner is also liable if damage is caused by someone else, when the other person – on behalf of the shipowner or the master – performs work in the vessel's operation.

47 In addition to the shipowner's liability for the fault of others, a shipowner is liable for damage caused by their own negligence.

48 The shipowner's liability is not, in a strict sense, vicarious in nature, since the work is not necessarily carried out with the shipowner as the employer. Instead, the responsibility is tied to the operation of the ship and thus is rather operating liability. Since the structure of ownership, operating responsibility, insurance policyholder, etc is rather intricate in maritime matters (as can be seen in this case), it seems to be a rather pragmatic approach to define liability in this way.

49 Since liability according to the Maritime Act to a great extent depends on who can be determined to be the shipowner, it became necessary for the Supreme Court to clarify which of the defendants was to be considered as such.

50 'Shipowner' ('redare') normally refers to the person, natural or legal, who initiates operations with a particular vessel, directs the operation and carries the financial risk, in other words, equips and conducts business with a particular vessel.

51 According to the Supreme Court, a typical feature of the person who is to be regarded as the shipowner is that they, by equipping the vessel, also exercise the operational management. This includes being responsible for manning the vessel, and thereby the shipowner exercises the right of instruction over the work, and is ultimately the person responsible for the ship's nautical management.

52 As a starting point, it is the vessel's owner who is to be considered the shipowner, unless the possession and disposal of the vessel has been transferred from the owner to someone else. The person who then assumes the role of shipowner must therefore derive their powers from the owner, which is usually done by a contract.

53 Considering the division of functions that occurs in maritime transport, there must be an overall assessment of the individual circumstances when concluding who has the role as shipowner. The party on which the majority of the typical shipowner functions rests is then considered the shipowner.

54 In such an assessment, the various shipowner functions can, with consideration of the context in which they occur, take on varying meanings. This means that the concept of shipowner can change depending on the context in which it is to be assessed.

55 In this case, SS was the sole owner of the vessel. The two companies (A and B), who had ownership connections to one another and with SS, could not be considered as owners of the vessel. The two companies had different functions: company A was considered to be more or less an agent acting on SS's behalf, and company B

merely served as a financial hub for the business, not in any way involved in the operation of the vessel.

The employment contracts between company C and the captain, first mate and the chief engineer provided no reliable conclusion that this company was the employer at the time of the incident. It was also noted that all the captain's contacts by reason of the machine failure were made with SS, and not with company C. 56

The conclusion from the Supreme Court was therefore that SS had the role of shipowner since he – in an overall assessment – was responsible for the majority of the typical functions of a shipowner. Thus, it was held that he was solely liable. 57

However, there was no substantial evidence to prove that anyone had acted with such qualified gross negligence that is required for an exemption of the right to a limitation of liability: there was no evidence of deficiencies in the access and use of maritime charts. Neither was there evidence to support the allegation that the defendants would have been aware of the conditions at the anchorage when instructing the anchor to be released with force. 58

c) Commentary

Much can be learned from this case when it comes to maritime law and how business at sea is normally organised and conducted, but, from a tort law point of view, the clarification regarding the assessment of a shipowner's liability is the most intriguing. As the Supreme Court also states, this liability is not vicarious in nature in a strict sense, as work is not necessarily carried out with the shipowner as the employer.[10] An overall assessment of the circumstances of the specific case must instead be made, taking into account the existing division of functions. Since operational management, insurance schemes, employment solutions and risk distribution can apparently vary to a great extent in the wide area of business at sea, the approach from the Supreme Court to make this type of individualised assessment seems to be the only way to strike a fair balance between potential tortfeasors and claimants. 59

The focus on typical features of the business in question, with particular attention to decisive authority in the matters leading up to the harm in question, is more accurate when weighing and balancing risk distribution. Different choices in company structures or contractual agreements may have been made with 60

10 In this case, the matter of employment contract did not bear much weight for the Supreme Court's assessment.

other purposes in mind and might therefore not be decisive when attributing liability.

61 Perhaps this type of liability assessment can be fair for other types of operational liability, where there may be a number of potential tortfeasors, at least if it is considered necessary to attribute liability to one tortfeasor instead of many, which – in this case – would have left the distribution of costs to the tortfeasors to administer between themselves.

5. Supreme Court (Högsta domstolen) 5 December 2023, Nytt Juridiskt Arkiv (NJA) 2023, 916: PFAS and Personal Injury

a) Brief Summary of the Facts

62 In 2013, it was discovered that the drinking water in the municipality of Ronneby contained very high levels of PFAS (per- and polyfluorinated alkyl substances). The pollution came from the fire training site at the Blekinge Wing base, where, since the mid-1980s, the Swedish Armed Forces used a special oil and petrol fire foam that contains PFAS for oil and gasoline fires. These substances have since spread from the fire drill area to the ground water and on to the drinking water.

63 A large number of residents in the area (the appellants) filed suit against the municipality's drinking water company, Miljöteknik AB. They demanded that the district court establish that the company was liable to compensate them for personal injury. They claimed that they had suffered personal injury because the water supplied by Miljöteknik AB had a safety defect due to the high levels of PFAS. The action was based on the provisions of the Product Liability Act (1992:18 PLA).

64 In its ruling, NJA 2018, 475, the Supreme Court established that the company's water supplied to the residents is a product, which is covered by the PLA.[11]

65 The district court determined that Miljöteknik is liable to compensate the plaintiffs for personal injury in the form of elevated levels of PFAS in the blood, involving increased health risks and physical changes and deterioration of the body. The Court of Appeal dismissed the action.

11 This case was discussed by *S Friberg*, Sweden, in: E Karner/BC Steininger (eds), European Tort Law (ETL) 2019 (2020) 647, nos 18–27.

b) Judgment of the Court

The Supreme Court granted leave to appeal based on the Court of Appeal's assessment that elevated levels of PFAS substances have been measured in the plaintiffs' bodies as a result of the drinking water supplied by Miljöteknik AB, which contained high levels of PFAS substances, and that each of the plaintiffs, because of this, runs – seen in relation to people who have *not* been exposed to the corresponding exposure – an increased risk of suffering such negative health effects and diseases that are associated with PFAS exposure. 66

The issue for the Supreme Court was to decide was if, due to the elevated levels of PFAS in their blood, the plaintiffs have suffered personal injuries. In other words, the question was whether liability as such can arise for damages. 67

The Court reiterates that the PLA is the implementation of the Product Liability Directive,[12] and that it regulates liability for damage caused by a product to someone or a thing other than the product itself. According to the PLA, damages are paid for, inter alia, personal injury that a product has caused due to a safety defect. Liability does not require negligence. 68

Neither the PLA nor its preparatory works contain any definition of personal injury. The Product Liability Directive is also silent on the matter of defining personal injury; it has been left to the Member States to determine the concept of personal injury and which damage is covered. However, the term shall, according to the European Court of Justice, be given a wide interpretation to ensure that injured parties receive adequate and full compensation for the damage they have suffered as a result of a defective product. 69

Since neither the PLA nor the underlying Directive provide any guidance for the interpretation of the term personal injury, it should, according to the Supreme Court, be given the same meaning as that stated in the Tort Liability Act. 70

The Supreme Court then moves on to interpret the term personal injury in the Tort Liability Act. There is no legal definition, but the term has been examined on numerous occasions in the preparatory works and in legal literature. 71

According to these sources, personal injury can be defined as physical and mental harm that has been caused by physical means or otherwise, eg a mechanically-induced injury to the body (a fractured foot, flesh wounds, internal bleeding, etc.) but also injuries caused by radiation, poisoning, etc (eg damaged tissues, sicknesses). 72

---

12 Council Directive 85/374/EEC of 25 July 1985 on the approximation of the laws, regulations and administrative provisions of the Member States concerning liability for defective products [1985] Official Journal (OJ) L 210/29.

73 In order for physical harm to constitute a personal injury, the Supreme Court states that there has to have been a change in or to a person's body and that this change results in a permanent or temporary worsening of an individual's health. It can be a visible external impact on the body, a state of disease or a reduced function of bodily organs. Such a reduced function can be a weakening of the immune system and an increased susceptibility to disease.

74 However, not all forms of bodily impact are compensable; liability for damages presupposes that the impact is *considerable* to the extent that it can be considered damage. Minor and quickly transient bodily reactions that only manifest themselves in mild pain or physical discomfort do not normally amount to personal injury.

75 Since tort liability also requires negligence or – as in this case – the deployment of a product with a safety defect and a causal link between this defect and the resulting harm, tortious liability does not, as a starting point, arise in relation to the common negative health effects that can result from normal exposure to commonly occurring substances in food or the environment.

76 The next question for the Supreme Court was if it is possible to establish liability merely due to an increased risk of future sickness. One argument in favour of such a position is to avoid claims becoming time-barred, but the Supreme Court acknowledged that, traditionally, there has been no such right in Swedish law and that the wording of the regulation almost speaks against such a development. A different approach would imply a fundamentally different view of the personal injury concept than the one that has been applied so far, which – in turn – would have implications for how fundamental principles of tort law are to be understood. Questions of principle that arise in tort law with liability based on risk are difficult to foresee and are therefore, according to the Supreme Court, best handled by the legislator.

77 The Supreme Court then reiterates that there are good reasons to distinguish between the harm in itself and its consequences: a finding that someone has suffered personal injury does not necessarily mean that this person is automatically entitled to damages. Chapter 5 of the TLA regulates the assessment and calculation of damages. What is compensated by applying ch 5 are rather the consequences of the personal injury (loss of income, costs, pain and suffering, etc), and not the personal injury as such.

78 When taking the high levels of PFAS in the residents' blood (among the highest ever to have been measured in the world) into consideration, in light of the fact that it will take many years before the levels have decreased to more normal ones, the Supreme Court concluded that the contaminated drinking water has had a substantial negative effect on the residents' bodies. Although the increased risk of future negative health effects is not in itself considered a personal injury,

the significant bodily deterioration manifested in the high levels of PFAS 'constitutes such a physical defective condition that constitutes a personal injury.'[13] The company was therefore held liable to compensate the residents for their personal injuries.

The Supreme Court had no possibility to judge on the matter as to the extent to which the personal injuries led to such consequences of the injuries entitling the appellants to compensation or the amount of any compensation. 79

c) Commentary

This ruling received considerable attention in the media and was a long-awaited relief for the residents of Ronneby, who have been involved in court proceedings for a decade. However, a few, important, questions remain to be answered. The ruling is merely a declaratory judgment on the prerequisite for the establishment of personal injury, and the residents now have to continue the process in specifying what consequences they have suffered that may lead to the payment of damages. By establishing that all the plaintiffs have suffered a personal injury, the more individualised examination of each individual's injury will be something to concretise within the levels of compensation; it remains to be seen what levels of damages might be appropriate and if the municipality's water company will offer a pragmatic solution out of court (which probably would be beneficial for everyone involved).[14] 80

Another question of perhaps more theoretical interest is of course the Supreme Court's discussion on a definition of personal injury. An important point is that the Supreme Court did *not* establish that risk of future injury can be considered as personal injury, but that an elevated *risk in itself* can constitute injury. This risk must be manifest and scientifically proven, and there are qualitative elements that must be met; the defective condition in or on the body must be substantial in both temporality and seriousness. 81

One remaining problem that the judgment does not solve is the matter of limitation periods in situations of delayed injuries. In the present case, the limitation period of ten years would have expired a couple of weeks after the judgment was passed by the Supreme Court. In Swedish law, the main rule is that the limitation period (ten years) starts from the time of the harmful act, regardless of the injured 82

---

13 The Supreme Court ruling, at 31.

14 The court costs for the claimants alone amounted to approx € 1,000,000.

party's knowledge of the injury.[15] There is, therefore, a risk that claims for compensation for delayed damage are time-barred before the damage is realised.[16]

83 The cause of delay can depend on: (a) the necessary accumulation of eg toxins before damage can be said to have occurred; (b) delayed discovery; or (c) (delayed) damage due to prior exposure of risk. The common feature is that the harm cannot be detected for a long period of time, although the time when the damage occurs varies. It has been argued that there are good reasons to separate between cases of damage that occurs with delay, and damage that is discovered with delay. The reason for this division is that the nature of the damage can influence the reasoning in a weighing of interests between the injured party and the tortfeasor.[17] While the injured party has a (justified) interest in an existing right to claim damages, the tortfeasor has a (justified) interest in predictability, in the sense of not having to be prepared to contest damage claims for all eternity.

84 In cases such as the present one, where people have been exposed to a substance that – much later – turns out (as a result of new, scientific findings or diagnostic methods) to be harmful, the general rules on limitation may provide unsatisfactory results. It can be questioned if the Swedish choice to let the general rule on limitation periods, without exception, run from the harmful act is in accordance with the right to a fair trial (art 6.1 European Convention on Human Rights).[18]

6. Personal Injury

85 The most important case on personal injury last year in Sweden was the Supreme Court case on 5 December: the *PFAS* case referred to above.

---

15 The PLA has a special rule on limitation (§ 12): the main rule is a limitation period of three years from when a party who seeks compensation received or should have received knowledge that the claim could be asserted. The claim for compensation must, however, be brought within ten years from the time the person who is allegedly liable for damages put the harmful product into circulation.

16 It seems like Sweden is rather exceptional from a European perspective, where most countries have, at least alternative, rules on limitation periods that start when the claimant becomes aware of the harm.

17 See *V Bolmgren*, Preskription vid fördröjda skador, Svensk Juristtidning (SvJT) 2023, 725–742.

18 See *Bolmgren*, SvJT 2023, 734–737.

C. Literature

1. *Stina Bratt*, Alternativa anspråksvägar i skadeståndsrätten – Om förhållandet mellan kontrakts- och deliktsansvar i avtalsförhållanden och kontraktskedjor [Alternative claim routes in tort law – On the relationship between contractual and tort liability in contractual relationships and contractual chains] (Jure, Stockholm 2023) 536 pp

The relationship between contractual and tort liability is a property law classic. In this doctoral thesis, alternative claim routes in tort law are examined. The book examines the opportunities which exist in Swedish law for an injured party to make a valid claim for damages according to both contract and tort rules. The main focus of the dissertation is claims for damages in contractual relationships and contract chains. 86

The book spans a wide field of different legal areas and deals with issues of damages in the event of, among other things, purchase, contracting and transport and addresses several central tort law themes, such as fault liability, strict liability, product liability and liability for pure property damage. In the thesis, comparative outlooks are also provided. 87

2. *Sören Öman*, AD om skadestånd, lön och preskription enligt LAS [AD on damages, salary and prescription according to LAS] (Åhnberg, 3rd edn Stockholm 2023) 107 pp

What has the Labour Court (AD) said about compensation to a person who was pressured to resign? What compensation levels apply in the event of wrongful terminations and dismissals? Does an individual have any possibility to receive damages or a salary even though the claim is time-barred? The answers to these and many other questions relating to damages, salaries and the statute of limitations according to the Employment Protection Act (LAS) can be found in this book. 88

The book presents the applicable rules as expressed by the Labour Court. The courts' judgments often contain guiding statements and educational summaries, and the court regularly follows what it itself says applies. The book contains 89 more than 140 selected quotations from guiding judgments, classified under various descriptive headings to enable easy access.

90 In the list of contents, there are questions on adjustment of damages when the employee has not done enough to reduce the damage, levels of damage and on the issue of whether prescription rules are applicable to claims that are not based directly on the Employment Protection Act.

3. *Bertil Bengtsson*, Miljöskadestånd och grannansvar [Environmental damage and neighbours' liability] (Norstedts juridik AB, Stockholm 2023) 162 pp

91 *Environmental damage and neighbours' liability* is an expanded edition of the author's previous book, *Damages for environmental damage.* The book deals with liability for environmental damage and certain other types of damage emanating from a business, where the legal situation has turned out to be surprisingly unclear. The legal area can be said to lie between tort law and environmental law, which has probably contributed to it often being overlooked in the jurisprudential debate, especially in recent years

92 This book primarily concerns the compensation rules in ch 32. of the Environmental Code (that is somewhat difficult to interpret) and the supplementary rules, the liability of neighbours, in ch 3 sec 1 of the Code of the Land.

4. *Måns Jacobsson*, Redarens rätt till ansvarsbegränsning – tolkning av internationella sjörättskonventioner [Shipowner's right to liability limitation – Interpretation of international maritime conventions], Svensk Jursttidning (SvJT) 2023, 50–58

93 In this article, the author discusses the question of whether national courts will follow the interpretation of the 1976 Convention on Limitation of Maritime Liability, as set out in the resolution by the International Maritime Organization, IMO. Among other things, the author highlights arguments on how the requirement of 'qualified gross negligence' should be interpreted, especially in relation to concepts such as 'intent' or 'wilful misconduct', but also that there is reason to assume that Swedish courts will interpret the Swedish provisions in the maritime law in accordance with what is stated in the resolutions of the IMO.

Together with the Supreme Court case from 14 November, 2023 (mentioned above), the article provides an interesting contribution to the interpretation of international conventions on maritime law, especially in relation to national legislation. 94

5. *Hannah Qvarsebo*, Det skadeståndsrättsliga föräldraansvaret och dess samspel med skadeståndets funktioner [Parental liability in tort law and the relationship with tort law functions], Juridisk tidskrift 2022/23, vol 4, 764–786

Anyone who has suffered damage as a result of a child's crime can choose to make a claim against the child's parents either based on vicarious liability, or with support of the independent liability for damage as a result of a lack of supervision over the child. These bases of liability differ in several ways. In this article, the author highlights some central differences between the bases of tort liability and discusses their interaction with the functions that damages are intended to have. 95

6. *Rebecca Larsson*, Särskild anhörigersättning – Stärkt rätt till ersättning för efterlevande anhöriga? [Särskild anhörigersättning – a strengthened right to compensation for close relatives?], Juridisk tidskrift 2023/24, vol 2, 284–311

On 1 July 2022, a new type of compensation was introduced in Sweden, special compensation to close relatives (*särskild anhörigersättning*). It is clear from the legal reasons that the purpose behind the introduction of this type of compensation was to strengthen surviving relatives' right to compensation. 96

In this article, the author aims to contribute to the discussion about how the *särskild anhörigersättning* strengthens close relatives' right to compensation. In her discussion, the question of how powerful the statutory right to compensation in practice can be, when it can involve a lengthy process for the person entitled to compensation to actually receive their compensation, with no guarantee of being ultimately fully compensated – and how this interacts with the functions of tort law – is examined. As part of this discussion, the author includes an overview of the compensation systems in Denmark, Finland and Norway. 97

7. *Håkan Andersson*, 14 articles on Tort Law, InfoTorg Juridik, infotorg.se

98 Over the years, faithful followers of this distinguished Yearbook have been able to read Håkan Andersson's in-depth and sharp reports on Swedish tort law. For a number of years, continuous reference has been made by the present reporter to the continuation of his close readings of Supreme Court rulings as presented in his publications on the online legal forum InfoTorg/Pointlex. Last year was no exception to his effort to incorporate the past year's rulings (sometimes together with other rulings from previous years) into a larger tort law context and to provide an explanatory framework through his much-appreciated analysis.

99 In this volume, it is not possible to give a full account of his articles, so I will have to succumb to a mere list of the articles, and provide follow-up information to anyone who would like a more detailed version:

(1) Frihetsberövandelagens ansvarsgräns vid falskt erkännande [Limit of liability under the Deprivation of Liberty Act in case of false confession], 1 March 2023
(2) Flerfaldig kränkningsersättning vid vidarespridning av förtalsuppgift, [Multiple infringement compensation in the event of dissemination of defamatory information], 10 March 2023
(3) Privatlivsskyddets utvidgning [The expansion of privacy protection], 31 March 2023
(4) Alternativa kravvägars temporalitet – sakrättsliga respektive skadeståndsrättsliga krav avseende samma egendom [Temporality of alternative claim paths – claims in rem and damages in respect of the same property], 1 June 2023
(5) Offentliga ersättningskrav och privaträttslig metodik [Public compensation requirements and private law methodology], 5 June 2023
(6) Den ideella humanjuridikens formalia – en disharmoni som upplöses i HD:s restriktiva tolkning av sig själv [The formality of non-profit humanitarian law – a disharmony that dissolves in HD's restrictive interpretation of itself], 15 June 2023
(7) Konstitutionalisering av ersättningsrätten (IV) – ersättningsprinciper vid rådighetsinskränkning pga miljöhänsyn (2:15 RF) [The constitutionalisation of the right to compensation (IV) – principles of compensation in the case of limitation of resources due to environmental concerns (2:15 RF)], 31 August 2023
(8) Val av ansvarsgrund vid myndigheters uppgiftsansvar [Selection of the basis of liability for authorities' data responsibility], 7 September 2023
(9) Försäkringsrättsliga komplikationer i anledning av covidpandemin [Insurance law complications due to the Covid pandemic], 13 September 2023
(10) Direktkravsdilemman (I) – kraven på kraven [Direct action dilemmas (I) – the requirements on the demands], 20 September 2023

(11) Direktkravsdilemman (II) – rättskraft och bevisverkan [Direct action dilemmas (II) – Binding effect and evidentiary effect], September 22, 2023
Skadeståndsansvar enligt allmänna principer i hyresförhållanden [Liability for damages according to general principles in tenancies], 8 November 2023
(12) Redaransvar respektive principalansvar – några jämförande konkretioner [Redaransvar and vicarious liability – some comparative concretnesses], 24 November 2023
(13) Risk för skada respektive risk som skada – kvalificering av personskadebegreppet [Risk of damage and risk as damage – qualification of the concept of personal injury], 15 December 2023.

Peter Loser

XXX. Switzerland

A. Legislation

1. Revision of Civil Procedure Act of 17 March 2023 to facilitate Liability Proceedings (with Collective Legal Protection for Liability Proceedings still to come)

On 17 March 2023, the Statute on Civil Procedure was partially revised.[1] The amendments will come into force on 1 January 2025 and are also relevant for liability proceedings. As a result, the new regulations on *legal costs and other formalities* may facilitate liability proceedings. 1

In particular, the legal costs are newly regulated. Under the current law, the plaintiff can be obliged to advance the estimated court costs in full. In principle, the advance payments will now amount to a maximum of half of the estimated total amount. In future, access to the court will also be made easier for persons who do not fulfil the requirements for the free administration of justice. The conciliation procedure is also strengthened in the revised Statutes on Civil Procedure. The out-of-court settlement of disputes is already successful in many cases today, as 50 % to 80 % of disputes can be settled in this way. In future, arbitration is to be used even more frequently. The conciliation authority will also be given additional powers. 2

Collective legal protection is still separate from the revision. The current status of the relevant legislative work is as follows:[2] 3

- In July 2023, the Grand Chamber of the Swiss Parliament took note of comparative law analyses. However, before making its decision, it requested an extended examination of possible security measures to prevent misuse of the class action instruments. These results have been available since February 2024. 4

---

1 See Press Release of Swiss Federal Council of 6 June 2023 (<https://www.admin.ch/gov/de/start/dokumentation/medienmitteilungen.msg-id-97610.html>). For a detailed analysis *D Staehelin/F von Mutzenbecher*, Die Revision der ZPO vom 17. März 2023, Schweizerische Juristenzeitung (SJZ) 2023, 815 ff.

2 See Press Release of Swiss Parliament 12 April 2024 (<https://www.parlament.ch/press-releases/Pages/mm-rk-n-2024-04-12.aspx>).

https://doi.org/10.1515/9783111376721-031

5 – This approach by Parliament has been criticised by consumer protection organisations as a delaying tactic.[3]

6 – However, following the recent judgment against Switzerland by the European Court of Human Rights (ECtHR) (*Verein KlimaSeniorinnen Schweiz and Others v Switzerland*)[4], the Parliamentary Commission sees a need for further clarification.

7 – The legislative project will therefore not be discussed by Parliament until the 2024 autumn session at the earliest.

2. Renewal of Project for Liability of Swiss Companies for Violation of Environmental Standards

8 In a sense, Switzerland was a pioneer in terms of corporate liability for damage caused by human rights violations and environmental offences abroad. A vote was held at the end of 2020 on such a legislative project as a popular initiative (known as the *Konzernverantwortungsinitiative* or 'Responsible Business Initiative'). The initiative was narrowly defeated.[5]

9 Following the failure of the referendum, a second initiative is now being launched to regulate liability.[6]

10 The reason for this is that the European Union has adopted a Directive with liability rules in the form of the Corporate Sustainability Due Diligence Directive (CSDDD)[7]. The new EU Directive establishes explicit civil liability for EU companies in the event of intentional or negligent breaches of due diligence obligations to prevent damage. However, the EU Directive is similar in some respects to the failed Swiss popular initiative. However, the EU Directive goes much less far when it comes to the burden of proof and the threshold values for the scope of applica-

---

3 Stiftung für Konsumentenschutz (Foundation for Consumer Protection) of 4 July 2023: 'Collective legal protection: The delaying tactics must come to an end!' (<https://www.konsumentenschutz.ch/medienmitteilungen/kollektivklage-tanzt-die-politik-nach-der-pfeife-der-konzerne/>).

4 Cf no 146 below.

5 Swiss Report in the Yearbook 2020: *P Loser*, Switzerland, in: E Karner/BC Steininger (eds), European Tort Law (ETL) 2020 (2021) 663, no 1, with further refs.

6 Compare the website of the 'Koalition für Konzernverantwortung' <https://konzernverantwortung.ch/>; and the report 'Zweiter Anlauf der Initiative', Tagesanzeiger 3 June 2024.

7 Directive (EU) 2024/1760 of the European Parliament and of the Council of 13 June 2024 on corporate sustainability due diligence and amending Directive (EU) 2019/1937 and Regulation (EU) 2023/2859; Text with EEA relevance [2024] Official Journal (OJ) L 1760. The proposal for the Directive was adopted by the European Commission on 23 February 2022. Cf European Commission website <https://commission.europa.eu/business-economy-euro/doing-business-eu/corporate-sustainability-due-diligence_en#documents>.

tion.[8] The Member States now have two years to transpose the Directive into national law.

The introduction of a new liability regulation in Switzerland is supported not only by the former group of initiators, but also by politicians who were originally against it.[9] A cross-party committee with politicians also from the bourgeois bloc and representatives from the business world is calling on the Federal Council and Parliament to introduce an internationally harmonised corporate responsibility law as quickly as possible. One of the main arguments against the Swiss popular initiative was that Switzerland would be at a competitive disadvantage if it adopted stricter regulation than other countries. The situation has now been reversed. 11

However, it should be noted that – at least according to some scholars – liability for breaches of due diligence can already be established under current law.[10] 12

B. Cases

1. Swiss Federal Supreme Court, 9 May 2023, Federal Supreme Court Decision (Bundesgerichtsentscheid, BGE) 4 A_18/2023: Definition of Damage – No Liability Claim for Car Buyers Affected by Incorrect Behaviour of Producers ('Dieselgate')[11]

a) Brief Summary of the Facts

A (plaintiff), domiciled in Switzerland, purchased a vehicle from C AG (seller), domiciled in Switzerland, on 3 February 2015 for the price of CHF 56,920.[12] This car was manufactured by B AG (defendant), based in Germany. 13

8 Compare the analysis 'Die EU beschliesst schärfere Regeln zur Konzernverantwortung – der Bundesrat wird wohl nachziehen müssen', Neue Zürcher Zeitung (NZZ) 30 May 2024.

9 Cf the 'Appell für Konzernverantwortung im internationalen Gleichschritt' of 1 June 2024 (<https://www.appell-konzernverantwortung.ch/>); and the report 'Zweiter Anlauf der Initiative', Tagesanzeiger 3 June 2024.

10 Cf no 151 f below; and 'Die EU beschliesst schärfere Regeln zur Konzernverantwortung – der Bundesrat wird wohl nachziehen müssen', NZZ 30 May 2024.

11 At <http://www.bger.ch/jurisdiction-recht>. Cf *V Jentsch/S Angliker*, Diesel emissions scandal before the Federal Supreme Court – judgments 4 A_17/2023 and 4 A_18/2023 of 9 May 2023, Anwaltsrevue 2023, 347 ff; *AF Rusch*, Haftpflichtrecht – Wichtige Urteile, Aktuelle Juristische Praxis (AJP) 2023, 1285, 1300 ff; *M Vischer*, Entscheidbesprechungen, AJP 2023, 1311 ff; *W Fellmann*, Entwicklungen im Versicherungs- und Haftpflichtrecht, Schweizerische Juristenzeitung (SJZ) 2024, 386 ff;

14 On 4 June 2020, the plaintiff filed a lawsuit against the defendant with the Commercial Court of the Canton of Zurich. He claimed that, due to software manipulation for which the defendant was responsible, unauthorised defeat devices such as switching logic and thermal windows had been used in his vehicle in order to comply with the emissions regulations during the standardised tests on the test bench. In normal operation on the road, however, his car had far higher exhaust emissions (diesel emissions scandal).

15 The plaintiff claims non-contractual damages, demanding the repayment of the purchase price of CHF 56,920 plus interest, simultaneously with returning the vehicle. He wants to be placed in the same position 'as if he had never concluded the purchase contract'; in other words, the purchase price should be reimbursed to him under the title of *Naturalrestitution* ie 'restitution in kind'. In his reply, the plaintiff stated that he had since sold the car (on 11 June 2020) for CHF 23,000 and was therefore reducing his main claim to CHF 33,920 (difference between the purchase price of CHF 56,920 and the resale price of CHF 23,000), whereby the return of the vehicle was no longer relevant.

16 Contingently, the plaintiff sought damages in the amount of 25% of the new price, ie CHF 14,230, plus interest. He is thus demanding the difference between the purchase price he paid and the 'hypothetical lower price' that he would have paid 'if all the information' about the manipulated software and the emissions values had been disclosed truthfully at the time the contract was concluded (referred to by the plaintiff as an 'overcharge').

17 By order and judgment dated 24 November 2022, the Commercial Court dismissed the proceedings in the amount of CHF 23,000 due to the withdrawal of the claim. It otherwise dismissed the action.

18 In his appeal in civil matters, the plaintiff demands that the judgment of the Commercial Court be set aside. The defendant should be ordered to pay him CHF 33,920 or CHF 14,230 in the alternative, plus interest.

b) Judgment of the Court

19 The Federal Supreme Court first clarified that the action was not brought against the seller (C AG), but against the defendant as the manufacturer of the vehicle, with whom he never had a contractual relationship. Accordingly, the claim is

S Greinig, Le dommage face au scandale du 'dieselgate', Haftpflicht und Versicherung (HAVE) 2023, 242 ff.

12 1 CHF = 1.03 € (therefore euro-equivalents are not cited hereinafter).

not based on the rules concerning the contractual warranty for defects in the purchased item and also not on the provisions concerning defects in consent upon conclusion of the contract. Rather, the plaintiff claims damages for alleged unauthorised acts.

The Federal Supreme Court then turns to the main issue: damage. A claim for damages in tort presupposes damage. The question under discussion is whether the plaintiff suffered damage because the vehicle he purchased and has since resold (allegedly) 'exhibited far higher exhaust emissions in normal road use'. 20

The Commercial Court as the lower court was unable to identify any relevant and proven damage.[13] According to the Commercial Court, with regard to the *in rem* restitution demanded in the main claim (repayment of the purchase price), damage in the amount of the purchase price would only have occurred if the plaintiff had not purchased a vehicle at all without the allegedly unauthorised actions of the respondent. Only in this case – according to the Commercial Court – would it have to be assumed according to the difference theory that he could still dispose of the purchase price amount in his current assets without the damaging event. According to general life experience, it is to be expected that the plaintiff would have purchased an alternative vehicle if he had been aware of the alleged software manipulation. Damage corresponding to the amount of the purchase price was therefore not proven. 21

According to the Commercial Court, the plaintiff had also not provided sufficient evidence with regard to an excessively high purchase price ('overcharge', ie the difference between the purchase price paid and the hypothetical price at the time when all information was disclosed). The plaintiff should have explained to what extent only a reduced resale price was achievable due to the alleged software manipulation. The difference between the actual resale price and the hypothetical resale price without the alleged manipulation would then have represented the realised reduced value as damage. Furthermore, the plaintiff did not take into account the fact that he had used the car intensively since purchasing it on 3 February 2015. 22

The Federal Supreme Court then clarified once again that the question is not whether the vehicle was defective according to the purchase contract ('unfavourable deviation of the actual condition from the target condition'). Nor is the issue whether the 'deceptions through misrepresentations and concealments' alleged against the defendant manufacturer in connection with the diesel emissions scandal would have permitted a rescission of the purchase contract concluded at the time (with C AG), including a reclaim of the purchase price. The sole subject of 23

13 BGE 4 A_18/2023, Consideration 4.4.

these proceedings is the question of whether the plaintiff has suffered damage in the sense of tort law as a result of the (allegedly) unauthorised conduct of the defendant manufacturer (use of software to manipulate the emissions values).

24 The plaintiff sees the damage in the conclusion of an 'unintentional contract'.[14] He referred to the judgment of the German Federal Court of Justice of 25 May 2020 regarding the diesel emissions scandal.[15] The Federal Court of Justice considered it decisive (in the context of an action for intentional damage pursuant to sec 826 of the German Civil Code [*Bürgerliches Gesetzbuch*, BGB]; corresponding to the provision of art 41 para 2 of the Swiss Code of Obligations [*Obligationenrecht*, OR]) that the buyer in that case had concluded a purchase contract that he would not have 'reasonably' entered into if he had known about the software manipulation. This 'unintentional obligation' constituted damage relevant under liability law. According to the Federal Court of Justice, the difference hypothesis must always be subjected to normative scrutiny because it represents a value-neutral calculation. What is required is an evaluative review of the result obtained on the basis of the difference hypothesis measured against the protective purpose of liability and the compensatory function of damages. The claim for damages does not only serve to compensate for a detrimental effect on the objective financial situation of the injured party. Rather, the injured party must be able to free himself from an 'unwanted' obligation, because it is not least a matter of protecting the general freedom of action and specifically the individual's right to economic self-determination.

25 The Federal Supreme Court cannot follow this view for Swiss law. It makes several fundamental statements on the concept of damage:[16] the Federal Supreme Court has consistently applied the difference theory to the concept of damage under tort law for many years. Accordingly, damage is deemed to be the unintentional reduction in net assets, corresponding to the difference between the current state of assets and the (hypothetical) state that the assets would have had without the damaging event. The damage may consist of an increase in liabilities, a reduction in assets or a loss of profit. It is therefore a purely economic concept of damage based on net assets. Impairments that do not affect assets are not relevant damage under liability law. This also applies in particular where a certain expense loses its intrinsic value because the purpose for which it was intended does not materialise or does not materialise in full. For example, loss of use or deprivation of use does not in itself constitute damage. According to case law, compensation for

14 BGE 4 A_18/2023, Consideration 5.2 and 5.3.3.
15 German Federal Supreme Court (Bundesgerichtshof, BGH) of 25 May, 2020 No VI ZR 252/19.
16 BGE 4 A_18/2023, Consideration 5.3.1.

so-called 'normative' damage – not based on a reduction in assets – is only awarded in two constellations, namely for household damage and care damage. Only in these cases is compensation payable even if there is no specific loss of assets. The Federal Supreme Court has expressly rejected the compensability of other types of normative damage.

26 Based on these principles, the Federal Supreme Court concludes that the 'unintentional' conclusion of a vehicle purchase contract does not in itself constitute compensable damage in the sense of tort law, provided that no concrete economic losses are associated with it. On the merits, the plaintiff is seeking 'disguised satisfaction for material defects'.[17]

27 The Federal Supreme Court also criticised the fact that the plaintiff wanted a 'penalty' as a result.[18] The plaintiff claims that the legal costs exceed the respective main claim. He complains of a 'lack of efficient instruments in collective legal protection' and the 'associated inefficiency in the legal protection system'. The 'preventive function of tort law against fraudulent damage to assets' must be helped to achieve a breakthrough. The general 'prohibition of enrichment' under tort law, which conflicts with this, must take a back seat in terms of value compared to these normative purpose aspects. For the Federal Supreme Court, this represents a criticism *de lege ferenda*; the Federal Supreme Court is bound by the applicable laws.

28 The Federal Supreme Court summarised that the plaintiff had not claimed damages in the sense of liability law. Rather, he is dissatisfied with the purchase agreement, which he would no longer conclude, or at least not on these terms. Contractual remedies are available for such a scenario. Liability law does not provide any means to financially compensate such non-economic disruptions and disappointments regardless of the damage.[19] The claim was therefore dismissed.

c) Commentary

29 The considerations of the Federal Supreme Court can be agreed with in several – but not all – points.

30 **Commentary 1: Punitive Damages**

31 Punitive damages are alien to Swiss law and introducing them would be within the competence of the legislator (it is also up to the legislator to introduce legal

---

17 BGE 4 A_18/2023, Consideration 5.3.3.
18 BGE 4 A_18/2023, Consideration 5.3.4.
19 BGE 4 A_18/2023, Consideration 5.4.

remedies for collective redress in order to make the legal protection system more efficient[20]). Such legal requirements apparently exist in European Union law. The EU Regulation, which is relevant to the *Dieselgate* judgments handed down within the EU,[21] states: 'The Member States shall lay down the provisions on penalties applicable for infringement by manufacturers of the provisions of this Regulation and shall take all measures necessary to ensure that they are implemented. *The penalties provided for must be effective, proportionate and dissuasive.*'[22] Current Swiss law cannot be reinterpreted in this way.[23]

32 The Federal Supreme Court is also rightly critical of the idea that a loss of use constitutes compensable damage.[24] In many cases, the award of damages for the impairment of property without the occurrence of financial loss would result in a form of satisfaction, which Swiss law only provides for restrictively in the case of personal injury or injury to personality.

33 Commentary 2: Unwanted Contracts

34 However, the conclusion of an unwanted contract is a different matter. If the Federal Supreme Court generally rejects compensation here because there is no impairment of assets, it is going too far.[25] However, such a remedy is not available per se if an unwanted contract is concluded. For a correct and value-compliant judgment, the background to the claim should be examined more closely.

35 This responsibility towards third parties in the case of 'unwanted' contracts can be seen as a special case of tort liability.[26] In my opinion, however, it is

---

20 Such a project is currently being discussed in Parliament: see no 3 above.

21 Cf CJEU 21.3.2023, C-100/21, *Mercedes Benz Group*, ECLI:EU:C:2023:229and the judgment of the German Federal Court of Justice BGH 26 June 2023 No VIa ZR 335/21.

22 Art 13 sec 1 of the Regulation (EC) No 715/2007 (emphasis added).

23 Generally critical of such reinterpretations, eg in the sense of an 'Americanisation' of liability law, *H Honsell*, Schweizerisches Obligationenrecht, Besonderer Teil (10th edn 2017) 94. In contrast, *AF Rusch*, Will das Recht, dass man klagt? in: P Breitschmid/I Jent-Sørensen/Hans-Schmid/M Sogo (eds), Tatsachen – Verfahren – Vollstreckung, Festschrift für Isaak Meier zum 65. Geburtstag (2015) 569 ff; *AF Rusch/A Schwizer*, Gewährleistung und Haftung bei abgasmanipulierten Fahrzeugen, AJP 2016, 1299 ff, 1309; *Rusch*, AJP 2023, 1304; *T Werlin*, Es braucht einen effektiven Zugang zum Recht für Geschädigte, HAVE 2023, 179 ff.

24 For restrictions, see *Vischer*, AJP 2023, 1314 f.

25 Cf also *Rusch*, AJP 2023, 1301 ff. Contra *Fellmann*, SJZ 2024, 387, who welcomes the Federal Supreme Court's restrictive view of normative damage, but does not address the special problem of the unwanted contract arising from the offence of *culpa in contrahendo* as described below; and *Jentsch/Angliker*, 9 May 2023, Anwaltsrevue 2023, 351.

26 *H Honsell* in: C Widmer Lüchinger/D Oser (eds), Basler Kommentar, Obligationenrecht I (7th edn 2020) art 197 no 7 in fine ('Deliktsanspruch gegen den Hersteller'). In conclusion also *Vischer*, AJP 2023, 1319 f.

more convincing if it is seen as an issue to be addressed in the *culpa in contrahendo* doctrine, ie as a sanction for breach of trust in the contractual environment (so-called *Vertrauenshaftung*, 'liability based on reliance').[27] Depending on who has committed the *culpa in contrahendo*, the sanction is directed against the contractual partner or against the third party. In other words:

– The problem of the unwanted contract as a result of deceptive behaviour concerns the issue of *culpa in contrahendo*. 36
– In the present case, however, we are dealing with the behaviour of third parties (manufacturers) who, although they are not parties to the contract, nevertheless influence the conclusion of the contract through the information they provide. 37
– In exceptional cases, such third parties can be held liable on the basis of *culpa in contrahendo*. The sanction in this case is so-called *negativer Vertrauensschutz*, 'the negative protection of legitimate expectations': the deceived party must be placed in the same position as if it had not relied on the incorrect information.[28] This results in restitution in kind (*Naturalrestitution*). 38

Commentary 3: Harmonisation with the *culpa in contrahendo* Doctrine 39

With this qualification, it is firstly clear that the sanction in the sense of the 40
negative protection of legitimate expectations can consist of the release from the unwanted contractual obligation.[29] On the other hand, however, it is also clear that the legislator's judgments and limitations in this area must be taken into account.[30] These arise from the regulations on the cancellation of contracts due to defects of consent and the regulations on the cancellation and reversal of purchase contracts due to defective goods. In the case of merely insignificant deviations and

27 Cf *P Loser*, Die Vertrauenshaftung im schweizerischen Schuldrecht (2006) no 858 ff (on reliance on product advertising no 797). Also *Vischer*, AJP 2023, 1316, 1319 f, points out the proximity to *culpa in contrahendo* and the protection of legitimate expectations as the material basis of responsibility, but rejects liability in reliance as an independent legal concept alongside the offence. Liability based on reliance was also mentioned by *Rusch/Schwizer*, AJP 2106, 1306 f, as a possible basis for liability; however, their reference to *CW Canaris*, Die Produzentenhaftung in dogmatischer und rechtspolitischer Sicht, Juristenzeitung (JZ) 1968, 494, 499 f, remains vague, especially since *Canaris* uses liability based on reliance as a basis for product liability in cases of damage caused by product defects (see *Loser*, supra, no 924 ff).

28 *Vischer*, AJP 2023, 1316; see already *Loser* (fn 27) nos 858, 1237.

29 Cf *Loser* (fn 27) nos 859, 861 in fine.

30 *Loser* (fn 27) nos 719, 732, 858 ('avoidance of contradictions with the legal institution of the contract') 861.

deceptions, a comprehensive cancellation of the contract is not possible, but only a correction of the price.[31]

41 It must also be taken into account that there are also and above all options for cancelling unwanted contracts in relation to the contractual partner (defects of consent, warranty in sales contract law). If the affected party voluntarily waives these options vis-à-vis the seller, it cannot seek compensation from the third party or the manufacturer (duty to minimise damage).[32]

42 In the case of the negative protection of legitimate expectations and when determining the hypothetical situation, it must also be taken into account – as the Commercial Court as the lower instance stated – whether the party concerned would not have purchased the vehicle at all or would have purchased a different vehicle if the correct information had been provided.

43 As a result, a claim for cancellation of the contract and reimbursement of the entire purchase price is likely to be rare. It will often be a case of reimbursement of a loss due to an excessively high purchase price or other damage (eg retrofitting costs or increased fuel consumption).[33] However, this requires the concretisation and proof of the corresponding financial loss, which the plaintiff did not provide in the present case.[34] In this respect, the rejection of the claim by the Federal Court is ultimately correct, but for different reasons.

---

31 According to art 205 sec 2 Swiss Code of Obligations (SCO), the judge can only demand a reduction or adjustment of the price instead of cancellation. Cf *Honsell* (fn 23) 94; *Loser* (fn 27) no 732 ('adjustment' instead of 'cancellation').

32 Cf *Loser* (fn 27) no 861.

33 Cf *Vischer*, AJP 2023, 1318 f ('price difference damage'); *Honsell* (fn 26) art 197 no 7 in fine; BGE 4 A_18/2023, Consideration 5.3.2.

34 *Rusch*, AJP 2023, 1303, on the other hand, is in favour of a damage estimate and wants to exempt the plaintiff from an exact damage calculation.

2. Swiss Federal Supreme Court, 16 November 2022, BGE 4 A_603/2020: Unlawfulness in Case of Pure Economic Loss – No Liability of a Bank for Money Laundering due to Organisational Deficiencies[35]

a) Brief Summary of the Facts

X was a Swiss citizen and opened an account with a bank in 1999 and a second account in 2004. X presented himself to the bank as an asset manager. Each time he claimed to be the Beneficial Owner of the deposited assets. The accounts were opened to hold money in the form of commission that he earned from his professional activities, but not his clients' money. He also claimed that he wanted to carry out transactions for his own account. 44

X convinced several clients to entrust him with money for various investments as their asset manager. He promised them an annual return of 10 % to 20 % and sometimes guaranteed 80 % or 100 % of the invested capital. The alleged asset manager deceived his clients for several years by making them believe that he was investing their money in profitable businesses, while in reality he used the money entrusted to him by 'new' victims to pay out other victims or to pay them alleged interest. 45

The bank had installed a computer monitoring system to recognise suspicious transactions. An alarm was triggered when various predefined criteria were met. In the case of the asset manager and his company, the system was set to a low-risk relationship; due to his Swiss citizenship and registered profession, the asset manager was categorised as a 'normal client', which generated fewer alerts. In fact, there were no alerts. 46

In 2004, the criminal prosecution authorities initiated a criminal investigation against X for money laundering. On 31 January 2006, they submitted a request for information to the bank. The bank complied with the request. The legal department forwarded the case to the compliance department for internal review. The investigation subsequently petered out and no written conclusions were reached. 47

35 At <http://www.bger.ch/jurisdiction-recht>. Cf inter alia *S Emmenegger/L Thévenoz/P Bürgi/ F Liégeois Fabien/T Brander*, Das schweizerische Bankprivatrecht 2022 – Le droit bancaire privé suisse 2022, 231 ff, 235 f, 254 f r33; *D Maritz/M Hochstrasser*, Entscheidbesprechungen, AJP 2023, 519 ff; *AF Rusch*, Haftpflichtrecht – wichtige Urteile, AJP 2023, 1285 f; *M Schaub*, Haftung einer Bank für Geldwäscherei durch Unterlassungen von Angestellten, Schweizerische Zeitschrift für Wirtschaftsrecht (SZW) 2023, 501 ff.

48 On 8 May 2013, the Supervisory Commission fined the bank CHF 230,000 for violating the Agreement on the Swiss banks' Code of Conduct with regard to the exercise of due diligence (CDB). The bank was accused of failing to correctly apply several regulations for the prevention and detection of money laundering activities.

49 Several defrauded customers subsequently sued the bank for damages.

b) Judgment of the Court

50 The central material question of the case was whether the requirement of unlawfulness for non-contractual liability of the bank was fulfilled. This was a case of pure financial loss. According to Swiss practice, it was therefore necessary for the bank to have violated a protective norm. Such protective norms can be found throughout the Swiss legal system (private, administrative or criminal law). The criminal provision of art 305bis Swiss Penal Code (SPC) on money laundering is such a protective norm.[36] As money laundering is only punishable in the case of intent, but not in the case of negligence, it was therefore necessary that liability be established and that evidence be provided that an intentional act of money laundering had taken place.

51 A bank as a legal entity can only be held liable in accordance with civil law standards if a governing body has committed an unlawful or, in this case, a criminal act of money laundering (art 55 Swiss Civil Code [SCC]).[37] A bank may also be liable if one or more employees have committed an unlawful act or, in this case, a criminal offence of money laundering (art 55 Swiss Code of Obligations [SCO]).[38]

52 It is therefore necessary for a governing body or an employee to have committed an unlawful act. As an act of money laundering is only punishable if committed with intent, it was therefore necessary for liability to be proven that an act of

---

36 Art 305bis sec 1 Swiss Penal Code (SPC): 'Any person who as part of his profession accepts, holds on deposit, or assists in investing or transferring outside assets and fails to ascertain the identity of the beneficial owner of the assets with the care that is required in the circumstances shall be liable to a custodial sentence not exceeding one year or to a monetary penalty.'

37 Art 55 secs 1 and 2 Swiss Civil Code (SCC): 'The governing bodies express the will of the legal entity. They bind the legal entity by concluding transactions and by their other actions.'

38 Art 55 sec 1 Swiss Code of Obligations (SCO): 'An employer is liable for the damage caused by his employees or ancillary staff in the performance of their work unless he proves that he took all due care to avoid a damage of this type or that the damage would have occurred even if all due care had been taken.'

money laundering had been committed with intent or at least with contingent intent (*dolus eventualis*).

The courts came to the conclusion that, from 2006 onwards, the bank should have suspected that X's behaviour was incorrect. In this case, however, it was not possible to establish exactly who had made a mistake. The bank was poorly organised, which is why it was very difficult to reconstruct the events. It was also not proven that an organ or an employee had deliberately committed an act of money laundering. 53

The plaintiffs had invoked the criminal liability of companies under art 102 of the Swiss Penal Code (SPC). According to sec 1, a company (and therefore also a bank) is liable to prosecution if a crime is committed in the exercise of its commercial activities and if it is not possible to attribute this act to any specific natural person due to the inadequate organisation of the undertaking.[39] According to sec 2, in the case of certain offences (including money laundering), the undertaking is also liable to prosecution alongside a known offender if it fails to take all the reasonable organisational measures that are required in order to prevent such an offence.[40] 54

However, the Federal Supreme Court stated that the provision of art 102 SPC is merely an attribution standard (*Zurechnungsnorm*, 'rule on the imputation of third party acts'), not an independent criminal provision. It is questionable whether a criminal attribution standard is suitable to establish civil liability.[41] An attribution standard for the civil liability of the company is generally to be found in civil law or tort law.[42] The question could ultimately be left open, because even if art 102 SPC could be considered to be a protective norm, intentional behaviour would have to be proven. The same is required for the civil law attribution standards of art 55 SCC and art 55 SCO. 55

In the present case, however, it was not proven that a governing body or an employee had intentionally committed an act of money laundering. Therefore, 56

---

39 Art 102 sec 1 Swiss Penal Code: 'If a felony or misdemeanour is committed in an undertaking in the exercise of commercial activities in accordance with the objects of the undertaking and if it is not possible to attribute this act to any specific natural person due to the inadequate organisation of the undertaking, then the felony or misdemeanour is attributed to the undertaking.'

40 Art 102 sec 2 Swiss Penal Code: 'If the offence committed falls under Articles 260ter, 260quinquies, 305bis, 322ter, 322quinquies, 322septies paragraph 1 or 322octies, the undertaking is penalised irrespective of the criminal liability of any natural persons, provided the undertaking has failed to take all the reasonable organisational measures that are required in order to prevent such an offence.'

41 Rejecting this, eg *DS Weber/L Baumgartner*, Zur Schutznormqualität von Art. 102 para. 2 StGB, AJP 2023, 437.

42 BGE 4 A_603/2020, Consideration 8; cf no 51 above.

there was no attribution in accordance with the civil law attribution standards. However, criminal attribution was also ruled out for this reason. The bank's liability was therefore rejected.

c) Commentary

57 The Federal Supreme Court repeatedly pointed out in the case that no intent or contingent intent (*dolus eventualis*) could be proven on the basis of the elements of the facts established. The elements were too 'nebulous' for any criminal intent to be inferred.

58 The Federal Supreme Court then also stated somewhat resignedly that the requirements for criminal liability or the civil liability of companies are difficult to fulfil if a lack of organisation prevents the perpetrator from being discovered. The doctrine has not yet really solved this dilemma.[43]

59 The described problem arises in particular in cases where wilful conduct is required for the establishment of liability. In practice, this requires that the behaviour of the specific persons can be reconstructed, which is difficult for the injured parties as outsiders due to a lack of insight into the specific organisation of the company. The result that liability is often denied is lamented in doctrine,[44] which has led to various solutions, some of which seem very creative.[45]

60 Another solution could be – but this was not done in the present case – for the plaintiffs to provide as detailed allegations and evidence as possible for specific circumstances and events.[46] In this way, the court can then be enabled to affirm an intentional act from the overall circumstances of the case. Direct proof of subjective intent is not always required for the existence of contingent intent (*dolus eventualis*).

---

43 BGE 4 A_603/2020, Consideration 8.
44 Cf *Rusch*, AJP 2023, 1303, 1285 f.
45 Cf the refs in *Rusch*, AJP 2023, 1303, 1286; and in *Maritz/Hochstrasser*, AJP 2023, 519, 523 f.
46 Convincing *Maritz/Hochstrasser*, AJP 2023, 519, 523.

3. Swiss Federal Supreme Court, 22 March 2023, BGE 6B_47/2021: Unlawfulness in the case of Omission – Voluntary Assumption of a Contractual Guarantor Position vis-à-vis Third Parties Not Party to the Contract[47]

a) Brief Summary of the Facts

On 26 May 2015, C, as an employee of painter D, was carrying out painting work on a box for compacting waste that was parked in front of bakery E. He asked technician F to help him open the waste container. He asked F, a technician employed by the bakery, to help him open the approx 220 kg unloading cap of the waste container. 61

The technician F asked his supervisor B whether F and the plant mechanic G could help the painter to open the hatch in question and whether they could use the forklift truck to do so. B was the safety officer at the bakery and was obliged by his employment contract to ensure safety in the company, to recognise dangerous situations and take the necessary measures. B authorised F and G to assist, stating that the unloading hatch had to be secured when it was opened. Painter C and mechanic G lifted the flap a little using muscle power. Technician F pushed the forks of the forklift truck under the flap so that it rested on the fork ends. F then lifted the flap further with the forks. Seconds later, the unloading flap slipped off the ends of the forks, slammed shut and hit C on the head. He suffered extremely serious head injuries and died at the scene of the accident. 62

b) Judgment of the Court

It was disputed before the courts whether the safety officer B employed by the bakery had a guarantor position (*Garantenstellung*, 'position with duties to prevent harm to others') not only towards the employees of the bakery, but also towards third parties. 63

The Federal Supreme Court ruled in favour of this: if B is asked for permission to perform a specific activity within the scope of his contractual duties as the company's safety officer, he assumes responsibility for this task as the company's safety officer by authorising or not prohibiting a specific activity. As the safety officer, B was also responsible in a qualified manner for the prevention of danger and the safety of the persons involved in this task. By authorising or not prohibiting the 64

47 At <http://www.bger.ch/jurisdiction-recht>. Cf *Fellmann*, SJZ 2024, 386, 387 f.

opening of the unloading hatch, he had (voluntarily) extended his contractual duty as guarantor to the other persons involved in this activity.[48]

c) Commentary

65 These were criminal proceedings. Nevertheless, the Federal Supreme Court's considerations are also likely to be relevant for civil liability, which was not conclusively assessed in these proceedings.[49]

66 A guarantor's liability for omissions can arise in particular from a contractual obligation (eg from an employment contract). Until now, however, the question of whether and when a contractual guarantor obligation can also give rise to duties to act and civil liability towards third parties – who are not contractual partners – remained unresolved. Following this ruling, it can be assumed – as *Walter Fellmann* rightly analyses – that the Federal Supreme Court now also considers the (voluntary) extension of a (employment) contractual guarantor position to third parties by the obligor himself to be possible in liability law if his conduct has a recognisable effect on third parties.[50]

4. Swiss Federal Supreme Court, 24 January 2023, BGE 4 A_314/2022: Liability for Motor Vehicles – House Fire Caused by a Heated Catalytic Converter does not Constitute an Operational Risk of the Vehicle[51]

a) Brief Summary of the Facts

67 Plaintiff A is a farmer who runs a farm in the canton of Schwyz in Switzerland.

68 On 29 October 2016, A had contract work carried out by C. C is the owner of a vehicle and he drove his van to the plaintiff's business twice. He parked his van in the plaintiff's barn each time to reload timber onto an agricultural transporter. After the timber had been reloaded, the van was left in the barn. A short time

48 BGE 6B_47/2021, Consideration 5.3.
49 Cf *Fellmann*, SJZ 2024, 386, 388.
50 Cf ibid.
51 At <http://www.bger.ch/jurisdiction-recht>. Cf *J Nef*, Fahrzeugbrand und Haftung nach Art. 58 Abs. 1 SVG, HAVE 2023, 251 ff; *M Spinner*, Keine Verwirklichung der Betriebsgefahr eines Lieferwagens, ius.focus 2023 No 66; *Fellmann*, SJZ 2024, 386, 390 f.

later, a smouldering fire broke out in the barn, causing considerable damage. Apparently, the heated catalytic converter of the van had ignited easily combustible hay lying on the floor in the barn close to the vehicle, causing the fire to break out. The heated catalytic converter of the van thus caused the fire.

The van was insured with B Insurance AG (the defendant). 69

A filed a claim for damages against B AG with the court of first instance. This 70
court considered that the fire in the barn had been caused by the operation of the van and upheld the claim. The court of second instance and the Federal Court, however, dismissed the claim.

b) Judgment of the Court

Strict liability under the Road Traffic Act (art 58 para 1 SVG) presupposes that the 71
damage was caused 'by the operation of a motor vehicle'.

According to the Federal Court, this requirement is not to be understood in a 72
traffic-related sense. In particular, it does not mean that a motor vehicle travelling on a public road is 'in use' as long as it is on such a road.

Rather, the concept of mechanical operation must be taken as the starting 73
point. The special requirement of strict liability is therefore only to be regarded as fulfilled if the accident, viewed in its entirety, is connected with the particular danger created by the use of the motor vehicle's mechanical equipment. If this is the case, it is irrelevant whether the motor vehicle was in motion or stationary at the time of the accident and whether its mechanical equipment was functioning properly or not. The decisive factor is therefore the nature of the motor vehicle, which the law presupposes as dangerous, ie the potential for damage that can be seen in the vehicle if it is travelling with independently developed and implemented forces

Although the catalytic converter was heated due to the previous journey and 74
was also the cause of the fire, the fire hazard was not inherent to the operation of the motor vehicle. In fact, any heated object stored in a highly flammable place presents a similar fire hazard. Therefore, a common danger that can occur in connection with objects stored in a place neither intended nor suitable for this purpose was realised. A fire would presumably also have occurred if a hot, non-motorised object had been stored in the barn (eg, a hot iron).

The concept of operation is to be interpreted in such a way that it includes the 75
creation of a danger that is permitted by the legal system in the public interest. The concept of operation and the associated strict liability is limited by this public interest. There is certainly a public interest in the motor vehicle being able to move, participate in traffic or be parked in a suitable place intended for this purpose.

76 The present fire, on the other hand, had no relation to these dangers.

c) Commentary

77 In its decision, the Federal Supreme Court described the reasons that prompted the legislator to introduce stricter liability for the vehicle owner in the form of no-fault liability.

78 Traffic with motor vehicles harbours particular dangers, which are mainly due to the high-speed propulsion of the motor vehicle and the resulting phenomena. These include difficulties in stopping and avoiding obstacles, lack of stability, noise and vibrations.

79 Due to the risk of many and sometimes very serious accidents associated with the operation of motorised vehicles, the operation of a motorised vehicle creates a danger that requires protective measures according to the so-called 'set of dangers'. From this perspective, the operation of a motor vehicle would in itself constitute fault if it were not permitted on the basis of the public interest in motor vehicle traffic. The introduced strict liability serves to compensate for this permitted danger, which was created with the authorisation of motor vehicle traffic.

80 The Federal Supreme Court therefore also correctly emphasised that the interpretation of the term 'operation' takes into account the creation of a danger permitted by the legal system for reasons of public interest and that this public interest limits liability.

81 The decisive factor for the operating risk is therefore not the fact that the motor vehicle is a machine, but that it is an object that moves by means of machine power. To decide otherwise would mean that, in principle, strict liability arises every time a moving motor vehicle is in any way the cause of damage.

82 By focussing on the characteristic risk of the dangerous activity or the vehicle, the Federal Supreme Court takes into account – as *Walter Fellmann* rightly points out[52] – the basic idea behind all forms of strict liability. The decision is therefore to be welcomed.

---

52 *Fellmann*, SJZ 2024, 386, 391.

5. Swiss Federal Supreme Court, 23 March 2023, BGE 2E_6/2021: State Liability for Pure Economic Loss – No State Liability due to Closure of Fitness Centres during the COVID-19 Pandemic[53]

a) Brief Summary of the Facts

This legal dispute concerns the State liability of the federal government as a result of the forced closure of fitness centres during the COVID-19 pandemic. 83

The Federal Council ordered a first mandatory closure of fitness centres from 13 March 2020 to 10 May 2020. A second forced closure took place from December 2020 to 19 April 2021. 84

The closure of fitness centres and other businesses was carried out by ordinances of the Federal Council. These were initially based directly on the Constitution (emergency law). Parliament subsequently passed an urgent federal law (Covid-19 Act) as the basis for the Federal Council ordinances. 85

A AG is a company, registered in the commercial register of the Canton of Bern since 2014, whose purpose is the operation of fitness centres. 86

In a submission dated 25 March 2021, A AG submitted a claim for damages in the amount of CHF 259,245 to the Swiss Confederation (Federal Department of Finance, FDF). It essentially claimed that the measures ordered by the Federal Council in connection with the fight against the Covid-19 pandemic were the reason why its business results had deteriorated by 48 % in 2020. The ordered temporary closure of fitness centres was unlawful in various respects, which is why the Swiss Confederation had to compensate A AG for the resulting damage. A AG had taken the measures available to it (withdrawal of Covid-19 credit, short-time working compensation, hardship aid). However, these measures would by no means cover the damage incurred. 87

A AG filed an action with the Federal Supreme Court on 11 November 2021. It claims that the Federal Council (Swiss Government) committed an unlawful act by issuing ordinance provisions. The federal government is therefore liable for the damage incurred. 88

---

53 At <http://www.bger.ch/jurisdiction-recht>. Cf *A Menzi*, No state liability due to forced closures of fitness centres, ius.focus 2023 No 176; and, for a broader view, the book *H Seiler*, Corona-Massnahmen und Verhältnismässigkeit (2024), where the author analyses how and with which arguments the highest courts in various countries have assessed the proportionality of the corona measures.

b) Judgment of the Court

89 The Federal Supreme Court first explains the legal basis and the principles of State liability for such cases of damage.[54]

90 Liability is based on art 3 of the Federal Act on the Liability of the Confederation and its Officials and Civil Servants (Liability Act, VG). Article 3 para 1 VG reads as follows: 'The Confederation shall be liable for any damage unlawfully caused to third parties by a civil servant in the performance of their official duties, irrespective of the fault of the civil servant.' This Law also applies to members of the Federal Council (art 1 para 1 lit b VG).

91 The issuance of legal acts (decrees or ordinances) by the Federal Council is one of the official activities that may fall under art 3 VG. In the present case, it is not a case of a decree by the Federal Council, but of an ordinance. Therefore, the provision of art 12 VG (no review of formally legally binding decrees, decisions and judgments in accountability proceedings) does not apply.

92 Article 3 para 1 VG provides for primary, exclusive and no-fault liability of the State. This means that the injured third party can only sue the State, but not the responsible official or the responsible member of the authority, and does not have to prove fault on the part of the latter. It is sufficient to prove an unlawful act, damage and a causal link between these two elements. These requirements must be met cumulatively.

93 The Federal Supreme Court then examines the criterion of unlawfulness.[55] According to art 3 para 1 VG, the infliction of damage is unlawful if the State, through its officials or members of the authorities, violates requirements or prohibitions of the legal system that serve to protect the infringed legal interest.

94 On the one hand, the plaintiff cited various provisions at the legislative level, including the Epidemics Act and the aforementioned Covid-19 Act. As a result, proportionality is relevant: 'The Federal Council is guided by the principles of subsidiarity, effectiveness and proportionality. Its strategy is geared towards the mildest and shortest possible restriction of economic and social life ....'.

95 On the other hand, the plaintiff claimed that provisions at the constitutional level had also been violated, in particular economic freedom and equality under the law. The Federal Supreme Court denied whether these norms were intended to protect assets in the case of economic freedom as a constitutional fundamental

54 BGE 2E_6/2021, Consideration 4.
55 BGE 2E_6/2021, Consideration 5.

right[56] and left the question open for the other legal norms. This is because it already denied unlawfulness for other reasons.

The following consideration is central here: a violation of a decree or ordinance of the Federal Council against overriding law is not sufficient to be able to conclude unlawfulness in the sense of State liability law. The authority must also be in breach of a material official duty.[57] According to the Federal Supreme Court, a distinction must be made as follows: 96

- If the alleged unlawful act consists of an individual legal act (eg an order or judgment), the material breach of official duty is an 'inexcusable error' that would not have been committed by a conscientious member of the authority or civil servant. 97
- If, on the other hand, liability is to be based on a general legislative activity of the Federal Council, the requirements are stricter. In this case, only a 'particularly blatant breach of official duty or a particularly serious error' can trigger liability. The Federal Supreme Court justifies this by stating that legislation is an important part of the Federal Council's activities, which must not be paralysed by the prospect of a liability claim.[58] 98

The Federal Supreme Court subsequently examined whether the Federal Council could be accused of such a breach of official duty in connection with the forced closure of fitness centres and answered in the negative: 99

- In particular, the applicant claimed that the forced closure of fitness centres was *disproportionate*. The Federal Council had inadequately clarified the risk of infection in fitness centres and had not relied on the current state of scientific knowledge. During the first lockdown in March 2020, milder measures than closing fitness centres were already available. During the second lockdown, it had been established that there was no increased risk of infection in fitness centres. 100
- However, this did not convince the Federal Supreme Court.[59] It pointed out that, in the case of newly emerging infectious diseases, there is typically a high degree of uncertainty about the causes, consequences and suitable control measures. The measures to be taken can therefore not be determined in advance with certainty by law, but must be taken on the basis of the current, usually incomplete, state of knowledge, which requires a certain degree of discretion on the part of the competent authorities. When it comes to potentially 101

56 BGE 2E_6/2021, Consideration 5.3.
57 BGE 2E_6/2021, Consideration 6.2.
58 BGE 2E_6/2021, Consideration 6.2.
59 BGE 2E_6/2021, Consideration 7.

significant risks, defence measures cannot only be taken when there is scientific clarity, but already when there is considerable plausibility. And then clearly: 'A measure cannot be regarded as unlawful simply because, with better knowledge, it may not appear to be optimal in retrospect. This would be an inadmissible retrospective error.'[60]

102 – The Federal Supreme Court's comments on unequal treatment are also interesting:[61] a certain schematisation in the closure of fitness centres appears permissible regardless of the specific spatial circumstances and does not exceed the discretion granted to the Federal Council in this area.

103 – Finally, the Federal Supreme Court also recognised a significant difference to the cases of the prohibition of assembly: Switzerland has been reprimanded by the European Court of Human Rights (ECtHR) because the bans on assembly in public spaces ordered by the Federal Council during the first lockdown violated art 11 European Convention on Human Rights (ECHR) (freedom of assembly and association).[62] The Federal Supreme Court was unable to derive unlawfulness as a criterion for liability from this. This is because the ECtHR judgment was concerned with examining the legality of a restriction of fundamental rights by the measures ordered by the Federal Council and not with examining the requirements for State liability for pure financial loss. The standard of review (here: particularly blatant breach of official duty) was therefore not comparable.

c) Commentary

104 The key finding of the case is that the liability criterion of unlawfulness is tightened in the case of State liability for conduct of the Federal Council or the government that is contrary to its duties.

105 In particular, when the government takes legislative action, it should have a great deal of room for manoeuvre ie wide discretion. Taking a wrong decision is therefore not enough. Rather, a particularly serious error in legislation or a blatantly disproportionate restriction of freedom is required.

---

60 BGE 2E_6/2021, Consideration 7.5.2. The focus of the judicial assessment of corona measures was mostly on proportionality: cf *Seiler* (fn 53).

61 BGE 2E_6/2021, Consideration 7.5.3.

62 ECtHR *Case of Communauté Genevoise d'action syndicale (CGas) v Switzerland*, 15.3.2022, no 21881/20, para 85 ff.

Such a far-reaching exemption from liability is obviously practical for the government. The Federal Supreme Court has also stated that the government should not be 'paralysed' in its legislative activities by liability risks. 106

However, such an exemption from liability would not be mandatory if the rule of law, rather than the financial consequences, were to take centre stage. 107

However, the described concept adopted by the Federal Supreme Court can be embedded in the constitutional requirements. According to the Swiss Constitution, federal laws are authoritative for the Federal Supreme Court (art 190 of the Swiss Federal Constitution). Switzerland has no constitutional jurisdiction and the federal government cannot be held responsible for legislative acts of Parliament, even if they would disproportionately restrict the fundamental rights of citizens. In this respect, it is consistent if the liability of the State for legislative activities of the government is not completely excluded, but at least considerably limited. 108

6. Swiss Federal Supreme Court, 7 December 2023, BGE 8C_128/2023: State Liability for Pure Economic Loss – No Protection of Reliance in Future Employment as a Professor[63]

a) Brief Summary of the Facts

Plaintiff A, born in 1958, worked as a research assistant (for 10 % from 1 October 2016 and for 20 % from 1 January 2018) for the E Medical Institute, which is a department of the F Institute of the University of Zurich (UZH) headed by Professor B. 109

The Head of Institute E, Professor C, proposed A to the Rector of the University as her successor for a period of five years in view of her retirement. According to her wishes, A was to succeed her as head of Institute E on an ad interim basis at the beginning of 2019 as part of a 50 % employment contract. Subsequently, Professor C repeatedly referred to A as her (designated) successor in her external correspondence. However, this did not materialise. 110

From the end of November 2018, various media reports appeared in connection with the so-called implant scandal. Plaintiff A was mentioned by name in some of them. The University refrained from transferring the management of the E Institute to A. On 21 August 2020, the University and A mutually agreed to terminate his employment as a research associate as of 30 November 2020, releasing him from work immediately. 111

63 At <http://www.bger.ch/jurisdiction-recht>.

112 Subsequently, plaintiff A asked the University of Zurich for compensation in the amount of CHF 750,000 due to his non-employment as head of the E Institute.

113 The University rejected the claim for damages. A subsequently filed a claim in court.

b) Judgment of the Court

114 The lawsuit concerns the State liability of the Canton of Zurich based on the liability law of the Canton of Zurich.

115 A claims that the former head of the institute, Professor C, had promised him employment as a professor. This had not been honoured, as a result of which he had suffered damage due to the unlawful behaviour of the mentioned officials (professors).

116 A thereby invokes the principles of the protection of legitimate expectations in public law. This is based on art 5 para 3 and art 9 of the Swiss Federal Constitution.

117 Article 5 para 3 of the Constitution states: 'State bodies and private individuals shall act in good faith.' Article 9 of the Constitution states: 'Every person has the right to be treated by State bodies without arbitrariness and in good faith.'

118 However, the Federal Supreme Court denied the protection of expectations in future employment as a professor at the E Institute for two reasons:

119 Firstly, the succession plan was not the responsibility of the former head of the institute, Professor C. She had also repeatedly expressed to A that she alone could not decide who would take over the management of the E Institute.

120 Secondly, the initial situation for the succession plan had changed with the implant scandal (faulty artificial discs). At the end of November 2018, several media reports appeared that mentioned A by name. In view of the undisputed negative media coverage, the appointment of A as head of the E Institute at the beginning of 2019 would have represented a reputational risk for the University of Zurich. Even if the University had previously assured A of his appointment as head of Institute E, it would no longer have been bound by this assurance due to the change in actual circumstances.

c) Commentary

121 The State can also be bound in its future decisions by behaviour that inspires expectations and reliance. However, the basis of reliance must be created by the competent authority. In addition, changed circumstances, in particular negative behav-

iour on the part of the person concerned, can eliminate the justification for such reliance.

7. Swiss Federal Supreme Court, 25 April 2023, BGE 149 (2023) I 366: State Liability as a Result of Excessive Detention until a Therapy Place is Organised[64]

a) Brief Summary of the Facts

On 9 December 2014, the court ordered A to undergo an outpatient measure. It found that the objective elements of several offences were fulfilled, but that A was not guilty at the time of the offence. The psychiatric report commissioned for the judgment diagnosed him with paranoid schizophrenia. 122

On 28 April 2015, A (plaintiff) was provisionally arrested on urgent suspicion of assault and was remanded in custody the following day. The expert opinion attested that A was at high risk of reoffending again with serious acts of violence. Accordingly, an inpatient therapeutic measure was the only suitable way to counteract the risk of further violent offences. According to the expert opinion, the inpatient measure should initially be carried out in a closed setting. Placement in a prison should be avoided if possible, as this would have an unfavourable effect on the course of the illness. 123

The early enforcement of measures began on 2 November 2015. A initially spent four months in a prison, where he received psychiatric counselling. Due to acute danger to himself and others, A was isolated in the security ward in February 2016. A then spent ten months in regional prisons, where he received basic psychiatric care. On 4 January 2017, A was again transferred to a security ward and then to another ward for three months. During this period, he received comprehensive psychiatric care. On 12 April 2017, A was finally transferred to a ward at the Königsfelden Clinic (not a prison). 124

A claimed damages and satisfaction from the Canton of Berne based on State liability. He applied for free legal aid, damages and satisfaction. He argued that from 2 November 2015 to 12 April 2017, he was placed in a facility that was unsuitable for the execution of inpatient therapeutic measures. 125

64 At <http://www.bger.ch/jurisdiction-recht>. Cf *J Huber/L Manz*, Staatshaftung infolge langer Organisationshaft, ius.focus 2023 No 202.

b) Judgment of the Court

126 The Federal Supreme Court ruled on the duration of the deprivation of liberty in accordance with art 5 para 1 lit e ECHR: 'Everyone has the right to liberty and security of person. Liberty may only be deprived in the following cases and only in the manner prescribed by law: e) lawful deprivation of liberty with the aim of preventing the spread of infectious diseases, as well as in the case of mentally ill persons, alcoholics or drug addicts and vagrants.'

127 The Federal Supreme Court stated that, in accordance with the practice under art 5 para 1 lit e ECHR, the State is obliged to provide a sufficient number of places in suitable facilities. A temporary stay in a penal or detention facility is only permissible in exceptional cases, as long as this is necessary to find a suitable facility (so-called 'organisational detention'). However, this is only permissible if the authorities endeavour to find a suitable place. The reasonable limit for a waiting period is deemed to be exceeded if the waiting period is due to a structural lack of facility capacity that has been known for years.[65]

128 The Federal Supreme Court considered that, given the notoriously long waiting times and a clear expert recommendation regarding a suitable placement, the efforts to find a place in therapy should have been all the more intensive in the specific case.[66] It also found that the temporary hospital stays during the period of organisational detention had not served to prepare for therapy, but were merely crisis interventions. As a result, these stays would not justify the long duration of 17 months of organisational detention. Difficulties caused by the person to be placed should be taken into account when determining the duration of organisational detention. However, due to his paranoid schizophrenia, A could not be blamed for the delays. Overall, the waiting period of 17 months was too long.

129 The Federal Supreme Court therefore referred the case back to the lower court for a new judgment.

---

65 BGE 2C_523/2021, Consideration 5.3.

66 BGE 2C_523/2021, Consideration 8.3.

8. European Court of Human Rights (ECtHR) *Jann-Zwicker and Jann v Switzerland*, 13 February 2024, application no 4976/20: Time-Barring of Asbestos Victim's Case Violated the European Convention on Human Rights[67]

Another case should be mentioned, although it concerns the 2024 reporting period: 130 on 13 February 2024, the European Court of Human Rights ruled that the Swiss rules on prescription are not compatible with the European Convention on Human Rights.

The case and its effects will be presented again in the ETL 2024 volume. I 131 would like to explain the key points here.

a) Brief Summary of the Facts

Marcel Jann was born in 1953 and died in 2006 from pleural cancer, allegedly from 132 exposure to asbestos. From 1961 until 1972, he lived in a house in the immediate vicinity of a plant in Niederurnen belonging to Eternit AG, where fibrous asbestos minerals were processed into cement panels. He stated that he had been regularly exposed to asbestos emissions.

In 2009, after Marcel Jann's death, his widow Regula Jann-Zwicker and his son 133 Gregor Jann brought an action against Eternit (Schweiz) AG (the alleged legal successor of Eternit AG) and others.

The first two court instances rejected the claims. They held that the limitation 134 period had expired: according to Swiss law, the limitiation period in this case began to run from the end of the alleged damaging action: 'The right to claim damages or satisfaction prescribes … in any event ten years after the date on which the harmful conduct took place or ceased' (art 60 sec 1 Swiss Code of Obligations [SCO]).

The applicants then appealed to the Swiss Federal Court. Shortly afterwards, 135 the European Court delivered its judgment in *Howald Moor and Others v Switzerland*,[68] in which Switzerland was condemned for insufficiently long limitation pe-

---

67 At <https://hudoc.echr.coe.int/eng>. Cf European Court of Human Rights Press Release no ECHR 034 (2024). Cf *C Widmer Lüchinger*, Verjährung und Asbest: Die Schweiz wird erneut durch den Europäischen Gerichtshof für Menschenrechte verurteilt, Jusletter 8 April 2024.

68 ECtHR *Case of Howald Moor and Others v Switzerland*, 11.3.2014, nos 52067/10 and 41072/11. Cf Swiss Report in the Yearbook 2013: *P Loser*, Switzerland, in: E Karner/BC Steininger (eds), ETL 2013 (2014) 673, no 21 ff.

riods in cases related to liability for asbestos damage. The Swiss Federal Court proceedings were suspended pending Parliament's debate on amending the statute of limitations for various civil law claims.[69]

136 Following the enactment of a new statute of limitations by Parliament, in 2018, the Federal Court resumed proceedings. It dismissed the applicant's claims:[70] the limitation period began to run when the injury to Marcel Jann had initially been caused. The Federal Court (1) held that the new limitation periods of 20 years for killing or causing bodily injury were not applicable to the case and also (2) noted that a compensation fund had been set up for asbestos victims (the *Entschädigungsfonds für Asbestopfer*, 'Compensation fund for asbestos victims' [EFA Foundation]).[71]

137 After the Swiss Federal Court decision, the widow and the son applied to the European Court of Human Rights. Relying on art 6 para 1 (right to a fair trial), the plaintiffs complained that they had been denied access to a court to hear their complaints on account of their claim being time-barred. Furthermore – but this will not be discussed in the following presentation – they complained that the proceedings before the courts had been excessively long.

b) Judgment of the Court

138 The European Court of Human Rights in *Jann-Zwicker* first discussed the relevance of the EFA Foundation as a supplementary compensation instrument alongside liability law. The Swiss Government argued that the plaintiffs could and should have applied to the EFA Foundation for benefits. The ECtHR noted that it was unclear if the plaintiffs could receive money from the EFA Foundation.

139 The ECtHR moreover noted that there was no scientifically recognised maximum latency period between exposure to asbestos and pleural cancer. Latency periods varied in the range of between 15 to 45 years (or more) after exposure. The ECtHR then stated its core conclusion that when it is scientifically proven that it is impossible for a person to know that they suffer from a certain illness, such a circumstance should be taken into account in setting the limitation period.

---

69 Cf Swiss Report in the Yearbook 2016: *P Loser*, Switzerland, in: E Karner/BC Steininger (eds), ETL 2016 (2017) 623, no 1 ff.

70 BGE 146 (2019) III 25 on Prescription of Liability for Asbestos-Related Disease in case Jann-Zwicker: ETL 2019 (2020) 659, no 61 ff.

71 Cf for the revised 'statute on limitation' Swiss Report in the Yearbook 2018: *P Loser*, Switzerland, in: E Karner/BC Steininger (eds), ETL 2018 (2019) 673, no 1 ff. Cf for the new 'EFA Foundation' Swiss Report in the Yearbook 2016: *Loser* (fn 69) no 3 ff.

Furthermore, the ECtHR held that, as Swiss domestic case law had placed more weight on giving legal certainty to those responsible for the damage than the victims' rights of access to a court, there had not been a reasonable proportionality between the aims sought and the means employed. 140

Therefore, according to the ECtHR, Switzerland had acted beyond the limits of its discretion ('margin of appreciation') in the case, in violation of art 6 para 1 of the Convention. 141

c) Commentary

The earlier *Howald Moor* judgment of 2014 was understood by the Federal Supreme Court to mean that it does not prohibit the setting of absolute limitation periods. Rather, the entire national regulation of damages must be considered. The new *Jann-Zwicker* judgment of 2024 appears to take a more restrictive view. 142

The *Jann-Zwicker* judgment – like the earlier *Howald Moor* judgment – was not handed down by the Grand Chamber, but by Section III. It would therefore have been possible to appeal the judgment before the Grand Chamber, but Switzerland did not do so. The judgment therefore became final on 12 May 2024. 143

This also meant that the objections of the Swiss Federal Court could not be re-examined in depth. In particular, the Swiss Federal Court had pointed out that the statute of limitations under Swiss law is not an institution of procedural law, but an institution of substantive law.[72] Article 6 para 1 ECHR grants everyone the right to assert their 'civil rights' in court, but does not itself establish these claims. The prerequisite for the applicability of art 6 para 1 ECHR is therefore the existence of a substantive claim under national law. The Grand Chamber has also confirmed this view in more recent judgments handed down after the *Howald Moor* judgment (as already mentioned, *Jann-Zwicker* was not a Grand Chamber decision). It must at least be possible to say in a justifiable manner (*de manière défendable*) that a claim recognised by national law exists. However, the *Howald Moor* judgment means that the interpretation of art 6 para 1 ECHR grants civil law claims that are not granted by substantive national law, not even in a justifiable manner (*de manière défendable*).[73] 144

The question therefore arises as to whether the ECtHR has gone beyond its competences in interpreting art 6 ECHR by deciding a substantive question of tort law. 145

72 BGE 146 (2019) III 25 (fn 70) Consideration 8.1.
73 BGE 146 (2019) III 25 (fn 70) Consideration 8.1.2.

146 This question of competence has now been explicitly raised following a decision by the ECtHR that was handed down shortly afterwards, even outside the legal community. In the decision *Verein KlimaSeniorinnen Schweiz*[74] Switzerland was found to have violated art 8 (right to respect for private and family life) of the ECHR for failing to implement sufficient legal measures to combat climate change. Following the judgment, a fierce political debate arose in Switzerland about the legitimacy of the judgment, which even led to parliamentary initiatives to practically 'ignore' the judgment.[75]

147 It remains to be seen what measures will now be taken in Switzerland to comply with the *Jann-Zwicker* judgment on the statute of limitations. On the one hand, it is conceivable that regulatory adjustments will be made to the statute of limitations in the Swiss Code of Obligations (SCO) or to the requirements for claims in accordance with the EFA Foundation. However, it is possible that the Federal Supreme Court will interpret the statutory provision on the suspension of the statute of limitations differently, thereby ensuring conformity with the ECHR and the case law of the ECtHR.[76]

---

74 ECtHR *Case of Verein KlimaSeniorinnen Schweiz and Others v Switzerland* [GC], 17.3.2024, no 53600/20. Cf European Court of Human Rights Press Release no ECHR 087 (2024); and ELI Webinar of 24 June 2024 on Assessing the Impact of KlimaSeniorinnen Case (<www.europeanlawinstitute.eu>; <https://europeanlawinstitute.eu/news-events/upcoming-events/events-sync/news/assessing-the-impact-of-klimaseniorinnen-and-associated-rulings-1/?no_cache=1&cHash=e882f804044079e26a9ed27283e06c26>).

75 Following the statement of the small Swiss Parliamentary Chamber (the Council of States, *Ständerat*) of 5 June 2024, the large Chamber (the National Council, *Nationalrat*) has also criticised the climate ruling of the European Court of Human Rights in a statement of 12 June 2024. According to the main arguments, the Court's judgment exceeded the limits of permissible legal development and disregarded Switzerland's democratic decision-making processes. The Swiss Federal Council has also criticised the broad interpretation of the Court in its declaration of 28 August 2024. It will now report to the Council of Europe. Cf <https://www.parlament.ch/de/services/news/Seiten/2024/20240612113101111194158159026_bsd076.aspx>; <https://www.admin.ch/gov/de/start/dokumentation/medienmitteilungen.msg-id-102244.html>; and the newspaper commentary 'Die Parlamentserklärung gegen Strassburg ist ein Gewinn für die Demokratie', NZZ 12 June 2024.

76 Cf *Widmer Lüchinger* (fn 67) Jusletter 8 April 2024, no 5.2 ff.

C. Literature

1. *Bernhard A Koch/Pascal Pichonnaz*, Der Entwurf einer neuen EU-Produkthaftungsrichtlinie aus schweizerischer Sicht [The draft of a new EU product liability directive from a Swiss perspective], Schweizerische Juristenzeitung (SJZ) 2023, 627 ff

This article begins with a very concise description of the provisions of the new **148**
Product Liability Directive, supplemented by indications of where the 2022 draft can still be improved. This is followed by an analysis of the need to adapt the Swiss regulation. The authors conclude that adjustments to Swiss law will be necessary in view of digitalisation.

As with the first Swiss Product Liability Act of 18 June 1993, this is a so-called **149**
freiwilligen Nachvollzug, 'voluntary replication', as Switzerland, as a non-EU member, is not formally obliged to implement the Directive.

2. *Valentin Jentsch/Syra Angliker*, Haftung für Nachhaltigkeitsinformationen [Liability for sustainability information], Zeitschrift für juristische Weiterbildung und Praxis (recht) 2023, 213 ff

In the course of the obligation to prepare a non-financial report and the increased **150**
awareness of sustainability in society, more and more questions are being asked about the consequences of misrepresenting sustainability information. This article examines the relevant civil law liability bases from a stakeholder perspective. Consumers, competitors and investors are dealt with. It is shown that contractual claims are the most promising, as they have lower substantive legal hurdles. Nevertheless, there are procedural difficulties.

3. *Daniel Daeniker/Karl Hofstetter*, Konzernhaftung nach Ablehnung der Konzernverantwortungsinitiative – Gibt es das nach geltendem Recht? [Corporate liability after the rejection of the Responsible Business Initiative – Does this exist under current law?], Zeitschrift für Gesellschafts- und Kapitalmarktrecht (GesKR) 2023, 13 ff

151 Even after the rejection of the so-called *Konzernverantwortungsinitiative* 'Responsible Business Initiative' in 2020 and the entry into force of the indirect counter-proposal to the Responsible Business Initiative in 2023, the debate on corporate liability in Switzerland has not abated.[77] In particular, there are conflicting opinions as to whether group liability already exists under the current legal system or whether it should be created. Karl Hofstetter is of the opinion that the Swiss legal system already provided for group liability before and even more so since the indirect counter-proposal came into force. Daniel Daeniker, on the other hand, is of the opinion that there is no actual group liability even under the new provisions following the revision of company law.

4. *Djamila Batache*, Künstliche Intelligenz in der Medizin aus haftungsrechtlicher Perspektive [Artificial Intelligence in medicine from a liability law perspective] (Dike Verlag AG, Zurich 2024)

152 In view of their technical ability to perform certain tasks autonomously, artificially intelligent systems are seen as having great potential in patient treatment. However, their use is also associated with new risks and legal challenges, especially as liability law generally assumes that autonomous actions are the sole responsibility of humans. In her dissertation, the author examines the extent to which the use of AI systems is permissible at all in view of the principle of personal fulfilment of services in contract law, specifically in medical treatment, which duties of care and in particular control duties are to be taken into account here and to what extent wrong decisions can be appropriately attributed. The underlying considerations and findings can, of course, also be used to categorise the use of AI systems in other areas in terms of liability law.

77 Cf no 8 ff above.

Bernhard A Koch and Thomas Thiede

XXXI. European Union

A. Legislation

The ongoing reform of product liability mentioned in last year's volume[1] was politically approved at the beginning of 2024[2] and will most likely be adopted formally in the first half of 2024. The new directive will therefore be presented in the next volume in this series. 1

B. Cases on Infringements of the GDPR

In 2023, the Court of Justice of the European Union (CJEU) came down with a remarkably high number of rulings on the interpretation of art 82 General Data Protection Regulation (GDPR).[3] Admittedly, each of these cases has its own peculiarities. Taken together, however, they reveal a common theme that will be familiar to readers. From a purely practical point of view, all cases oscillate between the needs of sometimes rather querulous claimants, business-driven law firms seeking fees by taking on high-profile cases, administrators and regulators seeking to leave a mark, overstretched technicians faced with new standards and, finally, the inevitable uncertainties of a relatively new area of the law. 2

As we have learned from the past, all of this is to be expected, and in the coming years, or perhaps decades, we will see – once again – an area of tort law taking shape, for example through a series of CJEU precedents aimed at balancing all of the above interests. 3

1 *BA Koch/T Thiede*, European Union, in: E Karner/BC Steininger (eds), European Tort Law (ETL) 2022 (2023) 695, no 1.

2 The Permanent Representatives Committee confirmed the agreement on 24.1.2024, 2022/0302(COD). The European Parliament adopted the draft with some linguistic amendments on 12.3.2024, P9_TA(2024)0132.

3 Regulation (EU) 2016/679 of the European Parliament and of the Council of 27 April 2016 on the protection of natural persons with regard to the processing of personal data and on the free movement of such data, and repealing Directive 95/46/EC, [2016] Official Journal (OJ) L 119/1.

https://doi.org/10.1515/9783111376721-032

1. CJEU 4 May 2023 – C-300/21, *UI v Österreichische Post AG*

a) Brief Summary of the Facts

4 From 2017, Österreichische Post, a company incorporated under Austrian law, inter alia an address broker, collected information on the political affinities of the Austrian population. Using an algorithm that takes into account various social and demographic criteria, it defined 'target group addresses'. The data thus generated were sold to various organisations, to enable them to send targeted advertising. In the course of that activity, Österreichische Post processed data which, by way of statistical extrapolation, led it to infer that UI had a high degree of affinity with a certain Austrian political party. That information was not communicated to third parties, but UI, who had not consented to the processing of his personal data, felt offended by the fact that an affinity with the party in question had been attributed to him. The fact that data relating to his supposed political opinions were retained within that company allegedly caused him great upset, a loss of confidence and a feeling of exposure. It is apparent from the order for reference that no harm other than those adverse emotional effects of a temporary nature was established.

5 UI brought an action before the Regional Court for Civil Matters Vienna seeking an injunction against Österreichische Post to cease processing of the personal data in question and an order requiring that company to pay him the sum of € 1,000 as compensation for the non-material damage which he claims to have suffered. That court upheld the application for an injunction but rejected the claim for compensation. On appeal, the Higher Regional Court Vienna confirmed that decision. The Austrian Supreme Court eventually did not uphold the appeal on a point of law against the injunction and referred to the CJEU inter alia the following questions regarding the claim for compensation:

> 'Does the award of compensation under Art 82 [GDPR] also require, in addition to infringement of provisions of the GDPR, that an applicant must have suffered harm, or is the infringement of provisions of the GDPR in itself sufficient for the award of compensation?
>
> Is it compatible with EU law to take the view that the award of compensation for non-material damage presupposes the existence of a consequence [or effect] of the infringement of at least some weight that goes beyond the upset caused by that infringement?'

b) Judgment of the Court

The CJEU held that art 82(1) GDPR cannot be interpreted as meaning that the mere infringement of GDPR's provisions is sufficient to confer a right to compensation as already the wording of art 82(1) GDPR speaks of 'damage' and the existence of an 'infringement' separately (para 32). Such a distinction would have been superfluous if the EU legislator had considered that violating the provisions of the GDPR could be sufficient, in and of itself and in any event, to support a claim for compensation (para 42). 6

Regarding some form and degree of 'seriousness' of non-material damage, the CJEU points to the lack of any such reference in art 82(1) GDPR (para 45) and to recital 146 GDPR stating that 'the concept of damage should be broadly interpreted ...'. The CJEU emphasises that it would be contrary to that broad notion of 'damage', favoured by the EU legislator, if that notion were limited solely to damage of a certain degree of seriousness (para 46). Moreover, any threshold of seriousness would risk undermining the coherence of the rules established by the GDPR, since the gradation of such a threshold would be liable to fluctuate according to the assessment of the courts seized (para 49). 7

The Court concedes, however, that the GDPR is silent on how to specifically compensate the losses covered by its art 82, leaving it to the Member States 'to prescribe the detailed rules governing actions for safeguarding rights which individuals derive from art 82 and, in particular, the criteria for determining the extent of the compensation payable in that context' (para 54). 8

c) Commentary

Compensation for non-pecuniary loss is perhaps one of the most disputed aspects of tort law throughout Europe, not only with regard to the amounts awarded.[4] Several jurisdictions have considered curtailing the compensability of minor harm.[5] In particular when there is no primary bodily injury, but only standalone immaterial harm such as in the case at hand, courts have shown reluctance to offer compensation. 9

It therefore came as no surprise (and is to be welcomed) that the Austrian Supreme Court tested this avenue by forwarding the question to the CJEU. The issue 10

4 Cf eg, *BA Koch*, The Dynamics of Tort Law in Europe – Two Decades of Accumulated Experience, in: E Karner/BC Steininger (eds), European Tort Law (ETL) 2021 (2022) 711, no 55 ff.

5 See eg, the German reform plans of 2001: *J Fedtke*, Germany, in: H Koziol/BC Steininger (eds), ETL 2002 (2003) 206, no 10.

of querulous plaintiffs may also have played a considerable role in this context as, from the perspective of a third party, the pain of being associated with a political party is unlikely to have comparable significance to, for example, an injury to one's body, health, freedom or sexual self-determination.

11 The freedom of the Member States to apply their own domestic rules on quantifying the losses and on determining the amounts awarded nevertheless gives them some leeway to prevent such claims from flooding the dockets, in particular if the monies paid out for secondary immaterial harm such as pain and suffering for bodily injuries are low: while they may not negate the compensability of the harm at stake in this case, they may still put a very nominal price tag on such losses, since otherwise EU law would interfere with domestic tort law principles without any authority to do so.

12 We would further like to note that the admissibility of marginal damages raises follow-up issues in practice: on the one hand, it gives rise to dispersed damages, the recovery of which has caused considerable problems in the past. Given the rational apathy of claimants, the only viable solution (in most cases) is the bundling of these claims, which in turn raises the question of the admissibility of such bundling and the often associated financing by litigation financing providers.

2. CJEU 5 December 2023 – C-807/21, *Deutsche Wohnen SE v Staatsanwaltschaft Berlin*

a) Brief Summary of the Facts

13 Deutsche Wohnen Group is a real estate company with its registered office in Berlin (Germany), holding indirectly approximately 163,000 housing units and 3,000 commercial units. As part of their business activities, Deutsche Wohnen Group processes personal data of tenants of the commercial and housing units, such as, for example, proof of identity, tax, social security and health insurance data of those tenants, as well as data relating to previous tenancies.

14 In 2017, the competent supervising authority informed Deutsche Wohnen Group during an on-the-spot inspection that companies within its group were storing the personal data of tenants in an electronic filing system in respect of which it could not be ascertained whether storage was necessary at all, or whether there were safeguards to ensure that data which are no longer required are deleted. The authority requested Deutsche Wohnen Group to erase those documents from its electronic filing system by the end of 2017 at the latest. In response to that request, Deutsche Wohnen Group stated that it was not possible for technical

and legal reasons to comply and announced that it intended to introduce a new storage system replacing the one which contained those documents.

Two years later, Deutsche Wohnen Group informed the authority that the electronic filing system in question had already been decommissioned and that the data would be migrated to the new storage system imminently. 15

Thus, the supervising authority held that Deutsche Wohnen Group had intentionally failed, between 2018 and 2019, to take appropriate measures necessary to allow regular deletion of personal data, and that it had continued to store the personal data of tenants even though such storage was not necessary. The authority therefore imposed an administrative fine of € 14,385,000 for intentional infringement of art 5(1)(a), (c) and (e) and of art 25(1) GDPR. 16

Deutsche Wohnen Group challenged that decision before the Regional Court Berlin. That court closed the proceedings without taking further action, holding that the decision at issue was vitiated by such serious defects that it could not serve as a basis for the imposition of a fine. 17

Berlin's Public Prosecutor's Office brought an appeal before the Berlin Higher Regional Court, which decided to stay proceedings and to refer inter alia the following question to the CJEU for a preliminary ruling: 18

> 'Is Art 83(4) to (6) of the GDPR to be interpreted as meaning that the undertaking must have intentionally or negligently committed the breach of an obligation vicariously through an employee ... or, is the objective fact of breach caused by it sufficient, in principle, for a fine to be imposed on that undertaking ("strict liability")?'

b) Judgment of the Court

In its judgment, the CJEU recalls that it is apparent from art 83(1) GDPR that administrative fines must be effective, proportionate and dissuasive. However, art 83 of the GDPR does not expressly state that the infringements referred to in art 83(4) to (6) may be penalised by such a fine only if they were committed intentionally or, at the very least, negligently (para 62). 19

The CJEU notes that art 83(2) GDPR lists the factors that the supervisory authority has to consider when imposing an administrative fine on the controller. Those factors include, in art 83(2)(b) GDPR, 'the intentional or negligent character of the infringement'. By contrast, none of the factors listed in art 83(2) GDPR mentions any possibility that the controller will incur liability in the absence of wrongful conduct on its part (para 66). Hence, the court concluded from the wording of art 83(2) of the GDPR that only wrongful and intentional violations of its rules can result in a fine being imposed upon the controller based on said provision 20 (para 68). Such sanction therefore requires proof of at least negligent infringement of the provision at stake (para 75).

c) Commentary

21 The case at hand could be categorised under the headings of authorities seeking to leave a mark, and of overstretched technicians faced with the new standards mentioned at the beginning of this report. Given that the Deutsche Wohnen Group's engineers were clearly not up to the task, it is highly commendable that the CJEU, in striking a balance of interests, upheld the oldest and most well-established tort standard on the books, that of fault.

22 As a result, the case law of the Member States will have to deal intensively with the requirements for such fault-based liability in the future. Most importantly, data protection authorities will have to prove negligent or intentional behaviour before they can impose a fine. A breach of the GDPR alone will therefore not be sufficient. At the same time, the requirements are not high. In particular, companies may find it more difficult in the future to demonstrate and prove that they could not have detected the GDPR breach.

3. CJEU 14 December 2023 – C-340/21, *VB v Natsionalna agentsia za prihodite*

a) Brief Summary of the Facts

23 NAP is an authority attached to the Bulgarian Minister for Finance which inter alia is charged with identifying, securing and recovering public debts. It is therefore a controller of personal data within the meaning of art 4(7) GDPR. In 2019, media revealed that an unauthorised access to the Network Access Protection (NAP) IT system had taken place and that, following that cyberattack, personal data contained in that system had been published on the internet. More than 6 million natural persons, of Bulgarian and foreign nationality, were affected by those events, including the claimant in the instant case.

24 VB brought an action before the Administrative Court Sofia seeking an order that the NAP pay her the sum of BGN 1,000 (approx € 510) on the basis of art 82 GDPR. This amount shall indemnify her non-material damage within the meaning of art 4(12) GDPR, incurred due to the breach of security that had been caused by NAP's failure to fulfil its obligations under, inter alia, art 5(1)(f) and arts 24 and 32 GDPR. She argues her non-material damage consists of the fear that her personal

data, having been published without her consent, might be misused in the future, or that she herself might be blackmailed, assaulted or even kidnapped.

In its defence, the NAP claimed that the appellant in the main proceedings had never asked for information concerning the precise data that had been disclosed. Next, the NAP produced documents intended to prove that it had taken all necessary measures to prevent the breach of the personal data contained in its IT system and, subsequently, to limit the effects of that breach and to reassure citizens. Furthermore, according to NAP, there was no causal link between the alleged non-material damage and that breach. Lastly, it argued that, since it had suffered a malicious attack by persons who were not its employees, it could not be held liable for the harmful consequences of that attack. 25

The Administrative Court Sofia dismissed the action brought by the appellant in the main proceedings. The court held, first, that unauthorised access to the NAP's database was the result of software piracy committed by third parties, and, secondly, that the appellant in the main proceedings had not proved that the NAP had failed to implement adequate security measures. In addition, it found that the appellant had not suffered any non-material damage that would give rise to a right to compensation. 26

On appeal, the Bulgarian Supreme Administrative Court submitted several questions to the CJEU for a preliminary ruling. First, in essence it asked whether the fact that a personal data breach has occurred may, on its own, trigger a presumption that the measures implemented by the data controller were not 'appropriate' within the meaning of arts 24 and 32 GDPR. If this question were answered in the negative, the referring court further inquires about the scope of the review that national courts must carry out in order to assess the appropriateness of the measures concerned and which rules of evidence must apply in that context, in particular regarding the burden of proof. In addition, the court wishes to know whether, in light of art 82(3) GDPR, the fact that the personal data breach is a result of an act committed by third parties, in this case a cyberattack, systematically exempts the controller from liability for the damage caused to the data subject. Lastly, the court asks whether a person's fear that their personal data might be misused in the future may, in and of itself, constitute 'non-material damage', within the meaning of art 82(1) of the GDPR. If so, that person would not have to establish that, prior to their claim for compensation, third parties made unlawful use of those data, such as misusing their identity. 27

b) Judgment of the Court

28 The CJEU first points out that arts 24 and 32 GDPR lay down a general obligation, on the part of the controller of personal data, not only to implement appropriate technical and organisational measures to ensure that the processing is performed in accordance with said regulation, but also to ensure that the controller is able to demonstrate this (paras 24, 26). Indeed, the reference in art 32(1) and (2) GDPR to 'a level of security appropriate to the risk' and to an 'appropriate level of security' shows that this regulation requires the establishment of a risk management system and that it in no way purports to eliminate the risks of personal data breaches (para 29). Thus, the CJEU held, it is apparent from the wording of arts 24 and 32 GDPR that those provisions merely require the controller to adopt technical and organisational measures intended to avoid, to the extent that it is at all possible, any personal data breach (para 30). Therefore, the unauthorised disclosure of personal data or unauthorised access to such data by a third party are not in and of themselves sufficient to trigger a presumption that the measures adopted by the controller concerned were not appropriate, within the meaning of those provisions, without even allowing that controller to rebut such a presumption by proving adequate measures (para 31). Such an interpretation is all the more necessary since art 24 GDPR expressly provides that the controller must be able to demonstrate that the measures it implemented comply with that regulation, a possibility which it would be deprived of if an irrebuttable presumption were accepted (para 32).

29 In lieu of a presumption, the CJEU calls for Member States' courts to examine whether the measures adopted by the controller are appropriate (para 43). In that regard, a national court must not confine itself to finding how the controller concerned intended to fulfil its obligations under art 32 GDPR, but must carry out an examination of the substance of those measures, in light of all the criteria referred to in said provision, the particular circumstances of the case and the evidence available to that court (para 45). Such an examination requires a concrete analysis of both the nature and the content of the measures implemented by the controller, the manner in which those measures were applied, and their practical effects on the level of security that the controller was required to guarantee, having regard to the risks inherent in that processing (para 46).

30 With regard to the burden of proving the appropriateness of the implemented measures in an action for damages under art 82 GDPR, the CJEU refers to art 5(2) GDPR and its principle of accountability, under which the controller is responsible for compliance with the rules governing the processing of personal data. The controller must therefore be able to demonstrate compliance with those principles (para 49). The same principle applies with a view to both art 24(1) and art 32(1)

GDPR, requiring the controller, in respect of any processing of personal data carried out by itself or on its behalf, to implement appropriate technical and organisational measures to ensure and to be able to demonstrate that the processing is carried out in accordance with that regulation (para 51). Hence, in an action for damages under art 82 GDPR, the controller bears the burden of proving that its security measures were appropriate (para 57). While the rules of evidence in each Member State apply (para 60), the CJEU indicated that 'an expert's report cannot constitute a systematically necessary and sufficient means of proof' (para 64).

On the question whether art 82(3) GDPR must be interpreted as meaning that 31 the controller is exempt from its obligation to pay compensation for the damage suffered by a data subject solely because that damage is a result of some unauthorised disclosure of, or access to, personal data by a 'third party' the CJEU, first, refers to the wording that an exemption would only be available if the controller proves that it is in no way responsible for the event giving rise to that damage (para 69). Only then will the exemption apply (para 70). A breach by cybercriminals cannot be attributed to the controller, unless the controller has made that infringement possible by failing to comply in particular with the data protection obligation (para 71), or if it can prove that there is no causal link between its possible breach of the data protection obligation and the damage suffered by the natural person (para 72).

Finally, the CJEU confirmed that fear experienced by a data subject with re- 32 gard to a possible misuse of their personal data by third parties following an infringement of the GDPR is capable, as such, of constituting 'non-material damage' within the meaning of that provision (para 86). While art 82(1) GDPR requires the existence of some 'damage' already 'suffered' (para 77), and any compensation for 'non-material damage', within the meaning of that provision, is subject to the condition that the damage incurred by the data subject has reached a certain degree of seriousness (para 78), the CJEU held that the wording of art 82(1) GDPR does not rule out the possibility that the concept of 'non-material damage' in that provision encompasses a situation in which the data subject invokes, in order to obtain compensation on the basis of that provision, the fear that their personal data will be misused by third parties as a consequence of the infringement of that regulation (para 83).

Thus, where a person claiming compensation relies on the fear of future data 33 misuse, the national court seized must verify that such fear can be regarded as well-founded, under the specific circumstances at issue and with regard to the data subject (para 85). Where a person meets that standard, fear can in itself constitute 'non-material damage' within the meaning of art 82 GDPR.

c) Commentary

34 The award of non-material damages for the mere fear of future misuse of data is certainly not surprising and is in line with previous rulings of the CJEU regarding immaterial harm.

35 We would nevertheless want to highlight an essential element of the present decision: the explicit emphasis on the burden of proof on the data processor. Of course, the CJEU also clarifies that courts must make a concrete assessment of the security measures taken by data processors. A data breach alone does not in and of itself show the inadequacy of those measures. More importantly, however, the CJEU stresses that data processors can also be held liable for unauthorised access to personal data by third parties unless the processor can prove that it is not responsible for that breach (at all). This (indirect) shift of the burden of proof will, therefore, be extremely important in the future.

4. CJEU 14 December 2023 – C-456/22, *VX, AT v Gemeinde Ummendorf*

a) Brief Summary of the Facts

36 In 2020, the Municipality of Ummendorf, Germany, without the consent of the participants, published on the internet the agenda of a meeting of the municipal council, in which the applicants' names were referred to on several occasions, and a judgment by an administrative court, which also referred to their full names and included the addresses of their domicile. These documents were accessible for three days after uploading.

37 Since the names of other parties in the published judgment had been redacted, the applicants argued that the Municipality of Ummendorf intentionally infringed the GDPR with that online publication and asked for compensation for the non-material damage which they had allegedly suffered. In essence, they submitted that the unlawful disclosure of personal data of an individual constitutes 'damage' within the meaning of art 82(1) GDPR, without any 'de minimis threshold' applicable, which would be contrary to the scheme of the GDPR and to the deterrent effect of that provision. The municipality of Ummendorf disagreed and held that compensation for 'non-material damage' within the meaning of art 82(1) GDPR requires proof of some noticeable disadvantage and an objectively comprehensible impairment of personal interests.

38 On appeal, the Regional Court of Ravensburg was uncertain whether the online publication at stake had caused the applicants non-material damage within

the meaning of art 82(1) GDPR and referred the following question to the Court of Justice for a preliminary ruling:

> 'Is the concept of non-material damage in Art 82(1) [GDPR] to be interpreted as meaning that the assumption of non-material damage requires a noticeable disadvantage and an objectively comprehensible impairment of personal interests, or is the mere short-term loss of the data subject's unfettered control over his or her data due to the publication of personal data on the internet for a period of a few days, which did not have any noticeable or adverse consequences for the data subject, sufficient for that purpose?'

b) Judgment of the Court

The CJEU responded that, in addition to the three conditions set out in art 82(1) **39**
GDPR, other conditions for establishing liability, such as the tangible nature of the damage or the objective nature of the infringement, may be added (para 17). Hence, art 82(1) GDPR does not require that the 'non-material damage' alleged by the data subject must reach a 'de minimis threshold' in order for that damage to be compensable (para 18). While the publication on the internet of personal data and the consequent loss of control over such data, even for a short period of time, may undoubtedly cause 'non-material damage' within the meaning of art 82(1) GDPR, giving rise to a right to compensation, those affected must nevertheless demonstrate that they have actually suffered at least some such harm (para 22). Therefore, while a 'de minimis threshold' would be incompatible with art 82 GDPR, claimants must still show at least some damage, however minimal.

c) Commentary

The CJEU complemented its earlier rulings on the notion of harm in art 82 GDPR by **40**
highlighting that there is no de minimis threshold for violations of the GDPR, not even for primary non-pecuniary harm. This strengthens the right to compensation for those affected, however querulous they may be. The balance of interests is achieved by the fact that those affected must prove that they have suffered at least some non-material damage as a result of the GDPR infringement.

5. CJEU 21 December 2023 – C-667/21, *ZQ v Medizinischer Dienst der Krankenversicherung Nordrhein*

a) Brief Summary of the Facts

41 The defendant (MDK) is a service affiliated with German medical insurance providers tasked inter alia with providing medical reports on the incapacity of the insured for work, including insured who are its own employees. In the latter case, only a special unit within MDK has access to a reserved segment of its IT system containing the relevant data. The claimant in the instant case worked for MDK's IT department before becoming incapable to work. His insurer asked MDK to produce a medical report assessing the claimant's condition. One of the experts involved in producing this report contacted the claimant's own doctor, who in turn informed the claimant. The latter then contacted a colleague in the IT department to take pictures of the expert's report stored in the electronic archives of MDK and to forward these pictures to him.

42 Upon receiving these screenshots, the claimant was of the opinion that his data had been processed in violation of the GDPR and claimed compensation for his ensuing losses, arguing inter alia that some other service should have been asked for such an expert report in order to keep his colleagues from seeing such information, and that the measures to prevent such access within MDK were insufficient.

43 After both first and second instance courts had dismissed the case, the German Federal Labour Court in third instance turned to the CJEU for a preliminary ruling on a series of questions. The referring court inter alia questions whether the exceptions of art 9(2)(b) or (h) – if any – applied in the instant case, since the controller was the claimant's employer and did not need the data (which had been requested by a third party, the claimant's insurer). The Federal Labour Court also questions whether the requirements of art 9(3) GDPR had been met in the instant case. If there had been a violation of the GDPR, the referring court asks whether the 'compensation' owed under art 82 GDPR is merely compensatory or whether it can at least include deterrent and punitive elements as well in order to be effective and equivalent. Furthermore, the court asks whether fault is a requirement for claims under art 82 GDPR, and whether the absence thereof impacts such claims.

b) Judgment of the Court

While the CJEU highlights the particularly sensitive nature of health-related data, it also underlines that the (exhaustive) list of exceptions in art 9(2) GDPR contains independent elements that have to be assessed individually and not cumulatively. Even if one of the exceptions should not apply, any other might instead, shifting the focus to the purpose of using the data. Therefore, the court concludes that art 9 GDPR does not prevent MDK from processing the data at stake here as long as the safeguards and other rules foreseen by the GDPR, in particular its art 9(3), are met (para 58). Furthermore, art 9(3) GDPR does not exclude that the employer of the person examined is the one who processes the latter's health data as long as the applicable safeguards are met (which the national courts need to assess). While Member States may impose such restrictions in their domestic laws, these must not impede the efficacy of the exceptional permissions granted in art 9(2) GDPR (para 67). 44

When it comes to the function of the compensation foreseen in art 82(1) GDPR, the CJEU insists that it only 'fulfils a compensatory function', allowing full compensation of the actual loss, but 'not a dissuasive or punitive function' (para 85). Therefore, the gravity of the infringement cannot influence the amount of compensation awarded, which is limited by the actual damage and the compensation needed to fully indemnify it (para 86). 45

After analysing the differing language versions of the GDPR, the Court came to the conclusion that fault 'is presumed unless the controller proves that the event giving rise to the damage is in no way attributable to it', which, according to the Court, ensures the balance of interests (para 98). However, art 82 GDPR does not call for the degree of seriousness of that fault to be taken into account when determining the amount of damages awarded as compensation (para 103). The CJEU made it therefore clear that art 82 GDPR does not foresee strict liability, but by shifting the burden of proving fault nevertheless facilitates access to compensation for victims. These no longer need to establish culpable wrongdoing within the sphere of the defendant, but it is rather the latter who has to rebut such presumption. 46

c) Commentary

47 A year of multiple rulings on art 82 GDPR was concluded by finally clarifying that it does not foresee strict liability,[6] but by shifting the burden of proving fault nevertheless some variant of strict*er* liability. This seems to strike a compromise between various opposing views in the Member States, which found support in (again) diverging language versions of the provision that seemingly allowed a much wider interpretation of para 3 than what it actually means according to the Court.[7]

48 Apart from repeating arguments used in earlier decisions, the ruling includes an important warning against querulous claims – all there is to gain from art 82 GDPR is a restoration of the status quo ante, ie compensation (only) for actual loss suffered. The provision does not include any punitive (or even deterrent) function, but is merely compensatory in nature. This is also an important clarification more generally with regard to EU tort law.[8]

C. Other Cases

1. CJEU 16 February 2023 – C-312/21, *Tráficos Manuel Ferrer SL, D. Ignacio v Daimler AG*

a) Brief Summary of the Facts

49 From 1997 to 2011, all European truck manufacturers had participated in a cartel, taking the form of a single continuous infringement of art 101 Treaty on the Functioning of the European Union (TFEU), concerning collusive arrangements on pricing and gross price increases for medium and heavy trucks in the European Economic Area. During that period, all Spanish applicants had purchased cartelized lorries and subsequently brought actions for cartel damages against Daimler based on the latter's wrongful infringement of art 101 TFEU.

---

6 The Attorney General was in support of such a conclusion, though; see the opinion of AG *Sánchez-Bordona* in this case at no 96: 'the model is not one based on fault (or even very minor fault) with reversal of the burden of proof'.

7 While the German version of para 2 speaks of 'a' processing ('eine' Verarbeitung), for example, the Spanish equivalent refers to 'the' processing ('el' tratamiento).

8 Cf *BA Koch*, Punitive Damages in European Law, in: H Koziol/V Wilcox (eds), Punitive Damages: Common Law and Civil Law Perspectives (2009) 197.

Both parties produced expert opinions on the overcharge. The claimants argued for approximately 16% overcharge, whereas the defendants argued that their infringement of art 101 TFEU did not result in any loss for the claimants. Following a preliminary hearing before the referring court, it was agreed between the parties that the claimants would have access to the data taken into consideration by the expert report submitted by the defendant, with the twofold aim of allowing a more thorough examination of those data and of leading to a possible reformulation of the expert report produced by the claimants. That access was provided in a data room at the defendant's offices. 50

After hearing the parties to the main proceedings discuss their respective expert reports and present their claims at the main hearing held before it, the referring Commercial Court No 3, Valencia (Spain), decided to stay the proceedings and to refer inter alia the following question to the CJEU for a preliminary ruling: 51

> 'Does the power of the national court to estimate the amount of damages enable those damages to be quantified in the alternative and independently, on the grounds that a situation of information asymmetry or insoluble difficulties regarding quantification have been identified which must not impede the right to full compensation of the person harmed by an anticompetitive practice as referred to in Art 101 TFEU,... including where the person harmed by an infringement of competition law consisting of a cartel generating [an overcharge] has had access during the course of the proceedings to the data on which the defendant based his [or her] expert report for the purpose of denying the existence of damage eligible for compensation?'

b) Judgment of the Court

The CJEU argues that the infringer by definition knows what it has done and or has been accused of doing, if anything. It also knows what evidence may have been used in such a case by the Commission or the national competition authority concerned to demonstrate its participation in anticompetitive conduct contrary to arts 101 and 102 TFEU, whereas the victim of the damage caused by that behaviour does not have such information (para 59). In order to counter-balance such asymmetry of information, the EU legislator therefore adopted a set of measures, since the need to undertake a judicial estimation of the harm may depend, in particular, on the result obtained by the claimant following a request for the disclosure of evidence (para 56). Thus, it is for the national court to determine, before proceeding to assess the harm, whether the claimant has made use of disclosure. If the practical impossibility of assessing the harm is the result of inaction on the part of the claimant, it is not for the national court to take the place of the latter or to remedy its shortcomings (para 57). 52

53 Article 17(1) Directive 2014/104 must be interpreted as meaning that a judicial assessment of the harm caused by the defendant's anticompetitive conduct is permitted as long as, first, the existence of that harm has been established and, second, that it is practically impossible or excessively difficult to quantify that damage with precision, which involves taking into consideration all the parameters leading to such a finding and, in particular, the unsuccessful nature of steps such as the request to disclose evidence (para 65). The fact that the defendant has itself made available to the claimant the data on which it relied in order to refute that claimant's expert report is not relevant for the purposes of assessing whether it is permissible for the national court to undertake an estimation of the harm (para 59).

c) Commentary

54 The compensation of cartel damage suffers from the asymmetry of information between cartel members and injured parties. At least in the laws of some EU Member States, this asymmetry is not taken into account when determining the burden of proof. For example, injured parties have to quantify the damage they have suffered, but of course they do not know about the unlawful agreement between the cartel members. Victims are therefore forced to commission (expensive) expert opinions, pursue discovery claims against the cartel members and reimburse their discovery costs. Given the obstructionist tactics of some defendant cartelists, courts sometimes tend to estimate the damage by reference to art 17 of Directive 2014/104.

55 In the present case, Daimler had in fact disclosed data, but the period during which it could be inspected was extremely short, and it was even forbidden to make copies. According to the opinion of Advocate General Kokott,[9] this did not fulfil the purpose of the disclosure rules. The claimant had made every effort to quantify the damage, and it could therefore be assumed that (additional) quantification was practically impossible or excessively difficult, and that an estimate by the court was therefore admissible.

56 In its judgment, the CJEU states the obvious, namely that claimants who have suffered damage as a result of a cartel cannot remain completely inactive to substantiate their claims. However, the courts of the Member States must take into account the fact and the manner of disclosure when determining whether it is excessively difficult in practice to quantify the loss. If that is to be answered in the affirmative, as it is here, and there is a reasonable, though unsuccessful attempt

9 Opinion of AG Juliane Kokott in Case C-312/21 *Tráficos Manuel Ferrer.*

to determine the amount, this can of course only mean that the court may proceed to make an estimate.

2. CJEU 21 March 2023 – C-100/21, *QB v Mercedes-Benz Group AG*

a) Brief Summary of the Facts

In 2014, QB purchased a used Mercedes-Benz vehicle with engine programming software that reduces the rate of exhaust gas recirculation when the outside temperature is below a certain threshold, resulting in an increase in NOx emissions. Accordingly, this recirculation is only fully effective when the outside temperature does not fall below this threshold (the 'temperature window'). QB brought an action before the Regional Court (*Landgericht*) Ravensburg (Germany) seeking compensation for the damage caused by Mercedes-Benz fitting the defeat device, prohibited by art 5(2) of Regulation No 715/2007, to the vehicle in question. 57

The Ravensburg court considers that the temperature window is a prohibited defeat device within the meaning of art 3(10), 5(2) Regulation No 715/2007. According to the court, QB may have a right to compensation under sec 823(2) German Civil Code, which requires only ordinary negligence. However, that provision presupposes the infringement of a law intended to protect others, which, according to the case law of the Federal Court of Justice, means that that law is intended to protect an individual or a group of persons. As the Ravensburg *Landgericht* is uncertain whether arts 18(1), 26(1), 46 of the Framework Directive and art 5(2) Regulation No 715/2007 are such laws intended to protect others, it decided to stay the proceedings and ask the CJEU for a preliminary ruling on whether these provisions are intended to protect the interests of individual purchasers of motor vehicles and are, thus, laws intended to protect others. 58

b) Judgment of the Court

The CJEU held that the unlawfulness of a defeat device equipped in a motor vehicle, discovered after the granting of EC type-approval for that vehicle, is capable of calling into question the validity of that type-approval and, by extension, the validity of the certificate of conformity intended to certify that that vehicle, belonging to the series of the type approved, complied with all regulatory acts at the time of its production. That unlawfulness thus leads to uncertainty as to the possibility of registering, selling or entering into service that vehicle, thereby ultimately harm- 59 ing the purchaser of a vehicle equipped with an unlawful defeat device (para 84). As a result, the CJEU interprets the above-mentioned provisions as protecting, in addition to public interests, the specific interests of the individual purchaser of a motor vehicle vis-à-vis the manufacturer of that vehicle where that vehicle is equipped with a prohibited defeat device (para 85, 88). In addition, the CJEU emphasised that it is for the Member States to determine the penalties for infringing the provisions of that framework directive. These penalties are to be effective, proportionate and dissuasive (para 90).

60 The purchaser of a motor vehicle equipped with a prohibited defeat device hence has a right to compensation from the manufacturer of that vehicle where that device has caused damage to said purchaser (para 91). In the absence of provisions of European law governing the detailed rules under which purchasers of such a vehicle may obtain compensation, it is for each Member State to determine such rules (para 92). National legislation may not make it, in practice, impossible or excessively difficult for the purchaser of a motor vehicle to obtain adequate compensation for the damage sustained (para 93).

c) Commentary

61 Temperature windows have been brought before the CJEU already several times in the past. Where the CJEU has had to rule on their legality, they have consistently been classified as an unlawful defeat device. In this respect, temperature windows are almost the proverbial old hat of European tort law.

62 In some Member States, one of the last remaining questions was whether the use of such thermal windows could give the purchasers of the affected cars direct claims against the manufacturers. So far, for instance, German plaintiffs have left German courts empty-handed, as the German Federal Court of Justice had argued that the relevant European provisions do not protect third parties, that is the purchasers within the meaning of sec 823(2) of the German Civil Code.

63 The CJEU has now clearly rejected this notion with regard to the effect the European type-approval regulations have to protect third parties. As a result, purchasers of cars fitted with thermal windows are now generally entitled to compensation.

3. CJEU 30 March 2023 – C-618/21, *AR et al v PK SA et al*

a) Brief Summary of the Facts

In the six cases at hand filed before the District Court for the Capital City of Warsaw (Poland), the claimants seek compensation for damage caused to their vehicles, in five cases as a result of a road traffic accident, in the sixth case due to a falling garage door.[10] All applicants in the main proceedings assessed their respective loss on the basis of repair costs corresponding to the estimated market value of the original parts plus the labour required to repair the damaged vehicle. Since the vehicles in dispute had not actually been repaired yet, the referring court classified those repair costs as 'hypothetical'. The defendants in the main proceedings, the insurers of those liable to compensate the damage, argue that compensation cannot exceed the amount of the damage actually suffered, which they calculate according to a 'differential' method, which determines the difference between the current value of the (damaged) vehicle with its hypothetical value had the accident not happened. The insurers argue that repair costs can only be claimed instead if such repair had actually been undertaken. 64

The referring court held that compensation for damage must not enrich the claimants, but merely restore the damage actually incurred, which, under domestic Polish law at least in theory, is the difference in value between the damaged and the non-damaged vehicle, since the provision of the Polish Civil Code applicable to direct claims against liability insurers only foresees monetary compensation rather than compensation in kind,[11] which is an alternative (only) available in cases of actions against the tortfeasor directly.[12] However, the referring court points to case law where such difference is calculated on the basis of (hypothetical or actual) repair costs instead, even if these amounts far exceed the mere difference in value, which the court deems unjust enrichment of the claimants, partic- 65

10 The referring court was aware that this sixth case does not fall within the scope of the MID, but believes that the same principles of assessing and calculating the property damage should apply in such cases as well. However, the CJEU – not surprisingly – held that sixth case to be inadmissible (para 31), which is why the following does not apply to this case.

11 Art 822(1) Kodeks cywilny provides: 'By a civil liability insurance contract, the insurer undertakes to pay compensation, as specified in the policy, for damage caused to third parties in respect of whom the policyholder or insured person bears liability.'

12 Art 363(1) Kodeks cywilny provides: 'Compensation for the damage should be effected, as the injured party chooses, either by restoration to the previous state or by payment of a corresponding sum of money. However, if restoration to the previous state is impossible or would involve excessive difficulty or costs for the party liable, the injured party's right of action shall be limited to a monetary payment.'

ularly in cases where the latter have already resold their car (as damaged) without actually paying for the repair. The court believes that such excessive compensation is effectively passed on to those insured via an increase in premia and is therefore detrimental to all policyholders.

66 The referring court wonders whether the special protection of victims of road traffic accidents under EU law justifies such excessive compensation, or whether capping it at the loss calculated according to the 'differential' method is nevertheless compatible with the Motor Insurance Directive (MID).[13] Also, the court questions what the nature of the insurer's obligation under the MID in a direct action is – is the victim owed whatever the (insured) tortfeasor would be obliged to offer as compensation (or at least the monetary equivalent thereof if this is compensation in kind), or is the payment to the victim by the insurer equivalent to the latter's obligation vis-à-vis the insured?

b) Judgment of the Court

67 The CJEU emphasised that art 3 MID requires each Member State, subject to art 5 of that Directive, to take all appropriate measures to ensure that civil liability in respect of the use of vehicles normally based in its territory is covered by insurance (para 33). Article 9 MID lays down the minimum compulsory cover in the form of minimum amounts of compensation (para 39).

68 As Member States may ensure that the protection of rights guaranteed under EU law does not result in unjust enrichment of the persons concerned (para 41). Member States are 'in principle' free to determine which damage caused by motor vehicles must be compensated, the extent of such compensation, and the persons who are entitled to claim it (para 44). Member States must not, however, thereby effectively exclude or limit the insurer's obligation to cover in full the compensation which the person responsible for the damage must provide to the injured party in respect of the damage suffered by the latter (para 47).

69 The Court therefore concludes that art 18 in conjunction with art 3 MID must be interpreted as not precluding national legislation foreseeing mere monetary compensation to be paid by the insurer in an *action directe*. However, national law must neither exclude nor limit 'the insurer's obligation … to cover all the com-

---

13 Directive 2009/103/EC of the European Parliament and of the Council of 16 September 2009 relating to insurance against civil liability in respect of the use of motor vehicles, and the enforcement of the obligation to insure against such liability (Codified version), [2009] OJ L 263/11.

pensation which the person responsible for the damage must provide to the injured party in respect of the damage suffered by that party' (para 48).

c) Commentary

Unfortunately, this is yet another example of a ruling where the CJEU misunderstood the civil law question posed (or at least failed to answer it), even though the Attorney General had tried his best to explain it to the court. Instead of the vague second half of the ruling presented supra in no 69, which misses the point, the Attorney General had proposed to state that 'the effectiveness of the direct right of action of the injured party would be impaired if it had to be limited or excluded because the damaged vehicle had not actually been repaired'.[14] 70

The Attorney General made clear that the rights of the injured persons in a direct action against the liability insurer are based on the contract of the insured party, so that 'they can only have the effect of awarding the injured party compensation that the insured party would have been entitled to claim from the insurance undertaking had he or she compensated the victim himself or herself, within the limits of the contract between them'.[15] However, the insurance contract must cover the civil liability of the insured tortfeasor (albeit subject to limitations). 'As such, the financial consequences of the civil liability are covered, as is personal injury, even if the insured party takes care of the repairs himself or herself' (no 49). In order to preserve an efficient system of indemnification, art 18 MID must not be (mis-)interpreted 'to mean that the insurer could be required to provide the compensation in kind that the injured party might obtain, under national law, from the person responsible for the accident. It is precisely a question of not confusing the direct relationship between the victim and the insurer with that between the victim and the person responsible' (no 55). The Attorney General was sympathetic to the referring court's concern that insisting on hypothetical repair costs may lead to over-compensation and therefore unjust enrichment of the injured persons, subject to the caveat that if the damaged vehicle is sold to a third party without being repaired, the ensuing price difference needs to be compensated by the tortfeasor (and hence also by the latter's insurer). 71

It is clear (as also confirmed by the Court in para 43 f) that EU law does not interfere with the Member States' autonomy to determine the rules of civil liability, including the details of calculating indemnifying losses. However, it would have 72

14 Opinion of AG Richard de la Tour in Case C-618/21, *AR v PK*, no 63.

15 This was also confirmed by the Court (para 36).

been helpful – in light of the enormous practical relevance of the question – if the Court had clarified in more detail what the Attorney General had outlined for it on a silver platter: full compensation yes, over-compensation no.

4. CJEU 17 May 2023 – C-264/22, *Fonds de Garantie des Victimes des Actes de Terrorisme et d'Autres Infractions (FGTI) v Victoria Seguros SA*

a) Brief Summary of the Facts

73 In the summer of 2010, a French swimmer was struck by the propeller of a boat registered in Portugal off a Portuguese beach, causing her serious physical injuries. The injured person claimed and subsequently received compensation from the French *Fonds de garantie des victimes des actes de terrorisme et d'autres infractions* (FGTI). The latter now seeks recourse from the Portuguese insurer of the tortfeasor.

74 The court of first instance, the Maritime Court of Lisbon (Portugal), dismissed FGTI's action, declaring that FGTI's right was time-barred since the three-year period laid down by the applicable Portuguese law had expired. On appeal, the *Tribunal da Relação de Lisboa* held that, in accordance with art 19 Rome II Regulation,[16] the applicable limitation period is not the one laid down by Portuguese law but was instead to be determined under French law. Since the latter had not yet expired, this court referred the following question to the CJEU for a preliminary ruling:

> 'Is the law applicable to the limitation rules for the right to claim compensation that of the place of the accident (Portuguese law), in accordance with Art 4(l) and [Art 15(h)] [Rome II] or, if the injured party's place is taken by subrogation, is the "law of the third person" subrogee (French law) applicable in accordance with Art 19 of that Regulation?'

b) Judgment of the Court

75 In its ruling, the CJEU points to art 4(1) Rome II and its primary reference to the law of the country in which the damage occurred (para 18), followed by some discussion of art 15(h) Rome II, stating that 'the law applicable to non-contractual ob-

16 Regulation (EC) No 864/2007 of the European Parliament and of the Council of 11 July 2007 on the law applicable to non-contractual obligations (Rome II), [2007] OJ L 199/40.

ligations under [that] Regulation shall govern in particular ... the manner in which an obligation may be extinguished and rules of prescription and limitation' (para 19). In combining these two, the CJEU identifies that rules of limitation at the place where damage occurred are generally applicable to the injured party's claim (para 20).

Next, the CJEU dissects art 19 Rome II and highlights the rules therein: the rule 76 on the law applicable to the relationship between the creditor (the injured party in the event of damage) and the third party subrogated to their rights, as well as the law governing the relationship between the creditor and its debtor, that is to say, in the event of damage, the relationship between the injured party and the person who caused that damage (para 21).

Thirdly, art 19 Rome II provides that the subrogee may exercise the rights of 77 the injured party under the law governing the relationship between that person and the person who caused the damage. It follows that the law applicable to an action by a third party subrogee against the person who caused the damage is the law applicable to an action brought by the injured party against that person who caused that damage, which is determined by art 4(1) Rome II Regulation.

As a result, a combined reading of all above provisions leads to the law which 78 governs an action of the injured party against the person who caused the damage and which determines, in particular, the rules on limitation periods in respect of that action. This is, in principle, the law of the country in which that damage occurs, and therefore also the law which governs the action of a third party subrogated to the rights of that injured party against the person who caused that damage (para 26).

The CJEU does not stop there, however, but verifies the prior conclusions 79 against the general structure of Rome II. Systematically, art 19 Rome II does not seek to determine the law applicable to the time-barring of an action relied on by a third party subrogee against the debtor referred to in that article (para 27). Indeed, the whole Chapter V of Rome II, which includes art 19, establishes common rules which apply to situations in which the law applicable to the non-contractual obligation at issue has, as such, already been determined. Such a determination is made in accordance with the rules set out in Chapter II of said Regulation (para 28).

Finally, the CJEU argues that it would run counter to the objective pursued by 80 Rome II to conclude from its art 19 that the law applicable to the duty of the third party subrogee to satisfy the creditor also determines the rules concerning the limitation period for that action, when the third-person subrogee brings an action against the debtor. As is apparent from recitals 6, 14 and 16 Rome II, that objective consists, inter alia, in ensuring certainty as to the applicable law, irrespective of the country in which the action is brought, thereby improving the foreseeability of court decisions and ensuring a reasonable balance between the interests of the person claimed to be liable and of the person who has sustained damage. Such foreseeability of the applicable law would, however, be undermined if, in cases of subrogation, the conditions for discharge and the manner in which the non-contractual obligation of the debtor towards the injured party may be extinguished were determined by the law applicable to the duty of the third person to satisfy that person. Under that interpretation, the law applicable and, therefore, those conditions for discharge and such manner of being extinguished, may vary according to whether or not subrogation has taken place (para 30).

81 Such an interpretation would also run counter to the objective of ensuring a reasonable balance between the interests involved as well as the very essence of the subrogation mechanism. The consequence of that interpretation would be that the person who caused the damage (the debtor), due to the fact that an action is brought against them by a third-person subrogee rather than the injured party (the creditor), would be placed in a different situation, which might be less favourable than the situation in which they would have found themselves had that creditor personally and directly exercised their rights against them. In so far as subrogation is intended in principle solely to enable the third-person subrogee to exercise the rights of the creditor, applying that mechanism should not have an effect on the legal situation of the debtor. Indeed, the debtor ought to be able to rely against the third-person subrogee on all the defences available to them against the injured party, in particular those relating to the application of the limitation rules (para 31).

c) Commentary

82 Even if the decision follows the already prevailing opinion in the literature, and if some may therefore be inclined to dismiss the CJEU's findings as quite obvious, the judgment has but to be welcomed, as it quite usefully supplements the earlier obiter dictum in the *ERGO Insurance* case[17].

83 Furthermore, the general statements on the scope of the recourse claim, which go beyond the specific question referred on the statute of limitations, are to also be welcomed. In the interests of legal certainty, the rather comprehensive clarifica-

17 CJEU 21.1.2016 – C-359/14 and C-475/14, *ERGO Insurance and Gjensidige Baltic v PZU Lietuva UAB DK*, ECLI:EU:C:2016:40, para 56 ff. On this case, see *BA Koch/T Thiede*, European Union, in: E Karner/ BC Steininger (eds), ETL 2016 (2017) 646, no 11 ff.

tion prevents the expected large number of individual requests for preliminary rulings on the individual aspects of art 15 Rome II Regulation in the future.

Practical consequences arise in particular for insurers settling claims with a foreign connection. As far as the avoidance of the statute of limitations of a subrogated claim is concerned, it is now finally clear that the law of the country in which the damage occurred is also the law which governs the action of a third party subrogated to the rights of that injured party against the person who caused the damage. 84

5. CJEU 6 June 2023 – C-510/21, *DB v Austrian Airlines AG*

a) Brief Summary of the Facts

In 2016, DB travelled from Tel-Aviv (Israel) to Vienna (Austria) on a flight operated by Austrian Airlines. During that flight, a jug containing hot coffee fell from the catering trolley and caused burns to DB. First aid was administered to him on board the aircraft. DB sued Austrian Airlines before the Commercial Court in Vienna (Austria), seeking, first, compensation for his injuries and, secondly, a declaration establishing that air carrier's liability for all future damage resulting from the aggravation of his burns due to the allegedly inadequate first aid administered on board the aircraft. 85

The action was dismissed at first instance, and the dismissal was upheld on appeal. DB brought the case before the Austrian Supreme Court (OGH). That court considers that injuries sustained due to hot liquid falling off a catering trolley aboard an aircraft constitutes an 'accident' within the meaning of art 17(1) Montreal Convention.[18] However, the Court was unsure whether the first aid administered on board the aircraft after the initial accident constitutes a separate harmful event, or whether those two events together constitute a single 'accident' within the meaning of that provision. The OGH therefore stayed proceedings and referred the following question to the CJEU: 86

> 'Is first aid which is administered on board an aircraft following an accident within the meaning of Art 17(1) of the [Montreal Convention] and which leads to further bodily injury to the passenger which can be distinguished from the actual consequences of the accident to be regarded, together with the triggering event, as a single accident?'

---

18 Convention for the Unification of Certain Rules for International Carriage by Air, concluded in Montreal on 28 May 1999, signed by the European Community on 9 December 1999 and approved on its behalf by Council Decision 2001/539/EC of 5 April 2001, [2001] OJ L 194/38.

b) Judgment of the Court

87 The CJEU emphasised that, according to art 17(1) Montreal Convention, the air carrier is liable to compensate the bodily injury of a passenger only if the accident which caused the injury took place on board the aircraft (para 21). The court also repeated that the concept of an 'accident' must be understood as an unforeseen, harmful and involuntary event which does not require that the damage be due to the materialisation of a hazard typically associated with aviation or that there be a connection between the accident and the operation or movement of the aircraft (para 22).

88 More importantly, it is not always possible to attribute the occurrence of damage to an isolated event where that harm is the result of a series of interdependent events. Thus, where there is a series of intrinsically linked events that take place successively, without interruption, in space and time, that series of events must be regarded as constituting a single 'accident' within the meaning of art 17(1) Montreal Convention (para 23). In view of the continuity in space and time between the burns sustained from the coffee and the subsequent first aid administered to the injured passenger, the CJEU confirms that there is a causal link between the fall of the cup of coffee and the aggravation of the ensuing bodily injuries due to the inadequate provision of first aid (para 24). Therefore, the latter forms part of the former, both jointly constituting the 'accident'.

89 This interpretation of an 'accident' within the meaning of art 17(1) Montreal Convention, according to the Court, facilitates passengers' claims for compensation without unduly increasing the compensation burden on air carriers (para 26).

c) Commentary

90 The outcome of the case is not surprising, but a useful clarification, preventing airlines in the future from delaying the process of compensating passengers injured aboard.

6. CJEU 12 October 2023 – C-286/22, *KBC Verzekeringen NV v P&V Verzekeringen CVBA*

a) Brief Summary of the Facts

91 In 2017, BV was riding an electric bicycle on a public road and was struck by a car insured by KBC. BV was seriously injured and died in 2018. As this was a 'commut-

ing accident', P&V, his employer's occupational accident insurer, paid compensation and was subrogated to the rights of the victim and those of the latter's successors in title.

P&V brought an action against KBC seeking reimbursement of its expenses. 92
KBC lodged a counterclaim requesting that P&V be ordered to reimburse a sum which allegedly should not have been paid. In its defence, P&V argued that the victim could not be regarded as having been the driver of a motor vehicle. The courts found that the driver of the car concerned was not responsible for the accident in question, but that KBC was nevertheless required to compensate the victim and P&V, which was subrogated to the rights of that victim, on the ground that the victim was not the driver of a motor vehicle and that he was therefore entitled to compensation.

Both parties lodged an appeal and cross-appeal, respectively. The appellate 93
court dismissed the main appeal, upheld the cross-appeal and held, inter alia, that the concept of a 'motor vehicle' corresponded to the concept of a 'vehicle' as set out in art 1 point 1 MID. Having found that the concept of 'mechanical power' was not defined by that Directive, it considered that this concept was nevertheless clear, and that the terms 'which may be propelled by mechanical power' had to be understood as meaning that a motor vehicle is a vehicle capable of movement without muscular effort. It concluded from this that a bicycle is not a motor vehicle, within the meaning of that law, if mechanical power cannot, by itself, start the bike's movement or maintain its movement despite being equipped with an auxiliary motor. On the face of the information provided by the manufacturer of the electric bicycle in question, the appellate court found that the motor with which that bicycle was equipped provided only pedal assistance, including the 'boost' function of that motor, and that this function could be activated only after the use of muscular power, whether by pedalling, by walking with the bicycle or by pushing it. The court concluded that the victim was not the driver of a motor vehicle and that he could claim compensation as a 'vulnerable road user', as could the occupational accident insurer, which was subrogated to the rights of that victim.

KBC brought an appeal before the Belgian Court of Cassation, which in turn 94
found that for the resolution of the dispute before it, a (further) interpretation of the notion of a 'vehicle' within the meaning of art 1 point 1 MID is needed, and referred the following question to the CJEU:

> 'Is [point 1 of Art 1] of [the MID], which defines [the term] "vehicle" as "any motor vehicle intended for travel on land and propelled by mechanical power, but not running on rails, and any trailer, whether or not coupled", [to] be interpreted as meaning that an electric bicycle (Speed-Pedelec) whose engine provides pedal assistance only, so that the bicycle does not

move autonomously, without muscular power, but only by means of engine and muscular power, and an electric bicycle which is equipped with a boost function, whereby the bicycle accelerates to a speed of 20 km/h when the boost button is pressed without pedalling, yet muscular power is required in order to be able to use the boost function, is not a vehicle within the meaning of [the MID]?'

b) Judgment of the Court

95 The CJEU first reiterates that, according to of art 1 point 1 MID, the term 'vehicle' refers to 'any motor vehicle intended for travel on land and propelled by mechanical power, but not running on rails, and any trailer, whether or not coupled'. Thus, in accordance with the usual meaning of those words in everyday language, that concept, insofar as it refers to 'any motor vehicle', necessarily relates to a device designed in order to allow travel on land by means of power produced by a machine, as opposed to human or animal effort, with the exception of vehicles running on rails (para 33). However, that wording is not sufficient, by itself, to provide an answer to the question referred, since it does not indicate whether such mechanical power must be exclusively responsible for the propulsion of the vehicle concerned (para 34).

96 The French, Italian, Dutch and Portuguese wordings encompass not only vehicles propelled exclusively by mechanical power, but also those which may be propelled by other means. However, in the Spanish, German, Greek, English and Lithuanian versions, that provision is drafted differently (para 35). Where there is a divergence between the different language versions of a provision of EU law, the provision in question must be interpreted by reference to the general scheme and purpose of the rules of which it forms a part (para 36).

97 Thus, as regards the general scheme of the MID, the CJEU notes, first, that according to recital 2 of said Directive, the compulsory 'insurance against civil liability in respect of the use of motor vehicles' provided for in that Directive refers to 'motor insurance', an expression which traditionally refers, in everyday language, to insurance against civil liability in respect of the use of devices such as motorcycles, cars and trucks which, unless they are out of order, are propelled exclusively by means of mechanical power (para 37).

98 In addition, art 13 MID specifies, in para 1(b) thereof, that each Member State is to take all appropriate measures to ensure that any statutory provision or any contractual clause contained in an insurance policy issued in accordance with art 3 is deemed to be void in respect of claims by third parties who have been victims of an accident where that statutory provision or contractual clause excludes from insurance the use or driving of vehicles by persons who do not hold a licence permitting them to drive the vehicle concerned. It follows from the wording of

art 4(1) Directive 2006/126/EC, that, in principle, only the driving of vehicles capable of running under their own power, other than rail-borne vehicles, is subject to a national driving licence (para 37).

As regards the objectives pursued by the MID, the CJEU notes that it is intended to ensure the free movement of vehicles normally based on EU territory and of persons travelling in those vehicles. It is further meant to guarantee that victims of accidents caused by those vehicles will receive comparable treatment irrespective of where in the European Union the accidents occurred, and it shall also ensure the protection of victims of accidents caused by motor vehicles (para 39). 99

Devices which are not propelled exclusively by mechanical power and which therefore cannot travel on land without the use of muscular power, such as the electric bicycle at issue, which, in addition, may accelerate to 20 km/h without pedalling, do not appear to be capable of causing bodily or material damage to third parties comparable, as regards gravity or scale, to the damage that may be caused by motorcycles, cars, trucks or other vehicles, travelling on land, propelled exclusively by mechanical power, which can reach a significantly higher speed and which, at present, predominate on the road. The MID's objective of protecting victims of road accidents caused by motor vehicles therefore does not require that such devices be covered by the concept of a 'vehicle', within the meaning of point 1 of art 1 of that Directive (para 40). 100

Hence, the concept of a 'vehicle' does not encompass a bicycle whose electric motor provides pedal assistance only and which is equipped with a function allowing the bicycle to accelerate to a speed of 20 km/h without pedalling, a function which may, however, be activated only after the use of muscular power (para 41). 101

c) Commentary

The problem of interpretation addressed in this preliminary ruling has meanwhile been resolved by an amendment to the MID[19] which expressly stipulates that a 'vehicle' within the meaning of the Directive is 'any motor vehicle which is propelled solely by mechanical means'. The updated art 1 point 1 MID also contains more detailed provisions on the weight and speed of vehicles. 102

---

19 Directive (EU) 2021/2118 of the European Parliament and of the Council of 24 November 2021 amending Directive 2009/103/EC relating to insurance against civil liability in respect of the use of motor vehicles, and the enforcement of the obligation to insure against such liability, [2021] OJ L 430/1.

7. CJEU 16 November 2023 – C-283/22, *DZ, EO, YV, YE, MP v Ministerstvo vnútra Slovenskej republiky*

a) Brief Summary of the Facts

103 In 2017, NK died following the crash of a helicopter owned and operated by the Ministry of the Interior of the Slovak Republic. The accident occurred during a specialised training of officers of the firefighting and rescue unit, which involved the evacuation and rescue of people from difficult to access terrain using an on-board hoist. At the time of that crash, the helicopter was in hovering mode, and NK was suspended from the hoist cable.

104 The applicants in the main proceedings seek compensation for their non-material damage sustained as a result of NK's death. They thereby rely on the relevant EU regulations in the field of civil aviation as well as the Montreal Convention. The Slovak first instance court stayed proceedings and asked the CJEU for a preliminary ruling, essentially on the question whether these EU and international instruments applied in the instant case.

b) Judgment of the Court

105 The CJEU held that the Montreal Convention requires some international carriage of goods of persons by air, which was not given in the instant case since the helicopter had remained within Slovakia.

106 However, neither did Regulation (EC) 2027/97 apply,[20] even though it extends the compensation regime of the Montreal Convention to domestic aviation within a Member State. After all, the helicopter had not been used for transportation from one point to another, but had remained locally on the spot for the training with the hoist.

107 Furthermore, the helicopter had been used in police services, and was therefore a 'State aircraft' within the meaning of art 2 para 2 lit a of Regulation 785/2004,[21] so it was also outside of the latter instrument's scope for that reason alone.

---

20 Council Regulation (EC) 2027/97 of 9 October 1997 on air carrier liability in respect of the carriage of passengers and their baggage by air, [1997] OJ L 285/1, as amended by Regulation (EC) No 889/2002 of the European Parliament and of the Council of 13 May 2002, [2002] OJ L 140/2.

21 Regulation (EC) No 785/2004 of the European Parliament and of the Council of 21 April 2004 on insurance requirements for air carriers and aircraft operators, [2004] OJ L 138/1.

c) Commentary

While it seems at first sight that all risks of aviation are addressed and covered by EU legislation and international instruments, the case at hand shows remaining gaps where victims lack such protection. 108

Ronen Perry

XXXII. Israel

A. Legislation

1. Compensation to Victims of Terror (Exemplary Damages) Bill, 2023 Hazaot Hok (HK) 142

Under Israeli law, victims of terror (or their family members in case of death) have two main avenues of legal redress. First, they can obtain some benefits from the state under secs 4 and 7 of the Benefits to Victims of Hostile Actions Act.[1] This scheme is operated by the National Insurance Institute. Second, victims can sue the perpetrators and their aides in torts. Victims of terrorist activities *must* choose between these two paths of redress, namely tort actions against the perpetrators and their aides or claims against the state.[2] When they choose the latter, they might undermine the deterrent effect of tort liability, to the extent that liability can deter terrorist activities. 1

In the case of *John Doe v The Palestinian Authority*,[3] reported in 2022,[4] the Supreme Court held that by offering special rewards (allowances and grants) to Palestinians tried and incarcerated in Israel for committing security offences and to family members of terrorists killed in action, the Palestinian Authority 'ratified' these acts and was therefore liable in torts as a 'ratifier' under sec 12 of the Civil Wrongs Ordinance (CWO).[5] The Court, however, held by a 2:1 majority that punitive damages cannot be imposed on those liable solely as 'ratifiers.' The reason, in a nutshell, was that two exceptional doctrines, foreign to the general principles of tort law, should not be conjoined. Ratifiers' liability is an exception to the general principles of tort law because there can be no causal link between the ratification, which applies to past conduct, and the commission of the tort or between the ratification and the victim's harm. Punitive damages are also an exception to the general principles of tort law because they do not aim to place the plaintiff in a 2

1 1970 Sefer Hahukim (SH) 126.

2 Benefits to Victims of Hostile Actions Act, § 17.

3 Civ App 2362/19, *John Doe v The Palestinian Authority*, Supreme Court, 10.4.2022.

4 *R Perry*, Israel, in: E Karner/BC Steininger (eds), European Tort Law (ETL) 2022 (2023) 729, nos 9–20.

5 1968 Nosah Hadash (NH) 266.

https://doi.org/10.1515/9783111376721-033

position equivalent to the one they would have been in but for the defendant's misconduct.[6]

3 In 2023, before the eruption of the Israel-Hamas war, the Knesset proposed to change this reality. The Compensation to Victims of Terror (Exemplary Damages) Bill[7] provided that if a person is killed by a terrorist act, the court shall award the estate at least NIS 10 million (approx € 2.5 million) in punitive damages against the entity ratifying the act by rewarding its perpetrators, as well as those aiding and abetting the perpetrators as per sec 12 of the CWO. If a person is injured by a terrorist act, the court shall award at least NIS 5 million in punitive damages against the same parties. Moreover, the Bill stated that a person claiming punitive damages under the proposed legislation will not be required to give up the statutory state benefits under the Benefits to Victims of Hostile Actions Act.[8] The Bill added that the punitive awards shall not be deducted from benefits paid by the state to the direct victims or their relatives.[9] It also enabled the victim (or the estate in case of death) to obtain the award from a defendant's assets seized or frozen by the state.[10] Note that the Bill ultimately passed the second and third readings with minor changes and entered into force in 2024 – outside the formal scope of this report.[11]

4 The Benefits to Victims of Hostile Actions (Amendment No 39) (Entitlement to Benefits in addition to Damages under Other Laws and Punitive Damages) Bill,[12] which passed the first reading a week before the Compensation to Victims of Terror (Exemplary Damages) Bill, was intended to allow victims of terror to receive partial tort damages in addition to statutory state benefits. The Bill offered to allow tort recovery, in addition to the statutory state benefits, in the amount of *either* 25 % of full compensatory tort damages *or* the difference between full compensatory tort damages and the statutory state benefits, whichever is greater. In addition, under this Bill, the victim (or the estate) would be able to recover punitive damages in a tort action. The National Insurance Institute would be able to claim reimbursement from the perpetrators for benefits it paid victims. This Bill has not yet passed the second and third readings, and it is unclear whether it ever will. Thus, while the right to claim punitive damages from the perpetrators in addition to statutory benefits from the state was ultimately established, victims

6 *R Perry*, It's a Wonderful Life, 93 Cornell Law Review 329, 381 (2008).
7 2023 HH 142, § 2(a)-(b).
8 Ibid § 3.
9 Ibid § 2(c).
10 Ibid.
11 Compensation to Victims of Terror (Exemplary Damages) Act, 2024 SH 594.
12 2023 HH 124.

are still not allowed to obtain even partial compensatory tort damages from the perpetrators in addition to statutory benefits from the state.

2. Benefits to Family Members of those Missing or Abducted in Hostilities or War Act, 2023 SH 64

On 7 October 2023, hundreds of terrorists led by Hamas carried out a surprise at- 5
tack against Israel from the Gaza Strip. They killed more than a thousand Israelis, injured thousands, raped, mutilated, and pillaged. More than 250 Israeli civilians and soldiers were abducted to the Gaza Strip and at the early stages dozens were unaccounted for. Under Israeli legislation, the state grants benefits to the families of people killed in hostilities and of security force members killed in war and to those injured in such circumstances. These social benefits offer some redress when it is impractical to sue the injurers in tort or enforce judgments against them. Yet until 2023, no law granted benefits to family members of Israelis missing or confirmed abducted in hostilities or war.[13]

The Benefits to Family Members of those Missing or Abducted in Hostilities or 6
War Act is the product of an unusual coalition-opposition cooperation. The Bill was signed and supported throughout the legislative process by members of almost all political parties represented in the Knesset. Section 2 of the new Act grants family members of hostages and missing persons, civilians and security force members, similar benefits to those currently granted to the families of people killed in hostilities and of soldiers killed in action, respectively. In the case of missing persons, these benefits continue until their fate is determined, and, in the case of hostages, until their release. The Act thus recognises new categories of cases in which the state, through its social security mechanisms, financially supports victims who cannot resort to tort law.

13 Some of the expenses of family members engaged in locating and releasing prisoners and absentees of war could be reimbursed. Funding Expenses of Families of Prisoners, Hostages, and Absentees Act, 2008 SH 837.

B. Cases

1. Leave Civ App 4244/20, *Shama-Hacohen v Revach*, Supreme Court, 2 January 2023: Defamation; Absolute Privilege

a) Brief Summary of the Facts

7 The appellant (defendant in the first instance), member of the Ramat Gan city council, alleged in the first meeting of the newly elected council that the appellee (plaintiff in the first instance), another council member whom the mayor intended to appoint as deputy mayor, was involved in criminal activities, and led his political party to a historical low. The court of first instance found the defendant liable for making the defamatory statements. An appeal to the Court of Appeals (the Tel Aviv District Court) was denied, and the defendant sought leave for appeal to the Supreme Court. He argued that any statement made by a city council member in a council meeting enjoys the 'permitted publication defence' under sec 13(9) of the Prohibition of Defamation Act,[14] and that this is an absolute privilege which applies even if the statement was not made in good faith.

b) Judgment of the Court

8 According to sec 13(9) of the Prohibition of Defamation Act, a publication that the publisher is legally obliged to make or either required or permitted by a legally competent authority to make cannot give rise to an action for defamation. All judges agreed, based on legislative history and prior case law, that the legal defence under sec 13 – including subsec 9 – is absolute, regardless of the accuracy of the statement, the defendant's fault or lack thereof, and the need for the publication.[15]

9 Justice Vogelman held in dissent that a municipality is a competent authority for the purpose of sec 13(9).[16] Section 13(9) applies only if the competent authority requires or permits the publication.[17] In other words, the defendant must establish

---

14 1965 SH 240.

15 Ibid, per Justice Barak Erez, para 4; Chief Justice Hayut, concurring, para 2; Justice Vogelman, dissenting, paras 19–25.

16 Paras 13–15.

17 Para 15.

a link between the competent authority and the publication.[18] In the case of statements made during a city council meeting, any statement made by a council member or a municipality employee in relation to any subject on the *official agenda* can be deemed 'permitted by the competent authority.'[19] The mayor granted the defendant permission to speak about the plaintiff's appointment, which was on the agenda, so the defendant's criticism was permitted by the competent authority.[20]

Justice Barak-Erez, with whom Chief Justice Hayut concurred, explained that according to Justice Vogelman's dissent, every statement made by a council member or a municipality employee during a council meeting in relation to any topic on the agenda is privileged.[21] She rejected this view, holding that sec 13(9) applies to (1) statements made by any person (not only 'insiders'), (2) under specific permission or requirement of a competent authority (3) which has a concrete power to require or permit such statements, not to all statements made with a wide-ranging permission of a generally competent authority.[22] The municipality cannot be said to permit or require, by setting the agenda or otherwise, all statements made in council meetings, definitely not the specific statement in hand. 10

According to Justice Barak-Erez, the proper defence with respect to statements made by city council members and municipality employees in council meetings is the 'good faith defence' under sec 15 of the Prohibition of Defamation Act, which requires that the critical statement be made in good faith.[23] This is consistent with the law in other common law jurisdictions, where qualified privilege (rather than absolute privilege) applies to local council meetings.[24] The fact that a statement does not concern any of the subjects on the agenda might indicate lack of good faith, but the opposite is not necessarily true.[25] The lower court must determine whether the good faith defence applies under the circumstances of this case. 11

Chief Justice Hayut added in her concurring opinion that sec 13(9), as opposed to other subsections of sec 13, does not apply to meetings of specific bodies, but to legally required or permitted statements. Thus, it cannot be invoked unless the defendant demonstrates that a particular law required or empowered the authority to instruct or permit the defendant to make the statement. Section 13(9) can apply, 12

18 Ibid.
19 Para 16.
20 Para 17.
21 Para 1 f.
22 Paras 9–22.
23 Paras 3, 30–34. For a discussion of sec 15 see Case 2 no 17 below.
24 Paras 23–29.
25 Para 35.

for example, when office-holders deliver or echo information provided by the competent authority with its specific permission in the course of fulfilling their duties.

c) Commentary

13 Section 13 of the Prohibition of Defamation Act provides that certain types of publications are permissible, that is, cannot generate a civil cause of action. These include statements made in the course of duty by public officials, statements made during a legal or a quasi-legal process (as explained below), copies of public registries, and – under subsec 9 – any publication required by law or required or permitted by a legally competent authority.

14 The absolute nature of the privilege under sec 13 was clarified in the case of *Khir v Gil*,[26] reported many years ago.[27] The plaintiff and the defendant in that case were lawyers representing the opposing parties in a labour law dispute. In one of the court sessions, the defendant hurled insults at the plaintiff, saying that the police launched an investigation against him, that an indictment was prepared, and that the ethics committee of the Israel Bar Association considered suspending him on this account. The plaintiff brought an action for defamation. The defendant invoked sec 13(5) of the Prohibition of Defamation Act, whereby no civil action can be brought for *publication in the course of legal proceedings* by (1) a judge, a member of a religious court, an arbitrator, or any other person vested with judicial or quasi-judicial authority; or (2) a party, a representative, or a witness in such a process. The Supreme Court held that sec 13 does not require that the statement be true or made in good faith. Even false statements made in bad faith are protected. Section 14 sets forth the truth defence (truthful publication in the public interest) and sec 15 lists circumstances in which publication in good faith constitutes a defence. Thus, truthfulness is required only by sec 14, good faith only by sec 15, and neither by sec 13. The Supreme Court in *Shama-Hacohen v Revach* upheld this view.

15 The applicability of sec 13 to city council meetings has never been addressed before. The Supreme Court held by a 2:1 majority that statements made in council meetings, even concerning subjects on the agenda, are not generally privileged. When the legislature wanted to afford an absolute privilege to specific public officials or specific forums, to enable a completely free exchange of ideas and information in areas of public interest, it did so explicitly. Thus, specific subsections

---

26 Leave Civ App 1104/07, *Khir v Gil*, 63(2) PD 511 (2009).

27 *R Perry*, Israel, in: K Oliphant/BC Steininger (eds), European Tort Law (ETL) 2011 (2012) 715, nos 44–49.

grant an absolute privilege to parliament members, ministers, the state comptroller, judges, and members of public inquiry committees, to the extent that their publications were made within their official roles or, in some cases, during a particular process.[28] Several subsections explicitly cover statements made by participants (with no public role) in government meetings and in judicial, quasi-judicial, and inquiry-committee proceedings.[29] Section 13 does not explicitly grant privilege to city council members or to participants in city council meetings. This is strong evidence that the legislature did not wish to grant such a privilege.

The Supreme Court refused to derive a council-meeting privilege from sec 13(9), which covers statements required by law or by a competent authority or permitted by a competent authority. The Court's interpretation of this subsection seems compelling. First, a competent authority does not have the power to require or permit every publication. The legislature probably considered public authorities that are empowered to make certain publications and require or allow other parties (such as employees) to make such publications on their behalf. Municipalities are not empowered to require or allow others to make defamatory statements about city council members. Second, even when the competent authority has the power to require or permit publication by the defendant, the latter must show that the former exercised its power to require or permit the specific publication or publications of a certain type. Allowing people to speak about a certain subject (eg by setting an agenda) is not a carte blanche to say everything about everyone. 16

2. Leave Civ App 817/23, *New Contract Association v Zohar*, Supreme Court, 30 May 2023: Defamation; The Fact/Opinion Distinction; Good Faith Defence

a) Brief Summary of the Facts

The plaintiff-appellee, who was the Minister of Culture and Sport at the time, criticised on social media (Twitter) the violent demonstrations near the Prime Minister's house, comparing them to the 6 January 2021 attack on the US Capitol building. A newspaper asked the defendant-appellant, an association playing a major role in the demonstrations, to respond. The association made the following statement: 17

28 Prohibition of Defamation Act § 13(1), (3)-(6).

29 Ibid § 13(2), (5)(6).

> '(The plaintiff) is a senior soldier in (the Prime Minister's) criminal organisation who never stops inciting and lying. The comparison between the violent American right-wing and law-abiding protesters is disturbed even by (the) distorted standards (of the Prime Minister's advisor). The protesters never tried to break into the Prime Minister's residence, but it appears that the obsessive preoccupation of the (Prime Minister's) propaganda machine with the demonstrations has generated a new record of delusion and fake news. (Prime Minister), incitement and lies will not help. We are determined and will not stop until you go.'

18 The plaintiff-appellee brought an action for defamation against the defendant-appellant. The court of first instance opined that only the first sentence in the defendant's statement refers to the plaintiff and may therefore be deemed defamatory of him. However, its first part ('the plaintiff is a senior soldier in a criminal organisation') is understood by the reasonable reader as a political metaphor rather than a statement of fact, and its second part ('the plaintiff never stops inciting and lying') is not unusual in Israeli heated political and public discourse. Thus, the statement is not defamatory, and the action must be denied. The Court of Appeals (the Central District Court) reversed, concluding that the abovementioned sentence was indeed defamatory and that none of the statutory defences applied. The defendant sought leave for appeal to the Supreme Court.

b) Judgment of the Court

19 Justice Sohlberg, with whom Justices Willner and Stein concurred, found that the first part of the first sentence in the defendant-appellant's response is not a factual statement but an expression of opinion.[30] A fact is an objective description of reality that can be verified or refuted. An opinion is a subjective impression that can be persuasive, reasonable, logical, etc, but does not fit the true/false categories. The classification of a particular statement is based on its understanding by the reasonable person. A statement phrased as factual can be an expression of opinion if it is perceived as such by the reasonable person.

20 In the case at bar, the expression 'senior soldier in a criminal organisation' is not understood as a factual statement but as a metaphor, hence a critical opinion about the plaintiff-appellee's behaviour.[31] The defendant did not attribute any specific criminal conduct to the plaintiff. The statement was made in the context of a political debate shortly before the general elections. The term 'criminal organisation' has been used very frequently in criticising political opponents. The expres-

---

30 Paras 18–25.

31 Paras 26–30.

sion 'never stops inciting and lying' is a response to the plaintiff's allegations within a public-political debate, and it does not cite specific incidents; it is therefore a critical opinion rather than a factual statement.[32]

The Court did not find it necessary to decide whether these expressions of opinion were defamatory because it concluded that the good faith defence applied. According to sec 15 of the Prohibition of Defamation Act, the defendant in an action for defamation has a legal defence if the publication was made in good faith under one or more of the circumstances enumerated in any of the eleven subsections. Subsection 4 covers 'expression of opinion about the plaintiff's behaviour in a judicial, official, or public role, in the public service or in relation to a public matter, or about their character, past, acts, or opinions as manifested in that behaviour.' The plaintiff was a minister and a member of parliament at the time of the publication, namely held senior public roles. The defendant responded to the plaintiff's allegations within a heated public debate. Therefore, the case neatly fits the 'expression of opinion about the plaintiff's behaviour in a public role' paradigm.[33] 21

As regards the requirement that the publication was made in good faith, sec 16(a) provides that if the defendant's publication was *reasonably* made under one of the circumstances enumerated in sec 15, *good faith* is presumed. Section 16(b) presumes *bad faith* if the publication was false and the defendant did not believe it was true or did not take reasonable measures to authenticate it, or if the defendant intended to cause harm greater than that reasonably required to protect the interests covered by sec 15. The Court explained that any presumption of bad faith based on the veracity of the publication does not apply here, because the statement in hand was an expression of opinion, not a statement of fact.[34] The presumption of bad faith based on intent to cause excessive harm does not apply because the potential harm within the current political climate was moderate and because the defendant's statement was a response to the plaintiff's equally harsh statements that cannot be actionable given parliamentary immunity.[35] In conclusion, the good faith presumption holds, and the good faith defence applies. 22

32 Para 31.
33 Paras 35, 40.
34 Para 36.
35 Para 37 f.

c) Commentary

23 The first and primary element in a cause of action for defamation is that the defendant's statement is defamatory (potentially harmful to the plaintiff's reputation). The judicial inquiry involves two steps – interpretive, whereby the court determines what the statement means, and evaluative, whereby the court determines whether the statement (as interpreted) has the tendency to harm the plaintiff's reputation.[36] Both rely on the views of the reasonable person: how would a reasonable person interpret the statement and what would a reasonable person's reaction to the statement as interpreted be?[37] *Shama-Hacohen v Revach* adds another role for the reasonable person in defamation law. The classification of a statement as one of fact or an expression of opinion is based on its understanding by the reasonable person. Apart from being relevant in determining whether the statement was defamatory (because a factual statement tends to have a different impact on the audience than an expression of opinion), this classification is crucial in deciding which of the two main defences may apply: the truth defence (which only applies to factual statements) or the good faith defence (which most frequently applies to expression of opinion).

24 In *Shama-Hacohen v Revach*, the Court concluded that the expression 'senior soldier in a criminal organisation,' though phrased as a factual statement, would be deemed a metaphor hence an expression of opinion by the reasonable person. The simple factual interpretation of these words (which was rejected by the Court) would not only constitute defamation but also give rise to liability because the only relevant defence could not apply (the statement is clearly not true). In contrast, interpreting the same words through the eyes of the reasonable person, as a metaphor in a heated political debate, made their defamatory nature questionable and, at any rate, enabled the defendant to invoke the good faith defence and avoid liability.

25 Section 15 lays down the good faith defence, whereby a defendant in an action for defamation will not be liable if: (1) they published the statement in good faith, and (2) one of the special circumstances enumerated in this section exists. The list of circumstances covered by sec 15 includes, inter alia, the existence of a legal, moral, or social duty to publish; the expression of opinion on the plaintiff's behaviour in a public role, in the public service or in relation to a public matter; the ex-

36 *LB Lidsky*, Defamation, Reputation, and the Myth of Community, 71 Washington Law Review 1, 3–4 (1996).

37 Civ App 6903/12, *Canwest Global Communications Corp v Azur*, Supreme Court, 22.7.2015, para 20; *AD Miller/R Perry*, A Group's a Group, No Matter How Small: An Economic Analysis of Defamation, 70 Washington & Lee Law Review 2269, 2270–2280 (2013).

pression of opinion about the conduct of a person whose matter is under investigation; and any criticism of a literary, artistic or scientific piece (subsecs 2, 4, 5, and 6 respectively). The case of a legal, moral, or social duty to publish (subsec 2) underlay the Supreme Court's recognition of the 'responsible journalism defence' in *John Doe v Dayan*,[38] as discussed in the 2014 report.[39] Most of the other circumstances enumerated in sec 15, including subsec 4, pertain to expression of opinion.

The applicability of the good faith defence to the facts of this case seems clear. 26
The first condition, that is, the existence of one of the circumstances enumerated in sec 15, was established once the classification of the statement as an expression of opinion had been decided. The publication complained of was an inimical response to the plaintiff's allegations against political opponents, while he was serving as a minister and a Knesset member. Subsection 4 covers 'expression of opinion about the plaintiff's behaviour in a judicial, official, or public role, in the public service or in relation to a public matter, or about their character, past, acts, or opinions as manifested in that behaviour.' The second condition, publication in good faith, was established through the statutory presumption. Section 16(a) provides that, if – as in the case at bar – the defendant's publication was reasonably made under one of the circumstances enumerated in sec 15, good faith is presumed. Unsurprisingly, therefore, a petition for rehearing was denied by the Chief Justice of the Supreme Court (*Esther Hayut*) later in 2023.[40]

Another important contribution of the case to the law of defamation is the un- 27
derstanding that the distinction between fact and opinion not only helps decide whether the publication was defamatory and ascertains which defence may be applicable (truth or good faith), but also determines whether the falsity-based presumptions of bad faith in sec 16(b) might apply and negate the good faith defence. If the statement is an expression of opinion, which can be neither true nor false, there is no point in testing if the statement was false and the defendant did not believe it to be true or did not take reasonable measures to find out if it was true (sec 16(b)(1)-(2)). In other words, the falsity-based presumptions of bad faith do not apply in the main realm of the good faith defence (expression of opinion).

38 Civ Rehearing 2121/12, *John Doe v Dayan-Orbach*, Supreme Court, 18.9.2014.

39 *R Perry*, Israel, in: E Karner/BC Steininger (eds), European Tort Law (ETL) 2014 (2015) 688, nos 28–42.

40 Civ Rehearing 4973/23, *Zohar v New Contract Association*, Supreme Court, 11.10.2023.

3. Civ App 3709/22, *State of Israel v Jane Doe*, Supreme Court, 8 June 2023: Negligence; Duty of Care; Pure Omissions; Discretionary Function Exemption

a) Brief Summary of the Facts

28 The plaintiff-appellee was riding a personal watercraft (jet ski) with her son and a licensed operator. The plaintiff fell off and was seriously injured by the high-pressure water jet propelling the watercraft. After the accident and three similar incidents, the Israel Port Authority informed the public of the potential risk from high-pressure water jets, started an investigation, and instructed operators of same-brand personal watercrafts to avoid taking passengers during the investigation. Following the investigation, the Port Authority published safety guidelines for riding and taking passengers on personal watercrafts. It subsequently initiated an amendment to the Port (Navigation Safety) Regulations, obliging all those riding personal watercrafts to wear wetsuit bottoms and operators to brief the passengers about possible risks, as well as avoidance and response methods, before the ride.[41]

29 The plaintiff-appellee brought an action against the operator, the watercraft's insurer, the watercraft manufacturer and importer, and the state (for the alleged misconduct of its agency – the Israel Port Authority). A settlement was reached with all parties but the state. The court of first instance discussed the remaining claim and found the state liable for failing to identify the risks from high-pressure water jets (that were mentioned in the manufacturers' manuals) and address them through proper safety guidelines prior to the accident. The state appealed to the Supreme Court.

b) Judgment of the Court

30 Justice Willner, with whom Justices Kasher and Ronen concurred, started with a reminder of the structure of the tort of negligence. To succeed in an action for negligence, the plaintiff must prove four elements: the defendant owed a duty of care to the plaintiff; the defendant breached that duty through unreasonable conduct; the plaintiff suffered harm; a causal link exists between the unreasonable conduct

41 See Port (Navigation Safety) Regulations, 1983 Kovets Hatakanot (KT) 387, as amended in 2012 KT 1472 (introducing secs 26I1 and 26I2).

and the harm.[42] To establish a duty of care, the plaintiff must show that the defendant *could* foresee that the conduct would cause harm to the plaintiff (as a factual-physical matter) and that the defendant *ought* to have foreseen this occurrence (as a normative matter). The normative component is examined in accordance with legal policy considerations.[43]

The defendant could foresee that improper safety regulation of watercraft activity might cause harm to users.[44] The question is whether the defendant ought to have foreseen such harm, and the Court concluded that policy considerations negate 'normative foreseeability' and hence the duty of care in this case. 31

First, the accident was directly caused by the operator's negligence. The state was sued for a pure omission, namely its failure to protect the plaintiff from the misconduct of a third party.[45] Imposition of liability for pure omissions must be cautious and restrained, particularly when the defendant is a public authority exercising public powers (given its limited resources and the numerous risks that others might create within its realm).[46] One possible reason is that liability for omissions dilutes the burden imposed on wrongdoers, the direct injurers in particular, and undermines its deterrent effect. 32

Second, liability might distort regulatory policy. On the one hand, accepting the argument that the state should be liable for failure to regulate a certain aspect of personal watercraft activities because it has already used its power to regulate these activities quite intensively might deter regulation (because more regulation increases the likelihood of liability for failure to address specific risks).[47] On the other hand, imposing liability might lead the regulator to prohibit risky but entertaining activities altogether to avoid the need to pay considerable damages for injuries attributed to imperfect regulation.[48] 33

Third, imposing liability on the state burdens taxpayers, and it seems unfair to burden the public at large with the costs of highly risky activities that benefit only the few (as opposed to the costs of activities that benefit everyone, which should not befall an unfortunate victim). The state is not a super-insurer of all risky activities. Rather, those engaged in the activity should secure private insurance coverage.[49] 34

42 Para 24.
43 Para 25.
44 Para 27.
45 Para 28.
46 Paras 29, 38.
47 Paras 31 f, 38.
48 Ibid.
49 Paras 33–35, 38.

35 In addition to all of the above, the state does not owe a duty of care due to the discretionary function exception laid down in *State of Israel v Levi.*[50] A public authority does not owe a duty of care with respect to decisions involving the exercise of a discretionary power, namely the power to choose among several ways of action, provided that the empowering legislation does not offer specific criteria to guide the decision maker and that the discretion is 'broad' (involves the consideration and balancing of competing social, political, and economic considerations).[51] The discretionary function exception hinges on legitimate policy considerations, such as the fear of opening the floodgates of litigation, the risk of over-deterring public officials, and the courts' inability to scrutinise certain types of decisions through the prism of reasonableness.[52] According to Justice Willner, this exception applies to the state's failure to set forth safety regulations concerning high-pressure water jets. In her view, regulation policy, including the regulation of watercraft safety, lies at the heart of the regulator's broad discretion. The Port Authority needs to choose among different regulatory schemes without statutory guidelines by balancing competing considerations.[53]

c) Commentary

36 The first point to be made about this case is that it joins others in revalidating the traditional structure of the tort of negligence, knows as the Gordon model.[54] Under the traditional approach, this tort has four elements: (1) a duty of care, (2) breach of duty through unreasonable conduct (fault), (3) harm, and (4) a causal relation between the breach and the harm. The duty of care is examined first, and this is done on two cumulative levels: conceptual (taking into account general categories of injurers, victims, activities, and harms) and concrete (taking into account the specific injurer, victim, activity, and harm). On each level, the duty is evaluated through the prism of foreseeability, which has two prongs: under factual foreseeability, a prima facie duty arises if the harm (or category of harms) was foreseeable; under normative foreseeability, the prima facie duty can be constrained or negated if policy considerations so require. Causation is also tested on two levels:

---

50 Civ App 915/91, *State of Israel v Levi*, 48(3) PD 45 (1994).

51 Paras 41, 46.

52 Paras 42, 46,

53 Paras 48, 57–59.

54 Civil Wrongs Ordinance §§ 35–36 as interpreted in Civ App 243/83, *Gordon v Municipality of Jerusalem*, 39(1) PD 113 (1985).

factual (determined by the *causa sine qua non* test) and legal (determined by the foreseeability, scope of risk, or common sense tests).

As previously reported, this structure was challenged by several judges. In a 2013 case, Justice Amit, who relied heavily on the writings of Israel Gilead, proposed an alternative model, whereby the element of fault (unreasonable conduct) is examined first, causation of harm is examined second, and the duty of care serves only as a means for policy-based screening at the third and last stage.[55] This model has not been endorsed by other members of the Supreme Court. In more recent decisions, judges used the Gordon model, either ignoring Justice Amit's proposal[56] or mentioning it while following the traditional approach.[57] 37

In a 2014 case, Justice Hendel rejected Justice Amit's proposal, but offered another modification.[58] In his view, there is no need to separately discuss the conceptual duty and the concrete duty in all cases. Instead, courts should distinguish between three types of cases: (1) The first comprises cases in which the conceptual duty has already been recognised, such as those involving doctor-patient or employer-employee relations. In those, the examination of duty shall only be made on the concrete level. (2) The second category consists of novel cases in which the conceptual duty is examined for the very first time, as where the court had to decide whether a kibbutz owed its member a duty to prevent a crime committed against him by a third party.[59] In these cases the examination of duty shall be on a general level and rely on justice principles and policy considerations. (3) The third category consists of 'borderline cases,' in which a conceptual duty has been recognised in some relevant contexts but denied in others. In these cases, the duty will be discussed on a middle level of abstraction by analogy to other cases in which it was recognised or precluded. Justice Hendel's proposal has also failed to take hold. 38

In this year's case of *State of Israel v Jane Doe*, the Supreme Court once again adhered to the traditional Gordon model, insisting on the primary and preliminary nature of the duty of care and emphasising that the inquiry involves an analysis of both factual and normative (policy-oriented) foreseeability. The Court did not explicitly distinguish between the conceptual duty and the concrete duty, seemingly 39

55 Civ App 4486/11, *Doe v Clalit Health Services*, 66(2) PD 682 (2013), reported in *R Perry*, Israel, in: E Karner/BC Steininger (eds), European Tort Law (ETL) 2013 (2014) 731, nos 16–28.

56 Civ App 8650/08, *Rafaelov v State of Israel*, Supreme Court, 17.7.2013; Civ App 9833/09, *Cohen v State of Israel*, Supreme Court, 25.8.2013; Civ App 1167/11, *Doe v Roe*, Supreme Court, 18.11.2013.

57 Civ App 6507/11, *Luki Construction Ltd v GD Ayit Services Company Ltd*, Supreme Court, 11.3.2014.

58 Civ App 3521/11, *Wagner v Abadie*, 67(1) PD 84 (2014), reported in *R Perry*, Israel, in: E Karner/BC Steininger (eds), European Tort Law (ETL) 2014 (2015) 688, nos 12–27.

59 Civ App 1167/11, *Doe v Roe*, Supreme Court, 7.11.2013, discussed in *Perry* (fn 55) nos 37–44.

injecting some uncertainty into the system. However, the analysis was carried out on the abstract conceptual level, and the negation of a duty of care on this level made any additional analysis on the concrete level redundant.

40 Next, the Court emphasised the cautious attitude of the common law to liability for pure omissions. Thus, liability for non-prevention of a third party's wrongdoing, which is an archetypal case of a pure omission (unless the defendant encouraged or assisted the third party), is traditionally limited to two categories of cases.[60] First, liability can be imposed if a special relationship existed between the victim and the defendant, so that the former had a reasonable expectation that the latter would take measures to prevent a third party's wrongdoing. Legally recognised special relationships include, for example, school-student, common carrier-passenger, business owner-customer, and landlord-tenant.[61] When a legally recognised relationship exists (so a conceptual duty is established), several factors should be considered in assessing foreseeability on the concrete level. Those include the defendant's awareness of the looming wrongdoing, past occurrence of similar wrongdoing at the same place, the prevalence of wrongdoing in the surrounding area, the nature of the wrongdoing (routine or exceptional), the defendant's control over the wrongdoer or the scene, the reasonableness of the plaintiff's reliance on the defendant given the nature of the relationship between them. Second, liability can be imposed if a special relationship existed between the third-party wrongdoer and the defendant, so that the latter had special knowledge about the risk that the third party posed or some level of control over the third party's conduct. A good example is a psychiatrist-patient relationship between the defendant and the offender.[62] Failing to exercise discretionary regulatory powers in the area of watercraft safety to prevent harm by third parties does not fit these categories.

41 Lastly, the Court also validated the *Levi* discretionary function doctrine. Under this thirty-year-old rule, which is somewhat similar to that recognised in the United States,[63] the state and its agencies owe no duty of care to potential victims of the exercise of governmental powers when three conditions are met: (1) the acts are carried out under a discretionary power; (2) the empowering legislation does

---

60 Civ App 3510/99, *Vales v Egged – Cooperative Society for Transportation in Israel*, 55(5) PD 826 (2001).

61 See eg *DB Dobbs*, Undertakings and Special Relationships in Claims for Negligent Infliction of Emotional Distress, 50 Arizona Law Review 49, 50 fn 1 (2008).

62 *Tarasoff v Regents of the University of California*, 551 Pacific Reporter, Second Series (P 2d), 334 (Cal 1976).

63 Federal Tort Claims Act, 28 United States Code (USC) § 2680, as interpreted in *United States v Gaubert*, 499 United States Supreme Court Reports (US) 315, 325 (1991).

not provide specific criteria to guide the decision maker; and (3) the discretion is broad. Thus, for example, the state's monetary authority (in Israel – the Bank of Israel) cannot be liable in negligence for harms caused by interest rate hikes; financial regulators cannot be liable for harms caused to customers of banks or insurers by business practices or insolvencies attributable to lenient regulation; and public health regulators cannot be liable for harms caused to businesses and individuals by measures taken to reduce infection rate during a pandemic.

The *Levi* rule was either completely ignored or narrowed in the early years of the 21st century, and on at least one occasion the Supreme Court called for its abolition.[64] However, it recently regained its original vitality and vigour. In a case reported last year, the plaintiff argued that the Ministry of Health was negligent in delaying the publication of a recommendation for women to use folic acid as a supplement shortly before and during the first months of pregnancy.[65] The Israeli Ministry of Health issued a recommendation only in 2000, eight years after the United States Centres for Disease Control and Prevention. The Supreme Court held that establishing a new practice for treating pregnant women is at the core of the Ministry's discretion and is therefore subject to the *Levi* rule. This year's *State of Israel v Jane Doe* applied *Levi* to the failure to exercise regulatory powers in the context of watercraft safety. Even though this was not a straightforward example of broad discretion, a petition for rehearing was denied by Deputy Chief Justice Vogelman later in 2023.[66] 42

4. Civ App 2959/22, *Jane Doe v Hadassah Medical Organisation*, Supreme Court, 18 June 2023: Medical Malpractice; Wrongful Birth

a) Brief Summary of the Facts

The plaintiff-appellant sought genetic counselling from the defendant-appellee in 2002. The genetic counsellor estimated the risk of her future child suffering 43

64 See eg Civ App 8500/06, *Tsabari Orly Farm Ltd v State of Israel*, Supreme Court, 27.8.2012, para 41 (describing the decline of the *Levi* rule and judicial calls for its abolition); Civ App 10078/03, *Shatil v Mekorot Water Co Ltd*, 62(1) PD 803, 845–849 (2007) (holding that the *Levi* rule should be abolished and preferring to limit state liability for implementing discretionary powers by expanding the boundaries of reasonable conduct).

65 Civ App 2829/21, *Jane Doe v State of Israel*, Supreme Court, 29.6.2022, reported above in *Perry* (fn 4) nos 25–31.

66 Civ Rehearing 4770/23, *Jane Doe v Israel Port Authority*, Supreme Court, 19.7.2023.

from a neurological disorder as 15 % at most. In 2005, the plaintiff-appellant gave birth to a daughter (also a plaintiff in this case) suffering from a rare genetic neurodegenerative syndrome (known as H-ABC) and serious disability. The court of first instance found that the counsellor was negligent in (1) providing a seemingly final estimate in her summary letter even though she believed additional tests to one of the mother's older children were required, (2) failing to separately emphasise the importance of the additional tests to the mother, and to remind and encourage her to take them, and (3) not forwarding the summary letter to the mother's doctors. The court of first instance also held that had an additional test been carried out, the higher risk would have transpired to the aspiring mother, and the disabled daughter would not have been born. Finally, the court attributed contributory negligence to the mother for failing to take additional medical tests as recommended by the counsellor.

b) Judgment of the Court

44 A medical practitioner must explain the medical condition to the patient and ensure that the explanation is understood. This is part of the duty of disclosure which also underlies the patient's right to informed consent. Justice Amit, with whom Justices Grosskopf and Kabub concurred, found that the genetic counsellor met this duty. She explicitly indicated in her letter that the summary was based on the information available at the time and that additional tests must be carried out. The plaintiff-appellant could easily understand this letter. She argued, however, that according to medical practice, the recommendations should be included in a separate section at the end of the letter, which did not exist here. The Supreme Court held that there is no single way to properly structure a medical summary letter, so the absence of a formal recommendations section does not constitute negligence insofar as the recommendations were clearly made in the letter.

45 Justice Amit also concluded that there was no negligence in failing to remind or encourage the mother to take the additional tests. A reasonable medical practitioner is not required to 'nag' the patient. This would absolve the patient of any responsibility for their own well-being. Neither was the counsellor negligent in failing to send the letter to the referring doctor whose identity was unknown to her.

46 Lastly, Justice Amit opined that the plaintiffs did not properly establish a causal link between the genetic counsellor's alleged negligence and the mother's pregnancy. First, the additional test that could be carried out would not reveal the risk of genetic disorder. At the relevant time, H-ABC was not known to be a genetic disorder so it could not be predicted through the additional tests recommended by the

counsellor. Thus, the mother could not receive a higher estimate of the risk. Second, the mother was reckless with respect to medical advice. In fact, she took none of the commonly recommended pregnancy tests. It is thus very likely that she was fully aware of the genetic counsellor's recommendation and simply ignored it. In other words, she would not have taken the recommended tests even if the counsellor reiterated the recommendation in a separate section in her letter, 'nagged' the mother about the tests, and forwarded the letter to the referring doctor. Third, even if the mother knew of the risk, it would be practically impossible to detect the disorder during pregnancy because H-ABC develops only after birth. No change in anyone's conduct could generate a diagnosis that would affect the mother's decision to continue the pregnancy.

c) Commentary

Even though the Court focused primarily on the mother's wrongful birth action, 47 her daughter was also a plaintiff in this case. The daughter's claim was for wrongful life. However, the Supreme Court repealed the previously recognised cause of action for wrongful life while maintaining the parents' cause of action for wrongful birth in the famous 2012 case of *Hammer v Amit.*[67] The Court explained there that the possibility of being harmed by being born, which underlies wrongful life claims, is a metaphysical matter that is normatively and institutionally unfit for judicial decision. Courts cannot compare life with disability to non-existence and should not engage in the social and moral debate on the question of whether life may be inferior to non-life.

The Supreme Court allowed wrongful life claims to be pursued during a well- 48 defined interim period to avoid the harsh reality that might occur if the child could no longer recover following *Hammer v Amit* and the parents' claim was already time-barred (note that the parents' claim for wrongful birth is usually barred seven years after birth, whereas the child's claim for wrongful life, when recognised, was barred seven years after reaching adulthood, namely 25 years after birth). The child's claim in the current case was not brought within this timeframe and was therefore invalid. The Court briefly mentioned this in a single paragraph midway through its decision.[68]

67 Civ App 1326/07, *Hammer v Amit*, Supreme Court, 28.5.2012, reported in *R Perry*, Israel, in: K Oliphant/BC Steininger (eds), European Tort Law (ETL) 2012 (2013) 745, nos 19–33.

68 Civ App 2959/22, *Jane Doe v Hadassah Medical Organisation*, Supreme Court, 18.6.2023, para 18.

49 The Court in *Hammer v Amit* counteracted the financial consequences of abolishing the wrongful life action by extending the scope of damages recoverable in a wrongful birth action. The Court held that for the duration of the disabled child's minority, the parents are entitled to damages for special expenses entailed by the child's disability (but not for ordinary child-rearing expenses). For the time after the child reaches adulthood, the parents are entitled to damages covering the child's normal cost of living, assumed to be equivalent to the average worker's wage, in addition to damages for disability-related costs. This important feature of Israeli wrongful birth law was irrelevant in the case at bar because, concluding that the defendant's conduct was not negligent and that causation could not be established, the Court did not reach the damages stage.

50 The *Jane Doe v Hadassah Medical Organisation* case also provides several important guidelines for determining whether medical practitioners met or breached the standard of care in negligence. In denying a petition for rehearing later in 2023, Deputy Chief Justice Vogelman held that these guidelines constituted application of existing law rather than new rules,[69] even though their relation to existing rules and principles differed.

51 First, medical summary letters are not subject to strict structural requirements, even when medical practice follows a specific structure. Medical practitioners meet their duty of care by clearly providing the relevant information, regardless of form. This guideline was not explicitly discussed before but seems to derive from the general principles of medical malpractice law. A medical practitioner is obliged to disclose information that the patient needs for an autonomous decision and to ensure that the patient adequately understands it. Once the practitioner discloses the required information and the patient can reasonably understand it, the purpose of disclosure (enabling an autonomous decision) is met. A specific structure of a medical summary letter is not essential for an autonomous decision and therefore not legally required.

52 Second, medical practitioners need to provide information about the possible courses of action that would be sufficient for patients' autonomous decisions; but they do not need to 'nag' patients about a course of action they deem appropriate. This ruling is indeed consistent with prior case law. In the comparable case of *Khalifa v State of Israel – Ministry of Health*,[70] the doctors recommended an alpha fetoprotein test to a pregnant woman. The woman rejected the advice and later gave birth to a child suffering from spina bifida. She argued that the doctors should have tried to persuade her to undergo the test. The Supreme Court held that 'nag-

69 Civ Rehearing 5012/23, *Jane Doe v Hadassah Medical Organisation*, Supreme Court, 23.10.2023.
70 Civ 119/05, *Khalifa v State of Israel – Ministry of Health*, Supreme Court, 10.9.2006.

ging' cannot be expected from reasonable doctors because it absolves patients of the responsibility to make informed decisions about their own medical treatment and might expose them to unwarranted pressure (undermining the voluntariness of consent). An obligation to 'nag' patients might also impose an unreasonable burden on medical practitioners.[71]

Third, while medical practitioners performing or analysing medical tests should generally send the summary letters to the referring doctor, they are not negligent in failing to do so when they cannot reasonably know the referring doctor's identity. Here, the Court distinguished prior case law. In *Taig v Glaser*,[72] the Supreme Court held that the practice of handing over medical test results to the patients and expecting them to bring the documents to their doctors is negligent. Generally, copies of the results letters should be directly sent to the referring doctors. The genetic counsellor in the *Hadassah Medical Organisation* case usually complied with this requirement but could not do so in the case in hand because she did not know the referring doctor's identity (and the patient did not disclose it). There is no negligence in failing to send a test summary to the referring doctor if the author of the summary cannot reasonably know the doctor's identity. In such a case, the patient is expected to give the letter to the relevant physician. 53

5. Personal Injury

a) Road Accidents Victims' Compensation

The interpretation and application of the Road Accident Victims' Compensation Act (RAVCA)[73] have been a recurring theme in Israeli case law since its enactment. Section 1 of RAVCA defines a 'road accident' as an event in which a person incurred bodily injury due to the use of a motor vehicle for transportation. This is known as the basic definition. Section 1 then adds that the term 'road accident' also includes: (1) an event caused by an explosion or combustion of the vehicle, caused by one of its components or by another substance which is crucial for its mobility, even if instigated by a cause outside the vehicle; (2) an event caused by hitting a vehicle 54

71 See also Civ App 2813/06, *Leumit Health Services v Zelig*, Supreme Court, 11.7.2010, para 34 (holding that once the doctor explained the appropriate course of action, they do not need to follow up with the patient and verify that this course of action was taken); Civ App 10218/08, *Abramowski v Ephraim*, Supreme Court, 23.8.2012, para 26 (same, citing *Khalifa v State of Israel* and *Leumit Health Services v Zelig*).

72 Civ App 6023/97, *Taig v Glaser*, 53(2) PD 840, 846–847 (1999).

73 1975 SH 234.

parked illegally; and (3) an event caused by using the vehicle's mechanical power without changing its original purpose. These are known as the inclusion presumptions/categories. Finally, the definition excludes an event caused by an act intended to cause harm to the body or property of the victim if the harm was caused by the act itself, and not by its impact on the use of the vehicle. This is known as the exclusion presumption/category.

55 Section 1 also defines the elements of the basic definition of a road accident – 'bodily injury', 'use of a motor vehicle', and 'motor vehicle'. 'Use of a motor vehicle' is defined as:

> 'driving/riding a motor vehicle, entering or exiting it, parking, pushing or towing it, roadside treatment or roadside repair of the vehicle performed by the user or by another person not in the course of his occupation, including the rolling down or turning over of the motor vehicle, disengagement or falling of a part of the motor vehicle or its cargo while in transit, as well as disengagement or falling off, as mentioned, from a standstill or parked motor vehicle, while not in maintenance of a person in the line of his business, and excluding the loading or unloading of cargo while the motor vehicle is standing still.'

56 In a recent case, the owner of a truck-mounted crane (powered by the truck engine) was hired to remove concrete pillars from a building. The crane was used to pull and stretch the pillars to prevent them from falling when they were cut, and one of the pillars sprang with the crane and injured the crane-truck owner. The Supreme Court held that this case was a road accident under the third inclusion presumption – an event caused by using the vehicle's mechanical power without changing its original purpose.[74] The Court explained that the presumption applies to accidents occurring when multi-purpose vehicles serve their *original non-transportation purpose*, provided that a causal link between the use of the mechanical power and the accident is established and that the vehicle's original purposes were maintained. The crane-truck in this case was a multi-purpose vehicle, and the use of its mechanical power caused the accident. The question was whether it served one of its *original* purposes. The Supreme Court rejected the lower court's finding that the crane's intended non-transportation use was only to load and unload the truck and concluded that as long as 'the crane remained a crane' the unusual use was still part of its original purpose.

57 Under sec 2 of RAVCA, in conjunction with the Motor Vehicle Insurance Ordinance (New Version),[75] if a road accident involves one vehicle, the user (driver) is liable for personal injuries arising from that accident, and the vehicle's insurer

74 Civ App 7592/22, *Doe v Roe*, Supreme Court, 27.4.2023.
75 1970 NH 320.

covers the driver's injuries and liability.[76] Under sec 3, in conjunction with the Motor Vehicle Insurance Ordinance, if a road accident involves two or more vehicles, each user is liable for injuries sustained by the passengers in their own vehicle, all are liable in equal shares for injuries sustained outside the vehicles, and the insurer of each vehicle covers its driver's injuries and liability.[77] In a 2023 case, the driver of car A pulled over at a bus lay-by to use a navigation app, staying buckled and leaving the engine running; car B crashed into car A.[78] The question was whether the accident involved *two* vehicles, A and B, or only car B, making car A the accident scene rather than an involved vehicle. In the former case, the driver of car A would need to recover from her own insurer, and in the latter case, she would be able to sue the driver and insurer of car B, as if she was a pedestrian hit by car B. The Supreme Court held that the short stop at the bus lay-by to use the navigation app (without unbuckling or turning off the engine) did not end the driving, so the driver of car A was still using the vehicle at the time of the accident. This interpretation is consistent not only with the common understanding of 'driving' but also with public policy: searching for a destination or a route on navigation apps without pulling over is undesirable as it increases the risk. Thus, car A was also involved in the accident and its driver had to sue her own insurer.

According to sec 12 of RAVCA, a road accident victim who is entitled to compen- **58**
sation under the Act but cannot recover from the injurer for lack of proper insurance can recover from the Road Accident Victims' Compensation Fund ('Karnit'). In a 2023 case, a motor vehicle owner permitted his employee to drive the vehicle. The employee, who did not have a valid driver's licence, was involved in an accident, in which two of his passengers were injured. Because the insurance did not cover non-licensed drivers, Karnit compensated the victims and sought reimbursement from the driver and the vehicle owner (who permitted the driving). One who pays damages under RAVCA, including Karnit, does not normally have a right to reimbursement against others. Section 9 contains several exceptions. Most notably, reimbursement is allowed against people who, according to sec 7, would have been barred from bringing an action under the Act had they been injured. Those include a person who drove the vehicle without mandatory insurance and the owner or possessor of the vehicle who permitted the driver to use it without such insurance.

The Supreme Court held in 2023 that the right to reimbursement from the **59**
driver who used the vehicle without insurance or the owner or possessor who permitted such driving hinges on their fault, namely knowledge or reasonable ability

76 RAVCA § 2.
77 RAVCA § 3.
78 Civ App 5903/22, *Clal Insurance Co v Jane Doe*, Supreme Court, 30.10.2023.

to know of the lack of insurance. The party seeking reimbursement must establish such fault based on the circumstances of the specific case. The court considers the nature of the indications for the lack of insurance. Where no insurance is attributed to the driver's lack of a driver's licence, the intensity of the prior acquaintance between the owner and the driver may indicate that the former could reasonably assume that the latter had a licence and vice versa. Other circumstances supporting the assumption that the driver had a driver's licence (when known to the owner) are prior employment as a driver, the driver's ownership of a car, the driver's confirmation that they have a licence, the driver's clean record, no past incidents of licence revocation or suspension, no unlawful presence in the country, etc.[79]

b) Personal Injuries Inflicted by Dogs

60 Sections 41A-41C of the Civil Wrongs Ordinance, enacted in 1992, set forth a special non-exclusive strict liability scheme for personal injuries caused by dogs. According to sec 41A, whenever a dog inflicts personal injury, its owner (or permanent possessor) must compensate the victim, whether or not the owner was at fault. Section 41B provides that the owner shall not have a legal defence against an action under sec 41A unless the injury was caused by (1) the victim's provocation of the dog; (2) the victim's assault of the dog's owner, their spouse, parent, or child; (3) the victim's trespass to the dog owner's land. In a 2023 case, the plaintiff was bitten by the defendants' dog when she was eight years old and brought a tort action many years later. The defendants argued that the plaintiff's parents were also at fault in letting their daughter play in the defendants' backyard knowing that they had a dog. While the contributory negligence defence is generally invoked only when the victim's fault contributed to the injury, if the victim is a minor, the parents' negligent contribution to the occurrence of the injury is also – somewhat confusingly – labelled contributory negligence. The Court concluded that there was no 'contributory negligence' on the parents' part. Given this factual conclusion, it left unanswered the question of the applicability of general tort law defences (contributory negligence, assumption of risk, etc) to actions under sec 41A.[80] This gives rise to unwarranted uncertainty, as sec 41B unequivocally states that there shall be no

79 Civ App 1872/22, *John Doe v Jane Doe*, Supreme Court, 10.7.2023; affirmed Civ Rehearing 5689/23, *John Doe v Jane Doe*, Supreme Court, 5.11.2023.
80 Civ App 7611/22, *John Doe v Jane Doe*, Supreme Court, 7.6.2023.

legal defence to an action under the special scheme other than the three defences listed therein.

c) Damages for Loss of Earnings

Several decisions in 2023 focus on the assessment of damages for loss of earning capacity. First, when a tort victim is an employee of a self-owned company, damages for loss of earning capacity should be assessed, in the absence of special circumstances or data, in accordance with the salary reported in pre-injury payslips or in the employer's annual report of the victim's salary to the revenue service ('form 106').[81] The company's profits and any benefits conferred on the employee but not reported as taxable income are not taken into account. The default rule is that the salary used to assess damages is the same as that reported for tax and national insurance purposes. 61

Second, the Supreme Court upheld an earlier decision whereby, in assessing damages for loss of earning capacity of self-employed victims, courts should assume that the victim would have worked to the age of seventy (which is higher than the statutory retirement age of 67 for men and 62–65 for women).[82] This assumption also applies to lawyers, even though many lawyers in Israel work past this age. The assumption can be rebutted based on concrete evidence pertaining to the special circumstances of the case and the special characteristics of the plaintiff, but such divergence is relatively rare. 62

Third, in a regular tort action, damages for loss of earning capacity are assessed in accordance with the victim's gross income even though the lump sum award is exempt from income tax. In an action under RAVCA, damages are assessed in accordance with the victim's net income (subject to a 25 % income tax cap). In 2023, the Supreme Court held by a 2:1 majority that the tax rate used to determine the victim's net income must be the rate applicable to their income when the court delivers its decision. Courts must disregard potential reforms in tax law as well as future changes, even certain, in the victim's personal circumstances which may affect tax rates.[83] 63

---

81 Civ App 8583/22, *John Doe v The Israeli Auto-Insurance Pool Ltd*, Supreme Court, 16.4.2023.
82 Civ Rehearing 2485/23, *John Doe v The Phoenix Insurance Co*, Supreme Court, 12.6.2023.
83 Civ App 4611/22, *The Israeli Auto-Insurance Pool Ltd v State of Israel – Ministry of Defence*, Supreme Court, 3.7.2023.

Corinne Widmer Lüchinger

XXXIII. Comparative Remarks

A. Introduction

1 Looking back over recent volumes of the European Tort Law Yearbook, there appears to be widespread agreement that it is both an honour and a pleasure to present the comparative report at the Annual Conference. However, it is also a challenging task – indeed, one might even call it daunting. A few years back, Olaf Riss described the comparative reporter's role as, in essence, providing a brief summary of the country reports, highlighting continuing trends and anticipating future developments. He very fittingly compared these trends and developments with guests whom we should welcome like the best of hosts, giving equal attention both to old friends and acquaintances, who return year after year, and to newcomers, who might over time turn into regular guests.[1] In the run-up to the Conference, it seemed to me that this approach, which I will call the 'perfect hostess approach', was better suited to the written report. It is harder to do justice to all the national reports in the oral presentation, not least because many of them – to stay with Olaf Riss's image – tend to turn up to the party very late. That is why I, as this year's hostess, set myself a more modest goal, which I called the 'sweet shop approach'.

2 What, you might ask, do sweet shops have to do with comparative tort law? While reading through the national reports, I felt transported back to my childhood. After school was over, my schoolfriends and I would often go to the sweet shop on our way home and stare in amazement at the rows of glistening sweets and chocolates, all displayed in large glass jars, all looking equally tempting, covering the shop's walls from top to bottom. How on earth, we asked ourselves, should we decide which sweets to choose and what to spend our pocket money on? Why could we not just have some of each? In the end, of course, our limited funds meant a choice was inevitable. In the same way, the comparative reporter also has to make a choice amongst the many exciting tort flavours, old and new, which run through the national reports. This choice will, of course, be influenced by one's personal taste in sweets.

3 Initially, I had thought that the perfect hostess might make a comeback for the written report. However, the many kind comments I received after the Conference

1 *O Riss*, Comparative Remarks, in: E Karner/BC Steininger (eds), European Tort Law (hereinafter: ETL) 2018 (2019) 743, no 1 f.

https://doi.org/10.1515/9783111376721-034

in Vienna persuaded me that I am not the only one with a sweet tooth. And so, the perfect hostess will have to wait for another year – and another party.

B. The Sweet Shop Selection

1. The Covid Pandemic

4 Let us turn to my first choice, the Covid pandemic. Last year, Andrew Bell noted in his comparative remarks that case law on the Covid-19 crisis had yet to rear its head across the European scene.[2] This has changed over the past year, with cases being reported from the Czech Republic, Switzerland, Lithuania, Austria, Sweden and Spain.[3]

5 With the exception of Sweden, where a claim was brought (unsuccessfully) by the owner of a nightclub against its insurer under an epidemic interruption insurance policy, all of the cases revolved around State liability. In several cases, service providers or retailers were seeking compensation for alleged loss of profits due to restrictions during national lockdowns.[4] However, damages were also sought by claimants who had become infected with the virus due to an alleged failure by the authorities to protect their citizens, such as in a case decided by the Austrian Supreme Court,[5] or, in one of the cases from Lithuania,[6] by a claimant whose mother had become infected with the virus while being treated in a State hospital, leading to the mother's death. In a Czech case, the claimants sought compensation for non-pecuniary damage caused by measures, subsequently declared null and void, which restricted their freedom of movement and required them to wear a face mask.[7]

6 In most of the reported cases, the issue of liability turned on the question of statutory interpretation. Given the differences in national legislation both with respect to State liability in general and with respect to the legal basis for Covid mea-

2 *AJ Bell*, Comparative Remarks, in: E Karner/BC Steininger (eds), ETL 2022 (2023) 761, no 53 ff.
3 SC 21.4.2023 and 31.8.2023 (Czech Republic, nos 27 ff and 4 ff); SC 23.3.2023 (Switzerland, no 83 ff); SAC 19.4.2023 and SC 15.6.2023 (Lithuania, nos 6 ff and 95 ff); SC 15.5.2023 (Austria, no 22 ff); SC 11.7.2023 (Sweden, no 32 ff); SC 31.10.2023 (Spain, no 63 ff).
4 Eg SC 31.8.2023 (Czech Republic, no 4 ff: trading company in the retail sector); SAC 19.4.2023 (Lithuania, no 6 ff: provider of dental and health services); SC 23.3.2023 (Switzerland, no 83 ff: fitness centre).
5 SC 15.5.2023 (Austria, no 22 ff).
6 SC 15.6.2023 (Lithuania, no 95 ff).
7 SC 21.4.2023 (Czech Republic, no 27 ff).

sures in particular, it comes as no surprise that outcomes varied, with a slight majority rejecting liability, for example in Switzerland, Austria and Spain.[8]

An interesting point was raised in one of the Czech cases where the claimant, 7
a trading company, sought compensation for lost profits in connection with State measures during lockdown. The Supreme Court clarified that a damages claim will not fail simply because the claimant complied with the very State measures which subsequently caused the damage.[9] In other words, submitting to State authority cannot be equated with the injured party's 'consent' to the injury. However, as highlighted in another Czech decision, the situation might change where the claimant would have been entitled to challenge *the measure itself* in court but failed to do so within the statutory period.[10]

I suspect that this new guest to the conference is likely to stay with us for a 8
few years yet, and it will be interesting to see whether common approaches to liability emerge across national borders. It is probably also just a matter of time before the first cases against *private* tortfeasors are adjudicated and reported. Absent a specific provision such as that in the Czech Crisis Act,[11] I expect that many courts will be reluctant to hold their governments liable for measures taken during such exceptional circumstances. The concern might be that they are straying too far into political territory. And this brings me to my second choice of sweet: the intersection of politics and tort.

2. Where Politics Meet Torts

State liability has been a regular guest at the conference for a number of years 9
now, and this year was no different. While all cases of State liability potentially raise the issue of separation of powers and the sometimes uneasy divide between the legal and the political, there are some where the boundaries of tort law are severely tested. This is particularly striking where tort claims appear to be less an instrument for compensating the harm suffered by an individual, and more a means to achieve a political solution by increasing political pressure.

A remarkable case in point is discussed in the French report. The claimants 10
brought an action in tort against the French state in the French overseas *département* of Martinique, seeking inter alia compensation for 'past, present and future

8 SC 23.3.2023 (Switzerland, nos 83, 89 ff); SC 15.5.2023 (Austria, nos 22, 24 ff); SC 31.10.2023 (Spain, no 64); see also SAC 19.4.2023 (Lithuania, nos 6, 9 ff).

9 SC 31.8.2023 (Czech Republic, nos 4, 11 ff, 15).

10 SC 21.4.2023 (Czech Republic, nos 27, 31 ff, 34).

11 Cf Czech Republic, nos 4 ff, 11 ff.

losses arising from slave trade and slavery committed by French public authorities', the funding of 'the repatriation to Africa of all descendants of deportees' who wish to be so repatriated, and the establishment of a fund of € 20 billion to cover future damages.[12] The claims failed in all instances, with the final appeal being rejected by the French Supreme Court (*Cour de Cassation*) last year.[13] The Court gave two reasons: first, whatever their legal merits, the claims brought by the descendants of slaves were time-barred. The Court reasoned that the descendants would have been in a position to file a claim against the State as soon as France had ratified international conventions which recognised slavery as a crime against humanity after the Second World War. It was at this point that the four-year limitation period had started to run. Secondly, the Court held that no certain, direct and personal loss to the claimants had been established.[14]

11 The Netherlands, in particular, already has experience of such lawsuits. In a paper published in 2020, the Dutch academic and former member of the Dutch Supreme Court, Marc Loth, highlights the difference between 'ancestor-based claims [which] are based on past harm, wrongfully inflicted upon the victim (slave) in the remote past', for which the claimant, as the descendant of the victim, seeks compensation now, and 'descendant-based claims' which are based on an alleged injustice or inequality from which the claimants themselves suffer in the present day.[15] Both types of claims raise distinct and particular problems – the first type with respect to the requirement of wrongfulness vis-à-vis the ancestor, as standards then were not the same as standards now, the difficulty of connecting today's claimants to the victims of the past and today's defendants to the perpetrators of the past, and the statute of limitations; and the second type also with respect to wrongfulness, but this time vis-à-vis the *descendant*, as well as the assessment of damage and causation.

12 The boundaries between the political and the legal can also be blurred in less remarkable circumstances, for example whenever the courts have the power to hold the State liable for wrongdoing of the legislative branch.[16] Coming from Switzerland, where federal laws passed by parliament are binding on the courts by virtue of a constitutional provision and where courts do not have the power to declare federal laws to be unconstitutional, I was particularly intrigued by recent

12 France, no 14.
13 SC (Cass Civ) 5.7.2023 (France, no 15 ff).
14 SC (Cass Civ) 5.7.2023 (France, no 16).
15 How Does Tort Law Deal with Historical Injustice? On Slavery Reparations, Post-Colonial Redress, and the Legitimations of Tort Law (2020) 11 Journal of European Tort Law (JETL) 181, 184 ff, <https://doi.org/10.1515/jetl-2020-0141> (5.8.2024).
16 See eg County Court Velika Gorica, 28.2.2023 (Croatia, no 21 ff).

developments in Belgium. In December 2022, the Belgian Supreme Court held that, where damage caused by the legislator is at issue, the State will be liable in tort if its conduct did not comply with the standard of the 'normally careful and prudent legislator'[17]. Deviation from this standard will constitute 'fault' for the purpose of tort liability.[18] It appears that this notion of fault was also sanctioned, at least indirectly, by the Belgian legislator itself when it adopted the text of the new Book 6 of the Civil Code on 1 February 2024 without addressing this issue.[19]

The interesting question is how to develop an objective standard of the 'reasonable legislator'. It seems clear that a court's own political leanings cannot provide the measure. Belgian academics have suggested that one criterion could be whether the legislator heeded or ignored justified criticism of the draft law by the Belgian *Conseil d'État.*[20] My understanding of the role of the *Conseil d'État* is that it has an advisory capacity during the legislative process, where it assists with legal advice. However, given that the advice is not binding, academics have raised concerns with regard to the separation of powers between the judicial and legislative branch.[21] 13

The Israeli Supreme Court showed more reluctance to wade into the political sphere in a case concerning the omission, by a State agency, to address the risks from jet skis through safety guidelines.[22] The claimant had been riding a jet ski with her son and a licenced operator when she fell off and sustained serious injury. The State was held liable for negligence by the court of lower instance. On appeal, the decision was reversed by the Supreme Court, confirming the rule, developed in case law, that the State does not owe a duty of care where it has broad discretionary power to choose between several courses of action (so-called 'discretionary function exception').[23] 14

A different aspect of the divide between the political and the legal is highlighted by the decision, in Germany, not to pursue a claim for damages against Andreas Scheuer, the former Federal Minister of Transport.[24] Scheuer is said to have caused damage to the German taxpayer to the tune of more than € 200 million by implementing a doomed road toll system despite strong doubts regarding its legality, doubts which were then confirmed in 2019 by a decision of the European Court 15

17 SC (Cour de Cassation/Hof van Cassatie) 15.12.2022 (Belgium, nos 5 ff, 16 ff, 22, 24).
18 Belgium, no 26.
19 Belgium, no 27 f.
20 Cf Belgium, no 24, with refs.
21 Cf Belgium, no 26, with refs.
22 SC 8.6.2023, *State of Israel v Jane Doe* (Israel, no 28 ff).
23 SC 8.6.2023, *State of Israel v Jane Doe* (Israel, nos 28 ff, 35, with commentary at no 41 f).
24 Germany, no 12 ff.

of Justice[25]. The German reporters point out that introducing a special scheme for ministers' liability might deter citizens from seeking political office, as the risk would be deemed too great, and that therefore, political solutions might be more appropriate. Shortly before the Conference, it was reported that Scheuer, perhaps wisely, had left the German Bundestag with immediate effect. The announcement was made on 1 April, which led to several inquiries being made as to whether it was an April Fools' joke (it was not).[26]

3. Tort Liability for Mere Increase of a Risk

16 A topic which I have long been fascinated by is the approach taken by courts with respect to tort claims for increasing the mere risk of disease.[27] This interest was fuelled once more by two decisions reported on this year. In Sweden, the Supreme Court was called upon to decide on the liability of a water company for drinking water contaminated by PFAS (per- and polyfluorinated alkyl substances) under product liability law. The water contamination had increased the risk of disease in the residents of the municipality of Ronneby.[28] In France, a case decided by the *Cour de Cassation* dealt with tort liability for the anxiety suffered by a woman who, as a foetus, had been exposed to the drug diethylstilbestrol (DES) taken by her mother during pregnancy, and who therefore had an increased risk of developing cancer.[29]

17 It is, perhaps, useful to place these decisions into a wider context. Taking a step back for a moment, two groups of cases can be distinguished where a tortfeasor has increased a risk.

18 In the first, the risk of disease has actually materialised, meaning that the claimant has become sick. If, in such a situation, the claimant can prove that the defendant caused his injury, no particular problems arise. Sometimes, however, because of the current limits of science, the claimant will be unable to prove that the defendant's conduct was indeed a *conditio sine qua non* of the claimant's injury. Whether the defendant can be held liable in such circumstances simply by virtue of having increased the risk is a question which has been raised sev-

---

25 CJEU 18.6.2019, C-591/17, *Austria v Germany*, ECLI:EU:C :2019:504.

26 Cf Frankfurter Allgemeine Zeitung 2.4.2024, "Jetzt geht Scheuer doch", <www.faz.net/aktuell/wirtschaft/unternehmen/leiser-rueckzug-des-csu-politikers-jetzt-geht-andreas-scheuer-doch-19626580.html> (5.8.2024).

27 See *C Widmer*, A Civil Lawyer's Introduction to Anglo-American Law: Torts (2008) 240 ff, 283 ff.

28 SC 5.12.2023 (Sweden, no 62 ff).

29 SC (Cass Civ) 18.10.2023 (France, no 20 ff).

eral times in English law in particular. Perhaps the most famous case is the decision of the House of Lords in *Fairchild v Glenhaven*,[30] where Mr Fairchild had developed mesothelioma caused by work-related exposure to asbestos, but was unable to prove, because of the limits of medical science, whether his disease was the result of exposure to asbestos during his employment with employer A, or during his employment with employer B, or during his employment with A and B taken together. A more recent case is the decision by the English Court of Appeal in *Holmes v Poeton*,[31] in which work-related exposure to unsafe levels of Trichloroethylene (TCE), an organic solvent, had at least *possibly* increased the claimant's risk of developing Parkinson's disease, from which he now suffers. The problem raised by these types of cases is essentially one of causation.

In light of both the Swedish and the French cases, however, I would like to 19
focus on the second group. In this group, unlike in the first, the risk has *not yet materialised*, and it is uncertain whether it ever will. The question here is whether an increased risk of future disease can, by itself, constitute actionable damage. Cases in this category generally involve claimants who have been exposed to toxic substances without any disease having manifested itself, and without it having been established that a disease related to the exposure will manifest itself in the future. At first glance, the problem is not one of causation, but of the notion of 'damage'. The two questions are, however, inextricably linked. For if the risk itself, on its own, is looked on as damage, the claimant who, at a later date, does indeed develop the disease, will no longer have to prove that their disease was caused by the person who wrongfully exposed them to the risk. Allowing such a claim introduces a speculative element into tort law.

Courts are generally reluctant to recognise claims for increased risk. However, 20
there are exceptions, and the American experience is particularly instructive. In the past, American courts sometimes allowed claims for increased risk. One of the reasons for this was to prevent tort claims from becoming time-barred under the so-called single-action rule. Under this rule, an injured party must claim damages in the same action for all the damage which they have suffered or will suffer as a consequence of the breach of duty.[32] A person who, for example, has developed pleural plaques[33] due to exposure to asbestos at their workplace has a significantly higher statistical risk of developing a malignant disease such as mes-

30 [2002] UKHL 22, [2002] 3 All ER 305, [2003] 1 AC 32, [2002] 3 WLR 89.

31 [2023] EWCA Civ 1377, [2024] KB 521, [2024] ICR 723.

32 Cf also *Johnston and NEI International Combustion Limited* [2007] UKHL 39 at [13] f ([2007] ICR 1745, [2007] 3 WLR 876, [2008] 1 AC 281). In the UK, the rule was modified for personal injury actions through legislation; see sec 32 A of the Senior Courts Act 1981.

33 See below at no 22.

othelioma.[34] If such plaques are considered an 'injury' for the purposes of limitation, and if they trigger the limitation period for all harm, both current and future, arising from the tortious exposure, then a claim might become time-barred long before the actual disease manifests itself. By allowing claims for increased risk, American courts were in effect mitigating these harsh consequences of the single-action rule.[35] The single-action rule has since been abolished in most, if not all, American states, at least with respect to asbestos litigation.[36] Since then, claims for increased risk have generally been rejected.[37] This link between increased-risk claims and limitation periods is also mentioned in the Swedish report.[38]

21 The Swedish Supreme Court differed from the approach previously taken by some American courts in that it held that under the Swedish Product Liability Act (based, in turn, on the EU Product Liability Directive), increase of risk alone does not constitute personal injury.[39] Instead, the Court focussed on the bodily change in the claimants' blood (which showed highly elevated levels of PFAS), even though this change alone did not appear to cause any symptoms.[40] This distinction between 'mere' increased risk on the one hand, and increased risk in combination with a physical change on the other, seems compelling at first. However, unless it is established that the physical change will, at some point, actually lead to a disease, the argument loses some of its force, as the speculative element remains. The claimants will, in effect, still be receiving compensation for their increased statistical risk of disease.

22 A counter-example can be found in the English case of *Johnston and NEI International Combustion Limited*, decided by the House of Lords in 2007.[41] The claimants had been exposed to asbestos through the negligence of their employers. As a

34 See below at no 22.
35 *Widmer* (fn 27) 285.
36 *JA Henderson/AD Twerski*, Asbestos Litigation Gone Mad: Exposure-Based Recovery for Increased Risk, Mental Distress, and Medical Monitoring, 53 South Carolina Law Review 815, 821 (2002), with refs.
37 See *AR Klein*, A Model for Enhanced Risk Recovery in Tort, 56 Washington & Lee Law Review 1173, 1176 (1999); *Henderson/Twerski*, 53 South Carolina Law Review 822 f (2002).
38 Sweden, no 76.
39 SC 5.12.2023 (Sweden, no 76).
40 Cf SC 5.12.2023 (Sweden, no 78, with commentary at no 81); cf also Swedish court ruling unlocks potential for more PFAS lawsuits, 5.12.2023, <https://chemsec.org/swedish-court-ruling-unlocks-potential-for-more-pfas-lawsuits> (5.8.2024), and Sweden: Supreme Court Declares High Levels of PFAS in Blood Constitutes Personal Injury, 7.3.2024, <www.loc.gov/item/global-legal-monitor/2024-03-06/sweden-supreme-court-declares-high-levels-of-pfas-in-blood-constitutes-personal-injury/> (5.8.2024).
41 See fn 32.

result, they developed pleural plaques, ie a fibrous thickening of pleural membrane surrounding the lungs. Such plaques do not, as a rule, cause any symptoms, nor do they cause other asbestos-related diseases such as asbestosis or mesothelioma. However, the statistical risk of developing such diseases is significantly higher in persons with plaques than in those who have been exposed to asbestos but have not developed plaques.[42] The House of Lords unanimously held that symptomless plaques, together with the increased risk of future injury, did not constitute actionable damage. An interesting question is whether the outcome in *Johnston* would have been different if the physical change in the pleural membrane had caused pecuniary damage. Depending on the type of disease, one could, for example, envisage a claim for the costs of periodic medical examinations that might help detect the onset of disease at an early stage, enabling beneficial medical intervention. In some American states, such so-called medical-monitoring claims have been more successful than increased-risk claims.[43]

The Swedish Supreme Court chose a different route to that of the House of 23
Lords in *Johnston* in that it accepted tort liability in principle where increased risk and physical change come together. However, the Court did not have to rule on the difficult question of damages.[44] Hopefully, there will be more to report on this question in the future.

In the DES case mentioned above,[45] the French *Cour de Cassation* went even 24
further than its Swedish counterpart. In holding that 'the anxiety resulting from exposure to a risk of harm is a compensable damage' under the general tort clause of the French Civil Code (art 1240), it refused to make compensation dependent on the existence of any physical deterioration.[46] It did so by focussing on the anxiety caused to the claimant by the increased risk, a risk which required the claimant to undergo periodic medical examinations. The costs of these examinations were not at issue; as reported, the claim was not concerned with the expenses of medical monitoring.

Whatever one's view of these controversial questions, the French approach of 25
allowing compensation for risk-related anxiety without any physical manifestation, as long as the anxiety is well-founded, has the benefit of being transparent.

---

42 *Johnston and NEI International Combustion Limited* [2007] UKHL 39 at [1], [78].

43 See eg, *Ayers v Township of Jackson*, 525 A2d 287 (NJ 1987); cf also *Widmer* (fn 27) 285 f with further refs.

44 SC 5.12.2023 (Sweden, no 79, with commentary at no 80).

45 See no 16.

46 SC (Cass Civ) 18.10.2023 (France, no 20 ff, with commentary at no 27).

However, the concern is that it might open the floodgates, with claimants seeking compensation although they might never become ill.[47]

26 In the final analysis, liability for increased risk, for medical monitoring or for mental distress are all creative ways of surmounting (or circumventing?) the obstacle of *causation.* It will often be easier to establish that tortious exposure to a harmful substance merely increased the claimant's risk of disease, caused the claimant anxiety or necessitated regular medical examinations than to prove that the subsequent disease itself (if it develops at all) would not have occurred but for the tortious exposure.

4. Causation

27 Leaving the question of increased risk aside, 'normal' issues of causation make a regular appearance at the Annual Conference. This year is no different, with several cases raising difficult questions of factual causation in particular. Many cases revolved around causation in the context of healthcare.[48] I found the following cases particularly noteworthy:[49]

47 Cf *Ayers v Township of Jackson,* 525 A2d 287 (NJ 1987) at 3 on increased-risk claims: 'A holding that recognizes a cause of action for unquantified enhanced risk claims exposes the tort system, and the public it serves, to the task of litigating vast numbers of claims for compensation based on threats of injuries that may never occur. It imposes on judges and juries the burden of assessing damages for the risk of potential disease, without clear guidelines to determine what level of compensation may be appropriate …'.

48 See CoA 31.5.2023 and 25.10.2023 (Malta, no 2 ff, regarding medical malpractice by two different dentists on separate occasions, and, no 46 ff, concerning medical malpractice by a chiropractor); SC 15.6.2023 (Lithuania, no 95 ff, regarding an alleged contamination with the COVID-19 virus during a hospital stay due to a failure to comply with health legislation); SC 6.7.2023 (Italy, no 59 ff, concerning the establishment of a causal link between an HIV infection and a blood transfusion); SC 14.6.2023 (Norway, no 37 ff, regarding 'adequate [or legal] causation' of harm suffered by a father whose daughter had committed suicide due to a failure in health care); Court of Session (Outer House) 6.1.2023, *Paterson v Lanarkshire Health Board* [2023] CSOH 1 (Scotland, no 2 ff, on liability of a health provider towards relatives of a patient who had committed suicide after being discharged from a psychiatric ward); SC Curia Pfv.III.20.287/2022/5. (Hungary, no 2 ff, on medical malpractice and loss of a chance); SC 1.3.2023 (Croatia, no 39 ff, on medical malpractice); SAC 14.9.2023 (Portugal, no 13 ff, regarding medical malpractice).

49 For further decisions on causation, see also SC 15.2.2023 (Bulgaria, no 52 ff, regarding damage allegedly caused by the State's failure to implement an EU directive); SC Curia Pfv.III.20.604/2022/5. (Hungary, no 12 ff, on liability of a lawyer towards his client for loss of a chance due to the belated submission of a claim); SC 1.2.2023 (Italy, no 2 ff, regarding liability of a landowner for environmental damage); Court of Session (Outer House) 9.5.2023, *Moray Offshore Renewable Power Ltd v Bluefloat Energy UK Holdings Ltd* [2023] CSOH 29 (Scotland, nos 18 ff, 20, 24, concerning alleged

In the DES case mentioned above,[50] the French *Cour de Cassation* not only decided that standalone anxiety due to increased risk is actionable damage, but also addressed the question of causation between the claimant's infertility and her mother's exposure to DES whilst pregnant with the claimant.[51] In the particular circumstances of the case, a different cause of the claimant's infertility (namely a chlamydia infection) could not be discounted; in fact, it was considered the more probable cause by medical evidence at trial. However, in the view of the Supreme Court (and contrary to the position of the lower court), this did not suffice to rule out causation. Rather, it was sufficient that the DES was a *possible* cause of the claimant's infertility, meaning that the manufacturer will be liable unless it can prove that its product could not have contributed to the claimant's condition. As pointed out in the French report,[52] this amounts to liability for alternative causation, but with the special feature that only one of the causes is tortious. 28

An illustration of how factual causation can be weakened beyond recognition comes from Israel in the form of the Compensation to Victims of Terror (Exemplary Damages) Act. This Act was proposed by parliament before the Hamas-led attack of 7 October and entered into force in 2024.[53] Under its provisions, if a person is killed or injured by a terrorist attack, the court shall award the estate or the injured person punitive damages against entities such as the Palestinian Authority who are considered to have 'approved' or 'ratified' the tort by giving financial support to the perpetrators *after* the act, despite there being no causal link between their approval and the harm caused to the victims. The Law expands a decision from 2022,[54] in which the Israeli Supreme Court introduced 'ratifiers' liability' in tort, to the exclusion of punitive damages.[55] 29

---

false claims in a consortium's contract bid), and 2.11.2023, *Ronnie O'Neill Freight Solutions Ltd v Macroberts LLP* [2023] CSOH 75 (Scotland, nos 32 ff, 35, 37, regarding the alleged professional negligence of a solicitor who had not advised about arguments which could have been made in litigation); SC 17.1.2023 (Portugal, nos 40 ff, 46, 48, 51, concerning the liability of an insurer for the insured party's loss of profits) and CoA Porto 12.7.2023 (Portugal, no 54 ff, on liability of the custodians of chattels and immovable property); CoA 23.2.2023, *Davey v Sligo County Council* [2023] IECA 39 (Ireland, no 16 ff, regarding a traffic accident and the defendant employer's alleged failure to provide sufficient protective measures).

50 See nos 16 and 24.

51 SC (Cass Civ) 18.10.2023 (France, no 20 ff).

52 France, no 26.

53 Israel, no 3.

54 SC 10.4.2022, *John Doe v The Palestinian Authority*, Civ App 2362/19; see *R Perry*, Israel, in: E Karner/BC Steininger (eds), ETL 2022 (2023) 729, no 9 ff.

55 Israel, no 2.

30 On a more light-hearted note, although clearly not for the defendant involved in the case, worrying news for tax lawyers comes from Denmark, where a law firm was held liable for the loss incurred by the Danish tax authorities due to fraud committed against the State by one of the law firm's clients.[56] Although the law firm was not held to have committed any criminal offence or to have been aware that its client intended to defraud the Danish State, the Supreme Court held it to be liable as it had 'unreasonably disregarded the interests of the tax authority'[57] when advising its client. The Supreme Court also found that there was a sufficient causal link between the law firm's advice and the loss suffered by the tax authorities. As pointed out in the Danish report, it appears doubtful that a bank intent on committing a criminal offence against the authorities would have acted differently based on a note of caution from its lawyers.[58] The law firm's brief had been billed at around € 13,000; the damages for which they were then held liable amounted to more than € 50 million (DKK 400 million).[59] At least they appear to have had good insurance coverage.

5. Vicarious Liability

31 One guest I would happily see the back of, but who is likely to stay with us in the foreseeable future, is sexual abuse and assault, with vicarious liability for an employee's conduct at the forefront of several recent cases. In particular, the requirement of a close connection with the abuser's employment continues to occupy the courts, with cases being reported from England,[60] Germany[61] and Scotland[62].

32 Drawing the line between conduct which is sufficiently connected to a tortfeasor's employment and that which is not is extremely difficult, and it is perfectly conceivable that courts presented with the same set of facts might reach different conclusions. In the German case, for example, the first instance court was con-

56 SC 20.11.2023 (Denmark, no 2ff).
57 SC 20.11.2023 (Denmark, no 4).
58 Denmark, no 8.
59 Denmark, no 8 f.
60 SC 26.4.2023, *BXB v Trustees of the Barry Congregation of Jehovah's Witnesses* [2023] UKSC 15 (England and Wales, no 53ff).
61 Landgericht Köln (Cologne) 13.6.2023 (Germany, no 49 ff).
62 Court of Session (Outer House) 2.3.2023, *X v Y & the Lord Advocate* [2023] CSOH 17 (Scotland, no 8 ff, regarding State liability for the alleged sexual assault against a legal practitioner by a judge); Court of Session (Inner House) 13.10.2023, *X & S v Shaw & another* [2023] CSIH 36 (Scotland, no 25 ff, concerning historical sexual abuse of two brothers by a caretaker employed by a sports centre).

cerned with historical sexual abuse suffered by the claimant as a child at the hand of a priest. The defendant archbishopric had retracted its defence of limitation, and it did not deny the acts of the priest (now deceased) who had perpetrated the abuse. The claimant had become acquainted with the priest when serving as an altar boy. He took part in all the camps offered by the priest as part of the archbishopric's youth and altar servers programmes. The Court held that the abuse suffered by the claimant while participating in these programmes was sufficiently connected to the priest's employment, but not, however, the abuse perpetrated during holidays which the priest had invited him on.[63]

A different conclusion was reached by the Swiss Federal Court in an old case concerning the liability of a psychiatric clinic for damage caused to a patient.[64] A doctor employed by the clinic had started a relationship with a 17-year-old girl while she was an in-patient at the clinic. Intimate relations continued during a three-week holiday which the doctor had suggested to the girl's parents to aid recovery, and which she ostensibly had spent on her own. In reality, the couple spent the entire three weeks together, as had been the plan all along. The defendant clinic was subsequently held liable not only for the doctor's conduct while the girl was staying at the clinic, but also for his conduct during those three weeks. The Court reasoned, inter alia, that the girl's medical treatment had not been completed when they went on holiday, and that the plan to go on holiday together had been taken during her stay at the clinic.[65] 33

It is not clear from the German case that tortious conduct by an employee during his holidays will never be sufficiently connected to their employment for the purposes of vicarious liability. In its decision, the Court pointed out that the claimant had failed to provide dates and further details relating to the alleged abuse suffered during his holidays with the priest. This allows the inference that the analysis might change if – to follow the line of reasoning of the Swiss Supreme Court – the plan to go on holiday together had, for example, been made and discussed while the claimant was still serving as an altar boy. 34

6. Wrongful Birth

Another guest who has kept courts busy this year is doctors' liability for wrongful birth, with decisions reaching us from Austria, Israel and, for the first time, the 35

63 Cf Germany, no 55.

64 SC 1.2.1966, BGE 92 II 15 ff.

65 SC 1.2.1966, BGE 92 II 15 at [5].

Czech Republic. The issues dealt with spanned from compensation for non-pecuniary damage caused by interference with the parents' right to reproductive self-determination and their private and family life;[66] a sibling's claim for compensation for mental distress due to the level of care required by her younger brother, who had been born with a heart defect, and the social isolation necessary to avoid additional risks to his health;[67] compensation for pecuniary damage where the parents would have terminated the pregnancy if they had known of their child's disability;[68] to the question whether a doctor is under a duty to remind and encourage a pregnant woman to take additional tests for neurological disorders during pregnancy.[69]

36 Two decisions are of particular interest. In the first, handed down by the Austrian Supreme Court, the parents had sued the defendant obstetrician not just for the disability-related increase in maintenance costs, but for the maintenance costs in full. The Court upheld the claim, reasoning that the purpose of the treatment contract had, inter alia, been to detect disabilities and to allow the parents to opt for a legally permissible abortion. The fact that the parents would have been willing to pay maintenance for a healthy child did not change this purpose, which had been thwarted by the defendant's failure to detect the defect. Accordingly, the Court concluded that compensation could not be limited to the additional expenses caused by the child's disability.[70]

37 The issue in the second case, decided by the Israeli Supreme Court, was whether a genetic medical counsellor had breached a duty of care toward the claimant during pregnancy. Based on the information at the time, the counsellor had estimated the risk of a neurological disorder of the claimant's unborn child at 15%, but had explicitly indicated in her letter to the claimant that additional tests ought to be carried out. The claimant failed to take these tests and subsequently gave birth to a severely disabled daughter who suffered from a rare genetic neurodegenerative syndrome. In her claim, the mother submitted, inter alia, that the counsellor's recommendations should have been placed in a separate section at the end of the letter, rather than in the body of the letter itself, and that the counsellor had failed to remind or encourage the claimant to take the additional tests.[71] The Court rejected the claim, holding that the recommendations had been made

66 SC 16.5.2023 (Czech Republic, no 106 ff).
67 SC 17.8.2023 (Austria, no 32 ff).
68 SC 21.11.2023 (Austria, no 56 ff).
69 SC 18.6.2023, *Jane Doe v Hadassah Medical Organisation* (Israel, no 43 ff).
70 SC 21.11.2023 (Austria, nos 56 ff, 62, 67).
71 The daughter herself had also brought a claim for wrongful life; this was, however, invalid under current Israeli law; see Israel, no 47 ff.

clearly in the letter and that a reasonable medical practitioner was not under a duty to 'nag' a patient.[72]

7. Limitation Periods

As always, many cases dealt with the matter of limitation, in particular with the question when such periods start to run[73] and the determination of the injured party's (actual or imputed) knowledge in the case of short (subjective) limitation periods.[74] 38

Although it does not date from the reporting period, given its importance and the fact that it was handed down shortly before the Conference, mention must be made of the latest decision of the European Court of Human Rights on limitation periods in case of delayed damage. The decision of *Jann-Zwicker*[75] is the second decision[76] in which Switzerland was held to have violated Art 6 of the European Convention on Human Rights with respect to limitation periods in case of asbestos-related diseases. Switzerland has two different limitation periods in tort claims. One period starts with the injured party's knowledge of the damage and the identity of the tortfeasor (the 'relative' or 'subjective' period). The other period starts on the date the duty was breached, even if the damage has not yet occurred (the 'absolute' or 'objective' period). This second period was at issue in the case of *Jann-Zwicker*. The European Court of Human Rights made it very clear that when it is *scientifically impossible* for a person to know that they suffer from a certain illness, this must be taken into account for the purposes of limitation. This can be done, for 39

72 SC 18.6.2023, *Jane Doe v Hadassah Medical Organisation* (Israel, nos 43 ff, 44 f, 50 ff).

73 Eg SC 10.5.2023, *Jalla v Shell International Trading and Shipping Co Ltd* [2023] UKSC 16 (England and Wales, no 26 ff, on the distinction between continuing nuisance and one-off events for the purposes of limitation in case of an oil spill).

74 On the latter, see, in particular, SC 19.7.2023 (Slovenia, no 16 ff: limitation period does not run separately for each individual item of non-pecuniary damage resulting from the same traffic accident, but only when the injured party is aware of the entire damage); SC 13.1.2023 (Greece, no 3 ff, on determining 'knowledge' in the case of damage suffered as a result of surgery whilst unclear which acts or omissions by which surgeon or nurse caused the damage); see also SC 21.7.2023 (Spain, no 35 ff: thalidomide) and 12.6.2023 (Spain, no 42 ff, with commentary at no 47 f: truck cartel); SC 21.4.2023 (Netherlands, no 26 ff); SC 10.5.2023 (Norway, no 14 ff).

75 ECtHR *Jann Zwicker and Jann v Switzerland*, 13.2.2024, no 4976/20.

76 The first was ECtHR *Howald Moor and Others v Switzerland*, 11.3.2014, no 52067/10 and no 41072/11; for a discussion from a Swiss law perspective, see *C Widmer Lüchinger*, Die Verjährung bei Asbestschäden: Eine Standortbestimmung nach dem EGMR-Entscheid Howald Moor et autres c. Suisse, ZBJV 2014, 460 ff, with further refs.

example, by adapting the starting point when the limitation period starts to run, or by suspending the running of the limitation period. Although one is never happy when one's own country is held to have violated the Convention, in my view, the decision was both inevitable and justified. It will likely have repercussions not only for Switzerland,[77] but also for other countries in Europe with similar laws, eg Sweden[78].

40 On a different issue, an interesting decision was also reported from Romania. The case involved an action for compensation for non-pecuniary damage suffered by a party as a result of deportation during the USSR regime on the basis of their ethnicity. The Supreme Court held that while no statute of limitations applies to genocide in criminal law, corresponding tort actions remain subject to the normal rules. Accordingly, 33 years after the event, the claim was time-barred. In the Court's opinion, the limitation period for the tort claim had started to run when it first could have been brought, ie after the fall of the Communist regime.[79]

C. Final Comments

41 And with that, my tour comes to an end. Of the many other sweets which would have deserved sampling, I would like to mention, in particular, the controversial threshold for liability in case of a breach of the General Data Protection Regulation (GDPR)[80] and the assessment of damages in the *Dieselgate* cases[81] – both topics which are likely to receive much attention elsewhere in legal literature.

42 Other interesting guests at this year's Conference included the limits of compensation for pain and suffering for the relatives of a deceased person;[82] the notion of damage in the case of deletion of data from a data carrier;[83] the requisite

77 For a discussion of this judgment, see *C Widmer Lüchinger,* Verjährung und Asbest: Die Schweiz wird erneut durch den Europäischen Gerichtshof für Menschenrechte verurteilt, Jusletter 8.4.2024; *C Müller,* Bis repetita placent: Der Europäische Gerichtshof für Menschenrechte verurteilt die Schweiz erneut wegen der absoluten Verjährung der Ansprüche von Asbestopfern, Jusletter 8.4.2024.

78 Cf Sweden, no 82.

79 SC 16.2.2023 (Romania, no 41).

80 CJEU 4.5.2023, C-300/21, *UI v Österreichische Post AG,* ECLI:EU:C:2023:370 (EU, no 4 ff); CJEU 14.12.2023, C-340/21, *VB v Natsionalna agentsia za prihodite,* ECLI:EU:C:2023:986 (EU, nos 23 ff, 32); CJEU 14.12.2023, C-456/22, *VX, AT v Gemeinde Ummendorf,* ECLI:EU:C:2023:988 (EU, no 36 ff); Oberlandesgericht Hamm 15.8.2023 (Germany, no 36 ff); CoA Warsaw 22.6.2023 (Poland, no 16 ff).

81 SC 9.5.2023 (Switzerland, no 13 ff); SC 28.9.2023 (Austria, no 45 ff).

82 See SC 15.11.2023 (Finland, no 25 ff).

83 SC 24.11.2023 (Estonia, no 2 ff, concerning the unlawful deletion of data from a data carrier).

connection, in the case of liability for dangerous operations or things, between the *danger* of the operation or thing and the *damage* caused by that operation or thing;[84] and liability towards third parties for breach of a duty owed to one's clients, patients or employees under a contract.[85] I expect we will all meet again.

84 SC 23.3.2023 (Czech Republic, no 54 ff, on liability for damage caused to forests by emissions released from factories); SC 24.1.2023 (Germany, no 29 ff, on liability of the keeper of a car in the event of explosion of a removed car battery); SC 24.1.2023 (Switzerland, no 67 ff, on liability of the keeper of a car in the event of fire caused by a heated catalytic converter).

85 CoA Athens 17.1.2023 (Greece, no 25 ff: liability of a bank); SC 17.8.2023 (Austria, nos 32 ff, 36 ff: ultimately unsuccessful claim against an obstetrician by the older sibling of a disabled child in a wrongful birth case, cf above at no 35); SC 22.3.2023 (Switzerland, no 61 ff: duty of a safety officer employed by a bakery extended to a third party not employed by the bakery); the Danish case on the liability of a law firm to the tax authorities because of advice given to a client (see above at no 30) also falls in this category.

Contributors

Ewa BAGIŃSKA

Faculty of Law and
Administration
Gdańsk University
Jana Bażyńskiego 6
80 – 309 Gdańsk
Poland
Tel: (+48) 58 523 2851
baginska@fulbrightmail.org

Ewa Bagińska (Prof Dr hab) holds the Chair of Civil Law at the School of Law and Administration of the University of Gdańsk. She was a Fulbright Visiting Scholar (1998/1999) and NATO Science Fellowship grantee (2000/2001) at the CUA Columbus School of Law, Washington, DC. She has authored a number of books on product liability, public liability and medical law, as well as over 200 other contributions in the area of civil law. She is the editor of 'Damages for Violations of Human Rights. A Comparative Study of Domestic Legal Systems', Springer Verlag (2016). Ewa Bagińska was a member of the Commission for the Codification of Civil Law. She is a member of the European Group on Tort Law, the International Academy of Comparative Law (of which she is currently vice-president) and the European Law Institute. She is also a member of several advisory boards of law journals in the field of comparative law (incl European Review of Private Law) and is editor of two national journals (State and Law and the Insurance Quarterly Review). She acts as a National Correspondent for the Journal of Civil Law Studies (Louisiana, US).

Marko BARETIĆ

Faculty of Law of the University of Zagreb
Trg Republike Hrvatske 3
10000 Zagreb
Croatia
Tel: (+385) 1 4597 561
mbaretic@pravo.hr

Marko Baretić is a tenured Professor of Civil Law and Consumer Protection Law at the Faculty of Law of the University of Zagreb. He obtained his LLM (Pre-Contractual Liability) and PhD (Liability for Defective Products) degrees from the University of Zagreb. He also studied at the Asser College Europe, Asser Institute, The Hague, The Netherlands. He publishes on various topics in the fields of civil law, predominantly the law of obligations (contract law and tort law) and consumer protection law. He was active in negotiations of the Republic of Croatia for accession to the EU as a member of the working group 28 (consumer protection and health). As a member of various legislative working groups, he actively participated in drafting the Croatian Obligations Act and the Consumer Pro-

https://doi.org/10.1515/9783111376721-035

tection Act. He was the representative of the Republic of Croatia in the working group III of UNCITRAL (online dispute resolution). He is also active in commercial arbitration.

Elena BARGELLI

Faculty of Political Science
Pisa University
Via Serafini 3
56126 Pisa
Italy
Tel: (+39) 50 2212458
bargelli@sp.unipi.it

Elena Bargelli is currently a full Professor of Private Law at the University of Pisa, Law Department. She was a Research Fellow of the Alexander von Humboldt Stiftung at the Max Planck Institut für ausländisches und internationales Privatrecht in Hamburg (2008–2009). She is a member of ECTIL, the International Academy of Comparative Law (IACL) and the European Law Institute. She is on the editorial board of several journals and book series. She has authored a number of books as well as numerous contributions in various fields of civil law. Her areas of interest are contract law, tort law and family law from a national, comparative and EU perspective.

Søren BERGENSER

Bergenser Advocate firma
Ostre Kanalgade 4
9000 Aalborg
Denmark
Tel: (+45) 21177472
sb@bergenserlaw.dk

Søren Bergenser is an Assistant Professor at the University of Aalborg, Institute of Private Law, where he deals with professional and product liability and the liability of public authorities. Søren Bergenser holds a PhD from the University of Copenhagen and he was a research fellow at Duke University School of Law and at the Max Planck Institute of Private Law in Hamburg. In 1999, Søren Bergenser graduated from Aarhus University, where he also worked as an Assistant Professor from 1997–1999. He is also a practising lawyer and liability and insurance law, litigation and arbitration are his areas of expertise.

Agris BITĀNS

University of Latvia
Faculty of Law
Raina bulvaris 19
Riga
Latvia, LV 1586
Tel: (+371) 67280102
agris.bitans@eversheds-sutherland.lv

Agris Bitāns graduated from the Faculty of Law at the University of Latvia with a Bachelor's degree in law in 1993 and with a Master's degree in law in 1995. As well as practising as an attorney-at-law, he continues his academic studies at the University of Latvia for a doctorate degree. He also lectures at the Civil Law Department, Faculty of Law, University of Latvia. His area of expertise is the law of obligations, with a focus on civil liability, contract law, tort law, intellectual property law and Roman law. He is a co-author of the commentaries on Obligation Law of the Latvian Civil Law and co-author of the commentaries on Sections 2 and 8 of the Latvian Constitution. He is the author of the book 'Civil liability and its kinds' ('Civiltiesiskā atbildība un tās veidi') and of many articles relating to law issues, as well as co-author of the book 'Problems of Contract Law and Tort Law in the European Union and Latvia' ('Līgumu un deliktu problēmas Eiropas Savienībā un Latvijā'). He is a member of the Latvian Bar, International Bar Association and AIPPI (International Association for the Protection of Industrial Property). From 2008 until 2014, Agris Bitāns was the Council's member of the Latvian Bar and since 2005 he has been the President of AIPPI Latvian National Group. Since his admittance to the Latvian Bar in 1998, he has been practising mostly in civil (contracts and tort), intellectual property, commercial and administrative matters. He is a managing partner of the Law Office 'Eversheds Sutherland Bitāns'. His fields of legal research include contract and tort law, personality law, medical law and media law. He is also a regular participant at international conferences and workshops dealing with civil law, intellectual property law, litigation and arbitration.

Lucian BOJIN

West University of Timisoara
Faculty of Law
Bd Eroilor de la Tisa no 9/A
300557 Timisoara
Romania
Tel: (+40) 256 592400
lucian.bojin@e-uvt.ro

Lucian Bojin was born in 1975 in Timisoara. He graduated from the University of Timisoara in 1998 and pursued postgraduate and PhD studies in Business Law. He is an Associate Professor at the West University of Timisoara where he teaches International Law and Human Rights. He is also a practising barrister and partner in the law firm 'Valentin & Asociatii'. He has authored three books and published over 40 papers on European Law, International Law, Business Law, Private Law and Human Rights.

Sergiu CĂILEANU

West University of Timisoara
Faculty of Law
Bd Eroilor de la Tisa no 9/A
300557 Timisoara
Romania
Tel: (+40) 256 592400
sergiu.caileanu@e-uvt.ro

Sergiu Căileanu graduated from the University of Timișoara in 2017 and obtained a Master's degree in Business Law in 2018. He is a PhD candidate in Civil Law, with a thesis on the relation between property and contract law in the field of securities. He has also been a practising barrister in the Timis Bar Association since 2017 and has published several papers in the field of contract law.

Giannino CARUANA DEMAJO

Judges' Chambers
Courts of Justice
Republic Street
Valletta VLT 2000
Malta
Tel: (+35) 6 2590 2281
giannino.caruanademajo@gov.mt

Giannino Caruana Demajo was born in Malta in 1958. He graduated in law (LLD) from the University of Malta in 1982 and was awarded a warrant to practise as Advocate in the Superior Courts in April of that year, after which he exercised the profession in private practice until 1994. He was appointed lecturer in Civil Law at the University of Malta in 1989 and Head of the Department of Civil Law in 1993. Between 1992 and 1994, he also served as Chairman of the Board of a commercial reinsurance company. In 1997, he was appointed Chairman of the Committee of Experts on Efficiency of Justice of the Council of Europe, a post he held until 1999, during which time he also served on the Committee of Experts advising on the drafting of the Enforcement Code of Bosnia-Herzegovina, the Code of Procedure of Moldova and the Civil Code of Ukraine. In December 1994, he was appointed Judge of the Superior Courts, where he is Senior Administrative Judge since 2007 and Vice-Chairman of the Judicial Studies Board since 2009.

Rui CASCÃO

Lusófona University of Porto
Faculty of Law and Political Science
Rua Augusto Rosa, nº 24
4000 – 098 Porto
Portugal
Tel.: (+351) 22 2 073 230
Rui.cascao@gmail.com

Rui Cascão (LLB Coimbra, PhD Tilburg, ECPC-B DPO Cert. Maastricht) is Professor of EU Law and Law of Succession at the Lusófona University of Porto and researcher at the Centre for Advanced Legal Studies Francisco Suárez (CEAD). He has taught and developed research in several teaching institutions: Centre for Biomedical Law of the University of Coimbra (since 2001); ISIT-University of Paris 2 Panthéon-Assas (since 2021); Higher School of

Management and Technology of the Polytechnic Institute of Leiria Portugal (2023 – 2024); Legal and Judicial Training Centre of Macau, China (2009 – 2016); Karl-Franzens-University of Graz, Austria (2006 – 2008); and Tilburg University, The Netherlands (2000 – 2005). Between 2008 and 2021, he was Senior Legal Advisor to the Government of Macau, China, responsible for legislative production, legal reform, and international law matters. He is a member of the board of the Portuguese Association of Health Law (ALDIS), as well as member of the European Law Institute (ELI) and the World Association for Medical Law (WAML). He is the author of several scientific texts in the area of private, European and healthcare law and has participated in high-impact international research projects, such as the Draft Common Frame of Reference (DCFR) and Shifts in Compensation between Private and Public Systems (Tort and Insurance Law vol 22). He is currently developing research on international and European health law, medical liability, European law of succession, law and technology, fundamental rights and private law.
Orcid: 0000 – 0001 – 9783 – 2337.

Michael CHATZIPANAGIOTIS

University of Cyprus
Department of Law
1 Panepistimiou Ave.
OED 02, office B126
2109 Aglantzia, Nicosia
Cyprus
Tel: (+357) 22892937
chatzipanagiotis.michael@ucy.ac.cy

Michael Chatzipanagiotis is an Assistant Professor in Private Law at the Department of Law of the University of Cyprus. He lectures on Torts, Insurance Law, Consumer Protection, Banking Law, European Private Law and Air Law. His main research interests are Legal aspects of Artificial Intelligence (AI), Torts, Air and Space Law, Insurance Law, Consumer Protection, Intellectual Property Rights (IPR), Banking Law and Alternative Dispute Resolution (ADR). He has also participated in various research and consulting projects of the European Commission on the digitalisation of justice, air law, space law and consumer protection. Before joining the University of Cyprus, he worked as a lawyer and a legal advisor in Cyprus, Greece and Germany.

Andrea CIONI

Faculty of Law
Pisa University
Via del Collegio Ricci 10
56126 Pisa
Italy
Tel: (+39) 3498509801
andrea.cioni@jus.unipi.it

Andrea Cioni is currently a postdoctoral researcher and adjunct professor at the University of Pisa. He is working on a project on artificial intelligence and medical liability. He graduated in law in October 2019 with a thesis in private law on the legal issues raised by genome editing technologies, with a grade of 110 cum laude. In June 2024, he obtained his PhD at the University of Pisa with the highest distinction, defending his thesis on civil liability for pharmaceutical damages. Andrea has conducted research at the Max-Planck-Institute in Hamburg and at the European Centre of Tort and Insurance Law in Vienna. His main areas of interest are tort law, product liability and the law of new technologies.

Emanuel GD VAN DONGEN

Utrecht Centre for Accountability and Liabilty Law
Molengraaff Institute for Private Law
Utrecht Law School
Achter Sint Pieter 200
3512 HT Utrecht
The Netherlands
Tel: (+31) 30 253 7179
e. g.d.vandongen@uu.nl

Emanuel van Dongen is an Associate Professor at the Molengraaff Institute for Private Law, Utrecht University, the Netherlands, and a Research Fellow at the Utrecht Centre for Accountability and Liability Law. He is also a deputy judge at the Court of Appeal, Arnhem-Leeuwarden. He studied law at Tilburg University and, partly, at the Catholic University of Nijmegen. He obtained his PhD at Maastricht University. In 2017 and 2019, he was a visiting scholar and professor at UISS Universita di Guido Carli, Rome. From 2018–2024, he was a visiting professor at Universita degli Studi di Torino. In 2019, he was a visiting fellow at Universita degli studi Roma Tre. In 2021 – 2022, he was a visiting professor at Ghent University.

Simona DRUKTEINIENĖ

Mykolas Romeris University
Ateities g 20
08303 Vilnius
Lithuania
Tel: (+370) 5 27 14 625
simona@mruni.eu

Simona Drukteinienė is Professor of Private Law at the Law School of Mykolas Romeris University, Vilnius. She studied law at Vilnius University and in 2002 obtained the Master of Laws degree. She completed and defended her thesis on public liability at Mykolas Romeris University in 2008. Her spheres of interest include tort law, contract law, public liability and personality rights issues. Simona Drukteinienė is also a practising lawyer and recommended arbitrator of Vilnius Court of Commercial Arbitration. Since 2010, Simona Drukteinienė has participated in the annual European tort law project organised by the European Centre of Tort and Insurance Law (ECTIL) together with the Institute for European Tort Law, as well as in other projects on various specific issues of tort law organised by the Institute for European Tort Law. She is also a Member of the committee supervising the Civil Code of the Republic of Lithuania appointed by the Minister of Justice. In 2021, Simona Drukteinienė was appointed for a period of six years to the ICSID Panel of Arbitrators for the Settlement of Investment Disputes by the Government of the Republic of Lithuania. In 2023, Simona Drukteinienė was designated by the Lithuanian Government as a member of the Permanent Court of Arbitration (The Hague).

Gregor DUGAR

University of Ljubljana
Faculty of Law
Poljanski nasip 2
SI – 1000 Ljubljana
Slovenia
Tel: (+386) 1 42 03 132
gregor.dugar@pf.uni-lj.si

Gregor Dugar is an associate professor at the Faculty of Law, University of Ljubljana. He studied in Ljubljana and obtained his Doctorate in Law (LLD) in 2013 with a degree thesis on the topic 'A company as common property of spouses'. He teaches and writes in the area of civil law and commercial law, especially in the areas of tort law and business contract law.

Anton DULAK

Law Faculty Pan-European University
Tomašikova 20
820 09 Bratislava
Slovakia
Tel: (+421) 2 4820 8834
dulak@sba.sk

After graduating in law in 1985, Anton Dulak started to work at the Department of Civil Law at Comenius University, Bratislava as an assistant. In 2001, he obtained his PhD degree. In 2003, Anton Dulak habilitated with a thesis on Product Liability Law and was promoted to an associate professor. He has attended courses at Cambridge University, the University of Oslo and University Louvain la Neuve. He is a member of the Slovak Bar Association. From 2007 until 2015, he was a member of the Ministry of Justice Recodification Commission for a new Civil Code. From 2013 – 2015, he was the Chairman of this Commission. Since 2018, he has been a full professor at the Law Faculty of the Pan-European University in Bratislava.

Isabelle C DURANT

Université catholique de
Louvain
Faculté de droit et de criminologie
Place Montesquieu 2 bte
L2.07.01
B-1348 Louvain-la-Neuve
Belgium
Tel: (+32) 10 47 47 41
isabelle.durant@uclouvain.be

Isabelle Claire Durant studied law at the Université catholique de Louvain (UCL), where she was a teaching and research assistant from 1991 until 2004. She obtained her PhD degree in law in 2003 at this university and is currently Professor at the Department of Private Law. She teaches real property law, security law and contract law. Her main fields of research are tort, contract and real property. She has also contributed to several research projects for the Institute for European Tort Law and for the European Centre of Tort and Insurance Law (ECTIL) in Vienna where she was on leave for work from October 2004 to March 2005. She is a member of ECTIL and is a guest of the European Group on Tort Law (EGTL). In addition, she was an attorney at the Brussels Bar from 1991 until 2004.

Andreas BLOCH EHLERS

Copenhagen University
Studiegaarden
Studiestraede 6
1455 Copenhagen
Denmark
Tel: (+45) 353 – 23103
andreas.ehlers@jur.ku.dk

Andreas Ehlers is Professor of Tort Law at the University of Copenhagen. He obtained his Master's degree from the University of Copenhagen in 2004 and subsequently worked for the law firm 'Kromann Reumert' in Copenhagen. In 2006, Andreas Ehlers was awarded the Sir Gerrard Brennan Scholarship at the University of Queensland (Australia) from where he obtained an LLM degree in 2007. In 2011, he published his PhD thesis, which deals with the doctrine of adequacy in tort law. In 2017, Andreas Ehlers published an LLD thesis on causation and personal injury.

Sandra FRIBERG

Juridiska institutionen
Uppsala universitet
Riddartorget, Trädgårdsgatan 1
751 20 Uppsala
Sweden
Tel: (+46) 18 – 471 71 44
sandra.friberg@jur.uu.se

Sandra Friberg is an Associate Professor of Tort Law at the faculty of law, University of Uppsala. She obtained her doctorate in law (LLD) at the end of 2010 after defending her thesis on Non-Pecuniary Damages to Victims of Crime. The thesis rendered her the Karnov prize (Thomson-Reuters Professional) and the Benzelius award (the Royal Society of Sciences at Uppsala). Her main research and teaching areas are tort law, civil law and criminal law. She is a board member of the Centre for Multidisciplinary Studies on Racism (Faculty of Theology, Uppsala University) and a part-time guest researcher at the Uppsala Religion and Society Research Centre.

Martin HOGG

Head of the School of Law and Established Professor
University of Galway
Galway H91 TK 33
Ireland
Tel: (+35) 3 91 524411
martin.hogg@nuigalway.ie

Martin Hogg is Head of School and Established Professor at the Law School of the University of Galway, having previously held a Chair at the University of Edinburgh. He has written and published extensively in the obligations field since 1992, from both a national and comparative legal perspective. He is a contributor to the Digest of European Tort Law, as well as to the European Tort Law Yearbook, and is a Member of the European Centre of Tort and Insurance Law (ECTIL). He is a non-practising member of the Scottish Bar (the Faculty of Advocates).

Jiří HRÁDEK

Charles University
Faculty of Law
Department of Civil Law
Nám.Curieových 901/7
116 40 Praha
Czech Republic
Tel: (+420) 728 228224
hradek@prf.cuni.cz

Jiří Hrádek is an Assistant Professor at the Department of Civil Law at the Faculty of Law of Charles University and a lawyer at Zeppelin CZ. He graduated in law from the Faculty of Law of Charles University (2002). Jiří Hrádek studied at the University of Hamburg (2000 – 2001), in the LLM programme at the Eberhard-Karls University in Tübingen (2002 – 2003) and in the post-graduate programme of the Charles University (2002 – 2009). In 2002 and 2003, he completed research stays at the European Centre of Tort and Insurance Law (ECTIL) in Vienna; in 2007, he received an internship at the European Commission, DG Health and Consumer Protection. Jiří Hrádek is a member of the editorial board of the Czech journal, Jurisprudence. He specialises in civil and procedural law, with a special focus on tort law. He is the author of a book on pre-contractual liability, co-author of a book on delict law as well as commentaries on the Czech Civil Code and the Czech Civil Procedure Code.

Zoé JACQUEMIN

University Toulouse Capitole
2 rue du Doyen Gabriel Marty
31000 Toulouse
France
zoe.jacquemin@ut-capitole.fr

After completing a double-degree (Master's in Law in Paris and LLM at Humboldt University in Berlin), Zoé Jacquemin engaged in a PhD under the supervision of Benedicte Fauvarque-Cosson (co-founder and Chair of the ELI French Hub) and Gerhard Dannemann (founding member of the Acquis Group). In September 2016, she became a permanent lecturer at the University Sorbonne Paris Nord. In January 2022, she joined the University Toulouse Capitole as a full Professor of Law. Her work focuses on contract law and civil liability, mostly from a European and/or comparative perspective. Her thesis on contractual liability in French, English and German law has been awarded several prizes. She has served as the President of Trans Europe Experts since 2022.

Ernst KARNER

Institute for European Tort Law
Reichsratsstraße 17/2
1010 Vienna
Austria
Tel: (+43) 1 4277 34880
ernst.karner@oeaw.ac.at

Ernst Karner is Director of the Institute for European Tort Law, Austrian Academy of Sciences and University of Graz, and of the European Centre of Tort and Insurance Law. He holds a chair in civil law at the University of Vienna. Born in 1969, he studied law in Vienna (Dr jur 1997 with distinction) and completed his habilitation in 2004 with a thesis on bona fide acquisition. He is co-editor of the Journal of European Tort Law (JETL) and a member of the European Group on Tort Law (EGTL) and the World Tort Law Society (WTLS). Furthermore, he was a member of the commission for the reform of Austrian tort law established by the Ministry of Justice in 2000. Ernst Karner has written extensively in the fields of Austrian and European tort law and has been granted several prizes including the Figdor-Preis of the Austrian Academy of Sciences and the Kardinal-Innitzer-Förderungspreis.

Anne LM KEIRSE

Utrecht Centre for Accountability and Liabilty Law
Molengraaff Institute for Private Law
Utrecht Law School
Newtonlaan 201

Anne Keirse is a judge at the Court of Appeal in Amsterdam and a professor of Private Law at the Utrecht Centre for Accountability and Liability Law (UCALL) of Utrecht University. She is a member of the European Group on Tort Law. Born in 1975 in

3584 Utrecht
The Netherlands
Tel: (+31) 30 253 7192
a.l.m.keirse@uu.nl

Oxford, she studied law at the University of Groningen (1993 – 1997), where she also obtained her doctorate and became a (senior) lecturer (1997–2006). Before becoming a professor in Utrecht (2008), she was appointed senior lecturer at the Radboud University of Nijmegen (2006–2008). In 2013 – 2104, she was a visiting professor at the University of the Free State, Bloemfontein, South Africa. The teaching and research activities of Anne Keirse are primarily focused on the law of obligations, with an emphasis on the field of (national and European) contract law, tort law, law of damages, prevention and mitigation of damage. Alongside her academic work, she has been engaged in judicial work, first as a registrar at the District Court in Assen, subsequently as a judge at the District Court in Groningen, thereafter as a judge at the Court of Appeal in Arnhem. She presently works as a justice at the Court of Appeal in Amsterdam and handles cases regarding commercial law and civil law, especially in the field of contract law, tort law, law of damages, and international and European private law.

Jonas KNETSCH

University Paris 1
Panthéon-Sorbonne
Sorbonne Law School
12, place du Panthéon
75231 Paris Cédex 05
France
Tel: (+33) 628 78 12 61
jonas.knetsch@univ-paris1.fr

Jonas Knetsch is a Professor of Civil and Comparative Law at the Sorbonne Law School (University Paris 1 Panthéon- Sorbonne). Before his PhD in Comparative Tort Law, he graduated from the University Panthéon-Assas and from the University of Cologne (Germany). He was a senior lecturer at the University Panthéon-Assas before being appointed full professor in 2013 following his success in the concours d'agrégation in private law. From 2013 to 2021, he held professorships at the University of Réunion Island and Jean Monnet University of Saint-Étienne. Jonas Knetsch has published extensively in tort and insurance law as well as in comparative law. Lately, he has conducted research projects on tort law and insurance law issues related to data protection and on the interplay of social security, private insurance and tort law compensation.

Bernhard A KOCH

University of Innsbruck
Innrain 52
6020 Innsbruck
Austria
Tel: (+43) 512 507 – 81210
bernhard.a.koch@uibk.ac.at
<www.zivilrechts.info>

Bernhard A Koch was born in 1966 in Feldkirch (Austria). He studied law in Innsbruck (Mag iur 1989), Tübingen (Germany, Dr iur summa cum laude 1992), and Michigan (USA, LLM 1993). He completed his habilitation for private law and comparative law in 1998. Bernhard A Koch started to work as an assistant at the University of Innsbruck in 1985, where he was awarded tenure in 1999. After two years on leave for work at the European Centre of Tort and Insurance Law (ECTIL) and the Austrian Academy of Sciences, he returned to Innsbruck in 2003, where he since holds a chair in civil law. He is currently the Dean of Studies of the Law Faculty and serves as the academic director of the faculty's medical law programme. From 2004 to 2010, Bernhard A Koch was also the Vice Director of the Austrian Academy of Sciences' Institute for European Tort Law (ETL). He was a member of the EU Expert Group on Liability for New Technologies. Bernhard A Koch's main fields of research are tort, contract, real property and family law. He is part of the European Group on Tort Law.

Päivi KORPISAARI

Professor in Communication Law
University of Helsinki
PO Box 4 (Yliopistonkatu 3)
FI – 00014 University of Helsinki
Finland
Tel: (+358) 50 4482617
paivi.korpisaari@helsinki.fi

Päivi Korpisaari is Professor in Communication Law at the Faculty of Law of the University of Helsinki. Before her career at the university, she worked (1993 – 2003) as a lawyer at a law firm, as a younger judge at the District Court of Riihimäki, as a presenting officer at the Court of Appeal of Helsinki and as a legal counsel at the Finnish Soil Mechanics Association. Päivi Korpisaari has worked at the university since 2003 and has published many books and articles in the fields of media and communication law, information law, tort law, criminal law and constitutional law. Her main fields of research are media and communication law, tort law, personal data protection law, constitutional law, human rights law, and criminal law in respect of 'freedom of expression offences'. She has been a national expert in studies in the field of media and communications.

Irene KULL

University of Tartu
Faculty of Law
Naituse 20
50409 Tartu
Estonia
Tel: (+372) 737 5060
irene.kull@ut.ee

Irene Kull is a Professor of Civil Law and holds the position of the head of the Private Law Department of the Tartu University Law School. She has participated in a number of international research groups. She lectures on contract law, the law of obligations and European contract and commercial law. She is a member of the group of authors of comments on the Estonian Civil Code Acts. Her main interests include the general principles of contract and tort law, the harmonisation of European private law and comparative contract law. She is an advisor on the civil chamber of the Estonian Supreme Court.

Janno LAHE

University of Tartu
Faculty of Law
Näituse 20
50409 Tartu
Estonia
Tel: (+372) 737 5992
www.oigus.ut.ee
www.ut.ee
Janno.Lahe@ut.ee

Janno Lahe is a Professor of Tort Law at the University of Tartu (since 2016). He obtained his PhD in Civil Law in 2005. Since 2006, he has worked as an advisor to the civil chamber of the Estonian Supreme Court. Among his publications there are a variety of journal articles on issues in tort and insurance law. He lectures on insurance law and non-contractual obligations. His main interests include the law of obligations, insurance law and harmonisation of European tort law.

Peter LOSER

University of Basel
Faculty of Law
CH - 4002 Basel

St Galler Kantonalbank AG
Legal & Compliance
St Leonhardstrasse 25
CH - 9000 St Gallen
Switzerland
Tel: (+41) 71 231 3131
peter.loser@sgkb.ch

Peter Loser, born in 1964, is a Professor at the University of Basel (Titular professor for Private, Commercial and Comparative Law), where he habilitated in 2006 with a comprehensive work on 'liability based on reliance', after studies in St Gallen and Lausanne, Switzerland (University of St Gallen HSG, lic iur 1990; Dr iur summa cum laude 1994). He was a visiting scholar at Yale University in 1992/93 and did research at the UNIDROIT in Rome and at the University of Oxford. Currently Peter Loser teaches private, tort and banking law at the Universities of Basel and St Gallen HSG. He is a Fellow of the European Law Institute (ELI, Brussels), member of the European Centre of Tort and Insurance Law (ECTIL, Vienna) and has been an active participant of the project 'The Common Core of European Private Law' (University of Torino, Italy). From 2006 to 2009, he was a member of the Board of the Swiss Lawyers' Association. Peter Loser has worked as a lawyer since 1995 and is a Member of Senior Management of a bank in Switzerland.

Indrė MACULEVIČIENĖ

Institute of Private Law
Mykolas Romeris University
Ateities g 20
08303 Vilnius
Lithuania
Tel: (+370) 5 271 4512
indremaculeviciene@mruni.eu

Indrė Maculevičienė graduated from Mykolas Romeris University in 2009 and obtained a Master's degree in Civil Law in 2011. She is a doctoral candidate in civil procedure law, with a thesis on the use of secret information as evidence in civil proceedings. She is also a lecturer at Mykolas Romeris University. She specialises in contract law, tort law and civil procedure. She worked as a judge's assistant and advisor at the Supreme Court of Lithuania (2012 – 2024) and currently works as a senior legal counsel at AB 'Via Lietuva'.

Inês de OLIVEIRA MARTINS

Faculty of Law of the University of Coimbra
Pátio da Universidade
3004 – 528 Coimbra
Portugal
Tel: (+351) 239 859 801
mivom@fd.uc.pt

Inês de Oliveira Martins is a Professor of Civil and Commercial Law at the Faculty of Law of the University of Coimbra and a private legal consultant in Portugal and Brazil. She was a visiting scholar at the Max-Planck Institut für ausländisches und internationales Privatrecht, Hamburg (2011, 2014/15, 2017/18), at Faculdade de Direito da Universidade de São Paulo (2016), and at the Centre de Droit Privé, Faculté de droit et de criminologie de l'Université Catholique de Louvain (2015/2016), and a speaker at conferences and post-graduate courses in the fields of insurance law, personal data and medical law in several countries. She is a member of the Supervisory Board of the Institute for Banking, Insurance and Capital Market Law of the Faculty of Law of the University of Coimbra (BBS), of the board of the general meeting of the Portuguese Chapter of the Association Internationale de Droit des Assurances (AIDA), of the Brazilian Institute for Insurance Law (IBDS), and of the German-Portuguese Legal Association (DLJV). She is also responsible for the Section of European Insurance Contract Law of the Institute of Iberian-American Law (IDIBE). Inês de Oliveira Martins has conducted research on contract and liability law and devoted a great amount of attention to insurance law, which she has always approached as a part of the general system of private law. She is also very interested in legal methodology, in the questions raised by big data and technology and, more recently, in company law, examining these fields through the lenses of comparative law.

Colm Peter McGRATH

The Dickson Poon School of Law
King's College London
Strand
London WC2R 2LS
United Kingdom
Tel: (+44 20) 7848 5013
colm.mcgrath@kcl.ac.uk

Colm Peter McGrath is a Senior Lecturer in Tort Law at the Dickson Poon School of Law, King's College London and an Academic Fellow of the Middle Temple. Prior to this he was the WYNG Research Fellow in Medical Law and Ethics at Trinity Hall in the University of Cambridge. He studied law as an undergraduate and as a doctoral student at the University of Cambridge. His research focuses on comparative private law and professional liability, particularly the liability and regulation of healthcare in both the modern and historical common law and civilian legal traditions. His monograph The Development of Medical Liability in Germany 1800 – 1945, (Klostermann, 2019) was selected by jury as one of the '2019 Legal Books of the Year' in the Neue Juristische Wochenschrift. Colm Peter McGrath is joint General Editor of the long-running Journal of Professional Negligence, Book Review Editor for the Journal of European Tort Law, and a Fellow of the European Centre of Tort and Insurance Law.

Attila MENYHÁRD

ELTE Faculty of Law
Civil Law Department
Egyetem ter 1 – 3
H-1364 Budapest
Hungary
Tel: (+36) 1 411 6510
menyhard@ajk.elte.hu

Attila Menyhárd works at the University of Eotvos Lorand, Faculty of Law, Civil Law Department (Budapest) as a full professor. He was the Dean of the Faculty from 2016 – 2019. His special research fields are: contract law, tort law and property law, company law, commercial law, law and economics, law and literature and human rights in private law as well as international commercial contracts, European business law and European company law. Upon the invitation of the Ministry of Justice, he contributed to the project on a new Hungarian Civil Code, being responsible for the provisions on property law and rent law. He is a registered member of the Arbitration Court of the Hungarian Chamber of Commerce and Industry, Budapest and the ICSID Panel of Arbitrators. He is a member of the Centre for Social Sciences, Institute for Legal Studies, the Hungarian Academy of Sciences Centre of Excellence, a fellow of ECTIL, a member of UNIDROIT Governing Council and Head of the New Civil Code Advisory Board to the Supreme Court. He is also the counsel to the Oppenheim Law Firm (Budapest).

David MESSNER-KREUZBAUER

Institute for European Tort Law of the Austrian Academy of Sciences and the University of Graz
Reichsratsstraße 17/2
1010 Vienna
Austria
Tel: (+43) 1 4277 29660
david.messner@oeaw.ac.at

David Messner-Kreuzbauer is a postdoctoral researcher at the Institute for European Tort Law of the Austrian Academy of Sciences and the University of Graz, which he joined in 2015. He studied law at the University of Vienna and Shanghai Jiao Tong University from 2011 – 2021 (Mag iur 2015, Dr iur 2021). During this time, he successfully defended and published his thesis on 'Permitted Acts of Necessity and Civil Liability' (Erlaubte Notstandshandlungen und zivilrechtliche Ausgleichsansprüche), published articles on various topics of civil law in highly regarded journals, and presented papers in Austria and abroad. He is a fellow of the Ars Iuris Vienna Doctoral School and the European Centre of Tort and Insurance Law (ECTIL) and was a guest researcher at Harvard Law School (USA) and Université Paris I Panthéon-Sorbonne (France).

André PEREIRA

University of Coimbra
Faculty of Law
3004 – 545 Coimbra
Portugal
Tel: (+351) 239 051725
andreper@fd.uc.pt

André Pereira is Professor of Law at the University of Coimbra (Portugal), Director of the Centre for Biomedical Law and Researcher at the University of Coimbra Institute for Legal Research. Pereira is a Vice-President of the National Council of Ethics for Life Sciences, President of the Institutional Review Board of AIBILI and member of the Ethics Committee of the National Institute of Legal Medicine and Forensic Sciences. At the international level, Pereira is Chair of the Educational Committtee of the World Association for Medical Law and he is a fellow of the European Centre of Tort and Insurance Law (Austria), member of the Brazilian Insti-

tute for Tort Law (IBERC), member of the Iberoamerican Law Institute (IDIBE), Founder of the Portuguese Speaking Association for Health Law (ALDIS), member of the Luso-Brazilian Institute for Comparative Law and he is member of the International Academy of Comparative Law.
Orcid: 0000 – 0001 – 9871 – 5298.

Ronen PERRY

University of Haifa
Faculty of Law
31905 Haifa
Israel
Tel: (+97) 2 4 828 – 8487
rperry@law.haifa.ac.il

Ronen Perry is a Professor of Law and Director of the Aptowizer Center for Risk, Liability, and Insurance at the University of Haifa, former President of the Israeli Private Law Association, and member of the World Tort Law Society, the European Centre of Tort and Insurance Law, and the Global Young Academy. Ronen Perry received his LLB magna cum laude from the Tel Aviv University (1996), where he studied in the special programme for excellent students (admitting 0.5 % of undergraduate students). He completed with distinction his LLM studies, as part of the direct doctoral track requirements (1997), and received his LLD summa cum laude from the Hebrew University (2001). Ronen Perry has been a visiting researcher at New York University, University of Oxford, Pompeu Fabra University, and the University of Vienna. He is one of the founding editors, and a senior editor of the Journal of Tort Law, the editor-in-chief of the Haifa Law Review, and member of the editorial board of the Asian Journal of Law & Economics and Law & Social Inquiry. Ronen Perry has published sixty articles on tort law, contract law, insurance, remedies, jurisprudence, and the legal process, and his book, Economic Ricochets, discusses relational economic loss from historical, comparative, and theoretical perspectives.

Eoin QUILL

University of Limerick
School of Law
Limerick
Ireland
Tel: (+35) 3 61 20 2220
eoin.quill@ul.ie

Eoin Quill was born in Limerick in 1965. He studied law at University College Cork, a constituent college of the National University of Ireland, between 1982 and 1988 obtaining two bachelors and a master's degree – BCL; LLB; LLM. He lectured at the School of Professional and Management Studies in Limerick from 1988 – 1990 and has been lecturing in the University of Limerick since 1991 in a variety of subjects including Tort, Commercial Law and International Tort Law & Business. His publications include Torts in Ireland (Gill & Macmillan 1999, 4th edn 2014), Tort Law in Ireland (Kluwer 2015), Damages and Compensation Culture: Comparative Perspectives (2016, co-edited with Raymond J Friel) and a variety of journal articles and chapters in edited books on issues in tort. He is currently an examiner in Tort for the Law Society of Ireland, a member of the International Commercial & Economic Law Group, University of Limerick and a member of ECTIL.

Lawrence QUINTANO

19 Gulio Cauchi Street
Balzan BZN 1130
Malta
lawrence.quintano@gov.mt

Lawrence Quintano is a retired judge. He is now chairman of the Permanent Commission Against Corruption. He also teaches Civil Law at the University of Malta with his areas of specialisation being Contract Law and the Law of Marriage and Betrothal. He also teaches that part in the Law of Obligations which is entitled 'Extinction of Obligations' and he also deals with the Law of Evidence in Civil Procedure. He has been selected as an examiner in the board which discusses the merits of dissertations or MA theses dealing with themes from the Civil Code. For a long time, he served as an advocate with the Attorney General's Office where his main areas were Constitutional Law, Human Rights, EU Law and International Law. He also served as an ad hoc judge in the European Court of Human Rights.

Nicolas RIEMANN

Universität Hamburg
Faculty of Law
Rothenbaumchaussee 33
20148 Hamburg
Germany
Tel: (+49) 40 42838-2498
nicolas.riemann@uni-hamburg.de

Nicolas Riemann is a Research Fellow at the University of Hamburg. He graduated from the University of Tübingen in 2020, having also studied at the University of Hong Kong. After completing his legal traineeship in 2023, he became a PhD candidate, with a thesis in the field of competition law. He also worked for several international law firms in Stuttgart, Hamburg and Brussels.

Albert RUDA

University of Girona
Facultat de Dret
Campus de Montilivi
C/ de la UdG 12
17003 Girona
Spain
Tel: (+34) 972 41 97 68
albert.ruda@udg.edu

Albert Ruda is an Associate Professor in Private Law and Dean at the Faculty of Law of the University of Girona. He is also a member of the Institute of European and Comparative Private Law of the same University, the European Centre of Tort and Insurance Law (ECTIL, Vienna), the Instituto Brasileiro de Estudos de Responsabilidade Civil (IBERC) and the Institute of Iberoamerican Law (IDIBE); research fellow of the Utrecht Centre for Accountability and Liability Law (UCALL), founding member and chair of the European Law Institute (ELI) Spanish Hub, chair of the ELI Special Interest Group on Global Private Law and member of the Commission of Codification of Catalonia. He is also a former scholar of the Japan Foundation and former van Calker scholar of the Swiss Institute of Comparative Law.

Barbara C STEININGER

Centre of European Private Law
University of Graz
Universitätsstraße 15 Bauteil D/IV
8010 Graz
Austria
Tel: (+43) 316 380 3585
barbara.steininger@uni-graz.at

Institute for European Tort Law/
ECTIL
Reichsratsstraße 17/2
1010 Vienna
Austria

Barbara C Steininger studied law and Dutch in Vienna and Leiden, obtaining Master degrees from the University of Vienna in both areas as well as a doctoral degree in law from the same university. During her studies, she was employed as a student assistant at the Institute of Roman Law of the University of Vienna. She worked as a researcher at the European Centre of Tort and Insurance Law, the Institute for European Tort Law, the University of Geneva and at the University of Graz, where she completed her habilitation in 2019. Since April 2020, she has been Associate Professor (tenured) in Civil and Comparative Law at the University of Graz. For her habilitation thesis, she was awarded the Kardinal-Innitzer-Förderungspreis, the VKB-Wissenschaftspreis and the Alois Mock-Wissenschaftspreis. In October 2020, Barbara C Steininger was appointed Vice-Director of ECTIL and since October 2023 she has been Director of the Centre of European Private Law of the University of Graz and Vice-Director of ETL. While (comparative) tort law remains her favourite, the law of obligations, property law and family law are also among her areas of interest. Barbara C Steininger is a Fellow of the European Law Institute.

Hristina TANCHEVA

Sofia University 'St. Kliment Ohridski'
Faculty of Law
15 Tsar Osvoboditel blvd
1504 Sofia
Bulgaria
Tel: (+359) 889954546,
hr.tancheva@gmail.com

Hristina Tancheva is a head assistant professor at Sofia University 'St. Kliment Ohridski', Department of Civil Law Sciences. She was born in 1988 in Ruse, Bulgaria. In 2012, she graduated with a master's degree in law from Sofia University 'St. Kliment Ohridski'. Since 2014, she has been an assistant professor in 'Obligation Law' and as, of 2022, also of civil law – general part. She is also a lecturer in commercial and tax law and foundations of civil law in English at the Faculty of Economics of Sofia University. In 2018, Hristina Tancheva acquired her PhD in civil law with a thesis on product liability, which was published in 2019. She has been a member of the editorial board of the science magazine 'Commercial Law' (ISSN 0861 – 6892) since 2018. As of 2019, she is a member of the Union of scientists in Bulgaria. Since 2014, she has been registered as a lawyer at the Sofia Bar Association specialising in civil and commercial law, including corporate law, contract law, tort law and bankruptcy. She is the author of a dozen articles dedicated to contract and tort law issues. She is also a judge at the disciplinary court of Sofia Bar Association.

Knut Martin TANDE

University of Bergen
Faculty of Law
Magnus Lagabotesplass 1
Bergen
Norway
Tel: (+47) 5 55589551
knut.tande@uib.no

Knut Tande is an Associate Professor and Vice Dean at the Faculty of Law of the University of Bergen. His main topics for teaching and research are copyright law, legal methodology and tort law. He has been the Vice Dean of Education and the Vice Dean of Digitalisation at the faculty and is now the head of the Learning and Communication Center. For several years he was a member of the National Committee for Research Ethics in the Social Sciences and the Humanities (NESH), and is now a member of the Research Ethics Committee of the Faculty of Medicine at the University of Bergen.

Thomas THIEDE

Derner Kippshof 23
44329 Dortmund
Germany
Tel: (+49) 231 95858 0
mail@thomasthiede.info
<www.thomasthiede.info>

Thomas Thiede studied Law, Economics and Political Sciences at the Ernst Moritz Arndt University of Greifswald, Germany where he obtained his Bachelor of Laws in 2003. He then went on to complete a Master of Laws (Comparative and EU Law) at the same institution. Following this and having taken a position as a scientific assistant at the Austrian Academy of Sciences' Institute for European Tort Law in Vienna, he began his doctoral studies. For his thesis he was awarded his doctorate with distinction as well as the 2011 Franz-Gschnitzer Award and promoted to a Junior Scientist at the Austrian Academy of Sciences. At the beginning of 2013, he joined the ranks of lecturers at the Institute for Civil Law, Foreign and Private International Law of the University of Graz, Austria; in addition, and since October 2016, he has been teaching at the Ruhr University Bochum, Germany. Since August 2017, he also practises as a lawyer in Germany.

Viktor TOKUSHEV

University of Sofia
Faculty of Law
15 Tsar Osvoboditel blvd
1504 Sofia
Bulgaria
Tel: (+359) 888 603 090
v.tokushev@law.uni-sofia.bg

Viktor Tokushev is Assistant Professor in Civil and Commercial Law at the Law Faculty of Sofia University. He was born in Sofia (Bulgaria) in 1978. He studied law at Sofia University and graduated with honours in 2002. In the following year, he specialised in 'Legal English and Writing for Global Lawyers' at the Boston University, London Center (London). He further developed his interest in private law by participating in the development of more than 50 legislation projects for the 39th National Assembly of Bulgaria. Since 2005, he has been running a law office, 'Tokushev and Partners' in which he is a managing partner. He acquired his doctorate degree in 2012 with a thesis on Special Purpose Investment Companies, which was published in the same year. From 2012, he has been a lecturer on Capital Markets Law at Sofia University. He is a fellow of the European Centre of Tort and Insurance Law (ECTIL, Vienna).

Zafeirios TSOLAKIDIS

Associate Professor of Civil Law,
Law School, National & Kapodistrian University of Athens
8, Vissarionos Str.
106 72 Athens
Greece
Tel: (+30) 210 3647397
zatsolak@law.uoa.gr

Zafeirios Tsolakidis was born in Athens in 1977. He graduated and received his doctorate with merits from the Law School of the National & Kapodistrian University of Athens. He is an Associate Professor of Civil Law at the National & Kapodistrian University of Athens Law School, where he teaches General Principles of Civil Law, Law of Obligations (General and Special Part), Family Law, Applications of Civil Law, as well as Banking Law, Land Register Law and Methodology of Law (in postgraduate courses). Zafeirios Tsolakidis is the author of six books (among which 'Compensation in Pre-Contractual Liability', 'Bank Transactions Law Pt I' and 'Contractual and Delictual Liability for Assistants') and more than 30 articles in legal journals and essays' collections. He is also a Member of the Parliamentary Committee of the Hellenic Republic for the Scrutiny of the Quality of the Legislative Process. Zafeirios Tsolakidis practises law in Athens, issues legal opinions and serves as an arbitrator.

Corinne WIDMER LÜCHINGER

Basel University
Peter Merian-Weg 8
4052 Basel
Switzerland
Tel: (+41) 612072553
corinne.widmer@unibas.ch

Corinne Widmer Lüchinger was born in Watford (UK) in 1974. She studied law in Basel and Neuchâtel, graduating in Basel in 1998 (summa cum laude) and subsequently completing her doctorate on pre-contractual liability (summa cum laude) in 2002. After passing her bar examination, she completed her habilitation in 2008 and was interim and guest professor at the University of Zurich in 2008/2009 while working as an attorney in private practice. In 2010, she was appointed to the Chair for Private Law, Private International Law and Comparative Law at the University of Basel, where she became Head of the Department of Private Law (2012 – 2015) and then Dean of Faculty (2015 – 2017). Corinne Widmer Lüchinger was Herbert Smith Freehills visiting scholar at the Law Faculty of the University of Cambridge in 2015. Her main fields of research are the law of obligations (torts and contracts) and private international law, areas in which she has published extensively and co-edited two comprehensive Commentaries. She has received prizes for her academic work and was shortlisted for the Credit Suisse Award for Best Teaching in 2020. She is, inter alia, a member of the ETL's Advisory Board, regularly provides expert advice to courts in Switzerland and other jurisdictions and has advised the Swiss parliament on legislative drafts in the area of the law of obligations. In 2021, she was a member of the Board of Electors for the Downing Professorship of the Laws of England at Cambridge.

Wolfgang WURMNEST

Universität Hamburg
Faculty of Law
Rothenbaumchaussee 33
20148 Hamburg
Germany
Tel: (+49) 40 42838 5999
wolfgang.wurmnest@uni-hamburg.de

Wolfgang Wurmnest has been a full professor of law at the University of Hamburg since 2021. Previously he served as a full professor at the University of Augsburg (2013 – 2021), Georg Wilhelm Leibniz University of Hanover (2009 – 2013), and as a Senior Research Fellow at the Max Planck Institute of Private International and Comparative Law, Hamburg (2004 – 2008). He studied law at the Universities of Hamburg, Lyon III and at the UC Berkeley (LLM). Wolfgang Wurmnest's main fields of research are comparative and international contract, tort and competition law.

Paulina WYSZYŃSKA-ŚLUFIŃSKA

Faculty of Law and
Administration
Gdańsk University
Jana Bażyńskiego 6
80 – 309 Gdańsk
Poland
Tel: (+48) 58 523 28 51
paulina.wyszynska-slufinska@ug.edu.pl

Paulina Wyszyńska-Ślufińska is an Assistant Professor in the Department of Civil Law at the Gdańsk University Law School. In 2014, she received her law degree from the University of Gdańsk. From September 2013 to February 2014, she attended the University of Sheffield, Law School. In July 2012, she took part in the Sommerschule Internationales Sportrecht und Schiedsgerichtsbarkeit, organised by Salzburg University. In the summer of 2013, she participated in the Catholic University of America's International Business and Trade Law Programme in Cracow, Poland. Since 2018, she has been a licensed attorney-at-law. She is an author and co-author of publications in the following areas of law: civil law, torts and insurance law. Paulina Wyszyńska-Ślufińska serves as a content supervisor of Wiadomości Ubezpieczeniowe (Insurance Review).

David E ZAMMIT

Department of Civil Law
Faculty of Laws
University of Malta
Msida – MSD2080
Malta
Tel: (+356) 2340 – 2758
david.zammit@um.edu.mt

David E Zammit is Head of the Civil Law Department of the University of Malta Law Faculty and Director of the University of Malta Law Clinic. He was born in 1969 and after graduating (LLD) from the University of Malta in 1993, he pursued further studies leading to his Doctorate in Legal Anthropology from the University of Durham, UK in 1998 and also a specialisation course (Diploma di Perfezionamento) in Tort Law at the 'La Sapienza' University of Rome in 1999. In 1996, David Zammit was appointed Assistant Lecturer at the University of Malta and is currently Senior Lecturer in Law and Anthropology at the same institution. In 2006, he was awarded a Fulbright research scholarship to study clinical law teaching at the University of Villanova Law School in the United States. His main fields of legal research include Tort Law, Legal Anthropology, Migration and Clinical Legal Education. David E Zammit is a Fellow of the European Centre of Tort and Insurance Law.

Index

The numbers given refer to marginal numbers, the letters refer to the reports. A stands for Austria, B for Belgium, BU for Bulgaria, CH for Switzerland, CR for the Comparative Report, CRO for Croatia, CY for Cyprus, CZ for the Czech Republic, D for Germany, DK for Denmark, E for Spain, EST for Estonia, EU for European Union, EW for England and Wales, F for France, FIN for Finland, GR for Greece, H for Hungary, I for Italy, IRL for Ireland, ISR for Israel, LT for Lithuania, LV for Latvia, MT for Malta, N for Norway, NL for the Netherlands, P for Portugal, PL for Poland, RO for Romania, S for Sweden, SCO for Scotland, SK for Slovakia, SLO for Slovenia.

access to justice CH 130–147; IRL 19–21; RO 1–4
aircraft *see* aviation
adequacy DK 2–10; N 37–77
administrative acts *see* public authority liability
administrative fines EU 16–22; IRL 22–24
alcohol FIN 25–46; SCO 50–57
animals BU 26–31; E 11–15; ISR 60
– wild ~ CRO 20
artificial intelligence E 26
asbestos *see also* toxic torts CH 130–147; CRO 82–93; E 1–5; F 2–9
assessment of damages *see* damages, assessment of ~
assumption of risk BU 17–25; IRL 3–4; SCO 50–57
aviation E 70; EU 85–89, 103–108

bankruptcy FIN 16–24; LV 81–93; RO 12; SLO 6–7
banks BU 52–64; CH 44–60; DK 2–10, 18–24, 25–44; GR 25–43, 57–70
bereavement A 44; BU 80–89; D 68; E 70; EU 103–108; FIN 25–46; GR 19–24; H 5–7; LT 107–109, 115–118; NL 42–49, 52–55; RO 5–22; SCO 2–7; SK 13–27
boats *see* water vessels
buildings CY 25–30, 31–41; EST 24–34; LV 100–109; NL 26–33; SCO 50–57
burden of proof A 2–13, 45–55; E 8, 44; EU 30, 35, 46–47; F 26; GR 50, 55; I 59–70; LT 84–85, 88; P 13–22, 54–68
business judgement rule DK 25–44

causation BU 52–64; CR 27–30; CRO 39–56; CZ 106–123; DK 2–10; F 20, 26; H 1–4, 12–14; I 2–20, 59–70; ISR 43–53; MT 2–26, 46–59; P 40–53, 54–68
– alternative ~ CR 28; MT 22–26
– chain of ~ IRL 17–18
– multiple ~ F 26
– proof of ~ F 22
cartel E 42–52; EU 49–56
church D 49–66
children *see* minors
civil procedure A 48; BU 52–64, 74–79; CH 1–7; CRO 9–11; CY 1–5; CZ 1–3; H 22–24; SLO 1
class action *see* collective action
collective action CH 1–7; CRO 1–8; CY 1–5, 6; D 1–11; F 33; IRL 10; LV 1–16; NL 1
compensatio lucri cum damno A 2–13; H 18–21
compensation scheme CH 130–147; E 1–5, 36; EU 73; F 2–9, 17, 40; GR 19–24; I 59–70; IRL 11; ISR 1–4; LT 1–5; LV 23–29; N 2–13, 37–77, 111–130
concurrence of tort claims
– with compensation schemes I 59–70
– with contractual liability F 10–13
– with restitution claims BU 5–16; I 21–44
conflict of laws EU 73–84
consent IRL 4; SLO 11–15
– informed ~ BU 65–73; CZ 106–123; H 5–7
constitutionality BU 5–16; CH 83–108, 130–147; CRO 67–81; CZ 124–134; LT 6–24; RO 23–37
consumer protection A 2–13, 45–55; BU 52–64; CRO 1–8; D 1–11; E 23, 30–34; I 45–58; LV 1–16; NL 1

https://doi.org/10.1515/9783111376721-036

contract
- breach of ~ CZ 78–90; GR 57–70; SCO 18–24
- relative nature of ~ A 32–38, 56–67; CH 61–66; NL 15, 20
contra bonos mores see morals, against good
contractual liability A 32–38; B 48–49; CH 13–43; CRO 57–66; CY 31–41; CZ 91–105; GR 25–43; MT 27–45; SCO 18–24; SK 2–12
contributory conduct B 50–59; BU 17–25, 43–51; CY 42–54; D 15–28; E 69; FIN 25–46; GR 44–56, 72–73; IRL 4; LT 26, 34; N 95–110; P 6–12; SCO 50–57; SLO 20–23
copyright *see also* intellectual property LV 34
corporate social responsibility CH 8–12
costs
- of maintenance A 56–67; CR 36
- of medical care E 66; H 18–21
- of repair EU 64–72
COVID-19 A 22–31; CH 83–108; CZ 4–26, 27–43; LV 23–29
criminal law CH 44–60; EST 2–14, 35–44; FIN 16–24; LV 94–99; P 23–39; S 19–31; SLO 1
criminal procedure LV 30–53; NL 42–49; RO 1–4, 23–37

damage
- definition of ~ CH 13–43; CR 19, 21–25; PL 44–45; S 62–84
- proof of ~ BU 74–79; MT 60–81; RO 23–37
damages
- assessment of non-pecuniary ~ *see also* non-pecuniary loss A 2–13; BU 32–42, 43–51, 52–64, 80–89; CRO 21–38; CZ 44–53, 135–137; E 70; EST 12, 15–23, 35–44, 45–58; EU 11; H 5–7; IRL 26, 30–35; LT 47, 51; LV 30–53; N 78–94; P 69–70; RO 5–22; SLO 11–15
- assessment of pecuniary ~ A 45–55, 56–67; CH 13–43; E 42–52; EST 2–14, 24–34; EU 49–56; EW 82; F 40–42, 43–44; FIN 47–65; H 22–24; I 82; LV 54–66; MT 2–26, 27–45; NL 18–19; P 69–70; SLO 24–27
- punitive ~ CH 31; CR 29; CY 20–24; ISR 1–4
data
- protection D 36–48; EU 2–3, 4–12, 13–22, 23–35, 36–40; LT 37–51; LV 30–53; RO 53–65
- loss of ~ EST 2–14
death *see also* suicide BU 80–89; FIN 25–46; H 5–7; LT 107–109; N 2–13; NL 21–25; P 6–12; RO 5–22; SK 13–27
- medically assisted P 1–3
defamation BU 32–42; CY 7–19; E 53–62; EST 15–23, 35–44, 45–58, 59–60; F 5, 8; ISR 7–16, 17–27; LT 76–94; LV 81–93
defences D 22, 26–28; EU 27, 31; IRL 3; ISR 7–16, 17–27; SLO 16–19
DES F 20–27; CR 24, 28
directors and officers DK 18–24, 25–44; FIN 16–24; LV 67–80; SLO 6–7
disability A 56–67; BU 43–51; CZ 106–123; GR 1–19, 71, 79; H 8–11; MT 2–26; N 111–130; P 23–39
discrimination E 16–17
duty
- of care CR 14, 37; CY 31–41, 42–54; D 69; E 22–23; EW 70–78, 81; GR 25–43; IRL 1–2, 36; ISR 28–42, 43–53; NL 14–20; P 6–12; SCO 2–7, 32–42, 43–49, 50–57
- to inform A 32–38; B 1–4; BU 65–73; EW 38–52; H 5–7; NL 16; P 40–53
- to mitigate the loss D 70; F 44
- to protect CH 61–66; IRL 18
- to secure A 14–21; BU 43–51; LV 100–109
- to supervise GR 44–56

ECHR *see* human rights
employers' liability CY 42–54; DK 45–54, 55–62; EW 53–69; F 2–9, 10–13; FIN 47–65; IRL 16–18, 25; LT 52–64; SCO 25–31, 43–49; SK 2–12; SLO 11–15, 20–23
environmental liability CH 8–12; CZ 54–65; I 2–20; P 6–12
EU law A 2–13, 45–55; BU 52–64, 74–79; CH 8–12, 13–43; CRO 12–13; CY 6, 7–19; D 1–11, 48; E 43, 47; EU 103–108; I 2–20, 45–58, 71–80; IRL 10; LT 64; LV 1–16; NL 1, 2

evidence IRL 37; MT 46–59; P 54–68; RO 23–37; SCO 32–42
excessive claims RO 5–22
excessive length of procedure CZ 124–134
experts *see* professional liability

family
- bond GR 22–24; H 5–7; PL 49–51; SK 13–27
- life A 39–44; CZ 106–123
fault B 20–28, 50–59; BU 54–68; CR 12–13; D 15–28; EU 19–22; F 30–37; LT 32; P 13–22
financial industry *see also* banks DK 2–10, 18–24, 25–44
firefighters EU 103
force majeure E 68
foreseeability *see also* adequacy A 32–38, 68–74; DK 2–10; IRL 18, 36; ISR 28–42; N 37–77; SCO 2–7, 50–57
fraud DK 2–10; FIN 16–24; GR 57–70
functions of tort law
- compensation A 45–55, 56–67; CH 13–43; CZ 135–137; EU 41–48; RO 5–22
- deterrence IRL 23; PL 12–14, 36
- punishment CH 31; CY 20–24; ISR 1–4; PL 12–14, 36

harmonisation of tort law PL 13, 36
health services CZ 106–123; H 1–4, 5–7, 15–17; ISR 43–53; LT 1–5, 6–24, 37–51, 95–103; MT 60–81; P 13–22; SCO 2–7
human rights A 22–31; CH 83–108, 122–129, 130–147; CR 39; CRO 67–81; CZ 134; H 12–14; IRL 12–15; LT 11–24; SLO 28–33
imprisonment CH 122–129; RO 1–4, 23–37
information-based liability *see* liability, information-based
insurance DK 45–54; FIN 47–65; N 2–13; P 1–3, 4–5; S 42–42
- compulsory ~ E 14; EU 64–72, 91–102
- first party ~ N 95–110; P 40–53
- liability ~ EU 64–72
- right of direct action EU 64–72
intellectual property LV 30–53
intent A 50–59; CH 44–60; FIN 25–46; S 19–31
internet BU 32–42; EST 45–58; RO 42–52

joint and several tortfeasors *see* liability, joint and several

labour law SLO 11–15, 20–23
land law A 14–21; CY 25–30, 31–41; SLO 2, 24–27
lawful alternative conduct A 45–55
lawyers CRO 57–66; DK 2–10; H 12–14; SCO 32–42
liability
- for dangerous activities CZ 54–65; P 54–68
- for lawful activities SLO 8–10
- for others CR 31–34; CY 42–54; D 49–66; EST 24–34; EW 53–69; F 10–13; S 48, 59; SCO 8–17, 25–31; SK 2–12
- for reliance CH 13–43, 109–121
- for things BU 17–25, 26–31; P 54–68
- information-based A 10, 22–31; BU 1–3; CZ 91–105
- joint and several ~ D 26; EST 24–34; GR 17–18; LT 52–64; MT 2–26
- limitation of ~ A 45–55; DK 45–54; N 78–94
loss
- of a chance B 32; H 1–4, 12–14; SCO 18–24
- of earnings DK 45–54; H 8–11; ISR 61–63; LT 52–64; MT 27–45
- of housekeeping capacity D 70
- of profits CRO 21–38; CZ 78–90; GR 74; LT 6–24, 25–36; LV 67–80; P 40–53; SLO 24–27
- of value LV 54–66
- working capacity LT 52–64
- pure economic ~ CH 44–60, 83–108, 109–121

malice CY 20–24
maritime law S 43–61
mass media BU 32–42; D 36–48; ISR 17–27
mass tort A 2–13, 27; CH 13–43
medical malpractice A 32–38, 56–67; BU 65–73; CRO 39–56; CY 57–61; CZ 106–123; EW 38–52; GR 1–18; H 1–4, 5–7, 15–17, 18–21; IRL 36–37; ISR 43–53; LT 95–103; MT 2–26, 27–45, 46–59, 60–81; SCO 2–7
mental harm *see* psychological harm
mental incapacity CH 122–129; MT 60–81; SCO 2–7

mental shock *see also* psychological harm
A 39–44, 68–74; H 8–11; NL 21–25, 42–49, 50–55
military LV 20–22
minors
– as tortfeasors FIN 25–46; N 78–94
– as victims A 32–38, 39–44; GR 44–56; N 78–94; SCO 25–31
morals
– against good ~ A 14–21; CRO 67–81; CZ 78–90
moral harm *see* non-pecuniary loss
motor vehicle liability B 50–59; CH 67–82; CZ 66–77; D 15–28, 29–35; E 67; EU 91–102; ISR 43–53; P 4–5

natural disaster SLO 8–10
negligence EW 70–78; IRL 2; ISR 28–42, 43–53; SCO 2–7, 32–42
neighbours and nuisance A 14–21; E 53–62; EW 2–12, 26–32
no-fault system *see* compensation scheme
non-pecuniary loss *see also* damages ~ assessment of non-pecuniary A 39–44; BU 32–42, 43–51, 52–64, 80–89; CRO 21–38; CZ 44–53, 106–123; D 44–45, 58–59, 71; EST 15–23, 35–44, 45–58; EU 23–35, 36–40; F 27; GR 36–37, 67, 75–80; LT 107–114, 115–118; LV 30–53, 81–93; PL 1–14, 16–23, 24–48; SK 2–12; SLO 11–15
nuclear liability E 18–21

occupational disease F 2–9; FIN 47–65; LV 17–19
omission A 14–21, 22–31; CH 61–66; GR 36; ISR 28–42

pain and suffering A 39–44, 68–74; CZ 44–53, 135–137
personal injury A 39–44, 68–74, 75; BU 17–25, 26–31, 90–93; CRO 82–93; CY 20–24, 55–73; CZ 66–77; D 67–71; E 66–70; EST 59–60; EU 85–89; EW 79–82; F 28–37, 38–44; FIN 25–46; GR 1–18, 71–80; H 5–7; I 45–58, 59–70, 71–80, 81–85; IRL 7, 25–37; ISR 28–42, 43–53; LT 52–64, 106–118; LV 23–29, 94–112; MT 27–45, 46–59, 82–88; N 111–130, 131–151, 152; NL 52–55; P 23–39, 69–70; RO 38–41; S 62–84; SCO 43–49, 58–62; SK 13–27; SLO 34
personality rights BU 32–42; CR 35; CY 7–19; CZ 106–123; E 27–29, 53–62; EST 15–23, 45–58; F 5,8; GR 25–43; H 15–17; ISR 7–16, 17–27; LV 30–53, 81–93; PL 1–14, 15, 16–23, 24–48, 49–51; SLO 11–15
PFAS *see also* toxic torts CR 16–26; S 62–84
pharmaceuticals F 20–27, 28–37
police FIN 4–15; IRL 7, 19–21, 25; S 5–18
politicians BU 32–42; ISR 7–16, 17–27
pre-contractual liability CH 13–43; CZ 78–90
prescription CH 130–147; CR 38–40; CRO 7, 57–66; E 10, 35–41; EU 73–84; EW 26–32; F 15–18, 30; GR 1–18; IRL 12–15; N 14–36; NL 3–12, 26–33; S 19–31, 82–84; SLO 16–19
principle of full compensation *see* functions of tort law, compensation
Principles of European Tort Law *see also* harmonisation of tort law E 52
privacy EW 2–25; PL 16–23; SLO 11–15
product liability E 30–34; F 28–37; I 45–58, 71–80; S 62–84
professional liability CRO 57–66; CZ 91–105; DK 2–10; H 12–14; LV 81–93; MT 46–59; SCO 32–42
property law CY 25–30; NL 3–12
prospectus E 9–10
protective purpose of the rule A 2–13, 22–31; CH 44–60; CRO 39–56; EU 57–63; F 20–27
psychological harm *see also* mental shock A 32–38, 68–74; F 20–27; H 8–11; IRL 36; N 37–77; NL 21–25, 42–49, 50–55; SK 13–27
public authority liability CR 4–8, 9–15; D 11–14, 49–66; E 63; EW 70–78; LT 22–23, 65–75, 76–94, 119–129; PL 16–23
– applicability of ~ ISR 28–42
– for administrative authorities A 22–31; BU 43–51; CH 109–121; CRO 14–19;

EST 2–14, 35–44; FIN 4–15; P 6–12; RO 1–4
- for breach of EU law BU 52–64
- for legislative acts B 5–28; BU 5–16; CH 83–108; CRO 21–38; CZ 4–26, 27–43; E 63–65
- for the judiciary BU 74–79; CH 122–129; CZ 124–134; RO 23–37; SCO 8–17
public procurement SCO 18–24
public servants CRO 14–19, 21–38; FIN 4–15
punitive damages *see* damages, punitive
restitution in kind A 2–13; B 29–49; CH 13–43; E 9; NL 3–12
right of recourse DK 11–17; EU 73–84; GR 49, 51–56
risk, exposure to ~ CR 16–26; F 20–27; S 62–84
road traffic accidents B 50–59; CY 70–73; CZ 66–77; DK 15–28; E 67; EU 91–102; FIN 25–46; GR 19–24, 44–56, 72–73; H 8–11; I 45–58; IRL 16–18; ISR 54–59; LT 115–118

secondary victim A 32–38, 39–44, 68–74; BU 80–89; D 68; FIN 25–46; GR 19–24; H 5–7; LT 115–118; NL 21–25; RO 5–22; SK 13–27
self-defence P 23–39
sexual abuse CR 31–34; D 49–66; EW 53–69; SCO 8–17, 25–31
social security scheme DK 11–17; F 38–39; ISR 5–6; LV 17–19
standard of care A 45–55; CR 12–13; CRO 39–56; IRL 1–2, 4, 18; ISR 43–53; LT 32, 45, 98; MT 27–45, 60–81
statutory duty A 2–13, 22–31; CH 44–60
stock company DK 18–24
strict liability BU 17–25; CH 67–82, 83–108; CY 31–41; CZ 4–26, 66–77; D 15–28, 29–35; E 30–34; EW 34; GR 11; I 2–20, 45–58, 71–80; LT 56, 95–105
suicide MT 60–81; N 37–77; SCO 2–7

tax law DK 2–10; LV 54–66; N 14–36
terrorism ISR 1–4, 5–6
tort law reform FIN 1–3
toxic torts CH 130–147; CR 16–26; CZ 54–65; E 1–5; F 2–9; S 62–84
trees A 14–21; RO 5

unjust enrichment B 5–16; EU 65–66, 71; I 21–44

vaccination LV 23–29

water vessels ISR 28–42
whistleblowers BU 1–3; E 6–8; IRL 6; SLO 3–5
whiplash EW 80
work accident CH 61–66; CY 42–54, 62–65, 66–69; DK 11–17, 45–54, 55–62; EU 91–102; FIN 47–65; GR 77; IRL 16–18; LT 52–64; LV 17–19; SCO 43–49; SLO 20–23
wrongful birth A 32–38, 56–67; CR 35–37; CZ 106–123; ISR 43–53
wrongful conception A 56–67
wrongful life ISR 43–53
wrongfulness GR 42, 69–70; LT 32–33, 36, 70–75; NL 15

Publications

Principles of European Tort Law Series

Volume 1: *The Limits of Liability: Keeping the Floodgates Shut*
Edited by Jaap Spier
Kluwer Law International, The Hague
Hardcover. ISBN 90-411-0169-1
1996, 162 pp

Volume 2: *The Limits of Expanding Liability: Eight Fundamental Cases in a Comparative Perspective*
Edited by Jaap Spier
Kluwer Law International, The Hague
Hardcover. ISBN 90-411-0581-6
1998, 244 pp

Volume 3: *Unification of Tort Law: Wrongfulness*
Edited by Helmut Koziol
Kluwer Law International, The Hague
Hardcover. ISBN 90-411-1019-4
1998, 144 pp

Volume 4: *Unification of Tort Law: Causation*
Edited by Jaap Spier
Kluwer Law International, The Hague
Hardcover. ISBN 90-411-1325-8
2000, 161 pp

Volume 5: *Unification of Tort Law: Damages*
Edited by Ulrich Magnus
Kluwer Law International, The Hague
Hardcover. ISBN 90-411-1481-5
2001, 225 pp

Volume 6: *Unification of Tort Law: Strict Liability*
Edited by Bernhard A Koch and Helmut Koziol
Kluwer Law International, The Hague
Hardcover. ISBN 90-411-1705-9
2002, 444 pp

Volume 7: *Unification of Tort Law: Liability for Damage Caused by Others*
Edited by Jaap Spier
Kluwer Law International, The Hague
Hardcover. ISBN 90-411-2185-4
2003, 335 pp

Volume 8: *Unification of Tort Law: Contributory Negligence*
Edited by Ulrich Magnus and Miquel Martín-Casals
Kluwer Law International, The Hague
Hardcover. ISBN 90-411-2220-6
2004, 300 pp

https://doi.org/10.1515/9783111376721-037

Volume 9: *Unification of Tort Law: Multiple Tortfeasors*
Edited by WV Horton Rogers
Kluwer Law International, The Hague
Hardcover. ISBN 90-411-2319-9
2004, 313 pp

Volume 10: *Unification of Tort Law: Fault*
Edited by Pierre Widmer
Kluwer Law International, The Hague
Hardcover. ISBN 90-411-2098-4
2005, 391 pp

Tort and Insurance Law Series

Volume 1: *Cases on Medical Malpractice in a Comparative Perspective*
Edited by Michael Faure and Helmut Koziol
Verlag Österreich, Vienna
Softcover. ISBN 978-3-7046-6056-5
2001, 331 pp

Volume 2: *Damages for Non-Pecuniary Loss in a Comparative Perspective*
Edited by WV Horton Rogers
Verlag Österreich, Vienna
Softcover. ISBN 978-3-7046-6057-2
2001, 318 pp

Volume 3: *The Impact of Social Security Law on Tort Law*
Edited by Ulrich Magnus
Verlag Österreich, Vienna
Softcover. ISBN 978-3-7046-6083-1
2003, 312 pp

Volume 4: *Compensation for Personal Injury in a Comparative Perspective*
Edited by Bernhard A Koch and Helmut Koziol
Verlag Österreich, Vienna
Softcover. ISBN 978-3-7046-6082-4
2003, 501 pp

Volume 5: *Deterrence, Insurability and Compensation in Environmental Liability. Future Developments in the European Union*
Edited by Michael Faure
Verlag Österreich, Vienna
Softcover. ISBN 978-3-7046-6891-2
2003, 408 pp

Volume 6: *Der Ersatz frustrierter Aufwendungen. Vermögens- und Nichtvermögensschaden im österreichischen und deutschen Recht*
by Thomas Schobel
Verlag Österreich, Vienna

Softcover. ISBN 978-3-7046-6093-0
2003, 342 pp

Volume 7: *Liability for and Insurability of Biomedical Research with Human Subjects in a Comparative Perspective*
Edited by Jos Dute, Michael G Faure and Helmut Koziol
Verlag Österreich, Vienna
Softcover. ISBN 978-3-7046-5812-8
2004, 445 pp

Volume 8: *No-Fault Compensation in the Health Care Sector*
Edited by Jos Dute, Michael G Faure and Helmut Koziol
Verlag Österreich, Vienna
Softcover. ISBN 978-3-7046-5821-0
2004, 492 pp

Volume 9: *Pure Economic Loss*
Edited by Willem H van Boom, Helmut Koziol and Christian A Witting
Verlag Österreich, Vienna
Softcover. ISBN 978-3-7046-5790-9
2004, 214 pp

Volume 10: *Liber Amicorum Pierre Widmer*
Edited by Helmut Koziol and Jaap Spier
Verlag Österreich, Vienna
Softcover. ISBN 978-3-7046-5792-3
2003, 376 pp

Volume 11: *Terrorism, Tort Law and Insurance. A Comparative Survey*
Edited by Bernhard A Koch
Verlag Österreich, Vienna
Softcover. ISBN 978-3-7046-5795-4
2004, 313 pp

Volume 12: *Abschlussprüfer. Haftung und Versicherung*
Edited by Helmut Koziol and Walter Doralt
Verlag Österreich, Vienna
Softcover. ISBN 978-3-7046-5822-7
2004, 180 pp

Volume 13: *Persönlichkeitsschutz gegenüber Massenmedien/The Protection of Personality Rights against Invasions by Mass Media*
Edited by Helmut Koziol and Alexander Warzilek
Verlag Österreich, Vienna
Softcover. ISBN 978-3-7046-5841-8
2005, 713 pp

Volume 14: *Financial Compensation for Victims of Catastrophes. A Comparative Legal Approach*
Edited by Michael Faure and Ton Hartlief
Verlag Österreich, Vienna
Softcover. ISBN 978-3-7046-5849-4
2006, 466 pp

Volume 15: *Entwurf eines neuen österreichischen Schadenersatzrechts*
Edited by Irmgard Griss, Georg Kathrein and Helmut Koziol

Verlag Österreich, Vienna
Softcover. ISBN 978-3-7046-5865-4
2006, 146 pp

Volume 16: *Tort Law and Liability Insurance*
Edited by Gerhard Wagner
Verlag Österreich, Vienna
Softcover. ISBN 978-3-7046-5850-0
2005, 361 pp

Volume 17: *Children in Tort Law. Part I: Children as Tortfeasors*
Edited by Miquel Martín-Casals
Verlag Österreich, Vienna
Softcover. ISBN 978-3-7046-5848-7
2006, 476 pp

Volume 18: *Children in Tort Law. Part II: Children as Victims*
Edited by Miquel Martín-Casals
Verlag Österreich, Vienna
Softcover. ISBN 978-3-7046-5869-2
2007, 320 pp

Volume 19: *Tort and Regulatory Law*
Edited by Willem H van Boom, Meinhard Lukas and Christa Kissling
Verlag Österreich, Vienna
Hardcover. ISBN 978-3-7046-5870-8
2007, 477 pp

Volume 20: *Shifts in Compensating Work-Related Injuries and Diseases*
Edited by Saskia Klosse and Ton Hartlief
Verlag Österreich, Vienna
Hardcover. ISBN 978-3-7046-5913-2
2007, 236 pp

Volume 21: *Shifts in Compensation for Environmental Damage*
Edited by Michael Faure and Albert Verheij
Verlag Österreich, Vienna
Hardcover. ISBN 978-3-7046-5911-8
2007, 338 pp

Volume 22: *Shifts in Compensation between Private and Public Systems*
Edited by Willem H van Boom and Michael Faure
Verlag Österreich, Vienna
Hardcover. ISBN 978-3-7046-5912-5
2007, 246 pp

Volume 23: *Tort Law of the European Community*
Edited by Helmut Koziol and Reiner Schulze
Verlag Österreich, Vienna
Hardcover. ISBN 978-3-7046-5935-4
2008, 693 pp

Volume 24: *Economic Loss Caused by Genetically Modified Organisms. Liability and Redress for the Adventitious Presence of GMOs in Non-GM Crops*
Edited by Bernhard A Koch

Verlag Österreich, Vienna
Hardcover. ISBN 978-3-7046-5937-8
2008, 747 pp

Volume 25: *Punitive Damages. Common Law and Civil Law Perspectives*
Edited by Helmut Koziol and Vanessa Wilcox
Verlag Österreich, Vienna
Hardcover. ISBN 978-3-7046-6117-3
2009, 335 pp

Volume 26: *Aggregation and Divisibility of Damage*
Edited by Ken Oliphant
Verlag Österreich, Vienna
Hardcover. ISBN 978-3-7046-6116-6
2009, 568 pp

Volume 27: *Damage Caused by Genetically Modified Organisms. Comparative Survey of Redress Options for Harm to Persons, Property or the Environment*
Edited by Bernhard A Koch
De Gruyter, Berlin/New York
Hardcover. ISBN 978-3-89949-811-0
eBook. ISBN 978-3-89949-812-7
2010, 954 pp

Volume 28: *Loss of Housekeeping Capacity*
Edited by Ernst Karner and Ken Oliphant
De Gruyter, Berlin/Boston
Hardcover. ISBN 978-3-89949-813-4
eBook. ISBN 978-3-89949-814-1
2012, 339 pp

Volume 29: *Medical Liability in Europe. A Comparison of Selected Jurisdictions*
Edited by Bernhard A Koch
De Gruyter, Berlin/Boston
Hardcover. ISBN 978-3-11-026010-6
eBook. ISBN 978-3-11-026016-8
2011, 701 pp

Volume 30: *Tort Law in the Jurisprudence of the European Court of Human Rights*
Edited by Attila Fenyves, Ernst Karner, Helmut Koziol and Elisabeth Steiner
De Gruyter, Berlin/Boston
Hardcover. ISBN 978-3-11-025966-7
eBook. ISBN 978-3-11-026000-7
2011, 906 pp

Volume 31: *Employers' Liability and Workers' Compensation*
Edited by Ken Oliphant and Gerhard Wagner
De Gruyter, Berlin/Boston
Hardcover. ISBN 978-3-11-026996-3
eBook. ISBN 978-3-11-027021-1
2012, 619 pp

Volume 32: *Medical Malpractice and Compensation in Global Perspective*
Edited by Ken Oliphant and Richard W Wright

De Gruyter, Berlin/Boston
Hardcover. ISBN 978-3-11-026997-0
eBook. ISBN 978-3-11-027023-5
2013, 573 pp

Volume 33: *Proportional Liability: Analytical and Comparative Perspectives*
Edited by Israel Gilead, Michael D Green and Bernhard A Koch
De Gruyter, Berlin/Boston
Hardcover. ISBN 978-3-11-028253-5
eBook. ISBN 978-3-11-028258-0
2013, 376 pp

Volume 34: *Mass Torts in Europe: Cases and Reflections*
Edited by Willem H van Boom and Gerhard Wagner
De Gruyter, Berlin/Boston
Hardcover. ISBN 978-3-11-034945-0
eBook. ISBN 978-3-11-034946-7
2014, 311 pp

Volume 35: *Compulsory Liability Insurance from a European Perspective*
Edited by Attila Fenyves, Christa Kissling, Stefan Perner and Daniel Rubin
De Gruyter, Berlin/Boston
Hardcover. ISBN 978-3-11-048469-4
eBook. ISBN 978-3-11-048617-9
2016, 564 pp

Volume 36: *Directors' & Officers' (D & O) Liability*
Edited by Simon Deakin, Helmut Koziol and Olaf Riss
De Gruyter, Berlin/Boston
Hardcover. ISBN 978-3-11-048971-2
eBook. ISBN 978-3-11-049149-4
2018, 1008 pp

Volume 37: *Civil Liability for Artificial Intelligence and Software*
Edited by Ernst Karner, Bernhard A Koch, Mark A Geistfeld and Christiane Wendehorst
De Gruyter, Berlin/Boston
Hardcover. ISBN 978-3-11-077534-1
eBook. ISBN 978-3-11-077540-2
2023, 407 pp

European Tort Law Yearbook

European Tort Law 2001
Edited by Helmut Koziol and Barbara C Steininger
Verlag Österreich, Vienna
Softcover. ISBN 978-3-7046-6085-5
2002, 571 pp

European Tort Law 2002
Edited by Helmut Koziol and Barbara C Steininger
Verlag Österreich, Vienna

Softcover. ISBN 3-211-00486-6
2003, 596 pp

European Tort Law 2003
Edited by Helmut Koziol and Barbara C Steininger
Verlag Österreich, Vienna
Softcover. ISBN 978-3-7046-5825-8
2004, 493 pp

European Tort Law 2004
Edited by Helmut Koziol and Barbara C Steininger
Verlag Österreich, Vienna
Softcover. ISBN 978-3-7046-5847-0
2005, 674 pp

European Tort Law 2005
Edited by Helmut Koziol and Barbara C Steininger
Verlag Österreich, Vienna
Softcover. ISBN 978-3-7046-5871-5
2006, 711 pp

European Tort Law 2006
Edited by Helmut Koziol and Barbara C Steininger
Verlag Österreich, Vienna
Hardcover. ISBN 978-3-7046-5908-8
2008, 576 pp

European Tort Law 2007
Edited by Helmut Koziol and Barbara C Steininger
Verlag Österreich, Vienna
Hardcover. ISBN 978-3-7046-5938-5
2008, 661 pp

European Tort Law 2008
Edited by Helmut Koziol and Barbara C Steininger
Verlag Österreich, Vienna
Hardcover. ISBN 978-3-7046-6120-3
2009, 708 pp

European Tort Law 2009
Edited by Helmut Koziol and Barbara C Steininger
De Gruyter, Berlin/New York
Hardcover. ISBN 978-3-11-024606-3
eBook. ISBN 978-3-11-024607-0
2010, 735 pp

European Tort Law 2010
Edited by Helmut Koziol and Barbara C Steininger
De Gruyter, Berlin/Boston
Hardcover. ISBN 978-3-11-023941-6
eBook. ISBN 978-3-11-023942-3
2011, 706 pp

European Tort Law 2011
Edited by Ken Oliphant and Barbara C Steininger

De Gruyter, Berlin/Boston
Hardcover. ISSN 2190 – 7773
eBook. ISSN 2190 – 7781
2012, 789 pp

European Tort Law 2012
Edited by Ken Oliphant and Barbara C Steininger
De Gruyter, Berlin/Boston
Hardcover. ISSN 2190 – 7773
eBook. ISSN 2190 – 7781
2013, 816 pp

European Tort Law 2013
Edited by Ernst Karner and Barbara C Steininger
De Gruyter, Berlin/Boston
Hardcover. ISSN 2190 – 7773
eBook. ISSN 2190 – 7781
2014, 824 pp

European Tort Law 2014
Edited by Ernst Karner and Barbara C Steininger
De Gruyter, Berlin/Boston
Hardcover. ISSN 2190 – 7773
eBook. ISSN 2190 – 7791
2015, 758 pp

European Tort Law 2015
Edited by Ernst Karner and Barbara C Steininger
De Gruyter, Berlin/Boston
Hardcover. ISSN 2190 – 7773
eBook. ISSN 2190 – 7791
2016, 764 pp

European Tort Law 2016
Edited by Ernst Karner and Barbara C Steininger
De Gruyter, Berlin/Boston
Hardcover. ISSN 2190 – 7773
eBook. ISSN 2190 – 7781
2017, 747 pp

European Tort Law 2017
Edited by Ernst Karner and Barbara C Steininger
De Gruyter, Berlin/Boston
Hardcover. ISSN 2190 – 7773
eBook. ISSN 2190 – 7781
2018, 762 pp

European Tort Law 2018
Edited by Ernst Karner and Barbara C Steininger
De Gruyter, Berlin/Boston
Hardcover. ISSN 2190 – 7773
eBook. ISSN 2190 – 7781
2019, 803 pp

European Tort Law 2019
Edited by Ernst Karner and Barbara C Steininger
De Gruyter, Berlin/Boston
Hardcover. ISSN 2190 – 7773
eBook. ISSN 2190 – 7781
2020, 797 pp

European Tort Law 2020
Edited by Ernst Karner and Barbara C Steininger
De Gruyter, Berlin/Boston
Hardcover. ISSN 2190 – 7773
eBook. ISSN 2190 – 7781
2021, 778 pp

European Tort Law 2021
Edited by Ernst Karner and Barbara C Steininger
De Gruyter, Berlin/Boston
Hardcover. ISSN 2190 – 7773
eBook. ISSN 2190 – 7781
2022, 785 pp

European Tort Law 2022
Edited by Ernst Karner and Barbara C Steininger
De Gruyter, Berlin/Boston
Hardcover. ISBN 978-3-11-124019-0
eBook. ISBN 978-3-11-124124-1
2023, 817 pp

European Group on Tort Law

Principles of European Tort Law. Text and Commentary
Edited by the European Group on Tort Law
Verlag Österreich, Vienna
Softcover. ISBN 978-3-7046-5837-1
2005, 282 pp

The Liability of Public Authorities in Comparative Perspective
Edited by Ken Oliphant
Intersentia, Cambridge/Antwerp/Portland
Softcover. ISBN 978-1-78068-238-9
2016, 887 pp

The Borderlines of Tort Law: Interactions with Contract Law
Edited by Miquel Martín-Casals
Intersentia, Cambridge/Antwerp/Portland
Softcover. ISBN 978-1-78068-248-8
2019, 846 pp

Prescription in Tort Law. Analytical and Comparative Perspectives
Edited by Israel Gilead and Bjarte Askeland
Intersentia, Cambridge/Antwerp/Portland

Softcover. ISBN 978-1-78068-963-0
2020, 746 pp

Digest of European Tort Law

Volume 1: *Essential Cases on Natural Causation*
Edited by Bénédict Winiger, Helmut Koziol, Bernhard A Koch and Reinhard Zimmermann
Verlag Österreich, Vienna
Hardcover. ISBN 978-3-7046-5885-2
2007, 632 pp

Volume 2: *Essential Cases on Damage*
Edited by Bénédict Winiger, Helmut Koziol, Bernhard A Koch and Reinhard Zimmermann
De Gruyter, Berlin/Boston
Hardcover. ISBN 978-3-11-024848-7
eBook. ISBN 978-3-11-024849-4
2011, 1175 pp

Volume 3: *Essential Cases on Misconduct*
Edited by Bénédict Winiger, Ernst Karner and Ken Oliphant
De Gruyter, Berlin/Boston
Hardcover. ISBN 978-3-11-053434-4
eBook. ISBN 978-3-11-053567-9
2018, 1286 pp

Sino-European Legal Studies

The Aims of Tort Law. Chinese and European Perspectives
Edited by Helmut Koziol
Jan Sramek Verlag, Vienna
Hardcover. ISBN 978-3-7097-0127-0
2017, 230 pp

The Legal Protection of Personality Rights. Chinese and European Perspectives
Edited by Ken Oliphant, Zhang Pinghua and Chen Lei
Brill | Nijhoff, Leiden/Boston
Hardcover. ISBN 978-9-0042-7629-1
eBook. ISBN 978-9-0043-5171-4
2018, 227 pp

Tortious and Contractual Liability. Chinese and European Perspectives
Edited by Ernst Karner
Jan Sramek Verlag, Vienna
Hardcover. ISBN 978-3-7097-0275-8
2021, 263 pp

World Tort Law Society

Product Liability. Fundamental Questions in a Comparative Perspective
Edited by Helmut Koziol, Michael D Green, Mark Lunney, Ken Oliphant and Yang Lixin
De Gruyter, Berlin/Boston
Hardcover. ISBN 978-3-11-054600-2
eBook. ISBN 978-3-11-054581-4
2017, 610 pp

Others

European Tort Law. Basic Texts
Edited by Ernst Karner, Ken Oliphant and Barbara C Steininger
Jan Sramek Verlag, Vienna
Softcover. ISBN 978-3-7097-0170-6
2018, 2nd Edition, 466 pp

Grundfragen des Schadenersatzrechts
by Helmut Koziol
Jan Sramek Verlag, Vienna
Hardcover. ISBN 978-3-902638-28-1
2010, 371 pp

Grundfragen des Schadenersatzrechts aus rechtsvergleichender Sicht
Edited by Helmut Koziol
Jan Sramek Verlag, Vienna
Hardcover. ISBN 978-3-7097-48-8
2014, 941 pp

Basic Questions of Tort Law from a Germanic Perspective
by Helmut Koziol
Jan Sramek Verlag, Vienna
Hardcover. ISBN 978-3-902638-85-4
2012, 380 pp

Basic Questions of Tort Law from a Comparative Perspective
Edited by Helmut Koziol
Jan Sramek Verlag, Vienna
Hardcover. ISBN 978-3-7097-0040-2
2015, 867 pp

Comparative Stimulations for Developing Tort Law
Edited by Helmut Koziol
Jan Sramek Verlag, Vienna
Hardcover. ISBN 978-3-7097-0060-0
2015, 273 pp

Harmonisation and Fundamental Questions of European Tort Law
by Helmut Koziol
Jan Sramek Verlag, Vienna
Hardcover. ISBN 978-3-7097-0128-7
2017, 168 pp

Austrian Private Law. An Overview in Comparison with German Law and with References to English and French Law
by Gabriele Koziol and Helmut Koziol, in cooperation with Andrew Bell and Samuel Fulli-Lemaire
Jan Sramek Verlag, Vienna
Softcover. ISBN 978-3-7097-0156-0
2017, 119 pp

Grundzüge des japanischen Schadenersatzrechts
by Keizo Yamamoto
Jan Sramek Verlag, Vienna
Softcover. ISBN 978-3-7097-0102-7
2018, 220 pp

Basic Features of Japanese Tort Law
by Keizo Yamamoto
Jan Sramek Verlag, Vienna
Softcover. ISBN 978-3-7097-0188-1
2019, 202 pp

Tort Liability Law of China
by Lixin Yang
Jan Sramek Verlag, Vienna
Softcover. ISBN 978-3-7097-0088-4
2018, 384 pp

Essays in Honour of Helmut Koziol
Edited by Ernst Karner, Ulrich Magnus, Jaap Spier and Pierre Widmer
Jan Sramek Verlag, Vienna
Hardcover. ISBN 978-3-7097-0228-4
2020, 262 pp

Essays in Honour of Jaap Spier
Edited by Helmut Koziol and Ulrich Magnus
Jan Sramek Verlag, Vienna
Hardcover. ISBN 978-3-7097-0101-0
2016, 325 pp

Politikerhaftung. The Liabilities of Politicians
Edited by Helmut Koziol
Jan Sramek Verlag, Vienna
Hardcover. ISBN 978-3-7097-0242-0
2020, 487 pp

Die Haftung von Eisenbahnverkehrs- und Infrastrukturunternehmen im Rechtsvergleich
Edited by Helmut Koziol
Jan Sramek Verlag, Vienna

Softcover. ISBN 978-3-7097-0191-1
2019, 318 pp

Schadenersatzrechtliche Verantwortlichkeit im internationalen Eisenbahnverkehr
by Gregor Christandl and Olaf Riss
Jan Sramek Verlag, Vienna
Softcover. ISBN 978-3-7097-0273-4
2021, 161 pp

Die Vereinheitlichung der Haftung von Eisenbahnunternehmen in der Europäischen Union
by Helmut Koziol
Jan Sramek Verlag, Vienna
Softcover. ISBN 978-3-7097-0274-1
2021, 229 pp

Medienpolitik und Recht. Media Governance, Wahrhaftigkeitspflicht und sachgerechte Haftung
Edited by Helmut Koziol, Josef Seethaler and Thomas Thiede
Jan Sramek Verlag, Vienna
Hardcover. ISBN 978-3-902638-36-6
2010, 214 pp

Medienpolitik und Recht II. Presserat, WikiLeaks und Redaktionsgeheimnis
Edited by Helmut Koziol, Josef Seethaler and Thomas Thiede
Jan Sramek Verlag, Vienna
Hardcover. ISBN 978-3-902638-63-2
2013, 216 pp

Tatsachenmitteilungen und Werturteile. Freiheit und Verantwortung
Edited by Helmut Koziol
Jan Sramek Verlag, Vienna
Hardcover. ISBN 978-3-7097-0171-3
2018, 197 pp

Österreichisches Haftpflichtrecht Band I. Allgemeiner Teil
by Helmut Koziol
Jan Sramek Verlag, Vienna
Hardcover. ISBN 978-3-7097-0225-3
2020, 4th Edition, 1002 pp

Österreichisches Haftpflichtrecht Band II. Haftung für eigenes und fremdes Fehlverhalten
by Helmut Koziol
Jan Sramek Verlag, Vienna
Hardcover. ISBN 978-3-7097-0173-7
2018, 3rd Edition, 1074 pp

Österreichisches Haftpflichtrecht Band III. Gefährdungs-, Produkt- und Eingriffshaftung
by Helmut Koziol, Peter Apathy and Bernhard A Koch
Jan Sramek Verlag, Vienna
Hardcover. ISBN 978-3-7097-0022-8
2014, 3rd Edition, 596 pp

Mangelfolgeschäden in Veräußerungsketten. Am Beispiel der Aus- und Einbaukosten
by Ernst Karner and Helmut Koziol
Jan Sramek Verlag, Vienna

Softcover. ISBN 978-3-902638-84-7
2012, 96 pp

Zur Anwendbarkeit des UN-Kaufrechts bei Werk- und Dienstleistungen. Am Beispiel der Maschinen- und Industrieanlagenlieferungsverträge
by Ernst Karner and Helmut Koziol
Jan Sramek Verlag, Vienna
Softcover. ISBN 978-3-7097-0052-5
2015, 91 pp

Obsoleszenzen im österreichischen Recht. Geltendes Recht, Schutzlücken und Reformbedarf
by Helmut Koziol
Jan Sramek Verlag, Vienna
Softcover. ISBN 978-3-7097-0108-9
2016, 137 pp

Vertragsstrafe und Schadenspauschalierung
by Ernst Karner and Alexander Longin
Jan Sramek Verlag, Vienna
Softcover. ISBN 978-3-7097-0234-5
2020, 240 pp

Haftungsfreizeichnungen zulasten Dritter. Im Zwischenbereich von Vertrag und Delikt
by Johannes Angyan
Jan Sramek Verlag, Vienna
Hardcover. ISBN 978-3-7097-0257-4
2021, 351 pp

Recht auf Anpassung des Werkvertrags
by Alexander Longin
Jan Sramek Verlag, Vienna
Hardcover. ISBN 978-3-7097-0258-1
2021, 396 pp

Mehrstufiger Warenverkehr. Spezifische Probleme bei Vertragsketten
by Helmut Koziol
Jan Sramek Verlag, Vienna
Hardcover. ISBN 978-3-7097-0284-0
2021, 317 pp

Rechtsunkenntnis und Schadenszurechnung
by Helmut Koziol
Jan Sramek Verlag, Vienna
Hardcover. ISBN 978-3-7097-0309-0
2022, 189 pp

Erlaubte Notstandshandlungen und zivilrechtliche Ausgleichsansprüche
by David Messner-Kreuzbauer
Jan Sramek Verlag, Vienna
Hardcover. ISBN 978-3-7097-0314-4
2022, 448 pp

Baumgefahren-Management in Österreichs Nationalparks. Zugleich ein Beitrag zu den Grundlagen der Baum- und Forsthaftung samt Entscheidungsübersicht
by Ernst Karner and Karoline Zsak

Jan Sramek Verlag, Vienna
Hardcover. ISBN 978-3-7097-0322-9
2023, 159 pp

Rechtszuweisung, Güterzuordnung und deren Schutz
by Helmut Koziol
Jan Sramek Verlag, Vienna
Hardcover. ISBN 978-3-7097-0367-0
2024, 314 pp

Die Ehre Verstorbener und ihr Schutz
by Helmut Koziol
Jan Sramek Verlag, Vienna
Softcover. ISBN 978-3-7097-0374-8
2024, 108 pp

Journal of European Tort Law

The Journal of European Tort Law (JETL) is published three times a year. The General Editor is Professor Ken Oliphant, University of Bristol.

Further information, including subscription details and instructions for authors, is available on the JETL website <http://www.degruyter.com/view/j/jetl>.

Queries may be addressed to <information@jetl.eu>. Articles, comments and reviews should be submitted for consideration to <submissions@jetl.eu>. The Journal applies a policy of double-blind peer review.

Eurotort

EUROTORT is the first comprehensive database of European cases on tort law. Access to the database is free (subject to prior registration) at <www.eurotort.org>.